Philosophical Foundations of Precedent

Philosophical Foundations of Precedent

Edited by
TIMOTHY ENDICOTT,
HAFSTEINN DAN KRISTJÁNSSON, AND
SEBASTIAN LEWIS

OXFORD
UNIVERSITY PRESS

Great Clarendon Street, Oxford, OX2 6DP,
United Kingdom

Oxford University Press is a department of the University of Oxford.
It furthers the University's objective of excellence in research, scholarship,
and education by publishing worldwide. Oxford is a registered trade mark of
Oxford University Press in the UK and in certain other countries

© The several contributors 2023

The moral rights of the authors have been asserted

First Edition published in 2023

All rights reserved. No part of this publication may be reproduced, stored in
a retrieval system, or transmitted, in any form or by any means, without the
prior permission in writing of Oxford University Press, or as expressly permitted
by law, by licence or under terms agreed with the appropriate reprographics
rights organization. Enquiries concerning reproduction outside the scope of the
above should be sent to the Rights Department, Oxford University Press, at the
address above

You must not circulate this work in any other form
and you must impose this same condition on any acquirer

Public sector information reproduced under Open Government Licence v3.0
(http://www.nationalarchives.gov.uk/doc/open-government-licence/open-government-licence.htm)

Published in the United States of America by Oxford University Press
198 Madison Avenue, New York, NY 10016, United States of America

British Library Cataloguing in Publication Data

Data available

Library of Congress Control Number: 2022947941

ISBN 978–0–19–285724–8

DOI: 10.1093/oso/9780192857248.001.0001

Printed and bound in the UK by
TJ Books Limited

Links to third party websites are provided by Oxford in good faith and
for information only. Oxford disclaims any responsibility for the materials
contained in any third party website referenced in this work.

In memory of Joseph Raz

Contents

Homage to Bruno Celano	xi
List of Contributors	xiii
Introduction: The Central Question and Its Ramifications	1
Timothy Endicott, Hafsteinn Dan Kristjánsson, and Sebastian Lewis	

I. THE NATURE OF PRECEDENT

1. Precedent: The What, the Why, and the How *Larry Alexander*	11
2. The Doctrine of Precedent and the Rule of Recognition *Grant Lamond*	21
3. On the Nature of *Stare Decisis* *Sebastian Lewis*	35
4. Why Precedent Works *Nicholas W Barber*	49
5. Precedent and Legal Creep: A Cause for Concern? *Adam Rigoni*	62
6. Elements of Precedent *Hafsteinn Dan Kristjánsson*	75
7. Precedent and Paradigm: Thomas Kuhn on Science and the Common Law *Leah Trueblood and Peter Hatfield*	89
8. Supplanting Defeasible Rules *Barbara Baum Levenbook*	101

II. PRECEDENT AND LEGAL ARGUMENT

9. The Uses of Precedent and Legal Argument *Claudio Michelon*	117
10. The 'Expiscation' of Legal Principles *Luís Duarte d'Almeida*	130
11. The Hermeneutics of Legal Precedent *Ralf Poscher*	143
12. Do Precedents Constrain Reasoning? *Emily Sherwin*	158
13. Precedent, Exemplarity, and Imitation *Amalia Amaya*	171

viii CONTENTS

14. How Does Precedent Constrain?   185
John Horty

15. Precedent, Contest, and Law: A Logocratic Agony That Fits   198
Scott Brewer

16. *Dog Law*: On the Logical Structure (or Lack Thereof) of *Distinguishing*   214
Bruno Celano

17. Analogical Reasoning and Precedent   227
Cass R Sunstein

18. Precedent and Similarity   240
Frederick Schauer and Barbara A Spellman

III. PRECEDENT AND LEGAL THEORY

19. Presumptive Reasons and *Stare Decisis*   255
Andrei Marmor

20. An Artefactual Theory of Precedent   268
Kenneth M Ehrenberg

21. The Gravitational Force of Future Decisions   281
Nina Varsava

22. A Precedent-Based Critique of Legal Positivism   296
John CP Goldberg and Benjamin C Zipursky

23. Realism About Precedent   312
Brian Leiter

24. Precedent and the Source–Norm Distinction   320
Fábio Perin Shecaira

25. Precedent as Generalized Second-Order Reasons   335
Stephen Perry

26. Reasons Holism and the Shared View of Precedent   350
Torben Spaak

IV. PRECEDENT AND JUDICIAL POWER

27. Should Courts Follow Mistaken Statutory Precedents?   367
Dale Smith

28. Precedent and Law-Making Powers   380
Mikołaj Barczentewicz

29. Shaping Our Relationship: The Power to Set a Precedent   392
Maris Köpcke

30. Constitutionally Erroneous Precedent as a Window on Judicial
Law-Making in the US Legal System   405
Richard H Fallon, Jr

CONTENTS ix

31. Statutory Interpretation and Binding Precedents in the Civil Law Tradition   418
Lorena Ramírez-Ludeña

32. The Oracles of Codification: Informal Authority in Statutory Interpretation   431
Nils Jansen

33. Predictability and Precedent   443
Hillary Nye

V. EFFECTS OF PRECEDENT IN MORALITY AND LAW

34. Precedent Slippery Slopes   459
Katharina Stevens

35. 'A Previous Instance': Yamamoto and the Uses of Precedent   475
Jeremy Waldron

36. Consistency in Administrative Law   488
Adam Perry

37. Escaping Precedent: Inter-Legality and Change in Rules of Recognition   498
Nicole Roughan

38. Hoary Precedents   511
Matthew H Kramer

39. Partnering with the Dead to Govern the Unborn: The Value of
Precedent in Judicial Reasoning   523
Heidi M Hurd

40. Emotions and Precedent   537
Emily Kidd White

Index   551

Homage to Bruno Celano

Palermo, 1961–2022

To our great sorrow, our colleague Bruno Celano died in May 2022, during the production of this book.

We are proud to publish Professor Celano's essay, 'Dog Law: On the Logical Structure (or Lack Thereof) of *Distinguishing*' (Chapter 16). His accomplishment in completing his contribution to this book in circumstances of adversity was one instance in a sustained pattern of fortitude that we can only describe as heroic, lived out over many years by a brilliant philosopher. We honour his courage and we celebrate his camaraderie with us. We also salute the rare combination of original ideas and rigorous argumentation that you will find in all of his work and in his essay in this volume in particular.

His friend Professor José Juan Moreso concluded a beautiful tribute to Professor Celano with the following words from the poet Miguel Hernández.[1] With thanks to Professor Moreso, we join him in offering those words as our homage to Bruno Celano:

> *A las aladas almas de las rosas*
> *del almendro de nata te requiero*
> *que tenemos que hablar de muchas cosas*
> *compañero del alma, compañero.*

The Editors
June 2022

---

[1] https://www.upf.edu/web/lphi/home/-/asset_publisher/B8ZD0QMBzXVe/content/id/257968166/maximized#.Yo4-Hi8w3fB.

List of Contributors

Larry Alexander is the Warren Distinguished Professor of Law at the University of San Diego School of Law.

Amalia Amaya is the British Academy Global Professor in the School of Law at the University of Edinburgh and Research Professor of Philosophy at the National Autonomous University of Mexico.

Nicholas W Barber is Professor of Constitutional Law and Theory at Trinity College, University of Oxford.

Mikołaj Barczentewicz is Senior Lecturer in Law at the University of Surrey.

Scott Brewer is Professor of Law at Harvard Law School.

Bruno Celano was Professor of Philosophy of Law at the University of Palermo.

Luís Duarte d'Almeida is Honorary Professorial Fellow at the University of Edinburgh, and Aggregate Associate Professor and Director of CEDIS—R&D Centre in Law and Society at NOVA University's School of Law, Lisbon.

Kenneth M Ehrenberg is Professor of Jurisprudence and Philosophy, and Co-Director of the Surrey Centre for Law and Philosophy at the University of Surrey School of Law.

Timothy Endicott is the Vinerian Professor of English Law at the University of Oxford.

Richard H Fallon, Jr is the Story Professor of Law at Harvard Law School.

John CP Goldberg is the Carter Professor of General Jurisprudence at Harvard Law School.

Peter Hatfield is Hintze Research Fellow in the Department of Physics at the University of Oxford.

John Horty is Professor of Philosophy at the University of Maryland.

Heidi M Hurd holds the Ross and Helen Workman Chair in Law and is Professor of Philosophy at the University of Illinois.

Nils Jansen holds the Chair for Roman Law, Legal History, German and European Private Law at the Westfälische Wilhelms-Universität, Münster.

Emily Kidd White is Assistant Professor in Osgoode Hall Law School at York University.

Maris Köpcke is Lecturer at the Faculty of Law of the University of Barcelona.

Matthew H Kramer is Professor of Legal and Political Philosophy at the University of Cambridge and Fellow of Churchill College, Cambridge.

Hafsteinn Dan Kristjánsson is Assistant Professor of Law at the University of Iceland and Stipendiary Lecturer at Balliol College as well as St Anne's College, University of Oxford.

Grant Lamond is University Lecturer in Legal Philosophy at the University of Oxford and Fellow in Law at Balliol College, University of Oxford.

Brian Leiter is Karl N Llewellyn Professor of Jurisprudence and Director of the Center for Law, Philosophy, and Human Values at the University of Chicago.

xiv   LIST OF CONTRIBUTORS

Barbara Baum Levenbook is Professor Emerita at North Carolina State University.

Sebastian Lewis is Lecturer in Law at Oriel College, University of Oxford, and Global Associate Professor of Law at the University of Notre Dame in England.

Andrei Marmor is the Jacob Gould Shurman Professor of Philosophy and Law at Cornell Law School.

Claudio Michelon is Professor of Philosophy and Law and Director of the Edinburgh Centre for Legal Theory at the University of Edinburgh.

Hillary Nye is Assistant Professor at the Faculty of Law of the University of Alberta.

Adam Perry is Associate Professor at the Faculty of Law of the University of Oxford and Fellow and Tutor at Brasenose College, University of Oxford.

Stephen Perry is John J O'Brien Professor of Law and Professor of Philosophy Emeritus at the University of Pennsylvania Law School.

Ralf Poscher is Director of the Department of Public Law, Max Planck Institute for the Study of Crime, Security and Law and Honorary Professor at the Faculty of Law, University of Freiburg.

Lorena Ramírez-Ludeña is University Lecturer in Legal Philosophy at the Department of Law, Universitat Pompeu Fabra, Barcelona.

Adam Rigoni is Associate Teaching Professor at Barrett, The Honors College at Arizona State University.

Nicole Roughan is Associate Professor at the Faculty of Law at the University of Auckland.

Frederick Schauer is David and Mary Harrison Distinguished Professor of Law at the University of Virginia.

Fábio Perin Shecaira is Professor at the Faculty of Law at the Federal University of Rio de Janeiro.

Emily Sherwin is Frank B Ingersoll Professor of Law at Cornell Law School.

Dale Smith is Professor at Melbourne Law School at the University of Melbourne.

Torben Spaak is Professor of Jurisprudence in the Department of Law at Stockholm University.

Barbara A Spellman is Professor of Law and Professor of Psychology at the University of Virginia.

Katharina Stevens is Assistant Professor in the Department of Philosophy at the University of Lethbridge.

Cass R Sunstein is the Robert Walmsley University Professor at Harvard Law School.

Leah Trueblood is Career Development Fellow in Public Law at Worcester College and British Academy Postdoctoral Fellow at the Bonavero Institute of Human Rights.

Nina Varsava is Assistant Professor of Law at the University of Wisconsin-Madison.

Jeremy Waldron is Professor in the School of Law at New York University.

Benjamin C Zipursky is Professor of Law at Fordham Law School, where he holds the James H Quinn '49 Chair in Legal Ethics.

Introduction

The Central Question and Its Ramifications

Timothy Endicott, Hafsteinn Dan Kristjánsson, and Sebastian Lewis

You have no general reason to do the same thing today that you did yesterday. Let alone the same thing that *someone else* did yesterday. So why should a judicial decision today depend on what a court decided in the past? That is the central question concerning precedent in law.

This book offers a broad array of philosophical investigations into the central question, and into the multiple, ramified issues that arise from efforts to answer it. By 'philosophical' we mean, in this context, having to do with basic aspects of the nature and authority of precedent and of the forms of reasoning that it involves, and with fundamental normative principles as to how and when to act in accordance with precedent.

We will not summarize the forty original contributions to the subject that this book presents. We aim to set the scene by pointing out reasons for the range and the depth of the investigations offered here. And we will explain the way in which the project has developed.

The chapters discuss and criticize a variety of practices of adhering to past decisions or precedents (we think of a precedent as a previous decision, considered under the aspect of its potential use as a guide to action). The chapters address precedent in the common law, the civil law, and allied fields of practical reasoning. Those varied practices all presuppose an answer to the central question. Without an answer, we would seem to end up with a sort of pragmatic paradox: a putative argument for the conclusion that courts cannot rationally act on the basis of precedent. On this view, you *should* do the same thing today that you did yesterday, if there were reasons that required it yesterday, and the same reasons require it today. If a court did its duty in yesterday's case, today's court ought to do something similar in a relevantly similar case (unless its duty has changed). But then, it is enough for today's court to act on the grounds that also required that same decision in yesterday's case. Today's court need not treat the mere fact of yesterday's decision as a ground of decision. Conversely, if yesterday's court made the wrong decision, then it seems that today's court should do something different (that is, it should act on the grounds that yesterday's court ought to have acted on in a relevantly similar case). Precedent, it would seem, makes no rational difference, whether yesterday's decision was right or wrong. It appears that courts should never act on the basis of precedent. A precedent, you might say, can only have independent force when it was decided incorrectly, and then today's court should depart from it!

That argument needs to be met if the practice of precedent is to be justified. In this book you will see resolutions to this apparent paradox offered from diverse perspectives, and you will see arguments that it is irresolvable.

Timothy Endicott, Hafsteinn Dan Kristjánsson, and Sebastian Lewis, *Introduction* In: *Philosophical Foundations of Precedent*. Edited by: Timothy Endicott, Hafsteinn Dan Kristjánsson, and Sebastian Lewis, Oxford University Press. © Timothy Endicott, Hafsteinn Dan Kristjánsson, and Sebastian Lewis 2023. DOI: 10.1093/oso/9780192857248.003.0001

1. Surely Like Cases Should Be Treated Alike?

The answer to the central question may seem to be obvious because judicial decision is a matter of right, and in matters of right, like cases should be decided alike.

But put that way—in the passive voice—there cannot possibly be such a general principle: if there were any genuine principle, it would have to be a principle that *a particular agent or agency* ought to decide like cases alike. The unity that legal systems tend to impose on themselves offers a crucial initial step in a justification of following precedent in law. The legal unification of judicial agency may involve a hierarchy, and may allow dissenting judgments, but it secures finality and a non-contradictory form of ordering. In that unification of agency, judges tend not to be free to disregard what other judges have done. The judges who serve on a court tend to act as representatives of a single, institutional agency. That tendency generates expectations that the court will act consistently, and a sense of responsibility on the part of judges to do so. The decision of the court is seen as an action of the same agency that reached a decision yesterday, or years ago. Adherence to precedent not only makes the system look *unified*; it tends to make the system look *timeless*, conferring the stability, reliability, and consistency that are crucial elements in the rule of law. This institutional unification is crucial to making sense of precedent in law.

2. Answers to the Central Question Generate a Central Tension

And then, if an agent ought to treat like cases alike, that seems to answer the central question. And yet, even if an agency has reason to take the same action in the same circumstances, it does not actually follow that it should do the same as it did in the past. What if the agency acted improperly in the past, ignoring the reasons for action that apply in the case it decided and in all relevantly similar cases? Systems that give legal force to precedent seem to act on a presumption that what has been done has been rightly done, and because no such presumption is perfectly reliable, a tension arises between reasons for acting consistently, and reasons for reform. A court may have to choose whether to perpetuate a mistake, or to act differently today. Judges very often feel an impulse to buttress the credibility and the prestige of their institutions by adhering to what has been done before (we will call this the 'prestige impulse'). The presumption that the court has acted rightly in past decisions becomes an element in the good repute of the court. But of course, like any responsible agent, a court should not *only* aim for consistency; it ought to be prepared to improve, and to learn from past mistakes.

The value of readiness to reform is endangered by a practice of strict adherence to precedent. A rule requiring decisions that accord with precedent creates a potential tension with justice: both with general justice (because a bad precedent may generate an unjust general rule) and with equity (because there may be some special reason of justice in a new case for departure from a general rule). All the reasons for precedent have a poignant frailty, insofar as the court that decided the earlier case was fallible. Conversely, the fallibility of the later court counts in favour of precedent. The result is a tension within the law's effort to regulate its own content and development in a way that manages imperfections in its institutions and in its rules. Adhering to precedent promotes the rule of law, insofar as its rule-like constraint distinguishes judicial decision in a new case from the arbitrary say-so of today's court. But a strict doctrine of precedent can also pose a threat to the rule of law, insofar as it gives legal effect to wayward and wilful decisions, generating the arbitrariness of governance by the mere say-so of a court in an earlier case. Acting by precedent, Jeremy Bentham wrote, 'is acting without reason, to the declared exclusion of reason, and thereby in declared opposition to reason'.[1]

The reasons for treating the mere fact that a court decided *this* in the past as a norm for today are very different from the reasons for treating the mere fact that a legislature (or the framers of the constitution, or the maker of a will, or the parties to a contract) decided *this* in the past as a norm for today. Yet the central question about precedent is an instance of the general question of why the community today should pay attention to what was decided on behalf of the community in the past. So it is an instance of the question of why there should be law. And therefore, the central tension is an instance of the general tension between the value of the rule of law and the demands of justice. The central tension is the very epitome of that broader tension. And because justice can require that officials and institutions adhere to the rule of law instead of presuming to act on their own conception of justice, the central tension is a tension *within* the principle that a state must act justly.

The central tension can be managed to some extent by a variety of judicial techniques. These techniques have the potential to make various practices of precedent more just:

- overruling (typically by higher courts);
- an *obiter dicta* rule (giving the effect of precedent only to the earlier court's rationale for its decision in the case—the *ratio decidendi*—and not to other statements of law made by the judges along the way);
- distinguishing a precedent (confining its effect to some new, restrictive specification of the basis on which it was decided, so as to justify a different decision in a new case);
- a *per incuriam* rule (a doctrine that a decision does not have the legal effect of a precedent insofar as it was decided on a basis that was legally mistaken, if it is incontrovertible that the court in that case would have decided differently, if the mistake had been pointed out);
- innovative techniques of interpreting precedents: the effect of a precedent can evolve (or even change radically) because of the legal effect of later decisions that interpret it or reinterpret it or misinterpret it; and
- treating precedents as sources of persuasive authority only, as is done in many civilian jurisdictions.

Because of these management techniques, the central tension is a dynamic tension with reflexive aspects. The system's management of its practice can itself generate problems. A doctrine of precedent can create a danger of hidebound, merely conformist adherence to stupid decisions, but a doctrine of precedent can also create a danger of lawless judging: the judges in a later case sometimes honour the judges in a precedent by treating the earlier judgment as if it had established whatever rule the judges in the later case would prefer.

Moreover, a legal system may use legislation as a technique to respond to perceived injustices resulting from precedent, through the legislature's capacity to reform the law made by precedent (at least, if the precedent does not change constitutional rules that are beyond the competence of the legislature!). But lawmakers may be accused of disrespect for the rule of law if a legislature reverses the particular effect of a judicial decision. The law may prevent

---

[1] J Bentham, *Constitutional Code for the Use of All Nations and All Governments Professing Liberal Opinions* (Robert Heward 1830) 566.

them from doing so. And lawmakers are sometimes accused of disrespect for the rule of law even when the legislature enacts a prospective departure from a rule that was made by precedent—a fascinating result of the prestige impulse, which for many generations supported a rule that statutes would be presumed not to change the common law.

3. Against a Negative Model of Precedent

If the rival risks of hidebound decisions and lawless decisions make you sceptical about precedent, let us offer you an experiment. We recommend it, at the outset of this book, as a reminder of the possibility that a doctrine of precedent might promote justice and the rule of law. Imagine an anti-precedent doctrine: when a court decides a new case in which the facts are the same as those of an earlier case, this doctrine requires the court to give an outcome that is *different* from the outcome that it gave in the earlier case. Please do not spend too much time imagining it—a moment is enough to see that an anti-precedent doctrine would be deranged (Lewis Carroll might have made it into a doctrine of the Queen of Hearts' legal system). A rule that a court should decide like cases alike has advantages and drawbacks; a rule that courts should decide like cases differently would be irrational. The community would be subjected to governance that is organized against reason. It really would involve what Bentham said a doctrine of precedent involves: acting in declared opposition to reason.

In adjudication, as in other areas of human action, there is a radical asymmetry between doing the same thing this time as you did before, and doing something different this time. The former, adopted as a general policy, involves the tensions that you will encounter in the chapters of this book. You can see that it may be worth trying to resolve those tensions, because deciding a new case differently from an earlier case cannot possibly be your general policy.

4. The Book

There are new things to be said about the role of precedent in law. Old questions can be addressed in new and different ways, and new issues are waiting to be brought into the daylight. We embarked on this project because we thought that there was an opportunity for established writers and for new voices to make original contributions to the field in a collegial and interactive project.

We had to make a strategic decision: whether to try to cover the area by commissioning people to write on particular topics, or whether to invite them to decide for themselves. We wholeheartedly took the latter approach. Our priority was for the authors to decide what would be worthwhile, in a landmark collection that would involve an inclusive and balanced group of authors coming from both the civil and the common law tradition. Although the challenge remains, we hope to continue working towards a more inclusive and interconnected community of legal philosophers.

We invited the authors to address problems of doctrine, of history, and of comparative law, using any of the methodologies appropriate to dealing with such problems. But the central purpose of each contribution was to be philosophical (in the broad sense explained earlier, which includes much of what is sometimes called 'jurisprudence' or 'legal theory'). The focus of the book is on the role of precedent *in law*, but we have also taken a broad approach to the connection to law. We simply asked the authors to say something new and worthwhile in the philosophy of precedent in law.

That approach explains why the book is arranged in five rather fluid parts: (I) the Nature of Precedent, (II) Precedent and Legal Argument, (III) Precedent and Legal Theory, (IV) Precedent and Judicial Power, and (V) Effects of Precedent in Morality and Law. We could well have arranged the essays differently within those parts, and several of the essays deal with all five of those matters. Our allocations of essays to those parts of the book are impressionistic, reflecting our sense of each author's focus of attention. And all of the essays address the central question and the central tension, to some extent, and from very different directions.

We set out to arrange for each author to receive critical feedback from at least one of their fellow authors. To kick off that process in a convivial fashion, we organized a two-day online workshop in October 2021, in which we discussed twenty-one of the chapters offered here. We are very grateful to the authors for the responses they gave each other in the workshop, and also by correspondence.

A significant part of the value of the resulting volume lies in the diversity of problems that the authors chose to address, and in the diversity of perspectives and methods that they have brought to their work, and in their diverse opinions. As you can see, this diversity in the work did not arise from central planning, but from the variety of the authors' own ideas and approaches. It has been a pleasure to see the results of the authors' lateral thinking. Again and again we have found them working out what they might bring to the project that is original and different from what anyone else would do. It actually came as a relief to us that the essays in this unregulated array do not all simply address the central question and the central tension in the same way. You might say that we were lucky, but it isn't exactly luck: it is the result of forty-three authors asking themselves what they have to say that will shed new light on issues resulting from the central question, and from the tensions generated by ways of approaching it.

In lieu of a summary, consider the following forty questions—each of which we have drawn from one of the forty essays—as a glimpse of those ideas and approaches:

Can precedents really be distinguished, or can they only be followed or overruled? (Larry Alexander)

Can the law-creating aspect of precedent be explained in terms of criteria provided by a social rule? (Grant Lamond)

What is the relation between moral and legal grounds for following precedent? (Sebastian Lewis)

What is the relation between legal duties to follow precedent and non-legal social rules of the legal community? (Nicholas Barber)

Should findings of fact ever be treated as having precedential effect in later cases? (Adam Rigoni)

Is *stare decisis* a norm for the recognition of law, or a norm governing institutional decision-making? (Hafsteinn Dan Kristjánsson)

Does setting a precedent amount to establishing a paradigm? (Peter Hatfield and Leah Trueblood)

What forms of argument do courts use when they rely on precedent? (Claudio Michelon)

Does distinguishing a precedent amount to replacing one original rule with two new rules? (Barbara Baum Levenbook)

Can courts extract an underlying principle from a string of previously decided cases? (Luís Duarte d'Almeida)

Do the intentions of the court determine the content of the law that is made by its decisions? (Ralf Poscher)

Can precedent constrain judicial decision-making in any way other than by laying down determinate, authoritative rules? (Emily Sherwin)

Are precedents exemplars, so that reasoning by reference to precedent is a form of imitative behaviour? (Amalia Amaya)

Is it possible for a doctrine of precedent to constrain courts when they can distinguish earlier cases? (John Horty)

What is the relation between power and reason in precedential decision-making? (Scott Brewer)

Does the norm applied in a precedent remain essentially the same (changing only by specification) in a later case? (Bruno Celano)

What is the role of analogy in precedent-based decision-making? (Cass R Sunstein)

Can perceptions of similarity lead a later court to reason from particular to particular, without the mediation of any rule or principle? (Frederick Schauer and Barbara A Spellman)

Does a doctrine of precedent impose a duty either to follow a horizontal precedent, or to explain a departure? (Andrei Marmor)

Is the use of precedent compatible with the idea that law is an artefact? (Kenneth M Ehrenberg)

Do judges have a duty to decide in a way that will accord with future decisions? (Nina Varsava)

Does a doctrine that precedents may be distinguished empower courts to amend the law? (John CP Goldberg and Benjamin C Zipursky)

Is law capable of constraining the judgment of a court as to whether an earlier case was relevantly similar to a new case? (Brian Leiter)

Is it true that precedents are binding (and are sources of law) in the common law but not in the civil law? (Fábio Perin Shecaira)

Should precedents be understood as giving second-order reasons to treat first-order reasons as having a greater weight than they would otherwise have? (Stephen Perry)

Are the reasons for following precedent genuine, or merely conventional? (Torben Spaak)

Should courts follow a mistaken interpretation of a statute in an earlier case, or should they adopt the true interpretation that the statute ought to have been given? (Dale Smith)

Can a court in a jurisdiction with a doctrine of precedent choose *not* to set a precedent when it decides a case? (Mikołaj Barczentewicz)

What kind of power do we exercise when we set a precedent? (Maris Köpcke)

Does a doctrine of precedent in constitutional cases mean that a court's erroneous interpretation of the Constitution can displace the supreme law of the land? (Richard H Fallon, Jr)

Can precedents have binding force in countries where the courts and the jurists claim that judges must not make law but only apply it? (Lorena Ramírez-Ludeña)

If a civil law jurisdiction imposes no obligation on judges to decide in accordance with earlier decisions, but it is the judges' regular and accepted practice to do so, how should we describe the law of their jurisdiction? (Nils Jansen)

To what extent is predictability a value that calls for adherence to precedent? (Hillary Nye)

When judges know that their decision will set a precedent, should they be concerned that their decision may start future courts down a slippery slope? (Katharina Stevens)

How, if at all, can non-judicial precedents justify state action? (Jeremy Waldron)

Should the law require administrative agencies to treat their previous decisions as precedents? (Adam Perry)

How do judges escape from precedent (and utilize precedent) in deciding claims that they should give effect to the norms of indigenous legal orders such as *tikanga Māori* in Aotearoa New Zealand? (Nicole Roughan)

Can it be the case that judicial decisions made long ago (and never overturned) are not legally binding as precedents? (Matthew H Kramer)

Does the justification of a doctrine of precedent depend on arguments—aesthetic, psychological, or moral—for living in the past? (Heidi M Hurd)

What roles can precedent play in the judge's emotional engagement with legal concepts and doctrines? (Emily Kidd White)

Given the many connections among the questions the authors address, you will frequently find one benefiting from the views of another. You will also find one author disagreeing deeply with another. The book could not give a clear portrayal of the state of the discipline if it were not full of controversy. But we encouraged the authors to prioritize the articulation and defence of original claims, over taking further incremental steps in established debates.

Like law in general, the practice of following precedent can flourish without consensus on crucial questions concerning its nature and value. As ever in legal philosophy, it turns out that the controversial issues tend to be basic issues. We hope that readers will gain from discovering the various forms of convergence and divergence among authors in this volume, and we would only add this caveat: not every claim by one author is challenged by another. Perfect dissensus is not attainable in a collaborative project of this kind! It is just where you find the authors agreeing with each other that we hope you will be especially prepared to disagree, and to bring to the issues your own contrary-minded thinking.

5. A Note About Joseph Raz

Just weeks before his untimely death at the age of eighty-three in May 2022, Joseph Raz agreed that we could use one of his photographs on the jacket for this book. That makes this book part of a proud tradition of books with cover photographs by Professor Raz, published by the university presses of Cambridge, Harvard, Oxford, and Yale.

The photograph that Joseph gave us portrays the connection between the roots and the ramifications of a dynamic organism. We knew that the beautiful and evocative image, and the simple fact that it was Joseph who created it, would mean something to many readers whose understanding, like ours, has been influenced and shaped through our responses to Joseph's pioneering work on precedent, on the nature of law, and on practical reasoning in general. We have all gained from his patient and brilliant and unyielding determination to situate philosophy of law in the philosophy of practical reason. That is why we dedicate this book to Joseph's memory.

6. And Finally

We thank the authors. We did not know, when we started, what a pleasure it would be to watch this unprecedented collection of original philosophical investigations come together.

Timothy Endicott
Hafsteinn Dan Kristjánsson
Sebastian Lewis

PART I
THE NATURE OF PRECEDENT

1
Precedent
The What, the Why, and the How

Larry Alexander

1. Why Have the Practice of Following Precedent?

What is the doctrine of following precedent or *stare decisis*? To put it tersely, the doctrine refers to a court's having taken itself to be bound, in deciding the case before it, by an earlier decision or set of decisions by a court or courts. In describing a court as 'bound' by earlier judicial decisions, one means that the bound court is constrained by the earlier decisions in a way that prevents it from deciding the present case as it would have in the absence of those earlier decisions.

The doctrine of precedent applies to courts' determinations of *law*. It is those determinations that bind later courts. The doctrine of precedent is not to be confused with the doctrine of *res judicata*, which dictates that courts do not allow relitigation of particular lawsuits after they have been decided. *Res judicata* applies only to the particular parties to a lawsuit and only with respect to the factual issues that were raised or should have been raised in their lawsuit. Nor is the doctrine of precedent to be confused with the doctrine of collateral estoppel, which prevents the relitigation in a second lawsuit of the factual issues that were decided in the first lawsuit, even if the second lawsuit is distinct from the first (it is based on a different claim) and, in certain circumstances, even if the parties are different.

So the doctrine of precedent deals with determinations of law, not fact. And it is those determinations by the earlier courts—the precedent courts—that bind the later courts—the constrained courts. In what ways the precedent courts bind the constrained courts will be discussed at some length later. First, though, why have a doctrine of precedent at all? Why constrain courts so that they cannot decide cases how, in the absence of precedents, they believe those cases should be decided?

One reason to do so is based on authority. If the precedent court is ranked higher in authority than the constrained court, then the hierarchy of the courts and their relative authority is preserved. When we speak of a lower court being bound by earlier decisions of higher courts, we are referring to *vertical precedent*. Vertical precedent is to be contrasted with *horizontal precedent*, where a court of equal authority nonetheless acts as if it were bound by an earlier decision.

The benefit of vertical precedent is that of having a judicial hierarchy, that is, a system of courts in which some courts are subordinate in authority to other courts, and the former must rule in accordance with what the latter have held. What I have to say about the scope of precedential constraint applies to both vertical and horizontal precedent. What I have to say about the strength of precedential constraint applies only to horizontal precedent, as vertical precedent's strength is essentially absolute.

Larry Alexander, *Precedent* In: *Philosophical Foundations of Precedent*. Edited by: Timothy Endicott, Hafsteinn Dan Kristjánsson, and Sebastian Lewis, Oxford University Press. © Larry Alexander 2023. DOI: 10.1093/oso/9780192857248.003.0002

12 LARRY ALEXANDER

What then are the benefits of courts being constrained by horizontal precedents? One obvious benefit is convenience. Instead of trying to figure out the merits of the case before it, the constrained court can merely cite the precedent decision and declare that the merits are what the precedent court declared them to be. Precedential constraint thus economizes on the scarce judicial resources of time and effort.

Another benefit of precedential constraint is that of settlement of contested legal matters. I have taken the position in other writings that law's primary function is to settle controversies over what must be done and avert the moral costs those controversies threaten to impose. Through settlement of controversies about what must be done, law promotes coordination, planning, and peace. And just as law settles moral controversies, precedential constraint settles legal controversies. And that settlement promotes liberty-enhancing reliance and planning.

2. What Does Following Precedent Require? Three Models of Precedential Constraint and Its Scope

Precedential constraint has two aspects. The first is its *scope*. How many potential decisions are affected by the precedent? Put differently, questions of scope ask: how broad or narrow are the legal issues that precedent court's decision has settled?

The second aspect of precedential constraint is its *strength*. The strength of the constraint refers to the reasons the constrained court must have to justify refusing to be bound by the precedent and thus overruling it. I will discuss overruling at the conclusion of this chapter. Overruling precedents turns out to be only an instance of the more general problem associated with legal transitions and the rationality of rule following.

A. The Natural Model of Precedential Constraint

How is it that a decision by a court at T1 is supposed to affect a court at T2, so that the T2 court is constrained to decide its case differently from how it would have decided it in the absence of the T1 decision? One way the decision at T1 can affect the T2 case is by changing the facts on the ground. Suppose, for example, that in the T1 case of *A v B*, the decision is in favour of A. And suppose, had the T2 court decided *A v B*, it would have decided in favour of B. In other words, the T2 court believes the T1 court decided *A v B* incorrectly. Still, now that *A v B* has been (incorrectly) decided in favour of A, people, including A', may have relied on that decision in arranging their affairs. If the T2 court decides *A' v B'* in favour of B'—as it would have in the absence of the earlier decision—A' will suffer a loss because of their reliance on the decision in *A v B*. On balance, then, the case of *A' v B'* may now tip in favour of a decision for A' because of the erroneous decision in the T1 case.

In previous works I called this way in which an incorrect decision might constrain subsequent ones the *natural model of precedent*.[1] I labelled it 'natural' to emphasize the fact that the later court—the constrained court—is merely deciding its case as it naturally should, that is, by taking into consideration all relevant facts and then reaching a decision it deems correct

---

[1] See L Alexander, 'Constrained by Precedent' (1989) 63 So Cal L Rev 1; L Alexander and E Sherwin, *The Rules of Rules: Morality, Rules and the Dilemmas of Law* (Duke University Press 2001), ch 8.

in the light of those facts. The precedent decision—or, more precisely, the behaviour induced by it—is a fact, though it is just one fact among many that might be relevant.

The natural model of precedential constraint is not the model Anglo-American courts employ. Although they may look at reliance on precedents in deciding whether to *overrule* precedents—something I take up in the discussion of precedential strength—they do not look at reliance in determining the scope of precedential constraint. In other words, Anglo-American courts view precedential constraint to be broader than the natural model would entail.

B. The Rule Model of Precedent

A second model of precedential constraint is one that I have labelled the *rule model of precedent*.[2] It can be easily described. On this model, when the precedent court decides *A v B*, it announces and promulgates a rule—'if X, Y, and Z, then decide for the party analogous to A'—and subsequent courts are bound to follow this rule unless and until the precedent is overruled by a court or other body with the authority to do so.

The rule model of precedent views a precedent court as a legislative body as well as an adjudicative one. The precedential constraint in *A v B* is not located in the decision in favour of A but in the rule promulgated in the precedent that purports to justify that decision ('if X, Y, Z, then decide for the party analogous to A'). The rule promulgated is the precedent case's 'holding'. Everything else said by the court is 'dicta' and has no binding effect.

There are three principal objections to this model. One objection is that courts are not competent to or not authorized to legislate. I am not saying that courts do not legislate rules. The common law belies such a statement. Rather, what I am voicing is the criticism that even if courts are quite competent to assess the merits of the cases that come before them, they are far less competent in fashioning rules to govern future cases. That is the competence complaint regarding the rule model.

A second objection is that it is often difficult or impossible to locate a 'rule' in a court's opinion.[3] On the rule model, if no rule can be located in the precedent court's opinion(s), then the case stands only for its decision based on its facts.

A third objection is that the rule model obliterates one feature that is thought to be present in a system of precedent, namely the feature of *distinguishing* prior decisions as opposed to overruling them. For the later court either follows the rule laid down in the precedent case or else overrules or amends it (which is a partial overruling).

Joseph Raz disagrees with this last point.[4] He suggests that precedent rules can be distinguished without being overruled. According to Raz, a judge seeking to distinguish a precedent rule must restate the rule in a way that meets two conditions: the modified rule must be the precedent rule with some further condition added and the modified rule must support the outcome of the precedent case. He illustrates with an example in which the precedent case involved facts a, b, c, d, and e, the result was X, and the opinion announced a rule 'if A, B, and C, then X'. The new case involves facts a, b, c, d, and f, but not e. The court can distinguish

---

[2] See Alexander (n 1).

[3] See, e.g., K Stevens, 'Reasoning by Precedent—Between Rules and Analogies' (2018) 24 Legal Theory 230–34; RC Williams, 'Plurality Opinions and the Ambiguity of Precedential Authority' <https://ssrn.com/abstract=3816 564> accessed 23 January 2022.

[4] See J Raz, *The Authority of Law: Essays on Law and Morality* (1st edn, OUP 1979) 183–89.

14 LARRY ALEXANDER

the new case and announce a modified rule 'if A, B, C, and E, then X', or a modified rule, 'if A, B, C, and not F, then X'. But it cannot announce a modified rule, 'if A, B, C, and not D, then X', because this rule does not support the outcome of the precedent case.

This constraint is illusory, however. Assume a precedent rule, 'Wild animals in residential neighbourhoods are nuisances.' And suppose it is announced in a case involving a pet bear. In a later case, Jerome is keeping a crocodile in his house and the court, in response to a suit seeking to enjoin Jerome from doing so, and sympathetic to Jerome, announces its modification of the precedent rule, 'Furry wild animals in residential neighbourhoods are nuisances.' This rule may not be ideal and it authorizes a result that seems contrary to the values the precedent rule was designed to protect, but it meets Raz's two conditions: it is the precedent rule with a condition added and it justifies the outcome of the precedent case. Nor do Raz's conditions guarantee that the modified rule will be similar in effect to the precedent rule. The later court could announce a rule, 'Wild animals that are not three-year-old ocelots with one lame foot are nuisances', without running afoul of the supposedly constraining conditions. But the pattern of future nuisance decisions under the rule will be radically different from the pattern one would have expected under the earlier court's rule, 'Wild animals are nuisances.'

Raz might object that although these new rules would produce the same result in the precedent case as did the rule announced in that case, they do not *justify* that result. That is true. But remember, the constrained court does not believe the decision in the precedent case *was* justified. It disagrees with the rule announced in the precedent case. That is why it is not really distinguishing its case but is instead partially amending and thus partially overruling the precedent rule.[5]

Precedent rules cannot therefore be 'distinguished'. They can only be followed or overruled, either in whole or in part. So all three of the stated objections to the rule model of precedent are valid.

Despite these objections, the rule model is the only model of precedent that can constrain a later court to decide a case in a way that it believes is incorrect at the time it decides it. (The natural model does not do this because it asks the later court to reach the correct all-things-considered decision in the case before it in light of the effects of the precedent decision.) However, in order to show that only the rule model of precedent can constrain, I need to put on the table a third model of precedent, one that seems to possess all the features that we associate with a system of precedent. Its only problem is that it is conceptually confused.

C. The Result Model of Precedent

This third model is what I have labelled the *result model of precedent*.[6] On this model, the constraint imposed on later courts by the precedent decision comes from its having decided in favour of A in a case in which the facts were F1, F2, and F3. Suppose in the latter case of *A' v B'*, the facts are F1, F2, F3, and F4. Suppose the later court believes that these facts in total weigh in favour of a decision for B'. However, F4 is a fact that weighs in favour of a decision for A'. Therefore, the later court believes that although in the absence of the *A v B* precedent, it should decide the case in favour of B', the facts weigh more heavily in favour of a decision for A' than they did for A in *A v B*. And because the precedent court decided for A on weaker

---

[5] I thank Andrei Marmor for pressing me on this point.
[6] See Alexander (n 1) 28–44.

grounds than exist for A', *A' v B'* is an a fortiori case for a decision for A'. In other words, if the precedent decision is to be followed, then *A' v B'* must be decided in favour of A' even though in the absence of *A v B* the decision would be in favour of B'.

The result model of precedent appears to possess all of the features we commonly associate with a system of precedent. Unlike the natural model, the result model's constraint does force subsequent courts to decide differently from how they would decide even after considering reliance on the precedent. In other words, the result model views precedent decisions as themselves constraining even in the absence of any reliance or other relevant effects. Unlike the rule model, the result model does not view precedent courts as legislating rules. And also unlike the rule model, the result model retains the distinction between overruling a precedent and distinguishing it. For a precedent can be distinguished by citing some fact in the present case that did not obtain in the precedent case and that counts in favour of a decision in favour of the party analogous to the losing party in the precedent case. (If F5, a fact in the case of *A' v B'* that was not present in *A v B*, counts in favour of B', then the present court might decide for B' and cite F5 as the fact that distinguishes *A v B*.)

The only problem with the result model is that it cannot work. To begin with, the later court has only filtered access to the facts of the precedent case. It knows only what the precedent court has told it. A precedent court that wanted to bind subsequent courts quite broadly could just cite a few facts, described at a high level of generality. In other words, it might issue the following kind of opinion: 'In *A v B*, B made a promise to A, supported by consideration, and B breached it. Decision for A.' The later courts would know nothing of the particulars of B's promise, A's consideration, or B's breach. In another case involving a promise, consideration, and breach, but one in which the court believes the promisor should prevail, how can the court distinguish *A v B*, given that it knows only the generalities and not the particulars of that case?

There is a way for a court to distinguish a precedent despite the precedent court's spare and highly abstract recitation of the facts it considered material. The later court might assume the presence of an unmentioned fact in the precedent case, a fact that would have justified the precedent court's decision and that is absent in the present case. Suppose, for example, that the precedent court's decision for A in *A v B* would have been correct if a decision for B would have triggered a great calamity. (Nuclear terrorists would have detonated an atom bomb had the decision been for B.) Call that fact, unmentioned by the precedent court, F6. If the precedent court recites facts F1, F2, and F3, in support of its decision for A, the later court can read the precedent as F1, F2, F3, and F6. And because F6 does not exist in *A' v B'*, the precedent court can decide for B' and distinguish *A v B* on that ground.

This tack, however, makes precedents incapable of constraining, as one can always produce some fact, unmentioned in a precedent case, which would have justified its decision, even if one has little reason to surmise such a fact was present. On the other hand, it seems quite uncharitable towards the precedent court to assume that it would fail to mention those facts that would have justified its decision while mentioning facts that did not by themselves do so.

But instead of distinguishing *A' v B'* on the ground that a fact that was possibly present in *A v B* is absent in *A' v B'*, the court in *A' v B'* might distinguish *A v B* on the ground that a fact that is present in *A' v B'* was not mentioned in *A v B* and can therefore be assumed to have been absent in that case. This seems more charitable to the precedent court than assuming it failed to mention a fact that was present and necessary for justifying the outcome. But it leads to the same result, namely that the court in *A' v B'* is unconstrained by *A v B*. For if the court believes *A' v B'* should be decided in favour of B', it believes the facts justify that result.

16 LARRY ALEXANDER

And because the facts justify it, the court can assume that at least some of them were absent in *A v B*.

All of this is quite abstract, so let me try to give a concrete example. Suppose in *A v B* A sought to enjoin B's keeping a caged pet bear in a residential neighbourhood, and the court sided with A, finding a bear to be a dangerous nuisance. Suppose in *A' v B'* a similar injunction is sought, but the court believes that, in the absence of *A v B*, B' should win. In other words, it does not believe keeping a caged bear in a residential neighbourhood to be a nuisance. Suppose there is evidence in *A' v B'* that many neighbourhood children enjoy seeing the bear. No such evidence is cited in the opinion in *A v B*. The court in *A' v B'* can then distinguish *A v B* on that ground and avoid the precedent's constraint. *And it will always be able to do so if it describes the facts in its case with sufficient particularity.*

Is it true, however, that the later court can always find facts that would justify distinguishing the prior case? Suppose, for example, that the precedent court did mention that neighbourhood children enjoyed seeing the caged bear but found the bear to be a nuisance, nonetheless. And suppose, moreover, that there were more potentially disappointed children in the first neighbourhood than in the second. This would mean that the second court could not cite the disappointment of the children as a distinguishing fact. That would not, however, leave the second court without any basis for distinguishing the precedent case. It could, for example, note that the bear's cage in its case is very secure and then, because the nature of the cage in the precedent case was not mentioned, assume that the cage in that case was less secure than the cage in its case. Unless the precedent court mentions the absence of every conceivable fact that would have justified its (from the later court's perspective) otherwise incorrect decision, or mentions the presence of every conceivable fact that would have undermined its decision, the later court will be able to distinguish the precedent decision and reach what it thinks is the correct result.

Grant Lamond gives what I believe is the best defence of the reasons version of the result model. That version requires later courts to adhere to the reasoning of the precedent court. Lamond cites as a good example of a court's properly distinguishing a precedent the case in which threats of death or serious injury, which an earlier criminal case had held to suffice for the defence of duress, were held not to afford the defence when the defendant belonged to a criminal gang and had been threatened by fellow gang members.[7] Suppose, however, that the earlier courts had not mentioned whether the defendant had belonged to a gang and had been threatened by other members even though those facts were present in that case. Let us suppose that the court did not mention those facts because it did not believe they were or should be relevant to eligibility for the excuse of duress. If that is true, then the later court, in refusing to grant the excuse, is not actually distinguishing the precedent or its reasons but only distinguishing the precedent as reported. For the earlier court had in fact reasoned that threats of death or injury suffice for duress irrespective of whether they come from fellow gang members, reasoning that the later court rejects. The later court only appears to be distinguishing the reasons of the precedent court because the latter failed to mention facts that given its *actual* reasons were irrelevant.

If, despite what I have argued, the later court cannot escape the constraint of the precedent by assuming either the presence or the absence of unmentioned facts in the precedent case, then it must assume that the reasoning of the precedent court—that (mentioned) facts F1, F2, and F3 by themselves justified a decision for A—is correct reasoning, even though,

---

[7] G Lamond, 'Revisiting the Reasons Account of Precedent' in M McBride (ed), *New Essays on the Nature of Legal Reasoning* (Bloomsbury Publishing 2021), citing *Sharp* [1987] 1 QB 853 (CA).

in the opinion of the later court, it is not. The later court then must ask, what would be correct outcomes if the incorrect reasoning of the precedent court were correct? I do not think that such a question is coherent. It is like asking how seals should be classified if hippos were correctly deemed to be mammals but whales were incorrectly deemed to be fish. Or what the correct view of discrimination against Roma would be if discrimination against Jews were correctly deemed immoral but discrimination against Hispanics were incorrectly deemed morally proper. The reasoning of an incorrectly decided precedent cannot cohere with other normative views, at least some of which are correct. It is like a misshapen piece in a jigsaw puzzle. To fit it in renders other pieces incapable of fitting. Moreover, any case that is an a fortiori case for following an incorrect precedent can also be an a fortiori case for following other precedents that were correctly decided, resulting in contradictory prescriptions for the constrained court.[8]

I received considerable pushback on this point.[9] Can we not apply and extend reasoning that we believe is incorrect? Don't we try to understand—and teach our students to understand—points of view with which we ultimately disagree? I agree that we can do so when we assess full-blown normative theories. A deontologist can understand how a utilitarian would decide a case and vice versa. But where the mistaken reasoning is not part of coherent normative theory, I am doubtful that we can know how to extend it to new cases. If the court's reasoning were muddled when it decided that discrimination against Jews was wrong but discrimination against Roma was not, I am doubtful that one would know how to extend that reasoning to deal with discrimination against Hispanics. Moreover, a precedent based on incorrect reasoning will conflict with precedents based on correct reasoning; and presumably there will be some precedent decisions that are reasoned correctly. The later court will rightly regard those decisions based on reasons with which it agrees as the precedents it should follow.

The result model of precedent is the model Ronald Dworkin appears to endorse. Dworkin distinguishes between a precedent's *enactment force*—its rule—and its *gravitational force*.[10] The latter refers to the precedent's result, which now constrains future courts along the axis of *fit*. Future courts must make their decisions the best they can be, but they must also 'fit' their results with the precedent results. Yet that approach is tantamount to courts asking what results would be correct were certain earlier *incorrect results correct*, a question that I do not believe can be coherently answered.[11]

My conclusion then is that although the result model has all the features we associate with a system of precedent—on it, precedents constrain more than they do on the natural model and, unlike precedents on the rule model, they can be distinguished as well as overruled—it suffers from the fatal defect of incoherence. There is no sensible answer to the question that the result model asks a court to pose: what would the correct decision in our case be should an earlier incorrect decision have been correct? Only the rule model survives as a truly constraining model of precedent.

---

[8] The 'reasons' version of the result model has been advocated by Grant Lamond, John Horty, and Robert Mullins, though each elaborates his model differently from those of the others. See, e.g., ibid and G Lamond, 'Do Precedents Create Rules?' (2005) 11 Legal Theory 1; J Horty, 'Rules and Reasons' (2017) 17 Legal Theory 1; R Mullins, 'Protected Reasons and Precedential Constraint' (2020) 26 Legal Theory 40. I believe that the first of the Lamond articles cited is the best defence of the reasons version of the result model—though, as I have argued, I do not believe it is ultimately successful.

[9] Especially from Heidi Hurd and Jeremy Waldron.

[10] See R Dworkin, *Taking Rights Seriously* (1st edn, Harvard UP 1977) 110–15.

[11] See Alexander (n 1) 36.

3. Interlude: Precedential Constraint Under Statutes and Constitutions

How does precedential constraint work when the precedent deals with a statutory or constitutional text? There are two aspects to such precedents. The first is the interpretation of the statutory or constitutional text. That amounts to the precedent court substituting its language for the language of the text. The court's language is supposed to clarify the meaning of the text and not alter it, as when the court substitutes an unambiguous term for the text's ambiguous one.

The precedent court's new formulation of the text constrains later courts to treat that formulation as the text's correct interpretation even if the later courts disagree that it is. The precedent court's formulation is now the *rule* the later courts must follow in place of the later court's own interpretation of the statutory or constitutional text. The rule model of precedent captures this aspect of precedential constraint in interpreting statutory and constitutional texts.

The second aspect looks at what the precedent court does once it has interpreted the text. If it has interpreted the textual provisions to be a determinate rule, then it will have applied the rule in the precedent case. Presumably that will not be the aspect of the precedent case with which the later court disagrees.

On the other hand, if it interprets the textual provision to be a vague standard, then either it will have merely decided the case in all its particularities under that standard, or it will have created rules for implementing the standard and decided the case under such rules. The later courts would be bound by both the interpretation of the text and by the implementing rules announced by the precedent court. If no implementing rules were announced, and the precedent case was merely decided directly under the announced standard, only the interpretation of the text to be a standard would constrain later courts. The precedent court's decision implementing the standard in the case before it could only constrain later courts if the result model were a tenable model of constraint.

4. The Strength of Precedential Constraint

The question of strength is a question of when precedents are properly overruled. An answer of 'never' is too extreme, as it could entrench catastrophically poorly decided cases. On the other hand, an answer of 'whenever following the precedent decision leads to an incorrect result' reduces precedents to their status under the natural model, which is one of complete non-entrenchment. Too little entrenchment results in too little settlement of issues that need to be settled, just as too much entrenchment results in too many potentially disastrous mistakes.

The question of how much to entrench precedents against overruling is one aspect of the more general issue of legal transitions. Law should be changeable in order to adapt to new circumstances and information and to purge itself of past errors. But law should also be relatively stable and predictable so people can confidently plan their affairs. The problem of legal transitions appears in controversies over what changes in regulations of property and contracts should lead to compensation. Such controversies surface in constitutional litigation in the US under the takings clause, the impairment of obligations of contracts clause, and the due process clauses.[12]

---

[12] See US Constitution, Art I, § 10; US Constitution, amend V; US Constitution, amend XIV, § 1. See also Symposium, 'Legal Transitions: Is There an Ideal Way to Deal with the Non-Ideal World of Legal Change?' (2003) 13 J Contemporary Legal Issues 1.

At the deepest level, these controversies boil down to the problem of the rationality of rule following: for although law's primary moral function is to settle moral controversies, and law achieves this settlement through determinate rules ('standards' leave matters unsettled), determinate rules' determinacy comes from their bluntness and thus their over- and under-inclusiveness vis-à-vis their background moral justification. This in turn means that some applications of legal rules will depart from what an all-things-considered direct application of the background moral norms would require, leaving actors with moral reasons for departing from rules that they have moral reasons to maintain.[13]

But the problem of legal transitions also appears in other guises, including the question of the proper strength of precedential constraint, that is, the question of when precedents should be overruled. I know what the wrong answers to this question are: that we should never overrule precedents is wrong and that we should overrule precedents whenever we disagree with them. (I should say that the latter answer is not wrong if you do not believe precedents should constrain in the domains of statutory and constitutional adjudication, and there are vocal opponents of precedential constraint in those domains, especially the latter.[14] I just happen to disagree, at least to some extent, with those people. For the logic of the argument that erroneous judicial interpretations of statutes and constitutions should never bind later courts also entails that misinterpretations by higher courts should not bind lower courts—a repudiation of so-called *vertical precedent*—and, even more radically, that judicial misinterpretations should not bind *anyone*, officials and citizens alike, which would undermine all principles of repose, including *res judicata* and the force of judicial orders.)

5. Conclusion

Let me summarize. I have argued that the rule model of precedent is the only model of precedent that is capable of constraining later courts. On the rule model, the holding is the announced rule, and the dicta are everything else said by the court. Moreover, the holding, if it applies, must either be followed or overruled, at least in part. It cannot be distinguished.

The result model of precedent, on the other hand, is incapable of constraining in any coherent way. Although it, unlike the rule model, leaves room for distinguishing precedents, it in fact leaves room for extinguishing them through distinguishing them.

Finally, with respect to the strength of precedential constraint, I have argued that precedent rules should be overrulable, at least by certain bodies. Absolute entrenchment is too strong. But no entrenchment is also ill-advised. And there can be no algorithm for determining when erroneous precedents should be overruled. For if a court is instructed to overrule erroneous precedent rules whenever, all things considered, the costs of overruling are less than the benefits of doing so, then the rule model of precedent would collapse into the natural model, under which the only 'constraint' is 'do the right thing'.[15] Moreover, if a judge concludes that, all things considered, doing the right thing requires entrenching

---

[13] See Alexander and Sherwin (n 1) ch 4.

[14] See MS Paulsen, 'The Intrinsically Corrupting Influence of Precedent' (2005) 22 Const Comment 289; G Lawson, 'The Constitutional Case Against Precedent' (1994) 17 Harv J L & Pub Pol'y 23. See also L Alexander, 'Did *Casey* Strike Out? Following and Overruling Constitutional Precedents in the Supreme Court' in CJ Peters (ed), *Precedent in the United States Supreme Court* (Springer 2013) 47–61 (making a qualified argument against precedential constraint at the US Supreme Court level in constitutional cases).

[15] See Alexander and Sherwin (n 1) ch 4.

rules more than the natural model would dictate, the natural model would collapse back into the rule model, thus generating a practical paradox.[16] To avoid the Scylla of absolutely entrenching mischievous rules and the Charybdis of undermining the entrenchment of rules and thus the value of rules, courts must rely on a presumption in favour of following even mischievous rules the strength of which cannot be captured in any formula.[17]

---

[16] See Alexander (n 1) 15–16, 48–51.

[17] See Alexander and Sherwin (n 1) ch 8 (but see ch 4, discussing presumptive positivism).

2

The Doctrine of Precedent and the Rule of Recognition

*Grant Lamond**

1. Introduction

The doctrine of precedent is a fundamental part of the common law.[1] In the first part of this chapter two aspects of the doctrine as it is understood by common lawyers are highlighted: the law-creating nature of judicial decisions and the ways in which precedents bind courts. The second, longer, part of the chapter considers whether the doctrine can be given a satisfactory philosophical analysis in terms of HLA Hart's rule of recognition, and what light the doctrine sheds on the rule of recognition itself. It defends the view that the law-creating aspect of precedent can be explained in terms of criteria in the rule of recognition against claims that there is too much disagreement over the criteria for this conception to be plausible. It goes on to argue that the rule of recognition is not simply a social rule of officials but a customary law of the system, and a detailed account of such customary law is proposed. Finally, it suggests that the existence of other customary laws that do not owe their existence to the rule of recognition militates against the idea that every legal system necessarily has just one (often highly complex) rule of recognition. Instead, legal systems contain as many rules of recognition as there are ultimate sources of law.

2. The Doctrine of Precedent

The standard view among lawyers and officials in the common law world is that the doctrine of precedent has at least two important components. The first and most basic part of the doctrine is that the decisions of superior courts create law. The second additional part of the doctrine is that courts are bound by the decisions of courts higher in the judicial hierarchy and also (to a more limited extent) by their own earlier decisions. Each of these elements contains further complications that will be considered in turn.

---

[*] I would like to thank Hafsteinn Kristjánsson, Barbara Levenbook, and Sebastian Lewis for their very helpful comments on earlier drafts of this chapter.

[1] There is, of course, some variation *within* the common law legal family, but the analysis captures features that are fairly standard: see R Cross and J Harris, *Precedent in English Law* (4th edn, OUP 1991) ch 1 and (for the US) BA Garner and others, *The Law of Juridical Precedent* (Thomson Reuters 2016) 1–44.

Grant Lamond, *The Doctrine of Precedent and the Rule of Recognition* In: *Philosophical Foundations of Precedent*. Edited by: Timothy Endicott, Hafsteinn Dan Kristjánsson, and Sebastian Lewis, Oxford University Press. © Grant Lamond 2023. DOI: 10.1093/oso/9780192857248.003.0003

A. Precedents as an Independent and a Dependent Source of Law

In the common law, precedent can operate both as an independent and a dependent source of law. Sources of law are those materials and practices from which legal considerations are derived.[2] What makes a source a source *of law* is that officials regard the source as *authoritative*, that is, that there are reasons for using the source (and the considerations derived from the source) in official decision-making irrespective of officials' views about the *merits* of the source.[3] So what makes statutes and precedents sources of law is that officials treat them as authoritative sources in their decision-making. This does not mean that officials may not also believe there are good merit-based reasons for using the source (e.g., in the case of statutes, that they have democratic legitimacy). It is just that officials believe that they (and other officials) have reasons to use the source independently of their views about such merits: there are merit-independent reasons for using the source.[4] In addition, those merit-independent reasons are themselves sufficient to justify official use of the source.

Precedent constitutes a source of law in the common law because the judgments of superior courts of record are treated by officials as authoritative sources of considerations to be used in official decision-making. Nonetheless, there are two different ways in which precedents can be a source of law, which might be described as 'independent' and 'dependent'. An 'independent' source of law is one that is independent of other sources of law. As is well known, many major parts of the law in common law jurisdictions are based primarily on case law (e.g. contract, trusts, administrative law). By contrast, a 'dependent' source of law is one which is dependent on another source of law. In the case of precedent, the most obvious example is statutory interpretation: those decisions of courts which provide an authoritative interpretation of a statute. A dependent source of law determines the legal effect of another source of law; and its legal effect depends upon the continued existence of the other source. Thus, if a statute is repealed, the judicial decisions interpreting that statute also cease to have legal effect (though they may be relied upon by courts to assist in the interpretation of other statutes).[5]

B. Individual Precedents as Sources of Law

Another characteristic feature of the common law is that it regards *individual* court decisions as law-creating. A single decision of an appellate court can create law. There are two notable features of this practice. The first is simply the obvious one that the judicial decision does not have to be endorsed or followed by other courts before it creates law. By contrast, before the mid-nineteenth century the common law seems to have had a more relaxed view about the significance of individual decisions. A doctrine that had been accepted in many other cases was regarded as established and settled, whereas a doctrine supported by a single outlier decision was not.[6] The early common law, then, had a degree of affinity with the approach

---

[2] The term 'consideration' is used throughout this chapter to refer to the full gamut of normative factors relevant to decision-making, e.g. rules, reasons (both operative and auxiliary), principles, conditions, etc.

[3] This is a rough characterization: see G Lamond, 'Sources of Law in Common Law Analytical Jurisprudence' in L Burazin and others (eds), *Jurisprudence in the Mirror* (OUP, forthcoming).

[4] On merit-independence, see J Gardner, *Law as a Legal of Faith* (OUP 2012) 30–31.

[5] This is akin to the use of analogies in case law reasoning.

[6] See JH Baker, *An Introduction to English Legal History* (5th edn, OUP 2019) 207–12 and FG Kempin, 'Precedent and *Stare Decisis*: The Critical Years, 1800–1850' (1959) 3 Am J Legal Hist 28–54.

in some civilian legal systems which attach significance to a series of cases (a *jurisprudence constante*) endorsing a legal doctrine, rather than to a solitary decision doing so.

Secondly, in the earlier stages of the common law's development the courts in England regarded judicial decisions as, at most, *evidence* of the common law, rather than as creating the common law.[7] This was, of course, another way in which individual decisions carried less weight than in contemporary law: they could be treated as wrongly decided on the basis that the judge had misstated the law. The 'law' was based on the judiciary's *collective* understanding of legal doctrine. Individual judges could err, whereas the judiciary collectively could not.[8]

C. How Judicial Decisions Create Law

Judicial decisions can create law, akin to the law created by legislation. Nonetheless, precedents are not statutes, and they create a distinctive sort of law in a distinctive manner. First of all, courts are normally reactive rather than proactive.[9] They make decisions on cases that are brought before them by other parties, rather than by initiating the law-creating process. Unlike legislatures, they do not decide for themselves whether an issue should be addressed by the court, but must wait for the issue to be brought before them.

Secondly, judicial law-making is constrained by the issues put before it by the parties. In the common law, the primary function of courts is to resolve disputes between parties and determine the law that is applicable to that dispute. It makes general law *en passant*, as a side effect of settling the dispute between the parties. It is only the rulings on those issues of law that were used to resolve the dispute between the parties that create binding law.[10] Consequently, not all decisions of superior courts create law. In many first instance (i.e. trial) courts, the disputes between the parties are purely about the facts of the case, rather than the applicable law. The only questions, ultimately, are evidentiary: has it been proved (on the balance of probabilities or beyond reasonable doubt) that the defendant acted in the way that it is alleged they did? It is only where there is a dispute about the applicable law that the court needs to make a ruling.

Thirdly, precedents decide issues by reference to existing law, rather than *de novo*. A legislature can usually base a novel legal arrangement entirely on non-legal grounds (e.g. the moral desirability of the new arrangement), so long as the legislation is within the scope of the legislature's powers and does not conflict with a constitutional restriction. Courts, by contrast, seek some guidance in existing case law for their decision, even when they are dealing with an entirely novel question. Underlying legal principles, analogous legal doctrines, and persuasive authorities from other common law jurisdictions are prayed in aid, though non-legal considerations such as fairness and justice also have a role to play. Courts see their creative role as adapting the law to new circumstances, rather than starting afresh.

Fourthly, unlike statutes, precedents can be *distinguished* by later courts (including by courts lower in the hierarchy of courts). Even when a precedent makes a ruling that is (*pro*

---

[7] See, e.g., *Blackstone's Commentaries on the Laws of England* (OUP 2016 [1783]) vol 1, 53.

[8] Or at least did not: it is unlikely that early common lawyers regarded their collective understanding as constitutive of the law, but simply as an accurate view of it. See JH Baker, *The Oxford History of the Laws of England, Vol VI, 1483–1558* (OUP 2003) 486–89.

[9] There are a few established exceptions, such as contempt of court.

[10] These rulings are often referred to as the *ratio decidendi* of a case. Strictly speaking, it is only the ruling *on the facts of the specific case* that is law-creating.

tanto) applicable to a later case, the later court may point to some significant factual difference between the cases to justify not following the precedent. The main restriction on distinguishing is that the later court must treat the earlier case as having been correctly decided. The later decision must neither be inconsistent with the earlier case nor imply that the earlier case was wrongly decided. Thus, the law created by a precedent is highly context-dependent: it must be understood by reference to the facts of the case in which it was created.[11] Statutes, by contrast, are generally far more context-independent, their interpretation and application depending primarily on the text of the statute (though the background facts that led to their enactment may play a subsidiary role).

For all this, precedents, like statutes, create law. A precedent is a decision that must either be followed or distinguished in later cases (unless the court has the power to overrule). So precedents have (practical) *authority* for courts: a later court has a sufficient reason to follow an indistinguishable precedent independently of the merits of the decision.

D. Courts are 'Bound' by the Decisions of Higher Courts (and Their Own Decisions)

A further element of the doctrine of precedent in the common law, and one which is sometimes taken to be the gist of the doctrine, is that lower courts are 'bound' by the decisions of courts higher in the appellate hierarchy and by their own, earlier, decisions. This is not a doctrine about the law-creating effect of precedent, however. It is a doctrine about where the power to *overrule* a precedent lies.

The common law view that courts are 'bound' by their own decisions and the decisions of higher courts covers two types of situations. The first, and simplest, concerns the relationship between lower courts and higher courts. The basic rule is that lower courts are *strictly* bound by the decisions of higher courts. They must treat those decisions as correctly decided, and have no power to overrule them. Lower courts must follow such precedents unless they are distinguishable in the case at hand.

On the other hand, courts are 'bound', but *not* strictly bound, by their own earlier decisions.[12] Although they have the power to overrule their own decisions, there is a presumption against doing so. It is not a sufficient ground for overruling a decision that the court thinks the decision was wrongly decided (i.e. that the presently constituted court would have decided the case differently) or that changes in surrounding circumstances mean that the decision would not be reached if it was decided now. There must be stronger grounds than this for overruling, for example that the decision is regarded as 'clearly' wrong and overruling it would clearly improve the law.[13]

By contrast, courts are *not* bound by decisions of lower courts, for instance the UK Supreme Court is not bound by decisions of the Court of Appeal. What this means is that the Supreme Court may overrule decisions of the Court of Appeal (and courts below the Court of Appeal) simply on the basis that the decision was wrongly decided or is no longer correct.

---

[11] For a more detailed discussion of this aspect of precedents, see G Lamond, 'Do Precedents Create Rules?' (2005) 11 Legal Theory 1.

[12] An anomaly here is the English Court of Appeal, which treats its decisions as strictly binding subject to a small number of exceptions: *Young v Bristol Aeroplane* [1944] KB 718. Similarly, the House of Lords, from (at least) 1898 until 1966, treated its own decisions as strictly binding: *Practice Statement (Judicial Precedent)* [1966] 1 WLR 1234.

[13] See, e.g., Cross and Harris (n 1) 138–43.

There is no presumption against doing so. But until a precedent is overruled by a court or overridden by statute, it remains the law.

3. The Nature of the Doctrine of Precedent

The preceding section has sought to capture the standard view of common lawyers about the doctrine of precedent. That view sees individual precedents in some areas of legal doctrine as independent sources of law. Legal philosophers differ on the question of how exactly such precedents create law. Precedents involve courts making rulings on legal issues disputed by the parties before the court. On some views precedents create law because (i) the ruling amounts to a legal *rule* created by the case.[14] On other views precedents create law because (ii) the ruling represents a legally *sufficient reason* for the decision on the facts of the case.[15] Alternatively, some views regard precedents as law-creating by virtue of (iii) the underlying *principles* that justify the body of decisions to which the precedents belong. It is these principles that constitute the law.[16]

In this section I will focus on (i) the rule and (ii) the sufficient reasons account, which regard the ruling in the case (the *ratio decidendi*) as having a distinct significance in legal reasoning, since this reflects the standard view of common lawyers.[17] On these two approaches, the 'doctrine of precedent' is a legal doctrine that provides, among other things: (a) that the judicial decisions of superior courts are a source of law; and (b) that the rulings in such decisions are authoritative considerations that must be followed or distinguished by courts of equivalent or inferior status (and by other officials).

The doctrine of precedent thus understood raises two further questions: (1) how does the doctrine work; and (2) what is the legal basis for the doctrine? The most sophisticated philosophical response to these questions is provided by Hart's theory of the 'rule of recognition'.[18] According to Hart, the law-creating aspect of the doctrine of precedent is *part* of the rule of recognition.[19] And the rule of recognition is a social rule of officials that provides criteria for the identification of standards as valid legal standards. The rule of recognition itself, on the other hand, is neither valid nor invalid. Its legal status derives from the role it plays in official

---

[14] e.g. N MacCormick, *Legal Reasoning and Legal Theory* (rev edn, OUP 1994) 213–28; J Raz, *The Authority of Law* (rev edn, OUP 2011) ch 10; F Schauer, *Playing by the Rules* (OUP 1991) 181–87; L Alexander and E Sherwin, *Demystifying Legal Reasoning* (CUP 2007) ch 2.

[15] e.g. Lamond, 'Do Precedents Create Rules?' (n 11); J Horty, 'Rules and Reasons in the Theory of Precedent' (2011) 17 Legal Theory 1; and R Mullins, 'Protected Reasons and Precedential Constraint' (2020) 26 Legal Theory 40.

[16] e.g. S Perry, 'Judicial Obligation, Precedent and the Common Law' (1987) 7 OJLS 215, especially 234–43; and M Moore, 'Precedent, Induction, and Ethical Generalization' in L Goldstein (ed), *Precedent in Law* (OUP 1987). Although Ronald Dworkin partly fits this approach, he also takes precedents to have 'enactment' force: see, e.g., R Dworkin, *Taking Rights Seriously* (rev edn, Harvard UP 1978) 118–23 and R Dworkin, *Law's Empire* (Harvard UP 1986) 401–02.

[17] These views need not deny the significance of legal principles, but they do regard the ruling in a precedent as itself a legal consideration.

[18] HLA Hart, *The Concept of Law* (3rd edn, OUP 2012) chs 5 and 6. My discussion does not follow Hart in every respect. For a more detailed account of the rule of recognition, see G Lamond, 'The Rule of Recognition and the Foundations of a Legal System' in L Duarte d'Almeida and others (eds), *Reading HLA Hart's The Concept of Law* (Hart 2013).

[19] Hart, *The Concept of Law* (n 18) 101 and 294 (and see 95). The question of overruling, on the other hand, would seem to be (on Hart's view) part of the rule of *change* (ibid 95–96), though Hart says very little about this rule. I will put to one side the question whether common law courts have a law-*creating* power. For an argument that, strictly speaking, they do not, see Lamond, 'Do Precedents Create Rules?' (n 11) 24–26.

26   GRANT LAMOND

decision-making. In the following two subsections I will consider the adequacy of each of these responses.

A. The Doctrine of Precedent in the Rule of Recognition

Precedent, on Hart's theory, is a source of law because it is identified by the rule of recognition. But it can be questioned whether the rule of recognition adequately accounts for the doctrine of precedent. There are two prominent interpretations of the way in which the rule of recognition functions, and both present difficulties in accommodating the doctrine of precedent. The first interpretation is that the rule of recognition simply identifies *sources* of law, rather than the legal considerations created by those sources.[20] So in the case of precedent, it would identify the judgments of superior courts of record as sources from which the law can be derived. Those judgments (like statutes) have a status that other materials (such as Law Commission Reports) lack, since they are a source of valid legal considerations. But if this is the case, the rule of recognition does not identify the law created by judgments, because it does not identify the legal considerations created by sources of law.

A second interpretation of the rule of recognition is that it both identifies the sources of law and also the methods by which the legal considerations are derived from those sources.[21] So in the case of the doctrine of precedent, the rule of recognition includes the criteria for the identification of the binding legal considerations created in court judgments. The method by which the ruling is derived from a judgment is provided by the rule of recognition, not simply the criteria for identifying judgments as a source of law. This view of the rule of recognition is, however, vulnerable to arguments that it cannot accommodate 'theoretical disagreements' between legal officials.[22] It is not uncommon for officials (particularly judges) to disagree about the precise methods to be used to derive legal considerations from the source material. In the case of the doctrine of precedent, for instance, there is some disagreement in the literature on how to determine the *ratio* of a precedent.[23] Why is theoretical disagreement a problem for this account of the rule of recognition? Because the rule of recognition is proposed as a convergent practice of officials. Officials are supposed to accept and follow the *same* practice, and to believe that all officials should do likewise.[24] It is the officials' consistent practice that gives the rule of recognition its existence, since it is essentially an official custom.[25]

Is there an alternative to these two approaches? One possibility is this. The doctrine of precedent (understood as part of the rule of recognition) provides the *criteria* for what constitutes a valid legal consideration, but not the *method* for applying those criteria. So in the case of precedent the rule of recognition does more than simply identify court judgments as sources of law. But it does less than providing the exact way to identify valid legal considerations.

---

[20] e.g.J Raz, 'Dworkin: A New Link in the Chain' (1986) 74 Cal L Rev 1103, 1107. On some views, such as Raz's, the rule of recognition identifies law-creating *acts*, such as enactment. The alternative view, adopted here, is that it identifies the materials enacted: see Lamond (n 3).

[21] e.g. S Shapiro, 'What Is the Rule of Recognition (and Does It Exist?)' in MD Adler and KE Himma (eds), *The Rule of Recognition and the US Constitution* (OUP 2009) especially 248–50.

[22] See Dworkin, *Law's Empire* (n 16) 31–43.

[23] For an overview of some different methods that have been proposed, see Cross and Harris (n 1) 52–71.

[24] Hart, *The Concept of Law* (n 18) 116.

[25] ibid 256.

How would this work? As noted earlier, the legal considerations created by precedents are the *rationes* of judgments of superior courts of record.[26] The criterion in the rule of recognition provides that the *rationes decidendi* of judgments of superior courts of record constitute legal considerations. This criterion can be understood in more detail. The *ratio decidendi* of a judgment is the court's ruling on a legal issue that was relied upon in reaching the conclusion on the facts of the case.[27] And superior courts of record are those courts with particular legal features, such as their decisions being binding on parties even if made in excess of jurisdiction (unless and until overturned on appeal).[28]

On the other hand, *applying* the criterion to determine the *ratio* of a judgment is a *skill*.[29] This is why a great deal of time is spent in law schools reading and discussing cases. Students need to learn *how* to ascertain the *ratio* of a judgment, and that can only be achieved through the practice of reading cases and discussing their significance. Students are often taken aback, even when they have had the idea of the *ratio* carefully explained to them, just how difficult they find it (initially at least) to identify the *ratio* of a case they are reading. To put it in other terms, ascertaining the *ratio* of a case is a form of know-how, rather than know-that: it involves being able to competently perform a task rather than simply understand what the task involves.[30] Much of the disagreement in the literature over how to ascertain the *ratio* of a case derives from the difficulty of discursively describing the exercise of a skill, and the impossibility of reducing the exercise of this type of skill to a decision procedure that could be followed by those untrained in the skill. Another source of disagreement is an assumption that *rationes* can always be characterized with a high level of specificity, whereas there is often a significant leeway for later courts due to a degree of imprecision in how the *ratio* is to be understood.[31] Appreciating that there is such a leeway is part of the understanding of precedent that common lawyers possess.

So there is a plausible account of how Hart's rule of recognition can accommodate the doctrine of precedent.[32] The doctrine of precedent is *part* of the rule of recognition. The rule of recognition provides the ultimate criteria for identifying considerations as valid legal considerations. The criteria in the rule of recognition are ultimate because their status as law-creating criteria is not conferred by a further legal standard. All legal standards derive their validity (directly or indirectly) from the criteria in the rule of recognition. (Indirectly when

---

[26] I am oversimplifying here: the law created by a precedent is more complex than the *ratio*, but the basic point still stands. For the more complex account, see Lamond, 'Do Precedents Create Rules?' (n 11) and G Lamond, 'Revisiting the Reasons Account of Precedent' in M McBride and J Penner (eds), *New Essays on the Nature of Legal Reasoning* (Hart 2022).

[27] Something along these lines is widely endorsed as an account of the *ratio*: see Cross and Harris (n 1) 72–75; J Bell, 'Sources of Law' in A Burrows (ed), *English Private Law* (3rd edn, OUP 2013) 24–27 and, for the US, Garner and others (n 1) 44–46.

[28] See *R v Chancellor of St Edmundsbury and Ipswich Diocese, ex p White* [1948] 1 KB 195 (CA).

[29] As AWB Simpson observed, there is a difference between *defining* the *ratio* and *determining* it; see AWB Simpson, 'The Doctrine of Binding Precedent' in AG Guest (ed), *Oxford Essays in Jurisprudence* (OUP 1961) 159.

[30] On know-how, see C Pavese, 'Knowledge How', *The Stanford Encyclopedia of Philosophy* (Summer edn, 2021) <https://plato.stanford.edu/archives/sum2021/entries/knowledge-how/> accessed 31 March 2022. There is some dispute in the philosophical literature on whether know-how can be reduced to particular types of know-that. The key point, however, is that even if this is true (in some interesting sense), it is only those with the know-how who can possess the relevant know-that.

[31] On some of the ways in which the common law reduces the leeway, see Gardner (n 4) 77–79.

[32] This approach has some affinities to Jules Coleman's contrast between the content and the application of the rule of recognition: J Coleman, *The Practice of Principle* (OUP 2001) 116–18, but it attributes disagreements over the methods for applying the criteria to a mischaracterization of what is involved in doing so. It is worth emphasizing that officials need only roughly agree about the criteria and how they apply in practice, so long as they understand each other to be following a common approach to precedent. And ascertaining the *ratio decidendi* of a case is, of course, only one step in the process of deciding a new case.

28   GRANT LAMOND

they are validated by a standard that is itself validated by the criteria in the rule of recognition, or a standard validated by another standard that is itself validated by the rule of recognition, and so on.) The rule of recognition itself, on the other hand, is neither a valid nor an invalid legal standard according to Hart, because its status as law does not depend upon it being validated by a further standard.[33] Instead, the legal status of the rule of recognition is due to its role in validating other legal standards: it is part of the system of interconnected standards as the apex standard in the system.[34]

But the rule of recognition does more than (1) provide the criteria for the identification of considerations as valid legal considerations (with each criterion representing a different source of law).[35] It also (2) provides criteria for resolving conflicts between legal considerations created by *different* criteria (i.e. laws having different sources)[36] and (3) imposes a duty on all officials to follow and apply the considerations identified (directly or indirectly) by the criteria in the rule of recognition.[37] The rule of recognition can be, on Hart's reckoning, a very complex standard indeed.[38]

B. The Legal Status of the Doctrine of Precedent

According to Hart, the doctrine of precedent is a legal doctrine because it is part of the rule of recognition, and the rule of recognition is a legal rule because it is the basis on which all considerations are given (directly or indirectly) their status as valid law.[39] The rule of recognition itself, on the other hand, is regarded as binding by officials because they practise and accept it. The rule of recognition is, in Hart's terms, a 'social rule' of officialdom.[40] Hart was led to this conclusion by the fact that the doctrine of precedent, like the doctrine of parliamentary supremacy (in the UK), is a legal doctrine that is not validated by any other law. Both precedent and statute therefore are ultimate sources of law.

Is this the right way to understand the legal status of the doctrine of precedent, however? It is, of course, true that common law systems do not give the doctrine of precedent its legal status by some other law such as statute (and that it could not have that status as a result of precedents themselves, since the law-creating effect of precedents presuppose the doctrine). But statute and precedent are not the only sources of law in the common law. The other significant type of law is customary law. As Bentham noted, there are in fact two different types of customary law.[41] The first is customary law *in pays*, that is, the customs of legal subjects that are given legal effect by the law. So if fishermen have for many generations dried their

---

[33] Hart, *The Concept of Law* (n 18) 109.

[34] ibid 111–12.

[35] ibid 100–10, 294.

[36] ibid 95, 101, 106. And presumably criteria for resolving conflicts between laws with the *same* source. Perhaps (2) means that the criteria of validity in (1) are more precisely criteria of *pro tanto* validity: the validity of the standard can be defeated by conflicting standards (or by being repealed or overruled). It could be argued that (2) simply provides *additional* criteria for the validity of particular sources, and could be subsumed into (1). Although I cannot pursue this point here, the distinction between (1) and (2) should be preserved. E.g., to incorporate (2) into (1) would efface the contrast between a statute that is invalid because it conflicts with a constitutional right and a 'statute' that is not valid law because it has not been enacted in the prescribed manner.

[37] Hart is not clear about this in ch 6 of *The Concept of Law* (n 18) (see, e.g., 115–16)—though it is supported by what he says about international law at 235–36—but he is explicit about its duty-imposing role in HLA Hart, *Essays on Bentham* (OUP 1982) 155–56, 160.

[38] As Hart acknowledged: HLA Hart, *Essays in Jurisprudence and Philosophy* (OUP 1983) 359–61.

[39] Hart, *The Concept of Law* (n 18) 111.

[40] ibid 55–57.

[41] J Bentham, *A Comment on the Commentaries* (JH Burns and HLA Hart eds, OUP 1977) 180–85.

nets along a stretch of beach unchallenged, and done so in the belief that they have a right to do so, then that right may be legally valid, despite the lack of any statutory authorization or judicial decision establishing such a right.[42] If the system has some existing criteria by which officials can identify certain customs of its *subjects* as legally valid, then it recognizes customary law *in pays*.[43] The second type of customary law, less frequently discussed, is customary law *in foro*, that is, customary law of the *officials themselves*.[44] These are standards that are not validated by any other legal standard, but are treated as legally binding by officials in their official roles. In the common law, the most obvious example of customary law *in foro* is the royal prerogative—prerogative rights and powers of the Crown that have been long established as parts of the laws of England, such as the power to enter treaties and issue passports,[45] but which rest on neither statute nor precedent.[46] From this perspective, the doctrine of precedent can also be understood as a form of customary law *in foro*.

But is this really fundamentally different to Hart's view? Some theorists have argued that the rule of recognition just *is* a form of customary law (*in foro*).[47] If the rule of recognition can be understood as a form of customary law *in foro*, what is Hart's account of such law? It would seem to be this:

(1) Official practice exhibits a pattern of behaviour.[48]

(2) Officials regard the pattern of behaviour in (1) as a standard of behaviour.[49]

(3) Officials 'accept' the standard in (2) as a *common* standard to be followed by all officials; that is, they have a 'critical reflective attitude' towards the standard.[50]

(4) The critical reflective attitude in (3) is manifested in a number of ways, for example by officials demanding conformity to the standard, criticizing deviations by other officials from it (and regarding those criticisms as justifiable), and treating criticisms of their own deviations from it as justified.[51]

So far, this provides an account of official customary standards. But what makes a social standard followed by officials customary *law*? The social standard must somehow be connected to the law. Officials, after all, might be subject to *non-legal* social standards in their official roles; for example, standards of decorum, collegiality, or efficiency, that satisfy conditions (1)–(4). Hart only discusses the rule of recognition, and says that it is a *legal* standard because:[52]

---

[42] *Mercer v Denne* [1904] 2 Ch 534, especially 551–52.

[43] This is the only sort of customary law that Hart explicitly discusses in *The Concept of Law* (n 18) 44–48, 100, 101.

[44] Bentham (n 41) 182–84. It is possible that there might be a custom *in pays* of the officials, which satisfied the same criteria of identification as customs of non-officials. Customary law *in foro*, by contrast, relates to the practices of officials in performing their official roles.

[45] See D Feldman (ed), *English Public Law* (2nd edn, OUP 2009) 181–86.

[46] As the UK Ministry of Justice commented in *The Governance of Britain: Review of the Executive Royal Prerogative Powers: Final Report* (Ministry of Justice 2009): 'there are many prerogative powers for which there is no recent judicial authority and sometimes no judicial authority at all', 7 (§ 27).

[47] e.g. J Raz, 'Legal Principles and the Limits of Law' (1972) 81 Yale LJ 823, 851–54 (though without using the expression '*in foro*'); and to similar effect, J Raz, *Practical Reason and Norms* (2nd edn, Princeton UP 1990) 147; Raz, *The Authority of Law* (n 14) 96–97; and Gardner (n 4) 70, 83–84, 102. Hart himself later referred to the rule of recognition as a 'judicial customary rule': Hart, *The Concept of Law* (n 18) 256; see also Hart, *Essays on Bentham* (n 37) 156.

[48] Hart, *The Concept of Law* (n 18) 55, 57.

[49] ibid 56.

[50] This is what Hart dubs the 'internal aspect of rules': see ibid 56–57, 116.

[51] ibid 55–57.

[52] ibid 111.

(5) The standard identifies other standards[53] and places officials under a duty to apply those standards when acting in their official roles.[54]

Since (5) is closely tailored to the nature of the rule of recognition, a different type of element would be needed for customary law such as the royal prerogative.

I will propose an alternative account of customary law. It takes as its starting point the fact that there are legal doctrines like the doctrine of precedent and the royal prerogative that are not validated by any other legal standard in common law systems, and asks what makes them legal standards as opposed to non-legal standards for officials. An account along these lines looks like this:[55]

A standard *S* constitutes customary law (*in foro*) in legal system *L* if:
(1) *S* is used in official practices in *L*;
(2) *S* is used as an *authoritative* standard in official practices in *L* (e.g. as an authoritative duty-imposing, power-conferring, disability-creating, or immunity-granting, etc, standard);
(3) *S*'s use as an authoritative standard in official practices in *L* is not due to its being validated by another legal standard *R*; and
(4) *S* is used as an authoritative standard in the reasoning of judicial decisions in *L*, independently of other legal standards.

This approach has a number of virtues. It locates customary law firmly in the practices of officials. It does not make any claims to be a general account of customary standards that might be found in non-legal settings (or at least in non-institutional settings). And it relates the legal status of such customary standards to the features that they share with other legal standards.

Let me consider each element in turn. The first simply requires that the standard is actually used in official practice, that is, by officials in the performance of their official roles. As *S* is a customary standard its existence depends upon being practised by officials. If officials stop using the standard, it ceases to be a legal standard. Unlike validated standard, which exist in the system if they satisfy some criteria of validation, whether or not they are practised (unless being practised is one of the criteria of validation), non-validated standards must be practised in order to exist as part of the system.

But official use plays an additional role, in helping to determine the content of *S*. A standard may be used explicitly or implicitly in the practice of officials. They may state that they are following the standard in question, describing it in some way, whether very generally or in more detail. Alternatively, their conduct may rely on the standard without it being referred to, with it simply being assumed in what officials are doing. What matters in the end is how the officials *understand* what they are doing. Would they (at least on reflection) understand their conduct to be guided by standard *S*; and if so, what is the content of that standard? If their conduct *is* guided by *S*, then it will be possible to explain to a new official joining an ongoing practice that the practice involves following *S*. It may not always be

---

[53] ibid.

[54] ibid 115–16, 235–36 and Hart, *Essays on Bentham* (n 37) 155–56, 160.

[55] This account obviously assumes that a satisfactory account can be given of 'legal systems' and 'officials'. For an earlier attempt to characterize customary law *in foro*, see G Lamond, 'Legal Sources, the Rule of Recognition, and Customary Law' (2014) 59 Am J Juris 25, 43–47.

possible to explain very precisely the content of S, but those involved in a practice will still have a sense that the practice requires S to be followed, as opposed to their conduct simply being what tends to be done in certain circumstances. Legal practices, like institutional practices generally, are highly articulated and self-conscious practices, and so participants are (ordinarily) well aware of what is required by the practice and what is not. They are also normally able to give some formulation of the standards that they are following. A verbal formulation of S helps to capture its content, but understanding S requires an appreciation of how S applies to particular circumstances. This explains the attention paid to what officials have done in following the standard: it helps to give the standard its content. (What officials have 'done' includes what they have *said* when they are doing what they are doing: both are relevant to helping to understand the content of S.) What matters in the end, therefore, is that officials understand themselves to be following a common standard S, and that their individual understandings of S overlap sufficiently.

The second element of the account of customary law is that the standard is used as an *authoritative* standard in the practice of officials. What does this mean? That a standard is authoritative means that there is (believed to be) (sufficient) reason to apply it independently of the decision-makers' views of the merits of the standard, that is, whether or not they regard it as a desirable standard to have. It is a characteristic feature of legal standards that they are authoritative in this way. Not all standards followed by officials are regarded as authoritative. The most obvious example are the standards that officials endorse purely because they believe them to be desirable. For example, officials may think that judges should give judgment in their cases within a reasonable time. This may be reflected in official practice, for example in judgments generally being delivered in this time frame, and in the criticism of judges who exceed it. Whether such a standard is part of the law depends upon *why* it is used by officials. If it used simply because the officials who rely on it think it is desirable for the health of the legal system to act in such ways, then it is not an authoritative standard. Were the officials to come to the view that it was better to have accurate decisions than speedy decisions, then it would no longer be followed.[56] In addition, an individual judge will regard themselves as at liberty to depart from the common view. They will be criticized by their colleagues for doing so and for not appreciating the importance of speedy justice, but not for acting against the law. But if the requirement is regarded as authoritative, then it is to be followed by officials whether or not they agree with the merits of the consideration. A failure to follow it involves a failure to act as officials legally should.[57]

What determines whether the standard is authoritative is how the officials treat the standard. This is a further way in which official practice is relevant to customary law. If there is some question over whether a standard is a legal standard or simply a widely endorsed view, officials will examine their practice to ascertain why it has been followed. If officials have treated the standard as applicable to them in their official activities, irrespective of its merits, then it will be regarded as authoritative. What matters, then, is whether officials have treated those who depart from the standard as simply wrong about its merits, or have regarded the standard as applicable to others independently of its merits. In some cases it may not be clear which approach has been taken. After all, if officials think that a standard *is*

---

[56] The view, apparently, of Lord Eldon in the Court of Chancery at the start of the nineteenth century: see 'Scott, John, Lord Eldon' in DM Walker, *The Oxford Companion to Law* (OUP 1980) 1120.

[57] Assuming, of course, that the other elements for customary law are satisfied. This requirement might instead amount to a judicial *convention*: authoritative but non-legal. See the later discussion of element (4) and constitutional conventions.

meritorious, they are very likely to point this out, and so it may be unclear whether it is *also* regarded as applicable independently of its merits. So although the distinction between authoritative and non-authoritative standards is clear in principle, it may be difficult to determine in practice. This underlines another important point. That a standard is regarded as authoritative, that is, as applicable independently of its merits, does not exclude it from *also* being regarded as meritorious. It is simply that its authoritativeness is regarded as a sufficient reason for using it, whatever its merits.[58]

The third element in the account is the obvious point that the use of the standard as an authoritative standard in the practices of officials is not due to the standard being validated by another legal standard. Customary law is a form of law whose use does not depend on validation.[59] This last point, while self-evident, is often obscured in the common law. It can sometimes seem as if there is no customary law *in foro*, save perforce the ultimate criteria of validity. The reason for this is that such customary law is often described as part of the 'common law', and it is supposed that the common law means the law based on precedent, as opposed to the law based on statute. But there are in fact two different senses of the 'common law' here. 'Common law' may mean case law, that is, the law based on precedent. But 'common law' may also mean 'non-statutory law', which includes, but is not exhausted by, case law. Such non-statutory common law includes both case law and customary law. The thought that customary law is a form of case law also owes something to its use in judicial decision-making. Sometimes customary law is relied upon implicitly, for example when it is taken for granted that the royal prerogative is law, and the only question is whether some issue falls within the scope of a prerogative power. Sometimes it is relied upon explicitly, for example where a court justifies its decision on the basis of the 'inherent jurisdiction' of the courts.[60] When a court explicitly justifies its decision on a customary legal doctrine, the case provides 'authority' for the existence of that doctrine, but the decision does not create or establish the underlying doctrine. The decision merely acknowledges its existence.[61] It is 'authority' for the doctrine in the sense that it is a clear example of its existence, rather than because it puts the doctrine on a case law footing. On the other hand, if it is uncertain whether or not a standard has been used as an authoritative standard (element (2)), then a court considering the issue may resolve the question by ruling one way or the other. In this situation, the status of the standard will henceforth be determined by the court's ruling, and whether it is law will now turn on precedent rather than custom.

The fourth element addresses the fact that customary law only exists when it is used as an authoritative standard in the reasoning of judicial decisions. The ultimate criteria for various sources of law, for instance, are treated by the courts as authoritative. Other officials also use these criteria as authoritative standards in identifying the rules they are to apply.[62] In the case of the royal prerogative, non-judicial officials exercise various rights and powers, and the courts treat those exercises as creating enforceable rights and duties. But not all authoritative

---

[58] The merits of the standard also matter for questions of whether the standard should be expanded or whether it should be understood more narrowly.

[59] Note that even if, coincidentally, the standard *does* satisfy the criteria of validity in another legal standard, the question is whether the officials regard that as the basis for following it, or simply consider it to be incidental.

[60] For a classic discussion of inherent jurisdiction, see IH Jacob, 'The Inherent Jurisdiction of the Court' (1970) 1 CLP 23.

[61] e.g. *R v Forbes, ex p Bevan* (1972) 127 CLR 1, 7 (Menzies J) (High Court of Australia).

[62] The relationship between the practices of judicial and non-judicial officials over criteria of validity is discussed in more detail in Lamond, 'The Rule of Recognition and the Foundations of a Legal System' (n 18) 108–10. It is important to emphasize that the functioning of a legal system depends upon non-judicial as well as judicial officials using the criteria of validity.

official practices amount to customary law. Constitutional conventions (as they are understood in the UK and many Commonwealth jurisdictions) are regarded as binding by officials in their official roles, but are not used in judicial reasoning as authoritative standards.[63] Equally, the rules governing parliamentary practice in the UK (the *lex parliamentaria*) are not amenable to judicial scrutiny.[64] It is, of course, possible for *other* laws to require the courts to use constitutional conventions or the *lex parliamentaria* in reaching a decision. But the law can direct courts to use any set of standards in this way (e.g. the rules of an association): it does not turn those standards into law.[65]

On this account, then, the doctrine of precedent is part of the customary law *in foro* of common law systems because: (1) it is used in the practice of officials (providing the criteria for the *rationes* of cases that officials follow and apply); (2) it is used as an authoritative standard in those practices; (3) it is not validated by another legal standard; and (4) it is used as an authoritative standard within judicial decision-making. In effect, the doctrine of precedent is both a duty-applying and a constitutive standard: it constitutes other standards as those to be applied by officials.[66]

How does the account of customary law *in foro* bear on an understanding of the rule of recognition? From the point of view of the rule of recognition, the doctrine of precedent provides one of the criteria of validity for standards that are binding on officials. So it is part of the rule of recognition. But the preceding account of customary law casts doubt on the idea that the rule of recognition is a single (albeit internally complex) standard. The laws of a legal system are composed of both customary and validated standards, including customary standards (such as some parts of the royal prerogative and the inherent jurisdiction of superior courts) that do *not* provide criteria of validity. The fundamental appeal of the idea that there is a single rule of recognition, on the other hand, lies in the thought that the laws of a system are exhaustively composed of the rule of recognition and all of the standards validated (directly or indirectly) by the criteria in the rule of recognition. On this picture, the rule of recognition gives the law its internal unity.[67] But if one concedes that there can be other instances of customary law *in foro* besides the ultimate criteria of validity, then the rule of recognition does not play this unifying role. So there is no need to combine the different ultimate criteria of validity (plus the rules for resolving conflicts between standards validated by different ultimate criteria) into a single rule. Instead, each ultimate criteria of validity can be regarded as a separate rule of recognition, with additional customary and validated legal

---

[63] See N Barber, *The United Kingdom Constitution: An Introduction* (OUP 2021) ch 6. Constitutional conventions can, however, be used in ancillary ways: see F Ahmed, R Albert, and A Perry, 'Judging Constitutional Conventions' (2019) 17 Int'l J Const L 787.

[64] There is some argument that the status of the *lex parliamentaria* today rests on art 9 of the Bill of Rights 1689, restating the 'privileges' of Parliament. But even if this is so, art 9 does not cover all of the privileges of Parliament. On parliamentary privilege generally, see Barber (n 63) 46–53.

[65] Note that whilst element (3) emphasizes that customary law is not *validated* by another legal standard—i.e. does not owe its status as law to another legal standard—element (4) emphasizes that customary law is used in judicial decision-making as a self-sufficient basis for reaching a decision, rather than being used as the result of another law directing its use. A further refinement to (4), which I cannot develop here, is that a customary legal standard may be *non-justiciable*, i.e. unenforceable in court. So it may be that a standard amounts to customary law *in foro* because it *would be* used in the decision-making of the courts, absent another legal doctrine requiring courts not to do so.

[66] On constitutive standards, see E Bulygin, 'On Norms of Competence' in his *Essays in Legal Philosophy* (OUP 2015) and A Marmor, *Social Conventions* (Princeton UP 2009) 31–36.

[67] See Hart, *The Concept of Law* (n 18) 95, 233–36. Hart also relies on there being standards for resolving conflicts between laws from different sources as a ground for speaking of a single rule of recognition: Hart, *Essays in Jurisprudence and Philosophy* (n 38) 360. But this does not seem to be as significant as the unifying aspect. For arguments in favour of Hart's view (and against other objections to the unity of the rule of recognition), see MH Kramer, *HLA Hart: The Nature of Law* (Polity Press 2018) 84–91.

standards to deal with issues such as how to resolve conflicts between laws.[68] What unifies the legal system must be sought elsewhere, for instance in the relationship between the law-applying institutions (including courts) that use the customary and validated standards that make up the law.[69]

4. Conclusion

The doctrine of precedent in the common law involves both the law-creating role of the decisions of superior courts and the varied powers of those courts to overrule earlier decisions. This chapter has focused on the law-creating aspect of the doctrine, and considered what light Hart's rule of recognition can shed on precedent, and what light can be shed on the rule of recognition by the doctrine of precedent. It has defended the idea that precedents create law by virtue of satisfying one of the ultimate criteria of validity in common law systems, as Hart proposed. It has also argued that the rule of recognition amounts to customary law *in foro*, and not simply to a social rule of officials. Finally, it has argued that the existence of customary laws *in foro* besides the rule of recognition supports the idea that there can be multiple rules of recognition in a legal system—one for each ultimate source of law.

[68] Note three points here: (1) conflict resolution standards are not criteria of validity but defeating conditions, e.g. the Law Reform (Year and a Day Rule) Act 1996 (UK) abolished the common law doctrine that to be guilty of homicide a victim must die within a year and a day of the act causing death, but only from 1996; (2) some conflicts can occur between laws from the same source, as well as laws from different sources; and (3) some conflict resolution standards are not customary law, e.g. the UK standards over conflicts between 'constitutional' statutes and other statutes is a case law doctrine: see *R (HS2 Alliance) v Secretary of State for Transport* [2014] UKSC 3.

[69] Raz suggests something along these lines in *Practical Reason and Norms* (n 47) 147.

3

On the Nature of *Stare Decisis*

Sebastian Lewis[*]

1. Introduction

The question of why courts in the common law must follow precedent can be analysed from two different but ultimately complementary approaches. Someone could say, first, that courts must follow precedent because they have a duty to give effect to the law—and precedents, or at least many of them, are sources of law. Assuming that legal sources are capable of producing binding legal requirements, it follows that whenever a later court is confronted with a relevant precedent the court is confronted with relevant law. The court must therefore follow precedent just because its duty is to give effect to the law. The question, secondly, can also be approached by identifying specific moral values that can ground sufficiently strong moral reasons for following precedent. Consider Gerald Postema:

> What accounts for the moral force of precedent? My project is to explain in moral terms why we believe that the fact that a decision of a certain sort was taken in the past provides a sound reason for reaching a similar decision in the situation currently facing us.[1]

On this view, if the advancement of specific moral values is important enough to ground a judicial obligation to follow precedent, then we have a second, moral answer to our question. Crucially, a judicial obligation to follow precedent might be justified on moral grounds, even if the law does not make it legally obligatory that judges follow precedent. Conversely, the law may place courts under a legal obligation to follow precedent, even if that is not what the later court (morally) ought to do. Hence the two conceptually distinct, but ultimately complementary, approaches to the question under analysis. In the former, what grounds judicial duty is a *legal* obligation, and that is why I will call this approach 'juridical'. In the latter that duty is *moral* and not necessarily legal; accordingly, I shall call this approach 'moral'.

Although this view may sound familiar, it is not uncontroversial. Proponents of a new and distinctive approach to jurisprudence, namely the so-called 'one-system view',[2] might disagree with the analysis just sketched. Roughly, under the one-system view, a question of law (e.g. about legal rights and obligations) should be understood as a moral question, that is, as a question that ought to be answered on moral grounds. Since the law is, on this view, conceived of as a subset of political morality,[3] it follows that an individual's rights and obligations under the law are crucially a subset of her rights and obligations under political

---

[*] I would like to thank Jeremy Waldron, Nina Varsava, Hillary Nye, Timothy Endicott, Fábio Shecaira, and Paolo Sandro, for excellent comments on previous versions of this chapter, and participants of the international workshop for this collection.

[1] G Postema, 'On the Moral Value of Our Past' (1991) 36 McGill LJ 1153, 1158.

[2] As opposed to the 'two-systems' view that R Dworkin, *Justice for Hedgehogs* (Harvard UP 2011) ch 19 firmly rejects.

[3] ibid 405.

Sebastian Lewis, *On the Nature of* Stare Decisis In: *Philosophical Foundations of Precedent*. Edited by: Timothy Endicott, Hafsteinn Dan Kristjánsson, and Sebastian Lewis, Oxford University Press. © Sebastian Lewis 2023. DOI: 10.1093/oso/9780192857248.003.0004

morality.[4] Proponents of this view might object that, by treating the moral and juridical approaches as conceptually different and metaphysically independent, I have treated law and morality as separate domains, whereas they are in fact part of the same domain.

I will address this objection in section 4. Before doing so, I will offer, in sections 2 and 3, an interpretation of *stare decisis* that benefits from distinguishing the moral and juridical approaches. I will argue that these approaches provide a full grasp of *stare decisis*: while the moral approach offers the basic moral input to justify *stare decisis*, the juridical approach conceptualizes the legal output created by the law.[5] Both approaches are necessary to get a full grasp of *stare decisis*. The moral approach is not enough, for it does not tell us much about one essential feature of legal practice—that many courts (particularly in the common law) follow precedent *because* it is the law. Likewise, common law lawyers look for precedents because their *rationes* constitute legal authorities supporting a particular decision. The juridical approach, on the other hand, does not tell us much about *why* these courts and lawyers do what they do. Crucially, the moral approach cannot, by itself, account for central features of *stare decisis*, such as the rules on vertical and horizontal precedent, the distinction between the *ratio decidendi* and *obiter dicta*, and the grounds on which courts may overrule otherwise binding precedent. These are central features of precedent-following that any account should accommodate—thus, I am not making an arbitrary selection of the data.[6]

2. The Moral and Juridical Approaches

The common law literature on precedent has traditionally focused on two questions: first, what moral values, if any, justify placing courts under an obligation to follow precedent? Secondly, granted that case law constitutes a source of law, and that certain precedents might thus give rise to binding legal requirements, how should we understand the constraining effect of precedent?

The first type of inquiry typically aims to justify (sometimes merely to evaluate without necessarily endorsing) the practice of precedent in the common law—particularly vis-à-vis its counterpart in the civil law. On the cliché (increasingly being undermined by important legal reforms),[7] precedents in the civil law tradition are not sources of law,[8] and thus later courts are not legally bound by precedent. If many civil law jurisdictions share this specific, non-binding practice of precedent, then arguably there are good reasons for it. Some of these reasons were well known to legal philosophers working in the common law tradition, such as Thomas Hobbes, Jeremy Bentham, and John Austin.[9] How can we then explain the common

---

[4] ibid 404–05.

[5] I have borrowed the expressions 'moral input' and 'legal output' from E Monti, 'On the Moral Impact Theory of Law' (2022) 42 OJLS 298, 301, who refers to the debate between legal positivism and natural law theories as involving two different questions—one of 'legal input' and another of 'legal output'.

[6] In the common law literature on precedent, the methodological constraint imposed by practice is often known as the 'minimum descriptive requirement'. It was arguably G Lamond, 'Do Precedents Create Rules?' (2005) 11 Legal Theory 1, 15, who first warned about the fundamental constraint imposed by the practice of distinguishing on any account of precedent-following in the common law. This minimum descriptive requirement has been endorsed, among others, by A Rigoni, 'Common-Law Judicial Reasoning and Analogy' (2014) 20 Legal Theory 133, 135 and K Stevens, 'Reasoning by Precedent—Between Rules and Analogies' (2018) 24 Legal Theory 216, 219.

[7] See, e.g., new legislation passed in Mexico on 11 March 2021, amending art 94 of the Mexican Constitution. According to the amended constitutional provision, the reasons supporting a decision adopted by eight judges of a Plenary Supreme Court (or by four judges sitting as a Supreme Court Chamber) are binding upon all federal jurisdictional authorities and federal entities.

[8] See, e.g., JH Merryman and R Pérez-Cardozo, *The Civil Law Tradition* (4th edn, Stanford UP 2019) 23.

[9] See, e.g., N Duxbury, *The Nature and Authority of Precedent* (CUP 2008) 17.

law's robust idea of precedential constraint? And we can find a generous menu of values supporting *stare decisis*,[10] from rule-of-law accounts stressing the values of stability, reliance, equality, and so on,[11] to epistemic defences of precedent,[12] and Dworkinian integrity.[13] We can also add Randy Kozel's 'second-best' approach to *stare decisis* to the list—precedent facilitates convergence of judges who are deeply divided in law, morality, and politics.[14] I will return to some of these values in section 3.

The point is that, except perhaps for the case of Ronald Dworkin—for whom moral and legal practice are on a continuum[15]—those moral values, which give rise to moral reasons, can remain intelligible without the need to collapse them into legal values—giving rise to legal reasons. Put differently, there can be moral values triggering moral reasons—and eventually grounding a moral obligation to follow precedent—even if the law remains silent or prohibits courts from following precedent. That moral input can exist regardless of whether it is legally recognized by law. Admittedly, at some point that moral input—if it is going to give rise to a widespread and systemic judicial practice—will most likely receive legal recognition. And then the reasons for following precedent will be moral and legal. But the point is that a moral answer to the question of why certain courts must follow precedent is intelligible without the need for appealing to the rather uninformative answer 'because precedents are part of the law'. Call this the 'moral approach'.

The second type of inquiry, which I call the 'juridical approach', usually accepts (or takes for granted) that precedents are sources of law, and that they are thus capable of producing binding legal requirements. The question is not so much about the values that justify *stare decisis* but about how best to capture and conceptualize the constraining effect that, in virtue of *stare decisis*, precedents have. Thereby the juridical approach seeks to understand other crucial aspects of adjudication according to precedent. For example, what is the part of a precedent that binds later courts? How should that part, namely the *ratio decidendi*, be both defined and determined?[16] How should we account for the normative but not binding effect of a *dictum*? 'Do Precedents [borrowing the title of Grant Lamond's seminal essay] Create Rules?'[17] What is the relation between precedential reasoning and analogical reasoning?[18] And so on. Assuming that precedents are sources of law, how can this reality (its central features and practical consequences) be usefully conceptualized?

Now I want to be careful in one thing. I am not suggesting that authors grouped under the juridical approach think that the obligation to follow precedent cannot be explained in moral terms. They may well think so. Likewise, I am not suggesting that these authors think that this obligation is ultimately *legal*, not moral. They may well think that such an obligation is ultimately moral and not legal. The point, again, is that the project underlying the juridical approach is very different from the evaluative inquiry concerning what justifies *stare decisis*. For the juridical approach, there is no need to tackle the moral question since there is already

---

[10] For an excellent study, see N Varsava, 'How to Realize the Value of *Stare Decisis*: Options for following Precedent' (2018) 30 Yale J Law & Humanities 62.

[11] I myself have argued for this view elsewhere; see S Lewis, 'Precedent and the Rule of Law' (2021) 41 OJLS 873.

[12] See, e.g., D Hellman, 'An Epistemic Defense of Precedent' in CJ Peters (ed), *Precedent in the United States Supreme Court* (Springer 2013) ch 4.

[13] See, e.g., S Hershovitz, 'Integrity and *Stare Decisis*' in S Hershovitz (ed), *Exploring Law's Empire: The Jurisprudence of Ronald Dworkin* (OUP 2006) ch 5.

[14] RJ Kozel, *Settled vs Right: A Theory of Precedent* (CUP 2017).

[15] A point which I will further elaborate in section 4.

[16] For an excellent discussion, see Duxbury (n 9) 67–92.

[17] Lamond (n 6).

[18] See the contributions to this volume by Luís Duarte d'Almeida (Chapter 10), Cass Sunstein (Chapter 17), and Frederick Schauer and Barbara A Spellman (Chapter 18).

38 SEBASTIAN LEWIS

a workable answer at hand. It is a brute fact from the reality of the common law that precedents, in general, constitute sources of law. Courts must follow precedent because it is part
of their duty to give effect to the law. Why should we care about the moral question if there
are plenty of other equally challenging problems ahead? In fact, the moral question is for the
most part not even asked. If the question does bubble up, it is many times for the sake of intellectual rigour—which can be safely met by providing a working assumption, as Katharina
Stevens does:

> I will assume that if the use of the doctrine of binding precedent is justified, then that is be-
> cause it produces a balance between stability and flexibility in the development of the law,
> and that such a balance would in fact justify adopting the doctrine of binding precedent.[19]

Thereby, Stevens argues in favour of the analogical approach—that is, that it can be amended
to allow later courts to receive as much precedential constraint as they do under the rule-
based approach. But, again, there is no need for Stevens to argue in support of a moral obligation to follow precedent: a *legal* obligation already exists or is assumed to exist. This legal
obligation can be grounded in customary legal practice, as the work of Brian Simpson would
suggest,[20] or in any other legal source, such as statutory law. Thus, whatever the ultimate nature of the obligation to follow precedent—moral or otherwise—the reality of the common
law already provides a working answer to our question. Courts have a legal obligation to
follow precedent because they have a duty to give effect to the law—and precedents constitute, in general, sources of law. Since courts have this legal obligation—regardless of its moral
merits—let us focus on understanding the constraining effect of precedent in the common
law. That is, in a nutshell, what I have in mind with the juridical approach.

3. The Legal Doctrine of *Stare Decisis*

In this section I offer an interpretation of *stare decisis*. I argue that the moral and juridical
approaches are both indispensable for getting a full picture of *stare decisis*. While the moral
approach, on the one hand, provides the basic moral input for justifying *stare decisis*, the
juridical approach, on the other, aims to conceptualize the legal output created by the law on
the basis of the moral input. To be sure, I shall not make any historical claim whatsoever on
the chronology of *stare decisis*—in England or elsewhere. I remain agnostic as to the historic
point of whether the justification of *stare decisis* came before or after courts started practising
this doctrine.[21]

A. Moral Input

Stare decisis needs justification—and constant justification—if it is to appear legitimate
in the eyes of law's subjects. Consider two recent examples showing the major systemic

---

[19] Stevens (n 6) 219.
[20] To be sure, according to Simpson the common law (with its distinctive approach to precedent) forms a body
of customary legal practice. See AWB Simpson, 'The Common Law and Legal Theory' in W Twining (ed), *Legal
Theory and Common Law* (Basil Blackwell 1986) 20.
[21] For an overview of the history of *stare decisis*, See Duxbury (n 9) ch 2.

implications of having a system of *stare decisis*. In the UK, the Supreme Court recently changed the legal status of thousands of workers by declaring that Uber drivers are 'workers' under the Employment Rights Act 1996—and thus entitled to statutory rights.[22] And in the US, as it is well known, the reproductive rights of thousands of women suffered major changes after the Supreme Court decided to overrule *Roe v Wade*.[23]

By setting binding precedents, courts affect the content of the law, sometimes intentionally and other times as a by-product.[24] Thereby, courts have the power to affect the legal rights and obligations of people who are not parties to a dispute. This striking feature demands constant justification. Why does a very small group of non-elected officials, who often come from a highly privileged and unrepresentative part of society, have the power to affect the legal rights and obligations of people who are not parties to a dispute? Does a court with such a power have both the institutional capacity and democratic pedigree to affect the content of the law by handing down binding precedents? What if the court gets things wrong? Do we have to bear the costs of the court's mistake until Parliament repeals the bad precedent—or a court with sufficient power overrules it? And who bears the economic costs of litigation aimed at repealing a decision that causes 'judicial regret'—as Rupert Cross and Jim Harris would put it?[25]

These are important questions. Hence, the moral approach aiming to justify *stare decisis* on moral grounds. To be sure, these questions raise fundamental concerns—moral, political, and otherwise. As such, a juridical answer providing that 'courts must follow precedent because they have a duty to give effect to the law' is as unsatisfactory as it is misplaced. We need non-legal reasons supporting *stare decisis*. Only then can we start giving legal shape to this striking practice. Typically those reasons include: (a) epistemic considerations—later courts may receive useful epistemic guidance from precedent; (b) efficiency reasons—a legal system can better allocate resources (particularly spend less time) when judges rely on precedent instead of reinventing the wheel; (c) pragmatic considerations—deferring to precedent is a way to avoid substantive first-order disagreement between judges; and (d) moral reasons—like cases can be treated alike, Dworkinian integrity demands institutional consistency with the past, and the rule of law can be advanced by precedent-following. The literature is vast.

I have always tended to pay more attention to the moral reasons supporting *stare decisis*—and to the moral reasons *against* this practice—than to those other considerations mentioned previously. It is not that I think those other considerations are not important; it is only that I think we have second-order reasons suggesting we should pay more attention to moral reasons. 'Justice [writes John Rawls] is the first virtue of social institutions, as truth is of systems of thought. A theory however elegant and economical must be rejected or revised if it is untrue; likewise laws and institutions no matter how efficient and well-arranged must be reformed or abolished if they are unjust.'[26] This is a remarkable opening by Rawls, which captures very nicely the thought of those of us who give priority to morality in the evaluation of social institutions—and, if I may add, of social practices as well. That is why, in what follows, I would like to focus exclusively on the moral reasons supporting the practice of *stare decisis*.

As said, these moral reasons usually include the maxim that like cases should be treated alike, Dworkinian integrity, and rule-of-law values such as stability, reliability, and equality

---

[22] *Uber BV v Aslam* [2021] UKSC 5.
[23] *Dobbs v Jackson Women's Health Organization*, No. 19-1392, 597 U.S. ___ (2022).
[24] See, e.g., Lamond (n 6) 25; J Gardner, *Law as a Leap of Faith* (OUP 2012) 79–81; and the contribution to this volume by Hafsteinn Dan Kristjánsson (Chapter 6).
[25] R Cross and JW Harris, *Precedent in English Law* (4th edn, Clarendon Press 1991) 36.
[26] J Rawls, *A Theory of Justice* (Harvard UP 1971) 3.

in the application of the law. As a principle of morality, however, the maxim of like cases has been severely criticized.[27] Also, as David Lyons and Frederick Schauer have argued,[28] this principle does not provide a solid foundation for *stare decisis* either. Dworkinian integrity, on the other hand, may be an attractive idea—for its emphasis on equal treatment and political consistency.[29] But even setting aside the fact that Dworkinian integrity is a contested theory of law,[30] Dworkin's one-system view (favoured, if not entailed,[31] by law-as-integrity) is also hard to reconcile with the central features of *stare decisis*—a point I shall articulate in section 4.

So we are left with the rule-of-law values of legal stability, reliability, and equality in the application of the law—the latter should be understood as a moral constraint on the exercise of lawful discretion by judges.[32] Possibly the wisest approach to justifying *stare decisis* on these values acknowledges a *ceteris paribus* caveat: all else being equal, *stare decisis* is a distinctive means for advancing these moral values.[33] At the same time, these values impose constraints on how judges should set precedents *today*—that is, the so-called 'forward-looking' aspect of precedent.[34] But does this *ceteris-paribus* advancement justify *stare decisis*? What about the moral costs of this practice, such as the possibility of entrenching morally deficient decisions in the law? Notice also that there are political and institutional objections to *stare decisis*. Judges, who often are non-elected officials, are given the power to create (again, intentionally or as a by-product) law of general application with major systemic consequences—see the two decisions mentioned earlier. And it is also debatable whether courts have the proper institutional capacity to undertake this law-creating task—a point which was acknowledged by the House of Lords when dealing with the Human Rights Act 1998.[35] So the question is: do the moral values outweigh the moral costs?

A thought experiment might help to elucidate. Suppose you are in a situation akin to Rawls' original position,[36] and you are asked to design a legal system from scratch. By virtue of the veil of ignorance, you don't know anything about the culture that has shaped your legal, moral, and political mindset. Would you argue in favour of implementing *stare decisis* as a general rule? If so, courts would have a *general* obligation to follow precedent—the obligation is general because not every court is bound by precedent; and while every court can

---

[27] See, e.g., P Westen, 'The Empty Idea of Equality' (1982) 95 Harv L Rev 537.

[28] D Lyons, 'Formal Justice and Judicial Precedent' (1985) 38 Vand L Rev 495; F Schauer, 'On Treating Unlike Cases Alike' (2018) 33 Const Commentary 437.

[29] See R Dworkin, *Law's Empire* (Harvard UP 1986) chs 6 and 7.

[30] Not everyone agrees with the claim that 'propositions of law are true if they figure in or follow from the principles of justice, fairness, and procedural due process that provide the best constructive interpretation of the community's legal practice' (ibid 225).

[31] cf C Crummey, 'One-System Integrity and the Legal Domain of Morality' (2022) Legal Theory (online version).

[32] A point which I have elaborated in Lewis (n 11) 883–84.

[33] Accordingly, a *ceteris paribus* caveat acknowledges that there might be cases in which following precedent will *not* advance the values of *stare decisis*. cf Lyons (n 28) 511–12; F Schauer, 'Precedent' (1987) 39 Stan L Rev 571, 597–98; Duxbury (n 9) 163 and S Lewis, 'Towards a general practice of precedent' (2022) Jurisprudence (online version).

[34] On which, see discussions by N MacCormick, *Legal Reasoning and Legal Theory* (rev edn, Clarendon Press 1994) ch IV; Schauer, 'Precedent' (n 33) 572–75; J Waldron, '*Stare Decisis* and the Rule of Law: A Layered Approach' (2012) 111 Mich L Rev 1; K Stevens, 'Setting Precedents Without Making Norms?' (2020) 39 Law and Philosophy 577. In her contribution to this volume (Chapter 21), Nina Varsava argues that it is not only past judicial decisions that can ground obligations but also judges' reasonable predictions of *future* judicial decisions.

[35] *Ghaidan v Godin-Mendoza* [2004] UKHL 30. According to the Law Lords, UK courts cannot, under s 3(1) of the Human Rights Act 1998, interpret Convention rights in a way 'for which they are not equipped' insofar as that requires 'legislative deliberation' [33] (Lord Nicholls).

[36] Rawls (n 26) ch 3.

distinguish precedent,[37] only some of them may overrule it. Or would you rather consider a hybrid approach—one where the obligation to follow precedent is both targeted (for certain courts only) and piecemeal (for certain areas of law)? Perhaps you would consider inverting the default rule, as happens in many civilian jurisdictions, where courts are not obliged to follow precedent unless doing so is expressly required by law.

In Rawls' original position, it is debatable whether *stare decisis* would be chosen as the general rule. But the common law is an ongoing reality; thus, the threshold for not wanting *stare decisis* is more demanding vis-à-vis Rawls' original position. There are significant costs associated with stopping the machine—that is, with changing or abolishing *stare decisis* in the common law. There is, to begin with, a cost in general reliance—people and officials already know that courts adjudicate under *stare decisis*. And arguably there are important costs (economic, institutional, and otherwise) associated with codifying common law rules. It is a reality that in systems where *stare decisis* does not exist codification tends to be the general rule. If judges are to stop receiving authoritative guidance from precedent, then they must get it elsewhere. The natural candidate appears to be codification—for its virtues of democratic pedigree, systematicity, and clarity, among others.[38] The costs associated with stopping the machine in order to effect major changes in the legal system (to change or abolish *stare decisis*, again a reality of the common law) thus invert the *onus*. If *stare decisis* is to be abolished or otherwise changed, then this must be so in virtue of very compelling arguments. Yet none of the arguments canvased so far (e.g. lack of both democratic pedigree and institutional capacity, entrenchment of morally deficient decisions in the law, etc) warrant this major change. The upshot is that the common law can tolerate these costs and move on with a non-ideal, perfectible *stare decisis*. The benefits of *stare decisis* outweigh the costs given the heightened burden for changing the *status quo*.

In this justificatory process, *stare decisis* receives fundamental moral input. Yet that moral input is not enough, by itself, to make *stare decisis* a workable and effective practice within a complex, modern legal system. Consider the distinction between the *ratio decidendi* and *obiter dicta*—the former being the binding part of a precedent, the latter its non-essential part, which can nevertheless be treated as persuasive by later courts. As Neil Duxbury observes:

> If, within the common law tradition, the distinction between *ratio decidendi* and *obiter dicta* was not recognized, judges would be able to create a more or less unlimited amount of new law and courts would be overwhelmed by precedent; everything within a previous decision—and not necessarily just the decision on materially identical facts—would be potentially relevant to the case at hand.[39]

Without the help of the *ratio/obiter* distinction, *stare decisis* would face some serious practical difficulties in accomplishing what it has promised to deliver. Consider another example, the rules of vertical and horizontal *stare decisis*. It is plausible to think that the moral values advanced by *stare decisis* do not, in principle, require a strict separation between vertical and horizontal *stare decisis*. Put differently, these moral values do not themselves tell us, for instance, that the precedents of lower courts are not to be binding upon higher courts, but that the reverse holds. Another, final example—I shall elaborate these claims in section 3.B.

---

[37] A point made long ago by J Raz, *The Authority of Law* (2nd edn, OUP 2009) 186.
[38] cf P Yowell, 'Legislation, Common Law, and the Virtue of Clarity' in R Ekins (ed), *Modern Challenges to the Rule of Law* (LexisNexis 2011) 121.
[39] Duxbury (n 9) 90. See also N Duxbury, *The Intricacies of Dicta and Dissent* (CUP 2021) 5.

The specific grounds on which courts can overrule precedent. We know that it is part and parcel of the idea of a binding precedent that it takes more than a good ground for a court to overrule it. That good ground must be *legally* recognized. For example, the House of Lords 1966 Practice Statement allowed that court to depart from precedent when 'it appears right to do so'. And the limited instances in which the highest court (today the Supreme Court) has overruled precedent[40] are judicial (and thereby legal) instantiations of the meaning of this provision. Again, the moral values of *stare decisis* do not themselves tell us on which specific grounds courts may overrule precedent. Do these moral values require the Supreme Court to overrule precedent only when it appears 'right to do so'? The answer to this question is left for a later stage of specification.

B. Legal Output

In order for a legal system to work out the moral input in a coordinated and effective way, we need what Maris Köpcke has recently called 'specific convergence'. According to Köpcke:

> Specific convergence is required, as a matter of justice, where some needed state of affairs is most appropriately brought about through the convergent conduct of a large number of persons, and that conduct could in principle follow any one of several available and appropriate but incompatible patterns.[41]

Consider again the distinction between vertical and horizontal precedent. It is a central feature of *stare decisis* that later courts are only bound by the precedents of higher courts and of courts of coordinated jurisdiction. Conversely, higher courts are never bound by lower court precedent. But does this distinction respond to *moral* value?[42] Take the rule-of-law values of stability, reliability, and equality—often, as we saw, supporting *stare decisis*. Do these moral values recommend implementing a strict separation between vertical and horizontal precedent? Surely if the lower courts have constantly upheld a particular doctrine, and if they have thus promoted the values of stability and reliability, there can be situations where a higher court can be morally required to defer to lower court precedent. As one commentator has argued:

> there are circumstances in which the decisions of sister and lower courts may well generate substantial reliance, and in these circumstances, they should be accorded precedential weight. For example, if the courts are unanimous or near-unanimous in their opinions concerning a particular issue, if these decisions are longstanding, and if they have become woven into the fabric of a larger body of law, then people may justifiably rely on these decisions. Under these circumstances, such decisions should be considered precedential even among higher courts and courts of other jurisdictions.[43]

---

[40] cf Duxbury (n 9) 128 and W Twining and D Miers, *How to Do Things with Rules* (5th edn, CUP 2010) 283–85.

[41] M Köpcke, *Legal Validity: The Fabrics of Justice* (Hart 2019) 72–73.

[42] It is admittedly possible, although I shall not examine the matter here, that epistemic considerations alone may justify a system of vertical *stare decisis*. Since higher courts are, on this view, more likely to get things right than lower courts, their precedents merit deference. Hershovitz (n 13) 108 argues for this view. But a careful analysis of this question needs to consider empirical data as well as the fact that lower courts may have expertise in a particular field—vis-à-vis higher courts that usually have general jurisdiction.

[43] HY Levin, 'A Reliance Approach to Precedent' (2013) 47 Ga L Rev 1035, 1075.

And yet it is a central feature of *stare decisis* that higher courts are never *legally* bound to follow lower court precedent. I am, of course, not arguing that higher courts should be legally bound by lower court precedent. All I am saying is that if we focus on the specific moral values often relied on to justify *stare decisis* (such as reliability), it is plausible to think that some cases might arise where a higher court can be *morally* required to defer to lower court precedent, but that moral requirement would *not* translate into legal obligation. For the law would still allow the higher court to follow such a precedent as a permissive and non-mandatory legal source, borrowing HLA Hart's famous terminology.[44]

Once we set aside the precedents of lower courts, why should we include, in the category of binding precedent, the decisions of courts of coordinate jurisdiction? Why not instead give deference to the precedents of higher courts only? More radically, why not eliminate vertical *stare decisis* altogether, and require instead that each court act consistently with its own previous decisions?

Answers to these questions do not seem to hinge on the idea of advancing the moral values of *stare decisis*. More precisely, if they do hinge on such an idea, it is far from clear that the answer requires a patchwork between moral input and legal output—*stare decisis*. Now, it may seem as though lower courts must follow higher court precedent (but not the other way around) because there exists a relation of authority between them. This is, I think, Frederick Schauer's justification for vertical precedent. According to Schauer:

> the justifications ... are fairly obvious. Just as children are expected to obey their parents even when they disagree, as privates are expected to follow even those orders from sargeants they believe wrong, as Catholics are expected to follow the dictates of the pope even if they think those dictates mistaken, and as employees are expected to follow the instructions of their supervisors, lower courts judges are expected to follow the 'instructions' of those courts above them in what the military calls the 'chain of command.'[45]

But it is doubtful that authority entails that one should follow precedent as a matter of obligation. If I work in a company and face a difficult decision, the fact that my boss (an authority over me) has decided X in a previous similar case is normatively significant for me. But there is an important difference between that scenario, on the one hand, and my being bound by my boss's precedent, on the other. My action will be judged on its own merits—most likely for the good or bad consequences it produces. But there would be something utterly unfitting if my boss criticized me for not doing as she did before. To say that someone is under an obligation to follow precedent is to say that such a person can be criticized (and be held responsible) on the sufficient ground that she has failed to follow precedent *even when* her action brought about good results. In many contexts where authoritative relations exist, failing to follow a superior's precedent is not sufficient for holding someone responsible. Admittedly, the story is different if, in the earlier example, it is part of my job description to follow the precedents that my boss sets. But this proviso does suggest that authoritative relations do not themselves mandate following precedent; an authoritative and intentional prescription is required to that effect.

Specific convergence is required in order to work out a system of *stare decisis*. We need specific convergence at least on what counts as the *ratio* and *obiter*, on the specific precedents

---

[44] HLA Hart, *The Concept of Law* (3rd edn, Clarendon Press 2012) 294.
[45] F Schauer, *Thinking Like a Lawyer* (Harvard UP 2009) 41–42.

that later courts must follow (the rules on vertical and horizontal *stare decisis*), and on the grounds on which later courts may overrule binding precedent. Without an intentional choice aimed at specific convergence we are left with the underdetermination of the moral input. Law's contribution is precisely to make *stare decisis* possible by reducing such a moral underdetermination via intentional choice aimed at specific convergence. Part of the result is: 'it is the *ratio*, not the *obiter*, that binds later courts, and this is how the *ratio* is to be determined'. Likewise, 'only the precedents of higher courts and those courts of coordinate jurisdiction bind'. Finally, 'the grounds on which a court may overrule precedents are X'. This intentional choice reflects the law's voice. But this is not a conceptual claim as to the nature of law (or *stare decisis*), for what the law has authoritatively determined may change across various jurisdictions. In the US, for example, the rules for determining the *ratio* may be different from those in Australia—and even within the US those rules may change between states.[46] The rules on vertical and horizontal *stare decisis* may also vary; the law may provide that not all the precedents of higher courts must be followed, but only those that are reached by, say, a unanimous court. And the grounds on which the UK Supreme Court may overrule its precedents are clearly different from those that apply to the Supreme Courts of New Zealand or Canada.

Intentional choice aimed at specific convergence brings about a legal doctrine of *stare decisis*—a doctrine quite unique to each legal system, despite the central features that may be shared. What appears to be more common to all legal systems is the moral input offered to justify *stare decisis*. But this moral input is messy and cannot provide a workable foundation upon which courts may adjudicate. The law, accordingly, filters out part of the moral input in order to produce a more coordinated and specified legal output. Among what is left out of this legal output is the intelligible but arguably unworkable notion that, in order to advance the moral values of *stare decisis*, lower court precedent should bind higher courts. However attractive this idea might be (if it is attractive in particular circumstances), it is arguably unfeasible for the law to implement it. Whatever the force of lower court precedent, it is up to higher courts alone to assess it.

Does the choice aimed at specific convergence need to have a specific legal form? In some jurisdictions, that choice can have the form of codified rules.[47] In others, the choice can be identified as a matter of convergent judicial practice.[48] In others still, we can carve out specific rules from relevant case law in order to see what the law has determined.[49] Whatever the form picked by the law, it is sensible to think that the content of law's choice must be both accepted and practised by courts.[50] It is because of this acceptance and critical convergence of judicial behaviour that we could think of *stare decisis* as a legal doctrine setting out the fundamental rules on precedent-following. That doctrine tells us, among other things, what specific precedents are legally binding, what is the binding part of a precedent, and what are the legal grounds on which later courts can overrule precedent.

---

[46] See, e.g., N Varsava, '*Stare Decisis* and Intersystemic Adjudication' (2022) 97 Notre Dame L Rev 1207—see the section titled 'Intersystemic Interpretation in Practice'.

[47] cf the case of Mexico (n 7).

[48] cf Simpson (n 20).

[49] In England, see, e.g., *Young v Bristol Aeroplane Co Ltd* [1944] KB 718, the decision of the Court of Appeal (Civil Division) setting out the grounds for overruling its past decisions.

[50] It may be tempting to see in this judicial practice the root of a specific rule of recognition. But I shall avoid pursuing this strategy. See Grant Lamond's contribution to this volume (Chapter 2) for an analysis along these lines.

4. The One-System View Objection

But someone might object that I have begged too many questions—and too many important questions—in adopting a two-systems view whereby we can distinguish the moral input and the legal output.[51] My analysis might be said to be problematic since both moral input and legal output should be understood as forming part of one domain. Thus, we should not analyse questions of law as though they were distinct, and metaphysically independent, from questions of morality. Ronald Dworkin, for one, has explicitly rejected the two-systems approach to jurisprudence. In *Justice for Hedgehogs*, he argued that:

> Once we take law and morality to compose separate systems of norms, there is no neutral standpoint from which the connections between these supposedly separate systems can be adjudicated.[52]

For Dworkin, an analysis aiming to isolate the moral reasons for following precedent from the legal reasons is question-begging. For this type of analysis would presuppose a form of legal positivism that treats questions of law as distinct, and metaphysically independent, from questions of morality. According to Dworkin, positivism considers a question of law as one that can be answered by looking at the relevant legal rules *exclusively*—that is, without attending to 'the principles necessary to justify those rules'.[53] Thus, an analysis on which purely legal grounds—ultimately to be explained by social facts—can ground, say, legal obligation is a positivist analysis. For this analysis would treat moral facts as neither necessary nor sufficient to ground legal obligation—thus establishing a sort of metaphysical independence between legality and morality. By treating moral facts, such as justifying moral principles, as neither necessary nor sufficient to ground legal obligation, I have begged an important question: why did I exclude the justifying moral principles in the first place? That is why Dworkin argues that we should reject this type of two-systems analysis and treat questions of law *as* moral questions. According to Dworkin:

> The doctrinal concept of law can only be understood as an interpretive concept ... defending an analysis of that interpretive concept can only mean defending a controversial theory of political morality. An analysis of the concept [of law] *must assume from the start an intimate connection between law and morality.* The supposed escape from the circularity problem is no escape at all.[54]

There are two different issues at stake. One concerns the conceptual possibility of distinguishing a question of law from a question of morality; the other consists in explaining a legal fact (such as legal obligation) by reference to social facts alone, or by reference to a mix of both social facts and moral facts. Call the former the 'Difference Thesis' and the latter the 'Metaphysical Independence Thesis'. A natural lawyer can agree that a question of law is conceptually different from a question of morality, and thereby subscribe to the Difference Thesis. At the same time, she will most likely be sceptical that we can explain legal facts by

---

[51] Although I have made no claim whatsoever about whether law and morality are necessarily connected—the famous 'no-necessary connection' thesis.
[52] Dworkin (n 2) 402.
[53] ibid 403.
[54] ibid 404 (emphasis added).

reference to social facts alone, and would thus reject the Metaphysical Independence Thesis. A positivist, on the other hand, would distinguish a legal question from a moral question—thus endorsing the Difference Thesis—but maintain that legal facts are ultimately explainable by social facts alone.[55] In doing so, the positivist would subscribe to the Metaphysical Independence Thesis. While the natural law theorist and the legal positivist disagree on the Metaphysical Independence Thesis, they agree on the Difference Thesis. On Dworkin's view, however, the Difference Thesis must also be resisted. As Hillary Nye puts it:

> In *Justice for Hedgehogs*, Dworkin claims that we cannot accept the 'two-systems view', which treats law and morality as separate domains. Rather, we must adopt the 'one-system view', according to which law is a branch of morality. This means legal questions must be understood as moral questions. It is not that answering legal questions requires taking a moral stance, but that to understand legal questions at all we have to frame them as *questions in morality*.[56]

Yet according to some scholars, Dworkin's invitation—to embrace the one-system view from the outset—is as question-begging as the two-systems approach he firmly criticizes.[57] Why should we assume that the only non-circular answer rests in treating legal questions as moral questions? Shouldn't this correspondence—between law and morality—be established as well? Dworkin thinks there is no need for this, since his alternative, namely the one-system view, is the only approach that can remain immune to what we could call the 'Neutrality Objection'. To cite Dworkin again:

> Once we take law and morality to compose separate systems of norms, there is no neutral standpoint from which the connections between these supposedly separate systems can be adjudicated.[58]

If someone asked me, 'how can we know whether a court is legally bound by precedent', and I responded, 'by looking at the relevant legal rules', my answer would be, on Dworkin's view, biased. For I have excluded moral reasons from the picture. If, on the other hand, I answered, 'by looking at the moral reasons the court has for following precedent', my answer would be equally biased. For I have excluded the relevant legal rules. Either answer, says Dworkin, 'yields a circular argument with much too short a radius'.[59] The only way to escape from this self-defeating scenario is, for Dworkin, by collapsing both questions into the one-system view: 'The supposed escape from the circularity problem is no escape at all.'[60] Otherwise we are confronted with the Neutrality Objection, accusing us of being non-neutral adjudicators.

To be sure, what is at stake is neither Dworkinian integrity nor a debate concerning the ultimate grounds of law. We have, rather, a debate concerning the conceptual possibility of distinguishing a question of law from a question of morality—the Difference Thesis. And the

---

[55] This formulation can make room for Inclusive Legal Positivism as well: if some moral grounds are also necessary for grounding legal obligation, that necessity ultimately obtains by virtue of some more fundamental, grounding social facts.

[56] H Nye, 'The One-System View and Dworkin's Anti-Archimedean Eliminativism' (2021) 40 Law & Philosophy 247, 250 (emphasis in original).

[57] See, e.g., L Sager, 'Putting Law in its Place' in W Waluchow and S Sciaraffa (eds), *The Legacy of Ronald Dworkin* (OUP 2016) 118. I owe this reference to Nye (n 56) 259.

[58] Dworkin (n 2) 402–03.

[59] ibid 403.

[60] ibid 404.

main problem with endorsing the Difference Thesis is, as seen earlier, Dworkin's Neutrality Objection, stressing the importance of remaining neutral (of not begging the question) when it comes to theory-adjudication. But it is far from clear whether this neutrality has any value in its own right. If someone has, on good grounds, sided with one of two competing theories, it is no objection (against her) to say that she has lost the neutrality necessary to adjudicate whether that theory should, after all, be preferred to the competing candidate. That claim simply does not pass muster.[61]

Now even granting, for the sake of the argument, Dworkin's Neutrality Objection, it should be noted that his proposal faces serious challenges as well. The main problem with the one-system view rests in what Hasan Dindjer has recently called the 'Correspondence Thesis'.[62] According to Dindjer, the Correspondence Thesis, entailed by Dworkin's one-system view, provides that:

> wherever one has a legal obligation, there exists a moral obligation with the same content ... For legal and moral obligation to correspond is just for them to have the same content.[63]

The Correspondence Thesis, Dindjer argues, is entailed by the 'Identity Thesis', in virtue of which there exists 'a metaphysical connection between legal and moral norms: the former just are (a type of) the latter'.[64] For Dindjer, the Identity Thesis is endorsed by proponents of the one-system view, who by implication must also subscribe to the Correspondence Thesis. The upshot is that if one has a legal obligation to pay a certain tax, one not only has a correlative moral obligation but *both obligations also have the same content*. If the Correspondence Thesis were false, then according to Dindjer the Identity Thesis could not be true: 'For there could then be a legal obligation that corresponded to no moral obligation, and hence could not be a moral obligation.'[65]

If a court is legally required to follow precedent, then the court is also, on the Correspondence Thesis, morally required to follow precedent—both obligations having the same content. Yet, at least as applied to precedent, the Correspondence Thesis is false. In a nutshell, there can be situations in which a court is legally required to follow precedent without being morally bound to do so. This is the case of many common law courts. Conversely, a court may be morally required to follow precedent, without being legally obliged to do so. This is the case of many civil law courts. But even setting aside these cases, the mismatch between moral input and legal output becomes even more apparent once we consider the rules on vertical and horizontal *stare decisis*. As suggested earlier, in certain cases, where the lower courts have consistently upheld a particular doctrine—and where thus there might be a pressing need to protect the values of stability and reliability—a higher court may be morally required to defer to lower court precedent. Yet under *stare decisis* that court would never be *legally* bound by lower court precedent.

---

[61] And if the objection bites, wouldn't it also apply, by extension, to other areas? If someone asked me, 'How can I know the time' and I answered, 'By looking at the watch', wouldn't I also be taking a stance between two rival theories as to how to know the time? Dworkin could, of course, object that whereas nobody denies that we know the hour by looking at the watch, things are notoriously more controversial when it comes to the concept of law. But this move wouldn't take us too far either. Things wouldn't be any different if we could, indeed, find two rival theories as to how to know the time.

[62] H Dindjer, 'The New Legal Anti-Positivism' (2020) 26 Legal Theory 181, 185.

[63] ibid.

[64] ibid.

[65] ibid.

This mismatch puts proponents of the one-system view in a difficult position: how can they account for the non-correspondence between moral and legal obligation in cases such as these? More generally, how can they account for the fact that many judges are torn between their moral and legal obligations? If for any legal obligation there exists a correlative moral obligation of equal normative content, it is doubtful that both obligations might conflict. Yet we know that judges do experience this type of normative conflict. One answer is to say that while judges believe they are torn between their moral and legal obligations, their belief is mistaken. If a higher court judge is morally required to follow lower court precedent, that judge is also legally obligated to do so—and if she thinks she is not, then that belief is mistaken. Another answer is to say that current practice is deficient or needs serious reinterpretation. Although a rigorous answer to these replies would take me too far,[66] I fear both moves would come at too high a price. They are difficult to reconcile with central features of practice—the minimum descriptive requirement.[67] Thus, we could reply in the same way Adam Rigoni objected to some philosophers arguing for a strict rule-based approach to precedent, such as Larry Alexander and Emily Sherwin.[68] Proponents of the one-system view would, as Rigoni puts it, 'miss the mark', as they would ignore 'too much of judicial practice'.[69] Given the centrality of the data that proponents of the one-system view need to account for, I am inclined to think that the burden lies with them.

5. Conclusion

The grounds on which a court may be morally required to follow a particular precedent need not be the same as those on which the same court may have a general legal obligation to follow precedent—*stare decisis*. That is why I have distinguished between the moral input and the legal output—and thereby between the moral and juridical approaches to the question of why certain courts must follow precedent. Both approaches, I have argued, are crucial for attaining a full grasp of *stare decisis*. The moral approach alone is not sufficient because it cannot account for central features of *stare decisis*: the distinction between the *ratio* and *obiter* of a precedent; the rules on vertical and horizontal precedent; and the grounds on which courts may overrule binding precedent. *Stare decisis* is a legal doctrine because that underdetermined moral input needs to be filtered by an intentional choice aimed at specific convergence. That is precisely law's contribution. The Correspondence Thesis, entailed by Dworkin's one-system view, is difficult to reconcile with central features of practice, such as the rules on vertical and horizontal precedent. Proponents of the one-system view need to show how this view can account for these central features while also being compatible with the Correspondence Thesis.

---

[66] For careful criticism of the one-system view, see Dindjer (n 62).
[67] See n 6.
[68] L Alexander and E Sherwin, *Demystifying Legal Reasoning* (CUP 2008) 122–23.
[69] Rigoni (n 6) 135.

4
Why Precedent Works

Nicholas W Barber[*]

Precedent turns on the capacity of one judge to effectively constrain another. In a telling phrase, it has been described as 'strongly coercive',[1] yet while precedent is experienced as coercive by lawyers and judges, this experience is hard to explain. There are two features of precedent that make its coercive aspect hard to understand. First, the legal rules of precedent are often insufficiently specific to ground such constraint. Secondly, compounding this, the formal mechanisms that back it up are too weak to explain its effectiveness; much of law is coercive because it is backed by force, with fines and imprisonment underpinning its commands, but aside from the risk of being criticized by a higher court there are no obvious legal sanctions attached to the rules of precedent in many legal systems. These two challenges combine to present a paradox: while experienced as coercive, precedent seems to lack the form and institutional backing that would grant this character. This chapter argues that the answer to the paradox is to be found in the social dimension of precedent. Precedent should be understood as a social practice, a mode of argumentation partly structured by non-legal rules that operate within social groups, and social expectations are key to the effectiveness of these rules. This chapter concludes by considering some of the problems raised by the roles of social groups in the operation of precedent and suggests ways in which these problems may be mitigated.

1. The Paradox of Precedent

There have been many attempts to identify the *ratio* of cases, that is, to pick out the authoritative proposition of law for which the case stands. In some instances, this appears easy. Where a case turns on a binary question, the decision of the court can provide a clear answer. In *Gilham v Ministry of Justice*, for example, a question was raised whether a district judge was a 'worker' within the scope of the Employment Rights Act 1996, and so entitled to the protections given by that statute to whistle-blowers.[2] The Supreme Court decided that she did fall within that category, and was entitled to the protection. If the same question were to arise in a later case, *Gilham* would apply: district judges are included in the category of 'workers'. In the literature on precedent, many tests are suggested by scholars to identify the *ratio* of a case.[3] Some of these exercises embody the hope that if we are able to extract *rationes* reliably and consistently from cases, then the practice of law will start to look more like a science than an art, with legal uncertainty narrowing over time as skilled lawyers extract binding

---

[*] I would like to thank Hafsteinn Kristjánsson, Maris Köpcke, Sebastian Lewis, and Julius Yam.
[1] R Cross and J Harris, *Precedent in English Law* (4th edn, OUP 1991) 3. See also N Duxbury, *The Nature and Authority of Precedent* (CUP 2008) 13–17.
[2] *Gilham v Ministry of Justice* [2019] UKSC 44.
[3] Cross and Harris (n 1) ch 2; Duxbury (n 1) 67–92.

Nicholas W Barber, *Why Precedent Works* In: *Philosophical Foundations of Precedent*. Edited by: Timothy Endicott, Hafsteinn Dan Kristjánsson, and Sebastian Lewis, Oxford University Press. © Nicholas W Barber 2023. DOI: 10.1093/oso/9780192857248.003.0005

propositions from a growing range of judgments. However, any scientific model of precedent is likely to remain an aspiration for three reasons: the difficulty of extracting a *ratio* from a case, the limited significance of these binding *rationes* to precedent as a practice, and the practical capacity of a judge, if she wished, to evade the constraints of precedent.

Extracting the *ratio* from a simple case like *Gilham* might seem easy, but it requires lawyers to distinguish between relevant, irrelevant, and ambiguous factors. The *ratio* of the case is not just the bare conclusion it reached, that the statute extended to Gilham, but the reason that led to that conclusion.[4] That Gilham held judicial office is plainly relevant, her name and gender are plainly irrelevant but other factors are ambiguous: did it matter that she was specifically a *district* judge or does the *ratio* of the case apply to any judicial office holder? A competent lawyer, reading the case, will be able to place many of the factors into one of these three categories easily, almost without thinking: some are just obviously relevant, others obviously irrelevant, and others, equally obviously, require further thought. A problem for the scientific model of precedent, though, is that it is often not obvious *why* it is clear which factor falls into which category and, indeed, judges and lawyers may struggle to provide an explanation if asked to do so. Furthermore, the boundaries between these three categories are soft: a persuasive lawyer, arguing a case before a later judge, might be able to push a factor from one category into another. Even in a simple case like *Gilham*, the identification of the *ratio* requires decisions that are hard to explain, and the reach of the *ratio* can be ambiguous and disputed. Things become even more complicated when there are multiple judgments or multiple issues in the case on which the decision could turn. In *Gilham*, the core *ratio* is easy to identify, even if its reach is ambiguous, but in other cases even the extraction of the core *ratio* maybe debatable.[5]

While the courts' capacity to produce decisions that bind other courts, decisions those courts are obliged to follow, is an important part of precedent, it is only one aspect of that practice. In addition, elements of past judgments that are not binding on a judge may be persuasive: *rationes* of cases that are not formally binding, or other elements of legal reasoning within cases, may need to be considered.[6] Lawyers and judges commonly talk of these elements of precedent as having weight; even if they do not formally bind, they possess, to steal a term from Ronald Dworkin, 'gravitational force'.[7] Once again, appreciating which elements of a past decision possess weight and, even more delicately, how much weight those elements should or will be accorded, is not easy to explain. Both lawyers and judges have a sense of the elements of past decisions that affect the present case. When these have considerable weight, they may effectively constrain the judge or at least demand that the judge provide a careful explanation of why she is not following precedent. Departure requires effort from the lawyers and judges; the easy (though not necessarily the correct) path is to follow these past decisions. Precedent can exert so powerful a gravitational pull that the line between the binding and the persuasive, though conceptually sharp, becomes blurred. A judge may find it easier to navigate around an ambiguous binding *ratio* than to set aside a piece of reasoning from a past decision that is strongly persuasive. This sense of weight, of gravitational pull, is key to the successful operation of precedent and to the law-making function of the court. In assessing weight, lawyers and judges gauge something that exists separate from them,

---

[4] F Schauer, *Thinking Like a Lawyer. A New Introduction to Legal Reasoning* (Harvard UP 2009) 50–51.
[5] AWB Simpson, 'The Common Law and Legal Theory' in AWB Simpson (ed), *Oxford Essays in Jurisprudence: Second Series* (OUP 1973) 89–90.
[6] Cross and Harris (n 1) 4.
[7] R Dworkin, 'Hard Cases' in R Dworkin, *Taking Rights Seriously* (Duckworth 1978); Duxbury (n 1) 23–27.

they do not *ascribe* weight to past reasoning, they instead *identify* the weight that the past reasoning possesses. This opens the possibility of mistake, the assessment can be wrong, and can fail to accord a past decision its proper weight. But the criteria for this assessment are only partially, if at all, articulated in judgments: it seems to be something competent lawyers just know how to do, even if they would struggle to explain their reasoning.[8]

The last two paragraphs have argued that attempts to produce a scientific model of precedent are unlikely to succeed because of the nature of this process of law-making. Extracting a binding *ratio* from a case and assessing its scope are matters of judgment, over which skilled lawyers can disagree, and, moving beyond the *ratio*, the identification of the elements of past decisions which possess a gravitational pull (despite not being strictly binding), and the estimation of the weight those elements possess is a process as unclear as it is commonplace. These two features of precedent are compounded by a third: the efficacy of precedent appears to depend on the willingness of those bound by precedent to accept its demands. It is the judge who must decide what precedent requires, and the judge who must then follow it—yet it is the judge who is bound by its requirements. Taken in purely legal terms, the successful operation of precedent appears to depend on the good faith of the judge. As Carleton Allen, somewhat bemusedly put it, judges are 'only bound intellectually' to precedent.[9] A judge who wished to avoid its constraints has a range of options to choose from. She could manipulate the findings of fact to get the outcome she wanted by distinguishing the present case from the precedent, she could recite the law as found in past cases while covertly applying a different rule, she could wilfully misinterpret past case law, or, most crudely of all, she could just ignore the past decisions. All of these possibilities are rendered easier for the judge by the ambiguities around precedent; it is hard to distinguish between reasonable disagreement, a mistaken decision about the law, and one taken in bad faith. The formal sanctions that could be brought against the maverick judge are few and difficult to deploy and, given the limited capacity of appeal courts to re-hear cases, many of the judge's decisions would probably stand.

2. The Social Model of Precedent

Judges are people and, like everyone else, they live and work within communities that shape their action. In his analysis of the motivation of judges, Lawrence Baum has written of the multiple audiences to which they speak, both inside and outside the court, and the ways in which these audiences condition their behaviour.[10] Baum identifies judicial colleagues, pressure groups, and legal academia, among other possible audiences, as groups that judges may address, and which can shape the way judges make and justify their legal decisions. Baum has little to say about precedent directly, but his work provides a starting point for an account of this form of reasoning; in common law systems precedent is commonly used by judges to justify their decisions, and it seems that this form of explanation carries weight with the judges' audiences. Such an account of precedent would treat the practice as, in part, a social one; a mode of argumentation conditioned by the expectations of a group or groups.[11] Under

---

[8] J Hutcheson, 'The Judgment Intuitive: The Function of the "Hunch" in Judicial Decision' (1929) 14 Cornell L Quarterly 285.

[9] CK Allen, 'Precedent and Logic' (1925) 41 LQR 329, 333.

[10] L Baum, *Judges and Their Audiences* (Princeton UP 2008).

[11] Duxbury (n 1) 151.

the social model of precedent, precedent is effective because it operates within communities that condition how legal argument should proceed, and which determine what counts as a good legal argument. The legal rules of precedent, such as the rules of judicial hierarchy, are complemented by non-legal, social rules, and it is in these social rules that we find the answers to the challenges raised in the previous section.[12] Three elements of the social model of precedent require consideration: the groups within which precedent operates; the non-legal rules of precedent that supplement the legal rules; and the pressures which tie judges to these rules.

A. Social Groups and Precedent

Baum writes of 'audiences' to which judges speak, but it might be better to think of these as groups of which the judge is a member. Talk of an audience suggests that judges are speakers addressing listeners, outsiders communicating with insiders, but in the examples Baum gives the judge is invariably an insider talking to fellow group members. As an insider, the judge cares about what these people think because they identify as a member of the group, consciously or unconsciously accepting that the group's evaluation determines their success as a judge, and using the expectations of the group as criteria which condition their arguments.[13] So, for example, when a judge frames their reasoning in a way which will appeal to the other judges sitting in the case, she treats that set of judges as the group which tests the success of her argument, while when she addresses her remarks to lawyers more generally, it is the wider legal community's standards to which she appeals. In each case, the judge cares about their reaction because she understands her office as a judge as being constructed, in part, by these groups.

It is a strength of Baum's analysis that he identifies a range of possible audiences judges might speak to, and which might then condition her decisions. Put in terms of groups, there are multiple groups which might shape the reasoning of the judge. These groups overlap, can contain subgroups, and frequently have vague or disputed boundaries. To give some examples, there is the group of judges in the court in which the judge is sitting, the set of judges in the court system as a whole, the professional legal community in which the courts operate, and the constitutional community in which the legal system is located. These are distinct but interconnected groups. There are also subgroups within these groups of which the judge may be a member, or which may be part of a wider group to which the judge belongs. For instance, legal academia is a group of which some judges are members while others are not, but all judges are members of the wider legal community of which legal academia is a subgroup. All of these groups may help to shape the operation of precedent.

Social groups contain, create, and are created by social rules, rules which determine the purpose of the group and which set standards for successful (and unsuccessful) conduct inside the group.[14] These social rules are artefacts of the group; it is the group that, more or less clearly, formulates the rules and the group that, more or less effectively, enforces them,

---

[12] Even the legal rules of hierarchy can be unclear in some situations: NW Barber, *The United Kingdom Constitution: An Introduction* (OUP 2021) 22–24. See further the contribution to this volume by Sebastian Lewis (Chapter 3).

[13] R Brown and S Pehrson, *Group Processes* (3rd edn, Wiley Blackwell 2020) ch 3.

[14] ibid; NW Barber, *The Constitutional State* (OUP 2010) 25–31. See further the contribution to this volume by Maris Köpcke (Chapter 29).

responding to their breach with criticism and censure.[15] The ambiguity over the nature and boundaries of the groups to which the judge, as judge, belongs may make it hard to determine how those rules apply to the judge. Membership of some of these groups is, for the judge, non-optional. Rules of the legal order specify that the judge is a member of a bench deciding a case and a member of the judiciary more generally—a judge that doubted if she were part of these groups would just be making a mistake. Membership of other groups may be unclear. Some judges might consider themselves members of the Bar or the international set of judges by virtue of their office, other judges might consider themselves outside these groups.

That this chapter is concerned with precedent allows us to narrow down the range of social groups we are interested in. The legal and non-legal rules of precedent relate to how a judge, as a judge, *should* decide a case. This allows us to cut away group memberships that are matters of personal attachment rather than linkages that exist by virtue of the judicial role. A judge who is a staunch supporter of a political party or a pressure group may, officially or not, be a member of these groups and the social rules of these groups may then shape how the judge decides cases. For instance, a judge who is a member of an environmental pressure group may feel the weight of expectations of that group when deciding a case over pollution legislation, and the fear of what her fellow group members will think may affect her decision. However, the judge is a member of these groups in a private capacity, and not in her capacity as a judge. While knowing that she belongs to these groups may both explain and help us to predict her decisions, these are not ties that *should* shape her decision-making in her judicial role; the rules of these social groups are irrelevant to her conduct as a judge. The task of identifying the social rules of precedent is distinct from the task of predicting the outcome of cases.[16] The rules of precedent are rules that apply to the judge because of her occupation of that legal role: consequently, the rules of precedent must apply to all judges, not just to judges with special private connections.[17]

While we can narrow the range of groups to a certain extent, it remains the case that there are multiple, linked, groups in which we might find social rules of precedent. The rules are likely to increase in quantity and precision as the groups become more legally specialized: the judiciary is likely to have a far richer set of rules determining how cases should be decided than, say, the citizenry as a whole. But it also raises the possibility that there will be conflicting rules. There is no reason to assume that the various groups of which judges are members necessarily agree on the content of the rules determining precedent.

The office of the judge, then, has a social, as well as a legal, dimension. Judges, in their capacity as judges, belong to social groups, and these groups contain rules which apply to judicial decision-making. The identification and delineation of these groups can be tricky. It can be unclear which groups the judge belongs to by virtue of her judicial role and which she belongs to in a private capacity, and, even once those social groups that shape the office of the judge have been identified, the rules of those groups may be disputable within the group or in conflict with the rules of other groups.

---

[15] HLA Hart, *The Concept of Law* (3rd edn, OUP 2012) 56–59.

[16] Another reason why computers may struggle with precedent: artificial intelligence might be great at predicting what a judge *will* decide, but struggle to determine what a judge *should* decide. See J Yam and M Verhagen, 'The Law of Attraction: How Similarity Between Judges and Lawyers Helps Win Cases in the Hong Kong Court of Final Appeal' (2021) 65 Int'l Rev L & Econ 105944.

[17] On the interaction of roles and precedent, see Köpcke (n 14).

B. The Social Rules of Precedent

While many legal rules are also social rules, operative within the communities whose conduct they purport to regulate, not all social rules are also legal rules. These non-legal social rules are not found in legal sources, but exist because of broad consensuses within the groups in which they operate.[18] Because of the ways in which they are created, non-legal social rules can lack the clarity and certainty which often characterize laws. But this need not be the case; some social rules can be as clear and as certain as their legal counterparts. While some of the social rules of precedent are unclear, and some may be disputed, in many instances their implications are uncontested, even if they may prove hard to apply. There are at least two sets of social rules that determine the operation of precedent: rules that relate to the identification of the *ratio* of a case, and rules that attribute weight to a past decision or pronouncement.

The first part of this chapter discussed the problems of extracting a *ratio* from a judgment. The identification of the *ratio* required a distinction to be drawn between relevant and irrelevant factors, but the test of relevance was unclear. Competent lawyers will often agree on identification of the *ratio* of a case because they share a broad agreement over the aim of law. At the most general level, lawyers recognize that law is an institution which aspires to be as good, morally speaking, as it can be. Though the defining point of law is so obvious it is often forgotten by formalists, it animates legal reasoning and can be seen in the arguments of both lawyers and judges. The content of the *ratio* is, as a consequence, determined by a test of perceived moral salience. We know, for example, that the gender of the judge in *Gilham* was irrelevant because, unless there are good reasons to the contrary, we would not expect employee's rights to be limited on grounds of sex. On the other hand, the value of whistle-blowing—and the broader importance of protecting people from bullying in their workplace—was relevant to the decision to class district judges as 'workers' who fell within the protection of the legislation: it is (morally) valuable to enable workers to expose problems in their workplace, and it is (morally) valuable to prevent abuses of power occurring between employers and employees. This pushes towards a broader interpretation of the *ratio*, it is likely that all judges would count as 'workers' for this reason. Lawyers and judges can identify a case's *ratio* because they possess a shared set of moral beliefs about the aims of the law, and these moral beliefs help them to pick out the salient features of a decision that constitute the *ratio*.

While law aspires to meet the requirements of morality, it is not morality that, directly, serves to identify the salient elements of a decision but, rather, the beliefs of lawyers and judges about what morality requires. These shared beliefs take the form of social rules. These rules specify that the law ought to pursue or respect a given end and, as an implication of this, that judges ought to recognize some factors as salient within legal decisions and competent lawyers should pick out these in arguments to the court. Those who ignore or misunderstand these rules will be criticized and corrected by others in the group.

An objection might be made at this point. Are these rules purely social, non-legal, or are they, in fact, legal? An alternative approach to the delineation of the *ratio* would argue that these unspoken assumptions are legal principles, broad rules of law that are grounded in the past decisions of judges and statutes. These are, perhaps, the principles Dworkin talks of when he speaks of 'justification' standing alongside 'fit' in legal reasoning.[19] But these assumptions are not normally understood by lawyers as derived from legal sources. If a lawyer

---

[18] On social rules, see Barber, *The Constitutional State* (n 14) 58–67.
[19] R Dworkin, *Law's Empire* (Hart 1998) ch 7.

in the course of argument claimed that the *ratio* of *Gilham* was confined to female judges, for instance, they would be corrected, but it is unlikely that those who corrected them would feel the need to point to a statute or case countering their claim. These are not source-based rules. As a result, these rules can change without necessarily requiring a change in the law or, indeed, any formal decision. The beliefs that legal rules should treat men and women equally and that homosexual relationships are as morally valuable as heterosexual relationships, for instance, have emerged slowly, pivoting the underlying assumptions of lawyers in these areas. While these changes to beliefs within the legal community may have been reflected in, or even spurred by, changes in the law, they were not dependent on legal change but were manifestations of changes in society more generally. Unlike changes to legal rules, which must be brought about through, or at least recognized by, other legal rules, changes to non-legal social rules can occur without any formal process of alteration. A second, related, line of challenge would point to AWB Simpson's brilliant, but underdeveloped, paper on the common law, 'The Common Law and Legal Theory', in which he argues that the common law should be understood as customary law, as 'the body of practices observed and ideas received by a caste of lawyers'.[20] Perhaps the social rules described in this chapter are in fact elements of customary law. Customary law exists when a rule requires the judges to look at the customs of a group and the practices, the conduct, of this group are accorded legal force.[21] However, the social rules discussed in this chapter are not generated out of practice, but are grounded in consensus: the judge, when applying these rules, does not look back at the past conduct of the legal community. And, moreover, the judge is a member of the group whose rules she applies; she does not apply these rules because she is required to render legally binding the custom of the group, she applies these rules because she is a member of the group which is bound by the rule. It is a direct, rather than indirect, obligation.[22]

A second area in which non-legal rules supplement the legal is in the attribution of weight, giving precedents their gravitational pull. There are at least two, interconnected, reasons why weight might be given to past decisions.[23] First, to maintain confidence in the law by providing litigants with guidance as to the rules that are likely to be applied in their case and, in addition, by requiring judges to explain their decisions to litigants when that guidance is not followed. Secondly, where relying on material from past cases makes it more likely the judge will reach the optimal outcome in the case before them, perhaps because the earlier decision was made by a judge with expertise in the area, or because the reasoning in the earlier decision was especially legally strong. There is a circularity here: where the earlier decision is accorded weight because of its inherent quality, its likelihood of being followed increases and, as a result, the expectations of litigants that it will be followed are raised. The combination of these two considerations entails that this is not merely a situation in which a future court looks back at a past decision for inspiration or to benefit from the learning of the previous judge.[24] The court might examine many types of legal material that are not accorded precedential weight, such as academic articles or foreign judgments, but is not, normally, required to do so. The gravitational pull of precedent is something that judges are required to

---

[20] Simpson (n 5) 94.

[21] On customary law, see J Gardner, *Law as a Leap of Faith* (OUP 2012) 65–74.

[22] It is also worth noting that these rules cannot be customs *in foro*, that is, the customs of a group of legal officials, as they are grounded in groups which extend beyond constitutional office holders. See J Bentham, *A Comment on the Commentaries and a Fragment on Government* (JH Burns and HLA Hart eds, The Athlone Press 1977) 182–84.

[23] See further S Lewis, 'Precedent and the Rule of Law' (2021) 41 OJLS 873.

[24] Schauer, *Thinking Like a Lawyer* (n 4) 39–40.

honour and which litigants are entitled to expect will sway the court; even if the judge doubts there is anything to be gained from the earlier ruling they must still examine and engage with it. The assessment of the significance of the elements that feed into the pull of precedent is, in large part, a function of non-legal social rules. There are social rules which determine the reputation of judges and past cases and, moreover, some social rules which establish the methods by which these reputations can be created. These rules embody assessments of the likely value of the earlier decision and, connectedly, the likelihood of the earlier case being followed.

The reputation of a judge will depend, in part, on the collective perception of their general legal ability and their ability in the particular area in which the case was decided. For example, Lord Goff and Sir John Laws both have strong general reputations as judges but are also particularly highly regarded in certain areas of law. Goff's reasoning would be especially powerful in a restitution case, an area in which he was recognized as an expert, but might be regarded as having less force in administrative law. Laws, in contrast, has a strong reputation in administrative law but is not so highly regard as a commercial law judge. The general standing of a judge is also significant and can shift over time. The pronouncements of judges who are found to have undertaken wrongdoing outside the court are less likely to be cited and, where cited, are less likely to be engaged with by the court. It is hard to imagine, for example, Lord Devlin's judgments now carrying much weight.[25] Individual cases can also have reputations that give them precedential weight. Cases can be regarded as strong, likely to be followed, or weak, embodying mistakes. Crucially, this assessment of the case is distinct from their legal position within the court hierarchy. A Supreme Court decision might be regarded as poorly reasoned and lawyers might be slow to cite or place weight on its reasoning in subsequent cases, while a High Court decision might be regarded as path-breaking, a model that the law is likely to follow.

Reputations, including those of judges and their decisions, are artefacts of groups. The reputations discussed in the previous paragraphs are established within the legal community, the products of discussions between judges, lawyers, and, to an extent, legal academics. Of course, not everyone will agree about the reputation that judges and cases should possess, but their reputation exists separate from the views of any individual within the group, and is set through social rules. The rejection of the bare existence of the reputation is treated as a simple mistake, a failure to recognize one of the group's artefacts; however, those within the group can dispute the foundations or extent of the reputation without breaching that social rule. A lawyer who claimed Laws was a poor administrative law judge would face staunch disagreement from within the legal community, but the claim would be accepted as one that could be debated within the group, while a lawyer who denied Laws possessed a reputation as a strong administrative law judge would have broken a rule of the group, the rule attributing the reputation to Laws, and, in failing to comply with this rule, shown themself to be a less competent lawyer.

While the gravitational pull of precedent most obviously applies to the parts of precedent that are not formally binding, it also affects the delineation of the scope of the *ratio*.[26] The *ratio* of a case can be interpreted broadly or narrowly, and the stronger the reputation of the case and judge, the more likely it is that the *ratio* will be given a broad formulation. If a Supreme Court judge were to reveal misconduct in the Supreme Court, and attempted to

---

[25] B Campbell, "'Our Silence Permits Perpetrators to Continue': One Woman's Fight to Expose a Father's Abuse' *The Observer* (25 July 2021).

[26] Cross and Harris (n 1) 69–74.

argue the decision in *Gilham* required that they, too, be treated as a 'worker' for the purposes of labour law legislation, the question of whether the *ratio* in *Gilham* applied to all judges or just to district judges might, in part, be determined by the reputations attached to that ruling: that is, by the standing of the judges in the case and the way in which the case had been received by the legal community.

C. Why These Rules are Effective

The social dimension of precedent also helps to explain why precedent is effective, why it is that precedent is experienced by those in the court, lawyers and judges, as coercive, both in terms of being effectively binding in some instances and requiring the judge to treat it as possessing gravitational weight in others. The overarching explanation of the force of precedent is simple: those who occupy the roles of judges and lawyers want to succeed in these roles.[27] At the most basic level, those within the legal community want to be effective, to win cases and to shape the law, and they want the material rewards that accompany success, such as wealth and power.[28] But, for many, these immediate motivations will be nested within a broader desire to be acknowledged as successful by the groups of which they are members.[29] As social psychologists have long recognized, our identity and self-esteem is, in large part, built within those social groups of which we are members.[30] It is these groups which provide us with social roles to occupy, and these groups which then determine whether we have succeeded or failed in these roles.[31] Just about everyone cares what others think of them, and the more significance a person places on their membership of a group, the more they are likely to care about their standing within that institution. The high social status of the legal community in general, and the judicial community in particular, ensures that being seen as successful within the terms of these groups is particularly attractive.[32] Adhering to the legal and social rules of precedent makes all of this more likely, the rules of precedent are part of the rules of the group which determine success in office. The ability to use these rules successfully shows that the lawyer or judge is able to exercise their office successfully—and, as a product of this, is likely to achieve the more immediate benefits of shaping the law and boosting their pay.

Precedent works because a judge who accepts the constraining force of rules of precedent is more likely to succeed in their role than a judge who rejects it. A judgment which uses precedent skilfully is more likely to persuade others in the legal community that the decision is correct, that it should be accepted and followed, than one which fails to use precedent. The skilful use of precedent provides a justification of the decision that, by following the rules of the group, is reasoned in the forms of argumentation contained within the legal community or, to make the point another way, is an explanation expressed in the language of the group. Reasoning with precedent then presents the judgment as a product of the legal community

---

[27] See the discussion in Duxbury (n 1) 153–59. Brown and Pehrson (n 13) ch 2.

[28] Though, as Richard Posner notes, the likelihood of success in this context generating material rewards for the judge is quite small: R Posner, 'What Do Judges and Justices Maximise? (The Same Thing Everybody Else Does)' (1993) 3 Supreme Ct Econ Rev 1, 5–7.

[29] H Tajfel and J Turner, 'The Social Identity Theory of Intergroup Behaviour' in S Worchel and W Austin (eds), *Psychology of Intergroup Relations* (Nelson Hall 1986) 15–19.

[30] D Abrams and M Hogg, 'Collective Identity: Group Membership and Self-Conception' in M Hogg and S Tindale (eds), *Blackwell Handbook of Social Psychology: Group Processes* (Blackwell 2001); Tajfel and Turner (n 29).

[31] Baum (n 10) 22.

[32] Tajfel and Turner (n 29) 17–19.

as a whole, rather than as the judge's personal decision, it is a decision that builds upon the past decisions of other judges, as refined and evaluated by the broader legal community.[33] As a product of this group, the use of precedent signals that the decision was predictable, as it forms a coherent part of the course of the development of the law, and is likely to be correct, as it builds on the past wisdom of earlier judges and lawyers. Where the judge departs from previous decisions that have precedential weight, the rules of precedent direct the judge to explain this departure, an explanation that both acknowledges the weight of precedent and explains why the earlier reasoning should not be followed.[34] This act of explanation can be, in itself, a way of satisfying the rules attributing weight to the earlier reasoning; the judge complies with the rules giving weight to the precedent by expending the time and effort to explain why she is declining to follow it.[35] By reasoning within the language of the legal community, the judge makes it more likely that her decision will be accepted by the parties and more likely that it will sway future judges. Each of these two outcomes is relevant to the evaluation of the judge within the legal community: a judge whose decisions are rarely disputed and whose decisions are often influential in the development of the law is succeeding within their role.

3. Implications of the Social Model

This chapter started out with a puzzle. Precedent is experienced by lawyers and judges as coercive, as providing a framework for judicial reasoning that effectively constrains how judges develop the law. Yet if we treat precedent as a purely legal phenomenon, it lacks the form to constrain, it is unclear, as a legal matter, how *rationes* can be extracted from cases or how the 'weight' of precedent is assessed. And even if these problems could be overcome, there is no formal enforcement mechanism to ensure judges stick to precedent; taken in purely legal terms, the effectiveness of precedent appears to turn on the goodwill of the judge. The answer to this puzzle lies in seeing precedent as mix of legal and non-legal rules that exist within social groups, primarily, though not exclusively, the legal community. It is these groups that formulate the social rules which supplement the legal aspect of precedent, clarifying the content of *rationes*, giving weight to reasoning in past cases, and it is these groups which apply the pressure that constrains judges to precedent by determining what constitutes success in the judicial role.[36]

Seeing precedent as a practice located within, and shaped by, the legal community, a mode of argumentation structured by the rules of that group, presents it as a form of 'groupthink'. The concept of groupthink, originally drawn from George Orwell's dystopia, was developed by the psychologist Irving Janis and is normally presented in purely negative terms.[37] Groupthink arises where a group develops a set of rules which frame its decision-making.

---

[33] Baum (n 10) 106–09.

[34] F Schauer, 'Precedent' (1987) 39 Stan L Rev 571, 580; S Condor, C Tileagã, and M Billig, 'Political Rhetoric' in L Huddy, D Sears, and J Levy (eds), *The Oxford Handbook of Political Psychology* (2nd edn, OUP 2013) 273–74; M Billig, *Arguing and Thinking* (CUP 1996) 49–55, 117–23.

[35] This squares with Grant Lamond's view of elements of precedent as acting as 'theoretical' authorities, giving the judge reason to think there are reasons for the law to take a certain form: G Lamond, 'Persuasive Authority in the Law' (2010) 17 Harv Rev Philosophy 16, esp 25–26.

[36] This may also help to explain the emergence of the legal doctrines of precedent: in its early stages, common law was able to function without legal rules of precedent, perhaps because the social rules were powerful enough to bring consistency and certainty: Duxbury (n 1) 31–37.

[37] I Janis, *Groupthink* (2nd edn, Houghton Mifflin 1982) ch 8.

These rules are enforced through pressure within the group—those who challenge these rules are criticized by their fellow group members—and the rules stand, within the group, as tests of the correctness of the decision. Normally, groupthink is undesirable, and used to explain poor decision-making—it can result in important considerations relevant to the decision being ignored, and critical voices in the group being excluded—but precedent shows that groupthink can sometimes have a positive effect. By narrowing the range of accepted reasons for decisions, precedent makes legal reasoning more predictable, and by putting pressure on those who develop the law to adhere to these reasons, it makes legal decision-making more stable. However, there is a downside to precedent. Like other examples of groupthink, there is a risk that the group generates suboptimal rules, either by excluding relevant considerations from deliberation or by building in error, and the cohesiveness of the group, on which the group depends for its effectiveness, marginalizes dissenting voices. These negative aspects of groupthink may be a feature, on occasion, of legal reasoning. It is, for instance, a curious feature of legal education, experienced by many who have gone through that process, that it sometimes seems to be trying to stop its students from thinking critically about the law, shutting out certain avenues of criticism while encouraging others. The limitation of the range of critical engagement is reinforced, and doubtless partly caused by, the reasoning that is acceptable with a courtroom. After all, a lawyer who sought to argue that the institution of property was inherently oppressive, that much of what the law identifies as negligence is simply bad luck, or that it is unfair to place weight on the words of a contract one of the parties had not read, would not prove a success before a judge. There is a danger, then, that some considerations that are relevant to the development of the law are systematically overlooked by the group. Given that the legal community is also involved in the development of the law through statute, there is a risk that the narrowness of reasoning on which precedent rests may spill over to law reform more generally, and inhibit the improvement of the law. When reflecting on the hazards of precedent, there is a fine line to tread. The problems that it brings are the counterparts of its strengths, and trying to mitigate its costs without impairing its benefits will be tricky. Nevertheless, there are steps we can take to reduce the dangers of groupthink, through the use of precedent, within the legal community.

Perhaps the best guard against the evils of groupthink is diversity. Though not the only social group that plays a role in the formulation of precedent, the legal community is the most significant, refining the moral beliefs and social rules on which precedent rests, and debating and gauging the reputations of judges and cases. Ensuring that there is diversity of experiences within this group—a diversity which includes, but is not limited to, gender, race, and economic background—is of exceptional importance. Partly, diversity is needed to guard against moral error. These different backgrounds can provide differing perspectives on moral issues and, indeed, can lead to differing evaluations of reputations. While there is no reason to suppose that any one perspective should be privileged over another, discussion within a diverse group may help members of that group to refine their positions. Sometimes this might lead to attitudes shifting; a person's appreciation of the demands of morality might alter because of this dialogue. Sometimes even if the substance of beliefs is not changed, an awareness of disagreement may, itself, be of value: those within the group will become aware that what might have seemed obvious is in fact contested and requires explanation, even if consensus cannot be reached.

In addition, diversity within the group is important to ensure that the rules and assessments of the legal community have a relationship with those that are found in society as a whole, or perhaps would be found if those outside the legal community directed their minds to the issue. The non-legal rules discussed in this chapter lack a democratic foundation. They are not the products of a legislature, they are not even the products of a constitutional institution, the legal community as an entity being part of the environment in which the state operates, rather than an element of the state itself. Nevertheless, these rules have a significant impact on the formulation and development of the law. If the composition of the legal community resembles that of society more generally, this provides a link, however weak, between the law and the people it governs. For diversity to succeed in shaping the beliefs of the group, members of the legal community must be brought together, there must be interaction between its members. Without this interaction, the benefits of diversity are lost. The flummeries of the legal world, the dinners in the Inns of Court, the Law Society's summer party, those strange little ceremonies with judges in fancy dress, alongside the more obvious virtues of conferences, magazines, and workshops, may play a role in bringing together members of the group, enhancing group cohesion and providing forums through which social interaction can defuse tensions within the group.[38]

It is worth noting that while the demand for diversity is irresistible, it might come at a cost in terms of group cohesion and, by derivation, to the capacity of the group to pressure its members to adhere to its rules. Having a legal community that was almost exclusively white, male, educated at public school, and drawn from a narrow socio-economic background was patently unjust and probably generated many poor legal decisions as a result, but it may have added to the cohesion of the group, creating multiple points for group identification and reinforcing group boundaries. If the cohesiveness of the legal community weakens, precedent could fragment, with different groups of judges adopting different sets of precedential rules.[39] One of the core challenges for the legal community over the next few decades will be to find ways of maintaining group cohesion while diversifying its membership.

Legal academia also has a particular role to play in shaping the attitudes of the legal community. Legal academics are probably best considered a subgroup of the legal community as a whole, part of the group, but distinct from practising lawyers and judges. One of the tasks of legal academia is to educate law students. Part of this is the inculcation of the social rules on which precedent rests, giving students a sense of the arguments and forms of reasoning that will prove successful in court. But another equally important task should be to encourage students to be aware of, and to take a critical attitude towards, these rules. If we think, for example, questions about social inequality should not be relevant to judicial decisions about company law or tort, this is a claim that needs to be examined and explained, not simply assumed. Encouraging criticism can help to build dissent into the legal community, dissent that can counter some of the unhealthy pressure towards consensus that is a standing risk of groupthink.[40] Furthermore, as Tarunabh Khaitan has argued, legal academia has a vital part to play in scrutinizing and critiquing judicial reasoning.[41] Academics can act as a bridge between the broader public and practising lawyers and judges, explaining legal decisions to the public and scrutinizing the content and assumptions of judicial reasoning. They also have a role to play in ensuring that considerations relevant to an area of law that are excluded from judicial reasoning for institutional reasons—such as the inability of judges to research the economic impact of their decisions—are nevertheless included in the development of the law at the legislative level.

---

[38] Brown and Pehrson (n 13) 41–42.
[39] S Choi and G Mitu Gulati, 'Bias in Judicial Citations: A Window into the Behavior of Judges?' (2008) 37 J Legal Stud 87.
[40] C Sunstein, *Why Societies Need Dissent* (Harvard UP 2003) ch 1.
[41] T Khaitan, '*Koushal v Naz*: Judges Vote to Recriminalise Homosexuality' (2015) 78 MLR 672, 678.

4. Conclusion

This chapter has argued that a legalistic approach to precedent is unable to explain its coercive nature and that to understand the operation of precedent we must recognize that its legal rules are supplemented by non-legal rules, generated within social groups of which judges and lawyers are members. Though this interpretation of precedent may depart from others developed in this volume, it might be less novel than it first appears. The tight connection between the development of the common law and the legal practice of precedent is comparatively recent; the common law operated for centuries without a doctrine of precedent. Instead, it was the common learning of the legal profession developed within the Inns of Court that shaped the law and it was not until the end of the eighteenth century that something like our modern system of precedent emerged.[42] Before this period, the common learning—which, in the terms of this chapter, comprises the rules generated by the legal community outside the courts—provided enough certainty to allow the common law to operate. While the legal aspect of precedent has grown in importance over the last two hundred years, it has been built on top of, rather than replaced, this social practice and its operation cannot be understood without reflection on its social dimension.

---

[42] Duxbury (n 1) 31–37; Simpson (n 5) 77–78.

5
Precedent and Legal Creep
A Cause for Concern?

Adam Rigoni[*]

1. Introduction

Precious little attention has been paid to the role of the law–fact distinction in theories of precedent, though the law–fact distinction itself hardly lacks discussion.[1] There seems to be consensus in both the US and the UK that precedent, whatever else it may be, is something that stems only from determinations of 'matters of law' and that judicial or jury-made decisions regarding 'matters of fact', whatever else they may be, are not precedential. One might therefore expect significant discussion of matters like how to distinguish legal conclusions from factual conclusions within an opinion, when is an appellate case limited to its facts, and so on. What one finds is a bit of that on the UK side, and nearly none of that in the US. Instead, the trend in the US in legal practice and globally in legal theory is towards what I call 'legal creep': treating more and more of the factual conclusions within an opinion as precedential, with the result that what was once 'factual' is now 'legal'.

My purpose in this chapter is neither to argue for a particular explanation of the law–fact distinction nor to criticize legal creep itself. Rather, I want to stress that legal creep is happening and that a number of factors, including the prevailing trends in theories of precedent in jurisprudence and artificial intelligence (AI), make it highly likely to continue at an increasing pace. Since legal creep clearly at least *might* be bad, those of us working on theories of precedent should be cognizant of how our own work might accelerate it.

This chapter proceeds as follows. The next section offers evidence for the relationship between the law–fact distinction and precedent as alleged earlier. It also details the paucity of discussion the distinction has received. Section 3 introduces my working example of legal creep: the concept of negligence in tort actions. In tort law in both the UK and the US, the determination of whether a party was negligent is treated as a factual determination and hence should not, outside exceptional instances, establish a precedent. And yet, as section 3 shows, this area has been subject to legal creep. UK judges have explicitly pushed back against this tendency, while most lawyers in the US seem to be either unaware of or indifferent to it. Section 4 then identifies the factors that will encourage and accelerate legal creep now and ever more so in the future. My particular focus there is on the role of AI and law and theories

---

[*] This essay is indebted to conversations with and the memories of Judge Richard J Celello.
[1] See, e.g., RJ Allen and MS Pardo, 'The Myth of the Law–Fact Distinction' (2003) 97 Northwestern U L Rev 1769; DP O'Gorman, 'Contract Law's Predominant Purpose Test and the Law–Fact Distinction' (2018) 45 Fla State U L Rev 443; SA Weiner, 'The Civil Jury Trial and the Law–Fact Distinction' (1966) 54 Cal L Rev 1867; RH Warner, 'All Mixed Up about Mixed Questions' (2005) 7 J Appellate Practice and Process 101; AO Larsen, 'Factual Precedents' (2013) 162 U Penn L Rev 56; DW Robertson, 'The Precedent Value of Conclusions of Fact in Civil Cases in England and Louisiana' (1968) 29 Louisiana L Rev 78; T Endicott, 'Questions of Law' (1997) 114 LQR 292.

Adam Rigoni, *Precedent and Legal Creep* In: *Philosophical Foundations of Precedent.* Edited by: Timothy Endicott, Hafsteinn Dan Kristjánsson, and Sebastian Lewis, Oxford University Press. © Adam Rigoni 2023. DOI: 10.1093/oso/9780192857248.003.0006

of precedent, as that is my area of expertise. Finally, section 5 provides a summary and some closing thoughts on how we might slow legal creep.

However, having claimed that legal creep at least *might* be bad, I should offer some justification for being concerned about it. After all, if two cases have the same (or essentially the same) facts, legal creep will help to ensure that judges decide them the same way, and shouldn't we want that? And isn't this consistency and predictability a standard justification for precedent? Against this view, I suggest five considerations that provide a prima facie case against legal creep, which justifies further scrutiny.

First, legal creep is contrary to the value of transparency of a legitimate legal system. Even assuming that expanding the scope of precedent to include more factual determinations is desirable, I struggle to see why it would be desirable to make this change unwittingly rather than consciously. The relevant legal systems draw this distinction between law and fact; they still pay lip-service to the idea that precedent binds the later court on questions of law and not on questions of fact. If we ought to change the relationship between the two, we should do so after considering the process itself and the reasons for or against it.

Secondly, there is the issue of expertise and perceived legitimacy. The judge is (supposedly) an expert in the law, and future judges and citizens are only required to give deference to the judge's decision within his or her area of expertise. The deference of future judges cannot be justified by expertise, since they too are legal experts, but the deference of the public certainly is, because the judge knows the law better than them. This grants rules of precedent some degree of legitimacy in the eyes of the governed. Faced with a legal determination they suspect is incorrect, they may nonetheless (perfectly rationally) accept it as correct on the basis of deference to the experts. But factual determinations do not work that way. The judge is no better than John Q Public when it comes to factual determinations, such as deciding how a reasonable driver responds to sudden fog, or how many drinks it takes to make someone drunk. Many members of the public may in fact have more expertise on these issues than the judge. Hence these rules could carry an air of illegitimacy or arbitrariness.

Thirdly, the law–fact distinction is extensively intertwined with the distinction between the province of the judge and that of the jury. Juries simply are not bound by past cases—in theory, precedent does not bind the determinations that they make. If judges feel they are bound by legal rules that would not apply to juries, then bench trials apply different laws than jury trials. This is not a matter of procedure but a matter of different legal rules being applied to decide the case. Again, we might think that having these two different options is beneficial, but, returning to transparency, the choice between them should be explicit, not hidden behind claims that the only difference is who finds the facts. I should add that the Anglo-American legal systems will permit two juries to reach different conclusions from (essentially) the same facts in two cases, provided both sets of conclusions are reasonable. We may chafe at the idea of two judges doing the same thing—reaching different conclusions from the same set of facts—but perhaps that feeling is misguided. At the very least, it needs a justification.

Fourthly, it is well known that appellate courts give more deference to findings of fact than matters of law. There are a number of justifications for this, but the most compelling is that the lower-level court is in a better position to evaluate the evidence, especially testimony, since it experiences it directly. Expanding the scope of legal determinations threatens to undermine this. Appellate courts would be increasingly empowered to overturn findings that lower courts are better positioned to make.

Finally, we can question the degree of predictability that legal creep can realistically provide. Probably the easiest way to think of factual determinations as precedent is to think of

64 ADAM RIGONI

them as providing rules requiring a certain factual inference from some set of facts. To be usefully guided by such rules, an agent has to be somewhat confident that they know all or most of the applicable ones. As we will see, factual determinations (and hence the rules) are large in number, but mostly small in scope, dealing only with very specific facts. On the one hand, the rules' narrowness means that in many future cases none or only a few of the rules will apply. Their narrowness also means that in other future cases, a great many rules will be applicable, providing guidance only if one has a good deal of knowledge. On the other hand, their considerable number makes it unlikely that many agents will be confident they know all the applicable rules for a given situation. Practically speaking, legal creep may enable experts in narrow specialties (and those willing to pay them) to predict a few results, but they do not seem likely to offer useful general guidance.

2. Precedent and the Law–Fact Distinction

In both the UK and the US it is well accepted that only conclusions on the law side of the law–fact distinction in a past case can be treated as precedent. In the US, often the distinction itself is presupposed in statements about precedent, such as variations on 'a court's prior statement of law is a holding',[2] where the implied contrast is with statements of fact. At other times, the distinction is explicit, for example, Garner and others write, 'for stare decisis to apply, a decision … must involve an issue of law not fact',[3] and they are sure to distinguish holdings, which are the basis for precedent, from findings, which are 'a trial court's determination of facts'.[4] Abramowicz and Stearns, in one of the most thoroughly developed theories of precedent in the US, note that 'A satisfactory definition of holding and *dicta* must therefore examine the reasoning that connects the material facts to the result',[5] but not the reasoning that establishes those material facts.

On the other side of the pond, the matter is more clearly stated. Here Cross and Harris speak so directly to this point that I must quote them at length:

> It is not everything said by a judge when giving judgment that constitutes precedent. In the first place, this status is reserved for his pronouncements on law, and no disputed point of law is involved in the vast majority of cases that are tried in any year. The dispute is solely concerned with the facts. For example, the issue may be whether a particular motorist was driving carelessly by failing to keep a proper look-out or travelling at an excessive speed. No one doubts that a motorist owes a legal duty to drive carefully, and, very frequently, the only question is whether he was in breach of that duty when he caused damage to a pedestrian or another motorist. Cases in which the only issues are questions of fact are usually not reported in any series of law reports, but it is not always easy to distinguish law from fact and the reasons which led a judge of first instance or an appellate court to come to a factual conclusion are sometimes reported at length. For example, an employer is under a legal duty to provide his employees with a reasonably safe system of working. The question whether that duty has been broken is essentially one of fact, but the law reports contain a number of cases in which judges have expressed their views concerning the precautions

---

[2] CW Tyler, 'The Adjudicative Model of Precedent' (2020) 87 U Chi L Rev 1551, 1552.
[3] BA Garner and others, *The Law of Judicial Precedent* (Thomson Reuters 2016) 6.
[4] ibid 77.
[5] M Abramowicz and M Stearns, 'Defining Dicta' (2005) 57 Stan L Rev 953.

which an employer should have taken in particular instances. When an injury would not have occurred if a workman had been wearing protective clothing it has been said that his employer ought to have insisted that such clothing should have been worn instead of merely rendering it available for those who desired to wear it, but the House of Lords has insisted that observations of this nature are not general propositions of law necessarily applicable to future cases and the decisions based upon them do not constitute a precedent [citing *Qualcast (Wolverhampton) Ltd v Haynes* [1959] AC 743]. There is no point in endeavouring to ascertain the *ratio decidendi* of such cases.

Similarly, Gardner notes:

A ruling which is arrived at 'on the facts' is to that extent not subject to legal generalization. Even when the ruling is by a higher court, and hence capable of altering the law, the reasons for it include some reasons that are not thereby adopted into the law for re-use in later cases ... So once the question ... is classified as a question of fact, the generalizations made ... are not legal generalizations. They do not enter the law.[6]

Likewise, Endicott writes, 'the common law distributes decision-making power by enabling the court that set the precedent to bind a later court on questions of law, but not on questions of fact.[7] I suspect that the comparative ease of finding exact statements on the distinction in the UK is in part due to *Qualcast (Wolverhampton) Ltd v Haynes*,[8] a case in the House of Lords that explicitly discussed the distinction and its impact on precedent. I'll consider *Qualcast* in greater detail in the next section.

Although Anglo-American common law takes the law–fact distinction as crucial for understanding *stare decisis*, as we have just seen, that distinction is seldom discussed in detail in the context of precedent. The distinction has been examined in the abstract, on the question of whether the law is factual,[9] as well as in very specific applications, such as the precedential status of empirical data in US Supreme Court decisions.[10] The bulk of the discussion of the distinction is focused on either standards of review or the proper allocation of duties between judge and juries.[11] In Endicott's treatment of it with respect to standards of review, he rightly points out that the distinction poses different difficulties in the context of *stare decisis*. Of course, the allocation of duties to juries is relevant to precedent, as jury verdicts have no precedential value whatsoever.

Nonetheless, once the duties are allocated to a jury, they pose few problems for a theory of precedent, since the determinations made by a jury are clearly marked as such and treated with great deference by appellate courts. The real trouble stems from bench trials, where the judge takes on the role of fact-finder. While in theory this does not change the precedential status of the factual determinations—those are still factual regardless of who the fact-finder is—now those conclusions are embedded in an opinion alongside legal conclusions and judges appear to feel increased pressure to maintain consistency between judicial opinions.[12]

---

[6] J Gardner, 'The Many Faces of the Reasonable Person' (2015) 131 LQR 563, s 2.

[7] Endicott (n 1) 294.

[8] *Qualcast (Wolverhampton) Ltd v Haynes* [1959] AC 743.

[9] Allen and Pardo (n 1).

[10] Larsen (n 1).

[11] Weiner (n 1); O'Gorman (n 1); Warner (n 1). Endicott (n 1) is an exception in that he explains that the context of *stare decisis* is rather different than that of precedent.

[12] For a striking example of this, see *Mamiye Bros v Barber Steamship Lines, Inc* 360 F2d 774, 777 (2d Cir 1966) ['It would be shocking if contrary decisions of two district judges in this circuit on exactly the same facts had to be left standing, although there would be no similar shock if such a divergence should happen as a result of the

66 ADAM RIGONI

Further, these determinations are now laid out with justifications and details not present in jury verdicts, which enables appellate courts to more freely discuss, examine, support, or criticize these decisions in their own opinions.[13] These are the preconditions for legal creep.

3. Legal Creep: The Example of Negligence

Legal creep, as I define it, occurs when the sphere of 'matters of law' creeps into and gradually swallows up parts of the sphere of 'matters of fact', that is, when what was once 'fact' is increasingly governed by legal precedent. For my purposes in this chapter, it does not matter whether one thinks this process results in improvement or deterioration of the law. Nor am I concerned with whether there is a legitimate or analytic or functional basis for sorting issues into the bins of law and fact or judge and jury in the way that Anglo-American systems do.[14] All that matters to me is that those systems *do in fact* (pun intended) label some issues as factual (and hence possibly for a jury and not precedential) and other issues as legal (and hence never for a jury and precedential).

Probably the best and most discussed example of legal creep is in determinations of negligence. Determinations of negligence are 'universally considered a jury question'[15] and hence should not create precedential rules. As Alldridge writes, 'in deciding these questions of reasonableness ... a court cannot rely upon the decision of another court that particular conduct was, in different (however similar) circumstances, reasonable. This is a question of fact, and will in all cases be ex post.'[16] Nonetheless, there is an exception for when an appellate court decides to impose a fixed rule in certain circumstances: 'where human experience uniformly suggests the amount of care a reasonable man should exercise in a given set of circumstances, the courts may properly fix the amount of care as a matter of law, thus taking from the jury the factual inquiry ordinarily left with it'.[17] Notably, the appellate rules considered here are not standards that courts may direct a jury to apply, but rules that explicitly state that certain conduct is or is not reasonable, rules that would allow a judge to by-pass the jury altogether.

Despite the general status of findings of negligence, within the applicable legal standard (e.g. reasonable person standard, negligence per se), as factual determinations, at some point in time judges and litigants in both the US and the UK increasingly treated findings of negligence from bench trials/appellate opinions on bench trails as creating horizontal/vertical precedent on the issue of negligence. Judges and lawyers saw rules of 'negligence as a matter of law' in seemingly every appellate opinion on a negligence case, even when the appellate court itself was only examining the determinations of the fact-finder. For example, one finds cases citing as precedent affirmations of trial court findings of negligence.[18]

---

deliberation of two different juries']. However, this is a minority viewpoint, as it was even when *Mamiye* was decided. See *Pacific Boat Two v State Marine Corp* 276 F2d 745, 752 (9th Cir 1960); *Imperial Oil v Drlik* 234 F2d 4, 10 (6th Cir), cert denied 353 US 941 (1956); *Merritt v Interstate Transit Lines* 171 F2d 605, 608–09 (8th Cir 1948).

[13] See the discussion from Lord Somervell in *Qualcast (Wolverhampton) Ltd v Haynes* [1959] AC 743, 757–58.

[14] On that topic, see, e.g., Allen and Pardo (n 1); Warner (n 1).

[15] Warner (n 1) 119.

[16] P Alldridge, 'Rules for Courts and Rules for Citizens' (1990) 10 OJLS 487, 498.

[17] *Ambrose v Cyphers* 29 NJ 138, 145, 148 A2d 465, 469 (1959).

[18] See *Ardoin v Southern Farm Bureau Cas Ins Co* 133 So 2d 129, 131 (La Ct App 1961), citing *Ervin v Burns* 126 So 2d 805 (La Ct App 1961). *Ervin v Burn* itself cites *Butler v Fry* 36 So 2d 69 (La Ct App 1948), which is another appellate court affirmation of a trial court finding of negligence, for support. While a reversal of trial court finding probably always creates a rule of negligence as a matter of law, no one would think that an affirmation has the same effect.

In *Qualcast*, the House of Lords felt compelled to weigh in. The case dealt with whether an employer had been negligent in not advising or ordering his employee to wear certain protective clothing. The trial judge felt that he was bound by findings of negligence in past cases to find negligence here, although he would have found none if he were not so bound. The House of Lords explained that he was not so bound. Gerald Dworkin summarized the holding thus:

> The House of Lords in *Qualcast (Wolverhampton) Ltd.* v. *Haynes* recently emphasised that all courts, including the House of Lords, are not so tied to precedent as had been thought by some. Since the decline of juries in civil cases, particularly in negligence actions, the judges have included in their judgments findings of fact, and often give reasons for their findings, whereas juries gave no reasons. [Quoting *Qualcast* at 758:] 'It may sometimes be difficult to draw the line, but if the reasons given by a judge for arriving at the conclusion previously reached by a jury are to be treated as "law" and citable, the precedent system will die of a surfeit of authorities.' Thus, quite properly, the power of precedent has been weakened in this field.[19]

Regarding the justification for agreeing with the trial judge's initial impulse, Lord Somervell noted that he 'will not elaborate these reasons or someone might cite my observations as part of the law of negligence'.[20] Lord Denning added that we ought:

> to beware of allowing tests or guides which have been suggested by the court in one set of circumstances, or in one class of cases, to be applied to other surroundings, and thus by degrees turn[ing] that which is at bottom a question of fact into a proposition of law ... lest we be crushed under the weight of our own reports.[21]

Qualcast thus explicitly railed against legal creep with respect to negligence. Yet we can see flickers of legal creep in *Qualcast* and its commentary. Properly understood, *Qualcast* is about the difference in kind discussed in section 2: findings of negligence are (typically) matters of fact and hence findings of it do not create precedent. But Lord Denning's remark could be interpreted to instead suggest a difference of degree: findings of negligence do create precedent, but they are very narrow and fact-specific rules and therefore unlikely to bind future courts. On this reading, Lord Denning's remark cautions not against treating these conclusions as rules of precedent but against applying them 'in other surroundings'. Although these two interpretations are particularly similar, they are not equivalent. On the second reading of *Qualcast*, past findings of negligence *could* bind if the present case were sufficiently similar. This understanding has been taken up by a number of commentators. For example, we see *Qualcast* summarized as holding that 'no situation is precisely the same as another; previous cases may therefore be cited as a guide only and not as a rule'.[22] Aubrey Diamond's gloss of *Qualcast* explicitly countenances treating findings of negligence as binding in cases that are sufficiently similar:

I should also stress that these cases are from Louisiana, which is the only US state that comes from a civil rather than common law tradition. As such, it should be the most resistant to legal creep, as the constraining force of precedent should be less pronounced. Tellingly, we still see fact-finding in negligence cases swallowed up by rules even in that environment. See Robertson (n 1).

[19] G Dworkin, '*Stare Decisis* in the House of Lords' (1962) 25 MLR 163.
[20] *Qualcast (Wolverhampton) Ltd v Haynes* [1959] AC 743, 759.
[21] ibid 761 (quotation marks omitted).
[22] BMJ Legal Correspondent, 'Precedent and the Duty of Care in Negligence' [1959] BMJ 1595, 1594.

68   ADAM RIGONI

> [In *Qualcast*] The House of Lords emphasised that whether an employer has broken his
> duty of care is a question of fact, the answer to which depends entirely on the circum-
> stances of each case, and that, therefore, what one court decides on the facts of one case
> cannot bind another court confronted with the facts of a later case.
>
> This is technically impeccable. However, the possible combinations of factors in em-
> ployment situations are not infinite. Situations keep recurring that are, for all practical pur-
> poses, similar in the risk involved, the experience of the workman, his appreciation of the
> risk, the amount of warning or advice received.[23]

This view of negligence as creating narrow rules can still be found today. Lunney and
Oliphant explain, 'as decisions on breach of duty are decisions of fact, and negligence actions
almost inevitably have slightly different facts, it follows that the ruling in one case has no
precedential value in another case, even if the facts are superficially the same'.[24] On the US
side, in their tome on precedent Garner and others write, 'a ruling that specific facts do or
do not amount to negligence is by its very nature narrowly limited', rather than stating that it
is conclusion of fact rather than law. A full review of how effective *Qualcast* was at stopping
legal creep is outside the scope of this chapter, but the persistence of this view of negligence
suggests that it was not entirely successful.

Effective or not, at least the UK legal system has a case like *Qualcast* addressing this issue.
The US system lacks any major case specifically addressing legal creep and negligence in the
way that *Qualcast* did.[25] While a finding of negligence is still acknowledged as a matter of
fact within the applicable standard of negligence, one can find many cases where this does
nothing to halt an onslaught of narrow precedential rules. Consider *Ardoin v Southern Farm
Bureau Cas Ins Co*,[26] wherein the court cited ten cases in support of the proposition that it is
negligent to drive in excess of the speed at which the vehicle can be stopped given the limits
of visibility, distinguished two cases of drivers striking stationary vehicles at night on the
basis that those stationary vehicles were on a curve and hence not illuminable by headlights,
and finally granted a rehearing during which two more cases were produced in support of
the quotidian proposition that it is unreasonable to travel at excessive speed when visibility is
reduced.[27] Crushed under the weight of their reporters, indeed. There is a single law review
article from David Robertson in 1968 ringing the alarm bell, but with only seventeen citations it appears to have fallen on deaf ears.[28] This chapter does not attempt a comprehensive
study of how far legal creep has extended (or, less likely, receded) in this domain. The law of
negligence is merely one example of how legal creep can arise and significantly impact, for
good or bad, an area of the law.

---

[23] AL Diamond, 'Notes of Cases' (1959) 22 MLR 416, 430.

[24] M Lunney and K Oliphant, *Tort Law: Text and Materials* (3rd edn, OUP 2008) 162.

[25] One can, of course, find cases asserting that negligence is a factual determination. Yet these same cases also
typically work to distinguish past findings of negligence, even though such distinguishing should not be needed
if the determination is a matter of fact. See the examples discussed in Robertson (n 1). On occasion, the consequences of legal creep bleed into jury trials. See *Northern Pacific Railroad Co v Mitchell* 80 Ariz 50 (1956), which
distinguishes four past negligence cases dealing with vehicles at railroad crossings and supportively cites three
more such cases, all to justify the trial court judge's decision to let a jury decide the question of negligence.

[26] *Ardoin v Southern Farm Bureau Cas Ins Co* (n 18).

[27] *Northern Pacific Railroad* (n 25) 96–97.

[28] Robertson (n 1).

4. Cause for Concern? Factors Encouraging Legal Creep

Our example of negligence has shown how legal creep can arise imperceptibly and continue at least until legal actors start to recognize what is happening. Many of the examples in the previous section come from the mid-twentieth century (*Qualcast* is from 1959, for instance). The legal landscapes in the UK and (perhaps more so) the US have become much more fertile ground for legal creep since then, for a number of reasons. This section discusses four such reasons: (A) the increasing availability, length, and detail of opinions and the research practices associated with electronic case databases; (B) the increasing prominence of 'the inclusive paradigm of precedent'[29] in courts and the related use of findings of legislative facts as precedent; (C) the current direction of scholarship theorizing or modelling precedent; and (D) in particular the direction of current research in AI and law.

A. Opinions: Everyone's Got One and It's Searchable

On the US side, it is well established that the numbers of court cases and opinions have been increasing, some say exploding.[30] In the UK, the introduction of neutral citations and online access to cases that are not published in reports has greatly increased the number of available precedent cases.[31] US federal court opinion-writing tends to imitate, in weaker forms, Supreme Court opinion-writing, and opinions at both levels have consistently become longer and longer.[32] Longer opinions mean more room for extensive explanation of the underlying facts, including the factual conclusions drawn and the reasons for them. There is just more factual discussion available for counsel to cite and for courts to potentially follow.

This abundance of material is also searchable using the electronic methods familiar to all. As Stinson notes, 'electronic word searching emphasizes, by its very nature, particular words over concepts'.[33] Advocates and clerks are tempted to search until they find the sentence stating the conclusion they want regardless of the surrounding context of the case.[34] Kuh and Huab summarize the current scholarship on the impacts of electronic legal research as follows:

> Scholars have also posited that the shift [to electronic search methods] makes it difficult to research abstract concepts and thus encourages an emphasis on case facts at the expense of principles, leads to 'rapid rule extraction' and shallow legal reasoning and analysis.[35]

Rapid rule extraction with focus on facts is precisely what is needed to catalyse legal creep.

---

[29] RJ Kozel, 'The Scope of Precedent' (2014) 113 Mich L Rev 180, 199.

[30] See RA Posner, *The Federal Courts: Challenge and Reform* (Harvard UP 1996) 62; S Lavie, 'Appellate Courts and Caseload Pressure' (2016) 27 Stan L and Pol'y Rev 57, 58–59; see also FAO Schwartz, Jr and David Greenwald, 'The Censorial Judiciary' (2002) 35 Davis L Rev 1133–74, 1145–47; AC Stucky, 'Building Law, Not Libraries: The Value of Unpublished Opinions and Their Effects on Precedent' (2006) 59 Okla L Rev 403, 403; J Stinson, 'Why Dicta Become Holdings and Why It Matters' (2010) 76 Brook L Rev 247 and citations therein.

[31] 'BAILII—Citations' <https://www.bailii.org/bailii/citation.html> accessed 12 September 2021.

[32] M Penrose, 'Enough Said: A Proposal for Shortening Supreme Court Opinions' (2018) 18 Scribes J Legal Writing 50–59; A Feldman, 'Empirical SCOTUS: An Opinion Is Worth at Least a Thousand Words' <https://www.scotusblog.com/2018/04/empirical-scotus-an-opinion-is-worth-at-least-a-thousand-words/> accessed 13 September 2021. For evidence of increases in appellate opinion length, see Posner (n 30) 146.

[33] Stinson, 'Why Dicta' (n 30) 253.

[34] TL Fowler, 'Holding, Dictum ... Whatever' (2003) 25 North Carolina Central L Rev 139, 141.

[35] K Fischer Kuh, 'Electronically Manufactured Law' (2008) 22 Harv J L & Tech 223, 237–38.

B. Holding, Dicta, and Factual Precedents

A substantial number of American commentators have noted a trend towards what Kozel calls 'the inclusive paradigm of precedent',[36] that is, treating more of an opinion as binding precedent.[37] Recent empirical work provides further evidence of this trend.[38] Much of the discussion on this point focuses on the distinction between dicta and holdings, and if we define dicta as everything in an opinion that is not the (or a) holding, then legal creep is just one example of this larger trend. However, legal creep is a bit more pernicious than many of the standard examples of dicta precisely because many of the standard tests will not identify it as dicta, as we shall see. Regardless of whether legal creep is strictly speaking an example of this larger trend towards an inclusive paradigm of precedent, the trend itself suggests that legal creep will be increasingly common.

One sees this inclusive trend at work in the precedential treatment of what Davis called 'legislative facts', which differ from the 'adjudicative facts' at issue in legal creep regarding negligence. Davis, explaining the distinction, writes:

> When an agency finds facts concerning immediate parties—what the parties did, what the circumstances were, what the background conditions were—the agency is performing an adjudicative function, and the facts may conveniently be called adjudicative facts. When an agency wrestles with a question of law or policy, it is acting legislatively, just as judges have created the common law through judicial legislation, and the facts which inform its legislative judgment may conveniently be denominated legislative facts.[39]

As early as 1955, Davis was able to claim, 'Whatever the theory about *stare decisis* may be, the tendency of the courts to apply that principle to findings of [legislative] fact is a rather substantial one.'[40] This tendency seems to have continued, as in 2011 Gorod notes:

> Whatever the law might require, lower courts will, as a practical matter, often reflexively follow a statement by a higher court, even if the statement is only dictum or a factual finding that perhaps ought not be binding ... Indeed, in the aftermath of *Citizens United*, numerous courts have treated as gospel the Court's factual claim that independent expenditures do not result in corruption.[41]

Even more recently, Larsen identified a host of instances of lower courts making use of factual precedents from empirical data found in US Supreme Court opinions.[42]

---

[36] Kozel (n 29) 199.

[37] Stinson, 'Why Dicta' (n 30); JM Stinson, 'Preemptive Dicta: The Problem Created by Judicial Efficiency' (2021) 54 LA L Rev 587. PN Leval, 'Judging Under the Constitution: Dicta about Dicta' (2006) 81 NYU L Rev 1249–82; Fowler (n 34); Kozel (n 29) 184 ('the prevailing definition of precedent is capacious and inclusive, imbuing a wide range of judicial propositions with binding effect'). Stinson, 'Why Dicta' (n 30) 250–55 and Fowler (n 34) 140–43 attribute this in part to the same facts about access to opinions and electronic research discussed in section 4.A.

[38] D Klein and N Devins, 'Dicta, Schmicta: Theory Versus Practice in Lower Court Decision' (2012) 54 Wm & Mary L Rev 2021–54; N Devins and D Klein, 'The Vanishing Common Law Judge?' (2017) 165 U Pa L Rev 595; Tyler (n 2).

[39] K Culp Davis, 'An Approach to Problems of Evidence in the Administrative Process' (1942) 55 Harv L Rev 364, 402.

[40] K Culp Davis, 'Judicial Notice' (1955) 55 Colum L Rev 945–84, 970.

[41] BJ Gorod, 'The Adversarial Myth: Appellate Court Extra-Record Factfinding' (2011) 61 Duke LJ 64–5.

[42] Larsen (n 1).

This is another type of legal creep, insofar as it involves findings of facts being treated as precedent. However, it is very different from the kind of legal creep discussed earlier, which hinged on the distinction between matters for a jury and matters for a judge—legislative facts are found only by judges or their administrative equivalents and do not derive from the particular facts of an individual case. They are also somewhat rarefied, usually only appearing in US Supreme Court opinions or prominent opinions of federal appellate courts.[43] Nonetheless, their existence raises similar questions regarding the proper understanding of precedent and its limits,[44] and their frequency and acceptance makes it all the easier to accept adjudicative factual precedents, furthering legal creep.

C. Theories of Precedent

The previous catalysts of legal creep are all features of the practice of law, which are unlikely to be affected by any academic article. However, legal creep is also being unwittingly encouraged by developments in legal theory, and here this chapter might make a bit of a difference. The primary trend in recent theorizing is towards more expansive conceptions of precedent and away from accounts centred on necessity. The wizened necessity model proclaimed that a statement of law in an opinion can be a holding if and only if it was necessary to the outcome of the case.[45] However, the 'adjudicative model' repudiates that model and makes precedent out of 'any ruling on an issue that was directly involved in the issues of law raised by the [case]'.[46]

The necessity model, and the slightly more expansive facts-plus-outcome model, are similarly targeted for criticism by Abramowicz and Stearns.[47] Abramowicz and Stearns are motivated to capture the importance of the line of reasoning provided within an opinion and define a holding as consisting 'of those propositions along the chosen decisional path or paths of reasoning that (1) are actually decided, (2) are based upon the facts of the case, and (3) lead to the judgment'.[48] Duxbury disclaims any attempt at a 'satisfactory overarching theory of precedent',[49] but also makes it clear that necessity models will 'provide only inadequate conceptions of'[50] precedent. In the other direction, many commentators have criticized courts for treating dicta, characterized as unnecessary statements of law, as precedent.[51] While not explicitly adopting the necessity model, these criticisms show the force of the intuition that only the essential or important parts of an opinion are binding precedent.

What is notable in all of this is that it has nothing to do with legal creep. Even a focus on necessity, which we have already seen is criticized as too restrictive, will not exclude the factual findings that legal creep is concerned with. It's not hard to think of cases where things like the inference from the fact that the plaintiff passed a field sobriety test to the conclusion that plaintiff was sober are necessary for the result in the case. In an even more obvious

---

[43] Although see *Perry v Schwarzenegger* 704 F Supp2d 921, 953–91 (ND Cal) for a famous example, discussed in Dahlia Lithwick, 'A Brilliant Ruling', SLATE (4 August 2010) <http://www.slate.com/id/2262766>.

[44] Larsen (n 1); Gorod (n 41).

[45] Tyler (n 2) 1552, quoting *Schmidt v Prince George's Hospital* 784 A2d 1112, 1121 (Md 2001), quoting *Carstairs v Cochran* 52 A 601, 601 (Md 1902).

[46] ibid 1554.

[47] Abramowicz and Stearns (n 5) 92–109.

[48] ibid 1065.

[49] N Duxbury, *The Nature and Authority of Precedent* (CUP 2008) 109.

[50] ibid 78.

[51] Leval (n 37); Stinson, 'Preemptive Dicta' (n 37); Stinson, 'Why Dicta' (n 30).

example, nobody thinks a finding of negligence is unnecessary to an ordinary tort judgment. The necessity approach presupposes the law–fact distinction, as both holdings as to the law and findings of fact are necessary to the court's decision in any case. It is the necessary propositions of law that count as the *ratio*. This same presupposition underlies the alternative models as well—notice, for example, that Tyler's 'adjudicative model of precedent' defines a holding as resolving an 'issue that was directly involved in the issues of *law*'.[52] The difficulties the distinction raises are simply not addressed in discussions on theories of precedent. To wit, Abramowicz and Stearns expertly and thoroughly work through more than a hundred pages of addressing difficulties in separating dicta from holding, but say nothing about the difficulties in sorting fact from law.[53] As mentioned earlier, equally silent are those advocating for less inclusive paradigms of precedent, as they are concerned with necessity or at least the importance of the supposed holding to the result of the case, which will not distinguish law from fact.[54]

D. AI and Law

AI and law, I think, merits a special notice because of its potential influence. That influence is unlikely to be direct: I doubt scholarship in AI and law is well known by practitioners and many legal decision-makers. Rather, its massive potential influence lies in how it is operationalized in programs that are used by practitioners. I am (sadly) confident that more lawyers and judges read *The Harvard Law Review* than read *AI and Law*, but I am certain that they all use the search programs on Westlaw or LexisNexis. A change in the Westlaw interface is likely to have greater impact than hundreds of articles, and changes in those programs are a product of the environment of AI and law. Although we are probably a long way away from an overhaul of how Westlaw represents cases, when that does eventually happen, I suspect it will greatly accelerate legal creep.

In AI and law, much of the earlier work on case law was devoted to explaining the reasoning within cases (often for instructional purposes).[55] This, of course, does not mean only explaining the 'legal' or precedential portion of the reasoning, since you can hardly make sense of that without the factual portion. Eventually, as those systems became more sophisticated, the focus expanded to generating predictions about future cases[56] and even to explicitly addressing precedent.[57] However, outside machine-learning predictive programs, there is often very little difference between work on precedent and work aiming for predictive accuracy, and for good reasons. It's very difficult to make accurate predictions without understanding the binding rules requiring a certain decision. It's very difficult to know if

---

[52] Tyler (n 2).

[53] Abramowicz and Stearns (n 5).

[54] But see Larsen (n 1) and Gorod (n 41) for concern for legal creep in the limited context of legislative facts.

[55] KD Ashley, 'Reasoning with Cases and Hypotheticals in Hypo' (1991) 34 Int'l J Man-Machine Studies 753; V Aleven and KD Ashley, 'Evaluating a Learning Environment for Case-Based Argumentation Skills', 6th International Conference on Artificial Intelligence and Law (ACM 1997).

[56] KD Ashley and S Brüninghaus, 'Automatically Classifying Case Texts and Predicting Outcomes' (2009) 17 Artificial Intelligence and Law 125; H Prakken and others, 'A Formalization of Argumentation Schemes for Legal Case-Based Reasoning in ASPIC' (2015) 25 J Logic and Computation 1141.

[57] A Rigoni, 'An Improved Factor Based Approach to Precedential Constraint' (2015) 23 Artificial Intelligence and Law 133; JF Horty and TJM Bench-Capon, 'A Factor-Based Definition of Precedential Constraint' (2012) 20 Artificial Intelligence and Law 181.

you've got the right understanding of those binding rules if your theory doesn't accurately predict case outcomes.

Case-based theories in AI and law typically represent legal cases as consisting of some bundle of facts and rules, or of a bundle of things roughly equivalent to those (like statements and supports), as extracted from the relevant opinion. The extraction process is quite difficult, as one might suppose, and the prevailing pressure is to pay greater attention to the details[58]—after all, the end user can simply choose to ignore the more granular stuff, but if that's left out, it's gone for good. Hence, if the opinion says 'the plaintiff was inebriated' without explanation, then that gets represented as a brute fact, but if the judge gives some reasons for that 'factual' determination, then that gets represented as a decision made based on some rule or rules, maybe entailing some weighing of pro and con reasons. As computational power continues to increase, programs will be able to model more and more of those detailed determinations. To my knowledge, no system attempts to go through and label some of those rules 'non-precedential', again for good reason: those rules are essential to explaining the opinion and are predictively valuable.

One might wonder how those rules can be predictively valuable without being precedential. The answer is that they may capture a commonly shared understanding of some concept. For example, Judge One might write, 'the plaintiff was inebriated, as he had at least six drinks in the preceding hour', and later judges might quite reasonably conclude that other people having had six (or more) drinks in an hour were inebriated as well. The 'six-drink rule' will do a good job predictively but only because it states the shared sentiment of common sense that six drinks in an hour will make someone drunk, not because it has any legal force as precedent. These sorts of common-sense rules are, as I have noted, essential to the decision in a case and cannot be ignored by anyone or anything trying to predict a future decision. But they are not precedent.

That pesky one might continue, 'okay, we have this six-drink rule floating in a sea of algorithms in a computer program, so what?' My worry (and prediction) is that eventually programs like Westlaw will use the representations of cases as facts and rules to further enhance searching databases of opinions for rules on specific topics, such as 'inebriation'. Then the six-drink rule and its siblings will all appear on screens and eventually appear in briefs and then opinions as law, and we're back at *Qualcast* again, having converted a factual determination within the judge's discretion into a legal one that she is bound to decide according to precedent.

In general, my concern is that the trend in AI and law towards more granular representations including factual rules (i.e. rules governing factual determinations, such as the six-drink rule) will eventually be operationalized on a large scale. Once that happens, it is not just that the parties will have strong incentives to o cite favourable factual rules as precedent. That might be stopped by the opposing parties arguing against such attempts or by judges refusing to be persuaded. Rather, the presentation in Westlaw and other databases of these factual rules along with genuine rules of precedent as the rules of a case will blur the distinction between the two, and do so on a large scale. I can point to the large literature on default effect for evidence,[59] but the phenomenon is easy to identify in our everyday lives. Just as we rarely second-guess Google's report of the weather, even those with training often will not second-guess Westlaw's report of the law.

---

[58] Ashley and Brüninghaus (n 56).

[59] For a meta-analysis that covers much of the data, see JM Jachimowicz and others, 'When and Why Defaults Influence Decisions: A Meta-Analysis of Default Effects' (2019) 3 Behavioural Public Pol'y 159.

If we in AI and law want to avoid facilitating legal creep, we have to be very explicit that not all the rules that capture the reasoning within a case are precedent. Since the law–fact distinction is so muddy and controversial, attempting to definitively label or exclude certain rules (or inferences) may do more harm than good. But we can make sure to stress that end users must use their judgment, considering the relevant opinion and legal context, to determine whether a rule or inference is precedential rather than factual. We should also consider methods of flagging inferences that appear to fall on the factual side to attract the attention of users. For example, rules involved in what could reasonably be understood as factual inferences should be flagged as potentially problematic so the end user is encouraged to review the rule as it appears in the full context of the case.

5. Conclusion

I have introduced legal creep as a phenomenon that is worthy of our attention. Many of the costs of shifting towards codifying factual determinations as legal rules are discussed by the bench in *Qualcast*. Yet it's worth noting that there may be benefits associated with that practice as well. It may make decisions more predictable, increase public confidence that judges are constrained by law, and increase consistency across cases within a system. This chapter makes no attempt at weighing these costs and benefits. Instead, it stresses that we should attempt such a weighing *before* allowing our legal system to shift in that direction . The danger of legal creep is that it 'creeps in this petty pace'[60] unnoticed, making changes that perhaps no one in the legal system would consciously approve.

I have discussed examples of legal creep, identified some of its catalysts, and offered some inhibitors. Whether it ultimately should be inhibited is an open question, but the answer won't matter much if it continues to proceed rapidly and unnoticed. The most important step now is increasing awareness. This is something that theorists of precedent should take seriously; even if one's project is not specifically directed at the law–fact distinction, it's worth discussing how that distinction might fit with the relevant theory. Even just reminding readers that the distinction is relevant can be valuable, especially in AI and law, where the relevant theories are more likely to be operationalized in programs for the legal community.

---

[60] William Shakespeare, *Macbeth* (first published 1623, Simon & Schuster 2013), 177.

6

Elements of Precedent

*Hafsteinn Dan Kristjánsson**

1. Legal Method and the Significance of Precedent

The goal of this chapter is to lay down a framework within which many issues about legal precedent can be analysed and understood in general, that is for all legal systems. To focus on a more concrete topic and demonstrate the usefulness of the framework, the chapter will address the following question: what legal significance or effects can precedent have?

Familiar distinctions have been made to highlight the legal effects of precedent and explain the differences between them, for example in some common law and civil law jurisdictions. It is said that some precedents are binding (or authoritative) but others are persuasive.[1] Some precedents are binding *de jure* but others are binding *de facto*.[2] Even in those jurisdictions where precedents are not binding, there may be a presumption that they are to be followed or taken into account in practice. It is also said that precedents are sources of law in some jurisdictions but sources of knowledge or evidence about the law in others.[3] These distinctions (and others) capture something important: precedents can have different roles. The distinctions are helpful to an extent; but they are too crude or binary to explain the versatile and even nuanced legal effects of precedent in different jurisdictions and circumstances.

The legal significance or effects of precedent will here be viewed from the perspective of legal method. What is that? Legal method is an array of techniques for determining (identifying) the applicable law and applying it in a particular legal system. Legal methods vary between legal systems. The legal method in a jurisdiction is used to answer a legal question, that is a question about what the law is on some subject matter.[4] Even though a legal method is a way to work out what the law is in a particular legal system, its main elements can be analysed in general, that is for all legal systems.[5] In light of this, legal significance or effects will refer to the possible roles of precedents in determining and applying a legal norm according to the legal method in the jurisdiction.

---

* I would like to thank Grant Lamond for very helpful comments in relation to the workshop held in preparation for this volume as well as Timothy Endicott, John Goldberg, Sebastian Lewis, Lorena Ramírez-Ludeña, Fábio Perin Shecaira, Joshua Pike, and Nina Varsava, who gave very helpful comments on drafts of the chapter.

[1] See, e.g., JW Salmond, *Jurisprudence* (6th edn, Sweet & Maxwell 1920) 163–64.

[2] See, e.g., A Peczenik, 'The Binding Force of Precedent' in DN MacCormick and RS Summers (eds), *Interpreting Precedent* (Routledge 1997) 461–63.

[3] For these and other distinctions, see, e.g., F Schauer, *Thinking Like a Lawyer. A New Introduction to Legal Reasoning* (Harvard UP 2009) 62 and 67–70.

[4] See, e.g., S Vogenauer, 'Sources of Law and Legal Method in Comparative Law' in M Reimann and R Zimmerman (eds), *The Oxford Handbook of Comparative Law* (OUP 2008) 870, 885. For Icelandic law, see, e.g., HD Kristjánsson, *Að iðka lögfræði. Inngangur að hinni lagalegu aðferð* (BC 2015).

[5] The discussion about legal method and its norms is based on my DPhil thesis, HD Kristjánsson, *Philosophical Foundations of Norms of Legal Method* (University of Oxford 2022).

Hafsteinn Dan Kristjánsson, *Elements of Precedent* In: *Philosophical Foundations of Precedent.* Edited by: Timothy Endicott, Hafsteinn Dan Kristjánsson, and Sebastian Lewis, Oxford University Press. © Hafsteinn Dan Kristjánsson 2023. DOI: 10.1093/oso/9780192857248.003.0007

Legal methods have at least three elements. The first of these is legal materials, practices, or factors on which the law is based. They are the raw ingredients of the law, so to speak. Statutes, judgments, and *travaux préparatoires* are illustrations of legal materials. Some are sources of law but others are interpretive factors. The second element is norms of legal method. They regulate the determination and application of the applicable law. They regulate, among other things, the role and relevance of legal materials, practices, and other factors for the law. To give examples, some norms identify sources of law, others identify interpretive factors and specify their use, yet others regulate conflicts of law. The third element is legal reasons. Applying norms of legal method to legal materials, practices, and factors in order to determine the applicable law involves reasoning.

Precedents can be analysed in light of these elements. First, we can ask: what sort of legal material is a (written) precedent? Secondly, we can ask how norms of legal method can apply to a precedent. Thirdly, we can ask how to reason with precedent. Due to space constraints, the last question will be left untouched here. By answering these questions, we learn about elements of precedents and their potential legal significance or effects.

2. What Sort of Legal Material?

A. The Concept of Legal Precedent

The term 'precedent' has many meanings, even in legal practice. Very broadly speaking, it refers to a past decision or an example, which is, may, or should be followed (in some way) when a new decision is made or an action is taken.[6] So understood, the term captures binding and persuasive precedents, for instance. The term 'legal precedent' will be used here for past decisions that matter for what the law is in a legal system and how it should be applied. A legal precedent in a narrow sense is a source of law. In a wide sense, it refers to all past decisions that are relevant for determining the law and even applying it according to the legal method in the jurisdiction. Past decisions that are, for example, only persuasive, sources of knowledge, or actually followed in practice (*de facto* binding) can be considered precedents in some sense but they are not *legal* precedents because they do not determine the law or the legal position in this sense.[7] References to 'precedent' in what follows are (usually) to 'legal precedent'.

A precedent is a decision made by an institution or a person in a case. Decisions of different kinds of institutions can possibly be precedents. They include decisions of courts or tribunals, administrative organs, parliamentary ombudsmen, and other organs of the legislative branch. Conceivably, they can also include decisions of private persons. Commonly, the focus is on the decisions of courts and tribunals and the same applies here. Nevertheless,

---

[6] For examples of definitions, see, e.g., AL Goodhart, *Precedent in English and Continental Law* (Stevens & Sons 1934) 8; A Ross, *On Law and Justice* (2nd edn, OUP 2019) 100.

[7] Heuristics, rules of thumb, practical guidelines, or 'how-to' rules for ascertaining or applying the law may refer to past decisions but they are not norms of legal method. They do not constitute the law or make the decisions, e.g. sources of law. For heuristics and rules of thumb in law, see, e.g., F Schauer, *Playing by the Rules. A Philosophical Examination of Rule-Based Decision-Making in Law and in Life* (OUP 1991) 5, 104–09; M Greenberg, 'The Moral Impact Theory of Law' (2014) 123 Yale L Rev 1288, 1335–36; M Greenberg, 'Natural Law Colloquium. Legal Interpretation and Natural Law' (2020) 89 Fordham L Rev 109, e.g., 116. Additionally, there may be various social norms, expectations, etc among judges and others that are not a part of the legal method in a jurisdiction. They matter for understanding and analysing *de facto* precedents.

it is fruitful to keep in mind, when thinking about the concept of legal precedent, that there can, for example, be precedents of administrative organs.

Another thing to be mindful of is that judicial precedents are not all the same. Courts have dissimilar powers and roles, and they operate in different ways.[8] Some courts decide on disputes, others can only hear appeals on points of law, yet others answer questions about the compatibility of law with the constitution and have the power to strike down unconstitutional statutes, and others still answer legal questions referred to them without applying the law to the facts of the case.

B. Precedent as a Source of Law

The term 'source of law' has multiple meanings as well.[9] Here it will refer to an aspect of legal material or practice (or some factor) that is a basis or a reason for the existence of a legal norm. Statutes, judgments, and practices are examples of sources in this sense. They are bases or reasons for the existence of statutory law, case law, and customary law.[10] A norm cannot be a law of a legal system without having a sufficient basis in one or more sources of that legal system. A source is like a frame within which a legal norm must fit to be a law of the legal system.[11] Even though the legal norm is distinct from the source, there is an inseparable connection between them since the former must have a sufficient basis in the latter to exist as the law of the legal system.[12]

Some precedents are sources of law in this sense. The reason why a particular legal norm exists is because the precedent exists and has the content it does.[13] If, say, the judgment did not exist, then the legal norm, too, would not exist unless it has a basis in a different source in the legal system. As a source *of law*, a precedent is the kind of thing that could be a reason for the existence of a legal norm. Law can have a basis in the precedent. Of course, it could fail as a source, for example because it is too unclear.

In at least some situations, a legal norm is determined by interpreting a source of law. An interpretation is here understood in a wide sense. The source is the object of interpretation and the legal norm is the outcome. For example, a statutory provision is interpreted in its context and the outcome is a statutory law. The same applies to precedent. The precedent is the object of interpretation and the legal norm, which has its basis in the precedent, is the outcome.[14] However, this does not mean that an interpretation is the only sort of legal reasoning that can be relevant in relation to a precedent. Overruling is not (only) an interpretation, for example.[15]

---

[8] See, e.g., J Raz, *The Authority of Law. Essays on Law and Morality* (2nd edn, OUP 2009) 180.

[9] See, e.g., R Cross and JW Harris, *Precedent in English Law* (4th edn, OUP 1991) 166–67.

[10] For 'sources of law', see, e.g., Ross (n 6) 89–93; Schauer (n 3) 66–67. My use of the term is (slightly) different than its use in HLA Hart, *The Concept of Law* (3rd edn, OUP 2012) and Raz (n 8) 45–52, 62.

[11] The metaphor is inspired by H Kelsen, 'On the Theory of Interpretation' (1990) 10 Legal Studies 127, 128–31, 133; H Kelsen, *Pure Theory of Law* (Max Knight tr, The Lawbook Exchange 2005) 245.

[12] To clarify, this is not the same view as that of JC Gray and R Gray, *The Nature and Sources of the Law* (2nd edn, The MacMillan Company 1948) 124–25. See also in this context, J Gardner, *Law as a Leap of Faith* (OUP 2012) 58.

[13] Salmond (n 1) 163; N MacCormick, *Rhetoric and the Rule of Law* (OUP 2005) 144. For a discussion of different models of precedent, see G Lamond, 'Do Precedents Create Rules?' (2005) 11 Legal Theory 1–26; N MacCormick, 'The Significance of Precedent' (1998) Acta Juridica 174, 178–83.

[14] See, in this context, e.g., Raz (n 8) 184; Gardner (n 12) 57–58.

[15] See, in this context, CK Allen, *Law in the Making* (7th edn, OUP 1964) 260, 415. See also, in part, Raz (n 8) 184. See though AWB Simpson, 'The *Ratio Decidendi* of a Case and the Doctrine of Binding Precedent' in AG Guest (ed), *Oxford Essays in Jurisprudence* (OUP 1961) 158.

The relationship between a precedent as a source of law, interpretation, and legal norm can cast a light on some issues about precedent. Among them is the question of what counts as the *ratio decidendi*, the holding, or the proposition of law; is it the law stated by the precedent court or the law interpreted by the instant court?[16] In line with what has been said, the instant court needs to interpret the precedent in order to determine the law based on it. That does not mean that what the precedent court wrote in the judgment concerning the law does not matter, since the legal norm is an interpretation *of the judgment*. Even if a specific rule is formulated in a judgment, the judgment still needs to be interpreted and the rule-formulation is only a part of the object of interpretation. However, where there is only a single precedent, a rule-formulation is likely to be an important part of the interpretation.

C. The Law Used as a Source of Law

In what way is a precedent a source of law? Or what is characteristic about a precedent as a source? A precedent is a past decision where a case was decided on the basis of some law. Often the law was applied to the facts of the case to decide a dispute. It is an example of the use of law in some instance. To follow a precedent is to decide a case or to use the law in the same or a similar way as it was used in the past. As was said earlier, judicial precedents are not all the same. In the focal case, a judgment or a legal decision consists of (proven) material facts, law, the application of the law to the facts, which determines the legal position of some person or persons (usually the parties to the case), and an outcome, often called a ruling or an order. The reasoning of a judgment is typically focused on these elements and the arguments and claims of the parties.[17]

So, which part of a judgment or a decision is the basis for the law? A ruling or an order tends to be an individual or a particular norm, such as: 'Peter shall pay Sandra one million in damages.' The individual norm is usually binding between the parties and it has certain legal effects commonly referred to under the label of *res judicata*.[18] The individual norm is not the (more general) legal norm based on the judgment as a precedent. The same goes for the legal position but that is the conclusion of applying the law to the facts. Often, it is the rights or duties of the parties in light of the factual circumstance. In our example, the legal position could be that Peter is liable for Sandra's loss and should pay her damages that cover that loss. The ruling is based on the legal position, the power of the court to decide the case in a certain way, and the relevant procedures. A court orders Peters to pay Sandra damages because of its conclusion about their respective legal positions, its power to do so, and procedural matters, such as the fact that Sandra made a claim for damages. But the legal position as such is not the law for which the precedent stands.

The core part of the judgment is the use of law to decide the case. The law used in the judgment to decide the case becomes a source of law, that is a part of a legal material (the judgment) which is a reason for the existence of a legal norm (henceforth). The judgment is not mere evidence for what was decided but the content and form of the decision. Therefore, it would not matter if it came to light that a court had 'actually' based its decision on some other

---

[16] G Marshall, 'What is Binding in a Precedent?' in MacCormick and Summers (n 2) 511–12.

[17] For the structure of a typical judgment, see, e.g., Cross and Harris (n 9) 39–42. See also in this context, Kelsen, *Pure Theory of Law* (n 11) 237ff.

[18] See Gardner (n 12) 76. See also H Kelsen, *General Theory of Law and State* (A Wedberg tr, The Lawbook Exchange 2007) 134, 144–46; T Endicott, 'How Judges Make Law' in Elizabeth Fisher and others (eds), *The Foundations and Future of Public Law. Essays in Honour of Paul Craig* (OUP 2020) 129–31.

law than that reflected in the judgment. Conceptually speaking, the use of law in a judgment could be broad. An example is when a court restates the law on some subject matter in a general fashion before deciding the case with reference to a specific (part of the) law. However, a norm (or norms) could exist in a legal system that narrows what is relevant. For instance, there could be norms about necessary premises and what counts as necessary. The norms are, though, not conceptually necessary.

Sometimes a court explicitly identifies or determines the law for the purpose of the case. For example, a court interprets a statutory provision, perhaps in light of the facts of the case, in order to determine a legal norm. Then it applies the legal norm to the facts of the case to determine the legal position and to support its ruling, which is the individual norm. In so doing, the court may concretize, clarify, or dispel doubts and settle what the law is. The decision on what the law is in the case becomes the basis for what the legal norm is henceforth.[19]

In some instances, the use of a (specific) legal norm is implicit. It is not clearly identified or stated in the judgment. Also in this situation, the law that is understood to have been used to decide the case is the (core part of the) source. This applies as well to situations where a court has *created* the law used to decide the case. The law used to decide the case is a more general norm than the individual norm of the ruling. Even when courts only decide on points of law, answer reference questions, or decide on the constitutionality of the law, it is the use of law, that is the decision on what the law is in the case, which becomes the source for what the legal norm is henceforth.

Other parts of a judgment are not irrelevant. The argument of a judgment is interpreted with an eye to identifying the law used.[20] This means that the material facts, legal position, outcome of the case or ruling, reasoning of the judgment, and the parties' arguments and claims can matter for interpreting the precedent. The same goes for other factors, such as the relevant procedural laws and competences of the court. For example, the reasoning about the law (*ratio*) and the material facts can matter for deciding the level of generality of the legal norm for which the precedent stands. Depending on the legal system, *obiter dicta* and dissenting and separate opinions may also matter for interpreting the argument of a judgment.

3. How Do Norms of Legal Method Apply?

A. Norms of Recognition

Precedents are not necessarily sources of law just because there is an institution like a court with a jurisdiction to determine conclusively and finally whether the law has been violated.[21] Whether or not a precedent is a source in a legal system is a contingent matter. It depends on whether there is a norm of recognition that identifies a precedent as a source, such as 'Judgments of the Supreme Court are sources of law.' Norms of recognition regulate the existence conditions of a legal norm in a legal system by identifying sources.[22]

---

[19] Gardner (n 12) 75–79; MacCormick, *Rhetoric and the Rule of Law* (n 13) 154. For precedent as an example, see Hart, *The Concept of Law* (n 10) 124–25.

[20] Gardner (n 12) 79. See also Lamond (n 13) 24.

[21] See Hart's remarks in Hart, *The Concept of Law* (n 10) 97, in this context.

[22] The norms are based on and closely related to Hart's rules of recognition, see, e.g., Hart, *The Concept of Law* (n 10) 94–95, 99–110, but there are some differences, which will not be elaborated due to space constraints.

A norm of recognition can identify a precedent as a source by pointing to it or providing criteria for the identification of any precedent, for example by describing its general characteristics or identifying marks.[23] While identification by ostension (or reception of a single judgment) is rare, such as 'This judgment of the Supreme Court is a source', it is possible. Norms of recognition can provide criteria in different ways. A norm can, for example, refer to norms about a particular court, that is norms of adjudication, as a part of its criteria. It is a part of the criteria because the law is not whatever is created according to norms of adjudication. That is typically the individual norm of the ruling. The relationship between norms of recognition and adjudication is therefore looser than the relationship between norms of recognition and change, which will be discussed later.

A norm can also lay down other identifying marks, conditions, or considerations, such as 'The *ratio decidendi* of a judgment of the highest court of the land, which is supported by the opinion of the majority of the judges and so on, is a source (or the law).' The conditions or considerations can be more or less vague or open-ended. This is part of the reason why it can be hard to formulate fixed rules for identifying the *ratio*. Another part is that the interpretation required to determine the legal norm is context-dependent.[24]

While there may be a single norm identifying a precedent in a legal system, there may also be many, in which case they need to be applied together to identify the source. Norms of recognition can also be of the same or different kinds. Some may be legal norms just like any others, that is have a basis in a source identified by a norm of recognition, but other norms may be so-called ultimate norms.[25]

Norms of recognition can also be positive or negative.[26] Positive norms identify sources and negative norms state what does not count as a source. An example of the latter is 'Judgments are not sources of law.' Therefore, it would be a mistake to think that there cannot be norms of recognition about judicial precedents in those legal systems where they are not considered to be sources. Precedent as sources can, furthermore, be mandatory (must be used) or permissive (may be used).[27]

Two complications are worthy of being mentioned. First, while a single precedent can be a source, many precedents can be relevant for determining a legal norm.[28] Why does it matter? A single precedent may be interpreted in a certain way. The legal norm with a basis in the precedent may be relatively concrete (stick closely to the factual circumstances of the case) and even rule-like. Remarks in the judgment may be interpreted as supporting the legal norm having a certain content. When faced with multiple precedents, all relevant as sources of law in the context, they may be interpreted together instead of being treated as supporting distinct legal norms, which may conflict. A legal norm can have bases in multiple sources. Whereas the object of interpretation was a single precedent before, now it is multiple precedents, which may address (slightly) different factual circumstances and have (slightly) different arguments. Since the object of interpretation has changed and become more complex, so too can the legal norm. As precedents are added, the 'original' legal norm may expand or contract. Its scope may become wider and/or qualifications or exceptions to it may be

---

[23] See ibid 94–95.

[24] See, in this context, e.g., Raz (n 8) 184; Hart, *The Concept of Law* (n 10) 55.

[25] See, in this context, Hart's ultimate rule of recognition, Hart, *The Concept of Law* (n 10) 106–07.

[26] See, in this context, JW Salmond, *The First Principles of Jurisprudence* (Steven & Haynes 1893) 220; Schauer (n 3) 77.

[27] For permissive sources, see, e.g., Hart, *The Concept of Law* (n 10) 294; L Green, 'Positivism, Realism and Sources of Law' in T Spaak and P Mindus (eds), *The Cambridge Companion to Legal Positivism* (CUP 2021) 51–56.

[28] Lamond (n 13) 20–21.

recognized. Whereas a single precedent supported a particular conclusion about the legal norm, other precedents may 'pull' in a different direction. While a rule-formulation in a single judgment may be a weighty factor in its interpretation, it may have less weight when a line of precedents is interpreted. Eventually, many precedents may support a legal principle, that is a (very) general norm. This may partly explain the sense that the common law is fluid, the legal rules are modified as they are applied and a principle may 'grow' or be 'built' from concrete decisions.[29] A precedent, which usually involves identifying and applying the law, becomes a source of law relevant for the future determination of the law.

Secondly, the law used to decide a case often depends on other sources of law and is determined by using the legal method in the jurisdiction. For example, a decision is based on the constitution, a statute, a precedent, or a custom. These sources, which will be called 'underlying sources', were already in existence when the case was decided. In this situation, the precedent involves a decision on what the law is according to those other sources. This raises the following question: what is the relationship between the precedent and the underlying source?

Sometimes a precedent 'replaces' the underlying source. A precedent may overrule another precedent, which may have similar effects to repeal. It may also distinguish or narrow its scope and simultaneously replace a part of it with a different legal norm. Moreover, a precedent may have a higher rank in the legal system than the underlying source. For instance, a precedent may be ranked higher than the legal custom on which the decision was based. Whereas the legal norm was based on practice alone before, now it has a new source of law with a higher rank. Depending on the legal system in question that may entail that, after the judgment is rendered, a judge or a lawyer relies on the precedent as the higher ranking source and does not 'fall back on' the legal custom except where the precedent runs out.[30]

A precedent can also add to the underlying source in various ways. As was said earlier, the precedent becomes a new source, which is relevant for the determination of the law henceforth. A norm of recognition can identify a precedent as a source (relatively) independently of its treatment of the underlying source. A precedent as an 'independent' source becomes a new source of law whether or not it is based on, for example, a convincing interpretation of the underlying source, stays within its boundaries, or identifies the law correctly. Crudely put, it becomes a source even if it is (clearly) wrong (unless there is a *per incuriam* doctrine).[31]

In contrast, a precedent can be identified by a norm of recognition in a way that depends on its treatment of the underlying source. A precedent as a 'dependent' source only becomes a source if the law used to decide the case has a basis in the underlying source and is identified in accordance with the legal method in the jurisdiction. The law used in the precedent must be within the (fuzzy) boundaries of, for example, the statutory provision on which it was based. The legal norm must, at the very least, be a possible interpretation of the statutory provision according to norms of legal method. If it is not, then the precedent does not become a source independently of the underlying source. It is an error to be overlooked when the law is determined henceforth. In that situation, it is not identified by a norm of recognition as a source.

---

[29] See, e.g., E H Levi, *An Introduction to Legal Reasoning* (University of Chicago Press 1949) 3–4; Schauer (n 3) 105–13; J Holland and J Webb, *Learning Legal Rules* (9th edn, OUP 2016) 155, 194–200, 228, 232. See also Raz (n 8) 195.

[30] Goodhart (n 6) 15.

[31] For *per incuriam*, see, e.g., Cross and Harris (n 9) 148–49; I McLeod, *Legal Method* (9th edn, Macmillan 2013) 151.

Even though a precedent can depend on the underlying source, it does not mean that it does not add to the law. A precedent can, for instance, concretize, clarify, or settle the law.[32] After the judgment has been rendered, a judge or a lawyer needs to look at both sources, that is the statutory provision and the precedent in the earlier example, to determine the law despite the need of the latter to be in accordance with the former.[33] As precedents for the interpretation of the statutory provision pile up, so do the sources that need to be taken into account when the law is determined. Sometimes this situation gives the sense of there being a 'layer' of precedents on 'top' of the statutory provision. Even when a precedent does not add any content to the law based on the underlying source, it is still a source. The sources can overlap.[34]

The distinction between precedents as independent and dependent sources is a matter of degree and sources can be (in)dependent in different ways. It mainly turns on the way in which a precedent is identified by a norm of recognition in the situation or the legal system in question. The distinction may be among the explanatory factors of different treatments of precedents in different situations and jurisdictions. A precedent may be a source even though it does not have all the same characteristics as the prime examples of precedents, which we observe, for example, in English common law. This may be the case in those legal systems where there is a legal norm or a view that judges cannot create the law; they should only identify and apply it; or where a precedent interacts with a higher ranking source, such as the constitution or a statute. Possibly, precedents of the UK Supreme Court about the common law are relatively independent sources. But precedents of the Supreme Court of Iceland are relatively dependent sources. Where precedents are dependent sources, it may cause some to state that a precedent gets its force from the underlying source or to be hesitant about claiming that precedents are 'really' sources.

B. Norms of Change

Norms of change confer a power on someone to create, change, or cancel laws.[35] They are those power-conferring norms that norms of recognition refer to as (a part of) the criteria for identifying sources or that stand in certain relations to such norms.[36] Norms of change and recognition interlock in this way.[37] Examples of norms of change are amendment clauses in constitutions and articles conferring a legislative power on Parliament or Congress. A norm of recognition identifies what is created according to the power-conferring norms as sources.

Precedents can be sources without judges having a law-making power in a certain sense. A norm of recognition can identify a source without referring to or relying on a norm of change (a norm that confers a power to create the general norm for which the precedent stands). A court can have a jurisdiction or a legal power to decide a case according to norms of adjudication without having a specific power to make a new (general) legal norm

---

[32] For precedent having force when it is considered to be wrong, see, e.g., F Schauer, 'Precedent' in A Marmor (ed), *The Routledge Companion to Philosophy of Law* (Routledge 2015) 123, 131. A precedent can have force even though it is not considered to be wrong, strictly speaking. It may concretize, clarify, and settle. A precedent may also be more or less convincing given the underlying source and the legal method in the jurisdiction.

[33] See, in this context, Gardner (n 12) 58–59.

[34] Salmond (n 1) 161.

[35] They are based on Hart's rules of change, see Hart, *The Concept of Law* (n 10) 95–96, but there may be some differences depending on the proper understanding of the relationship between rules of recognition and change.

[36] For power-conferring rules, see ibid, e.g., 27–38.

[37] See, in this context, ibid 96.

according to some norm of change. It suffices that a norm of recognition identifies the precedent as a source of law. In that way, judges can make law, without being specifically empowered to do so, by deciding a case that becomes a source of law. That is one of the ways they can be in a different position from the legislature.[38]

However, there could be a norm of change conferring a power on a court to create, change, or cancel laws. For example, there might be a norm conferring an incremental or piece-meal law-making power on a particular court, that is to create new law (of general application) insofar as it is necessary to decide the case. Or there might be a norm empowering a court to overrule a precedent, where the legal effect is to cancel (or 'repeal') the previous law. Moreover, there might be a norm conferring a power to distinguish cases, where the legal effect is to change and narrow the law but is not merely a conclusion that the facts of the instant case do not fall within the ambit or scope of the legal norm of the precedent.[39] And there might be a single norm of change covering these situations. Nevertheless, there need not be a specific norm conferring a power to overrule or distinguish precedents. All of this is contingent; it depends on the power-conferring norms and norms of recognition in the legal system.

Sometimes a constitutional court is specifically empowered to strike down unconstitutional statutes. In that case, the constitutional court acts according to a norm of change to cancel laws, that is to repeal or derogate the law. It acts as a 'negative' legislature.[40] In this situation, it can be difficult to distinguish between norms of change and adjudication. Whether or not the judgment becomes a source of law still depends on there being a norm of recognition with that effect. The individual norm that (expressly) repeals the statute is not a precedent just because it has legal effects or is binding for people other than the parties to the case any more than a statute which repeals another statute.[41]

Finally, past decisions can matter because of analogy. Despite the great importance of analogy for understanding precedents, the nature of analogy and the norms governing it will not be discussed here aside from stating that not all legal systems allow the use of analogy from precedents.[42]

C. Norms of Institutional Decision-Making

Norms of institutional decision-making concern the role of a *particular* institution, or the way in which such an institution can and should decide a case, including how 'far' it goes.[43] For example, sometimes there are norms of deference that demand that a court defer to or grant another institution, such as another court or other branches of government, discretion or a margin of appreciation. Norms of institutional decision-making include institutional considerations and duties imposed, for example, on courts to adjudicate. They also include the law-applying powers to decide a case. However, they do not include other types

---

[38] See, e.g., Gardner (n 12) 74, 79. See also, in this context, Lamond (n 13) 24–26.

[39] Raz (n 8) 185–92, 196, 200; Gardner (n 12) 74, 80. For interstitial legislation by judges, see, e.g., BN Cardozo, *The Nature of The Judicial Process* (Quid Pro Law Books 2010), e.g., 41; Justice Holmes in *Southern Pacific Co v Jensen* 244 US 205, 221.

[40] See Kelsen, *General Theory of Law and State* (n 18) 267–69.

[41] See ibid 268.

[42] For analogical reasoning, see, e.g., Raz (n 8) 201–06.

[43] They are based on and inspired by Hart's rules of adjudication, see Hart, *The Concept of Law* (n 10) 96–98 and in part 29 and 285, but as a category they are both wider and narrower: for example, they include certain duty-imposing norms.

of norms of legal method. Whereas norms of recognition identify sources, norms of institutional decision-making concern the duties and powers of a *particular* institution in deciding a case. Norms of institutional decision-making can be further categorized, depending on the type of law-applying power or type of institution, into norms of adjudication (courts), norms of executive action (administrative organs),[44] and other law-applying powers and duties, including those of parliamentary ombudsmen and legislative organs.[45]

The nature of *stare decisis et non quieta movere* (or, alternatively, *stare rationibus decidendi* or the doctrine of binding precedent) is interesting in this respect. Here it is taken to be a norm (or a bundle of norms) the content of which is that lower courts are bound by decisions of higher courts (vertical) and some courts are bound by their own decisions (horizontal), either absolutely (strong/strict) or with exceptions or limitations (weak). Therefore, there is a need to look at which court is bound by which court and to what extent. Accordingly, *stare decisis* is a norm that imposes a duty on a court to follow a past decision of a higher court or its own past decision.[46]

A lot depends on how *stare decisis* is characterized (in different legal systems). Understood as a duty on a court to follow a past decision of a higher court or its own past decision, it is a norm of institutional decision-making, more specifically a norm of adjudication. It imposes a duty on a court to decide a case in a particular way.[47] It does not as such identify precedents as source of law in the sense used here. If it did, then it would be a norm of recognition.[48] And it does not impose a duty on other officials to recognize precedents as sources. Instead, it imposes a duty on particular institutions to decide cases in a certain way and these duties may differ between courts. How courts, especially higher courts, decide cases matters of course for other officials and the people in the jurisdiction. But that alone does not make it a norm of recognition.

There is an intimate connection between *stare decisis* and norms of recognition that identify precedents as sources. A norm of recognition may identify that part of the judgment that concerns the law used to decide the case as the source and then what is binding according to *stare decisis* is the *ratio* (i.e. the law for which the precedent stands).[49] The two can be virtually indistinguishable in many situations. However, precedents can be sources in legal systems where there is no *stare decisis*. In this situation, it is sometimes said that a court is not strictly bound to follow its own precedents. There are no institutional norms with that effect. And a past decision is not a source of law just because there is an institutional duty to follow it. Sometimes an administrative organ is bound by past decisions of a higher administrative

---

[44] T Endicott, 'The Generality of Law' in L Duarte d'Almeida and others (eds), *Reading HLA Hart's The Concept of Law* (OUP 2013) 20, points out that Hart is missing executive rules.

[45] Norms of discretion are closely related to law-applying powers. An institution may have a power to decide a case even though it is a (partly) unregulated dispute. Norms of discretion direct or guide the use of the discretion. They are not simply norms of change since they do not empower institutions to create laws as such. See, in this context, Raz (n 8) 96–97.

[46] See, e.g., Cross and Harris (n 9) 6, chs 3 and 4; McLeod (n 31) 125–26, 156, 164; Holland and Webb (n 29) 155, 157–58; Schauer (n 32) 124; S Hershovitz, 'Integrity and *Stare Decisis*' in S Hershovitz (ed), *Exploring Law's Empire. The Jurisprudence of Ronald Dworkin* (OUP 2006) 103–04.

[47] According to Hart's scheme, it would not be a rule of adjudication but a supporting duty, see Hart, *The Concept of Law* (n 10) 97. Gardner (n 12) 84, says that the doctrine of *stare decisis* 'regulates the extent to which and the way in which later courts may overrule earlier courts'. It protects against overruling. Simpson (n 15) 173, says that a court's law-making power is limited by the duty to follow or distinguish.

[48] See, in this context, an interesting discussion about the House of Lords Practice Statement of 1966 in Cross and Harris (n 9) 104–08; R Cross, 'The House of Lords and Rules of Precedent' in PMS Hacker and J Raz (eds), *Law, Morality, and Society* (OUP 1977) ch 8. See also Raz (n 8) 184.

[49] See, e.g., Cross and Harris (n 9) 6, 97.

organ, such as a ministry or an appeal committee. The duty to follow, or the bindingness of those past decisions, is not enough to make them sources.[50] The past decisions need to be identified as such by a norm of recognition of the legal system even though they are binding. Given the existence of institutional duties that are not duties to identify sources of law, it is clearer to keep them distinct from norms of recognition even though the two may be entangled in practice and literature.

Norms of recognition are also qualifying norms at their core, that is norms about what counts as something for some purpose. They come in the following form: 'Precedents of the Supreme Court are/count as sources of law in this legal system.'[51] *Stare decisis* is not a qualifying norm but a duty-imposing norm.[52] Even if norms of recognition are duty-imposing norms that does not make *stare decisis* into one. Not every duty imposed on institutions (namely, courts) in deciding a case is a norm of recognition. In order to be a norm of recognition, at the very least, there must be a duty to treat certain characteristics as identifying marks of legal standards (or primary rules of obligation).[53] *Stare decisis* does not do that even though it is closely connected to a norm of recognition that does. If *stare decisis* is a norm of recognition, then it is submitted that its content should be described differently than usual: that is, the norm identifies precedents as sources of law and courts are bound by case law in the same way as they are bound by other laws of the legal system. Vertical and horizontal *stare decisis* would, then, be described by saying, for example, that a court has or lacks a power to overrule its own or other courts' past decisions, and *stare decisis* would not be considered a special duty limiting that power where it exists.

Now, it might be wondered whether *stare decisis* adds something to a norm of recognition that identifies precedents as sources. An institutional duty to follow past decisions can reinforce and entrench precedents as sources by forbidding or limiting departure from them. Also, it may make precedents more rigid than they would otherwise be, especially for lower courts. It regulates the relationship between courts.[54] To illustrate, the situation could arise in a legal system, especially where precedents are dependent sources, where a lower court departs from a precedent of a higher court because it considers the precedent to be wrongly decided. Or the lower court might depart from the precedent because it considers multiple sources to be relevant and the underlying source, such as a statute, which is of higher rank, leads to a different outcome than the precedent. An institutional duty to follow a past decision might change the situation by demanding that the lower court follow the precedent even if it considers it to be wrongly decided, or if it considers that the statute, in the example, should be interpreted differently. The court would be under a duty to decide the case in a certain way, that is according to the precedent, irrespective of, for example, whether the court considers the law to be otherwise. It is under a duty to treat the precedent as correctly decided.

---

[50] See Gardner (n 12) 84. He says that a precedent can be binding without the doctrine of *stare decisis*. That is true, but there still needs to be a norm of recognition identifying it as a source in order for it to be a basis for a legal norm.

[51] They are related to constitutive rules but (slightly) different. For constitutive rules, see, e.g., JW Searle, *The Construction of Social Reality* (The Free Press 1995), e.g., 27–29; 43–44. For constitutive conventions, see A Marmor, *Social Conventions: From Language to Law* (Princeton UP 2009), e.g., 32–34.

[52] For duty-imposing rules, see Hart, *The Concept of Law* (n 10), e.g., 27–38.

[53] See, in this context, HLA Hart, 'The New Challenge to Legal Positivism' (2016) 36 OJLS 459, 464; Gardner (n 12) 69.

[54] For a discussion of the possible difference that *stare decisis* makes, see, e.g., Hershovitz (n 46) 106, 108–09.

Assuming that *stare decisis* is a norm of institutional decision-making, four situations can arise. First, there may be a duty on some institutions to follow a past decision without it being a source of law. This can be the case for some administrative organs. Secondly, a precedent might be a source without there also being an institutional duty to follow it. This may be the case in some civil law jurisdictions like Iceland. Thirdly, a precedent might be a source and, in addition, there might be an institutional duty to follow it. This might be the case in some common law jurisdictions today. Fourthly, a past decision may not be a source, and there might be no institutional duty to follow it. This is the situation in some civil law jurisdictions, such as possibly in France.[55]

In those situations where there is no institutional duty to follow a past decision, there might, nonetheless, exist institutional considerations or norms, such as a presumption that a past decision is to be followed, or that it should be taken into account where possible. There might be institutional considerations based on stability, predictability, and clarity that recommend that the institution follow past decisions even though it is not under a duty to do so. There might also be various other institutional considerations, such as reasons to respect decisions of other courts because of convenience, coordination, comity, or professional courtesy.

D. Norms of Interpretation

Norms of interpretation regulate legal interpretation or the interpretation of a source. They regulate the (more exact) content of a legal norm.[56] They identify interpretive factors and specify their uses, statuses, and interrelationships. An interpretive factor is an aspect of legal material, practice, or other factor that can partly determine the content of a legal norm. Examples of interpretive factors in the case of statutes are other statutes *in pari materae*, *travaux préparatoires*, purpose, and history. Interpretive factors form the context of a statutory provision within which it is interpreted. While a source furnishes the main content of a legal norm and is its existence condition, interpretive factors shape which norm actually exists within the source's frame. Even though both matter for the existence and content of the law in a sense, they stand in different relations to it. A legal norm cannot exist if it only has a basis in an interpretive factor. For example, a norm that only has a basis in *travaux préparatoires*, where it only counts as an interpretive factor but not a statutory provision, does not exist as law in the legal system.

A precedent can be an interpretive factor for another precedent.[57] In this case, two precedents are not treated as sources for one legal norm, but one precedent is interpreted in the context of another (or, more precisely, the law based on it). This can happen, for instance, when a precedent relates to a connected legal norm. This includes the situation where *obiter dicta* in one precedent are used to interpret another precedent.

A precedent can also be an interpretive factor for other types of sources when it is identified by norms of interpretation that apply to them. To give an example, a norm concerning statutory interpretation can identify a precedent as an interpretive factor. When this happens, a precedent is 'taken into account' and, possibly, weighed against other interpretive

---

[55] For precedent in France, see M Troper and C Grzegorczyk, 'Precedent in France' in MacCormick and Summers (n 2) 103–37. The complication of precedent as an interpretive factor is left untouched here.

[56] See, in this context, Salmond (n 26) 226–27.

[57] See, in this context, '*res interpretata*', for example in Troper and Grzegorczyk (n 55) 126.

factors that point in a different direction. A precedent can also be an interpretive factor for one statutory provision, which is considered to be in pari materae, when another statutory provision is interpreted. The distinction between a dependent source and an interpretive factor can sometimes be difficult to discern in practice, but it depends on the precedent's role in determining the law.

A 'foreign' precedent can also be (indirectly) relevant because of a norm of interpretation. For example, a statute incorporating the European Convention on Human Rights could be interpreted in concordance with the Convention according to a domestic norm of interpretation with that effect. Precedents of the European Court of Human Rights can be relevant insofar as they matter for what the Convention law is according to a (foreign) norm of recognition or a norm of interpretation of the Convention. In this situation, the precedents are indirectly relevant for the interpretation of the statute because they matter for what the law of the Convention is.

E. Norms of Subsumption

Norms of subsumption can regulate the application of a legal norm to the facts. This is sometimes the case for evaluative legal standards and legal principles. An example of such a standard is 'the best interests of the child'. For example, there can be norms as to how to identify and weigh considerations that are relevant for applying an evaluative legal standard.[58] The views expressed in past decisions can be identified as or be relevant for considerations that are evaluated to determine the standard's application to the facts. It might even be the case in some legal systems that the tort law standard bonus pater familias makes past decisions relevant in some instances, such as when officials undertake administrative acts.

Past decisions can also matter for the application of legal norms without being identified by norms of subsumption. A prime example is the principle of equality. An institution, such as a court or an administrative organ, may be bound to treat similar cases in the same way. That means they must follow their past decision in order to not discriminate. In that way, the principle operates in a similar way to stare decisis. The past decision does not determine the content of the principle of equality as such but is relevant for its application to the facts and, thereby, the legal position of some person(s). Nonetheless, the decision is not a source of law unless it is identified by a norm of recognition as such. Another example is professional duties, such as those that require lawyers to advise their clients with reference to precedents.

F. Norms of Applicability

Norms of applicability regulate the status of a legal norm, its relationship with other norms, as well as other conditions for its applicability, such as promulgation.[59] Very briefly put, some norms govern the status of a legal norm and its relationship with other legal norms of the system whereas other norms govern the status of a legal norm and its relationship with norms of other systems, such as foreign or international law. The latter can regulate the applicability of a foreign precedent within a legal system. The legal effects of judgments of the European Court of Justice in an EU Member State's legal system can depend on such norms.

[58] More on this in, e.g., Kristjánsson (n 4) 176–79.
[59] See, in this context, Salmond (n 26) 223–26.

4. The Various Legal Effects of Precedent

As should be clear from the foregoing, the familiar distinctions that have been made to eluci-date the different roles of precedents can be too crude or binary. To give an example, it is not sufficient, at least not in many circumstances, to contrast binding (or authoritative) and per-suasive precedents. As we have learned, precedents can be binding in different ways. There could be an institutional duty to follow a precedent. Even where there is no such institutional duty, there might be various institutional considerations that support taking the precedent into account where possible. An institution or a person might also be required to follow a past decision because of, for example, the principle of equality, *bonus pater familias,* or pro-fessional duties or because it matters in other ways for considerations relevant for applying an evaluative legal standard or a legal principle. Moreover, the precedent could be binding in the sense that it is a source of law or an interpretive factor.

Another example is the distinction between sources of law and sources of knowledge. Even where a precedent is a source of law, it should be kept in mind that not all sources of law are the same. Some are independent but others are dependent. And some are manda-tory but others are permissive. The multitude of possible roles can also make it hard in some instances to draw a distinction between *de jure* and *de facto* precedents, for example where institutional considerations, presumptions, and permissions are relevant.

In light of all this, we should be wary about making simplistic claims, such as that pre-cedents are sources of law or binding (*de jure*) in common law but not in (some) civil law jurisdictions.

7

Precedent and Paradigm

Thomas Kuhn on Science and the Common Law

Leah Trueblood and Peter Hatfield

1. Introduction

In the *Structure of Scientific Revolutions* (*The Structure*), Thomas Kuhn uses an analogy with the common law to help to explain the nature of scientific progress. He says that:

> In science … a paradigm is rarely an object for replication. Instead, like an accepted judicial decision in the common law, it is an object for further articulation and specification under new or more stringent conditions.[1]

While Kuhn employs this analogy to explain the nature of science, this chapter argues that the analogy helps to understand the philosophical foundations of precedent as well. This is for three reasons. First, in this passage, Kuhn offers a serviceable—although non-exhaustive—definition of precedent as, inter alia, 'an object for further articulation and specification under new or more stringent conditions'. Such a definition is helpful because it helps to clarify what is at stake in the project of judicial interpretation. Secondly, his account helps to explain when and why precedents must be overturned. This is not because precedents are 'mistaken' exactly but rather because, as in science, 'malfunctions' arise in the process of solving legal problems. Kuhn's theory explains the two types of change which are necessary for the common law to progress: cumulative and paradigmatic. Thirdly and finally, Kuhn's analogy shows that, while progress in the law is not linear, this complexity is to the law's advantage. Sometimes it is necessary, and even helpful, for the common law to move backwards to move forwards.

This chapter has five sections. Section 1 explains both Kuhn's account of science and the analogy he draws with common law. Section 2 traces the way in which Kuhn's analogy does and does not translate to the law. The focus then moves on to the value of Kuhn's analogy for understanding the philosophical foundations of precedent. Section 3 argues why the definition Kuhn offers—a precedent as an object for further articulation and specification under new or more stringent conditions—is both accurate and helpful. Section 4 shows that Kuhn's use of the term 'malfunction' articulates when and why precedents must sometimes be overturned. Both cumulative and paradigmatic change are necessary for the common law to progress. The fifth explains why Kuhn is correct that theories of paradigms are principally theories of agreement.

---

[1] T Kuhn, *The Structure of Scientific Revolutions* (50th anniversary edn, University of Chicago Press 2012) 23.

Leah Trueblood and Peter Hatfield, *Precedent and Paradigm* In: *Philosophical Foundations of Precedent*. Edited by: Timothy Endicott, Hafsteinn Dan Kristjánsson, and Sebastian Lewis, Oxford University Press. © Leah Trueblood and Peter Hatfield 2023. DOI: 10.1093/oso/9780192857248.003.0008

2. Kuhn on Scientific Progress

It is perhaps surprising that Kuhn begins his analysis of progress in science by drawing a parallel with the common law. *The Structure* is a work in the history and philosophy of science. The master thesis of Kuhn's book is that one kind of science—normal science—involves the gradual accumulation of knowledge within a fixed paradigm.[2] These periods of normal science are interrupted by revolutionary science, which is the result of new paradigms.[3] Examples of these paradigm shifts include the move from Aristotle's analysis of motion[4] to classical mechanics (and then later from classical mechanics to a relativistic view of space, time, and motion), steady-state theory to Big Bang cosmology,[5] miasma theory to germ theory, and phlogiston theory to Lavoisier's application of chemical balance.[6]

The parallel Kuhn draws between the common law and normal science is that normal science operates by accumulation within a fixed paradigm. A paradigm offers the prospect of success and is then applied to a series of questions and problems through normal science. In this way, Kuhn argues that a scientific paradigm acts like a precedent or 'accepted judicial decision'. In drawing this parallel, Kuhn argues that a paradigm gets off the ground because of its potential for success. Almost all science is the 'normal science' of experimenting and observing within the broad set of assumptions of the assumed paradigm. 'Inevitably, however, paradigms have their limits. Normal science leads to experimental results which are not explicable in the current paradigm.'[7] Eventually, a tipping point is reached where a paradigm fails to solve problems in a sufficient number of situations that a new paradigm competes. This new paradigm becomes the dominant paradigm if it is consistently able to produce better results in a broader range of contexts than the previous paradigm. Kuhn draws a connection here with political revolutions arguing that in both political and scientific revolutions, there is a 'growing sense ... that an existing paradigm has ceased to function adequately in the exploration of an aspect of nature to which that paradigm itself had previously led the way'.[8] Kuhn says this 'malfunction' is a prerequisite to a revolution in both these scientific and political cases.[9] While the analogy Kuhn draws between science and law is imperfect, it is nevertheless helpful. The next section will explain how Kuhn's analogy translates, and does not translate, to the common law.

3. Precedent as Paradigm

What is a paradigm in a legal context? In explaining the nature of science, Kuhn uses the idea of paradigm in a range of different ways.[10] He says it can be a framework or mindset.[11] It may

---

[2] ibid ch III.

[3] ibid ch VII.

[4] ibid 121–25.

[5] W Marx and L Bornmann, 'How Accurately Does Thomas Kuhn's Model of Paradigm Change Describe the Transition from the Static View of the Universe to the Big Bang Theory in Cosmology?' (2010) 84 Scientometrics 441, 441.

[6] Kuhn (n 1) 54–57.

[7] 'A novel theory emerged only after a pronounced failure in the normal problem-solving activity', ibid 75.

[8] ibid 92.

[9] ibid, 93.

[10] Indeed, it is a familiar critique of Kuhn's theory that he uses the idea of 'paradigm' in a wide range of ways. M Masterman, 'The Nature of a Paradigm' in I Lakatos and A Musgrave (eds), *Criticism and the Growth of Knowledge* (CUP 1970) 59.

[11] Kuhn (n 1) 85.

also be a way of 'solving puzzles'.[12] These multiple uses of the word paradigm are a familiar criticism of Kuhn's account but, in drawing the parallel with law, the flexibility of the idea of a paradigm is advantageous. A legal paradigm may take different forms but at root, as in science, a legal paradigm is a method or test for solving a legal problem. This method can be an approach or philosophy, as in the case of textualism[13] or common law constitutionalism.[14] A paradigm may also be a legal doctrine if the doctrine, such as *Wednesbury* unreasonableness[15] or the tort of negligence,[16] is also a method or test for solving legal problems. Further, they are methods which adopt a particular philosophy or approach. They are not neutral; they are driven by a hypothesis about how a legal problem should be solved. Now, Kuhn's analogy does not hold perfectly because, on Kuhn's account, all precedents are paradigms.[17] This cannot be correct. Precedents and paradigms are not synonymous. In law, not all precedents are paradigms and not all paradigms are precedents. Not all paradigms are precedents because a way of solving a legal problem may not have been adopted, or adopted yet, in a particular jurisdiction. Originalism is a paradigm of constitutional interpretation, for instance, but it is not a precedent in Canada. Additionally, not all precedents are paradigms. An accepted judicial decision is not necessarily a method or test for solving a legal problem. An accepted judicial decision may instead be the equivalent of an experiment in science: one instance of the application of a paradigm to a particular case. Any precedent may, however, become a paradigm over time, depending on how it is used in the common law. A precedent may well become a method for solving a legal problem if the issues raised by a particular case raise issues that arise more generally.

To help to clarify the way in which process in science sometimes traces progress in law, Table 7.1 compares the two domains. The table demonstrates both the cumulative process which occurs through ordinary science and judicial decisions, and well as the—necessarily—disruptive process which sometimes occurs through overturning precedents too.

Tracing these parallels between progress and science and in the common law does not mean that Kuhn was correct in all respects. Kuhn himself made material revisions to his account.[18] This chapter is also not the first to pick up on this parallel Kuhn draws between

---

[12] ibid 52.

[13] 'Textualism does not admit of a simple definition, but in practise is associated with the basic proposition that judges must seek and abide by the public meaning of the enacted text': JF Manning, 'Textualism and Legislative Intent' (2005) 91 Va L Rev 419, 420.

[14] Common law constitutionalism is a theory of public law which has achieved prominence in the UK. There are different versions, but the core idea is that constitutional courts are guardians of fundamental democratic values such as the rule of law. For a helpful account of the theory, see T Poole, 'Back to the Future? Unearthing the Theory of Common Law Constitutionalism' (2003) 23 OJLS 435, 440. Indeed, Kuhn's account of paradigms also helps to explain the work that these two theories of law are doing. It articulates that these are methods or tools for solving particular legal problems.

[15] *Associated Provincial Picture Houses Ltd v Wednesbury* [1948] 1 KB 223 [234] (Lord Greene): 'It may be still possible to say that, although the local authority have kept within the four corners of the matter which they ought to consider, they have nevertheless come to a conclusion so unreasonable that no reasonable authority could ever have come to it. In such a case, again, I think the court can interfere.'

[16] *Donoghue v Stevenson* [1932] UKHL 100. Lord Atkin: 'You must take reasonable care to avoid acts or omissions which you can reasonably foresee would be likely to injure your neighbour. Who, then, in law, is my neighbour? The answer seems to be—persons who are so closely and directly affected by my act that I ought reasonably to have them in contemplation as being so affected when I am directing my mind to the acts or omissions which are called in question.'

[17] This must be what Kuhn means because he draws an equivalence in the original analogy: 'In science … a paradigm is rarely an object for replication. Instead, like an accepted judicial decision in the common law, *it is* an object for further articulation and specification under new or more stringent conditions.' Kuhn (n 1) 23 (emphasis added).

[18] Particularly his 1969 postscript to *The Structure*.

Table 7.1 Science Law

Normal Phase	Classical mechanics; using Newton's equations to calculate motion of planets, etc.	Uncontroversial judgments based on previous precedents, e.g. application of Lord Atkin's 'neighbour principle' from *Donoghue v Stevenson*.
Extraordinary Anomalies or Malfunctions	Lack of Galilean invariance of Maxwell's equations, orbit of Mercury.	Cases arise giving contradictory, unsound, or unjust outcomes, e.g. the test in *Anns v Merton*[a] for establishing the existence of a duty of care in the tort of negligence in the UK.
Adoption of Paradigm	Special and general relativity seem to explain a number of observational anomalies (e.g. orbit of Mercury) well, in addition to satisfying a range of desirable theoretical properties, and achieve broad acceptance.	A higher court employs a new test, legal doctrine, or approach as a method for solving a legal problem, e.g. overturning the *Anns* test in *Murphy v Brentwood*.[b]
New Normal	Using equations of general relativity to solve problems of motion on a day-to-day basis, and it is well understood when Newtonian approximation is appropriate.	Judgments applying the new three-stage test which includes proximity, rather than the two-stage test of *Anns*. Although the meaning of proximity is itself a source of ongoing debate.

[a]*Anns v Merton* [1977] AC 728.
[b]*Murphy v Brentwood* [1991] 1 AC 398.

science and law. The analogy Kuhn makes has been applied to debates both about positivism[19] and critical legal theory.[20] The scope of this chapter is narrow. The focus here is only on the value of the analogy Kuhn draws between science and the common law for the philosophical foundations of precedent. Consider now three reasons why Kuhn's analogy is helpful for understanding progress and precedent in the common law.

4. Kuhn's Definition of Precedent

In drawing his analogy between precedent and paradigm, Kuhn provides a serviceable— although non-exhaustive—definition of precedent. Kuhn's definition has three parts. He says that a precedent is (i) an object, (ii) for further articulation and specification, (iii) under new or more stringent conditions. Consider each part of this definition in turn.

A. Precedents as Objects for Further Articulation

A precedent is an object. That is not to say precedent is just an object, but it is an object insofar as it is an artefact. That a precedent is an object, or artefact, comes from the written nature of the common law. The common law is a textual type of reasoning. Accepted judicial

---

[19] N Sidorova, A Zeldner, and V Osipov, 'The Paradigm of Law (In Honor of Thomas Kuhn)' (2020) International Scientific Conference 626, 632.
[20] JH Schlegel, 'Of Duncan, Peter, and Thomas Kuhn' (2000) 22 Cardozo L Rev 1061, 1062.

statements necessarily take the form of written reasons. This form and publicity are essential for the efficacy of the common law, for precedents to be applied and applied again. This textual nature of precedents holds even for different kinds of precedents. Even if, for instance, a precedent is drawing on an academic account—for example, Dicey's definition of parliamentary sovereignty—Dicey's definition too is an artefact. What matters here is that precedents can be different types of objects but, given the textual nature of the common law, Kuhn's first insight is correct: they are objects.

The second part of Kuhn's first claim is that precedents are objects for 'further articulation'. This is helpful because the word 'further' draws out that the meaning of precedent is a dynamic process. Precedents have some meaning before they are applied, but this meaning is both backward- and forward-looking. The dual directions of precedent are helpfully captured by Kuhn's use of the word 'further'. The meaning of the *Case of Proclamations*,[21] for example, both shapes and is shaped by its application in the cases of *Miller I*[22] and *Cherry/Miller II*.[23] Just as with scientific experimentation in normal science, every time a paradigmatic precedent is applied it achieves greater meaning in and through its application. A paradigm is not a paradigm if no one is using it. Kuhn is right to say that the process of articulation, in science and law, is both ongoing and iterative.

B. Precedent as Specification

Precedents are particular. This is the second part of Kuhn's definition of precedent: a precedent is an object for specification. This idea of specification, on the Kuhnian account, is analogous to experimentation. This idea of specification is helpful because it captures the particularity of precedents in the common law. The paradigm of the *Case of Proclamations* may be applied in a range of different circumstances, as seen earlier in the two *Miller* cases, but this application occurs in a way that is sensitive to sets of facts. Further, there is no single precedent governing constitutional interpretation, the tort of negligence, or the limits of prerogative powers. The question of application is one of specification: is this precedent applicable in these particular and specific circumstances? This process of specification is not identical to normal science, but it does have many of the same features. Most notably, specification is cumulative in that it builds on what has come before. Case law is a series of precedents which are followed and refined over time. This leads to the final part of Kuhn's definition.

C. More Stringent Conditions

As common law systems evolve, the conditions under which precedents are applied become more and more demanding. The range and types of considerations change, and the number

---

[21] *Case of Proclamations* [1610] EWHC KB J22: 'The King has no prerogative but that which the law of the land allows him.'

[22] *R (Miller) v Secretary of State for Exiting the European Union* [2017] 2 WLR 583. The Secretary of State did not have the power under the prerogative to give notice under art 50 of the Treaty on European Union that the UK would withdraw from the European Union.

[23] *R (Miller) v The Prime Minister* and *Cherry v Advocate General for Scotland* [2019] 3 WLR 589. Prorogation was an unlawful use of the prerogative because it had the effect of frustrating, without reasonable justification, the ability of Parliament to carry out its dual constitutional roles of legislating and scrutinizing the executive.

of objects that may (or indeed must) be drawn on by judges in their reasoning become increasingly diverse. In this way, the conditions under which judges are using precedents as objects for further articulation and specification become more complex. This is true in normal science as well. As the volume and scope of experiments within paradigms each increase, the conditions under which paradigms are tested become more and more demanding. Sometimes this process of normal science can continue indefinitely, but sometimes the progress that can be achieved within a paradigm reaches its limit. This is when paradigms must be overturned for progress to occur. Kuhn is right that sometimes this kind of disruption is necessary for progress in science, and the next section argues that this is true in law as well. Sometimes the applications of precedent under increasingly stringent conditions lead to unacceptable outcomes. The law has malfunctioned and there is a need to move backwards and revisit the paradigm or method for solving the legal problem, to move forwards.

5. Mistakes and Malfunctions

The question of when a precedent must be overturned is a challenge for the law. By definition, a precedent is an authoritative determination of the law by a court. How, then, can a decision be overturned on the basis that it is 'mistaken'? Kuhn's idea of paradigms can help to make sense of this kind of challenge. This is because, on Kuhn's account, precedents are not overturned because they are 'mistakes', but rather because they are 'malfunctions' of the current paradigm. Kuhn's idea of malfunction better captures the nature of progress in science and the common law than the idea of a mistake. Consider first an instance of a paradigm shift, the overturning of the test in *Anns v Merton* for establishing a duty of care in the tort of negligence, and then a potential paradigm shift in the move from *Wednesbury* to proportionality in determining whether a public authority has acted unlawfully. Both of these cases demonstrate why this idea of a malfunction is so helpful.

Let's return to the table from section 2 and to the overturning of the test *Anns v Merton* for establishing a duty of care in the tort of negligence. In *Murphy v Brentwood*, the House of Lords concluded that the *Anns* test was too broad to perform the necessary legal work, and so the House of Lords shifted from a two-stage test to a three-stage test.[24] The third stage of the new test added a requirement of 'proximity'. While there were clearly challenges in applying the *Anns* test before it was overturned, it is misleading to characterize the *Anns* test as 'mistaken'.[25] *Anns* was cited in '189 English cases in only 13 years (and until recently mostly with approval)'.[26] That is to say: the test in *Anns* was doing a great deal of legal work, it was being applied a great deal. The question was: was this legal work itself working? This was a paradigmatic change in the tort of negligence and an instance where 'something extraordinary happened'.[27] The House of Lords unanimously concluded that a new test was necessary. It is important too that the new paradigm, including the test of proximity, is also

---

[24] 'In my opinions there can be no doubt that *Anns* has for long been widely recognised as an unsatisfactory decision. In relation to the scope of the duty owed by a local authority it proceeded upon what must, with due respect to its source, be regarded as a somewhat superficial examination of principle and there has been extreme difficulty ... in ascertaining upon exactly what basis of principle it did proceed. I think it must now be recognized that it did not proceed on basis of principle at all, but constituted a remarkable example of judicial legislation': *Murphy v Brentwood DC* [1991] 1 AC 398 [15]–[16] (Lord Keith).

[25] Howarth uses the word 'unsound', for instance, in D Howarth, 'Negligence After *Murphy*: Time to Rethink' (1991) 50 CLJ 58, 58.

[26] ibid.

[27] ibid. Extraordinary, as Howarth says too, in that the decision was 7:0.

an imperfect and contested solution. It is possible, perhaps even likely, that this paradigm will be overturned in the future. Doubtless the replacement and modification of tests creates legal challenges, but it is neither surprising nor problematic that the law goes through paradigmatic upheaval to find better solutions to the sticky legal problem of establishing a duty of care in negligence.

A second example of competing paradigms that demonstrates the helpfulness of Kuhn's idea of malfunctions is the debate in UK administrative law about whether *Wednesbury* unreasonableness should be supplanted with the alternative doctrine of proportionality. There are numerous and long-standing challenges to *Wednesbury* unreasonableness. These challenges include, for instance, that it is tautological, unclear, or an inappropriate standard of review.[28] Despite these serious challenges to the helpfulness of the doctrine, the challenges are not that *Wednesbury* must be overturned because it is *mistaken*. The debate is instead about, for instance, whether it is the most effective means available of solving a legal problem. Perhaps because it treats certain kinds of public wrongs differently without sufficient justification.[29] A legal test can cease to be the right test without being a test that is straightforwardly wrong. So it is not that *Wednesbury* should be displaced by proportionality because the doctrine itself is incorrect, but rather because the tool is not doing the legal work required. The test in *Anns* was not wrong, it was just overinclusive and so the House of Lords (attempted) to rein it in through adding a requirement of proximity to the test for establishing a duty of care in negligence. Again, in this way, paradigmatic change in the law broadly reflects paradigmatic change in science. At a certain point, the limits of a hypothesis are reached. The results a paradigm yields are unacceptable and so it is necessary to modify the fundamental approach to solving problems.

Similarly, it is not that Newtonian gravity is 'wrong' or that astronomers had incorrectly calculated its predictions in the case of the orbit of Mercury, it is simply that it wasn't appreciated that Newtonian gravity becomes inaccurate for higher gravitational fields, and was not appropriate for the orbit of Mercury (for the degree of precision to which it had been measured). Newtonian gravity is now understood as an approximation of general relativity, that holds to an extraordinary degree of accuracy under a well-understood specific range of conditions (namely, weak and slowly changing gravitational field strengths, and low velocities). However, Newtonian gravity is still extremely widely used, in circumstances for which it is likely to be the most effective tool for the problem at hand (if it will be computationally easier, which would usually be the case, and the aforementioned physical conditions are met).

Comparing *Anns*, *Wednesbury*, and the relationship between special and general relativity is helpful too because malfunctions should not be disregarded altogether. Even when paradigms are replaced, they still have value. The limits of the test remain instructive in understanding why the law is the way it is. Even if *Wednesbury* is replaced, the evolution of the law will itself be instructive for evaluating the lawfulness of actions by public authorities. In this way, a paradigm that has been replaced still has epistemic value. Similarly, even though general relativity is generally understood theoretically to encompass and replace Newtonian

---

[28] 'The general criticisms of unreasonableness as a basis of review are well-known and often repeated: it is a circular definition; it is an uncertain guide as to the extent of the "margin of discretion" to be permitted to a public authority in any given situation or (the flip side of the coin) the intensity of review to be conducted by the court; it is a cloak which may tempt lawyers and courts to deal with the merits of grievances rather than questions of legality. These conceptual weaknesses have led to proposals for the common law to recognise a number of *substantive* principles in place of unreasonableness (e.g., equality) or for the replacement of the reasonableness test with one of proportionality': A Le Sueur, 'The Rise and Ruin of Unreasonableness' (2005) 10 Judicial Review 32, 32.

[29] P Craig, 'Proportionality, Rationality and Review' (2010) NZ L Rev 265, 276.

gravity, as mentioned earlier, Newtonian gravity remains in wide use where appropriate (which is in fact most situations). Newtonian gravity also illustrates some aspects of gravity more intuitively perhaps than general relativity (which is typically extremely hard to visualize), and is important pedagogically for a number of reasons (e.g. illustration of inverse square law). The point is this: in both science and in law, students are not only taught the current paradigm but previous paradigms too. This is for good reason. The common law, as has been argued, is a textual mode of reasoning. In textual reasoning, the progress is part of the point. The progress helps to explain the current paradigm. The value of Kuhn's account is in showing why legal paradigms sometimes need to be overturned. Kuhn usefully shifts the debate about the question of whether a legal doctrine, test or method is mistaken, to asking instead whether the law is malfunctioning. The idea of malfunctions speaks to the larger value of Kuhn's theory: demonstrating that sometimes it is necessary for both science and law to move backwards to move forwards.

The power of Kuhn's theory of paradigms is not only in offering a serviceable definition of precedent and the helpful idea of malfunctions but also in demarcating the two kinds of change that are necessary for progress in both science and law: cumulative change and paradigmatic change. Progress in law and science happens gradually, all at once, and sometimes requires revisiting fundamentals. This dual method of progression is not straightforward, but the resilience of both the scientific method and the common law demonstrates its advantages. Cumulative change is necessary for progress both in science and in the common law. This is the process of further articulation and specification under more stringent conditions. This kind of progress is necessary for practical and theoretical reasons. It is necessary practically as a matter of application. Statutes cannot anticipate all possible eventualities, there is a need for responsiveness to circumstances, which the common law allows in increments. It is also philosophically necessary to consider different kinds of questions on their own terms. There is, however, also a need for paradigmatic change when fundamental approaches must be revisited. This process is risky. Paradigmatic change, and the overturning of precedents, is more difficult to justify because the consequences—as the next section shows—can be severe. Normal science from previous paradigms may be superfluous or create conceptional confusion. A change in legal paradigms, on the other hand, may result in arbitrariness or retrospectivity. None of this is to trivialize that disruption. Nevertheless, as cases like *Anns* demonstrate, sometimes legal conclusions are untenable. Sometimes cases can be distinguished away, but sometimes it is necessary to revisit the foundations of an approach. Kuhn's theory is valuable in helping to explain why and when this kind of paradigmatic change is necessary.

6. The Risks and Rewards of Upheaval

Much is at stake in overturning legal precedents that are paradigms. There is the potential for unfairness in the form of arbitrariness and retrospectivity. The rule of law, of course, requires that the law must be clear, intelligible, and constant. The overturning of precedent can, of course, throw this all into doubt. Nevertheless, not overturning precedents can raise challenges too. The law may be overinclusive, creating floodgate problems, as in *Anns*. The role of the state may have evolved as is arguably the case with *Wednesbury*. Thirdly and finally, the law may be morally or socially out of step with society. So, on the one hand is the need for evolution, on the other is the certainty that citizens place on law that is essential to its legitimacy. When does the case for evolution outweigh the need for reliance? That is not a question that can be answered in general, but Kuhn's theory of paradigms is nevertheless helpful. When weighing up these possibilities, Kuhn helps to clarify what is at stake in three ways. This clarification helps to lead to better legal outcomes and a stronger legal system overall. The first way that Kuhn's theory helps to balance evolution and certainty is this: the idea of paradigm shifts moves the debate about overturning a precedent away from the *content* of the law toward the *form* of the law. The debate then becomes less about whether the law in question is just or unjust, which is particularly difficult under circumstances of reasonable disagreement, and moves instead towards the legal work that a paradigm is doing. This entails less consideration about the content of the paradigm and more about whether it is succeeding in achieving its intended effect. So, in the case of *Wednesbury*, for instance, it means less debate about whether the test itself is circular or tautological and instead asking whether the *results* are circular or tautological.

The second way in which Kuhn's theory is helpful is in stressing the necessity of agreement in both science and the common law. Kuhn's theory is, at root, a theory of agreement, and again this emphasis on agreement helps to shift debates about the content of law towards the form of the law. The question at stake in cases of deep disagreement is: what legal test or tool can be agreed on and applied? This softens the edges of overturning well-established precedents if the focus is on where judges do agree. If the foundation of new legal tests is alternative areas of agreement, then the foundation on which future precedents agree will be stronger.

These two benefits of Kuhn's theory—the move from form to content and placing emphasis on the importance of agreement—may be seen in the pending US Supreme Court case of *Dobbs v Jackson Women's Health Organization*.[30] This section will briefly introduce the arguments in the case which concern the nature of precedent, before arguing the two ways in which Kuhn's theory is helpful for making sense of those arguments.

A. *Dobbs v Jackson Women's Health Organization*

Dobbs v Jackson Women's Health Organization asks whether the paradigmatic case of *Roe v Wade*[31] should be overturned. In his opening remarks in the case, the Solicitor General of the State of Mississippi argued that *Roe v Wade* was straightforwardly incorrect. Abortion, he argued, was a political issue which was best left to democratic law-makers rather than unelected judges. The case should be overturned, he says, because it was mistaken and has undermined the law and the US Constitution.[32] The Solicitor General never questioned that *Roe* and *Casey* were good law in the sense of being precedents, he argued instead that they were bad law altogether. By contrast, the Solicitor General of the Government of the US argued for the importance of upholding precedent. She said that the reliance interests of women would be undermined by overturning fifty years of precedent, particularly a precedent of such significance.[33] At the root of the debate in *Dobbs* is a disagreement about the

---

[30] *Dobbs v Jackson Women's Health Organization* 597 US __ (2022).

[31] *Roe v Wade and Planned Parenthood v Casey* 505 US 833 (1992).

[32] '*Roe v Wade* and *Planned Parenthood v Casey* haunt our country. They have no basis in our constitution. They have no home in our history or traditions. They have damaged the democratic process. They have poisoned the law. They have choked off compromise. For fifty years they have kept this court at the center of a political battle that it can never resolve. And, fifty years on, they stand alone. Nowhere else does this Court recognize the right to end human life': *Dobbs* (n 30) 4, 11–21.

[33] 'There has been profound reliance. And it's certainly not the case that every woman in the United States has needed to exercise this right or wanted to, but ... the right secured by *Roe* and *Casey* has been critical in ensuring

justness of abortion. Oral arguments from the state of Mississippi claimed that sometimes precedents must be overturned because the law was straightforwardly unjust, as in *Brown, Griswold, Lawrence, Obergefell*,[34] and that *Roe* and *Casey* are such cases as well. In response to questioning from Justice Kavangh, Jackson Women's Health argued that *Roe* did not belong in this category, and further that *Brown, Griswold, Lawrence, Obergefell* did not overturn precedents to extinguish, but rather to expand, constitutional rights.[35] Kuhn's theory, of course, offers no help on the substance of the justness questions at stake in *Dobbs*. What it does do, however, is helpfully frame the question of what legal paradigms can and cannot accomplish.

B. The Form and the Content of the Law

On Kuhn's view, the proof of legal paradigms is in the pudding. The success of legal paradigms is determined by the work they are doing. Paradigms can be more or less successful in solving legal paradigms. These paradigms have skin in the game. If they are not working, solving the problems they need to solve in a defensible way then they need to be overturned. The better questions in *Dobbs* focused on the test at stake itself and the defensibility of the viability test for human life. Of course, larger questions about justice which concerned the petitioners, and the respondents as well, shape questions about legal tests. Further, a salient question for a legal test, law, or paradigm is also whether its outcomes align with prevailing social views. Nevertheless, to frame a question as the state of Mississippi did as a straightforward question of justness is less helpful. Under conditions of reasonable pluralism there will be deep disagreement about justice. Adopting Kuhn's theory of precedent helpfully moves the debate about overturning a precedent away from the question of whether it is straightforwardly a good or bad law to the question of whether it is doing the work that law and society need it to do. The question of whether a legal paradigm is producing good results is a question that judges are far better equipped to answer than the question of whether a law is substantively just or unjust.

To emphasize again: none of this is to suggest that the justness of a contested social issue cannot, and should not, ever be at issue in a case like *Dobbs*. The point is instead this: when the matter of overturning a precedent is at stake, questions of *form* should motivate questions of *content*. The question for judges is whether a legal paradigm is working and performing the role it needs to; whether the cumulative process of legal evolution can continue within the existing paradigm. The question is not whether the paradigm is good or bad. In science, for instance, the question is not whether a paradigm is a good or bad idea. The question is whether it is breaking down through the process of normal science and experimentation. It is leading to unacceptable, contradictory, or arbitrary results. Similarly, the justness of the law is a question which is better cast in terms of the work the law needs to do. In the case of *Dobbs*, this would have been accomplished, for instance, by focusing instead on

---

they can control their bodies and control their lives. And then I think there's a second dimension to it that *Casey* properly recognised. That's the—understanding of our society, even though it's been a controversial decision, that this is the liberty interest of women': ibid 96–97.

[34] ibid 25, 27, 36.
[35] 'The Court has never revoked a right that is so fundamental to so many Americans and so central to their ability to participate fully and equally in society. The Court should not overrule this component of women's liberty': ibid 85.

the tenability of the viability test for life at twenty-one weeks established by *Roe* and upheld in *Casey* and particularly its application in the law over the past fifty years. Arguing that a precedent should be overturned because the petitioners disagreed with it is incredibly unhelpful. The focus should be instead on areas of agreement about the functions of law, as Kuhn's theory also demonstrates.

C. Agreement, Precedent, and Paradigm

Kuhn's theory of science is, he says, at root a theory of agreement. While there need not be deep rationalizable agreement on the theory behind the science, there must be agreement on the paradigm itself.[36] Without this agreement, the normal science of experimentation cannot get off the ground. As in science, the law is composed of all kinds of agreement. Without these agreements, there would be no possibility of responding to different facts and solving problems. When that agreement breaks down, severe problems of legitimacy can arise in a scientific endeavour. The parallels between the importance of agreement in law and science are clear. A paradigm in law, as in science, cannot operate without agreement that is indeed the paradigm to be applied. Further, the common law cannot operate without agreement through precedent. Without the agreement that precedent provides, the common law could not fulfil its functions. If it were necessary for judges to reason from first principles in every case, it would be impossible to apply the law to the facts. That precedents evolve and are even occasionally overturned is a clear demonstration of why they are necessary in the first place.

It is particularly important that Kuhn emphasizes that deep, rationalizable agreement is not required either in science or in law. What is required is the following: (i) agreement about what kind of exercise is being engaged in, and then (ii) agreement to participate in that exercise. With this kind of agreement in place, it is possible and defensible to overturn legal paradigms when they are failing to do the necessary legal work. That is because there is a larger agreement in place—such as *stare decisis*—which hold despite occasional turbulence in overturning precedent. Further, Kuhn's emphasis on agreement rightly makes the case for incremental change, even when paradigmatic shifts in the law are occurring. Focusing on areas and the importance of agreement helps to maintain the viability of the doctrine of precedent. Focus on where there is agreement creates the stability for precedents to occasionally be overturned in limited ways. Finally, emphasizing areas of agreement and application, rather than disagreement, supports the overall project and progress of the law.

7. Conclusion

In *The Structure*, Kuhn offers a theory of scientific progress. He offers a theory for both the cumulative progress which occurs through normal science and the disruption that periodically occurs through paradigm shifts as well. Kuhn's insight about scientific paradigms, for which he is rightly famous, captures that a framework for solving a problem can be both accepted as workable at one point but open to necessary revisions in the future. This chapter has argued that Kuhn's analogy helps to clarify the conceptual foundations of precedent for

---

[36] Kuhn (n 1) 48–49.

three reasons. First, Kuhn offers a serviceable definition of precedent as 'an object for further articulation and specification under new or more stringent conditions'. Secondly, his account helps to explain when and why precedents must be overturned. As in science, paradigms must be revised because of 'malfunctions' in the process of solving legal problems. This process of paradigm-revision shows the two types of change which are necessary for the common law to progress: cumulative and paradigmatic. Thirdly and finally, Kuhn's account helps to make sense of when the upheaval of a paradigm is justified. While neither process in science nor law is linear, this is to the advantage of both disciplines. While the parallel Kuhn draws between science and the common law may possibly be prima facie surprising, this surprise is perhaps unwarranted. Science and the law are two of the most enduring and important vehicles of human progress. This is because of, not despite, periodic paradigmatic upheaval.

8

Supplanting Defeasible Rules

Barbara Baum Levenbook[*]

One of the leading accounts of what it is to follow precedent is a rule model, on which following precedent is applying the rule laid down or referred to by the source court. Decades ago, I argued that following precedent ought not to be conceived of as applying a rule, except in the limiting case.[1] Rather, precedent is more fruitfully conceived of as laying down an example, which may have partial categories.

Since then, a handful of writers have developed what Stevens classifies as an amended rule model, designed to meet the objection that the rule model is unable to account for the practice of distinguishing a precedent.[2] The amended model employs the notion of a defeasible rule. The idea is that a court bound by precedent is following precedent whenever the court applies a rule provided by a source court case. A court is distinguishing precedent whenever a source court provides an applicable precedential rule that is treated as defeated (but not rejected) in the case before the target court; and, if there are only two choices of result, the target court reaches the opposite result in a way that does not challenge the source court result. Both of these ideas assume that there is a satisfactory rule individuation that produces distinct and determined—if defeasible—rules from source court cases.

Two quick clarifications are in order here. First, a rule is individuated by its content. Secondly, as I am using the terms, a rule may be *distinct* and (its content) *determined* though it has borderline cases of application.

In this chapter, I will probe further and ask if the defeasible rule account can be combined with a satisfactory account of rule individuation to be explanatorily adequate—that is, fit precedential practice in legal systems. Can an enhanced defeasible rule account plausibly maintain that generally courts required to follow precedent do so but sometimes distinguish, and that other courts authorized to overrule sometimes do so as well? The answer, I shall argue, is no. Precedential practice is better explained by development and application of my earlier idea of exemplar grouping on a salience account.

The structure of this chapter is as follows. Section 1 clarifies a background motivation for the defeasible rule account. Its problem concerning rule individuation and explanatory adequacy is explained in section 2. Section 3 and some of section 4 explore possible solutions. The failure of the most promising is instructive and motivates the alternative outlined in section 4.

---

[*] I would like to thank Timothy Endicott, Katherina Stevens, Dale Smith, and Hafsteinn Kristjansson for helpful comments on this chapter.

[1] BB Levenbook, 'The Meaning of a Precedent' (2000) 6 Legal Theory 185–240.

[2] For a list of the writers, an argument for classifying them this way, and a summary of the approach, see K Stevens, 'Reasoning by Precedent—Between Rules and Analogies' (2018) 24 Legal Theory 216–54, especially 223 fn 25. Though I will follow Stevens in taking Lamond as holding this view, Lamond would deny that he has any sort of rule account. See G Lamond, 'Revisiting the Reasons Account of Precedent' in M McBride and J Penner (eds), *New Essays on the on the Nature of Legal Reasoning* (Hart 2022).

Barbara Baum Levenbook, *Supplanting Defeasible Rules* In: *Philosophical Foundations of Precedent.* Edited by: Timothy Endicott, Hafsteinn Dan Kristjánsson, and Sebastian Lewis, Oxford University Press. © Barbara Baum Levenbook 2023. DOI: 10.1093/oso/9780192857248.003.0009

1. Clarifying Motivations

Defeasible rules make sense when formulating rules about an objective reality only partly grasped, the rules are formulated for (what are) normal conditions (from our perspective), it is unclear what all those normal conditions are, and future experience may reveal them. An everyday example sometimes given is, 'Birds fly.' On some views of morality, a defeasible rule is, 'If you make a promise, then you ought to keep it.' Applying this idea to law, courts setting precedent are giving a rough approximation that is provisional because of epistemic limitations. It is because of epistemic limitations that a defeasible legal rule drawn from precedent is 'subject to implicit exceptions that cannot be exhaustively listed'.[3]

However, this idea is not appropriate for precedent in law. Even if one assumes, with Dworkin, that in mature legal systems there is always an antecedent right answer to a legal question before a court, a model of precedent in law is not for mature legal systems only. It is logically possible to follow precedent, distinguish it, or overrule it in a legal system so immature that there fails to be an antecedent right answer to every legal question; and so, sometimes no objective legal reality that the source court imperfectly grasps.

Moreover, even if there is an antecedent right answer, a source court may give the wrong answer and nonetheless set precedent.

A better motivation for adopting a defeasible rule model comes from the idea that law is incomplete. The law at certain points is being constructed, diachronically, by judges setting out defeasible rules and later modifying (or replacing) them. A defeasible legal rule's list of exceptions is both legally and metaphysically underdetermined. This is why a defeasible legal rule from precedent is 'subject to implicit exceptions that cannot be exhaustively listed'.[4] In this chapter, I will assume this second motivation for the defeasible rule model.

2. The Problem of Indeterminacy

I start by explicating the defeasible rule model with more specificity than it is usually given, in order to reveal the centrality and importance of a problem. In this task, I will follow the example of some defeasible rule theorists in imagining that the alleged defeasible legal rule is a conditional. In order to present the defeasible rule model in its most plausible form, I will take the consequent of the conditional to be the outcome of the case without personal identifiers, where the outcome is the answer to a binary legal question—for example, 'the plaintiff has a right to recover damages', 'the conduct was illegal within the meaning of the Mann Act', 'no duty of care was breached with regard to the plaintiff', and so on. (Formulating the consequent requires a certain amount of legal education and legal literacy, but I will help the model by assuming that the consequent is always determined and that ordinarily, recognizing it creates no controversy among legal experts.) I will further suppose, following a simplifying convention, that a case has only two possible outcomes for each legal issue raised.[5] Following Lamond, I will let S and $\sim S$ stand for these outcomes.

---

[3] Phrase from JL Rodriguez, 'Against the Defeasibility of Legal Rules' in JF Beltrán and GB Ratti (eds), *The Logic of Legal Requirements: Essays on Defeasibility* (OUP 2012) 89–105, 105.

[4] ibid. To the idea that the courts are together working out a more complete law one should add that the members of this team are not co-equals in the process.

[5] An appellate case may raise several legal issues at once, as law students well know. A party may prevail on only one of them and fail on the others.

What is in the antecedent? That, I contend, is a difficult question for the defeasible rule theorist. Note, first, rules that can be followed in subsequent cases are not confined to bare particulars—what philosophers call 'tokens'. Such rules make use of types or, as I prefer to say, categories with a certain level of generality.[6] This is true even of defeasible rules. I will use the word 'elements' to refer to what these categories in a defeasible rule pick out in a case, real-world facts and properties. According to a defeasible rule, certain elements support a particular outcome.[7] I will follow Lamond and use capital letters J through N to represent the categories in an antecedent of a defeasible rule and, when this will not cause confusion, to represent elements in a case.

Defeasible rule theorists assume that the defeasible rule model either has resources to (metaphysically) determine the categories of a defeasible rule or is compatible with such a determination. It is a crucial assumption and one that I will challenge. Note that if—and only if—we make this assumption, we can represent the view as follows. Suppose the source court's original precedent's defeasible rule is formalized as

$$R1 = \text{If } \{J, K, L\} \text{ then } S.$$

As a rough approximation, we can say that a subsequent court distinguishing R1 might set a new defeasible rule on the basis of an element, M, present in the target case but absent in the source case. Following Lamond's notation, the new defeasible rule would be represented as

$$R2 = \text{If } \{J, K, L, M\} \text{ then } \sim S.$$

This account of distinguishing needs immediate refinement. As Lamond points out, 'what matters is not the true facts of the case, but the facts as recorded in the judgment'.[8] So, rather than describing distinguishing in terms of the absence of an element in the source case, we should say that, according to the source court opinion (or implied in it), the element is absent.

This discussion has now introduced an entry point for indeterminacy. If it is indeterminate whether according to the source opinion M is absent in the source case, or if it is indeterminate whether the absence of M is implied in the source case, then it is indeterminate on this model whether the target court allegedly setting R2 has distinguished the target case from the source case or has done something else—erred in failing to apply R1 (because M is either irrelevant to the decision or relevant to outcome S).[9] Moreover, if the target court has the authority to overrule, it is indeterminate whether the target court has (implicitly) overruled R1.

How pervasive is this indeterminacy? In order to be explanatorily adequate, a theory of precedent cannot afford a truly pervasive indeterminacy. Even an extremely

---

[6] Levenbook (n 1).

[7] Each of the considerations referred to in the antecedent of a defeasible rule severally need not be a legal reason to reach a particular outcome. See Horty's discussion of Dancy's 2004 *Ethics Without Principles* distinction between reasons for action and other sorts of considerations crucial to the conclusion in practical reasoning such as enablers, intensifiers, and attenuators in JF Horty, *Reasons as Defaults* (OUP 2012) s 5.3.3. One might argue that there can be legal enablers, intensifiers, and attenuators.

[8] Lamond (n 2) 15.

[9] This suggestion from Timothy Endicott, private correspondence.

widespread indeterminacy would challenge the claim that the theory fits the facts of precedential systems that the model was designed to explain: namely, that in a precedential system precedent is commonly either followed or distinguished, and sometimes overruled.

An account of the determination of the content of the antecedent—and thus of defeasible rule individuation—would settle the matter. There is a second reason that such an account is needed. There is an activity that Lamond calls 'reinterpretation'.[10] In some of the 'reinterpretation' cases, a target court with the authority to overrule claims that the source court's rule was never what it has been taken to be, for example,

$$R1 = \text{If } \{J, K, L\} \text{ then } S$$

but rather

$$R1^* = \text{If } \{J, K, L^*\} \text{ then } S,$$

where L^* is a narrower category than L, L^* is entirely subsumed in L, and L^* is applicable to the source case but inapplicable to the target case. For example, in *Parker v Brown*[11] a defeasible rule might have been contended to be:

> Any actor relying on the state's authority to regulate local matters in a way that does not materially obstruct commerce has an immunity from lawsuit under a federal anti-trust law (Sherman Act) authorized by the commerce clause of the U.S. Constitution.

In a later Supreme Court case,[12] however, five justices can be read as suggesting that the following is *Parker*'s defeasible rule:

> *State* actors relying on the state's authority to regulate local matters in a way that does not materially obstruct commerce have an immunity from lawsuit under a federal anti-trust law (Sherman Act) authorized by the commerce clause of the U.S. Constitution.

According to this 'reinterpretation', *Parker*'s rule was inapplicable to the case before the later court, as that case involved only private actors. 'Any actor' is, of course, a broader category than one of its proper subsets, 'state actors'.

'Reinterpretation' can go the other way. The rule stated in *Barwick v English Joint Stock Bank*[13] was:

> [T]he master is answerable for every such wrong [fraud] of the servant or agent as is committed in the course of the service and for the master's benefit, though no express command or privity of the master be proved.

---

[10] Lamond (n 2) 16–17.
[11] *Parker v Brown* 317 US 341 (1943).
[12] *Cantor v Detroit Edison Co* 428 US 579 (1976).
[13] *Barwick v English Joint Stock Bank* (1867) LR 2 Ex 259.

Goodhart says:

> It was generally believed that this statement of the law was correct until, forty-five years later, the House of Lords ... held that it was too narrow. The words 'and for the master's benefit' were merely descriptive of the facts in the *Barwick* case ... [14]

On the defeasible rule model, is the 'state actors' 'reinterpretation' of the *Parker* case distinguishing (on the basis of a new element)? A faithful following? An overruling (albeit implicitly)? Something else not traditionally recognized in the discussion of precedent? It isn't immediately clear; because it isn't obvious what the source case defeasible rule is. A theory of precedent on which it is always indeterminate whether a reinterpretation is a following is unacceptable. So once more, a defeasible rule model requires an account of rule individuation that determines the categories.

This brings us to overruling on the defeasible rule model. A subsequent court with the authority to do so might overrule R1 (If {*J, K, L*} then *S*). How should that be represented? Here, defeasible rule theorists are remarkably silent. This claim seems to be embraced by the overruling court

$$C1 =\sim\left(\text{If } \left\{J,K,L\right\} \text{ then } S\right).$$

But the overruling court also reached the outcome $\sim S$; and on the defeasible rule model, $\sim S$ is the consequent of a defeasible rule set therein. The rule cannot be C1, for C1 entails no conditionals.[15] How might the rule be represented?

Note that it might not be:

$$R3 = \text{If } \left\{J,K,L\right\} \text{ then } \sim S.$$

For an overruling court may treat at least some of the elements, *J*, *K*, and *L*, as irrelevant to legal outcomes in a case like this, and might introduce others. An example could be the overruling of *Swift v Tyson*[16] by the *Erie R Co v Tompkins*[17] court. On the defeasible rule model, we might say, simplifying a little, that this is the defeasible rule in *Swift v Tyson*:

> If a lawsuit is brought in federal court that the Federal Judiciary Act requires to be decided by state law, and if there is no state statute on point, if the general common law contains a rule that favours one party, then that party wins the lawsuit.

In contrast, since the *Erie* majority declared that a state's law cannot be found in general common law, the replacement rule in *Erie* is more like this:

> If a lawsuit is brought in federal court that the Federal Judiciary Act requires to be decided by state law, and if there is no state statute on point, if the state's highest court set down a rule that favours one party, then that party wins the lawsuit.

---

[14] A Goodhart, 'Determining the *Ratio Decidendi* of a Case' (1930) 40 Yale LJ 161–83, 167. See also Cardozo's admission in *MacPherson v Buick Motor Co* (217 NY 382, 387 [1916]) that subsequent cases 'may have extended the rule' of an earlier case, *Thomas v Winchester* 6 NY 37 (1852).

[15] In propositional logic, R3 is equivalent to: {*J, K, L*} and $\sim S$. It *isn't* equivalent to another conditional.

[16] *Swift v Tyson* 16 Pet 1 (1842).

[17] *Erie R Co v Tompkins* 304 US 64, 58 S Ct 817, 82 L Ed 1188 (1938).

In non-monotonic logic, designed for reasoning with defeasible rules, one cannot 'strengthen the antecedent'. In other words, if the overruling court held that L was irrelevant, but set this rule

$$\text{If } \{J,K\} \text{ then } \sim S$$

it does not follow that

$$\text{If } \{J,K,L\} \text{ then } \sim S.$$

Clearly, the answer to the question about how to formulate the rule set in overruling awaits an account of the determination of categories in a defeasible precedential rule.

There is a further problem. I have mentioned that it might be indeterminate whether, according to the source court case opinion, an element picked out by a target court—M—is present or absent in a source court case where it was assumed that the antecedent of the source court rule has elements J, K, and L. I have also mentioned that it might be indeterminate whether those elements were not J, K, and a narrower L^*. We must now ask: can the entire antecedent of a source court rule be indeterminate, and if so, how pervasive is this indeterminacy? An indeterminacy that is prevalent should not be tolerated by a defeasible rule theorist, for reasons previously rehearsed. So, there is a third reason to ask for an account of the determination of the categories in a defeasible rule.

The examination of the defeasible rule model has brought us to this crucial question: can the defeasible rule model be consistently augmented with an account of the determination of categories in a defeasible precedential rule that avoids pervasive indeterminacy? The assumption that it can has not, as far as I know, been challenged. In the remaining sections, I shall challenge it.

3. Accounting for Determined Categories

Borrowing from the literature on recognizing relevant similarities in analogy, we might consider these three ideas:[18]

(1) The categories (in the antecedent of a defeasible rule) are those that jointly provide the best available justification for the outcome of the source case, consistent with the information in the opinion.

(2) The categories are the ones that the source court thought jointly provide the best available justification for the outcome of the source case.

(3) The categories are all and only the ones that the source court cited in the precedential opinion as legally relevant in support of the outcome of the source case.[19]

---

[18] Recognizing is an epistemic endeavour. The three possibilities are inspired by an epistemic suggestion about extracting relevant similarities made by K Stevens, 'Case-To-Case Arguments' (2018) 32 Argumentation 431–55, 441 and a suggestion about modifying a rule approach in Stevens (n 2).
[19] Stevens, 'Case-to-Case Arguments' (n 18) 442.

The first option has a Dworkinian flavour. However, apart from Dworkin's idiosyncratic ideas about what interpretation amounts to and its role in legal content, which have been well criticized in the literature, this option remains unmotivated. It looks like a confusion between the rule—assuming there is a rule—that was set down by the source court with the rule that ought to have been set down; a conflation of 'is' and 'ought'. Moreover, this option is prey to a problem analogous to the one Finnis found in Dworkin:[20] 'best available justification' can be gauged legally or morally; but if we try to combine the two dimensions (or the two sets of criteria) we may find them to be incommensurable.

The second option initially seems better, for it is consistent with the assumption that the alleged defeasible rule is authoritatively set by the authorities deciding the case. Further, it might be argued that such judges are, if even minimally competent, infallible about the outcome they have reached, from which it follows they are infallible about the consequent of the defeasible rule. But when we turn to the antecedent, difficulties appear.

The second option inherits the incommensurability difficulty, but let us set that aside. The main problem is that, given that the idea of genuine reinterpretation of precedent is not incoherent, it is perfectly conceivable that judges fail to precisely set the rule they think they do in deciding a case. The setting down, if there is any, is done through a written (or oral) opinion, not through what judges think.

The third option is also consistent with the assumption that the alleged defeasible rule is authoritatively set by the authorities deciding the case. Moreover, the third option avoids the problem of determining the best justification. In addition, this third option makes sense of the traditional epistemological procedure of searching for the rule of a precedential case by careful reading of the written opinion. For to identify what is cited, one needs to read the deciding judges' descriptions for the level of characterization of elements treated as part of the argument for the outcome.

The following seems to be a good illustration of this third view:

> So when, for example, the Supreme Court decided *New York Times Co. v. Sullivan,* [note omitted] which dramatically revamped American libel law on First Amendment grounds, it described the plaintiff, Commissioner Sullivan, not only as a police commissioner (which itself would have been an abstraction from Sullivan himself and from Sullivan's particular job), but also as a "public official." And it described the *New York Times* not just as the single *New York Times,* and not even just as a newspaper, but as "the press." As a result, *New York Times v. Sullivan,* from the beginning, stood as a precedent for all libel cases involving public officials suing the press, and that is precisely because, and only because, the Supreme Court *said* just that.[21]

Unfortunately, proponents of the rule account who want to embrace this third option encounter two immediate difficulties. First, its application is problematic to many cases that seem to have operated as precedent. There are, for example, British precedents in which there is no majority consensus on the reasoning, but rather a varied set of rationales for the ruling.[22] It is difficult to see how the third option can be applied to case reports containing

---

[20] JM Finnis, 'On Reason and Authority in Law's Empire' (1987) 6 Law and Philosophy 357–80, 372.

[21] F Schauer, *Thinking Like a Lawyer: A New Introduction to Legal Reasoning* (Harvard UP 2009) 54.

[22] As many readers know, for a considerable period until fairly recently the House of Lords, operating as the highest court in the UK, published individual opinions (called 'speeches') without a statement of consensus on the supporting reasoning. See R Cross, 'The *Ratio Decidendi* and a Plurality of Speeches in the House of Lords' (1977) 93 LQR 378–85.

only a statement of the facts and a judicial order, and to instances in which a majority judicial opinion explicitly decides the outcome for a multiplicity of incompatible reasons.[23] Whether or not all cases like these are binding precedent, I will argue in the next section that we should resist the conclusion that such cases cannot be followed, distinguished, or overruled. Yet on the defeasible rule model, that appears to be the conclusion if such cases lack a single determined defeasible rule.

Secondly, background assumptions and legal presumptions about the absence (or presence) of an element will not be cited in the source court's opinion. Do they not belong in the antecedent of the alleged defeasible rule? They may turn out to be part of the source court's rationale for the outcome, as a later court thought was true in the *Parker* decision.

So, suppose the third option is refined—or perhaps the better word is 'abandoned'—to permit elements legally presumed or rational to assume to have been (implicitly) relied on. The result is that sometimes the alleged defeasible rule will not be formulated, or not accurately formulated, anywhere in the source court opinion(s); and it must be reconstructed from the opinion(s) in order to be identified.

Plainly, this move merely pushes the problem back a level. For it leaves unanswered the question of what determines which elements (including the absence of an element) were implicitly relied on, or legally presumed, with all the level-of-generality issues that brings. The answer must not be ad hoc. It also must not make every alleged defeasible rule from a source court open to being distinguished on the basis of an implicit element so concrete as to obtain only in the source case. If in all cases, the antecedent of an alleged source court rule can fail to apply to a new case, we have left the idea of a rule altogether.

Suppose, on the other hand, that the defeasible rule theorist holds that necessarily all the elements (including the absence of an element) are explicitly characterized at the correct level of generality in the source court opinion.[24] The first problem is that often there are several characterizations at varying levels of generality in a single source court opinion (as the previous quotation about the *New York Times* case illustrated—'*New York Times*', 'newspaper', 'the press').[25] Are all of the rules it is possible to string together using these various levels to be considered defeasible rules set by the source court? If so, it follows that a later court can at the same time and with the same decision both correctly find a precedent court rule inapplicable (by applying one of the narrower rule candidates) and (given the authority) overrule that same precedent court (by failing to apply one of the applicable broader rule candidates). A second implication is that a later court can at the same time and with the same decision both be bound by and follow a precedent court (by correctly applying one of the applicable broader rule candidates) and also be unbound by that court (but use one of its narrower rule candidates as a persuasive reason to expand the law by argument by analogy). Both implications are absurd.

Suppose we narrow the view to the claim that the source court sets a precedent if and only if there is a unique defeasible rule present (in its language) in the opinion. Judicial language is now being treated as canonical regarding the identity of categories.[26] The occurrence of unique, explicitly formulated, rules in judicial opinions in precedential systems is

---

[23] In these last two remarks, I am indebted to Salmond's critique of a suggestion for identifying the *ratio decidendi*. PF Fitzgerald, *Salmond on Jurisprudence* (12th edn, Sweet & Maxwell 1966) 179–80. Cross suggests that cases without a *ratio* can be followed. Cross (n 22) 379.

[24] Schauer remarks that in the vast majority of cases courts will describe the facts of the case in justifying their decisions in terms of type (or category). Schauer (n 21) 53–54.

[25] I am hardly the first to make this point. See, e.g., J Stone, *Legal Systems and Lawyers' Reasonings* (Stanford UP 1964) 269.

[26] This is strikingly at variance with much of avowed legal practice. See, e.g., AWB Simpson, 'The *Ratio Decidendi* of a Case and the Doctrine of Binding Precedent' in AC Guest (ed), *Oxford Essays in Jurisprudence* (OUP 1961)

so infrequent[27] that the view under consideration threatens to reduce the number of cases in which precedent has been or can be followed (and also distinguished or overruled) to the point that following precedent is a peripheral feature of familiar common law systems, rather than a central one.

The upshot of these reflections is a failure to find an acceptable account of category (and thus rule) individuation such that generally in its opinion(s) a source court sets a single defeasible rule with distinct and determined categories. If such an account cannot be given, the defeasible rule model is in more trouble than merely not being able to answer the question of what some alleged reinterpretation amounts to (and thus whether some target courts followed or distinguished or implicitly overruled a precedent). For there would then be nothing to justify the assumption—vital to the defeasible rule model—that indeterminacy is the exception, rather than the rule. There would be nothing to justify the assumption that it is seldom indeterminate what it would be like to follow the source court precedent. (It is important to recall that it is metaphysical indeterminacy that is at issue, not merely epistemic indeterminacy.) One could not even claim that overruling and distinguishing were rare or peripheral activities at the appellate level in a common law system.

4. A Last Attempt and the Salience Account

As many readers know, those with legal training who look for rules select some of the descriptions and levels of generality over the others. For instance, they read *New York Times v Sullivan*[28] as setting a defeasible rule about *the press's* liability for libel for false statements about *public officials*. They read *Riggs v Palmer* as setting a defeasible rule about the right to inherit under state law when *a legatee* has *murdered* the *testator* (rather than the very broad maxim, 'No one shall be permitted to ... take advantage of his own wrong, or to found any claim upon his own iniquity, or to acquire property by his own crime', stated in the majority opinion[29]). In so doing, perhaps they are relying on a particular feature created by the judicial opinion and its context to select descriptions and levels of generality—that is, to identify the categories in the defeasible rule. Perhaps they are relying on what I will call *contextual salience*.

In a previous work,[30] I introduced the notion of salience to explain, among other things, how informal reports of decided cases can guide lay law conduct. Three clarifying points about salience are in order. The first is that the kind of contextual salience postulated here is common to a group and interpersonal.[31] The second is that it is the contextual salience of a grouping of individual instances (tokens)—of a 'this belongs with that'. Salient groupings depend upon the (known or perceived) context in which they are made. So, the third point is that their salience is context relative. The context may include, among other things, purpose, special information or interest, and culture or subculture. Children in Canada who are asked what dessert belongs with Thanksgiving turkey will usually answer, 'Apple pie', but children

---

148–75, 162. I am indebted to the contribution to this volume by Luís Duarte d'Almeida's (Chapter 10) for this reference.

[27] See, e.g., Goodhart (n 14) 167; J Stone, 'The Ratio of *the Ratio Decidendi*' (1959) 6 MLR 597–620, 605.

[28] *New York Times v Sullivan* 376 US 254 (1964).

[29] *Riggs v Palmer* 115 NY 506, 511 (1889). They also read the case as setting a rule about when a court may deviate from the clear language of a statute it is asked to apply.

[30] Levenbook (n 1).

[31] I also assumed mutual knowledge or mutual expectation.

asked that same question in most of the US are likely to say, 'Pumpkin pie'. (Children asked this question in parts of the southern US will probably say, 'Pecan pie'.[32]) For the purposes of espionage in the old Soviet Union, a spy staying in a Moscow hotel would (if he were prudent) group the lay floor-charge woman, the *dejournaya*, with members of the KGB as potential enemies and therefore dangerous to his mission. However, for purposes of Soviet pay and privileges, the *dejournaya* would not have been grouped with employees of the KGB.

When persons who are similarly socialized (and hence share a language) share information about the context and sufficient empirical information in order to make a grouping with an exemplar, they will be disposed to group new items with the exemplar in the same way. (Sometimes this requires some reasoning.) It will be contextually salient that this belongs with that.

Contextual salience explains how persons approximately equally socialized and with approximately equal information about the context and other relevant empirical information converge on a grouping of this with that. Contextual salience operates in the following example adapted from Schauer: a faculty decision that a male student may be excused from an examination to attend the funeral of his sister is taken as precedent for allowing a female student to be excused from an examination to attend the funeral of her brother.[33] There are many other examples of contextual salience commonly at work: children 'following the leader' in a wordless game, one child learning from the punishment of their sibling without explicit rules from the parents, the 'modelling' of interpersonal relationships between the parents that occurs without explicit instruction in a child's home (and which can be quite psychologically powerful in the child's future behaviour and expectations). Contextual salience explains why it is reasonable in the current climate in the US to worry that a verdict of not guilty on all charges in a well-publicized case in which a vigilante took a high-powered gun to a political protest and killed two unarmed men in alleged self-defence will be taken (in the larger society) as legal permission by those so inclined to arm themselves and seek out trouble from political opponents.[34]

As is well known, legal opinions in precedential jurisdictions typically describe the facts, the who-did-what-to-whom and who-is-asking-for-what, in fairly concrete, and in broader, terms. Legal opinions also often give reasons, explaining why the result was reached. Now consider the idea that the groupings we are envisaging take place under the assignment of what Schauer calls 'headings',[35] so that in each instance a category is named—for example, *students* may be excused from examinations for the death of *siblings* (or maybe *immediate family members*). The focus is on the contextual salience not of a partial grouping but of a category. With this idea, might contextual salience—to the legally trained—be used in an account of metaphysical determination of categories in a defeasible rule to solve the problem of indeterminacy?

There is, of course, the immediate problem of the makeup and limits of the context in question. To what extent does the context include understandings and perspectives of lay members of the broader culture? Does the context include previous legal cases in the branch

---

[32] <https://www.foodandwine.com/news/most-popular-thanksgiving-pie-every-state> accessed 14 December 2021.

[33] F Schauer, 'Precedent' (1987) 39 Stan L Rev 571–605, 578.

[34] I refer to the verdict in the 2021 trial of Kyle Rittenhouse, Kenosha County (Wisconsin) Circuit Court. See <https://theintercept.com/2021/11/19/kyle-rittenhouse-acquittal-trial-ahmaud-arbery/> and <https://www.pbs.org/newshour/show/does-the-rittenhouse-acquittal-set-a-precedent-two-experts-weigh-in> accessed 17 December 2021.

[35] Schauer, 'Precedent' (n 33).

of law? Does it include the reports of legislative committees when the issue is the application of a statute? Does it include judicial opinions in other branches of law that might make the limits of application of a key concept salient—for example, possession?[36] Let us set this issue aside, as it requires considerably more attention than is possible to provide here.

A defeasible rule theorist might say that the categories of the defeasible rule set by a court are all and only those that are contextually salient upon the reading of the opinion(s). On this view, salience supplies the appropriate categories—not only for a source court decision but for target court decisions as well.

We are considering the view that when those with legal training see *New York Times v Sullivan* as laying down a rule regarding the liability of the press for libel of a public official, and when those with legal training reject the idea that *Riggs v Palmer* lays down a rule that no one may profit from his or her own wrong, they are using a common contextual salience derived from the opinions in the lawsuit of Sullivan (a police officer) and the demand for inheritance by the poisoner of Grandfather Palmer (his grandson Elmer) to select categories for a defeasible rule. They will be doing so correctly, according to the version of the defeasible rule theory currently under consideration. So long as in the vast majority of cases there are salient categories for everything in the antecedent of a defeasible rule, on this account the defeasible rules for source and target courts will be largely distinct and determined; and so, it will be largely determinate whether a target court is following, distinguishing, or overruling a source court decision.

I do not think we can be sanguine that in the vast majority of cases there are sufficient salient categories such that exactly one defeasible rule emerges that would be converged upon by the legally trained, but I will not press this point here.

The aforementioned account represents my best attempt to save the defeasible rule theory from too pervasive an indeterminacy. Unfortunately, for reasons now to be elucidated, if it does so, it does so at too high a cost. First and least important, the model is conceptually cumbersome in explicating the activity for which the idea of defeasible rules was designed, namely distinguishing. On this account, distinguishing amounts to replacing an original rule with two others. So distinguishing expands the number of rules.

Here is why: suppose contextual salience determines that the following is the rule of a source court case

$$R1 = \text{If } \{J,K,L\} \text{ then } S.$$

Suppose, further, that contextual salience determines that a target court, holding that M was absent in the source court case, sets this rule:

$$R2 = \text{If } \{J,K,L,M\} \text{ then} \sim S.$$

Note that $\sim M$ could not have been contextually salient as an element in the source court case antecedent to the target court decision, or R1 would not have been the rule facing the target court. But suppose that it is now contextually salient that M was absent in the source court case. (Perhaps the target court opinion has made $\sim M$ contextually salient in the source

---

[36] See the discussion of 'concepts, which ... figure in several of the different branches' of law in Fitzgerald (n 23) 187.

112 BARBARA BAUM LEVENBOOK

court case.) Then the target court has replaced R1 with another rule. For now, the source court rule is

$$R1^{***} = \text{If } \{J,K,L,\sim M\} \text{ then } S. \text{ [37]}$$

There is no equivalence between R1 and R1*** or R1*** and R2.

Thus, in the case of distinguishing, we go from one rule—R1—to two—R2 and R1***. The model is proliferating rules. What is to be gained from this proliferation?

Secondly, this account is in tension with the notion of a defeasible rule. A defeasible rule persists even in the face of discovered or created exceptions. The rule is defeated in some cases, but holds good in others. 'If you have made a promise, you ought to keep it' is a default rule, though there are many exceptions. A parental rule for children, 'Bedtime is at 9 pm on school nights', persists as a default rule once an exception or two is made for special conditions. But once the target court has set R1***, nothing remains of R1. That for which the source court case is precedent has changed. No longer is it true that if J, K, and L, presumably S. S is now presumed if four, not three, elements obtain: J, K, L, and $\sim M$. So, the default has changed. For this reason, it aids clarity to deny that R1 has been defeated in a new case—and so, was defeasible in the first place. It is not merely that R1 does not, we now decide, properly apply to the new situation. On this account, we have decided that it is now not the rule for the past situation as well.

Thirdly and perhaps most important, the model is blind to the possibility of following precedent when there is no single defeasible rule that emerges from a source case. I have developed the idea that examples (established, I maintain, by precedents) can be followed in the work referred to at the beginning of this chapter, so I will only illustrate it now. It may be that *Donoghue v Stevenson*[38] had no single defeasible rule on this model for a considerable time after its decision was handed down (and especially one year later) because categories weren't uniquely picked out by contextual salience. As many readers know, the decision was not unanimous. The result allowed a lawsuit (and thus recognized potential tort liability) of a manufacturer for an ultimate consumer's illness following the ingestion of ginger beer in an opaque bottle containing the remains of a decomposing snail. After reading the judicial opinion(s), one may be able to make a case for categories of a defeasible rule being variously:

> dead molluscs in opaque ginger beer bottles, or dead animals in carbonated beverages, or 'noxious physical foreign agents' in 'beverages', or 'noxious foreign elements' in any container of foodstuffs or in any 'container of commodities for human consumption', and so on. (There is a similar list of the categories of who is liable for injury therefrom— manufacturers of foodstuffs, 'manufacturers of goods nationally distributed through retailers', etc.—of the plaintiff's 'relationship to the vehicle of harm', and so on.[39])

---

[37] On the other hand, suppose that it is not now contextually salient that M was absent in the source court case. Then the target court isn't distinguishing. It can be overruling—if, that is, it has the authority to do so. (Alternatively, it can be plainly in error and failing to follow a precedent it is bound to apply.) For the target court is refusing to find S when the antecedent of R1 obtains, and that is refusing to apply R1.

[38] *Donoghue v Stevenson* [1932] AC 562.

[39] Some of these suggestions are from Stone (n 25) 269–70.

At least some of the candidates may have seemed equally contextually salient; or perhaps none of them may have risen to the level of contextual salience in 1933.

Yet if categories weren't uniquely set by contextual salience, nonetheless, partial groupings, falling far short of categories, do seem to have been set by contextual salience—indeed, I suggest, by a salience that would be shared by many, not just the legally trained, if the facts and some of the reasoning were known to them. For even if, relying on contextual salience, it was unclear whether or not an alleged defeasible rule of the case is *confined* to liability for illness caused by dead animals in beverages, it was clear that the case stands as a precedent for finding a manufacturer's tort liability for illness following the ingestion of lemonade sold in an opaque container adulterated with snails or dead mice or other vermin. A court in 1933 confronted with a tort liability claim against the manufacturer of lemonade containing the decomposing remains of a dead mouse unlikely to be immediately detected by the ultimate consumer would clearly have been following the *Donoghue v Stevenson* precedent in allowing the lawsuit.

This brings us to my proffered replacement for the defeasible rule model: a salience account. In the work referred to at the start of this chapter, I offered a salience account of following (the guidance of) a precedential case, chiefly for lay law subjects, in the central case. Now I will say that a court follows precedent when it reaches the source case result in a case that contextual salience groups with the precedent case.[40] In some instances, particularly when a string of cases is in the context, that grouping may be the result of applying categories that are the only ones salient. An entire rule may be contextually salient.[41] However, not in other cases, and these are the ones I find most interesting. There can, as I have remarked, be contextually salient partial groupings, even when there is also a range of competing salient categories just where a rule would require a choice among them.

On the salience account, there is, antecedent to a case that distinguishes, a range of salient category candidates for the source case. (For those who think of conditional rules, imagine a range of equally salient rules sharing a consequent—the outcome of the source case—but differing in antecedents.) The candidates get winnowed when the distinguishing court reaches the opposite result in a case falling under some—the broader—of them. This refusal to group the instant case with the source case may leave other category candidates still salient for the source case and still viable for directing decisions towards the source court outcome. For example, 'all actors' drops out but 'state actors' remains. (In other terms, distinguishing leaves some salient rule candidates for the source court case viable.) In other reinterpretation, the rejected category candidates are among the narrower ones.

When a court has the authority to overrule, it does so by reaching an outcome opposite to that of a source case in a case that contextual salience groups with the source case. For example, think of grouping *Erie R Co v Tompkins* with *Swift v Tyson*.[42] What is salient in the context is that both were lawsuits brought in federal court that the US Federal Judiciary Act required to be decided by state law, with no state statute on point. For those who think in terms of rules, overruling removes viability from all of the equally salient rule candidates for the source court case. (If there were several equally salient rule candidates for the source

---

[40] See BB Levenbook, 'The Law of the Street' in M McBride and J Penner (eds) (n 2) for the complication introduced when the salience for lay law subjects diverges from the salience for the legally informed or legally trained.

[41] That rule will not be defeasible, for reasons just rehearsed. For those same reasons, I am inclined to agree with Emily Sherwin, in her contribution to this volume (Chapter 12), that there can be no distinguishing once a rule is established by precedent; though there can be subsequent rejection of the rule, both authorized and unauthorized.

[42] *Erie R Co v Tompkins* (n 17); *Swift v Tyson* (n 16).

court case prior to the target case, the antecedents of each of these rules apply to the target case.) There may be just one salient rule candidate; in explicit overruling, the court will sometimes state the—that is, a determined—rule that is rejected. (Let us set aside the question of whether overruling must be explicit.)

Suppose only a partial grouping for the source case is contextually salient and there are no categories that come close to salience. (There are no contextually salient rule candidates.) Then a subsequent judicial decision, in addition to following (and perhaps overruling) the precedent, might group a target case with the source case and thereby make one or more category candidates for the source case salient. To adapt an example provided by Stevens: *Dillon v Legg*[43] upheld tort liability for emotional distress for injury to another, but the majority opinion explicitly refused to provide a rule.[44] We can imagine that a subsequent case provides sufficient focus to provide one category—the victim and claimant are immediate family members—but not others (leaving open questions such as: how physically proximate to the claimant must the event that injured the victim be? How temporally proximate must the start of the emotional distress be to the injury?). This is one way that subsequent cases can develop the law.

One advantage of the salience account is that it can explain everything the defeasible rule theory does while avoiding its difficulties. Moreover, the salience account can explain more, namely the instances previously mentioned of following precedent where there appears to be no distinct and determined rule, not even a defeasible one.[45] Finally, the salience account offers a plausible and attractive account of the process of the development, through precedential decisions, of much of the common law.

On the salience account, it is contextual salience that constrains, insofar as precedent constrains. I think it is highly plausible that the foregoing account of distinguishing is applicable to enough instances so that the proposed model fits the practice of distinguishing in existing legal systems; though I can offer no proof. I also think, but cannot prove, that there is contextual salience, at least of partial groupings, in so many cases that the salience account fits the practice of following in existing legal systems—including the mundane followings of precedent that are uncontroversial in myriad trial courts.

---

[43] *Dillon v Legg* 68 Cal 2d 728 (1968).

[44] K Stevens, 'Setting Precedents Without Making Norms' (2020) 39 Law and Philosophy 577–616, 577–578.

[45] The salience account is compatible with an analogical account of precedential reasoning in working towards contextual salience of groupings, even partial ones. Suggestion by Katharina Stevens, private correspondence.

PART II
PRECEDENT AND LEGAL ARGUMENT

9

The Uses of Precedent and Legal Argument

Claudio Michelon[*]

It is a truth universally acknowledged that courts, sometimes, claim to rely on the authority of previously decided cases to justify their decisions. These justifications take the form of arguments, explicitly or implicitly presented. It is also common knowledge that courts deploy different types of argument that, they claim, build on the authority of precedent. So far, so uncontroversial. Often, however, the price to pay for widespread agreement is a lack of clarity about what has been agreed upon. In what follows, I intend to unpack the claim that courts rely on authoritative judicial precedents. They do so by deploying different *types* of argument. Each different argument type, I will argue, leaves a distinctive argumentative footprint: they are deployed for different reasons, possess different structures, rely on different assumptions, and, crucially, offer different support to different types of claims. Lack of attention to the differences between such arguments can blur our understanding of the different ways precedent might support a judicial decision. Unpacking the nearly consensual claim that courts argue diversely from authoritative precedent will allow us to see a more interesting underwater seascape than we could have suspected by gazing on these calm surface waters. Moreover, it will help us to develop a more subtle theory of precedent.

The general claim that there is an important connection between the way courts argue from precedent and the adequacy of a theory of precedent is not new. Neil MacCormick, for one, made this point persuasively in an article published over three decades ago.[1] But the past few years have seen a growing literature containing detailed analysis of canonical varieties of legal argument employed by courts. My main concern here is to demonstrate that these developments in the theory of legal argumentation allow for a sharper understanding of judicial precedent. In turn, and unsurprisingly, this sharper understanding of the use of precedent in argumentation creates significant room for disagreement.

Among many other argumentative uses of authoritative precedents, courts *apply* the *ratio decidendi* of previous cases to an instant case, deploy legal analogies, argue a fortiori, argue *a simile*, and infer that a specific principle should be followed in deciding an instant case. My strategy in what follows is to present three types of judicial precedent-based argument and contrast them. These are not the only types of precedent-based arguments utilized by courts, but their distinctiveness should be sufficient to achieve my main purpose here of demonstrating that a satisfactory theory of authoritative judicial precedent should take account of the different ways in which precedent is used in legal argument.

The three precedent-based argument types I intend to contrast are (i) arguments by which a court purports to *apply* a precedent, (ii) precedent-based legal analogies, and (iii) precedent-based inferences to the best legal explanation. After presenting and comparing

---

[*] I would like to thank Timothy Endicott, Cormac MacAmhlaigh, and George Dick for helpful comments on an earlier version of this chapter.

[1] N MacCormick, 'Why Cases Have Rationes and What These Are' in L Goldstein (eds), *Precedent in Law* (OUP 1987) 155.

Claudio Michelon, *The Uses of Precedent and Legal Argument* In: *Philosophical Foundations of Precedent*. Edited by: Timothy Endicott, Hafsteinn Dan Kristjánsson, and Sebastian Lewis, Oxford University Press. © Claudio Michelon 2023. DOI: 10.1093/oso/9780192857248.003.0010

118   CLAUDIO MICHELON

them in sections 1, 2, and 3, I will proceed to draw some conclusions from these comparisons for a theory of precedent (in section 4).

An initial difficulty in following this strategy is the fact that there are different accounts of each of those arguments. Discussing each rival account of each of the three argument types I intend to compare would take much longer than I can afford here. Instead, I have opted for choosing one or two representative accounts of each argument type and I proceed to compare these (admittedly controversial) accounts. The argument type by which courts follow precedents that I will be discussing in the next section is the popular (but question- able) one centred around the so-called 'legal syllogism'. I shall make some of my misgivings about the legal syllogism clear as I present it but, in spite of its shortcomings, focusing on this account of precedent application will help to identify central aspects of the footprint left by precedent-application arguments. In section 2, I will briefly discuss the traditional account of legal analogy (and in particular Golding's canonical presentation of it), but I will contrast it with the erotetic account of legal analogies that Luís Duarte d'Almeida and I put forward. Both rival accounts converge on some aspects of precedent-based legal analogies and that would be sufficient to identify central aspects of a legal analogy's argumentative footprint. Finally, I will present, in section 3, the account of an inference to the best legal explanation on which I have been working over the past few years (which is far from being uncontrover- sial, as readers of Chapter 10 of this book will not fail to notice). Despite these accounts being controversial, they will allow me to demonstrate how attention to the different types of argu- ment allows us to develop a more wholesome theory of precedent.

1. Applying Precedent

Routinely, courts need to decide cases that they take to be on all fours with an authoritative legal precedent. Some of those cases include features that justify a court in distinguishing it from the authoritative precedent and some courts might have the legal power, and good reasons, to overrule an authoritative precedent. In many cases, however, there would not be either sufficient reason to distinguish the instant case, or power (or reason) to overrule the earlier decision. In such cases, and assuming no other legal sources bear on the case, the doc- trine of precedent obligates the court to apply the authoritative precedent.

However, what precisely it means to 'apply' a precedent is not immediately transparent. Some of it is, of course, clear. First, it is apparent that a court, in relying on an authoritative precedent, is trying to support its *particular* decision settling a *particular* issue raised by the case at hand. Courts decide a variety of issues: they decide on the issue of whether an appeal should be allowed, on whether they should order someone to do, or abstain from doing, something, on whether they should award damages, on whether a putatively valid contract should be declared to be null and void, inter alia. For each such decision, an authoritative precedent that is on all fours with the case the court is charged with deciding would provide support, according to the doctrine of precedent. Secondly, it is clear that whatever else might be involved in this 'support' relationship, an authoritative precedent that is on all fours with the case at hand furnishes the court with a legal reason to decide the issue at hand in a par- ticular way. This relationship between a previous decision and the decision to be taken in the instant case is part of the *explanandum* of a theory of precedent.

Additionally, the application of a precedent comes with its own conceptual apparatus and vocabulary. What is said to be authoritative is the *ratio decidendi* of the previous case, not its *obiter dicta* (even though *obiter dicta* of previous decisions might play a role in future decisions).[2] The *ratio decidendi* of the authoritative precedent is said to bind the court in its decision of the instant case (unless the court is able to distinguish the instant case or over-rule the precedent). Within the set of cases over which the authority of precedent binds the court, the law is said to be 'settled'.[3] There are, of course, complications that might arise, for instance, when two different putatively authoritative cases' *rationes* point in diametrically opposed directions—and I shall return to them later. For now, it suffices to keep in mind that this conceptual apparatus, often employed in the practice of applying precedent-based arguments, is another part of the *explanandum* of a theory of precedent.

My use of the phrase 'on all fours with' in the previous paragraphs was, of course, a procrastination strategy. For things become complicated when we start trying to unpack what it means to say that a case is on all fours with another, authoritatively decided, case. Yet the question cannot be avoided indefinitely and, if I am correct, the key to a sufficiently subtle theory of legal precedent is attention to the argument types that best represent the diverse ways in which previous cases have been used by lawyers as sources of legal authority.

In the article mentioned earlier, Neil MacCormick has provided a prime example of how looking into the structure of judicial argument relates to the core problem of a theory of precedent, to wit: what makes two cases sufficiently close to demand the same legal solution. Like many others,[4] he believed that the arguments deployed by courts when they 'apply' precedents possess the same basic form. They are instances of the so-called 'legal syllogism', an argument form in which (i) the 'major premise' is the statement of a legal rule and (ii) the 'minor premise' is a statement of facts present in the instant case, yielding (iii) a conclusion about how the court should decide, according to the law.

In the legal syllogism, the legal rule is presented in conditional form, with an antecedent that comprises a series of facts (or types of facts), and a consequent that contains the legal consequences that should follow from the occurrence of those facts. If the facts described in the minor premise match the facts in the antecedent of the conditional, then the conclusion will simply be that the legal consequences contained in the consequent of the rule should apply to the instant case.[5] The traditional, if embattled,[6] conception of the *ratio decidendi* as a legal rule helps to put the argument by which the court applies the authoritative precedent into syllogistic form.

Here is one way of representing the legal syllogism:

(1) For every x, if x has properties A, B, C, ..., then the court ought to render decision D.
(2) The instant case has properties A, B, C, ...

---

[2] R Cross, *Precedent in English Law* (OUP 1961) 33.

[3] 'Settled law' here is used as a term of art, defined in the earlier text. I am not concerned here with the notion of settled law discussed in GA Nunn and AM Trammell, 'Settled Law' (2021) 107 Va L Rev 57.

[4] e.g. H Hart, *The Concept of Law* (3rd edn, OUP 2012) 126; J Gardner 'The Legality of Law' in J Gardner, *Law as a Leap of Faith: Essays on Law in General* (OUP 2012) 186.

[5] MacCormick (n 1) 159–60.

[6] This is what Lamond calls the 'traditional view' of precedent: G Lamond, 'Do Precedents Create Rules?' (2005) 11 Legal Theory 1, 1. Lamond, of course, objects to this characterization of the *ratio decidendi*. Although a discussion of this point would carry me far from the path of my argument here, I am not convinced that the foil to Lamond's reasons conception is in fact the rule conception. Lamond's view is best contrasted with a particular version of rule conception in which the rules created by precedent cannot contain in their antecedents a set of facts that are not sufficient to justify distinguishing the precedent. But this seems to be the wrong way to think of rules. Logically at least, there is plenty of space to include in the antecedent of a legal rule all the facts that the previous court did not consider sufficient reasons to defeat the reasons that justified its decision.

120 CLAUDIO MICHELON

Therefore (from (1) and (2)):

(3) In the instant case, the court ought to render decision D.

Courts, according to MacCormick, do not often deploy this argument explicitly, but this is both the ideal type they should aim at in the presentation of their arguments and the best way to understand what is really going on underneath the (often good and necessary) rhetoric of legal opinions.[7] From this characterization of the argument by which a court follows an authoritative precedent, stems an account of the deeper theoretical structure of authoritative precedents, including conceptions of the *ratio decidendi*, of *obiter dicta*, and of how exactly the source and the target cases can be said to be similar.

If MacCormick's account is correct, in applying an authoritative precedent a court would be committed to the existence of a particular set of generic properties (positive and negative) that occur in both cases and that, in both cases, would justify making the same type of decision. But in a legal syllogism, the court would not only be relying on *there being a legal* rule covering both cases but also on a particular *formulation* of that legal rule (however imperfectly presented in the judge's opinions). As we have seen, the 'major premise' of the legal syllogism is a legal rule. It is a claim that 'for every x, if x has properties A, B, C, [...], then the court should render decision D'. If the legal syllogism were the type of argument courts employ in following precedents, 'being on all fours' would simply mean that the antecedent of the rule used by the court in the previous authoritative decision also covers the facts in the instant case.

MacCormick offers a paradigmatically clear articulation of a popular conception of what courts do when they 'apply' an authoritative precedent. I do not want to defend this conception here and, in fact, I share some of Duarte d'Almeida's worries regarding the claim that the legal syllogism is an apt model to explain law application.[8] Notice, first, that the major premise of a legal syllogism is a very bold claim for a court (and indeed for anyone arguing *sub specie humanitatis*) to make. In fact, it is unclear that courts do (or even should) commit to such claims.[9] As with any conditional statement, it affirms a relationship between the antecedent and the consequent in which the truth of the antecedent is *sufficient* to establish the truth of the consequent. Such claims discount the possibility of riders, countervailing legal reasons, undercutters, conflicting rules, inter alia. Justifying such a claim would be a very tall order indeed but, if the legal syllogism were the right account of an argument that applies a precedent, that is what the court would be committed to defending. Notice that, in principle, a court could be committed to *there being* a legal rule that covers both cases without having to commit to *a particular formulation* of it. In fact, a court could even argue meaningfully in favour of there being a rule that covers both cases, without having to settle for a particular formulation of that rule. If the argument by which courts apply precedents is indeed a legal syllogism, the court would be required to go one step further: it would have to commit to a particular formulation of a legal rule.

Be that as it may, an account of precedent application in general (and the legal syllogism in particular) operates under the assumption that there is 'settled law' that covers the case at hand, however hard it might have been to unearth it through research into and interpretation of authoritative sources. This is in contrast with what is sometimes called a 'case of first

---

[7] MacCormick (n 1) 159.
[8] L Duarte d'Almeida 'On the Legal Syllogism' in D Plunkett, SJ Shapiro, and K Toh (eds), *Dimensions of Normativity* (OUP 2019).
[9] ibid.

impression', that is to say, a case where the court cannot identify settled law that covers the case at hand and, accordingly, needs to reach out for other argumentative resources. This difference is not meant to imply any deeper legal metaphysical position and in particular it is not meant to deny (or affirm) that there is always a legal norm that covers the case at hand. It is simply meant to identify different ways in which courts see themselves as operating: they sometimes see themselves as operating within the domain of established legal norms; sometimes, in contrast, they see themselves as unable to rely on established legal norms in order to decide the case at hand. The application of a precedent, as modelled in the legal syllogism, is the process of bringing that settled law to bear on the instant case. But any account of the argumentative form of law application that improves on the legal syllogism would also be an account of this process. As we will see in section 2, that is not the only way in which courts argue from precedent.

The legal syllogism argument type makes it clear that precedent application is primarily concerned with offering an answer to the question of how *this* court ought to decide *this* particular case. In doing so, courts are often aware of the wider implications of the decisions they are taking and those legal consequences might (and often do) play a role in the court's reasoning aimed at formulating the right major premise in a syllogism, for instance when they try to interpret a previous decision whose *ratio decidendi* they intend to apply to the instant case.[10] But the conclusion of the syllogism is a conclusion about what should be done in the particular case that is presented to the court. The question that this conclusion is trying to settle, directly or indirectly, is not a general question about the meaning of a previous case or about whether a particular rule belongs to the legal system. Surely courts argue about general legal questions in applying precedents, but precedent application comes downstream from those arguments.

Notice that, in the legal syllogism model, precedent application yields a particular type of conclusion. The consequent of the rule in the major premise is a type of decision that *ought* to be taken whenever all facts contained in the antecedent obtain (a contract should be declared null and void, an order should be issued, etc). Accordingly, the conclusion of the syllogism is that the court *ought* to decide the case at hand in a particular way (contract C ought to be declared null and void; P ought to be ordered by the court to do A). In other words, the court has a *duty* to decide in a particular way. This is stronger than, say, a conclusion according to which the court has *a reason* to decide in a particular way. Duties are *mandatory reasons* that possess a special type of force. They are both (a) reasons to do something and (b) reasons not to act on a given set of countervailing reasons.[11] This means that the duty-reason is insulated from certain types of reason, no matter how strong they might be.[12] Accordingly, if two previous authoritative cases point in opposite directions, the reasons they provide cannot be weighed against one another. They cannot both control the decision, so the court must find another way to dismiss at least one of them as not applicable to the case.

An illustration of this argumentative dynamic can be found in the well-known Scottish case of *Morgan Guaranty*.[13] When the Scottish Court of Session decided that case, the

---

[10] Such consequences might also play a role beyond the practice of precedent application. Consequences might be one of the main arguments in cases of first impression, when authoritative sources are either lacking or are not clearly articulated. See N MacCormick, *Legal Reasoning and Legal System* (2nd edn, OUP 1994) 129; see also N MacCormick, 'On Legal Decisions and Their Consequences: From Dewey to Dworkin' (1983) 58 NYU L Rev 239.

[11] J Raz, *Practical Reasons and Norms* (2nd edn, OUP 1999) 58–59; J Gardner and T Macklem, 'Reasons' in JL Coleman, KE Himma, and SJ Shapiro (eds), *The Oxford Handbook of Jurisprudence and Philosophy of Law* (OUP 2004) 466.

[12] Raz (n 11) 35ff.

[13] *Morgan Guaranty Trust Company of New York v Lothian Regional Council* 1995 SC 151.

122 CLAUDIO MICHELON

Senators of the College of Justice were presented with two putatively binding decisions whose respective *rationes* required the court to make two incompatible decisions. The first was the 1959 Court of Session decision in *Glasgow Corporation*,[14] in which the pursuer was trying to recover an amount paid by mistake to the defender. The pursuer's mistake, however, was not a mistake about facts but a mistake about the law. The court in *Glasgow Corporation* decided that mistakes in law, in Scots law, were not sufficient grounds on which to ask for the money back and, accordingly, found in favour of the defender. The second was *Stirling*,[15] a poorly reported case, pieced together by the pursuer's legal team in *Morgan Guaranty* (with the help of legal historians). There, the Court of Session had decided that mistakes in law were perfectly good grounds to claim back money paid. In *Morgan Guaranty*, the court argued that the precedent set in *Stirling* should be followed, and the one set by *Glasgow Corporation* should be ignored.

Many arguments were produced to favour one or another of the putative authorities, but the material facts that constituted the *rationes* of each respective precedent case were not weighed against each other. Instead, the arguments presented were reasons for or against taking one (or the other) decision as the right authority applicable to the case. In *Stirling*'s favour, for instance, were the facts that (a) it was decided before *Glasgow Corporation*, thus taking temporal precedence, (b) it was more coherent with the rest of the law of Scotland under a principle of *unjustified enrichment*, and (c) *Glasgow Corporation* was wrongly decided perhaps under the (in this instance) unwelcome influence of English law, and without the benefit of more complete information about *Stirling*, that had since been unearthed. In favour of *Glasgow Corporation* was the fact that, as the most recent decision, (a) it had been effectively taken to be the law on the matter for a generation of jurists (and that, as a result, at the time of deciding *Morgan Guaranty*, there was no doubt in most practitioner's minds that mistakes in law could not justify repetition), and that (b) *Stirling* was so poorly recorded that it left room for conjecture about the actual points of law settled in its decision.

Notice that the *rationes* of the two competing precedents were not taken by the court to be, each, reasons to be weighed against one another. Instead, each precedent was taken to imply a duty by the court. The reasons that were (perhaps) balanced concerned which of the available 'authorities' should take precedence; once that question was settled one way or another, the court would have a duty to decide in a particular way by force of a specific 'application' argument. An application argument (such as the legal syllogism), if sound, supports a claim that the court is under a duty to decide in a particular way.

Before we move to the last aspect of the argumentative fingerprint of the legal syllogism, it is worth asking if a tweak to the legal syllogism would not allow for a less strong conclusion. Perhaps the conclusion that the legal syllogism establishes, contra MacCormick and others, is simply that whenever the antecedent of the rule obtains, the court 'has an authoritative reason' to make a certain decision (but no reasons not to act on other reasons). This would be a roundabout way of claiming that the facts contained in the antecedent of the conditional in the major premise of the legal syllogism are, taken together, a reason in favour of making a particular decision. That might be so, but notice how this is not really a minor tweak. With that change, the legal syllogism would no longer allow the court to settle the matter, as one cannot simply assume that there are no other reasons bearing on the case. New premises (including either a premise that there are no other reasons bearing on the matter, or a premise that all other reasons bearing on the matter are outweighed by the reason given by

---

[14] *Glasgow Corp v Lord Advocate* 1959 SC 203.
[15] *Stirling v Earl of Lauderdale* (1733) Mor 2930.

the precedent) would be needed in order to reach the stronger conclusion that a court ought to decide in a particular way. That would also apply to other acceptable attempts to model precedent application.

Finally, the legal syllogism is a deductive argument and, as such, the truth of the conclusion would follow necessarily from the truth of the premises. The conclusion that the court 'ought to render decision D' is supported by the premises as a matter of logical necessity (rather than, say, probability).

So, to sum up, if the precedent-application argument is modelled on the legal syllogism, what we obtain is a type of precedent-based argumentation practice (i) that relies on a formulation of a legal rule, (ii) in which the court believes itself to be operating within the realm of settled law, (iii) which is exclusively trying to answer the question of how to decide the case at hand, (iv) which supports a conclusion to the effect that the court ought to decide in a particular way, (v) as a matter of logical necessity (if major and minor premise are both true).

Before I move on to our two other comparators, let me come back to my misgivings about the legal syllogism and explain why these are of limited importance in the present context. As mentioned earlier, a court that applies a precedent does not need to have clarity about all necessary elements of the legal rule that covers the case, including all possible riders, undercutters, and other properties that would need to be included in the antecedent if the court were to provide a complete formulation of the rule it is applying. That is not to say that there is no rule of law that covers the case, but courts do not need to have clarity about all elements of the antecedent of that rule. Many, often the majority, of these elements are simply not at issue in a case. Moreover, and *pace* MacCormick, it is not clear why a court should always aim for that. That means that the argument type that a court employs to follow a precedent would not need to commit to a particular formulation of the legal rule that, ultimately, determines whether the application of the authoritative decision to the instant case is legally correct.

But notice that a better account of the argument type that is used by courts in precedent application would still share a number of features with the legal syllogism, in particular features (ii), (iii), and (iv). These three features will be enough for my purposes here. An adequate analysis of arguments that rely on a legal analogy between the case at hand and an authoritative precedent would conclude that they share feature (iii) with the law-application argument type, but not features (ii) and (iv). Inferences to the best legal explanation, in turn, do not share feature (iii) with either legal application arguments or legal analogical arguments.

2. Precedent-Based Analogies

Sometimes, courts have to decide cases that are not 'on all fours' with a precedent and do not fall squarely within the scope of any other authoritative legal norm. Courts decide those cases in a number of different ways. Sometimes they investigate the 'juridical consequences'[16] of their decisions when searching for reasons to decide one way or another; sometimes they draw inspiration from solutions found in sources that do not possess practical

---

[16] I use the phrase 'judicial consequences' in the sense in which it is employed by B Rudden, 'Consequences' (1979) Juridical Review 24, 197; MacCormick, 'On Legal Decisions and Their Consequences' (n 10). Roughly as the consequences of the envisaged decision across a range of future cases that would fall under whatever rule is left behind by the decision.

124   CLAUDIO MICHELON

authority (*obiter dicta* or foreign law, for instance); sometimes they argue from authoritative legal sources that, albeit not being 'on all fours' with the case they are charged with deciding, are sufficiently similar to offer support to their decision. The latter can give rise to a legal analogy.

References to analogy are common in accounts of judicial precedent, but my concern here is with a particular *argument type*. Courts deploy this argument type when an authoritative precedent, in spite of not being applicable to the case at hand, is somehow similar to it. From that similarity, they conclude that there is a legal reason to decide the 'target case' in a way similar to the 'source case'. When courts apply this (and other types of comparative argument, such as the argument *a fortiori* or the *e contrario*), they produce legal arguments that are based on authoritative legal sources, but that are not reducible to law application.

In the dominant account of legal analogy, certain features (F, G, ...) are shared between the authoritative precedent (source case) and the case at hand (target case). The source case has an additional feature: it was decided in a particular way (call it feature H). From the similarities (F, G, ...), it is inferred that source and target should also share another feature (i.e. H), that we know the source to possess. Hence, the target case should also possess feature H. In other words, it should be decided in the same way the source case was decided. Martin Golding provides the best-known formulation of this account of a legal analogy. According to him, an analogical argument has the following structure:

(1) x has characteristics F, G ...
(2) y has characteristics F, G ...
(3) x also has characteristic H.
(4) F, G ... are H-relevant characteristics.

Therefore (from (1)–(4)),

(5) Unless there are countervailing considerations, y has characteristic H.[17]

Notice that, for Golding, the inference would only run if it were assumed that the features that we know to be shared (F, G, ...) are 'H-relevant'. So, the inference supposes that there is a connection between a certain number of 'operative facts' and the decision, in a way that is suspiciously similar to the conditional structure of a rule ('If F, G ... then H').

In a paper published a few years ago, Duarte d'Almeida and I take issue with the dominant account of legal analogies and provide an alternative erotetic account.[18] We do not believe that the legal analogical inference needs to rely on an explicit enumeration of the particular H-relevant features present both in the source case and in the target case (as in premises (1), (2), and (4) of Golding's scheme). In our account, all a court needs to commit to is the claim that the normative questions raised by source and target cases are themselves sub-questions of a more general normative question (one which admits a uniform answer). Such claim can be made even if the court does not provide an articulation of what that more general question actually is. As a matter of fact, courts do, sometimes, provide an articulation of what

---

[17] See M Golding, 'The Logical Force of Arguments by Analogy in Common Law Reasoning' in C Farelli and E Pattaro (eds), *Reason in Law: Proceedings of the conference held in Bologna, 12–15 December 1984*, vol 3 (Giuffrè 1988). I have changed the graphic representation of the argument slightly from Golding's (as I did in L Duarte d'Almeida and C Michelon, 'The Structure of Arguments by Analogy in Law' (2017) 31 Argumentation 377), but the contents are quoted verbatim.

[18] Duarte d'Almeida and Michelon (n 17).

they believe to be the more general normative question that covers both analogized cases, but faced with a convincing objection to their formulation of that question, a court does not need to withdraw the claim that there is a more general normative question covering the questions raised by source and target cases.

Both the traditional account and the erotetic account of legal analogies share a number of features. Attention to those shared features suffices to demonstrate particular differences in what an authoritative precedent means when a court *applies* it and when a court *uses it as the source of an analogy*.

Let me start with a similarity between the law-applying arguments and the legal analogical argument. Both are aimed at justifying a decision in a particular case. Not all arguments put forward by courts, including those grounded on the authority of precedent, have the same aim and in fact I will claim in section 3 that this is not the (primary) point of a court's deployment of an inference to the best legal explanation.

But the contexts in which a law-applying type of argument is useful are very different from the contexts in which a legal analogical argument is useful. The former is an attempt to relate settled law to the instant case; the latter is useful in contexts in which there is no settled law. This relates to a third feature of legal analogies: their conclusion is not the claim that there is a duty for the court to follow the decision that was taken in the source case; rather, it simply tries to establish that there is *a reason* to do so. As we have seen in section 1, the conclusion of an argument type that captures the rational move from settled law to court decision is one in which what is justified is a claim that the court has a *duty* to decide in a particular way.

This becomes clear if we compare the conflict of authorities in *Morgan Guaranty* (discussed in section 1) with conflicting analogies. In what is perhaps the most discussed judicial example of an analogical argument,[19] the Court of Appeals of New York had to decide whether it was necessary to establish negligence for a steamboat company to be held liable for money stolen from a passenger's cabin. In that case, there were two sources of analogy pulling in opposite directions. On the one hand, the case had similarities with the well-established rule that innkeepers should be held responsible (without negligence) for money stolen from their guests' rooms (discussed at pages 166–68 of the decision in *Adams*); on the other hand, there was an authoritative precedent pointing in the opposite direction in *Carpenter*, a case concerning theft in railroad sleeping coaches.[20] Each 'analogue' had points of similarity with the situation in *Adams* and, accordingly, each could have grounded a legal analogy. Each of these analogies generated a reason for the court to decide in a particular way. The court weighed those reasons and concluded that the reason provided by the analogy with the doctrine of innkeepers' strict liability was stronger than the reason provided by *Carpenter*. But there was no need to dismiss the authority of *Carpenter* altogether in the way the Scottish Court of Session, in deciding *Morgan Guaranty*, needed to dismiss the authority of *Glasgow Corporation* in order to favour the precedent established by *Stirling*.

So, authoritative precedent does not always possess the same strength. In some contexts (the ones in which the court believes the law to be settled), a law-applying type of legal argument is appropriate and the conclusion this argument yields concerns a court's *duty* to decide

---

[19] *Adams v New Jersey Steamboat Company* 151 NY 163 (1896). Besides Golding, many others have discussed this particular case, including J Hall (ed), *Readings in Jurisprudence* (Bobbs-Merrill 1938) 577–78; S Brewer, 'Exemplary Reasoning: Semantics, Pragmatics, and the Rational Force of Legal Argument by Analogy' (1996) 109 Harv L Rev 923; L Weinreb, *Legal Reason: The Use of Analogy in Legal Argument* (CUP 2005); F Schauer, 'Analogy in the Supreme Court: *Lozman v City of Riviera Beach*' (2013) Supreme Court Rev 405; Duarte d'Almeida and Michelon (n 17) 363ff.

[20] *Carpenter v New York NY, NH HRR Co* 124 NY 53 (1891).

in a certain way. In other contexts (in which there is no settled law), an analogical legal argument might, given some additional conditions, be available, but its conclusion does not concern a duty of the court; it just provides an authoritative reason to decide in a certain way.

Before we conclude this section, let me just say a word about the different commitments implied by each type of argument. As is manifest in the structure of the legal syllogism, law application is committed to there being a rule of law that covers the case at hand. In the legal syllogism, we find this rule in the major premise, but even if, more generally, the argument type that best explains how courts apply such precedents were not predicated on a *clear articulation of a legal rule*, that is not to say that the whole enterprise of authoritative precedent application is not predicated on *the existence* of one such legal rule that covers the case. Contrast that with the legal analogical argument: the inexistence of a settled legal rule is what gives rise to the need to employ the analogical argument. While precedent might be predicated on (and is certainly not incompatible with) the existence of a legal rule covering the case at hand, legal analogies are not so.

With this short but, hopefully, informative comparison between law-applying arguments and legal analogies in place, we can now move on to our third argument type, the inference to the best legal explanation.

3. Inferences to the Best Legal Explanation

That courts use anything like inferences to the best legal explanation (hereinafter, IBLE) is controversial. I believe they do[21] and in what follows I will present a brief account of what I believe they are doing when they employ this type of argument. But regardless of whether or not I am right, it is abundantly clear that courts often *appear* to be inferring that there are reasons for a court to decide according to a particular norm that they *infer from a string of cases or other legal norms*. In fact, this argumentative move is made in many celebrated decisions and opinions, including Lord Atkin's opinion in *Donoghue v Stevenson*,[22] Lord Denning's dissenting opinion in *Lloyds Bank v Bundy*,[23] Lord Rodger's opinion in *Shilliday v Smith*,[24] and Lord Goff's opinion in *Lipkin Gorman v Karpnale Ltd*.[25]

An account of the IBLE's structure needs to meet some desiderata. *Inter alia*, it needs to represent the 'explanatory' relationship between the norm the court intends to apply to the instant case and the positive norms that it takes to be (non-controversially) a part of the legal system, and it also needs to reflect how identifying this norm helps to decide the instant case.

Here is one possible scheme that tries to capture the argument and achieve these two desiderata:

(1) If there were a Norm N_1, then there would be a reason to act as required by Legal Norms LN_1, LN_2, ... LN_n.

---

[21] As I have explained in C Michelon, 'The Inference to the Best Legal Explanation' (2019) 39 OJLS 878. A good example of the opposite view can be found in the contribution to this volume by Luís Duarte d'Almeida (Chapter 10).
[22] *Donoghue v Stevenson* [1932] AC 562, 582.
[23] *Lloyds Bank v Bundy* [1974] 3 All ER 757, 763.
[24] *Shilliday v Smith* 1998 SC 725.
[25] *Lipkin Gorman (a firm) v Karpnale Ltd* [1991] 2 AC 548.

(2) No other norm is better than N_1 at providing a reason to act as required by each LN_1, LN_2, ... LN_n.

(3) If (if there were a Norm N_1, then there would be a reason to act as required by each LN_1, LN_2, ... LN_n) and no other Norm is better than N_1 at providing a reason to act as required by each LN_1, LN_2, ... LN_n, then there is a reason to act according to N_1.

Therefore, from (1), (2), and (3):

(4) There is a reason to act according to N_1.[26]

Put to the side for a moment the question of whether this is indeed the best scheme to represent the structure of an IBLE. The scheme represents the 'explanatory' relation as a justificatory relationship: the norm the argument tries to establish we have a reason to act on is the one that best *justifies* the existence of the legal norms LN_1, LN_2, ... LN_n in the legal system. Now this justification is merely conjectural. There would be no contradiction in holding that (i) the principle of Change of Position (that Lord Goff tries to establish in *Lipkin Gorman*) is both the best conjectural justification for the two groups of precedent cases he mentions in the decision[27] and (ii) a norm with no actual value, or even a bad norm for a legal system to contain. We would only have a reason to act according to it because of the explanatory relationship it has with positive law.

Before we move on, three observations are in order. First, IBLE does not need to be based on authoritative precedents. Any other authoritative legal source would do and, indeed, there is a close relation between the structure of an IBLE and traditional legal arguments like those that appeal to the will of the 'rational' legislator. Secondly, general inferences that one has a reason to adopt a certain norm because it is the best 'explanation' (i.e. justification) for a series of authoritative cases are not only employed by courts but also commonly found in non-judicial legal activities, such as doctrinal scholarship and legal advice. In legal scholarship, the reason to adopt the norm is not connected to any particular case. Doctrinal scholars often claim that a certain norm should be treated as a reason for action in an unspecified number of cases. That unjustified enrichment is a general source of obligations in Scots law was thought by Lord Rodger to underlie the presence of various specific authorities normally grouped around the so-called 'three Rs' (recompense, restitution, and repetition) in *Shilliday*.[28] Thirdly, a court's use of the IBLE to decide cases is *often* supererogatory: for reasons I have explained elsewhere,[29] in every case in which a court could infer a principle (soundly) from a set of authoritative precedents, another argument would also be available to resolve the case—a legal analogy between the source cases and the instant case. Moreover, as we have seen, a legal analogy can run perfectly well without an articulation of the 'rule' or 'norm' that covers the analogized cases. Hence, it is worth asking: why should courts embark on this supererogatory argumentative exercise?

The reason for a court to do so is not primarily to resolve the case at hand (which they could do without having to infer the general norm) but to resolve the case in a way that tries to vindicate the practical force of a legal norm that is not part of settled law. Lord Atkin argued for the *Neighbour Principle*, and in doing so changed the law of negligence; Lord

---

[26] This mirrors, with some minor nomenclature changes, a scheme I put forward in Michelon (n 21).
[27] *Lipkin Gorman* (n 25) 578G.
[28] *Shilliday* (n 24) 728.
[29] Michelon (n 21).

Denning argued for the principle that *inequality of bargaining power could render an otherwise legally binding agreement unenforceable* and, in doing so, had great impact in the law of contract; Lord Rodger argued in favour of a *general principle that unjustified enrichment is a source of obligations* and, in doing so, was at the centre of the 'enrichment revolution' in Scotland; Lord Goff argued for the principle that *Change of Position* is a valid defence and, in doing so, had significant impact in the English law of restitution. One might disagree with the previously mentioned assessments about these decisions' impacts, but generating such an impact is the point of each of them. In their IBLEs, these courts were addressing not only the parties to the case at hand but also future courts in a way that is different from setting an authoritative precedent that binds them.

So, in deploying an IBLE a court has the double objective of (i) giving reasons to decide the case at hand, and (ii) giving general reasons for future courts to decide in ways that are not covered by the precedents it is setting through the facts of the case they are deciding. That *double aim* is one of the features that distinguishes their deployment from the deployment of a legal analogy. Another distinguishing feature is the reliance on an explanatory/justificatory relation between a set of settled legal rules and another (not legally settled) norm. They do have in common, however, that they are called for only in contexts that are not covered by settled law and that they only produce a reason (rather than a duty) to decide in a particular manner. The latter two features set them apart from precedent-application argument types, like the legal syllogism.

With this sketch of three argument forms in place, let me now explain how the analysis in sections 1, 2, and 3 should affect a theory of legal precedents.

4. Argument and Precedent

Attention to the argumentative structures in which legal precedent possesses a central role allows us to see how precisely the authority of precedent operates in ways that are not reducible to the doctrine of precedent. According to the doctrine of precedent, authoritative decisions by previous courts are binding on the courts subject to them, that is to say, the court in the latter case has a duty to either follow or distinguish the precedent. But we saw that in arguing analogically from an authoritative precedent, courts are using content-independent reasons for action provided by authoritative precedent in a way that does not generate a duty to decide in any particular way, only a reason in favour of a particular decision. The doctrine of precedent concerns a duty which the court has to apply authoritative precedents to *decide a particular case*. But we saw that when courts put forward IBLEs, they are attempting to support general claims about how certain types of cases should be decided.

The analysis in this chapter can be made more complex along two different vectors. In order to make my point, I have only discussed three argumentative uses of authoritative precedent, but the analysis could be expanded to incorporate other canonical legal argument types, such as the *a fortiori*, the *e contrario*, and the *a simile*, among many others. In addition, each argument type discussed is, as I have tried to make clear along the way, controversial. Regarding each of the argument types discussed, I have tried to rely on features that rival conceptions of that argument type might agree on. Thus, for instance, I have relied on features of legal analogies that both the traditional account and the erotetic account agree they possess. A satisfactorily complex theory of precedent should not shy away from a more complete discussion of the rival versions of each argument type.

The complexity revealed by a close attention to the uses of precedent in legal argument helps us to reframe the desiderata of a satisfactory theory of precedent: instead of conceiving it simply as an account of how and when the existence of an authoritative precedent binds future courts (and when it does not), a theory of precedent should also account for all the other argumentative uses of authoritative precedent in legal argument. In other words, a satisfactory theory of precedent should also account for the widespread practice of legal decision-making in which courts purport to be still producing genuine legal arguments (and not simply general moral arguments) in the space beyond settled law.

10

The 'Expiscation' of Legal Principles

Luís Duarte d'Almeida[*]

1. Introduction

The unusual word in my title comes from a 1991 essay by Neil MacCormick.[1] There he discusses one way in which courts are said to rely on precedent: they sometimes 'search for underlying principles' they take to be common to a line of previously decided cases.[2]

MacCormick's main example is *Donoghue v Stevenson*, and he quotes this well-known excerpt from Lord Atkin's opinion:

> It is remarkable how difficult it is to find in the English authorities statements of general application defining the relations between parties that give rise to the duty [of care]. The Courts are concerned with the particular circumstances which come before them in actual litigation, and it is sufficient to say whether the duty exists in those circumstances. ... And yet the duty which is common to all the cases where liability is established must logically be based on some element common to the cases where it is found to exist.[3]

MacCormick writes that Lord Atkin:

> saw the negligence cases as grounded in a principle that was more implicit in them than as yet fully explicated. His effort was to construct this underlying principle. ... [T]his effort of Lord Atkin's strikes me as of the very essence of the process of the evolution or indeed expiscation of legal principles.[4]

'To expiscate' is not a common verb. (Merriam-Webster calls it 'chiefly Scottish.') It does capture nicely, though, one way of thinking about what judges do when they formulate a principle they take to underlie a string of previous decisions. The word comes from the Latin *expiscari*—to 'fish out'. (*'Piscari'* means 'to fish'.) To 'expiscate' legal principles is to

---

[*] I would like to thank Maria Alvarez, Gianluca Andresani, David Duarte, John Gardner, Chris Himsworth, Martin Kelly, Euan MacDonald, Cláudio Michelon, Ezequiel Monti, José Juan Moreso, Serena Olsaretti, Connie Rosati, Fábio Shecaira, Federico Samudio, Sebastian Lewis, Stephen Perry, Andrew Williams, audiences in Edinburgh, Barcelona, and Lisbon, and participants in the authors' workshop for this volume in October 2021, for very helpful comments and suggestions.

[1] N MacCormick, '*Donoghue v Stevenson* and Legal Reasoning' in PT Burns and SJ Lyons (eds), *Donoghue v Stevenson and the Modern Law of Negligence* (The Continuing Legal Education Society of British Columbia 1991) 191–213. MacCormick had first engaged with this topic in *Legal Reasoning and Legal Theory* (Clarendon Press 1994) 152–94.

[2] MacCormick, '*Donoghue v Stevenson* and Legal Reasoning' (n 1) 201.

[3] *Donoghue v Stevenson* [1932] AC 562, 579–80 (HL).

[4] MacCormick, '*Donoghue v Stevenson* and Legal Reasoning' (n 1) 201.

Luís Duarte d'Almeida, *The 'Expiscation' of Legal Principles* In: *Philosophical Foundations of Precedent*. Edited by: Timothy Endicott, Hafsteinn Dan Kristjánsson, and Sebastian Lewis, Oxford University Press. © Luís Duarte d'Almeida 2023.
DOI: 10.1093/oso/9780192857248.003.0011

THE 'EXPISCATION' OF LEGAL PRINCIPLES   131

metaphorically fish them out of a pool of past decisions. The 'expiscated' principle, once made explicit, can then be applied to new cases.[5]

This is not something that courts do very often, but there are a few other well-known examples of the expiscatory move. One comes from Lord Denning's opinion in *Lloyds Bank Ltd v Bundy*.[6] Denning points out that the 'general rule' in English law is that 'a customer who signs a bank guarantee or a charge cannot get out of it'.[7] But he notes that 'there are exceptions to this general rule', and says that although 'hitherto these exceptional cases have been treated each as a separate category in itself', 'the time has come when we should seek to find a principle to unite them'.[8] He then reviews five classes of exceptional cases—duress of goods, expectant heir, undue influence, undue pressure, and salvage agreements[9]—and says this:

> Gathering all together, I would suggest that through all these instances there runs a single thread. They rest on 'inequality of bargaining power.' By virtue of it, the English law gives relief to one who, without independent advice, enters into a contract on terms which are very unfair or transfers property for a consideration which is grossly inadequate, when his bargaining power is grievously impaired by reason of influences or pressures brought to bear on him by or for the benefit of the other. ... I hope this principle will be found to reconcile the cases.[10]

The expiscatory move has not received much attention from legal theorists. There is, however, a general picture on which authors who have written on the topic seem to agree. This standard view—as I will call it—is that courts are drawing an *inference* that proceeds *from* the previous decisions *to* a more general conclusion about a principle that governs a broader class of cases (including, characteristically, the case in hand).

There is debate on how to specify this general picture. Some see the inference as a legal analogue of induction. Some think of it as a kind of inference to the best explanation. Some seem to think that the conclusion of the inference is a first-order statement *of* the unifying principle itself. Others see it instead as a second-order statement that there is reason to decide in accordance to that unifying principle.[11] Whatever the details, though, there appears

---

[5] Elsewhere, MacCormick uses a different metaphor: he says that such unifying principles are formulated 'by way of *extrapolation* from atomic or fragmentary rules already settled': see *Legal Reasoning and Legal Theory* (n 1) 160 (emphasis added). (In *Haseldine v Daw & Son Ltd and Others* [1941] 3 All ER 173F, Scott LJ said that Atkin in *Donoghue* was 'engaged in extracting the true metal of principle from the ore of the particular cases'.) The underlying thought is the same.

[6] *Lloyds Bank Ltd v Bundy* [1974] 3 All ER 757. Another famous example is Cardozo J's opinion in *MacPherson v Buick Motors* 217 NY 382 (1916), which, indeed, Atkin in *Donoghue v Stevenson* (n 3) 598 refers to as 'illuminating'.

[7] *Lloyds Bank Ltd v Bundy* (n 6) 763. Denning's approach diverged from the majority's, who reached the same conclusion but on different, narrower grounds.

[8] ibid.

[9] In *Avon Finance Co Ltd v Bridger* [1985] All ER 281, Denning claims to have found a sixth category.

[10] *Lloyds Bank Ltd v Bundy* (n 6) 765.

[11] Authors who endorse (some version of) the standard view include D Hunter, 'No Wilderness of Single Instances: Inductive Inference in Law' (1998) 48 J Legal Education 365; JB Downard, 'The Common Law and the Forms of Reasoning' (2000) 13 Int'l J Semiotics of Law 377, 389–98; G Tuzet, 'Legal Abduction' (2005) 6 Cognitio 265, 272; G Pino, 'Principi e argomentazione giuridica' (2009) Ars Interpretandi 131, 150–51; KJ Vandevelde, *Thinking Like a Lawyer: An Introduction to Legal Reasoning* (2nd edn, Westview 2011) 67–68; G Tuzet, 'L'Abduzione dei Principi' (2009) 33 Ragion Pratica 517; A Amaya, 'Coherencia, Justificación y Derecho' (2011) 10 Discusiones 217, 228; A Amaya, *The Tapestry of Reason: An Inquiry into the Nature of Coherence and its Role in Legal Argument* (Bloomsbury 2015) 503–20; JSA Maranhão, 'Conservative Coherentist Closure of Legal Systems' in M Araszkiewicz and K Płeska (eds), *Logic in the Theory and Practice of Lawmaking* (Springer 2015) 123–25; B Schafer and C Aitken, 'Inductive, Abductive and Probabilistic Reasoning' in G Bongiovanni and others, *Handbook of Legal Reasoning and Argumentation* (Springer 2018) 275–313; C Michelon, 'The Inference to the Best Legal Explanation' (2019) 39 OJLS 878; and B Askeland, 'The Potential of Abductive Legal Reasoning' (2020) 33 Ratio Juris 66, 69.

to be agreement that (a) the formulations of the relevant principle are to be somehow *supported*, argumentatively, by the fact that there is a line of cases that have been authoritatively decided in a certain way, and that (b) the fact that those cases were authoritatively decided in *that* (rather than some other) way determines, at least in part, the content of the relevant principle. The standard view, then, in short, is that courts move argumentatively *from* past decisions *to* general unifying principles. And that too is the idea that MacCormick's use of the word 'expiscation' calls into mind.

But the standard view, I argue in this chapter, is wrong. My own view is that the fact that there is a consistent line of previous cases authoritatively decided in a certain way is inferentially irrelevant to the claim that there is a broader principle that both subsumes those previous cases and prescribes the same decision for a larger class of cases. We should *not* understand the judicial formulation of such unifying principles as being in any way supported, argumentatively, by the contingent fact that the previous cases happen to have been decided in a certain way. And, indeed, we find in opinions like Atkin's or Denning's no distinctive inference drawn—or argument given—from past cases to general principle. The relation between the two elements must therefore be explained in a different way.

When I say the expiscatory move involves no *distinctive* inference from past cases to general principle, what I mean is that it does not amount to any specific way of relying on precedent decisions as sources of content-independent practical reasons. There are two main ways in which a judicial decision can bear normatively on some future court's decision. If the previous decision is precedent-setting, the future court typically has a duty to decide in the same way if the new case falls under the *ratio* of that previous decision. And if the new case does not fall under the *ratio* of a previous decision but is still relevantly analogous to a previously decided case, then the new court has a reason (although not a duty) to decide the analogous case in the same way.[12] Now, a court that decides either by following precedent or by extending it analogically will in each case offer an argument of a distinctive kind showing its decision to be justified by reference to that past decision. One might thus think that when a court adopts the expiscatory move, we have a *third* characteristic way by which past decisions can normatively constrain, as sources of content-independent reasons, the decision-making procedure of a court. What I want to suggest is that this is not the case. There is no such third way.

Indeed, my strategy will be to begin by making some remarks about both following precedent and arguing by analogy from precedent, relying on a theoretical framework that, together with Cláudio Michelon, I have developed in previous work.[13] It is an erotetic framework that conceptualizes judicial decisions in terms of the relevant *questions* courts can be said to face and the different answers they can give. In section 2, I will introduce and expand on some aspects of this framework. In section 3, I show how the framework can help us to characterize both the judicial practice of following precedent and that of extending it by analogy. And then, in section 4, I will argue that, once we are minimally clear about what each of those two distinct ways of relying on previous decisions involves, the expiscatory move becomes relatively easy to understand and demystify.

---

[12] This basic distinction is commonly accepted (and does not mean that analogical *reasoning* is not at play in both cases). For just a couple of examples—one old, another recent—see AL Goodhart, 'Determining the *Ratio Decidendi* of a Case' (1930) 60 Yale LJ 161, 180–81 n 73; G Lamond, 'Precedent and Analogy in Legal Reasoning' in EN Zalta (ed), *The Stanford Encyclopedia of Philosophy* (Spring 2016 edn) <https://plato.stanford.edu/archives/spr2016/entries/legal-reas-prec/> accessed 5 March 2022.

[13] L Duarte d'Almeida and C Michelon, 'The Structure of Arguments by Analogy in Law' (2017) 31 Argumentation 359.

THE 'EXPISCATION' OF LEGAL PRINCIPLES   133

2. An Erotetic Framework of Questions and Sub-Questions

Courts typically face what I will call *particular questions*.[14] A particular question is a norma-tive question asked wholly with regard to a particular situation, and it concerns some action by a court. Here is a simple working example of a particular question:

(Q1) Should we (the court) enforce this contract?

There are two noteworthy features of particular questions. The first concerns the *universal-izability* of answers to particular questions. The point is that whoever endorses (as courts must) an answer to a particular question is rationally committed to the view that *all* cases that are similar in all relevant respects to the particular case in hand ought to be settled in the same way. But what exactly does 'settled in the same way' mean? One way of clarifying this notion, and the universalizability point more generally, is by appealing to the idea of a *general question*.

Suppose that a court is concerned with (Q1), and believes that the answer to (Q1) is 'Yes'. Then that court is rationally committed to the view that there is a question with the *form* of (Q2) below and to which the answer is also 'Yes':

(Q2) Should we (the courts) enforce contracts that have features x, y, and z?

A question of this form is a *general question*: it is a question, not about this or that particular contract but about *any* contract that satisfies the relevant description—the description speci-fied by whatever actual features we substitute for 'x', 'y', and 'z'.

A court that answers (Q1) affirmatively, then, is rationally committed to the claim that there is a general question of this form in which the features we substitute for 'x', 'y', and 'z' will be all and only the normatively relevant features of the particular contract that (Q1) is about, and to which the answer is also affirmative. The court's rational commitment, in other words, is to the existence of a general question of which (Q1) happens to be a *sub-question*, and to which the answer is 'Yes'.

In fact, the court will be committed not only to that but also to the view that, for all con-tracts that satisfy the relevant description, the answer will be 'Yes' *for the same reason*. Call this a *uniform* answer: one that is not to be further qualified by saying, 'but for different reasons depending on the type of contract' (or something to the same effect). And a uniform answer to a general normative question is what I will call a *rule*.

So the first relevant point—the universalizability point—can be reconstructed as the point that whoever answers 'Yes' (or 'No') to (Q1) is rationally committed to the view that there is a *general question* of the form of (Q2) to which there is a *uniform* 'Yes' (or 'No') *answer*, and of which (Q1) is a *sub-question*.

It doesn't mean, though—and this is the second point to raise with regard to particular questions—that the decision-maker who adopts an answer to a particular question will herself necessarily be fully clear about what exactly that *general* question is, about how *exactly* it is to be formulated. Indeed, she may be hard-pressed to come up with a precise formulation of that question herself. The point here is that one may be able to recognize, and even feel certain of, an answer to a certain particular question, while not being fully clear about what the relevant

---

[14] Throughout this section, I use italics to introduce some relevant terminology.

134 LUÍS DUARTE D'ALMEIDA

features of the particular situation are that would justify that answer. One may have a strong intuition, for example, that the answer to a question like (Q1) should be 'Yes', and indeed be able
to say something by way of indicating in general terms some of the features of the particular
situation that are relevant to that answer; but still have only a relatively diffuse understanding
of how to formulate the corresponding *rule*. That a judge should 'have a rule in mind' when she
'decides to act', as Simpson puts it, does not mean that she 'should have in mind a precise formulation of a rule; a person may act upon a rule without thinking out the draft of a rule'.[15]

To give a simple example (based on the well-known 1896 US case of *Adams v New Jersey
Steamboat Company*[16]), suppose that G, a hotel guest, had money stolen from her room
without negligence on either her part or on the part of H, the hotel owner; and that a court
faces the following particular question:

(Q3) Should we hold H liable for the money stolen from G's room?

Now a court may be clear that its answer to (Q3) is 'Yes', but still be unclear whether its own
justification for that answer would be that there is a uniform 'Yes' answer to (Q4) below; or to
(Q5); or to (Q6); or to any other of a number of general questions that could be asked and of
which (Q3) would be a sub-question:

(Q4) Should we hold *hotel owners* liable for money stolen from guests' rooms without
negligence on the part of either the guest or the owner?
(Q5) Should we hold *providers of closed accommodation* liable for money stolen from
guests' rooms without negligence on the part of either the guest or the owner?
(Q6) Should we hold *providers of accommodation* liable for money stolen from guests'
rooms without negligence on the part of either the guest or the owner?

The obvious risk when considering how exactly to understand the relevant general
question—and therefore the relevant *rule*—is that of over-inclusion; any rule-formulation
that the court might decide to adopt may turn out to have instances that *by the court's own
lights* ought *not* to be decided in the same way.

The court could, of course, invest time in considering all kinds of hypotheticals and testing
different candidate formulations of different rules against its own intuitions. But since all the
court is standardly required to do is to settle the *particular* question before it, there is no
reason why it should put itself through the time-consuming exercise of coming up with a
formulation of the relevant rule that it could confidently believe not to be over-inclusive.[17]

That is why courts often intentionally refrain from giving crisp statements of the rule—
the *ratio decidendi*, as it is normally called—they take to justify their decision;[18] and, in any
event, even if or when they do offer statements of what they take to be the *rationes* of their

---

[15] AWB Simpson, 'The *Ratio Decidendi* of a Case and the Doctrine of Binding Precedent' in AC Guest (ed),
Oxford Essays in Jurisprudence (OUP 1961) 162.

[16] *Adams v New Jersey Steamboat Company* 151 NY 163 (1896).

[17] It would certainly be reckless to adopt a strict rule-formulation having considered carefully only a *single*
case, the particular case in hand; and it is quite possible to give a satisfactory justification—in general terms—
of a decision without going through the motion of explicitly articulating any such watertight rule. See also N
MacCormick, 'Why Cases have Rationes and What These Are' in L Goldstein (ed), *Precedent in Law* (Clarendon
Press 1987) 162–65.

[18] The idea that the *ratio decidendi* of a case can be understood as *rule*, while widespread in the jurisprudential
literature, is not uncontroversial: see, for discussion and criticism of what he calls the 'rule-based' model of precedent (and for a defence of an alternative, reasons-based account), G Lamond, 'Do Precedents Create Rules?' (2005)
11 Legal Theory 1; and G Lamond, 'Precedent' (2007) 2 Philosophy Compass 699. By endorsing, for the purposes

decisions, such statements are not authoritative and do not bind future courts. The *ratio* of a precedent-setting decision is left to be reconstructed by future courts—and these too will often themselves refrain from giving tight formulations of the *rationes* of the very precedents that they take themselves to be following. It is not the function 'of any judges to frame definitions or lay down hard and fast rules', as Lord Reid put it: 'and much they say is intended to be illustrative or explanatory and not to be definitive'.[19]

Importantly, though, to say that the *ratio decidendi* of a judicial decision has no canonical, authoritative formulation, and is open to reconstruction by future courts—or indeed by anyone—is not to say that the exercise of reconstructing it is a fully creative one. It is, rather, an *interpretative* exercise: the goal is still to articulate a rule the previous court can be said to have in fact been committed to. As such, the reconstruction of the *ratio* is constrained by what the previous court may have said. (Of course, if the previous court *did* give a formulation of what it took to be the *ratio* of its decision, then that will matter interpretatively; as will the language and level of generality at which a court will have described the relevant facts, and so on.) Generally speaking, though, there seems to be a commonly adopted interpretative principle of parsimony according to which a court should usually be taken to have been committed to the *least general* version of a *ratio* that is consistent with the relevant interpretative material.

3. Applying the Framework: Precedent and Analogy

The framework just introduced allows us to characterize both the practice of following precedent, and that of extending precedent by analogy. We can think of a precedent-setting decision as a decision that settles authoritatively, not only the particular question it is directly addressing, but the general question that corresponds to its *ratio*—the general question, that is, to which the *ratio* (understood as a rule) is an answer. So a future court follows precedent when it takes the particular question in hand to be a sub-question of a general question that has been authoritatively settled by a previous court.[20]

As to arguments by analogy, they presuppose that there is no previous decision whose *ratio* directly applies to the case in hand: they presuppose, that is, that the particular question faced by the second court is *not* a sub-question of any general question that has been authoritatively settled. But there may be a relevantly analogous case, and what that means is that there is a further, more general question of which both (a) the general question that *has* been

---

of this chapter, the view that the *ratio decidendi* of a decision can be properly thought of as a rule, though, I do not mean to endorse all the particulars of how Lamond depicts what *he* takes a 'rule-based' model to be.

[19] *Cassell & Co Ltd v Broome* [1972] 2 WLR 645, 681–82. And see also Simpson (n 15) 162: 'Even where a judge does take some peculiar care to formulate a rule accurately and precisely, we do not usually treat such a formulation in the same way as a section in a statute, for the prerogative of judges is not to confer binding force upon a rule by formulating it and submitting the formulated rule to some procedure, but rather to decide cases by acting upon rules, without settling for the future the verbal form of the rule on the basis of a single application of it.'

[20] What of distinguishing? It involves two claims: that (1) although the particular question at hand is indeed a sub-question of a general question that has been authoritatively settled by a previous court, (2) the *ratio* of that previous decision is over-inclusive *relative to the previous case*: that (more precisely) the *previous* court's own understanding of the general question raised by the particular case it was addressing failed to take into account a *relevant* feature of that particular case, which feature is not present in the case at hand. When this is true, the second court is at liberty—and perhaps even under a duty—*not* to follow the previous decision, and to *narrow* the previous decision's *ratio*. It means also that the ascription, by a future court, of a *binding ratio* to a previous decision involves the second court's agreement that that previous court's understanding of the general question raised by the previous particular case was correct.

136 LUÍS DUARTE D'ALMEIDA

authoritatively settled and (b) the general question that the second court takes to be raised by the particular case before it are *themselves* sub-questions; and to which there is a uniform answer.

To give an example: in the already mentioned *Adams v New Jersey Steamboat Company* case,[21] it seems fairly clear that the court took itself to be concerned with the following general question:

> (Q7) Should we hold steamboat companies liable for money stolen from guests' rooms without negligence on the part of either the guest or the owner?

There was no directly applicable authority that could be appealed to in order to answer this question. But there was authority—a previous judicial decision[22]—settling the following general question in the affirmative:

> (Q8) Should we hold *hotel owners* liable for money stolen from guests' rooms without negligence on the part of either the guest or the owner?

The *Adams* court answered (Q7) affirmatively too, by analogy with that previous court's answer to (Q8); and to say that the two questions are analogous is to say—or rather, it is a thought that can be, under the proposed erotetic framework, reconstructed as meaning—that there is a further, *more* general question of which both (Q7) and (Q8) are themselves sub-questions and to which there is a uniform answer.

The crucial feature of arguments by analogy, though—the feature roughly captured by the popular notion that arguments by analogy proceed *from case to case* without the identification of an overarching rule—is that a court that argues from analogy will claim (however implicitly) that there is such an overarching more general question, but *refrain from attempting to formulate it*.[23]

One way of reconstructing the scheme of arguments by analogy that does justice to these considerations, then, is the following:

> (1) G_T (the 'target' question) is a general question that is not authoritatively settled.
> (2) G_S (the 'source' question) is a general question that is authoritatively settled.
> (3) There is a (more) general question of which both G_T and G_S are sub-questions, and to which there is a uniform answer. (Call this more general question 'G_C.')
> (4) For every x and every y, if (a) x is a general question that is not authoritatively settled, (b) y is a general question that is authoritatively settled, and (c) there is a (more) general question ('G_C') of which both x and y are sub-questions, and to which there is a uniform answer, then there is reason to adopt, with regard to x, the answer that

---

[21] *Adams v New Jersey Steamboat Company* (n 16).

[22] *Hulett v Swift* 42 Barb 230 (1864).

[23] On this feature of arguments by analogy—which I regard as part of the data (or the *explanandum*, if you want) that any theoretical account of such arguments needs to reflect—see, e.g., EW Patterson, 'Logic in the Law' (1942) 90 U Pa L Rev 875, 903–04; T Halper, 'Logic in Judicial Reasoning' (1968) 44 Indiana LJ 33, 42; JR Murray, 'The Role of Analogy in Legal Reasoning' (1982) 29 UCLA L Rev 833, 847–48; U Klug, *Juristiche Logik* (4th edn, Springer 1982) 115–16; D Hunter, 'Reason is Too Large: Analogy and Precedent in Law' (2001) 50 Emory LJ 1197, 1208, 1252; F Schauer, *Thinking Like a Lawyer: A New Introduction to Legal Reasoning* (Harvard UP 2009) 98–100; see also WV Quine and JS Ullian, *The Web of Belief* (2nd edn, McGraw-Hill 1978) 90–95; and T Govier, 'Analogy and Missing Premises' (1989) 11 Informal Logic 141, 147–48.

THE 'EXPISCATION' OF LEGAL PRINCIPLES   137

is implied by the same uniform answer to G_C that implies the authoritatively adopted answer to y.

Therefore (from (1)–(4)):

(5) There is reason to adopt, with regard to G_T, the answer that is implied by the same uniform answer to G_C that implies the authoritatively adopted answer to G_S.
(6) The answer that is implied, with regard to G_T, by the same uniform answer to G_C that implies the authoritatively adopted answer to G_S, is answer A.

Therefore (from (5) and (6)):

(7) There is reason to adopt, with regard to G_T, answer A.

There is no need to go into this in any further detail.[24] What matters now is to highlight that the most distinctive feature of arguments by analogy is the one captured by the claim in premise (3). This premise asserts that there is a more general question of which both the *target* question (the general question the second court faces) and the *source* question (the general question that is authoritatively settled by a previous decision) are sub-questions; this more general question, note, is itself left unarticulated. And what we might call the *analogy principle*—a notion to which I will return in section 4—is the normative claim made in premise (4), which states that when this is the case, then there is *reason* (a coherence-based reason) to decide the second case in the same way.[25]

Let me, then, sum up the relevant points so far. Courts compare questions *both* when they follow precedent and when they extend it by analogy. When they follow precedent, they take the particular question they need to answer to be a sub-question of a general question that has been authoritatively settled—in which case they are, according to the doctrine of *stare decisis*, typically duty-bound to answer their own question in the same way. When they extend precedent by analogy, they take their particular question to be a sub-question of a general question that is not authoritatively settled; but they take both that general question and the authoritatively settled general question to both be sub-questions of a further, more general question to which there is a uniform answer—and that gives them a reason to decide their own particular question in the same way.

Why would a court that argues by analogy refrain from attempting a precise formulation of that broader general question? For precisely the same reason that courts typically refrain, as I mentioned towards the end of section 2, from giving precise formulations of the *rationes* of their own decisions: because of the risk of over-generalization, of over-inclusion. This risk cannot easily be allayed when a court is closely considering only one or two possible cases—rather than a large range of possible cases, real or hypothetical—as a means of testing and refining different candidate rule-formulations. And this means that the court is also communicating that it takes the *ratio* of its own decision—the decision that it justifies on the basis of the analogy—to be an answer to the *narrower* general question mentioned in

---

[24] For a full discussion and defence of this reconstruction of the structure of arguments by analogy (as well as a critical discussion of competing accounts), see Duarte d'Almeida and Michelon (n 13) 376–91.

[25] Why is there such a reason? Because of the normative importance of coherent decision-making in law, and of associated considerations of equality as expressed in the also popular idea that 'like cases' should be treated 'alike'. But this reason can, of course, be countervailed by reasons to decide in a different way. Conflicting analogies, for instance; or the second court's own view that the previous case was wrongly or unjustly decided on the merits.

premise (1) (the court's 'target' question), and not to the broader, overarching one referred to in premise (3).

4. Legal Principles

We are now well placed to come back to decisions like *Donoghue v Stevenson* or *Lloyds Bank v Bundy* and try to get a clearer understanding of what the 'expiscatory' move involves. My impression is that there are two independent aspects of what judges like Atkin or Denning are doing; and that once we clarify them, it will become apparent that there really is nothing going on that could plausibly be described as an 'expiscation' or 'extraction' of legal principles from past decisions.

A. Can Broader Questions Be 'Expiscated' from Past Cases?

What are these two aspects of what judges like Atkin or Denning are doing?

First, they are looking at a range of previously decided cases, none of whose *rationes* is directly applicable to the particular case in hand. What this means, in the more precise language of the framework presented earlier, is that they are looking at a range of authoritatively decided general questions, but do not take the particular question raised by the case before them to be a sub-question of any one of those general questions. Nevertheless, Atkin and Denning clearly take *all* those authoritatively settled general questions to be themselves sub-questions of an even more general question, itself not authoritatively settled, of which the particular question before them is *also* a sub-question, and to which there is a uniform answer. In other words, they take every single one of these cases to be *analogous*, in the relevant sense, to any of the others. And what this entails is that they might just as well have chosen to decide the case in hand by analogy—either by analogy from any one of those previous cases, or even by analogy from *all* of them, since the scheme of arguments by analogy can easily accommodate, by logical extension, analogies from more than one source at the same time.

And yet they decided *not* to simply argue by analogy. To argue by analogy would have meant—as we saw in section 3—that they would have refrained from formulating the broader general question of which they take all those previous decided general questions to be sub-questions. Instead, they actually took the bold step of formulating that broader general question. Atkin's view, for example, was that all those authoritatively decided general questions were sub-questions of the following more general question (to which a uniform answer could, according to them, be given):

> (Q9) Should we hold a person liable if they act in such a way as to cause injury to their neighbour (i.e. to anyone who is so closely and directly affected by that person's acts that they—the agent—ought reasonably to have them in contemplation as being so affected when that person is directing their mind to the acts or omissions which are called in question)?[26]

---

[26] While this formulation follows closely Atkin's own language—see *Donoghue v Stevenson* (n 3) 580—I give it purely for illustration purposes: it doesn't matter whether it really captures what Atkin thought or would have said had he undertaken to actually phrase his views in the form of a question (together with its uniform answer).

We already know why this is step is a bold one: because of the risk of over-inclusion. As Atkin himself puts it in *Donoghue v Stevenson*, 'to seek a complete logical definition of the general principle is probably to go beyond the function of the judge, for the more general the definition the more likely it is to omit essentials or to introduce non-essentials'.[27] But it does makes sense for a court to feel more confident in actually endorsing as correct a formulation of such a general question—as one to which a uniform answer can be given—when they have in fact considered, not just one or two cases, but a long string of cases against which they can test and refine different candidate formulations and intuitions. The wider the pool of cases that one carefully considers, the less likely it is that one's adopted formulation will turn out to be over-inclusive. And this is the first aspect of what is going on in decisions like *Donoghue v Stevenson* or *Lloyds Bank v Bundy*.[28]

But the important thing to realize is that this exercise is not that of *looking for* a general question that successfully captures a line of previously decided cases. Rather, the role that those previously decided cases play has nothing to do with the fact that they are *previously decided* cases. Their role is simply that of providing examples for consideration in the process of testing, revising, and refining possible formulations of a general question that one takes to have a uniform answer. As far as the exercise is concerned, the cases could have come from textbooks, from other non-judicial sources, even from the judge's own imagination; and, indeed, could and should have been considered alongside any relevant hypothetical cases. The previous decisions are being relied on purely as a *database* of cases; and because this first element of what Atkin or Denning are doing concerns the formulation of a *question*, it is irrelevant that these previous cases have been decided in a certain way, let alone that they have been decided all in the *same* way. Atkin's claim that all the previous cases he is considering are instances of the broader question in (Q9) would hold (if it holds) even if all (or even only some) of those cases had been decided in a different way.

So—and this is the first point I want to stress—there is no sense in which Atkin's or Denning's general questions (or their view that these *are* correctly formulated general questions that capture the relevant features of the previously decided cases) are 'extracted' or 'expiscated' *from* the previous court's decisions. What matters is that Atkin and Denning are *considering* those cases; not that previous courts did the same.

B. Can Answers to Broader Questions Be 'Expiscated' from Past Cases?

The second noteworthy aspect of judgments like Atkin's or Denning's is that they go on to note that all those past cases they are considering have in fact been decided by previous courts *in the same way*. What this means, more precisely, is that each of the general questions raised in each of the previous cases has been answered by a court—and therefore

---

[27] *Donoghue v Stevenson* (n 3) 580.

[28] Whether the line of cases either Atkin or Denning considers is wide enough, and whether their consideration of such cases is sufficiently careful, is another matter; but this is in any case what they purport to be doing. Denning's opinion was criticized in *National Westminster Bank plc v Morgan* [1985] 1 All ER 821, where Lord Scarman questions (at 830d) not only 'whether there is any need in the modern law' for Denning's 'inequality of bargaining power' principle but also whether the principle was even accurate in its statement of existing law. Denning's own formulation of this 'principle' was actually *not* satisfied by some of the very cases that it was presented as 'uniting': see LS Sealy 'Undue Influence and Inequality of Bargaining Power' (1975) 34 CLJ 21, 23.

140 LUÍS DUARTE D'ALMEIDA

authoritatively settled—and that each of those answers is implied by the *same* uniform answer to the broader general question that Atkin and Denning venture to formulate.

That the previous courts all answered their general questions in this way is, of course, a contingent fact; and the question to ask now is whether in decisions like *Donoghue v Stevenson* or *Lloyds Bank v Bundy* this fact is being accorded any particular normative weight as at least a content-independent reason for Atkin or Denning to answer their own broader questions the way they did. And my suggestion is that it isn't. For the reason-giving significance of the fact that previous courts have given consistent answers to that line of general questions is exhausted by what at the end of section 3 I called the *analogy principle*—the principle captured by premise (4) of the scheme, given earlier in that section, of arguments by analogy.

Here is why. Atkin and Denning, I noted, acknowledge—or would acknowledge: they are committed to the view—that all the cases they are considering, including the new one before them, are relevantly analogous. It means that they acknowledge that they have, per the analogy principle, a reason—a coherence-based reason—to decide the new case *in the same way*. So they *could*, as I pointed out, have given an argument by analogy, and decided the case in hand in that way—and that, crucially, is all that coherence, as a source of practical reasons, requires of them.

Coherence with previous decisions does not require them to formulate their broader general questions, nor does it require them to endorse, as they did, a broader answer to any such broader question. A decision like *Donoghue v Stevenson* would not have been less coherent with the previous line of cases had Atkin decided to simply offer an argument by analogy and refrained from formulating his broader question together with its answer—for there are no grounds on which to ascribe to any previous court (or even to all of them taken collectively) a view on that general question. None of the previous courts can be said to have authoritatively answered Atkin's or Denning's general question: for if any had, then *that* would have been the *ratio* of that previous court's decision—which is something that Atkin's and Denning's opinions *ex hypothesi* exclude.[29]

So it is not merely that Atkin's or Denning's formulation of their broader general questions is not derived or 'expiscated' from any line of previous decisions; their *answers* to those broader question are themselves also not normatively determined by any line of previous decisions. To repeat the point: the fact that each previous court gave the 'same' answer to each of the general questions they took themselves to be addressing does *not* give Atkin or Denning a reason to give the 'same' answer to the *broader, all-encompassing questions* that they venture to formulate. It only gives them a reason to decide the new case in hand, by analogy, in the same way.

What this shows is that Atkin's or Denning's answer to their broad general questions must be one that they endorse *on its merits* rather than on the basis of authority. What they are

---

[29] Nor would those courts have typically expressed their views on the matter. (The principle Denning claimed to have 'found' in *Lloyds Bank v Bundy* was 'yet unknown', as Slayton notes: see P Slayton, 'The Unequal Bargain Doctrine: Lord Denning in *Lloyds Bank v. Bundy*' (1976) 22 McGill LJ 94, 99.) But it *could* have been the case, of course, that any of the previous courts had stated that they took the *ratio* of their decision to settle only their own low-level general question, while simultaneously declaring that they believed there was a broader question that should be uniformly answered in the same way, and even going as far as giving their own formulation of that broader question. But then that declaration would by definition be *obiter*, and as such normatively inert, except, potentially, as *theoretically* authoritative claim: an instance of what is normally referred to as 'persuasive' (as opposed to 'binding') judicial authority; it would again not have authoritatively settled the broader general question. On the common contrast between 'binding' and 'persuasive' authority, see F Schauer, 'Authority and Authorities' (2008) 94 Va L Rev 1931; and G Lamond, 'Persuasive Authority in the Law' (2010) 17 Harv Rev Philosophy 17.

THE 'EXPISCATION' OF LEGAL PRINCIPLES   141

doing, I suggest, is either adopting the broader answer—the broader rule or principle—as the *ratio* of their own judgment (as Denning does)[30] or putting it forward as dictum accompanying an argument by analogy (as Atkin can also, and indeed came to, be interpreted to be doing).[31]

C. Consistency with Past Cases as a Mere Enabler

This doesn't mean that the fact that the previous cases happen to have been decided in a certain way is normatively irrelevant to Atkin's or Denning's *endorsement* of the broader principle that they choose to adopt. But the normative relevance of those past decisions does not lie in any justificatory authoritative support *for* those answers; they lend those answers no such support. (The opposite is true: it is those principles that, once adopted, present the past answers as justified.) Rather, the fact that the previous courts have all decided in that way works normatively purely as an *enabler* (if that is the right word) of Atkin's and Denning's decisions.

The reason is that Atkin's and Denning's proposed principles are such that every single one of the previously decided cases satisfies them. But no court can simply propose a principle, and especially adopt a *ratio*, that is inconsistent or conflicts with the *ratio* of a previous decision. That means that if even a single one of the previous cases that Atkin or Denning looks at had been decided in the contrary way, Atkin or Denning would not have been at liberty to base their decisions on the broad principle that they proposed. So the role that is being played by the contingent fact that every one of those cases was consistently decided is not that of providing *justification* for Atkin's or Denning's decisions, but merely the enabling role of making it the case that they are *permitted* to adopt them.[32]

Once they *have* adopted their broad rules, of course, they will be able to *show* that their decision in the case in hand coheres with those previous decisions. But here coherence, or its demonstration, is an outcome of, rather than a driving reason for, their decision to adopt the relevant principle. The principle, once formulated, allows judges like Atkin or Denning to retrospectively refer to those past cases as examples *avant la lettre* of its application; as 'determinations or concretizations' of the principle, as MacCormick says.[33] The formulation of the principle itself, however, is itself not authoritatively guided by those precedent cases—and therefore not an aspect of the common law doctrine of judicial precedent. And indeed one

---

[30] A hypothetical *ratio*, in this case, since, as I mentioned earlier (n 7), the majority in *Bundy* reached the same particular decision on narrower grounds.

[31] 'It is at least arguable,' Cross and Harris write, 'that Lord Atkin considered the neighbour principle which he enunciated in *Donoghue v Stevenson* to be the *ratio decidendi*': see R Cross and JW Harris, *Precedent in English Law* (4th edn, Clarendon Press 1991) 73–74. And Hueston, for example, says that 'the neighbour principle is part of the *ratio decidendi* of Lord Atkin's judgment' (although not part of the *ratio decidendi* of the court's decision, 'for the two other members of the majority seem to have been careful to avoid expressing their concurrence with it'); see RFV Heuston, '*Donoghue v Stevenson* in Retrospect' (1957) 20 MLR 1, 7–8. But future courts treated it instead as dictum; and Atkin did also formulate at the very end of his opinion a narrower proposition, specifically about manufacturers, answering the (narrower) general question specifically raised by the case, and which came to be taken to express that the *ratio* of *Donoghue v Stevenson*. Even regarded as dictum, though, Atkin's principle did still provide guidance for future courts as they went on to develop the law of negligence, by making 'explicit', as MacCormick says, 'a ground for treating as relevantly analogous cases similar in some respects to *Donoghue v Stevenson*': see MacCormick, *Legal Reasoning and Legal Theory* (n 1) 186; 159–61 for a discussion of how, over time, the normative weight attributed to the neighbour principle increased.

[32] By the same token, a single recalcitrant case would not 'falsify' their principles; it would only make it the case that they would not be permitted to adopt them as the basis of their own decisions.

[33] N MacCormick, *Rhetoric and the Rule of Law: A Theory of Legal Reasoning* (OUP 2005) 199.

142 LUÍS DUARTE D'ALMEIDA

could be excused for wondering, as Slayton does, whether such a unifying impulse is not more aptly regarded as, in a sense, a codificatory one:

> Cases are treated not as *sui generis,* standing by themselves and supported by the doctrine of precedent, but as *examples* of the application of a great principle. Here, in some measure, are civilian tendencies at work, not in the sense of the unthinking use by a judge of a rule laid down by the legislature, but in the sense of an impetus to synthesize or codify. Dare one suggest that Lord Denning is a civilian at heart?[34]

5. Conclusion

My conclusion is that there is nothing that can helpfully be thought of as an 'expiscation' of legal principles in decisions like these. That Atkin's or Denning's principles 'unite' a line of previous cases is a condition of their being permitted to adopt those principles; but provides no authoritative, content-independent support to the actual formulation or endorsement of the principles themselves.

There is therefore—as far as I can see—no distinct kind of argument that moves *from* the fact that those past cases were authoritatively decided in a certain way, to the formulation or adoption of such principles. The 'expiscation' metaphor, lovely as it is, is not, it turns out, a fruitful one.

---

[34] Slayton, 'The Unequal Bargain Doctrine' (n 29) 95. In *National Westminster Bank plc v Morgan* (n 28) — where, as I have already mentioned, Denning's principle is criticized—Lord Scarman also suggests (at 830d) that formulating such a principle would be 'essentially a legislative task'; and Tiplady says of Denning's approach, more bluntly, that it 'deserves the description of unstructured judicial paternalism': D Tiplady, 'The Limits of Undue Influence' (1985) 48 MLR 579, 584.

11
The Hermeneutics of Legal Precedent

Ralf Poscher[*]

1. Introduction

There are many ways to approach differences between common law and continental law traditions of precedent. One fairly clear-cut formal difference between the two types of legal systems lies in their differing authoritative quality, owing to the emergence of the *stare decisis* maxim into the common law in the early nineteenth century. In common law systems, precedents of a higher court are binding for lower courts—and to some extent also precedents of the same appellate level. Decisions of lower courts that neither follow precedent of a higher court nor distinguish it violate the law solely because of this deviation, irrespective of the merits of their substantive arguments. In the continental tradition, such binding force of precedents is rare.[1] In a continental system like Germany, precedents are generally said to have merely 'persuasive' force. This persuasive force, however, has to be qualified. It does not stem solely from the 'non-coercive force of the better argument';[2] the persuasive force of vertical precedents is instead supported by all the other functions attributed also to the binding character of precedents, such as an epistemic division of labour, the equal administration of justice, the predictability of the law, the predictable fruitlessness of a lower court's effort at 'blowing in the hurricane'.[3] There are even some secondary legal obligations with respect to precedents in German law, such as the professional duty of lawyers to consider and to advise their clients on precedents even if they deem them incorrect.[4]

Thus, often the difference in formal bindingness is not considered to make a vast difference for the practical importance of precedents in common law and continental systems. From a birds-eye perspective, there is definitely something to this harmonizing picture. It should not, however, distract us from more subtle differences.[5] The continental approaches to precedents are already less sophisticated because they are not as subtle in determining the holding of a decision and in distinguishing parts of a decision that are formally binding from those of only persuasive force. This comes with a lesser focus on the facts of the case. Facts are not irrelevant to continental lawyers; they, too, distinguish between the persuasive force of the *ratio decidendi* and *obiter dicta*, but they need not be as meticulous about the relation between the facts of the case and the court's reasoning. A precedent's persuasive weight is a gradual phenomenon that hinges on many factors, of which importance of the dicta for the

---

[*] I would like to thank Randall Stephenson not only for his edits but also for guiding me through some of the common law literature and most of the cases.

[1] e.g. decisions of the German Federal Constitutional Court are given the force of law by statute: § 31 s 2 Procedural Code of Federal Constitutional Court.

[2] J Habermas, *The Theory of Communicative Action*, vol 1 (Thomas tr McCarthy tr, Beacon 1984) 24.

[3] *Jaffree v Board of School Commissioners* 554 F3d 1104 (SD Ala 1983); using the quote to illustrate the point, see BA Garner and others, *The Law of Judicial Precedent* (1st edn, Thomson Reuters 2016) 32.

[4] See the contribution to this volume by Nils Jansen (Chapter 32).

[5] See, e.g., the subtle explanation of the importance of facts in the common law by G Lamond, 'Do Precedents Create Rules?' (2005) 11 Legal Theory 1, 21–26.

Ralf Poscher, *The Hermeneutics of Legal Precedent* In: *Philosophical Foundations of Precedent*. Edited by: Timothy Endicott, Hafsteinn Dan Kristjánsson, and Sebastian Lewis, Oxford University Press. © Ralf Poscher 2023. DOI: 10.1093/oso/9780192857248.003.0012

case is only one; others are the number of decisions that relied on the reasoning, the passage of time, the comparability of contexts, and general historical circumstances. Further, there is a generally more system-based approach to the law in the continental tradition, which places less emphasis on the facts of individual cases and more on developing a system of rules. These subtle differences are well worth exploring in more depth and with greater accuracy for different common law and continental jurisdictions.

This chapter, however, does not expand on these differences but rather investigates the fundamental methodology of precedents. What is this methodology in theoretical terms? What types of cognitive and creative activities do lawyers engage in when they rely on precedents for their case? How does the application of precedents relate to statutory interpretation and construction? For these types of questions, however, the formal bindingness of precedents is of no particular import. Whether or not lawyers rely on precedents because of their formal bindingness or because of their persuasive and quasi-authoritative force does not seem to change the *way* they rely on them. It follows that the methodological perspective relates both to formally binding and to persuasive, quasi-authoritative precedents. This holds true for common law and continental legal systems and, within both cultures, for both formally binding holdings and merely persuasive judicial dicta. The methodological inquiry is interested in how lawyers apply precedents, not in whether they are legally bound to apply them.

The general methodological approach to the application of precedents will be discussed on the basis of a general methodological theory, which has been developed with mainly statutory interpretation in mind.[6] Confronting the analytical reconstruction of legal hermeneutics with the role of precedents in adjudication will serve as a test case for the scope of the hermeneutical approach. Will its most basic tenet—namely, that the application of the law, in contrast to the exercise of discretion or legislation, is hermeneutical in an intentionalist interpretative sense even in hard cases—also hold true for precedents? Section 2 lays the groundwork for the answer to this question by recapitulating the most basic structure of legal hermeneutics and its theoretical motivations. Section 3 investigates how this theoretical framework applies to the application of precedents. Taking a piecemeal approach, section 3 begins by reviewing statutory and constitutional law precedents. Since hermeneutics developed with statutory law in mind, statutory precedents are closest to or even inherent to the original statutory context (section 3.A). The real test for the hermeneutical approach, however, is presented by common law precedents that do not relate to statutory law (section 3.B). The third step shifts from the application of precedents to the creation of precedents in common law systems. On the one hand, the *creation* of precedents goes beyond the methodological theory focusing on the *application* of the law. On the other hand, legal hermeneutics aims to explain the adjudicatory process in general. So, it is pertinent to explain its relation to this aspect of the common law, too (section 4). Finally, section 5 summarizes the role of precedents for a more general analysis of legal hermeneutics.

2. An Analytical Reconstruction of Legal Hermeneutics

The general theoretical framework from which the methodology of precedents will be explored relies on an intentionalist conception of meaning and interpretation. The only way

---

[6] For an outline of this approach, see R Poscher, 'Hermeneutics and Law' in M Forster and K Gjesdal (eds), *The Cambridge Companion to Hermeneutics* (CUP 2019).

we can conceive of meaning entering the world is via the intentions of intentional subjects. As offensive as it might seem to humanity's sense of exceptionalism, the universe does not care. It can only be bestowed with meaning via the intentions of an intentional subject such as a goddess. As for utterances, this implies that they, too, can acquire their meaning solely via the intentions of an intentional subject. As Donald Davidson succinctly put it: 'So in the end, the sole source of linguistic meaning is the intentional production of tokens of sentences.'[7] This insight is illustrated by Paul Grice's distinction between natural 'meaning' and non-natural meaning:[8] smoke *signals* fire due to the causal relationship between the two, but to shout 'Fire!' *means* fire only because of the intention the shouting person connects with it. Interpretation in its most basic sense involves reconstructing the intentions of an utterer via the utterance and its context.

The Davidsonian point to add would be that neither meaning nor interpretation depend on conventional language:[9] conventional language is a powerful tool to facilitate the production of meaning and interpretation, but it is not necessary for communication. In Jorge Luis Borges's short story 'The Garden of Forking Paths', a German spy communicates the target for the next attack against the German forces by murdering a famous academic whose last name matched that of the target, speculating correctly that the papers read by his handler would report on his crime.[10] The relation between—in Gricean terms—sentence and speaker's meaning, or—in more linguistic terms—semantic and pragmatic meaning, is a serving one. The semantic meaning of terms helps the interpreter to use his knowledge of terminological conventions and common usages to decipher the speaker's intentions. In turn, semantic meaning also helps the speaker to communicate her intentions by facilitating the interpreter's ability to understand her communicative intentions. There is nothing mysterious about meaning, interpretation, and their relation in this account along the lines of Grice and Davidson. In a nutshell, this is how communication and language in their most basic structure work. This basic structure can be used to create much more complex linguistic phenomena such as figurative speech, implicature, metaphorical expressions, irony, and so on. All these more complex phenomena, however, must be explained theoretically as variants of this basic structure—just as the most complex computer programs can be explained in binary code as a specific sequence of zeros and ones.

What does this mean for legal interpretation of statutes? In a straightforward theoretical sense, interpretation of statutory law aims to reconstruct the intentions of the legislator. This was already Savigny's position at the dawn of modern legal methodology. Legislative intent was not one of his famous interpretive canons, but the *aim* of all the others—namely: semantics, systematic context, legislative materials, historical background, and (reservedly) *telos*.[11] And there might be occasions, even in contemporary legal systems, in which such a theoretically straightforward interpretive model could work. The meaning of a by-law issued by a mayor can be inferred from the mayor's actual intentions.

In most cases, however, things are much less simple. Complications already arise with the intentional subject required by the theoretical model. Most laws are not issued on the basis of an actual intention of an intentional subject but rather in complex processes involving multiple institutions, each comprising multiple intentional subjects with different, sometimes

---

[7] D Davidson, 'The Social Aspect of Language' in D Davidson (ed), *Truth, Language, and History* (Clarendon Press 2009) 120.

[8] HP Grice, *Studies in the Way of Words* (Harvard UP 1989) 217–23.

[9] D Davidson, 'Communication and Convention' (1984) 59(1) Synthese 3, 15–17.

[10] A Kemmerling, 'Meinen' in N Kompa (ed), *Handbuch Sprachphilosophie* (Verlag JB Metzler 2015) 231.

[11] FC von Savigny, *System of the Modern Roman Law*, vol 1 (J Higginbotham 1867) 37–39, 172 f.

even opposing, communicative intentions concerning the original statutory text. As with more complex uses of conventional language, however, the more complex institutional backgrounds of modern legislation cannot divert from the theoretical model. If statutory application is to be understood as an interpretation of a statute's meaning, it must be conceptualized as the reconstruction of communicative intentions, since we have to rely on intentions to make sense of meaning and interpretation.

To preserve the hermeneutical character of statutory application, legislative intent must be constructed by the statute's interpreter. This construction is only implicit in our talk of legislative intent. Again, in a nutshell, we seem to rely on the meaning a diligent legislator involved in the process of deciding on the statute would have connected with the text.[12] Thus, legislative intent is not the actual intent of an actual intentional subject but an interpreter's construction. Interpretation in the theoretical sense, however, relies on such intentions even if they must be constructed. Because of the lack of theoretical alternatives to generate meaning, we are so desperate to follow the intentionalist account of meaning and interpretation that we even construct an intentional subject when one is actually missing.

The construction of legislative intent, however, is not the only construction that statutory application relies on. Another type of construction becomes necessary when the interpreter is confronted with a case that the actual or constructed intention of the legislator does not resolve, either because that type of case was not reflected in the legislative process or because, despite being reflected, we are unable to uncover its precise meaning for epistemic reasons. For example, the German Constitution incorporated some regulations of the Weimar Constitution of 1919. Some questions regarding the meaning of these provisions cannot be answered by referring to the intent of the Constituent German National Assembly in Weimar because many protocols of their deliberations were lost during the Second World War. In these cases, lawyers must revert to what has traditionally been called legal construction for epistemic reasons.[13] The interpreter must incrementally amend the law. However, legal construction also requires a relationship to the statutory text if it wants to count as an instance of its application. Again, in a nutshell, it seems that legal construction in modern, liberal legal systems can be best construed as the interpreter relying on the intentions a rational legislator would have connected with the text regarding the case at hand.[14] Even though the interpreter constructs an intention that he then treat as a reconstruction of the statute's meaning, legal construction is not akin to legislation. Contrasted with legislation, legal construction is restricted by the text and its context. Even though legal construction amends the law, it is limited by the meaning that a rational legislator could have sensibly given to the text in the legislative context. Legal construction, in this way, retains a hermeneutical character. It adheres to the basic theoretical structure of meaning and interpretation.

An intentionalist account of meaning and interpretation following Grice and Davidson provides a theoretically productive framework for understanding the application of statutes by lawyers as a hermeneutical activity. Most importantly, it accurately describes what distinguishes legal construction from legislative discretion methodologically, even though, like legislation, legal construction amends the law.

---

[12] A more detailed account can be found in R Poscher, 'The Normative Construction of Legislative Intent' (2017) 9 Droit & Philosophie 1, 107; cf also, grounded in an intentionalist theory of meaning, R Ekins, *The Nature of Legislative Intent* (OUP 2012).

[13] F Lieber, 'On Political Hermeneutics, or on Political Interpretation and Construction, and Also on Precedents' (1837) 18 Am Juris & L Mag 37.

[14] For a more detailed account, see R Poscher, 'The Hermeneutic Character of Legal Construction' in S Glanert and F Girard (eds), *Law's Hermeneutics: Other Investigations* (Routledge 2017).

3. The Hermeneutics of Precedent

Methodological considerations are not at the forefront of legal scholarship about precedent. There are, however, scholars who explain the emergence of *stare decisis* through methodological considerations. MacCormick suggested that *stare decisis* was embraced as a reaction to positivism's critique of the declaratory theory, according to which judges simply 'declared' a pre-existing common law: 'The real reason for the modern development of *stare decisis* was the destruction of the foundation on which the old attitude to precedent rested. When judges could no longer argue that in rejecting previous decisions they were merely restating the "true" common law, they chose not to grasp the nettle and concede that their function was to improve the law by remaking it.'[15] According to MacCormick, courts shifted to *stare decisis* to avoid the impression that they were legislating when they amended the law by overturning precedent. By following the maxim of *stare decisis*, they could maintain that they were simply applying pre-existing law. Understood in this way, *stare decisis* is a reaction to the very issue that the analytical reconstruction of legal hermeneutics is meant to explain. Specifically, how can the creation of law by courts in hard cases be considered a specifically legal enterprise and not the exercise of political discretion? That is, how does it differ methodologically from legislation? Even though MacCormick's thesis is criticized from a historic perspective,[16] it points to the systematic issue that connects the theory of precedent with a broader hermeneutical perspective.

As for statutory and constitutional cases, the specific legal structure of adjudication can be explained by the hermeneutical methodology of justification. For adjudication on the basis of precedent, the question turns into whether the reliance on precedents shares the same hermeneutical structure or relies on a different methodology. The latter has sometimes been suggested by scholars who see a fundamental methodological difference between the application of statutory law and precedents. 'Case-law, we might say, unlike statute law, tends to be analogized rather than interpreted.'[17]

A. Collective Intentionality of Courts

One issue that precedents share with statutes is the communicative intention that is required if the application of a precedent is to be understood in hermeneutical terms. Whereas modern legislation regularly involves many intentional subjects and thus requires the legal construction of legislative intent, the situation is more differentiated for courts. If the court consists of a single judge or if the precedent consists of a single judge's opinion, the precedent is created by actual intentions of an actual intentional subject. In such cases, there is no need to construct the required intention. The interpretation could aim at the actual intention of the deciding judge.

Even where the court consists of multiple judges, the situation can still be different from that in legislation. Philosophers such as John Searle[18] or Michael Bratman[19] have offered

---

[15] N MacCormick, 'Can *Stare Decisis* be Abolished?' (1966) 11 Juridical Review 197, 206.
[16] N Duxbury, *The Nature and Authority of Precedent* (CUP 2008) 42–45.
[17] ibid 59.
[18] JR Searle, 'Collective Intentions and Actions' in PR Cohen, J Morgan, and ME Pollack (eds), *Intentions in Communication* (MIT Press 1990).
[19] ME Bratman, *Faces of intention: Selected Essays on Intention and Agency*, Cambridge Studies in Philosophy (1st edn, CUP 2004) 125–29, 142–61.

reductive accounts of collective intentionality, which provide reductive descriptions of what we mean when we talk about group intentions. These reductive theories have been developed for small-sized groups such as loggers collectively felling a tree or people taking a walk together. The quite challenging interconnectedness of individual intentions that has to obtain according to such reductive accounts of collective intentions is not fulfilled in legislative processes, which not only involve hundreds of assembly members but also countersigning ministers and proclaiming presidents. For panels such as the full bench of the European Court of Justice, which comprises twenty-seven judges, things might not be materially different from a legislature. Benches, however, are usually much smaller and consist of only three or five judges. In such smaller panels, it is possible that a 'collective intention' (in the sense of parallel and interconnected communicative intentions of all judges) is connected with a text. At least this is how some courts perceive themselves. For example, the First Circuit Court of the US references the 'collective mind'[20] of a circuit court.

Respecting the intentional subject targeted by every hermeneutical effort, the courts might, in some cases, have actual individual communicative intentions or actual collective intentions in the sense of reductive accounts. In these cases—unlike in most cases of modern legislation—it would be possible for the later court to rely on the actual individual or actual collective intentions of the precedent court.[21] Precedents can provide the intentions that make it theoretically possible to take a hermeneutical approach to precedents that relies not on constructed but on actual communicative intentions. In cases in which there is no actual collective intent, however, the construction of an intention probably follows the lines of constructing legislative intent. Judges are effectively assigned the communicative intention that a diligent judge would have assigned to their endorsed text, given full knowledge of the court proceedings. Thus, if one of the twenty-seven judges on the European Court of Justice misread a passage or misunderstood it, whether through inattention during proceedings or during deliberations, he would still be assigned the communicative intentions that a diligent judge would have connected with it. He could not claim that he issued a dissenting or concurring opinion if he connected a different communicative intention with the opinion that he formally endorsed.

Needless to say, courts can also rely on constructed intentions in cases in which there is an actual communicative intention on the part of the court issuing the precedent. The actuality of intentions only provides the theoretical basis for relying on them. Whether or not courts actually make use of this potential (an empirical question) and whether they should (a normative question) are both questions beyond the scope of this chapter, which is focused on the reconstruction of the theoretical options.

B. Precedents on Statutory Law

Even in common law systems, statutory law covers ever more regulatory ground. In these areas of the law, courts must decide cases on the basis of written law. Precedents in such cases are based on statutory texts. Further, in some legal systems, written constitutions play an

---

[20] *United States v Rodriguez-Pacheco* 475 F3d 434, 442 (1st Cir 2007).
[21] I follow the terminology proposed by Lamond, 'Do Precedents Create Rules?' (n 5) 5: 'I use the term "precedent court" and "precedent case" to refer to the earlier court and dispute; and I speak of "later courts" and "later cases" to refer to those courts and disputes which are bound by the precedent.'

increasing role, a tendency described sometimes described as 'constitutionalization'.[22] More and more cases involve questions of constitutional law and fundamental rights and thus apply precedents that turned on constitutional provisions.

From a hermeneutical perspective, precedents on statutory law or on constitutional provisions are legal interpretations or constructions of these texts. They assign meaning to legal texts as far as it is necessary to decide the case at hand. If courts rely on these precedents in later decisions, they rely on and endorse specific legal interpretations or constructions of the underlying legal provisions. So far, precedents do not seem to challenge the hermeneutical perspective sketched earlier. Even when courts are bound by or just apply precedents on statutory laws or written constitutions, their decisions must ultimately be justified as an interpretation or construction of a legal provision. Thus, for most areas of continental law and for at least large parts of the law in traditionally common law systems, the hermeneutical explanation of adjudication is not disturbed by reliance on precedent—be it binding or merely persuasive.

C. Precedents in the Common Law

Things are less obvious for common law adjudication that is not grounded in statutory or constitutional provisions. In these cases, the practice of precedents cannot be regarded as hermeneutical simply because of a connection to a legal provision that the precedent is but an interpretation or construction of. The application of the precedent only fits the hermeneutical model if the precedent itself is interpreted or constructed by the court applying it.

Whether or not precedents are interpreted and constructed by the later courts might depend on what the precedent consists in. With variations in detail, there seem to be at least two basic conceptions. One regards the precedent as the holding of the decision, which is derived from the reasons of the decision and the facts of the case. '[T]he reasons given in the judgment ... constitute the ratio decidendi'[23] as put concisely by a South African judge cited by Duxbury as an ideal statement of this position.[24] The opposing conception rejects this idea: 'It is clear therefore, that the first rule for discovering the ratio decidendi of a case is that it must not be sought in the reasons on which the judge has based his decision.'[25] According to this view, a precedent consists not in the reasons given by the judges in that case, but is determined by the facts of the case and the court's decision. 'The judge, therefore, reaches a conclusion upon the facts as he sees them. It is on these facts that he bases his judgment, and not on any others. ... It is by his choice of the material facts that the judge creates law.'[26] The reasons given only illustrate the precedent, but they are not essential to it.[27] The test case for

---

[22] GF Schuppert and C Bumke, *Die Konstitutionalisierung der Rechtsordnung: Überlegungen zum Verhältnis von verfassungsrechtlicher Ausstrahlungswirkung und Eigenständigkeit des 'einfachen' Rechts*, Forum Rechtswissenschaft Band 29 (1st edn, Nomos Verlagsgesellschaft 2000); cp also M Loughlin, *Against Constitutionalism* (Harvard UP 2022), forthcoming.

[23] *Pretoria City Council v Levinson* 1949 (3) SA 305, 317 (A) (Schreiner JA); on this statement, see Duxbury (n 16) 84.

[24] ibid 85.

[25] A Goodhart, 'Determining the *Ratio Decidendi* of a Case' (1930) 40 Yale LJ 161, 164; on the development of Goodhart's theory of precedent, see Duxbury (n 16) 80–85.

[26] Goodhart (n 25) 169.

[27] For a middle-of-the-road view between the two positions, see R Cross and JW Harris, *Precedent in English Law* (4th edn, Clarendon Press 2004) 67, generally agreeing with Goodhart but insisting that determining the *ratio* requires taking into account the reasons for knowing 'what portions of the law were in the mind of the court when the selection [of facts] was made', ibid 70.

150 RALF POSCHER

this conception is a legal decision for which no reasons are given by the court. According to this second conception, decisions for which no judicial reasons are provided can be precedents.[28] For reasons of brevity, these decisions are called 'bare precedents'.

As a continentally trained lawyer, I am in no position to opine on which of the two conceptions is correct. From a theoretical perspective, they are both interesting. From the perspective of the hermeneutical approach, bare precedents present the more challenging case. Therefore, it seems wise to start with the conception that relies on the documented reasoning of the court.

(i) Precedents as holdings in the reasons of a decision

If one regards the holding of a precedent to reside in the reasons that the court provided for its decision, the most obvious examples are cases in which the reasons contain a passage that is qualified explicitly or implicitly by the court as its holding.[29] Such a designated holding has a rule-like character.[30] One example would be *Donoghue v Stephenson*, in which the court states an entire ensemble of material and evidentiary rules in its reasoning, which then became the law of the land for a manufacturer's liability.[31] The hermeneutical character of relying on such a precedent seems obvious. The later court will attempt to reconstruct the meaning that the precedent court has connected with the text of the holding. In these cases—at least according to the self-understanding of the courts—the holding is the precedent court's holding, not the holding that the later court assigns to it. As Duxbury rightfully notes, this is also presupposed by the idea that precedents could be misunderstood by later courts:

> It is doubtful that there is any common law court which would accept as a convention the blunt proposition that the ratio of a case is created retrospectively. One reason judges might be expected to resist such a convention is that accepting it would make it difficult to argue that a court had misunderstood the ratio of an earlier case.[32]

At least in the case of an explicitly stated holding, the later court aims to decipher the intentions that the precedent court connected with the formulation in the holding.

One important precisification and two 'reminders' are in order regarding a holding's explicit formulation. The precisification concerns the manner in which the holding must be understood in relation to the legal rule created by a precedent. Lamond rightly observed that the holding of a precedent is conditioned by the facts, even if it is explicitly formulated as an abstract rule.[33] Taking the abstract formulation of the holding as the legal rule created by the precedent would not consider the power of the later courts to distinguish it. They have the power to do so if there are facts in the later case that justify diverging from the holding and if these facts were not reported in the precedent case. The holding only applies to cases fulfilling the conditions of the antecedent holding *and* containing no new material facts that justify distinguishing the later case. As Lamond shows, the latter condition explains the

---

[28] Duxbury (n 16) 83.

[29] cf Garner and others (n 3) 59, 57.

[30] ibid 45; J Austin, *Lectures on Jurisprudence or the Philosophy of Positive Law*, vol 2 (R Campbell ed, 5th edn, John Murray 1885) 622.

[31] [1932] AC 562, 622 (HL). Further examples from the House of Lords are *R v Millis* (1844) 8 ER 844, 889 (HL) and *Beamish v Beamish* (1861) 9 HL Cas 274, 11 ER 735 (HL), establishing the necessary presence and intervention of a priest for a valid marriage.

[32] Duxbury (n 16) 74.

[33] Lamond, 'Do Precedents Create Rules?' (n 5) 22f.

importance of the facts in the common law. Common law judges only have the power to create new, binding law under the restriction that comes with the later courts' power to distinguish, which in turn is limited by the facts of the precedent case. Compared to a general legislator, the law-making power of courts is systematically restricted. Much like federal restrictions on laws passed by state legislators, the common law courts' law-making power is circumscribed—not by federal restrictions but much more narrowly by the facts of the instant case.

Due to this fact-based restriction, Lamond suggests that it may be more helpful to understand precedents as protected reasons, not as rules.[34] It seems, however, that rules are flexible enough to embrace a specific, fact-based condition that takes the mechanics of distinguishing into account. This is not to deny that the fact-based condition would make them a specific type of rule. To adapt Lamond's semi-formalizations, in which uppercase letters stand for fact types and lowercase letters for fact tokens, a rough reconstruction of the precedent mechanism for simple constellations[35] could be as follows:[36]
A precedent P_1 with the facts

F_1: $\{g_1, h_1, i_1, j_1, k_1, l_1\}$
has the holding
H_1: If $\{J, K, L\}$ then C.
If the later court decides a case P_2 with the facts
F_2: $\{h_2, i_2, j_2, k_2, l_2\}$

it must follow the precedent, since the later court has to assume the precedent case was decided correctly.[37] The antecedent conditions of the holding $\{J, K, L\}$ are met. The later court cannot rely on the other facts present in the precedent case $\{H, I\}$ to deny C, because $\{H, I\}$ were also present in P_1 and the precedent court did not regard them sufficiently to deny C. Further, it cannot rely on the lack of facts that were present in the precedent case $\{\sim G\}$, since the precedent court did not regard $\{G\}$ as necessary for C. Thus, the *rule* R_1 that corresponds to the holding H_1 must include the condition that C only applies if there are no facts different from $\{G, H, I\}$ that justify $\sim C$

R_1: If $\{J, K, L\} \land \sim(\text{facts} \neq \{G, H, I\})$ that justify $\sim C$ then C.

The negative condition that there are no facts different from $\{G, H, I\}$ that justify $\sim C$ partially defeats the rule character of R_1, since it makes the holding defeasible by a vast array of reasons based on facts different from $\{G, H, I\}$. Thus, the application of R_1 is only partially different from an all-things-considered judgment based on the balance of all relevant reasons. This motivates Lamond's reason-based account of precedent.[38] Rules similar to R_1 are, however, not unusual in statutory law. At the peaks of the recent pandemic waves, most German states issued ordinances that prohibited going outside except for grocery shopping,

---

[34] ibid 23f.
[35] For more complex constellations, see G Lamond, 'Revisiting the Reasons Account of Precedent' in M McBride and JE Penner (eds), *New Essays on the Nature of Legal Reasoning* (Hart 2022) s 2.2.
[36] Lamond, 'Do Precedents Create Rules?' (n 5) 19–21.
[37] ibid 25.
[38] ibid 8–11.

152   RALF POSCHER

medical appointments, or for 'similarly weighty reasons'.[39] Such open-ended hardship clauses are quite common in statutory systems of rules without questioning their character. The fact-based negative condition in R_1 is at least similar to such hardship clauses.

The following scenarios exist for a precedent P_1 with the facts

F_1: $\{g_1, h_1, i_1, j_1, k_1, l_1\}$
and the holding
H_1: If $\{J, K, L\}$ then C.
In a later case P_3 with facts that correspond exactly to the fact type of precedent P_1
F_3: $\{g_3, h_3, i_3, j_3, k_3, l_3\}$

the later case P_3 has to follow the precedent and rule C. The decision adds nothing to the law. Thus, it seems an overstatement to say that each new case following a precedent adds something to the law.[40]

In a later case P_4 with additional facts

$$F_4: \{g_4, h_4, i_4, j_4, k_4, l_4, x_4, y_4\}$$

the decision of the later court will depend on whether the additional facts justify ~C. If they do not justify ~C, the later court must follow the precedent. The decision, however, will change the law insofar as the additional facts $\{X, Y\}$ and their absence are added to the list of facts that do not justify ~C, given the antecedents of the holding $\{J, K, L\}$.

$$R_4: \text{If } \{J, K, L\} \wedge \sim(\text{facts} \neq \{G, H, I, X, Y\}) \text{ that justify } \sim C \text{ then C.}$$

In both of the first two scenarios, deciding not to follow the precedent would constitute an overruling—a power only higher courts are entrusted with. Should the later court regard the additional facts $\{x_4\}$ as justifying ~C, then it must distinguish, adding a new precedent to the law and creating a new holding

$$H_{4^*}: \text{If } \{J, K, L\} \wedge X \text{ then } \sim C.$$

and a new rule

$$R_{4^*}: \text{If } \{J, K, L\} \wedge X \wedge \sim(\text{facts} \neq Y) \text{ that justify C then } \sim C.$$

The interpretation of the precedent aims at the holding. The fact-based condition added to the holding that, together with the holding, constitutes the legal rule of the precedent is not the result of interpreting the precedent but a general restriction on the law-making power of common law courts that applies to all holdings.

The two reminders regarding the interpretation of the holding are the following. First, similar to a statute, the *formulation* and semantics of a holding is not necessarily the holding of the case. The semantics of a holding might precisely fit the meaning that the court intended to communicate. This, however, is not necessarily so. Thus, if its semantics do not

---

[39] On the constitutionality of these provisions, Federal Constitutional Court, Order of 19 November 2021, 1 BvR 781/21 and others, paras 263–66.
[40] But cp Lamond, 'Do Precedents Create Rules?' (n 5) 22.

track the holding that the precedent court intended, the intended holding, which differs from the semantics of its formulation, can be the holding of the case. The semantics of the explicit formulation is not authoritative. In these cases, the court's intention can be gleaned especially from the justification of the holding and from contextual factors. As generally explained by the theory of meaning underlying the analytical reconstruction of hermeneutics: semantics is always only the stepping stone for our interpretative inferences as to the utterer's intentions.

Secondly, just like a statute, an explicitly stated holding might be indeterminate regarding the instant case. The indeterminacy can have two causes: epistemic and substantive. The court employing the precedent might be uncertain about the precedent court's intentions. This might especially hold true if cases like the instant one were known to the precedent court but the passage stating the holding is indeterminate on whether the holding is supposed to apply to these cases.

The indeterminacy can especially arise regarding the scope of the precedent's holding. Garner illustrates the point with a hypothetical example.[41] If the court stated, 'cats cannot inherit money under a will', it might be a judicious interpretation of the communicative intentions to not only rule out inheritance by cats but also by dogs and even all animals. But what about an animal that a human has promised to care for? Did the court intend to rule out inheritance by animals under any circumstances? It either did or did not intend it. The hurdles in deciphering the intentions behind a precedent can even cause epistemic exasperation. In *Great Western Railway Co v Owners of the SS*,[42] Lord Atkin simply gave up evaluating the opinion of Lord Hatherley in *River Wear Commissioners v Adamson*:[43]

> Lord Hatherley's judgment I pass over, because I really do not know, after reading it very carefully, what the view was that he formed about the matter. ... Whether he really was concurring in the appeal being allowed, or the appeal being dismissed, or whether he was concurring in the opinion given by Lord Cairns, I do not know.[44]

The epistemic uncertainty of Lord Atkin concerns the communicative intentions of Lord Hatherley. He did not think that Lord Hatherley did not rule on the matter; he just could not figure out what he meant to say. If the intention cannot be deciphered by the court that wants to rely on the precedent, that court would have to construct a holding.

The indeterminacy might also be substantive in nature. The precedent might formulate a holding that could apply to a case that the court could not have foreseen. For example, due to technological developments, many cases could not have been envisaged at the time the precedent was set. In statutory interpretation, cases of substantive indeterminacy might require the legal construction of a hypothetical legislative intent. It could even be that the legislators counted on the legal constructions of the courts. When designing a statute, all kinds of fringe and possible future cases might come up during debates. The legislators might see that the regulation they drafted is indeterminate for some of these fringe and possible future cases. For various reasons, however, they might opt for not amending their statute, since they count on the courts to resolve such issues should these cases actually arise. The legislators might prefer judicial constructions over statutory amendments as a dilatory compromise

---

[41] Garner and others (n 3) 59f.
[42] *Great Western Railway Co v Owners of the SS* [1927] P 25 (CA).
[43] *River Wear Commissioners v Adamson* (1877) 2 AC 743 (HL).
[44] *The Mostyn* [1927] P 25, 37–38.

if they encounter difficulty agreeing on an amendment, in order to save time, or to avoid encumbering statutory regulation with excessive detail.

It seems, however, questionable whether such rationales could also apply when constructing the holding of a precedent. In a common law system, the law evolves through the incremental development of judicial precedents. Functionally, the courts also perform a law-making role. There seems to be no necessity to engage in the legal construction of precedents in cases that are not covered by previous precedent, since the later court can always draw on its own power to create a new precedent for a later case not covered by the precedent's original intent. There might be strategic reasons to portray a new precedent as a legal construction of an older one, but normatively such a motivation seems dubious. From a normative standpoint, there seem to be good reasons to limit the construction of precedent to epistemic uncertainties. Several courts seem to see this similarly. In *King v State ex Rel Murdock Acceptance Corporation*, when confronted with new forms of electronic evidence, the Supreme Court of Mississippi held that in 'admitting the print-out sheets reflecting the record stored on the tape, the Court is actually following the best evidence rule. We are not departing from the shop book rule, but only extending its application to electronic record keeping.'[45] The court did not try constructing the previous precedents to make them fit the new technological development, but assumed responsibility for creating a new precedent of its own.

This is also how the application of a precedent and its analogous application can be distinguished. The application of a precedent consists in the application of the precedent case's *ratio* to the later case. This is possible when the later case falls under the antecedents of the rule of the precedent case. In cases of an analogous use of a precedent, the later case does not fulfil the conditions of the antecedents of the rule of the precedent case. Instead, the analogous application relies on a more abstract rule that covers both the precedent and the later case.[46] The analogous use of a precedent creates a new precedent with the more abstract rule as its holding.

Epistemic uncertainties, and with them the need for legal construction, might especially arise for precedents that provide reasons for judgment but not a paragraph containing a concise formulation of the holding. In these cases, the precedent's holding must be derived from the entirety of the court's reasons and the facts of the case. From a hermeneutical perspective, the text to be interpreted is the whole of the reasons. The facts are the context that provide decisive clues on what holding the court wished to communicate with its reasons. If both can be deciphered and are taken for the holding, the later court can interpret the precedent. As long as the holding remains unclear, the court relying on the precedent must construct a holding attributable to the precedent and thus to the intentions of the issuing court.

When constructing hypothetical intentions, the later court faced with epistemic uncertainties has at least two options. It can either hypothesize about how the original court would have decided the later case, considering the general jurisprudential outlook and doctrinal inclination of its actual judges. Or it can construct an idealized, rational court's intentions by

---

[45] *King v State ex Rel Murdock Acceptance Corporation* 222 S2d 393 (Miss Sup Ct 1969); for a similar decision by the Tennessee Supreme Court, see *Davis v Davis* 842 SW2d 588 (Tenn Sup Ct 1992), which resisted extending the existing precedent on persons or property to cryopreserved embryos and created a legal category of its own (ibid 597).

[46] Cp the contribution to this volume by Luís Duarte d'Almeida (Chapter 10, fn 25), phrasing it not in terms of rules but in terms of answers to more or less abstract 'questions'; Lamond, 'Do Precedents Create Rules?' (n 5) 22; more generally on the structure of analogies, see L Duarte d'Almeida and C Michelon, 'The Structure of Arguments by Analogy in Law' (2017) 31 Argumentation 359.

asking what intentions this court would have intended to communicate, given the precedent's factual context. It would take a deeper study of a given common law jurisdiction to see whether one of the two approaches prevails, or whether there is some eclectic or systematic mix of both models. In the continental tradition of German law, *ad hominem* arguments do not seem to be employed; however, some common law jurisdictions hold some of their most influential judges in high esteem and assign special authority to their precedents. Thus, it would at least seem consistent to bring knowledge about their personal jurisprudential and doctrinal outlook to bear when the holdings of their precedents require construction.

(ii) Bare precedents

The toughest challenge for a hermeneutical perspective is presented by bare precedents, that is, decisions without stated reasons, when the application of a precedent requires reliance on the decision and the facts alone. In these cases, the notion that applying precedent does not rely on interpretation but on analogical reasoning is quite plausible. How else could the precedent be followed than by comparing the facts of the cases? Bare precedents seem to leave us with nothing to work with but simple factual comparisons.

Comparisons, however, involve a three-way relationship. They not only require two *comparata* but also a property or relation that serves as a comparative parameter.[47] We cannot compare two tomatoes without specifying what properties of the tomatoes we are comparing: colour, weight, taste, and so on. The same holds true for the material facts of cases. When discussing precedents, it has often been remarked that no two cases are identical.[48] Thus, in comparing them, we must discern the relevant facts (the 'material' in Goodhart's sense) and why they are relevant. Garner's hypothetical case can illustrate the point.

According to the hypothetical facts, a testator bequeathed $10,000 to his cat Sylvester. To make it a bare precedent, let us suppose that the court simply rejected Sylvester's $10,000 inheritance without providing any reasons.[49] How can a court confronted with a new case in which a testator bequeathed $5,000 to her dog Hasso use Sylvester's case as a precedent? It cannot merely compare the facts because even a different cat would make Sylvester's case different: different cat, different testator, different sum, different time, different place, and so on. The court faced with Hasso's case can only compare it to the precedent if it uses the precedent's facts and decision to come up with a holding such as 'animals cannot inherit'. For the holding, it has to determine the fact type that corresponds the fact tokens of the precedent case at the right level of abstraction. Only such a holding relying on fact types makes it possible to compare both cases. Sylvester and Hasso are alike because they are both animals in the sense of the implied holding; the difference in the bequeathed sum does not matter, since animals are in principle excluded from inheritance.

The assumption of a holding would not be hermeneutical if it were not attributable to the precedent court's communicative intentions. Such an assumption, however, would be very plausible. It would only be different for a court acting like a Weberian kadi:[50] a court that

---

[47] R Weber, 'Comparative Philosophy and the Tertium: Comparing What with What, and in What Respect?' (2014) 13 Dao 151.

[48] e.g. *Begin v Drouin* 908 F3d 829, 836 (1st Cir 2018); CM Oldfather, 'Methodological Pluralism and Constitutional Interpretation' (2014) 80 Brook L Rev 1, 13; D Song, 'Judicial Pragmatism: Strengths and Weaknesses in Common Law Adjudication, Legislative Interpretation, and Constitutional Interpretation' (2018) 52 UIC John Marshall L Rev 369, 380.

[49] Garner and others (n 3) 59.

[50] M Weber, *Wirtschaft und Gesellschaft* (Mohr 1922) 467ff.; M Weber, *Economy and Society: An Outline of Interpretive Sociology* (G Roth and C Wittich eds, University of California Press 1968) 976–78.

does not intend to issue generalizable decisions; one that decides each case according to the outcome most beneficial to its community considering the power structures behind the parties, the contingent and ever-changing circumstances, the time of the year, the weather, and so on. In short, a court that does not want to create precedents. That, however, does not seem to be the way common law judges view their decisions and, if they do, it is widely regarded as an anomaly. When the majority of the US Supreme Court in *Bush v Gore* insisted that their decision on federal powers should be understood as a singular decision from which no further conclusions could be drawn,[51] even the justices themselves regarded this as a rare exception and not as the way a western legal system usually works.

In the context of precedents, the generalizability of court decisions is often captured by the principle that like cases are to be treated alike. To provide a standard of alikeness and a parameter of comparison, courts need to communicate a generalizable holding with their decision. The relationship between this holding and the principle of treating like cases alike is not that the principle generates holdings. It is the other way around: the generalizations in the holdings that are communicated by the precedent provide the *criteria* for discriminating between alike and unalike cases.[52] The decision on Sylvester is only a precedent for Hasso's case because the precedent court is understood to have communicated with its decision the holding that animals cannot inherit. The Sylvester decision can serve as a precedent for Hasso's case only if the precedent court intended to communicate such a generalization. If the court decided the Sylvester case like a Weberian kadi or if it made the same explicit reservation as the US Supreme Court in *Bush v Gore*, it could not have precedential import. Decisions are precedents because courts decide and communicate them as such. To do so, however, implies communicating a rule-like generalization as its holding.

Like the case in Louis Borges's story of the 'The Garden of Forking Paths', a court delivering a bare precedent does not explicitly state its communicative intent. The interpreter must reconstruct the court's intentions using the facts of the case, the decision, and some common (including common legal) sense. Thus, in the Sylvester case, another theoretically possible generalization would be to only exclude cats from inheritance. However, to suppose that the court aimed only at such a narrow generalization is neither supported by common sense nor by any other legal rules, since they do not differentiate between the legal powers of cats and dogs. It follows that the most plausible reconstruction of the court's intention requires broadening the holding to the level of animals.

4. The Creation of Precedents

The creation of precedent in common law systems functionally resembles legislation with the caveat described earlier. Setting a precedent promulgates law, the application of which is justified in a hermeneutical manner in later decisions. In the same way that the discretionary creation of new legislation does not place the hermeneutical character of its later application into question, the creation of precedent—whatever its nature—does not challenge the hermeneutical character of its application.

Whether or not the creation of precedents is in itself a hermeneutical practice depends on what sources it draws from. It would not be an interpretative practice if it merely relied on

---

[51] *Bush v Gore* 531 US 98, 109 (2000).

[52] Cp F Schauer, 'On Treating Unlike Cases Alike' (2018) 33 Constitutional Commentary 437, 446, who stresses the attributive role of the later court.

general practical reasoning about the best decision for a certain type of case. It would, however, be an interpretative practice in itself if it relied on an intentional subject's normative creation. If judges relied on religious texts such as the Ten Commandments, their decisions would depend on interpreting God's communicative intentions. Also, reliance on customs would have a hermeneutical nature, since it would interpret the normative intentions of certain community members, which become apparent in their practice. Thus, while the practice of precedent can be hermeneutical in full—including the creation of precedent—the creation of precedent does not necessarily have a hermeneutical structure.

5. Conclusion

So where does this exploration into the territory of precedents leave the hermeneutical approach? The application of precedents shares the intentionalist, hermeneutical character of the application of statutes. There are, however, some hermeneutical particularities when compared to the interpretation and construction of statutory law. Firstly, due to the restricted power of common law courts to create law via precedent, which is limited to the facts of the case at hand, the interpretation does not pertain to the legal rule created by the precedent but only to the holding, the generalizability of which is restricted by later courts' powers to distinguish. Secondly, in the face of complex, modern legislative procedures, legal interpretations of statutes must rely on a construction of their intentional subject. In contrast, due to the fact that court decisions and opinions are sometimes issued by single judges or a small bench, it is at least theoretically conceivable that the interpretation of a ruling relies on the actual intentions of the judges. This is obviously the case for individual judges. However, it is also conceivable for a small body of judges, since it seems possible that they—unlike legislatures—fulfil the conditions that reductive accounts of collective intentionality presuppose. A third difference pertains to the necessity of legal construction in cases of substantive indeterminacy of a holding. In statutory cases, the courts are forced to revert to legal construction in a case of legal indeterminacy, since the legislature cannot step in. The situation is different, however, for a court confronted with a substantive indeterminacy in a precedent. Unlike the legislature, the later court in a common law system can step in and create a new legal rule for the instant case. Hence, there is no need for the later court to construct a communicative intention of the precedent court if the latter did not reflect on the later case. Fourthly, even the application of bare precedents is hermeneutical in nature. Treating like cases alike presupposes a standard of alikeness that is implicit in the decision of a bare precedent as its holding. Lastly, even though every *application* of a precedent follows the structure of interpretation in the intentionalist sense, the *creation* of precedent is only hermeneutical if it draws on the communicative intentions of authorities such as revelations or the common normative intentions of a shared practice. The creation of precedent is not necessarily hermeneutic, however, since it can also draw on general practical reasoning. Thus, it is not necessarily 'turtles all the way down'.[53]

---

[53] *United States v Rapanos* 547 US 715, 754 (2006).

12

Do Precedents Constrain Reasoning?

Emily Sherwin[*]

1. Introduction

In recent years, there has been a resurgence of interest in the nature of *legal* reasoning, meaning reasoning that is specific to law and imbedded in legal practice. In an effort to capture the distinctive character of common law decision-making, scholars have attributed a variety of special forms of reasoning, not found in other areas of life, to judges resolving legal disputes. Legal reasoning has been characterized as analogical reasoning from case to case, as a fortiori reasoning based on the comparative strength of facts present in past and present cases in favour of an outcome, as identification of 'legal reasons' for decision imbedded in the facts and outcomes of prior cases, and as construction of 'legal principles' from an array of prior decisions. All of these methods are particularly associated with law and are thought to differ from reasoning about, for example, what to eat for dinner, whether to help a stranger, or what to do with a small business loan. All are familiar to any law student in the US, the UK, or the British Commonwealth.

The effort to describe and defend uniquely legal reasoning continues, in creative ways. The common theme is that current judicial decision-making is constrained, not by rules announced in prior cases, but by the cases themselves. The decisions past judges have reached, in response to particular assortments of facts, bind current judges. At the same time, judges are free to adapt the 'law' embedded in past decisions to the new circumstances that current parties bring before them. In this way, law is both authoritative and open to improvement.

In this chapter, I will argue that the only viable form of precedential constraint is a determinate judicial rule that requires a particular outcome in response to a particular set of facts. In the absence of legislation, the alternative to application of determinate rules is all-things-considered reasoning by the judge about what outcome is best on the facts presented by the current case. Ideally, judicial reasoning follows the method of reasoning to reflective equilibrium, with allowance for the exigencies of dispute resolution. In the process of reasoning, judges can and should study the facts and outcomes of past cases and the reasons given by past judges. By following this methodology, they can check the conclusions of their own reasoning and better anticipate the effects of any rule they propose to announce. In the absence of a determinate precedent rule, however, the current decision is not *constrained* given by prior cases but instead rests with the current judge.[1]

More specifically, I will also argue that various proposed forms of precedent-based decision-making, including analogical reasoning, deductive reasoning from the facts and

---

[*] I would like to thank Sebastian Lewis and Fabio Schecaira for excellent comments.
[1] In the case of a judicial panel, the decision ultimately represents consensus among a majority, each negotiating from a reasoned position.

Emily Sherwin, *Do Precedents Constrain Reasoning?* In: *Philosophical Foundations of Precedent*. Edited by: Timothy Endicott, Hafsteinn Dan Kristjánsson, and Sebastian Lewis, Oxford University Press. © Emily Sherwin 2023. DOI: 10.1093/oso/9780192857248.003.0013

outcomes of prior cases, and distinguishing prior cases, and reasoning from 'legal' principles, are not meaningful methods for resolving legal disputes. Analogical reasoning may be useful for the purposes of discovery or rational comparison, and possibly for rule-making, but it does not provide legal answers to disputes. Deduction from prior facts and outcomes cannot settle non-identical cases. Distinguishing prior decisions is a deceptive practice that undermines the benefits of reliable rules. Legal principles impose little if any constraint on decision-making.

2. Reasoning to Equilibrium

As just described, I believe that sound judicial decision-making must rest either on authoritative rules or, in the absence of a rule, on the current judge's own unconstrained reasoning.[2] Judicial reasoning is sometimes inductive, but the practical and moral aspects of judicial reasoning are best understood on the 'model of reasoning to wide reflective equilibrium'.[3] The reasoner begins with a specific problem, such as which party should prevail in a legal dispute. They make an initial judgment about how the dispute should be resolved and formulate a tentative principle to support their judgment. Next, they tests her principle by imagining how it might resolve other specific disputes, either actual or hypothetical.

If the principle yields outcomes that appears to be wrong when applied to test cases, the judge must refine her analysis. She can do this either by rejecting both her tentative principle and her initial judgment about the current dispute and beginning again; by rejecting the tentative principle but affirming her initial resolution of the current dispute and formulating a new principle; or, if she is convinced that both her initial resolution and her tentative explanatory principle are correct, by reconsidering her judgments about how the principle might apply to her test cases. In this way, the reasoner moves back and forth between general principles and specific applications to reach a better understanding of both the practical and moral values at stake and their implications for the case she must decide.

In legal contexts, the reasoning process will seldom be ideal because the reasoner must resolve a concrete problem within a limited period of time. This does not mean, however, that judges should give up on reasoning towards equilibrium and turn instead to intuition or to formulaic treatment of precedent decisions. It means only that, in law as in many other areas of life, the outcome will be the best the reasoner can do given limited time and resources.

Judicial reasoning is constrained only by legally authoritative rules, including precedent rules announced by prior judges. In my conception of the common law, judicial rules are binding on later courts except that a court operating at the same level of judicial authority can overrule a precedent rule it deems to be unwise, as a rule. I use the phrase 'as a rule' because a fundamental feature of authoritative rules is that they operate as a whole. They must be judged, and either followed or overruled, based on the sum of results they produce over time rather than the result they require in a particular case. In the context of judicial rules, it

---

[2] See L Alexander and E Sherwin, *Advanced Introduction to Legal Reasoning* (Elgar 2021) 87–145; L Alexander and E Sherwin, *Demystifying Legal Reasoning* (CUP 2008) 31–63; L Alexander and E Sherwin, *The Rule of Rules: Morality, Rules, and the Dilemmas of Law* (Duke UP 2001); N MacCormick, *Legal Reasoning and Legal Theory* (rev edn, Clarendon Press 1994); F Schauer, *Playing By the Rules: A Philosophical Examination of Rule-Based Decision-Making in Life and Law* (Clarendon Press 1991).

[3] Reasoning to reflective equilibrium is described, most notably, in J Rawls, *A Theory of Justice* (Harvard UP 1971) 43–53, 114–21, 578–82); N Daniels, 'Wide Reflective Equilibrium and Theory Acceptance' (1979) 76 J Phil 256; H Klepper, 'Justification and Methodology in Practical Ethics' (1995) 26 Metaphilosophy 201, 205–06.

160 EMILY SHERWIN

follows that overruling is appropriate only if a new rule, or no rule at all, will produce a better sum of outcomes over time than regular application of the existing rule.

It also follows that 'distinguishing' rules is not a legitimate practice. If a new case presents facts that are covered by the terms of the rule but were not present in the case in which the rule was announced, the court must either follow the rule or overrule it and return to unconstrained reasoning.[4] Carving out an exception that replaces the original rule with a new rule that no court has announced, and that may not produce an equally good sum of results over the full range of its application, is inconsistent with the nature of and justification for authoritative rules.[5]

3. Decision by Analogy

The view just described is not the conventionally accepted view of how the common law works. One traditional explanation of common law reasoning is that current judges 'reason by analogy' from prior cases. Analogical decision-making is attractive because it appears to constrain decision-making and maintain continuity with past decisions without treating prior judges' verbal formulas as binding on current judges. Judges can develop the law, but they must develop it consistently with what other judges have decided in the past. For reasons set out in what follows, I believe this understanding of the common law is illusory.

A. Analogy as an Intuition of Similarity

The simplest account of analogical decision-making, defended at length by Lloyd Weinreb,[6] is that judges look for factual likeness between current cases and past cases and, upon finding likeness, reach parallel results. Analogical decision-making, on Weinreb's view, does not require a supporting general principle to establish the likeness of one event to another. Likeness is something a judge can perceive or somehow understand from experience.[7]

I question whether two things can be similar or dissimilar in the abstract without background assumptions about the purpose of the comparison. Even if I am wrong about this as a psychological matter, intuitive similarity is not a valid basis for legal decision-making. Picture three objects: a pen, a pencil, and a ruler. Which two are most alike? If the aim is to write a letter, the pen and the pencil are relevantly similar because both could be used for this purpose. If the aim is business planning for a lumber yard, the pencil and the ruler may look

---

[4] A rule, on my view, is 'announced' when it appears in determinate form in an opinion.

[5] But cf A Rigoni, 'Common-Law Judicial Reasoning and Analogy' (2014) 20 Legal Theory 133, 138–39 (criticizing rule-based theories of decision-making on the ground that they do *not* sufficiently accommodate the practice of distinguishing rules). In my view, distinguishing is inconsistent with the nature and function of authoritative rules. Rigoni, however, favours a descriptive rather than a normative approach to discussion of judicial reasoning; my own approach clearly is normative.

[6] LL Weinreb, *The Use of Analogy in Legal Argument* (CUP 2005); see SJ Burton, *An Introduction to Law and Legal Reasoning* (Little Brown & Co Law Business 1995) 25–41; EH Levi, *An Introduction to Legal Reasoning* (University of Chicago Press 1948) 1–6.

[7] Weinreb cites *Adams v New Jersey Steamboat Co* 151 NY 163 (1896), in which the New York Court of Appeals held a steamboat owner who let staterooms to passengers strictly liable for property stolen from a room. Precedent cases held that (1) innkeepers are strictly liable for thefts from guest rooms but (2) railroads with sleeper cars are not. The court concluded that steamboats are more like railroads than like inns, and therefore not strictly liable for theft, without citing any principle to support its conclusion.

similar because both are potential products. Without a purpose in mind, objects or actions do not speak for themselves.

Questions about purpose are common in law. Suppose that in a precedent case, the owner of a laundromat signed a written contract to sell the property to a buyer for $100,000. The seller was busy at the time and failed to read the contract document. The value of the laundromat was later appraised at $150,000 and the seller claimed that he had discussed a higher price with the buyer. There was no evidence of fraud, although negotiations were complicated. On these facts, the seller sued to rescind the contract on the ground that he was mistaken about the price. The court upheld the contract, stating that the seller's unilateral mistake was not a defence against the written agreement.

A second case arises in which the owner of a home signed a written contract to sell the home for $100,000. The seller is an elderly carpenter; the buyer is a neighbour, who discussed the purchase with the seller's wife. The wife, who is not a native English speaker, claims to have named a price of $170,000; the appraised value is $150,000. The buyer's lawyer drafted the contract and provided a copy to the seller but made no effort to ensure that the seller had read and understood the paperwork.[8]

Are these two cases analogous, or is the second case importantly different? If protecting the reliability of written contracts is the dominant purpose of contract law, then the cases look alike. If enforcing agreements that are fundamentally fair is the dominant purpose of contract law, the two cases may look different.

Judgments of likeness between two legal cases may also depend on moral judgments. Suppose a white defendant is on trial for shooting a black victim in a dark alley at night. The defendant claims that she acted in self-defence, citing a prior case in which a defendant who shot a victim because she reasonably but wrongly believed the victim was about to attack her was excused from criminal liability on the ground of self-defence. The prosecution in the current case claims that the defendant's belief that she was in danger was not reasonable because it was based on implicit racial bias: bias of which the defendant was not aware, but which caused her to react as she did.[9] Similarity, or lack of similarity, cannot determine the outcome of this case without a judgment about whether an actor is *morally* responsible for actions motivated by an unconscious but otherwise unreasonable bias.

B. Analogy as Incompletely Theorized Decision-Making

Analogical reasoning has sometimes been explained as a compromise between intuition and fully considered practical and moral reasoning. Cass Sunstein in particular accepts that intuitive similarity is not an acceptable basis for legal decision-making but argues that reasoning to full reflective equilibrium is not practical in law.[10] Reasoning to equilibrium is too ambitious, it does not allow for compromise on disputed questions, and it cannot give weight to prior decisions. Analogical reasoning, he suggests, avoids these difficulties by resting legal decisions on lower level 'incompletely theorized' principles of similarity. Sunstein is right about the difficulty of reasoning to reflective equilibrium in legal contexts, but he fails to explain the process by which judges arrive at lower level principles to support analogies.

---

[8] These facts are based loosely on *Panco v Rogers* 87 A2d 770 (NJ Ch 1952), in which the court denied rescission but refused to enjoin performance of the contract.

[9] See SP Garvey, 'Implicit Racial Attitudes and Self-Defense' (draft).

[10] CR Sunstein, 'On Analogical Reasoning' (1993) 106 Harv L Rev 741.

162   EMILY SHERWIN

Putting the problem another way: what exactly counts as reasoning that is incompletely theorized but adequate for the purpose of legal decision-making? If incompletely theorized reasoning is reasoning that follows the model associated with reflective equilibrium but is truncated for practical reasons, then it is no different from any human reasoning that culminates in action. If it is something different—a form of reasoning special to law—then its nature, and also the justifications for whatever analogical conclusions follow, remain mysterious.

A related difficulty is that analogies are affected by the level of generality at which similarity is determined. Eugenia Chen discusses this problem in a book on logical conundrums in modern life.[11] One of her examples involves two individuals who want to marry. If marriage is understood as a relation between an unrelated adult man and woman, then a heterosexual couple and a gay couple are distinguishable and only the heterosexual couple can 'marry'. If marriage is understood more generally as a relation between two unrelated adults, the heterosexual couple and the gay couple are alike, but two first cousins are distinguishable. If marriage is a relation between two adults, then heterosexual marriage, gay marriage, and incest are alike, but paedophilia is distinguishable. And so forth up the ladder of generality.[12] The point she makes is that in assessing any judgment of similarity, it is important to understand not only what principle of comparison is at work but also at what level of generality the principle is operating.

One possible explanation of what goes on when judges reason by analogy is that their seemingly intuitive conclusions about similarity are actually based on professional know-how.[13] There is something to this idea: long familiarity with legal arguments and legal decisions may allow judges to 'see' relevant similarities among disputes without reflecting deeply on the principles that tie the examples together. If so, then analogical decision-making may be more principled than it seems. Yet, legal know-how is at best an aid to ordinary reasoning, not a special legal form of reasoning. Substantively, decision-making continues to be a process of testing moral and practical principles against examples, even if training and experience allow judges to follow shortcuts.

C. Analogy as Mapping

Other writers, most recently Katherina Stevens, have relied on discussions of 'analogical mapping' in the field of cognitive science to explain and defend analogical decision-making in law.[14] One source is Dedre Gentner, who examines the process of mapping analogies in several non-legal settings.[15] For Gentner, factual similarities between two phenomena do not count as analogies; analogy is concerned only with relational similarities within the source and target examples. In her leading illustration, a hydrogen atom is analogous to our solar system because components of the atom and the solar system share an important relation: electrons revolve around the nucleus of an atom, just as planets revolve around the sun.

---

[11] E Cheng, *The Art of Logic in an Illogical World* (Basic Books 2018) 228–34.

[12] ibid (discussing implicit and explicit levels of analogy); see also KJ Vandevelde, *Thinking Like a Lawyer* (Westview Press 2011) 115–24.

[13] cf JE Penner, 'Working with a Body of Rules: On the Nature of Doctrinal Legal Disagreement in Common Law and Equity,' in M McBride and J Penner (eds), *New Essays on the Nature of Legal Reasoning* (Hart 2022).

[14] See, e.g., K Stevens, 'Reasoning by Precedent—Between Rules and Analogies' (2018) 24 Legal Theory 216. Cf D Hunter, 'Reason is too Large: Analogy and Precedent in Law' (2001) 50 Emory LJ 1197.

[15] See in particular D Gentner, 'Structure Mapping: A Theoretical Framework for Analogy' (1983) 7 Cognitive Science 155.

At a higher, causal, level, electrons revolve around the atom's nucleus because the nucleus attracts the electrons and planets revolve around the sun because the sun attracts the planets.

Gentner's aim is to show how analogical mapping can play a role in creative thought. At least in scientific contexts, the objective of mapping analogies is to reveal relational similarities that may in turn be useful in discovering general principles. Comparing atoms and solar systems, we learn that peripheral objects revolve around a central object if the central object attracts the peripheral object. Gentner's analysis does not, however, suggest that analogies constrain reasoning. To the contrary, the structural rules for analogical mapping are independent from other criteria for decision-making 'such as appropriateness, insightfulness, or correctness' of the resulting analogies.[16]

Stevens relies more directly on work by Keith Holyoak and Paul Thagard.[17] Holyoak and Thagard use a mapping strategy for analogy that is somewhat different from Gentner's. Analogical thinking, for these authors, is based on a combination of direct similarity between elements of the source and elements of the target; 'structural' parallels between the source and the target, including parallel relations among the elements of each; and the purpose for which the reasoner is pursuing the analogy.[18] Holyoak and Thagard describe a wide range of examples in which analogical mapping has played a part in human decision-making. At the same time, they emphasize that analogies must be used with caution, checked against alternative comparisons, and applied with careful attention to the purpose the analogy is intended to serve.[19] Their examples include cases in which analogical comparisons have led to important discoveries and guided strategic decision-making, as well as cases in which analogical thinking without comparison and reflection has led to costly mistakes.[20]

Holyoak and Thagard suggest that analogies can be useful in the area of law, particularly when opposing lawyers propose multiple prior cases as potential analogies, and in this way broaden the judge's thinking about a current case.[21] But they caution that judges need to combine analogical thinking with 'legal principles, empirical facts, social needs, and so on'.[22] They also suggest that when a legal case raises difficult practical and moral questions, 'it is crucial to get beyond the mere swapping of alternative analogs ... the key question to ask is: what it is about the analog that makes you intuitively reach certain conclusions?'[23] In other words, analogies may be an aid to reasoning, but they are not a substitute for reasoning or a constraint on reasoning.

Although Holyoak and Thagard emphasize repeatedly that analogies, including legal analogies, must be guided by and checked against reasoning, they also maintain a distinction between analogical thinking and the Rawlsian method of reasoning to reflective equilibrium. Analogical reasoning, they suggest, has independent value in a legal setting because it allows courts to reach practical solutions without resolving controversy at the level of principle. This suggestion appears to support the claim that analogical reasoning from precedent

---

[16] ibid 165 and fn 11.

[17] KJ Hoyoak and P Thagard, *Mental Leaps: Analogy in Creative Thought* (MIT Press 1995).

[18] ibid 5–6.

[19] See, e.g., ibid 7 ('The success of an analogy must finally be judged by whether the conjectures it suggest about the target analog prove accurate and useful'); ibid 30 ('the best one can do is select a source analog with sufficient correspondences to generate inferences about the target, and then check whether these inferences actually hold up when the target domain is directly investigated').

[20] See, e.g., ibid 7 ('Franklin was right: lightening really exhibited all the properties that were predicted by his analogy to electricity. But Johnson was wrong: Vietnam not a domino whose fall would trigger the spread of communism to Thailand and India').

[21] ibid 151.

[22] ibid.

[23] ibid.

164 EMILY SHERWIN

is distinct from unconstrained practical and moral reasoning, and more appropriate than unconstrained reasoning in the context of legal decision-making. The primary source for Holyoak and Thagard's comments on analogical reasoning in law, however, is not an insight from cognitive science but the previously mentioned essay by Cass Sunstein, in which Sunstein maintains that legal questions should not be decided at the level of abstract principle. As I have already argued, Sunstein identifies no reasoned basis for mid-level decision-making of this kind.

Returning to Katherina Stevens, Stevens uses the analogical mapping strategy described in cognitive science literature to argue that analogical reasoning imposes precedential constraint on legal decision-making. Stevens's mapping method begins with common facts ('surface similarities'), then maps relations among these facts as well as 'higher order' relations among relations. In her lead example, the question is whether a kindergarten teacher who has witnessed an injury to a child in her care should have a damage claim against the injurer, by analogy to a prior case that allowed the claim of a parent who witnessed an injury to her child.[24] Witnessing the injury is a common fact, the relation of caretaker to ward maps from parent–child to teacher–student, and love for the child arguably maps as a higher order relation associated with both parent–child and parent–teacher relationships.

An important part of Stevens's discussion relates to the third component of Holyoak and Thagard's analogical method, which is the purpose of the analogy. In other areas of life, the purpose of an analogical map may be to put scientific knowledge to new purposes, or to predict the consequences of an action. In the area of law, Stevens assumes that the purpose of analogical mapping between cases is to show '*that the two cases are legally the same*'.[25] A bit later she clarifies that the mapping process aims to show that two cases are 'similar in the legally relevant ways and that there is no relevant difference'.[26]

This last statement, referring to legal relevance, incorporates the notion of precedential constraint into the mapping comparison. Stevens explains that in mapping a prior case to a current case, the precedent judge's descriptions of the prior case—including, notably, remarks about the importance of particular facts to the outcome of the case—are authoritative for the current judge, whether or not the prior judge's assessments appear to be correct. Accordingly, the current judge scans the prior opinion for descriptions of operative facts, relations among facts, and the legal implications of facts. Then, constrained by the prior judge's characterizations, the current judge maps the prior facts to the current case with the aim of establishing *legal* similarity between the cases.[27]

Stevens concedes, however, that if the legal implications of particular facts remain vague after careful study of the prior opinion, the current judge must engage in independent reasoning to complete the mapping process. She also indicates that it is up to the current judge to determine the legal significance of differences between cases—facts that are present in the new case and were not mentioned in the prior opinion. Thus, two very common occurrences—indeterminacy in the prior opinion or the presence of novel facts in the current case—call for new and unconstrained reasoning by the current judge.[28]

In my view, this last concession undermines the claim that precedential constraint can be achieved through analogical mapping. If the prior judge and the current judge agree on legal

---

[24] Stevens (n 14) 236ff. See *Dillon v Legg* (1968) 441 P2d 912.
[25] Stevens (n 14) 240–41 (emphasis in original).
[26] ibid 242.
[27] ibid 242–46.
[28] ibid 246.

implications of shared facts, and if the cases present no differences that appear important to the current judge, analogical mapping can proceed smoothly. In this situation, however, the current judge would have reached the same result independently of the prior decision and consequently there is no constraint.

Suppose, however, that the current judge disagrees with the prior outcome. In this case, Stevens's approach to precedent imposes an illogical set of tasks on the judge. If the prior opinion is vague about operative facts and their implications, the judge must elaborate a rationale for a prior decision she believes to be wrong. If the current case presents a combination of similar facts and different facts, the judge must weigh similar facts that, in her view, did not support the prior decision against new facts that, in her view, support a different decision. Either way, she will not find an answer in the prior decision itself; instead, she must rely on her own independent reasoning to compare facts and outcomes.

Suppose, for example, that the current judge believes the prior case allowing a tort claim by a parent who witnessed an injury to a child was mistaken. In the current judge's view, this expansion of tort liability probably is unwarranted, and if the tortfeasor's liability is nevertheless expanded to cover new parties, recovery should turn on proof of emotional harm to the claimant rather than the fortuity of the claimant's having been at the scene. Stevens's analysis indicates that the current judge must weigh the special impact of being at the scene, which the first judge clearly valued but the second judge believes is nonsense, against the first judge's own judgment that, in any event, a parent is much more likely to be emotionally affected by a child's injury than a teacher. Proximity clearly mattered to the first judge, but how can the second judge conscientiously compare the *weight* of the prior judge's conclusion that proximity matters, which she believes to have been wrong, with the weight of her own assessment that teachers differ from parents, which she believes to be correct?

My concern with analogical mapping as a means of achieving continuity in legal decision-making is not that current judges will use mapping as a strategy to obtain desired results[29] but that mapping past decisions to current cases does not supply enough information to constrain current reasoning. Mapping may suppress reasoning by encouraging hasty conclusions of similarity between past and present cases. Alternatively, it may confuse reasoning by requiring the current judge to weigh the implications of prior reasoning the current judge believes to be wrong against the implications of her own current reasoning on a matter not covered by a precedent opinion. Either way, it does not achieve a sensible form of precedential constraint.[30]

Cognitive science confirms that analogical reasoning is a feature of human thought. It also provides an organizational scheme for analogical reasoning, which is useful in science and other areas in which comparisons among facts, and among relations between facts, can yield new insight. Consideration of multiple possible analogies is especially helpful because it provides multiple checks on possible solutions to practical and moral problems. In my view, however, analogical mapping does not support the claim that conclusions of likeness can constrain decision-making, particularly in a high-stakes area such as law.

---

[29] Stevens refers to this possibility but confines her discussion to judges who respect precedent; ibid 240.

[30] For what seems to me an irrefutable argument that analogical mapping should not be confused with precedential constraint in law, see F Schauer, 'Why Precedent in Law (and Elsewhere) is Not Totally (or Even Substantially) About Analogy' (2008) 3 Persp Psych Sci 454.

D. Analogy as Deduction of 'Legal Reasons' from Prior Decisions

Several writers, beginning with Grant Lamond, have developed a deductive analogical approach that nicely captures the traditional understanding of how common law decision-making works.[31] As in other forms of analogical decision-making, the precedential force of prior judicial decisions lies in the facts and outcomes of those decisions rather than any rule-like statement appearing in the precedent opinion. The process by which current judges determine outcomes is one of fact-to-fact matching and distinguishing, comparing salient facts of the current case with salient facts of a prior case they deem to be comparable. If the current case presents the same set of facts that justified the prior decision, and presents no significant additional facts, then the current judge must reach a parallel outcome. In other words, sets of facts favouring the outcome of a prior case provide precedential 'reasons' for the outcome and, in the absence of distinguishing facts, are binding on future judges.

In the example Lamond provides, case 1 involved a set of facts F1, such that F1 = {g1, h1, i1, j1, k1, l1}. The judge in case 1 reached outcome S, and we know from the reason for decision stated in the opinion that the judge considered the combination of j1, k1, and l1 sufficient to justify S. We also know that in the judge's view, g1, h1, and i1 supported ~S, but were not sufficient to overcome j1, k1, and l1. From this information, a new judge in case 2 can deduce that the set {J, K, L} justifies S, and S is not defeated by the set of {G, H, I} or by any subset of {G, H, I}. This is exactly what case 1 settles; and all that it settles.

The attraction of this system of reasoning is that if case 2 presents all of {J, K, & L}, and does not present any additional facts that differ from {G, H, & I}, then case 1 settles case 2, even if the court in case 1 did not announce a discernible rule. At the same time, there is room to adapt the law to new circumstances if not all of {J, K, & L} are present or if facts other than {G, H, & I} are present and tend to support a different result. There is no need to grapple with problems such as whether the first court intended to state an authoritative rule, what the content of such a rule might be, or whether a later court has power to distinguish or overrule a rule announced in a prior case.

The 'reasons' approach is a pleasing way to explain the precedential effect of prior decisions because it treats law as both binding and organic. It also appears simple to apply. As a description of a form of constraint on judicial decision-making, however, it fails on several grounds. A preliminary problem is that, in the absence of an authoritative precedent rule, it may be hard to determine the grounds for decision in the precedent case. A rule names a set of relatively determinate conditions and prescribes an outcome whenever those conditions are met. Without a rule, the current judge, rather than the precedent judge, effectively determines which precedent facts make up the set that counts as a binding reason for decision.

More significantly, it is not clear how the current judge should assess the relative weight of the facts supporting the precedent decision and new facts present in the current case that favour a different result. As I have already argued at some length, a fact has no weight in itself; it has weight only when placed in a context and coupled with a moral or practical principle that the fact's presence might advance. Because the force of a precedent case, on the 'reasons'

---

[31] G Lamond, 'Revisiting the Reasons Account of Precedent' in McBride and Penner (n 13); G Lamond, 'Do Precedents Create Rules?' (2005) 11 Legal Theory 1; see JF Horty, 'Grant Lamond's Account of Precedent' in McBride and Penner (n 13); JF Horty, 'The Result Model of Precedent' (2004) 10 Legal Theory 19; JF Horty, 'Rules and Reasons in the Theory of Precedent' (2011) 17 Legal Theory 1; A Rigoni, 'An Improved Factor Based Approach to Precedential Constraint' (2015) 23 Artificial Intelligence & L 133. I characterize this approach as analogical because it is fact-based and does not rely on authoritative rules announced in prior opinions. But cf Stevens (n 14) 223 fn 25.

approach, comes from the facts and outcome of the prior case rather than rules stated in the prior opinion, it is up to the current judge to formulate whatever principles are needed to give weight and directional pull to particular facts.

For example: a case arises in which plaintiffs, homeowners in a residential neighbourhood, sue to enjoin the opening of a halfway house for prisoners released on parole, on the ground that the halfway house would constitute a nuisance.[32] Defendants, proprietors of the planned halfway house, cite a prior decision in which the court held that a day-care centre was not a nuisance in a residential neighbourhood. Evidence presented in the two cases shows that the day-care centre cares for twenty children, while the halfway house would hold only six parolees at a time. Parents drop their children at the day-care centre in the morning and pick them up in the evening; parolees occupying the halfway house would not be permitted to drive vehicles. The day-care centre is located three blocks from a school; the halfway house would also be located three blocks from a school. Day care enables parents to work and provides early education for children. Halfway houses have been found to increase the chances that parolees will reintegrate successfully into society after serving time in jail. Parolees would remain under close supervision at all times.

These two cases are not far apart on a map of legal subject matter, but reasons for and against allowing the activities in question are quite different. The first difficulty is that none of the facts or, in Lamond's phrasing, 'features' connected to these two nuisance cases are identical; at best they are comparable. The day-care centre has more occupants than the halfway house would have, although for less time per day. The day-care centre increases traffic in the area, the halfway house would not. Proximity to a school plays a role in the assessment of both uses, but their locations differ. Both uses are associated with social benefits, although the benefits are not the same.

A much greater difficulty is that, even assuming that the facts presented are comparable, nothing about these facts, in themselves, tells the current judge which outcome they favour (nuisance or no nuisance) or how much weight they carry in the direction assigned to them. Possibly the current judge can infer from the outcome of the day-care case (no nuisance) or from remarks by the day-care judge that high occupancy and the possibility of traffic congestion favour the complaining residents. Then judge might also infer that these considerations carry only moderate weight, given that they were outweighed in the day-care case by the social value of day care and the defendant's interest in making productive use of its property. A further possible inference is that a day-care centre's proximity to a school is not highly relevant, except perhaps as it bears on the problem of traffic congestion. But there is simply no basis in the precedent case for assigning relative weight to the social value of a halfway house, the presence of parolees at night, or the proximity of parolees to a school. Only the current judge can make these determinations and, when she does so, the facts and outcome of the prior day-care case will not control her decision.

A precedent *rule*, in contrast, provides more definite guidance to the current judge. If the opinion in the day-care case had announced that 'other than private residences, land uses that do not serve the educational needs of young children are nuisances when located within three blocks of a school', then, for better or worse, the fate of the halfway house at the planned location would be settled. But in the absence of a rule, the decision rests ultimately on moral, practical, and empirical reasoning by the current judge about whether and why a halfway

---

[32] This example is based, loosely, on *Nicholson v Connecticut Half-Way House, Inc* 218 A2d 383 (Conn 1966).

house should be treated as a nuisance. The nuisance precedent involving day care may be a useful point of comparison, but it is not a source of constraint.

John Horty has proposed a variant of the 'reasons' approach that appears designed to explain more precisely the effect of precedent decisions.[33] Horty endorses much of Lamond's account, but suggests that the 'reasons' that determine the precedential effect of a prior decision, or a set of prior decisions, lie in 'factors' rather than 'features' of a case base. 'Factors' are not simply facts present in prior cases, but 'legally significant fact[s] or patterns of facts', which possess 'polarities' favouring plaintiff or defendant.[34] Factors found in precedent cases may support a parallel outcome, or may support a distinction that leads to a different result in the current case.

Yet, for the reasons just discussed in relation to Lamond's 'features', the weight assigned to precedential 'factors' in the decision of a current case depend ultimately on original, unconstrained reasoning by the current judge. Horty indicates at one point that factors 'naturally' possess directional polarities.[35] This remark is mysterious: in the context of a new case it is the current judge who must identify the factors that were determinative in prior decisions and, more importantly, must weigh them against new factors present in the current case. Consequently, 'factors' drawn from a precedent case impose no greater constraint on current judges than 'features' of the case impose.

The 'reasons' account of precedent articulates what many consider the genius of judge-made law: a deductive methodology that imposes case-to-case constraint but also allows for incremental modification. Ultimately, however, the constraint this method imposes is illusory and the application and evolution of law continue to depend on the sound reasoning of judges. Meanwhile, legal 'reasons' exclude the possibility of settlement through authoritative rules because only facts are binding and new facts always provide an opportunity for distinction.

4. Construction of Legal Principles

For those who view common law decision-making as a process in which current judges are bound by past decisions but retain some power to innovate, another possibility is decision according to 'legal principles'. Analogies and legal reasons, as described in previous sections, are derived from the particular facts and outcomes of prior cases. Legal principles, in contrast, are principles immanent in the array of past judicial decisions.

Ronald Dworkin, a prominent advocate for legal principles, refers to this method of decision-making as a key element of 'integrity'.[36] In Dworkin's description of the common law, a judge called on to decide a current case surveys prior judicial decisions and constructs the morally best principle capable of explaining those decisions. A legal principle is not a rule: it is a principle constructed by the current judge, which determines the outcome of the

---

[33] Horty, 'Grant Lamond's Account of Precedent' (n 31); and Horty and Bench-Capon (n 31) 4.

[34] Horty, 'Grant Lamond's Account of Precedent' (n 31) 7.

[35] Horty, 'Rules and Reasons in the Theory of Precedent' (n 31) 4. Horty acknowledges that the polarities associated with factors may sometimes be 'variable'; ibid 30.

[36] R Dworkin, *Law's Empire* (Harvard UP 1986) 228–23, 240–50, 254–58; R Dworkin, *Taking Rights Seriously* (Harvard UP 1978) 22–31. Similar accounts include Burton (n 6) 105–11; H Hart and A Sacks, *The Legal Process: Basic Problems in the Making and Application of Law* (WN Eskridge Jr and PP Frickey eds, Foundation Press 1994) lxxix–lxxx, 545–96; R Pound, *An Introduction to Legal Philosophy* (Yale UP 1922) 56.

current case. Rules are fixed and authoritative until overruled. Legal principles are organic, drawn by each judge from past legal material and changeable from one case to the next.

At the same time, legal principles are different from ordinary practical or moral principles. In Dworkin's description, a legal principle must meet two criteria: moral appeal and 'fit' with prior decisions. The requirement of fit means that judges are not free to arrive at a principle they believe to be intrinsically morally correct if prior decisions conflict with that principle. This limitation ensures that legal principles will often, if not always, differ from morally ideal principles.

The promise of legal principles is that judges who construct legal principles will work from and contribute to an internally coherent body of law. Legal principles allow judges to exercise their powers of reason and moral judgment but also ensure that the conclusions they reach have a basis in pre-existing law. The difficulty with legal principles is that sound reasoning and institutional history cannot be blended in this way: the result of a decision based on legal principles is a nearly right outcome that almost but not quite fits the institutional history of the law.

Some might say that this type of compromise is acceptable in order to preserve the internal coherence, and also the reliability, of the common law. This defence of legal principles, however, assumes that decision-making according to legal principles places meaningful constraints on judicial decision-making that will in fact yield coherence and reliability. The problem with this assumption, at least under Dworkin's description of legal principles, lies in the requirement of fit and the related idea that judges must 'weigh' competing principles found in prior law.

Fit between a legal principle currently under consideration and the body of prior law is determined by the current judge. The judge's task is to balance defects in fit against the moral attractiveness of the principle in some reasonable way. How the balancing works is not clear: conceivably, a judge who believes that a principle immanent in prior law is seriously unjust could maintain fit by applying an ideal moral principle to all cases except those whose facts precisely match the facts of the prior cases that departed from it.[37] Dworkin indicates that this type of move would not be legitimate, but he fails to identify the line between legitimate and illegitimate compromises in fit.

The task of assessing the relative weight of principles immanent in prior law is also a task for the current judge. Prior law, taken as a whole, typically supplies multiple principles that might be pertinent to a current case. To determine which eligible principle should predominate, the judge must weigh their importance in context. The problem here is not just that the current judge has no algorithm for weighing principles that point in different directions. Given that legal principles are, by definition, different from ideal moral principles, the judge is asked to assign comparative weight to principles believes to be morally incorrect: what weight should one morally flawed principle have in comparison with another morally flawed principle? In answering this question, the judge cannot rely on moral principles the judge believes to be correct, because a correct moral principle will always dictate that an incorrect principle carries no moral weight at all.

A supporter of legal principles might respond that the alternatives I propose—deductive reasoning from authoritative rules and unconstrained practical, moral, and empirical reasoning in the absence of a rule—are also imperfect. Because rules are general and determinate, rule-following inevitably will lead to some particular outcomes that are practically,

---

[37] See L Alexander and K Kress, 'Against Legal Principles' in A Marmor (ed), *Law and Interpretation: Essays in Legal Philosophy* (Clarendon Press 1995) 301–06.

morally, or empirically incorrect. Unconstrained judicial reasoning will sometimes lead to incorrect results because judges are not perfect reasoners.

At the same time, however, there are other safeguards or compensating benefits associated with deductive reasoning from rules and unconstrained reasoning. Rules settle practical and moral controversies in an authoritative way and they allow actors to make legally dependable plans, either for their own projects or in their interactions with others. Meanwhile, if circumstances change so that the sum of results a rule produces over time is no longer preferable to no rule at all, judges with appropriate authority can overrule it. In the absence of a rule, judges may make reasoning mistakes, but they generally have substantial knowledge of the legal background and of the pattern of prior decisions, and so are equipped to reason effectively toward reflective equilibrium in legal matters.

In contrast, legal principles do not predate particular decisions and so are not a good source of settlement and guidance. Nor are they likely to be practically, morally, or empirically correct. Instead, the requirement of fit ensures that they will incorporate at least some of the errors made by past decision-makers.

5. Conclusion

Attention to the past is an important feature of legal decision-making. Judges should treat the law as a discipline developed over time. They should understand its history and recognize that its social functions include settling practical and moral disagreement and providing a reliable basis for future decision-making. They should test their reasoning, and the principles they rely on, against prior decisions.

In this chapter, I have argued that predominant theories of judicial decision-making are misguided. Past judicial decisions are not binding on present judges, except insofar as they announce authoritative rules for future cases. Analogies, legal reasons imbedded in the facts and outcome of particular past decisions, and legal principles immanent in the body of past decisions do not impose meaningful constraint on current decisions. The legal past, in other words, should always play a vital role in legal reasoning, but in the absence of a rule it does not and should not *constrain* legal reasoning.

13

Precedent, Exemplarity, and Imitation

Amalia Amaya[*]

1. Introduction

Exemplarism—which takes exemplars to be central to explaining normativity—has had little influence in legal studies.[1] Yet there are various ways in which exemplars are relevant in law. The law may itself function as an exemplar; exemplary jurists play a central, constitutive, role in legal communities; legal education and, more broadly, the transmission and reproduction of legal culture depends heavily on the successful imitation of relevant exemplars; and the law embodies exemplary practices and institutions in important ways.[2] In this chapter, I aim to examine precedent from an exemplarist perspective. This perspective, I will argue, illuminates some important dimensions of precedent and precedential reasoning, and provides an interesting stance for examining the role that precedent plays in the development of the law.

The chapter is structured as follows. In section 2, I will situate precedents within the broader framework of exemplarism and inquire into the kind of exemplars they embody. Precedents, like other exemplars, are objects of imitation, and this leads to conceptualizing following a precedent as a case of imitating an exemplar. Section 3 identifies and examines some critical features of reasoning by precedent that an analysis of its imitative dimensions brings to light. Section 4 argues that an exemplarist approach to precedent provides important insights into the distinctive way in which precedents contribute to the development of the law. Section 5 concludes.

2. Exemplarity and the Nature of Precedent

Precedents may be viewed as a kind of exemplar: they set an example to be followed in other, subsequent, cases.[3] This brings precedents in law together with precedents in non-legal

---

[*] I would like to thank Daniel Arjomand, Timothy Endicott, Claudio Michelon, and Katharina Stevens for extremely helpful comments on an earlier draft.

[1] For a highly influential contemporary articulation and defence of exemplarism, see L Zagzebski, *Exemplarist Moral Theory* (OUP 2012).

[2] See K Brownlee, 'What's Virtuous about the Law?' (2015) 21 Legal Theory 1 (claiming that the law models virtue by setting a moral example that is worthy of emulation); J Waldron, 'Torture and Positive Law: Jurisprudence for the White House' (2005) 105 Colum L Rev 1681 (claiming that some rules and institutions, such as the prohibition against torture, are 'legal archetypes', i.e. provisions that are emblematic or iconic of whole areas of the law); A Amaya, 'Imitation and Analogy' in H Kaptein and B van der Velden (eds), *Analogy and Exemplary Reasoning in Legal Discourse* (Amsterdam UP 2018) (arguing that exemplary judges are central to legal education and the development of legal culture).

[3] For a defence of the claim that precedents set an example, see BB Levenbook, 'The Meaning of Precedent' (2000) 6 Legal Theory 185. On the conception of precedents as exemplars, see A Amaya, 'Exemplarism and Judicial Virtue' (2013) 25 Law and Literature 428. For a discussion of the connections between exemplarity and precedent, see M Lowrie and S Lüdemann (eds), *Exemplarity and Singularity: Thinking through Particulars in Philosophy*

Amalia Amaya, *Precedent, Exemplarity, and Imitation* In: *Philosophical Foundations of Precedent.* Edited by: Timothy Endicott, Hafsteinn Dan Kristjánsson, and Sebastian Lewis, Oxford University Press. © Amalia Amaya 2023. DOI: 10.1093/oso/9780192857248.003.0014

domains, heroic actions, saints and sages, canonic literary texts, social media influencers, paradigmatic cases in science, role models, and iconic artistic representations. Exemplarity comes in different varieties. Which kind of exemplar do precedents embody? There is, first, a distinction between object-based exemplarity and subject-based exemplarity.[4] Objects, such as a decision, a political action, or a work of art, as well as subjects, such as a parent, a rockstar, or a teacher, can be said to be exemplary. Both kinds of exemplarity are relevant in law: there are, arguably, exemplary judges and legislators—for example, Deborah and Justinian—as well as exemplary constitutions and legal institutions—for instance, the 1812 Spanish Constitution, the French Cour de Cassation, or the Magna Carta. Precedents are an instance of object-based exemplarity: just as the 1812 Spanish Constitution or the Magna Carta set an example for other constitutions to follow, so do precedential cases set an example for other cases to follow.

Of course, there are important connections between subject and object exemplarity. On a virtue-based approach to exemplarity, a person's virtue is the primary conceptual bedrock upon which all kinds of exemplarity are to be explained. In this view, an exemplary act is an act that an exemplary subject (i.e. a person who possesses a large share of virtues to a high degree) would have performed. Similarly, an exemplary decision is one that an exemplary judge would have taken. Because exemplary judges would characteristically behave virtuously, it is highly likely that their decisions will also be exemplary. There is, however, the possibility that non-virtuous courts take a decision that an exceptionally virtuous judge would have taken. Virtuous judges are also fallible, which opens the possibility that their judgments fall short of exemplarity. Subject exemplarity is thus neither necessary nor sufficient for object exemplarity. Nonetheless, virtuous judges would be reliably successful in achieving virtuous outcomes. So it should come as no surprise that landmark cases are often decided by great judges. In previous work, I have explored subject-based exemplarity in judging.[5] Here, I will focus on case-based exemplarity, but it is worth keeping in mind the extent to which these two versions of legal exemplarism are importantly interrelated.

Secondly, there is an important distinction to be made between illustrative and injunctive exemplarity.[6] Examples may serve to illustrate the force of a claim that has been independently made or a previously defined concept. One can say, for example, that Spain, the Netherlands, or Mexico are examples of civil law systems. But examples may also be deployed in a way that establishes a model, rather than merely illustrates it—as when one says that the Code Napoleon is an example of a civil law code, in that it set the norm for other codes to follow. Examples thus embody a distinctive kind of normativity, one that has been interestingly described as a 'concrete abstraction'.[7] In their particularity, examples bring the

---

(Routledge 2015); A Condello and A Ferrara (eds), 'Exemplarity and its Normativity' (2018) 30 Law and Literature 1; A Condello (ed), *New Rhetorics for Contemporary Legal Discourse* (Edinburgh UP 2020). Waldron takes some precedents to be kinds of 'archetypes' (Waldron (n 2) 1725). Ferrara includes precedents among the main categories of public exemplars, see A Ferrara, 'Exemplarity in the Public Realm' (2018) 30 Law and Literature 387.

[4] See Amaya, 'Exemplarism and Judicial Virtue' (n 3) 439. See also Zagzebski's related distinction between exemplarist ethical theories that make persons the primary exemplars, exemplarist act-based theories, and exemplarist outcome-based theories. See L Zagzebski, *Divine Motivation Theory* (CUP 2004).

[5] See Amaya, 'Imitation and Analogy' (n 2) and 'Exemplarism and Judicial Virtue' (n 3).

[6] See M Roller, 'Exemplarity in Roman Culture: The Cases of Horatius Cocles and Cloelia' (2004) 99 Classical Philology 52.

[7] See A Condello and M Ferraris, 'La normatività esemplare: una prospetiva filosofico-giuridica' (2015) 46 Politica del Diritto 621. On the kind of normativity involved in exemplarity, see Condello and Ferrara (n 3; A Condello, *Between Ordinary and Extraordinary: The Normativity of the Singular Case in Art and Law* (Brill 2018).

general home, either by illustrating a general norm or value, of which they are an instance, or by playing a constitutive role in enacting a general norm of value, of which they become the exemplar.[8] Thus, examples mediate between the particular and the general, for they embody a mode of normativity that is anchored to the particular, but that reaches beyond the particular to illustrate or constitute a general norm or value. The force of the example as both an illustrative and a normative tool are interconnected.[9] An illustrative example may subsume a normative element, in that it may single out some specific features of a class as prototypical, and thus as a model for other elements belonging to the class: as when one exemplifies the category of chair with a four-legged chair, rather than a wheelchair, which is thereby viewed as a deviant case. An example used injunctively may also serve illustrative aims: by setting a standard, its user also aims to generate a new series of objects like it, so that it will ultimately become illustrative of a class. The placement of precedents alongside other kinds of examples vividly brings to light the way in which, far from merely being an instance of a rule or value, they exemplify rules or values in an injunctive mode.

Thirdly, a related distinction between normal and surprising—typical and unique—examples, is also helpful for understanding the exemplary dimensions of precedent. Examples can be typical of a series of similar objects—as is characteristically the case when one invokes an example in an illustrative way. They may also be unique, unlike other cases, outstanding, in that they either significantly surpass any other examples within the series when assessed against the normative standard in place, or are 'unprecedented', as they are the first of a series or category, which significantly diverges from previous categories either in the normative standard it sets up or the way in which it specifies a previously established standard. It is possible therefore to distinguish between two kinds of exemplarity: 'ordinary' exemplarity and 'extraordinary', or 'revolutionary', exemplarity.[10] Interestingly, the phenomenology of the two kinds of exemplarity is different. Whereas in the former, one has a 'normal experience', which repeats itself within an accepted framework, in the latter one has a 'surprising encounter', which defies a given order and is 'unparalleled' in its singularity.[11] This distinction may be connected to yet another distinction, between the *exemplum* and the *exceptio*—between the singular as a rule-case and the singular characterized as 'ruleless'.[12] As with the distinction between illustrative and injunctive uses of example, the distinction between ordinary and extraordinary exemplarity, while important, is also porous: examples have a 'Janus-headed' form in that the typical and the unique, the ordered and the extraordinary, merge.[13] It is also one of degree, just as 'ordinary heroes', may carry out the most extraordinary deeds, ordinary examples may prompt, incrementally, radical changes of the accepted order over time. Precedent in law embodies both kinds of exemplarity and clearly exemplifies the complex relation between the two: landmark cases embody a 'revolutionary' kind of exemplarity, while other cases, as the practice of distinguishing shows, have specific

---

[8] See S Clark, 'Neo-Classical Public Virtues: Towards an Aretaic Theory of Law-Making (and Law-Teaching)' in A Amaya and HL Ho (eds), *Law, Virtue and Justice* (Hart 2012) 87–88 (arguing that exemplary people do not merely 'represent' character traits but rather are 'vessels' through which these traits are constructed).

[9] See Roller, 'Exemplarity in Roman Culture' (n 6) 52.

[10] See R Langlands, 'Roman Exemplarity: Mediating between General and Particular' in M Lowrie and S Lüdemann (eds), *Exemplarity and Singularity: Thinking through Particulars in Philosophy, Literature, and Law* (Routledge 2015) 78; D Llyod, 'Kant's Examples' (1989) 28 Representations 42; and R Warnick, *Imitation and Education: A Philosophical Inquiry into Learning by Example* (State University of New York Press 2008) 116.

[11] On the different phenomenology of kinds of exemplarity, see B Waldenfels, 'For Example' in Lowrie and Lüdemann (n 10).

[12] See M Möller, 'Exemplum and Exception: Building Blocks for the Rhetorical Theory of the Exceptional Case' in Lowrie and Lüdemann (n 10).

[13] See Waldenfels (n 11) 43.

174 AMALIA AMAYA

features that lead to a gradual change of framework, within which other established precedents fall.

Fourthly, a significant distinction has been drawn between 'dogmatic exemplarism' and 'critical exemplarism'. Whereas the dogmatic strand of exemplarism is typically associated with medieval exemplification and Christian examples, the critical strand is associated with pagan examples and (controversially) viewed as linked to what has come to be known as the Renaissance crisis of exemplarity.[14] In contrast to dogmatic exemplarism, critical exemplarism makes room for criticism of the example, which is viewed as a source for ethical self-reflection. The Roman discourse of exemplarity is a case of critical exemplarity that is particularly interesting for the purpose of characterizing the kind of exemplarity embodied in legal precedent.[15] Such discourse has specific features that enable it to mediate between the general and the particular in a way that integrates adherence to communal normative standards with the exercise of individual critical judgment. More specifically, the Roman discourse of exemplarity was marked by indeterminacy (i.e. there was a diversity of meanings associated with any single exemplar, instead of a straightforward mapping of each exemplar into a single moral category) and multiplicity (i.e. exemplars always appeared in a series, as multiple examples of the same abstract concept). It embodied a spatial conception of virtue, which envisages a virtue as possessing a breath that encompasses variety; it explored and contested the boundaries between virtue and vice; it communicated situational sensitivity; and it aimed to inculcate creativity and independent thinking when following examples.[16] The practice of legal precedent, as a kind of exemplary discourse, shares some important features of the critical exemplarity characteristic of the Roman discourse, and similarly allows for socially constrained, albeit flexible, individual judgment.

Lastly, precedents embody a kind of public exemplarity. Exemplars play an important role across both private and public domains, for example science, friendship, education, ethics, parenting, and the arts. Precedents, like other kinds of legal exemplars, are public, rather than private, exemplars. Ferrara distinguishes between four kinds of exemplarity in the public realm: exemplary deeds (e.g. Seneca's death), exemplary personalities (e.g. Martin Luther King), exemplary legal notions such as landmark statues (e.g. the New Deal legislation), and exemplary constitutional orders.[17] 'Exemplary superprecedents', in Ferrara's terminology, fall within the third kind of public exemplarity (which, along with exemplary deeds and exemplary constitutional orders, would be cases of object-based exemplarity, as stated earlier). The classification could be extended, I believe, to encompass all precedents, not only landmark cases, given the previously mentioned dialectic between conformity and exceptionality that is inherent in exemplarity. It is worth inquiring into what makes these different kinds of public exemplarity public. What quality is one ascribing to landmark precedents, and precedents more generally, by describing them as public exemplars? Exemplars may be, as stated earlier, defined in terms of virtues, for example a heroic exemplary action manifests to a high degree the virtue of courage, an exemplary scientific theory, for example Newton's dynamics, exhibits to a high degree the virtues of simplicity and consistency, or an exemplary judge possesses a large share of the virtues of justice, wisdom, and compassion.

---

[14] See F Rigolot, 'The Renaissance Crisis of Exemplarity' (1998) 59 J Hist of Ideas 558, fn 5.

[15] Roman exemplarity was traditionally conceived as uncritical, univalent, and doctrinaire, and it was frequently lumped together with the medieval, tightly controlled, exegetical use of exemplars. However, as Rebecca Langlands has persuasively shown, the Roman discourse of exemplarity was, to the contrary, extremely rich, nuanced, and critical. See R Langlands, *Exemplary Ethics in Ancient Rome* (CUP 2018).

[16] See Langlands, 'Roman Exemplarity' (n 10).

[17] Ferrara (n 3).

Public exemplars embody public virtues, that is, the kind of virtues that are constitutive of, and help to advance, the common good. These virtues include, among others, virtues related to public goods (e.g. self-restraint or moderation), virtues of public deliberation (e.g. open-mindedness and intellectual sobriety); virtues concerning public relationships (e.g. humility and respectfulness); virtues related to public participation (e.g. civic activism and generosity); and virtues related to public institutions (e.g. law-abidance and loyalty).[18] Thus, a number of public virtues bestow precedents with exemplary force.

To sum up the discussion thus far, precedents embody a distinctive kind of exemplarity: it is an object-based, critical, and public kind exemplarity, which blends both illustrative and injunctive modes of exemplarity with ordinary and extraordinary, or revolutionary, modes. An exemplarist perspective further brings to light some interesting aspects of precedent that are marginal, at best, in most discussions. As exemplars, precedents share several features that are characteristic of all variants of exemplarity.

First, precedents, like other exemplars, prompt a specific emotional response. Admiration has been singled out as the most important emotion to which (positive) exemplars may give rise. In fact, in a highly influential exemplarist theory, developed by Linda Zagzebski, admiration provides the foundation for exemplarity.[19] In this view, admirability provides the criterion for identifying exemplarity. Certainly, admiration is central to exemplarity, but the claim that judgments of admirability are prior to judgments of exemplarity seems to have things backwards. It is not that an action, an artwork, or a rock star is exemplary because they give rise to admiration, rather they give rise to admiration because they are exemplary. The source of exemplarity is to be located, in keeping with the classic exemplarist tradition, in the virtues of the exemplar. Furthermore, the claim that admiration plays a foundational role in exemplarism is not only problematic, but also restrictive in that there are emotions other than admiration that are highly relevant to exemplarity. Positive exemplars also give rise to other positive emotions, such as awe and respect, as well as negative ones, such as envy, contempt, and resentment. Interestingly, mixed emotions, such as ambivalence, are also likely to emerge when facing exemplars.[20] Precedents, as exemplars, trigger the emotional reactions associated with encountering exemplarity—among which admirability retains a particularly important, albeit neither foundational, nor exclusive, place.[21] Indeed, some precedents are widely celebrated and admired within the legal community and beyond; some stand out as egregious negative exemplars that prompt repudiation; and precedent cases involving serious value conflict often give rise to mixed feelings in both the primary audience (the judiciary) and the secondary audience (the legal community and society at large).[22]

Secondly, precedents, like other exemplars, have a monumental quality.[23] Exemplars, their evaluation, and their consequences for the community are commemorated through monuments, which include narratives, statutes, scars, toponyms, and cognomina among others. For many exempla, and indeed, for precedents, narratives are the most important

---

[18] On this characterization and taxonomy of public virtues, see A Amaya, 'Vicios públicos' in C Pereda, *Diccionario de injusticias* (UNAM-Siglo XXI 2022).

[19] See Zagzebski (n 1).

[20] See E Sullivan and M Alfano, 'Negative Epistemic Exemplars' in BR Sherman and S Goguen (eds), *Overcoming Epistemic Injustice: Social and Psychological Perspectives* (Rowman & Littlefield 2019).

[21] On the relevance of admiration in legal exemplarism, see A Amaya, 'Admiration, Exemplarity and Judicial Virtue' in A Amaya and M Del Mar (eds), *Virtue, Emotion and Imagination in Law and Legal Reasoning* (Hart 2012).

[22] See Levenbook (n 3) 207.

[23] See Roller, 'Exemplarity in Roman Culture' (n 6). See also M Roller, *Models from the Past in Roman Culture: A World of Exempla* (CUP 2018).

monumental form.[24] These narratives include, most prominently, the narrative of the precedential decision itself, but also the subsequent decisions which it grounds, as well as those in which it is mentioned, alluded to, or cited. Scholarly pieces of writing are also central commemorative narrative devices, among which casebooks are particularly important. Exemplars—in law as everywhere else—are selected, cited, assembled, and classified.[25] The exemplary catalogue, such as the traditional book of *exempla virtutis* and the law casebook, brings different exemplars within the same category, providing thereby a context for their interpretation.[26] In addition to legal narratives, narratives in mass media and social media are also important vehicles of commemoration. Interestingly, however, other monumental forms are also associated particularly with landmark precedents. *Brown v Board of Education* provides an exemplary example.[27] It has been commemorated in architectural form, as in the National Historic Site in Topeka, pictorial representation, such as Michael Young's mural at Kansas State Capitol, figurative public sculpture, for example Antonio Tobias Mendez's children's statues in Annapolis, and medals, like the Congressional Gold Medal. In a diversity of forms, narrative and otherwise, monuments interpret and reify the exemplary force of precedents, and are an important resource for preserving collective and institutional memory.[28]

Last, and relatedly, precedents, like other exemplars, have an important aesthetic dimension.[29] Selection is central to the process of exemplification, and aesthetic criteria—I would like to argue—are highly relevant to this process. The particularly strong exemplary force that some exempla enjoy and their success as models for others to follow partly depend on their aesthetic qualities. In the case of a legal precedent, the aesthetic aspects of the narrative form, the judicial 'style', enhances its attractiveness, and gives rise to the admiration that is central to its success as a model.[30] The appreciation of the aesthetic dimensions of precedent also brings to light that they set up not only an example for others to follow when resolving future cases, but also an example of how to set an example: that is to say, an example of how best to follow previous cases and how to be a successful model for future ones.

Thus, precedents have, like other exemplars, emotional, monumental, and aesthetic dimensions. Different functions are associated with exemplars, which precedents, and other

---

[24] On the complex problems arising from the narrativization of exemplars, see S Goldhill, 'The Failure of Exemplarity' in IJF de Jong and JP Sullivan (eds), *Modern Critical Theory and Classical Literature* (Brill 1993).

[25] On the relevance of selection and compilation to the process of exemplification, see M Jeanneret, 'The Vagaries of Exemplarity: Distortion or Dismissal?' (1998) 59 J Hist of Ideas 578. Interestingly, anthologies and compilations of historical exemplars, like law casebooks, are not structured chronologically, but thematically, see A Eriksen, 'Time and Exemplarity' (2017) 6 J Early Modern Studies 183.

[26] On the relevance of the 'list' of exemplars to their interpretation, see M Roller, 'Between Unique and Typical: Senecan Exempla in a List' in Lowrie and Lüdemann (n 10) 578.

[27] *Brown v Board of Education of Topeka* 347 US 483 (1954).

[28] Precedents, in addition to having a monumental quality in that they are commemorated through different kinds of monuments (narrative and otherwise), may also be said to have such quality insofar as some of them stand in the legal landscape as monuments. I thank Katharina Stevens for this suggestion.

[29] On the aesthetics dimensions of moral exemplarity, see IJ Kidd, 'Admiration, Attractiveness, and the Aesthetics of Exemplarity' (2019) 48 J Moral Education 369; P Paris, 'The Aesthetics of Ethics: Exemplarism, Beauty and the Psychology of Morality' (2021) J Value Inquiry 601; M Summa and C Mertens, 'Exemplarity: A Pattern of Thought for Aesthetic Cognition' (2021) 1 Discipline Filosofiche 152. On exemplarity as a feature of aesthetic traditions and its relevance to legal thought, with a focus on the declamatory tradition, see M Del Mar, 'The Declamatory Tradition of Normative Inquiry: Towards an Aesthetic Theory of Legal and Political Thought' (2019) 1 Ius Cogens 151.

[30] e.g. the distinctive style and powerful rhetorical qualities of Benjamin Cardozo's judicial opinions is an important factor that makes these opinions important and influential. See AL Kaufman, *Cardozo* (Harvard UP 1998) 436–55; RA Posner, *Cardozo: A Study in Reputation* (University of Chicago Press 1990) 33–57.

legal exemplars, are also meant to perform.[31] First, exemplars are central to processes of identity-formation of both individuals and communities. Landmark cases—like landmark statutes, and exemplary jurists or institutions—are pivotal in shaping law's identity. They also provide, as argued earlier, concrete normative ideals, which outstrip what may be captured in the form of rules and principles. In addition, they are important pedagogical tools, as is vividly shown by the prominence of exemplary catalogues, in the form of the casebook, in legal education. Besides, insofar as they not only transmit previously held values but rather flesh out value, they are useful theoretical tools which help to refine, revise, and advance new legal concepts, values, and frameworks.[32] Finally, they contribute significantly to law's development and to the evolution of legal culture. Imitation is the central mechanism whereby these functions are performed. In the next section, I subject imitation to a close analysis and explain following a precedent as an instance of imitative reasoning. With an account of precedential reasoning as imitation in hand, I will return—in section 4—to explain the way in which an understanding of the common law system as an exemplary system may yield some insights into how precedents may perform the foregoing functions, with a special focus on the way in which they contribute to the growth of the law.

3. Reasoning by Precedent as Imitation

On the view that precedents are exemplars, reasoning by precedent amounts to following an example.[33] What kind of reasoning is involved in following an example? How could we characterize this process? Exemplars are first and foremost objects of imitation. One follows an example by imitating it. Thus, precedential reasoning, from an exemplarist perspective, involves imitation. What is the nature of the process of imitation that is central in this view to the practice of precedent? On a prominent approach, imitative reasoning is a matter of analogy. More specifically, an imitative inference schema would have the following form:

> One should emulate P.
> P did x in situation y.
> A situation similar to y obtains.
> Therefore, one should do x.[34]

The analogical approach to imitation brings to light the extent to which imitation, far from being a mechanical, mindless activity, is a reason-guided one—a point that was obvious to the classical writers, but that is worth remembering given the disdain of imitation in modern times. However, this approach, as I have argued elsewhere, faces significant problems and is, at best, partial, for it fails to account for some critical aspects of the process of imitation.[35] Here, I would like to turn my attention to the way in which imitation has been understood in classical reception studies. The suggestion is that we can gain some insights into the

---

[31] Amaya, 'Imitation and Analogy' (n 2).
[32] See Clark (n 8); Amaya, 'Exemplarism and Judicial Virtue' (n 3).
[33] For a discussion of precedent's exemplar force in legal reasoning, see Levenbook (n 3).
[34] See S-H Tan, 'Imagining Confucius: Paradigmatic Characters and Virtue Ethics' (2005) 32–33 J Chinese Philosophy 414. See also K McGreggor, 'Imitation as Analogy', unpublished manuscript.
[35] Amaya, 'Imitation and Analogy' (n 2).

imitation that is involved in precedential reasoning in law by linking it to the wider process of imitating authors.

Imitation—of which the imitation of the classics is a particularly relevant case—is central to literary writing.[36] When imitating (in particular when imitating the classics), authors, far from merely copying in a subservient way, recreate previous texts in a way that both preserves the literary tradition and innovates. Judges in a system of precedent may be viewed as similar, in some central respects, to imitating authors. In following precedent, they imitate former judgments by creatively re-enacting the values embodied in previous cases, thereby contributing to the development of the law. The insertion of the process of imitation that is involved in precedential reasoning in law into the larger context of imitative writing reveals significant features of the process and allow us also to see problems concerning precedential reasoning in law, for example the vexed issue of freedom vs constraint, in a different light.

A first aspect that an examination of precedent as a piece of imitative writing reveals is that reasoning by precedent is a multi-vocal process. Authors often imitate more than one earlier writer, given that the imitated text is also interconnected with other source texts that it, in turn, imitates. In addition, when authors imitate another author, their work is often mediated by previous imitations. Exemplars, as mentioned earlier, often appear in a list and are compiled, systematized, and preserved in exemplary catalogues. Series of exemplars, with their corresponding categories, frame their meaning and use as objects of imitation. Imitation is thereby a collective process, which involves multiple intertextual relations.[37] Similarly, precedential reasoning, as a form of imitative reasoning, does not merely establish a dyadic connection between a source case and a target case. Rather, the imitation of a previous case is a mediated one—it is mediated by previous judicial decisions for which it also served as a precedent, by 'window references' to yet other precedents, by other precedents within the same line of precedent, as well as by precedents that are taken to pertain—in scholarly discussions and pedagogical materials—to the same normative category.[38] Thus, a dyadic approach to the relation between a precedent case and a new case underplays the important sense in which there is an important collective dimension to the use of precedent.

Imitative writing, of which precedential judgment, as claimed, is a species, comes in different varieties. It can be overt, that is, it may explicitly acknowledge the texts it seeks to imitate, by providing 'allusions' or 'references'. Or it can be concealed, in that it may leave implicit the debt to the original—with plagiarism being an extreme case of textual appropriation.[39] The degree of explicitness of the imitative nature of a piece of writing is the result of a balance between the authority that the *imitand*, that is, the object of imitation, confers, and the limits on freedom it imposes—which explains the enduring attractiveness of the 'lost *imitand*' for imitative writers, including, of course, forgers.[40] In the case of precedents,

---

[36] On imitative literary writing, see Burrow's impressive study: C Burrow, *Imitating Authors: Plato to Futurity* (OUP 2019).

[37] See Goldhill, 'The Failure of Exemplarity' (n 24). On law as an intertextual practice and the role of precedent therein, see A Steel, 'Intertextuality and Legal Judgments' (1998) 2 Macarthur L Rev 87–108; TO Beebe, *Citation and Precedent* (Continuum 2012); TO Beebe, 'Intertextual Relations in the Judgment of the Court of Appeals' 11 (2018) XLinguae 301–10.

[38] *Fairchild v Glenhaven Funeral Services Ltd* [2002] IRLR 533 provides a good example of the sense in which the use of precedent is a mediated imitative practice that has significant collective dimensions. In *Fairchild*, two of the judges applied *McGhee v National Coal Board* [1972] 3 All ER 1008, and to do so they discussed *Wilsher v Essex Area Health Authority* [1988] AC 1074, which said that *McGhee* did not create any new rule as the rule was already present in an earlier case, *Bonnington Castings Ltd v Wardlaw* [1956] AC 613—even though the judges in *McGhee* used *Wardlaw* in different ways to justify their conclusions.

[39] See Burrow (n 36) 16, 146–55.

[40] See Burrow (n 36) 17.

imitation is typically overt, with the precedent conferring authority and binding the present case. Nonetheless, judges cannot possibly escape the very many ways in which imitation may be unreflective, rather than deliberate, that is, the result of a conscious selection of models.[41] There may be imitative forces at work in judicial writing that, although not concealed, are unreflective, and remain thereby implicit. A judge may imitate in a less than conscious way the judicial style of previous decisions or deployments of normative categories in previous decisions which may, nonetheless, lack precedential force. In addition, there may be imitative influences that, although deliberate, are not explicitly acknowledged, for example foreign judicial decisions or scholarly writing. Precedents thus work as examples for other cases to follow in a variety of ways—beyond the replication involved in explicitly redeploying a previously stated rule.

Another important distinction between kinds of imitation that is relevant for characterizing the imitation involved in precedential reasoning is that between adaptative and formal imitation.[42] Adaptative imitation happens when an author aims at adapting the text which is to be imitated so that it is apt to the present time and circumstances. In formal imitation, the author imitates the form of the imitated text, broadly understood as encompassing the structure of arguments, figures of speech, patterns of rhetorical configuration, the shaping of sentences, and the general method of combining and ordering materials. Often, imitating authors combine both imitative practices. Judges, as imitating authors, are arguably similarly eclectic. Past cases set an example that needs to be adapted to the current, new circumstances of the present case, which endow precedential reasoning, as is well known, with a high degree of flexibility and attunement to the times. In addition, the judicial style, the argumentative structure, and the deployment of certain types or rhetorical figures in precedents are also the object of imitation in subsequent cases.

Imitation always present authors with a conflict between two sets of values that compete for realization: freedom and faithfulness, autonomy and authority, differing and deferring. Imitating authors must find a compromise between 'respectful transmission' and 'transformative invention', and produce an object that is 'both old and new at the same time'.[43] A transaction needs to be made between the two poles as adherence to just one of them leads to a failure in imitation. On the one hand, imitation that aims at replicating the model degenerates into a subservient exemplarity or pedantic methodology, which does not advance knowledge but merely 'transport[s] it profitlessly from the past into the present'.[44] On the other, absolute disregard for previous models not only seems impossible (at the very least, if imitating authors are to retain their role as participants in a practice) but would also deprive authors of the resources of the past. Precedential reasoning, as an imitative practice, similarly requires a transaction between the demands imposed by following previous examples and the demands deriving from the need to attend to the novel features and circumstances of the present case.[45] Of course, the balance between the two poles differs with the practice— different transactions will be appropriate to judicial opinions in a system of precedent and to

---

[41] See S Hurley and N Chater, 'Introduction: The Importance of Imitation' in SL Hurley and N Chater (eds), *Perspectives on Imitation: From Neuroscience to Social Science* (MIT 2005) 37; AJ Dijksterhuis, 'Why We are Social Animals: The High Road to Imitation as a Social Glue' in ibid 207–21; R Compaijen, 'Recognizing and Emulating Exemplars' (2017) 24 Ethical Perspectives 569–70.

[42] See Burrow (n 36) 9.

[43] See Jeanneret (n 25) 567.

[44] ibid 577.

[45] Thus, an account of precedential reasoning as imitative reasoning realizes a balance between stability and flexibility, which is a requirement that, as Stevens has argued, a theory of precedent should satisfy. See K Stevens, 'Reasoning by Precedent—Between Rules and Analogies' (2018) 24 Legal Theory 219–20.

literary recreations of classic works. Nonetheless, the success of imitative practices—in law and elsewhere—depends on finding a balance between respect for the past, which guarantees continuity, and allowing for difference and deviance—which enables change.

Imitation, as should be obvious by now—interacts with temporality in a complex way. Any encounter with an exemplar produces a 'temporal dislocation' in that the exemplar draws the imitating author to the past and back to the present.[46] Exemplars 'interrupt context' insofar as they imbricate the past with the present—they dislodge the present time by bringing in the claims of another, earlier, time.[47] Exemplars reach across time in a way that requires that both the situatedness of the model and the situatedness of the reader/writer be appropriately taken into account.[48] Judges, both as readers of previous, precedent, cases and as writers of present cases are constantly experiencing the temporal dislocation that is characteristic of imitative writing. Precedents are historically situated yet reach through time, and this makes both the context of the precedent as well as that of the court in the present case relevant to precedent use. Interestingly, exemplars not only connect past and present, by transporting the reader/writer to another time which has a claim upon the present, but also to the future. When imitating past models, imitating authors are themselves setting an example for the future. Thus, imitation is not only backward-looking but it also has a forward-looking dimension, in that it is concerned with the subsequent imitations of itself.[49] Imitation in a system of precedent has similarly a bidirectional character as the resolution of a present case follows previous examples, that is, precedential cases, but also sets an example for the future, in that it becomes a precedent for subsequent cases.[50]

Temporality impinges in the practice of imitation in yet another way. Imitation, interestingly, can be self-referential in that the object of imitation may be the process of imitation itself, that is, a meta-imitation. Authors imitate not just pieces of writing but also previous authors' 'modes of imitating'.[51] There are, as mentioned, different strategies, techniques, and forms of imitation whereby authors create new pieces of writing in ways that assimilate previous work. When imitating, authors also imitate the practice of imitation that is embodied in the imitated text. As sixteenth-century humanist Roger Ascham put it, 'the one who intelligently observes how Cicero followed others will most successfully see how Cicero himself is to be followed'.[52] Practices of literary imitation change through time, as do practices of precedent. What it takes to follow a precedent, what counts as a departure, how precedential force is acknowledged and registered, which imitative influences are to be left implicit, are also—like modes of literary imitation—historically contingent. Thus, in precedent-following, judges similarly imitate the ways in which precedents are to be followed—which, like the precedents themselves, also evolve and are transformed as they are imitated.

To sum up, the imitation of precedent cases is a complex, reasoned-guided process that involves both reflective and unreflective components, combines formal reproduction with adaptation, aims at striking a balance between freedom and constraint, has an important temporal, bidirectional, dimension, and, by being itself an object of imitation, also varies

---

[46] Roller, 'Exemplarity in Roman Culture' (n 6) 32.

[47] S Goldhill, 'The Limits of the Case Study: Exemplarity and Reception' (2017) 48 Literary History 422.

[48] See C Gütenke, '"For Time is / Nothing if Not Amenable"—Exemplarity, Time, Reception' (2020) 12 Classical Reception Journal 46; Goldhill (n 47) 422–23.

[49] Burrow (n 36) 13.

[50] For a defence of a bidirectional model of precedent, see the contribution to this volume by Nina Varsava (Chapter 21).

[51] Burrow (n 36) 14.

[52] ibid.

through time. I have thus far discussed the imitative component of precedential reasoning as a case of imitative writing, but imitation is a broad phenomenon, which extends far beyond the domain of classical reception in literature. Indeed, imitation has been claimed to be central, among other fields, in education studies, machine learning, neuroscience, and social psychology.[53] Particularly relevant for the study of precedent is the work done on the role that imitation of exemplars plays in cultural evolution. This body of work provides, as I will argue in the next section, an interesting angle from which to explore the way in which precedent contributes to the growth and development of the law.

4. Exemplary Cases and the Development of the Law

Imitation is a driving force of cultural evolution which allows for, and enables, innovation. In the previous section, we saw how imitation in the reception of the classical tradition involves both faithful transmission and creation. This dynamic of literary imitation is also characteristic of imitation as a central mechanism for the development of human culture.[54] Imitation helps to transmit with a very high degree of fidelity through generations insights about how to achieve goals that could hardly be rediscovered through trial-and-error learning. Imitation not only helps to preserve cultural artefacts that would otherwise be lost but it also spreads these discoveries, which, in turn, form a platform for future developments. Thus, the unique evolution of human culture is characterized by a 'ratchet effect' in which 'modifications and improvements stay in the population fairly readily (with little loss or backward slippage) until further changes ratchet things up'.[55] This process relies both on inventiveness and faithful transmission, but while inventiveness is quite widespread among primates, humans transmit cultural items with a much higher degree of fidelity. Thus, it is the faithful transmission (the ratchet) that explains the unique human form of cumulative culture evolution.

The evolution of legal culture is, I would argue, similarly driven by imitation. The common law, as a cultural artefact, evolves through a cumulative process which preserves previous successes and makes novelty and change possible. The common law may be viewed as a repository of exemplars, which grow and mutate through a process of imitation. This process is not revolutionary—although it does have its revolutionary moments. Landmark cases embody the kind of 'exemplary originality', creative or revolutionary exemplarity, that triggers major change.[56] It is also this kind of precedent case that is more likely to perform the inspirational functions that are characteristic of exemplars as normative ideals and that is particularly relevant for the constitution of the identity of a legal system—and more broadly of the political community it sustains. Nonetheless, the kind of revolutions that the common law undergoes are best described as 'emplacement' rather than 'replacement', or Kuhnean, revolutions.[57] Law is closer in this sense to chemistry than it is to physics as the introduction

---

[53] See Hurley and Chater, *Perspectives on Imitation* (n 41); C Heyes, *Cognitive Gadgets: The Cultural Evolution of Thinking* (Harvard UP 2018); Warnick (n 10).

[54] See M Tomasello, *The Cultural Origins of Human Cognition* (Harvard UP 1999); C Tennie, J Call, and M Tomasello, 'Ratcheting Up the Ratchet: on the Evolution of Cumulative Culture' (2009) 364 Philosophical Transactions of the Royal Society Biological Sciences 2405.

[55] See ibid.

[56] Langlands, 'Roman Exemplarity' (n 10) 48.

[57] See I Hacking, 'Was there a Probabilistic Revolution, 1800–1930?' in L Krüger, L Daston, and M Heidelberger (eds), *The Probabilistic Revolution* (MIT Press 1987); I Hacking, 'Language, Truth and Reason: 30 Years Later' (2012) 43 Studies in History and Philosophy of Science 599; SS Schweber, 'On Kuhnian and Hacking-Type Revolutions' in A Blum and others (eds), *Shifting Paradigms: Thomas S Kuhn and the History of Science* (Max Plank Institute for the History of Science 2016); P Humphreys, 'Computational Science and Its Effects' in M Carrier

of novel forms of reasoning, new arguments, and original concepts does not amount to a wholesale replacement of one paradigm by another, but rather to the piecemeal revision and improvement of the body of knowledge.[58] This continuity, however, is not secured by a process of mere reproduction. The imitative chain that joins together precedents through time is not the result of mechanical replication or parrot-like repetition. 'Simulacra'—which mimic the superficial features of a previous model—are to be distinguished from the 'living revival' that a good imitation achieves. In the course of reasoning with precedent, imitation, when successful, engenders a living assimilation of the institutional past. Thus, imitation propels law's development in a way that is both constrained by and free from the exemplary force of the past.

This exemplarist approach to law's development, and the role that precedent plays therein, draws attention to some complexities of the process. The law evolves through imitative reasoning in less than a linear, straightforward, fashion. First, some exemplary cases remain hidden—there are cases that never make it into the canon and fall into oblivion. In science, there are important findings and theories that never made their way into the accepted body of scientific knowledge, which significantly altered the course of scientific development. Similarly, there are cases in law that are overlooked, and the recognition of which might have had an important impact on the way in which the law could have evolved.[59] These *hidden exemplars* could but did not become full exempla as they failed to be used as such. There is a sense in which an unfollowed precedent is not properly speaking a precedent, at least to the extent that it does not function as such. The exemplary quality that is attached to some objects—such as prior decisions in a system of precedent—is the outcome of a process of exemplification. Central to this process, as mentioned earlier, is the process of collection, categorization, and monumentalization. Of course, precedents will—in contrast to other exemplars, such as heroic figures, real or fictional, be monumentalized—at least, in modern legal systems—in narrative written form. It is also unlikely—although neither impossible nor unprecedented—that one should face in the legal context the problem of lost *imitanda*. Nonetheless, precedents may fail to be picked on, they may fail to be identified, cited, registered, used, and included in judicial opinions, compilations, scholarly writing, and case-books. As a result, these cases end up not playing their part in the chains of imitation driving the development of the common law.

Secondly, there are also *negative exemplars*, or anti-exemplars, that is, examples that are avoided, rather than followed, and which give rise to contempt rather than admiration. Overturned precedents may be viewed as a case of negative exemplarity. In law, as everywhere else, negative examples also play an important function. They signal disvalue, and in triggering avoidance rather than imitation, have a significant impact on the development of the law. They effectively signpost the paths that are best not pursued and the values—or specifications thereof—that should be set aside. One reason for their displacement as exemplars to be followed can be traced to the temporal dimensions of exemplarity mentioned

---

and A Nordmann (eds), *Science in the Context of Application* (Springer 2011). For a discussion of the relevance of emplacement revolutions to law, see A Amaya, 'The Explanationist Revolution in Evidence Law' (2019) 23 Int'l J Evidence and Proof 60.

[58] See J Chamizo, 'About Continuity and Rupture in the History of Chemistry: The Fourth Chemical Revolution' (2019) 21 Foundations of Chemistry 11. But (for an exploration of the relevance of Kuhnian revolutions to the development of the common law) see the contribution to this volume by Leah Trueblood and Peter Hatfield (Chapter 7).

[59] See SJ Gould and others, *Hidden Stories of Science* (New York Review of Books 1995).

earlier. Every act of imitation—or precedent use—recognizes the import of the past for the present and brings together the context of the exemplar with that of the new case. Exemplars may become obsolete in that they may embody values that are no longer recognized as one's own. Imitation presupposes 'ethical continuity', a sharing of ethical standards between the past and the present, which does not obtain when exemplars are perceived as belonging to an 'else-when' or being anachronistic.[60] In these cases, the past is not only distant but also foreign, and its imitation would amount to an act of alienation, rather than autonomous recreation. In addition to contributing to legal development by providing examples to be repudiated, instead of followed, negative exemplars in law, like in other domains, also have a pedagogical value, as they help to transmit—by contrast—the normative commitments, forms of reasoning, and ways of doing that are distinctive of a particular legal community.

Thirdly, exemplars are often mixed, in that they combine features worthy of imitation with undesirable qualities, thereby providing partial models. These *mixed exemplars* prompt 'ambivalent' emotions or mixed feelings, instead of outright admiration or abhorrence. Interestingly, mixed exemplars are particularly productive from a developmental point of view, in that they set up models that are easier to be followed and prompt critical engagement and contestation. The common law, as a collection of exemplars, also includes mixed kinds of exemplars—and deploys different strategies for following a precedent in a way that only partly reproduces it, thereby deviating from the model while acknowledging its exemplary force.

Fourthly, imitation is not always productive from a developmental point of view. Imitation may degenerate into copying, which reproduces superficial features, thereby creating, as mentioned earlier, a mere *simulacrum*. By iterative repetition, exemplars may become fossilized, and incapable of mobilizing change. The process of imitation—as Burrow has noted—has had 'long associations with necromancy and with the uncanny reawakening of the dead'.[61] The living assimilation of the past stands, however, in sharp contrast with the still, dead, ideal embodied in *fossilized exemplars*. A 'living revival', as opposed to a 'simulacral replication', provides 'blood for the ghosts', in Wilamowitz's famous expression, as it revivifies the past.[62] The routinized deployment of precedent, in a way that fixes its meaning instead of adapting and recreating it, does not animate the past but stultifies it. When downgraded to mere replication, imitation is inert as a mechanism that keeps the common law alive and growing.

Lastly, there are *unconceived exemplars*, that is, precedents that never came into being. Alongside the dead—and the dead ends—there are the unborn, or the paths that were not taken. In past cases, decisions could have been otherwise: just as in science there are unconceived alternatives, theories that could have been, but were not, articulated to explain the body of evidence available, so too there are in law unimagined examples, decisions that could have, but did not, result from a different rearrangement of the relevant facts or from a refashioning of the available theoretical framework.[63] Sometimes alternative scenarios leave a 'trace' in that arguments or concepts other than those deployed are hinted at, but not developed, in the judicial opinion, or are articulated, only to be subsequently rejected. Dissenting opinions are a particularly robust form in which alternative models may leave a

---

[60] Roller, 'Exemplarity in Roman Culture' (n 6) 38.

[61] Burrow (n 36) 22.

[62] See Gütenke (n 48) 54.

[63] On the problem of unconceived alternatives in science, see PK Stanford, *Exceeding Our Grasp: Science, History, and the Problem of Unconceived Alternatives* (OUP 2006); S Bhakthatsalam and IJ Kidd, 'Realism and Unconceived Alternatives' (2019) 196 Synthese 3911.

trace. Interestingly, dissenting judgments are sometimes objects of imitation, and reach an exemplary status, thereby also contributing to the development of the law.[64]

In short, imitation is a driving force of human culture, which has a distinctive cumulative form. Imitation through precedent, in a less than linear fashion, secures a thread of continuity within the legal system—thereby preserving identity between past and present—but also allows for change. Law, as a cultural artefact, evolves, mutates, and grows as the result of a collective effort, which brings together the living with the dead, in a creative cycle of cultural reproduction.

5. Conclusion

Exemplarism, as a mode of apprehending, reading, and employing the past is, as I hope to have shown in this chapter, a fruitful paradigm for examining precedent in law.[65] I have first claimed that precedents may be viewed as exemplars. More specifically, precedents are a case of object-based, public, and critical exemplarity. Like all exemplars, they mediate between the universal and the particular and, insofar as they have a dual ontology as both typical and unique, they also mediate between conformity and exceptionality, thereby embodying a specific type of normativity. The conceptualization of precedents in terms of exemplarity, I have argued, discloses the monumental, emotional, and aesthetic dimensions of precedent, and draws attention to the variety of functions that, as other exemplars, they may be capable of performing.

I have then explained reasoning by precedent as an imitative kind of reasoning. More specifically, I have explored the process of imitation involved in reasoning from precedent by linking it with imitative writing in classical reception theory. This examination of the imitative component of the practice of precedent highlights the extent to which precedent use is a collective process that involves various elements beyond the target and the source—such as cases within a series as well as the texts wherein these are collected and discussed; is directed at diverse objects of imitation -at the source case, but also its formal features and the process of imitation itself; aims at both faithful transmission of the model and its adaptative transformation; and intersects with temporality in complex ways.

Lastly, I have argued that an exemplarist perspective also sheds light on the way in which precedents contribute to the development of the law. The common law may be viewed as a repository of exemplars—just as history may be viewed as a collection of *magistra vitae*—which, like all human cultural artefacts, evolves cumulatively though a process of imitation. Placing the evolution of the law, and the role of precedents therein, in the larger context of cultural evolution and recent arguments about the relevance of imitation in this process, also directs attention to the complexity of the process whereby precedent drives legal change. A variety of precedents—hidden, negative, mixed, fossilized, and unconceived precedents—contribute (or fail to contribute) to law's development in diverse ways. Thus, seeing precedents within the framework of exemplarity helps us to tell a story of law's development as a process that is less streamlined than a genealogical approach (with its focus on tracing precedential lines) may convey.

---

[64] As, e.g., Denning's celebrated judgments in *Candler v Crane, Christmas & Co* [1951] 2 KB 164 and in *Lloyds Bank v Bundy* [1974] EWCA Civ 8. On the relevance of dissenting judgments for the development of the law, see A Spies, 'The Importance of Minority Judgments in Judicial Decision-Making: An Analysis of *Minister of Justice and Constitutional Development v Prince*' (2019) 35 South African J Human Rights 429–40.

[65] On an understanding of exemplarity as a strategy for reading the past, see Gütenke (n 48).

14
How Does Precedent Constrain?

*John Horty**

1. Introduction: Three Problems

This chapter describes three conceptual problems presented by a standard picture of precedential constraint, suggests that two of them have now been solved, and begins to explore a solution to the third.

We start with the familiar—and very natural, though not uncontroversial—position that constraint in the common law depends on rules. A precedent case normally contains not only a factual description of some situation together with a decision on the basis of those facts but also some particular rule through which that decision is justified, the *ratio decidendi* of the case. And according to the position under consideration, it is this rule that carries precedential constraint. Just as statutory and regulatory law are based on statutes and regulations, the common law is likewise thought to be based on rules, except that common law rules are formulated by courts, rather than legislators or administrative agencies.

This general position—that precedential constraint depends on rules—can be developed in at least two ways, depending on the conventions governing the use of these rules. On one view, defended with great force by Larry Alexander and Emily Sherwin, a common law rule introduced in an earlier case must govern any later case in which it is applicable, unless the court in the later case wishes to overrule the earlier decision and has the authority to do so.[1] According to a second view, however, although only certain courts, depending on their place in the judicial hierarchy, have the authority to overrule earlier decisions, all courts have the power of *distinguishing* a new case from previous cases in which a rule was formulated or applied—the power, that is, of identifying important, or material, differences between the facts of the two cases, and so modifying the earlier rule to avoid an inappropriate application in the present situation. The idea that common law rules can be adapted to fit new situations is, arguably, the most prevalent position among legal theorists, and provides what I will call the *standard model* of precedential constraint.[2]

The process of rule-modification underlying this standard model could be illustrated by tracing the development of an actual legal doctrine, but it will be simpler to concentrate on a more ordinary example. Suppose, then, that Jack and Jo are the parents of two

---

[*] I would like to thank Sebastian Lewis and Adam Rigoni for generous and helpful comments.
[1] See L Alexander, 'Constrained by Precedent' (1989) 63 S Cal L Rev 1, 64 ; L Alexander and E Sherwin, *Demystifying Legal Reasoning* (CUP 2008).
[2] Versions of this position have been developed by E H Levi, 'An Introduction to Legal Reasoning' (University of Chicago Press 1950); AWB Simpson, 'The *Ratio Decidendi* of a Case and the Doctrine of Binding Precedent' in AG Guest (ed), *Oxford Essays in Jurisprudence* (OUP 1961) 148–75; J Raz, *The Authority of Law* (OUP 1979); M Eisenberg, *The Nature of the Common* Law (Harvard UP 1988); F Schauer, 'Is the Common Law?' (1989) 77 Cal L Rev 455–71; F Schauer, *Playing by the Rules: A Philosophical Examination of Rule-Based Decision-Making in Law and Life* (OUP 1991); along with many others.

John Horty, *How Does Precedent Constrain?* In: *Philosophical Foundations of Precedent*. Edited by: Timothy Endicott, Hafsteinn Dan Kristjánsson, and Sebastian Lewis, Oxford University Press. © John Horty 2023. DOI: 10.1093/oso/9780192857248.003.0015

186   JOHN HORTY

children—Emma, who has just turned nine, and Max, aged twelve—and that they have agreed to respect each other's decisions concerning the children, treating these decisions, in effect, as precedents. And imagine that one night, Emma, who has completed both her chores and her homework but did not finish dinner, asks Jo if she can stay up to watch TV. This is like a legal case: a situation is presented to an authority, Jo, who must make a decision and, ideally, provide a rationale for her decision. Suppose that Jo resolves the case by granting the request, stating that Emma can stay up to watch TV since she is now nine years old. This decision can be seen as introducing a household version of a common law rule— perhaps, 'Children aged nine or greater can stay up and watch TV'—fashioned in response to a particular set of circumstances, but applicable to future situations as well.

Now imagine that the next day, Max, who has likewise completed his chores and failed to finish his dinner, but who has, in addition, failed to complete his homework, asks Jack whether he can stay up and watch TV. And suppose that, in this case, Jack refuses, on the grounds that Max has not completed his homework. Max might reasonably appeal Jack's decision with the complaint, 'Ah, but given the precedent established last night, in the case of Emma, our household is now governed by a rule according to which children aged nine or greater can stay up and watch TV.' The standard model of constraint, however, allows Jack to defend his decision by distinguishing the two cases, arguing that the previous rule should not apply to the new case of Max, since this new case, unlike the previous case of Emma, presents the additional feature that the child in question has not completed his homework. An effect of Jack's decision would be that the rule set out by Jo in the case of Emma is modified to avoid application in the case of Max—perhaps now understood to mean, 'Children aged nine or greater can stay up and watch TV, unless they have failed to complete their homework.'

Various proposals have been offered about how exactly Jack's modification of Jo's previous rule might be justified. Regardless of justification, however, the fact that the standard model of constraint allows Jack to modify Jo's rule at all leads to the first of our conceptual problems concerning constraint. If Jack is indeed able to reformulate Jo's earlier rule to avoid its unwanted application in a later case, it is hard to see how he can be thought of as constrained by that rule. More generally: if later courts are free to modify the rules set out in the decisions of earlier courts, then how can those rules carry any constraints at all—how can courts be constrained by rules that they are free to modify at will?

In fact, the literature already contains a response to this initial conceptual problem—first set out explicitly by Joseph Raz, although, as Raz notes, it owes much to the previous work of AWB Simpson.[3] The central idea is that although later courts are indeed free to modify the rules introduced by earlier courts, they are not free to modify those rules entirely at will. Any later modification of an earlier rule must satisfy the two *Raz/Simpson conditions* on rule-modification. First, the modification can consist only in the addition of further restrictions, narrowing the original rule. Secondly, the modified rule must continue to support the original outcome in the case in which it was introduced, as well as in any further cases in which this rule was appealed to as a justification.

If we understand the standard model as including the Raz/Simpson conditions on rule-modification, then a response to the first conceptual problem presented by the notion of constraint is at hand: even though later courts are free to modify the rules set out by earlier courts, they are still constrained by these rules, since they can modify them only in certain ways, those satisfying the Raz/Simpson conditions. This response to the first conceptual

---

[3] See Raz (n 2) 180–209; Simpson (n 2).

problem, however, leads at once to a second. Presumably, even if some modification of an earlier rule satisfies the Raz/Simpson conditions, a later court would, all the same, choose not to modify the rule in that way unless the court believed that it could actually improve the rule by doing so. But if a later court believes that it can improve an earlier rule through modification, why should it limit itself to modifications that satisfy the Raz/Simpson conditions? Why should the court not be free to modify the rule in any way at all that leads to an improvement, or if rule-modification must be subject to conditions, then why these conditions and not others—in short: what is the justification for this particular set of conditions, the Raz/Simpson conditions, on rule modification?

What I want to suggest is that this second problem, too, has now been solved. In recent work, motivated by ideas from the field of artificial intelligence and law, and by an earlier proposal due to Grant Lamond, I developed a model according to which precedential constraint is not a matter of rules at all, but of reasons.[4] On this view—which we can call the *reason model* of constraint—what matters about a precedent case is the earlier court's assessment of the balance of reasons presented by that case; later courts are then constrained, not to follow some rule set out by the earlier court, or even to modify this rule only in certain ways, but simply to reach decisions that are consistent—in a sense to be explained shortly— with the earlier court's assessment of the balance of reasons. Although the reason model was originally developed as an alternative to the standard model, it turns out that the two models are, in a precise sense, equivalent. The reason model can therefore be interpreted as providing a semantic justification for the standard model, with its Raz/Simpson conditions on rule-modification.

This equivalence between the reason model and the standard model of constraint is not something I can review here, since the arguments are complex and somewhat technical, re- quiring a precise formulation of the standard model as well as the reason model.[5] Instead, I want to focus in this chapter on a third conceptual problem presented by the notion of constraint, reflecting what may be the deepest, or at least the most frequent, objection to the idea that common law rules are malleable. The objection is that, as long as the rules set out by courts can be modified—even if the modifications involved are required to satisfy the Raz/ Simpson conditions—it may nevertheless seem that common law decisions cannot really constrain at all, since no two situations are ever entirely alike: there will always be features

---

[4] See G Lamond, 'Do Precedents Create Rules?' (2005) 11 Legal Theory 1 for his initial presentation of this general idea, and G Lamond, 'Revisiting the Reasons Account of Precedent' in M McBride and J Penner (eds), *New Essays on the Nature of Legal Reasoning* (Hart 2022). The first version of the account presented here is found in J Horty, 'Rules and Reasons in the Theory of Precedent' (2011) 17 Legal Theory 1, later developed in J Horty, 'Constraint and Freedom in the Common Law' (2015) 15 Philosopher's Imprint 1; J Horty, 'Reasoning with Precedent as Constrained Natural Reasoning' in E Lord and B Maguire (eds), *Weighing Reasons* (OUP 2016) 193–212; a more detailed exposition is contained in J Horty, *The Logic of Precedent: Constraint and Freedom in Common Law Reasoning* (CUP forthcoming). This account has been related to research in artificial intelligence and law in J Horty and TJM Bench-Capon, 'A Factor-Based Definition of Precedential Constraint' (2012) 20 Artificial Intelligence and Law 181 , compared to arguments from analogy and enriched in various ways in A Rigoni, 'Common-Law Judicial Reasoning and Analogy' (2014) 20 Legal Theory 133; A Rigoni, 'An Improved Factor Based Approach to Precedential Constraint' (2015) 23 Artificial Intelligence and Law 133, and explored from a formal perspective in H Prakken, 'A Formal Analysis of Some Factor and Precedent-Based Accounts of Precedential Constraint' (2021) 29 Artificial Intelligence and Law 559. More recently, a different interpretation of Lamond's original proposal, and one that connects more closely with traditional ideas from legal theory, has been presented in R Mullins, 'Protected Reasons and Precedential Constraint' (2020) 26 Legal Theory 40; interestingly, Mullins also shows that his alternative interpretation is, in a precise sense, equivalent to that presented here.

[5] See Horty, 'Constraint and Freedom' (n 4) for an initial presentation of the equivalence result; see Horty, *The Logic of Precedent* (n 4) for a more careful analysis.

188 JOHN HORTY

available for future courts to use in distinguishing the situations they face from those confronted earlier. What I hope to show is that, in addition to providing a semantic justification for the Raz/Simpson conditions, the reason model can help us to formulate a response to this third problem as well.

The chapter is organized as follows. After introducing basic concepts and notation in the following section, I define the reason model of constraint itself in section 3— these two sections can be read as a self-contained introduction to the reason model. In section 4, with the reason model before us, we then return to the third conceptual problem presented by the notion of constraint, that any fresh situation will always be distinguishable.

2. Basic Concepts

A. Factors and Facts Situation

We will suppose that a situation presented to a court for decision can be represented as a set of *factors*, where a factor is a legally significant fact or pattern of facts bearing on that decision. In our domestic scenario, the legal, or quasi-legal, issue at hand is whether a child can stay up and watch TV, and the factors involved might reasonably include those already considered—whether the child has reached the age of nine, completed chores, eaten dinner, finished homework—as well as countless others.

Many factors can naturally be taken to have polarities, favouring one side or another. In our domestic example, being older than nine or completing chores strengthens the child's claim, as plaintiff, that he or she should be allowed to stay up and watch TV; failing to finish dinner or homework strengthens the parents' claim, as defendants, that the child should go to bed immediately. As a simplification, we will assume here, not just that many, or even most, factors have polarities, but that all factors are like this, favouring one particular side. In addition, we rely on the further simplifying assumption that the reasoning under consideration involves only a single step, proceeding at once from the factors present in a situation to a decision—directly in favour of the plaintiff or the defendant—rather than moving through a series of intermediate legal concepts.

Formally, then, we start by postulating a set F of legal factors bearing on some particular issue. We will let $F^\pi = \{f_1^\pi, \ldots, f_n^\pi\}$ represent the set of factors favouring the plaintiff and $F^\delta = \{f_1^\delta, \ldots, f_m^\delta\}$ the set of factors favouring the defendant. Given our assumption that each factor favours one side or the other, the entire set of legal factors will be exhausted by those favouring the plaintiff together with those favouring the defendant: $F = F^\pi \cup F^\delta$. As this notation suggests, we take π and δ to represent the two sides in a dispute, plaintiff and defendant, and where s is one of these sides, we let $\bar{s}$ represent the other: $\bar{\pi} = \delta$ and $\bar{\delta} = \pi$.

Given this collection F of factors, a *fact situation* X, of the sort presented to the court for judgment, can be defined simply as some particular subset of these factors: $X \subseteq F$. And where X is a fact situation of this kind, we let X^s represent the factors from X that support the side s, so that: $X^\pi = X \cap F^\pi$ and $X^\delta = X \cap F^\delta$. Of course, any interesting situation will contain factors favouring both sides of a given dispute. For example, the situation $X_1 = \{f_1^\pi, f_2^\pi, f_1^\delta, f_2^\delta\}$ contains two factors each favouring the plaintiff and the defendant, with those factors favouring the plaintiff contained in $X_1^\pi = \{f_1^\pi, f_2^\pi\}$ and those favouring the defendant contained in $X_1^\delta = \{f_1^\delta, f_2^\delta\}$.

B. Reasons, Rules, Cases, Case Bases

When presented with a fact situation, the court's primary task is to reach a decision, or determine an outcome. Given our assumption that reasoning proceeds in a single step, we can suppose that the *outcome* of a case is a decision either in favour of the plaintiff or in favour of the defendant, with these two outcomes represented as π or δ respectively.

In addition to deciding for one side or the other, we generally expect the court to supply a rule, or principle, to serve as justification for its decision. Rules of this kind will be characterized in terms of reasons, where a *reason for a side* is some set of factors uniformly favouring that side; a *reason* can then be defined as a set of factors uniformly favouring one side or another. To illustrate, $\{ f_1^\pi, f_2^\pi \}$ is a reason favouring the plaintiff, and so a reason.

Since reasons, like fact situations, are sets of factors, we can stipulate that a reason U *holds* in a situation X just in case each factor from U belongs to X, so that U is a subset of X, or $U \subseteq X$. And we can also define a relation of strength among reasons for a side according to which, where U and V are reasons for the same side, then V *is at least as strong a reason as U for that side* just in case U is a subset of V, or $U \subseteq V$. To illustrate: we can see, first, that the reason $\{ f_1^\pi \}$ holds in the previous fact situation $X_1 = \{ f_1^\pi, f_2^\pi, f_1^\delta, f_2^\delta \}$, since $\{ f_1^\pi \} \subseteq X_1$. And we can see that, of the two reasons $\{ f_1^\pi \}$ and $\{ f_1^\pi, f_2^\pi \}$, the second favours the plaintiff at least as strongly as the first, since $\{ f_1^\pi \} \subseteq \{ f_1^\pi, f_2^\pi \}$.

Given this notion of a reason, a rule can now be defined as a statement of the form $U \rightarrow s$, where U is a reason supporting the side s. For convenience, we introduce two auxiliary functions—*Premise* and *Conclusion*—picking out the premise and conclusion of a rule, so that, if r stands for the rule just mentioned, we would have $Premise(r) = U$ and $Conclusion(r) = s$. And we will say that a rule is applicable in a situation whenever the reason that forms its premise holds in that situation. To illustrate: the statement $\{ f_1^\pi \} \rightarrow \pi$ is a rule, since $\{ f_1^\pi \}$ is a reason supporting the plaintiff. If we take r_1 to stand for this rule, we would have $Premise(r_1) = \{ f_1^\pi \}$ and $Conclusion(r_1) = \pi$. And r_1 is applicable in the situation X_1 earlier since $Premise(r_1)$ holds in this situation.

The rules defined here are to be interpreted as defeasible, telling us that their premises entail their conclusions, not as a matter of necessity, but only by default. Continuing with our illustration: what the rule $r_1 = \{ f_1^\pi \} \rightarrow \pi$ means, very roughly, is that, whenever the premise $\{ f_1^\pi \}$ of the rule holds in some situation, then, as a default, the court ought to decide that situation for the conclusion π of the rule—or perhaps more simply, that the premise of the rule provides the court with a *pro tanto* reason for deciding in favour of its conclusion.[6]

Given the concepts introduced so far—fact situations, rules, outcomes—a *case* can be defined as a situation together with an outcome and a rule through which that outcome is justified: such a case can be specified as a triple of the form $c = X, r, s$, where X is a situation containing the factors presented to the court, r is a rule, and s is an outcome.[7]

For illustration, consider the case $c_1 = X_1, r_1, s_1$, where the fact situation of this case is the familiar $X_1 = \{ f_1^\pi, f_2^\pi, f_1^\delta, f_2^\delta \}$, where the case rule is the familiar $r_1 = \{ f_1^\pi \} \rightarrow \pi$, and where the outcome of the case is $s_1 = \pi$, a decision for the plaintiff. This particular case, then,

---

[6] On the relation between reasons and default rules, see Horty and Bench-Capon (n 4).
[7] Our representation of cases embodies the simplifying assumption that the particular rule underlying a court's decision is plain, ignoring the extensive literature on methods for determining the *ratio decidendi* of a case; and, we suppose, as a further simplification, that a case always contains a single rule, ignoring situations in which a court might offer several rules for a decision, or in which a court reaches a decision by majority, with different members of the court offering different rules, or in which a court might simply render a decision in a case without setting out any general rule at all.

190   JOHN HORTY

represents a situation in which the court, when confronted with the fact situation X_1, decided for the plaintiff by applying or introducing the rule r_1, according to which the presence of the factor f_1^π—that is, the reason $\{ f_1^\pi \}$—leads, by default, to a decision for the plaintiff.

Finally, with this notion of a case in hand, we can now define a *case base* as a set Γ of precedent cases. It is a case base of this sort—a set of precedent cases—that will be taken to represent the common law in some area, and to constrain the decisions of future courts.

3. Constraint by Reasons

According to the reason model, what matters about a precedent case is the precedent court's assessment of the relative strength of the reasons presented by that case for each of the opposing sides. This assessment is represented as a priority ordering on reasons; later courts then required to reach decisions that are consistent with the priority ordering derived from the decisions of earlier courts.

In order to develop this idea, we need to explain how a priority ordering on reasons can be derived from the decisions of earlier courts, and then what it means for the decision of a later court to be consistent with that ordering.

A. A Priority Ordering on Reasons

To begin with, then, let us return to the case $c_1 = X_1$, , r_1, s_1 —where $X_1 = \{ f_1^\pi, f_2^\pi, f_1^\delta, f_2^\delta \}$ where $r_1 = \{ f_1^\pi \} \to \pi$, and where $s_1 = \pi$—and ask what information is carried by this case; what is the court telling us with its decision? Well, two things. First of all, with its decision for the plaintiff on the basis of the rule r_1, the court is registering its judgment that $Premise(r_1)$, the reason for its decision, is more important—or has higher *priority*—than any reason for the defendant that holds in X_1, the fact situation of the case.[8] How do we know this? Because if the court had viewed some reason for the defendant that held in the situation X_1 as more important, or higher in priority, than $Premise(r_1)$, the court would have found for the defendant on the basis of that reason, rather than for the plaintiff on the basis of $Premise(r_1)$. Secondly, if the court is telling us explicitly that the reason $Premise(r_1)$ itself has higher priority than any reason for the defendant that holds in X_1, then, the court must also be telling us, at least implicitly, that any other reason for the plaintiff that is at least as strong as $Premise(r_1)$ must likewise have a higher priority than any reason for the defendant that holds in this situation.

We can recall that a reason U for the defendant holds in the situation X_1 just in case $U \subseteq X_1$. And a reason V for the plaintiff is at least as strong for the plaintiff as the reason $Premise(r_1)$ just in case $Premise(r_1) \subseteq V$. If we let the relation $<_{cl}$ represent the priority ordering on reasons derived from the particular case c_1, then, the force of the court's decision in this case is simply that: where U is a reason favouring the defendant and V is a reason favouring the plaintiff, we have $U <_{cl} V$ just in case $U \subseteq X_1$ and $Premise(r_1) \subseteq V$. To illustrate: consider the

---

[8] When comparing the relative importance of reasons, it is more common to say that one carries greater weight than the other, or that one is weightier than the other. I prefer to speak in terms of priority, rather than weight, for two reasons: first, the priority ordering on reasons to be defined here is non-linear, while the concept of weight tends to suggest linearity; secondly, the ordering to be defined here allows only ordinal comparisons among reasons, while the concept of weight suggests that cardinal comparisons must be available as well.

reason $\{f_1^\delta\}$ for the defendant and the reason $\{f_1^\pi, f_2^\pi, f_3^\pi\}$ for the plaintiff. Here, we have $\{f_1^\delta\} \subseteq X_1$ as well as $Premise(r_1) \subseteq \{f_1^\pi, f_2^\pi, f_3^\pi\}$. It therefore follows that $\{f_1^\delta\} <_{c_1} \{f_1^\pi, f_2^\pi, f_3^\pi\}$—the court's decision in the case c_1 entails that the reason $\{f_1^\pi, f_2^\pi, f_3^\pi\}$ favouring the plaintiff is to be assigned a higher priority than the reason $\{f_1^\delta\}$ favouring the defendant.

Generalizing from this example, we reach the following definition of the priority ordering among reasons derived from a single case:

> **Definition 1 (Priority ordering derived from a case)** Let $c = X,r,s$ be a case, and let U and V be reasons favouring the sides $\bar{s}$ and s respectively. Then the relation $<_c$ representing the priority ordering on reasons derived from the case c is defined by stipulating that $U <_c V$ if and only if $U \subseteq X$ and $Premise(r) \subseteq V$.

Once we have defined the priority ordering on reasons derived from a single case, we can introduce a priority ordering $<_\Gamma$ derived from an entire case base Γ by stipulating that one reason has a higher priority than another according to the case base whenever that priority is supported by some particular case from the case base:

> **Definition 2 (Priority ordering derived from a case base)** Let Γ be a case base, and let U and V be reasons. Then the relation $<_\Gamma$ representing the priority ordering on reasons derived from the case base Γ is defined by stipulating that $U <_\Gamma V$ if and only if $U <_c V$ for some case c from Γ.

And using this concept of the priority ordering derived from a case base, we can now define a case base itself as inconsistent if its derived ordering yields conflicting information about the priority among reasons—telling us, for some pair of reasons, that each has a higher priority than the other—and consistent otherwise:

> **Definition 3 (Inconsistent and consistent case bases)** Let Γ be a case base with $<_\Gamma$ its derived priority ordering. Then Γ is inconsistent if and only if there are reasons U and V such that $U <_\Gamma V$ and $V <_\Gamma U$, and consistent otherwise.

B. Constraint

We now present the reason model of constraint itself, building on the concept of case-base consistency. The guiding idea, once again, is that, in deciding a case, a constrained court is required simply to preserve the consistency of the background case base. Suppose, more exactly, that a court constrained by a consistent background case base is confronted with a new fact situation. Then, what the reason model tells us is that the court is permitted to reach a particular decision only if that decision is consistent with the background case base:

> **Definition 4 (Reason model)** Let Γ be a consistent case base and X a fact situation confronting the court. Then against the background of Γ, the reason model of constraint permits the court to base its decision in X on a rule r, applicable in X and supporting the side s, if and only if the augmented case base $\Gamma \cup \{X,r,s\}$ is consistent.

192   JOHN HORTY

How do we get from this to notion of what a court is permitted to do to a notion of *constraint*, or of what the court is required to do? Simple: we stipulate that a court is required, or constrained, simply to reach some permitted decision.

The reason model can be illustrated by assuming as background the case base $\Gamma_1 = \{c_1\}$, containing as its single member the familiar case $c_1 = X_1$, r_1, s_1 —where, again, $X_1 = \{f_1^\pi, f_2^\pi, f_1^\delta, f_2^\delta\}$, where $r_1 = \{f_1^\pi\} \to \pi$, and where $s_1 = \pi$. Suppose that, against this background, the court confronts the fresh situation $X_2 = \{f_1^\pi, f_2^\pi, f_1^\delta, f_2^\delta, f_3^\delta\}$, and considers finding for the defendant in this situation on the basis of the reason $\{f_1^\delta, f_2^\delta\}$, leading to the decision $c_2 = X_2$, r_2, s_2 where X_2 is as given earlier, where $r_2 = \{f_1^\delta, f_2^\delta\} \to \delta$, and where $s_2 = \delta$. Is this decision permitted, by the reason model?

Well, as we can see, $Premise(r_1) = \{f_1^\pi\}$, the reason for the decision in the initial case, holds in the new situation X_2 as well, since $\{f_1^\pi\} \subseteq X_2$. And, of course, the new reason $Premise(r_2) = \{f_1^\delta, f_2^\delta\}$ favours the defendant at least as strongly as itself—that is, $Premise(r_2) \subseteq Premise(r_2)$, or $Premise(r_2) \subseteq \{f_1^\delta, f_2^\delta\}$. It therefore follows from Definition 1 that c_2, the court's envisaged decision, would assign the reason $\{f_1^\delta, f_2^\delta\}$ for the defendant a higher priority than the reason $\{f_1^\pi\}$ for the plaintiff—that is, $\{f_1^\pi\} <_{c_2} \{f_1^\delta, f_2^\delta\}$. But Γ_1 already contains the case c_1, from which, in a similar fashion, we can derive the priority relation $\{f_1^\delta, f_2^\delta\}$ $<_{c_2} \{f_1^\pi\}$, telling us exactly the opposite. Since the augmented case base

$$\Gamma_2 = \Gamma_1 \cup \{c_2\}$$
$$= \{c_1, c_2\}$$

resulting from the court's envisaged decision contains both these cases, we would then have both $\{f_1^\delta, f_2^\delta\} <_{\Gamma_2} \{f_1^\pi\}$ and $\{f_1^\pi\} <_{\Gamma_2} \{f_1^\delta, f_2^\delta\}$ by Definition 2, so that, by Definition 3, this augmented case base would be inconsistent. By Definition 4, then, we can conclude that the court is not permitted to carry through with its plan of deciding for the defendant in the situation X_2 on the basis of the rule r_2, since c_2, the resulting decision, would introduce an inconsistency into the background case base.

Of course, it does not follow from the fact that the court cannot decide for the defendant in the situation $X_2 = \{f_1^\pi, f_2^\pi, f_1^\delta, f_2^\delta, f_3^\delta\}$ on the basis of the particular rule r_2 that it cannot decide for the defendant in this situation at all. Suppose, for example, that the court appeals to the reason $\{f_1^\delta, f_3^\delta\}$ to justify its decision for the defendant, leading to the case $c_3 = X_3$, r_3, s_3, where $X_3 = X_2$, where $r_3 = \{f_1^\delta, f_3^\delta\} \to \delta$, and where $s_3 = \delta$. The augmented case base

$$\Gamma_3 = \Gamma_1 \cup \{c_3\}$$
$$= \{c_1, c_3\}$$

resulting from this decision would then be consistent. As before, the previous case c_1 supports the priority $\{f_1^\delta, f_2^\delta\} <_{c_1} \{f_1^\pi\}$, and the new decision c_3 would now support the priority $\{f_1^\pi\} <_{c_3} \{f_1^\delta, f_3^\delta\}$, so that we would then have both the case base priorities $\{f_1^\delta, f_2^\delta\}$ $<_{\Gamma_3} \{f_1^\pi\}$ and $\{f_1^\pi\} <_{\Gamma_3} \{f_1^\delta, f_3^\delta\}$. But there is nothing inconsistent about this pair of priorities, as we can see, informally at least, with another homely example: one can easily imagine a teenager thinking, and thinking consistently, that going to the movies is more fun than

HOW DOES PRECEDENT CONSTRAIN? 193

going to the beach with their parents, but that going to the beach with their friends is more fun than going to the movies.

C. The Domestic Scenario

All of this has been very abstract. For a more concrete illustration, we return to the domestic example set out in section 1. The example centred around a situation in which Jack and Jo have two children: Emma, who has just turned nine, completed her chores, failed to finish her dinner, but completed her homework, and Max, aged twelve, who also completed his chores, but neither finished his dinner nor completed his homework. Both children wanted to stay up to watch TV. We imagined that Emma first asked Jo, who granted the request to watch TV, justifying her decision with the rule, 'Children aged nine or greater can stay up and watch TV.' Next, we imagined that Max asked Jack, who denied the request to watch TV, distinguishing this case from that of Emma by appeal to the fact that Max had failed to complete his homework, and introducing the new rule, 'Children who have not completed their homework cannot stay up and watch TV.'

With Max and Emma as plaintiffs, and with Jack and Jo functioning—as parents do—both as defendants and adjudicators, this scenario can be cast in our framework by letting the factor f_1^π represent the fact that the child in question is at least nine years old, by letting f_2^π represent the fact that the child in question completed chores, and then letting f_1^δ and f_2^δ represent, respectively, the facts that the child failed to finish their dinner and failed to complete their homework. The initial situation presented by Emma to Jo can then be represented as $X_4 = \{ f_1^\pi, f_2^\pi, f_1^\delta \}$, which Jo then decided for Emma on the basis of the rule $r_4 = \{ f_1^\pi \} \to \pi$, leading to the decision $c_4 = X_4, r_4, s_4$, where X_4 and r_4 are as given earlier, and where $s_4 = \pi$. As a result of this initial decision, the case base representing the common law of the household, at least as it pertains to staying up to watch TV, is $\Gamma_4 = \{c_4\}$, with $<_{\Gamma 4}$ as its associated ordering on reasons.

Next, the situation presented by Max to Jack can be represented as $X_5 = \{ f_1^\pi, f_2^\pi, f_1^\delta, f_2^\delta \}$. In keeping with our story, we can suppose that Jack would like to decide against Max on the basis of the rule $r_5 = \{ f_1^\delta \} \to \delta$, leading to the decision $c_5 = (X_5, r_5, s_5)$, where X_5 and r_5 are as given earlier, and where $s_5 = \delta$. Is he permitted to do so, according to the reason model, against the background of the case base Γ_4? The answer is yes. From Jo's earlier decision, we can conclude that the reason $\{ f_1^\pi \}$ is to be assigned a higher priority than the reason $\{ f_1^\delta \}$ —that $\{ f_1^\delta \} <_{c_4} \{ f_1^\pi \}$, so that $\{ f_1^\delta \} <_{\Gamma_4} \{ f_1^\pi \}$ as well. And Jack's decision would force us to conclude that the reason $\{ f_2^\delta \}$ must be assigned a higher priority than the reason $\{ f_2^\pi \}$— that $\{ f_2^\pi \} <_{c_5} \{ f_2^\delta \}$. But there is no conflict between this priority statement and the previous priority statement, derived from Jo's decision—a reasonable individual might, for example, prefer chocolate ice-cream to vanilla and vanilla to strawberry. And because the background case base Γ_4 currently contains only Jo's decision, it follows that Jack's decision in the case of Max is consistent with this case base as well. The reason model thus permits Jack to carry through with his decision, resulting in

$$\Gamma_5 = \Gamma_4 \cup \{c_5\}$$
$$= \{c_4, c_5\}$$

194 JOHN HORTY

as the updated case base now representing the household common law, with $<_{r_5}$ as its strengthened ordering on reasons.

4. The Real Mechanism of Constraint

A. The Alligator and the Ocelot

We now return to the third conceptual problem presented by the standard model of constraint—that, if distinguishing is allowed, then real constraint is impossible, since there will always be features available for future courts to use in distinguishing the situations they face from those confronted earlier, and in which earlier rules were formulated.

This problem is set out forcefully by Alexander and Sherwin, who illustrate the point with their story, adapted here, of the alligator and the ocelot.[9] Imagine, first, that Albert, as defendant, wishes to keep a pet alligator on his property, but that the local neighbourhood association, as plaintiff, brings suit against Albert asking him to remove the alligator on the grounds that it is a dangerous wild animal. Albert argues that he should be allowed to keep his alligator, since it resides on private property, but the court is not convinced, and justifies its decision for the plaintiff with the rule, 'Residents are not allowed to keep dangerous wild animals.' Next, suppose that another resident, Olive, acquires a pet ocelot, and the neighbourhood association again brings suit for removal. This time, however, imagine that the case comes before a court that is sympathetic to the ocelot, wishes to arrive at a decision for the defendant in the case at hand, but is aware that it must distinguish the current situation from the previous case of the alligator in order to do so. The court therefore notes that ocelots, but not alligators, are furry, and proceeds to distinguish on that basis, modifying the previous rule to read, 'Residents are not allowed to keep dangerous wild animals, unless they are furry', and, we might as well suppose, justifying its own decision for the plaintiff with the new rule, 'Residents are allowed to keep furry wild animals.'

By modifying the earlier rule in this way, the later court renders it inapplicable to the case of the ocelot, providing itself the freedom to decide the new case as it wishes, without constraint from the rule. And as Alexander and Sherwin emphasize, this instance of rule-modification satisfies the Raz/Simpson conditions, merely narrowing the previous rule, and narrowing it in such a way that the modified rule continues to support the decision arrived at in the previous case. The example thus highlights the fact that distinct cases can be differentiated in any number of ways, even if many of these differences are either entirely incidental or of only marginal importance—that one dangerous wild animal but not the other is furry, or that the defendant in one case but not the other has freckles, or plays the harmonica, or has an aunt living in Idaho. And if all a court needs to do in order to shield the decision it wishes to reach from some previous rule is to narrow that rule by appeal to one of these incidental or marginal differences, it really does begin to seem, from the perspective of the standard model, that the decisions reached in earlier cases cannot constrain later courts at all.

But let us look at the example more closely. Suppose the court considering Olive's ocelot actually does believe that the ocelot's furry nature provides a reason for allowing Olive to keep it on her property, and indeed a stronger reason than that provided for the opposite conclusion by the fact that it is a dangerous wild animal. In that case, it would be right, at

---

[9] See Alexander and Sherwin (n 1) 84–86.

least from an internal perspective, for the court to reach exactly the decision described in the example—that the new situation should be distinguished, and the ocelot allowed because it is furry. The court, after all, has an obligation to reach the decision it sincerely thinks is best.

What is so odd about this result, and what gives the example its force, is not some problem with the idea of distinguishing, but simply the assumption that the court might actually conclude, in all sincerity, that this particular decision is best—that the court could somehow conclude that the ocelot's furry nature, even if it is a reason at all, is a strong enough reason that it should outweigh important reasons favouring the other side. How could this conclusion be justified? Surely a court that reasoned its way to a conclusion like this would be subject to criticism, just as those who engage in poor reasoning in any other domain are criticized.[10]

And it is by focusing on this idea—that common law decisions require justification, or otherwise are subject to criticism—that we can locate a response to the objection that, if distinguishing is allowed, then any situation can be distinguished from any other, so that constraint is illusory. In fact, this line of response has already been explored by Simpson, who notes that when we ask whether or not a court can distinguish a case, we are not asking about the 'can' of human ability.[11] Instead, he writes, we are asking about the 'can' of permissibility. What we want to know is not just whether it is possible for a court to find some factual difference between two cases—of course it is—but whether, in distinguishing on the basis of this difference, the court's action will be seen as permissible, in the sense that the factual distinction highlighted by the court will be accepted as a justification for failing to follow a binding rule, or whether, instead, the court will be subject to criticism, by the standards at work in the legal system or in society at large:

> From this [factual difference] it does not follow that it is always permissible for a judge to distinguish a case; that he can do so whilst conforming to the rules of the legal system, or that he can do so without becoming liable to be criticized for having acted improperly. Distinguishing does not simply involve pointing out a factual distinction between two cases; it involves further the use of this factual distinction as a justification for refusal to follow the earlier case.[12]

It is important to emphasize, and to tease apart, two distinct notions of permissibility at work in this passage, and in Simpson's paper more generally. There is, first, a notion according to which a decision is permissible if it satisfies the relevant legal norms—it is this notion that is explicated by the reason model, which classifies a decision as permissible if it is consistent with the existing case base. But, secondly, there is also a notion according to which a decision is permissible if it can be justified by the standards of society at large. In the remainder of this chapter, I refer to the first of these notions of permissibility as 'formal permissibility' and to the second as 'social permissibility', and try to show how the real mechanism of constraint arises from an interplay between these two notions.[13]

---

[10] There is also the suggestion in Alexander and Sherwin's own presentation of the example that the court, by introducing the ocelot's furry nature as a consideration at all, is being disingenuous. But then, this move would be criticizable as well—not in the way that poor natural reasoning is criticized, but in the way that the misrepresentation of important information can be criticized.

[11] See Simpson (n 2).

[12] ibid 175.

[13] The contrast between formal and social permissibility, and its use here, is related to the distinction between doctrinal and social propositions, and to the use of this distinction, in Eisenberg (n 2).

B. Two Notions of Permissibility

We begin by coding the alligator/ocelot example in our representational framework, taking f_1^π as a factor, favouring the neighbourhood association as plaintiff, that a wild animal is dangerous, and taking f_1^δ as the factor, favouring the resident as defendant, that the wild animal is kept on private property. The initial situation presented by Albert's alligator, a dangerous wild animal kept on private property, is therefore represented as $X_6 = \{ f_1^\pi, f_1^\delta \}$. And let us assume that the background case base concerning animals in the neighbourhood is initially empty, so that the alligator poses a case of first impression.

Now suppose that, of the two conflicting reasons that hold in this situation, danger and private property—that is, $\{ f_1^\pi \}$ and $\{ f_1^\delta \}$—neither is generally recognized as more important than the other: the priority relation between these reasons is a matter about which reasonable people can disagree. Imagine, however, that the case of Albert's alligator comes before a court that, while recognizing the matter as one of legitimate disagreement, itself happens to assign greater priority to the danger posed by the alligator—imagine, that is, that this court prioritizes $\{ f_1^\pi \}$ over $\{ f_1^\delta \}$. Given its own priorities, we can suppose therefore that the court finds in favour of the plaintiff in the case of the alligator on the basis of its danger, leading to the decision $c_6 = X_6, r_6, s_6$ —where X_6 is as given earlier, where $r_6 = \{ f_1^\pi \} \rightarrow \pi$, and where $s_6 = \pi$—and resulting in $\Gamma_6 = \{c_6\}$ as the augmented case base on the issue.

In rendering this decision, the court introduces a legal proposition. This proposition, according to the reason model, is not a rule, like 'Residents are not allowed to keep dangerous wild animals', but instead a statement about the relative priority of various reasons—the proposition that, as a matter of law, danger as a reason for the plaintiff carries a higher priority than private property as a reason for the defendant, or that $\{ f_1^\delta \} <_{\Gamma_6} \{ f_1^\pi \}$. Since, in introducing this proposition into the law, the alligator court simply elevates its own particular opinion concerning the relative priority of reasons to the status of legal doctrine, it is necessary to ask whether this decision is permissible, in each of our two senses: is it socially permissible? Is it formally permissible?

The answer is that, at least given a certain sensible assumption, the decision is indeed socially permissible. We have already stipulated that the priority relation between danger and private property is a matter about which reasonable people can disagree. So all we need to assume—sensibly, it seems—is that it is socially permissible for a court to take some particular side on a contentious issue about which reasonable people can disagree. And, of course, the alligator court's decision is formally permissible as well, since the initial case base is empty and any decision at all is consistent with an empty case base.

Next, we turn to Olive's ocelot—like Albert's alligator, a dangerous wild animal kept on private property, but one that is, in addition, furry. In representing this example, we will assume that the ocelot's furry nature, here taken as f_2^δ, is a factor that favours the defendant, though very weakly. (Furry wild animals, especially large furry felines, tend to be beautiful in a way that, for most people, alligators are not; and we can assume that preservation of beauty in the neighbourhood is at least a weak reason for allowing the ocelot.) The situation presented by the ocelot is therefore $X_7 = \{ f_1^\pi, f_2^\pi, f_2^\delta \}$.

Since we have assumed that the priority between considerations of danger and private property is a matter about which reasonable people can disagree, let us now imagine that the ocelot case comes before a court that happens to prioritize property rights over danger—we imagine, that is, that this court, unlike the previous alligator court, prioritizes $\{ f_1^\delta \}$ over $\{ f_1^\pi \}$. Given its own priority ordering, the current ocelot court would prefer to find for the

HOW DOES PRECEDENT CONSTRAIN? 197

defendant on the basis of private property, leading to the decision $c_7 = X_7, r_7, s_7$, where X_7 is as given earlier, where $r_7 = \{ f_1^\delta \} \to \delta$, and where $s_7 = \delta$. And, of course, by an argument exactly parallel to that just offered for the alligator court, this decision, taken on its own, would have been socially permissible. Unfortunately for the ocelot court, however, it is not considering the new situation against the background of an empty case base, but against the background of the case base $\Gamma_6 = \{ c_6 \}$ containing the previous alligator decision. In this context, the ocelot court's preferred decision is not formally permissible, since it would introduce an inconsistency into the background case base—the new priority $\{ f_1^\pi \} <_{c_7} \{ f_1^\delta \}$ resulting from the ocelot court's preferred decision would conflict with derived priority $\{ f_1^\delta \} <_{\Gamma_6} \{ f_1^\pi \}$ already established in the case of the alligator.

The effect of the alligator decision, then, is to prevent, on formal grounds, the ocelot court from reaching a decision for the defendant in what would have been, from the social standpoint, the most straightforward and easily justifiable way, on the basis of private property. But does the court have another option? Yes, at least from a purely formal perspective. As Alexander and Sherwin suggest, the ocelot court might decide for the defendant on the grounds of the ocelot's furry nature, leading to the decision $c_8 = X_8, r_8, s_8$ —where $X_8 = X_7$, where $r_8 = \{ f_2^\delta \} \to \delta$, and where $s_8 = \delta$—resulting in $\Gamma_7 = \{ c_6, c_8 \}$ as an augmented case base. This new case base is consistent, so that the court's decision would be permissible by the formal standards of the reason model. But it is hard to imagine how such a decision by the ocelot court could ever be classified as socially permissible: the proposition that the court would then introduce into the law—that a furry nature as a reason for the defendant has higher priority than danger as a reason for the plaintiff, or $\{ f_1^\pi \} <_{\Gamma_7} \{ f_2^\delta \}$—is so peculiar that it would surely be subject to intense criticism on substantive grounds.

This particular example illustrates the general mechanism of common law constraint, which relies on two notions of permissibility that work together. Decisions must be both formally permissible and socially permissible—neither is sufficient alone. Without the requirement of social permissibility, nothing prevents the ocelot court from reaching the decision c_8, allowing Olive to keep her ocelot on the grounds that it is furry. But without the requirement of formal permissibility, nothing prevents the decision c_7, allowing Olive to keep her ocelot on the grounds that it is kept on private property—even though the ocelot is also dangerous, and it was already decided by the alligator court in c_6 that danger is prioritized over private property.

According to the reason model, then, earlier courts constrain later courts, not by preventing these later courts from reaching decisions for a particular side entirely through the application of formal standards, but by restricting the formally permissible decisions for that side to those that are more difficult to justify in a satisfactory way. Each decision settles the priority relations among certain reasons and so, on formal grounds, restricts later courts from making decisions that would introduce conflicting priorities. After a sufficient number of decisions have been reached, the formal priority relations among the important reasons in some domains are settled to the extent that—as in our example—it becomes difficult to distinguish later cases without introducing further claims of priority among reasons that are harder to justify on social grounds, and so more likely to be classified as socially impermissible.

15

Precedent, Contest, and Law

A Logocratic Agony That Fits

Scott Brewer

1. Introduction: Precedented Contests in Legal Argument

During the writing of this chapter, in *Dobbs v Jackson*,[1] the US Supreme Court overturned *Roe v Wade*,[2] a precedent that had stood for fifty years. The dissenting opinion in *Dobbs* quoted the opening sentence of an earlier dissent, Justice Thurgood Marshall's final opinion as a full sitting justice. Justice Marshall opened his dissent in *Payne v Tennessee* thus:

> Power, not reason, is the new currency of this Court's decisionmaking. Four Terms ago, a five-Justice majority of this Court held that 'victim impact' evidence of the type at issue in this case could not constitutionally be introduced during the penalty phase of a capital trial. *Booth v. Maryland*, 482 U.S. 496 ... (1987). By another 5–4 vote, a majority of this Court rebuffed an attack upon this ruling just two Terms ago. *South Carolina v. Gathers*, 490 U.S. 805... (1989). Nevertheless, having expressly invited respondent to renew the attack, 498 U.S. 1076 ... (1991), today's majority overrules *Booth* and *Gathers* and credits the dissenting views expressed in those cases. Neither the law nor the facts supporting *Booth* and *Gathers* underwent any change in the last four years. Only the personnel of this Court did.[3]

Justice Marshall's dichotomy of 'power' and 'reason' (echoing Lon Fuller's distinction of 'reason and fiat'[4]), however rhetorically attractive, neither offers nor relies upon a distinction that is defensible on the best understanding of the nature of legal argument.

According to the theory I present in this chapter, legal arguments from precedent, like all legal arguments, and indeed all arguments, take place in contests, and understanding the nature of these contests is the key to understanding legal precedential arguments. I shall refer to an explanation of some concept or phenomenon that sees a central role for contest as 'agonophilic' ('contest loving'). This chapter offers an agonophilic explanation of the nature of legal precedential argument. Such a theory well explains the argumental phenomena animating the dichotomy of 'power' and 'reason' that Justice Marshall advanced in *Payne* and that the dissent in *Dobbs* also invoked in quoting it. What is wanting in the dichotomy is a recognition that, in legal argument, 'reason', in the form of *arguments* (including but not limited to precedential arguments), is the instrument by which authorized legal officials

---

[1] *Dobbs v Jackson Women's Health Org* 597 US __ (2022).
[2] *Roe v Wade* 410 US 113 (1973).
[3] *Payne v Tennessee* 501 US 808, 844–45 (1991) (Marshall J, dissenting).
[4] LL Fuller, 'Reason and Fiat in Case Law' (1946) 59 Harv L Rev 376.

Scott Brewer, *Precedent, Contest, and Law* In: *Philosophical Foundations of Precedent*. Edited by: Timothy Endicott, Hafsteinn Dan Kristjánsson, and Sebastian Lewis, Oxford University Press. © Scott Brewer 2023. DOI: 10.1093/oso/9780192857248.003.0016

exercise the 'power' to make and remake law. The life of the law is power exercised by the instrument of argumental reason.

It's worth pausing briefly to note that agonophilic currents of argument and understanding course through thousands of years of culture. Heraclitus is perhaps the most obvious reference ('One should know that war is common, and justice strife; and that everything comes about in accordance with strife and what must be'),[5] but easily as important for the history of philosophy were the practices of the ancient Pyrrhonians (a great deal of philosophy is footnotes to Pyrrho), who made the generation of argument contests 'on any matter whatsoever'[6] the core of their practice of the flourishing life as that life seemed to them. Recognition of widespread political, social, moral, and religious contestation was also central to the teachings and theories of the Sophists, early philosophers and the first western professors of law.[7] Jumping millennia forward, Nietzsche offered thorough-goingly agonophilic explanations of the genealogy of morality specifically, and of philosophy, religion, and culture more generally, in his contentions that in the wake—literally (albeit figurally)—of the death of God, the route to human flourishing lay through the contests of (some select) human beings striving against others in various settings to reach great dancing play-filled heights of mastery and also within and against themselves to become *Übermenschen*. More recently still, and perhaps closest to the domain of legal theory that this volume inhabits, there is at least one prominent agonophilic conception of the concept of justice,[8] and agonophilic explanations of law are prominent among legal realists, so-called 'critical' legal scholars, and some other prominent jurisprudes.[9]

The agonophilic explanation I offer in this chapter relies on a theory of the nature of argument, the Logocratic Method (LM), that is itself energetically suffused with an agonophilic approach to argument, informed by precursory sources in other philosophical theories of argument and human cognitive practices.[10] I've offered the precise details of LM elsewhere,[11] and, within the prescribed scope of this chapter, I'll mention only those that are strictly needed to present cogently (I hope!) the logocratic agonophilic explanation of legal argument by precedent. In so doing, I'll provide a logocratic agony that fits the facts of legal argument by precedent.[12]

---

[5] εἰδέναι δὲ χρὴ τὸν πόλεμον ἐόντα ξυνόν, καὶ δίκην ἔριν, καὶ γινόμενα πάντα κατ᾽ ἔριν καὶ χρεών. I use the translation from J Barnes, *The Presocratic Philosophers* (rev edn, Routledge & Kegan Paul 1982) 45 (citing fragment B80).

[6] See S Empiricus, *Outlines of Skepticism* (J Annas and J Barnes eds, 2nd edn, CUP 2000) Book 1 ch 12.

[7] See R Waterfield, *The First Philosophers: The Presocratics and Sophists* (OUP 2000).

[8] See S Hampshire, *Justice is Conflict* (Princeton UP 2000); and, of course, the positions advanced by Thrasymachus in Plato, *The Republic* (D Lee and M Lane trs, Penguin 2007) and by Gorgias in Plato, *Gorgias* (W Hamilton and C Emlyn-Jones trs, Penguin 2004).

[9] See AA Leff, 'Unspeakable Ethics, Unnatural Law' [1979] Duke LJ 1229; RM Cover, 'Violence and the Word' (1986) 95 Yale LJ 1601, 1601 ('Legal interpretation takes place upon a field of pain and death').

[10] Briefly two Menschen: Stephen Toulmin's logic–jurisprudence analogy in SE Toulmin, *The Uses of Argument* (CUP 2003) 7–8 ('A sound argument, a well-grounded or firmly-backed claim, is one which will stand up to criticism, one for which a case can be presented coming up to the standard required if it is to deserve a favourable verdict'); and Wilfrid Sellars' inferentialist explanation of conceptual thinking in W Sellars, *In the Space of Reasons: Selected Essays of Wilfrid Sellars* (Harvard UP 2007) 374 ('[A]nything which can properly be called conceptual thinking can occur only within a framework of conceptual thinking in terms of which it can be criticized, supported, refuted, in short, evaluated').

[11] Two recent expositions are S Brewer, 'First Among Equals: Abduction in Legal Argument from a Logocratic Point of View' in M McBride and J Penner (eds), *New Essays on the Nature of Legal Reasoning* (1st edn, Hart 2022) and S Brewer, 'Logic and the Life of the Law (Professor): A Logocratic Lesson from Hohfeld' in S Balganesh, TM Sichelman, and HE Smith (eds), *Wesley Hohfeld A Century Later: Edited Work, Select Personal Papers, and Original Commentaries* (CUP 2022). An overview is in the earlier paper S Brewer, 'Interactive Virtue and Vice in Systems of Arguments: A Logocratic Analysis' (2020) 28 Artificial Intelligence and Law 151.

[12] Cf L Carroll, *The Hunting of the Snark: An Agony in Eight Fits* (J Tannis and J Dooley eds, William Kaufmann Inc 1981).

200 SCOTT BREWER

I present my theory in three main steps, anchoring it from the start in concrete, typical, and illustrative examples of legal reasoning by precedent in the Anglo-American tradition.[13] First, I introduce three closely related cases in US contract law, all decided by the Supreme Court of the US state of New Hampshire from 1974 to 1981. These cases, though presenting issues and argument contests that are perhaps not as dramatic as those found in *Payne* and *Dobbs*, nevertheless provide illuminating and exemplary (in both senses) illustrations of the agonophilic nature of legal precedential argument—of, that is, the use of argumental reason to exercise power. Secondly, I use these cases both to present and to illustrate what is, from a logocratic point of view, the correct explanation of the logical form of legal argument by precedent, namely, that the 'mode of logical inference' (in logocratic terms) that best models such arguments is abduction, and more specifically, legal abduction. Thirdly and finally, having presented the logocratic meta-abduction (abduction of abduction), I apply the model to the *Monge* trilogy to advance and exemplify the logocratic agonophilic abduction of legal argument by precedent.

2. Precedent *Monge*-ring: Contests over Employment-at-Will in US Contract Law

A. First Case in the *Monge* Trilogy: *Monge v Beebe Rubber Co*

In *Monge v Beebe Rubber Co*,[14] Olga Monge, a factory worker at the Beebe Rubber Company in New Hampshire (US), brought an action for breach of contract against her employer. She claimed that she had been fired because she had declined to accept her factory foreman's invitation to 'go out' with him. A long line of precedents, both in New Hampshire and in other US states, specified that an employee who was hired under a contract for an indefinite period of time was an 'employee-at-will'. These precedents also specified that all employees-at-will either could themselves quit, or could be fired—that is, such a quitting or firing would not constitute a breach of contract—for 'any reason,' that is, not only for cause. Despite having been hired for an indefinite period of time, and thus being an employee-at-will (or seeming to be; she seems to have challenged that classification of her status[15]), not only did she *not* lose her case in the early procedural stages as one might have expected, but her case went to trial and she won a jury verdict. Moreover, when the defendant company appealed, Olga Monge won a partial but substantial victory (or perhaps the other way around—the Supreme Court reduced the amount of damages the jury had awarded her by a little less than half) in a decision that divided the New Hampshire Supreme Court by a margin of three to one, with one of the usual five justices not sitting.

---

[13] My examples are from US law which, undoubtedly, has features that distinguish it from both civil law systems and the systems of some other common law jurisdictions. I believe, though I shall not argue in this chapter, that this account also well explains the nature or legal reasoning by precedent when it is deployed in other systems.

[14] *Monge v Beebe Rubber Co* 114 NH 130 (1974).

[15] One of her arguments was that hers was a satisfaction-clause contract (because she had been told that she would be promoted if she did a good job). Although the trial judge instructed the jury on this theory of the case, the Supreme Court whose arguments concern me did not accept or even mention this argument. We cannot tell from the record whether the jury accepted this argument.

PRECEDENT, CONTEST, AND LAW   201

B. Second Case in the *Monge* Trilogy: *Howard v Dorr Woolen Co*

Six years after Olga Monge's (partial) victory, the administrator of the estate of an employee of the Dorr Woolen Company brought a suit against the company, specifically arguing a claim for breach of contract under the *Monge* case, decided by the same court.[16] In an opinion unanimously endorsed by the five-member New Hampshire Supreme Court, Justice Bois substantially cut back on *Monge*'s expansion of employee protections, logically narrowing the *Monge* court's newly articulated rule and thereby also holding against the employee's estate administrator.[17]

C. Third Case in the *Monge* Trilogy: *Cloutier v The Great Atlantic & Pacific Tea Co*

One year after *Howard* and seven years after *Monge*, the New Hampshire Supreme Court decided *Cloutier*, in which a long-term employee brought an action against his employer for wrongful discharge.[18] Both *Monge* and *Howard* were authoritative precedents for *Cloutier*. A trial had resulted in victory for the employee. Centrally at issue in the losing defendant company's appeal to the state Supreme Court was whether the narrowing predicate that the *Howard* court read into the *Monge* precedent rule was satisfied by the trial court's jury instruction. A majority of three justices, outvoting one dissenting justice, made two rulings (described later) that supported the jury finding in favour of the employee. Not coincidentally, the one dissenting justice in *Cloutier*, Justice Bois, was the author of the majority opinion in *Howard*.

D. The Agonies of Argument in the *Monge* Trilogy

These cases illustrate and typify the contests that constitute legal arguments (and, understood properly, arguments more generally). There is a contest of arguments between plaintiff and defendant in each of the three cases, in each of which the contest is between an employee (or an employee's representative) and the company that employed him or her. In each case, the employee (or representative) uses the tool-weapon (all weapons are tools) of legal argument to try to establish the conclusion that he or she was entitled under the law to damages for breach of contract. Two of the cases, *Monge* and *Cloutier*, also exhibit argument contests among members of the appellate panel (the state Supreme Court) to which the cases had been appealed. (*Howard* was a unanimous decision.) One of the cases, *Monge*, also exhibits an argument contest between the appellate panel and the trial-judge-cum-jury, specifically regarding the amount of damages Olga Monge was due from her opponent, the Beebe Rubber Company, for breach of contract.[19] Finally, there was a clearly identifiable *axiological*

---

[16] *Howard v Dorr Woolen Co* 120 NH 295 (1980).

[17] The posture of the case at the New Hampshire Supreme Court was an interlocutory appeal from the trial judge's granting of the defendant company's motion to dismiss.

[18] *Cloutier v A & P Tea Co, Inc* 121 NH 915 (1981).

[19] Juries issue no official arguments to support their conclusions, but we do know what legal *conclusions*—conclusions of legal abductions—they endorse (see n 15), and it is with those conclusions that appellate courts can and do disagree, often also making inferences about the premises of the legal abductions whose conclusions juries endorse. The *Monge* majority did exactly that regarding the issue of the damages the jury awarded to Olga Monge.

202   SCOTT BREWER

contest—advanced by means of *argument* contests—among the New Hampshire Supreme Court justices both within and across the *Monge* trilogy cases. A concise genealogy of that axiological-argument contest is as follows.

(i)   Pre-*Monge*: very broad power of an employer to terminate an employee under the employment-at-will rule

Before *Monge*, for many years in New Hampshire (and many other US states), an employment contract that did not specify a duration was presumed to be 'at will', which meant that the employer could fire the employee, and the employee could quit 'at any time ... regardless of motive for "good cause, bad cause or no cause" and for "any reason" ',[20] without either legal agent thereby committing breach of contract. This rule is referred to as the *employment-at-will* rule.

(ii)   *Monge*: narrowing employment-at-will rule to prohibit firings in bad faith, malice, or retaliation

The *Monge* Supreme Court majority, contesting against one dissenting justice and citing two non-New Hampshire cases and a law review article, explicitly narrowed the scope of the employer's power to fire an employee:

> We hold that a termination by the employer of a contract of employment at will which is motivated by bad faith or malice or based on retaliation is not the best interest of the economic system or the public good and constitutes a breach of the employment contract.[21]

(iii)   Post-*Monge*: *Howard*, narrowing *Monge*'s expansion of employee protection from firing

Howard, reading *Monge* as an authoritative precedent, significantly narrowed the scope of *Monge*'s limitation on the employer's legal (Hohfeldian) power to terminate. This narrowing re-broadened the scope of the employer's termination power. Using argument by disanalogy within a legal abduction (see section 3.B), a unanimous *Howard* court 'construe[d] Monge to apply only to a situation where an employee is discharged because he performed an act that public policy would encourage, or refused to do that which public policy would condemn'.[22] Thus, from a logical point of view (specifically, using the grammar of truth-functional propositional deduction), whereas the *Monge* majority adopted a new authoritative rule under which an employee could show breach of contract by an employer who had fired her in bad faith or in malice or in retaliation (i.e. these were disjointly sufficient conditions[23]), after *Howard*, an employee had to show *both* that he was fired for one of those disjointly sufficient conditions *and* that he was fired 'because he performed an act that public policy would encourage, or refused to do that which public policy would condemn'.

---

[20] See *Monge* (n 14).

[21] ibid 133.

[22] *Howard* (n 16) 297.

[23] The court seems to have presupposed, or perhaps mandated, that there are no internal inferential connections among these three predicates, such that, e.g., every malicious firing is in bad faith, or vice versa. Both the *Cloutier* and *Howard* courts also seem to have assumed—contrary to a plausible intuition—that being fired *for* doing (or refusing to do) something that public policy required (or prohibited) was *not* a sufficient condition for being fired in retaliation. Otherwise there would be no need for the two prongs of the rule that *Cloutier* specified in light of *Monge* and *Howard*.

PRECEDENT, CONTEST, AND LAW   203

(iv) Post-*Howard*: *Cloutier* offers a more employee-friendly interpretation of the
      Howard narrowing condition

Only one year after the unanimous decision in *Howard*, a divided New Hampshire Supreme
Court in *Cloutier v Great Atlantic & Pacific Tea Co*, reading both *Monge* and *Howard* as authoritative precedents,[24] gave an employee-friendly reading of *Howard*'s narrowing condition on *Monge*, thereby expanding employee protections that *Howard had narrowed*, though
not to the extent of *Monge*'s original protections. Specifically, the *Cloutier* majority contested
two arguments offered by the dissenting justices. First, the majority rejected the dissent's
argument that the 'public policy' that *Howard* specified (recall that *Howard* required an employee who sought the protection of the *Monge* rule must show that she was fired because
she had 'performed an act that public policy would encourage, or refused to do that which
public policy would condemn') could be established only by evidence from a statute. For the
Cloutier majority, the public policy could be evidenced by common law as well.[25] Second, the
Cloutier majority rejected the position that a jury was *not* competent to determine whether
the requisite public policy existed.[26]

(v) Precedential arguments in the *Monge* trilogy

Arguments from precedent are central to all three cases in the *Monge* trilogy, as follows:

Precedents operating in the arguments of Monge

1. The long-standing employment-at-will precedent that the *Monge* majority significantly narrowed.
2. *Kline v Burns*,[27] a New Hampshire case decided three years before *Monge*—and written,
   one must note, by the same justice (Justice Lampron) who wrote the majority opinion
   in *Monge*. *Kline* is a *tenancy*-at-will case in which the court changed then-existing precedent by adopting an implied warranty of habitability and also establishing a tenant-
   friendly measure of damages for breach of that warranty.
3. *Sargent v Ross*,[28] decided with no dissents and one concurrence in the result one year
   before *Monge*. *Sargent* is also a landlord–tenant case and held a landlord responsible for
   the death of a four-year-old girl, a tenant, under the newly adopted rule requiring that,
   'A landlord must act as a reasonable person under all of the circumstances including
   the likelihood of injury to others, the probable seriousness of such injuries, and the
   burden of reducing or avoiding the risk.'
4. *Frampton v Central Indiana Gas Co* and *Petermann v International Brotherhood*,[29] on
   both of which the *Monge* majority relied in arguing for the new rule the court adopted
   limiting the scope of an employer's power to terminate, despite the fact that neither
   was a New Hampshire case. The dissenting justice in *Monge* argued against the relevance of both cases.

---

[24] See *Cloutier* (n 18) 920.
[25] ibid 922.
[26] ibid 924.
[27] *Kline v Burns* 111 NH 87 (1971).
[28] *Sargent v Ross* 113 NH 388 (1973).
[29] *Frampton v Central Indiana Gas Co* 297 NE2d 425 (Ind 1973); *Petermann v International Brotherhood* 344 P2d
25, 27 (Cal Dis Ct App 1959).

204 SCOTT BREWER

Precedents operating in the arguments of Howard
For the purposes of my analysis, by far the most important precedent for *Howard* is *Monge* itself. As noted, the unanimous opinion in *Howard* 'construes' *Monge* in such a way as to impose an additional requirement on any employee who sought *Monge*'s protection. The opinion does also cite two precedent cases, neither from New Hampshire, to illustrate the kinds of circumstances the opinion regards as the proper limitation on *Monge*.

Precedents operating in the arguments of Cloutier
For the purposes of my analysis, *Monge* and *Howard* are the most important precedents for *Cloutier*. Additionally, *Cloutier* is, like *Monge*, a divided opinion, with interesting realignments compared to *Howard* and *Monge*. The sole dissenter in *Cloutier* is Justice Bois, the very same author of the *Howard* opinion that, as we've noticed, significantly limited the protections that *Monge* had provided. Majority and dissent both cite several precedents each to support their contesting contract-axiologies (see discussion in section 4).

3. The Unprecedented Logocratic Abduction of Abduction

I turn now to presenting the model of abduction that is central to my explanation of legal precedential argument. This model does a good deal of work in my argument in this chapter, providing an explanation of the general structure of abduction (an abduction *of* abduction) as well as two specific types of abduction that are important for understanding legal precedential argument: legal abduction, and interpretive abduction.

A. The Logocratic Enterprise-Conception of Explanation

Abduction is a type of argument, and *argument* is defined (in logocratic theory) as a set of premises that are or could be offered to provide evidential support for a set of conclusions.[30]

A successful meta-abduction—abduction of abduction—must have or rely on some cogent conception of the speech-act of explanation. Central to the logocratic account of abduction is an account of explanation as the application of a *point of view*. Abductive reasoners invoke points of view, sometimes explicitly, always at least implicitly, to try to justify some claim either about what one (or a group) ought to believe (a theoretical claim) or about how one (or a group) ought to act (a practical claim). Each claim is thus explicitly or implicitly a claim that a certain belief or course of action is justified. The logocratic account of abduction fashions and relies upon an *enterprise conception* of a *point of view*. This conception posits that an intellectual enterprise that produces distinctive justificatory claims may be dissected into three separate components: (i) *factual judgments*; (ii) the distinctive *methods* that the enterprise uses to generate those factual judgments; and (iii) the distinctive *axiological aims* that the methods are chosen to advance and serve. The logocratic *enterprise conception of point of view* provides this specification of the identity criteria for an individual point of view:

---

[30] For discussion of the 'chiasmic' relation of evidence and argument—argument is evidence and evidence is argument—see Brewer, 'First Among Equals' (n 11). Note that LM keeps rigidly separate the identification and the evaluation of arguments.

The *point of view* of enterprise E consists of the factual judgements, produced by the methodological rules, that are adopted to serve the axiological goals of E.

It is a matter for philosophical–anthropological empirical investigation[31] to determine, for actual abductive enterprises—in law, science, morality, philosophy, religion, and politics—what the participants and, as it were, administrators of those enterprises, accept as the axiological–cognitive aims, the methods used to serve those aims, and the factual judgments that issue from application of those methods. Practitioners within a single abductive enterprise will sometimes contest claims about *who is a member of the enterprise*, as well as judgments about what are the proper methods of the enterprise, what are its proper axiological aims, and what factual judgments are properly produced by applications of the methods chosen to serve the aims. Thus, abductive reasoners within a single enterprise can and do share beliefs about the methods, axiological aims, and factual judgments of the enterprise, but they also can and do disagree among themselves about any one or all three of these components. Larry Laudan, from whose model of scientific explanation, consensus, and dissensus the LM of abduction draws, calls attention to the fact of disagreements among scientists and philosophers of science about the methods, aims, and factual judgments of science. There is, to take one example, an identifiable *philosophical point of view*, but it is also clear that there are agreements among some and disagreements among others about what are the proper methods, aims, and judgments of the enterprise of philosophy. These disagreements surface not only in the sometimes-splashier contests between so-called 'analytic' and 'continental' philosophers[32] but also among members within each side of this divide—for example, among analytic philosophers who believe that philosophical methods, axiological–cognitive aims, and judgments should not countenance abstract entities, and those who reject such scruples.[33] Similarly, there are debates among legal philosophers about the nature of legal philosophy. From a logocratic point of view, these are debates about the proper aims, or the proper methods, or the proper factual judgments issuing from the methods of legal philosophy, and they occupy a central part of jurisprudence (e.g. contesting theories of Natural Law and Legal Positivism).

B. Goals, Purposes, and Truth

The logocratic meta-abduction shares with most accounts of abduction its structure as an argument that contains three types of premises offered as support for one type of conclusion. The argument begins with the articulation of some phenomenon to be explained, an *explanandum*. This serves as the first premise of the argument, often in the form of one complex proposition comprised of a conjunction of component propositions. The second premise is a statement of one or more hypotheses that might *explain* the phenomenon whose explanation the abducer seeks to provide. With one very important departure, LM accepts part of

---

[31] I understand philosophical anthropology to be a type of philosophical abduction that explores and explains the conceptual relations and commitments of the contingent methods of reasoning of cognitive agents. The domain of pragmatics is one type of this kind of inquiry, focusing on linguistic practices. The LM focuses even more specifically on one type of linguistic practice, the practice of making arguments.

[32] See, e.g., the discussion in R Moati, *Derrida/ Searle: Deconstruction and Ordinary Language* (T Attanucci and M Chun trs, Columbia UP 2014).

[33] See, e.g., I Scheffler, *Beyond the Letter: A Philosophical Inquiry into Ambiguity, Vagueness, and Metaphor in Language* (Routledge & Kegan Paul 1979).

206   SCOTT BREWER

the basic conception of the inferential process operating in abduction that Gilbert Harman (along with Charles Peirce, one of the pioneers of the study of abduction) articulated in his pioneering work:

> In making this inference one infers, from the fact that a certain hypothesis would explain the evidence, to the truth of that hypothesis. In general, there will be several hypotheses which might explain the evidence, so one must be able to reject all such alternative hypotheses before one is warranted in making the inference. Thus one infers, from the premise that a given hypothesis would provide a 'better' explanation for the evidence than would any other hypothesis, to the conclusion that the given hypothesis is true.[34]

Third, there is a step in the abductive argument in which such competing hypotheses as the abductive reasoner believes worthy of consideration (those that are in the reasoner's judgment, *serviceably plausible*—see the later discussion) are evaluated, some being rejected, leaving one hypothesis as the explanation that the abductive reasoner endorses.

Despite sharing the view that abductions contain these three types of propositions, LM differs substantially from many conceptions and discussions of this logical form, including Harman's conception just noted, in four principal ways.

First, taking the form to be, as Harman conceives it, an inference to an explanation that is 'best' among several possibly competing explanations of a given *explanandum*, the logocratic (and proto-logocratic) theory of abduction has always maintained that it is a condition of adequacy on any account of this logical form that it provide an accompanying account of what it is to explain. The LM has developed and defended the view that all explanations are offered from a *point of view* that has the identity criteria noted earlier (section 3.A). Second, LM's explanation of both abduction and of the concept of explanation is rooted in pragmatics, emphasizing the context-dependency of abduction as a type of speech-act (the speech-act of arguing to an explanation). Third, one structural feature of this context-dependency is described by a network of intensional concepts—interests, purposes, goals, and values—that I refer to as *axiological aims*, which vary from arguer to arguer. Fourth, the choice of which of the possible alternative explanations an arguer actively considers, and also the judgment of which of those alternatives she consider to be the best among those considered, are also a function of the arguer's axiological aims. The upshot of this difference is that, in the logocratic view, the inference in an abduction is not to the explanation that is most likely to be *true* (as Harman conceives it) but instead the explanation that best serves the arguer's axiological aims.

LM thus explicates abduction-cum-inference to the best explanation as being guided by a norm that directs abductive arguers to consider only those alternative hypotheses that are *serviceably plausible* given their axiological aims. This is a slight but improving and clarifying sharpening of the concept of 'plausibility' that is found in much of the literature on abduction and has also been central to prior logocratic accounts of abduction. It connects to the process of abduction the axiological-aim relativity of explanations on which LM relies. It also provides a criterion, surely crucial to any adequate conception of abduction, of the criteria of 'bestness', namely, best according to the abductive arguer's axiological aims. (For example, in legal abduction, what is best from the point of view of a plaintiff is different from what is best from the point of view of a defendant, and, as I shall discuss later, what is best

---

[34] GH Harman, 'The Inference to the Best Explanation' (1965) 74 Philosophical Rev 88, 89.

from the point of view of a 'romantic' contracts judge is different from what is best from the point of view of a 'classical' contracts judge—see section 4.)

In its account of abduction, LM recognizes both reason and emotion (the common colloquial sense of these two terms will suffice for my present purposes) as among the axiological goals that operate to guide abductions. The ever-growing literatures on motivated and other kinds of tribe-and-affect-driven reasoning[35] suggest that an account of explanatory arguments, and arguments in general, that is not sensitive to the driving force of affect in argument generally, and abductive arguments specifically, suffers considerably in explanatory scope and power.[36]

One consequence of this model of abduction is the contention that abductive reasoners sometimes, but by no means always, choose and follow axiological aims that include a norm requiring production of only factual claims that are true. In a nutshell, there are many instances in which an abductive arguer seeks to produce an argument for a conclusion that will be accepted by the judge (what LM calls the 'dialectical-rhetorical referee') of an abductive argument but whose conclusion the abductive reasoner does not himself accept or to whose truth or likely truth he is indifferent. There are several important examples of settings of abductive argument in which the abductive reasoner offers an argument with an axiological aim other than truth-telling, such as garnering votes (LM models the dialectical–rhetorical referee of elections as the electorates to whom abductive arguments are made by the candidates regarding, for example, why the candidate or his policies are the best among those of the electoral contestants) or winning a litigative contest (LM models the dialectical–rhetorical referee of litigation as the judge or the judge along with a jury in a division of legal decision-making authority guided by rules). This kind of argument behaviour is not rare, and it may be a type of argumental speech-act behaviour that neither obeys the Gricean conversational implicature maxim of quality (don't say what you know to be false or that for which you lack relevant evidence) nor flouts the maxim in a way that will be evident to the audience.[37] (Donald Trump, to take but one example, seems quite often to offer explanations that neither obey nor flout the quality maxim and other of the Gricean maxims, where he is seeking to achieve litigative or electoral success and the norms of the explanations—the abductions—he offers are often insensitive to empirical warrant.[38])

C. Interpretive Abduction

The logocratic model of abduction recognizes interpretation as one of the distinctive logical species of abduction—*interpretive* abduction—which is a central part of *legal* abduction

---

[35] To toe-dip in the vast pool: DM Kahan, 'Ideology, Motivated Reasoning, and Cognitive Reflection' (2013) 8 Judgment and Decision Making 407; Z Kunda, 'The Case for Motivated Reasoning' (1990) 108 Psychological Bulletin 480.

[36] Peirce offers a suggestive abduction of emotion as abduction: 'Now, when our nervous system is excited in a complicated way, there being a relation between the elements of the excitation, the result is a single harmonious disturbance which I call an emotion. Thus, the various sounds made by the instruments of an orchestra strike upon the ear, and the result is a peculiar musical emotion, quite distinct from the sounds themselves. *This emotion is essentially the same thing as an hypothetic inference, and every hypothetic inference involves the formation of such an emotion.*' C Sanders Peirce, *The Collected Papers of Charles Sanders Peirce*, vol 1 (C Harthsorne and P Weiss eds, Harvard UP 1931) para 2.643 (emphasis added).

[37] See HP Grice, 'Logic and Conversation' in JL Morgan, P Cole, and P Grice (eds), *Syntax and Semantics 3: Speech Acts* (Academic Press 1975).

[38] See the vast assembly of examples documented and collected in The Washington Post Fact Checker Staff, *Donald Trump and His Assault on Truth: The President's Falsehoods, Misleading Claims and Flat-Out Lies* (Scribner 2020).

208   SCOTT BREWER

generally and legal argument by precedent specifically. Recall that the logocratic model of abduction presented earlier maintains that explanations are always offered from a point of view that has a three-part structure: (i) factual judgments; (ii) the distinctive methods that the enterprise uses to generate those factual judgments (methodological rules); and (iii) the distinctive axiological goals that the methods are chosen to advance and serve. On the logocratic account of *interpretive abduction*, interpretation is a dyadic relation between a text being interpreted (an *interpretandum*) and a text doing the interpretation (the *interpretans*). The predicate for the dyadic relation is, *is the meaning of*. To take a simple example, if the *interpretandum* is

(1) Reading the *Tractatus Logico-Philosophicus* is no day at the beach

we might offer

(2) Reading the *Tractatus Logico-Philosophicus* is not easy and pleasant but is instead stressful and difficult

as the *interpretans*, where our justificatory claim in offering (2) as the interpretation of (1) is that (2) is the meaning of (1). On the logocratic model of interpretive abduction, the *interpretandum* is the *explanandum* and the *interpretans* is the *explanans*. On this model of interpretive abduction:

- The factual judgments interpreters make are their statements (to others or to themselves) of the meaning of texts being interpreted—that is, the *interpretantia* (*explanantia*) that are the conclusions of their interpretive abductions.
- The distinctive methods that interpreters use to generate those factual judgments are many and varied among interpreters and contexts of interpretation. These methods are discovered by the empirical study of interpreters' interpretive behaviour, one domain of the broader study of *argumental* behaviour in the philosophical anthropology of argument that comprises the LM. The previously mentioned example (regarding reading the *Tractatus*) resorts to interpreting (1) metaphorically. By contrast, a method of literal interpretation would read (1) as a literal assertion that reading the *Tractatus* is not a day at the beach (a so-called twice-true metaphor—if the sentence is true under the metaphorical interpretation—true both literally and metaphorically[39]). Among the common methods interpreters use are interpreting literally, interpreting figuratively (treating texts, e.g., as metaphors, metonyms, synecdoches, or other tropes), and interpreting in accord with the intent of a text's author or authors (and there are typical methods for doing this depending on the context and the author—typical methods, for example, of interpreting in accord with legislative intent). One noteworthy and quite common method of interpreting vague predicates in authoritative legal texts is by using argument by analogy.[40]

---

[39] *Pace* Davidson's claim that there is no distinctive metaphorical meaning. See D Davidson, 'What Metaphors Mean' in D Davidson (ed), *Inquiries into Truth and Interpretation* (OUP 1981).

[40] See the discussion in S Brewer, 'Exemplary Reasoning: Semantics, Pragmatics, and the Rational Force of Legal Argument by Analogy' (1996) 109 Harv L Rev 923, 937–38, 962–63. For details of the logocratic account of the role of analogy within interpretive abduction (an instance of the 'dynamic interactive virtue' of arguments), see S Brewer, 'Interactive Virtue and Vice in Systems of Arguments: A Logocratic Analysis' (2019) 28 Artificial Intelligence and Law 151; Brewer, 'First Among Equals' (n 11).

- Just as the methods of interpretive abduction vary from interpreter to interpreter and from context to context of interpretation, so also the axiological goals interpreters choose to advance and serve are many and varied among interpreters and contexts of interpretation. In some domains of interpretation, including the domain of legal interpretation, there are ongoing debates about which methods of interpretation are appropriate for interpretation in that domain. Here one finds, for example, debates about the appropriacy of literal interpretation vs interpretation in accord with the intent of the author vs purposive or teleological interpretation.

As claimed, *interpretive* abduction is a vital part of *legal* abduction—that is, in the application of potentially applicable authoritative legal texts to actual or hypothetical fact patterns. Interpretive abduction also plays a vital role within the logocratic analysis of arguments more generally. The core of LM is the *identification* and the *evaluation* of arguments. The identification step, which necessarily (logically) precedes the evaluation step, consists of the interpretation—the interpretive abduction, the explanation of the meaning—of the natural language texts that is the medium of the argument that is to be evaluated at a later stage. To explain this step of interpretive reasoning, LM has developed and relied upon a conception of the enthymeme that extends and adapts the classical conception of the enthymeme (a syllogism with one or another of its three steps unexpressed but assumed). On the logocratic conception, enthymemes are of two basic types (logical species). One is the *rule-enthymeme*, the other, the *argument-enthymeme*. The defining feature (the logical genus) of both types is this: an enthymeme is a sentence (for rule-enthymemes) or set of sentences (for argument-enthymemes) *whose logical form is not explicit in its original* mode of presentation. Both occur in natural languages in whatever is the domain of argument. When the domain is legal argument, the 'mode of presentation' of rule-enthymemes are such sources as statutes, administrative regulations, constitutional provisions, executive orders (in the US legal system at least), judicial opinions, official or unofficial compendia of legal rules such as the US *Restatements* series, lawyers' briefs, scholars' publications. The 'mode of presentation' of argument-enthymemes includes several of these sources as well, especially judicial opinions, lawyers' briefs, and scholars' publications and students' proffers in papers and exams.

The interpretive process central to LM's evaluative procedure is giving a *fair formal representation* to the rule-enthymemes (for rule-driven argument-enthymemes, including but not limited to legal arguments) and argument-enthymemes. Here LM relies on an *interpretive* axiological aim, a particular version of the principle of charity. Importantly, this is not the influential version one finds in work in philosophy of language, philosophy of mind, and epistemology, including variants in the content of the norm such as *interpret or translate what the person says and does so as to make the person as rational as possible* (David Lewis, Richard Grandy, and Donald Davidson) and *interpret so as to make the interpreted text 'the best it can be'* (Ronald Dworkin). By contrast, relying on a trenchant critique by Robert Nozick of these formulations of the norm, LM is committed to the axiological aim within interpretive abduction of a version of the principle of charity that directs the interpreter (interpretive abducer) of a rule-enthymeme or argument-enthymeme to interpret it so as to make as intelligible as possible the fact that in that context that person (or persons) promulgating the rule or making the argument promulgated it or made it. This accords well with the leading role of pragmatics in the logocratic approach to the interpretation of rules and arguments. By contrast to this axiological interpretive norm, the 'maximize agreement' (or 'maximize rationality') norm would, for example, seem always to counsel that one find another way to interpret an argument-enthymeme if it seemed prima facie that it might be

210   SCOTT BREWER

offering a deductively invalid argument. But some arguers (actual or hypothesized[41]) do offer argument-enthymemes that are accurately represented as invalid, and a principle of fair formal representation should not hide that possibility.[42]

One other logocratic adaptation of the concept of the enthymeme is worth mentioning, namely, the distinction between *specific* enthymemicity and *structural* enthymemicity. *Specific* enthymemicity is the phenomenon in which a rule-enthymeme or argument-enthymeme occurs in a natural language text (such as judicial opinion, statute, lawyer's brief) and the interpreter's task is to give a fair formal representation to *that* specific enthymeme. *Structural* enthymemicity is the phenomenon in which the theorist addresses the question, what is the structure of enthymematic arguments *in general*? So, for example, one interesting debate engaged by American legal realists is whether legal arguments *in general* are properly represented as deductions (some legal realists have argued, albeit not always clearly, that the answer is *no*, whereas LM argues that the answer is *yes*). This very chapter, whose topic is the best understanding of the logical form of legal precedential argument, is a sustained exercise in *structural enthymemicity*, maintaining that, in general, legal arguments from precedent are best interpreted as inferential steps within legal abductions. More generally, many of LM's core distinctive ideas are (philosophical-abductive) arguments about structural enthymemicity. The distinctive LM claims, for example that all abductive arguments and all analogical arguments have within them an inferential step within either of induction or deduction, and that all inductive arguments also include an inferential step of abduction,[43] are both claims about structural enthymemicity.

4. The Agonies of Legal Precedential Argument, From a Logocratic Point of View

On the logocratic view, abduction ramifies and proliferates—a reason for treating it as 'first among equals' in the four modes of logical inference.[44] The foregoing logocratic meta-abduction (abduction of abduction) now allows me to abduce legal argument by precedent as itself part of abduction, and to do so in a way that also explains, agonophically (see section 1), the role of contest in such arguments.

Recall that on the Logocratic enterprise conception of abduction (see section 3.A), abduction is an inference to the most serviceably plausible explanation from a point of view that is structured in three steps: (i) assertion of *factual judgments* specific to the domain of the enterprise within which the abduction is being made (thus, empirical facts when the enterprise is explanation from an empirical point of view, legal facts when the enterprise is explanation from a legal point of view, Hohfeldian facts with the enterprise is explanation

---

[41] LM's definition of 'argument', see text at n 31, allows that one might seek to make sense of a hypothetical arguer when giving a fair formal representation of a rule-enthymeme or argument enthymeme, although very often a logocratic analyst is applying the norm to an actual judge or lawyer who has uttered that argument enthymeme.

[42] The version of the principle of charity on which Dworkin relies in *Law's Empire*, which his central to his theory of 'law as interpretation', conflates interpretation (on the LM view, stating the meaning of a text) with advocacy.

[43] See Brewer, 'Interactive Virtue' (n 11); Brewer, 'First Among Equals' (n 11); see text at n 41. I cannot within this chapter's scope explain in detail why this does not occasion any problems of vicious circularity. I can, though, point to my reliance on the vital contention by Bryan Skyrms that: 'Deductive and inductive logic are not distinguished by the different types of arguments with which they deal, but by the different standards against which they evaluate arguments.' B Skyrms, *Choice and Chance: An Introduction to Inductive Logic* (4th edn, Wadsworth 2000) 22.

[44] As characterized in Brewer, 'First Among Equals' (n 11).

from a Hohfeldian point of view, moral facts when the enterprise is explanation from a moral point of view, and so on for every distinctive realm of explanation[45]); (ii) factual judgments are produced by the distinctive *methods* of the enterprise within which the abductive arguer offers the abduction; which methods are in turn chosen to serve (iii) the distinctive *axiological aims* of the enterprise, *as understood by the individual abductive reasoner*. This last qualification is vital to the *agonophilic* explanation of abduction in general, legal abduction specifically, and legal argument from precedent which always operates within legal abduction, still more specifically. Contest is always possible in principle, and very often occurs actually, at each abductive step. Larry Laudan, whose model of scientific explanation LM adapts to its account of the basic structure of abduction, aims to provide a model of scientific explanation that allows one to explain two facts—they seem to be facts—about the behaviour of scientists in offering scientific explanations: they sometimes agree (achieve consensus) and sometimes disagree (encounter dissensus). Laudan argues, cogently, that some models of scientific explanation (such as those of Feyerabend and Kuhn) cannot well explain *both* of these observed scientific explanatory behaviours, whereas his model can. But in providing an explanation of agreement Laudan does not try to explain away disagreement, dissensus, or, as I might characterize the same phenomenon, *contest* among scientific abducers. As noted earlier, Laudan calls attention to the fact of disagreements among scientists and philosophers of science about the methods, aims, and factual judgments of science.[46]

And, as Laudan also acknowledges, even scientists using the same methods, chosen to serve the same cognitive aims, can and do disagree on the factual judgments that those methods produce. Thus, to take an example that straddles scientific explanation and legal fact-finding, two geneticists called as expert witnesses might (there are many examples in which they do) use the same methods to arrive at competing factual judgments about the provenance of a given DNA sample.

What are examples of the kinds of factual judgments, methods, and cognitive aims that comprise legal abduction? In the *Monge* case (within the *Monge* trilogy, see section 2.D), there were two factual judgments. One was that the employer had (in fact) breached its contract with Olga Monge. The other was that the jury had (in fact) given an improperly large damages award to her for the company's breach. In *Howard*, the factual judgment was that the employer had not breached its contract of employment with the (deceased) employee on whose behalf the administrator brought the contracts action. In *Dobbs* (see opening discussion in section 1), the factual judgment (or one of the central ones) of the majority is that the US Constitution provides no right of abortion.

Here at last we arrive at the logocratic explanation of legal argument from precedent. Among the *methods* that comprise legal abductions in modern legal systems in which precedents are authoritative sources of law are the identification and (inextricably related)

---

[45] LM endorses a disquotational conception of the truth predicate, so that the factual judgment is logically equivalent to an assertion of the proposition, and those are assertions of fact. Thus, in identifying 'moral facts' as the conclusion of a given moral abduction (explanation from a moral point of view), this account neither presupposes nor is committed to moral realism. To offer a factual judgment from a moral point of view is to assert some moral proposition, for example 'slavery is wrong', as true, which is equivalent to asserting that slavery is wrong. Cf J Raz, *Practical Reason and Norms* (2nd edn, OUP 1999) 18 ('By "fact" is meant simply that which can be designated by the use of the operator "The fact that …" In this sense facts are not contrasted with values, but include them'). Meta-ethical commitments and disagreements among moral theorists, occur at both the level of moral methods— e.g. application of a categorial imperative vs application of a principle of utility vs application of phronesic virtue-judgments—and the level of axiological aims endorsed and relied on by these competing moral abductive arguers. The same is true for the abductions offered from the point of view of different religions.

[46] See, e.g., L Laudan, *Science and Values: The Aims of Science and Their Role in Scientific Debate* (University of California Press 1984) 138.

interpretive abductions of authoritative texts, principally, cases (precedents), statutes, administrative regulations, constitutions, and in some systems (such as in US law) executive orders, *and* also cases that interpret each of those sources. Thus, for example, *Howard* used the tool of reasoning by disanalogy as part of its interpretive abduction to read and narrow the rule the *Monge* court had articulated, while *Cloutier* read both *Monge* and *Howard* to offer a limitation on employers' power to fire employees that is closer to the broadened protections *Monge* had offered and that *Howard* sought to limit. (See sections 2.D.(ii), 2.D.(iii), 2.D.(iv).)

The *Monge* trilogy also exhibits the *contests of axiological aims* that typify legal abductive arguments in US contract law, and properly understood it also exemplifies the kinds of contests that comprise legal abductions in other doctrinal areas. A cogent philosophical–anthropological investigation[47] of the argument practices of American contract law judges reveals that they may usefully be sorted into two main 'tribes' with regard to the axiological goals that they use legal methods to serve. Fairly tracking the literature of US contract jurisprudence, I label one set of rationales 'classical' and the competing set of rationales 'romantic'. A judge who endorses classical axiological goals in his contract law legal abductions relies on a strong presumption that the parties should be given very wide latitude to arrange their contractual deals themselves, without modification by judges; presumes against using the tools of contract law legal abduction to redress inequalities between the parties to a contract (such as inequalities in bargaining power, information, and resources); and similarly presumes against reallocating the risk that a more or less literal interpretation of the transaction has imposed on the parties. By contrast—and contest—judges who endorse romantic axiological goals in their contract law legal abductions give much narrower latitude to the parties to arrange their contractual deals themselves without modification by judges; are quite ready to use the tools of contract legal abduction to redress inequalities between the parties to a contract; and are quite ready to reallocate the risk that a more or less literal interpretation of the transaction has imposed on the parties, including by resorting to non-literal interpretations of the terms of the transaction.

The *Monge* trilogy pellucidly displays the classical–romantic contest of axiological values. The long-standing employment-at-will rule reflects a paradigmatically classical contracts axiology. The *Monge* majority opinion used its legal abduction, in a manner that paradigmatically relies on a romantic contracts axiology, both to *narrow* the broad classical employment-at-will rule and also, and thereby, to contest against the classically oriented dissenting opinion. *Howard*, decided only a few years after *Monge*, relied in its legal abduction on classical contract axiology to narrow the expanded protections *Monge* had offered. And then *Cloutier*, decided a few years after *Howard*, relied on a romantic contract law axiology to re-expand the limits on an employer's power to terminate an employee.

The contest of axiological values displayed by the *Monge* trilogy is obviously specific to the doctrinal domain of contract. But contests at all three levels of legal abduction—factual judgments, both selection and application of methods, and selection and reliance of axiological aims—pervade legal abductions in all legal systems and include contestable and actually contested judgments about matters including proper judicial role, the ways in which a

---

[47] See n 32 for my conception of philosophical anthropology.

rule of law is to be preserved and heeded, and norms and methods more specifically linked to different doctrinal areas of law.

It is in this way that legal arguments from precedent, as one central method of legal abduction, exhibit the Logocratic-Heraclitan truth about law: for better and worse, law is argument, argument is contest, and precedential arguments are potent weapons in the contests that give law its life.

16

Dog Law

On the Logical Structure (or Lack Thereof) of *Distinguishing*

Bruno Celano

[T]he act of hanging, for example, is no definition of the act of stealing, and ... a blow which is given to a dog (for here dogs and men are put upon the same footing) is no lesson to the dog who is in the next yard, or to the whelp that will have been begotten by one of them a year hence.[1]

1. Introduction

Imagine you are at an intersection, and there is a traffic light. Usually (or 'under normal conditions'), if the traffic light is red, then you ought to stop. But what if an ambulance, sirens wailing, suddenly arrives behind you?

This is, in a nutshell, the problem I shall be discussing in this chapter.

A central issue both for the theory of law and for legal practice is whether, or to what extent, the law is *certain*, in the sense of being *predetermined*: given a case, we already know in advance how it ought to be decided—what the correct judgment is, how the case ought to be resolved (which normative solution is the right one, to be adopted by the relevant decision-maker)—according to the law.

In the *civil law*, legal certainty is supposed to be ensured by authoritative texts, containing canonical formulations of the norms which ought to be applied ('legal provisions').

In the *common law*, we find a further institutional device, *binding precedent* (*stare decisis*): later cases of the same type as previous ones ought to be decided in the same way.

In both the civil and the common law, the crucial condition, as far as the predetermination of the decision which ought to be adopted is concerned, is that the norm to be applied in later, future, cases remains the same (I shall call this the 'identity—*scil* of the norm to be applied—condition'): the condition, that is, that the norm to be applied has a definite identity, and it remains the same on each and every later decision-making (judgment, application) occasion. Or perhaps, even when the norm to be applied in later cases is different from the one which was applied in the previous case, may we at least say that the initial norm changes only *partially*, not in its entirety? (Some authors claim that, in such cases, later decision makers *specify* the initial norm. Or, in other words, later decision-makers apply the same norm, adapting it, however, to novel, more specific, cases as these come under their consideration.)

---

[1] J Bentham, *Of Laws in General* (Bloomsbury 1970) 184.

Bruno Celano, Dog Law In: *Philosophical Foundations of Precedent*. Edited by: Timothy Endicott, Hafsteinn Dan Kristjánsson, and Sebastian Lewis, Oxford University Press. © Bruno Celano 2023. DOI: 10.1093/oso/9780192857248.003.0017

I said that in the civil law legal certainty is supposed to be ensured by canonical formulations of the norms to be applied. It is well known, however, that things are not quite so simple: problems of interpretation of the canonical formulations arise, leading to interpretative conflicts; interpreters find a rich repertoire of interpretative strategies, techniques, and arguments available to them; they invoke doctrines and dogmatic constructions; they indulge in ingenious, sometimes reckless, interpretative acrobatics. The outcome of these operations is far from being predetermined.

In the common law, I said, legal certainty is supposed to be ensured, instead, by binding precedent. In this case too, however, things are not so simple, for at least two reasons.

(1) Interpretative problems arise here, too. What is binding for later judges is the norm on the basis of which the former case was decided, which is its *ratio decidendi*. But— and here is where problems arise—how are we supposed to extract the *ratio decidendi* from the text of a decision?[2]

(2) A further problem arises with regard to the identity condition: precedent is binding, true, but later judges have the power (i.e. they are empowered and authorized) to *distinguish* the case at hand from the previous case—i.e. later decision-makers have the power, and are authorized, to adopt, in the case at hand, a decision which is different from—and incompatible with—the decision adopted in the previous case.

The requirement of conforming to precedent (*stare decisis*) is typically understood in fact as a disjunctive obligation: *either* follow the precedent *or* distinguish the case at hand from the previous one.

2. Distinguishing: A First Approximation

What is *distinguishing*? As a first approximation: a later judge decides a new case of the same kind as a previous case in a different way.[3]

What sort of argumentative acrobatics is this? At first sight, it looks like pure and simple judicial arbitrariness, that is, pure and simple creation of law *ex nihilo*. Is it really so?

The principle underlying the requirement of *stare decisis* is that similar cases (that is, cases of the same type) ought to be treated in the same way (i.e. they should be decided in the same way). But which cases are similar?

Given any two cases, it is always possible to find respects in which they are similar, and respects in which they are not. An example: male adultery vs female adultery; adultery committed by a human being weighing less than 200 pounds vs adultery committed by a human being weighing more than 200 pounds. Are these four cases similar—of the same type—or not? In one respect, yes: they are all cases of adultery. In other respects—the sex or weight of the adulterous party—they are different.

---

[2] In principle, the formulation of the norm expressed in the text of the previous decision is not itself binding on later decision-makers.

[3] It makes no difference, for present purposes, whether it is the same judge deciding two or more individual cases on different occasions, or different judges are involved. In particular, I shall not consider relationships of superordination or subordination of one court with respect to another.

216   BRUNO CELANO

The problem therefore is this: similar cases ought to be decided in the same way; thus, if the case at hand and the previous case are similar, they must be decided in the same way. However, there are never two *absolutely* similar (i.e. identical: the same in every respect) cases. Given any two cases, the issue is whether their traits of similarity or dissimilarity are *normatively* (or, specifically, *legally*) *relevant*—that is, whether they should make a difference as far as the solution to be adopted is concerned—or not.

For example, is the gender of the adulterous party a normatively relevant trait? It is not difficult to imagine a patriarchal society in which only female adultery, but not male adultery, is a crime. Is the weight of the adulterous party a normatively relevant trait? Imagine a healthist society, in which overweight people are treated unfavourably. Adultery committed by an overweight person, male or female, is a crime. Adultery committed by a slim person is not. Finally, we can easily imagine a social context in which the 'adultery' trait is not, in general, regarded as normatively relevant.

The judgment—the *correct* judgment (the issue we are discussing is, recall, normative) — depends, in short, on which properties of the cases under consideration are normatively relevant; that is, which properties should make a difference as to the decision that ought to be adopted in each case.

The basic idea—the *rationale*—underlying the practice of *distinguishing* is this: a later judge has the power, and is authorized, to adopt, in the case at hand (i.e., the case they now have to decide), a solution which is different from, and incompatible with, the one adopted in the previous case, *if* and *because* the case at hand presents, compared to the previous one, new properties that are normatively relevant and justify a solution different from, and incompatible with, the solution adopted in the previous case. For this reason, some authors argue, this is not pure and simple arbitrariness, or pure and simple creation of law *ex nihilo*. At most, some claim, in such cases later decision-makers progressively specify, determine, the initial norm, so as to adapt it to the new circumstances (this stance is usually called 'specificationism').

But which properties are normatively relevant? Is a judge's decision to treat some properties as irrelevant, while treating others as relevant, arbitrary? Can it be other than arbitrary?

There is, according to some authors, one constraint at least: later judges cannot—that is, they are not empowered or permitted to—treat as irrelevant properties that were deemed relevant by the previous judge; nor can they treat as relevant properties that were deemed irrelevant by the previous judge.

This is in fact a constraint. But how stringent a constraint is it?

This is, specifically, the problem I want to discuss: whether, and to what extent, where precedents are binding and *distinguishing* is practised, the law is certain, or predetermined.

More precisely, the question is, in later cases, does the norm to be applied remain the same, or not? And if it changes, does it change entirely, or only in part (by a progressive specification of the initial norm)?

The problem does not only affect the common law. According to some authors, this—*distinguishing*—is the way in which constitutional courts proceed (or they can only, or even ought to, proceed) whenever they, as it is usually said, 'balance' constitutional norms (in particular when they balance principles, which confer rights), which conflict with each other.[4]

---

[4] But, one may wonder (Timothy Endicott wonders, thanks to him for this remark), how could *distinguishing* be the way in which constitutional courts proceed (or they can only, or even ought to, proceed), if constitutional courts are not under the obligation of respecting precedent? My reply is this: true, but the logical structure (or lack thereof) is, it seems to me, the same in the two cases.

And, as is well known, this balancing of conflicting constitutional norms is a widespread phenomenon—and one of the utmost importance, both theoretical and practical.

3. Definitions and Assumptions

Let me introduce some definitions, and a few (hopefully non-controversial) assumptions.

(1) *Conditional proposition*: a proposition having the form 'if … then …' ('if p, then q').

(2) *Norm (Normative conditional)*: a conditional proposition, which connects to a generic case, the condition (or 'antecedent'), a normative solution, as a consequence (the 'consequent'): 'if p, then it is Obligatory to do A' ('if p, then OA', where the letter 'A' designates a generic action; for instance, 'if the traffic light is red, then it is obligatory to stop').

(3) *Normative solution*: roughly, the deontic characterization of a certain generic action— that is, its characterization as Obligatory, Forbidden, or Permitted: OA, FA, PA (or, indifferently, Op, Fp, Pp, where lowercase letters designate propositions).[5]

(4) *Obligatory, Forbidden*, and *Permitted* are the basic *deontic modalities*. These are inter- definable: each one of them can—with the aid of negation (designated by the tilde, '~')—express the other two.

(a) Definitions in terms of the Obligatory:

$$Fp = df. \ O \sim p$$
$$Pp = df. \sim O \sim p$$

(b) Definitions in terms of the Permitted:

$$Op = df. \sim P \sim p$$
$$Fp = df. \sim Pp$$

Note that this use of 'Permitted' —the standard definition of permission in deontic logic— diverges from common usage: Permitted (in this sense) to do A is compatible with Obligatory to do A (i.e. permission is not, as it is usually said, 'bilateral'). The conjunction of the permission to do and the permission not to do one and the same action is a fourth deontic modality, the *Optional* (bilateral permission).

(5) The so-called *square of opposition* (Figure 16.1) illustrates some of the main logical relationships between deontic modalities—and therefore between norms. In particular this diagram illustrates two types of normative conflicts (conflicts between norms): conflicts between contrary and between contradictory norms.

---

[5] The distinction between *Tun-Sollen* (ought-to-do) and *Sein-Sollen* (ought-to-be) norms is irrelevant for our purposes.

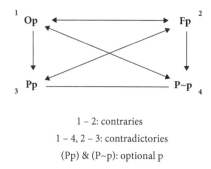

1 – 2: contraries
1 – 4, 2 – 3: contradictories
(Pp) & (P~p): optional p

Figure 16.1 The square of opposition

Two contrary or contradictory norms are *logically inconsistent* (I shall call such conflicts 'antinomies'). Roughly, two norms are logically inconsistent if and only if they cannot be jointly satisfied: there is no possible world in which both the actions they prescribe are performed.[6] (By 'satisfaction' of a permission, I mean the performance of the action, or the omission, which is permitted.[7])

(6) Let's go back to the notion of norm (or normative conditional): 'If p, then OA.' For our purposes, it is irrelevant whether legal norms are conceived as directives addressed to the application organs, prescribing to them the adoption, under certain conditions, of certain measures (e.g. the imposition of a certain sanction), or they are conceived, instead, as directives addressed to citizens, or to those who are subject to the legal system, generally, characterizing their behaviour as Obligatory, Forbidden, or Permitted.

We may understand—this, too, makes no difference for our purposes—the conditions (the antecedent), which a norm connects a normative solution to, both as—and this is what we have done so far—atomic or molecular propositions (designated by lowercase letters: p, q, z, etc, and their combinations), and as generic cases (C, where appropriate indexed with a number: Cn) defined by sets of normatively relevant properties (designated by capital letters: P, Q, Z, etc, and their combinations).

We thus obtain an alternative representation of the same normative conditional: 'if C(P), then OA.'

(7) In a conditional proposition the antecedent *implies* the consequent. It is possible to distinguish different implication relationships. In standard logic (by 'logic' I mean the

---

[6] R Barcan Marcus 'Moral Dilemmas and Consistency' (1980) in CW Gowans (ed), *Moral Dilemmas* (OUP 1987).
[7] Here's why, a few lines earlier, I said 'roughly'. The definition of a logical inconsistency between norms (antinomy) which I just gave in the text entails that the permission to do A and the permission not to do A are logically inconsistent, and their conjunction—the Optional—is an antinomy. (On this point, I am indebted to Giulia Sajeva.) This is obviously wrong. It is therefore necessary to amend the definition. One could say: two norms are logically inconsistent (antinomic) if and only if (1) at least one of the two norms is a norm in terms of obligation (be it positive or negative—Forbidden), and (2) they cannot be jointly satisfied. Permissions are never in an—intrasubjective—conflict. On the possibility of intersubjective normative conflicts, see B Celano, 'Col senno di poi. Perplessità, elucubrazioni, ritrattazioni (poche, non molto importanti, tranne una) e repliche' in P Luque Sánchez and MM Muñoz (eds), *Discutendo con Bruno Celano* (Marcial Pons 2020) s 5.4.3.3, with references.

theory of deductively valid inferences[8]) implication is expressed by (or, better, some of these different relationships are expressed by) *logical connectives*.

(8) The weakest logical connective for the representation of a conditional proposition is *material implication* ('⊃'): 'if p, then q' is represented as 'p ⊃ q'.

Material implication is defined by the following property: a proposition that has this logical form is false if and only if p is true and q is false. In every other model—that is, for any other possible attribution of a truth-value to the propositions p and q (p and q both true, or both false, or p false and q true)—it is true.

For our purposes, it will not be necessary to look at other forms of implication in logic (e.g. so-called 'strict implication': roughly, the consequent *necessarily* follows from the antecedent). What is of interest for us is, specifically, two properties that implication relationships possess in (standard) logic.

(9) Implication in (standard) logic—that is, implication as a (standard) logical connective—satisfies two conditions.

(a) It may be applied by *modus ponens* ('p ⊃ q; p; therefore, q') or by *subsumption* of an individual (an individual entity) under the concept—that is, by inclusion of an individual in the set—which is the antecedent of the conditional.

Examples: (i) 'if it rains, then it is windy; it is raining; therefore, it is windy' (*modus ponens*); (ii) 'all stars emit light; the Sun is a star; therefore the Sun emits light' (subsumption).

That *modus ponens* is a scheme of deductively valid inferences means that in inferences having this form (i.e. if the premises are true, then the conclusion is also true) the conclusion is predetermined, certain: given the premises, the conclusion is given, too. The same is true of those deductively valid inferences, such as the one just given ('all stars …'), which hinge on the subsumption of an individual under a concept (i.e. on the inclusion of an individual entity in a set).

(b) Implication in (standard) logic conforms to the law of *antecedent strengthening*:

$$p \supset q$$
$$\dots \dots \dots$$
$$(p \,\&\, z) \supset q$$

(The dotted line represents the 'therefore': the propositions above the line are the premises, the proposition below the line is the conclusion. The symbol '&' stands for *conjunction*: the conjunction of two atomic propositions, p, q, is a molecular proposition—p & q—which is true if and only if both conjuncts, p and q, are true.)

That is, given a deductively valid inference, if we add to the set of its premises any other premise, the resulting, new set of premises, too, implies the conclusion.

For example, given the conditional 'if it rains, then it is windy' we can validly infer that 'if it rains, and the Moon is round, then it is windy'.

---

[8] An inference is deductively valid if and only if, if the premises are true, then the conclusion is also true; it is not the case that the premises are true and the conclusion false.

220 BRUNO CELANO

(10) We can now transpose implication, understood as a (standard) logical connective, to normative discourse: 'p ⊃ OA' (or alternative representation—earlier, in this section, *sub* (6)—'C(P) ⊃ OA').[9]

(11) Normative conditionals too—if they are expressed, or expressible, through (standard) logical connectives (i.e. if they are understood as the expression of an implication relationship according to standard logic)—satisfy the two conditions indicated earlier.

(a) They may be applied by *modus ponens*, or by subsumption of an individual case under the generic case which is the antecedent of the norm. Roughly: 'if the traffic light is red, then it is obligatory to stop; the traffic light is red; therefore it is obligatory to stop' (*modus ponens*); 'if someone commits a theft, then he should be punished with n years of imprisonment; John has committed a theft; therefore John should be punished with n years of imprisonment' (subsumption).

(b) Antecedent strengthening: given the norm 'if the traffic light is red, then it is obligatory to stop', we can validly infer that 'if the traffic light is red, and the Moon is round, then it is obligatory to stop'.

Normative conditionals which meet these two conditions predetermine the normative solution to be adopted in all subsequent cases of the same type—in all cases, that is, that instantiate the antecedent of the conditional (or in all individual cases which can be subsumed under the generic case which is the antecedent of the norm). In other words, given the norm, and given the facts of the case at hand, we already know what the normative solution to be adopted in the case at hand is.

4. The Structure of Distinguishing

Let us now use these notions, these assumptions, and these symbols to represent the structure of *distinguishing*. Consider Figure 16.2.

In this tree diagram, each numbered circle (each 'node') represents a case (an individual 'decision-making occasion'). To each one of these cases the normative conditional is to be applied (recall that we are talking about *correct* normative solutions according to the law), the antecedent of which is the set of conditions (in this case propositions) to the left of the circle, and whose consequent is the normative solution specified to the right of the circle.

This is the structure of *distinguishing*. To fix ideas: (1) (*First node*) here we are at the intersection; the traffic light is red (p); therefore it is obligatory to stop (OA). (2) (*Second node*) Here we are at the intersection, once again; this time, too, the traffic light is red (p); this time, however, an ambulance, sirens wailing, suddenly arrives behind us (q); therefore it is permitted not to stop (P~A). (3) (*Third node*) Again, the intersection; again, the traffic light is red (p); this time, however, no ambulance with sirens wailing suddenly arrives behind us (~q); therefore it is obligatory to stop. (4) We are at the intersection for the fourth time; the

---

[9] There is, in deontic logic circles, a long-standing controversy about whether the logical form of conditional norms should be represented by the formula in the text, 'p ⊃ Oq' (the so-called 'narrow scope'—*scil* of the deontic operator—rendering) or by the formula 'O(p ⊃ q)' (the 'wide scope' rendering). Thanks to José Juan Moreso for reminding me of this complication. Fortunately, we do not have to settle this issue here, for two interrelated reasons. (I shall simply state them, rather dogmatically; a discussion would require a lengthy and, I believe, useless digression.) First, the argument to be presented in the following pages might be restated—albeit rather clumsily—in terms of the wide scope rendering. Secondly, the wide scope reading is, in crucial respects, quite counter-intuitive.

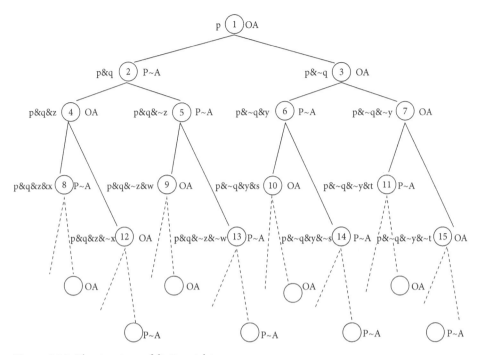

Figure 16.2 The structure of distinguishing

traffic light, as usual, is red (p); suddenly, an ambulance arrives behind us, sirens wailing (q); this time, however, there is, in front of us, an elderly lady who is crossing the street (z) —if we do not stop, we would most likely hit her; therefore it is obligatory to stop. (5) Here we are at the intersection for the fifth time; the traffic light is red (p); an ambulance suddenly arrives behind us, sirens wailing (q); this time, however, no old lady is there (~z); therefore it is permitted not to stop (P~A). (6) The same intersection, for the sixth time; the traffic light, unfortunately, is red (p); no ambulance suddenly arrives behind us (~q); but this time we are chased by a killer, who is about to reach us (y); therefore it is permitted not to stop. (7) The same intersection, once again; the traffic light is red (p); no ambulance suddenly arrives behind us (~q); no killer is chasing us (~y); therefore it is obligatory to stop. (8) The usual intersection, the traffic light is red (p) (*I have the feeling of having been here before*); an ambulance suddenly arrives behind us, sirens wailing (q); an elderly lady, in front of us, is crossing the street (z); this time, however, a fire truck suddenly arrives behind us, engaged in a rescue operation that will save many human lives (x); therefore it is permitted not to stop. (12) (*Twelfth node*) Twelfth time: the intersection, red light (p) (*here we are, stuck by this river*); ambulance (q); elderly lady (z); but this time no fire truck arrives (~x); therefore it is obligatory to stop. (9) I remember, however, that a few days ago I found myself (it was the ninth time, if I am not mistaken) at this intersection; the traffic light was red (p); there was an ambulance, sirens wailing behind me (q); there was no old lady crossing the street (~z); there was, however, a fire truck that was coming to the intersection from my right, sirens wailing (w); therefore OA. (13) And here we are at the intersection for the thirteenth time; for the thirteenth time, the traffic light is red (p); there is an ambulance behind us (q); there is no elderly lady who is crossing the street in front of us (~z); there is no fire truck that is coming to the intersection on our right (~w); therefore it is permitted not to stop. (10) Now let's go back to the possible world where the traffic light is red (p) (*we will never get out of this room*), but there is no

222 BRUNO CELANO

ambulance with sirens wailing behind us (~q); also this time (the tenth time we arrive at the intersection) a killer is about to reach us (y); but there are schoolboys crossing the street in front of us (s); therefore we ought to stop. (14) This time, the fourteenth, everything is like a few days ago—the tenth time we arrived at this intersection—only that the schoolboys are not there (~s); therefore it is permitted not to stop. (11) Red light (p), no ambulance (~q), no killer threatening us (~y), but this time we are in pursuit of a UFO, which is quickly moving in the direction of the White House (everything suggests that the aliens want to kidnap the President) (t); therefore it is permitted not to stop. This time again (*node 16*), however, the traffic light is red (p), there is no ambulance behind us (~q), no killer (~y), there are no aliens (~t); therefore we ought to stop, and wait patiently for the green light. And so on. (*How many more times will we find ourselves at this intersection, in front of this red light? But is it really, then, the same intersection, and the same traffic light? And are we—have we been, will we be, will we have been—the same?*[10])

An analogous phenomenon occurs in descriptive discourse.[11]

1. If I strike this dry, well-made match, then it will light. $(p \supset q)$
2. If p and the match is in a very strong electromagnetic field, then it will not light. $(p \& r \supset \sim q)$
3. If p and r and the match is in a Faraday cage, then it will light. $(p \& r \& s \supset q)$
4. If p and r and s and the room is evacuated of oxygen, then it will not light. $(p \& r \& s \& t \supset \sim q)$

Now consider the diagram in Figure 16.3 (it is the same decision tree).

The diagram in Figure 16.3 differs from the diagram in Figure 16.2 in that it uses the alternative representation of applicable norms, which was introduced in section 3 (6)): the antecedent is represented as a generic case, defined by a set of properties ('Cn(P , Q)').

Note that, in this diagram—as, indeed, in the previous diagram (Figure 16.2)—each subsequent case (Cn) logically implies (by material implication) the initial case (C1). (Whatever else happens in a case when there is a red light at the intersection—ambulances, old ladies crossing the street, schoolboys, aliens—any subsequent case is still a red-light case.) Or, in other words, any subsequent case, Cn, is an instance of the initial case, C1: it falls under it. It would follow—were the implication of the consequent by the antecedent one of the implication relationships in (standard) logic (a relationship, i.e. expressible through one of the standard logical connectives: material implication, strict implication, or other) —that the normative solution to be adopted for the initial case, C1, should be adopted also in any subsequent case, Cn.

It is easily seen, however (consider Figures 16.2 and 16.3 once again), that in *distinguishing*, things are different. Given any node, the normative solution adopted, and to be adopted, in many of the subsequent cases is different from, and incompatible with, the normative solution adopted, and to be adopted, in the preceding cases. The two diagrams represent antinomies by contradiction only. But we could easily integrate them by adding branches that lead to contrary normative solutions. For example, if the traffic light is red and there is an ambulance with sirens wailing behind us (case number 2), then it is not only permitted but also obligatory to stop.

---

[10] At this point, the reader may have the impression of being *l'année dernière à Marienbad*.
[11] RB Brandom, *Articulating Reasons. An Introduction to Inferentialism* (Harvard UP 2001) 88.

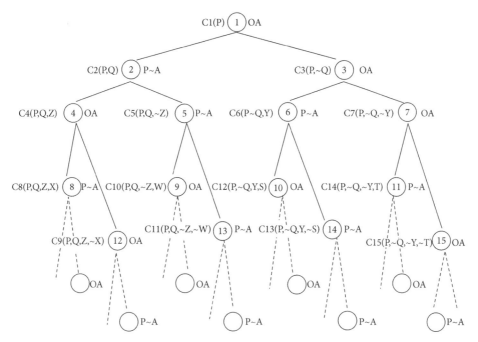

Figure 16.3 The structure of distinguishing, using the alternative representation of applicable norms

In particular, in *distinguishing* the normative conditionals (i.e. the norms), applied and to be applied, in each case differ from conditionals expressible through one of the (standard) logical connectives (implication in standard logic; section 3 (8)) in a crucial respect: they do not satisfy the two conditions (application by *modus ponens* or subsumption; antecedent strengthening) which, as we have seen, characterize implication in (standard) logic.

Keeping the latter consideration in mind, let us finally consider the diagram in Figure 16.4.

It is, once again, the same decision tree; and, indeed, the same diagram as in Figure 16.3. The only difference is that '(successive) decision levels' are now marked, by Roman numerals.

Note that at each decision level, cases—C2, C3, and so on—of the same type as the initial case, C1 (i.e. cases that logically imply, or are an instance of, C1), have different, and antinomic, normative solutions. The same holds of the relationship between each case, Cn, and subsequent cases, Cn + m, in each of the branches of the tree.

Two questions arise. When we go down along the different branches of this tree, introducing exception after exception—moving, that is, in the series of subsequent cases of the same kind (in the sense specified earlier: cases which imply, or are instances of, the initial case) from one decision-making level to the next—reversing from time to time, thanks to the detection of new normatively relevant properties of novel cases, the normative solution for the case at hand (jumping, that is, from one normative solution to the contradictory—or, it may easily be imagined, contrary—normative solution); when we do this:

(1) Is there any plausible sense in which we are applying the same norm—that is, adopting the same normative solution, or at least compatible normative solutions—for subsequent instances of the initial case (or in general the norms at upper decision levels)? Recall the first question posed earlier (when I introduced the 'identity condition' in section 1): are we, in subsequent cases, applying the same norm?

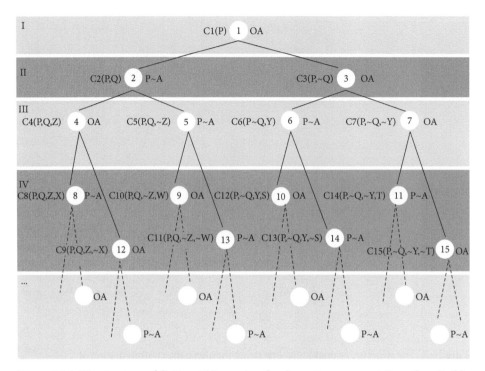

Figure 16.4 The structure of distinguishing, using the alternative representation of applicable norms and with '(successive) decision levels' marked by Roman numerals

(2) Is there any plausible sense in which we can say that, by distinguishing (in proceeding, that is, as indicated earlier), we are progressively specifying one and the same norm, adapting it to new circumstances as they arise?

Recall the second question posed in section 1: granting that, in subsequent cases, the norm does not remain the same, but changes, does it change entirely or only in part?

It seems to me that the answer to both questions is negative: we are not applying the same norm, nor are we progressively specifying the initial one. What happens is, trivially, this: node after node, we change our mind, as new circumstances arise, as to how cases of a given kind—cases, that is, falling under the antecedent of the initial norm (cases that logically imply, or are instances of, the initial case), or, in general, under the antecedent of the previous norms (i.e. those at the previous decision-making level: the norms adopted, and to be adopted, in previous decision-making occasions) along the same branch of the tree—should be decided (what the normative solution is, i.e. to be connected to cases of that kind), substituting old norms with new, less general, ones, some of which are incompatible with the former ones. We leave the initial norm behind us (at each subsequent node, we leave the previous norm behind us), proceeding in no definite direction (*no direction home*), at the mercy of contingencies—when new normatively relevant properties present themselves in unexpected new generic cases.

More precisely: if the set of normatively relevant properties (i.e. which items are included in the set of normatively relevant properties) for any given normative conditional is finite and predetermined, or at least predeterminable, then we shall have a finite number of decision levels, and once we reach the lowest decision-making level we shall finally have a finite set of *fully detailed* norms—that is, norms whose antecedent is fully specified, and, thus, can be applied by *modus ponens*, or by subsumption. If not—if, that is, the set of normatively relevant properties is neither predetermined nor predeterminable—we will go *ad infinitum*: we will never reach a fully detailed (in the sense just defined) norm, predetermining the normative solution to be adopted in subsequent cases of the same type (i.e. cases which fall under its antecedent); to be applied as new cases of the same type present themselves on subsequent decision-making occasions, by *modus ponens* or subsumption (a conditional proposition, i.e. expressible through one of the standard logical connectives).

In sum: if the set of normatively relevant properties is 'open'—that is, not susceptible of being previously delimited: neither predetermined nor predeterminable—what we are doing, node after node, proceeding from one decision level to the next is in fact replacing the previous norms with new, less general, norms. Indeed, as I said a few lines earlier, we left the initial norm behind us (at decision level after decision level we leave behind us the norms at the immediately superior decision level), proceeding in no definite direction (*no direction home*), at the mercy of contingencies—when new normatively relevant properties present themselves in unexpected new generic cases.

5. Conclusion

Recall our problem (section 2): can we say that, in a legal system where precedents are binding and *distinguishing* is practised (and, if this is in fact the way in which constitutional courts proceed in constitutional democracies, in constitutional adjudication), the normative solution to be adopted by the relevant decision-maker in subsequent cases which are instances of the initial case—or, in general, of the previous cases—is predetermined, or at least partially predetermined (specificationism)? Or is this pure and simple arbitrariness, or pure and simple creation of law *ex nihilo*?

At this point, you, the reader, can judge for yourself.[12]

6. *Coda*

But, it will now be objected,[13] in common law jurisdictions normative generalizations embodied in lines of precedents often display a remarkable inertia. Indeed, they look like enduring, predetermined norms, applied, and to be applied, by *modus ponens* or by subsumption, to subsequent cases of the same type as the ones previously decided.

---

[12] For my part, I have repeatedly argued that the set of normatively relevant properties for any given normative conditional is—for a reasonable decision-maker—neither predetermined nor predeterminable (B Celano, '"Defeasibility" e bilanciamento. Sulla possibilità di revisioni stabili' (2002) 18 Ragion pratica 223; B Celano, 'Possiamo scegliere fra particolarismo e generalismo?' (2005) 25 Ragion pratica 469; B Celano 'Pluralismo etico, particolarismo e caratterizzazioni di desiderabilità: il modello triadico' (2006) 26 Ragion pratica 133; B Celano 'True Exceptions. Defeasibility and Particularism' in J Ferrer Beltrán and GB Ratti (eds), *The Logic of Legal Requirements. Essays on Defeasibility* (OUP 2012)). HLA Hart, *The Concept of Law* (Clarendon Press 1961) 139 writes: 'a rule that *ends* with the word "unless..." is still a rule' (emphasis added). But what if the rule does *not* end, having an indefinite number of 'unless...' provisos, which cannot be previously or exhaustively determined?

[13] Thanks to Giorgio Pino for pressing this point on me.

True. The aim of the present chapter, however, is to show what this inertia is *not*. Whatever it may be, it is not the enduring identity of one and the same norm, applied, and to be applied, by *modus ponens* or by subsumption, to an indefinite series of individual instances of one and the same generic case. Granted, this is what these normative generalizations *look like*. They must, however, be something else.

17

Analogical Reasoning and Precedent

Cass R Sunstein[*]

In many nations, much of legal reasoning is analogical: is case A like case B? Or instead like case C? Is a ban on obscenity like a ban on political speech, or instead like a ban on bribery? Is a prohibition on abortion like a prohibition on murder, or like a compulsory kidney transplant? Ordinary people often make sense of the world by discerning patterns rooted in analogical thinking. The patterns found in the law also have analogical sources.

In ordinary discussions of political and legal questions, people often proceed analogically, and do so by reference to precedent. A court has ruled that same-sex marriage is protected by the constitution. Does this mean that government has to recognize polygamous marriages? A familiar argumentative technique is to show inconsistency between someone's claim about case X in light of their views on case Y, or in light of the fact that case Y is settled. The goal is to reveal hypocrisy or confusion, or to force the claimant to show how the apparently firm commitment on the case about which the discussants agree can be squared with the claimant's view about a case on which they disagree.

In analogical thinking as I understand it here, deep theories about the good or the right are not deployed. (Of course, it would be possible to reason analogically to justify or to build a large-scale theory, in science or ethics.) In many legal systems, such theories seem too sectarian, too large, too divisive, too obscure, too high-flown, too ambitious, too confusing, too contentious, too abstract, or in arguable or evident tension with much that is settled. On the other hand, analogizers cannot reason from one particular to another particular without saying something at least a little abstract. They must say that case A was decided rightly *for a reason*, and they must say that that reason applies, or does not apply, in case B. I will try to show that this method of proceeding is ideally suited to a legal system consisting of numerous judges who disagree on first principles, who lack scales, and who must take most decided cases as fixed points from which to proceed.

1. In General

A. Analogies Outside of Law

Everyday thought is informed by analogical thinking; we see things as we do partly because of analogies. Much creativity depends on seeing patterns, or likenesses, where these had not been seen before. Advances in science are often founded on discerning new patterns of

---

[*] I would like to thank participants in the authors' workshop for this volume in October 2021, and in particular Hafsteinn Dan Kristjánsson for superb comments and suggestions; I am acutely aware that I have not adequately responded to them here.

Cass R Sunstein, *Analogical Reasoning and Precedent* In: *Philosophical Foundations of Precedent.* Edited by: Timothy Endicott, Hafsteinn Dan Kristjánsson, and Sebastian Lewis, Oxford University Press. © Cass R Sunstein 2023. DOI: 10.1093/oso/9780192857248.003.0018

228   CASS R SUNSTEIN

commonality. Human creativity might even be defined as 'the capacity to see or interpret a problematic phenomenon as an unexpected or unusual instance of a prototypical pattern already in one's conceptual repertoire'.[1] The point is not limited to human beings. Even non-human animals think analogically.[2]

Analogical reasoning helps to inform our judgments about factual issues on which we are uncertain. I have a Labrador Retriever dog, and I know that she is gentle with children. When I see another Labrador Retriever dog, I assume that she too will be gentle with children. I have a Toyota Camry, and I know that it starts even on cold days in winter. I assume that my friend's Toyota Camry will start on cold winter days as well. (Let us stipulate that in these cases, people are not reasoning deductively, by defining Labrador Retrievers and Toyota Camrys as having certain characteristics, and really are working by analogy.) There is a simple structure to this kind of thinking. (1) A has some characteristic X, or characteristics X, Y, and Z. (2) B shares that characteristic or some or all of those characteristics. (3) A also has some characteristic Q. (4) Because A and B share some characteristic or characteristics, we conclude what is not yet known, that B shares characteristic Q as well.

This is a usual form of reasoning in daily life, but it raises many questions. The problem or 'target' case B has something in common with many possible 'source' cases; sometimes it is a great puzzle how we decide what we will choose as the relevant source or prototypical case for comparison. Perhaps I should compare the unknown Labrador Retriever not with my own dog, but with some other Labrador Retriever in the neighbourhood, who is not so gentle with children. Or perhaps I should compare the unknown Labrador Retriever not with other Labrador Retrievers at all, but with a dog owned by someone 'like' the person who owns that Labrador Retriever. Or perhaps I should look to another of the innumerable facets of the situation. In law and elsewhere, there is often a simple, intuitive understanding that the target case B is analogous to source cases A and C, but not to D and E. But greater reflection may show mistakes, bias, or inadequate care in the selection of source cases.

It will readily appear that analogical thinking does not guarantee truth. The existence of one or many shared characteristics does not mean that all characteristics are shared. Some Labrador Retriever dogs are not gentle with children. (Very few, undoubtedly.) Some Toyota Camrys do not start on cold days in winter. For analogical reasoning to work well, we have to say that the relevant, known similarities give us good reason to believe that there are further similarities as well and thus help to answer the open question.

Of course, this is not always so. Sometimes the very thought is absurd. South Korea is a country in Asia, and the second word in its name is 'Korea', and it is a democracy; North Korea is also a country in Asia, and the second word in its name is also 'Korea', but it is hardly a democracy. With respect to facts, analogical thinking can give rise to a judgment about probabilities, and these may be of uncertain magnitude. With respect to some questions, use of analogies is justified in probabilistic terms, at least if the similarity is relevant to the issue that concerns us. With Labrador Retrievers, analogical thinking works, because Labrador Retriever-ness is relevant to gentleness with children. The most disciplined way to proceed would be to identify the probability, asking: in view of characteristic Z, shared by X and Y, what is the likelihood that because X also has characteristic A, Y will have that characteristic as well? Sixty percent? Seventy-five percent? Ninety-five percent?

---

[1] PM Churchland, *The Engine of Reason, the Seat of the Soul* (MIT Press 1995) 278.
[2] See KJ Holyoak and P Thagaard, *Mental Leaps: Analogy in Creative Thought* (MIT Press 1995).

B. Analogical Thinking in Law: Its Characteristic Form

Analogical reasoning has a simple structure in law. Consider some examples. We know that an employer may not fire an employee for agreeing to perform jury duty; it is said to 'follow' that an employer is banned from firing an employee for refusing to commit perjury. We know that in the US a speech by a member of the Ku Klux Klan, advocating racial hatred, cannot be regulated unless it is likely to incite and is directed to inciting imminent lawless action; it is said to follow that the government cannot forbid members of the Nazi Party to march in Skokie, Illinois. We know that there is no constitutional right to welfare, medical care, or housing; it is said to follow that there is no constitutional right to government protection against domestic violence.

From a brief glance at these cases, we can get a sense of the characteristic form of analogical thought in law. When an analogy is found, the process appears to work in five steps. (1) Some fact pattern A—the 'source' case—has certain characteristics; call them X, Y, and Z. (2) Fact pattern B—the 'target' case—has characteristics X, Y, and Q, or characteristics X, Y, Z, and Q. (3) A is treated a certain way in law. (4) Some principle or rule, announced, created, or discovered in the process of thinking through A, B, and their interrelations, explains why A is treated the way that it is. (5) Because of what it shares in common with A, B should be treated the same way. It is covered by the same principle.

It should be clear that the crucial steps, and often the most difficult, are (4) and (5). It should also be clear that much might be said about the relationship between (3) and (4). We need to get clear on the meaning of (3). We also need to get clear on what it means to say that A and B share something in common. If what they share is relevant, it is because of the governing principle, not because of brute facts. Suppose that it is clear that if an employee is fired for seeking workers' compensation benefits; suppose that the question arises whether an employee can be fired for blowing the whistle on criminal wrongdoing by an employer. To know whether the second case is 'covered' by the first, the court must choose the principle that best accounts for the ruling in the first. There are, of course, many possible candidates.

Some people think that analogical reasoning is really a form of deduction, but this is a mistake. To be sure, analogical reasoning cannot proceed without identification of a governing idea—a principle or rule, discovered in (4)—to account for the results in the source and target cases. But the governing idea is not given in advance and simply applied to the new case. (If it is, we have a simple case of rule application.) Instead, analogical reasoning helps to identify the governing idea and is indispensable to the identification; we do not know what the idea is until we have assessed the cases. It is not wrong to say that once the principle or rule is identified, it can be applied. The only point is that it is not known in advance. Analogy and disanalogy are created or discovered through the process of comparing cases, as people discern a principle or rule that makes sense of their considered judgments.

Of course, we can imagine a legal system that would resolve these cases by rule and which would have no need for analogical reasoning. If clear rules pre-existed cases, and if people agreed on them, analogical reasoning might turn out to be beside the point (except if the domain of the rule were in doubt). That might be true in some jurisdictions, including civil law nations. But for many questions, it is very hard to devise clear rules, and even if one thinks that one has them, one might turn out to be surprised. Life turns up a host of new problems that rule-makers could not anticipate.

We can now see an important difference between analogical reasoning with respect to facts and analogical reasoning in law and ethics. For facts, people often use some case A to produce a probabilistic judgment that they think bears on case B. If dropped objects fall in New York, dropped objects will probably fall in London too. But to know whether this is so, people might not need analogies at all; an understanding of gravity will suffice, and it will be a lot better. If we had a full sense of causal mechanisms, we would not need analogies, though analogies might serve a heuristic function. The use of analogies in law and ethics is different. Here the key work is done not by a probabilistic judgment (based on known similarities), but by development of a normative principle (also based on known similarities).

It should readily appear that analogical reasoning does not guarantee good outcomes in law. For analogical reasoning to operate properly, we have to know that cases A and B are 'relevantly' similar, and that there are not 'relevant' differences between them. Even seemingly similar cases are always different from each other and along innumerable dimensions. The key task for analogical reasoners is to decide when there are relevant similarities and differences. Of course, the judgment that a distinction is not genuinely principled requires a substantive argument of some kind. What, then, are the characteristics of a competent lawyer's inquiry into analogies?

C. The Features of Analogy

In law, analogical reasoning typically has four different but overlapping features: *principled consistency, a focus on particulars, incompletely theorized judgments, and principles operating at a low or intermediate level of abstraction*. Taken in concert, these features produce both the virtues and the vices of analogical reasoning in law. I emphasize the word 'typically'; for example, incompletely theorized judgments, and principles operating at a low or intermediate level of abstraction, are not intrinsic to, or a necessary part of, analogical reasoning. The point is that as it operates in law, these features are typical. Here are some brief remarks on each of them.

First, and most obviously, judgments about specific cases must be made consistent with one another. A requirement of principled consistency is a hallmark of analogical reasoning (as it is of reasoning of almost all sorts). It follows that in producing the necessary consistency, some principle, harmonizing seemingly disparate outcomes, will be invoked to explain the cases. The principle must, of course, be more general than the outcome for which it is designed.

Secondly, analogical reasoning is focused on particulars, and it develops from concrete controversies. Holmes put the point in this suggestive if somewhat misleading way: a common law court 'decides the case first and determines the principle afterwards'.[3] Holmes's suggestion is misleading since in order to decide the case at all, one has to have the principle in some sense in mind; there can be no sequential operation of quite the kind Holmes describes. If anything, the principle comes first (or ought to). But Holmes is right to say that ideas are developed with close reference to the details, rather than imposed on them from above. In this sense, analogical reasoning, as a species of casuistry, is a form of 'bottom-up' thinking. Unlike many kinds of reasoning, it does not operate from the top down.

Despite the analogizer's focus on particulars, we have seen that any description of a particular holding inevitably has some more general components. We cannot know anything

---

[3] O Wendell Holmes, 'Codes and the Arrangements of Law' (1931) 44 Harv L Rev 725 (reprinted from 5 Am L Rev 11 (1870)).

about case X if we do not know something about the reasons that count in its favour. We cannot say whether case X has anything to do with case Y unless we are able to abstract, a bit, from the facts and holding of case X. The key point is that analogical reasoning involves a process in which principles are developed from and with constant reference to particular cases.

Thirdly, analogical reasoning in law operates without anything like a deep or comprehensive theory that would account for the particular outcomes it yields. The judgments that underlie convictions about the relevant case are incompletely theorized. Of course, there is a continuum from the most particularistic and low-level principles to the deepest and most general. I suggest only that analogizers in law avoid those approaches that come close to the deeply theorized or the foundational, and that to this extent, lawyers are generally analogizers and hence casuists.

Lawyers might firmly believe, for example, that the Constitution does not create a right to welfare, that political speech cannot be regulated without a showing of immediate and certain harm, or that government may impose environmental regulations on private companies. But usually lawyers are not able to explain the basis for these beliefs in great depth or detail or with full specification of the theory that accounts for those beliefs. Lawyers (and almost all other people) typically lack any large-scale theory. They reason anyway, and their reasoning is analogical.

Fourthly, and finally, analogical reasoning produces principles that operate at a low or intermediate level of abstraction. If we say that an employer may not fire an employee for accepting jury duty, we might mean, for example, that an employer cannot fire an employee for refusing to commit a crime. This is a standard, perhaps even a rule, and it does involve a degree of abstraction from the particular case, but it does not entail any high-level theory about labour markets, or about the appropriate relationship between employers and employees. If we say that a Nazi march cannot be banned, we might mean that political speech cannot be stopped without a showing of clear and immediate danger; but in so saying, we need not invoke any large theory about the purposes of the free speech guarantee, or about the relation between the citizen and the state. People can converge on the low-level principle from various foundations or without well-understood foundations at all.

If we put interpretation of rules to one side (while noting that analogical thinking may crop up even there), reasoning by analogy, understood in light of these four characteristics, is the mode through which ordinary lawyers operate. They have no abstract theory to account for their convictions or for what they know to be the law. But they know that these are their convictions or that this is the law, and they are able to bring that knowledge to bear on undecided cases. For guidance, they look to areas in which their judgment is firm.

2. Fixed Points

Thus far, I have suggested that analogical thinking operates by taking some precedents or judgments as 'fixed points' for analysis. But the idea is more complex than it first appears. Begin by distinguishing three possibilities. (1) Some decided cases cannot legitimately be overruled by some judges. They must be taken as authoritative; they are truly 'binding'. This is the case with respect to lower court receptions of US Supreme Court decisions. (2) Some cases can be overruled—they are not 'binding'—but only in quite exceptional circumstances. This is the ordinary view about the responsibilities of the Supreme Court with respect to its own precedents. (3) Some judgments are not embodied in cases at all. They are not precedents, but they seem so obvious and irresistible that they have the status of a decided case. Consider the idea that government may not jail Christians because of their religion or force Hispanics alone to donate blood to people who need blood to survive.

These distinctions may clarify matters, but a problem remains. Even if we know that some cases are authoritative in the sense that they are binding, and that others must be respected except in extreme circumstances, how do we know what past cases 'stand for'? The distinction between a case's 'holding' and the court's mere 'dicta' is designed to handle this problem. The holding is usually described as the outcome in the case, accompanied by the narrowest rationale necessary to defend it. By contrast, the dicta consist of language in the opinion that is not necessary to the outcome. This distinction works, but it is not always simple to apply, and to that extent, it may not be so clear what it means to say that a holding is authoritative. Often we come to see that a court originally justified an outcome by a rationale that turns out to be too broad once other cases are brought forward. As a result, the rationale is scaled back. Often we conclude that the argument in favour of a certain outcome was too narrow, in the sense that once we consult other cases, we see that a broader principle will do much better. Those who come up with rationales for outcomes are rarely able to anticipate the full range of cases to which those rationales might apply.

The subsequent court's characterization of any 'holding' in a past case is a constructive act, not a simple matter of finding something. Holdings may not be fully given in advance. At the same time, one cannot characterize any holding absolutely any way at all, and the constraints on characterization are enough to undergird the enterprise of analogy.

3. Precedents as Rules and Analogies

A precedent can serve as *either a rule or an analogy*. It serves as a rule to the extent that it governs all identical cases, that is, all cases that are 'on all fours' with it, in the sense that it is obvious that they are relevantly similar and there are no relevant differences between them.

A precedent serves not as a rule but as an analogy to the extent that it is at least plausibly distinguishable from the case at hand, but potentially suggestive of a more general principle or policy that seems relevant to that case. Members of the Ku Klux Klan cannot be stopped from speaking. Does it not follow that members of the Nazi Party cannot be stopped from marching? Often it is hard to distinguish precedents as rules from precedents as analogies; we can see what we have only after we start to think and talk. We might ultimately conclude that a precedent that appears to be a mere analogy for case X is actually a rule for case X because there are clearly no differences between the precedent and case X—because the analogy is obviously 'apposite'. The subsequent court may therefore have to construct—to create for the first time—the precise factual predicate for the outcome in the course of deciding the subsequent case.

All this is a matter of shared understandings, and nothing more. When a precedent is said to be a rule, it is because it is believed to be so closely analogous to the case at hand, or because there are so clearly relevant similarities without relevant differences, that people agree that it 'binds', and no one wants to suggest that it is 'merely' an analogy. In 2015, the US Supreme Court struck down bans on same-sex marriage. If a new case arises in which members of a same-sex couple are over the age of sixty, or in which there is a big age spread between them, everyone will agree that the precedent creates a rule and is binding; the age of the would-be spouses is not relevant (unless they are too young under state law).

When a precedent is said to be an analogy and not a rule, it is because there is at least plausibly a relevant difference between the two cases, and so it is too simple to say the precedent 'covers' the case at hand. Suppose that three people want to marry each other, and that they claim that they are protected by the same-sex marriage ruling. It is far from clear that their claim is convincing. Under existing law, it is not; the analogy fails. In the course of deciding the case, we might or might not conclude that the analogy is 'apposite', and here what emerges will be no simple (in the sense of obvious) statement of pre-existing law, but instead a rule or a principle whose content was determined amid controversy and not given in advance.

All cases are potentially distinguishable; when we say that case B (involving, say, a march by Nazis) is identical to case A (involving a speech by members of the Klan), we have selected some characteristics that are shared and treated as irrelevant those characteristics that are unshared. When two cases appear obviously identical to us, it is because we have disregarded, as irrelevant, their inevitable differences. It is the subsequent court that makes judgments about relevant similarities and relevant differences. And it will be readily apparent that because of the importance of shared understandings, whether the precedent is a rule or an analogy is an artefact of substantive ideas of some sort. We could imagine a community in which the Nazi speech was plausibly or even obviously different from the Klan speech (and so unprotected). Or we could imagine a community in which a threat to assassinate the president is obviously similar to the Klan speech (and so protected).

4. Analogical Confusion

Analogical reasoning can, of course, be done poorly. Sometimes the selection of a particular 'source' case is wrong or inadequately justified; sometimes judges treat some case A as the obvious basis for analogical thinking, even though cases B and C would be a much better place to begin. Sometimes case A and case B are unified by some principle, when another, better principle would distinguish them. Sometimes the creative dimensions of analogical thought are downplayed, as people simply announce that case A is analogous to case B, when an unarticulated supplemental judgment is necessary and not defended. William James described a related phenomenon as 'vicious abstractionism':

> We conceive a concrete situation by singling out some salient or important feature in it, and classing it under that; then, instead of adding to its previous characters all the positive consequences which the new way of conceiving it may bring, we proceed to use our concept privatively; reducing the originally rich phenomenon to the naked suggestions of that name abstractly taken, treating it as a case of 'nothing but' that concept, and acting as if all the other characters from out of which the concept is abstracted were expunged. Abstraction, functioning in this way, becomes a means of arrest far more than a means of advance in thought. It mutilates things.[4]

Different factual situations are inarticulate; they do not impose order on themselves. The method of analogy is based on the question: is case A relevantly similar to case B, or not? To

---

[4] W James, 'The Meaning of Truth' in AJ Ayer (ed), *Pragmatism and the Meaning of Truth* (Harvard UP 1978) 136, 302.

234   CASS R SUNSTEIN

answer such questions, one needs a theory of relevant similarities and differences. Everything is similar in innumerable ways to everything else, and different from everything else in the same number of ways. In the face of this fact, formalist analogical thinking—resting on an argument that is not offered—is no better than any other kind of bad or dishonourable formalism. Courts should always stand ready to explain and justify the claim that one thing is analogous to another.

Analogical reasoning can go wrong not simply because it is dishonourably formalistic but also because it rests on an inadequately defended judgment about relevant similarities and differences. Consider, for example, Justice Holmes's notorious argument in *Buck v Bell*,[5] the case upholding compulsory sterilization of the 'feeble-minded':

> We have seen more than once that the public welfare may call upon the best citizens for their lives. It would be strange if it could not call upon those who already sap the strength of the State for these lesser sacrifices, often not felt to be such by those concerned. . . . The principle that sustains compulsory vaccination is broad enough to cover cutting the Fallopian tubes. Three generations of imbeciles are enough.

Holmes is arguing that if people can be conscripted during wartime or forced to obtain vaccinations, it follows that the state can require sterilization of the 'feeble-minded'. But this is a casual and unpersuasive claim. Many principles cover the first two cases without also covering the third. We might think that a vaccination is far less intrusive than sterilization, and that conscription is plausibly a unique problem, unlike sterilization, growing out of a nation's fundamental need to defend itself under conditions of war. Holmes does not explore the many possibly relevant similarities and differences among these various cases. He does not identify the range of possible principles, much less argue for one rather than another. Instead he invokes a principle of a high level of generality—'the public welfare may call upon the best citizens for their lives'—that is quite crude, and not evaluated by reference to low- or intermediate-level principles that may also account for or explain the apparently analogous cases without covering the sterilization problem.

The example shows that analogical reasoning can go wrong (1) when one case is said to be analogous to another on the basis of a unifying principle that is embraced without having been tested against other possibilities, or (2) when some similarities between two cases are deemed decisive with insufficient investigation of relevant differences. These are, of course, pervasive problems, and they are the distinctive illogic of bad analogical reasoning.

A final problem is that analogical reasoning can distract attention from the essential features of the particular matter at hand, by persuading judges to grapple with other cases and hypothetical examples that actually raise quite different issues. For a long time, bans on same-sex marriage were (in my view) evaluated poorly, because people focused on bans on incest and polygamy, which are hardly the same. If done poorly, analogical thinking can deflect the eye from the specific problem and thus induce a kind of blindness to what is really at stake. Note here Bishop Butler's phrase, 'Everything is what it is, and not another thing', which Wittgenstein considered as a motto for *Philosophical Investigations*.

---

[5] *Buck v Bell* 274 US 200 (1927).

5. Analogies and Precedent-Following

Why might we think analogically? Would it not be better to choose the right theory and simply apply it? Why not develop and apply rules? Would it not be better to proceed directly to the merits, rather than to compare cases with one another? There is no simple answer to these questions. We need to know something about institutions and their capacities.

In some areas of morality and law, a problem lies in the nature of human cognition; there may be no such thing as proceeding 'directly to the merits' to the extent that moral and legal thought is pervaded by prototypical cases. In law, the case for analogies, which places a large emphasis on precedents, is provisional, contingent, humble, and pragmatic; it points to an array of diverse social interests.

First, the analogizer is committed to consistency and equal treatment. A litigant in case A may not be treated differently from a litigant in case B unless there is a relevant difference between them. This idea operates as a barrier to certain forms of prejudice, hostility, randomness, and irrationality. The conception of equal treatment underlying respect for precedent is closely related to the rule-of-law aspirations of analogical thinking. In fact, equal treatment and analogical thinking march hand in hand, at least when the system is working well.

Secondly, analogies can be a source of both principles and policies. A judge may not know which principles are best unless she investigates an assortment of apparently similar cases. The investigation can help to refine principles and to show where plausible candidates go wrong. It can have epistemic value. A judge who looks at a stock of precedents should be able to learn a great deal by seeing what others have found persuasive. It is important to emphasize that investigation of analogies is hardly the best way to do policy science or to investigate issues of principle. But it may contribute to that process.

Thirdly, the resort to decided cases, as analogies, helps judges to avoid hubris. A judge who respects what others have done is less likely to overstep, by invoking theories that are confused, idiosyncratic, highly divisive, or sectarian.

Fourthly, analogical reasoning, if based on precedent, promotes the important interests in fostering planning, maintaining predictability, and protecting expectations. If past rulings are entitled to respect, they allow people to believe that the law is a certain way, and that they may act safely on that belief. A commitment to following precedent, and to reasoning analogically, enables those expectations to be vindicated and in that sense too it is associated with the rule of law. We might distinguish here between the interest in liberty, which entails predictability in law and hence the capacity to plan, and the interest in protecting against unfairness, which occurs when government ignores people's reliance on previous decisions. Both interests argue for respecting precedent, and in that sense for thinking analogically.

Fifthly, and relatedly, analogical thinking saves a great deal of time. If judges had to start from scratch in each case, the legal system would be overwhelmed. This might well be so even if the legal system consisted of a single judge. The project of putting one's own convictions into genuine order is (to say the least) time-consuming, and ordinary people often do well to think of their own past practices as precedents. This is all the more certainly true for a legal system consisting of thousands of people operating in a decentralized but mostly hierarchical judiciary. Following precedent enables judges to avoid recreating the law from the ground up, and thus ensures that people of limited time and capacities can take much for granted.

Finally—to return to our main theme—precedents and analogies facilitate the emergence of agreement among people who diverge on most or many matters. Judges A, B, and C may disagree on a great deal. They may start from significantly different premises. And agreement is not a transcendent value. If people disagree, perhaps they should have it out. But to say the least, it is helpful if judge A can invoke certain fixed points for everyone's analysis, so that judges B and C can join the discussion from shared premises. Perhaps judge B can invoke some fixed points that argue in a surprising direction. We cannot exclude the possibility that ultimately the judicial disagreements cannot be bridged. But with analogies, at least they can begin to talk. That is no small virtue.

6. Top Down, Bottom Up

An important challenge, traceable to Jeremy Bentham, is that the method of analogy is hopelessly unreliable—insufficiently scientific, unduly tied to existing intuitions, and partly for these reasons static or celebratory of existing social practice.[6] On this view, analogical reasoning works too modestly from existing holdings and convictions, to which it is unduly attached. It needs to be replaced by something like a general theory—in short, by something like science. For the critics, analogizers are extreme or fanatical Burkeans, and their approach suffers from all the flaws said to be associated with Edmund Burke's celebration of the English common law. It is too insistently backward-looking, too sceptical of theory, too lacking in criteria by which to assess legal practices critically. It's a mess.

To be fair, let's allow Burke to speak for himself:[7]

And first of all, the science of jurisprudence, the pride of the human intellect, which, with all its defects, redundancies, and errors, is the collected reason of the ages, combining the principles of original justice with the infinite variety of human concerns, as a heap of old exploded errors, would no longer be studied. Personal self-sufficiency and arrogance (the certain attendants upon all those who have never experienced a wisdom greater than their own) would usurp the tribunal.

Burke can be seen to be arguing that the process of analogical reasoning, attending to 'the infinite variety of human concerns', has major advantages over the use of any theory, which would not be founded on experience, and which would reflect some kind of arrogance. In a Burkean vein, Chief Justice John Roberts said, 'I tend to look at the cases from the bottom up rather than the top down. … In terms of the application of the law, you begin, obviously, with the precedents before you.'[8] We can easily see Roberts as a kind of Burkean minimalist, avoiding large-scale theories in favour of analogical reasoning. From the Benthamite point of view, that is disturbing and even appalling. Why not develop and use the right theory? Why (again) does agreement matter so much?

The general objection includes several different claims, and it seems simultaneously convincing and a bit mysterious. Begin with the claim of excessive conservatism. True, analogical reasoning cannot work without criteria. One more time: in the absence of principles, it cannot get off the ground. But whether analogical reasoning calls for the continuation of existing practice turns on the principles, convictions, or holdings from which analogical

---

[6] This sort of attack on analogy is traceable to Plato and to ancient attacks on 'casuistry'. See A Jonson and S Toulmin, *The Abuse of Casuistry* (University of California Press 1991).

[7] E Burke, 'Reflections on the Revolution in France' in I Kramnick (ed), *The Portable Edmund Burke* (Penguin Classics 1999) 456–57.

[8] Text of Hearing of John G Roberts to be Chief Justice of the United States, part 3, <http://transcripts.cnn.com/TRANSCRIPTS/0509/13/se.01.html> accessed 20 December 2021.

reasoning takes place. Without identifying those principles, convictions, or holdings, we cannot say whether existing practices will be celebrated or instead abandoned. The process of testing initial judgments by reference to analogies can produce continuation of current practices (and that might be a good idea), or instead sharp criticism of many social practices and, eventually, can yield reform (and that too might be a good idea). Legal holdings that are critical of some social practices can turn out, through analogy, to be critical of other practices as well.

In the abstract, it is far from clear whether analogical reasoning is conservative or not. In numerous cases, it has produced large-scale change. In the US, the Supreme Court's decision in *Brown v Board of Education* invalidated racial segregation in education.[9] By analogy to *Brown*, US courts invalidated racial segregation elsewhere too. Even more than that, they reformed prisons and mental institutions; struck down many racial classifications, including affirmative action programmes; invalidated sex discrimination; and prevented states from discriminating on the basis of alienage and legitimacy. The requirement that states must recognize same-sex marriage can easily be seen as an outgrowth of *Brown*. The analogical process has hardly run its course. Whether analogical reasoning is conservative or not depends not on the fact that it is analogical, but on the nature of the principles brought to bear on disputed cases.[10]

On the other hand, analogical reasoning does start from existing convictions or holdings, and judgments of sameness or difference receive their content from current thinking. In this way, analogical reasoning can have a backward-looking, conservative, and potentially incremental character. Whether this is a bad thing for courts depends on the virtues and vices of different institutions of government, on the society in question, and on the weight to be accorded to stability. But insofar as analogical reasoning takes current legal materials as the basis for reasoning, it might indeed be an obstacle to justified change through law. Thus, Jonathan Swift's Gulliver comments:

> It is a maxim among ... lawyers that whatever hath been done before may legally be done again; and therefore they take special care to record all the decisions formerly made against common justice and the general reason of mankind. These, under the name of precedents, they produce as authorities to justify the most inequitous opinions; and the judges never fail to direct accordingly.[11]

The most important lesson to draw from this objection is that a full theory of legal reasoning should make it possible to say which holdings are wrong, and which holdings should be overruled because they are wrong. Analogical reasoning, at least as thus far described, is unhelpful here. It might therefore be said that efforts to reason from analogies are stuck in existing holdings or convictions, which are sometimes a morass, and that such efforts are for this reason severely deficient in comparison to forms of reasoning that provide better

---

[9] *Brown v Board of Education* 347 US 483 (1954).

[10] J Raz, *The Authority of Law: Essays on Law and Morality* (OUP 1979), defends analogical thinking as a response to the problem of 'partial reform', that is, the risk that piecemeal reforms will fail to serve their own purposes because public or private actors will adapt (as in the idea that the minimum wage decreases employment). In Raz's view, analogical thinking responds to this risk by ensuring that any 'new rule is a conservative one, that it does not introduce new discordant and conflicting purposes or value into the law, that its purpose and the values it promotes are already served by existing rules': ibid 204. There is truth in this claim, but if the purpose or values are described in certain ways, the analogical process may lead in highly non-conservative directions, with no abuse to analogies themselves.

[11] J Swift, *Gulliver's Travels*, IV, 5, in *The Writings of Jonathan Swift* (Norton 1973) 216.

resources for critical evaluation. This is not at all a complaint about excessive conservatism. It is more Benthamite in spirit. It is an argument for some kind of theory, such as utilitarianism, from which we can ground our judgments. In short, we need a foundation, not a bunch of conclusions accompanied by unambitious, low-level justifications.

There is truth in this complaint. As I have noted, analogical reasoning is especially unlikely to help us in figuring out the consequences of legal rules, and knowledge of consequences is crucial. We would not want administrative agencies—the Environmental Protection Agency, the Occupational Safety and Health Administration, the Food and Drug Administration—to make their judgments by analogy. Thank goodness, they do not do that. They do much better to investigate consequences, above all by assessing costs and benefits. They ask: how many lives would a regulation save? How many illnesses would it prevent? What would be its costs? Cost–benefit analysis, rather than analogical thinking, is the best way for agencies to decide what kinds of regulations make sense. It would be preposterous to say that rules governing air pollution, water pollution, and silica in the workplace should be made by analogical reasoning.

For courts, cost–benefit analysis can also be an excellent idea and, occasionally, it has a significant role. But judges may lack the tools to quantify costs and benefits, and reasoning by analogy has significant virtues, because it helps to clarify and improve thinking. Reference to other cases can show us that our initial intuitions are unreliable and inconsistent with what we actually think. Much of legal education, and much of lawyering, consists in the testing of initial judgments by reference to other cases, and sometimes it can be shown that those judgments must yield. If those judgments are reflected in judicial holdings, then it is necessary for courts to decide whether to overrule them. Of course, every legal system must make many decisions on how to weigh the interest in stability against the interest in getting things right (with the acknowledgement that what is now thought to be right might not in fact be right).

Nothing in these remarks suggests that analogical reasoning is superior to a general theory. If we have the right theory and if we can apply it, we should do so. In antitrust law, judges have generally converged on the view that the goal is to promote consumer welfare, defined in economic terms, and that view allows judges to use economic analysis across a wide terrain, with reduced emphasis on analogical thinking. That is a terrific development, and it might be replicated in other areas. But we have seen that in many areas of the law, use of a general theory might not be feasible or desirable. When it is not, we will usually benefit from thinking analogically.

Of course, many people do seek to replace legal reasoning with highly general non- or extra-legal approaches, especially those that apply a broad theory 'top down' to particular legal disputes. The advantage of economic analysis of law is that it casts a critical light on ordinary intuitions, showing that they are too crude to be a basis for law. Intuitions about the effects of legal rules may be completely wrong; a significant increase in the minimum wage, for example, could increase unemployment, and in that sense hurt many of the people one is trying to help. In a sharp restatement of Bentham's attack on the common law, economic analysts sometimes claim that traditional legal reasoning is not reasoning at all, but instead an encrusted system of disorganized and perhaps barely processed intuitions.

Judge Richard Posner uses ideas of this kind against analogical reasoning. In his view, we cannot really reason from one particular to another. Instead, we need to give an account of the policy that underlies the first particular. Once we are doing this, we are engaged in 'policy science'. 'One can call this reasoning by analogy if one likes but what is really involved is querying (or quarrying) the earlier case for policies that may be applicable to the later one and then deciding the later one by reference to those policies.'[12] In Benthamite fashion, Judge Posner's complaint is that if we are going to do policy science, we should really do it, rather than investigate prior cases, which 'often constitute an impoverished repository of fact and policy for the decision of the present one'. In his view, analogical reasoning is pervasively formalistic, that is, it treats law as a self-contained system, when legal decisions should be based on an investigation of what really matters, on which policy analysts would be far more helpful.

Judge Posner is right to insist that insofar as we are doing policy analysis, past legal decisions are at best a start. But as it occurs in courts, law is not always or only policy analysis, for which judges are imperfectly equipped; and we should not undervalue the process of ordering judgments about legal problems by seeing if one's judgment in the case at hand can be squared with judicial or hypothetical judgments in other cases. This process is especially well adapted for the context of adjudication, in which current judges seek to produce consistency and equal treatment, to save their own time and resources, to protect expectations and reliance, and to avoid hubris and sectarianism.

From these points, we can offer a general conclusion. Analogical reasoning lies at the heart of legal thinking, and for good reasons. It is admirably well suited to the particular roles in which lawyers and judges find themselves—to a system in which heterogeneous people must reach closure despite their limitations of time and capacity, and despite their disagreements on fundamental issues. There is nothing static to the analogical process; it leaves room for flexibility and indeed for an enormous amount of creativity.

Much creativity in law comes from the ability to see novel analogies. Precedents are often like poems or novels, in the sense that they come to have entirely fresh and unexpected meanings. And no matter how sophisticated a legal culture becomes, and no matter how committed it is to the rule of law, it is likely to make a large space for analogical thinking. The persistence of analogical thinking in day-to-day life is thus mirrored in law.

---

[12] RA Posner, *Overcoming Law* (Harvard UP 1995).

18
Precedent and Similarity

Frederick Schauer and Barbara A Spellman

A common defence of constraint by precedent is that it is justified by the seemingly obvious virtue of deciding like cases alike.[1] But, of course, no two cases are exactly alike. Any two acts or events differ in time and place, no matter how small those differences may be and no matter how many points of similarity there may be. And even if we examine the question in a less philosophically esoteric way, we can still note that the set of events in some case now before a court will almost always vary in more than microscopic respects from the set of events in some previous case. Accordingly, precedential constraint necessarily involves not a chimerical search for identity between the case now before the court and an earlier alleged precedent case, but, rather, an attempt to locate a *relevant similarity* between different cases taking place at different times and arising out of different situations.[2] Once we are in the realm of similarity between non-identical cases, however, the difficulties multiply. This chapter seeks to examine the question of precedential similarity, exploring the various ways in which similarity and difference might manifest themselves in any regime of precedential constraint.

1. Precedent: The Fundamental Norms

The foundational principle of precedent is that judges should decide some case—call it the *instant case*—so that its outcome is the same as the outcome had been in some previous case—the *precedent case*.[3] Often the precedent case is a decision of a higher court in the same jurisdiction, and in such instances of *vertical* precedent the obligation of a court in the instant case to follow the precedent case of a higher court follows from the typically hierarchical way in which most courts in most common law jurisdictions are organized.[4] The obligation of the Court of Appeal in the UK to follow the UK Supreme Court and the obligation of the federal Courts of Appeal and the federal District Courts to follow the decisions of the Supreme Court of the US represent a straightforward application of the vertical and

---

[1] Among the more iconic sources, see BN Cardozo, *The Nature of the Judicial Process* (Yale UP 1921) 149; R Cross and JW Harris, *Precedent in English Law* (4th edn, Clarendon Press 1977) 4; N MacCormick, *Legal Reasoning and Legal Theory* (Clarendon Press 1978) 73–99. See also AR Miguel, 'Equality Before the Law and Precedent' (1997) 10 Ratio Juris 373; recently, the opinion of Chief Justice Roberts in *June Medical Services LLC v Russo* 140 S Ct 2103 (2020), observing that '*stare decisis* requires us, absent special circumstances, to treat like cases alike'.

[2] See D Lyons, 'Formal Justice and Judicial Precedent' (1985) 38 Vand L Rev 495; F Schauer, 'On Treating Unlike Cases Alike' (2018) 33 Const Commentary 437; KI Winston, 'On Treating Like Cases Alike' (1974) 62 Cal L Rev 1.

[3] On this terminology, see F Schauer, 'Precedent' (1987) 39 Stan L Rev 571.

[4] On characterizing precedent as vertical and horizontal, see L Alexander, 'Constrained by Precedent' (1989) 63 So Cal L Rev 1. See also M Abramowicz and M Stearns, 'Defining Dicta' (2005) 57 Stan L Rev 953.

Frederick Schauer and Barbara A Spellman, *Precedent and Similarity* In: *Philosophical Foundations of Precedent*. Edited by: Timothy Endicott, Hafsteinn Dan Kristjánsson, and Sebastian Lewis, Oxford University Press. © Frederick Schauer and Barbara A Spellman 2023. DOI: 10.1093/oso/9780192857248.003.0019

hierarchical nature of the court systems in those countries. In some respects, therefore, the obligation of a lower court to follow the decisions of a higher court is closely analogous to the obligation of sergeants in the military to follow the orders of lieutenants, and the obligation of lieutenants to follow the orders of captains, majors, colonels, and generals.

Somewhat less obvious, and also more controversial,[5] is the idea of *horizontal* precedential constraint, often labelled as *stare decisis*.[6] Here the obligation of a court is to follow the previous decisions of that same court,[7] even when the precedent case was decided by different judges at an earlier time, and thus was decided by judges not hierarchically superior[8] to the judges deciding the instant case. Nevertheless, it is often maintained that the virtues of reliance, predictability, stability, consistency for consistency's sake, and collective and accumulating wisdom, among others, justify the existence of an obligation to treat earlier decisions, even and especially earlier decisions that the instant court believes mistaken, as having precedential force.[9] The instant court is thus expected to treat precedent cases as having content-independent authority,[10] thereby creating presumptive or absolute[11] (depending on the norms of the jurisdiction) obligations to follow the precedent cases even for courts that believe that the precedent decisions they are expected to follow have been wrongly decided.[12]

---

[5] Famously, the late Justice Antonin Scalia of the Supreme Court of the US expressed grave doubts about the obligations to *stare decisis*, believing that his obligation in constitutional cases was to the Constitution and decidedly not to what other and previous justices had believed the Constitution required. 'The whole function of [*stare decisis*] is to make us say what is false under proper analysis must nevertheless be held to be true.' A Scalia, *A Matter of Interpretation: Federal Courts and the Law* (Amy Gutmann ed, Princeton UP 1997) 197. And on Justice Scalia's views, see also A Coney Barrett, 'Originalism and *Stare Decisis*' (2017) 92 Notre Dame L Rev 1921. The doctrine of *stare decisis* is a relatively recent development in the history of the common law, although the timing of its origins is also controversial. See GT Evans, 'The Development of *Stare Decisis* and the Extent to Which It Should Be Followed' (1946) 23 Denver L Rev 32; T Healy, '*Stare Decisis* as a Constitutional Requirement' (2001) 104 West Va L Rev 43; FG Kempin, Jr, 'Precedent and *Stare Decisis*: The Critical Years, 1800 to 1850' (1959) 3 Am J Legal Hist 28; TR Lee, '*Stare Decisis* in Historical Perspective: From the Founding Era to the Rehnquist Court' (1999) 52 Vand L Rev 647; T Ellis Lewis, 'The History of Judicial Precedent' (1930, 1931) 46 LQR 207, 341, 47 LQR 411.

[6] Recently, the use of the term '*stare decisis*' to refer to both vertical and horizontal precedent has become more common, but traditional usage restricts *stare decisis* to horizontal precedent only (see CE Nelson, *Statutory Interpretation* (Foundation Press 2010) 420) and that is the usage we follow here.

[7] The extent to which that obligation extends also to hierarchically equivalent courts of coordinate jurisdiction within the same system varies among legal systems. The issue is especially complex in the US, where, for example, the twelve federal Courts of Appeal, some containing more than twenty judges, sit and decide in panels of three, with a panel decision only rarely being subject to further affirmation, reversal, or modification by the full court. For discussion, see HJ Dickman, 'Conflicts of Precedent' (2020) 106 Va L Rev 1345; JW Mead, '*Stare Decisis* in the Inferior Courts of the United States' (2012) 12 Nevada LJ 787.

[8] Except insofar as a regime of *stare decisis* serves to *make* earlier judges hierarchically superior by virtue of being earlier.

[9] RJ Kozel, *Settled Versus Right: A Theory of Precedent* (CUP 2017); F Schauer, *Thinking Like a Lawyer: A New Introduction to Legal Reasoning* (Harvard UP 2009) 36–44; S Lewis, 'Precedent and the Rule of Law' (2021) 41 OJLS 873. See also, famously, Justice Louis Brandeis's observation that 'in most matters it is more important that [the question] be settled than that it be decided right'. *Burnet v Coronado Oil & Gas Co* 285 US 383, 406 (1932) (Brandeis concurring). See also Justice John Marshall Harlan's opinion in *Moragne v States Marine Lines, Inc* 398 US 375 (1970), emphasizing the role that *stare decisis* plays in facilitating guidance by law, and noting (more controversially) its role in fostering public confidence in the law and in the courts.

[10] On content-independence, the authority of a rule or other directive on account of its source (or provenance or pedigree, more broadly), see, seminally, HLA Hart, 'Commands and Authoritative Legal Reasons' in HLA Hart, *Essays on Bentham: Jurisprudence and Political Theory* (OUP 1982) 241–66. See also RA Duff, 'Inclusion and Exclusion' (1998) 51 Current Legal Problems 247; KE Himma, 'HLA Hart and the Practical Difference Thesis' (2000) 6 Legal Theory 1; F Schauer, 'The Questions of Authority' (1992) Geo L Rev 95. A sceptical challenge to the idea is P Markwick, 'Independent of Content' (2003) 9 Legal Theory 43.

[11] On the weight of a norm of precedent, see Lewis (n 9).

[12] Indeed, the bite of *stare decisis*, and precedent more broadly, occurs largely when the instant court believes a precedent court mistaken. If the instant court believes that some previous decision was sound, then the instant court's reasons for believing that earlier decision sound will make reliance on the authority of the precedent case superfluous. See F Schauer, 'Precedent' in A Marmor (ed), *Routledge Companion to Philosophy of Law* (Routledge 2012).

All of this is familiar, but complexities arise in attempting to determine exactly what is a precedent for what. Of course, not every previous case is a precedent for every subsequent case. Beneath this triviality, however, lie a host of difficulties in determining which previous decisions count as the precedent cases that judges in the instant case are (at least presumptively) expected to follow.

2. The Questions of Identity

Confronting the question of which previous decisions have precedential authority for which subsequent ones requires determining which previous decisions are relevantly *similar* to which subsequent ones. But addressing this question requires, in turn, distinguishing relevant similarity of *questions* from relevant similarity of *facts*.

On occasion, a court may frame the question in the precedent case in terms so abstract as to make it possible for the *identical* question to be posed in the subsequent instant case.[13] Consider, for example, an especially prominent question now before the US Supreme Court as this chapter is being written. In *Roe v Wade*,[14] the Supreme Court faced and answered the question, 'Is it permissible for a state to make illegal all abortions (except possibly to preserve the life or health of the mother)?' In answering 'no' to that question, the Supreme Court added some number of criteria about whether and when abortion could be made criminal, but there was no doubt that the Court answered the question whether all abortions could be criminalized in the negative.

Almost fifty years later, the Supreme Court was faced with a case in which a virtually identical question was before the Court – the identity of the questions in the precedent case and the instant case being a consequence of the way in which the advocates and the lower courts had framed the issue.[15] As is now widely known, the Supreme Court answered the question differently in 2022 than it had in 1973, but the point here is that the abstract question before the Court in 2022 – Is it constitutionally permissible for a state to prohibit all abortions? - - was identical to the abstract question asked and answered half a century earlier. Insofar as the constraints of precedent apply,[16] the Court would be under a (presumptive) obligation to reach the same result it reached before, and that is because the question before the Court in the later case was identical to the question that was earlier before the Court.

We can observe the same phenomenon in the context of questions of statutory interpretation. Consider, hypothetically, HLA Hart's iconic example of a regulation prohibiting

---

[13] '[F]aced with a rule squarely applicable to the case before him, [the judge] has no need to gauge the similarity of his case to some other case.' RA Posner, *How Judges Think* (Harvard UP 2008) 180. Much the same can be said about a 'squarely applicable' answer to a previously squarely formulated question. And on understanding precedential similarity in terms of *questions* posed and answered, see also the contribution to this volume by Luís Duarte d'Almeida (Chapter 10).

[14] *Roe v Wade* 410 US 113 (1973).

[15] *Jackson Women's Health Organization v Dobbs* (5th Cir, 2019) 945 F3d 265, reversed by the Supreme Court at 142 S. Ct. 2228 (2022). As here, whether the putative similarity between a precedent case and the instant case is a similarity of question or a similarity of fact turns largely on how the issues are framed by the parties in the precedent and instant cases, and to some extent how the issue is framed in the precedent court's decision and opinion.

[16] With respect to the Supreme Court of the US, justices of the Supreme Court regularly speak as if they operate under a norm of *stare decisis*, but whether, as an empirical matter, they actually do so is far from clear. See S Brenner and HJ Spaeth, *Stare Indecisis: The Alteration of Precedent on the Supreme Court, 1946–1992* (CUP 1995); J Knight and L Epstein, 'The Norm of *Stare Decisis*' (1996) 40 Am J Pol Sci 1018; F Schauer, '*Stare Decisis*: Rhetoric and Reality in the Supreme Court' (2018) 2018 Sup Ct Rev 121.

vehicles in the park.[17] And suppose that a court must decide whether a conventional two-wheeled, non-motorized bicycle counted as a vehicle for the purposes of that regulation. If the court in some earlier case—the precedent case—had answered that question, then it is possible that what is genuinely the identical question would be presented in some subsequent case. In that subsequent case—the instant case—the court would then have to decide whether its obligation to precedent required it to give an identical answer now to the identical question presented in the past.

Far more commonly, however, neither the precedent court nor the instant court frames the issue in such abstract terms. Rather, the precedent court will have made a decision with respect to a specific set of facts—a specific bicycle in a specific portion of a specific park at a specific time on a specific day when operated by a specific cyclist for a specific purpose—and the instant court will have to decide whether the specific and technically different set of facts now before it is or is not *relevantly similar* to the specific set of facts in the putatively germane and thus putatively controlling (or at least constraining) precedent. And now things become more difficult. And the difficulty arises precisely because the notion of similarity is substantially more slippery than the notion of identity. Even if at some level of philosophical naivete two things are either identical or they are not, and even if at a perhaps higher level of philosophical sophistication it is obvious that similarity is a matter of degree, it remains centrally important to recognize that similarity is necessarily a function of which properties we take to be germane and which we can safely ignore.[18]

Once we are no longer speaking of identity, therefore, we confront the question of the posited similarity between two different acts, events, situations, or objects that will always be in some respects different but will also be, in other respects, the same. The bicycle whose presence in the park is now at issue is not the same bicycle that was present in the previous case of some years ago, and so too with many other aspects of the two situations. But it is still a bicycle. Having departed the realm of abstract questions in favour of facts, acts, events, and situations, we have also left the realm of identity and entered the domain of similarity. And then we must determine when two different events are sufficiently similar that we can conclude that the decision with respect to the earlier event has (or ought to have) precedential constraining force on the decision in the later.[19] To put it differently, when do we treat different acts, events, or objects as the same even when they are different?[20] Or to put it differently yet, sameness and thus identity are in most contexts importantly ascriptive and not descriptive, and the question then is to determine the criteria by which we *ascribe* sameness and thus *relevant* similarity when, as is almost always the case, complete sameness or identity does not exist. It turns out, therefore, that much of the history of theorizing about precedent

[17] HLA Hart, 'Positivism and the Separation of Law and Morals' (1958) 71 Harv L Rev 593, 606–15. The example is reprised and modified in HLA Hart, *The Concept of Law* (PA Bulloch, J Raz, and L Green eds, 3d edn, OUP 2012) (1961) 125–27. A (too) lengthy exploration of the example and its implications is F Schauer, 'A Critical Guide to Vehicles in the Park' (2008) 83 NYU L Rev 1109.

[18] *Attributing* similarity to pairs that are similar in some respects and different in others necessarily involves goal-based and contextual choices, as recognized as far back as Aristotle, and as prominently analysed more recently in A Tversky, 'Features of Similarity' (1977) 84 Psych Rev 327; A Tversky and I Gati, 'Similarity, Separability, and the Triangle Inequality' (1982) 89 Psych Rev 123.

[19] Sebastian Lewis raises in comments on a draft of this chapter—and see also, again, the contribution to this volume by Luís Duarte d'Almeida (Chapter 10)—the query that genuine precedential obligation presupposes identity between the precedent case and the instant case, such that mere similarity substantially weakens the obligation to follow the earlier decision. But once we understand that genuine identity is almost always absent, then the implication would be that genuine constraint—obligation—is almost always absent as well, a conclusion that I and most of the history of precedent as practised and theorized would resist.

[20] Suppose that you have a red 2014 Honda Civic. If I say to you that 'I had the same car', I am not accusing you of theft.

3. On Relevant Similarity

A. Two Traditional Views

The question of relevant or sufficient (or insufficient) precedential similarity, as posited at the conclusion of the previous section, is hardly a new one. But the answers that have been given over the years remain unsatisfying. The early traditional answer to the question of what makes some earlier decision a controlling precedent for some question presented in some non-identical instant case is not a direct perception of similarity, but, rather, that it is the *rationale*, or *ratio decidendi*, in a precedent case that determines whether it should be considered binding in some subsequent instant case.[21] More precisely, the rationale of the earlier decision—the *principle* that determined the outcome in the earlier case—has been thought to control subsequent decisions within the scope of that rationale. This was the view of Salmond, who deemed the controlling feature of a controlling earlier decision as 'the underlying principle which ... forms its authoritative element'.[22] So too with John Chipman Gray, who described the controlling feature of a precedent in much the same way,[23] and, even earlier, John Austin, who used the terms 'grounds' and 'reasons' to make much the same point.[24]

This traditional view has long been challenged, perhaps most prominently in a 1930 article by Arthur Goodhart.[25] Goodhart, correctly recognizing that a reason (or rationale, or *ratio*) is necessarily broader than the outcome that the reason is a reason for,[26] worried that locating the constraining force of an earlier case in its rationale not only made that constraining force of that case unnecessarily broad but also left too much of the determination of that constraining force in the discretion of subsequent courts. And thus, to the extent that the scope and strength of the constraining force was to be determined by the instant court and not the precedent court, the very idea of being constrained by past decisions was undercut. Accordingly, Goodhart urged that the constraining or precedential force of the earlier decision be located more narrowly in the conjunction of the material facts of the earlier case, as identified by the judge in the earlier case, with the outcome that the earlier case had reached based on those material facts.

Goodhart's view spawned a spirited debate, with some commentators believing that Goodhart merely repeated the traditional or classical view in different terms[27] and others believing that he had indeed offered an account different from the classical account, but that

---

[21] Cross and Harris (n 1) 42–52.

[22] J Salmond, *Jurisprudence* (7th edn, Sweet & Maxwell 1924) 201.

[23] J Chipman Gray, *The Nature and Sources of Law* (2nd edn, Little Brown 1921) 261.

[24] J Austin, *Lectures on Jurisprudence* (R Campbell ed, 5th edn, Murray 1885) 627. And see also C Kemp Allen, *Law in the Making* (2nd edn, OUP 1930) 155; E Wambaugh, *The Study of Cases* (2nd edn, Little Brown 1894) (describing the background principle that determines the outcome as the 'general doctrine').

[25] AL Goodhart, 'Determining the *Ratio Decidendi* of a Case' (1930) 40 Yale LJ 161.

[26] On this point, see F Schauer, 'Giving Reasons' (1995) 47 Stan L Rev 633.

[27] Especially because it appears that it is something like the *ratio* that enables us to determine which facts are material and which are not.

this different account was deficient on either descriptive or normative grounds, or both.[28] Yet even Goodhart's responses made clear what he had noted in his original article—that in the almost universal absence of genuine identity between either the facts or the rationale in the earlier case and those of some latter case, the question was not one of identity but of similarity.[29] Indeed, even modern entries in this debate, especially those arguing that the language of the earlier decision should be understood as equivalent to a rule set forth in canonical language and subject to interpretation as such,[30] have not succeeded in avoiding the basic problem, for even authoritative language remains subject to a considerable amount of discretion by the court in the instant case as to whether the facts of the instant case do or do not fall within the language set forth in the precedent case.

B. The Legal Realist Challenge

At about the same time that Goodhart was offering his own objection to the traditional view that it was the *ratio decidendi* that determined the scope of precedential constraint, the American legal realists offered a quite different challenge.[31] For Karl Llewellyn,[32] Herman Oliphant,[33] Jerome Frank,[34] and others, the search for genuine precedential constraint was largely a fool's errand. Because judges in the instant case could typically choose among a multiplicity of earlier cases to decide just which earlier cases would be considered precedential, because the set of available earlier cases would often or even typically contain cases supporting opposing results in the instant case, and because the facts of the earlier case would never be identical to the facts of the instant case, the realists insisted that the degree of constraint exercised by earlier cases was at least exaggerated and to a significant extent largely illusory. At least in cases likely actually to be contested, as Llewellyn so limited his claims,[35] the alleged force of precedent disappeared, with judges in the instant case determining, on

---

[28] See G Dworkin, '*Stare Decisis* in the House of Lords' (1962) 25 MLR 163; JL Montrose, '*Ratio Decidendi* and the House of Lords' (1957) 20 MLR 124; JL Montrose, 'The *Ratio Decidendi* of a Case' (1957) 20 MLR 587; AWB Simpson, 'The *Ratio Decidendi* of a Case' (1957) 20 MLR 413; AWB Simpson, 'The *Ratio Decidendi* of a Case' (1958) MLR 155; J Stone, 'The *Ratio* of the *Ratio Decidendi*' (1959) 22 MLR 597.

[29] AL Goodhart, 'The *Ratio Decidendi* of a Case' (1959) MLR 117.

[30] Alexander (n 4). Relatedly, see Schauer (n 9); CW Tyler, 'The Adjudicative Model of Precedent' (2020) 87 U Chi L Rev 1551. Challenges to the so-called rule-model include W Twining and D Miers, *How to Do Things With Rules* (4th edn, Butterworths 1999) 313; J Horty, 'Rules and Reasons in the Theory of Precedent' (2011) 17 Legal Theory 1; J Horty, 'The Result Model of Precedent' (2004) 10 Legal Theory 19; G Lamond, 'Do Precedents Create Rules?' (2005) 11 Legal Theory 1.

[31] See the contribution by Brian Leiter in this volume (Chapter 23).

[32] KN Llewellyn, *The Theory of Rules* (F Schauer ed, University of Chicago Press 2011) 124–25.

[33] H Oliphant, 'A Return to *Stare Decisis*' (1928) 14 Am Bar Assoc J 71.

[34] J Frank, *Law and the Modern Mind* (Brentano's 1930).

[35] In modern language, Llewellyn had limited his often misunderstood (and undoubtedly, often rhetorically exaggerated) claims by reference to what is now known as the selection effect. KN Llewellyn, *The Bramble Bush, On Our Law and Its Study* (Columbia Law School 1930) 58; KN Llewellyn, 'Some Realism about Realism— Responding to Dean Pound' (1931) 44 Harv L Rev 1222, 1239. If easy cases are disproportionately likely to be settled or even earlier not to be contested at all, then the non-contested or non-settled cases—the ones that end up contested in court—will represent a skewed sample of legal events. Accordingly, it is a mistake to generalize from the indeterminacy of litigated (or, even worse, appellate) cases to claims about the indeterminacy of field of legal rules or doctrines or precedents from which the litigated or appellate cases emerge. See especially GL Priest and B Klein, 'The Selection of Disputes or Litigation' (1984) 13 J Legal Stud 1. See also L Lederman, 'Which Cases Go to Trial?: An Empirical Study of Predictors of Failure to Settle' (1999) 49 Case West Res L Rev 315; JP Kastellec and JR Lax, 'Case Selection and the Study of Judicial Politics' (2008) 5 J Empirical Legal Stud 407. And on the relationship between precedent and the selection effect, see F Schauer, '*Stare Decisis* and the Selection Effect' in CJ Peters (ed), *Precedent in the United States Supreme Court* (Springer 2013) 121.

non-legal or at least on non-precedential grounds, what outcome would be best, and then selecting a precedent as professed justification—or rationalization—for a result that was not in fact determined by the precedent.

For the realists, therefore, the question of similarity, as distinguished from any question of identity, provided the entering wedge into the world of non-constraint. Once judges found themselves looking for points of similarity between non-identical cases, they found themselves free to decide which points of similarity were important and which could safely be ignored.[36] This process, in turn, was driven by a judge's outcome preferences and not by pre-existing identity, nor even by pre-existing fundamental similarity. For the realists, similarity did not exist antecedent to particular cases. Instead, similarity was imposed by judges on the basis of their views about how they wanted the cases before them to come out or, in the less extreme version, on how they reacted to categories or types of acts and situations.[37] And even judges' reactions to situation types and not particular situations would likely be, for the realists, driven by a judge's broader policy view about how situations of that type ought to be resolved. Similarity was thus not an *ex ante descriptive* attribute of two different sets of facts, but was, rather, an *ascriptive* and *ex post* attribution based on a judge's outcome or policy preferences.

C. Challenging the Challenge

Although the realist challenge to the traditional view about precedential constraint offered a valuable corrective to a range of traditional views, and to subsequent views similarly emphasizing a considerable degree of robust constraint, it suffered, ironically, from its frequent lack of 'realism'. It is admittedly almost certainly true that US Supreme Court justices often have (typically controlling[38]) pre-legal or extra-legal outcome and/or policy preferences for the seventy or so self-selected cases they decide every year out of the more than seven thousand they are asked to decide.[39] With a self-selected docket for which public policy importance is one of the principles of selection, it should come as no surprise that Supreme Court justices will have their own pre-legal or extra-legal moral and policy preferences, as even the briefest recognition of issues such as abortion, affirmative action, immigration, the place of religion in public life, and the scope of the power of the President should make clear.

Although it is also true that judges below the Supreme Court sometimes have outcome preferences as well, it is an empirical claim, and a different empirical claim, that judges below the level of apex courts have outcome preferences in many or most of the cases that they are asked (and, importantly, compelled) to decide. The outcome preferences of judges other than Supreme Court justices may arise when those judges are presented with cases whose resolution raises and depends on issues of extra-legal policy as to which the judges have antecedent political, social, or moral attitudes. Controversies about salient policy issues such as the respective rights of workers and employers, for example, would fit this description,[40] and so too would issues potentially involving environmental protection or the respective

---

[36] E Levi, *An Introduction to Legal Reasoning* (first published 1949, University of Chicago Press 2013).

[37] As described and analysed in B Leiter, *Naturalizing Jurisprudence: Essays on Legal Realism and Naturalism in Legal Philosophy* (OUP 2007).

[38] Brenner and Spaeth (n 16).

[39] See F Schauer, 'Judging in a Corner of the Law' (1988) So Cal L Rev 1717.

[40] As in the running example in modern realist D Kennedy, 'Freedom and Constraint in Adjudication: A Critical Phenomenology' (1986) J Legal Educ 518.

rights of consumers and manufacturers. Most judges, as socially aware human beings and not only as judges, are likely to have opinions about, for example, whether the purchaser or the dealer or the manufacturer of an automobile with a defectively manufactured component should bear the costs of damages or injuries causes by the defective component.[41] And even when questions of policy do not produce antecedent outcome preferences, the equities of the particular situation may have the same effect. As a pre-legal matter, it is hard to imagine that there would be very many judges who would be comfortable with allowing beneficiaries who have murdered the testator to recover under the will as against the innocent residuary legatees, to take a particularly well-known example.[42]

It is a mistake, however, to take such cases as more representative than they are. In most cases below the level of the Supreme Court, judges will have little reason, apart from the law, to prefer one party or outcome to another. When one bank sues another regarding some technicality in the law of bills and notes, or when one insured driver sues another insured driver on the basis of an accident that left both drivers equally injured and equally compensated by insurance, judges may often, as a pre-legal matter, not care who wins.

Moreover, and as Judge Richard Posner has argued, most judges have a genuine liking for the law in its technical dimensions, and often *for* its technical dimensions, leading Posner to conclude that most judges have an attraction to judging simply because it is an outcome-independent satisfying and gratifying enterprise.[43] To use Posner's analogy, most or at least many judges are attracted to judging as an activity in the same way that most chess players are attracted to chess as an activity.[44] Accordingly, for most judges the technical or formal or doctrinal aspects of judging likely represent an independent preference and an independently satisfying activity. That does not mean, of course, that a judge who believes that abortion is murder will subjugate that pre-legal preference to the pleasure of figuring out the legal doctrine, and much the same likely applies to the judge who believes as a matter of morality and policy that sex discrimination is evil or that non-unionized workers are typically exploited by their employers. But in cases with substantially lower social, moral, political, or other ideological extra-legal ideological valence, even a judge with a slight outcome preference will likely see that preference as existing in competition with various non-ideological professional and other personal preferences.

The American legal realists were characterized by their commitments to two different propositions. One was a belief that a host of extra-legal, pre-legal, or non-legal factors commonly determined judicial outcomes in litigated, and especially appellate, cases. And the other was the commitment to the belief that assessing what judges actually did in the cases before them or predicting what they would do in future ones were in the final analysis empirical exercises. But once we understand that in many cases judges do not have extra-legal views about who ought to win, and that in many others the professional preferences of judges for working with and within legal doctrine will compete with weak outcome preferences, we can understand that these two realist commitments may often conflict. Consequently, to the extent that believing that extra-legal outcome preferences would often make doctrine of lesser or no importance, the realist view about precedent at least is open to the charge that

---

[41] *MacPherson v Buick Motor Co* 111 NE 1050 (NY 1916) (Cardozo).
[42] *Riggs v Palmer* 22 NE 188 (NY 1889).
[43] RA Posner, 'Social Norms and the Law: An Economic Approach' (1997) 87 Am Econ Rev 365.
[44] And if the analogy rings false because the player who plays chess has an opportunity to win in a competition, much the same can be said for rule-governed activities that do not so plainly have winners and losers.

the realist view about the constraints of precedent were empirically *un*realistic, and thus inconsistent with one of the principal commitments of American legal realism.

4. On Determining Relevant Similarity: The View from Cognitive Science

In treating the outcome preferences of judges as dominant and the constraining power of previous decisions as minimal, the realist account of precedent is, as just noted, open to the charge that it is potentially unrealistic, or at least demands more empirical support than the realist tradition has thus far provided. There is another view, however, that accepts the realist position that non-legal, extra-legal, or pre-legal factors have a role to play, but that recognizes as well that these factors are not simply preferences for how particular cases or even types of cases (and situations) ought to be resolved. And this view draws on what cognitive science can tell us about determinations of similarity.

Recall that when we leave the domain of potentially identical *questions* presented first in a precedent case and then in the instant case, the question will be one of similarity between non-identical facts, situations, events, or acts. And then the question is how these determinations of similarity between non-identical particulars will be made. Realism insists that these determinations are often a function of a judge's precedent-independent outcome or policy preferences. But another perspective, still a contrast with the traditional view of precedent, would posit that many of these determinations of similarity are made not on the basis of potentially non-existent or weak outcome or policy preferences, not by reference to a rationale or principle, and not by reference to some fictitious objective similarity between the facts of the precedent case and the facts in an instant case, but rather by a judge's pre-legal—or at least pre-doctrinal—attribution of similarity between the two particular situations.

But where do these extra-doctrinal attributions of similarity come from? If the attributions are not based on some metaphysical objective similarity between the two situations (as some versions of the traditional view seem to presuppose), and if they might not be based (as most of the realists argued) on constructing or ascribing similarity based on a judge's outcome or policy preferences, then what might be left? And here the answer to that question lies more in human psychology than in legal doctrine. What is it that leads people to identify similarity when any two particulars will have multiple points of similarity but also multiple points of difference? Given that any two things or situations 'have indefinitely many common properties',[45] how does a legal decision-maker determine which similarities will be controlling and which discarded as irrelevant?

Of course, policy considerations in a particular case or even more general policy considerations might sometimes assist in making that determination, as realism claims. Some judge might, for example, treat the presence of an opaque bottle in a case involving full-fat milk as similar to (and potentially controlled by) the presence of an opaque bottle of ginger beer in the earlier case of *Donoghue v Stevenson*[46] despite the differences between milk and ginger beer. And that determination might be based on that judge's policy view about the importance of consumer awareness of the products they purchase and thus on the way in which the opacity of the container would interfere with that awareness.

---

[45] KJ Holyoak and P Thagard, *Mental Leaps: Analogy in Creative Thought* (MIT Press 1995) 22. Holyoak and Thagard give as an example the act that 'this book and your shoes are both a million miles from Venus'.

[46] *Donoghue v Stevenson* [1932] AC 562 (HL).

It is also possible, however, that some judge would not consider this particular policy question important, in which case the realist claim would recede into the background. The replacement, however, might well not be the traditional view that the determination would be made by the rationale offered by the judge in the precedent case, nor the material-facts-plus outcome in the precedent case, as argued by Goodhart and others. Instead, an alternative view—perhaps it could be called 'cognitive realism'—would suggest that the determination of relevant similarity would be made on the basis of the judge's non-policy (and non-particular-outcome) preferences, but nevertheless on pre-legal or extra-legal perceptions about which pairs of acts or events are similar and which are different in which circumstances.

It is time to explain in more detail the position suggested at the end of the previous paragraph. The basic idea is that determinations of similarity are often a function not of *ex post* attributions of similarity based on a judge's outcome or policy preferences, as realism would maintain. Rather, determining similarity would be a function of a judge's initial and outcome-independent perception of what is similar to what, with the outcome following rather than determining the attribution of similarity. In some respects, this understanding resembles the naive view according to which similarity is the object of direct perception by the decision-maker. Edward Levi, for example, offered what is substantially a realist account of the use of precedent and analogy in judicial decision-making but nevertheless described the first step as one in which a 'similarity is *seen* between cases'.[47] And we can observe related beliefs in the direct perception of similarity—a perception not mediated by an outcome preference—in the work of many others who have put forth one or another version of the traditional view.[48]

With a crucial qualification to be discussed presently, it turns out that much of the experimental cognitive psychological research on similarity supports this version of the traditional view. In fact, people faced with two items whose similarity (or not) is at issue will turn initially not to the consequences of the determination, but, rather, to their initial consequence-independent perception of similarity and difference—the *original encoding*, in technical cognitive science terminology.[49]

Although it seems well established in the experimental literature that people assess similarity more directly and less by conscious consideration of the consequences of an attribution of similarity or not than either the sceptics or the realists suppose,[50] the claim is not that

---

[47] Levi (n 36) 2.

[48] See SJ Burton, *An Introduction to Law and Legal Reasoning* (Little Brown 1985) 25–40; SJ Burton, 'On "Empty Ideas"' (1982) 91 Yale LJ 1136; EC Clark, *Practical Jurisprudence: A Comment on Austin* (CUP 1883) 251 (observing that identifying similarity or analogy involves 'a sense of likeness' and not an 'intellectual process'); CR Sunstein, 'On Analogical Reasoning' (1993) 106 Harv L Rev 741; LL Weinreb, *Legal Reason: The Use of Analogy in Legal Argument* (CUP 2005) 111–12.

[49] See Holyoak and Thagard (n 45) 5, discussing a perception of 'direct similarity'. See also RL Goldstone and JY Son, 'Similarity' in KJ Holyoak and RG Morrison (eds), *Cambridge Handbook of Thinking and Reasoning* (CUP 2005); DL Medin, RL Goldstone, and D Gentner, 'Respects for Similarity' (1993) 100 Psych Rev 254.

[50] Although reasoning by analogy is in important respects not identical to constraint by precedent, see F Schauer, 'Why Precedent in Law (and Elsewhere) is Not Totally (or Even Substantially) about Analogy' (2008) 3 Perspectives on Psych Science 454, much of the research on similarity in law, research almost completely applicable to questions about precedent, is situated within discussions of analogical reasoning. See BA Spellman, 'Judges, Expertise, and Analogy' in D Klein and G Mitchell (eds), *The Psychology of Judicial Decision-Making* (CUP 2010). Among prominent and sophisticated efforts to defend legal reasoning by analogy by understanding it as abductive reasoning or its close companion, inference to the best explanation, are S Brewer, 'Exemplary Reasoning: Semantics, Pragmatics, and the Rational Force of Legal Argument by Analogy' (1996) Yale LJ 923; FM Kamm, 'Theory and Analogy in Law' (1997) 29 Ariz St LJ 405. Such efforts, like the more traditional ones, still accept that there is an initial perception of similarity, one that precedes the development of an inference or theory that would explain the perception.

such an assessment is an innate or genetic talent of human beings nor that there is some variety of primary or ontological similarity that either exists or not. Rather, although similarity is not ontologically primary, and although people acquire perceptions of similarity rather than being born with them, the central claim here is that those perceptions, no less real, are substantially a function of the informational and experiential background (and baggage) that the perceiver brings to the task of perceiving the existence of non-existence of similarity.

Consider, to take a hypothetical example, the question of whether insects are similar to chocolate. For those of us for whom insects are not part of our daily (or even yearly) diet, the two are unlikely to seem similar. But where and when insects are regularly consumed by human beings, whether as a delicacy or for essential nutrition, the similarities between insects and chocolate will be more salient than they are to those of us with different tastes. Or, to offer another example, the title of George Lakoff's *Women, Fire and Dangerous Things*,[51] although largely about metaphor, nevertheless offers a striking illustration of the cultural contingency of categorization, and thus of the way in which assimilating multiple items in the same category—seeing those items or even multiple questions as similar—is largely determined by what the assimilator knows, which is in turn determined by the assimilator's culture, experiences, and much else.

Much of this can be made more concrete by bringing it back to the culture, background, education, and experiences of lawyers and judges. Consider, for example, the question of whether a defect in the design and manufacture of an automobile wheel—as in *MacPherson v Buick*—would present an issue similar to that presented in *Donoghue v Stevenson*. And although it is highly unlikely that a layperson would think that automobile wheels are in any interesting way similar to decomposed snails in bottle of ginger beer, or that wheels are similar to snails, or that automobiles are similar to glass bottles, most lawyers with a common law background, even without knowing of the actual *MacPherson* decision, would see its facts as almost intuitively similar to those in *Donoghue*. The lawyer would initially perceive (or retrieve, in the proper technical terminology) a similarity that most non-lawyers would miss.[52]

Or consider the comparison between Nazis and those who would protest against racial segregation. To most laypeople, any suggestion of similarity would be at least peculiar and more likely offensive. But to an American lawyer, and especially one knowledgeable about the US First Amendment tradition, both groups have been famously protected in their ability to conduct protest marches in public places. Against this background, the similarity between the otherwise different groups would be as immediately obvious to those aware of First Amendment doctrine as it would be strange to those without that awareness.

As these examples illustrate, people with certain types of backgrounds and experiences will perceive, from the virtually unlimited universe of similarities and differences between two acts, events, or situations, those that others with different backgrounds and experiences will not notice at all. And although these examples are about lawyers and judges, they are but the legal embodiment of a phenomenon that exists throughout the universe of human cognition and thus of human determinations of similarity.

To repeat, the claim that judges will see similarities because of their pre-existing knowledge, training, and experience is importantly different from the realist claim that judges see

---

[51] G Lakoff, *Women, Fire and Dangerous Things: What Categories Reveal about the Mind* (University of Chicago Press 1990).

[52] The examples in this and the following paragraphs are adapted from F Schauer and BA Spellman, 'Analogy, Expertise, and Experience' (2017) U Chi LR 249.

similarities and differences because of their case-specific outcome preferences or their more general and not case-specific policy preferences. Judges will sometimes, as the realists claim, see similarities because of such preferences, but the point here is that in identifying the similarities and differences that are essential to the operation of a system of precedent, judges are often also likely to make, contrary to the realist claim, outcome- and policy-independent judgments. But because such experience- and background-infused judgments are based neither on natural similarity nor on probing for the legal reasoning in the precedent case, they are as different from the traditional picture as they are from the realist one.

5. Conclusion: From Particulars to Particulars

None of the foregoing denies that perceiving similarity between snails and automobiles, or between Nazis and civil rights marchers, is entirely devoid of some principle or rule identifying the relevant similarities. It does take a rule or principle of some sort to say that my blue car is similar to your red car but not to your blue jacket, and often that rule or principle will be relative to some goal—are you choosing a paint colour or going for a ride?

That determinations of similarity are rule- or principle- or theory-dependent does not mean, however, that such rules or principles or theories are consciously perceived or consciously applied. Rather, such determinations, as multiple behavioural and neuroscientific studies have established, are often not perceived by the reasoner.[53] Rather, determinations of similarity do not consciously go from precedent case to rationale (or theory or principle or rule) to instant case but instead go from precedent case to instant case without the decisionmaker consciously perceiving the generality that supports the determination of similarity. In other words, at the level of consciousness, determinations of similarity often go directly from particular to particular. And in still other words, determinations of similarity are *sticky*, in the sense that initial and general perceptions of similarity carry over with only limited modification to more particular applications and situations.

The principal message here is that in going from particular to particular, judges are influenced by their own backgrounds, training, and experience and not only by their conscious views about which party ought to win or which policy it would be best for the legal system to adopt. The realists were undoubtedly correct in insisting that such outcome factors were sometimes the key determinants of judicial decisions about precedent. But how often such factors, and for which judges, in which courts, and in which kinds of cases, actually do control is an empirical question, the answer to which cannot be given without more empirical evidence than can be offered here, and that in fact thus far exists.

---

[53] See AE Green and others, 'Neural Correlates of Creativity in Analogical Reasoning' (2012) 38 J Experimental Psych: Learning, Memory & Cognition 1264; AE Green and others, 'Connecting Long Distance: Semantic Distance in Analogical Reasoning Modulates Frontopolar Cortex Activity' (2010) 20 Cerebral Cortex 70.

PART III
PRECEDENT AND LEGAL THEORY

19

Presumptive Reasons and *Stare Decisis*

Andrei Marmor[*]

It would be very difficult to imagine our practical reasoning without reliance on general-izations about reasons that normally or typically apply under the circumstances, even if not always. When somebody makes a promise, we would normally assume that the promisor ought to keep it; when someone is asked a simple question, we would normally assume that they ought to reply truthfully; and so on and so forth. We know that all these reasons for action that normally apply may have exceptions, they may not apply in this case, or even if they do, they may be defeated by conflicting reasons. And yet, practical reasoning without reliance on such generalizations would be almost impossible or, at the very least, hugely in-efficient. Notice, however, that the generalizations about reasons that we frequently rely on are just that, generalizations; by themselves, they carry no normative weight. The fact that a reason for action happens to apply frequently in a given context does not add anything to the weight of the reason. Furthermore, people are not generally expected to explain or to justify why a reason for action that would normally apply to them either does not apply or is defeated in their particular instance. However, I would like to focus here on one type of case in which an expectation to explain one's failure to comply with a reason that would have nor-mally or generally applied, is warranted; I call them *presumptive reasons*.

My purpose in this chapter is to use the idea of presumptive reasons to elucidate the practical reasoning that underlies the legal doctrine of *stare decisis* in horizontal (i.e. non-binding) precedents. I will therefore begin by explaining the idea of presumptive reasons and how they structure some familiar types of practical reasoning.[1] Next I move to the legal doc-trine of *stare decisis*, arguing that presumptive reasons can be employed to explain the prac-tical reasoning behind horizontal precedent. Let me state from the outset, however, that it is not my aim here to show how legal precedents are binding, legally or otherwise. On the con-trary, my main interest is in the force of precedents that are not considered strictly binding on the court that is supposed to apply them. I will explain this in greater detail when we get to section 2. First, however, we need to see what presumptive reasons are and how they struc-ture certain aspects of practical reasoning.

1. Presumptive Reasons for Action

Suppose that you ask your best friend for help with a minor errand. Let us make two as-sumptions about this request. First, we assume that your friend would have no other reason,

---

[*] I would like to thank Bill Watson for excellent research assistance, and Emad Atiq, Scott Brewer, David Enoch, Hafsteinn Dan Kristjánsson, David Shoemaker, and Ben Zipursky for very helpful comments on earlier drafts.
[1] I first presented the idea of presumptive reasons in the context of explaining the practical reasoning involved in so-called 'soft law'. The label 'presumptive' comes from an analogy with rebuttable presumptions in law. See A Marmor, 'Soft Law, Authoritative Advice & Nonbinding Agreements' (2019) 39 OJLS 507.

Andrei Marmor, *Presumptive Reasons and* Stare Decisis In: *Philosophical Foundations of Precedent*. Edited by: Timothy Endicott, Hafsteinn Dan Kristjánsson, and Sebastian Lewis, Oxford University Press. © Andrei Marmor 2023. DOI: 10.1093/oso/9780192857248.003.0020

256   ANDREI MARMOR

besides your request, to do what you ask for. Secondly, we assume that complying with the request is not particularly burdensome, just the kind of thing that friends ask of each other routinely. The request, we would assume, gives your friend a reason to comply; she wouldn't be your friend if it didn't. But we also know that the reason is defeasible; perhaps your friend happens to be ill, or is otherwise engaged, and cannot be expected to help you. Is this just one of those familiar cases where reasons for action conflict? I don't think so. We should think that even if your friend has a very good reason not to help you in this case, she needs to explain it to you. She needs to tell you what the reason is and why it prevents her from helping you this time. Even if the reason is one that your friend would not be comfortable disclosing, she needs to say something by way of explanation. It is not good enough that there is, actually, a defeating reason, unless she also tells you what it is (or something close enough to that).[2]

I hope we can see from this mundane example that there are many cases in which one is expected to do something or else explain why they wouldn't (or couldn't). This is, roughly, what I call presumptive reasons. Notice, however, that presumptive reasons do not change, by themselves, the balance of reasons in play. What they bring to the table, so to speak, is something like a 'burden of proof'. Your friend may not need particularly weighty reasons to defeat the reason to help you; what she needs, however, is to explain the defeat, at least to tell you about it. That is the additional burden, as it were, that comes with presumptive reasons, and I will call it the *burden of explanation*. Thus, a presumptive reason is in place when an expectation is warranted that the subject either comply with a reason for action that would normally apply to them, or else explain why not.[3] Two immediate questions arise here. First, what is this need for explanation: where does it come from, and is it necessarily an obligation? Secondly, there is a question about directionality: who do you owe this explanation to? Is it necessarily tied to some form of second-personal accountability, owed to someone else who gives you a reason for action? Or is the burden of explanation more general, wider in scope, not necessarily tied to second-personal accountability?

I will get to these questions and a few others shortly. Before that, let me give a few more examples of presumptive reasons and formulate the idea more precisely. In previous work I have argued that practical authorities sometimes issue advisory directives, not intending them to be binding or obligatory, and that such authoritative advice is best explained by the idea of presumptive reasons. An authority may simply point out a reason for action that applies to you, expecting, however, that you either comply with the reason or explain to the authority why the reason is defeated in your particular circumstances.[4] Regardless of authoritative contexts, however, presumptive reasons are rather ubiquitous in our daily lives. Consider, for example, someone who is late to a meeting at work. Let us assume that there are reasons not to be late; but, of course, sometimes those reasons are defeated. Perhaps John was late to the meeting because his daughter got sick and he needed to make sure that she was OK before leaving home. That is a perfectly acceptable defeat; but, again, it's not enough that the defeating reason is there. When John shows up at the meeting half an hour late, he needs to

---

[2] There are borderline cases, of course; the friend could tell you, e.g., 'I had a good reason, just trust me on this.' In some contexts, this might be good enough, in others, perhaps not.

[3] I am assuming here that we are talking about ordinary moral reasons for action; whether similar considerations apply to purely prudential reasons, or other kinds of practical considerations, I am not sure. But I am also not assuming that there is a clear or sharp boundary between morality and other practical domains. Be this as it may, thinking about ordinary moral reasons for action should be good enough for our purposes here.

[4] Authoritative advice is not very common in domestic legal contexts, but it is used extensively in international law. A great deal of international law is 'soft law', which is the paradigmatic case of authoritative advice. I explain all this in detail in Marmor, 'Soft Law' (n 1).

say something about it to his colleagues, he needs to give some explanation. The explanation, by itself, does not change the nature, strength, or validity of the defeating considerations. If John was late because he fancied a fresh croissant on his way to work, that might not do it, it might not be the right kind of defeating reason. Explaining it does not change anything in that respect.[5] Either way, in these types of cases, apart from the direct normative question of whether a reason was actually defeated or not, there is also the burden of explanation; if you rely on a defeating consideration, you need to explain that.

In case you are wondering why this isn't always the case, the simple answer is that we are not generally expected to explain to other people our failure to comply with moral reasons for action that apply to us, whether the failure was warranted under the circumstances or not. Life would be insufferably oppressive if people generally made it their business to mind others' compliance with reasons for actions that apply to them. Ordinarily, absent some special relationships, it's just none of our business whether someone else fails comply with a reason for action, and therefore none of our business to know whether their reason has been defeated or not.[6] In other words, it is just not generally the case that reasons for action involve the kind of disjunctive structure, expecting you to do or to explain why not, which is the case with presumptive reasons for action. Presumptive reasons would normally come into play when there is, already, an accountability relation between the relevant agents relative to the relevant reasons for action. As I will argue later, the accountability relation does not have to be second-personal; it may be wider in scope. But the idea is that presumptive reasons are in play only when the expectation to explain one's failure to comply with a reason for action that applies is a warranted expectation in the circumstances.

Of course, I am not assuming that the need for explaining one's failure to comply with reasons for action is confined to presumptive reasons. Far from it. There are many situations in which one would be rightly expected to explain to others some aspect of their behaviour; the need for explanation does not necessarily derive from presumptive reasons. Presumptive reasons pertain to those cases in which the expectation is to explain why reasons that typically or putatively apply to you are defeated in your particular circumstances. In other words, we use presumptive reasons in our practical reasoning when the warranted expectation is, from the start, disjunctive in nature: you are expected to φ in C *or else*, if the reason to φ in C is defeated in your case, you are expected to explain or demonstrate the defeat. To whom this explanation is owed is a complex question and I will get to it shortly.

So, let's formulate this a bit more precisely. We can say that R is a presumptive reason for A to φ in C, if and only if

(1) R is generally or typically a defeasible (*pro tanto*) first-order reason for A to φ in C.
(2) If R is defeated for A in C, there is a warranted expectation from A to explain the defeat and justify it as such.
(3) A's failure to either φ in C or demonstrate that φ-ing in C is defeated in this case is pro tanto wrong.

---

[5] Presumably in this case an apology is called for, but that's a different kind of explanation. As I will argue shortly, discharging a burden of explanation is very different from apology.

[6] This is one of the main critical points raised by J Raz, 'On Respect, Authority and Neutrality: A Response' (2010) 120 Ethics 279–301, against S Darwall, *The Second-Person Standpoint: Morality, Respect, and Accountability* (Harvard UP 2006), a second-personal standpoint account of moral reasons for action, that it overplays the accountability element in our interpersonal relations. I agree with Raz on this point.

Notice that presumptive reasons require the defeat to be justified; not excused or forgiven. People often explain their failure to comply with a reason for action that had applied to them by way of an apology or by pointing to an excuse. Excuses and apologies, however, share the admission by the agent that they had done some wrong; they express some admission of error. This is not the kind of explanation that the idea of presumptive reasons assumes. When your friend declines your request for help because they are sick or have some other conflicting engagement, they do not seek to be excused or forgiven; they point to the fact that though your request would normally or typically give them a good reason for action, it is defeated in this case.[7]

There are two main ways in which such reasons can be defeated. By way of a useful analogy, let me draw on a distinction long held by epistemologists between *rebutting* defeats and *undercutting* defeats. Something very similar also applies to reasons for action. Let me digress a little to explain. Suppose you are told that 'Tweety is a bird'. Normally, you can infer from this that 'Tweety can fly'. But, of course, this is a defeasible inference; if you get the additional information (henceforth: superseding premise) that 'Tweety is an ostrich', you can no longer infer that 'Tweety can fly'—ostriches cannot fly. Thus, the superseding premise here is a rebutting defeat, it negates the conclusion of the inference. In other cases, however, the superseding premise might be such that it undermines the initial evidence we had for the conclusion. For example, suppose an object in front of me looks red. Under normal conditions what looks red is red, and thus I may conclude that the object is red. However, suppose I learn the superseding fact that I was given a drug that makes me see many things in red. This superseding premise undercuts my evidence for concluding that the object in front of me is red. Notice that it does not necessarily negate the conclusion that the object is red; for all I know, it might be red. What is defeated here is the reliability of the initial evidence I had for concluding that the object is red. These are called undercutting defeats.[8]

Now think about the ways in which general, *pro tanto*, reasons for action can be defeated. A rebutting defeat is closely analogous to cases in which a reason for action is defeated by *a conflicting reason* that also applies in the circumstances, outweighing the original reason for action. Your friend's request for help would normally or typically give you a reason to help; but if you have a prior engagement to do something else at the relevant time, you have a conflicting reason that may outweigh the reason to help your friend; I will call these kinds of cases *conflicting defeats*. The equivalent of the superseding premise here is a conflicting reason that outweighs the original reason under the circumstances. But now consider cases in which your friend's request is such that it is not the kind of request that they should have made from the start. Suppose, for example, that your friend lied to you about their need for a loan, telling you some sad story that had not really happened. In this case, the general reason to help is such that it is undercut *ab initio*, as it were; what is normally a reason for action in similar circumstances, namely, helping a friend in need turns out not to be a reason in this case. The relevant *pro tanto* reason is undercut by defeating considerations that are present from the start, as it were. I will keep referring to these kinds of defeat in practical reasoning as undercutting defeats.

---

[7] I will say a bit more on this later.

[8] The idea of undercutting defeats was probably presented first by J Pollock, 'The Structure of Epistemic Justification' (1970) 78 Am Philosophical Quarterly 62–78. It has been widely used since. The distinction between undercutting and rebutting defeats is often utilized in the context of non-monotonic logic, as the examples in the text show. On the application of non-monotonic logic in practical reasoning and defeasibility in law, I elaborated elsewhere: A Marmor, 'Defeasibility and Pragmatic Indeterminacy in Law' in A Capone and F Poggi (eds), *Pragmatics and the Law, Philosophical Perspectives* (Springer 2016) 15.

The importance of the distinction between conflicting and undercutting defeats will become clear in section 2. For now, suffice to note two points. First, we should acknowledge that in the realm of practical reason the distinction between conflicting and undercutting defeats is not always very sharp; some borderline cases are to be expected. Suppose, for example, that what your friend is asking from you is to hear a juicy piece of gossip that you happen to know. And suppose that it relates to information that you really should not be revealing to anyone, it is none of your friend's business to know. There are many possible nuances here. There might be cases in which the defeat is clearly of the undercutting type; your friend should have known better than to ask at all. There are cases in which the defeat is clearly a conflicting one: your friend could not have guessed that you have reasons not to reveal the information, but the fact is that you do, and that is a conflicting defeat. Between such clear cases, however, there might be all sorts of borderline cases where it is neither clearly one or the other but some fuzzy mixture of both.

Secondly, we should bear in mind that both types of defeat are such that when they apply they justify the failure to comply with the reason for action. A defeat, as I use the term here, is not an excuse or a plea for forgiveness. It is the rebuttal of any failure. I may regret the fact that I cannot help my friend because I have a conflicting engagement that is more pressing or urgent, but I am not seeking to be excused or forgiven when I point this out to them.[9] The conflicting engagement defeats the reason to help, and thus the failure to help is not something that I need to genuinely apologize for. I do not fail to adequately respond to reasons in such cases, on the contrary, I would have failed otherwise.[10]

To recap thus far: we have a presumptive reason for action when there is a warranted expectation that the subject either comply with a reason for action that applies to them or else explain why the reason is defeated under the circumstances—if it is. The explanation for not complying with the reason needs to justify non-compliance, which is to say, it needs to demonstrate that the reason is defeated in this case—if it is. The defeat can either be of a conflicting kind or an undercutting one. The important point to bear in mind, however, that presumptive reasons are in play if and only if it is the case that the warranted expectation is initially of a disjunctive nature: the agent is expected to comply with a general reason that applies to them, *or else* explain why it is defeated in their particular circumstances.

What would generally make it the case that such a disjunctive expectation, to do or to explain, is appropriate? There is a wide range of cases and their rationales might differ. The recognition that reasons for action are defeasible, that even when they generally or typically apply, in particular circumstances they may be defeated, is certainly an essential part of it. But that, as we noted, is not enough. People cannot generally be expected to explain their failure to comply with a reason for action, or even with obligations, that apply to them; the burden of explanation applies only when you actually owe that explanation to someone. Which would suggest that the idea of accountability plays a key role here.[11] And there is a

---

[9] Note that regret is not necessarily agent regret. In other words, we can regret things that happen to us (or to others) even if there is nothing we could have done about it, or nothing wrong with what we have done.

[10] I use the expression 'genuine apology' advisedly. We often express apologies not by way of acknowledging any wrongdoing on our part, but just as a matter of politeness or kindness, and sometimes even to deflect responsibility, as if to say, 'I'm sorry but it's really not my fault!' Apology is genuine, as it were, when it does intend to express some acknowledgement of wrongdoing.

[11] According to Darwall (n 6), there is an identity relation between accountability and second-person perspective; one *just is* the other. Darwall regards all moral reasons for action to be of the second-personal type, and thus subject to accountability relations. I do not share this view. In fact, there are two points of disagreement here. First, I will argue here that accountability relations may obtain even in the absence of second-personal relations that give rise to the relevant reasons for action. Secondly, but this is not directly relevant to our concerns here, I am also

260 ANDREI MARMOR

great variety of facts that can ground accountability relations between people. Accountability can arise from promises and agreements, from special relationships like friendship or family, from institutional roles or functions, from certain forms of shared or collective agency, and so on and so forth. The circumstances are varied and the kind of reasons that ground the burden of explanation are multifarious. But there are two questions about the burden of explanation that we do need to address. First, is it an obligation to explain and, if not, what else could it be? And, secondly, to whom is it owed? Let me take up these two questions in turn.

It might be tempting to think that the question of whether the expectation to explain a defeat amounts to an obligation or not would depend on the nature of the initial reason for action that the agent failed to comply with. If A had an obligation to φ, and A failed to φ for defeating reason X, then A would have an obligation to explain X to B. And then we might think that if the reason to φ was not an obligation or a duty to begin with, some weaker sense of an expectation to explain the defeat is all that is warranted. But I doubt that this is the case; the burden of explanation does not necessarily track the strength or structure of the initial reason for action. It may stand on its own, as it were, sometimes more and sometimes perhaps less stringent than the relevant first-order reason for action. Consider this example: suppose I tell my graduate student that I will try to read their paper by next Friday. Let us assume that it is clear to my student that this is not a promise, I did not undertake this deadline as a matter of obligation. Let us also assume that there are reasons to try to make it by Friday, it would be helpful to them to get my comments before the weekend. Now suppose that I had tried to read the paper on time, but something much more urgent unexpectedly came up, and I could not finish the task in time. It does seem to me sensible to maintain that I actually have an obligation to explain the defeat to my student. I am not suggesting that my explanation needs to be detailed or exhaustive. But some explanation is owed, I think, as a matter of obligation. Anything less than that would betray their trust and the respect she is owed in our professional relations. In other words, the expectation to explain a defeat when the subject relies on it, might be morally or otherwise obligatory, even if the initial reason for action was not an obligation.

Whether this holds in the other direction as well, I am less certain. Either way, the important point to realize here is that the burden of explanation in presumptive reasons for action may or may not amount to an obligation. Sometimes it is an obligation to explain, and sometimes it is no more than a warranted expectation, something we would regard as the appropriate or the decent thing to do, even if the failure to explain would not amount to violation of an obligation. Let us draw a distinction, then, between strong and weak presumptive reasons for action: the presumptive reason would be strong when the burden of explaining the defeat is an obligation, and weak if it is no more than a warranted expectation but not of an obligatory nature.[12]

Presumptive reasons for action tend to be of the strong kind in institutional settings. It is often the case that an agent acting in some official capacity is expected to do something or

---

very doubtful about the idea that all moral reasons for action are generally second personal. See, e.g., RJ Wallace, 'Reasons, Relations, and Commands: Reflections on Darwall' (2007) 118 Ethics 24–36; Raz, 'On Respect' (n 6).

[12] Of course, I am assuming here that obligations or duties are distinguishable from first-order reasons for action. The assumption is hardly controversial. How to account for the nature of moral obligation is beyond the scope of this chapter. I am assuming, however, that something along the lines of the account in J Raz, *Practical Reason and Norms* (2nd edn, OUP 1990) of a combination between first-order and second-order exclusionary reasons, is going to be part of it. But maybe that's not quite enough. Perhaps also, as Raz, 'On Respect' (n 6) seems to have thought, the first-order reasons need to be of a categorical kind.

else explain why not, and this burden of explanation is obligatory. You are expected to teach your classes, it is your official duty as a professor; and if the fulfilment of your duty is defeated on an occasion, as it might be, due to illness or some other urgent need, you are under an obligation to explain the defeat. The obligation to explain is *pro tanto*, of course, and like any other obligation, it might also be defeated. But, in this case, an obligation it is; you can't just skip a class and keep quiet about it, even if the reason that kept you from teaching is compelling under the circumstances. In less formal or institutional contexts, we often encounter weak presumptive reasons. In the example I started with, asking a friend to help with some trivial errand to run, the expectation is for the friend to either comply or to explain why she cannot, but the burden of explanation here is hardly an obligation. If she don't bother to tell you why she cannot help you this time, you are likely to be disappointed, perhaps even begin to doubt the strength of the friendship, but it does not seem to me that you can blame your friend for violating an obligation (assuming that she did rely on a sound defeating consideration). The various expectations and mutual commitments that come with friendship are not necessarily of an obligatory nature.

I realize that some readers might disagree with my intuitions here. The main argument does not depend on sharing intuitions about the examples. My main point is only to suggest that the expectation to explain a defeat if and when it is present is sometimes no more than that, a warranted or appropriate expectation, and sometimes it is an obligation to explain. As long as you agree with the distinction, its application to particular cases is of secondary importance. I will return to the distinction and its institutional importance in section 2.

An important issue we have not yet addressed concerns the question of who is owed the relevant explanation when presumptive reasons are in place. Many cases are pretty straightforward, in which the presumptive reason for action is a reason given by one agent to another. People often give each other reasons for action. By *giving* a reason I mean to refer to those cases in which an exercise of agency, typically expressive in nature, like a request or a directive, gives another person a reason for action that he or she would not have had otherwise. Generally, A's φ-ing gives B a reason to X if and only if B would not have had the complete reason to X without A's φ-ing.[13] Why 'complete reason'? Because there are cases in which A's φ-ing only completes a reason for action that applies to B without creating it *ab initio*. Solutions to coordination problems are often of this nature. Suppose A and B want to meet for coffee; they have a reason to meet in the same café, but no particular reason to meet at *Chez Andre*, of all available places. By telling B 'Let's meet a *Chez Andre*', A gives B a reason to be at *Chez Andre*; but this reason depends on the reasons to meet and have coffee together.[14]

Be this as it may, people often give reasons to each other. Not all reason-giving involves presumptive reasons for action, but many cases do. If A and B agree to meet at *Chez Andre* at a certain time, the mutual expectation would be to show up on time or else explain why you couldn't. So, in these kinds of cases, it is pretty obvious to whom the explanation is owed, to the other party to the agreement. Generally speaking, when A gives a reason for action to B, and the reason is of the presumptive kind, the expectation to explain a defeat, if it arises, is owed to A. I say that this is obvious because from the start, as I mentioned earlier, the idea

---

[13] There are bound to be exceptions and some difficult cases here. Consider, e.g., A putting B in harm's way only to force C to help B. Would we say that A gave C a reason for action? In some sense, clearly yes, but in another sense, not so. Dealing with these types of case, however, is not needed here. We are not trying to analyse what it is to give people reasons for action, just to demonstrate the relevant notion of accountability.

[14] See D Enoch, 'Giving Practical Reasons' (2011) 11 Philosophers Imprint; A Marmor, *Philosophy of Law* (Princeton UP 2011) ch 3.

of presumptive reasons is closely aligned with the idea of accountability. We are not generally expected to account for failing to comply with a reason for action that applies to us. An expectation to account for failure to comply with a reason is warranted if there is some accountability relation between the relevant agents. Thus, it seems unproblematic to assume that if and to the extent that A is in a position to give a reason to B, B would be accountable for complying with the reason to A or else explain to A why the reason to comply is defeated in this case.[15]

It would be a mistake, however, to think that presumptive reasons for action arise only in contexts of second-personal relations of reason-giving. Our relations of accountability to others is much wider in scope. You may owe me an explanation for failing to comply with a reason that generally applies to you even if it is not a reason I have given you. For example, putting certain people at serious risk of injury makes you accountable to them, simply by virtue of your moral responsibility to avoid causing unnecessary harm to others. Or, to take an example which would be closer to our concerns in this chapter, think about institutional duties. People occupy various institutional roles that come with duties or obligations to perform certain tasks on behalf or others, and people generally rely on the performance of those institutional duties. Though failure to discharge an obligation in these contexts can be justified on occasion, there is normally a warranted expectation of explanation; the official would need to explain to the parties concerned why what is normally expected of them is defeated in this case. In other words, the kind of accountability relations presupposed by the idea of presumptive reasons are not confined to cases of (second-personal) reason-giving situations; they are often grounded in institutional settings. The score keeper in a tournament is accountable for the accuracy of the scores not only to the players or the teams but also to the audience or spectators at large.

2. Horizontal Precedent and Presumptive Reasons

Now that we have the tools in our hands, let us put them to use in the context of the legal doctrine of precedent, or *stare decisis*. In most jurisdictions that recognize an official doctrine of precedent, a distinction can be drawn between those that are considered legally binding and those that are not, or not quite. The distinction usually tracks the hierarchical structure of the courts: decisions of higher courts are binding on lower courts that are subject to their appellate jurisdiction, whereas previous decisions of the same court, or decisions of another court at the same level in the hierarchy, are not normally considered legally binding. For the sake of simplicity, we can use the terms *vertical* and *horizontal* precedent. Vertical precedent is binding, whereas horizontal precedent is not considered strictly binding on the court that is meant to apply it. I will assume here that a precedent is binding when there is a legal obligation to apply it, or else to show that the precedent does not apply by way of distinguishing it.[16] My interest in this chapter is confined to horizontal precedent. From the perspective

[15] There are varying accounts of what constitutes moral accountability relations and what morally grounds accountability. See, e.g., G Watson, 'Two Faces of Responsibility' (1996) 24 Philosophical Topics 227–48. I don't think we need to go into all of that. One idea shared by all those who write on accountability, and I certainly endorse it here too, is that accountability is always directional; an agent is accountable to another agent, something A owes to B. There is no such thing as accountability to nobody in particular.

[16] I am using the terms 'binding' and 'obligatory' interchangeably here. On the logic of distinguishing precedent, see J Raz, *The Authority of Law* (2nd edn, OUP 2009) ch 10. I am aware of the fact that some of the contributors to this volume do not agree with Raz's analysis of a binding precedent and the logic of distinguishing it. I do not share those misgivings, but defending Raz's account is not part of my task here.

of practical reasons, the idea of a precedent that is 'not quite binding', so to speak, is rather puzzling. We understand, more or less, the idea of an obligation to follow the ruling of a previous decision; a binding precedent is one that the court needs to apply or else distinguish from its present case. But what is the structure of practical reasoning that underlies the idea of a precedent that is not binding?

The easy suggestion that a precedent that is not binding gives the court only a reason, a legal reason, to decide the case accordingly, is not convincing. Reasons come cheap, any fact that counts in favour of deciding the case one way or the other is a reason. To suggest that a non-binding precedent is just a legal reason for a decision would put precedent on par with any other legal reason, often easily defeasible by conflicting reasons. But this is not how courts normally regard horizontal precedent; it would hardly be worth the name of *stare decisis* if they did. To work with a concrete example, I will focus on the doctrine of *stare decisis* applied by the US Supreme Court with respect to its own prior rulings.[17] As we will see shortly, there are some interesting disagreements between justices on the court about the constraints imposed by their previous rulings, different understandings, as it were, of what the doctrine of *stare decisis* actually entails for the US Supreme Court. But it seems that all members of the Court, past and present, share the assumption that the doctrine of *stare decisis* imposes some constraints on their legal decisions, even if, as most justices assume, those constraints do not quite amount to a legal obligation. So the challenge here is to explain this idea that previous rulings of the Court constrain the court's decision but not in a binding or obligatory sense.[18]

The fact that the US Supreme Court does not see itself legally bound by its previous rulings is nicely attested to by the fact that there are very few cases in which the Court engages in reasoning that purports to distinguish a precedent. If you are looking for textbook examples of distinguishing precedents in the US Supreme Court's decisions, you will come up almost empty-handed. When the Court wants to deviate from its previous rulings, it normally just deviates, sometimes explicitly justifying the deviation, sometimes more surreptitiously, but attempts to engage with detailed distinguishing are quite rare. Nevertheless, justices often see themselves constrained by previous ruling of the Court; they often council against deviations from established precedents, even if they would have preferred a different result. So it is this idea that horizontal precedent constrains judicial decisions without being considered to be binding that I find puzzling and in need of explanation.

Before we delve into the philosophical explanation here, however, let me first acknowledge that the political rationale for horizontal precedent, at least in the context of appellate courts, is fairly straightforward. Higher courts have an interest in the continuity of their legal decisions because it enhances their law-making powers. There is a great deal of law that the US Supreme Court gets to make by its rulings. But the Court's law-making power would not amount to much without a certain level of guaranteed stability. There is not much point in making new law if the law you enact can be changed easily by any subsequent decision. By recognizing and, more importantly, actually practising a doctrine of *stare decisis*, the justices

---

[17] Which may be, actually, the only case of horizontal precedent in the US Federal system. Generally speaking, with few exceptions, decisions of federal courts at the same level of hierarchy are not considered as precedents. It is, in fact, one of the interesting ideas of federalism that circuit courts of appeal (and state jurisdictions, of course) should be allowed to reach different, even opposing, legal conclusions on same issues, allowing experimentation with different legal regimes. The working assumption is that if conflicts become too inconvenient or problematic, the issue will find its way to the US Supreme Court.

[18] I cannot justify, beyond constraints of personal competence, only to apologize for this US-centred focus. It is certainly not my intention to imply that the US model applies to other jurisdictions. I am sure that there are many doctrinal and practical differences between legal systems on these matters.

264 ANDREI MARMOR

strive to ensure that their legal decisions have some long-lasting effect, that they remain relatively stable over time. Which is precisely why it often makes sense for the Court to abide by
its previous rulings even if the present Court would have preferred a different legal outcome;
if the Court makes it a practice to ignore its previous rulings it would undermine its own law-
making powers. Thus, there is no great mystery about the politics of horizontal precedent at
the appellate levels. What we see in practice is how the Court engages in a delicate balancing
act between securing its own law-making powers and reaching outcomes it favours. The
balance sometimes tilts in the direction of favouring the outcome, sometimes in the direction of favouring stability. Either way, the politics of it is clear enough.

How does the US Supreme Court present its own doctrine of *stare decisis*? The Court
consistently treats its own past rulings as settled law, particularly when the precedent concerns statutory interpretation cases. There is greater hesitation when the cases are constitutional and, for the simple reason that Congress cannot modify the Court's decision on
constitutional matters, that would take a constitutional amendment (which is not easily
accomplishable in the US). In non-constitutional cases, the Court sometimes goes so far
as to follow its own precedent even when it would clearly prefer not to, sometimes inviting
Congress to intervene and change the law. In constitutional cases, there is a greater willingness to overrule past decisions.[19] Either way, the Court normally treats its own decisions as
decisions that have settled the law on the particular legal issue decided, but it also allows
itself the freedom to change the ruling and, in effect, overrule its own precedent.[20] But not
without good reason. And then the debates usually concern the question of what kind of
reason is good enough to deviate from a prior decision. The debate, or rather, the disagreement between some of the justices on the Court, concerns the following question: is the fact
that a precedent that bears on the present case had been wrongly decided at the time a good
enough reason to overrule it?

In other words, using the terminology we introduced in section 1, the Court seems to be
conflicted on the question of whether an undercutting defeat is legitimately considered a
defeat or not. This came up, for example, in the recent decision of the Court in *June Medical
Services v Russo*,[21] where the Court struck down a Louisiana law imposing restrictions on
abortion clinics, practically identical to restrictions imposed by Texas that had been struck
down earlier as unconstitutional by the Court in *Whole Woman's Health v Hellerstedt*.[22] Not
surprisingly, the liberal justices on the Court ruled to uphold the recent precedent of *Whole
Woman's Health*. The conservative justices, in their dissent, argued that *Whole Woman's
Health* was wrongly decided and should not be followed. Chief Justice Roberts swayed the
decision in favour of the liberals' ruling exclusively for reasons of *stare decisis*. He shared the
view of his fellow conservatives that *Whole Woman's Health* was wrongly decided. But, he
says, 'for a precedent to mean anything, the doctrine must give way only to a rationale that
goes beyond whether the case was decided correctly'. He therefore declined to overrule the

---

[19] In the words of Justice Kavanaugh: 'In statutory cases, *stare decisis* is comparatively strict, as history shows and
the Court has often stated. That is because Congress and the President can alter a statutory precedent by enacting
new legislation. To be sure, enacting new legislation requires finding room in a crowded legislative docket and
securing the agreement of the House, the Senate (in effect, 60 Senators), and the President. Both by design and as a
matter of fact, enacting new legislation is difficult—and far more difficult than the Court's cases sometimes seem to
assume. Nonetheless, the Court has ordinarily left the updating or correction of erroneous statutory precedents to
the legislative process.' *Ramos v Louisiana* 590 US __ (2020).

[20] Treating the law as settled normally means that it would take an act of legislation (or constitutional amendment, as the case may be) to modify the law.

[21] *June Medical Services v Russo* 591 US __ (2020).

[22] *Whole Woman's Health v Hellerstedt* 579 US __ (2016).

precedent and sided with the liberal justices granting them the majority to strike down the Louisiana law. The position taken by Chief Justice Roberts in *June Medical Services* is not necessarily the general practice. For example, in the famous case of *Citizens United v FEC*[23] concerning campaign finance restrictions, the Court overruled its precedent in *Austin v Michigan Chamber of Commerce*[24] and largely because the majority thought that *Austin* had been wrongly decided. So, there is this ongoing wavering about the question of whether a defeat of the undercutting type can be relied upon to overrule the precedent or not. Sometimes, perhaps in most cases, the fact that the precedent was wrongly decided is not good enough, but on other occasions, it is.

What about conflicting defeats? Here the Court is more unanimous, as it were, in seeing conflicting defeats as acceptable reasons for ignoring or overruling its previous decisions. As I mentioned earlier, there might be some difference between constitutional and non-constitutional cases. When the Court is dealing with constitutional decisions, it seems more willing to overrule precedents on grounds of conflicting defeats. And this makes a lot of sense, actually, given the fact that in constitutional cases the Court is, in effect, the final arbitrator of the law. In such cases, there is a greater incentive to try to get things right than to uphold stability and predictability.

The patient reader might complain at this point that the argument started from the middle somehow. We saw that there is an ongoing controversy among justices on the Court about the legitimacy of relying on undercutting defeats, and a greater consensus on the legitimacy of modifying or overruling precedents on grounds of conflicting defeats. But then the question arises as to why this would matter to begin with. Why bother distinguishing between different kinds of potential defeats if the Court undeniably has the power to ignore its previous rulings or modify them at will? It's like stretching yourself to come up with an excuse when you've done nothing wrong; there is no need, is there? Well, there is, if the reason for action is of the presumptive kind. When you are expected to do or else to explain why not, then the need to explain is there from the start. Presumptive reasons have this disjunctive structure, expecting the agent to either comply with the relevant reason for action or else explain why it is defeated in this case. In other words, if we think that the Court's understanding of its doctrine of *stare decisis* comports with the idea of presumptive reasons, then the question of what counts as a legitimate defeat makes perfect sense.

The basic idea I am suggesting here is that the rationale of horizontal precedent is best seen as a form of presumptive reasons. There are generally good reasons for the Court to follow its own past decisions. Those reasons are grounded both in the legitimate reliance expectations of potential litigants and in the power of the Court to shape the law for the future. These general reasons to treat precedent as settled law are sometimes defeated by other considerations, but then, if the Court relies on a defeat, it is under an obligation to explain. The Court needs to demonstrate that the reasons to respect its precedent are defeated in the case under consideration. I think that the presumptive reasons in this case are what I called *strong presumptive reasons*; the burden of explanation is a legal obligation. Even if the Court does not see itself legally bound by its prior decisions, it is legally obliged to explain the defeating considerations when it relies on them to overrule its prior decisions.

Why should we think that the burden of explanation amounts to an obligation? The main reasons have to do with the legitimate expectations of potential litigants and others who would have relied on the precedent in their understanding of what the law is. When the

---

[23] *Citizens United v FEC* 558 US 310 (2010).
[24] *Austin v Michigan Chamber of Commerce* 494 US 652 (1990).

Supreme Court renders a decision that affects the law on a given issue, people would normally assume that it is now settled law and conduct their affairs accordingly. Even if potential litigants, particularly those who tend to be professionally well informed, know that the Court may change its mind in the future, they can hardly rely on changes that have not yet occurred and may never materialize. In other words, even if the general legal power of the Supreme Court to set aside its own precedents is common legal knowledge, as it is, potential litigants cannot afford to ignore the relevant precedents; they need to treat them, practically speaking, as settled law. And this puts a significant burden on the Court to explain its deviation from its own precedents, a burden that we can rightly assume to be legally binding.

I hope that it is now clear enough that the debate between the justices about the question of what counts as a legitimate defeat finds its place in this framework. Precedents are treated by the Court as strong presumptive reasons: the Court is expected to follow the precedent or else explain why it doesn't. And then all sorts of questions can arise about the kind of defeating considerations that the Court should be willing to rely upon. In particular, as we saw, justices disagree about the question of whether undercutting defeats are legitimately relied upon or not. When Justice Roberts says that the reason to follow a precedent cannot be defeated by the fact that it was mistaken, he essentially argues against the general legitimacy of relying on undercutting defeats. I doubt that he is right about this. If horizontal precedent was treated on a par with vertical precedents, that is, if it was regarded as legally binding, then it would have made a lot of sense to assume that certain types of considerations are to be excluded from counting as potential defeats. Vertical precedent is legally binding; plausibly, this means that there is a legal obligation to follow it or else show that the precedent does not actually apply by way of distinguishing it. At least on one plausible understanding of the nature of obligations, an obligation would normally consist of first-order reasons for action and second-order reasons to exclude certain considerations from counting as potential defeats. If this or some similar understanding of obligation is correct, then it makes perfect sense to assume that there are likely to be certain kinds of reasons that a binding precedent excludes from counting as potential defeats. But if the reasons to follow horizontal precedent are not of the obligatory kind, if they are treated as presumptive reasons, then nothing is in principle excluded from potentially defeating the first-order reasons. Presumptive reasons only add the burden of explanation, they do not change the balance of reasons in play.

I am not suggesting that these conceptual considerations show Justice Roberts to be wrong about the specific point he makes. My point is that excluding the mistake of the precedent from counting as a potential defeat does not follow from the rationale of horizontal *stare decisis*, as Roberts seems to assume. But it may still follow from other considerations. Perhaps it is a bad idea to allow the mistake of the precedent to count as a potential defeat because it would substantially increase the level of instability of judicial decisions, rendering their fate too dependent on the personal composition of the Court at any given time and the justices moral–ideological views. Perhaps it is a bad idea because it lays bare the fallibility of the Court itself. If the Court is all too ready to admit that it was mistaken in the past, what assurances would we have that it got it right this time? So there might be all sorts of reasons to be suspicious of the kind of undercutting defeats that rely on facts about the Court's prior errors. But there is nothing in the structure of the practical reasoning underlying the rationale of horizontal precedent to entail such conclusions. If the Court essentially treats the reasons to follow precedent as strong presumptive reasons, no considerations are excluded *ex ante* as potential defeats.

Now you might worry that my construal of horizontal precedent in terms of (strong) presumptive reasons is too weak. If the only practical constraint that is imposed on the Court by a horizontal precedent is the burden of explanation, you might think that it is not much of a constraint. After all, courts need to explain their decisions anyway, it is an integral part of the common law tradition. But this would be a misunderstanding of the practical import of presumptive reasons. The idea of a presumptive reason for action is not that you can do whatever you want as long as you explain it to the relevant parties. As I mentioned earlier, presumptive reasons do not change the balance of reasons in play. When A has a presumptive reason to φ, A is rightly expected either to φ or else to demonstrate that φ-ing in the circumstances is actually defeated by X; the defeat needs to be justified, it needs to be a sound defeat. What is added by the presumptive nature of the reasons is only the burden of explanation. And I think this is precisely the burden that courts assume in the context of horizontal precedent: they need to follow the precedent, treat is as settled law, unless there are good reasons not to do so, but then the burden of proof, as it were, to demonstrate that the precedent is defeated in this case, is on the Court to discharge. The Court needs to explain why what is normally required, to follow the precedent, is not required in this case. And this, I think, shows nicely how horizontal precedent constrains the practical reasoning of the Court without being binding; there is no legal obligation to follow the precedent, but there is a legal obligation to explain the relevant defeating considerations if and when they are present. But again, bear in mind that the burden of explanation does not change the substantive normative issue of whether the relevant defeating considerations are indeed justified or not.

20
An Artefactual Theory of Precedent

Kenneth M Ehrenberg[*]

1. Introduction

Across the jurisprudential spectrum, there is wide agreement that law is best understood as some kind of artefact. Where there is doubt or criticism of the notion that law is a kind of artefact, it is usually in the context of explaining the role of precedent that the critics say they find reasons to pause. One example of this is a paper by Dan Priel claiming that common law cannot be understood as an artefact (though he admits that other aspects of law can be).[1] As someone who has developed an explanation of how law is to be understood as an artefact,[2] I here develop and defend the claim that the understanding still applies to precedent. Since the issues with understanding the role of precedent in common law systems pose the greatest challenge to an artefactual understanding of law in general, I will focus more on those arguments with the expectation that my solutions and replies can be used *mutatis mutandis* to apply to any issues with precedent in civil law systems.

While I will use Priel's paper as a foil against which to develop my ideas of the artefactual nature of precedent, his paper is just one example applied directly against the artefactual understanding of law of an old problem for legal positivists, that of customary law.[3] The problem is that whether we say that law is the command of a sovereign[4] or a union of primary and secondary rules validated by a rule of recognition,[5] it is hard to deny that custom can be a source of law. Yet it does not appear to be entirely captured by these descriptions. With customary law, it is hard to identify a commanding moment of creation, even if we could overcome the hurdle of trying to identify its creation with the act of a sovereign. And although the customary rule may be primary or secondary, the usual criteria of validity we expect to see in a rule of recognition must be stretched beyond recognition to accommodate the murky sources of custom.

While we might be tempted initially to leave custom aside as a problematic addendum, once we start thinking clearly about precedent, custom seems to have an outsized role. Many early decisions, especially in common law jurisdictions, cite custom directly. Those decisions then form the basis of further decisions that maintain the authority of that custom, even as

---

[*] I would particularly like to thank Corrado Roversi, Luka Burazin, and Sebastian Lewis, though constraints of space did not allow me to employ all of their suggestions. Further thanks are given to the audience members who heard a very early version of this chapter at the International Conference on Collective Intentionality 2021.

[1] Dan Priel, 'Not All Law Is an Artifact: Jurisprudence Meets the Common Law' in Luka Burazin, KennethEinar Himma, and Corrado Roversi (eds), *Law as an Artifact* (OUP 2018).

[2] Most completely in Kenneth M Ehrenberg, *The Functions of Law* (OUP 2016).

[3] Another use of the customary nature of common law to attack legal positivism is Brian Simpson, 'The Common Law and Legal Theory' in William Twining (ed), *Legal Theory and Common Law* (Basil Blackwell 1986), with thanks to Sebastian Lewis for pointing out the reference.

[4] John Austin, *The Province of Jurisprudence Determined; and the Uses of the Study of Jurisprudence* (HLA Hart ed, first published 1832, Hackett 1998) 32.

[5] HLA Hart, *The Concept of Law* (3rd edn, first published 1961, OUP 2012) 79ff.

Kenneth M Ehrenberg, *An Artefactual Theory of Precedent* In: *Philosophical Foundations of Precedent*. Edited by: Timothy Endicott, Hafsteinn Dan Kristjánsson, and Sebastian Lewis, Oxford University Press. © Kenneth M Ehrenberg 2023.
DOI: 10.1093/oso/9780192857248.003.0021

the later decisions now cite the precedent rather than the custom directly. Furthermore, the weight afforded to precedent and justification for doing so can both be seen as aspects of custom and so resistant to artefactual analysis.[6]

I will begin by giving a thumbnail sketch of my understanding of how law is an artefact, focusing on those elements that are of most relevance to addressing the issues with precedent. Then I will address the concerns that Priel raises, showing that the theory is robust enough to accommodate his concerns and precedent more generally.

2. Law is a Genre of Artefact

When we say that law is a kind of artefact, in order for this claim to be explanatorily useful, we must be saying something more than simply that it is a product of human behaviour, even if we limit this to say that it is responsive to our interests.[7] In this Priel and I agree.[8] For it to be explanatorily useful (and apparently controversial), he says that the claim must be '(roughly) that law is the product of purposive action, that it is the product of design'.[9] While I think it is a mistake to equate purposive action with design,[10] I agree that artefacts are generally designed to serve a purpose.

More specifically, the notion of artefact that I employ in explaining law is that of a 'public artefact'. Amie Thomasson explains public artefacts are 'intended to be recognizable as artefacts of that kind by a certain intended audience'.[11] While I might invent some new artefact for my own personal use (knowing how to use it simply because I invented it), a public artefact must be designed to be recognizable to others so that they understand its use by understanding what kind of artefact it is. She and I therefore follow Randall Dipert in understanding artefacts generally to be tools that signal their identity by communicating their purpose and how they are to be used.[12] (Of course, that communication could fail. When we dig up an ancient artefact, we try to identify it by trying to figure out what its purpose was, which we do by examining its form and other clues from the context in which it was found.) Artefacts are therefore a sub-class of tools, which according to Dipert are instruments that have been adapted to serve some purpose. Instruments are simply objects that are used to serve some purpose.[13]

I believe law is a genre of institutionalized abstract (public) artefact. I say it is a genre of artefact in order to respect the type/token distinction;[14] it is not clear that the most general

---

[6] Priel (n 1) 245. See also Simpson (n 3) 20, defining common law as 'a customary system of law' in the sense of 'a body of practices observed and ideas received over time by a caste of lawyers, these ideas being used by them as providing guidance in what is conceived to be the rational determination of disputes litigated before them, or by them on behalf of clients, and in other contexts' (NB the functional element in the definition).

[7] *Contra* Brian Leiter, 'Legal Positivism About the Artifact Law: A Retrospective Assessment' in Burazin, Himma, and Roversi (n 1) 10–11.

[8] Priel (n 1) 239–40.

[9] ibid 240.

[10] Priel himself mentions the path created by many different hikers, which seems to be a result of purposive action (though not directed at the result) but not design, ibid 248. The hikers are each purposely choosing a given route, which happens to be the same as the others. This results in a path, though no hiker designed the path.

[11] Amie L Thomasson, 'Public Artifacts, Intentions and Norms' in Maarten Franssen and others (eds), *Artefact Kinds: Ontology and the Human-Made World* (Springer 2013) 50.

[12] Randall R Dipert, 'Some Issues in the Theory of Artifacts: Defining "Artifact" and Related Notions' (1995) 78 Monist 119, 127–29.

[13] ibid 121–23. See also Ehrenberg, *The Functions of Law* (n 2) 29–32.

[14] This is the distinction between a general sortal and its instances. See Linda Wetzel, 'Types and Tokens' in Edward N Zalta (ed), *The Stanford Encyclopedia of Philosophy* (2014) <http://plato.stanford.edu/archives/spr2014/entries/types-tokens/> accessed 20 June 2015.

type itself has all the properties of an artefact, even though its token legal enactments, judicial decisions, and even entire legal systems do.[15] It's abstract because it isn't to be equated with any particular recording and we could imagine legal norms that are never recorded (e.g. in verbal contracts). Explaining what it means to say that it is institutionalized is a bit more complicated and carries much more of the weight of the theory, showing more of what makes law special. Institutions are a sub-class of artefacts that operate primarily by creating and assigning artificial statuses where those statuses purport to carry deontic powers to change people's rights and responsibilities (giving new reasons for action), enabling them to perform specified functions within that institutional context.[16] Institutions are therefore themselves abstract artefacts that aid people in the attainment of certain goals by manipulating their reasons for action.[17] Putting this discussion together with the typography we started with from Dipert, we can say that each of the following (except the first) is a sub-class of the previous: instrument—tool—artefact—institution—law.

Take the example of a hospital as an institution. It is not identical to the building that houses it since a given hospital can move or have the building torn down and rebuilt. It is not identical to the doctors, patients, and administrators that populate it, as those are constantly in flux. Rather, it is an organization of elements with rules for assigning statuses to people, places, and perhaps even objects and events (like 'doctor', 'nurse', 'orderly', 'patient', 'administrator', 'visitor', 'operating theatre', 'waiting room', 'emergency room', 'nurses' station', 'doctors' rounds', etc). In order to facilitate the healing of the sick and injured, those statuses alter the rights and responsibilities of the people who interact with the institution. I use the verbal adjective 'institutionalized' to emphasize that the establishment of institutions is something that must be done (and can be done to a pre-existing artefact). As might be guessed from the example of the hospital (though hospitals could be developed prior to or outside legal systems), law is somewhat special in that it is quintessentially an institution for generating other institutions, potentially giving their purported changes to people's reasons for action greater social weight. An administrator ordering all visitors to leave the hospital has likely given those visitors a strong reason to leave, even if we imagine the hospital in an area with no law. But if we imagine it as organized under the rules of a legal system, that order might carry even more weight and the potential backing of wider social norms or enforcement.

Given this analysis, there is one sense in which an artefactual understanding of precedent should be relatively uncontroversial. That is in the basic sense of precedent as a prior judicial decision used by a later decision-maker to guide or control the later decision. That is an artefactual understanding since it sees the precedent as a human creation that serves the purpose of guiding or controlling those later decisions (and was likely at least partially written

---

[15] One might wonder if any type *qua* type can be an artefact, as types are perhaps merely conceptual groupings. While taking a position on that is not necessary for this chapter, it does appear that concepts can have the properties of public artefacts (to the extent that they are capable of being shared), having the function of organizing our experience of the world. But most amenable to this analysis are concepts developed as a result of conceptual engineering, or by an inventor designing a new class of thing, and it is not clear that LAW falls into those categories.

[16] Ehrenberg, *The Functions of Law* (n 2) 32–36, citing Neil MacCormick and Ota Weinberger, *An Institutional Theory of Law: New Approaches to Legal Positivism* (D Reidel 1986); Neil MacCormick, 'Norms, Institutions, and Institutional Facts' (1998) 17 Law and Philosophy 301; Seumas Miller, 'Social Institutions' (2007) <http://plato.stanford.edu/archives/fall2012/entries/social-institutions/> accessed 2 December 2021; Dick WP Ruiter, 'Structuring Legal Institutions' (1998) 17 Law and Philosophy 215; John R Searle, *The Construction of Social Reality* (Free Press 1995) and *Making the Social World: The Structure of Human Civilization* (OUP 2010); Amie L Thomasson, 'Realism and Human Kinds' (2003) 67 Philosophy and Phenomenological Research 580, among others.

[17] Admittedly, this makes calling law an 'institutionalized *abstract* artefact' somewhat redundant, but it helps for people accustomed to thinking of artefacts only as physical objects.

in order to serve that purpose).[18] It is institutional since its ability to serve that purpose depends upon its membership in the legal system as a valid decision. This sense of precedent can be contrasted with *stare decisis* (a principle of using precedents as generally controlling, rather than merely guiding) and common law (a body of law or kind of legal system characterized partially by a use of *stare decisis*, building up legal norms over time from precedent).[19] The problems tend to arise when we consider the role or strength of precedent within a legal system (which may be customary) and whether we can still think of them as artefacts when seen in that light. I will therefore focus on the role of precedent in common law as raising the most potential problems for the artefactual analysis.

3. Artefacts and Customs

If artefacts are generally intentionally designed to serve a purpose, it might seem that customs cannot be artefacts. After all, we usually don't think of customs as being designed consciously. This is precisely the argument Priel makes against seeing customs as artefacts. 'Unlike legislation, social norms (customs) are also a kind of order (design), but it is not typically conscious. Such norms typically emerge without any conscious decision by any single person to adopt them.'[20] He goes on to give the example of the norm of putting one's property on a table in a cafeteria-style eatery to signal that the table is 'taken'. Perhaps no one ever 'authored' this norm, and others may follow it without even realizing it.

The problem with this line of reasoning is that it views custom monolithically, suggesting all customs have a very narrow and circumscribed set of properties. Even if we admit that some customs are developed without conscious intention or design, it is far from clear that this is true of all customs. To understand this, we have to delve more deeply into the development of customs, particularly how they acquire their normative character. With the reserved table custom, there are several possibilities for its development. It is entirely reasonable to believe that, prior to the development of the custom, someone first put their property on the table to signal to others that the table was taken, and others recognized this signal and that someone was thereby requesting them not to sit at the table. Even if there were several people who independently developed this signal, such an explanation would easily be in keeping with an artefactual understanding of this norm. The custom was invented by the people who first devised the signal, even if they did not realize they were inventing a custom by doing so. The key for designers and inventors is to develop something that signals its purpose; they need not be self-aware that they are thereby creating an artefact of a given type. Hence, one can start a new custom without realizing that what one is doing is authoring a custom. Now, of course, in this story a lot of work is done by the people who receive and understand the

---

[18] It's possible that the very earliest precedents were not written partially to guide or control future decisions on similar cases. But we can then treat the earliest decisions as tools used by those who later used them to guide or control their decisions, who in turn began crafting their decisions with the likely intention that they guide or control others, and the artefactual analysis can begin there.

[19] I do realize that the principle of *stare decisis* and the particular weight now given to precedent within common law are comparatively recent developments when considering the history of the common law as a whole. But as that weight is itself an integral part of arguments against the common law's artefactual nature and our focus is on precedent in its most binding form as presenting the greatest potential challenge to its artefactual analysis, we can leave this consideration aside.

[20] Priel (n 1) 245. I believe a charitable interpretation here is not to think Priel is attempting to equate all social norms with customs by his use of the parenthetical, but rather to understand the parenthetical to indicate he is attempting only to capture the subset of social norms that are also customary.

272 KENNETH M EHRENBERG

communicated request and are the first to respect it. As with many social norms, the first fol-
lowers might in some ways be even more important to the story than the inventors. They had
to recognize the presence of the property on the table as a signal for the wishes of its owner,
understand that the wish was being communicated to them, and therefore to be giving them
a reason to comply. But so far this story is in perfect step with the development of other
public artefacts: an inventor develops a new kind of tool (possibly by modifying existing
designs), something about which communicates to the audience of potential users what the
tool is for and how to use it.[21] In this case the property on the table carries the clear signal
that the table is occupied and if the recipients of the signal wish to respect that request, they
do so by not occupying the table themselves. Of course, this is a very easy tool to replicate;
once people see that it is effective, they easily adopt it for reserving their own tables and the
custom spreads.

Now Priel might complain that this is a very self-conscious kind of story to tell about the
development of a custom and it might have developed in a much less self-conscious fashion.
Of course, he's right, but it's important to see that the self-conscious method is one way for
custom to develop and hence it is not enough to say simply that common law is custom.
There are at least two other possibilities Priel might suggest: that it developed from a more
inadvertent action, and that it developed from a habit. To understand the inadvertent action
possibility, let's imagine another scenario. A woman puts her belongings down on a table in
the eatery because it was a convenient place to put them. Perhaps she did intend to sit there
after getting her food, but she didn't have any intention to signal this to anyone. (We are
again imagining this taking place in an area where the custom is not yet established.) Perhaps
when she first arrived at the eatery there weren't many customers and so there was no need
to give any thought to 'reserving' the table. As she was getting her food, however, more customers came in and she noticed that they were avoiding the table on which she had placed
her belongings. To respect the analysis of artefacts preferred by Priel (and myself), perhaps
we should say that the norm is not yet an artefact. But after noticing the effect it has on
others, she (or someone else) begins to use the reserve-table-with-property technique intentionally. This would now be the first time someone uses it to send a signally intentionally and
we could then call the custom an artefact, since the technique is being adopted and refined
to send that signal.[22]

Finally, let's imagine that there is a widespread habit that people have of placing their belongings on tables when they come into an eatery and then they return to those tables to eat.
No one thinks of this behaviour as normative yet; it's just a habit that lots of people share,
like tying one's shoes in a certain order. At some point, however, someone starts to express
some kind of negative judgment when others take a table with someone else's property on

[21] The fact that audience members may then use it in a different way than the one envisaged by the inventor
doesn't detract from this picture, nor does it (immediately) change the identity of the artefact (though it may do
so eventually if enough people consistently use it in a specific different way). See Kenneth M Ehrenberg, 'Law Is an
Institution, an Artifact, and a Practice' in Burazin, Himma, and Roversi (n 1) 184–86.

[22] That there may be a period where people are respecting a norm (by avoiding tables occupied by personal
property) without anyone signalling them to do so does not prevent the norm from being ripe for artefactual analysis once the signal is intentional. We might also prefer to say that the first person to use the signal intentionally
is adapting something found, rather than creating something new, and therefore the norm is more akin to a tool
in Dipert's taxonomy, rather than an artefact. But since it is precisely this tool's signalling function that makes it
useful, it would still seem to be a borderline case between a tool and an artefact. Richard Grandy makes it clear that
where a subsequent user recognizes a function for an artefact that was not intended by the original inventor and
that later function comes to be closely associated with the artefact, we simply analyse it as an artefact with multiple designers. Richard E Grandy, 'Artifacts: Parts and Principles' in Eric Margolis and Stephen Laurence (eds),
Creations of the Mind (OUP 2007) 28.

it. A similar story likely explains the development of the norms about where to put the silverware when setting the table. At first, it was probably just widespread regularity of behaviour. But at some point one or more people started seeing departures from this behaviour as justifying negative judgments about such departures. Once those judgments are expressed, some might ignore or reject them. But others see those judgments as reasons for conformity to the behavioural pattern, changing the understanding of the behaviour from habit to norm. Again, the person or people who first begin to use the pattern of behaviour as the basis for negative judgments about departures from the pattern can be understood to be developing a new artefact out of the pattern.

Admittedly, the reserving-table norm may have developed in any of these ways, and possibly in multiple ways in different places. And I also admit that the final two ways do not sit quite as comfortably with an artefactual understanding as the first one (though not entirely uncomfortably either). But the key elements for Priel's attack on an artefactual explanation of custom are that customs are not the product of 'functional conscious design'.[23] However, once we realize that these three elements can come apart in time or person, yet we would still be confronting an artefact,[24] then custom need not always present a serious challenge to artefactual analysis. Designers frequently adapt and repurpose what they find to make those findings fit new functions or perform their original functions better. The fact that the original item that the designer is adapting was not the result of functional conscious design does not change the fact that the new item the designer creates is now the result of functional conscious design. The fact that the designer may not be the same person as the one who first consciously uses the item to serve that function is similarly of no consequence (though we might prefer to think of the first conscious user as the designer in that case), as is the fact that the identities of the first designers or users are lost in the mists of history.

4. From Custom to Precedent

As noted earlier, there are at least two aspects of common law precedent that are understood to be customary: the use of customs by early common law judges as sources for their decisions, and the weight or bindingness afforded to precedent (and the justification for doing so) in common law countries. While Priel is mainly concerned with the latter,[25] it pays to take a moment to discuss the first.

Even if we do not think that the customary norms employed by early judges as the basis for some of their decisions are ripe for artefactual analysis, it is unproblematic to give an artefactual analysis for these norms once they are used as the basis for a legal judgment. Something has changed once the norm is incorporated into law via the judicial decision: it has been institutionalized. Whereas before the decision, there may have been strong social pressure behind the norm, once it is the basis of a legal decision it now has an official imprimatur.

---

[23] Priel (n 1) 245. Priel further distinguishes between 'teleological' functions and 'cultural' functions, ibid 243–44, 245–46, in order to claim that the different functions justify their *explanans* differently and have 'different notions of success'. But it is not clear to me why cultural functions are not simply one sub-class of teleological functions, ones with the end of providing some cultural value or something analogous. The fact that the cultural value it provides may be conventional or culture-dependent is neither here nor there. I have been unable to find this distinction elsewhere in the analytic literature on functional explanations. Dan Sperber would agree with my suggestion that what Priel calls cultural functions are merely a sub-class of teleological functions, which Sperber calls 'cultural teleofunctions'. Dan Sperber, 'Seedless Grapes: Nature and Culture' in Margolis and Laurence (n 22) 128.

[24] See, e.g., Grandy (n 22) 28.

[25] Priel (n 1) 248.

274   KENNETH M EHRENBERG

Whereas before, sanctions for violations of the norm were mainly meted out by self-help among members of the community, now there will likely be officially specified sanctions to be given by people filling official roles. Where the norm violation involved a personal dispute, the incorporation into case law now means there is an official venue and means for redressing it. The judge who cites custom directly as the basis for a legal judgment is simply akin to a designer who is adapting an instrument or tool found 'in the wild', improving its functionality or giving it a new one.

Priel's focus is more on the common law itself or, as we might understand it, the practice of affording precedent a certain weight or authority in the making of current legal decisions. About this aspect of common law, his argument is that it resists artefactual analysis because its 'design level is low, whatever design it has is not conscious, and a teleological function does not often play a significant role in its design and development'.[26] He also argues that the incrementalism associated with artefact development is not of the same kind as that associated with the development of the common law.[27] I will address these points in the order he does: (1) low design; (2) lack of teleological functionality; (3) incrementalism; and (4) lack of consciousness in design.

Priel admits that the common law does have enough design to provide an artefactual analysis with regard to that element (if the other elements had been met), but that 'its design level is quite low'.[28] Since he admits that there is a design element (even if it's low), we don't have to spend too much time with this step of the argument. But it pays to note that his evidence for the low design level is the 'obscurity, confusion, and contradiction within the common law'.[29] Of course, this refers to the *content* of the common law rather than its justification, weight, or authority and hence in citing it Priel is failing to maintain the focus he promised on the common law as a whole rather than the particular customs that might have been the basis of its content.[30] More importantly, as anyone who has confronted a buggy software program or attempted to muddle through the overly complex rules of certain board games can attest, many artefacts are regretfully designed with lots of obscurity, confusion, and contradiction. Those failures are not themselves evidence of a low design level if we understand that to mean 'not much design went into it'. Heavily and perhaps especially over-designed artefacts can exhibit the same failures. And if we understand 'low design level' to mean instead simply 'poorly designed', then it would no longer be a point in favour of claiming that the *explanans* resists artefactual analysis.

Priel's next argument is that the common law lacks (the right kind of) '*functionality*'.[31] To begin with, Priel notes that a central element of common law is the use of existing or prior practices to settle novel questions with similar elements. Even where direct goal-oriented policy considerations are used in judicial decisions, they tend to be trumped by any persuasive arguments that the instant case is sufficiently similar to an existing practice noted in a prior decision.[32] That appears to put functionality lower on the list and to privilege a given outcome because it was done that way in the past. This privilege itself is then a 'tradition' or 'custom' and the attendant rejection of functionality in judicial decision-making suggests to

---

[26] ibid 247–48.
[27] ibid 251.
[28] ibid 249.
[29] ibid.
[30] While many of these problems likely arise as a result of the inadequacies of the judicial decisions that form the common law, some not insignificant part of those inadequacies can themselves be traced to the customs that early decisions used as source material.
[31] Priel (n 1) 249 (emphasis in original).
[32] ibid 250.

Priel that common law is resistant to artefactual analysis. But the mere fact that direct policy arguments are fewer and further between masks a more fundamental truth that the law is structured to value those traditional practices in order to enable it to fulfil a wider function relating to stability, settled expectations, and other values we associate with the rule of law.[33] That is, the weight given by common law as a whole to precedent enables the legal system to perform a function that would otherwise be difficult to meet, or would need other mechanisms to meet. Achieving that end might often be more important (to those tasked or faced with making such decisions, and even to those feeling the result of those decisions) than getting the best outcome for policy purposes in the instant case.[34]

Hence, the reliance upon practice over policy is not a rejection of functionality, but rather in pursuit of a wider functionality. This is true both of common law when considered as a whole, and of individual judicial decisions. Each decision contributes to the legal system's ability to pursue the goals of regularity, upholding settled expectations, and other values of legality (though some might uphold certain values at the expense of others). While individual judges may not be crafting their decisions with the conscious goal of upholding stability and settled expectations (though nothing prevents that either), we have seen that they need not have a self-aware conscious intention to design something with a specific wider function for the result to be ripe for artefactual analysis using that wider function.[35]

One might wonder why in cases of first impression there would be a need for stability and settled expectations. Yet it seems like the cases that are most open to success by either side are the ones in which the judges are most keen to cite precedent (a point Priel notes).[36] This is perhaps due to 'the threat of novelty' that striking out on one's own holds for judges who are systemically induced to hand-wringing at the slightest hint that they are straying into the domain of legislation. For our purposes, it suffices to note that it is precisely in the most novel cases that we would expect to see the most citation of precedent in order to shore up the system's ability to promote stability and uphold settled expectations. The more distinct the case is from what has come before, the less the result will be something that fits the pattern set by past decisions. But if continuity is of high value to those who design and use the institution, then they will do more to discover and emphasize any elements of continuity they can uncover. Hence, against Priel's claim to the contrary, this incorporation of prior decisions into novel cases in order to emphasize and uphold continuity is even greater evidence of the artefactual nature of common law since judges are using prior decisions as tools to perform the function of upholding continuity and settled expectations in the legal system.

Priel also claims that the incrementalism seen in common law is distinct, and even in opposition to, the incrementalism that is seen in artefact development:

---

[33] The fact that the common law enables the pursuit or attainment of rule of law values via *stare decisis* is not meant to suggest that there are no other effective methods for doing so. Civil law countries pursue the same values (though possibly giving slightly different relative weights to them) without the same emphasis on precedential weight.

[34] Simpson himself notes 'a customary system of law [such as the common law] can function only if it can preserve a considerable measure of continuity and cohesion, and it can do this only if mechanisms exist for the transmission of traditional ideas and the encouragement of orthodoxy': Simpson (n 3) 21.

[35] On the other hand, the role their decisions have in systemically upholding or pursuing certain rule of law principles provides strong reasons for judges to carefully consider the messages they are sending to future readers who will rely upon their decisions. Frederick Schauer, 'Precedent' (1987) 39 Stan L Rev 571, 572–73; Jeremy Waldron, 'Stare Decisis and the Rule of Law: A Layered Approach' (2012) 111 Mich L Rev 1, *passim*.

[36] Priel (n 1) 250, noting that appellate cases have more citations to prior decisions.

[A]rtifact design is often based on attempts to identify problems with past design and solve them; common law justification typically involves the opposite approach of acting in a particular way because of past practice. In the former, past design is relevant in that it may limit one's design space, it is an unfortunate constraint. In the latter, on the other hand, the past may be a reason in itself to do certain things in a particular way. The difference is that only in the latter the fact that things have been done in a certain way confers normative value on them.[37]

But seeing the past only as a constraint to be loosened and overcome is a very narrow and limiting view of artefact design, and certainly not something essential to the nature of artefacts. Corrado Roversi suggests the helpful example of a Gothic cathedral, which takes generations to build and undergoes many incremental changes in design.[38] Any definition of artefact that would exclude such a building would clearly be misguided.

Very often inventors and designers of even more mundane artefacts will view the history of an artefact with appreciation for the ways in which previous designers overcame challenges, seeing those innovations as valuable elements to be maintained and guides in the move forwards, refining the design already laid down. What's more, once we are confronting the institutional dimension of an artefact that has been institutionalized, we see that the use of prior practice to justify the retention of certain design elements is quite common and for good reason. When developing a new kind of chair, some designers might feel past choices as constraints to overcome if doing so will enhance the value of the new chair. But when designing the new line of Herman Miller-brand chairs, previous design choices provide strong reasons *against* their rejection in order to maintain the recognizable design elements associated with the brand. This kind of 'internal' or 'cultural' justification for the retention of design elements merely because of an existing practice is antithetical neither to an artefactual analysis nor to understanding institutionalized artefacts in terms of their design functions. In general, institutions will place a strong emphasis on continuity and recognizability in the properties of their members and instances in order to succeed better in the performance of the functions for which they were developed. Since the developers of the particular institution believed that those functions are best served by creating and assigning statuses that carry deontic powers (to change some reasons for action of people interacting with the institution), there is generally good reason for stability and predictability in what people and things carry those statuses and what is expected of people encountering them.

Priel's final argument is short but perhaps the most intuitively appealing. The final element of artefacts that he believes common law lacks is *conscious* design. The evidence for this lack is the 'messiness, confusion, contradictoriness, and obscurity of many of [its] constituent parts', indicating the absence of a clear plan.[39] But, once again, these deficiencies are found in the *content* of the common law, rather than in its weight or authority.[40] And again, absence of

---

[37] ibid 251.

[38] Corrado Roversi, 'On the Artifactual—and Natural—Character of Legal Institutions' in Burazin, Himma, and Roversi (n 1) 94–95.

[39] Priel (n 1) 251–52.

[40] One might be tempted to argue that these deficiencies are found in the justifications offered for that weight or authority, but that claim isn't borne out by the cases themselves. To the extent that judicial decisions offer any justifications for the practice of *stare decisis* and the authority of precedent, they are fairly uniform and consistent, though usually little more than a presumption. The complaints of confusion, obscurity, and contradiction, even when made by the judges themselves, are mainly focused on the content of decisions rather than on the practice of giving weight to precedents. Even where there is inconsistency in how much weight is given to precedent, it tends to be in contexts where there are competing precedents such that giving more weight to one line of decisions is to give less to another (which is therefore still a complaint about content).

evidence of a good plan is not evidence of the absence of a plan altogether. Notwithstanding these considerations, however, when we think about the common law it's hard to imagine a conscious designer for something that has developed over centuries, with the contributions of countless judges along the way.

We must be careful, however, not to misunderstand the distributed nature of the common law's development for the lack of any conscious design whatsoever. To adapt Dworkin's metaphor of the chain novel (in which each chapter is written by a different author, seriatim)[41] to a use of which he would likely not approve, we would not say of the resulting manuscript (or indeed of the very book you read at this moment) that it was not an artefact merely because many authors contributed to it. Even as all the authors have their individual plans and purposes for their contributions, they are aware of contributing to something larger, with a purpose somewhat distinct from their own individual ones. Of course, all those authors are contributing to the content of the book with their individual choices. But whether they are buying into a shared vision of the volume articulated by the editors or understanding that they are each contributing to the development of that vision by trying to make their chapter fit with what has come before, they are also jointly in control of how the volume communicates its significance. When we say that our relevant notion of artefact must include conscious design, we cannot mean to exclude those artefacts that are designed by a group, even where group members are all working on separate design tasks that contribute to the whole.

To apply this analysis back to the common law, perhaps there was some early judge who first considered himself bound by the decisions of prior judges he consulted in making his decision. He then communicated his sense of the bindingness of those earlier decisions in his decision and other judges followed. This would be akin to the first story we told about the custom to use one's property to reserve a table at the eatery. There is much less doubt in this story that the bindingness and authority of precedent in common law are the product of conscious design. Once again, the designer need not have consciously understood that he was undertaking a new practice that would be emulated by others for the result to be an artefact. And again, those who first internalize and follow the norm may be as important to the story as those who develop it.[42]

It is more difficult to imagine an application of the inadvertent action story to the development of the common law. One would have to say that a judge somehow accidentally relied upon prior decisions and that this was then emulated by other judges. This is difficult to imagine in that the prior decisions need to play the role of justifications for the judge's decision in the instant case. An only slightly more plausible story would be that the practice was originally a mistake, with one judge somehow mistakenly believing himself bound by prior decisions. Then other, subsequent judges might initially mistakenly follow the lead of that original judge, but some eventually come to see that there was actually great value in the practice and adopt it intentionally.

That an initial design was the result of a mistake does not necessarily defeat the presence of conscious design. As with all institutions, the normative structure of a given legal system is a web of interdependent recognitions of validity, and *stare decisis* in a common law system is an aspect of that system's criteria of legal validity. Where a mistaken understanding of the

---

[41] Ronald Dworkin, *Law's Empire* (Belknap Press 1986) 229.

[42] These considerations help to defeat Simpson's dismissive attitude towards the idea that common law can be understood on the 'legislative' model of early decisions setting down principles and rules that are then followed by later judges. Simpson (n 3) 14. The institutionalized artefact model accommodates Simpson's concerns perfectly (notwithstanding his refusal to countenance 'judicial legislation') by explaining the rule's inception artefactually and its continued reception institutionally.

278 KENNETH M EHRENBERG

system's legal validity is introduced by a given official, one of two things will happen. Either other officials will decline to recognize the validity of the mistaken holding and the norms that follow from it will not be considered valid members of the system, or other officials will recognize the validity of the holding, propagating the 'mistake' and incorporating it into the legal system. Where the mistake has implications for the criteria of validity themselves, these will have been adjusted when the mistake is incorporated. What this shows is that individual decision-makers, making conscious decisions but not aware of their mistakes, can introduce design changes to institutionalized artefactual systems. Those design changes are the result of conscious choices even if the choices are not aimed at effecting a change in design, but this does nothing to undermine the artefactual nature of the system.[43]

The final possibility we considered about the table-reservation custom was where it is more akin to a habit that gains normative significance. At first blush, this is not applicable to the common law in that the citation of earlier decisions must perform a justificatory function for the instant decision. That normativity is inherent in the behaviour itself in its need to serve as a justification means that it cannot be something that is habitual in the sense of a mere regularity of behaviour. The closest we can come might be to imagine some lazy early judge developing a habit of relying on the arguments in similar earlier decisions, rather than developing his own based only on the circumstances of the instant case. He would still be treating the earlier decisions as justificatory (of his own decisions), but he would not be implying anything normative (for others) about the practice of doing so. Once again, however, the practice itself begins to be seen as normative and instances of departure from it as deserving censure. We could analyse this similarly to that of an accident in that the original developer didn't intend the practice to be normative, or we could say that those who first treated the practice as normative are to be understood as the designers. Either way, it doesn't undermine seeing common law precedent as a kind of artefact.

5. Concluding Musings about Precedent's Institutionality

The role of judges in developing precedent could suggest a possible tension in seeing law as both an institution and an artefact. They appear to be simultaneously developing and using

---

[43] This helps to undermine Priel's argument that the claim practitioners are mistaken in their understanding of common law as custom is self-defeating. Priel (n 1) 253–54. I am not claiming that practitioners are mistaken in saying common law is custom. But it is not self-defeating to do so because the conscious intention of the original designer need not be focused on the actual function that the artefact will eventually serve for it to be meaningfully understood as an artefact. Later, Priel reformulates this consideration in a dig at John Gardner's claim that laws are artefacts but that some laws can also be a result of accidents. Priel cites Hilpinen's counter-example that the wood shavings formed in the process of making a wood carving would then be artefacts on Gardner's view: ibid 256 fn 27, citing John Gardner, *Law as a Leap of Faith: Essays on Law in General* (OUP 2012) 70–71, 193; Risto Hilpinen, 'Authors and Artefacts' (1993) 93 Proceedings of the Aristotelian Society 155, 159–60. The problem with his reply is that it again misses the possibility that the original (mistaken) designer can be distinct from the first person to identify the function the artefact will eventually come to be identified with. The wood shavings are not artefacts because they have no function and were not designed at all. They are a by-product. But *some* (though not all) 'accidental products of intentional action' can become artefacts when a use-function comes to be associated with them. On the distinction between design-functions and use-functions and how use-functions can change the identity of artefacts even when intentionally designed to serve a different function, see Ehrenberg, *The Functions of Law* (n 2) 12 fn 24, 24, citing Peter Achinstein, 'Function Statements' (1977) 44 Philosophy of Science 341, 349; Peter McLaughlin, *What Functions Explain: Functional Explanation and Self-Reproducing Systems* (CUP 2001) 54; Karen Neander, 'The Teleological Notion of "Function"' (1991) 69 Australasian J Philosophy 454, 462.

the artefact. As noted earlier, I generally think of institutions as a subset of artefacts.[44] Hence, if there is a tension in seeing law both as an institution and as an artefact, that would strongly suggest either that it is neither or that I am wrong in thinking of institutions as kinds of artefacts.

Artefacts clearly have histories of development and adaptation (Beth Preston calls it 're-production with variation').[45] They are adapted and developed in response to circumstances that change; their functions may be refined or revised over time. That suggests a flexibility that is not overly constrained by a set of rules for alteration of the artefact. There may be norms of usage and identification that the creator communicates with the artefact to her in-tended audience.[46] But as Priel noted, in altering existing artefacts and developing new ones, authors generally have a free hand. Common law precedent seems to cut against that as it is a way for the law to fix its application and usage over time. Since we generally say of most arte-facts that their norms of usage are quite weak, we think of their users as having a relatively free hand to use them in whatever way they need, but precedent binds the judge to a much more specific usage.[47] So, in a non-common law system, the role of precedent may be more in line with what would be expected from a system of artefacts: prior applications of law would be like prior uses of the artefact in that they would be helpful guides to current usage, but not necessarily binding. But in common law systems, prior applications of law are under-stood to be more binding than we would expect with artefacts more generally. It's not that this is necessarily a problem as we could likely imagine artefacts for which the norm of usage is more stringent: items of symbolic or ritual value come to mind. But given that elsewhere I rely upon the weakness of the norm of usage in the law to allow for flexibility in interpretive strategies,[48] this could be somewhat troubling.

The solution is in the institutionality of law, which explains the greater constraints that we see in it. Institutions constrain their members to uses of the institution in keeping with its rules for which actions or instances are to be considered bona fide. The rules of institutions generally tell us what counts and what doesn't, the proper way to confer the status that carries deontic powers and how to deploy those powers. So, the greater constraints on future deci-sions that precedent imposes (especially in common law jurisdictions) can be understood as one facet of the way the institution of law deploys its institutional rules about what counts.

---

[44] So, it is actually a bit redundant to say law is a genre of institutionalized abstract artefacts but there is utility in focusing separately on the properties of institutions and on the properties of artefacts, so this redundancy is justified.

[45] Beth Preston, 'Philosophical Theories of Artifact Function' in Anthonie Meijers (ed), *Philosophy of Technology and Engineering Sciences* (Elsevier 2009) 216–17. See also Lynne Rudder Baker, 'The Metaphysics of Malfunction' (2009) 13 Techne 82, 84.

[46] Since an artefact is a tool that communicates its usage, I have elsewhere (Ehrenberg, 'Law Is an Institution, an Artifact, and a Practice' (n 21) 185–86) distinguished between a norm of usage (or treatment) and a norm of identification (or recognition), which are understood to be communicated requests from the artefact author (com-municated via the artefact). The norm of usage is usually very weak in that it is easy to justify departures from it whenever I need the artefact to perform a function other than the one for which it was designed (though this can be stronger for certain artefacts—like national flags). The norm of identification (that the artefact be recognized as belonging to the class of artefacts of which the creator intended to create an example) is stronger in that it is harder to justify departures from it, but very little is required to comply with it other than recognizing the artefact to be a member of the class (even if I'm using it for something else).

[47] Nevertheless, Raz argues that judges are less bound by precedent than they are by statutory law since they have more ability to distinguish the case in front of them from the precedents. Joseph Raz, *The Authority of Law: Essays on Law and Morality* (Clarendon Press 1979) 183–89.

[48] This is why the theory does not imply an originalist interpretive strategy. See Ehrenberg, 'Law Is an Institution, an Artifact, and a Practice' (n 21) 187 fn 27; KennethM Ehrenberg, 'Intentions in Artefactual Understandings of Law' in Luka Burazin and others (eds), *The Artifactual Nature of Law* (Edward Elgar 2022).

The problem is that while the norms which underlie the legal doctrines that are being applied in judicial decisions are subject to the constitutive rules that specify their validity conditions and functional uses, the decisions themselves are more easily understood as applications of the surface-level legal rules. To employ an overworked analogy to games, the decisions of judges are more like moves in the game rather than setting forth the constitutive rules by which the game is supposed to be played. If the decisions are moves in the game, then it makes sense to say that those moves are constrained by the rules of the institution, but it is again harder to see those moves as imposing further constraints on future decisions.

Unlike moves in a boardgame, however, every judicial decision that carries precedential value is *also* a validity determination. In every case that has at least two sides to the issue at hand, the judicial determination that sets a precedent for future decisions about how to avoid running afoul of the law, and how to apply it when someone is thought (publicly, privately, or tortiously) to have run afoul of it, is impliedly or explicitly stating that the losing side's argument (or action) is legally invalid. More precisely, the decision (except where the decision is merely one of criminal guilt)[49] is that the losing side's argument is not a correct application of the law and hence not a valid 'move' in the legal system. Hence, if the law is like a game, it is more like the game Nomic, in which players make moves by making or changing the rules of the game (which renders the analogy unhelpful in that Nomic was designed to model or mimic legal systems).[50] It's not quite that the judges are changing the basic rules by making validity determinations. But each determination does purport to set forth a pattern by which future actions or arguments can be measured for legal validity (which could certainly be described as a rule).

Each precedential decision does seem, then, to be an institutionalized abstract artefact. Each precedent is a tool that is intended by its author to perform a function and to communicate that function to an audience of users (laypeople who may find themselves in similar situations, lawyers who are advising clients in similar situations, and judges who adjudicate similar situations). It is very much institutional as it is a decision partially about assigning a status (legally valid or not) to each side of the issue applying pre-existing standards of validity, and those statuses carry deontic powers or responsibilities within the context of the wider institution.

Beyond each decision, however, the fact that each one is both a validity determination and a potentially new application of legal norms to facts helps to show how the common law of a given legal system itself is an artefact, perhaps an iteration of the original or the development of the original, built and honed (not without setbacks) over generations.

---

[49] If we are keeping the status-conferral notion of law's institutionality, the need for criminal acts to be defined by law suggests that legal validity encompasses the attachment of criminal status. So, if the determination at issue is simply one of legal guilt for a criminal act, then we would not be able to say that the determination is itself also a validity determination. Of course, appellate cases are not usually simply about legal guilt for a criminal charge (though there are jurisdictions in which appellate courts must ratify guilty verdicts in serious cases).

[50] Douglas R Hofstadter, 'Metamagical Themas: About Nomic: A Heroic Game That Explores the Reflexivity of the Law' (1982) 246 Scientific American 16; Peter Suber, *The Paradox of Self-Amendment: A Study of Logic, Law, Omnipotence, and Change* (Peter Lang 1990).

21
The Gravitational Force of Future Decisions

Nina Varsava[*]

1. Introduction

The doctrine of precedent requires judges to treat like cases alike, so that similarly situated individuals receive the same treatment under the law. The doctrine has been said to serve a variety of purposes, including predictability, efficiency, and sociological legitimacy. But under Ronald Dworkin's theory of law as integrity, the primary value of precedent is equality or formal justice. The idea is that our legal institutions ought to recognize and enforce rights equally within their jurisdiction; if no principled justification is available for denying relief to one individual while granting it to another, then relief must be granted to both or neither, even if one dispute is adjudicated by different judges or at a different time than the other.

My aim in this chapter is not to defend Dworkin's theory of law, but rather to explore how that theory can ground a type of judicial obligation that has not been addressed in the literature. This obligation calls for a new model of case-based adjudication, which I begin to develop here. I'll suggest that law as integrity compels us to take seriously the possibility that judges have a duty to aim for consistency with not only past decisions but also future ones, and that the law is actually constituted by both.[1] If judges aim for the consistent enforcement of rights and duties, then they should indeed be concerned with following precedent in the conventional sense of abiding by past decisions. But judges should also be concerned with treating individuals in the present the same as similarly situated individuals will be treated in the future. This is because equality is an atemporal ideal; it does not discriminate based on the order of treatment. Accordingly, judges should afford weight to future judicial decisions and aim for principled coherence with them. In this sense, judges are duty-bound to predict, as best they can, future decisions and, to the extent that those decisions are reasonably foreseeable, to aim for consistency with them. This is not so different from the duty that judges have under law as integrity with respect to past cases: a duty to seek out those cases and aim to decide new cases consistently with them.

Suppose a US federal court—the Seventh Circuit Court of Appeals, for example—is charged with deciding a question of Wisconsin state law. Suppose further that the Wisconsin Supreme Court decided the very question at issue ten years prior, but that a majority of the state court's current justices have expressed credible intentions to overrule the case, such that we are able to predict with high certainty that they will not follow it in the future. On the traditional model of precedent, the past case represents Wisconsin law and the federal court would seem to have a duty to follow it. In contrast, on the model that I present here, future Wisconsin cases also have a claim over present disputes arising under Wisconsin law; if those

---

[*] I would like to thank Felipe Jiménez, Hafsteinn Dan Kristjánsson, Sebastian Lewis, Adam Perry, Ben Zipursky, and participants of the international workshop for this volume in October 2021 for feedback on earlier drafts.

[1] Law as integrity is not the only theoretical basis for attributing a precedent-like effect to future decisions, however, as I hope to show in future work.

Nina Varsava, *The Gravitational Force of Future Decisions* In: *Philosophical Foundations of Precedent*. Edited by: Timothy Endicott, Hafsteinn Dan Kristjánsson, and Sebastian Lewis, Oxford University Press. © Nina Varsava 2023. DOI: 10.1093/oso/9780192857248.003.0022

282 NINA VARSAVA

future cases are inconsistent with past ones, the federal court may be required to depart from the latter. In this hypothetical, then, the federal court might be duty-bound to depart from the past state decisions, on the ground that it is reasonably foreseeable that Wisconsin courts will do so themselves.

Although we can safely call the retrospective model of adjudication the standard view, others have proposed prospective or forward-looking accounts that are conceptually distinct from the one I propose here. Let me clarify at the outset, then, that when I refer to the gravitational force of future decisions I do not mean that when judges decide cases they do or should take into account their decisions' effects on future decision-makers who will regard those decisions as precedential, although my account does incorporate that insight.[2] Nor do I mean that legal rights and duties are 'nothing but prophecies' about how courts will or would decide disputes; my view is not a version of—and is actually opposed to—the latter view of law.[3]

On my account, future judicial decisions (so far as these are accessible—i.e. predictable) hold sway over present adjudication just as past ones (so far as these are accessible) do. If judges do their best to realize law as integrity, they will be moved by both past and future adjudication. This doesn't mean that in all cases judges will be duty-bound to conform their decisions to future decisions of like cases. The same goes for past precedent. But law as integrity does ground a duty to attend to future decisions and sometimes a duty to abide by them. Because past decisions might conflict with future ones, under the bidirectional model of case-based adjudication that I propose judges will sometimes have to determine whether past or future decisions weigh more heavily on the present. This will depend on various factors, but will ultimately come down to whether, in that instance, consistency with the past or future decisions better serves the integrity of the legal system as a whole.

In section 2, I begin by summarizing Dworkin's account of precedent as he presented it. I then turn to my two core arguments for the gravitational force of future decisions under law as integrity. In the first, I suggest that, if fairness or equality represents the main justificatory principle underlying our system of precedent, then judges should be concerned with forward-looking (just as they are with backward-looking) consistency. In the second, I draw on Dworkin's chain novel analogy to show how his idea of constructive interpretation is best understood to require construction of not only past decisions but also predictions of future ones. Then, in section 3, I spell out the bidirectional model more concretely, explaining what recognizing the gravitational force of future decisions would mean for adjudicative practice. Finally, in section 4, I respond to some objections to my central claim that future decisions carry gravitational force.

2. Integrity and Judicial Decisions

A. Dworkin on Precedent

Under law as integrity, it is a kind of equality—'the fairness of treating like cases alike'—that justifies the pressure, in Dworkin's terminology the 'gravitational force', that past cases put

---

[2] See, e.g., F Schauer, 'Precedent' (1987) 39 Stan L Rev 571, 573, 589; J Waldron, '*Stare Decisis* and the Rule of Law: A Layered Approach' (2012) 111 Mich L Rev 1; N MacCormick, *Legal Reasoning and Legal Theory* (Clarendon Press 1994) 75.

[3] OW Holmes, 'The Path of the Law' (1897) 10 Harv L Rev 457.

on new ones.[4] For Dworkin, this value of equality, which we might also conceive in terms of formal or comparative justice, 'offers the only adequate account of the full practice of precedent', and demands that legal institutions and their officers treat all individuals within their jurisdiction according to the same principles, whatever those principles may be.[5] The judicial obligation to follow precedent flows from the government's general obligation to 'treat its citizens as equals, as equally entitled to concern and respect'—its 'obligation to extend whatever political order it ... create[s] equally and consistently to everyone'.[6] Accordingly, we can assess the 'weight' of a precedent case on a present dispute by asking 'whether it is fair for the government, having intervened in the way it did in the first case', not to do the same in the second.[7]

On Dworkin's view, judges are in the business of constructive interpretation. This means that they identify the law by determining the principles that 'provide the best—morally most compelling—justification of legal practices as a whole'.[8] But Dworkin counts only past decisions, and not future ones, as possible sources of legal rights in present disputes:[9] the legal material that judges must interpret, he writes, 'continues [only] to the moment when [they] must decide what it now declares'.[10] So Dworkin adopts the traditional view that only past decisions exert force over present adjudication. But he doesn't justify this stopping point, and his theory of law as integrity ultimately doesn't warrant it but, rather, compels us to recognize the precedent-like effect of future decisions.

I'll make the case for the gravitational force of future decisions in two ways: first, in section 2.B, by appealing to the timeless or atemporal aspect of equality; and, second, in section 2.C, by showing, with recourse to Dworkin's chain novel analogy, how constructive interpretation at its best would recognize the force of future decisions.

B. Equality

The best interpretation of the kind of equality that, for Dworkin, underlies the doctrine of precedent would conceive of this value as an atemporal or timeless ideal—that is, two individuals should get the same treatment whether or not they were treated at the same time and regardless of the order in which they were treated. Suppose that you are a plaintiff in a lawsuit today, that you are denied relief based on a high court precedent, and that the high court declines to take your case on appeal for whatever reason. And suppose further that the judge deciding your case reasonably foresees that in the future courts will decline to follow the precedent that favours defendants in cases like yours. You have a plausible complaint, then, based on likely unequal treatment: you are denied a right that similarly situated fellow citizens are likely to be granted in the future.

For an example outside the law, imagine that a family has two children, and even though the parents know they should not have favourites, they in fact favour the second child and have a hard time resisting that child's requests. The parents reasonably believe that in the

---

[4] R Dworkin, *Taking Rights Seriously* (Harvard UP 1978) 113.

[5] R Dworkin, 'Hart's Postscript and the Character of Political Philosophy' (2004) 24 OJLS 1, 29.

[6] Some theorists reject the value of this kind of equality. This is not the place to mount an affirmative argument for it. My argument here is more limited. I claim that, *if* we accept something like Dworkin's conception of formal justice, then the force of future decisions follows.

[7] Dworkin, *Taking Rights Seriously* (n 4) 113.

[8] R Dworkin, *Justice in Robes* (Harvard UP 2008) 144.

[9] Dworkin, *Taking Rights Seriously* (n 4) 113; R Dworkin, *Law's Empire* (Harvard UP 1986) 99.

[10] Dworkin, *Law's Empire* (n 9) 316.

future they will spend a considerable sum of money on a university education at some expensive private school for their second child, who has persistently expressed an interest in that kind of educational experience. Suppose that—second child aside—they would not pay for their first child to go to a fancy school, regardless of that child's expressed interests, because they believe that a less expensive alternative would provide a fully adequate education and they have their own retirement to worry about. However, if they realize far enough in advance that they won't be able to resist supporting their second child's expensive university education, then they have a reason to also support their first child's like education (at least assuming that their first child has similar interests in such an education). This reason may not be dispositive; perhaps, all things considered, even if the parents will fund an expensive education for their younger child, they do not have an obligation to do so for their first child. But they do have a reason—grounded in equality and specifically the parental duty to refrain from exercising favouritism in the treatment of their children—for affording their older child the same educational opportunity as their younger one. The decision regarding the first child's education comes first, but it is informed by their prediction of the decision that they will make in the future regarding their second child's education. The latter decision tugs on the former one, even though the former one comes first. In the adjudicative context, the gravitational force of future decisions operates in the same kind of way.

What if a particular decision is incorrect or suboptimal on the merits? Does the decision-maker still have a reason, based on equality, to follow it? Other theorists have taken up this issue with respect to past precedent, and views differ sharply on whether equality provides any reason to repeat a decision that was substantively unjust.[11] This chapter is not the place to wade into that debate. For those who believe that there is no reason to repeat incorrect decisions, my argument will have more limited scope of applicability—but it will still have bite, because it suggests that decision-makers should not prioritize consistency with past decisions over future ones just because the latter happen to be in the past. For those who take the more conservative view of equality (i.e., that equality does not provide a reason for following an erroneous decision), a present decision-maker will still have a reason to follow future decisions. The reason exists to the extent that the future decisions will not be erroneous or the present decision-maker is not in an epistemic position to adequately assess their merit.[12] For Dworkin, however, even erroneous decisions possess gravitational force; indeed, equality might require a court to follow as precedent a decision that is 'now regretted', in which case judges will 'feel obliged to command what [they] wish [they] did not have to command'.[13]

This is not to say that all decisions exert meaningful gravitational force in present cases. Under law as integrity, following a past decision as precedent is to discover the principles that support and justify it, and that also fit with other legal practices, and to apply those principles to the present case. Extending this idea, following future decisions likewise requires discovering principles underlying those decisions and applying them to the present case. If there are no such principles to be discovered with respect to a decision, whether a past or future one, then integrity may justify, or even require, a decision-maker to depart from

---

[11] For example, in his contribution to this volume (Chapter 36), Adam Perry claims that '[i]t is simply not true that a wrong decision in one case is *any* reason, of any weight, to treat a like case wrongly as well.' Larry Alexander has likewise argued that equality generally does not provide any reason to repeat a morally incorrect decision. L Alexander, 'Constrained by Precedent' (1989) 63 So Cal L Rev 1, 10–12. For theorists taking an opposing view, in addition to Dworkin, see DN MacCormick, 'Formal Justice and the Form of Legal Arguments' (1976) 19 Logique et analyse 103, 109; J Feinberg, 'Noncomparative Justice' (1974) 83 Philosophical Rev 297.

[12] See the contribution to this volume by Adam Perry (Chapter 36) on the relevance of this epistemic issue to the obligation to follow past decisions.

[13] R Dworkin, *Justice for Hedgehogs* (Harvard UP 2011) 409.

the decision. In this way, the appropriate 'interpretive attitude may isolate [a particular decision] as a mistake because it is condemned by principles necessary to justify the rest of the [system]' and thus is 'not a real requirement'.[14] Law as integrity, then, does not require judges to conform their decisions to all reasonably foreseeable future decisions in like cases, just as it does not require them to do so with respect to all like past cases.

To return to our hypothetical family, in deciding whether to fund their first child's expensive university education, the parents should appeal to principled reasons that they will be prepared to act on in the future when it comes time to make a decision regarding their second child's education. Suppose that, considered as a one-off decision, the parents would decide against funding an expensive education for their child today, perhaps to ensure that they have sufficient savings to support their own autonomy and dignity in retirement or because they value affordable and accessible public school. If the parents rely on those reasons to support their decision today, then they should be prepared to rely on the same reasons in the future when they decide on their second child's education.

In the adjudicative context, this means that judges should try to predict how future decision-makers—themselves, current judges on other courts in the system, and subsequent judges—will decide future cases, and what principles those future decision-makers will be prepared to follow. Neil MacCormick pointed, I believe, to something like the gravitational force of future decisions when he wrote that a court ought to base its decision on 'reasons which will be acceptable as reasons for giving the same decision at a later point in time if a similar case should subsequently arise'.[15] A decision is not 'adequately justified,' he elaborated, 'unless it is justified by reference to reasons of general principle which the decision maker is prepared to commit himself to applying in future relevant situations'.[16] If a present court predicts that some principle it now finds appealing will be rejected by future courts, then the present court has a reason to refrain from relying on that principle itself. If future decisions will not be consistent with a contemplated present one, then that is a problem, counting against the contemplated one.

It is because equality in the sense of formal justice is atemporal or timeless in nature that, assuming we care about that value, we ought to recognize the precedent-like force of future decisions alongside the precedential effect of past ones. Individuals have a right that the government treat them under the same norms as their co-citizens. All else being equal, the sequence of treatment is morally irrelevant for the purposes of equality. This imposes on judges an obligation to aim for consistency with not only past decisions but also future ones, and it means that adjudication ought to be more prospective and predictive than Dworkin imagined. The same 'fairness of treating like cases alike' that he took to justify the gravitational force of past cases compels us to recognize the gravitational force of future ones too.[17]

C. Constructive Interpretation

In this section I draw on Dworkin's chain novel analogy to show how the input of the constructive interpretation enterprise is best understood to include future decision-making. Recall, under Dworkin's theory of law and adjudication, that judges have a duty to realize,

---

[14] Dworkin, *Law's Empire* (n 9) 203.
[15] MacCormick, 'Formal Justice' (n 11) 110.
[16] ibid.
[17] Dworkin, *Taking Rights Seriously* (n 4) 113.

and optimize, the integrity of their legal system. Dworkin says that judges fulfil that duty by deciding new cases according to the legal principles that provide the best 'constructive interpretation' of previous legal practices: this means that the principles they apply to new cases should both fit with and justify as much of political history as possible. But a judge's legal system and the body of law they are responsible for administering extend not only into the past but also indefinitely into the future. If judges look not only to political history but also to political future, including future judicial decisions, then they can arrive at a better constructive interpretation of their system's law than if they look to the past only. Since it is the integrity of the legal system as a whole that judges should strive to optimize, the proper domain of constructive interpretation includes future adjudication.

In an extended metaphor, Dworkin likens judges to creative writers working on a chain novel. The chain novel enterprise requires that any given writer, as one of many writers contributing sequentially to a single novel, ought to build on past contributions in a way that makes the novel the best it can be. In describing this enterprise, Dworkin vacillates between referring to the novel 'so far' and the novel 'as a whole'. Consistent with the novel-so-far point of view, Dworkin asserts that 'each novelist in the chain interprets the chapters he has been given in order to write a new chapter'.[18] But Dworkin also at times suggests that contributors must take the view of the novel *as a whole*: they must ask themselves 'which interpretation makes the work of art better *on the whole*'.[19]

These are very different things: the content of the optimal contribution will depend on which vantage point we take. Suppose that the first three chapters of a novel have been written, each by different authors, and that the novel will have some unknown number of chapters greater than four. If the next contributor, the author of chapter four, endeavours to create the best possible novel so far, they need only take account of what has already been written; their chapter, then, must continue the narrative in a way that coheres with the first three chapters and shows them in the best possible light, but beyond that they have free rein to shape the story as they see fit. If each contributor's only objective is to create the best novel so far, then they have no reason to give any consideration to the content of future chapters.

This novel-so-far perspective reflects Dworkin's view of the judicial role with respect to precedent: '[a] judge's decision—his postinterpretive conclusions—must be drawn from an interpretation that both fits and justifies *what has gone before*, so far as that is possible'.[20] Accordingly, the judge must consider 'what other judges *in the past* have written ... to reach an opinion about what they have collectively *done*, in the way that each of our novelists formed an opinion about the collective novel *so far written*'.[21]

A capable contributor to a chain novel, though, should consider not only what has already been written before their turn to contribute but also what will be or is likely to be written subsequently. Dworkin seems to recognize this at one point, but only in passing, when he writes that, '[e]ach novelist aims to make a single novel of the material he has been given, what he adds to it, and (so far as he can control this) *what his successors will want or be able to add*'.[22] The qualification about the control that a contributor may have over future contributors is mysterious, because even if the novelist has little or no control over future content, he ought to take that content into account when determining what shape the present chapter should

---

[18] Dworkin, *Law's Empire* (n 9) 229.
[19] R Dworkin, ' "Natural" Law Revisited' (1982) 34 U Fla L Rev 165, 169.
[20] Dworkin, *Law's Empire* (n 9) 239 (emphasis added).
[21] Dworkin, 'Natural Law Revisited' (n 21) 168 (emphasis added).
[22] Dworkin, *Law's Empire* (n 9) 229 (emphasis added).

take. In his consideration of the kind of effect that future contributions should have on the present decision, then, the main contingent factor is not the degree of control the present novelist has over his successors, but rather his knowledge of, or ability to predict, what they will do. Although he might have a better ability to predict future chapters if he can control his successors' contributions, he ought to aim for coherence with subsequent material *regardless of his ability to control or influence it.*

If a present contributor is able to predict to some extent the form that future contributions will take, then this prediction ought to inform the present contribution. A writer who cares about the quality of the novel will care about how their chapter fits in with the text that has already been written as well as the text that will be written. We might reasonably evaluate some version of the fourth chapter as the best one possible when considering only the first four chapters (the novel so far), but might rightly perceive that same version as highly problematic when considering, together with the first four chapters, the likely content of subsequent ones (the novel as a whole).

For example, Dworkin asks us to imagine that Charles Dickens never wrote *A Christmas Carol* and that the work is currently being written in chain novel fashion by multiple authors. Suppose, he says, that you 'have been given only the first few sections of *A Christmas Carol*' and that you have the task of writing the next section.[23] Suppose you think that in the best possible version of the novella, holding the first few sections constant but all else open, Scrooge would grow only colder and more callous over the course of the narrative. If you thought that your successors would feel the same way, you would proceed to develop Scrooge's character in that direction.

But suppose further that you know that your successor novelists have bleeding hearts and will ultimately seek to redeem Scrooge regardless of the content of your section. That reality ought to inform your contribution. Perhaps you should foreshadow Scrooge's redemption— as in fact the early sections of *A Christmas Carol* do (e.g. when Scrooge expresses regret at having shut out the Christmas caroller who shows up at his home).[24] In so doing, you would construct a sort of bridge between the cold, miserly, and mean Scrooge we see in the first pages of the novella and the warm, generous, and kind Scrooge that you predict we will see by the end. You are not permitted to stick to your conviction and characterize Scrooge as irredeemable; doing so would make it impossible for your successors (again, assuming they were committed to redeeming him) to do a good job, since their sections would inevitably be inconsistent with yours.

A contributor aiming for a coherent plot, then, ought to view their own contribution in the context of the novel as a whole, and not only in the context of the novel so far. Dworkin fails to acknowledge or recognize the implications of the difference between these two vantage points, for the writer in the context of the chain novel and for the judge in adjudication. A writer might take a chain novel in some direction that appears appropriate to the novel so far (i.e. if we consider only what has come before) but is patently detrimental to the novel as a whole (i.e. if we consider the shape that future contributions are likely to take).

A writer might reasonably disregard the future only if their chapter will be the final one in the novel, marking its completion, or perhaps if they have no idea whatsoever (and no reasonable means of ascertaining) what subsequent chapters will look like. In the adjudicative context, however, a judge is relatively unlikely to encounter either of these scenarios.

---

[23] ibid 232.
[24] C Dickens, *The Illustrated Christmas Carol: 200th Anniversary Edition* (SeaWolf 2020) 32.

Because the point of constructive interpretation is the integrity of the legal system *as a whole*, and not just particular snapshots of its history, and because the legal practices of a system typically extend into the future and that future is to some extent predictable, a constructive interpretation of judicial decisions should not end with past cases. An indefinite number of future cases looms over every present decision, and judges can more fully realize law as integrity by attending to that reality.

To summarize: so far I've argued that Dworkin's theory of law as integrity compels us to recognize the gravitational force of future decisions. To make my case, I appealed to the value of equality in the form of treating like cases alike and to the idea of constructive interpretation. In section 3, I show more concretely what it means for future decisions to exert gravitational force in adjudication. I also suggest that the bidirectional model I propose is not as radical as it may seem; judges already and widely recognize, through various adjudicative practices, the precedent-like effect of future decisions on the present.

3. The Bidirectional Model

A given decision in the present is typically part of a pattern of decisions that extends backwards but also forwards—and so a court that cares about the integrity of its legal system ought to aim for coherence with both the past and future of adjudication. If it foresees that future courts will depart from past cases, then it ought to decide the present case with that in mind; this would require considering what kind of decision today would make future decisions seem less capricious and more coherent when those decisions come to pass.

The task that confronts the judge is like the one that confronts the interim chain novelist: that contributor has a responsibility to make the novel as a whole the best it can be, which means that their own contribution will be shaped by both their best understanding of previous contributions and their best prediction of subsequent ones. If judges 'should speak with one, morally consistent, voice',[25] then judges should aim to adjust their voices not only to the tune of their predecessors but also to that of their successors. Because the law is an ongoing project, a judge should take the point of view of an interim contributor, somewhere in the middle or perhaps early on (depending on the age and life-expectancy of the legal system). This is what the best interpretation of law as integrity itself demands.

The claim that a decision at T2 (D2) exerts force over a decision in a like case at T1 (D1) means that the T1 judge ought to do their best to anticipate how D2 will be decided and then take that prediction into account when they decide D1. What does it mean to take the future decision into account? That will depend heavily on where the T1 judge is situated in the judicial hierarchy, but may involve considering various counterfactuals along the lines of, *if I decide this case in favour of the defendant, is the T2 judge likely to do the same?* The duty to serve systemic consistency does not mean that the T1 judge necessarily has an obligation to decide the case the same way that the T2 judge will decide D2. As with past precedent, sometimes judges will be justified in departing from a decision in a like case.[26] Integrity provides only a reason to consider past and future decisions and to reason with them, where reasoning with them means searching for the principles that would best justify and fit with those decisions together with other relevant legal materials.

---

[25] SR Perry, 'Two Models of Legal Principles' (1977) 82 U Iowa L Rev 787, 812.
[26] See section 1.B. for discussion of this point.

Further, the set of relevant materials will differ between T1 and T2. And so the second judge's decision might depart somewhat from the first's without either judge having done anything wrong. Perhaps the first judge foresees that decisions will take a particular and desirable direction in future cases and makes D1 with that in mind, appealing to principles that would support those future decisions. This might help to enable the second judge to go even further in pushing the law in a positive direction. That judge relies on some of the same principles as the T1 judge but can also rely on principles that weren't available at T1—for example, principles that the second judge discovers in other cases that have been decided in the interim and that the judge can foresee, from their T2 vantage point, will shape future legal practices as well.

An important difference, of course, between past and future decisions from the point of view of a judge in the present is that the judge's present decision can (and often will) affect future decisions but not past ones. Returning to the chain novel analogy, if it is my turn to contribute to *A Christmas Carol* and I believe that in the best possible version of the novel Scrooge would not be redeemed, then I might decide to write my chapter in such a way that would make it very difficult for future contributors to redeem him and at the same time maintain coherence with the previous chapters. A judge aiming to decide a case consistently with past and future decisions must consider how their own imminent decision may affect future ones. And a judge might reasonably decide a present case with the aim of nudging future adjudication in a direction that will ultimately make for a more coherent and justified body of law overall. The degree to which a given judge's decision is likely to influence their successors depends on many factors, including their position in a judicial system—for example, whether the judge serves on a trial court or an appellate one—and the judge will have to take these factors into account when assessing what subsequent adjudicators are likely to make, if anything, of their imminent decision.

On the bidirectional model, judges will likely be required to set aside more past judicial decisions than they would on the traditional view of precedent. My modification of law as integrity, then, makes it less susceptible to the criticism that it is overly conservative or deferential to tradition.[27] If a judge perceives a previous line of decisions as mistaken on grounds of substantive justice and reasonably predicts that regardless of how they currently treat that line of decisions future judges are likely to reject it, then departing from the line of decisions today will not seem as costly in terms of consistency as it would on a purely backward-looking approach to constructive interpretation. We would sacrifice some consistency with the legal system's past, but we would gain consistency with its future. To the extent that judges recognize the precedent-like effect of future decisions, then, the legal system is less likely to suffer from the entrenchment of erroneous decisions or a perverse commitment to political history.

The bidirectional model helps to explain, and justify, various predictive practices that judges already engage in. For example, when US federal courts decide questions arising under state law, they often apply a predictive approach to a state's case law: they adjudicate the dispute in accord with their predictions of how the state's courts will decide similar cases in the future. Although federal courts often purport to resort to the predictive approach only when they find that state law is unclear or indeterminate, they have also been known to prioritize predictions of future decisions over clear past ones when they are reasonably confident that the state's courts will decline to follow those past cases in the future. Expressing

---

[27] On Dworkin's conservatism, see, e.g., A Marmor, 'Integrity in *Law's Empire*' (2019) Cornell Legal Studies Research Paper No 19-28 <https://ssrn.com/abstract=3422173> accessed 1 July 2021.

290　NINA VARSAVA

support for the latter practice, the US Supreme Court has declared that previous 'rulings of the Supreme Court of Florida ... must be taken as controlling ... *unless it can be said with some assurance that the Florida Supreme Court will not follow them in the future*'.[28] The Court not only acknowledged the gravitational force of future cases over current disputes, then, but also suggested that this force can outweigh that of inconsistent past cases.[29] Courts have also used prediction to guide adjudication outside the inter-systemic context; for example, courts sometimes follow vacated decisions and various types of dicta, and have even cited the predictive power of these materials as justification for relying on them.[30]

So far I've made an affirmative argument for the precedent-like force of future decisions under law as integrity (section 2) and elaborated on what that force might look like in practice (section 3). Although I do not have the space here to address all reasonable objections, in section 4 I take up a few that seem especially pressing and introduce some qualifications to my central claim along the way.[31]

4. Objections

A. Strategic Decision-Making

Judges and scholars alike have suggested that predictive approaches to adjudication are strategic, extra-legal, and illegitimate. For example, criticizing his court for taking a predictive approach to federal law, a California Supreme Court justice asserted that 'nose-counting is a job for litigators, not jurists' and that 'our role is not simply to determine what outcome will likely garner five votes on the high court' but rather 'to render the best interpretation of the law in light of the legal texts and authorities binding on us'.[32] Empirical evidence indicates that federal appellate courts also 'engage in prognostication' of Supreme Court decisions and are less likely to follow past cases if they suspect that the current Court disapproves of them—a phenomenon that scholars describe in terms of psychological incentives as opposed to legal obligations.[33] According to Michael Dorf, predicting how future cases will be decided is a categorically distinct enterprise from ascertaining '*what the law is*'.[34] '[W]hat makes a course of conduct unlawful' on a predictive account of adjudication, says Dorf, 'is not some metaphysical property of unlawfulness, but the fact that a court will impose sanctions for engaging in the conduct'.[35] On this commonly held view, predictive approaches to adjudication are incompatible with norm-based decision-making.

Under my predictive model, however, the impact of a judge's predictions on present adjudication is norm-based just as the impact of a judge's understanding of past decisions is. Although the judge might well consider the likely composition of future courts in the

---

[28] *Meredith v City of Winter Haven* 320 US 228, 234 (1943) (emphasis added).

[29] For another example, see *Mason v American Emery Wheel Works* 241 F2d 906, 909–10 (1st Cir 1957) (predicting that Mississippi state precedent would be overruled and following its prediction of the state's future decisions).

[30] See, e.g., *United States v Anderson* 705 F Supp 2d 1, 7 (DDC 2010) (following a vacated opinion on the ground that it likely represented how future cases would be decided).

[31] Note that I don't attempt to address objections that are really objections to Dworkinian law as integrity itself, such as the positivist claim that legal validity is ultimately a matter of social fact alone and not moral principle.

[32] *People v Lopez* 286 P3d 469, 485 (Cal 2012) (Liu J dissenting).

[33] SM Benjamin and Georg Vanberg, 'Judicial Retirements and the Staying Power of US Supreme Court Decisions' (2016) 13 JELS 5, 22.

[34] MC Dorf, 'Dicta and Article III' (1994) 142 U Pa L Rev 1997, 2027 (emphasis added).

[35] MC Dorf, 'Prediction and the Rule of Law' (1995) UCLA L Rev 651, 656–57.

process of predicting how future decisions will come out—for example, maybe the judge reasonably predicts that women will enjoy greater representation on courts in the future, which will influence case outcomes—the judge still has to determine or find the principles that best fit with and justify future decisions, and not only those but past ones too. Judges, then, can and probably should take into account the 'prejudices, pathologies, and ideologies' of judges in their efforts to predict future decisions; but this approach does not necessarily 'show[] disrespect for [the] law by treating it as unprincipled',[36] at least not any more so than the traditional, past-oriented approach. Past decisions, after all, are also affected by the biases and personal policy preferences of judges. Compared to the traditional model that Dworkin hangs on to, according to mine a judge just takes a more capacious view of the legal practices that are relevant to the process of constructive interpretation.

That said, decisions that are the product of political or results-oriented judging are likely to be more difficult to justify using a set of principles that also fits with the rest of the law, since those decisions themselves were not decided in that way; such decisions, accordingly, might carry less weight, or even none at all (if they can be written off as mistakes). This goes for past and future decisions alike. Nevertheless, once a judge predicts how future judges will decide cases similar to the present one, they ought to attempt to justify the future decisions with legal principles. It is those principles that have gravitational force over the present case.

The predictive model of adjudication that I propose, then, is fully consistent with a norm-based system of law: those norms are simply informed by predictions of future cases together with understandings of past ones and other conventional legal materials. To the extent that judges are able to predict the shape that future decisions in similar cases will take, they have a duty to take future adjudication into account and aim for consistency with it. This is because judges have a duty to ensure that their legal system treats like cases alike. There is nothing cynical or improper, then, about judges forming predictions, based on any evidence available, of future decision-making and using those predictions to inform their decision-making in the present.

On my version of the predictive model, future adjudicative events affect the content of existing legal norms: the legal content of future actions of judges just are properties of lawfulness. What is that legal content? It is the set of principles that would best fit with and justify the future decisions together with all other legal materials. The legal content of the future decisions, then, like that of past decisions, is interpretive and evaluative, and judges need to factor in both kinds of content if they wish to realize the full value of integrity. In this way, both past and future exercises of judicial authority have normative implications for how judges should exercise their authority today.

B. Redundancy

If a judge at T1 has a duty to follow the decision of a judge at T2 and the T2 judge has a duty to follow the T1 decision, then shouldn't the first judge just decide the present case as she sees fit on the merits, knowing that the second judge will follow that decision as a precedent?

If a future judge will perfectly follow a present decision, whatever shape the current decision takes, then it would indeed be redundant for the present judge to worry about following the future decision; after all, that decision will end up matching the present one

---

[36] MS Green, 'Horizontal Erie and the Presumption of Forum Law' (2011) 109 Mich L Rev 1237, 1251.

anyway! This objection has bite, but I don't think it's fatal to the bidirectional model, for a few reasons.

First, the objection supposes a highly unrealistic adjudicative setting. In reality, judges do not follow past precedents perfectly, whether because they are unwilling or unable to do so. And so the first judge has to consider the extent to which future judges would follow her decision in the event that she decides one way rather than another—the extent to which the principles she would now rely on are likely to be relied on in the future. The preferences, priorities, and biases of future judges will influence their decisions. And the content of the T1 decision will affect whether future judges decide to follow it, or instead disingenuously distinguish, ignore, or (if they have the power) overrule it. Given that judges have a responsibility to try to prevent this kind of inconsistency in adjudicative practice, which amounts to unequal treatment of individuals under the law across time, they should not simply assume that whatever they decide today will be followed as precedent in the future. Sometimes judges will have a duty to intentionally align their decision with future ones because they reasonably believe that future judges, for whatever reason, will not follow the present decision as precedent.

Further, background conditions change over time, and so an optimal one-off decision on the merits today might look different than an optimal decision in a similar case in the future. If a judge today decides a dispute as she sees fit on the merits without considering future decisions, then future decision-makers might be compelled to sacrifice consistency with the past case because the value of that consistency is outweighed by other factors. And so, even if those other factors—which might include new social conditions and further judicial decisions—have not yet come to pass at T1, they may nevertheless appropriately influence the T1 judge's decision.

Second, the first judge might not be sure about the best way to decide her case on the merits. Suppose that she is relatively certain that future courts in like cases will believe, for whatever reason, that the correct judgment on the merits is for the plaintiff. But suppose that the T1 judge does not know how the case should come out, or that she determines that the parties have equally strong arguments or that the defendant's position is just slightly stronger than the plaintiff's. If the judge decides for the defendant, then future courts will face pressure from her decision. They may follow it and decide in a way they believe is otherwise mistaken on the merits, or instead ignore or (if they have the power) overrule it. Either scenario is regrettable in its own way. Because the T1 judge has no reason to think that the future courts will be incorrect or that she knows better than them, she should abide by the decisions that those future courts would wish to make and decide the present case in favour of the plaintiff, thus sparing future courts (and her legal system) from a cause for regret.

Third, the objection loses much of its bite when we focus on the vertical context of a judicial hierarchy. Since higher courts generally do not follow lower court decisions, attempts on the part of lower courts to follow future higher court decisions are not superfluous. A higher court might decide some type of case in a particular way in the future regardless of how lower courts decide similar cases today. For the sake of equality, then, lower courts ought to predict and follow the higher court's future decisions.

C. Epistemic Asymmetry

Since judges do not know how future courts will decide cases, perhaps they ought to concern themselves with past decisions only.

The predictive enterprise, of course, involves considerable judgment, and a federal court might get its prediction wrong. To the extent that judges have a better grasp on past cases than future ones, they might have a better chance of achieving consistency with the past than the future, and so past-oriented efforts might be more likely to pay off than future-oriented ones. This kind of asymmetry should inform their approach to adjudication and might indeed warrant giving greater weight to past decisions than anticipated future ones.

Of course, predictions come with varying degrees of certainty, and a judge should consider their level of uncertainty when determining how to weigh future cases relative to past ones. For example, if a judge has a mere inkling that courts will depart from some line of precedent in the coming years, that prediction should not play much of a role in their adjudication of a present dispute, whereas if the judge is relatively certain in their prediction then it should have greater force. If a judge has no reasonable basis whatsoever on which to predict how future judges will handle a past line of cases, then speculation about the future of those cases should probably have no bearing at all on the present decision. If some decisions in similar cases are utterly inaccessible to a judge, those decisions still exert pressure in a sense. It would be better if the judge knew about them and took them into account. But the judge would not be abdicating her duties by failing to recognize decisions that she cannot possibly access. The same goes for past precedent—and we should keep in mind that judges do not have perfect access to past instances of adjudication either—although problems of accessibility admittedly loom much larger with respect to future decisions.

D. Notice and Fairness

One might contend that law as integrity requires judges to place more, or even exclusive, weight on past decisions because the community has notice of past decisions and therefore can and, in fact, does rely on them.

For Dworkin, judges need to consider the possibility of unfair surprise in the process of adjudication. This factor will figure in a judge's overall determination of whether a decision in favour of one party and against another is fair and thus legally correct. As Dworkin explains, 'if the court believes that the plaintiff has a right, then it believes, all things considered, *including the question of surprise*, that a decision against the plaintiff would be, at least *prima facie*, unfair'.[37]

This does not mean that a judge adjudicating a given dispute should refrain from giving weight to their predictions of how future judges will decide similar disputes. However, it does mean that a judge ought to consider the extent to which people might have reasonably relied on a past decision before departing from it in favour of consistency with future cases, and should consider as well the extent to which people would reasonably predict a departure from the past decision. It is possible that some rule would be the law were it not for the unfair surprise that applying the rule would create. Because individuals are likely to have better access to past decisions than future ones, all else being equal past decisions weigh more heavily than future ones on present adjudication.

However, even non-judges and non-lawyers can and do predict (whether or not with the help of legal experts) the direction that judicial decisions will take going forwards, including departures from past cases, and they might reasonably rely on those predictions

---

[37] Dworkin, *Taking Rights Seriously* (n 4) 336 (emphasis added).

in planning their affairs. As AM Honoré explained, 'the idea of protecting reasonable expectations[] is consistent with change, since when reasonable notice of changes in rules or habits has been given, then the unfairness of departing from rules previously accepted disappears'.[38] Further, because reliance interests constitute one of the primary factors that weigh against overruling a past case, a court's reasonable prediction of future courts' treatment of a past case will involve an assessment of the extent to which people have reasonably relied on the case.[39]

The extent to which people rely on any given past case changes over time, of course, and judges might sometimes be in a unique position to predict that future courts will depart from a previous decision. It is certainly possible that the reliance interests at stake at a given moment are too great to permit overruling some past case, even though the court accurately predicts that going forwards reliance on the case will diminish such that those interests will not prevent a future court from overruling it. In this scenario, judges might have a duty to continue following the past case rather than their prediction of future ones. Whatever gravitational pull the future decisions have would be outweighed by the push of past cases once we factor in the value of notice and the risk of upsetting reasonable expectations.

E. Feedback and Tradition

The prevailing approach to adjudication at any given time—and, in particular, the extent to which judges are influenced by past and future decisions—will affect people's reasonable expectations. As Stephen Perry explains, 'once a practice of following precedent is in place, there may be a kind of feedback effect: the justified expectations and the reasonable reliance to which the practice gives rise are first-order reasons that [judges] should [take] into account in the overall balance of principles'.[40] If the existing practice of precedent is primarily past-oriented, then judges might be required to weigh past decisions more heavily than future ones, all else being equal, given the fairness cost of upsetting reasonable expectations.

However, judges already recognize the gravitational force of future decisions. In various adjudicative contexts in the US at least, judges seek consistency with not only past cases but also future ones. They aim to interpret the law in such a way that shows the totality of legal practices—past, present, and future—in the best light possible, which is just what law as integrity ultimately demands. People's reasonable expectations in litigation will be informed by that reality. The more prediction that judges pursue, the more prediction they might be justified, or required, to pursue, because people will increasingly come to expect it.

To sum up, then, the objections considered here show the force of past and future decisions to be asymmetrical in various ways. But my responses to the objections suggest that there is nevertheless space for future decisions to exert meaningful precedent-like effect on the adjudication of present cases.

---

[38] AM Honoré, 'Social Justice' (1962) 8(2) McGill LJ 77, 100.
[39] See, e.g., *Planned Parenthood v Casey* 505 US 833 (1992) ; *Ramos v Louisiana* 590 US __, 140 S Ct 1390 (2020) .
[40] Perry, 'Two Models of Legal Principles' (n 27) 800.

5. Conclusion

For Dworkin, law itself is an interpretive concept and the best description of law will be the one that 'best captures or realizes [its] value'.[41] 'We prefer an account of what law is, and how it is to be identified,' wrote Dworkin, 'that incorporates the value—integrity—whose pertinence and importance we recognize.'[42] Here I have argued that, if law's value lies in integrity, then an account of law that includes future decisions better captures law's value than the standard picture of case-based adjudication that excludes them.

[41] Dworkin, 'Hart's Postscript' (n 5) 9.
[42] Dworkin, *Justice in Robes* (n 8) 177.

22
A Precedent-Based Critique of Legal Positivism

John CP Goldberg and Benjamin C Zipursky

1. Introduction

Early versions of legal positivism offered by the likes of Hobbes and Bentham were developed in large part out of impatience with common law. It is thus unsurprising to find critics of Hart, Raz, and other latter-day positivists claiming that it is a weakness of their theories that they cannot make sense of common law decision-making. Dworkin's *The Model of Rules* is illustrative.[1] One line of argument that he and those following his lead have offered asserts that precedent-based adjudication cannot be accurately represented as a matter of rule application, but must instead give substantial place to legal principles. Courts invoke these principles, they say, in accordance with the doctrine of precedent, which itself cannot be represented as a rule or set of rules.

Careful readers will have noticed an ambiguity in the preceding paragraph. It can be read to say that *the content of common law precedents cannot be represented adequately in the kind of framework advanced by many positivists* or it can be read to say that *the doctrine of precedent itself cannot be fully captured in a positivistic framework*. The former is a first-order critique of positivism. The latter is a second-order critique. Unlike *The Model of Rules*, this chapter focuses largely on the second-order critique.

In what follows, we will deliberately pluralize the word 'doctrines' in the phrase 'doctrines of precedent'. We do so because there are at least two such doctrines, each with complexities of its own.[2] The first doctrine holds that an apex court is required to adhere to its prior decisions absent certain kinds of reasons. Following the lead of others, we shall call this the doctrine of 'horizontal' precedent.[3] The second holds that lower courts within a jurisdiction are required to follow the relevant decisions of the courts above them, which means that, while they may distinguish such decisions, they are not permitted or empowered to overrule them. Again following others, we shall call this the doctrine of 'vertical' precedent.

While Dworkin aimed his critique at Hart's form of legal positivism, our critique will focus specifically on Raz's form of exclusive legal positivism. And while Dworkin relied upon the distinction between rules and principles, we instead will rely on a distinction between norms that satisfy the sources thesis and norms that do not. Finally, while we will review a prior debate between Stephen Perry and Raz over the ability of exclusive legal positivism to make sense of the doctrine of horizontal precedent, we will focus on the doctrine of vertical precedent. In a nutshell, we contend that the latter doctrine consists in part of a norm that fails to satisfy the sources thesis, that this norm is part of the law of common law legal systems,

---

[1] RM Dworkin, 'The Model of Rules' (1967) 35 U Chi L Rev 14.

[2] As we discuss in section 4, a law of precedent also governs the permissibility and nature of apex court decisions, even if it does not fit neatly into either the 'vertical' or the 'horizontal' category.

[3] See, e.g., AC Barrett, 'Precedent and Jurisprudential Disagreement' (2013) 91 Tex L Rev 1711, 1712 (distinguishing horizontal and vertical versions of *stare decisis*).

John CP Goldberg and Benjamin C Zipursky, *A Precedent-Based Critique of Legal Positivism* In: *Philosophical Foundations of Precedent*. Edited by: Timothy Endicott, Hafsteinn Dan Kristjánsson, and Sebastian Lewis, Oxford University Press.
© John CP Goldberg and Benjamin C Zipursky 2023. DOI: 10.1093/oso/9780192857248.003.0023

and that the cost of denying the status of 'law' to this norm is accepting the claim that the common law is not law at all.

Section 1 outlines Perry's important Dworkinian critique of Raz's treatment of horizontal precedent, as well as Raz's ingenious response.

Section 2 turns to vertical precedent, offering a critique analogous to Perry's, then considering how the response Raz offered to Perry plays out when applied to this doctrine. Raz's key move, we argue, would be to insist that what looks like a duty-imposing legal rule (specifying that lower courts must follow relevant decisions of higher courts in the same jurisdiction) is actually a power-conferring rule. According to this envisioned rule, lower courts enjoy a power to make new law whenever they have grounds for distinguishing binding precedents. Thus, according to Raz, although a lower court decision that distinguishes a binding higher court precedent might appear to consist of law *application* that involves moral reasoning— that is, identifying what is morally distinctive about the case before the lower court, such that the holding of the precedent does not apply—it is actually an instance of moral reasoning in *law-making*. As we explain, this elaborate recharacterization is untenable as an account of the doctrine of vertical precedent.

Section 3 discusses a line of decisions within the state of Indiana's common law of torts to demonstrate our conceptual point in more concrete terms. Section 4 concludes by considering some of the implications of our analysis.

2. Legal Positivism and the Doctrine of Horizontal Precedent

More than thirty years ago, Stephen Perry provided a powerful critique of Raz's exclusive positivism based on the claim that it cannot account for the doctrine of *stare decisis*.[4] Although we understand our argument as a descendant of Perry's, for reasons explained later we frame it somewhat differently.

Perry argued that *stare decisis* in common law jurisdictions takes the following form (this is our reconstruction). Courts of final resort must adhere to their own prior rulings unless a condition of type T is satisfied. The difference he articulates between his anti-positivism and Raz's positivism is reflected in the different answers they give to the question: what is type T?

On Raz's view, as expressed in *Practical Reason and Norms* and (in a considerably more qualified form) in *The Authority of Law*,[5] a type-T condition must be such that its satisfaction or non-satisfaction is ascertainable without reference to the underlying merits of the rule or standard put forth by the precedential decision whose validity is in question. The contention that type T has this attribute can be labelled as 'the merits-independence conjecture for allowing overruling' (MICAO). An example of a condition that satisfies MICAO would be this: 'underlying conditions have changed dramatically since the precedent was decided, and there has not in the meantime been overwhelming reliance upon it'.

The motivations for Raz's acceptance of MICAO is perhaps clear. On his view, the norms of some area of the common law (e.g. torts) constitute exclusionary reasons for courts responsible for applying that law to rule in a particular way. For areas of the law that call for the application of precedents, precedents must be exclusionary reasons for courts. However, for

---

[4] SR Perry, 'Judicial Obligation, Precedent and the Common Law' (1987) 7 OJLS 215.
[5] J Raz, *Practical Reason and Norms* (2nd edn, OUP 1999) 140–41; J Raz, *The Authority of Law: Essays on Law and Morality* (OUP 1979) 180–209.

apex courts, what makes prior decisions exclusionary reasons is the doctrine of horizontal precedent, and under standard iterations of this doctrine, precedents are *not* inevitably binding: overrulings are sometimes allowed. This appeared to be a problem for Raz, for it seems to suggest that apex courts will have to rely on non-source-based considerations when they overrule prior decisions. However, according to Raz, the problem could be solved if the conditions that must be present to justify an overruling could be ascertained independently of an assessment of the merits of the decision(s) being overruled. Hence MICAO.

Against Raz, Perry argued that the correct description of type T for most common law jurisdictions is provided by what he calls the 'strong Burkean account'.[6] According to this account, an apex court is entitled to overrule a precedent based on the existence of compelling substantive considerations. If Perry is correct about this, then what we have called MICAO is false for these legal systems: in them, an apex court's decision to overrule a precedent will sometimes turn on a judgment that its prior decision was badly wrong on the merits. In other words, the doctrine of horizontal precedent in some jurisdictions seems to be: follow precedent, unless: (i) underlying conditions have changed dramatically and there has not been overwhelming reliance; or (ii) the precedent is, on the merits, badly wrong.

Perry's critique can be seen as challenging Raz's exclusive positivism in two interrelated ways. As mentioned earlier, the precedential decisions themselves seem not to be actually duty-imposing on courts if they are not mandatory, not mandatory if they are not binding, and not binding (in the appropriate way for Raz) if a court's view on the merits of the rule can defeat the rule's applicability. Relatedly, the doctrine of horizontal precedent is itself a piece of law, and an important one at that. Yet the application of the doctrine (and, in one important sense, its content) is not determined by sources in the Razian sense, but instead requires substantive moral decision-making by judges.

Although the preceding paragraph does not invoke Dworkin's rules/principles distinction, it should be evident that the relation between Perry's critique of Raz and Dworkin's *The Model of Rules* critique of Hart is quite close. After all, an apex court's decision-making about whether a precedent is 'badly wrong' would be characterized by Hart as 'discretionary', just as it would be by Raz. In both cases, this would defeat the idea that the doctrine of precedent yields *law*, and—on Dworkinian terms—put the positivist (Hart or Raz) in the awkward position of having to question whether the common law is law at all.

Over time, Raz developed a response to Perry, one that unsurprisingly matched his overall response to Dworkin's principles-based critique of Hart in *The Model of Rules*. In order to reply to Perry's initial critique and a subsequent elaboration,[7] Raz constructed a rather striking view of high courts' power.[8]

On the empirical question of whether there exist legal systems in the Anglo-American tradition that have a strong Burkean version of the doctrine of horizontal precedent, Raz agreed with Perry: such systems do exist. And on the question of how to characterize a decision of an apex court that a precedent was badly wrong and so should be overruled, Raz unsurprisingly characterized it as discretionary, refusing to treat it as an application of the law as such. However, he argued that all of this is consistent with exclusive legal positivism and the sources thesis because the doctrine of horizontal precedent is properly understood to have a power-conferring dimension to it. Apex courts enjoy a power to *revise* the law, which power they exercise when they overrule precedent. In other words, an overruling is an authorized

---

[6] Perry, *Judicial Obligation* (n 4) 239.
[7] SR Perry, 'Second Order Reasons, Uncertainty and Legal Theory' (1989) 62 So Cal L Rev 913.
[8] J Raz, 'Facing Up: A Reply' (1989) 62 So Cal L Rev 1153.

act of judicial legislation. Raz acknowledged, of course, that apex courts do not exercise this discretionary power indiscriminately. But this, he said, is because there are, in most common law systems, norms about how and when courts should exercise this power, and what sorts of value-considerations courts should attend to when they legislate by overruling.

In sum, like Hart, Raz does not deny that common law judges engage in first-order normative reasoning when they are doing their job, and he does not claim that judges should always refrain from doing so. Indeed, as evidenced by his famous critique of Dworkin in *Legal Principles and the Limits of Law*,[9] Raz in some ways goes further than Hart did. As noted, he claims that some legal rules empower or even require judges to craft new legal rules, and indeed some legal principles may be fruitfully understood as doing so, too. As we have also noted, Raz tempers the potential radicalism of this claim by arguing that judges are subject to various kinds of norms governing how they go about exercising their power to legislate. Exclusive positivism is nonetheless preserved because, while such norms are in a loose sense part of the legal system, they are not law, strictly speaking. This point was later developed elegantly by John Gardner, who argued that norms of legal reasoning explain why the power to create law is exercised differently by courts than by legislatures.[10]

Looking back, one can trace an admirable continuity between Raz's argument, made in response to Perry, that apex courts' authority to overrule precedents is explained by their enjoying a power to legislate, and the model of the doctrine of horizontal precedent he put forward in *The Authority of Law*. It comes to this: the "law," proper, includes those precedents that are binding on lower courts, and if the apex court chooses not to overrule the precedent, it is applying the law (i.e. treating precedent as an exclusionary reason). However, the apex court also has a legal power to craft new law. The overturning of precedent is an exercise of this power, not an application of law. Likewise, the crafting of a new rule in place of the old one is an act of law-making, and the normative decision-making judges engage in to craft the best new rule is itself deliberation about law-making, not about the content of law that already exists.

3. Legal Positivism and the Doctrine of Vertical Precedent

We turn now from horizontal to vertical precedent. For a lower court adjudicating a case that presents a legal issue on which a higher court in the same jurisdiction has previously ruled, the doctrine of vertical precedent holds that the lower court must decide the legal issue in the same way as the higher court did, unless the case before it is distinguishable from the case in which the higher court's decision was issued. While there are likely to be indefinitely many facts that render a case different from a prior case, factual differences alone do not suffice to make the prior case distinguishable. What matters, of course, is whether the current case and the precedent are factually different *along some relevant dimension*.

As with the doctrine of horizontal precedent, the positivist here seems to run into trouble. For the inquiry into whether the precedent is distinguishable would seem to be (or at least could be in some legal system) an inquiry into the reasons the precedent case was rightly decided. Simply put, it appears that a lower court cannot determine whether higher court precedent demands the same result in a case before it unless the lower court determines whether the precedent is distinguishable, but distinguishability turns on the merits and the

---

[9] J Raz, 'Legal Principles and the Limits of Law' (1972) 81 Yale LJ 823.
[10] J Gardner, 'Legal Positivism: 5½ Myths' (2001) 46 Am J Juris 199.

justifiability of retaining the precedent decision on its facts while rejecting the same disposition on the factually different case before the lower court.

In *The Authority of Law*, Raz's strategy for dealing with the phenomenon of distinguishing precedent runs parallel to his strategy for dealing with overruling precedent. Just as legal systems empower courts to overrule cases, they empower them to distinguish cases. The rule allowing lower courts to distinguish higher court decisions is thus cast as a rule of legal change. Secondly, he thinks that, insofar as the rule of change is a part of the law, it is formal: it is not the case that the conditions triggering the lower court's power to amend the law are merits-based. Thirdly, he acknowledges that a lower court judge engages and ought to engage in first-order normative reasoning when deciding to distinguish precedent; indeed, he asserts that lower court judges have an obligation to improve the law when they exercise this power to amend the rule. But the obligation to improve the law comes from norms applicable to courts that are not necessarily laws as such.

On this account, a lower court's power to distinguish precedent, like an apex court's power to overrule precedent, is a power to produce a new rule that preserves the disposition of the prior ruling on the prior facts while inserting a condition that rejects that disposition for cases missing a fact that was present in the precedent case. Distinguishing a case, in other words, is an instance of law-amendment: 'Since "distinguishing" means changing the rule which is being distinguished, the power to distinguish is the power to develop the law even when deciding regulated cases and even by courts which have no power to overrule.'[11] As Grant Lamond has observed, this characterization of the power to distinguish renders it extremely broad:[12] Raz appears to view lower court judges as having the power to distinguish a wide range of cases. The reality of practice and the reality of what a well-regarded judge does (including normative reasoning) may be, on this view, a display of a norm applicable to judges, but this norm is not itself part of the law.

While we are inclined, with Perry, to doubt that Raz has a satisfactory rendering of the doctrine of horizontal precedent, we think it is considerably clearer that his law-amendment/law-creation strategy cannot work for the doctrine of vertical precedent. There is simply no reason to believe that, for example, a trial court who distinguishes a precedent issued by the jurisdiction's apex court is 'amending' a legal rule announced by the apex court. Lower courts have no such power. Perhaps one can say that an instance of this sort of distinguishing involves the lower court proposing that the legal rule contained in the precedent is narrower than it was understood to be when the high court first issued its decision. And, by hypothesis, the lower court is resolving the dispute before it in the manner in which it would come out were the rule the one hypothesized. In doing so, however, the lower court does not purport to amend or change a legal rule adopted by the high court (or purport to have the power to do so). It instead claims the power to adopt an available interpretation of the high court's legal rule and to apply it according to that interpretation.

In sum: the awkwardness of Raz's description of *distinguishing as law-making* resides in his effort to convert a permission into a power. The doctrine of precedent, insofar as it

---

[11] Raz, *Authority of Law* (n 5) 185. Raz's account seems clearly meant to explain what lower courts are doing when they distinguish a precedent decided by a court above them within a court system. And he needs to provide such an account, because lower courts are understood to be permitted to distinguish even precedents from the apex court in their jurisdiction. Unless Raz means to provide one account of distinguishing for lower courts and one account for high courts—which he plainly does not—it seems entirely appropriate to understand his account as one that should apply to lower courts.

[12] G Lamond, 'Do Precedents Create Rules?' (2005) 11 Legal Theory 1.

concerns distinguishing, is not about judicial *empowerment*; it is about what courts are *permitted* to do in the face of precedent and when they are permitted to do it.

A defender of Raz might suggest that we are pointing out a mere technical misclassification, from a Hohfeldian vantage point, that does not matter to the plausibility of accounting for the doctrine of precedent from within Raz's positivistic framework. In fact, Raz's choice of empowerment over permission in characterizing the doctrine of precedent is key to his whole strategy. When he sets forth his theory of what a court must do to be successful in distinguishing a case, the conditions he sets forth are entirely formal:

(1) The modified rule must be the rule laid down in the precedent restricted by the addition of a further condition.
(2) The modified rule must be such as to justify the order made in the precedent.[13]

From this perspective, as Lamond has pointed out, a wide range of judicial decisions distinguishing precedents are possible, including some that would be inane (e.g. the events of the precedent case happened on a Tuesday; the events in the case before the lower court happened on a Wednesday). Courts, on Raz's view, have the power to create an amended rule like this, even if it would be unwise to do so. He recognizes, of course, that legal scholars will object that courts have an obligation to do better when it comes to distinguishing, but he accommodates this fact by asserting that there is a norm that governs law-making by lower court judges: they are obligated to do their best to improve the law, from a first-order normative point of view, when they are amending it. This second-level norm, utilizing first-order reasons in amending the law, is not itself law.

Raz's two-level strategy cannot work, however, because the description offered at the first level is not viable. Distinguishing (overwhelmingly) is not amending. The ability to distinguish is not a legal power. The facets of legal doctrine that allow distinguishing are permissive, not power-conferring. So the question becomes whether the normative framework that governs this question is plausibly regarded as Raz regards it, once we see it is about permission rather than empowerment. Our answer is that it is not.

A Razian might respond by arguing that there is a way to re-run his two-level approach by casting it in terms of permissibility. On this version, there is at level 1 a rule permitting a lower court to distinguish binding precedent as long as Raz's two formal conditions apply. At level 2 are the norms for the appropriate exercise of the (privilege) of distinguishing cases, and the latter norms are not themselves law. Decisions at level 1 are not discretionary, and a mistake at level 1 is a mistake of law; a failure to apply the law correctly. Level 2 is important and also relates to permission, but judgments at level 2 are discretionary, and when a higher court reverses a lower court because of disagreement at level 2, it is, at root, criticizing the lower court's decision-making about what counts as the best normative judgment regarding how the legal system should resolve the case at hand and cases like it in relevant respects; it is not saying that the lower court has misapplied the law.

There are two reasons to reject this reconstruction. Our principal point is that lower courts, in distinguishing precedent and deciding a case differently than the rule embedded in the precedent might seem to require, are not actually changing the law. Indeed, the reason we are so interested in pointing out that they lack the power to change the law is not that we

---

[13] Raz, *Authority of Law* (n 5) 185. Note that the accompanying discussion by Raz reveals that he is using the clause 'the modified rule must be such as to justify the order' to mean that it must be the case that if the modified rule had been in place when the precedent case was decided, the order would have come out as it in fact did.

are interested in the power of lower courts per se; it is that recasting what those courts are doing from applying the law to *changing* the law is Raz's strategy for explaining why what they are doing need not count as applying the law. Because that move does not work, we are inclined to return to the conventionally accepted understanding: when lower courts distinguish a precedent in the course of resolving the case before them, they do so in the context of *applying the law*. For obvious reasons, this tends to cut against the sources thesis and the Razian model more generally. The two-level solution reproduces a distinction between application at level 1 and level 2, but does not actually say what is occurring at level 2 if it is not applying the law or amending the law.

There is a second problem, and it relates to the first. Translating Raz's formal conditions for distinguishing cases from empowerment conditions into permissibility conditions leaves the theoretical model unacceptably and conspicuously awkward, even if it is formally possible (and even if Raz were able to find a suitable mid-level description for what courts are doing at level 2 if they are neither applying nor amending the law). For one must now say that the norms governing how judges are required to go about crafting distinctions are not part of the law, even though they too are about which sorts of distinctions it is permissible for a court to make. There will be two levels of permissibility; permissibility of a sort that actually counts as applying the law or staying within the law or taking precedent sufficiently seriously, and permissibility of a sort that has to do with dealing appropriately with precedent as a judge. This seems an artificial distinction, one motivated solely by the desire to preserve an exclusive positivistic position at all costs. And the problem is even worse than this, for it appears that when an appellate court (say, a mid-level appellate court) rules that a trial court erred in concluding that a precedent ought to have been distinguished because the grounds for distinguishing invoked by the trial court did not warrant a different result, the trial court is best described as actually *not having been permitted* to distinguish the case. Yet some criticisms of a lower court's distinctions deemed impermissible will be considered misapplications of the law or incorrect applications of the law, while others will be deemed impermissible and reversible but not misapplications of the law.

4. Determining Distinguishability: Some Examples

Our analysis to this point has taken Razian analysis on its own terms, at a high level of abstraction. To illustrate and elucidate our core claims, we turn to a set of decisions in which lower courts were faced with the task of applying apex court precedent to resolve an issue of negligence law under the law of the state of Indiana. Specifically, these decisions called for a determination of when a business has a duty to aid a person who is injured or becomes ill while on the business's premises.

We start with the apex court decision: *LS Ayres v Hicks*, issued in 1942 by the Indiana Supreme Court.[14] Suit was brought on behalf of a six-year-old boy who, while riding with his mother on an escalator in the defendant's store, fell and caught his hand in the escalator. The escalator could be turned off by switches that employees had been trained to use and to which employees stationed near the escalator had access. However, it took several minutes after the boy's fingers became trapped for the escalator to be deactivated. A jury found that the employees' negligent delay exacerbated the boy's injuries.

---

[14] *LS Ayres v Hicks* 40 NE2d 334 (Ind 1942).

On appeal to the state's high court, the defendant argued that this verdict rested on a finding of liability for non-feasance (failure to rescue), and that, as such, it was legally erroneous because Indiana negligence law contained a general rule of no duty to rescue. Relying in part on a Minnesota case and language from a prior Indiana appellate decision that it had affirmed, the court rejected this argument:

> From the above cases it may be deduced that there may be a legal obligation to take positive or affirmative steps to effect the rescue of a person who is helpless and in a situation of peril, when the one proceeded against is a master or an invitor or when the injury resulted from use of an instrumentality under the control of the defendant. Such an obligation may exist although the accident or original injury was caused by the negligence of the plaintiff or through that of a third person and without any fault on the part of the defendant. Other relationships may impose a like obligation, but it is not necessary to pursue that inquiry further at this time.
>
> In the case at bar the appellee was an invitee and he received his initial injury in using an instrumentality provided by the appellant and under its control. Under the rule stated above and on the authority of the cases cited this was a sufficient relationship to impose a duty upon the appellant.[15]

Sixty years later, an Indiana trial court and intermediate appellate court—both of which sit below the Indiana Supreme Court in the state judiciary's hierarchy—were faced with a negligence suit similar in some respects to *Ayres*. In *Baker v Fenneman & Brown Properties, LLC*,[16] a customer in the defendant's fast-food restaurant fainted, fell backwards, hit his head on the floor, and experienced convulsions while unconscious. After regaining consciousness, he stood up, only to fall again. The second fall resulted in serious injuries. The customer's suit was predicated on the alleged failure of restaurant employees to come to his aid after he first fell. They were legally obligated to do so, he argued, and had they done so he would not have fallen the second time.

Accepting the plaintiff's allegations as true for the purposes of a motion for summary judgment, the defendant argued that its employees were under no duty to render assistance to Baker after he fainted. On this issue of law, the defendant invoked *Ayres*, arguing that the high court's recognition in 1942 of an affirmative duty owed by a business to a stricken invitee was limited to cases in which (in the words of the *Ayres* court) the invitee's need for assistance 'resulted from the use of an instrumentality under the control of the [business]'.

The trial judge granted judgment for the defendant without a trial. Here is the entirety of the trial judge's ruling granting summary judgment to the defendant:

ORDER GRANTING DEFENDANTS' MOTION FOR SUMMARY JUDGMENT
Comes now the plaintiff Aaron Baker ... and come now the Defendants Fenneman & Brown Properties, LLC and Southern Bells of Indiana, Inc., all d/b/a Taco Bell ... on August 28, 2002, for argument on defendants' motion for summary judgment and plaintiffs [sic] opposition to the same. And now the court, having considered the arguments of counsel, the materials designated by the parties for the court's consideration in ruling upon

---

[15] ibid 337. In another part of its decision, the court found error in the damages instruction given by the trial judge and reversed the verdict on that ground, ordering a new trial.
[16] *Baker v Fenneman & Brown Properties, LLC* 793 NE2d 1203 (Ind App 2003).

304   JOHN CP GOLDBERG AND BENJAMIN C ZIPURSKY

the defendant's motion for summary judgment, having considered the authorities cited
by counsel, having taken this matter under advisement, and being duly and sufficiently
advised in the premises, finds there is no genuine issue of material fact in dispute between
these parties at this time, and defendants are entitled to judgment as a matter of law.

...

Dated this 5th day of September, 2002.
Robert R. Aylsworth, Judge
Warrick Superior Court No. 2[17]

As it indicates, this order was issued on the basis of briefing and oral argument. Yet, as is clear
from the parties' subsequently filed appellate briefs, both the parties and the trial judge—in
keeping with the rule of vertical *stare decisis*—concerned themselves almost exclusively with
how *Ayres* applied to the facts of the case.[18] Judge Aylsworth accepted the defendant's contention that *Ayres* had identified a relatively narrow exception to the general rule of no duty
to rescue—one that applies only when an instrumentality of the defendant-business causes
an invitee's peril—and hence did not cover the facts of *Baker*, which instead fell under the
general no-duty rule. Nothing here indicates a lower court legislating a new rule that partially exempts businesses from the duty to assist stricken customers. Quite the opposite, it
reveals a lower court endeavouring to determine whether a binding precedent controlled
the outcome of the case or was distinguishable because of some normatively salient factual
difference: namely, the difference between a customer whose on-premises peril is caused by
an instrumentality of the business and a customer who merely happens to face a peril while
on the business's premises. The trial court distinguished *Ayres* because it was persuaded that
a business that does nothing to help its customer in need of assistance is no more responsible
for the customer's need than would be another patron who happened to be present when
the customer came to be in need. Morally, there is all the difference in the world—the court
reasoned—between merely being situated so as to be able to provide assistance, on the one
hand, and having caused the need for assistance, on the other.

   The Court of Appeals reversed Judge Aylsworth's ruling. In doing so, it nowhere suggested
that the problem with his decision was that it was an *unwise bit of law-making* (as one might
have expected to find, implicitly or explicitly, if Raz's account of distinguishing were correct).
Instead, its reversal was grounded on a judgment that Judge Aylsworth's interpretation of
Ayres was erroneous, and that *Baker* was not distinguishable from *Ayres*.

   In standard fashion, the appellate court's reasoning proceeded as follows. Under Indiana
precedents, the plaintiff was required to establish that the defendant was under a duty to
conduct itself with due care for plaintiff's well-being, that the defendant breached that
duty, and that the breach was a proximate cause of the plaintiff's injuries. Focusing on the
duty element, the court then explained, quoting horizontal precedent, that '[t]o determine
whether a duty exists, we must balance three factors: "(1) the relationship between the parties; (2) the reasonable foreseeability of the harm to the person injured; and (3) public policy
concerns".[19] However, it then qualified this broad description of how to structure its duty

---

[17] Brief of Appellant, *Baker v Fenneman & Brown Properties, LLC* (31 January 2003) 2003 WL 25266434 *2.
[18] ibid *6–*12; Brief of Appellees, *Baker v Fenneman & Brown Properties, LLC* (5 March 2003) 2003 WL
25266432 *4–*15; Reply Brief of Appellant, *Baker v Fenneman & Brown Properties, LLC* (21 March 2003) 2003 WL
25266431 at *2.
[19] *Baker* (n 15) 1206 (quoting *Ind State Police v Don's Guns & Galleries* 674 NE 2d 565, 568 (Ind Ct App 1996),
trans denied 683 NE2d 592 (Ind 1997).

inquiry by invoking the particular duty rule that was recognized in—and served as the premise of the legal analysis provided by—the *Ayres* court, along with an acknowledgement that the rule has exceptions:

> As a general rule, an individual does not have a duty to aid or protect another person, even if he knows that person needs assistance. *L.S. Ayres v. Hicks*, 40 N.E.2d 334, 337 (1942) ... However, both common law and statutory exceptions to the general rule exist. ... See also *L.S. Ayres*, 40 N.E.2d at 337 ('under some circumstances, moral and humanitarian considerations may require one to render assistance to another who has been injured, even though the injury was not due to negligence on his part ...').[20]

From here, the court offered several reasons why, even though *Ayres* involved an invitee being injured by an instrumentality of the defendants, the state Supreme Court's decision was not properly interpreted to limit the application of its exception to the no-duty-to-rescue rule to that precise situation. First, the *Baker* court noted that the Minnesota case that *Ayres* had cited had recognized a duty to rescue even though the defendant in the Minnesota case had done nothing to bring about the peril that put the plaintiff in need of rescue. It further observed that the Indiana Supreme Court, in another decision that it had also issued in 1942, summarized the rule of *Ayres* without referring to the qualification that the defendant in *Baker* proposed to read into it. It next pointed out that the recognition of a duty owed based on the business–invitee relationship, irrespective of the role played by an instrumentality of the defendants, would render Indiana law consistent with the rule articulated in Section 314A of the American Law Institute's *Second Torts Restatement* and by other states' courts. Finally, the *Baker* court reasoned that some considerations of justice favoured the broader rendition of the *Ayres* rule while others that could in principle disfavour it—such as the injustice to businesses of facing burdensome affirmative duties of conduct—were not likely to result from its adoption.[21]

The appellate court judges in *Baker*, like the trial judge, were bound to apply and did apply precedents defining the negligence tort, precedents describing at a general level the nature of the inquiry into that tort's duty element, and the specific precedent of *Ayres*. This is why the litigants framed the appeal of *Baker* as raising the question of how the court should decide the case *under Ayres*—that is, on the assumption that the court's job in this case was to apply *Ayres*. Of course, the appellate court towards the end of its legal analysis offers policy or merits-based analysis. But this analysis is offered as one of several grounds *for adopting a particular interpretation of the* Ayres *rule*—that is, the rule taken to govern the disposition of the case at hand. In that respect, *Baker* simultaneously attests to the vertical doctrine of precedent as a legal rule, and as a vindication of the idea, articulated in different ways in the work of Dworkin and Perry, that common law reasoning calls on judges to do something beyond source-based legal analysis when deciding whether and how to distinguish precedents.

Of course, *Baker* is just one case featuring two lower court decisions. And yet, based on our experience reading thousands of US court decisions, we are confident that it is completely mainstream in its treatment of precedent.[22] And—to return, finally, to the critique of

---

[20] ibid.

[21] Although the *Baker* court did not make anything of it, language in *Ayres*, as we note later, makes clear that the Indiana Supreme Court had not limited its duty-to-rescue holding to instances in which the defendant's instrumentality imperilled the plaintiff. See n 34 and accompanying text.

[22] Indeed, it is so nicely representative of how a court in a common law case addresses precedent that it has for years been a staple in our torts casebook. JCP Goldberg and others, *Tort Law: Responsibilities and Redress* (5th edn, Aspen Publishing 2020) 80.

306   JOHN CP GOLDBERG AND BENJAMIN C ZIPURSKY

positivism—everything about that treatment indicates that it would be erroneous to believe that either of the lower courts were legislating: that is, exercising a broad, legally conferred power to change the rule in *Ayres* according to their best judgment about what would make for good policy.

We now introduce a third Indiana court decision: *Estate of Short v Brookville Crossing*.[23] The plaintiff's decedent David Short was a guest at the defendant's budget hotel. At some point on a frigid night, Short left the hotel. As footage from a security camera later revealed, Short returned at around 3 am, fumbled with his room key to gain entrance to one of the hotel's side doors, then collapsed, hitting his head against the exterior wall, and falling to the ground. Short's dead body was discovered early the next morning by a maintenance worker. The same footage established that there was no other activity in the vicinity of the door between the time of Short's collapse and when his body was discovered.

The plaintiff's negligence suit alleged that the hotel had failed in its duty to rescue Short and that, had it not so failed, he would have survived. For the purposes of ruling on the defendant's summary judgment motion, the following additional facts were assumed. When Short collapsed and fell to the ground, he remained visible to the security camera located by the side door. That camera was one of sixteen, each of which provided a live feed into a single monitor located in the general manager's office, which office was located adjacent to the hotel's front desk. On the night in question, there was one overnight clerk on duty, stationed at the front desk. The clerk did not inspect the grounds during the night, in part because hotel protocols called for the overnight clerk to remain at the front desk except for brief periods when necessary to use the restroom or to respond to particular guest requests. (No such requests that night gave the clerk occasion to go to the area of the side door.) The clerk did walk by the monitor in the general manager's office during the period in which the side-door security camera would have shown Short lying on the ground. However, given that there were images from sixteen cameras appearing simultaneously on the single, 19-inch monitor, and given that the clerk passed the monitor from a distance of 10 to 12 feet, he did not notice the image of Clark lying on the ground outside the door.

Based on these facts, the trial court granted summary judgment for the defendant and issued an order nearly identical in form to the one issued by Judge Aylsworth in *Baker*. In sum, the trial judge accepted the defendant's argument that, as a matter of law, the hotel owed Short no duty to assist him under *Ayres* and *Baker* because those cases 'involve[d] situations where the premises owners were undeniably aware of the invitees' need for assistance and failed to provide it'. '*Unlike the foregoing cases*,' the defendant continued, the evidence in *Short* 'establishe[d] that until approximately 7 a.m. on January 4, 2009, no employee of the defendants was aware Mr. Short had collapsed and required assistance.'[24] The defendant further argued that neither *Ayres* nor *Baker* could be read to have recognized a duty requiring the hotel to check its video feeds to see whether patrons might be in need of assistance, both because the language in *Ayres* suggested otherwise and because any such reading of precedent might have the perverse effect of discouraging businesses from installing security cameras.[25]

---

[23] *Estate of Short v Brookville Crossing* 972 NE 2d 897 (Ind App 2012).

[24] Defendant's Memorandum in Support of Summary Judgment at 9, *Estate of Short v Brookville Crossing* (2 September 2011) No 49D03-0911-CT-52090 (emphasis added) (on file with authors).

[25] ibid 12 (noting a passage from *Ayres* stating that, 'One is not bound to guard against a happening which there is no reason to anticipate or expect').

As in *Baker*, the arguments to the trial court in *Short* correctly assumed that the duty issue turned on the question of whether there was a factual difference between the case at hand and binding precedents that had defined an exception to the no-duty-to-rescue rule, such that the trial court was required to apply the general rule rather than the exception. Of course, this question did not admit of mechanical resolution—credible arguments were made on both sides. And in that sense the trial court enjoyed a certain degree of *interpretive discretion*. But, again, nothing in the records suggests that this sort of discretion should be confused with the power to legislate a new rule.

Things proceeded in much the same manner at the intermediate appellate court level, except here, unlike in *Baker*, the higher court concluded that the trial court had correctly interpreted precedent. The appellate court accepted as a matter of horizontal precedent *Baker's* rule that the duty of a business to rescue an invitee who is stricken while on the premises extends beyond cases in which the defendant's instrumentality contributed to the invitee's predicament.[26] Nonetheless, it held that the trial court was correct to distinguish *Ayres*, *Baker*, and other duty-to-rescue precedents on the ground that all had presupposed that a business's duty to rescue a stricken invitee becomes operative 'only after it knows or has reason to know that [an invitee on the premises] is ill or injured'.[27]

Importantly, the court also relied on Section 314A of the *Second Torts Restatement*, a provision that (as the *Short* court pointed out) *Baker* had essentially incorporated into Indiana law. Unlike prior Indiana cases, Section 314A explicitly states that, in the absence of actual or constructive knowledge of the victim's predicament, the defendant is not under a duty to rescue the victim.[28] According to the *Short* court, in *Ayres*, *Baker*, and other precedents that recognized liability for failure to rescue, the defendant had been alerted or should have alerted it to the patron's injury or imperilment.[29] Because, in the court's view, there was no evidence that the clerk actually knew of Short's predicament, and because the evidence failed to establish that the clerk had reason to know of it, the trial court properly concluded that these cases were all *distinguishable*.

Much of what we said previously about the *Baker* court's treatment of precedent applies to *Short*. There is every indication that, in distinguishing precedents, the *Short* courts devoted themselves to considering whether there was a normatively salient factual difference that warranted a different decision under the *Ayres–Baker* framework than did *Baker* itself. Underlying this mode of analysis was the assumption that Indiana's lower courts were operating under a duty to apply the rule fashioned by the state's apex court, not a power to change the rule because such changes would improve the law. On this point, the concluding language of the *Short* court (discussing the *Restatement* provision noted earlier) is revealing:

> The rule advocated by [plaintiff] would have the effect of *expanding the scope of the 'have reason to know' element of [Restatement] § 314A* to instances in which the owner did not have knowledge of the situation of peril, *rather than instances currently within its scope* in which the owner knew of the situation but failed to recognize the peril attached.[30]

---

[26] *Short* (n 22) 905.
[27] ibid.
[28] ibid 902, 905.
[29] ibid 907.
[30] ibid (emphasis added).

308   JOHN CP GOLDBERG AND BENJAMIN C ZIPURSKY

Clearly, the court was endeavouring to determine how properly to *apply* the rule, *not* whether to change it. That is, the court was inquiring whether the facts of the *Short* case brought the case within the scope of a legal rule, established by precedent, that imposes a duty to rescue on certain actors in certain situations. Of course, it is possible that even though the *Short* court was correct to view the facts of the case before it as distinguishable (such that *Ayres* was not controlling), it would have been a better decision to recognize a duty of care in *Short*, too, notwithstanding its distinguishability (e.g. perhaps the court too narrowly construed the conditions that should be required for a business's duty to rescue to kick in). But that is a different question.[31]

We now turn now to a fourth decision, issued not by an Indiana court but by a federal appellate court responsible for reviewing the decisions of federal district courts in several states, including Indiana.

In *Stockberger v United States*, the plaintiff's decedent, Maurice Stockberger, a diabetic employee of a federal prison, was prone to hypoglycaemic episodes that caused him to experience dramatic personality changes.[32] Stockberger's co-workers were aware of his condition. Thus, when he experienced a hypoglycaemic episode, they would urge him to eat or drink to correct for his low blood sugar. On one such occasion, a co-worker successfully convinced Stockberger—who was complaining about feeling ill and, because of that, wanting to leave work to go home—to consume a beverage. Although doing so made Stockberger feel somewhat better, he still insisted on driving home against the advice of co-workers. None of the co-workers attempted to take away Stockberger's car keys, offered him a ride, or contacted his supervisor or his wife. And, while the prison had sometimes provided rides home to ill employees, it did not do so on this occasion. On his way home, Stockberger drove erratically and died when his car collided with a tree.

Stockberger's widow brought a negligence claim against the US Bureau of Prisons, which is why the case was filed in federal court. Under well-settled rules established by the US Supreme Court's 1938 *Erie* decision,[33] the federal courts hearing the case were required to resolve its substantive legal issues by applying the tort law of the relevant state, which, as it turns out, was Indiana. Applying Indiana law, the federal trial judge granted summary judgment for the defendant and the Seventh Circuit, in an opinion by Judge Richard Posner, affirmed.

With characteristic bravado, Judge Posner—arguably violating the letter and spirit of *Erie*—cited dozens of decisions from courts around the nation to support his preferred account of exceptions to the rule of no-duty to rescue. Courts, he concluded, were prepared to recognize duties to rescue only 'when the rescuer either has assumed explicitly or implicitly a duty to rescue, or has caused the injury [that placed the victim in need or rescue]'.[34] Neither of these conditions were present in the case before his court: there was no promise from the prison to protect Stockberger from the consequences of his hypoglycaemia, nor did it force him to drive home. A contrary result, Posner further reasoned, would thus require a rule of duty according to which the owner of premises owes a duty to rescue any invitee in peril, regardless of whether the owner contributed to creating it. After noting that some states seemed inclined to adopt this rule and suggesting that such a rule might be justified

---

[31] As the foregoing qualifications indicate, we do not believe our account in any way commits us to a 'one right answer' thesis.

[32] *Stockberger v United States* 322 F3d 479 (7th Cir 2003).

[33] *Erie Railroad Co v Tompkins* 304 US 64 (1938).

[34] ibid 482.

by reference to 'hypothetical contract' (cost–benefit) analysis, Posner stated confidently that Indiana courts had not adopted it.[35] Reversing the trial court's judgment would therefore require his federal court to make a prediction that Indiana's high court would legislate such a rule, and he was not prepared to hazard such a guess, especially in this factual scenario. Writing for the three-judge panel, Posner thus affirmed the dismissal of the case.[36]

Judge Posner's opinion is doubly unfaithful to binding vertical precedent: he failed to follow *Erie* and *Ayres*. Under *Erie*, his job was to apply Indiana tort law. Instead, he offered a national survey of case law in aid of developing a distinctive rule of federal common law, according to which a duty to rescue is owed only if the defendant has undertaken to rescue or caused the plaintiff's predicament. He then misread the leading Indiana case on the issue—*Ayres*—a misreading evidenced by the Indiana state appellate court's nearly contemporaneous decision in *Baker*. Unlike *Stockberger*, *Baker* addressed several features of *Ayres* that weighed in favour of the characterization of *Ayres* as holding that inviters have an affirmative duty of care to imperilled invitees. Judge Posner's opinion does not acknowledge any of these. Additionally, it failed to address a key passage in *Ayres* that plainly speaks disjunctively rather than conjunctively:

> there may be a legal obligation to take positive or affirmative steps to effect the rescue of a person who is helpless and in a situation of peril, when the one proceeded against is a master or an invitor *or* when the injury resulted from use of an instrumentality under the control of the defendant. Such an obligation may exist although the accident or original injury was caused by the negligence of the plaintiff or through that of a third person and without any fault on the part of the defendant.[37]

Our point is not that judicial text is always by itself the key to characterizing a precedent, but that the many features (apart from these particular words) of the *Ayres* court's opinion that were quoted or cited in *Baker*, in addition to these words, demonstrate convincingly the content of the rule that the *Ayres* court had adopted, and that the *Baker* court faithfully followed. In short, it was not justifiable for Judge Posner to take the position that the Indiana Supreme Court had not opined on whether inviters have affirmative duties to invitees, and doubly so that he took his court to be left to 'predict' what rule that court might adopt.

For the reasons just articulated, it is correct to say that Judge Posner failed to apply Indiana law on the issue of whether a business owes a duty to assist an invitee who is stricken while on the business's premises. This does not mean, however, that his resolution of the case was ultimately wrong. Ironically, there were at least two tenable ways to distinguish *Stockberger* from *Ayres* and thereby (perhaps) affirm the lower court's dismissal. One would have been to rule that, while a duty to assist was owed, an employer does not count as having breached this duty by failing to take steps to prevent an ailing but mentally unimpaired adult worker from acting on his choice to drive himself home. (While 'breach' is normally for the jury, it

---

[35] ibid 483–84.

[36] Although it might help our cause to do otherwise, our analysis declines to follow Professor Shugerman's informative prior treatment of *Stockberger*. JH Shugerman, 'Affirmative Duties and Judges' Duties: *United States v Stockberger*' (2007) 120 Harv L Rev 1228. Shugerman credits Judge Posner for exercising restraint by following Indiana law rather than adopting an alternative duty rule based purely on prescriptive considerations. In reaching this conclusion, Shugerman (in the context of a symposium honouring Judge Posner) is more generous in accepting Posner's narrow reading of *Ayres* than we think is warranted. As explained in the text, we think *Ayres* ought to have been read to signify Indiana's recognition of an affirmative duty to invitees. The Indiana appellate court's *Baker* decision, issued within weeks of *Stockberger*, strongly supports our analysis.

[37] *Ayres* (n 13) 337 (emphasis added).

was open to the court to say, 'no breach as a matter of law'.) Relatedly, Judge Posner perhaps could have maintained that the duty question in *Stockberger* was, after all, different and more challenging than the question in *Ayres*, because it concerned whether an employer's duty to assist or rescue includes a duty to protect employees against *self-injurious* conduct. These features of the case actually drew comment from Posner, and were part of his view about the weakness of the case as a whole. Yet he failed to recognize the analytically clear and candid path towards the conclusion he thought sound: namely, that Indiana had recognized a duty to aid that was owed by inviters to invitees, but it had not recognized a duty to shield them from harm they might inflict on themselves by their own poor judgment.

Does it really make any difference which path Judge Posner took, given that these different paths could reach the same result? It surely does. Had the *Baker* court selected Judge Posner's path, the plaintiff in that case would have lost. To broaden the point, on the Posner interpretation of Indiana law, an employer is not legally required to call an ambulance for an employee who, while at work, experiences a heart attack; the employer may leave the employee lying there without facing liability in negligence law. This is not Indiana law and was not at the time *Ayres* and *Baker* were decided.

Judge Posner's *Stockberger* opinion offers a sharp contrast with the opinions of the intermediate state appellate courts in *Baker* and *Short*. As such, it adds support for the core claim of this chapter. Judge Posner unapologetically embraced a conception of the judge as minimally constrained law-maker.[38] Thus, he claimed to reject the idea that his obligation was to apply binding legal rules and standards to the cases before him. To his credit, Judge Posner owned his identity as pragmatist-cum-legal realist. Our worry is that since it is incorrect to say that lower court judges are amending the law, other jurists who are flippant about the normative content of common law precedents will find themselves less self-consciously drifting towards Posnerian realism, at least about the common law. Presumably this is a prospect that positivists less enamoured of realism would find unappealing.

5. Implications

At one level, the argument of this chapter is quite limited: we have criticized Raz's account of the phenomenon of courts distinguishing vertical precedents. Our claim is that the relevant legal rule in most common law systems is this: in a case that falls within the terms of a higher court precedent, a lower court must follow the precedent unless there is adequate reason to distinguish the precedent case. Because of this rule, courts applying the common law must make decisions about whether distinctions between cases are justifiable, and in so doing they must delve into the normative grounds for the precedent decision, not simply the content of the precedent rule itself. We suggest that several additional implications follow from this argument: (a) some legal rules or principles (at least the one pertaining to vertical precedent) that are part of the law do not satisfy the constraints articulated by the sources thesis; (b) the manner in which higher court rulings impose obligations on lower courts regarding their decisions, in the common law, is not aptly characterized by Raz's exclusive positivist model; (c) courts' obligations to rely on moral grounds in deciding common law cases are sometimes incurred outside gap-filling cases; (d) courts are sometimes obligated to use moral

---

[38] J Masur, 'How Judges Think: A Conversation with Judge Richard Posner', University of Chicago Law School (20 August 2009) <https://www.law.uchicago.edu/news/how-judges-think-conversation-judge-richard-posner>.

reasoning in applying the law to cases before them; and (e) the content of the common law, as to its applicability to particular fact patterns, sometimes turns on moral reasons.

We have used the term 'suggest' because the Razian jurisprudential fortress is so elaborately constructed that it would be imprudent to use stronger language in the context of a short piece such as this one. Nonetheless, if these suggestions are along the right lines, it is likely that still stronger conclusions would follow, in at least three respects.

First, we have used the qualifying term 'sometimes' because we refer only to cases in which courts distinguish precedent, and there are, of course, many in which they do not. A more aggressive rendition of the views we have put forward might suggest a more ambitious claim: namely, that lower court decisions *refraining from* distinguishing precedent are themselves—at least implicitly—decisions that rest on a judgment that any distinctions one might plausibly draw are morally unjustifiable. On this account, the legal rule requiring courts to follow precedent, no less than the rule permitting them to distinguish precedents, calls on them to make normatively-laden decisions.

Secondly, while our argument is rooted in the common law, and statutory and constitutional law would seem to rely upon authoritative texts in a manner that sidesteps the problems we have been discussing, it is far from clear whether such a sharp contrast can be drawn. We are not referring here to the domains of constitutional law (such as the Establishment Clause of the US Constitution's First Amendment) notorious for generating elaborate doctrinal categories in a manner redolent of common law decision-making, or statutes onto which huge amounts of common law development have been grafted. We refer to something more basic: the reality that adjudication of any case in litigation—common law, statutory, or constitutional—inevitably involves a range of rules of interpretation, *res judicata*, recusal, and so on, which plainly come from judge-made law.

Thirdly, while Raz was, of course, a towering figure among legal positivists, there are many positivists (including Hart) who have resisted Raz's version, with its especially sharp form of separationism. It is not entirely clear whether other versions of positivism would be vulnerable to the criticisms set forth here. However, we are inclined to think so, for the simple reasons that: (a) the articulation and usage of rules of recognition will itself commonly involve adjudication; and (b) rejecting the pervasiveness of moral reasoning in day-to-day adjudication of ordinary cases in the law is plainly a central goal of the most prominent forms of legal positivism.[39]

Finally, while we have not set forth any affirmative model of adjudication here, it is worth noting that none of the features of our critique imports the most controversial features of Dworkin's jurisprudence. In particular, nothing in the chapter suggests a commitment to a right answer thesis, or requires us to adopt a sharp distinction between rules and principles. And nothing precludes our acceptance of Raz's quite powerful observation that lawyers distinguish settled from unsettled issues of law, or indeed the positivist inclination to recognize that *sometimes* the judicial role is to create law rather than apply it. Indeed, the analysis in this chapter is put forward in the spirit of agreement with those, like Raz, who believe a jurisprudential theory ought to be able to accommodate basic features of the ways in which down-to-earth judges and lawyers practise law.

---

[39] One of us has argued elsewhere that 'inclusive' legal positivism, if it relies for its positivistic credentials on a 'social facts' thesis rather than a 'sources thesis', must give up claiming to be a form of positivism at all, since the social facts thesis in its distinctively positivistic form is untenable. See BC Zipursky, 'Pragmatism, Positivism, and the Conventionalistic Fallacy' in JK Campbell and others (eds), *Law and Social Justice* (MIT Press 2005) 285, 307–08.

23

Realism About Precedent

Brian Leiter[*]

1. Introduction

In jurisdictions with a doctrine of precedent (or *stare decisis*), later courts are supposed to be bound by the decisions (the *ratio* or holding) of earlier courts, either those above them in a chain of authority (vertical precedent) or their own earlier decisions (horizontal precedent, where the later incarnation of the same court usually retains the option of overruling its earlier decision). The later court, in either the vertical or horizontal cases, is bound *only* by those decisions which are 'on point' or 'the same in relevant respects' to the case currently before the court. Since cases are never identical in all particulars, this always requires figuring out which general categories that subsume the particulars of different cases are the *relevant* ones: I will call this 'relevant similarity' in what follows. Relevant similarity is typically assessed in the light of either the reasons the earlier court actually gave for the decision or the reasons that can be imputed to the earlier court based on the legal decision that court reached.[1] Analogical reasoning figures crucially in ascertaining whether an earlier case that might be precedent is, in fact, 'relevantly similar'. Indeed, there is no doctrine of precedent without analogical reasoning,[2] since in any jurisdiction with a doctrine of *stare decisis*, any earlier decision by a court is a possible precedent for a later court considering the same legal question, and any earlier decision considering the same legal question is potentially distinguishable as involving facts that are not 'relevantly similar'. Uncontroversial judgments of relevant similarity deal with most of the former cases.

---

[*] I would like to thank Hafsteinn Dan Kristjánsson and Claudio Michelon for their helpful comments on an earlier version, and Sarah Cohen for research assistance.

[1] Joseph Raz suggests—*contra* sceptics about identifying the holding (*ratio*) of the case—that 'the *ratio* is the reason(s) by which the court justifies its decision' and this is 'partly a matter of the interpretation' of the written decision. J Raz, *The Authority of Law: Essays on Law and Morality* (Clarendon Press 1979) 184. That Raz thinks this is a response to scepticism is surprising. Indeed, Raz echoes Hart's mistaken confidence on this score: 'the identification of the *ratio* of a case is reasonably straightforward' (ibid). Raz does recognize the great 'freedom' courts have when it comes to precedent, and that it is 'unreasonable to attribute great weight to the actual formulation of the rule in the hands of the' earlier court (ibid 188). Raz suggests that sometimes the later court may try to formulate a 'modified rule that was really the rule the original court had in mind' (ibid).

[2] Grant Lamond understates this point in G Lamond, 'Precedent and Analogy in Legal Reasoning', *The Stanford Encyclopedia of Philosophy* (Spring edn, 2006) <https://plato.stanford.edu/entries/legal-reas-prec/> accessed 26 January 2022. He writes: 'Arguments by analogy complement arguments from precedent in two ways: (i) they are used when the facts of a case do not fall within the *ratio* of any precedent, in order to assimilate the result to that that in the analogical case; and (ii) they are used when the facts of a case *do* fall within the *ratio* of a precedent, as a basis for distinguishing the case at hand from the precedent' (ibid s 4). But whether the facts of a case actually fall within a *ratio* itself depends on at least *sotto voce* analogical reasoning, since no two cases are identical, and whether the particulars in a new case really do fall under the general categories of the prior case is often arguable—a point the realist approach to precedent calls attention to. We shall examine an instance of this in the text.

Brian Leiter, *Realism About Precedent* In: *Philosophical Foundations of Precedent*. Edited by: Timothy Endicott, Hafsteinn Dan Kristjánsson, and Sebastian Lewis, Oxford University Press. © Brian Leiter 2023. DOI: 10.1093/oso/9780192857248.003.0024

Realists about precedent—from Karl Llewellyn[3] to Julius Stone[4] to this author[5]—are sceptical that precedent really binds courts[6] (especially, as we will see, appellate courts). Realists are sceptical about the constraint of precedent not because they believe judges improperly disregard binding precedents (they may sometimes do so, but that would not be an interesting theoretical point); the worry, rather, is that judges can often properly distinguish precedents that might impede the decision they want to reach on moral or political grounds. They can do so precisely because judgments of 'relevant similarity' that are central to distinguishing are largely unconstrained by law. First, such judgments depend on inchoate and sometimes unconscious norms that govern general classifications of particulars, about which reasonable people can and do differ, and about which the law is mostly silent. Secondly, given the range of permissible characterizations of the earlier court's reasons in many instances, the requirement that the judgment of relevant similarity or difference be consistent with those reasons imposes only a limited constraint on the general classification employed.[7] This is particularly important in the cases that reach the stage of appellate review precisely because of selection effects: advocates often pursue cases through the stage of appellate review when the 'precedents' could go either way.[8]

A caveat at the start: legal systems with doctrines of precedent differ in important respects. Even Joseph Raz (decidedly not a legal realist) concedes, regarding his treatment of precedent in the English system, that it may not be representative: '[T]he English judiciary is small and highly centralized. It is recruited exclusively from the Bar (itself small), comes from a more or less homogeneous social background, and is unified by strong professional and social ties into a relatively cohesive social group.'[9] That is surely part of the explanation for why no legal realism movement developed in England.[10] Raz adds that his account is 'meant to be faithful to the accepted theory of the practice [of precedent] rather than to the

---

[3] KN Llewellyn, *The Bramble Bush: Some Lectures on Law and Its Study* (Oceana 1951) 56–69. I return to Llewellyn, later, in the text.

[4] J Stone, *Precedent and Law: Dynamics of Common Law Growth* (Butterworths 1985) 2. Stone notes that most studies 'tend to take for granted that the ambit of a precedent, that is, the range of circumstances for which it is binding, is normally clear and known. When this is taken for granted, all the sources of appellate leeways of choice to which this work is devoted are ... often ... ignored.' Stone references Rupert Cross as an example of those who take it for granted, but the same is true of HLA Hart, Joseph Raz, and many others. Stone identifies various sources of 'appellate leeways', including 'equally licit and competing methods of finding the purported *ratio decidendi* of a case, and of distinguishing *obiter dicta* from it. They include more than one—often many—alternative ratios which even a single method can reveal. They also include an array of levels of generality at which any "material" fact can usually be described, delimiting the purported *ratio* more widely as the level of generality of each such fact is raised.'

[5] See, e.g.,B Leiter, *Naturalizing Jurisprudence: Essays on American Legal Realism and Naturalism in Legal Philosophy* (OUP 2007); B Leiter, 'Constitutional Law, Moral Judgment, and the Supreme Court as Super-Legislature' (2015) 66 Hastings LJ 1601.

[6] More precisely, realists are sceptical about how often precedent really permits the court to justify one and only one decision on legal grounds. More often, precedent may *restrict* the range of possible decisions, but that is consistent with the realist point that legal reasoning is *under*determinate, not, strictly speaking, *in*determinate.

[7] Prior cases and legal experience can *influence* the unconscious norms governing classifications and the imputation of reasons, but that is a weak constraint. Still, when precedent is relevant for a court, it is more of a constraint than exists in a case of 'first impression'.

[8] This is why realists emphasize indeterminacy in appellate adjudication. See, e.g., Stone, *Precedent and Law* (n 4) ch 1; Leiter, *Naturalizing Jurisprudence* (n 5) 11–12, 20, 79–80. My view now is that it is not clear that this states any dispute with Hart's account of legal indeterminacy; see generally B Leiter, 'Legal Positivism as a Realist Theory of Law' in T Spaak and P Mindus (eds), *The Cambridge Companion to Legal Positivism* (CUP 2021).

[9] Raz, *Authority of Law* (n 1) 181.

[10] Other factors include: (1) the civil service system of the judiciary in England, where appointment and advancement depend on evaluation by other judges, who are likely to enforce adherence to norms of interpretation; and (2) the fact that English law students start studying law at age seventeen or eighteen, without exposure to other disciplines, so are presented with law as though it is actually a discipline unto itself. Theology students, e.g., tend

practice'.[11] The realist account of precedent concerns itself with the practice, not the theory, and its primary evidence is *the actual decisions of the courts*.[12] According to the realists, judgments about relevant similarity are sufficiently flexible that precedent is less a constraint on a decision than a tool that judges can either use to avoid decisions they would rather not reach on other normative grounds, or to justify decisions they want to reach on other normative grounds, but for which they need a legal precedent. How flexible judgments of relevant similarity are will depend, however, on the inchoate norms governing such judgments in a particular legal culture, as well as the norms governing the imputation of reasons to a prior court. The realistic view of precedent may have wider or narrower scope in different legal systems, depending on these factors.

2. A Non-Legal Example of the Problem Afflicting Judgments of 'Relevant Similarity'

Let us start with a non-legal example. Children often take parental decisions about siblings to have precedential force, mostly on the grounds of 'equal treatment': for example, claims of the form, 'why did my brother get to do X, but I can't?' (The general justification for a doctrine of precedent is not my concern here, but 'equal treatment' looms large in many accounts.) Suppose the father tells his fourteen-year-old son that he can stay up late in the evening on a school night to watch a movie, but forbids his eleven-year-old daughter from doing the same. The daughter objects: 'You are letting my brother stay up for the movie!' She here makes an appeal to precedent, one that assumes that the relevant general category covering the particulars of the case is 'child of the father'. The father, unlike a court, probably has said less that would illuminate his *reasons* for the prior decision about the brother. Here are some reasons that are compatible with—and thus perhaps imputable to (depending on what precisely was said)—the father's earlier decision about the brother:

(1) Older children need less sleep, so can stay up later than younger children and still perform adequately at school the next day.
(2) Younger children are more likely to wet their bed if they stay up late.
(3) Boys deserve more privileges than girls, since a boy's life is harder.
(4) The boy has fewer responsibilities than the girl, so if he is tired the next day it hardly matters.
(5) The boy has gone above and beyond the call of duty with regard to family responsibilities lately, and deserves the privilege.
(6) Past experience shows that the son needs less sleep than his sister.

---

not to attend to non-theological explanations for the beliefs of theologians, and perhaps something similar happens with law students in England.

[11] Raz, *Authority of Law* (n 1) 181.

[12] Raz puts to one side the question of what happens in practice by saying '[o]nly an empirical study' could settle the matter (ibid). Only a very sophisticated empirical study could settle the matter decisively, but familiarity with what courts do, emerging from practice or reading cases (or both, in the case of most realists), can surely suffice to suggest that the 'theory' may be bogus. The latter constituted the *actual*, and generally compelling, methods of the American legal realists. See B Leiter, 'Legal Realisms, Old and New' (2013) 47 Val U L Rev 67.

Appeals to 'equal treatment' are vitiated when the principle governing the treatment is of dubious moral merit (e.g. sexist assumptions about boys and girls, as in point 3), but that is most relevant in cases of (horizontal) precedent where overruling is an option.[13] Even putting point 3 aside, the reasons established by the father's precedent include subsuming the particulars of the precedent case under general categories like: 'ability to perform the next day' s duties' (point 1 and also point 4), 'avoiding wetting the bed' (point 2), 'desert based on merit' (point 5), and 'physical and psychological need' (point 6, although there is possible overlap with point 1). The choice of any one of these ways of characterizing the particulars of the precedent case will affect the application of the precedent to the present case, that is, the daughter's demand to stay up to watch the movie given the precedent. The daughter wins her 'appeal' if the only relevant category is 'child of the father', but she may lose her appeal on all of the other ways of stating the relevant similarity, *unless* she can argue that the general category does not in fact apply to her: for example, she doesn't need more sleep than her brother, she never wets the bed, and so on.

Perhaps the father gave reasons that rule out some of these possible descriptions of the categorization of the relevant facts justifying his decision. But it is a feature of precedent in ordinary life and in the law that parties can later raise distinctions that the precedent decision did not explicitly contemplate, subject to the constraint that these distinctions can be made consistent with the earlier outcome. Sometimes it is proper to identify the rule of the precedent by appeal to a pattern of decisions: for example, how has the father treated the fourteen-year-old vis-à-vis *his* older brother? But courts do this too when they locate a particular precedent in the context of related decisions, in order to elucidate the *real* or *more general* rationale at work in an area of law.

Much of the latitude in identifying the reasons and the 'relevant similarity' between cases arises from the fact that, as HLA Hart pointed out in Chapter VII of *The Concept of Law*, precedent is a form of instruction by 'example', rather than explicit linguistic guidance formulated in a rule, and, as a result, it 'may leave open ranges of possibilities, and hence of doubt, as to what is intended'.[14] Sometimes appeal to the reasons given in connection with the 'example' may help, but not always. Let us consider a US case from the US Supreme Court that illustrates the case for realism about precedent.

3. A Legal Example of Realism About Precedent

New York v United States from 1992[15] was one of the early cases[16] that signalled the intent of some members of the US Supreme Court to redraw the boundaries of federal power after an earlier incarnation of that Court—appointed in large part by President Franklin Roosevelt— redrew them in the late 1930s and early 1940s to make Roosevelt's New Deal possible.[17] *New York* concerned the Low-Level Radioactive Waste Policy Amendments Act of 1985,

---

[13] It is not wholly irrelevant in cases of vertical precedent, since courts, sometimes, should not do what the law requires, but that is a separate issue.

[14] HLA Hart, *The Concept of Law* (3rd edn, OUP 2012) 125. There are exceptions, of course, to the 'example' model of precedent.

[15] *New York v United States* 505 US 144 (1992).

[16] Earlier, see *Gregory v Ashcroft* 501 US 452, 461 (1991).

[17] The classic American realist example of scepticism about precedent is Edward Levi's discussion of *MacPherson v Buick Motor Co* 217 NY 382 (1916) and the privity doctrine in E Levi, *An Introduction to Legal Reasoning* (University of Chicago Press 1949) 8–10. For discussion, including contrast of Levi's and Cardozo's treatment with Dworkin's, see B Leiter, 'In Praise of Realism (and Against "Nonsense" Jurisprudence)' (2012) 100 Geo LJ 865, 878–84.

316   BRIAN LEITER

which the State of New York now challenged as betraying 'federalism' values—that is, the value of preserving certain regulatory questions for the states, and thus as beyond the reach of the federal government—by infringing upon state autonomy. Under what one might have thought the controlling precedent, *Garcia v San Antonio Metropolitan Transportation Authority*[18] just seven years earlier, this might have seemed an 'easy' case, that is, one in which the law clearly dictated that New York lose. *Garcia*, which concerned federal regulation of wages and working hours (including those of state and city employees), held that the only protection for federalism values, like state autonomy, came from the political process itself, that is, from the fact that the states were all represented in the US Congress; only if there were a breakdown in the political process, so the *Garcia* court suggested, would the Supreme Court intervene. *New York* seemed a clear case from the standpoint of *Garcia*: the Radioactive Waste Management Act had been enacted by Congress *after being drafted by the various states*: the states, in effect, wanted Congress to bind them to the agreement they had reached among themselves. This would seem to be a paradigmatic case of federalism values in action: autonomous states strike a bargain about how to dispose of their radioactive waste, and then ask Congress to enforce the bargain.

Because the 'doctrine of precedent' is malleable, once the Supreme Court agreed to review the case, everyone was on notice that what might have seemed clear as a matter of *stare decisis* was not. In the majority opinion, Justice Sandra Day O'Connor effectively took a page from the American legal realist Karl Llewellyn's explanation of the malleability of precedent from his 1930 book *The Bramble Bush*.[19] In Llewellyn's famous rendering, appellate courts approach precedents in one of two ways: they read 'unwelcome' precedents strictly, that is, they characterize their holding in a way that is highly specific to the facts of the earlier case in order to distinguish it from the case currently before the court. In Llewellyn's obviously facetious example, a strict reading of an earlier court's holding might be, 'This rule holds only of redheaded Walpoles in pale magenta Buick cars.'[20] By contrast, a 'loose' reading of a precedent abstracts away from the particular facts of the case in favour of a generic rule of law that the court would like to treat as binding in the present instance. Not every 'strict' or 'loose' reading is going to be plausible, but Llewellyn is plainly correct that in the US legal system the doctrine of precedent affords courts enough latitude in construing the holdings of earlier cases—in identifying the 'relevant similarity' between the earlier case and the present one—to make precedent a weak constraint on present decision in many cases. And that is precisely what happened in *New York*.

Justice O'Connor, in the majority opinion, faced a prima facie problem as mentioned already: under *Garcia*, the Federal Radioactive Waste Act looked like a clear case of the political process operating to protect the interests of the states—after all, the states had drafted the Act in negotiations with each other, and then asked Congress to enact it. Presumably O'Connor lacked the votes to overrule *Garcia*—a move that would have been unseemly, in any case, given that *Garcia* had overruled another case, *National League of Cities*,[21] from less than a decade before—and so, taking a page from Llewellyn, she set out to *distinguish Garcia* by reading it strictly. According to Justice O'Connor's majority opinion,[22] the rule

---

[18] *Garcia v San Antonio Metropolitan Transit Authority* 469 US 528 (1985).

[19] Llewellyn (n 3) 56–69.

[20] ibid 66–67. Llewellyn was an experienced lawyer, and obviously knew that limiting the *ratio* of a prior case by the names of the parties or the colour of their cars was not going to be effective. But rhetorical excess, rather than analytical precision, was Llewellyn's trademark.

[21] *National League of Cities v Usery* 426 US 833 (1976).

[22] *New York* (n 15) 149–88.

in *Garcia*—the rule that the only protection for federalism values comes from the political process itself—applies *only* in cases where the federal regulation applies to *both* public and private entities, as was true of the wage and hour regulations at issue in *Garcia*. *Garcia* itself did not make an issue out of this factual difference, but Justice O'Connor did: for the Federal Radioactive Waste Management Act applied only to public entities—namely, states—and so according to Justice O'Connor presented a different issue than in *Garcia*. In other words, the relevant similarity or difference is whether or not the challenged legislation regulated *only* state actors, or whether it regulated both public *and* private actors. With *Garcia* distinguished and left intact, Justice O'Connor proceeded to an historical analysis and ultimately invalidated a portion of the Act being challenged in *New York*. Those details do not matter for our purposes.

The dissenting opinion by Justice Byron White[23] can also be read as taking a page from Llewellyn: he effectively accused the majority of distinguishing *Garcia* on the basis of factual differences that did not make a difference. Justice White, we might say, complained that the majority opinion said the rule in *Garcia* applies only to 'redheaded Walpoles in pale magenta Buick cars',[24] that is, an irrelevant factual dissimilarity. From Justice White's perspective, the difference between a federal regulation that reached public and private entities as opposed to only public ones was irrelevant, *New York* was an easy case, and *Garcia* should have controlled the result.

Crucial to the interest of this example for my purposes is that I believe neither the majority nor dissent were right 'as a matter of law' in this case, that is, neither side had stronger legal reasons for their decision than the other. That the federal law at issue in *Garcia* applied to both public and private employers was not emphasized in *Garcia*, but the reasoning of the *Garcia* majority opinion is not inconsistent with that distinction. Undoubtedly, Justice O'Connor did a poor job of explaining why the factual difference between *Garcia* and *New York* actually mattered, but an explanation is not hard to come by: surely it is reasonable to worry that state autonomy might be more at risk when a federal regulation *only applies to the states*, as opposed to regulating activity, regardless of whether it is performed by public or private actors. Justice O'Connor's opinion says, in effect, when federal law controls only the operations of state governments, a different kind of judicial scrutiny is warranted to insure protection for federalism values. At the same time, Justice White's view was equally plausible as a matter of law: the *Garcia* rule emphasized the importance of the political process as a safeguard for state autonomy, and the underlying facts in *New York* seemed to indicate a political process functioning well, indeed, driven by the states themselves, until the state of New York had some buyer's remorse. Justice O'Connor and Justice White made different judgments about the 'relevant similarities' between *Garcia* and *New York*, and the law was compatible with both judgments. In that sense, precedent did not constrain the decision.[25]

---

[23] ibid 188–211.

[24] Llewellyn (n 3) 66–67.

[25] On the realist account, it is natural to ask what really explains the decision in *New York*. *New York*, as students of US federalism know, was near the beginning of a series of Supreme Court cases in which, for the first time since the triumph of the New Deal, the Court began placing some limits on the exercise of federal power. President Reagan, who appointed Justice O'Connor a decade earlier, ran partly on this issue, the issue of state autonomy from federal overreach. And so, for Justice O'Connor, a new-fangled conservative in the Reagan mould, *New York* presented an opportunity to state loud and clear that there really are limits on federal power. By contrast, for Justice White, an old-fashioned conservative, appointed by President Kennedy in the early 1960s, the New Deal revolution had settled all the questions about the scope of federal power; Justice White was a law-and-order conservative, sceptical of the expanding rights of criminal defendants, as well as of abortion rights, but he was fully accepting of the transformation of the constitutional system effected by the New Deal.

4. A Rejoinder to Realism About Precedent

A rejoinder to the realist account of precedent in *New York* must argue that in fact either Justice O'Connor or Justice White was *correct as a matter of law*, that is, that either Justice O'Connor found a relevant difference between *Garcia* and *New York*, or she did not (as Justice White argued). To make that case, one must show that the inchoate norms governing judgments of relevant similarity and difference are in fact governed (or constrained) by more demanding legally obligatory norms than the realist argument has so far allowed. The clearest (perhaps only) example of such an alternative account would be Ronald Dworkin's theory of law as 'constructive interpretation.'[26] According to Dworkin, judgments about the relevant similarity of a precedent are part of a broader 'constructive interpretation' of the prior case and (in principle) all other aspects of the prior institutional history of the legal system (although only a Hercules could do that): that is, an interpretation that both fits or explains some portion of the prior institutional history and shows it in the best moral light. A non-Herculean Dworkinian judge considering *New York* must ask whether distinguishing the facts in *Garcia* from the facts in *New York* (as Justice O'Connor did) is really part of the best constructive interpretation of (at least) the federalism line of cases: that is, whether a principled explanation of the distinction (between federal laws that apply only to public entities, as opposed to those that apply to all economic actors, regardless of public/private status) would provide the best moral justification for the law. Put more simply, the Dworkinian judge asks whether ours is a morally better legal system if it applies the *Garcia* rule in all federalism cases, or adopts a different approach (as Justice O'Connor would have it) when federal regulations target only state actors (on the assumption that both approaches fit well enough with some of the prior cases). On this approach, intuitive judgments about 'relevant' similarity and difference are now 'disciplined' by moral arguments about the merits and demerits of different approaches to federalism. The 'discipline' involved is, of course, only as compelling as the objective force of the moral arguments in question: if equally good moral arguments can be marshalled in favour of both Justice O'Connor's and Justice White's view, without any further way to adjudicate between them, then Dworkinian constructive interpretation imposes no additional constraint at all.

Legal realists like myself are inclined to think that the idea that judgments of 'relevant similarity' are constrained by 'moral argument' is comical: it is not only that there are arguments against Dworkinian optimism about moral argument[27] but also that it seems implausible that morality takes sides in the O'Connor–White dispute. One need not agree wholeheartedly with the legal realist's meta-ethical views to nonetheless concede that the proposed Dworkinian rejoinder to the realist argument about precedent requires several highly contentious assumptions: that the law depends on constructive interpretation; that there is an objective answer to the moral question about the different approaches to

---

[26] R Dworkin, *Law's Empire* (Belknap Press 1986). Scott Brewer suggests there is more constraint in reasoning by analogy than realist sceptics allow, but even he admits his preferred methodology is 'admittedly far from determinate' and that there is 'inevitably an uncodifiable imaginative moment in ... analogical reasoning'. See S Brewer, 'Exemplary Reasoning: Semantic, Pragmatics and the Rational Force of Legal Argument by Analogy' (1996) 109 Harv L Rev 923, 954–55. This is not surprising given the central role of abductive inference in his account (ibid 962), since inferences to the best explanation (in this case, of similarities and differences between cases) are hostage to a variety of values about what makes one explanation better than another. The evidence that Brewer thinks constrains (confirms or disconfirms) the abductive hypothesis is also quite flexible, as his extended discussion of 'pragmatics' makes clear (ibid 989–1003). Brewer's aim is, in any case, to show that analogical arguments can have 'rational force', not that they uniquely determine outcomes in a way that would defeat realist scepticism.

[27] See, e.g.,JL Mackie, 'The Third Theory of Law' in M Cohen (ed), *Ronald Dworkin and Contemporary Jurisprudence* (Rowman & Allanheld 1984); Leiter, *Naturalizing Jurisprudence* (n 5) ch 8; B Leiter, 'Disagreement, Anti-Realism about Reasons, and Inference to the Best Explanation' (2021) Ethic Theory & Moral Prac (forthcoming).

federalism in the O'Connor–White dispute; and that this answer, if it exists, constrains judgments of relevant similarity. Even though few legal philosophers now accept these latter assumptions, the possible Dworkinian rejoinder to the realist view underlines the point that realism about precedent, like any argument about the indeterminacy of legal reasoning, depends on a view (tacit if not explicit) about which norms are legally valid and thus prima facie binding on the courts.[28]

When the realist about precedent claims that judgments of relevant similarity and difference between cases are often indeterminate, that presupposes that valid legal norms are silent on the choice between, for example, Justice O'Connor's or Justice White's interpretation of *Garcia*. If valid legal norms were not silent on that point, then the choice would not be (what I call) 'rationally indeterminate', that is, indeterminate with respect to the reasons the court may properly invoke. Obviously, there are many norms for decision that are not silent on the choice confronting the US Supreme Court in *New York*: for example, the norm 'one ought to promote federal over state power whenever possible' would decide the case in favour of Justice White. The latter norm, however, is not legally valid in the US, even on Dworkin's view I suspect.[29]

Even if judgments about relevant similarity are at some point legally unconstrained, they are not wholly unconstrained: the demand for 'relevant' difference (or similarity) with regard to the reasons for the precedent operates in all legal systems, as in ordinary lives. The latitude a decision-maker has about 'relevance' will be constrained always by the inchoate norms governing those judgments, as our initial example of the father setting bedtimes suggests. The father could not justify (by his lights or the children's) his decision to the eleven-year-old daughter by appealing to her hair colour compared to her brother's, for example. Although this is a difference between the daughter's case and her older brother's case, it is not 'relevant' in the sense that there is no general principle that anyone accepts that would explain its relevance, unlike the examples given earlier.

That law depends in this way on non-legal norms of judgment should hardly be surprising. The normative force of grammar, maths, and deductive inference also constrain legal judgments, although none of the latter are legally valid norms. Unlike the norms governing judgments of 'relevant similarity', however, the norms of grammar, maths, and deductive inference impose more constraint, although grammar has a more dynamic element (dependent as it obviously is on practice) than the others. However, even grammatical norms are more demanding than norms about 'relevant similarity'. Grammatical norms may evolve over time given the linguistic practices of large groups of people, but 'relevance' norms are subject to extensive contestation in the present moment, as the non-legal example we began with illustrates. Analogical reasoning is central to legal reasoning and (as noted at the start) central to precedent, but it is also hostage to the norms governing judgments of relevant similarity. Since those norms are contested and fluid—meaning that the constraint imposed by them is quite limited—it should be unsurprising how often judicial decisions are underdetermined by the valid legal norms in the jurisdiction. That is the foundation of realism about precedent, although its scope may vary in different legal systems and different cultures as noted at the start.

---

[28] See Leiter, *Naturalizing Jurisprudence* (n 5) ch 2.

[29] Hart's 'Soft Positivism' in the 'Postscript' to *The Concept of Law* (n 14) does not help either, absent a showing that the moral considerations American judges treat as legally binding would have rendered *New York* an improper decision. But since *New York* was not met with a chorus of disapproval by American judges, it does not seem that Hart's one concession to Dworkin's early critique helps here. (Recall that American legal realists, at least, accept a positivist criterion of legal validity: cf Leiter, *Naturalizing Jurisprudence* (n 5) ch 2; Leiter, 'Legal Positivism' (n 8).)

24

Precedent and the Source–Norm Distinction

Fábio Perin Shecaira[*]

1. Introduction

It is often said that judicial precedents are binding in some jurisdictions and merely persuasive in others. In fact, this distinction has served as an important criterion for sorting legal systems into different families or traditions (civil law, common law, mixed, etc). But the 'binding-versus-persuasive' distinction can be misleading. Contemporary scholars who are wary of the distinction offer the following caveats and qualifications:

(i) One ought to realize that official pronouncements about the (binding or persuasive) character of precedent may sometimes misrepresent the role effectively played by past cases in judicial reasoning.

(ii) One ought to note that the 'binding-versus-persuasive' dichotomy does not exhaust all the possible roles of precedent and that some precedents may be considered more than merely persuasive even if not exactly binding.

(iii) One ought to note that jurisdictions that do not assign binding status to individual cases may still attribute that status to series of converging decisions.

There is much to be said in favour of the foregoing caveats, but there is also reason to be cautious about the implications that may be derived from them. As we will see in section 2, the caveats have often been put forward by authors who emphasize the functional similarities hidden behind the various styles of reasoning prevailing in different legal systems. In other words, their point is to show that past cases tend to play similar roles in legal decision-making even if they are not referred to or discussed in the same way by the officials of different legal systems. By contrast, one of the aims of this chapter is to block premature conclusions about functional similarity in respect of the practice of precedent in common law and civil law jurisdictions. The chapter pursues this goal, not by refuting any of the caveats, but by adding to them. The proposed supplement to the list of caveats comes in the form of the 'source–norm' distinction. This is a distinction between sources of law (e.g. statutory provisions or judicial opinions) and the legal norms that can be derived from such sources by means of interpretation.[1] When applied to the comparative study of precedent, the source–norm distinction brings to light important differences among legal systems.

---

[*] I would like to thank Guilherme de Almeida, Priscila Andrade, Michael Baumtrog, Luís Duarte d'Almeida, Lorena Ludeña, Lucas Miotto, Claudia Roesler, Katharina Stevens, Noel Struchiner, Wil Waluchow, and the editors of this volume for helpful comments.

[1] As I explain later in the chapter, the source–norm distinction may also be rendered as the threefold 'source–interpretation–norm' distinction. The latter emphasizes that interpretation inevitably mediates the relation between sources and norms.

Fábio Perin Shecaira, *Precedent and the Source–Norm Distinction* In: *Philosophical Foundations of Precedent*. Edited by: Timothy Endicott, Hafsteinn Dan Kristjánsson, and Sebastian Lewis, Oxford University Press. © Fábio Perin Shecaira 2023. DOI: 10.1093/oso/9780192857248.003.0025

Here is a sketch of the argument. Whenever a claim is made about the degree to which precedents bind or about the stringency of the local doctrine of *stare decisis*, it is important to be clear about which aspect of precedent is at issue. The fourth caveat I want to propose is that there are three elements of the doctrine of precedent that are often conflated in comparative analyses. Claims about the weight of precedent can be understood as claims about: (1) the *use of precedent*; (2) the *interpretation of precedent*; or (3) the *enforcement of the norms* derived from precedent through interpretation. Aspect (1) pertains to whether prima facie applicable past cases must be discussed in later cases and, if so, in how much depth. Aspect (2) pertains to whether judges are tied to the explicit judicial formulation of the precedent norm (i.e. the explicit *ratio decidendi*) as an object of interpretation or whether they are free to reformulate the precedent norm on their own terms. Aspect (3) pertains to whether the precedent norm (once derived through interpretation) is taken to be decisive and therefore immune from overruling and other kinds of departure. To say that a legal system adopts a strict (or a lax) doctrine of precedent, may be to say that it is strict (or lax) about (1), (2), and/ or (3). The variety of possible combinations shows that the doctrine of precedent admits of more versions than commonly acknowledged.

This chapter is structured as follows. Section 2 explains the three caveats briefly presented earlier. Section 3 introduces the source–norm distinction. Section 4 discusses the fourth caveat and the consequences of applying the source–norm distinction to the study of precedent. Although section 4 begins with a very general analysis of the notion of precedent, it eventually discusses how the relevant jurisprudential insights apply to the study of national legal systems, particularly those of England, the US, and Brazil. Section 5 concludes.

A terminological note is in order. In this chapter, a precedent is understood as any past judicial decision that is thought to be of some significance for later cases. Others would define it more specifically as 'a judicial decision that should be followed by a judge when deciding a later similar case'.[2] The trouble with such normatively loaded definitions is that they imply that precedents are necessarily binding (or at least weighty) sources of law. If precedents ought, by definition, to be followed, then we can hardly speak of precedents that do not constrain with any degree of authority. As the reader will see in section 2, this definition would make nonsense of some important uses of the word 'precedent' in the context of comparative law.

2. The Comparative Study of Precedent: Common Caveats

Neil MacCormick and Robert Summers introduce their important collection of essays on precedent with a familiar remark: 'It is trite learning that precedents count for less in civilian legal systems than in those of the common law, and it has sometimes been doubted whether they stand for anything much at all in the civilian systems.'[3] This juridical commonplace has taken other, subtly different forms. One such form refers to the 'binding-versus-persuasive' distinction introduced earlier. Precedents are thus said to be binding in common law systems but not in civil law systems, where judges may refer to, but are not constrained by, past decisions. Another way to formulate the commonplace is to say that past cases function

---

[2] This definition appears in the Merriam-Webster online dictionary <https://www.merriam-webster.com/dictionary/precedent> accessed 3 January 2022.

[3] DN MacCormick and RS Summers, 'Introduction' in DN MacCormick and RS Summers (eds), *Interpreting Precedents: A Comparative Study* (Routledge 2016) 1, 2.

as sources of law in common law systems but not in civil law systems, where they serve at best as sources of information about the content of other, genuinely authoritative sources of law (e.g. statutes). Call this the 'source-of-law-versus-source-of-information' distinction. Finally, to put it in Latin, it is often said that only common law systems abide by the doctrine of *stare decisis*.[4]

But does trite mean true? Though we still find sophisticated jurists who endorse some of the foregoing claims,[5] specialists in comparative law have often denounced them as misleading. These scholars have sought to render our understanding of precedent more accurate by introducing a series of caveats, three of which will be emphasized in this section.

Caveat 1: beware of legal discourse. Although this is not the place to discuss the ultimate foundations of the doctrine of precedent, it is important to give some idea of the sort of consideration that may ground a claim about the role of precedent in any given legal system. Some systems try to regulate the use of precedent by means of statutes and other canonical statements (e.g. the Practice Statement made in the House of Lords in 1966[6]). These official pronouncements about precedent are relevant to determining their role, but they are not conclusive. We cannot determine the significance of precedent in a legal system without paying attention to official practice, that is, to the way in which precedents are effectively used (invoked, interpreted, enforced) by legal actors, especially by the courts of law.

In other words, to assess the role of precedent in any given legal system we must not limit our gaze to abstract official statements. It is important to read cases systematically and look for patterns in judicial argumentation (while remaining aware, of course, that judges can also mislead us).[7] One should also be wary of the lessons of the standard textbooks. The discourse of textbook writers is often normative and aspirational, that is, they tend to present things as they ought ideally to be and not quite as they are. For instance, when a civil law teacher affirms that judges do not make law because only legislators *have that power*, one wonders whether to understand this as a (naive) description of legal practice or as the expression of a political ideal.

As these examples suggest, legal discourse may sometimes misrepresent the influence of precedent by either understating or overstating it. When we look under the surface of the most noticeable official and scholarly pronouncements about precedent, we may find that departures from precedent are not rare in the common law, and that many civil law judges follow precedent routinely. Among comparative lawyers, these points do not seem to be under serious dispute: 'Everybody knows that civil law courts do use precedents. Everybody knows that common law courts distinguish cases they do not want to follow, and sometimes overrule their own decisions.'[8]

Caveat 2: beware of dichotomies. A lawyer who is curious to understand a foreign legal system might ask the following questions: are precedents binding in this system or are they not? Are they sources of law or not? These questions are not senseless, but they rely on simple dichotomies that comparative lawyers tend to reject. To account for the various roles that a precedent may play in legal practice, the contributors to the collection of essays

---

[4] As we will see, these alternative formulations of the commonplace are close but not identical in meaning.

[5] See, e.g., A Rigoni, 'Common-Law Judicial Reasoning and Analogy' (2014) 20 Legal Theory 133, 133.

[6] Practice Statement [1966] 1 WLR 1234.

[7] e.g. some common law judges may make a show of respecting precedent in some cases while silently departing from precedent in others. On 'non-overt' departures from precedent, see RS Summers and S Eng, 'Departures from Precedent' in MacCormick and Summers (n 3) 519, 522–23.

[8] JH Merryman and R Pérez-Perdomo, *The Civil Law Tradition: An Introduction to the Legal Systems of Europe and Latin America* (3rd edn, Stanford UP 2007) 42.

edited by MacCormick and Summers devised a helpful typology. They distinguish precedents according to whether they are: (1) formally binding; (2) forceful (but not binding); (3) supportive (but not forceful or binding); and (4) merely illustrative. These categories are explained and further subdivided as follows:

(1) *Formal bindingness:* a judgment not respecting a precedent's bindingness is not lawful and so is subject to reversal on appeal.

Distinguish:

(a) formal bindingness not subject to overruling...
(b) formal bindingness... subject to overruling or modification.
(2) *Not formally binding but having force:* a judgment not respecting a precedent's force, though lawful, is subject to criticism on this ground, and may be subject to reversal...
(3) *Not formally binding and not having force (as defined in (2)) but providing further support:* a judgment lacking this is still lawful and may still be justified, but not as well justified as it would be if [based on the precedent].
(4) *Mere illustrativeness or other value.*[9]

Two related remarks are in order. First, notice that this typology is relevant not only for comparing the role of precedent across legal systems but also for indicating how it may vary within a legal system. The role of precedent in any system depends on factors pertaining to court hierarchy and composition, as well as age and subject matter (e.g. whether the precedent applies constitutional or statutory law).[10] Secondly, notice that such variation marks virtually every system, common law systems included. The latter do not currently treat their precedents as absolutely binding (as defined in point 1(a)) because they admit the possibility of overruling at least at the horizontal level (i.e. overruling of past decisions by the very court that made them).[11] Moreover, although lower courts in common law systems do not typically overrule precedents of higher courts, they can still find ways to circumvent those decisions by means of the elusive technique of distinguishing. As Randy Kozel puts it, 'If the first rule of precedent is that prior decisions warrant respect, a close second is that no decision is untouchable.'[12]

Caveat 3: remember that there is strength in numbers. The idea that precedents are not binding in civil law systems may appear to be directly contradicted by such current practices as that of according *erga omnes* effect to judgments delivered in abstract constitutional review. It could be argued, however, that judgments given in abstract review (i.e. independently of any concrete case or controversy) do not really constitute precedents in the Anglo-American sense of the word. Precedents are traditionally understood as past judicial decisions that have settled disputes between adverse parties. Although the effect of precedent is not exclusively *inter partes*, its focus on a concrete dispute is one of its defining features.

Be that as it may, there are older trends within the civil law that also belie the thought that precedents in that tradition never come close to being binding. Consider the doctrine of

---

[9] A Peczenik, 'The Binding Force of Precedent' in MacCormick and Summers (n 3) 461, 463.
[10] See ibid 477–78; RJ Kozel, *Settled vs Right: A Theory of Precedent* (CUP 2017) 25–28.
[11] It should be noted that some jurists in the US identify exceptional 'super-precedents' that are supposedly immune from overruling because of the firm social consensus that supports them.
[12] Kozel (n 10) 60.

jurisprudence constante, which is accepted in various civil law and mixed systems.[13] The doctrine states that precedents become weightier as they form series of converging decisions, so that a rule repeated in a long line of cases can even come to have great weight.[14] Some countries have enhanced the doctrine of *jurisprudence constante* by empowering the courts to summarize in canonical form the rules established by lines of precedent.[15] These authoritative summaries are entirely judge-made, though they may resemble statutory provisions in breadth and abstractness.

So, in civil law systems a series of cases may give rise to binding (or at least weighty) rules. It might be pointed out that this is still quite different from the common law doctrine of precedent, which treats individual cases as self-sufficient sources of law; but that too would be misleading. Although it is true that, as a matter of principle, one judgment can make law under *stare decisis*, the practice in common law systems is often more complicated than that. The rule contained in a case of first impression tends to be clarified, refined, and reshaped as it is applied, commented upon, and distinguished in subsequent cases. Common law judges often need to look at a line of cases to piece together the rule of law that unifies them all.[16] In practice, then, following precedent in common law systems is often a matter of reviewing sets of precedents, as opposed to focusing on a single landmark case.

The three caveats presented in this section have many merits. Together they improve our understanding of the judicial process by qualifying the simplistic generalizations that once prevailed about precedents and their value in different legal systems. We should be careful, however, about the implications that might be drawn from these caveats. We should be mindful of the risk of replacing a dubious emphasis on the differences between legal traditions with an equally dubious affirmation of their similarities. For it appears that in some circles the trope of difference has already been replaced by that of convergence.[17] As Summers puts it, 'There is today no sharp dichotomy here, but a continuum along which the systems are converging, though, of course, not all at the same pace.'[18] Section 4 will focus on the important differences that remain despite the similarities pointed out in this section. That will require, however, that we take a step back to consider the source–norm distinction.

3. The Source–Norm Distinction

A. The Distinction Explained

Sources of law, as I use the term, are the resources or materials on which courts regularly base their decisions.[19] There is, of course, an important distinction between material and

---

[13] See RL Henry, '*Jurisprudence Constante* and *Stare Decisis* Contrasted' (1929) 15 Am Bar Assoc 11.

[14] Notice that legal systems that accord great weight to lines of precedents will sometimes deny that they are sources of law. This is because they deem a judicial decision inadequate if grounded only on past cases, with no reference to legislation or custom. So, even when precedents add weight to a ruling, they may lack the self-sufficiency of other sources. This is a reason to distinguish the 'binding-versus-persuasive' distinction from the 'source-of-law-versus-source-of-information' distinction.

[15] See R Camarena González, 'From *Jurisprudence Constante* to *Stare Decisis*: The Migration of the Doctrine of Precedent to Civil Law Constitutionalism' (2016) 7 Transn'l Legal Theory 257.

[16] See R Cross and JW Harris, *Precedent in English Law* (4th edn, Clarendon Press 1991) 14–15.

[17] See, e.g., LM Soriano, 'The Use of Precedents as Arguments of Authority, Arguments *ab exemplo*, and Arguments of Reason in Civil Law Systems' (1998) 11 Ratio Juris 90, 94.

[18] RS Summers, *Essays in Legal Theory* (Springer 2000) 210.

[19] This section summarizes arguments developed in F Shecaira, 'Sources of Law Are not Legal Norms' (2015) 28 Ratio Juris 15.

formal sources of law, or sources of law in a material and a formal sense.[20] Materials sources of law are those that effectively (i.e. materially) motivate judicial decisions. Formal sources of law are those that are explicitly (i.e. formally) used by judges in their arguments. In other words, formal sources are those that courts regularly invoke as *reasons* for making their decisions. Some resources may play the role of both material and formal sources of law, but this combination of roles is by no means necessary. Some material sources may act silently because judges may be motivated by resources (e.g. newspaper editorials) that they prefer not to mention.

Take the sentence, 'in this legal system, judges regularly base their decisions on resource *r*' (where *r* could refer to statutes, precedents, textbooks, etc). This could mean either that *r* is what motivates judges to make their decisions or that *r* is regularly invoked by judges as part of their explicit arguments. I am interested in the latter meaning of the sentence. The word 'source' in the phrase 'the source–norm distinction' should be understood as referring to sources in the formal sense only. In modern national legal systems, this role is played primarily by official documents (such as statutes or judicial opinions) although certain unwritten social practices (such as customs or conventions) may also qualify. It is from these documents and practices that judges derive the norms on which they ground their decisions. To illustrate the source–norm distinction, in this section I will use examples pertaining to legislation. Section 4 will discuss the distinction as it applies to precedent.

To distinguish between sources of law (in a formal sense) and legal norms is to emphasize the ever-present possibility that different legal actors may derive different norms from the same source of law, even if these actors are equally well informed about the law and equally earnest in their attempts to discern its content. Other legal theorists may want to invoke the source–norm distinction in the service of a more abstract ontological point. For instance, it can be argued that statutes should not be confused with statutory norms because the former are sets of sentences (i.e. linguistic entities) while the latter are sets of propositions (i.e. semantic entities). I am sympathetic to this view, but here I will not dwell on the metaphysics of law. In this chapter, the source–norm distinction has a less abstract purpose, namely, to highlight the fact that sources of law may be understood differently by different interpreters without it being possible to say that any of the contending interpretations are unlawful.

But what makes this kind of interpretative disagreement possible? The answer is that most legal systems do not prescribe a single method of interpretation for all legal actors to use.[21] When judges read legislation, for instance, they are relatively free to opt between at least two or three methods of interpretation, such as textualism (which takes the words of the relevant provisions literally), intentionalism (which seeks to discern the intentions of the authors of the provisions), and purposivism (which assesses the goals most reasonably associated with the provisions).[22] Consider an example. Let us imagine a by-law prohibiting vehicles from entering a public park. Literally, all vehicles are banned by the by-law, including ambulances, garbage trucks, cars driven by individuals taking shortcuts to the hospital, and so on. But, of course, it might not have been the intention of the creators of the by-law to prohibit every one of these vehicles from entering the park. And even if it had been their intention to ban all vehicles, it could be argued that the by-law is more reasonably interpreted as banning only

---

[20] See, e.g., HLA Hart, *The Concept of Law* (2nd edn, Clarendon Press 1994) 294.

[21] Undoubtedly, even if a legal system did prescribe a single method (which is rare) there could still be disagreement about how to apply it in concrete cases.

[22] The number of admissible methods will vary, and so will their names. In Brazil, textualism, intentionalism, and purposivism are recognized as the grammatical, historical, and teleological methods (respectively).

those vehicles that detract from the safety and cleanliness of the park. So, the content of the norm that the by-law is thought to contain will vary depending on the interpreter's focus (e.g. text, intention, or purpose).

There should be nothing particularly controversial about acknowledging the possibility of interpretative disagreement among legal actors. Yet the source–norm distinction is sometimes viewed with suspicion for two different reasons. First, because of its association with sceptical theories of interpretation and with the view that judges have wide discretion to apply the law as they wish.[23] The sceptical argument contends that judges are not seriously constrained by any source of law because they are free to read the law as they like (or at least to choose the reading they prefer among the available options). I find this argument dubious because it suggests, not only that judges can choose among different methods of interpretation—which is true—but also that nothing pushes the disparate approaches to interpretation to converge toward the same results. Recall the ban on vehicles in the park. Some of the exceptional scenarios discussed (e.g. ambulances) do test our intuitions about the meaning of the by-law. But take the routine case of a driver who attempts to enter the park for a sightseeing tour. Taken literally, the by-law prescribes that this driver ought to be turned away. It is also likely that the creators of the ban would have intended that result. Moreover, it is clearly reasonable to turn away a driver who wants to enter the park for frivolous reasons. This kind of convergence of interpretative methods is admittedly contingent, but there is no reason to think that it is uncommon.

A second reason for suspicion about the source–norm distinction is that it looks too tidy. It is not the case, one might argue, that we first locate a source of law and *then* interpret it to find the legal norm that it contains. When an ambulance enters the park, for example, we only look to the by-law banning vehicles (as opposed to some other source) because we already have some idea about what it means and about its capacity to provide guidance about how to deal with the ambulance. Interpretation is pervasive and not something that we do only *after* locating the relevant sources of law. True, but the source–norm distinction is not meant to deny this—it only shows that legal actors who look to the same source (after some preliminary act of interpretation) can still diverge about what that source entails once they engage in a more methodical interpretative exercise.

B Implications of the Distinction

The source–norm distinction would perhaps be more aptly (though less elegantly) stated as a threefold distinction between *sources*, *norms*, and that which mediates their relation, namely, *interpretation*. It is only for the sake of brevity that I do not refer to the 'source–interpretation–norm' distinction. But it should be clear that the point of the distinction is to show that the connection between sources and norms is less simple and direct than it might be precisely because of issues pertaining to interpretation. The relation between sources and norms is made complicated by the fact that interpreters usually have more than one method at their disposal.

That is the point of the distinction. Let us now consider some of its implications. Judges have certain responsibilities with respect to the sources of law. Typically, their decisions ought to be grounded on one kind of source or another, and there are priorities among

---

[23] See, e.g., R Guastini, 'Fragments of a Theory of Legal Sources' (1996) 9 Ratio Juris 364.

the different kinds of sources available to the judges. Legislation usually takes precedence over case law, which usually takes precedence over legal scholarship, and so on. For related reasons, a decision that fails to refer to an applicable statute is more likely to be impugned for error *per incuriam* than one that fails to refer to an applicable precedent (although this depends, of course, on the local doctrine of *stare decisis*); and legal scholarship—though capable of adding weight to a ruling in many legal systems—is usually entirely optional. Aleksander Peczenik proposes a hierarchy of sources to account for these differences:

- 'Must-sources' [e.g. statutes] are formally binding *de jure*; 'should-sources' [e.g. precedents, in many jurisdictions] are not.
- The consequences of disregarding 'should-sources' are usually milder than the consequences of disregarding 'must-sources'.
- 'Must-sources' are more important than 'should-sources', which in turn are more important than 'may-sources' [e.g. academic writings about the law].[24]

According to Peczenik, then, legal systems differentiate sources of law according to their relative weight and importance. This point is well established among jurisprudents, but the picture is further complicated when the source–norm distinction is brought to the fore. Peczenik's typology pertains to the responsibilities of judges in relation to the various kinds of sources of law, but it does not address judges' responsibilities in relation to the norms derived from those sources.[25] Once sources are decoupled from norms, it become necessary to address these responsibilities separately. For example, the fact that judges have a stringent duty to address the existence of a statute in their reasoning does not necessarily mean that they have an equally stringent duty to enforce the norms derived from the statute. The duty to discuss the statute may be absolute (and judges who fail to discharge that duty may even be subject to sanction), while the statutory norms themselves may be subject to exception(s) or overridden by considerations of equity.

The point I want to make is that corresponding to the distinction between sources and norms, it pays to introduce a distinction between *use* (of a source) and *enforcement* (of a norm). In other words, it is important to note that judges' responsibilities relative to the use of a source are different from, and do not directly determine, their responsibilities relative to the enforcement of the norms contained in that source. Although one might think that must-sources always yield norms that judges are duty-bound to enforce, and that should- and may-sources yield correspondingly weaker norms, in fact other arrangements are possible. For example, it is conceivable—albeit very unlikely—that the use of a source might be entirely optional but that, once used, it may give rise to a duty that cannot easily be evaded. Think, for instance, of a scholarly treatise that need not be cited but whose prescriptions, once mentioned, are binding on the courts. Moreover, it is also conceivable—and, as we will see, much more likely—that the use of a source might be required, but that the source might yield weak norms that are easily defeated by other considerations. Think, for instance, of a precedent that judges must address but whose *ratio decidendi* they are under no obligation to follow. The existence of the precedent, in this scenario, cannot be ignored, but judges still have ample leeway to depart from what it prescribes. The latter possibility is important to keep in mind as we return to the topic of precedent in section 4.

---

[24] A Peczenik, *Scientia Juris: Legal Doctrine as Knowledge of Law and as a Source of Law* (Springer 2005) 16.

[25] Nor does it address the judges' ability to choose between interpretative methods, but I leave that complication aside for now.

4. Precedent as Source, Precedent as Norm

A. The Interpretation of Precedent

There are many jurisprudential quandaries that would have a better chance of being resolved if the source–norm distinction were given its due.[26] I want to show that the comparative study of precedent would also benefit from attending to the source–norm distinction. When applied to precedent, the distinction serves to emphasize the point that different norms may be derived from a single past judicial opinion (i.e. from the same precedent understood as a source of law), depending on the method of interpretation with which the opinion is approached.

Some authors think it is misleading to speak of the interpretation of precedent. For them, to interpret is to focus on the particular words of a canonical text and therefore it is a notion that applies more appropriately to statutes than to precedents.[27] These authors define interpretation more narrowly than I do. For our purposes, any act of deriving a general norm from a source of law counts as interpretation. On this broad view of interpretation, even unwritten sources like customs can be interpreted. So, precedents are possible objects of interpretation insofar as they may be said to contain general prescriptions whose content can be identified through different methods.

It should also be noted that the general norms that result from the interpretation of precedent need not be understood as 'rules' in the narrow sense of precise and conclusive directives. In this chapter, I assume the validity of the rule-model of precedent only in the broad sense that any approach to precedent counts as a rule-approach if 'it works by first establishing rules (whether they are strict or defeasible) and then uses these rules to determine the decision in the present-case'.[28] Excluded from the purview of this chapter are only those theories that understand precedents as grounds for reasoning processes that entirely dispense with general norms.[29] I take the idea that precedents contain rules (conclusive or defeasible) to be an element of the standard account of precedent—if not among legal philosophers, then among comparatists and jurists more generally. Indeed, this idea is implicit in the conventional view that the binding part of a precedent is its *ratio decidendi*, that is, the principle, rule, or doctrine that grounds the precedent decision.[30]

So, let us assume that precedents can function as sources of general norms. This is not to say, of course, that there will always be consensus about the content of such norms. On the contrary, my aim is to show that there are different ways to interpret a precedent. It may seem quite natural to think that precedent-interpretation requires looking for a norm that was clearly enunciated in the judgment of the precedent court. But there are other possible routes, such as looking for a norm implicitly used by the court as a necessary step in its reasoning or constructing a norm out of the material facts of the case together with the court's decision. The admissibility of these different methods will vary according to legal culture and convention. Take, for instance, the idea that future courts are constrained by

---

[26] I discuss these quandaries in Shecaira (n 19) 22–28.

[27] See, e.g., N Duxbury, *The Nature and Authority of Precedent* (CUP 2008) 59.

[28] K Stevens, 'Reasoning by Precedent—Between Rules and Analogies' (2018) 24 Legal Theory 1, 8.

[29] I am not necessarily excluding analogical theories of precedent, because such theories do not always associate precedents with utterly particularistic, case-by-case reasoning (e.g. Rigoni (n 5) 148). Also included within the purview of my analysis is Lamond's 'reasons account' of precedent (G Lamond, 'Do Precedents Create Rules?' (2005) 11 Legal Theory 1), which may be understood as a defeasible rule-approach (see Stevens (n 28)).

[30] See CW Collier, 'Precedent and Legal Authority: A Critical History' (1988) Wisc L Rev 771, 801–05.

the rule enunciated in the precedent case. This is a form of textualism with respect to judicial opinions that is probably more popular in the US than in England.[31] I will return to this point later, but notice for now how John Gardner (a Scot) describes the practice of precedent in the common law tradition:

> Where legislative law is concerned ... the legislative formulation is canonical. So long as one is applying the legislation one may not abandon the legislative formulation as an object of interpretation ... With case law the reverse is true: the rule that a case stands for is a rule that supports the ruling in the case, and is supported by the rationale in the case, *even if these cannot be reconciled with the judge's attempted formulation of the rule.*[32]

On Gardner's view, a judge may be mistaken about the rule that she created in her own legal opinion. She may give a formulation of the rule that is not compatible with her reasoning and thus is not constraining on future judges. Consider one of Gardner's examples of a simple legal argument that might be made by a judge:

> *Rule:* Any person who calls another person a liar has a duty to pay $50 to that other person.
>   *Fact:* Barnewall (a person) called Adolphus (another person) a liar.
>   *Ruling:* Thus, Barnewall has a duty to pay $50 to Adolphus.[33]

Let us assume that the *Rule* as formulated by the judge is incompatible with the judge's own reasoning in the case of *Barnewall v Adolphus.* Suppose that the judge preceded the formulation of the *Rule* with an argument to the effect that any insult gives rise to a duty to pay $50 because of the damage it may do to the other person's reputation. Given the existence of that argument, it might be said that the rule of *Barnewall v Adolphus* is not the *Rule* formulated by the judge but a significantly broader one, namely, *Rule**: 'Any person who insults another person has a duty to pay $50 to that other person.' Leaving aside the question of what is more common in each legal system, the basic idea is that two readers of *Barnewall v Adolphus* may in principle derive from that case two different norms—*Rule* and *Rule**.

From this it may be taken to follow that a precedent contains not just one rule, but rather different rules depending on the method of interpretation that is employed.[34] Indeed, to the extent that a legal system accepts more than one method for interpreting precedents, it will be quite common for interpreters to diverge about the content of the rule contained in these cases. I would only insist that this view does not have radical implications with respect to judicial discretion. Judges who diverge *in abstracto* about the content of the general norm contained in a past case will often be bound to agree *in concreto* about how the past case bears on the resolution of the instant case.[35] Imagine that I call another person a liar in the jurisdiction where *Barnewall v Adolphus* stands as authority. The difference between *Rule* and *Rule** will be immaterial in my case because they both imply that I should pay $50 to the person whose reputation I have attacked.

---

[31] See PM Tiersma, 'The Textualization of Precedent' (2006) 82 Notre Dame L Rev 1187); Collier (n 30) 814–16.
[32] J Gardner, *Law as a Leap of Faith* (OUP 2012) 79 (my emphasis). Gardner seems to use the word 'rule' loosely as a synonym of 'general norm'.
[33] ibid 76.
[34] For an argument to this effect, see J Stone, 'The *Ratio* of the *Ratio Decidendi*' (1959) 22 MLR 597.
[35] On this point, see R Sartorius, 'The Doctrine of Precedent and the Problem of Relevance' (1967) 53 Archiv für Rechts- und Sozialphilosophie 343, 358.

B. Practices of Precedent

How is any of this relevant to the comparative study of precedent? Let us recall that the source–norm distinction is an abbreviated formulation of the source–interpretation–norm distinction. This threefold distinction helps to reveal an ambiguity that affects many common claims about precedent—our three caveats included. Claims about the weight of precedent or about the degree of rigidity of the doctrine of *stare decisis* often fail to clarify what aspect of precedent is being thematized and where precisely the rigidity (or laxity) lies. Such claims may be understood in at least three ways, each of them focusing on a different element of the source–interpretation–norm distinction. They may be understood as claims concerned:

(1) with the *use of precedent* or, more precisely, with the stringency of the requirement that past cases be addressed in later cases (even if ultimately discarded);

(2) with the *interpretation of precedent* or, more precisely, with the admissibility of different methods of interpretation with which past cases may be approached; or

(3) with the *enforcement of the precedent norm* or, more precisely, with the possibility of departing from, creating exceptions to, or refuting that which the precedent prescribes.

Section 4.C will expand on the meaning of (1), but (2) and (3) deserve immediate clarification. (2) refers to the interpretative aspect of the doctrine of precedent. The doctrine is rigid with respect to (2) when it limits judicial freedom to choose among possible interpretative methods, for example by instructing judges to interpret precedents literally and thus in accordance with the rule enunciated by the court in the earlier case.[36] When judges are not instructed to interpret earlier decisions literally, they may seek to derive the precedent norm by other, more elusive means, such as seeking the 'material' facts of the case or otherwise parsing the text of the judicial opinion into its purportedly essential and non-essential parts. I think it is safe to assume that these subtle techniques of precedent analysis are more apt to create opportunities for the exercise of judicial discretion than the literal application of the rule enunciated by the precedent court (provided, of course, that the court is clear in its presentation of a unanimous, or at least majority, rule *as the rule for which the case officially stands*).[37]

Aspect (3), on the other hand, refers to the forcefulness or decisiveness of the norm that is derived from precedent. Suppose that there is significant agreement among judges about the content of the rule for which a precedent stands. That still says little about the conditions under which that rule may be suspended, overruled, or otherwise deemed inapplicable. Take the following questions as examples. To overrule a precedent, must it be shown that the precedent decision is mistaken as a matter of law, or is it sufficient to show that it is unworkable in the current context? Can a precedent be overruled on the same grounds originally adduced by the defeated party, or must the decision to overrule invoke new arguments? These are not questions about what the earlier decision means but rather about the ability of its prescriptions to constrain.

---

[36] This instruction is rarely absolute; see MA Eisenberg, 'The Principles of Legal Reasoning in the Common Law' in DE Edlin (ed), *Common Law Theory* (CUP 2007) 81, 92.

[37] For development of this idea, see ibid 88–92.

Once these possible understandings of binding precedent are clearly laid out, it becomes easier to perceive and describe certain variations in the doctrine of precedent. I have in mind not only the enduring differences between common and civil law systems but also some significant (and possibly growing) differences within each of these traditions. Let us begin by considering an example of the latter. It is sometimes said that the English doctrine of precedent is more rigid than the US doctrine of precedent because overruling of horizontal precedent is more common in the US than in England, and because judges in lower courts also depart from vertical precedent more often in the former than in the latter.[38] But this is not sufficiently nuanced. The rigidity of one aspect of the English version of *stare decisis* is arguably compensated by a laxity that characterizes a different aspect of the same doctrine. This is how Peter Tiersma makes this point:

> The fact that in England the common law has remained unwritten in a certain sense—that it is something to be extracted from the decisions of judges rather than ascertained by close reading of the text of a judge's opinion—may help explain why it is possible for the courts to believe themselves absolutely bound by their own previous decisions. In such a rigid system there has to be an escape valve. It turns out that English judges and lawyers have several ways to avoid the force of a precedent ... it is always possible to recharacterize the ratio decidendi retrospectively[39]

Another way to formulate Tiersma's point would be to say that the English doctrine of precedent is more rigid than the US doctrine with respect to (3) but not with respect to (2). In other words, English judges are not constrained by the text of past judicial opinions, and thus enjoy a significant amount of discretion at the point of interpretation. On the other hand, when there is consensus about the content of the rule for which precedent stands, that rule cannot be discarded lightly. US judges, in turn, are less free to depart from text but freer to conclude that a text-based precedent rule is defeated by countervailing considerations (hence their stronger disposition to overrule).

So, these two legal systems converge with respect to (1)—past cases must be addressed—and combine it with at least one other feature of binding precedent, pertaining to either (2) or (3). Traditionally, civil law judges are not under any of these obligations, that is, they are not even duty-bound to refer to precedent, much less interpret it strictly and follow it. This leads us to another major theme of this chapter. Some civil law systems have recently adapted their official discourse to embrace the doctrine of *stare decisis*. But what exactly does this mean in the minds of civil law judges? In which aspect(s) of precedent—(1), (2), or (3)—lies the emphasis of the civil law version of *stare decisis*?

C. *Stare Decisis* in Civil Law Systems

The civil law is obviously a large and heterogenous group of legal systems. Focusing on continental Europe (also a diverse group of legal systems), Jan Komárek argues that courts therein often present their holdings in concise, quasi-statutory language. Since the style of reasoning influences the way in which judicial decisions are read by other judges, the

---

[38] See, e.g., Cross and Harris (n 16) 19; Duxbury (n 27) 111.
[39] Tiersma (n 31) 1207.

quasi-statutory language of continental European judges tends to be taken literally.[40] This contrasts with English practice, where judicial opinions are written in a discursive style that is less amenable to textualist interpretation.

If Komárek is right, then it could be argued that some European courts (like US courts) practise a relatively rigid doctrine of precedent with respect to (2), that is, the interpretative aspect. Komárek has less to say about (1) and (3), and I will not speculate about European practice in those respects. Suffice it to discuss some possible scenarios. We have already seen that legal convention may leave relatively little room for choice about interpretative method-ology while granting wider discretion at the point of enforcement of the precedent norms. So, a legal system can be rigid about (2) while remaining lax about (3). On the other hand, it may seem paradoxical for a legal system to be rigid about (2) yet lax about (1). In any case, this is not a possibility that we should simply dismiss. It is at least imaginable that some courts are relieved from any obligation to address past cases at the same time as they are under pressure to abide by the text whenever they do decide to use a past case. The rationale for this practice would be that if a court is going to voluntarily engage in the tricky business of using past cases, then it should at least take their language seriously.

Another scenario worth discussing will draw our attention away from Komárek's analysis of European courts. This is the scenario in which courts are strict about (1) but only about (1). To be strict about (1) could mean a few, subtly different, things. For instance, it could mean that judges must mention past cases but that it suffices to refer to them by name or number. Alternatively, it could mean that judges must state the central facts and/or *rationes decidendi* of past cases—either in their own words or by reference to headnotes. In sum, the required depth of discussion of past cases is something that may vary among legal systems that are strict about (1).

The scenario where courts are only strict about (1) is that in which judges are expected to use past cases that are prima facie applicable—that is, they must relate the cases on which they rely and those from which they depart—but have considerable leeway to interpret those cases as they prefer and to declare that they (i.e. the norms that they contain) are not en-forceable. My impression is that this is all that is meant by 'binding precedent' in some civil law countries. In this scenario, courts take themselves to be bound to note how the present case relates to past cases but not to follow any past case. Again, the latter picture is not what Komárek has in mind, but it is not fanciful or even unlikely. Indeed, I submit that it is a plaus-ible description of current practice in Brazil. But before turning to the Brazilian legal system, it is important to consider a possible objection.

According to Harlan Cohen, '[i]n its weakest form, precedent simply supplies an argu-ment that one must respond to' by explaining why it is 'right, wrong, or distinguishable'.[41] If Cohen is right about this, then the use of past cases that I have in mind is weaker than the weakest conceivable form of precedent-following. If a legal system is strict about (1) but only about (1)—that is, if it requires judges to refer to past cases but allows them to inter-pret cases freely and to depart from them without justification—then it can be argued that this legal system does not adopt *stare decisis*, not even in its weakest possible version. I have no counter-argument to give. Although the notion of *stare decisis* is quite elastic, it is true that there must be some limit beyond which it cannot be stretched—and perhaps Cohen has

---

[40] See Jan Komárek, 'Reasoning with Previous Decisions: Beyond the Doctrine of Precedent' (2013) 61 Am J Comp L 149, 155.

[41] H Grant Cohen, 'Theorizing Precedent in International Law' in A Bianchi and others (eds), *Interpretation in International Law* (OUP 2015) 268, 275.

identified that limit. In any case, it is still noteworthy that some legal systems may purport to practise *stare decisis* while proceeding as I have suggested that they do, that is, by being strict only about (1). To understand the distinctive role that these legal systems assign to precedent, we ought to attend to what *they* mean by *stare decisis*.

The Brazilian legal system is an interesting case because the notion of binding precedent has only recently gained currency within the discourse of Brazilian jurists. This process began several decades ago but gained momentum with the advent of the new Code of Civil Procedure in 2015. Indeed, the Code seems to affirm the binding character of the decisions of high-level courts, apparently at both vertical and horizontal levels.[42] This has led some Brazilian jurists to conclude that *stare decisis* had finally come to Brazil.[43] The practice of the Brazilian courts, however, is more ambiguous than the text of the Code may suggest. Let us focus here on the country's most influential court, namely, the Supreme Federal Tribunal (or STF, the acronym current among Brazilians).

The first thing to note is that the court refers to its own precedents quite frequently.[44] Apart from numbers, the court has often affirmed that its precedents should not be taken lightly. At the same time, the justices handle past decisions in a surprisingly casual way. For the most part, past cases are not discussed in any detail. Justices often cite the headnotes of past cases and omit to give information about the underlying facts. Indeed, they rely on headnotes even though these are notoriously unreliable summaries of the court's reasoning.[45] When justices do cite from the body of past opinions, they do so with little regard for the distinction between *ratio* and *dictum*, often taking sentences out of context and sometimes invoking the same case in support of opposing conclusions.[46]

It is possible that the STF is going through a transitional period at the end of which it may come to adopt a version of *stare decisis* that will not be so different from the versions accepted in the US or England. But this is not how things currently stand. It could be argued that the frequent citations to precedent by STF justices are nothing but a show of faux concern for the ideals of judicial consistency and collegiality. The analysis I have been suggesting here is not so cynical. My hypothesis is that STF justices do accept an important responsibility regarding precedent, namely, to explain how their current decision relates to past cases. There is a burden of explanation to be discharged here, albeit a relatively light one. The burden does not go so far as to demand justification for departures from precedent, but it does require that departures be acknowledged.[47] It is important to insist that this is not a trivial requirement from the perspective of a civil law system, even if it seems weak from the Anglo-American point of view. If a decision that fails to explain its relation to existing case law is deemed faulty, then gone is the traditional idea that precedents need not be considered in

---

[42] See arts 489 (§1, IV and V), 926, and 927.

[43] See, e.g., D Mitidiero, 'Precedentes Jurisprudência e Súmulas no Novo Código de Processo Civil Brasileiro' (2015) 245 Revista de Processo 333; H Zaneti, Jr, 'Precedentes Normativos Formalmente Vinculantes: A Formalização das Fontes Judiciais' (2015) 1 Cuadernos Juridicos Ius Trib 31. Of course, I do not assume that the question of whether *stare decisis* has been introduced in Brazil rests solely on the correct interpretation of the Code. The actual practice of the courts is a crucial factor.

[44] In 2017, past cases were cited in roughly three out of four decisions of the court. See F Leal and others, *IX Relatório Supremo em Números: A Justificação de Decisões no Supremo* (FGV Direito Rio 2020) 84–88.

[45] See C Cutrupi Ferreira and others, 'Construção de Ementas das Decisões do Supremo Tribunal Federal' (2015) FGV Direito São Paulo Research Paper Series No 125.

[46] See F Leal, 'Força Autoritativa, Influência Persuasiva ou Qualquer Coisa: O Que É um Precedente para o Supremo Tribunal Federal?' (2020) 7 Revista de Investigações Constitucionais 205, 222.

[47] Justification is indeed required by art 489 of the Code of Civil Procedure; but here I am discussing the practice of the court, not the Code.

judicial opinions. Gone also is the idea that legislation is a self-sufficient source of law, that is, one that can be interpreted and applied without reference to precedent.

5. Conclusion

This chapter has mobilized a particular set of jurisprudential insights in the service of comparative law. The source–norm distinction has been used to explain versions of the doctrine of precedent whose particularities have often gone unnoticed. This applies not only to legal systems undergoing transitions on which international commentary is scarce—for example, the Brazilian legal system—but also to legal systems whose doctrine of precedent is supposedly well established and well understood—such as those of the US and England. The doctrine of precedent is varied and changeable. To explain this variety and changeability, comparative lawyers need a conceptual framework that is more subtle than the one that has been developed thus far (considering the three caveats). The subtlety that is lacking is precisely that which the source–norm distinction helps to introduce.

25

Precedent as Generalized Second-Order Reasons

Stephen Perry[*]

1. Introduction

Joseph Raz has offered by far the most plausible theoretical account of legal positivism, and in doing so he makes a powerful argument for positivism's jurisprudential claims. The core of his account is the proposition that the existence and content of every valid law is fully determined by social facts, such as facts about the actions of courts, legislatures, and other legal actors, without resort to moral argument.[1] Raz defends this proposition, which he calls the 'sources thesis', by arguing that law can only guide persons' conduct if it is publicly ascertainable by, and accessible to, all of a society's members. This would not be possible, he argues, if laws could in general be identified only by engaging in moral argument. Raz further holds that adherence to the sources thesis not only contributes to the public ascertainability and accessibility of law but also makes it possible for the law to hold all persons to be bound by legal standards without any of them being able to question the validity of a particular standard by challenging its moral justification.

Raz maintains that the sources thesis applies to all forms of law, including both laws enacted by legislatures and judge-made law. In this chapter, I shall argue that he is mistaken about judge-made law in common law jurisdictions, at least with respect to the manner in which such law binds the courts themselves. The sources thesis, Raz argues, requires that common law courts draw a hard-and-fast distinction between what he calls regulated cases (or disputes) and unregulated cases. Regulated cases fall under valid legal rules. Common law rules are, on Raz's view, valid legal rules just as much as rules laid down in statues are, and as such their existence and content can be determined by reference to social sources alone.[2] The relevant social sources in the case of common law rules are the various judicial activities that are associated with the doctrine of precedent. Unregulated cases, by contrast, are not governed by a valid legal rule, and as such they fall to be decided by the judicial exercise of discretion. Raz argues that, in exercising discretion, courts do and should draw upon extra-legal and non-source-based considerations, including in particular moral considerations such as values, rights, and principles. Once such discretion has been exercised and the doctrine of precedent has operated so as to give rise to a new legal rule, a court is obligated, according to Raz, to decide future cases that fall under the new rule on the basis of the rule

---

[*] I would like to thank Sebastian Lewis for very helpful comments on an earlier draft.

[1] J Raz, *The Authority of Law* (2nd edn, OUP 2009) ch III, especially 45–52. See also J Raz, 'Authority, Law and Morality' (1985) The Monist 285.

[2] Raz's most important discussion of precedent, and of judicial reasoning more generally, can be found in Raz, *The Authority of Law* (n 1) ch X.

Stephen Perry, *Precedent as Generalized Second-Order Reasons* In: *Philosophical Foundations of Precedent*. Edited by: Timothy Endicott, Hafsteinn Dan Kristjánsson, and Sebastian Lewis, Oxford University Press. © Stephen Perry 2023.
DOI: 10.1093/oso/9780192857248.003.0026

alone and thus without recourse to moral considerations, including those that led the court to formulate the rule in the first place. I shall argue that, contrary to Raz's view, common law courts do not draw such a hard-and-fast distinction between regulated and unregulated cases and that the doctrine of precedent both can and should be explained in a way that does not depend on the sources thesis. The result will be a theory of adjudication and judicial reasoning that is non-positivist in nature.

One element of Raz's account of common law precedent is a distinction that he draws, within his more general theory of practical reason, between first- and second-order reasons for action. Although Raz's introduction of this distinction is an innovation of the first importance for both jurisprudence and the philosophy of practical reason more generally, his characterization of second-order reasons is, at least in a formal sense, too narrow. Raz holds that a second-order reason is a reason to act upon or to refrain from acting upon a first-order reason. I shall argue instead that a second-order reason is a reason to treat a first-order reason as having a weight that differs from the weight it is ordinarily thought to possess. In other words, Raz's notion of a second-order reason can and should be *generalized*, and once that has been done it becomes clear that a second-order reason in Raz's sense is simply a special case of the more general concept. As I shall argue, this has important ramifications for the theoretical understanding of judicial reasoning in general and the doctrine of precedent in particular. The generalized notion of a second-order reason is, as we shall see, the basis of an account of precedent that is both empirically and theoretically superior to Raz's account. While the account I defend rejects any significant role for the sources thesis in a theory of judicial reasoning, I do not argue that the thesis has no role to play at all in the philosophy of law. Raz may well be correct, for example, that only source-based law can provide appropriate guidance for citizens. My arguments in this chapter are limited to the practical reasoning of courts.

2. Raz on Practical Reason

Before considering how the generalization of second-order reasons bears on judicial lawmaking and the common law doctrine of precedent, it will be helpful to discuss a few details of Raz's work on the general philosophy and logic of practical reason.[3] As already noted, he draws a distinction between first- and second-order reasons, which respectively correspond to two different modes of reasoning about what ought to be done. The first mode, which involves consideration of and action upon what Raz calls the 'balance of reasons', presupposes both that all the relevant reasons which bear on whether or not one ought to perform some action have a certain weight or strength and that, generally speaking, such reasons are at least roughly commensurable.[4] The reasons that figure in the balance of reasons can be called first-order reasons. A rational agent who is deliberating in accordance with this mode of practical reasoning first determines the aggregate weight of the various first-order reasons that favour or disfavour each possible course of action, and then decides to take that action which has the greatest overall support. For example, one might decide whether or not to carry an umbrella on a given day by weighing the chance of rain that day against the inconvenience of having to tote an umbrella around. The essential idea bears some resemblance to,

---

[3] See generally J Raz, *Practical Reason and Norms* (2nd edn, OUP 1999) 15–84; Raz, *The Authority of Law* (n 1) 16–25, 37–52.

[4] Raz, *Practical Reason and Norms* (n 3) 25–33.

though it is by no means identical with, the economic notion of always acting so as to maximize one's expected utility.

The second mode of practical reasoning that Raz distinguishes concerns acting on second-order reasons. Raz defines a second-order reason as a reason to act on or refrain from acting on a reason. In law, the most important category of second-order reasons is that of 'exclusionary reasons'.[5] An exclusionary reason is a second-order reason to refrain from acting on a reason, or on some specified category of reasons. For present purposes, we can assume that the reasons excluded by an exclusionary reason are always first-order reasons. An exclusionary reason can be a reason to refrain from acting on the balance of most, or even all,[6] of the relevant first-order reasons. If an exclusionary reason is general, in the sense that it applies not just to a one-off situation but across a specified range of situations, and if it is also itself a first-order reason to perform (or refrain from performing) a certain kind of action in those situations, then it is an exclusionary rule. (Raz calls exclusionary reasons that are also first-order reasons 'protected reasons'.[7]) If an agent begins consistently to act on the basis of an exclusionary reason across a range of situations, then he or she has, in those situations, replaced acting on the balance of ordinary first-order reasons with acting on an exclusionary rule. The rule stands in for the excluded first-order reasons, so that it would be a mistake to think that the agent has simply added a second-order reason to the balance of first-order reasons. Raz recognizes that an exclusionary rule can have a dimension of scope, which simply means that the rule might not exclude every relevant first-order reason. Thus, an exclusionary rule need not be absolutely exclusionary.[8]

Raz illustrates the difference between acting on the balance of reasons and following an exclusionary rule by discussing rules of thumb that one might adopt in one's personal life, such as a rule not to make a major investment decision when one is tired, under pressure or, more generally, in a condition of impaired rationality.[9] Adherence to this rule might sometimes mean forgoing an investment possibility entirely, and thus effectively amount to a decision on the substantive question of whether or not to invest at all in, say, corporation X. The decision would not have been taken on the balance of reasons, and it might be the case that, according to the balance of reasons, one ought to have made the investment. It may also be the case that, had the investment been made, it would have been a profitable one. The decision not to invest might nonetheless be justifiable, that is, rational, if the person would be better off in the long run by always following the rule. Note that the idea of being better off in the long run implies that the *generality* of an exclusionary rule, as discussed in the preceding paragraph, is critical in explaining why it can sometimes be rational, across a specified range of situations and over time, to follow such a rule instead of always acting on—or at least attempting to act on—the balance of reasons in each relevant situation as it arises.

Raz argues persuasively that personal rules of thumb can sometimes be justified on efficiency grounds. Calculating the balance of reasons involves costs, in the form of time and effort consumed, and one might well be better off in the long run if one avoids incurring these costs by adhering, within a specified type of situation, to a preconceived plan of action. For

---

[5] ibid 35–39; Raz, *The Authority of Law* (n 1) 16–18. Sometimes Raz calls exclusionary reasons 'preemptive reasons.' See, e.g., J Raz, *The Morality of Freedom* (OUP 1986) 60.

[6] By this, I mean it can exclude all 'regular' first-order reasons, meaning all such reasons apart from the exclusionary reason itself. Raz holds that an exclusionary reason can sometimes also be a first-order reason. As noted in the text, he calls such hybrid reasons 'protected' reasons.

[7] Raz, *The Authority of Law* (n 1) 17–25.

[8] ibid 22; Raz, *Practical Reasons and Norms* (n 3) 46–47.

[9] ibid 59–65.

example, an exclusionary rule never to check the accuracy of a bill that is presented to one in a restaurant might be justified as rational if any potential monetary savings would not, in the long run, outweigh the costs of time and effort required to make such a calculation on every occasion that one dines out. Raz's notion of 'scope' could be introduced here by supposing that a person who adopted this rule might also decide, in advance, that it excludes only monetary (or, more generally, economic) considerations and not reasons having to do with personal or social relations. So, for example, if the diner learns that the waiter would be offended, because of a local custom, if the diner did not check the bill, then he or she will do so, or at least will not feel bound by the rule not to do so.

Raz further argues that the distinction between acting on the balance of reasons and acting on an exclusionary rule can clarify, and perhaps resolve, important and long-standing questions in moral and political philosophy. For example, he argues that it is at least sometimes justified, both rationally and morally, for an individual to treat the directives of a de facto political authority as exclusionary rules—and thus as giving rise to an obligation to obey those directives—rather than attempt to work out for themselves, on the basis of the balance of reasons, what they ought to do on each and every relevant occasion.[10] If Raz is correct about this, then he has shown both that it is possible for a de facto political authority to be, at least sometimes, morally legitimate and, relatedly, that a certain brand of philosophical anarchism is mistaken. Even if he is not correct, his arguments in support of these conclusions have been highly influential and have sparked extensive further debate about the nature of political authority.

3. Practical Reason and Precedent

As the discussion in section 2 showed, Raz's distinction between acting on the balance of reasons and acting on the basis of an exclusionary reason is a powerful normative and conceptual tool in the analysis of practical reason.[11] It is important to note, however, that the distinction is not always exhaustive of the possible modes of practical reasoning that may be available to an agent. To see why this is so, it will be helpful to concentrate on the particular practical phenomenon that is of immediate concern, namely, the common law doctrine of precedent. Assume for the moment that we are concerned only with the decision-making process of a jurisdiction's highest court of appeal. In what ways could a previous decision of that court figure in a later decision such that the court could be said to be 'following precedent'? One possibility is that the *ratio decidendi* of the prior case gives rise to—or better, just *is*—an exclusionary rule in the sense discussed earlier. This is Raz's own positivistic interpretation of common law precedent. A second possibility would regard the court as bound by one of its previous decisions, itself decided on the basis of the balance of reasons, only until such time as it was convinced both that the balance of reasons had been wrongly assessed on the prior occasion and that the correct assessment leads to a different result. The court could not depart from its previous decision unless it had a reason for doing so, but that reason could be as simple as a different understanding of the ordinary balance of reasons.

---

[10] J Raz, *The Morality of Freedom* (n 5) 23–105.

[11] In this and the following two sections, I draw on previous work. See SR Perry, 'Judicial Obligation, Precedent and the Common Law' (1987) 7 OJLS 215; SR Perry, 'Second-Order Reasons, Uncertainty and Legal Theory' (1989) 62 So Cal L Rev 913; SR Perry, 'Two Models of Legal Principles' (1997) 82 Iowa L Rev 787.

On this second understanding of precedent, which in prior work I have called the 'weak Burkean conception',[12] it takes very little to overcome the binding force of the earlier case. Despite this evident lack of strength, the weak Burkean conception *is* a form of following precedent, since it is distinguishable from a system of adjudication based on the exercise of absolute discretion in every case. I have in mind here a system of absolute discretion of the sort Raz has described.[13] In such a system, a court is not obligated to take into account either the reasoning or the result of an earlier case. It need not even acknowledge the existence of prior cases. By contrast, the weak Burkean conception obligates a court to consider the reasoning of a relevantly similar prior case and to reach the same result unless it can formulate an assessment of the balance of reasons that points to a different result. It is true that the results reached under a weak Burkean conception and those reached under a system of absolute discretion might, as a practical matter, often converge. The difference between the two is, at least in part, one of process; a weak Burkean court is obligated to consider the reasoning of an earlier, relevantly similar case, whereas a court of absolute discretion is not.

The two conceptions of precedent just described correspond, in a fairly straightforward way, to the two modes of practical reasoning distinguished by Raz. The first conception regards precedents as giving rise to exclusionary rules, and the second regards them as giving rise to a certain kind of weak constraint on departing from past decisions that is at the same time consistent with a case-by-case consideration of the balance of reasons. There is a third conception of precedent, however, which corresponds to a mode of practical reasoning that Raz does not discuss. Consider a court which does not look upon its previous decisions as precluding it from taking account, in a later case, of any particular reason or set of reasons, as happens on the model of exclusionary rules, but which nonetheless will not depart from the *ratio* of a relevant earlier case unless it is satisfied that the aggregate weight of the reasons supporting a different result is of greater strength, to some specified degree, than what would generally be required to reach that result on the ordinary balance of reasons. The intuitive idea is that a court is bound by a previous decision unless it is convinced that there is a *strong* reason for holding otherwise. This conception of precedent, which I call the 'strong Burkean conception',[14] differs from the weak Burkean model in that one needs more than just a reason to overcome the binding force of a precedent, but at the same time it differs from the exclusionary model in that no relevant first-order reasons are excluded from consideration as a matter of course.

The mode of practical reason underlying the strong Burkean conception of precedent might be characterized as action in accordance with a *weighted* balance of reasons. One would be acting on this basis if one were to accept a second-order reason to assign one or more first-order reasons a greater or lesser weight than they would otherwise receive in an assessment of the ordinary balance of reasons. As was noted in section 2, Raz defines a second-order reason as a reason to act on or refrain from acting on a first-order reason but, I wish to suggest, that is too narrow. A second-order reason is better understood as a reason for treating a first-order reason as having a greater or lesser weight than it would ordinarily receive, so that an exclusionary reason is—or at least is extensionally equivalent to—the special case where one or more first-order reasons are treated as having zero weight. This conception of a second-order reason is, in effect, a generalization of Raz's conception. The two modes of practical reason that Raz distinguishes—viz acting on the balance of reasons

---

[12] Perry, 'Judicial Obligation' (n 11) 221–23.
[13] Raz, *Practical Reason and Norms* (n 3) 138.
[14] Perry, 'Judicial Obligation' (n 11) 221–23, 239–43.

340 STEPHEN PERRY

and acting on an exclusionary rule—can be thought of as points on a continuum. At one end, action is to be assessed on the basis of a balance of reasons in which no reason has been assigned anything other than its ordinary weight, while, near the other end, action is to be assessed on a balance of reasons where most first-order reasons have been assigned, on the basis of one or more second-order reasons, a non-ordinary weight of zero.[15] Between these two points lies an indefinitely large number of further possibilities, all of which are variations on the idea of a weighted balance of reasons.

Perhaps a second-order reason, as defined here, is a kind of function, in the mathematical sense, which takes first-order reasons as arguments. Whether that is true in a strict or formal way, this understanding of a second-order reason is, in at least one respect, more elegant than Raz's understanding. On Raz's account, an exclusionary rule is a second-order exclusionary reason which is also a first-order reason. Raz calls such hybrid reasons 'protected reasons'. [16] In contrast, the understanding of a second-order reason offered here does not require hybrid reasons. Second-order reasons have a systematic effect on the balance of first-order reasons without themselves being first-order reasons. It should be noted that reliance on a second-order weighting reason does not mean that the first-order reason (or set of such reasons) that is being 'assigned' a different weight actually *has* that different weight. Rather, the idea is that, under specified circumstances, one is to act *as if* that first-order reason (or set of such reasons) has a different weight, but only under the specified circumstances and not as a more general matter. The mode of acting on a weighted balance of reasons does not therefore simply collapse into the mode of acting on the ordinary balance of reasons.

Presumptions, as these arise in both law and ordinary life, are often second-order weighting principles of the kind just described.[17] The presumption of innocence in criminal law, which underlies the standard of proof beyond a reasonable doubt, is best understood in this way.[18] So is the presumption of death after seven years. Rebuttable presumptions usually require that the aggregate weight of reasons supporting a contrary result be of greater weight than would otherwise be required. (I say 'usually' because a rebuttable presumption might simply shift the burden of proof.) Irrebuttable presumptions assign zero weight to all reasons supporting a contrary result. Something similar to a presumption, understood as a second-order weighting reason, is at work in the many areas of law which require that a court not set aside a reviewable decision by another court (or by a tribunal, agency, or jury) if the decision of the latter was reasonable, and this is so even if the court believes that the decision being reviewed was wrong on the merits.[19] Once you begin to look for them, second-order weighting principles can be found in many places in the law.

4. Dworkin on Precedent

The conception of precedent that is suggested by Ronald Dworkin in his article 'The Model of Rules I' [20] must be understood, as I have argued

---

[15] Strictly speaking, the end of the continuum is a situation in which *all* first-order reasons have been assigned a non-ordinary weight of zero. That would seem, however, to be just a formal possibility.

[16] Raz, *The Authority of Law* (n 1) 17–18.

[17] See Perry, 'Second-Order Reasons' (n 11) 926, 933.

[18] It is important to remember that while reasons for belief and reasons for action are related to one another, they are not the same thing. The fact-finder in a criminal trial might have more than enough reason to believe that the accused committed the crime, but still not have sufficient reason to find the person guilty.

[19] See Perry, 'Second-Order Reasons' (n 11) 936–41.

[20] R Dworkin, 'The Model of Rules I' in R Dworkin, *Taking Rights Seriously* (2nd edn, Harvard UP 1978) 14.

before,[21] as a strong Burkean conception. In that article, Dworkin draws a logical distinction between rules and principles. A rule, which he describes as operating in an all-or-nothing fashion, gives rise to an obligation to perform (or refrain from performing) a specified action whenever the rule's conditions of application have been met, an account of rules that is, with regard to its logical character, similar in important respects to Raz's exclusionary account. A Dworkinian principle differs from a Dworkinian rule in that a principle favours one course of action over others but does not, by itself, require that that course of action be followed. It possesses, rather, a dimension of weight or importance, which is to be factored into the determination of what ought to be done whenever the relevant principles do not all point to the same result. Here, again, we find a similarity to Raz's account of practical reason, since weighing up and then acting on Dworkinian principles bears a clear resemblance, logically speaking, to Raz's notion of acting on the balance of reasons. For Dworkin, principles are, so far as content is concerned, reasons for action that are drawn primarily from morality, especially political morality.[22] Raz's understanding of the content of first-order reasons, as these figure in legal adjudication, is more complicated,[23] but what matters for present purposes are the logical similarities between his and Dworkin's accounts.

Dworkin argues that in law not only are there rules that are legally binding on judges but principles as well, meaning there are *moral* principles that courts are *legally* obligated to take into account when making their decisions.[24] He gives the example of the common law maxim, 'No one should profit from their own wrong.'[25] This is a legal principle, on Dworkin's view, and it can be recognized as such because, while it is evidently not an all-or-nothing rule, courts are nonetheless legally obligated to take it into consideration when deciding cases with facts to which it is relevant. They do so, according to Dworkin, by balancing the maxim's weight or importance against the weight of other legal principles that are also relevant on the facts. In weighing such principles against one another, a court is engaged in assessing the balance of reasons, in Raz's sense of that notion. A principle such as, 'No one should profit from their own wrong' is also clearly a first-order reason, again in Raz's sense. Since principles like this always point directly to a particular legal result—in the case of the principle under discussion, to a result in which a wrongdoer who has profited from his or her wrongdoing loses in court—they can be characterized as 'content-laden'.

Dworkin argues that, among the principles that courts are legally obligated to take into consideration, are a number that 'reflect ... the equities and efficiencies of consistency ... [and that] incline toward the status quo'.[26] This cluster of 'conservative' principles, as Dworkin calls them, is the foundation of his conception of precedent. The doctrine of precedent is not an all-or-nothing rule, in Dworkin's view, but rather a set of principles that judges must weigh into the general balance of principles when deciding cases at law. There is a puzzle here, however. 'Conservative principles' of the kind Dworkin envisages cannot be, logically speaking, ordinary first-order reasons, nor can they be content-laden reasons, in the sense of that term discussed earlier. This is because the doctrine of precedent cannot, on any plausible view, have independent, substantive content at the first-order level; the result

---

[21] Perry, 'Judicial Obligation' (n 11) 223–26.

[22] Dworkin, 'Model of Rules' (n 20) 41.

[23] See J Raz, 'Legal Principles and the Limits of Law' (1972) 81 Yale LJ 823.

[24] Dworkin, 'Model of Rules' (n 20) 40. For discussion of Dworkin's characterization of a legal principle, see Perry, 'Legal Principles' (n 11) 807–15. As is noted later in the text, Dworkin adopted, later in his career, a different understanding of legal principles.

[25] Dworkin, 'Model of Rules' (n 20) 23–25.

[26] ibid 37–38.

to which it points in any given case varies with the prior course of institutional history. The doctrine does not, in other words, invariably pull towards a particular result regardless of context; rather, it affects the balance of principles in a way that varies with what has been decided by courts in the past. To borrow a term from a different (but related) discussion in jurisprudence, the doctrine of precedent gives rise to content-independent reasons.[27] So, the puzzle is this: how can principles that are ordinary, content-laden, first-order reasons be weighed against principles that are none of these things?

The solution to this puzzle begins with the observation that a satisfactory explanation of the common law doctrine of precedent requires second-order as well as first-order reasons. I shall argue in section 5 that Raz's understanding of second-order reasons as reasons to act on or refrain from acting on first-order reasons does not provide an adequate account of the doctrine. What is required instead is the understanding of second-order reasons that is associated with the strong Burkean conception of precedent discussed in section 3. According to that understanding, a second-order reason is a reason to assign one or more first-order reasons a greater or lesser weight than it would otherwise receive in an assessment of the ordinary balance of reasons. So far as Dworkin's account of precedent is concerned, it is reasonable to regard it as theoretically sound, even though Dworkin does not explicitly distinguish between first- and second-order reasons. The principles that comprise his conception of precedent are best understood as second-order reasons for judicial action which direct that, when there exists an applicable precedent, the relevant substantive first-order principles must meet a higher threshold of aggregate weight to justify a contrary result than would have been required to reach that result in a case of first instance. This is precisely the strong Burkean conception of precedent. The puzzle posed in the preceding paragraph asks how principles that are ordinary, content-laden, first-order reasons can be weighed against principles that are none of these things. The answer given by the strong Burkean conception of precedent is that, strictly speaking, they cannot be weighed against one another. This is because, as was noted in section 3, second-order reasons of the strong Burkean sort have a systematic effect on the balance of first-order reasons without themselves being first-order reasons.

It is worth remarking that Dworkin's theory of judicial reasoning, understood as involving a weighted balance of principles in the strong Burkean sense, is not limited, in the 'The Model of Rules I', to cases at common law. Dworkin seems at times in the article to maintain that the balancing of principles is a source of judicial obligation *in addition to* that imposed by rules, but the theory can be seen, when properly understood, to be much more radical than this would suggest. Dworkin argues that the bindingness of a legal rule is nothing more than the collective normative weight of the principles that, taken together, justify the result expressed by the rule; when that support is considered to have evaporated, or never to have existed at all, then the rule no longer binds courts.[28] It would seem to follow that all-or-nothing, exclusionary-type rules in fact have no place in the theory of judicial reasoning that Dworkin advances here, appearances to the contrary notwithstanding.[29] The nature of judicial obligation is completely determined by a duty to act on the balance of first-order

---

[27] For a recent discussion of content-independent reasons in law, see NP Adams, 'In Defense of Content-Independence' (2017) 23 Legal Theory 143.

[28] Dworkin, 'Model of Rules' (n 20) 37–38, 44.

[29] See Perry, 'Judicial Obligation' (n 11) 224–25. A similar observation is made by T Endicott, 'Are There Any Rules?' (2001) 5 J Ethics 199 200–01. The point has recently been discussed in detail by M Berman, 'Dworkin versus Hart Revisited: The Challenge of Non-Lexical Determination' (2022) 42 OJLS 548. In that article, Berman develops a sophisticated new model of legal rules and principles and of the relationship between them.

principles, as modified by second-order weighting principles of the strong Burkean sort. Even statute law is apparently not considered to be obligatory in itself. Whatever binding force a legislative enactment possesses that is not attributable to its content, derives from certain conservative principles of 'legislative supremacy', which require no more than that the courts 'pay a qualified deference to the acts of the legislature'.[30] These principles of qualified deference to legislatures are best understood as second-order weighting principles of the same general sort as those that constitute, on the reading of 'The Model of Rules I' that I have offered, the doctrine of precedent.

Dworkin did not carry forward the understanding of judicial reasoning and precedent that he developed in 'The Model of Rules I' into his later work. In *Law's Empire*, he comes close to reversing the roles of rules and principles in both judicial reasoning and law generally. In 'The Model of Rules I', principles are foundational; legal rules derive from, and depend for their existence upon, underlying principles. In *Law's Empire*, by contrast, the starting point of analysis is 'legal practice as a whole' (approximately, existing legal rules plus facts about the nature and history of legal institutions).[31] Judges and legal theorists are meant to seek principles that best justify legal practice as a whole, which means showing the practice in its best moral light. Crudely put, in 'The Model of Rules I' principles have priority over rules, whereas in *Law's Empire* rules, as one element of legal practice taken as a whole, have priority over principles. Elsewhere, I have discussed at length the two quite different concepts of legal principles that emerge, respectively, from the theory of law Dworkin developed early in his career and the theory he developed later on.[32]

5. Precedent and Legal Theory

As was noted in section 1, Raz's positivist account of judicial reasoning and precedent requires a hard-and-fast distinction between regulated and unregulated cases, where regulated cases fall under a valid legal rule and unregulated cases do not. We are now in a position to see that, for Raz, the doctrine of precedent gives rise to valid legal rules, that valid legal rules are exclusionary rules, and that the sources thesis takes effect through these rules' exclusionary character. When a court applies a valid legal rule, it is precluded from taking moral considerations into account, including those moral considerations that presumably provided the rule's original justification.[33] In earlier work, I argued that a strong Burkean conception of precedent better captures the nature of the common law doctrine of precedent than does Raz's conception.[34] For present purposes, I will offer a few illustrative observations about overruling and then turn to a discussion of the common law practice of distinguishing a prior case.

According to Raz, the constraint that the highest court in England recognizes on overruling one of its own prior decisions is both consistent with, and requires, an exclusionary understanding of judge-made law.[35] The court may not, he says, modify the law to such an extent that a previous case would now be decided differently except on the basis of certain *sorts* of reasons, meaning reasons that fall outside the scope of an exclusionary

---

[30] Dworkin, 'Model of Rules' (n 20) 37–38.
[31] R Dworkin, *Law's Empire* (Belknap Press 1986) 90.
[32] Perry, 'Legal Principles' (n 11) especially 807–15.
[33] Raz, *The Authority of Law* (n 1) 37–52, 180–209.
[34] Perry, 'Judicial Obligation' (n 11) 234–48.
[35] Raz, *The Authority of Law* (n 1) 189–93.

reason. As was noted in section 2, Raz acknowledges that an exclusionary rule need not be absolutely exclusionary, since it might not exclude certain reasons that are properly regarded as falling outside the rule's scope. He accordingly argues that there is a 'permissible list' of non-excluded reasons for overruling a previous decision that includes—but is apparently not exhausted by— 'injustice, iniquitous discrimination, and being out of step with the court's conception of the relevant area of law'.[36] Quite apart from the fact that this list is stated at such a general level that it seems to capture many, if not most, of the reasons that a court would ever be likely to have for overruling a previous decision, so that an exclusionary prohibition would be left with little work to do and one would be led to expect overruling to occur more frequently than it does, common law courts do not appear to have even an implicitly limited category of non-excluded reasons in mind when they consider overruling an earlier case.

Judges in England's highest court thus tend to speak of the necessity for 'a very good reason' to overrule rather than for a reason of one or another sort.[37] That same court, like the highest courts in other common law jurisdictions, also emphasizes that it will not ordinarily consider overruling a prior case simply because it has come to think that the earlier case was wrongly decided; the prior decision must not only have been wrong but 'clearly wrong'.[38] What seems to be called for, then, is an account of precedent that does not treat prior decisions as giving rise to exclusionary rules, but that also does not permit a prior decision to be reversed simply because the present court holds a different view of the ordinary balance of reasons than did the earlier court. A middle course along just these lines is offered by the strong Burkean conception of precedent, which requires decisions about overruling to be made on the basis of a weighted balance of reasons rather than by seeking a reason that falls outside the scope of an exclusionary rule. The actual practice of overruling in common law courts is, I suggest, much closer to the strong Burkean model than it is to Raz's exclusionary account since the courts tend to ask whether the aggregate strength of *all* relevant reasons exceeds a certain threshold rather than asking whether there exists a reason within a distinct and limited category of supposedly non-excluded reasons.

The *ratio* of a case is to be regarded, on the strong Burkean conception, not as an exclusionary rule—or as an all-or-nothing rule in Dworkin's sense—but rather as a summary proposition of how the balance of the various reasons that figure in the court's judgment—in American terminology, in its opinion—both justifies the result in the instant case and would justify a similar result in cases that are, according to the court's reasoning, relevantly similar on their facts to the instant case. This understanding is consistent with Brian Simpson's observation that cases (and their associated *rationes*) are rarely said by judges to possess validity, which is a key all-or-nothing concept in legal-positivist thought, but are often said by judges to possess authority.[39] Authority, at least in this context, is not an all-or-nothing matter. A case can come to possess greater or lesser authority over time as later courts, in accordance with the strong Burkean conception, reassess the weight of the earlier court's reasoning and thus reassess the weight of the case's *ratio*. Even a case decided by a lower court can come to have sufficient authority that the jurisdiction's highest court will not consider overturning it.

---

[36] Raz, *Practical Reason and Norms* (n 3) 140; see also Raz, *The Authority of Law* (n 1) 114.

[37] *Knuller Ltd v DPP* [1973] AC 435, 455.

[38] *Fitzleet Estates Ltd v Cherry* [1977] All ER 996, 1000; *O'Brien v Robinson* [1973] AC 912, 930; *Jones v Secretary of State for Social Services* [1972] AC 944, 993.

[39] AWB Simpson, 'The Common Law and Legal Theory' in AWB Simpson (ed), *Oxford Essays in Jurisprudence, Second Series* (OUP 1973) 77, 86.

The strong Burkean conception of precedent is of a piece with a more general account of common law reasoning, which holds that even lower courts remain more closely in touch, so to speak, with the weighted balance of justificatory reasons than would be suggested by the exclusionary account. This emerges from an analysis not only of overruling but also of the judicial practice of distinguishing a prior case. In earlier work, I suggested that the *ratio* of a case decided by a higher court is exclusionarily binding on courts lower in the judicial hierarchy,[40] but in making that suggestion I did not pay sufficient attention to the nuances of the practice of distinguishing. Grant Lamond[41] and, more recently, John Goldberg and Benjamin Zipursky,[42] have offered powerful arguments in favour of the conclusion that distinguishing cannot readily be explained by an account of judicial reasoning based on rules. Their arguments cohere with, but are independent of, those I have offered for the strong Burkean conception of precedent. Lamond's and Goldberg and Zipursky's arguments regarding distinguishing, together with the arguments I have made in support of the strong Burkean conception, make a strong case for a non-positivist account of common law judicial reasoning.[43]

An earlier case may be distinguished not only by a court of the same or a higher level as the court that decided the earlier case, but also by a court lower in the judicial hierarchy. When a court distinguishes an earlier case, it holds that, even though the facts of the instant case fall within the *ratio* of the earlier case, there is some difference between their facts that permits the later court to reach a result that differs from the one reached in the earlier case. The reasoning of the later court must nonetheless be such as to support the result of the earlier case. Raz argues that when a court distinguishes a prior case, it is exercising a legal power to amend the *ratio* of the prior case by adding, to the conditions for applying the *ratio* that were explicitly enumerated by the earlier court, one or more new conditions.[44] Recall that, for Raz, the *ratio* of a case is an exclusionary, legally valid rule, so that when a court exercises the power to distinguish a prior case it is narrowing a legally valid rule and, in that way, amending the law. He is thus committed to the view that a lower court may amend law that was made by a higher court.

Lamond argues persuasively that the various arguments that have been offered in support of the view that common law cases give rise to rules, either in the form of their *rationes* or in some other way, are weak.[45] He also points out that common law courts do not characteristically approach distinguishing in the same spirit as they approach overruling; they do not proceed, as Lamond appears to suggest they do when considering overruling a case, as if there were a presumption against distinguishing.[46] They simply look to whether the facts of the precedent case can be distinguished in a morally plausible manner while also determining whether their proposed rationale for deciding the case before them would justify the result of the precedent case. Lamond's own understanding of the common law is that it operates on

---

[40] Perry, 'Judicial Obligation' (n 11) 237–39, 244.

[41] G Lamond, 'Do Precedents Create Rules?' (2005) 11 Legal Theory 1.

[42] The contribution to this volume by John CP Goldberg and Benjamin C Zipursky (Chapter 22).

[43] Lamond does not take a position on whether his arguments support a positivist or a non-positivist account of common law reasoning: Lamond, 'Precedents' (n 41). In my view, they point strongly to the latter.

[44] Raz, *The Authority of Law* (n 1) 183–89.

[45] Lamond, 'Precedents' (n 41) 7–15. It should be pointed out that the way Lamond understands 'rules' seems unavoidably to include exclusionary rules in Raz's sense, even though he makes a valiant attempt to argue that one permissible way to conceptualize precedents is to regard them as Razian 'protected reasons.' ibid 18–19. The notion of a protected reason is discussed, and criticized, in section 3.

[46] ibid 12. The idea that there is a presumption against overruling is consistent, for reasons discussed in section 3, with the strong Burkean conception of precedent.

a case-by-case basis, is 'reason-based' in character rather than 'rule-based', and, in cases not involving overruling, requires courts to treat earlier cases as correctly decided.

Goldberg and Zipursky are inclined to the view that the strong Burkean conception is correct regarding 'horizontal' precedent, by which they mean the legal doctrine governing how a jurisdiction's highest court of appeal is obligated to reason about its own prior decisions. They are not persuaded that the strong Burkean conception has direct application to 'vertical' precedent, by which they mean the legal doctrine governing how lower courts are bound by the decisions of higher courts, including, in particular, the doctrine governing the practice of distinguishing prior cases. They nonetheless present strong independent arguments that Raz's exclusionary account of distinguishing is mistaken and that common law judicial reasoning should be understood as non-positivist in character. They point out that factual differences do not, by themselves, suffice to make a prior case distinguishable, and that what surely matters is whether a proposed distinction is merits-based, by which I take them to mean whether it is grounded in plausible moral considerations. They argue that Raz's understanding of distinguishing as a legal power that is essentially formal in nature cannot adequately deal with this point. They further argue that it is problematic to think that lower courts have a power to amend law made by higher courts. They propose instead that courts have legal *permission*, not power, to distinguish prior cases, and that when they act in accordance with this permission they neither change the law nor purport to change the law.

To sum up, the *rationes* of earlier cases, as these are treated by common law courts with regard to both overruling and distinguishing, do not possess 'the relative independence ... from ... their justifying reasons' which Raz says is typical of exclusionary rules, and which explains why we 'hypostatize' rules and treat them as 'complete reasons in their own right'.[47] He acknowledges that, in practice, there are no pure law-creating cases and that, as a result, unregulated cases are in practice always only partly unregulated.[48] (By the same token, it would seem to be similarly true, although Raz does not expressly remark upon the point, that regulated cases are always only partly regulated.) Raz further acknowledges that the special revisability of judge-made law, which he thinks is due mainly to the ever-present possibility of distinguishing earlier cases, means that judge-made law 'has a different status from legislated law'.[49] He nonetheless maintains that, while judge-made law can be said to be metaphorically less binding than enacted law, 'strictly speaking judge-made law is binding and valid, just as much as enacted law'. Assuming *arguendo* that legislated law is best understood in terms of exclusionary rules, my suggestion is that judge-made law *really is* less binding than legislated law, because the bindingness of judge-made law rests on second-order weighting principles that need not take an exclusionary form. It is plausible to think that such second-order principles can assign a weight to a given first-order reason (or set of such reasons) that differs from one context to another, as determined by such factors as the length of time a precedent (or line of precedents) has gone unchallenged, the degree of public reliance it has induced, and the need, in a particular area of the law, for the *right* answer to a legal question, as opposed simply to *some* answer.[50] Common expressions to the effect that the law is more 'settled' in one area than it is in another, or that a particular principle, case, or line of cases is especially 'entrenched' or 'embedded' in the law, can be accordingly understood as meaningful.

---

[47] Raz, *Practical Reason and Norms* (n 3) 79.
[48] Raz, *The Authority of Law* (n 1) 195.
[49] ibid.
[50] See further Perry, 'Judicial Obligation' (n 11) 241–43, 248–50; Perry, 'Second-Order Reasons' (n 11) 968–72.

I hope enough has been said to motivate the thought that common law courts do not draw sufficiently clear a line between regulated and unregulated cases to justify, even as an ideal, a pervasively exclusionary account of judicial reasoning. One can still intelligibly call the *rationes* of common law cases rules, so long as it is understood that such rules stand in for a weighted balance of justificatory—and usually moral—considerations. There is no clear line, even in theory, between what Raz calls regulated and unregulated cases, and hence no clear line between source-based and non-source-based judicial reasoning in common law cases. Moral considerations inevitably enter into common law reasoning, sometimes implicitly but often explicitly, across the board. This fact undermines an important element of Raz's overall case for legal positivism. I have not taken a position on the question of whether or not the enactment of legislation by a legislature should be understood in terms of issuing exclusionary rules, nor have I taken a position on the related question of whether statutory interpretation is fundamentally different from common law reasoning. I have simply argued that common law reasoning eludes easy capture by the exclusionary model.

6. Justifying the Doctrine of Precedent

The question remains whether common law reasoning, understood as I have explained it, is a morally justified practice. Raz conceives of a second-order reason as a reason to act on, or refrain from acting on, one or more first-order reasons. I argued in section 3 that the notion of a second-order reason can be generalized in the following way: a second-order reason is a reason to treat a first-order reason as having, in specified circumstances, a weight that differs from the weight it is ordinarily taken to possess. Exclusionary reasons then become a special case of the more general concept, namely, the case where one or more first-order reasons are treated as having zero weight. Some of Raz's more convincing examples of exclusionary rules involve decision-making by individual human agents, such as a person who decides to adopt an exclusionary rule of thumb for a private purpose, or an individual citizen of a state who decides that he or she ought to treat the state's directives as morally binding across some specified range of situations. In circumstances involving individual decision-making, reliance on second-order reasons that have an exclusionary character might very well be rationally justified and, in some cases, such as that of the individual who decides to treat a state's directives as obligatory across a range of situations, it might be morally justified as well.

Recall that, as was remarked in section 1, Raz defends the sources thesis by arguing that law can only guide a person's conduct if it is publicly ascertainable by, and accessible to, all of a society's members. This would not be possible, he argues, if laws could in general be identified only by engaging in moral argument. The point is well taken as regards private citizens who are looking to the law for personal guidance. Courts, however, are not private citizens who are looking to their own earlier decisions for personal guidance. It is true that courts are agents, but they are agents of a special kind. First, they are institutions rather than individuals (or any other sort of private legal entity) and, secondly, they are public rather than private agents. As regards the first point, their institutional character is quite different from that of, say, legislatures. Common law courts are primarily charged with the task of settling specific disputes that arise between or among specific sets of litigants. From this perspective, it seems morally compelling to say that it is part of a court's job always to stay in touch with the balance of underlying reasons as these apply to particular cases, especially since the facts of superficially similar cases may actually differ quite substantially from one case to the next. As regards the second point, which is that courts are public institutions, meaning institutions of government, it also seems morally compelling to say that, for reasons having to do with fairness, consistency, efficiency, respect for individual autonomy, and, more generally, the various values that are associated with the rule of law, they ought to decide particular cases in a manner that provides some reasonably reliable measure of ongoing guidance for society at large.

Common law courts have a dual role as settlers of particular disputes and providers of more general public guidance. My suggestion is that the morally optimal way to balance these roles is neither to treat prior cases as giving rise to exclusionary rules that bind the courts themselves, nor to treat the results of prior cases as revisable whenever the current court holds a view of the ordinary balance of reasons which differs from that held by an earlier court. Courts ought, rather, to do what I have argued they already do, which is to adopt a doctrine of precedent that looks to a *weighted* balance of reasons. They ought, in other words, to adopt the strong Burkean conception of precedent. In addition, courts ought to be permitted, as in fact they are permitted, to distinguish prior cases on their facts. The practice of distinguishing gives courts a great deal of flexibility in rendering morally appropriate decisions on the facts of particular cases while at the same time maintaining a morally significant degree of consistency in their decision-making over time.

It bears emphasis that the practical reasoning of citizens vis-à-vis previously decided cases can be expected to be quite different from that of the courts. Citizens can find guidance in a body of case law that is, from their perspective, entirely source-based, while courts can, and should, find in that same body of law guidance of a different sort, meaning that the fact that earlier cases were decided in this or that way ought to provide only some of the reasons that figure in the disposition of new cases. That is not quite the right way to put the point since, as was noted in section 3, a strong Burkean doctrine of precedent has a systematic effect on first-order reasoning without itself being a first-order reason. The main point, though, is that courts reason about prior judicial decisions in a different way from citizens. It is true that citizens can be expected, for either prudential or moral reasons, to try to anticipate possible changes in the law and alter their current behaviour accordingly. But, generally speaking, the law does not demand that citizens engage in such anticipatory deliberation. It only demands, again generally speaking, that they act in accordance with the public, socially sourced decisions that the courts have issued to date. Herein lies the strength of Raz's argument for legal positivism based on the sources thesis. But the scope of the argument is limited. While it may well apply to the reasoning of citizens, it does not apply to the reasoning of courts.

7. Conclusion

I have not suggested in this chapter that Raz's argument for legal positivism, based on the moral significance of the sources thesis, is wrong-headed in its entirety, mainly because, as was noted at the end of section 6, it may not *be* wrong-headed in its entirety. There is a strong case to be made that his argument for positivism applies to the practical reasoning of citizens but, I have maintained, that case cannot be extended to the reasoning of common law courts. I have also not suggested that Raz is mistaken in claiming that courts are exclusionarily bound by statutes. Independently of whether that claim can ultimately be upheld, common law reasoning does not give rise to exclusionary rules. My overall conclusion is thus fairly modest. There may be some truth in legal positivism, but it does not offer the entire truth about law. More particularly, the common law doctrine of precedent, together with the related common law practice of distinguishing prior cases on their facts, must be understood in non-positivist terms.

26

Reasons Holism and the Shared View of Precedent

Torben Spaak*

1. Introduction

One may plausibly distinguish two different models of precedent, the common law model, according to which precedents have binding force and are sources of law proper, and the civil law model, according to which precedents have persuasive force only and are sources of law only in a weaker sense. Although the two models thus differ in certain respects, they both assume: (i) that a precedent is a precedent in relation to cases that are like the precedent case, and only in relation to such cases; (ii) that the *ratio decidendi* of a case is the general norm without which the precedent court could not rationally have decided the case the way it did;[1] (iii) that following precedent is acting in accordance with such a general norm; and (iv) that the general reasons for following precedent are that doing so is a matter of fairness, and that it is conducive to predictability, stability, and economy of effort. In what follows, I shall refer to this as the shared view of precedent, and the question I shall be discussing is whether the shared view can be squared with a theory called reasons holism. The reason why there may be a problem is that if reasons holism is correct, and if it applies to legal reasons, there can be no general legal norms; and if there can be no general legal norms, questions will arise about what, exactly, the *ratio decidendi* of a case is, about what it means to follow precedent, and about the binding, or persuasive, force of precedent.

But what is reasons holism? Reasons holism is a general theory of reasons, according to which a reason in favour of, or against, an action or a belief, need not have the same force or polarity (direction) in every situation in which it appears. For example, the fact that a man promised to do X may sometimes be a reason for him to do X and sometimes no reason for him to do X, and the fact that a person is the biological father of a child may sometimes be reason (for a court) to let him visit the child and may sometimes not be a reason for letting him visit the child. So, if legal or moral reasons function in this way, there can be no general legal or moral norms since the existence of such norms presupposes precisely that the reasons behind them function in the same way in every relevant situation—if the reasons

---

* I would like to thank the participants of the authors' workshop for this volume in October 2021 and in particular Jakob Holtermann, for helpful comments and questions on the text. I would also like to thank Brian Bix, Åke Frändberg, Tomas Mautner, Victor Moberger, JJ Moreso, and Jan Sieckmann, as well as the participants in the advanced seminar in practical philosophy at the Department of Philosophy, Uppsala University, for equally helpful comments on an earlier version of the text. Finally, I would like to thank Robert Carroll for checking my English. As always, the responsibility for any remaining errors and imperfections in the text rests with the author alone.

[1] As we shall see (in section 2), although one does not normally speak of the *ratio decidendi* of a case in civil law jurisdictions, one does seem to accept the idea that there is a general norm, or principle, at the core of every precedent, and that it is this norm that is to guide lower courts in their decision-making. For ease of exposition, I shall therefore speak of the *ratio decidendi* in both common and civil law jurisdictions.

Torben Spaak, *Reasons Holism and the Shared View of Precedent* In: *Philosophical Foundations of Precedent*. Edited by: Timothy Endicott, Hafsteinn Dan Kristjánsson, and Sebastian Lewis, Oxford University Press. © Torben Spaak 2023. DOI: 10.1093/oso/9780192857248.003.0027

behind the norms could change force or polarity from one situation to another, then a norm might require the agent to perform an action in a situation in which they do not have any reason to perform the action, or even have a reason not to perform it.

It is important to note, however, that reasons holism is a theory of genuine, not conventional, reasons, where a conventional reason is a reason that applies to, and has force for, an agent if and only if the agent has accepted a certain institution, such as the institution of law, or etiquette, and a genuine reason is a reason that applies to, and has force for, an agent, whether or not the agent has accepted such an institution. For if legal reasons are genuine, and if reasons holism is true, the question arises of whether we have to modify, or even reject, the shared view; whereas if legal reasons are merely conventional, the shared view will not be threatened.

The nature of legal reasons depends in turn on the nature of law. And it seems that if legal positivism is true, legal reasons will be merely conventional reasons, since this appears to follow from the separation thesis, which has it that there is no necessary connection between the content of law and true morality; if instead some version of non-positivism is true, legal reasons will be genuine reasons, since such theories reject the separation thesis and conceive of moral reasons as genuine reasons. But there are some complications. First, we need to inquire whether inclusive—as distinguished from exclusive—legal positivism might allow genuine legal reasons to enter into legal thinking in general. Secondly, we need to consider whether there might after all be some room for genuine reasons to enter into the interpretation and application of the law under exclusive legal positivism, too, since one could argue that neither exclusive nor inclusive positivism applies to the interpretation and application of the law and so cannot rule out the possibility that legal reasons that occur in the interpretation and application of law are genuine.

But, one may wonder, does it really make sense to bring the theory of reasons holism into the legal sphere? Whereas not many believe that *moral* reasoning involves the interpretation and application of general norms (people tend to believe that it involves figuring out which act-alternative would bring about the best consequences, or how a virtuous person would act, or something like that), *legal* reasoning is considered by almost everyone to be a matter of interpreting and applying general norms to the facts of the case. Could there really be room for reasons holism in law?

I think there might be some room. First, quite a few judges and legal scholars prefer a piecemeal, context-oriented approach to the interpretation and application of the law, an approach that sometimes licenses legal decision-making that goes against, or beyond, the applicable general norms. Daniel Farber, for example, sees legal reasoning as eclectic, anti-foundational, and respectful of legal tradition, claiming that it is about 'solving legal problems using every tool that comes to hand, including precedent, tradition, legal text, and social policy'.[2] As he sees it, a judge who is confronted with a case in which different considerations point in different directions ought simply to make the best decision possible under the circumstances.[3] And it seems to me that reasons holism, if true and if applicable to the legal sphere, could be at least part of the justification for such a pragmatic approach to legal reasoning.[4]

---

[2] DA Farber, 'Legal Pragmatism and the Constitution' (1988) 72 Minn L Rev 1331, 1332.
[3] DA Farber, 'Reinventing Brandeis: Legal Pragmatism for the Twenty-First Century' (1995) U Ill L Rev 163, 165.
[4] I discuss (what I call) a pragmatic approach to legal reasoning in T Spaak, *Guidance and Constraint: The Action-Guiding Capacity of Theories of Legal Reasoning* (Iustus 2007) 83–92.

352   TORBEN SPAAK

Secondly, one could argue that anyone who rejects reasons holism and subscribes instead to the view that reasons have the same force and polarity in all situations, will be forced to engage in a never-ending process of refining the relevant reasons, in order to be able to maintain that they will behave in the same way in all situations, thus making the reasons increasingly specific and hence increasingly complex and therefore increasingly difficult to handle. In my view, this argument is not without force.

Although I will later question this assumption, I shall begin by assuming that reasons holism is true and ask what the implications are of this assumption for the shared view of precedent. I shall argue: (1) that if the usual reasons for following precedent are genuine, then any of these reasons may favour following precedent in some situations, but may favour not following precedent in others, and that this would threaten the shared view. I will, however, also argue (2) that we may coherently conceive of these reasons as merely conventional reasons, and that therefore the shared view will not be threatened. Moreover, I shall argue (3) that if ordinary legal reasons are genuine, the *ratio decidendi* of a precedent cannot be conceived as a genuine general legal norm, that following precedent cannot therefore be understood as action in accordance with such a norm, and that no alternative analysis of the *ratio* in terms of legal rules of thumb, or supervenience likeness, could be successful. Finally, I will, however, also argue (4) that the theory of reasons holism turns out to be rather problematic; and (5) that even if it were not, exclusive legal positivists could still defend the shared view, on the grounds that legal reasons at all levels are merely conventional reasons.

I begin with a few words about the idea of precedent and the general reasons in favour of following precedent (section 2) and proceed to introduce some important concepts that we need to be able to discuss questions of reasons holism and the shared view in an illuminating way, namely, the concepts of fairness, universalizability, supervenience, and resultance (section 3). I then consider the theory of reasons holism in more detail (sections 4 and 5) and explain the difference between genuine and conventional reasons (section 6). Having done that, I discuss the implications of reasons holism for the usual reasons in favour of following precedent (section 7) and for ordinary legal reasons (section 8). The chapter concludes with a consideration of the question of whether reasons holism could be rejected, on the grounds that it depends on a doubtful division of relevant considerations into reasons and background conditions (section 9).

2. Precedent

According to the common law model of precedent, while courts decide cases by issuing an individual norm that concerns the parties and their legal issue, they are presumed to have based their decision on a general norm without which they could not rationally have decided the case the way they did.[5] This general norm is called the *ratio decidendi* of the case and is said to legally bind both citizens and legal officials in more or less the same way that statutes do. So, while a precedent clearly expresses an individual norm that deals with the issue between the parties, say, that Jones has sued Smith for damages of £10,000, on the grounds that Smith has damaged Jones's property, it also expresses a *general* norm (a 'principle'), that is, the *ratio decidendi*, such as, 'Whoever causes damage to another's person's property ought to

---

[5] See, e.g., J Chipman Gray, *The Nature and the Sources of the Law* (2nd edn, Macmillan 1921) 261–62; N MacCormick, *Rhetoric and the Rule of Law: A Theory of Legal Reasoning* (OUP 2005) 153; R Cross and JW Harris, *Precedent in English Law* (4th edn, OUP 1991) 40.

pay damages to the person whose property it is.' And even though judges and legal scholars in civil law jurisdictions rarely speak of the *ratio decidendi* of a case, it appears that similar considerations play a role in those jurisdictions, too.[6] For it seems that in those jurisdictions, too, one assumes that a precedent expresses a general norm, so that it will be relevant in later cases that can be subsumed under this norm, and only in such cases, or, if you prefer, will be relevant in later cases that are like the precedent case, and only in such cases. The above-mentioned differences notwithstanding, the two models of precedent are thus importantly alike.

A precedent, then, is an authoritative case, typically a case decided by the highest court (or courts) in the relevant legal order, the function of which is to guide and constrain the decision-making of the (lower) courts in later cases. The idea is that if the deciding court is faced with a case, B, which is like the precedent case, A, the court ought to decide B on the basis of the *ratio decidendi* of A,[7] where the normative force of the 'ought' is said to be either binding force or else persuasive force. If, instead, the deciding court finds that B differs in relevant ways from A, the court will simply proceed without giving A any further consideration. In the common law model, in such a situation, the court is said to have *distinguished* the precedent.[8]

The general reasons for following precedent are that doing so: (i) is a matter of fairness (or formal justice); and that it is conducive to (ii) predictability; (iii) stability; and (iv) economy of effort.[9] The reason why following precedent is a matter of *fairness* is that it involves treating like cases alike and that treating like cases alike is a requirement of fairness. The reason why following precedent is conducive to *predictability* is that in their efforts to predict, on the basis of the law, how courts and other law-applying organs will decide future cases, the citizens can assume that such organs will decide any given case in the same way that previous like cases were decided. The reason why following precedent is conducive to *stability* is that following precedent means that things will go on as before, in the sense that like cases will be treated alike, and thus will not change. And the reason why following precedent is conducive to *economy of effort* is that in following precedent the deciding court is adopting an already available solution to the relevant legal problem, in the sense that it will decide the case at bar in the same way that previous like cases were decided. We see, then, that the reasons for following precedent are reasons to *treat like cases alike*.

3. Fairness, Universalizability, Supervenience, and Resultance

I have said that one reason for following precedent is that doing so is a matter of fairness, in the sense of treating like cases alike. But what exactly does this mean? I believe we should make a distinction between fairness (or formal justice), on the one hand, and universalizability, on the other. As Wlodek Rabinowicz points out, whereas the principle

---

[6] See, e.g., R Alexy and R Dreier, 'Precedent in the Federal Republic of Germany' in DN MacCormick and RS Summers (eds), *Interpreting Precedents* (Ashgate 1997) 17–64, 47.

[7] For some attempts to explain what a precedent is understood to be in the authors' own jurisdiction, see ibid 17, 23; M Troper and C Grzegorczyk, 'Precedent in France' in MacCormick and Summers (n 6) 103–40, 111–12 and Z Bankowski, DN MacCormick, and G Marshall, 'Precedent in the United Kingdom' in ibid 315–54, 323.

[8] On this see, e.g., R Cross and JW Harris, *Precedent in English Law* (4th edn, Clarendon Press 1991) 40–41; Bankowski, MacCormick, and Marshall, 'Precedent in the United Kingdom' (n 7) 341–42.

[9] On this see, e.g., F Schauer, 'Precedent' (1987) 39 Stan L Rev 571, 595–602.

of fairness imposes on us a *categorical* moral duty to treat like cases alike (or similar cases similarly), the principle of universalizability imposes on us only a *conditional* moral duty to treat like cases alike, namely, in the following way: *if* one ought to act in a certain way in situation A, *then* one ought to act in this way in the relevantly similar situation B.[10] My own view is that the principle of universalizability fits our thinking about precedent better than the principle of fairness, though for my purposes in this chapter nothing much will depend on whether it is the one or the other principle that underlies the shared view of precedent.

What is the relation between universalizability and supervenience and between supervenience and resultance? As we have seen, whereas *universalizability* means that *if* A and B are alike, and if one ought to do X in A, *then* one ought to do X in B, *supervenience* can be understood in the following way: necessarily, if A and B are alike as regards natural properties, they are alike regarding moral properties, and if they differ as regards moral properties, they differ regarding natural properties.[11] The difference, then, is that whereas the latter is the idea that moral properties depend on natural properties, the former is the more demanding idea that moral properties depend on *universal* natural properties, that is, properties that can be specified without reference to particular individuals or groups of individuals.[12] The distinction between universalizability and supervenience is of interest in this context because while reasons holists reject universalizability, they need not (and do not) deny that moral properties supervene on natural properties.

As regards the relation between supervenience and resultance, whereas the supervenience relation holds between *all* non-moral properties of an action and the relevant moral property, the *resultance* relation holds between, on the one hand, those non-moral properties of an action that count *in favour of* the action (in the case of rightness), or *against* the action (in the case of wrongness), and, on the other hand, the relevant moral property. That is to say, the supervenience base includes the resultance base.[13]

The distinction between supervenience and resultance is important when discussing reasons holism, because Jonathan Dancy argues that any general norms ('principles') that we might be able to generate from the supervenience base, although true, would be far too unwieldy to function as moral norms, since they would include in their antecedents every single property that is part of the supervenience base, whether or not it is morally significant, and that no general norms that we might be able to generate from the resultance base would be genuine (or true), because of the distinction between favourers and enablers.[14] For, as we shall see (in section 4), whereas a favourer is a reason that favours performing a certain action, an enabler is not a reason but a background condition that makes it possible for the favourer to do its job, that is, to favour the action; and a favourer may change its force or polarity from one situation to another, depending on the presence or absence of enablers (and intensifiers).

One might be tempted to suggest that a reasons holist who accepts supervenience could defend a weaker conception of the concept of *treating like cases alike* than the one that is part

---

[10] W Rabinowicz, *Universalizability. A Study in Morals and Metaphysics* (Reidel 1979) 14–15.

[11] On supervenience, see J Dancy, *Moral Reasons* (Blackwell 1993) 77–79; S Blackburn, *Spreading the Word. Groundings in the Philosophy of Language* (OUP 1984) 182–87.

[12] On this, see ibid 220.

[13] J Dancy, *Ethics Without Principles* (OUP 2004) 85–86.

[14] ibid 8.

of the shared view. Whereas the latter conception has it that if one acts in accordance with a general norm that covers all and only the relevant cases, one is treating like cases alike, the former has it that if one treats cases alike that are alike as regards their *supervenience bases*, one is treating like cases alike. One may, however, wonder whether the latter conception could be of any practical use to an agent who wishes to follow precedent. For Dancy's point—that any general norms that we might be able to generate from the supervenience base would be far too unwieldy to function as principles—appears to mean precisely that a supervenience conception would be very difficult to handle and would therefore be of little or no practical use to the agent.

Alternatively, one might be tempted to suggest that a reasons holist could maintain that if one acts in accordance with a *rule of thumb*, one is treating like cases alike, the idea being that reasons holism does nothing to undermine rules of thumb. The fact remains, however, that rules of thumb are very different from norms. For whereas the latter are binding, the former allow us to deviate from them when we see fit to do so. And, clearly, we do not think of the principle of treating like cases alike, however we understand it, more precisely, as a rule of thumb, but as a binding rule (or principle).

4. Reasons Holism

To gain a good understanding of the theory of reasons holism, we can contrast it with its main competitor, which we may call *reasons atomism*, following Dancy. According to reasons atomism, a consideration that is a reason in one situation, with a certain force and polarity, will be a reason with the same force and polarity in any other situation.[15] For example, that one person promised another to do something is, on this view, always a reason with a certain force to require that the promisor do what he promised to do, and to hold that he acted wrongly and, perhaps, that he ought to be sanctioned, if he does not do what he promised to do; and that an act is one of gratuitous cruelty is always a reason with a certain force to hold that the agent's act was wrong, and to blame the agent and sanction her. By contrast, as we have seen, the central idea of *reasons holism* is that a reason in favour of, or against, an action (or a belief), need not have the same force or polarity in every situation.[16]

Focusing on *contributory* (or *pro tanto*) reasons, and insisting that they must be understood in their own right and not in terms of overall reasons, Dancy makes a distinction between three different types of considerations, namely: (i) favourers (and disfavourers); which are reasons, (ii) enablers (and disablers); and (iii) intensifiers (and attenuators), which are not reasons but background conditions.[17] His idea is that whereas a favourer favours (and a disfavourer disfavours) an action, an enabler enables (and a disabler disables) the favourer (or disfavourer) to favour (or disfavour) the action, and an intensifier intensifies (and an attenuator attenuates) the favourer (or disfavourer). Figure 26.1 illustrates these distinctions.

---

[15] ibid 7, 94–95.
[16] See also Dancy, *Moral Reasons* (n 11) 60.
[17] Dancy, *Ethics Without Principles* (n 13) 38–45.

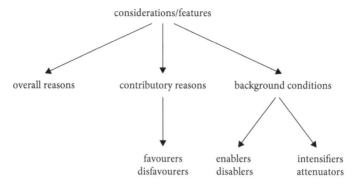

Figure 26.1 Types of considerations

To explain the concepts of a favourer and of an enabler, Dancy considers the following practical inference, which consists of four premises and a conclusion, and explains that whereas premise (1) is a favourer, premises (2)–(4) are different types of enablers:[18]

(1) I promised to do it.
(2) My promise was not given under duress.
(3) I am able to do it.
(4) There is no greater reason not to do it.
(5) So: I do it.

Dancy's idea is that whereas premise (1) *favours* (5), premises (2)–(3) *enable* (1) to favour (5), and premise (4) *enables* the move from (1) to (5):

> Premise (1) presents a clear favourer. That I promised to do it is (in this context at least) a reason in favour of doing it ... none of the other premises is a favourer. They play other roles; they are relevant, but not in the favouring way.[19]

Thus, (2)—that the promise was not given under duress—is not a reason that favours (5) but a consideration in the absence of which (1)—having promised to perform the action—would not favour (5). And (3)—that the agent is able to perform the promised action—is also not a reason favouring (5) but a consideration that enables (1) to favour (5). The main reason why (3) is not a favourer, Dancy explains, is that if it were, the agent's ability to perform the relevant action would always be a favourer; and this is clearly not so. And, as Dancy sees it, whereas (2) is a specific enabler, (3) is a general enabler.[20] Finally, he points out that (4)—that there is no greater reason not to perform the action—is also an enabler, though a different kind of enabler. For while (4) doesn't enable (1) to favour (5), it does enable the *move* from (1) to (5).[21]

Dancy proceeds to introduce the concept of an *intensifier* and its opposite, the concept of an *attenuator*, where an intensifier strengthens, and an attenuator weakens, a favourer

---

[18] ibid 38.
[19] ibid 39.
[20] ibid 40.
[21] ibid 40.

(or disfavourer). He introduces the following practical inference in order to clarify these concepts:

(1) She is in trouble and needs help.
(2) I am the only other person around.
(3) So: I help her.

As Dancy sees it, (1) is a favourer and (2) an intensifier, because whereas (1) would remain a favourer even if (2) were not present, (2) would not be anything at all if (1) were not present. The better view of the situation, according to Dancy, is to view (2) not as a consideration that favours (3) but as one that intensifies (1), which does favour (3).[22]

The distinction between favourers and enablers is crucial to Dancy's defence of holism and critique of atomism. For it is by invoking this distinction that Dancy can maintain what seems prima facie implausible, namely, that a given reason may speak in favour of performing an action in situation A and may speak against performing the same (type of) action in situation B. For example, a reasons atomist will argue that the fact that the agent promised their neighbour in a coercion-free situation, A, to pay back a loan in thirty days, is a reason to do so, whereas the fact that in B the agent was coerced into promising their neighbour to pay back the loan in thirty days does not provide the agent with a reason to do the promised act, and that what explains the difference is that uncoerced promises, but not coerced promises, are reasons to perform the promised act. On the atomist analysis, then, there are two *different* considerations at work in A and B, only one of which (the making of a coercion-free promise) is a reason, which means that the reasons atomist can maintain without contradiction that, when properly refined, a given reason always has the same force and polarity. A defender of reasons holism, on the other hand, will argue that the act of promising is the same reason, that is, the same *favourer*, in both A and B, that it favours the promised act in A, but not in B, and that this is so because there is a *disabler* (coercion) present in B, but not in A, or, if you prefer, because there is an *enabler* (the absence of coercion) present in A, but not in B.

We see that whereas the reasons atomist needs to refine the relevant reason by making it more and more specific, in order to be able to maintain that it always has the same force and polarity, the reasons holist can maintain, by distinguishing between favourers, enablers, and intensifiers, that a given, unrefined reason (a favourer) may have different force or polarity in different situations. We see, then, that both the atomist and the holist must refine the relevant considerations, though they do it in different ways. We might therefore say that the disagreement between holists and atomists concerns the most illuminating way to conceptualize the relevant considerations/features, and this is to say that the debate between holists and atomists is primarily a *conceptual* debate, and only secondarily, and indirectly, if at all, a substantive debate about how to act. It does not appear to be a debate about empirical matters.

5. Why Reasons Holism?

Dancy maintains that all types of reasons are holistic, and that it is difficult to understand why moral reasons should be different.[23] He begins by pointing out that *theoretical* reasons

---

[22] ibid 41–42.
[23] ibid 73–78.

are holistic, and that everyone accepts that this is so. Suppose, he says, that it seems to me that an object before me is red, and that I also believe that I have just taken a drug that makes blue objects look red and red objects look blue. In such a situation, that the object looks red to me is a reason to believe that there is a blue, not a red, object before me.[24] So if Dancy is right, the fact that an object looks red to the agent may in one situation be a reason for the agent to believe that the object is red and may in another situation (in which the agent has taken a drug) be reason for the agent to believe that the object is not red, but blue. He then points out that ordinary *practical* reasons, too, are holistic:

> For instance, that there will be nobody much else around is sometimes a good reason for going there, and sometimes a very good reason for staying away. That one of the candidates wants the job very much indeed is sometimes a reason for giving it to her and sometimes a reason for doing the opposite. And so on.[25]

And, he adds, *aesthetic* reasons, too, are holistic, so that, say, symmetry sometimes adds aesthetic value and sometimes takes aesthetic value away from an object.[26]

Having thus argued by way of examples that reasons in general are holistic, Dancy proceeds to argue that given that this is so, both (i) fundamental considerations about rationality and (ii) our inability to provide a principled explanation of the difference between moral and non-moral reasons speak in favour of conceiving of moral reasons, too, along holistic lines. As regards (i), he notes that there may be *invariant* reasons, typically connected with thick concepts such as those of generosity, cruelty, or bravery, but he concludes that the existence of some invariant reasons does not threaten reasons holism, provided that the invariance is not a matter of the logic of such reasons but of their *content*.[27] If it were a matter of the logic of such reasons, he points out, we would have to accept a hybrid conception of rationality, and this would be very unattractive.[28] As for (ii), he writes:

> Consider here the sad fact that nobody knows how to distinguish moral from other sorts of reasons; every attempt has failed. How does that fit the suggestion that there is this deep difference between them? Not very well at all.[29]

He does not, however, consider any failed attempts to distinguish between moral and non-moral reasons, which means that it is difficult to assess his claim.

6. Legal Reasons: Genuine or Conventional?

I have said that reasons holism is a theory of genuine reasons, and that if reasons holism is true there can be no genuine general norms because if reasons function holistically, they can change force or polarity from one situation to another, and because general norms provide that one always ought to (or may) act in a certain way in a situation of the relevant type. I have also said that reasons holism, being a theory of genuine reasons, might not apply

---

[24] ibid 74.
[25] ibid 74.
[26] ibid 76.
[27] ibid 77–78.
[28] ibid 77.
[29] ibid 76.

to *legal* reasons, which many think of as being merely conventional reasons. But this raises some questions:

(1) What exactly are genuine reasons, and what are conventional reasons?
(2) Why is reasons holism a theory of genuine, but not conventional, reasons?
(3) Are legal reasons really conventional reasons, and if so, then why?

I have said (in section 1) that whereas a conventional reason is a reason that applies to, and has force for, an agent if and only if she has accepted a certain institution, a genuine reason is a reason that applies to, and has force for, an agent, whether or not she has accepted any institution at all; and I have also said that since law is clearly an institution, it is tempting to assume that legal reasons are merely conventional reasons, at least on a positivistic analysis. I need to say a little more about this, however.

Richard Joyce observes that we typically think of *moral* reasons as genuine reasons, that is, as reasons that have categorical force, force that is independent of the agent's desires or interests.[30] To clarify the idea of a genuine, or, as he says, a real, reason, Joyce contrasts genuine reasons with institutional reasons. He considers a case in which a person, Celadus, has been forced to become a gladiator and finds himself in a precarious situation in a fight with a professional gladiator. He assumes that Celadus's only chance is to throw sand in his opponent's eyes. He points out, however, that throwing the sand would be a violation of the rules of gladiatorial combat and that therefore Celadus has an institutional reason not to throw sand in his opponent's eyes. He adds, though, that Celadus may nevertheless have a non-institutional reason to throw sand in the eyes of his opponent, if this is his only way to avoid death or defeat.

As Joyce sees it, the gladiator rules are *weak* categorical imperatives, in the sense that although they *apply* to Celadus independently of his desires or interests, they provide him with nothing more than institutional reasons, that is, reasons that depend for their *force* on his acceptance of the relevant institution. The non-institutional reason to throw sand in the eyes of his opponent, by contrast, Joyce explains, is a *strong* categorical imperative, in the sense that it applies to Celadus independently of his desires and interests *and* provides him with a genuine reason to throw the sand.[31]

But, one wonders, why is reasons holism a theory of genuine, as distinguished from conventional (or institutional), reasons? The idea, as I understand it, is that genuine reasons are independent of human institutions and simply function in a holistic way, and that in this regard they are importantly different from conventional reasons, which are reasons for us because we have (tacitly) agreed that they are reasons by accepting the relevant institution. Thus, whereas an agreement (or institution) can (tacitly or explicitly), and typically does, include the idea that conventional reasons never change force or polarity, the function of genuine reasons cannot be affected by agreement.

Should we think of *legal* reasons—such as reasons provided by statutes or precedents—as genuine or conventional reasons? As I have said, I believe the nature of legal reasons depends on the nature of law. And it seems that if legal positivism is a true theory of law, legal reasons will be *conventional*. For this seems to follow from the separation thesis of legal positivism— according to which there is no necessary connection between the content of law and true

---

[30] R Joyce, *The Myth of Morality* (CUP 2003) 34.
[31] ibid 37.

morality—conceived as a thesis about the content of (first-order) legal statements.[32] The separation thesis, thus conceived, has it that such legal statements do *not* entail moral statements. On this analysis, to maintain normatively that I have a legal duty to pay income tax, or to drive on the right-hand side of the road, is to make a legal, but *not* a moral, statement. If such a statement is true, one has a *legal*, but not necessarily a moral, reason to act accordingly; and, if this is so, legal reasons are merely conventional.

There is a problem, however, namely, that legal positivism comes in more than one form. While exclusive legal positivists argue that, properly understood, the so-called social thesis requires the use of *exclusively* factual criteria of legal validity, and that any reference to moral values is best understood as granting the judge power and discretion to create new law, inclusive legal positivists maintain instead that the criteria of validity can, but need not, be of a moral nature, provided that they are grounded in facts. That is to say, whereas inclusive legal positivists insist on a distinction between the basis and the content of criteria of validity and hold that the social thesis is satisfied if the basis of such criteria is (exclusively) factual, even if the content is not, exclusive legal positivists maintain that both the basis and the content need to be exclusively factual.

The distinction between inclusive and exclusive positivism is of interest in this context, because under *inclusive*, but not under exclusive, positivism legal reasons may turn out to be moral reasons. Assume that the rule of recognition in a given jurisdiction constitutes and identifies the usual sources of law—legislation, custom, and precedent—and also imposes a moral constraint on the norms that can be found in the sources of law. If it does, then morally acceptable and only morally acceptable (or morally good) norms can be legally valid, and this appears to mean that any given legal norm will provide the law subjects with a legal reason for action that is *also* to some extent a moral reason. Of course, such a relation between law and morality would be *contingent* only, but the theory of reasons holism would nevertheless get a foothold in law, and the shared view would therefore be affected to a corresponding degree.

Finally, if some form of non-positivism, including natural law theory, is a true theory of law, legal reasons will *necessarily* be genuine moral reasons. This is so because non-positivist theories all reject the separation thesis and conceive of legal rights and duties as a species of moral rights and duties and of legal statements as a species of moral statements, and because they think of moral reasons as genuine reasons.[33]

7. Implications: Reasons to Follow Precedent

I have identified (in section 2) four general reasons to follow precedent, namely, fairness, predictability, stability, and economy of effort (though I also have suggested that it is really the principle of universalizability—not the principle of fairness—that is part of the shared view). If these reasons are *genuine*, and if reasons holism is true, each reason may change its force or polarity from one situation to another, so that it may sometimes speak in favour of,

---

[32] On the separation thesis thus conceived, see T Spaak and P Mindus, 'Introduction' in T Spaak and P Mindus (eds), *The Cambridge Companion to Legal Positivism* (CUP 2021) 1–36, 7–12.

[33] See, e.g., M Greenberg, 'The Moral Impact Theory, the Dependence View and Natural Law' in G Duke and RP George (eds), *Natural Law Jurisprudence* (CUP 2017) 275–313; R Dworkin, *Law's Empire* (Belknap Press 1986); J Finnis, *Natural Law and Natural Rights* (Clarendon Press 1981).

and sometimes against, following precedent. For example, the fact that following precedent is conducive to stability may sometimes be a reason to follow precedent, and sometimes be no reason at all, or even a reason not to follow precedent. However, although it is a common observation that the force, but not the polarity, of the underlying reasons, such as predictability or stability, may vary somewhat from one area of law to another, the general idea is that one ought *pro tanto* to follow precedent. Hence, the shared view of precedent would be threatened.

Could we perhaps solve the problem by arguing that the four reasons to follow precedent are really *conventional*, and that therefore reasons holism does not apply to them? I think so. For given that the institution of law is sufficiently rich, in the sense that it includes much more than the institution of precedent, as it undoubtedly does, one could accept this institution as a whole, perhaps reasoning that civilized life presupposes the existence of a legal order; and if one did, one could think of the reasons to follow precedent as merely conventional reasons, as reasons that presuppose acceptance of the institution of law thus conceived. Of course, the price we would have to pay for this is that those reasons would not be reasons for those who did not accept the institution of law. As I see it, however, this is a price we could afford to pay, since there would be little point in arguing about whether one ought to follow precedent with someone who does not accept the institution of law.

Note here that even if our reasons to accept the very institution of law are, and have to be, genuine—since there does not seem to be any other institution from the standpoint of which we could accept the institution of law—it does not follow that our reasons to follow precedent cannot be conventional. For if this were so, it would mean that many, though perhaps not all, conventional reasons would turn out to be genuine reasons, after all, and that therefore the very distinction between genuine and conventional reasons would be threatened. But this does not seem right. Moreover, it seems to me that one might actually accept the institution of law for the wrong reasons or, perhaps, for no reason at all. I conclude that what is important is our acceptance of the institution of law, not our reasons for accepting it.

8. Implications: Ordinary Legal Reasons

I have said (in sections 1 and 6) that one may wonder whether reasons holism really applies to ordinary legal reasons, such as reasons provided by statutes or precedents, since one may suspect that legal reasons will be merely conventional. And I have said that the answer to this question appears to be that legal reasons will necessarily be conventional if exclusive legal positivism is true, that they might, as a matter of contingent fact, be genuine if inclusive legal positivism is true, and that they will necessarily be genuine if instead some form of non-positivism is true.

As it turns out, however, there is a further complication that we need to consider. For one might argue that, even under exclusive legal positivism, there might be some room for genuine reasons in the interpretation and application of the law. For example, a judge might argue that in a certain (type of) case, a given statutory provision should receive a literal, not a purposive, interpretation, on the grounds that predictability is (in general, or at least in this type of case) a more important interpretive value than legislative efficiency, or systemic coherence, or giving effect to the legislative purpose. One might therefore be tempted to believe that *if* the *ratio* of the decision thus depends on one or more genuine reasons, namely, ones that occur in the interpretation and application of the relevant norm, *then* one may find that in some situations the *ratio* of the case will require the agent to perform an action that they

362   TORBEN SPAAK

have no reason to perform, or even have a reason not to perform. That would not be acceptable, however.

The argument under consideration assumes, however, (i) that legal positivism is a theory of sources of law, or, if you prefer, a theory of legal validity, *not* (ii) a theory of sources of law (or legal validity) *and* a theory of interpretation and application of the law. This is so because under (i) the interpretation and application of legal norms does not come within the scope of the separation thesis, whereas under (ii) it does. For under (i) the separation thesis applies only to uninterpreted legal norms, that is, legal norms as they come from a source of law, whereas under (ii) it applies to both interpreted and uninterpreted legal norms. Thus, if interpretation (ii) is correct, a legal positivist can invoke the separation thesis to rule out the possibility that legal reasons that occur in the interpretation and application of the law are genuine reasons, whereas if interpretation (i) is correct, he cannot do so.

I myself prefer interpretation (i) because if one adopts this interpretation one can avoid having to say that judges create new law in most cases, and one can also steer clear of Ronald Dworkin's theoretical disagreement objection.[34] Let us assume, then, if only for the sake of argument, that interpretation (i) is the better interpretation. If we do, a further question arises, namely, whether—contrary to what the argument under consideration assumes—the interpretive arguments and other legal meta-norms that are part of (what we might refer to as) the legal toolbox may not actually be best conceived as providing the judge with merely conventional reasons.[35] In fact, I think so. For, as I see it, the tools in the legal toolbox have the legal status they do not because they are right but because of a tacit agreement (a convention) on the part of judges, legal scholars, and others. And if this is so, considerations of the above-mentioned type—that predictability is a more important interpretive value than legislative efficiency, or systemic coherence, or giving effect to the legislative purpose—will be conventional reasons, and this in turn means that reasons holism will not apply to interpretive legal reasons and will not threaten the shared view. I therefore conclude that even if reasons holism is true, exclusive legal positivists can defend the shared view, on the grounds that legal reasons at all levels are best conceived as merely conventional reasons.

9. Reasons and Background Conditions

So far, I have been assuming that reasons holism is a true theory. But is this assumption justified? I doubt it. One natural objection to Dancy's reasons holism is that it presupposes a doubtful division of relevant considerations into reasons and background conditions. More specifically, the objection is that when Dancy maintains that a favourer, f, may favour doing X in A, but not in B, on the grounds that there may be an enabler, e, present in A, but not in B, or that f may favour doing X in A more strongly than it favours doing X in B, on the grounds that there is an intensifier, i, present in A, but not in B, he is treating favourers as if they were (complete) reasons, f and (e or i), when in reality they are only reason fragments, f. Clearly, this division is very important, because while f can indeed change its force or polarity, f and (e or i) cannot.

Consider in this light the examples adduced by Dancy in support of the claim that reasons in general are holistic, considered in section 5. He maintains, as we have seen, that his examples make it clear that both theoretical and practical reasons can change polarity from one

---

[34] On this, see Spaak and Mindus (n 32) 443–64, 452–58.
[35] I discuss the ingredients in the legal toolbox in Spaak (n 4) 43–56.

situation to another. He is, of course, right. But this is so only because he has moulded the reasons, that is, the favourers/disfavourers, so narrowly that they exclude features of the situation that are highly relevant to the issue under consideration and that might for this reason naturally be thought of as being part of the relevant reasons, such as the circumstance that the observer has taken a drug that makes blue objects look red and red objects blue, or that the candidate is likely to work very diligently if she is hired, and so on.

Let us consider the colour example a little more closely. As I see it, the claim that a person's reason to believe that an object before him is red is that he is looking at it and can see that it is red, presupposes, in order to be meaningful, that the agent is perceiving the object in (what we may refer to as) standard conditions. Of course, the idea of standard conditions is not very precise, but most would agree that it includes, among other things, that the lighting is good, that the agent is healthy and has good eyesight, and that he has *not* taken a drug of the above-mentioned type. The question, then, is whether these standard conditions should be part of the relevant reason or not.[36] Clearly, if they are part of the reason, the latter cannot change its force or polarity from one situation to another, whereas if they are not part of the reason, it might do so. Given that the idea of standard conditions thus seems to be necessary to any meaningful discussion of these issues, I conclude that a (complete) reason must reflect a situation in standard conditions—if it doesn't, it will not be a reason but a reason fragment. Indeed, it is tempting to suggest that the reason why Dancy focuses on reason fragments instead of reasons is that he is presupposing the truth of reasons holism, specifically, the distinction between favourers and enablers, because, as we have seen, a favourer is a reason fragment and not a reason.

---

[36] Brad Hooker makes this objection to Dancy's example. B Hooker, 'Moral Particularism: Wrong and Bad' in B Hooker and M Little (eds), *Moral Particularism* (OUP 2001) 1, 14.

PART IV
PRECEDENT AND JUDICIAL POWER

27
Should Courts Follow Mistaken Statutory Precedents?

Dale Smith[*]

1. Introduction

Sometimes, when a court interprets a statute, it makes a mistake. For example, it might misunderstand what the statutory text says or may fail to apply a relevant principle of interpretation, and hence may misidentify the statute's legal effect. (By 'legal effect', I mean the contribution the statute makes to the content of the law, which we might understand in terms of the legal norms the statute creates, modifies, etc.) Where the court is an appellate one, the following question arises: should later courts follow the earlier court's mistaken interpretation of the statute or should they uphold the statute's legal effect?

Courts can also make mistakes about other sources of law, such as the common law, and similar questions arise as to whether later courts are bound by those mistakes. However, as we shall see, it makes a difference whether we are concerned with, say, a statute or the common law. I shall confine my attention to mistakes about statutes.

The question just posed can be understood as a question about what courts ought morally to do or as a question about what the law requires of them. I am interested in the second way of understanding the question: are later courts required *by law* to follow the earlier court's mistaken interpretation of the statute or to uphold the statute's legal effect? The answer to this question may vary between legal systems, and I shall focus on the position in the UK. However, I hope that some of the discussion is of broader interest.

It is not immediately clear what the law requires of courts in this situation. There is an apparent tension between the legal obligation to follow precedent and the legal obligation to uphold the law established by Parliament. I shall suggest that the tension is genuine. However, I shall also suggest that the law resolves that tension by requiring the court to uphold the statute's legal effect, rather than following precedent. In section 2, I clarify what type of judicial decision I am concerned with. In section 3, I argue that the court may have both a legal duty to follow precedent and a legal duty to uphold the statute's legal effect, but the principle of parliamentary supremacy requires the court to prioritize the latter duty. I discuss some qualifications in section 4, before considering an important objection in section 5.

However, this chapter offers only an initial exploration of what a later court should do when faced with an earlier court's mistaken interpretation of a statute. The question I address

---

[*] I would like to thank Andrea Dolcetti, Ken Ehrenberg, Patrick Emerton, Timothy Endicott, Jeff Goldsworthy, Nils Jansen, Hafsteinn Dan Kristjánsson, Matt Lister, Lorena Ramirez Ludena, Nicole Roughan, Julian Sempill, David Tan, Lulu Weis and especially Sebastian Lewis, Arie Rosen, and Leah Trueblood for very helpful comments. Thanks also to Tom Fletcher and the MLS Academic Research Service for excellent research assistance.

Dale Smith, *Should Courts Follow Mistaken Statutory Precedents?* In: *Philosophical Foundations of Precedent*. Edited by: Timothy Endicott, Hafsteinn Dan Kristjánsson, and Sebastian Lewis, Oxford University Press. © Dale Smith 2023. DOI: 10.1093/oso/9780192857248.003.0028

368 DALE SMITH

is a practical one, but we shall see that it raises theoretical issues which cannot be fully explored here. Moreover, while I contend that the principle of parliamentary supremacy requires later courts to uphold the statute's legal effect, there may be other legal norms—beyond the doctrine of precedent and the principle of parliamentary supremacy—which also bear on this issue (a possibility I return to in section 6).

2. Mistaken Statutory Precedents

There are at least two ways in which an appellate court may make new law when interpreting a statute. First, it may fill a gap in the statute. In these cases, the statute's legal effect is underdeterminate—the norm established by the statute rules out some courses of action while leaving others open—and the court's decision resolves the lack of determinacy (e.g. by stipulating that one of the open courses of action is legally required). I shall call decisions of this type 'gap-filling statutory precedents'.

The second type of case—the one I am interested in—arises where the statute's legal effect is determinate, but the court misidentifies that legal effect and the mistake forms part of the binding content of the court's decision. (I shall call a decision of this type a 'mistaken statutory precedent' or 'MSP'.) For my purposes, there are two important features of this type of case. The first, which I discuss later, is that the court misidentifies the statute's legal effect. The second is that the mistake forms part of the binding content of the court's decision. The second feature is perhaps most easily understood on the 'rules model' of precedent, according to which a precedent binds later courts by establishing a rule they are legally obligated to follow.[1] Where an appellate court misidentifies a statute's legal effect, the court may establish a new rule, which later courts are obligated to follow.[2] However, the issue with which I am concerned may also arise on understandings of precedent other than the rules model, provided they allow that a mistaken assessment of a statute's legal effect can play such a role in an appellate court's decision that the doctrine of precedent imposes a duty on later courts to act in accordance with that assessment. (As we shall see, this does not settle the question of what a later court is legally required to do, because the court also has a legal duty to uphold the statute's legal effect.)

A gap-filling precedent may be thought of as supplementing the statute, by rendering its legal effect more determinate. By contrast, an MSP is decided contrary to the statute because the court makes a mistake about the statute's legal effect.[3] This suggests that the case for following gap-filling precedents is stronger than the case for following MSPs. Nothing in what follows is intended to suggest that later courts should not follow gap-filling precedents, even if they would have preferred that the gap be filled in a different way.

There may be a third way in which a court can make new law when interpreting a statute. Legal and/or social developments that occur after a statute is enacted may mean that the interpretation the statute should be given changes over time, and a court may be authorized to offer a new interpretation in light of those developments.[4] However, this is not the issue

---

[1] Regarding the rules model of precedent, see G Lamond, 'Precedent' (2007) 2 Philosophy Compass 699, 700–02.

[2] It might be said that the court applies the statute to the facts of the case, rather than establishing a new rule. However, to apply the statute to the facts, the court may need to form a view about what norm the statute created. Where the court's view is mistaken, it may inadvertently establish a new legal rule.

[3] In section 3.B, I consider the possibility that the court's decision *changes* the statute's legal effect.

[4] See, e.g., J Raz, *Between Authority and Interpretation* (OUP 2009) 294–97. The legal developments of relevance here exclude changes to the statute itself, such as the introduction of amending legislation (or an MSP, if we assume

I am concerned with. I am interested in cases in which the legal reasons for a later court to offer a different interpretation from that offered by an earlier court follow from the fact that the earlier court's decision was mistaken about the statute's legal effect. I am not concerned with cases where legal and/or social developments that occurred between the earlier court's decision and the later court's mean that a different interpretation of the statute is now appropriate, so that whether the earlier court's decision was correct at the time it was made is a moot point. (I shall call such decisions 'outdated statutory precedents'.)

Even after distinguishing MSPs from gap-filling and outdated precedents, there is considerable scope for MSPs to occur. Any attempt to demonstrate this is complicated by the fact that there are competing accounts of how a statute's legal effect is constituted (though that may itself be a reason for thinking that courts will sometimes misidentify a statute's legal effect). However, I will mention two factors that any plausible account must recognize as contributing, in some way or other, to a statute's legal effect, and will briefly explain how those factors leave room for judicial error.

The first factor is the meaning of the words contained in the statute.[5] Ascertaining that meaning is often a complex process, requiring consideration of not just the literal meaning of the words but also the context in which they are used.[6] That context is multifaceted. It may include the other words used in the statute, the words used in other statutes, and extrinsic materials such as Hansard. Courts must then draw these elements together to reach an overall conclusion about what the words in the statute mean. There is significant potential for error here.

Secondly, to the extent that a statute's legal effect depends on the application of principles of statutory interpretation, there are many such principles, some of which are obscure or contested. The interaction between these principles is also complex, and may necessitate judges making difficult assessments of how much weight to accord to conflicting principles. Again, this leaves considerable room for judicial mistakes.

It might be objected that these considerations show that there is potential for disagreement about a statute's legal effect, but—where there is disagreement among judges—there cannot be a legally correct answer about which courts could be mistaken. If this were right, there might be little room for MSPs. However, there is reason to reject this suggestion. The type of disagreement about the meaning of words that is relevant to statutory interpretation is disagreement about what Parliament said when it enacted the statute. We do not normally think that disagreement about what someone said on a particular occasion precludes there being a right answer as to what was said. Indeed, if we thought this, we would struggle to make sense of the dispute, since the very fact of disagreement would falsify the disputants' claims to have identified the right answer.

Similarly, the content and application of principles of statutory interpretation are sometimes contested among judges, but judges do not take the fact that they disagree to indicate

---

for the moment that an MSP changes the statute's legal effect). In such cases, the statute has already been updated or changed, hence there is no need for a later court to do so (though the court may need to fill any gaps in the amending legislation).

[5] On some views, the meaning of the words is relevant in its own right; on other views, it is relevant as evidence of legislative intent or as a constraint on the intentions that can be ascribed to Parliament. (These options are not exhaustive.) Whatever role this factor plays, complexities about meaning are likely to contribute to difficulties in assessing a statute's legal effect.

[6] Not everyone agrees. Waldron argues that the legislature intends that statutory words be given 'their conventional English meaning': J Waldron, *Law and Disagreement* (OUP 1999) 143. This would likely increase the scope for MSPs, since judges often consider contextual factors of the sort discussed in the text.

370   DALE SMITH

that there cannot be a correct understanding of these principles, and for good reason. Consider the principle of legality. This is an important principle of statutory interpretation, but judges disagree about many aspects of that principle.[7] If its content was confined to whatever is agreed among judges, one might conclude that it has very little content.

These remarks are not intended to be conclusive. However, they do suggest that there can be a correct answer concerning a statute's legal effect even if judges disagree about the factors that help to constitute that legal effect.[8] Since the correct view is unlikely always to prevail, we can expect MSPs to arise.

3. Should Courts Follow Mistaken Statutory Precedents?

A. Judicial Practice and Its Limits

When confronted with an MSP, a court may be subject to conflicting legal duties. On the one hand, the doctrine of precedent, as it exists in the UK, applies to appellate court decisions, whether they involve statutes or the common law. A court lower in the judicial hierarchy must follow a decision of a higher court (vertical *stare decisis*) and some courts must follow their own earlier decisions (horizontal *stare decisis*).[9] Thus, when faced with an MSP, a later court may—depending on the respective standing of the earlier and later courts—have a legal duty to follow that decision.

On the other hand, the later court has a legal duty to uphold the statute's legal effect, as an instance of a general duty owed by courts to give effect to the will of Parliament.[10] In the case of an MSP, the norm established by the statute differs from the norm contained in the precedent (because the earlier court was mistaken about the statute's legal effect), and so the two duties conflict. The later court is obligated to uphold the statute's legal effect *and* to follow precedent, but it cannot do both.[11]

Unsurprisingly, judges disagree about what to do when faced with an MSP. We shall see that there is, perhaps, agreement among judges that vertical *stare decisis* must be respected, and so an MSP from a higher court must be followed.[12] Yet beyond that, judges disagree about what the relevant legal principles are.

Let me give a few examples to illustrate the disagreement. In *R v London Transport Executive, ex p Greater London Council*,[13] Kerr LJ stated that responsibility for interpreting statutes rests with the courts and that—once a statute has been authoritatively interpreted (at least by the House of Lords or, now, the Supreme Court)—that interpretation is the law, unless subsequently changed by Parliament. This suggests that statutory precedents—at least

---

[7] See, e.g., J Varuhas, 'The Principle of Legality' (2020) 79 CLJ 578.

[8] Things would be different if a statute's legal effect was not constituted by factors such as the meaning of the statutory text and relevant principles of statutory interpretation, but rather was whatever judges said it was. But that is not so: see n 34.

[9] For the distinction between vertical and horizontal *stare decisis*, see F Schauer, 'Precedent' in A Marmor (ed), *The Routledge Companion to the Philosophy of Law* (Routledge 2012) 124.

[10] This way of characterizing the general duty is common among judges (see, e.g., text for n 28). Readers who are sceptical about the existence of legislative intentions may wish to instead think of the duty as a duty to give effect to the law made by Parliament. I say more about the nature of the duty later.

[11] Even if the two norms support the same outcome in the case before the later court, it may need to specify which norm it is applying to reach that outcome.

[12] Despite this apparent agreement, I argue later that an MSP should *not* be followed even if it comes from a higher court.

[13] *R v London Transport Executive, ex p Greater London Council* [1983] QB 484, 490.

those of the Supreme Court—must be followed by lower courts, even if the decision was mistaken. Moreover, if the earlier interpretation offered by the Supreme Court is now the law, unless changed by Parliament, then it seems to follow that that interpretation must also be followed by the Supreme Court itself in subsequent cases.[14]

By contrast, in *Ogden Industries Pty Ltd v Lucas*,[15] the Privy Council stated:

> It is quite clear that judicial statements as to the construction and intention of an Act must never be allowed to supplant or supersede its proper construction and courts must beware of falling into the error of treating the law to be that laid down by the judge in construing the Act rather than found in the words of the Act itself.

This suggests that MSPs should *not* be followed. However, it was not intended to extend to vertical *stare decisis*, since the Privy Council added that '[n]o doubt a decision on particular words binds inferior Courts on the construction of those words on similar facts'.[16]

In one respect, though, the approaches taken in these cases converge. Each approach treats MSPs as belonging to a distinct category, while disagreeing about the principles that govern that category. Yet this, too, is contested. There are cases in which no distinction is drawn between MSPs and mistaken common law precedents. For example, the Supreme Court often invokes the 1966 Practice Statement when considering whether to depart from one of its own past decisions, whether that decision involved a statute or the common law.[17] On this approach, the Supreme Court can depart from its previous decision, but only when there is very good reason to do so. The fact that the court considers the decision to be mistaken is not sufficient.[18]

This is only a very brief survey. However, it might suggest the following conclusions. UK law requires that MSPs be followed by courts lower in the judicial hierarchy. However, in other contexts, the law does not specify whether later courts must follow an MSP, because judges disagree about what principles to apply.

These conclusions would be premature. It is not enough to consider judges' views about the foundational principles of their legal system. One must also look to the views of other legal actors, including legislators.[19] This is especially important in the present context, where the question is whether courts are ultimately bound by a statute's legal effect or their own past decisions (or perhaps neither, in the case of the Supreme Court). Appealing solely to *other* past decisions of the courts—this time, about whether MSPs are binding—risks begging that question.

---

[14] Notwithstanding the fact that the Supreme Court is not otherwise bound by its own past decisions: Practice Statement (Judicial Precedent) [1966] 3 All ER 77 (endorsed in *Austin v Mayor and Burgesses of the London Borough of Southwark* [2010] UKSC 28, [2011] 1 AC 355 [25]).

[15] *Ogden Industries Pty Ltd v Lucas* [1969] 1 All ER 121, 126.

[16] ibid.

[17] For a recent example involving a statute, see *Test Claimants in the Franked Investment Income Group Litigation v Commissioners for Her Majesty's Revenue and Customs* [2020] UKSC 47, [2020] 3 WLR 1369.

[18] ibid [245] (Lords Reed and Hodge). Nor is it necessary for the court to conclude that the previous decision was mistaken in order for the court to be entitled to depart from that decision. Under this approach, it may sometimes be appropriate for the court to overrule an outdated statutory precedent.

[19] J Goldsworthy, *The Sovereignty of Parliament* (OUP 2001) 240–42. Admittedly, this raises broader jurisprudential issues I cannot explore fully here. It is also the subject of disagreement among judges: compare Lord Bingham, *The Rule of Law* (Allen Lane 2010) 167 with *Jackson v Attorney-General* [2005] UKHL 56, [2006] 1 AC 262 [102] (Lord Steyn). However, as Goldsworthy shows, Hart's observations about the legal pathology of a system in which judges and legislators are fundamentally at odds about foundational legal principles provide a powerful reason not to overlook the views of legislators. See HLA Hart, *The Concept of Law* (2nd edn, Clarendon Press 1994) 122–23.

372   DALE SMITH

There is a lack of evidence concerning whether legislators regard MSPs as binding on later courts. In the absence of direct evidence, it is tempting to draw certain inferences. For example, it might be suggested that, when Parliament legislates, it does so in a legal system that is well known to contain the doctrine of precedent, and so Parliament can be taken to accept that its statutes are subject to that doctrine, and hence to accept that MSPs are binding on later courts (perhaps subject, on the Supreme Court, to the Practice Statement).[20]

However, even if Parliament is aware of the doctrine of precedent, it may not have considered whether that doctrine applies to judicial decisions that misinterpret its statutes. Further, if it *has* considered this issue, why think that Parliament accepts that its legislation is subject to the doctrine of precedent in this way? As we have seen, judicial practice on this point is not settled. Even if we focus on vertical *stare decisis*—which provides an obligation that judges do appear to agree extends to MSPs—why think that Parliament concurs? The fact that Parliament has not done anything about this judicial practice is, at best, only weak evidence that it endorses the practice. There are other possible explanations of Parliament's inaction. It may think that there are more important matters to which to devote limited legislative time. Or legislators may dislike the practice but disagree among themselves about what to do about it.[21]

B. Parliamentary Supremacy

I have suggested that, at most, judges agree that MSPs must be followed by courts lower in the judicial hierarchy. They disagree about whether MSPs should be followed in other contexts. I have further argued that we cannot even conclude that the obligation provided by vertical *stare decisis* applies to MSPs, since the legal position depends on the practices not just of judges but also of legislators.

At this point, one may be tempted to conclude that there is no determinate legal position concerning whether later courts must follow MSPs (or, in the case of vertical *stare decisis*, that the position is uncertain until we learn more about the views of legislators). However, that conclusion, too, would be premature since we have yet to explore the full implications for the present issue of the principle of parliamentary supremacy.

Consider two ways in which one might argue for the claim that later courts should follow MSPs. First, it might be contended that an MSP changes the statute's legal effect, so the statute now has the legal effect set out in the precedent. This appears to be Kerr LJ's view in *London Transport Executive*, at least with regard to decisions of the Supreme Court, when he states that a court's authoritative interpretation of a statute is the law unless subsequently changed by Parliament. On this view, a later court faced with an MSP is not confronted with conflicting legal norms because the earlier court's decision changed the statute's legal effect (so the decision states what the statute's legal effect is now, even though it was mistaken about what the statute's legal effect was *before* the decision was reached). Thus, the later court's duties to follow precedent and to uphold statutory norms require the same thing of it.

Alternatively, one might maintain that the legal norm established by the statute remains part of the law but now coexists with the norm introduced by the MSP, and later courts must

---

[20] This possibility was suggested by Jeff Goldsworthy. The suggestion presupposes that it is possible to ascribe views to Parliament as a whole. I shall not contest that presupposition, but rather will consider *which* views should be ascribed to Parliament.

[21] Similar points have been made in response to a related claim: see n 40.

uphold the latter. For example, it might be suggested that an MSP creates a protected (legal) reason—a reason to act in accordance with the norm contained in the precedent, and a reason not to act on certain other norms, including the norm contained in the statute. On this view, the statute and precedent give rise to conflicting legal norms, but the MSP resolves the conflict by providing later courts with a reason to follow the precedent plus a reason not to act on the statutory norm.[22]

These are two importantly different ways of arguing for the claim that later courts should follow MSPs. However, on either approach, the earlier court has the power to alter or exclude a statute's legal effect, and hence to override the legal norm established by Parliament. Indeed, the court can (and perhaps must) do so unwittingly. The court thinks it is correctly interpreting the statute but makes a mistake, and—without the court realizing—that mistake generates a new legal norm that replaces or excludes the statute's original legal effect.

This result is contrary to the principle of parliamentary supremacy. That principle does not just obligate courts to give effect to the will of Parliament. It also requires them to prioritize that obligation over competing claims. As the Supreme Court has stated, 'it is not open to a court to challenge or refuse to apply a statute, save to the extent that Parliament authorises or requires a court to do so'.[23] The Court did not have in mind MSPs when it made that statement, but the same principle applies. The earlier court does not deliberately refuse to apply the statute. However, if a later court concludes that the earlier court's decision is mistaken and yet follows that decision, it is either refusing to give effect to the statute or is treating the earlier court as having the power to change the statute's legal effect (without parliamentary authorization). Neither is compatible with the supremacy of Parliament.[24]

These considerations apply regardless of what type of mistake the earlier court made about the statute's legal effect. Certainly, they support a *per incuriam* doctrine, according to which blatant errors on the part of the earlier court—such as overlooking a clearly relevant statutory provision or making an obvious mistake about what the provision says—undermine the precedential effect of the court's decision.[25] However, the argument presented earlier goes further. It extends to cases where an error about what the provision says is not obvious, and to cases where the mistake involves a misunderstanding or misapplication of a valid principle of statutory interpretation. To the extent that what the statute says or what the principle of statutory interpretation requires contributes to the statute's legal effect, it goes to what law Parliament made. The principle of parliamentary supremacy requires later courts to uphold that law, rather than following an earlier court's misunderstanding of it. And it requires them to do so regardless of whether the matter is difficult or contested. The courts' duty to

---

[22] This suggestion borrows ideas from Raz, but I do not think it is Raz's view. He claims that when a court applies a legal norm—including a statutory norm—its decision is binding even if mistaken (J Raz, *Practical Reason and Norms* (rev edn, OUP 1990) 134–35). This means that the decision provides a reason that excludes not only contrary extra-legal reasons but also contrary legal reasons, including the statutory norm (ibid 145). However, Raz has in mind 'determinations of the rights or duties of individuals in concrete situations', which he distinguishes from 'creat[ing] precedent and lay[ing] down general rules' (ibid 136–37). This suggests that his claim is that the court's decision about the parties' legal rights and duties is binding, not that the court's decision generates a rule that is binding on later courts even if it is based on a mistaken interpretation of a statute.

[23] *Public Law Project v Lord Chancellor* [2016] UKSC 39, [2016] AC 1531 [20]. This was stated to be 'subject to arguable extreme exceptions', but it is clear that the Court did not have MSPs in mind. See also *Miller v Secretary of State for Exiting the European Union* [2017] UKSC 5, [2018] AC 61 [43], where the majority quoted Dicey's famous statement that 'no person or body is recognised by the law as having a right to override or set aside the legislation of Parliament' (AV Dicey, *Introduction to the Study of the Law of the Constitution* (8th edn, Macmillan 1915) 38).

[24] Similarly, it is problematic for the Supreme Court to invoke the Practice Statement when deciding whether to follow its own statutory precedents. This will sometimes require the court to follow a precedent it regards as mistaken, and hence to treat that precedent as replacing or excluding the statute's legal effect.

[25] See, e.g., *Rickards v Rickards* [1989] EWCA Civ 8, [1989] 3 WLR 748.

374   DALE SMITH

give effect to the will of Parliament does not end as soon as there is disagreement about what Parliament willed.

Similarly, these considerations apply to both vertical and horizontal *stare decisis*. To claim that a lower court should refuse to follow a higher court's decision may seem to strike at the heart of the doctrine of precedent. If that doctrine means anything, one might think, it means that lower courts must follow decisions of higher courts, even if they disagree with those decisions. Nevertheless, lower courts are bound to uphold a statute's legal effect, just as higher courts are. They are also required to recognize statute law as a higher source of law than judge-made law. This suggests that, when confronted with an MSP, a later court must uphold the statutory norm, rather than following precedent, even if the precedent comes from a higher court.[26]

Let us take stock. When faced with an MSP, a court may be subject to conflicting legal duties. On the one hand, the doctrine of precedent may obligate the court to follow the MSP. On the other hand, the court is obligated to uphold the statute's legal effect. However, the principle of parliamentary supremacy requires the court to prioritize its duty to uphold the statute's legal effect over its duty to follow precedent.

True, there may be a broad judicial consensus that courts are bound by vertical *stare decisis* in the statutory context. However, there is little evidence that Parliament agrees. Moreover, once we look beyond vertical *stare decisis*, there is disagreement even among judges. Against that is the general acceptance—including by judges—of the importance of parliamentary supremacy. The majority in *Miller* described parliamentary supremacy as 'a fundamental principle of the UK constitution'.[27] In *ZH and CN v London Borough of Newham and London Borough of Lewisham*,[28] Lord Neuberger described the duty 'to give effect to the will of Parliament as expressed in the statute' as 'the fundamental duty of the court'. If a later court follows an MSP, it fails to give effect to the will of Parliament, and so breaches this legal duty. It therefore acts inconsistently with legal principles that judges profess to hold—and treat as fundamental—in other contexts.

It has been suggested that parliamentary supremacy is subject to certain limits.[29] However, the focus has been on judicial review of executive action and the protection of fundamental rights. It is another thing to claim that a court's misunderstanding of a statutory norm can override that norm. Still, some judicial discussions of parliamentary supremacy might be thought to support that claim. In a passage in *Cart v The Upper Tribunal*,[30] which was cited with approval by Lady Hale on appeal to the Supreme Court,[31] Laws LJ emphasized the need for statute law to be 'mediated by an authoritative source' that is independent of both the legislature and executive—that is, a court. Statutes, Laws LJ maintained, are texts which often cannot speak for themselves, but rather must be interpreted. This interpretation cannot be undertaken by the legislature or executive, or else 'they ... would be judge in their own cause'.[32] Moreover, because judicial interpretation is necessary to prevent the statute's 'scope and content [from] becom[ing] muddied and unclear', the 'requirement of an authoritative judicial source for the interpretation of law' is not contrary to the principle of parliamentary

---

[26] I consider in section 4 what role this leaves for the doctrine of precedent to play.

[27] *Miller* (n 23) [43].

[28] *ZH and CN v London Borough of Newham and London Borough of Lewisham* [2014] UKSC 62, [2015] 1 AC 1259 [148].

[29] A possibility left open by the Supreme Court in *Public Law Project* (n 23).

[30] *Cart v The Upper Tribunal* [2009] EWHC 3052 (Admin), [2010] 2 WLR 1012 [36]–[40].

[31] [2011] UKSC 28, [2012] 1 AC 663 [30].

[32] *Cart* (n 30) [37].

supremacy, but rather is necessary to give effect to that principle (and so 'cannot be dispensed with by Parliament').[33]

Laws LJ was concerned with an ouster clause (i.e. a statutory provision that purports to exclude the jurisdiction of the courts to review certain administrative decisions), and his remarks could be understood as confined to that context. However, some of what he says seems to go further. Indeed, it might be thought to support the conclusion that, when faced with an MSP, a court should follow precedent, rather than upholding the statute's legal effect.

Laws LJ was clearly worried about the effect of disagreement on the operation of statute law, as indicated by his concern to prevent the scope and content of statutes from becoming 'muddied and unclear'. When he says that statutes are texts that often cannot speak for themselves, his point may be that—where there is disagreement about a statute's legal effect—that disagreement cannot be resolved by appealing to the statutory text, since what the text says is precisely what is in dispute.[34] By contrast, judicial interpretation *can* resolve the disagreement, and hence ensure that the statute is able to guide people's behaviour. However, a judicial interpretation can play this role only if later courts treat it as binding even if they think it is mistaken. One might conclude that the principle of parliamentary supremacy requires judges to uphold MSPs, because this is necessary to ensure that statutes are able to guide behaviour in the face of disagreement about their legal effect.

It is true that, when a statute's legal effect is disputed, a judicial interpretation will sometimes resolve that dispute. The law's subjects may then use that interpretation to guide their behaviour. However, if the interpretation is mistaken, they will not be guiding their behaviour in a way that conforms to the statute. In such cases, upholding the court's interpretation is not supported by the principle of parliamentary supremacy. That principle requires judges to give effect to each statute that comes before them.[35] It does not authorize them to refuse to uphold a statute's legal effect because they think that doing so will increase the law's ability, more generally, to guide people's behaviour.[36] (I consider a related suggestion—that it is more important to provide certainty about how a statute will be interpreted than it is to get that interpretation right—in section 5.)

4. Some Qualifications

Let us call the argument presented earlier 'the argument from parliamentary supremacy'. Before I consider further objections to that argument, I should mention some ways in which it is not as radical as it may appear. First, it leaves room for judicial decision-making to play an important role in the context of statute law. I have contended that the principle of parliamentary supremacy requires courts not to act contrary to a statutory norm, as they would if they followed an MSP. However, parliamentary supremacy may be consistent with courts filling gaps in statutes, where this is necessary to resolve a legal dispute. Thus, gap-filling statutory precedents may be binding on later courts, even though MSPs are not.

---

[33] ibid [38].

[34] Presumably, he is not suggesting that statutes cannot have a determinate legal effect until they are interpreted by a court. This would be to claim that statutes cannot make law—only judicial interpretations of them can. See further J Goldsworthy, *Parliamentary Sovereignty: Contemporary Debates* (CUP 2010) 230–31.

[35] Wherever possible. It may not be possible where two statutes conflict.

[36] The text speaks to the position at law, and so leaves open the possibility that it would be better (morally speaking) if legal officials rethought the principle of parliamentary supremacy to permit judges to act in a way that maximizes the law's ability to guide behaviour. I cannot assess this possibility here, though the discussion in section 5 may offer reasons for doubt.

376   DALE SMITH

Secondly, nothing I have said precludes the possibility that mistaken common law precedents are binding on later courts. The discussion in section 3 suggests that different considerations apply when considering MSPs from those that apply when considering mistaken common law precedents. The conflict of duties that arises in the former context does not arise in the latter context. This is not to deny that the principle of parliamentary supremacy is relevant in both contexts, but it is relevant in different ways.

Thirdly, before concluding that a statutory precedent is mistaken, a later court should consider what epistemic weight to give to the earlier court's decision. It may give greater weight to a decision of a higher court than to its own previous decisions or those of a lower court.[37] However, the principle of parliamentary supremacy means that a lower court cannot abdicate responsibility for deciding what the statute's legal effect is. If, after giving due epistemic deference to the higher court, the lower court concludes that the higher court's interpretation is mistaken, then—for the reasons given earlier—it is required to uphold the statute's legal effect, rather than following precedent.

Fourthly, the argument from parliamentary supremacy addresses what courts are legally required to do when faced with an MSP, not what they morally ought to do. There may be instances where the MSP is morally preferable to the statute's legal effect, so that a later court ought morally to follow the MSP. However, in these circumstances, the court is departing from the law (for good moral reasons). Legally, it is required to uphold the statutory norm.

Finally, there is a possible implication of the argument from parliamentary supremacy about which I wish to remain neutral. If the earlier court's mistaken interpretation of a statute is not binding on later courts, then is its decision about the rights and duties of the parties to the earlier case also not binding? Arguments can be made on both sides of this issue. On the one hand, we might think that there is an important difference between identifying the norm created by a statute and applying that norm to resolve a particular legal dispute, such that a court's resolution of the dispute must be binding even if its attempt to identify the statutory norm is not. On the other hand, we might think that if later cases must be decided by reference to the correct interpretation of the statute, then the legal rights and duties of the parties to the earlier case must also be assessed by reference to that interpretation, or else parties to different cases will be treated according to different standards, in a way that undermines equality before the law.[38] I shall not seek to resolve this debate here: I claim that a later court should not follow an MSP, but I leave open what implications that claim has for the legal standing of the earlier court's determination of the rights and duties of the parties to the earlier case.

5. Objections

In this section, I consider an important objection to the argument from parliamentary supremacy. First, though, I wish to set aside two other objections. It is sometimes pointed out that, if the legislature does not like a statutory precedent, it is free to override that precedent by introducing amending legislation.[39] This might suggest that where a later court follows an MSP, this does not breach parliamentary supremacy, because Parliament had the opportunity

---

[37] Perhaps due to the larger number of judges on the higher court and their greater eminence and/or experience. See further Lamond (n 1) 709.

[38] This way of expressing the concern was suggested by Sebastian Lewis.

[39] See, e.g., *Kimble v Marvel Entertainment* 576 US 446, 455–57 (2015).

to override the precedent. (I shall call this 'the legislative override argument'.) Further, if Parliament does not introduce amending legislation, this indicates that it is content with the court's decision, even if a later court thinks the decision was mistaken. Parliament may even agree that the decision was mistaken, and yet may prefer the MSP to the statute's true legal effect or may believe it is more important that the issue is settled than that it is resolved correctly. This suggests that later courts better conform to Parliament's wishes by following the MSP. (I shall call this 'the tacit acquiescence argument'.)

The legislative override and tacit acquiescence arguments have been subject to thorough criticism elsewhere.[40] In this section, I consider a different objection to the argument from parliamentary supremacy.

The crux of this objection is that the argument in section 3 overlooks the values that support the doctrine of precedent. Adhering to precedents—whether common law or statutory—promotes certain values. Moreover, the objector claims, this is true regardless of whether the precedent was correctly decided. The need to promote those values is such that later courts should follow a statutory precedent even if it is mistaken.

The values to which this objector might appeal are multitudinous, but I shall focus on three closely related values. First, the doctrine of precedent promotes certainty and predictability. If the law's subjects know that previous decisions will be followed by later courts, even if the court regards the decision as mistaken, then the law's subjects are able to predict future judicial decisions and plan accordingly.[41] By contrast, if courts were free to depart from previous decisions they regard as mistaken, it would be uncertain when a precedent will be followed.

Secondly, the doctrine of precedent promotes stability. It ensures that legal issues— including how particular statutes should be interpreted—can be settled over time. By contrast, if court B today was not legally required to follow the precedent established by court A yesterday, there would be nothing to stop court C overturning court B's decision tomorrow. The result would be that no legal issue could ever be regarded as settled.[42]

Thirdly, the doctrine of precedent protects reliance interests.[43] Once a precedent is decided, people may act in reliance on that precedent, and may suffer detriment if it is not followed in subsequent cases. To protect these reliance interests, the precedent on which they are based should be followed, even if that decision was mistaken.

It seems, therefore, that there are reasons to follow precedents, including statutory precedents, even if those decisions are mistaken. Some of these reasons derive from the interests of the law's subjects (in planning for the future or in being able to rely on existing plans); others reflect systemic considerations (e.g. the need for stability in the body of legal norms).

Recall, though, that our concern is with what courts are legally required to do, not what they morally ought to do. Thus, for the present objection to engage with our concerns, it must be the case that these values are *legal* values, in the sense that they bear on the question of whether courts are legally required to follow precedent. Otherwise, the preceding

---

[40] See, e.g., A Coney Barrett, 'Statutory *Stare Decisis* in the Courts of Appeals' (2005) 73 Geo Wash L Rev 317, 330–39; C Nelson, '*Stare Decisis* and Demonstrably Erroneous Precedents' (2001) 87 Va L Rev 1, 76–78; WN Eskridge, Jr, 'Overruling Statutory Precedents' (1988) 76 Geo LJ 1361, 1402–09. See also *ZH and CN* (n 28) [85] (Lord Carnwath) and [167] (Baroness Hale (dissenting)). Some of the criticisms are particular to the US context, but others apply more generally.

[41] *Telstra Corporation v Treloar* [2000] FCA 1170 [23] (Branson and Finkelstein JJ). The Practice Statement also notes the need for 'some degree of certainty upon which individuals can rely in the conduct of their affairs'.

[42] This argument is discussed in Nelson (n 40) 3. Nelson's response is considered later.

[43] S Lewis, 'Precedent and the Rule of Law' (2021) 41 OJLS 873, 881–82.

discussion may show that, morally speaking, judges ought to follow MSPs, but it does not speak to what the law requires.

However, let us concede, *arguendo*, that these values *are* legal values. Nevertheless, it is not clear that these values require courts to follow an MSP, rather than upholding the statute's legal effect. Discussions of these values that are framed with the common law in mind cannot be transposed to the statutory context without recognizing that there is an additional legal source—the statute—which affects what these values require.

Consider reliance. It is true that if the law's subjects act in reliance on an MSP, a refusal by later courts to follow precedent may undermine reliance interests. However, if the law's subjects instead rely on the statute, a refusal by later courts to follow an MSP may protect reliance interests.

A similar point can be made about certainty and predictability. If the law's subjects are aware only of the MSP, they will find subsequent judicial decisions to be more predictable if courts follow precedent.[44] However, if the law's subjects are aware only of the statute, they will find subsequent decisions to be more predictable if courts uphold the statute's legal effect.[45]

What of someone who is aware of both the statute and the MSP? We might think they will be better able to predict judicial decisions if judges follow the MSP, at least where there is disagreement about the statute's legal effect (and hence uncertainty about whether judges will identify the error in the MSP). However, this will depend on whether there is more uncertainty about what the statute requires than there is about what the MSP requires. (Precedents, not just statutes, can generate uncertainty.) We might expect that, as a general rule, there will be more uncertainty about what the statute requires in circumstances where the earlier court failed to correctly identify the statute's legal effect. However, even if this is so, whether following precedent better promotes certainty and predictability overall also depends on how many people are aware of both the statute and the MSP.

Thus, invoking these values appears to result in an impasse. One might think that resolving the impasse requires empirical investigation into whether the law's subjects are more likely to be aware of, and rely on, the statute or the MSP.[46] However, this would be a mistake. Courts lack the legal power to undertake such an inquiry and then, on the basis of their findings, to decide whether they will follow MSPs. Rather, courts are required by the principle of parliamentary supremacy to treat legislation as a higher source of law, prevailing over judge-made law—including MSPs—in cases of conflict. Ultimately, the court is bound by the statute, not by people's expectations or reliance interests.[47]

That courts are bound in this way may be no bad thing. Even if the values just considered support following MSPs, there may be other values that push in the opposite direction. If certainty is a legal value in the UK, then is democracy? If so, do democratic considerations support upholding a statute's legal effect (perhaps even when that legal effect is disputed)? If they do, which is more important, promoting certainty and predictability or respecting Parliament's democratic credentials?

These are difficult questions, and we may have reason to want legally settled answers to those questions, rather than courts being free to arrive at their own answers. We might think of the principle of parliamentary supremacy as providing that legal settlement, by treating

---

[44] Assuming that the law's subjects correctly identify the rule (or principle or reasons) supplied by the MSP.

[45] Assuming that the law's subjects correctly identify that legal effect.

[46] This may include an assessment of how likely the law's subjects are to correctly identify either.

[47] Which is not to say that predictability, reliance, etc are legally irrelevant. They may contribute to the existence of a legal duty to follow precedent. However, in the case of an MSP, this duty gives way to the duty to uphold the statute's legal effect.

democracy as prevailing over certainty and predictability to the extent that they conflict. Moreover, for the reasons given in section 3.A, judges alone cannot bring about a new legal settlement since it is not just judicial practice that matters for this purpose—the views of legislators also count.[48]

I have focused on certainty, predictability, and reliance, but similar remarks apply to the claim that the need for stability supports following MSPs. Caleb Nelson points out that this claim assumes that the mistake made by the earlier court cannot be demonstrated to the satisfaction of future courts.[49] If it can, then future courts will not be tempted to overturn the decision in which the MSP is rejected, and stability will be achieved. This is true, but the discussion in section 2 suggests that judicial errors concerning a statute's legal effect will not always be readily demonstrable. A more complete answer is that it is not left to judges to decide whether they should depart from a statutory norm. The judge's task is to uphold the statute's legal effect, not to act on their own assessment of the importance of stability in the law or of how best to achieve that stability.

6. Conclusion

I have suggested that when faced with an MSP, a court may be subject to conflicting legal duties. On the one hand, it has a duty to uphold the statute's legal effect. On the other hand, it may have a duty to follow precedent. I have also suggested that the law specifies how this conflict is to be resolved. The principle of parliamentary supremacy requires the court to prioritize its duty to uphold the statute's legal effect over its duty to follow precedent.

However, as mentioned in section 1, this chapter represents only an initial exploration of these issues. There may be other legal norms—beyond the principle of parliamentary supremacy and the doctrine of precedent—that bear on the question of what courts are legally required to do when faced with an MSP. An obvious candidate is the rule of law. It has been suggested that the doctrine of precedent safeguards the rule of law by promoting stability and protecting reliance interests.[50] This might suggest that the discussion of stability and reliance in section 5 is incomplete because it fails to take account of the way in which the rule of law—arguably, a norm of UK law as fundamental as the principle of parliamentary supremacy—supports following MSPs. I cannot fully assess that suggestion here, but let me offer two brief observations. First, we have seen that it is not clear that considerations of stability and reliance do support following MSPs. Secondly, the rule of law is a complex ideal. Even if it is concerned, in part, with stability and reliance, and even if those considerations support following MSPs, the rule of law also requires courts to apply the norms in the statute book.[51] This requirement is itself concerned, in part, with promoting reliance and stability. However, it may also be concerned with constraining the powers of judges, in ways that cohere—rather than conflict—with the principle of parliamentary supremacy.

---

[48] Courts sometimes claim that it is typically more important that an interpretation of the law provide certainty than that the interpretation be correct (see, e.g., *Rickards* (n 25) 755 (Lord Donaldson MR)). Whatever the merits of that view in other contexts, when it comes to statutory interpretation the view is inconsistent with the principle of parliamentary supremacy, which—by emphasizing the importance of the court's duty to uphold the will of Parliament—prioritizes correctness over certainty.

[49] Nelson (n 40) 3–4.

[50] Lewis (n 43). Laws LJ also appeals to the rule of law in *Cart* (n 30) [35]–[36] (in the context of considering an ouster clause).

[51] LL Fuller, *The Morality of Law* (rev edn, Yale UP 1969) 37–39.

28

Precedent and Law-Making Powers

Mikołaj Barczentewicz

1. Introduction

My main concern in this chapter is that some who argue that judges do exercise legal powers specifically to make (change) the law, may be implicitly using the concept of a legal power in a way that is inconsistent with the best general accounts of legal powers. My second concern is that perhaps the theorists should not be too fast to dismiss what the official stories of the various legal systems say about the limits of judicial power. Or at least to dismiss one aspect, that is, that judges do not have law-making powers to change the law in a similar way to how legislators change the law. It may very well be that in some legal systems judicial influence on legal change is realized through customary mechanisms or mechanisms closer to custom than to legislating. In this chapter, I try to identify the signs that would help us to make the distinction. My interest is not limited to common law jurisdictions: I accept that legal systems without an official doctrine of precedent may in fact have very similar mechanisms to common law systems.

This chapter begins, in section 2, with a discussion of the common features of the major general accounts of legal powers and their implications for different roles played by judges in legal change. First, I discuss what distinguishes the major conceptions of legal powers—focusing on the aspect of intentionality of exercises of legal powers (section 2.A). I consider what this means for the phenomenon of 'unprecedent'. In section 2.B, I argue that exercises of legal powers have normative, not merely causal, effect on legal change. I then show that this precludes, under most circumstances, the possibility of a legal power to change a customary rule and what this means for judge-led legal change (section 2.C). In section 3, I discuss some prominent views on whether judges exercise law-making powers in the UK, in France, and in Germany. I consider the issue of tensions related to existence and limits of judicial powers to make (change) the law between official stories (ideologies) of legal systems and second-order (e.g. academic) accounts of those legal systems.

2. The Limits of Legal Powers and Judge-Led Legal Change

A legal power to change the law allows an agent to create, remove, or otherwise modify laws (legal rules). Exercises of legal powers are not just actions, they are 'acts-in-the-law'.[1] Legal powers are more than abilities to bring about effects in the physical world (such as my power to move this glass in front of me) or 'powers-in-fact' (such as influence, social power, or political power).[2] Being able to exercise a legal power may require having those other powers, but

---

[1] HLA Hart, *The Concept of Law* (3rd edn, OUP 2012) 28.
[2] MacCormick defined the latter as 'power actually to change the factual situation so that another's interests are affected and thereby his or her reasons for action or inaction altered'; N MacCormick, 'Powers and

Mikołaj Barczentewicz, *Precedent and Law-Making Powers* In: *Philosophical Foundations of Precedent*. Edited by: Timothy Endicott, Hafsteinn Dan Kristjánsson, and Sebastian Lewis, Oxford University Press. © Mikołaj Barczentewicz 2023.
DOI: 10.1093/oso/9780192857248.003.0029

they are distinct.[3] Moreover, legal powers are not reducible to, do not require, or entail any legal rights, legal permissions, or legal duties. One can have a legal power to X without having a legal right or permission to X (also when doing X is legally prohibited).[4] Importantly, it is not the case that whenever an action has a law-changing effect, that action is an exercise of a legal power.[5] Even in that case, there is a need to show that the law considers the action as an exercise of a legal power. Sometimes the law enables by merely recognizing human action as law-affecting, without involving legal powers.

What I have said so far is common among the major modern conceptions of legal powers. One other notion that those conceptions share, at least implicitly, is that a legal power is an ability to change someone's legal situation by a volitional act.[6] Crucially, this excludes any legal effect (e.g. a change in the law) of a fact which is also not meaningfully under the control of an agent. Within the discussion of legal change there is a clear example of this sort: change in customary law.

A. Intentions: The Significance of Clear Contrary Indications

The spectrum of views on the role of intentionality in definitions of legal powers may be presented in the following simplified way. My argument in this chapter does not, for the most part, hinge on choosing any of the following positions and, when it does, I indicate that.

An action counts as an exercise of a legal power to X if that action results in a change X of a legal situation (legal position) and this action is ...

1. 'volitional',[7]
2. 'volitional' and desirable from the perspective of the person exercising the legal power,[8]

Power-Conferring Norms' in SL Paulson (ed), *Normativity and Norms: Critical Perspectives on Kelsenian Themes* (OUP 1999) 495. See also J Raz, *Practical Reason and Norms* (OUP 1999) 103; C Essert, 'Legal Powers in Private Law' (2015) 21 Legal Theory 136, 141–42.

[3] WN Hohfeld, *Fundamental Legal Conceptions as Applied in Judicial Reasoning* (W Wheeler Cook ed, Yale UP 1923) 58; MacCormick, 'Powers and Power-Conforming Norms' (n 2) 497; L Lindahl and D Reidhav, 'Legal Power: The Basic Definition' (2017) 30 Ratio Juris 158, 163.

[4] Hohfeld (n 3) 58; J Raz, 'Voluntary Obligations and Normative Powers' (1972) 46 Proceedings of the Aristotelian Society, Supplementary vols 59, 82; HLA Hart, 'Bentham on Legal Powers' (1972) 81 Yale LJ 799, 816; E Bulygin, 'On Norms of Competence' (1992) 11 Law and Philosophy 201, 205–06, 215–16; L Duarte d'Almeida, 'Fundamental Legal Concepts: The Hohfeldian Framework' (2016) 11 Philosophy Compass 554, 559; Lindahl and Reidhav (n 3) 163. Moreover, having a power by itself provides no reason for action (no reason to exercise the power), see Raz, *Practical Reason and Norms* (n 2) 106; J Gardner, 'Justification under Authority' (2010) 23 Can J Law and Jurisprudence 71, 78–79.

[5] And in general: 'not all abilities to change someone's normative position, even abilities to do so knowingly and intentionally, are normative powers'; ibid 87. See also Raz, *Practical Reason and Norms* (n 2) 98–99.

[6] In Wesley Hohfeld's famous formulation: 'some superadded fact or group of facts which are under the volitional control of one or more human beings'; Hohfeld (n 3) 50–51. This arguably excludes acts of non-human animals and quite clearly excludes acts of nature. However, Visa Kurki argued that both animals and infants can hold legal powers on a proper construction of the Hohfeldian position as they can act with volition; VAJ Kurki, 'Legal Competence and Legal Power' in M McBride (ed), *New Essays on the Nature of Rights* (Hart 2017) 46.

[7] 'Volitional' is used here as a term of art which does not mean 'with intention to X', see n 13; see also Hohfeld (n 3) 50–51; MH Kramer, 'Rights Without Trimmings' in MH Kramer, NE Simmonds, and H Steiner (eds), *A Debate Over Rights: Philosophical Enquiries* (OUP 2000) 104.

[8] Hart (n 1) 27. See also M Köpcke, *Legal Validity: The Fabric of Justice* (Hart 2019) 15–17. According to Kramer, Hart 'appeared to confine the category of powers to Hohfeldian powers that are normally beneficial for the people who are endowed with them'; MH Kramer, *HLA Hart: The Nature of Law* (Polity Press 2018) 37.

3. with intention to X and desirable from the perspective of the legal system,[9]
4. manifesting an (actual or imputed) intent to use the law to X,[10]
5. with intention to X or without (but in the latter case only if the agent's intention would have been 'minimally sufficient' for similar legal effect in other similar situations),[11]
6. with a (legally crucial) decision to exercise a legal power to X (real will theory).[12]

Overall, the fourth category—exercises of legal powers manifest intent to use the law to bring about some legal effect—includes conceptions of legal powers that are most plausible and closest to how the notion of legal powers is used in ordinary legal discourses. Those conceptions avoid the consequence of the volitional-only view that people exercise legal powers by actions such as committing crimes or committing suicide.[13] And, unlike the 'real will' theories, they can account straightforwardly for contracts by reliance—that is, contracts where at least one party did not *intend* to enter the contract but is taken by the law as having manifested intent to enter and is thus legally bound by the contract.[14]

Of course, these are not all the conceptions of legal powers available in the literature. But it is fair to say, Hohfeld and Kramer notwithstanding, that it is a dominant view that exercises of legal powers necessarily manifest (communicate) an intent to achieve the result of an exercise of the power.[15] For some legal powers, such as the power to contract, a merely imputed intent may suffice—there is no necessity for the agent to actually have the intent ('real will').[16]

Even if a merely imputed intent is sufficient for a particular legal power, it is still the case that an indication to the contrary entails that the legal power was not exercised.[17] For example, this may be the case when someone expressly claims that they are merely testing a pen and have no intent to enter a contract, while doing what otherwise appears to be signing a contract. Cases of clear contrary indication are *not* cases of leading or inducing a reasonable observer to believe that someone exercises a legal power. Whenever the law ascribes legal

---

[9] Raz, *Practical Reason and Norms* (n 2) 102. See also Köpcke (n 8) 20–23.

[10] N MacCormick, *HLA Hart* (2nd edn, Stanford UP 2008) 98; Lindahl and Reidhav (n 3) 169; Köpcke (n 8) 59.

[11] Kurki (n 6).

[12] A Halpin, 'The Concept of a Legal Power' (1996) 16 OJLS 129. See also A Reilly, 'Is the "Mere Equity" to Rescind a Legal Power? Unpacking Hohfeld's Concept of "Volitional Control"' (2019) 39 OJLS 779.

[13] Kramer, 'Rights Without Trimmings' (n 7) 104; Kurki (n 6) 43–44. Wesley Hohfeld's volitional-only notion of legal powers, adopted by Kramer, is the broadest among the major views; Hohfeld (n 3) 50–51. As long as a fact grounding the legal effect is under human volitional control, we are dealing with a Hohfeldian legal power. Even if, together with Kramer, we appreciate the analytical rigour and the corrective (not lexicographical) ambition of Hohfeld's conceptual engineering, there is clearly a rather large gap between Hohfeldian powers and how the notion of legal powers is used today, both in ordinary legal discourses and in academic legal writing. I consider it more confusing than useful to refer to Hohfeldian powers as 'legal powers' *simpliciter*.

[14] Köpcke (n 8) 59; Halpin (n 12) 146–47.

[15] See also T Spaak, 'Explicating the Concept of Legal Competence' in JC Haage and D Pfordten (eds), *Concepts in Law* (Springer 2009); Essert (n 2) 147–48.

[16] Essert (n 2) 154–54; Lindahl and Reidhav (n 3) 173–75.

[17] ibid 170–73. Kurki's account of legal powers ('legal competence') allows for exercises of legal powers in cases when an agent's intent to do so is legally irrelevant; Kurki (n 6) 38–39. On Kurki's view, for that to be the case it must also be that the same agent is capable of bringing about the same legal effect through the basic scenario (i.e. when their intention matters legally). Kurki did not confront the question of the necessary legal relevance of contrary indications (clear indications of no intent to exercise a legal power). Kurki suggested that taking someone to have exercised a legal power unintentionally can be justified (morally) in the following way:

> By not questioning whether an individual has actually intended the legal consequences of his or her act effects, we also abstain from questioning that individual's moral agency. (ibid)

It is difficult to see how this justification applies to situations where the individual clearly indicates that they do not intend to bring about certain legal consequences. If anything, we show less respect to the individual's moral agency by imputing to them an intent they clearly indicate they do not have. Lindahl and Reidav's account deals with this in a much more straightforward way.

consequences to voluntary action despite even the clearest protestations from the agent in question that she intends not to incur such consequences, we are not dealing with an instance of a legal power.

If someone (voluntarily) moves to a new city and the law thus applies local tax rules to that person—and if it is irrelevant whether she intends this legal consequence—she is not exercising a legal power to incur a new set of tax liabilities.[18] Another example of an action with legal effects, which is not an exercise of a legal power, is when a person who kills intentionally incurs legal liability irrespective of whether she intends to incur that liability. The issue is thus not whether the law considers *some* intentionality or voluntariness as relevant to ascribing legal consequences to an action (e.g. in the case of murder it does), but whether it takes as relevant an expressed lack of intent specifically to create those particular legal consequences (e.g. in the case of murder, it does not).[19]

How does this matter for legal change? Consider a change in the law initiated by a court. Many may be tempted to simply conclude that the court in question exercised a law-making power and legally *made* the change. However, what if the court expressly disclaimed any law-making power and went to some pains to present its decision as: (1) not departing from the law as it was before; or (2) not intended to have any legal effect beyond the case before the court (*inter partes*)? These type of claims are routinely made by courts in many legal systems, as I will show.[20] Such clear indications of no intent to exercise a law-making power strongly suggest that the law-changing effect happened without the exercise of a law-making power.[21]

Nonetheless, one should not be too quick to take what judges say at face value. There may be situations where there are good reasons to discount apparent indications of no intent. Such statements may be mistaken, even without being insincere.[22] That is, there may be reasons to believe that the law has a different standard for effective indications of no intent than it may seem.[23] For instance, it could be the case that some ritual claims of judicial restraint are legally irrelevant, but some kinds of technical expressions of intent not to change the law are actually legally effective—thus allowing for a possibility that the judges in question do have a legal power specifically to change the law not only on the broadest Hohfeldian view of legal powers.

A question remains whether it must be possible to cancel the implication of intent to exercise a law-making power while still effectively exercising a power to adjudicate. What if a legal system could confer on some judges a legal power to change the law by creating binding precedents, while at the same time treating almost any published judgment as having precedential force?[24] It could perhaps then be that only a court's decision not to publish its judgment or to publish something that is clearly not a judgment (but, e.g., a cooking recipe)

---

[18] Raz, *Practical Reason and Norms* (n 2) 103.

[19] I do not deny that sometimes it is possible to exercise a legal power insincerely, see K Kessler Ferzan, 'The Bluff: The Power of Insincere Actions' (2017) 23 Legal Theory 168. The issue I focus on here is whether it is possible to have a legal power when one's sincere and clear indication of not intending to bring about some legal effect is irrelevant to whether that legal effect occurs.

[20] See section 3.

[21] To say with Andrei Marmor that '[w]hether they recognize it as such or not, judges have the power to change the constitution' is to use 'power' in a broad Hohfeldian sense—or perhaps even beyond Hohfeld, see nn 13 and 17; A Marmor, *Interpretation and Legal Theory* (2nd edn, Hart 2005) 142.

[22] In general, for the court to be an authority means that its decisions bind even if they are mistaken and even if they do not change the legal situation; Raz, *Practical Reason and Norms* (n 2) 135–36. However, the issue here is that the law may deem some things said by the courts as not authoritative.

[23] Kimberly Kessler Ferzan discusses a case 'where a father claimed that creditors could not take furniture that his son had used as collateral because the father had never actually intended to give the furniture to the son, just to let the son use the furniture'; Kessler Ferzan (n 19) 180.

[24] I thank Kenneth Ehrenberg for pressing me on this point.

would count as not exercising the power to set a precedent. One way to look at that is to see it as insensitivity of legal consequences (of setting a precedent) to intent to bring the consequences about and thus not a case of a legal power to set a precedent. Nothing a court could try to do *specifically* to prevent setting a precedent (e.g. stating clearly that this is what they want to avoid) would matter legally. It could only refuse to adjudicate altogether (or at least to adjudicate in a way somehow departing from previous case law).

To use a concrete example, the US Supreme Court in its landmark *Bush v Gore* decision employed a tactic Josh Blackman labelled as 'unprecedent'.[25] The Court has written:

> [o]ur consideration is limited to the present circumstances, for the problem of equal protection in election processes generally presents many complexities.[26]

The idea of unprecedent is simply that a court tries to avoid setting a precedent, which later courts would follow. In other words, that a court aims to limit the legal effects of the case at hand to the parties involved. The problem is that it is doubtful whether even the US Supreme Court can successfully impose such a limitation.[27] Or, more precisely, whether the Court can simply say that its present decision is not a precedent, as opposed to trying to use other techniques of framing the judgment in such a way as to make it less likely it will be followed.[28] Similarly, in some legal systems, judges (especially judges of the highest courts) control which judgments are published and may decide not to publish a judgment formally, but at the same time be unable to prevent, for example, the parties from making the judgment public. It could be that such informally published judgments are treated in the legal system simply as authoritative as the formally published ones.

If later courts treat purported unprecedents (or informally published judgments) in the same way that they treat precedents, then this may suggest that in the legal system in question there is no legal power to make precedents (on a mainstream view of legal powers that requires at least imputed intent). There is no legal power because clear indications of no intent to exercise the purported power are not determinative of whether the legal effect obtains. Instead, there may be a legal power to adjudicate and a legal duty for judges to treat certain past court decisions as precedents.[29]

B. 'Volitional Control': Normative and Causal Effects on Legal Change

Setting aside the differences between major conceptions of legal powers, I will now focus on what I think they have in common. A key element implicit in Hohfeld's 'volitional control' and in other accounts focused on the intent of a power holder was helpfully framed by Adam Perry and Adam Tucker in the following way: 'your act must be recognized as creating a rule

---

[25] J Blackman, 'The Unprecedent' (Josh Blackman's Blog, 4 April 2013) <http://joshblackman.com/blog/2013/04/04/the-unprecedent/> accessed 1 December 2021.

[26] *Bush v Gore* 531 US 98, 109 (2000).

[27] J Blackman, 'Justice Thomas Cites the *Bush v Gore* 'Unprecedent' in Arizona Dissent' (Josh Blackman's Blog, 17 June 2013) <http://joshblackman.com/blog/2013/06/17/justice-thomas-cites-the-bush-v-gore-unprecedent-in-arizona-dissent/> accessed 1 December 2021.

[28] The latter is less like an exercise of a legal power and more like trying to predict something the court does not have direct control over; see the distinction between normative and causal influences on normative change later in this section.

[29] See also G Lamond, 'Do Precedents Create Rules?' (2005) 11 Legal Theory 1, 25.

because it is expected that, if it is so recognised, then you will tend to perform that act only when you intend to create a rule'.[30] Using Joseph Raz's phrasing, the exercise of a legal power has a 'normative', not merely 'causal', effect on the change of the legal situation.[31] Similarly, Lindahl and Reidhav have stressed that exercises of legal powers are to be seen in terms of 'characteristic legal consequence'—that is, when 'a legal result ensues in the case in which the person acts in a specified way'.[32] Importantly, the law-changing result is *in the case* where the purported holder of the legal power acts. Or, in other words, the 'requirement is that it is the behaviour of the power-holder that must be the legal ground for achieving the legal result'.[33]

Applied to legal change, this means that an exercise of law-making power must result in, or must end in, a change in the law—without further ('causal') intermediation. This is not a trivial requirement. It excludes all the cases in which an apparent law-maker merely influences someone else who then changes the law or when she contributes to a bottom-up process of legal change where no one can take the credit, legally speaking, for making the change.[34]

Consider the first type of case, that of influence. A simple example is that of an agent who convinces a power holder to exercise their power. For instance, a lobbyist who convinces a local authority to enact a regulation. Clearly, the action of the lobbyist is not a legal ground for that regulation. This is so even when the information that the lobbyist produces engages a legal duty for the local authority to enact the regulation (perhaps the authority has a legal duty so to act whenever it is informed of a certain kind of environmental risk).

Going back to the issue of unprecedent, depending on what precedent means in the legal system in question, it could be that a judgment of a higher court merely activates a duty of other courts to deem it as correctly decided on the facts, but the higher court has no legal power specifically to control whether and how it sets a precedent.[35] As noted earlier, the higher court may try to use language, as did the US Supreme Court in *Bush v Gore*, to influence the lower courts not to regard the judgment as precedent, but in that it is akin to the lobbyist trying to convince the local authority.

C. Precedent that Works Like Custom

As previously discussed, exerting influence over a power holder is not the same as exercising the power in question. Similarly causal, not normative, effects on legal (normative) situations also occur in some instances where legal change takes place through a process in which many agents are involved. Admittedly, some such changes are the result of exercising legal powers. A complex group such as a Parliament can be vested with legal power and can act jointly to exercise that legal power.[36] But the same cannot be said of most, if not all, changes in customs and conventions—that is, in social rules. A change to a social rule obtains by the virtue of a change in the underlying social practice. For a social rule to change,

---

[30] A Perry and A Tucker, 'Top-Down Constitutional Conventions' (2018) 81 MLR 765, 772. See also Raz, Practical Reason and Norms (n 2) 103; Raz, 'Voluntary Obligations' (n 4) 93–94.

[31] Raz, Practical Reason and Norms (n 2) 103.

[32] Lindahl and Reidhav (n 3) 161–62.

[33] ibid 160.

[34] See Raz, 'Voluntary Obligations' (n 4) 80; Lindahl and Reidhav (n 3) 177–78.

[35] For an argument that something like this is the case in English law, see Lamond (n 29).

[36] For a detailed discussion of how legislatures act jointly to make law, see R Ekins, *The Nature of Legislative Intent* (OUP 2012).

the thoughts and actions of a sufficient number of members of the relevant group involving the social rule actually have to change.

Sometimes, such change happens almost instantaneously and in response to the action of a single agent. A king, or a religious leader, or anyone else with social power, may be able to influence their community to change a social rule. But the crucial thing is that this influential person does not exercise a *normative* power to change the rule; they merely have a 'causal' effect on normative change, to use Raz's terminology. This is also the case with legal custom (customary law). To the extent that any legal rule is customary, it is unlikely to be a product of an exercise of a legal power to make that rule.

This is quite different from legal change through an exercise of legal power to change the law, as with the law-making power of a legislature. A legal power to change the law, when exercised, may have immediate and—in a sense—automatic law-changing effects. There is no need to wait and see whether anyone knows about the change, accepts the change, or adjusts their behaviour to take account of it (although such conditions could be part of some power-conferring norms).

Could it not be said that members of a group act jointly to exercise a normative power to change a social rule? After all, it is possible to come up with an account of joint (group) action that is sufficiently permissive to accommodate such bottom-up processes. This will not suffice, at least not for virtually all relevant cases. Normally, an intent that could plausibly be attributed to such a group agent would not be specific enough to constitute the relevant power-exercising intent.[37] In a typical situation of a change in custom, the change is hard to grasp, almost imperceptible. It is hard to know, even for a member of the group in question, when the process of change begins and when it is has concluded. Not uncommonly, members of the group are not aware of taking part in the change and would be surprised (or even in denial) when informed that they have done so.[38]

In situations such as this, the intent that can be attributed to the group members is an intent of some higher order: to live together, to undertake a particular project (e.g. to construct a building), and so on. And on that basis, one could try to say that the group together intends to exercise a power to change the custom. But the explanatory gap is too wide, the analogy (with an individual or an institutional group agent) too distant. As John Gardner remarked about custom (in the context of ultimate rules of recognition): '[t]his customary law is not the work of many working as one. It is the work of many acting as many.'[39]

My objection may not apply as forcefully to customary changes within a more cohesive group (e.g. within one organization) and where the group members are both aware of the past content of the customary rule and clearly intend to change it. In such circumstances, it might make sense to attribute to the group a joint intent to exercise a legal power to change the custom, and to accept that the group exercised that power. However, in relation to change, for example in customary areas of constitutional law, those conditions will rarely, if ever, obtain. And to the extent that they do not, I suspect that the chief motivation for positing the existence of 'customary powers' (legal powers to change custom) is a misguided intuition that it just must be the case that any effective change in the law is a result of an exercise of a legal power to make the change.[40]

---

[37] See J Gardner, *Law as a Leap of Faith* (OUP 2012) 72–73.

[38] See also ibid 70–72.

[39] ibid 73–74; Perry and Tucker (n 30) 783.

[40] The notion of 'customary powers' was used in this context in N Bobbio, 'Kelsen and Legal Power' in SL Paulson (ed), *Normativity and Norms: Critical Perspectives on Kelsenian Themes* (OUP 1999) 446. Interestingly, Bobbio concluded that Kelsen never articulated a position on this issue, so it is unclear whether he thought that custom changes by exercises of legal powers.

3. Official Accounts of the Law and the Legal Limits of Judicial Power

A perception of tension between the legal limits of judicial power and how judges in fact effect legal (and constitutional) change is very common in modern legal systems. For instance, Alec Stone Sweet in his *Governing with Judges* showed how the 'constitutionalisation' of law in several European countries in the twentieth century, in practice, undermined the traditional European model of the separation of powers, without displacing that model from the official accounts of those legal systems.[41]

The French case provides a very good illustration of this tension. As Mitchell Lasser has observed, in French law there is an 'official portrait' of the judicial role and an 'unofficial' one.[42] According to the official version, the judge is a 'kind of mechanical mouth; he does no more than apply legislative provisions.'[43] Furthermore, according to Troper and Grzegorczyk, in France 'courts are never bound by precedents' and 'statutes are the only source of law'.[44] However, this is viewed as a sort of fiction in French academic legal writing, where the much more prominent role of the judge in legal change is both admitted and endorsed.[45]

If the court's influence is through its contribution to customary law, then it would be inconsistent with the major accounts of legal powers to say that the court is exercising a legal power to change the law.[46] As argued earlier, in situations like these, we can speak of a causal influence over a custom ('social power'), but not of a legal (normative) power to change it. How much customary law there is, for example, in English common law today is controversial, but it is widely accepted that English common law *was* customary law 'with no firm doctrine of stare decisis' for a considerable length of time (until the eighteenth century).[47] Stephen Sachs has recently argued that it is both possible and desirable for adjudication in the US today to work more on the model of customary law ('finding' law) than that of judicial law-making.[48]

With regard to case law, John Gardner has defined it as law created by judges '*solo*, and instantaneously, by making legal rulings'.[49] On his view, case law can function without the doctrine of *stare decisis*, because, from the fact that a court can depart from a legal rule set in an earlier judgment, it does not follow that the legal rule does not exist until it is changed in a later judgment.[50] According to Gardner, English judges have a legal power to make case law.

Writing about precedent in the common law, Timothy Endicott has also argued that the powers of overruling or setting a precedent 'are instances of the power of judges to make new law'.[51] Grant Lamond has disputed this view, claiming that:

---

[41] A Stone Sweet, *Governing with Judges* (OUP 2000) 130–33.

[42] M Lasser, *Judicial Deliberations. A Comparative Analysis of Judicial Transparency and Legitimacy* (OUP 2004) ch 2.

[43] ibid 37.

[44] M Troper and C Grzegorczyk, 'Precedent in France' in ND MacCormick and RS Summers (eds), *Interpreting Precedents* (Routledge 1997) 111, 117.

[45] ibid 112–13, 119, 126, 137–38; Lasser (n 42) 38–61.

[46] See section 2.

[47] GJ Postema, 'Philosophy of the Common Law' in J Coleman, K Himma, and S Shapiro (eds), *The Oxford Handbook of Jurisprudence and Philosophy of Law* (OUP 2004) 589; see also Gardner, Law as a Leap of Faith (n 37) 82–85; SE Sachs, 'Finding Law' (2019) 107 Cal L Rev 527, 557–58.

[48] Sachs (n 47).

[49] Gardner, Law as a Leap of Faith (n 37) 74.

[50] ibid 84.

[51] T Endicott, 'Adjudication and the Law' (2007) 27 OJLS 311, 316.

the doctrine of precedent operates without giving the courts lawmaking power. What the doctrine does is this: it requires later courts to treat earlier decisions of certain courts as correctly decided. It does not give earlier courts the power to lay down legal rules, either for the cases before them or for other cases to be decided in the future.[52]

In the US context, Stephen Sachs has similarly resisted the conclusion that the Supreme Court and other appellate courts can make law (understood as general legal rules applicable in the whole legal system).[53] On Sachs's view, even though sometimes lower court judges are bound to treat Supreme Court decisions 'as if' they were law, there is still a categorical difference between 'as if' law and the law.[54] One good reason to think that was given by Caleb Nelson:

> modern lawyers conversing about constitutional law might say something like this: 'The Constitution plainly establishes Rule X, but the Supreme Court has interpreted it to establish Rule Y instead, and the Court is not going to overrule that interpretation.' All modern lawyers would understand the distinction that this statement draws, and relatively few would consider it completely artificial or incoherent.[55]

According to Sachs, it is not even the case that the US Supreme Court has a general power to bind all legal officials in the US, because some of its purported determinations of state law are not 'always binding on the courts of that state'.[56] What makes this particularly interesting is that some legal philosophers tend to see it as uncontroversial that the US Supreme Court has the power to bind all legal officials in the US by its authoritative determinations of the law.[57] Matthew Kramer went even so far as to say that:

> Whenever the [US Supreme] Court pronounces on the validity or invalidity of some norm as a law, its ruling settles the status of that norm (as a law or not) and also settles the status of any other norm which is relevantly similar and which is thus within the precedential ambit of the ruling. No minimally credible exposition of the Rule of Recognition in the United States could fail to acknowledge as much.[58]

It seems that at least some of the US constitutional scholars cited earlier do not share Kramer's certainty on this point. I will not attempt to settle the debates about US or English common law here; I only wish to point out that there is a live disagreement about the scope of judicial powers to make law, even in common law jurisdictions.

Furthermore, even if judges do have a legal power to change the law, it does not follow that the power is unlimited. Judge Pierre Leval argued that in the US the power is limited to making law through holdings, but not through dicta.[59] Thus, both attempting to make law

---

[52] Lamond (n 29) 25.

[53] Sachs (n 47) 561–67.

[54] ibid 561–63.

[55] C Nelson, 'A Critical Guide to *Erie Railroad Co v Tompkins*' (2013) 54 Wm & Mary L Rev 921, 937; see also Sachs (n 47) 564.

[56] ibid 563.

[57] See, e.g., K Himma, 'Understanding the Relationship Between the US Constitution and the Conventional Rule of Recognition' in M Adler and K Himma (eds), *The Rule of Recognition and the US Constitution* (OUP 2009) 102–05; MH Kramer, *Where Law and Morality Meet* (OUP 2008) 134.

[58] ibid.

[59] PN Leval, 'Judging Under the Constitution: Dicta About Dicta' (2016) 81 NYU L Rev 1249.

this way and accepting such attempts by other courts exceeds the powers given to US judges under the US Constitution. Furthermore, even if a judicial decision is within the scope of judicial power, it may still be in breach of some duty and thus unlawful, though effective.

Leaving aside the common law world, decisions of the German Federal Constitutional Court, the Bundesverfassungsgericht (Federal Court of Justice) are binding on all German state organs.[60] Some of the Bundesverfassungsgericht's decisions are even published in the Federal Register of Statutes, which—according to Alexy and Dreier—'extends the bindingness to all citizens'.[61] Can other German courts influence the content of German law? Yes, but not through the formal bindingness of a single court judgment.[62] On one prominent view in German jurisprudence, the higher German courts influence the content of the law through judicial custom (*Gewohnheitsrecht*).[63] Judicial development of the law (*richterliche Rechtsfortbildung*) occurs through establishing a stable lines of cases (stable interpretation or 'jurisdiction', *ständige Rechtsprechung*).[64] Or, as the Bundesverfassungsgericht puts it, by 'established jurisdiction of the highest judges' (*gefestigte höchstrichterliche Rechtsprechung*).[65]

However, the official account of German law holds that in areas of law governed by statute, it is not judicial precedent which is binding, but statute. As Alexy and Dreier have framed it:

> precedents in Germany derive their power from the power of the formal source of law they interpret. Formally, it is the statute which binds; substantially, the precedent.[66]

When, as in German labour law, statutory law (or customary law) is not well developed, the legal basis for judges to step in is a 'general foundations of law (*allgemeine Rechtsgrundlagen*)'.[67] But, importantly, this is not 'an undefined pure power of courts to create' binding precedents.[68] Hence, the official account of German law is careful not to turn judges into law-makers.

A similar custom-like mechanism by which judicial decisions have an effect on the content of the law is also at work in France. According to Troper and Grzegorczyk:

> the quality of being a precedent does not arise only from the character of the decision itself, but from a collection of decisions and from their interpretation by legal dogmatics.[69]

The French equivalent of the German 'established jurisdiction' is referred to as 'persisting jurisprudence' (*jurisprudence constante*).[70] If other courts and legal academics do not approve of a judgment, then that judgment is not likely to have much effect on legal change.[71] However, sometimes even a single judgment is taken as *jurisprudence constante*.[72]

---

[60] Though the exact scope of the bindingness is controversial, see R Alexy and R Dreier, 'Precedent in the Federal Republic of Germany' in MacCormick and Summers (n 44) 26.

[61] ibid.

[62] ibid 27–28, 45.

[63] This view is closer to being the official view, with a strong historical pedigree from the nineteenth-century Historical School and *Begriffsjurisprudenz*, but it is not without its academic critics; see, e.g., ibid 42–46.

[64] See, e.g., ibid 30, 35, 50–51.

[65] ibid 30, 51.

[66] ibid 33.

[67] ibid.

[68] ibid 34.

[69] Troper and Grzegorczyk (n 44) 123.

[70] ibid 122.

[71] ibid 124.

[72] ibid 130–31.

Endorsement by legal theory and sociology, or even by doctrinal legal literature, of the creative role of a judge in legal change, does not necessarily translate to an endorsement of such a role by the official account of the law as presented in court judgments and other normative texts. No doubt, in many contemporary legal systems there is a good deal of novelty emanating from the courts. This is so despite sometimes being in tension with the official account of the legal system in question—the official account which may be endorsed in the same judgment that appears to depart from it.

Is this type of legal change brought about by the exercises of law-making powers? If we take some of the official views of the limits of the judicial role at face value, then perhaps we should conclude that it is not. This is a common strategy propounded by critics of any court judgment. However, there is a need for a more systematic answer. There are simply too many cases in tension with the official versions. One response is to throw the official version under the bus and disavow it as outdated fiction. In other words, the strategy is to accept that the law does in fact give judges the law-making powers they already seem to be using.[73] This may be motivated by an enthusiasm towards judicial activism (or even judicial supremacy[74]) or merely by a desire to cleanse the official story of the law of features that are systematically contradicted in legal practice. A shortcut to this approach could be that if a legal change is effective, then it was legally authorized (as a result of an exercise of a legal power to make law).

This strategy at the very least shifts the balance in the debate of the limits of judicial power—but does so in the face of recalcitrant official accounts. The fact that some official versions still hold to a view of the judicial role having more limited legal powers suggests that those legal systems have yet to clearly align the law-changing effects of adjudication with the scope of judicial law-making power. There may be very good reasons for this.[75]

Another serious problem with admitting the sufficiently wide scope of judicial law-making powers to resolve 'the official version vs in practice' tension, is that there is considerable disagreement on the scope of the powers that should be accepted, even aside from the general debate regarding judicial activism and judicial supremacy. One seemingly attractive solution would be to accept that all court-led legal change that results in being effective in practice is due to the legal power to make the law. But, as I have argued in section 2, this is an ad hoc answer that confuses how legal powers work. For one thing, there is a significant difference between causal influence on legal change, which is only effective through acceptance of the particular change by the wider community (e.g. by other judges and legal academics) and between having a legal power to make law—a power effective from the moment it is exercised. John Gardner has argued that case law (at least in English law) works through the latter mechanism—the courts exercise legal powers to make (case) law.[76] I noted earlier that this characterization is controversial and disputed, for instance, by Grant Lamond. And even John Gardner has noted that UK (constitutional) law has a good deal of customary law, which—as long as it remains customary—must be changed otherwise than through the exercise of law-making powers. Even if Gardner is right about English law, this does not mean that judges have law-making powers in any other legal system—this is a contingent question.

---

[73] Stone Sweet (n 41) 132.

[74] On the notion of judicial supremacy, see, e.g., L Alexander and F Schauer, 'Defending Judicial Supremacy' (2000) 17 Constitutional Commentary 455; R Ekins, 'Judicial Supremacy and the Rule of Law' (2003) 119 LQR 127; B Leiter, 'Constitutional Law, Moral Judgment, and the Supreme Court as Super-Legislature' (2015) 66 Hastings LJ 1601.

[75] See, e.g., Ekins, 'Judicial Supremacy and the Rule of Law' (n 74); R Ekins, 'Acts of Parliament and the Parliament Acts' (2007) 123 LQR 91.

[76] Gardner, Law as a Leap of Faith (n 37) 74.

4. Conclusions

It was not my aim in this chapter to show that the practice of precedent (and, more broadly, direct judicial influence on the content of the law) does or does not involve judges exercising law-making powers in any concrete legal system. I aimed to clarify what may be entailed by taking one possible view. As I have argued, there may be a discrepancy between the law's official account (or ideology) of how judges are legally constrained, on one hand, and what the law really is, on the other.[77] The official view of the law, found in court judgments and other official texts, is likely to exaggerate the constraints and underestimate the effects of adjudication on legal change.[78] But just because the official story probably exaggerates the constraints, it does not necessarily follow that legally there are no limits to judicial power and, in particular, that judicial power includes the power to make (change) some or any law.[79] This is arguable even in common law systems.

[77] M Barczentewicz, 'The Illuminati Problem and Rules of Recognition' (2018) 38 OJLS 500.
[78] J Goldsworthy, 'Raz on Constitutional Interpretation' (2003) 22 Law and Philosophy 167, 176.
[79] See, e.g., J Goldsworthy, *Parliamentary Sovereignty: Contemporary Debates* (CUP 2010) 74.

29
Shaping Our Relationship
The Power to Set a Precedent

Maris Köpcke[*]

Precedents cannot be set outside relationships, only within them. In giving a coin to the charity collector on the corner, I do not set a precedent binding me to give a coin to the charity collector two streets down. But I do set a precedent when I offer cake to the babysitter who today has stayed beyond her finishing time. The precedent bears on what I ought to do next time she or the other babysitter stays longer. We set precedents in dealing with our children, and in dealing with our students. We set precedents relevant to students whom we may not even know at the time the precedent is set. There is something peculiar about the relational context or framework *within which* one event counts as a precedent for another. Reflecting on this trait of precedent helps to shed light, I will argue, on an embarrassing theoretical question with significant implications for institutional responsibilities in legal systems. The embarrassing theoretical question is whether, and in what sense, judges exercise law-making *power*.

I say that the question is embarrassing because prominent discussions of *legal power* either circumvent it or speak to it in wavering terms. Section 1 suggests why this is so: precedent does not fit in the received idea of legal power. This does not mean that the received idea is ill-conceived, or that precedent cannot plausibly be understood as an exercise of power. To show why it can and should, section 2 identifies some main features of precedent outside law, and section 3 argues that these features hang together to make up a morally distinct form of action with discernible uses. By thus considering not merely what precedent is *not*, but positively developing an understanding of its moral purpose, we will be able to articulate in section 4 the sense in which setting a legal precedent amounts to the exercise of a power, and the place of this power in a community's pursuit of justice.

1. Precedent and Legal Power

It is quite natural to say, and to hear, that judges have law-making power—at least in common law jurisdictions.[1] Precedents are sources of law, and it is judges who set them. In the last few centuries, it has become commonplace to refer to law-making acts as exercises of legal power.[2] Statutes, regulations, and by-laws, on this view, all issue from exercises of legal power.

---

[*] I would like to thank Crescente Molina, Nick Barber, Timothy Endicott, Fábio Shecaira, and Hafsteinn Dan Kristjánsson for greatly beneficial conversations and feedback.

[1] This chapter focuses on judges, but they are not the only ones who can set precedents in law (as noted, e.g., in the contribution to this volume by Hafsteinn Dan Kristjánsson (Chapter 6, section 2).

[2] On the history of the ideas of legal power and legal validity, see M Köpcke, *A Short History of Legal Validity and Invalidity: Foundations of Private and Public Law* (Intersentia 2019).

Maris Köpcke, *Shaping Our Relationship* In: *Philosophical Foundations of Precedent*. Edited by: Timothy Endicott, Hafsteinn Dan Kristjánsson, and Sebastian Lewis, Oxford University Press. © Maris Köpcke 2023. DOI: 10.1093/oso/9780192857248.003.0030

Legal power is an enlightening idea.[3] It captures a distinctive *way* of bringing about changes in legal duties, rights, and other legal positions. That way is a focally intentional act. Specifically, it is an act of expressing the normative changes one intends to bring about through that very act of expression.[4] 'It is an offence to hunt', uttered with requisite authority, *makes it the case* that it is an offence to hunt. The phrase, 'It is hereby made an offence to hunt' renders the underlying technique more overt. The offence is created *hereby*—that is, *by* doing what the agent does *here* and now, namely, uttering the sentence. Thus understood, of course, legal powers extend to private law as well. We enter contracts, make wills, and marry through exercises of legal powers. Such acts effect particular rather than general normative changes. But the *way* the changes are effected is akin to the way they are effected through legislation and other public powers. Yet public powers, too, may effect particular normative changes. In giving judgment in a case, a court makes a ruling which settles the legal position of the parties. Here, as well, 'A has a duty to pay €100 to B' *makes it the case* that A has a duty to pay €100 to B.

The literature on legal power converges on all the above-mentioned points. But its treatment of precedent is shy. Hart's discussion of precedent in Chapter 7 of *The Concept of Law* does not rely on the idea of legal power, central as the idea is to the understanding of law developed in his book.[5] Indeed, Hart is one of the writers who has contributed most to give currency to this idea. Raz[6] and Gardner,[7] in turn, speak generically of judges' 'powers' or 'power' to make law, but do not resort to this notion when spelling out the specifics of how judges make law—with two exceptions. The exceptions are two special techniques that may be involved in precedent-setting, which these authors, like others, consistently refer to as the 'power to distinguish' and the 'power to overrule'. It is no coincidence that precedent-setting which involves the exercise of either of these powers bears a closer resemblance to legislating than precedent-setting which does not. It is significant that Raz has expressed doubts on whether precedent can be said to set exclusionary reasons.[8] Marmor, for his part, offers an account of 'law-making acts' that is very much along the lines of the received idea of legal power.[9] He claims that his account also holds good about judicial law-making[10]—but his discussion focuses narrowly on legislative enactments. Other contributions on legal power ignore or gloss over law-making through precedent.[11]

The cause of such inconsistencies and silences is not hard to find. Precedent does not fit the received idea of legal power. This section outlines the main differences between these two ways of making normative changes in law. I will take as the standard case of judicial precedent a precedent set by a court deciding a dispute on the application of law to certain facts, and I will focus the contrast on legislation for ease of comparison.

For legislation and precedent have in common that they have general normative effects. That much is implied when we say that they are ways of making *law* (and when we refer to precedent's legal effect as *case law*). When a court sets a precedent, its decision bears not only

---

[3] See further M Köpcke, *Legal Validity: The Fabric of Justice* (Hart 2019), especially chs 2 and 3.

[4] The expression may be more or less articulate, and may involve a range of different formulations: see further, ibid 47–50; J Gardner, *Law as a Leap of Faith* (OUP 2012) 57–58.

[5] See HLA Hart, *The Concept of Law* (2nd edn, OUP 1994) especially chs 3 and 5.

[6] J Raz, *The Authority of Law: Essays on Law and Morality* (OUP 1979) 180ff ('powers').

[7] Gardner (n 4) 74ff ('power', 'legal power').

[8] J Raz, 'Facing Up: A Reply' (1989) 62 So Cal L Rev 1153, 1171–73.

[9] A Marmor, *The Language of Law* (OUP 2014).

[10] ibid 11.

[11] They include my own discussion in Köpcke, *Legal Validity* (n 3) 113–15, 147–48, and others surveyed in ibid 29–30.

on the legal position of the parties to the dispute but also on the legal position of persons in relevantly similar situations. It bears not only on a situation-token but also on a situation-type.[12] But the normative effect of precedent differs from that of legislation in two major respects, which I will call content and force.

The content of precedent is something that lawyers in common law jurisdictions characteristically spend a substantial part of their professional life quibbling about. It is variously referred to, more or less loosely, as the rule in the case, the proposition the case stands for, the *ratio*, or the case's legal meaning, among others. I myself will often speak of the content of precedent as the 'rule' a case creates, but I make no suggestion that this notion is exactly coextensive with the foregoing ones, or with all plausible conceptions of the content of precedent. This does not detract from my argument; in fact, it bolsters it. For the very existence of such different conceptions of the content of precedent is a symptom of the underlying difference from the content of legislation. The difference lies in the relationship the content bears to the language of the decision. The rule that a case creates does not have a canonical formulation.[13] The court may attempt to formulate the rule, but that formulation may not be decisive. The rule that a case creates is a rule that justifies the ruling, and is otherwise consistent with the court's argument as a whole.[14] Of course, the court's attempted formulation of the rule is part of that argument, but so are the reasons relied on by the court, and so is the ruling itself. The formulation, if there is one, is not uniquely decisive in the manner in which a rule's legislative formulation is. This is why precedents can create rules without formulating them, or even stating any reasons whatsoever for the judgment. Not so legislation. Legislated law is created by being expressed—typically articulated in language. Canons of legislative interpretation can be very varied, but they must answer to the legislative formulation of the rule. Case law is not made by being expressed, but by being used in argument.

It follows that legislation is a purposive way of making law, and precedent is not. Although a judge may know he is making law, and even purport to make it in doing what he does, his *way* of making law is not a purposive one. A legislator with the requisite authority makes the very law he articulates, in articulating it. That is the defining point of the act he is engaged in. The defining point of deciding a case is different. It is to give judgment. It is to settle particular legal positions. This, the court does in the manner of a legislator—by articulating the very normative changes he thereby brings about. But the court need not intend to make law in the process. Whether or not he intends to does not settle the question whether he does.

One might object that something similar is true of legislative law-making, indeed of any exercise of legal power. It is possible to exercise a legal power without meaning to—a slip of the tongue, one mouse click too many on eBay, the wrong ballot paper in a vote.[15] In these cases, the agent does not intend to make the normative changes he actually makes. But— this is the key difference with case law—he *appears* to intend to make them. The technique whereby legal power is exercised involves an *expression* of one's intent—an expression which,

---

[12] This paragraph and the next two build on Gardner (n 4) 74ff.

[13] ibid 79; in a similar spirit, R Dworkin, *Taking Rights Seriously* (Harvard UP 1977) 110ff; Frederick Schauer, 'Precedent' (1987) 39 Stan L Rev 571, 571–75, 579–81; N Duxbury, *The Nature and Authority of Precedent* (CUP 2008) 92, 107.

[14] Gardner (n 4) 79. On the elements of the argument and methodological constraints that go to determine the legal effect of precedent, see further ibid 78–79; T Endicott, 'How Judges Make Law' in E Fisher, J King, and A Young (eds), *The Foundations and Future of Public Law* (OUP 2020) 131. The individual relevance of these considerations may be jurisdiction-specific, within limits. If the trend that Tiersma predicted towards 'textualization' (canonical formulation) of US judge-made law were to take over (P Tiersma, 'The Textualization of Precedent' (2013) 82 Notre Dame L Rev 1187), US judges might cease to make law through precedent.

[15] On unintentional exercises of legal power, see further Köpcke, *Legal Validity* (n 3) 54ff.

under appropriate conditions, realizes that intent. This is why even an accidental exercise of legal power looks intentional. Sound doctrines on mistake and other impediments of the will ultimately hold us to the intention a reasonable observer would have attributed to us. The judge is in a different position. It may be plain that, in issuing his decision, he does not intend to make the law he actually makes, or to make any law at all. Judges' duty to keep faith with the law may even lead them to draft their opinions in a way that reinforces the extent to which they simply apply pre-existing law rather than make new law.[16]

All this renders the content of precedent distinctly open-ended.[17] It may be radically underdetermined, in working out the rule, whether more or less prominence should be given to the string of cases cited, to the court's stated reasons or formulations, and to some aspects of the facts rather than others. But it is not only the content of precedent that is open-ended—so, too, is its force. By this, I mean the degree to which a precedent binds, primarily future courts.[18] Content and force are rarely disaggregated in argument, but they are logically distinct.[19] We can imagine settling on the rule a case stands for, only to go on to ask how much weight we should assign that rule. Perhaps it is a precedent from a lower court. Perhaps it is an outlier in an otherwise contrary line of precedent. Perhaps it is very old. Perhaps it was decided *per incuriam*. Perhaps in this jurisdiction it is merely persuasive precedent. Or perhaps the precedent should be distinguished—in which case the content of the precedent will be modified after all, as the instant court narrows the earlier rule.[20] But even to understand distinguishing one needs to separate content and force: the rule is narrowed because it exerts enough force to be reckoned with, but not enough force to prevent it being changed.

The legal force of precedent may vary from jurisdiction to jurisdiction, and the legal force of any single precedent may depend on a range of factors. In this sense, the legal force of precedent is a matter of degree. It is inherently inconclusive. This may render it artificial even to speak of precedents creating 'rules', making 'law', or changing 'duties' and 'rights', as these ideas have an all-or-nothing ring that sits uneasily with precedent. Of course, rules setting out duties and rights may themselves conflict in various ways, and a rule may be void as a result (e.g. *an ultra vires* regulation, an unenforceable contract term). But void decisions are not sources of duties and rights *at all*. They have no *pro tanto* legal weight as legal reasons to be balanced with others.[21] Precedent is different. Courts may be bound to *either* follow *or* distinguish precedent, or even just to explain how their present decision relates to earlier ones.[22] In such cases, future litigants may have a right that the court should engage with the precedent in the legally prescribed manner, but they cannot be said to have a right, derived from the precedent, that the court should decide in a particular way. The precedent provides reason, in law, to change the parties' normative positions, but it may not amount to such change.

Precedent's inconclusive force reinforces the need not to treat as decisive a judge's attempted formulation of a rule, in terms of a statement of duties and rights. And it explains

---

[16] This makes it contrived to seek to determine the content of precedent by asking what the judge 'intended to communicate', as proposed in the contribution to this volume by Ralf Poscher (Chapter 11).

[17] On the open-endedness of the legal effect of precedent, see Endicott (n 14) 137–41.

[18] I am treating together precedent and *stare decisis*—the reason for this emerges in section 4.

[19] cf Schauer (n 13) 591–95.

[20] On distinguishing, see Raz, *The Authority of Law* (n 6) 185ff; Gardner (n 4) 80.

[21] Voidable or even void decisions may give rise to claims based on reliance, but these claims, too, are framed in terms of *either* the presence *or* the absence of rights, duties, etc. On voidable decisions, see Köpcke, *Legal Validity* (n 3) 111–13.

[22] Different possibilities in this regard are canvassed in the contribution to this volume by Fábio Perin Shecaira (Chapter 24).

396   MARIS KÖPCKE

why the idea of legal validity is fundamentally alien to the logic of precedent.[23] The open-endedness of the content and force of precedent stands in tension with legal validity's all-or-nothing character. Nothing is more or less legally valid. Unsurprisingly, legal validity is closely associated with the received idea of legal power.[24] Exercises of legal power are that *of which* we predicate legal validity—contracts, statutes, by-laws, wills, and so on. They are purposive ways of changing legal positions, which canonically articulate their legal effect. Not so precedent. For setting a precedent is not an exercise of a legal power in the received sense.

2. Five Features of Precedent

It is time to lift our outlook from law to social life more generally. Given the ubiquity of legal powers in contemporary legal systems, we are liable to approach legal precedent with the bias that it is not a proper or real way of making law. The fact that precedent is ancillary to a judicial ruling can be additionally distracting. These constraints vanish as we step out of legal reasoning. Precedents are mundane outside law. It is common to speak of persons setting precedents in a variety of situations. The common law doctrine of precedent is, moreover, relatively young.[25] It is plausible to surmise that at least part of the ordinary understanding of precedent, crystallized in our use of this term, has gone to frame the legal conception.

Examples of precedent-setting abound. Among writers on legal precedent, favourite non-legal examples involve students, children, and other household members. It is no coincidence that examples are drawn from such scenarios. It is a feature of precedents that they are always set within standing relationships. I set a precedent in relation to my students if I refuse to mark an essay that is submitted late.[26] I set a precedent in relation to my child if I let him stay up late today because a game is on. I set a precedent in relation to the babysitters if I give one of them a Christmas present. The relevant relationships need not have a triadic structure. They need not involve me, the precedent-setter, standing in a similar relationship towards more than one person—as does a teacher with several students, or a parent with several children. The ability to set a precedent extends beyond settings involving narrowly 'distributive' justice. I set a precedent if I refuse to mark an essay that is submitted late, even if the student is my only one, provided the predicament (an essay deadline) will recur in our relationship, yielding further opportunities for me to *do it again* (refuse to mark). Note, also, that the presence of more than one person with whom I stand in a similar relationship is not enough to yield an opportunity for me to set a precedent. In giving a friend an expensive birthday present, I am not setting a precedent binding me to give an expensive birthday present to another friend with whom I happen to be similarly close.

In order for a precedent to be set, some kind of unity of purpose or shared enterprise must exist, prior to setting the precedent, between all those in relation to whom the precedent is set. The shared relationship need not be formal, never mind legal. We could modify the last example to make it more precedent-apt. Perhaps we are a group of three friends and neighbours who tend to lend each other a hand on a range of matters. Instead of making one of them a gift, assume I house one of her children while the sibling recovers from Covid. Here

---

[23] As Duxbury ((n 13) 23, 58) stresses, but does not explain.
[24] Köpcke, *Legal Validity* (n 3) ch 2.
[25] For a short overview of its history, see Duxbury (n 12) 17–18.
[26] This is a simplification. I only set a precedent if all features of precedent identified in this section apply. For ease of exposition, I phrase my examples assuming that they do (unless otherwise noted).

it is more plausible to say that I am setting a precedent by housing the child, which bears (inter alia) on what I should do when one of my other friend's children catches the illness. Or take charitable giving. I do not set a precedent by giving €1 to a random beggar downtown, but things may be different if it is the beggar on my doorstep, with whom I have made some acquaintance by inquiring for his well-being, and who shows up every Sunday after church when I carry my change from the bakery.

It might be thought that the decisive element making these scenarios precedent-apt is the presence of expectations on the part of those I interact with. But neither are expectations unique to precedent, nor is it a necessary feature of precedent that those in relation to whom a precedent is set expect the original act to recur, or even know of its occurrence. University committees routinely set precedents unbeknown to students to whom the precedents might one day apply. What is decisive is not the expectations but that which justifies the expectations, or would justify them if they existed. The persons to whom the precedent is relevant have an interest in knowing of the precedent-setting act, and have reason to expect it to recur. The reason derives from that unity of purpose or common enterprise they participate in.

This is not to deny—in fact, it entails—that setting a precedent requires some kind of publicity. An act that sets a precedent, if not already known to those who partake in the enterprise, must at least be knowable by them in the normal course of that enterprise (whether or not under the description of an 'act that sets a precedent'). If I am involved in college admissions and I happen to detect a mistake my colleague has made in officially recording the panel's decision on an applicant, I have reason not only to correct that mistake but also to go over the records of the other applicants. My colleague might have messed them up as well, and I ought to be fair to all applicants. But by checking the first record I have not *set a precedent* binding me to check the others.[27] No one might ever come to know (except, perhaps, with a court order). Setting a precedent involves a degree of publicity, of action in plain sight. Sleepy committee members may not realize what we are deciding, or even *that* we are deciding something, but they can come to know in the normal course of business.

We can take provisional stock of the features of precedent unearthed so far. They include, *first*, a common purpose or shared enterprise in the context of which the precedent is set. I am using these ideas loosely, to extend even to highly informal relationships, and to relationships more or less voluntary in origin.[28] Crucially, they are relationships wherein the precedent-setter *can affect the interests of persons to whom he is related in a way that calls for his behaviour to be consistent or fair*, by treating like cases alike. *Secondly*, the act that sets a precedent must have a degree of publicity or recognizability as part of that same relationship. *Thirdly*, as is partly implicit in the first feature, there must be some continuity in the relevant relationship. The continuity is both backward- and forward-looking. The relationship predates the act that sets the precedent because a precedent is not set in a social vacuum. But the relationship also extends (or can be expected to extend) beyond the act that sets the precedent, because nothing is a precedent unless there can be a relevant situation which the precedent *precedes*.

A *fourth* feature of precedent is likewise implicit in my earlier remarks. The act that sets a precedent is an intentional act. By this, I mean an act that is performed for reasons. Slipping on a banana peel does not set a precedent. The agent's purpose in performing the

---

[27] If I told my colleague, I might set a precedent in relation to *her*, should we again be involved in a task requiring her to monitor databases.

[28] The related idea of social groups is discussed in the contribution to this volume by Nicholas W Barber (Chapter 4).

act, however, need not be to set a precedent. Many precedents are in fact set without the agent aiming to. This is why we often talk not of setting precedents but of *having set* them. Someone makes us aware that our act has set a precedent for the future ('You've now set a dangerous precedent!'). We did not appreciate this normative bearing of the act. The act itself may not have involved articulating any normative considerations. Precedents can be set other than by means of exercises of legal power or their analogues in moral life. I can set a precedent by playing football with my son or by buying him a bun. I can set a precedent by massaging or by consenting to be massaged. I can set a precedent by giving or by forgiving.

The above-mentioned four features go some way towards pinning down precedent. But they do not suffice. We can imagine predicaments in which all four of them hold but which would be ill-described in terms of precedent. You are my regular supplier and on this occasion you deliver late. You do not set a precedent by delivering late—although I do set a precedent by accepting the delivery. The babysitter asks for an advance. She does not set a precedent by asking—but I do set a precedent by giving her the advance. It is not immediately obvious where the relevant difference is found. In all these cases, you and I are part of a relationship—the same relationship—in which our acts can affect the interests of each other in a way that morally calls for us to display mutual fairness. Moreover, our dealings have publicity (we communicate), continuity, and involve intentional action.[29] To be sure, my actions, as opposed to yours, involve an exercise of legal power or something analogous to it. But we have just seen that this is not a distinguishing mark of precedent.

It might be thought that benevolence or benefit-conferral is the key. In fact, most of the examples of precedent we have brought up so far involved just that—favours, acceptances, gifts. This might also seem to explain why saying that someone (or oneself) has set a precedent often carries a negative connotation in ordinary talk. It is supposed be bad news for the precedent-setter; having conferred a benefit once, he is now bound to confer it again. But it would be a mistake to think of precedent as necessarily involving benevolence. I set a precedent either by accepting or by refusing your delivery, either by marking or by rejecting the essay. I set a precedent when I settle a dispute between the children, which entails ruling to one child's advantage and to the other's detriment. Of course, only those benefited by a precedent may wish to appeal to it in the future—when submitting another essay late, my student will not insist on *stare decisis* if I rejected his essay the first time round. Perhaps this renders benefit-conferring precedents more salient in practice.

But benefit-conferring precedents can steer us to the answer we are after, in a different way. You do not set a precedent by delivering late, not because the late delivery is disadvantageous to me, but because there is no *reason* to repeat it. A late delivery is a failure: it is wrong in principle, however excusable. No consideration of consistency or fairness in our relationship could warrant you delivering late again because you did so once. In fact, fairness may require making up for the delay in the future! My own act is different. Having accepted *this* late delivery, I have a reason to accept a late delivery again, perhaps in similar circumstances. The reason is derived from the value of predictability, which is an aspect of fairness in our dealings. The babysitter's request for an advance is not wrong, but it is analogous to the late delivery in the crucial respect. The fact of having asked for one advance does not provide reason to ask for another. In fact, it provides reason to be more restrained going forwards! But I have reason to be consistent in my pay policy, also as between babysitters.

---

[29] It makes no difference to the example whether lateness is accidental or deliberate.

This takes us to the *fifth* relevant feature of precedent. In order for an act to set a precedent, it is not enough that the act occurs within a relationship governed by requirements of fairness or consistency (feature 1). Something additional must be true of the act itself. The act must be such that, given those requirements, performing it once provides reason to perform it again. This must not be confused with the false claim that only morally admirable acts can set a precedent. I may set a precedent through a decision which was morally not the best one to have taken. Perhaps I ought to have rejected your delivery, or to have settled the quarrel among the kids in a different manner. But, *having* taken that course, there is a moral reason to stick to it. Of course, that reason is defeasible—it may be outweighed—and the merits of the decision may be among the defeating factors. Still, there is something there to be defeated. There is a reason now which did not exist before. The act's first performance provides reason for the second. The reason derives from the moral significance, to the purpose of the relationship, of the fact that the act has taken place.

3. The Point of Precedent

Reflection on the features of precedent, and on the last one in particular, serves to highlight that the judgment that someone has set a precedent is not a morally neutral diagnosis—at least outside law. When I say, 'You have now set a precedent', I normally imply that you are in a kind of relationship in which, on grounds of fairness or consistency, the fact that you did *this* on this occasion provides reason to do it again. This judgment, to repeat, is compatible with the view that the precedent is mistaken, even unjust. I imply that you ought to be fair in the relationship, not that you actually are. I imply that there is reason to do it again, not that you should or will act on that reason, or that you are likely to wisely ponder the considerations in conflict.

The way we speak about precedent has a rationale. As section 2 began to demonstrate, linguistic uses of the term 'precedent' track coherent settled understandings. The five features of precedent we have identified hang together by making up a distinctive way of changing reasons in shaping human relationships. I will argue in this section that the practice of precedent-setting has a distinctive moral point, to which precedent's five features answer. Precedent's moral point warrants speaking of a moral *power* to set a precedent.

Precedent creates a reason that did not exist before. It is a reason that makes a practical difference. I do not set a precedent by accepting an essay submitted on time, because I was already bound to do so as a result of my role in the relationship with the students. Being part of that relationship involves, among other things, being subject to a specific set of normative considerations, of reasons to act or forebear or tolerate, with respect to the students and others (feature 1). But these considerations leave us—perhaps especially me—some latitude in determining aspects of our relationship. The aspects in question are not just matters of detail or housekeeping, such as determining a cut-off time for essay submission. They may extend to the very content of what I teach. Having such normative latitude is crucial to the purpose of our relationship, as it is to the purpose of any of the relationships considered so far. That latitude enables us to truly partake in the common enterprise, to *make it ours*, by shaping it normatively through our interaction and associated expectations, dispositions, and understandings. One way such shaping can occur is by setting precedents.

This shows why it is reductionist to think of precedent, as Schauer does, as a mere external 'constraint' on reaching the 'optimal' result in new situations.[30] On Schauer's view,

---

[30] Schauer (n 13) 597–98.

whenever precedent makes a practical difference it leads to 'suboptimal' results. In so arguing, Schauer assumes that, independently of the precedent, particular cases have only one uniquely correct or superior ('optimal') answer. But that is unwarranted as a general assumption, and moreover it eclipses precedent's central creative role in shaping relationships *in the face of underdetermination*.[31] Very often, in the scenarios we have considered, one could have reasonably decided either way in the absence of precedent. There are good reasons for and against marking a late essay, for and against giving to charity, for and against housing the neighbour's child. The existence of latitude in our relationships is valuable partly for the very same reasons that call for sticking to the precedent once set (feature 5), indeed that may call for setting it in the first place. Setting a precedent in the face of underdetermination is a central case of setting a precedent, although a precedent may also be set, and can be valuable, when it commits to a course of action that goes against what morality would have otherwise required.

I have spoken of latitude to *determine*, or *shape*, the normative contour of our relationship. This is consistent with precedent not being a purposive way of doing this. Precedent shapes relationships, even though it is not a purposive way of shaping them. The act that sets a precedent is public and intentional (features 2 and 4), but it is not necessarily an act that articulates its own normative bearing. The fact that precedent is not a purposive way of shaping relationships does not preclude inquiring about the purposes *of* this way of shaping relationships. Indeed, the contrast with purposive techniques shows why and when this peculiar manner of making normative changes can be appropriate. It shows the distinct uses of precedent.

Compare marking a late essay with emailing students my essay submission policy. Compare giving a beggar €1 on Sunday with promising to give him €1 every Sunday. Compare giving an advance with announcing to babysitters under which circumstances advances will be available. The latter acts involve exercising legal powers or analogues thereof. They enable me to introduce normative changes in a targeted way. Assuming I have authority to make them, I can control their content on inception. Precedent does not give me such control. This is evident in the type of guidance the former acts provide to those I interact with. Students who know I marked a late essay may be left wondering just what the content is of the precedent I set. The facts may be compatible with various possibilities. Am I marking late essays when accompanied by a doctor's note? When the student has submitted early in the past? Whenever there is good reason to? Even if I would like to limit the range of plausible constructions, there is not much I can do to that end *in setting the precedent*. Telling the student why I marked his essay ('only because last week you submitted 30 minutes early') would not foreclose justified appeals to *similar reasons*, even *similarly good reasons*, for marking late essays in the future.[32] Nor does any of this yet settle the force my precedent carries—I may only be the lecturer's teaching assistant, after all. The guidance provided by precedent is different in kind from the guidance provided by an exercise of legal power or its analogues.

That may be why precedent suits me. Perhaps I do not have the time now to work out fair criteria for handling late essays in general, and would rather do this on the fly, in the light of what continuous interaction with students teaches me. I may feel that whatever criteria ought to govern our essay submission, they should warrant accepting *this* late essay. I may feel similarly in awarding the babysitter an advance. I may have reservations about giving

---

[31] I use 'underdetermination' (and 'latitude') in a sense compatible with the existence of better and worse reasonable options.

[32] If I added 'and this is the only reason why I will ever mark a late essay', I would be almost, or actually, legislating.

advances in the future, or giving them to the other babysitter. Perhaps the other babysitter is already well paid and does a different type of work anyway. I may sense that I *can* be fair to both babysitters by only giving advances to the former, or by only giving this advance, but I cannot at present articulate a criterion for payment that is compatible with this, and I am not sure there is one.

Precedent enables me to *defer decision*. This is an aspect of precedent's third feature, continuity. Through precedent I exercise less initial control over the shape of our relationship, but I have an ongoing control over it and the guidance it offers. Precedent has these advantages even over a vague essay submission or payment policy—one that does not go beyond an appeal to 'good reasons'. A policy stating that I shall mark late essays or give advances when there is 'good reason' to do so, does not commit me to a specific criterion. But, by the same token, it binds me to act for any good reason. Students or babysitters will be able to appeal to the full range thereof in vindicating their case. Of course, a vague policy can be amended, but so can a precise one, and they will bind me until amended. Precedent, by contrast, I can later narrow or otherwise balance against pertinent considerations, precisely because its content and force are open-ended in the sense portrayed in section 2. Moreover, precedent provides valuable *control over guidance* where the very existence of legislated policy is counterproductive. Students may be discouraged from trying their best to submit on time if they are certain of the existence and content of an exemption policy that their case could fit or be made to fit—especially when the policy is vague. For similar reasons, a teacher concerned about his workload may not publicly offer to mark practice essays, despite being disposed to mark essays whenever reasonably requested to.[33]

The distinct uses of precedent can be summed up as deferred decision-making and guidance control. They make up precedent's moral point, and show why precedent can be regarded as a moral *power*. This is so despite the fact that these uses entail risks. There may be no sound principle to reconcile my treatment of both babysitters after all, and I may find myself committed to either handing out copious advances or retracting the first one.[34] Or I may be a bad negotiator and strike a worse deal as a result of having postponed my decision instead of settling on a policy on advances right away. Or my mother may eventually develop the precedent in a direction I find unsuitable. I would not have taken these risks if I had chosen at once, but I would have taken others. Promises bind the promisor; legislated rules may be relied on until changed. Exercises of legal power (and their analogues) limit the agent's freedom of action. But they are no less exercises of power for that reason.

We are not less but more powerful as a result of having the ability to bind ourselves to others by taking on commitments, pursuing joint ventures, embarking on projects, or making bets. This ability is key to the development of our identity as individuals and groups, precisely because its reasonable exercise may constrain what we may reasonably choose in the future. Such ability is, in an important sense, conferred on us. It is *given* the practice of promising and the moral reasons supporting it that my uttering these words morally binds me. I exercise the power to promise in the context of a normative framework. So, too, the power to set a precedent. The framing relationship enables the precedent to be set and limits

---

[33] On the related yet different idea of 'acoustic separation' in a normative order, see M Dan-Cohen, 'Decision Rules and Conduct Rules: On Acoustic Separation in Criminal Law' (1983) 97 Harv L Rev 625.

[34] There is no general non-legal analogue to the legal power to overrule a precedent, that is, to cancel its normative effect by so saying (in the course of setting another precedent). Phrases like 'I will never do this again' may be ambiguous as between an attempt to overrule ('it was a mistake to give that advance') and an attempt to narrow the precedent ('it is unlikely or impossible that the justifying facts will recur'). Whether either attempt succeeds depends on the normative considerations governing our relationship.

402 MARIS KÖPCKE

what I can reasonably do, compatibly with my role. Both precedent and legal power (and its analogues) involve normatively shaping the future by doing something in the present. Not everyone *can* do that, and whether one can does not only depend on oneself. But they do not shape the future in precisely the same way, and are not power in the same sense. Precedent enables deferred choice, but no purposive shaping. It is a check on guidance, but not a boost thereof. It limits initial control, but facilitates an ongoing rule by all those discharging the role they share. This last consideration is critical to the point of precedent in law.

4. The Point of Legal Precedent

The moral point of precedent is also the general moral point of precedent in law. Legal (judicial) precedent is positively characterized by the five features outlined in section 2, albeit with peculiarities derived from the law's appropriation and regulation of the notion of precedent.

Perhaps the most obvious peculiarity is that to say that a court has set a precedent is not focally a moral diagnosis. 'The Supreme Court has now set a precedent' does not carry the same moral implication as my saying, 'You have now set a precedent', the first time you give a babysitter an advance. If asked to justify my claim, in the latter case I may point to the value of consistent behaviour towards household members, and note that other babysitters may be similarly deserving. In the former case, I may simply point to the fact that in English law what the Supreme Court decides is binding on the lower courts. In this important sense, a legal system takes over the task of determining who can set a precedent and how, and when there is good reason to do the relevant act again. Law identifies *legal* precedent and *legal* reasons. Yet the moral point of legal precedent is best understood by appreciating how it mirrors non-legal precedent.

Take, to begin with, the kind of act whereby legal precedent is set. The act is both public (feature 2) and intentional (feature 4): giving a ruling. Although it may not articulate its own general normative effect, it is an act performed for reasons, and those reasons go to determine the act's general normative effect. Hence the relevance of the court's stated reasons to discerning the rule in the case. Moreover, the act is such that, given the purpose of the relationship in which it occurs, there is a moral reason to do it again should a similar situation arise (feature 5). The act settles a dispute and disputes ought to be settled in a consistent manner. Writings on legal precedent characteristically appeal to the values of predictability, fairness between litigants, and efficiency, to explain why precedent ought to be followed. These are ultimately requirements of justice. Respect for people's expectations is important especially where expectations are *justified*, as here, given the judiciary's central role in acknowledging and giving effect to a community's shared standards, including by solving disputes. That role, in turn, calls for impartiality and thus consistency in applying general rules, minimizing both error and undue delay.

We have thereby touched on the nature of the relationship within which legal precedents are set (feature 1). It is a relationship uniting those setting precedent and those on whom precedent bears—in principle, the whole political community. That relationship is both represented and furthered by the community's legal system. The overall purpose or point of that relationship is to realize justice. Judges ought to act consistently given the way their behaviour can affect the interests of others in the relationship. But that behaviour is not limited to acknowledging *existing* law and solving disputes. There can be good reasons to legally bestow on (certain kinds of) judicial rulings the general normative effect we refer to as precedent. Judges may be better placed than legislators to give specific content to certain legal regimes, given judges' proximity to factual scenarios, their specialized legal expertise, and the flexibility of judicial law-making that results from precedent's open-ended content and force.[35] It may even be appropriate for legislators to leave open the specifics of legal regimes to that very end. Thus understood, the central case of legal precedent is precedent set in the face of legal underdetermination, even though decisions *per incuriam* may also set legal precedent, and can be morally binding (especially when they change bad law). The moral point of legal precedent is to supplement underdetermined law, in a manner that both provides control over guidance and facilitates deferred and so gradual and experience-sensitive choice.

Note that the earlier remarks have referred to judges jointly. I have spoken of the *judiciary's* role in supplementing existing law and solving disputes. Deferred choice, in particular, is only an exercise of power if it is the same agent choosing on the different instances. Otherwise, in choosing once and never again, one loses rather than acquires control, given the open-ended normative bearing of precedent. Individual judges sitting in the precedent-setting court may not be the same ones later bound to apply the precedent, just as the precedent I set as teacher may be developed by my fellow teacher or my teaching assistant. But we miss something important about precedent, both in law and outside it, if we let individual episodic action blind us to the fundamental unity of role among those liable, for that reason, to set a precedent and to be bound to apply it. Technically, legal precedent can exist without *stare decisis*,[36] but it is unsurprising that they tend to be found and discussed together. As I hope reflection on non-legal scenarios has helped to bring out, to set a precedent is not merely to change *your* normative positions. It is focally to shape *our* relationship, including my commitment to *treat you* in a certain way. The relationship's continuity (feature 3) is central to precedent.

Hart famously presents precedent as a way of communicating general standards of behaviour.[37] He describes a father taking off his hat on entering church, by way of teaching his son appropriate conduct. But that is misleading as a picture of precedent. The father sets an example, but not a precedent. One is bound to take off one's hat quite independently of the father's act. The father conveys to his son what is to be done, but does not bind himself in the process. He might not return to church again; his son should abide by the rule. Precedents focally involve acts that do something *to* someone—such as giving charity, extending bedtime, or settling a dispute. There is a crucial rational connection, in setting judicial precedent, between creating a standard for citizens and binding judges to hold citizens to that standard. Not only judges are bound but other officials as well. That is because of the *role* in which the individual judge acts, when he sets the precedent. He acts in the name of the unfolding community which he represents, for whose sake judicial office exists.[38]

Law-making through precedent is an exercise of power. The power is limited—any law-making power is. Even legislative power must be conferred on the individuals exercising it. Conferral determines the manner of its exercise and is liable to circumscribe its scope. The power to set a precedent is limited in an additional sense. As we have seen, the very idea of precedent presupposes that there is a relationship, hence a body of normative considerations, to which precedent-setting answers, primarily by way of specification of its requirements. Precedents create new reasons within a framework *very much determined* by reasons. The purpose of the relationship circumscribes what can reasonably be done by the

---

[35] See further Köpcke, *Legal Validity* (n 3) 113–15.

[36] See, e.g., Gardner (n 4) 84 and the contribution to this volume by Hafsteinn Dan Kristjánsson (Chapter 6, section 3.C).

[37] Hart (n 5) 124ff.

[38] Dworkin (n 13) 113 suggests a related understanding of precedent in terms of fair treatment by 'the government'.

precedent-setter and those bound to engage with the precedent. Doctrines of the separation of powers speak to these concerns. Legal systems may circumscribe judicial law-making power by means of positive legal regimes. But it is primarily incumbent on judges themselves to determine the limits of this power.[39] They should do so keeping in mind the moral point of legal precedent.

There is ample opportunity to bring to bear such moral considerations in reasoning in and about legal precedent. Legal systems can only go so far in regulating precedent's content and force. Moral judgment may be involved in interpreting legislation and any exercise of legal power, but the place of moral reasoning in engaging with precedent is prominent. That is a mark of the kind of power precedent-setters lack, and of the kind of power they wield.

[39] See further Endicott (n 14) 134–36.

30
Constitutionally Erroneous Precedent as a Window on Judicial Law-Making in the US Legal System

Richard H Fallon, Jr[*]

1. Introduction

Worries about erroneous constitutional precedent and the criteria that should govern their overruling are rampant in US constitutional law.[1] The problem arises when a majority of the justices of the Supreme Court—who alone can overrule the Court's prior decisions—think that an earlier case was wrongly decided. A stylized model captures the issue that the justices then must resolve: at Time One (T1), relevant constitutional language was drafted, and then ratified by the requisite number of states, and acquired a T1 meaning. At some subsequent Time Two (T2), the Supreme Court interpreted that language and assigned it a mistaken T2 meaning (as gauged by criteria that a subsequent majority of the justices endorses). Then, at Time Three (T3), the Court confronts a case in which one of the parties asks it to overrule the T2 decision that a majority of the current justices thinks was insupportable as an original matter, typically because a majority believes the T2 ruling deviated from the US Constitution's T1 meaning. At T3, should the Court adhere to its T2 ruling or decide on the basis of its current best judgment concerning how to interpret or specify the Constitution's original meaning?

In the US context, no one thinks that the Supreme Court must always adhere to erroneous constitutional precedents.[2] In the academic literature, a few originalists—who insist that the meaning or communicative content of constitutional language becomes fixed at the time of its ratification—have maintained that all erroneous T2 decisions ought to be overruled.[3] But

---

[*] I would like to thank Timothy Endicott, Nils Jansen, Hafsteinn Dan Kristjánsson, Sebastian Lewis, Nina Varsava, Ben Zipursky, and Jeremy Waldron for comments on an earlier draft and Mez Belo-Osagie, Max Bloom, and Abe Kanter for research assistance.

[1] The justices of the Supreme Court have engaged in extended debate and discussion in a number of recent cases. See, e.g., *Ramos v Louisiana* 140 S Ct 1390, 1402–08 (2020); ibid 1411–17 (Kavanaugh J concurring in part); ibid 1427–40 (Alito J dissenting); *Franchise Tax Board v Hyatt* 139 S Ct 1485, 1499 (2019); *Kisor v Wilkie* 139 S Ct 2400, 2422–23 (2019); *Knick v Township of Scott* 139 S Ct 2162, 2189 (2019) (Kagan J dissenting). The debate in the surrounding scholarly literature is even more extensive. Prominent recent contributions include RJ Kozel, *Settled Versus Right* (CUP 2017); RJ Kozel, 'Retheorizing Precedent' (2021) 70 Duke LJ 1025; RM Re, 'Precedent as Permission' (2021) 99 Tex L Rev 907; W Baude, 'Precedent and Discretion' [2019] Sup Ct Rev 313; F Schauer, '*Stare Decisis*—Rhetoric and Reality in the Supreme Court' [2018] Sup Ct Rev 121.

[2] See Baude (n 1) 316.

[3] See n 10 and accompanying text.

Richard H Fallon, Jr, *Constitutionally Erroneous Precedent as a Window on Judicial Law-Making in the US Legal System* In: *Philosophical Foundations of Precedent.* Edited by: Timothy Endicott, Hafsteinn Dan Kristjánsson, and Sebastian Lewis, Oxford University Press. © Richard H Fallon 2023. DOI: 10.1093/oso/9780192857248.003.0031

that remains a minority position to which none of the justices has subscribed so far.[4] Instead, most theorists and all of the justices believe that the Court, guided by applicable principles of *stare decisis*, must make case-by-case T3 choices about whether to adhere to T2 errors or to base its decision on correctly identified T1 meanings.[5]

Insofar as the doctrine of *stare decisis* authorizes the justices to make discretionary choices in T3 cases—by which I mean choices that the justices do not believe to be determined by any clearly controlling rule or principle—and insofar as the Supreme Court's decisions bind the lower courts until the Court reverses itself, the practical effect of constitutional *stare decisis* in the Supreme Court is to empower the Court to function as a constitutional-law-making institution. The Court gets to choose whether to make new constitutional law for the future (based on T1 meaning) or to adhere to and possibly extend law made previously by the Court that deviated from T1 meaning. That consequence raises jurisprudential puzzles in the minds of some and provokes rule-of-law-based anxieties among others, who view *stare decisis* as more properly a device for narrowing the scope of judicial discretion—by settling what previously was unsettled—than for broadening it by authorizing the Court either to hew to or reject what it believes to have been T2 mistakes.[6]

Although the principal ambition of this chapter is to explicate the doctrine of *stare decisis* as it operates in constitutional cases in the US, I hope that some aspects of my analysis may contribute to transnational discussions of *stare decisis*, comparative constitutional law, and jurisprudential theory. Section 2 seeks to explain, first, how the US Supreme Court's erroneous T2 precedents can acquire the ture of valid law despite the Constitution's self-identified status as 'the supreme law of the land'.[7] It then goes on to explain how and why, if T2 errors sometimes prevail over the Constitution's T1 meaning, they need not always do so. With respect to the first of these issues, my analysis suggests that the general jurisprudential framework introduced by HLA Hart in *The Concept of Law*[8] successfully dissolves what some have taken to be either a contradiction or a mystery. With respect to the issue of why T2 precedents are not always binding, I again rely on Hartian concepts, but suggest that a wholly successful analysis would require a fuller explanation than Hart offered of the relationship between what he characterized as 'rules of recognition' and 'rules of change'.[9] Consideration of that relationship may be especially important in understanding the role of apex courts. Section 3 uses section 2's analysis as a springboard for further, simultaneous reflections on the Supreme Court's authority to revise the constitutional law of the US and on the capacity of Hartian concepts to illumine that authority. Section 4 briefly addresses rule-of-law-based objections to a doctrine of *stare decisis* that accords substantial authority to the Supreme Court to revise US constitutional law.

---

[4] Justice Thomas has come closest. See *Gamble v United States* 139 S Ct 1960, 1984 (2019) (Thomas J concurring) ('In my view, if the Court encounters a decision that is demonstrably erroneous—*i.e.*, one that is not a permissible interpretation of the text, the Court should correct the error, regardless of whether other factors support overruling the precedent').

[5] See, e.g., *Seminole Tribe of Florida v Florida* 517 US 44, 63 (1996) ('[W]e always have treated *stare decisis* as a "principle of policy" and not as an "inexorable command" ' (citations omitted); first quoting *Helvering v Hallock* 309 US 106, 119 (1940); and then quoting *Payne v Tennessee* 501 US 808, 828 (1991)); *Kisor* (n 2) ('[A]ny departure from the doctrine demands 'special justification'—something more than 'an argument that the precedent was wrongly decided") (quoting *Halliburton Co v Erica P John Fund Inc* 573 US 258, 266 (2014)).

[6] See, e.g., Baude (n 1) 329–33.

[7] See US Constitution, Art VI, § 1, cl 2.

[8] See HLA Hart, *The Concept of Law* (3rd edn, OUP 2012).

[9] See ibid 94–95.

2. The Status and Weight of Constitutionally Erroneous Supreme Court Precedent

A. Mistaken T2 Rulings and Supreme Court Law-Making Authority

Within the US, some (but not all) constitutional originalists maintain that the Constitution's T1 meaning must always prevail over erroneous T2 Supreme Court interpretations.[10] Originalists who hold this view sometimes argue that their conclusions follow directly from Article VI of the Constitution, which picks out the Constitution itself—in asserted contrast with judicial interpretations of it—as 'the supreme law of the land'.[11]

But originalists who maintain that the Supreme Court should overrule all T2 errors occupy a minority position. The Supreme Court says recurrently that mere error is not a sufficient ground for overruling.[12] It has adhered to this view openly and insistently since early in constitutional history.[13] The lower courts, moreover, have overwhelmingly acceded to the Supreme Court's claim of authority.

The widely recognized status of erroneous T2 rulings as furnishing eligible grounds for decision at T3 implies that the Supreme Court, operating at T2, occupies the status of a legitimate constitutional law-making authority capable of establishing its holdings as part of the constitutional law of the US.[14] There are two plausible routes to this conclusion.

The more convincing holds that the authority of T2 precedents arises directly from acceptance of their authority by the justices, lower court judges, and other officials.[15] That rationale is classically Hartian, reflecting Hart's central premise that the foundations of law lie in official acceptance, exhibited in what Hart called the rule of recognition.[16] Although Hart most often spoke of the rule of recognition as singular, he sometimes wrote of rules in the plural.[17] If there are diverse rules of recognition, some may trace their validity to more ultimate rules. But Hart insisted that the ultimate rule or rules of recognition were social rules that exist only insofar as they actually guide the practice of relevant actors.[18]

Once it is recognized that the foundations of law lie in social facts involving contemporary acceptance—as I shall assume without arguing that Hart demonstrated to be the case—the authority of erroneous T2 precedent depends on current practices and attending attitudes, not the bare language of the written Constitution proclaiming itself 'supreme'. When judged by the former gauge, the claim that judicial precedent cannot establish valid law contrary to what otherwise would be the best interpretation of the written Constitution appears insupportable. Even critics of judicial reliance on non-originalist precedent acknowledge that

---

[10] See, e.g., RE Barnett, 'Trumping Precedent with Original Meaning: Not as Radical as It Sounds' (2005) 22 Const Comment 257, 269; G Lawson, 'The Constitutional Case Against Precedent' (1994) 17 Harv J L & Pub Pol'y 23, 24; M Stokes Paulsen, 'The Intrinsically Corrupting Influence of Precedent' (2005) 22 Const Comment 289, 291.

[11] US Constitution, Art VI, § 1, cl 2.

[12] See, e.g., *Halliburton* (n 5) 266.

[13] See TR Lee, '*Stare Decisis* in Historical Perspective: From the Founding Era to the Rehnquist Court' (1999) 52 Vand L Rev 647, 662–81 (tracing the history of constitutional *stare decisis* from the founding through the Marshall Court).

[14] See Schauer (n 1) 123 ('The idea of precedent is fundamentally about authority, and authority is, in the context of law, about the source of a directive and not about its content').

[15] See, e.g., K Greenawalt, 'The Rule of Recognition and the Constitution' (1987) 85 Mich L Rev 621, 641, 654.

[16] See Hart (n 8) 79–99. Within Hart's conceptual framework, the rule of recognition is the ultimate criterion by which officials within a legal system differentiate law from non-law. See ibid 92, 94–95, 100–10.

[17] See, e.g., ibid 92, 95.

[18] See ibid 256 ('[T]he rule of recognition ... is in effect a form of judicial customary rule existing only if it is accepted and practised in the law-identifying and law-applying operations of the courts').

'[t]he idea that "[t]he judicial Power" establishes precedents as binding law, obligatory in future cases', began to take root no later than the early nineteenth century.[19] Since then, the Supreme Court has invoked *stare decisis* with great frequency, seldom if ever apologetically. So far as I am aware, no justice up until and including those currently sitting has persistently questioned the legitimacy of *stare decisis* or failed to apply it in some cases.[20] As others have emphasized, moreover, the doctrine of *stare decisis* is strictly necessary to support T3 results only in cases involving erroneous T2 decisions. When prepared to endorse the correctness of T2 rulings, justices at T3 have no need to invoke *stare decisis* as a ground for their decisions.[21] For this reason, I infer that under the ultimate rules of recognition existing in the US, which are accepted and practised by the courts and enable them to identify valid legal norms (even if those rules lack agreed, canonical formulations), erroneous T2 precedents can acquire the force of law and justify judicial rulings contrary to the T1 meaning of constitutional language.

The other plausible ground for recognizing the law-changing authority of erroneous T2 decisions appeals to Article III of the Constitution. According to this account, Article III vests the Supreme Court with law-establishing authority by conferring 'judicial power' on the Court.[22] As a historical matter, the argument runs, the judicial power has always included an authority to establish subsequently binding interpretive precedents.[23] Although this argument puts the text of the Constitution in the foreground, the best background account of why the Constitution's text and history should control legal decisions is Hart's. To the extent that the Constitution's text and history are legally authoritative in the US, it is because they are accepted as such. The Constitution that is accepted as law is a constitution that somehow authorizes or at least tolerates T3 decision-making based on T2 precedents that diverge from the T1 meaning of constitutional language.

B. Do T2 Meanings Obligate the Justices?

The exact status of T2 precedents under the rule of recognition poses further questions and raises further anxieties about the nature of US constitutional law and about the judicial role in applying and shaping it. The traditional understanding of *stare decisis* makes T2 meanings a source of legal obligation, binding on the justices in at least some cases.[24] But the nature and strength of this obligation are much disputed. The justices frequently disagree about which erroneous decisions to adhere to and which to overrule.[25]

In response to controversy about the precise contours of practice-grounded rules of recognition, a Hartian framework encourages empirical examination of judicial practice, not just

---

[19] M Stokes Paulsen, 'Abrogating *Stare Decisis* by Statute: May Congress Remove the Precedential Effect of *Roe* and *Casey*?' (2000) 109 Yale LJ 1535, 1578 fn 115 (second alteration in original) (quoting US Constitution, Art III, § 1).

[20] There have been occasional complaints and expressions of doubt, including a suggestion by Chief Justice Taney that the Supreme Court might dispense with *stare decisis* in constitutional cases. See *The Passenger Cases* 48 US (7 How) 283, 470 (1849) (Taney CJ dissenting). But Taney's suggestion came in a solitary dissent, and he subsequently appeared to apply a more standard position. See Lee (n 13) 717–18 and fn 377.

[21] *Kimble v Marvel Entertainment LLC* 135 S Ct 2401, 2410 (2015) ('[S]*tare decisis* has consequence only to the extent it sustains incorrect decisions; correct judgments have no need for that principle to prop them up').

[22] See, e.g., RH Bork, *The Tempting of America: The Political Seduction of the Law* (Simon & Schuster 1990) 157; JO McGinnis and MB Rappaport, 'Reconciling Originalism and Precedent' (2009) 103 Nw U L Rev 803, 823–25.

[23] See, e.g., C Nelson, '*Stare Decisis* and Demonstrably Erroneous Precedents' (2001) 87 Va L Rev 1, 5.

[24] See, e.g., L Alexander, 'Constrained by Precedent' (1989) 63 So Cal L Rev 1, 4; Schauer (n 1) 125–26.

[25] For examples of recent disputes, see cases cited at n 1.

judicial rhetoric. An inquiry of this kind yields complex and in some respects equivocal results. There appears to be consensus, adhered to out of a sense of obligation, that overruling a T2 precedent requires more justification than 'mere' error.[26] Relatedly, the evidence strongly suggests that the justices observe a norm that forbids calling large numbers of T2 decisions into question all at once.[27] Another norm that can be identified based on a mixture of the justices' rhetoric and their practice calls for unusual deference to T2 rulings that have engendered massive reliance, such as those establishing the permissibility of paper money and the Social Security system.[28]

But once the issue of T2 error is pressed with respect to a particular decision that has not generated overwhelmingly strong reliance interest, there is little evidence that the justices feel obliged to adhere to precedents that they think both originally mistaken and seriously regrettable from a legal, moral, or policy perspective. On average, the modern Supreme Court overrules two precedents per year.[29] Prior to the 2020 appointment of Justice Amy Coney Barrett, all of the sitting justices had voted to overrule at least some T2 decisions during their tenures on the Court.[30] Absent behavioural evidence that the justices feel compelled to 'accept the bitter with the sweet'[31] in their professed acknowledgements of precedent's binding force, Professor Frederick Schauer maintains that the norm of horizontal *stare decisis* in the Supreme Court—governing when the Court binds itself as distinguished from courts that are lower down in the judicial hierarchy—is almost vanishingly weak.[32]

In his contribution to this volume, Professor Andrei Marmor seeks to explicate the doctrine of *stare decisis* as reflecting an obligation of courts either to follow an on-point precedent or to articulately justify any deviation.[33] Although I do not disagree, a norm of *stare decisis* that cashes out in these terms would add little to the general judicial obligation of candour in articulating the grounds for a decision,[34] at least in the absence of substantial agreement about which proffered justifications for deviations from precedent are legally adequate.

Persuasively, in my view, Professor Richard Re maintains that the justices much more commonly experience T2 precedents as conferring a permission for them to adhere to past errors, if they should choose to do so, than as binding them to perpetuate their past mistakes.[35] On this account, the Court's precedents are binding on the lower courts but not in subsequent Supreme Court cases—beyond, we might add, the weak obligation to explain any decision to overrule a constitutional precedent on some further basis than 'mere error'.

If this analysis is correct, erroneous T2 precedents have major legal and jurisprudential significance, even in the Supreme Court, though not the same significance as a more robustly

---

[26] See cases cited at n 1.

[27] RH Fallon, Jr, *Law and Legitimacy in the Supreme Court* (Belknap Press 2018) 79.

[28] See, e.g., RJ Kozel, 'Original Meaning and the Precedent Fallback' (2015) 68 Vand L Rev 105, 126; *Leegin Creative Leather Products Inc v PSKS Inc* 551 US 877, 906 (2007); *Payne v Tennessee* 501 US 808, 827 (1991).

[29] See Congressional Research Service, 'Table of Supreme Court Decisions Overruled by Subsequent Decisions' (*Constitution Annotated*) <https://constitution.congress.gov/resources/decisions-overruled> accessed 12 February 2021 (showing 108 decisions overruled in the last fifty years).

[30] See *Knick* (n 1) (Roberts CJ and Thomas, Alito, Gorsuch, and Kavanaugh JJ, voting to overturn *Williamson County Regional Planning Commission v Hamilton Bank of Johnson City* 473 US 172 (1985)); *Alleyne v United States* 570 US 99, 116 (2013) (Thomas, Ginsburg, Breyer, and Sotomayor JJ, voting to overturn *Harris v United States* 536 US 545 (2002)).

[31] Schauer (n 1) 141.

[32] ibid 132, 135, 137.

[33] See the contribution to this volume by Andrei Marmor (Chapter 19).

[34] See generally RH Fallon, Jr, 'A Theory of Judicial Candor' (2017) 117 Colum L Rev 2265.

[35] See Re (n 1); cf J Raz, *The Authority of Law* (2nd edn, OUP 2009) 67, 117 fn * (labelling legal permissions 'explicit' and 'strong' when resulting from an authorizing norm, not just the absence of a relevant prohibition).

obligation-creating doctrine of *stare decisis* would have. Absent one or more relevant T2 pre-cedents, I assume that the justices would have no legally adequate justification for rendering a decision incompatible with the best specification of the Constitution's T1 meaning.[36] If an erroneous T2 ruling can alter that obligation, it must be because of the legitimate authority of the justices as T2 decision-makers, within vaguely marked limits, to alter legal obligations that would exist otherwise.[37]

In *The Concept of Law*, Hart distinguished among rules of recognition, rules of adjudi-cation, and rules of change.[38] On the account that I am offering here of the role of constitu-tional *stare decisis* in the Supreme Court, T3 cases involving erroneous T2 decisions reveal a practical overlap in the US legal order between a rule of recognition and a rule of change: er-roneous T2 precedents are law under the rule of recognition applying in the Supreme Court, but their erroneous status triggers the applicability of a rule of change, under which the just-ices have a permission, but not an obligation, to overrule precedents at T3 and revise the law for the future if they so choose.

Insofar as the authority of the Supreme Court is concerned, characterization of erroneous T2 precedents as permission-conferring is more illuminating than their traditional charac-terization as robustly obligation-creating in three respects. First, it should be uncontrover-sial as an empirical matter that an on-point T2 precedent grants permission to the justices not to inquire at all into T1 constitutional meaning in a T3 case unless they choose to do so, even if they have strong dispositions to believe that a particular T2 decision was mistaken as gauged by the Constitution's T1 meaning.[39]

A few examples should suffice to make the point. In the view of many observers, many of the most important elements of current US constitutional doctrine would be impossible to support based on the Constitution's T1 meaning. Without endorsing specific claims, I note the confident pronouncements of leading scholars that decisions and doctrines potentially vulnerable to overruling by the Supreme Court on the ground that they deviate from T1 con-stitutional meanings include those establishing all of the following:

- The constitutional validity of paper money as legal tender.[40]
- The permissibility of the Social Security system and other features of the modern ad-ministrative state.[41]
- The Fourteenth Amendment prohibition against racial discrimination in public schools.[42]

[36] In framing the point this way, I adhere to the view, which I have expressed elsewhere, that the original public meaning of constitutional provisions will often be vague or indeterminate and thus capable of being given more than one legal meaning by courts. See RH Fallon, Jr, 'The Chimerical Concept of Original Public Meaning' (2021) 107 Va L Rev 1421.

[37] See n 14 and accompanying text.

[38] See Hart (n 8) 95–97; see also J Gardner, 'Can There Be a Written Constitution' in L Green and B Leiter (eds), *Oxford Studies in Philosophy of Law: vol 1* (OUP 2011) 162.

[39] Because the Supreme Court has nearly complete discretion to determine which cases to hear, it can and fre-quently does use the *certiorari* process to reject calls to reconsider T2 decisions that petitioners claim were erro-neous. See A Coney Barrett, 'Precedent and Jurisprudential Disagreement' (2013) 91 Tex L Rev 1711, 1731–33; F Schauer, '*Stare Decisis* and the Selection Effect' in CJ Peters (ed), *Precedent in the United States Supreme Court* (Springer 2013) 121.

[40] See, e.g., HP Monaghan, '*Stare Decisis* and Constitutional Adjudication' (1988) 88 Colum L Rev 723, 744–45 (asserting the inconsistency of the *Legal Tender Cases* 79 US (12 Wall) 457 (1871), with the Constitution's original meaning).

[41] See ibid 739.

[42] See DA Strauss, *The Living Constitution* (OUP 2010) 12–13.

- The application of 'equal protection' norms against the federal government, to which the Equal Protection Clause does not apply, via the Due Process Clause of the Fifth Amendment.[43]
- The application of the Bill of Rights to the states via the Due Process Clause of the Fourteenth Amendment.[44]
- The one person, one vote principle.[45]
- The right of indigent defendants to appointed lawyers and waivers of applicable fees in a variety of contexts.[46]
- Numerous rights of criminal suspects, including the protections afforded by *Miranda* warnings and the exclusionary rule.[47]
- Modern, stringent protections against content-based regulation of any category of speech that was not historically recognized as specifically beyond the protective reach of the First Amendment.[48]

With regard to each of these matters, the Supreme Court routinely accepts the doctrine as settled without bothering to re-examine the correctness of T2 decisions as measured against T1 meanings.

Secondly, a permission-granting theory accords well with the justices' patterns of actually voting to reverse only those T2 decisions that they regard as normatively unattractive from a forward-looking perspective.[49] I can think of no case in which a justice has ever professed a felt obligation to overrule a T2 decision despite a confessed apprehension of significantly undesirable forward-looking consequences.

Thirdly, viewing T2 precedents as granting permissions of adherence explains how justices can concur in opinions that apply precedents that they think ought to be overruled if a majority of their colleagues were prepared to take that step.[50] A justice might reasonably believe that in the light of known divisions within the Court, it would be better, all things considered, to apply a T2 precedent until a majority is ready both to reconsider a T2 holding and adopt the correct T1 meaning.

---

[43] See ibid 13.

[44] See ibid 14.

[45] See ibid.

[46] See ibid 107.

[47] See A Reed Amar, 'Fourth Amendment First Principles' (1994) 107 Harv L Rev 757, 793 fn 135 ('[I]f we look at the original design of the Fourth Amendment, we see that its text, history, structure, and early implementation do not support the exclusionary rule').

[48] Historians of the First Amendment have characteristically maintained either that the Founders predominantly understood the Free Speech Clause as having a narrow reach (by modern standards), see, e.g., LW Levy, *Emergence of a Free Press* (Ivan R Dee 1985) xii–xv, or that they widely viewed the Free Speech Clause as broad in scope but readily tolerating restrictions that served the public interest, see, e.g., J Campbell, 'Natural Rights and the First Amendment' (2017) 127 Yale LJ 246; G Lakier, 'The Invention of Low-Value Speech' (2015) 128 Harv L Rev 2167.

[49] See Schauer (n 1) 129–30 (reporting that '[t]he conventional empirical' conclusion of 'those who study Supreme Court decision making systematically' is that the justices' 'prelegal ideologies play[] a larger role than *stare decisis* in determining and predicting Supreme Court outcomes').

[50] See, e.g., *Gundy v United States* 139 S Ct 2116, 2130–31 (2019) (Alito J concurring in the judgment) (stating that, 'because a majority is not willing' to reconsider the Court's approach to legislative delegation, 'it would be freakish to single out the provision at issue here for special treatment'); *McBurney v Young* 569 US 221, 237 (2013) (Thomas J concurring) (joining the Court's opinion because it 'properly applied our dormant Commerce Clause precedents' while objecting to the doctrine as a whole and indicating that it should be abolished).

3. Erroneous T2 Constitutional Precedent, Hartian Concepts, and the Role of the Supreme Court Within the US Legal System

The functional role of the Supreme Court's erroneous T2 constitutional precedents—both in altering constitutional obligations and in permitting the Court to choose the applicable rule for the future—opens a window through which to examine the Court's distinctive place within the US legal system. In looking through that window, this section toggles between examination of phenomena within the US legal system and consideration of the capacity of Hart's conceptual framework, which I found to be so useful in analysing the issues discussed in section 2, to achieve a perspicuous understanding of further aspects of the Supreme Court's role.

A. Multiple Institutions, Partially Divergent Rules of Recognition: The Supreme Court vs the Lower Courts

As I noted in section 2, the phenomenon of erroneous T2 constitutional precedents by the Supreme Court, which alter the constitutional law of the US but do not bind the Court irrevocably, reveals a significant overlap between the rule of recognition in the Supreme Court and US rules of legal change. Insofar as the doctrine of *stare decisis* permits the Court either to adhere to erroneous T2 precedents or to revise the constitutional law of the US, it invites reflection on the extent to which the Court—in significant contrast with other US courts—functions as a constitutional law-maker. As debates about the binding authority of erroneous T2 rulings by the Supreme Court bring out, the US has a substantially two-tiered legal system, in which the rule of recognition in the Supreme Court differs materially from that which applies in other courts. While debate rages about when the justices should reject T2 precedents in favour of T1 constitutional meanings, the rule in the lower courts is settled and categorical: lower courts must adhere to the Supreme Court's T2 decisions, however demonstrably erroneous they may be, until the Court reverses those decisions.[51]

The implications of this disparity between the law-revising capacity of the Supreme Court and that of lower courts are far-reaching. As the Supreme Court bluntly put it in *Camreta v Greene*, '[a] decision of a federal district court judge is not binding precedent in either a different judicial district, the same judicial district, or even upon the same judge in a different case'.[52] Federal circuit courts of appeals occupy an intermediate position with respect to authority to establish binding law. Their decisions bind district courts within their circuits. In addition, rulings by ordinary three-judge panels are typically horizontally binding on future

---

[51] See, e.g., *Rodriguez de Quijas v Shearson/American Express Inc* 490 US 477, 484 (1989); *Hohn v United States* 524 US 236, 252–53 (1998). Despite the rarity of Supreme Court review of lower court decisions, 'most systematic studies have found defiance to be rare and compliance the norm'; PT Kim, 'Lower Court Discretion' (2007) 82 NYU L Rev 383, 395 and fn 4. But cf RM Re, 'Narrowing Supreme Court Precedent from Below' (2016) 104 Geo LJ 921, 971 (maintaining that lower courts can sometimes evade the full effect of Supreme Court precedents through narrowing interpretations); J Blackman, 'Originalism and *Stare Decisis* in the Lower Courts' (2019) 13 NYU J L & Liberty 44, 46 (arguing that lower court judges can and should 'decline to extend a constitutional rule to brand new circumstances, if the binding precedent is completely unmoored from the Constitution's original public meaning').

[52] *Camreta v Greene* 563 US 692, 709 (2011) (quoting JW Moore and others, *Moore's Federal Practice* (3rd edn, Matthew Bender 2011) vol 18, § 134.02[1][d]).

panels within the circuit unless overruled by extraordinary meetings of most or all appellate judges in the circuit, sitting *en banc*.[53] Even in that situation, however, law-making capacity for one panel implies incapacity for future panels, which typically lack the authority to overrule their predecessors' decisions.

Earlier I cited numerous examples of cases and doctrines that commentators think insupportable as a matter of T1 constitutional meaning. For the lower courts to be absolutely bound by these decisions, while no past precedent is theoretically immune from reconsideration by the Supreme Court, locates the Court in a unique status within the US legal system.

At one point in *The Concept of Law*, Hart said that the existence of a rule of recognition requires its acceptance or practice by an apparently broad cohort of officials.[54] In a postscript to the second edition, he maintained more specifically that the rule of recognition is 'a form of judicial customary rule existing only if it is accepted and practised in the law-identifying and law-applying operations of the courts'.[55]

In the US context, both formulations are misleading. To put the point slightly more sharply, the Hartian model encourages false impressions not only about the nature of the rule or rules of recognition in the US, but also about the unique role of the Supreme Court and about the scope and nature of law-altering authority in different tiers of the judicial system. The discontinuity between the Supreme Court and lower courts illustrates the need—which I am hardly the first to notice—for a friendly amendment to Hart's account of the rule of recognition: it should be emphasized that different officials, including the judges of different courts, can be subject to different rules of recognition.[56]

A closely related lacuna in Hart's account arises from his failure to follow through on his own insight—to which I alluded earlier—that a legal system will normally include rules of adjudication and rules of change as well as rules of recognition. In the Supreme Court, the rule of recognition that makes erroneous T2 precedents a permitted but not obligatory basis for T3 decisions stands in a close but non-obvious conceptual relationship with rules of adjudication and change by abetting the Supreme Court, much more than the lower courts, in revising the constitutional law of the US. Without attempting to work out all of the conceptual relationships among rules of recognition, adjudication, and change, I would simply note that their elucidation may be crucial to developing a satisfactory account of the Supreme Court's role within the general outlines of a Hartian framework.

I would also offer the relatively summary observation that the Supreme Court's law-changing prerogatives have spillover effects that render its constitutional decision-making substantially less rule-bound than that of other courts—which typically must resolve

---

[53] ibid § 134.02[1][c]; see, e.g., *Payne v Taslimi* 998 F3d 648, 654 (4th Cir 2021) ('[U]nlike the discretionary application of *stare decisis* by the Supreme Court, we are bound by prior panel decisions'). Somewhat diminishing the stringency of this rule, a majority of the circuits have adopted some form of a 'mini *en banc*' procedure, under which a panel can overrule circuit precedent after giving notice to the other judges in the circuit and receiving an indication that the circuit would not vote to rehear the panel's decision *en banc*. See N Devins and A Orr Larsen, 'Weaponizing En Banc' (2021) 96 NYU L Rev 1373, 1422–23; see generally AE Sloan, 'The Dog that Didn't Bark: Stealth Procedures and the Erosion of *Stare Decisis* in the Federal Courts of Appeals' (2009) 78 Fordham L Rev 713, 725–41.

[54] See Hart (n 8) 116 ('[R]ules of recognition specifying the criteria of legal validity and [the legal system's] rules of change and adjudication must be effectively accepted as common public standards of official behaviour by its officials').

[55] ibid 256.

[56] See, e.g., J Raz, *Practical Reason and Norms* (2nd edn, OUP 1990) 146; Greenawalt (n 16) 636; KE Himma, 'Making Sense of Constitutional Disagreement: Legal Positivism, the Bill of Rights, and the Conventional Rule of Recognition in the United States' (2003) 4 J L Soc'y 149, 162.

414 RICHARD H FALLON, JR

constitutional cases within a dense network of Supreme Court precedents—along multiple dimensions. Precisely because the choice to overrule T2 precedents is always open to it, the Court routinely needs to confront a significant range of divisive issues—not determined by rule or a rule-mandated decision procedure—that the lower courts face only much more rarely, if at all. Three examples will illustrate the point.

First, in order to determine what authority to accord to erroneous T2 precedents, the Supreme Court needs criteria by which to identify T2 error. Those criteria depend on standards for ascertaining T1 meanings that are notoriously unsettled by rules and are highly divisive.

Secondly, after original meanings are identified and T2 errors marked, the justices must determine which erroneous rulings should be reversed and which retained. The Supreme Court's most familiar formulations of its criteria for overruling or affirming erroneous T2 precedents—once they have been marked as erroneous—characterize the issue as pragmatic or prudential.[57]

As a further ground for disagreement, most justices' criteria for determining whether to reverse or uphold erroneous precedents appear to depend partly on whether T1 meanings or T2 holdings are more normatively attractive.[58] Divisions on this score appear intractable. Although a number of the justices have recently advanced proposals to govern future applications of *stare decisis* in the Supreme Court,[59] the chances of their bargaining to agreement seem poor.

Thirdly, recent Supreme Court decisions reflect deep disagreements about the jurisprudential status of erroneous T2 precedents that the Court has declined to overrule. Some justices appear to believe that initially mistaken decisions that the Court declines to overrule possess the same scope of precedential authority as other T2 precedents. In their view, if the rationale of an erroneous T2 decision applies to the new facts of a T3 case, that rationale should control.[60] By contrast, other justices appear to believe that erroneous T2 precedents, or at least some of them, should not be extended to new facts or new contexts, even if they are not to be overruled immediately and even if their articulated rationales would apply.[61]

Overall, the contrast between the Supreme Court and the lower courts highlights a vast disparity in their constitutional functions and in the extent to which their constitutional decision-making is meaningfully constrained by rules. Beyond identifying and applying sources of law picked out by rules of recognition, and even beyond resolving disputes between particular parties, much if not most of the business of the Supreme Court involves the consideration and effectuation of constitutional change.

---

[57] See, e.g., *Planned Parenthood of Southeastern Pennsylvania v Casey* 505 US 833, 854–55 (1992).

[58] See, e.g., Schauer (n 1); Baude (n 1) 330–33.

[59] See, e.g., *Ramos* (n 1) 1414–16 (Kavanaugh J concurring in part); *Gamble* (n 4) 1984–86 (Thomas J concurring).

[60] See RE Barnett, 'No Small Feat: Who Won the Health Care Case (and Why Did so Many Law Professors Miss the Boat)?' (2013) 65 Fla L Rev 1331, 1346–49 (asserting that liberals generally hold this attitude towards precedents recognizing congressional power under the Commerce Clause that go beyond the clause's original meaning).

[61] See, e.g., *Ocasio v United States* 136 S Ct 1423, 1437 (2016) (Thomas J dissenting) (noting that *Evans v United States* 504 US 255 (1992) made the Court's holding 'plausible' but maintaining that, '[r]ather than embrac[ing] that view, I would not extend *Evans*' errors further'); cf B Friedman, 'The Wages of Stealth Overruling (with Particular Attention to *Miranda v Arizona*)' (2010) 99 Geo LJ 1, 8–13 (contending that the Supreme Court silently overrules cases by failing to extend precedents where they logically would apply or by limiting earlier cases to their facts).

B. Rules of Recognition as Social Rules: The Case of the Supreme Court

Hart depicted rules of recognition as social rules, partly enforced by expectations and social pressure in the form of criticism, if not by stronger sanctions.[62] Debates about appropriate overruling of T2 precedents by the Supreme Court, among other phenomena, suggest that characterization of the justices as bound by social rules may be potentially misleading even if not literally inaccurate.[63] Depiction of rules of recognition as social rules practised by all officials or at least by all judges may imply the existence of a highly cohesive group whose members have a strong influence over one another in identifying controlling legal norms. The Supreme Court deviates from this picture in several ways.

First, the justices operate in a variety of professional, cultural, and social matrices in which many of those with whom the justices interact may contest prevailing or once-prevailing views within the Supreme Court concerning the justices' role-based obligations. The justices are nominated and confirmed by political officials, often with an agenda of altering the Court's interpretive understandings. As electioneering debates about nominations to the Court make manifest, questions involving appropriate standards of Supreme Court decision-making are both politically salient and highly contestable. Both political leaders and academic theorists anticipate that justices can, and frequently should, resist any social pressures that their colleagues might exert on them. Accordingly, justices who attempt to move the law in one or another direction are likely to find admiring academic or political constituencies to support their endeavours. Under these circumstances, the justices seem unlikely to recognize the practice of their colleagues as uniquely authoritative in fixing their role-based responsibilities.

Secondly, because the Supreme Court is a small institution—comprising only nine members—presidential appointments of new justices can provoke rapid and occasionally profound shifts in prevailing interpretive understandings. One day's outlier justice may be the next day's centrist. During the New Deal era, a series of appointments by President Franklin Roosevelt—following a failed attempt to expand the Court's membership—produced a dramatic overhaul of leading substantive precedents and interpretive frameworks.[64] More recently, conservative justices have brought originalist and textualist interpretive methodologies into the mainstream of arguments in and before the Court.[65]

Thirdly, as the Court decides one case after another, justices tend to form ad hoc coalitions, united on results if not on the deep bases for their conclusions, and to paper over even fundamental differences about the ultimate grounds of law. Although there are possible sanctions against justices who fail to conform to rules of recognition that their colleagues accept, the costs of attempted discipline are likely not to seem worth bearing in many cases.

---

[62] See Hart (n 8) 55–61, 254–59.

[63] For discussion of rules of precedent as social rules elsewhere in this volume, see Nicholas W Barber (Chapter 4). Others have argued that the rule of recognition is better characterized as a 'convention' or 'Lewis-convention', see, e.g., MD Adler, 'Popular Constitutionalism and the Rule of Recognition: Whose Practices Ground US Law?' (2006) 100 Nw U L Rev 719, 730–31 (explicating but not endorsing this view); a 'shared cooperative activity', see, e.g., SJ Shapiro, 'Law, Plans, and Practical Reason' (2002) 8 Legal Theory 387, 394–401; or a 'constitutive rule', see A Marmor, 'Legal Conventionalism' (1998) 4 Legal Theory 509, 521–27.

[64] See generally WE Leuchtenburg, *The Supreme Court Reborn* (OUP 1995).

[65] In a widely noted tribute to that influence, Justice Elena Kagan has asserted that 'we're all textualists now'; Justice Elena Kagan, 'The Scalia Lecture: A Dialogue with Justice Elena Kagan on the Reading of Statutes' (17 November 2015) 8:09 <http://today.law.harvard.edu/in-scalia-lecture-kagan-discusses-statutory-interpretation> (https://perma.cc/3BCF-FEFR).

Justice Clarence Thomas may furnish a case in point. In a number of cases, he has written solitary concurring opinions calling for reconsideration of issues, based on T1 meanings, that most or all of his colleagues view as settled.[66] Justice Scalia reportedly once compared himself with Justice Thomas by asserting, 'I am an originalist … , not a nut.'[67] Yet Justice Thomas's most extreme pronouncements seldom draw rebuke.

Nothing that I have said in this subsection may be flatly incompatible with the Hartian account of rules of recognition as social rules. If one takes a sufficiently relaxed view of what rules of recognition are and of how they are fixed, disagreement and shifting understandings may involve the rules' proper interpretation or application, not their existence or even their core of agreed content. Nevertheless, the characterization of the rule of recognition as a social rule seems likely to create misleading expectations concerning, if not to encourage distorted perceptions of, the functioning of the Supreme Court. Once again, the hazy outlines of a more accurate portrait may begin to emerge if we imagine the Supreme Court as operating much of the time pursuant to rules of change that empower the Court to function as a law-making institution, even in constitutional cases.

4. Conclusion: *Stare Decisis* in the Supreme Court and the Rule of Law

The account of the role of *stare decisis* in the US Supreme Court that I have offered in this chapter, as one abetting the Court's exercise of substantial law-making prerogatives in constitutional cases, invites normative objections, perhaps most saliently including one that appeals to the ideal of the rule of law. According to this objection, the function of *stare decisis* should be to constrain judicial discretion, including that of the Supreme Court, whose justices should be ruled by law, not empowered to decide cases based on their contestable moral and political views.[68]

I shall not attempt a full appraisal of this normative argument. But two analytical points may be in order. First, law-making by a court, including the Supreme Court, differs dramatically from law-making by a legislature or an initial constitution writer. Legislatures, including Congress, can develop new rules on an entirely forward-looking, ad hoc basis. By contrast, the Supreme Court's role in constitutional cases is limited to interpretation of language adopted on past occasions by others, even though it also features important forward-looking aspects.

Secondly, as I have meant to signal, constitutional law-making by the Supreme Court has important effects in making adjudication by the lower courts much more rule-bound, determinate, and predictable than it would otherwise be. By nearly all accounts, the lower courts take very seriously their obligation to adhere to Supreme Court precedent.[69] Available data

---

[66] See, e.g., *American Legion v American Humanist Association* 139 S Ct 2067, 2094–95 (2019) (Thomas J concurring) (suggesting that the Establishment Clause 'should not be incorporated against the States' and may only apply to legislative enactments); *McDonald v City of Chicago* 561 US 742, 806 (2010) (Thomas J concurring in part and concurring in the judgment) (suggesting that the Court should incorporate provisions of the Bill of Rights through the Privileges or Immunities Clause, rather than the Due Process Clause); *United States v Morrison* 529 US 598, 627 (2000) (Thomas J concurring) (suggesting that the Court 'replace[] its existing Commerce Clause jurisprudence with a standard more consistent with the original understanding').

[67] J Rosen, 'What Made Scalia Great?' *The Atlantic* (15 February 2016) <http://www.theatlantic.com/politics/archive/2016/02/what-made-antonin-scalia-great/462837>.

[68] See Baude (n 1) 329–33.

[69] Kim (n 51) 395 and fn 4.

suggest that ideological differences among lower court judges have far less influence on outcomes than comparable differences among Supreme Court justices.[70]

In my view, nothing inherent in the ideal of the rule of law, as defensibly explicated, precludes the assignment of substantial law-changing authority to an apex court.[71] As Hart noted, any complex legal system requires rules of legal change, including authorizations to clarify vague or disputable meanings and to resolve conflicts among applicable norms. Whether assignment of even further law-changing authority to a court is normatively desirable or defensible seems to me to depend on a complex mix of factors, some involving empirical variables, including contingent likelihoods that other institutions would deal sensibly with previously unforeseen or otherwise changed circumstances if an apex court did not step into the breach. But no sensible account of the ideal of the rule of law could preclude the possibility of legal and constitutional change based on the exercise of law-making discretion by one institution or another, including an apex court.

That said, both concerned citizens of particular regimes and students of comparative jurisprudence should be clear-eyed about how legal systems allocate law-making and law-revising powers and about the devices through which relevant allocations occur. In the US legal system, the doctrine of constitutional *stare decisis* as it applies in the Supreme Court substantially abets constitutional law-making by the justices. In the lower courts, rules of constitutional *stare decisis* are discretion-limiting. In the Supreme Court, by contrast, *stare decisis* norms are part of a network of rules of recognition and of change that, for better or worse, effectively confers substantial law-revising responsibilities on nine unelected justices.

---

[70] See L Epstein, WM Landes, and RA Posner, *The Behavior of Federal Judges* (Harvard UP 2013) 168–69 (finding that ideology had a significant impact in producing divisions in the courts of appeals only in 'cases that politicians and segments of the public feel strongly about, as opposed to the routine and technical legal cases that dominate the dockets of those courts').

[71] For general discussion of the rule of law as a concept in US constitutional debates, see RH Fallon, Jr, '"The Rule of Law" as a Concept in Constitutional Discourse' (1997) 97 Colum L Rev 1.

31

Statutory Interpretation and Binding Precedents in the Civil Law Tradition

Lorena Ramírez-Ludeña[*]

1. Introduction

In countries that belong to the continental tradition, it is frequently claimed that past judicial decisions do not have binding force, and that judges do not create law but *merely* apply it.[1] Binding precedents are associated with the creation of case law by judges, which contrasts with the role assigned to them in the civil law tradition.[2] In countries like Spain, law is considered to be created by the legislature. What place would precedents have if it is the legislature, and not judges, who create general norms? This set of claims is related to the selection and training of judges in many countries in the civil law tradition, who often have to overcome a rote-based education, where candidates have to memorize all the details of the written rules that they will simply apply when they have to decide particular cases.[3] Although formalist conceptions are rejected at the theoretical level, there is no doubt that in the continental tradition certain formalist assumptions are still present in the general understanding of the activities performed by judges and in their own style of expression.

At the same time, it is generally accepted that the decisions of the higher courts play an important role in the interpretation of the law by the lower courts.[4] But, again, because of the entrenched image of judges as merely applying the law, these interpretations are usually expressed and often perceived as discoveries of pre-existing law. For this reason, the importance of precedent in systems such as the Spanish one continues to be denied. It is assumed that what is decisive is still the statutory law, which all courts, including the Spanish Supreme Court, merely discover. Interpretation by the higher courts is considered not to be a source

---

[*] I would like to thank Sebastián Agüero, Timothy Endicott, Hafsteinn Dan Kristjánsson, Genoveva Martí, Jose Juan Moreso, Álvaro Nuñez, Diego M Papayannis, Giovanni Ratti, and Josep M Vilajosana for their comments on a previous version of this chapter.

[1] Analysing the relation between the binding force of precedents and the creation of law by judges, M Orozco Muñoz, *La Creación judicial del derecho y el precedente vinculante* (Aranzadi 2011). Rejecting the view that judges merely apply the law, P Chiassoni, *La Giurisprudenza civile* (Giuffrè 1999).

[2] In the common law tradition, the declaratory theory, according to which judges identified pre-existing law, is regarded by many as obsolete. In contrast, it is now generally held that judicial decisions are law precisely because they are created by judges, not because they conform to the uses and customs that make up the common law. See R Cross and JW Harris, *Precedent in English Law* (4th edn, Clarendon Press 2004) ch 1.

[3] L Ramírez-Ludeña, 'Las teorías del derecho en la formación de los jueces' (2014) 30 Cuadernos Electrónicos de filosofía del Derecho 37–59.

[4] Once the idea of consulting the legislature to clarify interpretative doubt was overcome, and cassation was consolidated as part of the judiciary, the higher courts were given an important interpretative role. For the development of cassation in Spain, see S Díez Sastre, *El precedente administrativo. Fundamentos y eficacia vinculante* (Marcial Pons 2008) 89–196, MJ Falcón y Tella *La jurisprudencia en los Derechos romanos, anglosajón y continental* (Marcial Pons 2010); L Moral Soriano, *El precedente judicial* (Marcial Pons 2002) ch VII.

Lorena Ramírez-Ludeña, *Statutory Interpretation and Binding Precedents in the Civil Law Tradition* In: *Philosophical Foundations of Precedent.* Edited by: Timothy Endicott, Hafsteinn Dan Kristjánsson, and Sebastian Lewis, Oxford University Press.
© Lorena Ramírez-Ludeña 2023. DOI: 10.1093/oso/9780192857248.003.0032

of law, but merely the identification of the content of real sources (statutes), so that there are no binding precedents.[5] These statements refer to three questions that will be distinguished in this chapter: the existence of genuine precedents that carry out a certain creative activity, their binding character, and whether they are sources of law.

Here I will argue that interpretation undertaken by judges involves, to a large extent, creative activity, so that it makes sense to speak of genuine precedents that govern legal interpretation. I will also try to show that in contrast to what is usually assumed, the binding force of these precedents may be quite robust, mainly because of features related to the legal culture of many civil law countries. And this is independent of their status as sources of law. My analysis will reveal not only a kind of normative tension in countries like Spain,[6] but also a stark contrast between theory and practice.

It is important to note that in this chapter I will largely leave aside the problems of identification of the *ratio decidendi*, that is, the problems related to the interpretation of the interpretation adopted by the higher court. In precedents related to the interpretation of statutory law, these problems may seem less severe than in cases in common law systems in which no legislation is in issue, but doubts can and often do arise. However, these will not be the focus of my analysis. Moreover, although regulation and legal practice may confer special significance on the existence of repeated decisions, I will leave this element aside, even though it may increase the complexity of extracting the *ratio*. I will refer to individual decisions, assuming that my analysis can also be extended to situations where two or more earlier decisions are deemed relevant.

The analysis I will carry out will enable me to identify certain peculiarities of the continental systems in relation to precedents, and of the Spanish system in particular, but also to reflect more generally on the role of precedents in the interpretation of the law, their binding force, and their status as a source of law.

2. Interpretation and Creation of Law

Decisions related to the interpretation of statutes enacted by the legislature are increasingly important in countries in the civil law tradition, such as Spain. In particular, I will focus on decisions of higher courts in individual cases, which apply a general norm that presupposes a certain specification of the content of the law.[7] In Spanish criminal law, for example, the

---

[5] In other words, they are seen as sources of knowledge of pre-existing law.

[6] Francisco Laporta makes reference to a kind of normative schizophrenia, which is shown by facts such as the following: according to the Civil Code, jurisprudence is understood only as a complementary source, but the law recognizes that the decisions of the Supreme Court have a unique authority; under the Spanish Constitution, judges are subject only to the law, not to the decisions of other judges, but the Supreme Court has a clear role in unifying legal doctrine; there are decisions of the Constitutional Court which state that judges are bound by the (statutory) law and not by precedent, but this contrasts with the fact that there are provisions that recognize that jurisprudence can constitute autonomous grounds for appeal. See F Laporta, 'La fuerza vinculante de la jurisprudencia y la lógica del precedente' in V Ferreres and JA Xiol (eds), *El carácter vinculante de la jurisprudencia* (Fundación Coloquio Jurídico Europeo 2010) 11–42.

[7] Although much of what I will point out can be extrapolated to decisions that, in the abstract, are made by the higher courts with respect to interpretation. Precedents that focus on resolving interpretative disputes in the abstract may involve the choice of one interpretation, but also the choice of a range of interpretations as admissible and/or the exclusion of other possibilities. Precisely because they do not deal with a concrete case, they do not raise some of the difficulties to which I will refer. In mentioning the general norm, I am not referring to an interpretative norm about which tool should be used to interpret a statement, nor to a rule about what interpretative result should be achieved, but to the interpretation as a product itself. See R Guastini, 'Interpretaciones precedentes' in R Guastini, *Ensayos escépticos sobre la interpretación* (Zela 2018); Álvaro Núñez Vaquero, 'Interpretaciones

interpretation of the term 'violence' used in the article on coercion (art 172 of the Spanish Penal Code) has been the subject of intense controversy.[8] In particular, it has been debated whether the provision includes only physical violence against persons or also psychological coercion and the use of force on things (as opposed to persons), which are considered to be covered by the terms 'intimidation' and 'use of force' in other criminal offences. The problem stems from the fact that the legislature has not included these other expressions ('intimidation' and 'use of force') in the definition of coercion, while it has done so in other definitions such as sexual assault and robbery. In deciding cases, the Supreme Court has moved to a so-called 'spiritualization' of the word 'violence' for coercion, understanding it in a broad way. In this regard, the Supreme Court has decided that it includes cases in which there is no physical violence but psychological coercion or use of force on things. My analysis will address this type of Supreme Court decision, in which controversies are resolved by applying a general rule in a way that implies a certain specification of the law.[9]

If, independently of the question of precedent, the problem of the creation of law by judges in resolving individual cases arises, different meanings of 'creation' can be distinguished. On the one hand, when they decide a particular dispute, judges create an individual norm (the individual norm of the ruling) in relation to the persons who have been involved in the proceeding. This decision involves the application of a generic norm (an interpretation as a product), which is the normative premise of the legal syllogism. Furthermore, as part of the external justification of the normative premise, judges take into account certain methods and tools related to the determination of this normative premise.[10] When we are dealing with a normative gap, it is usually assumed that judges create the general norm that they apply. But do the judges create law when the case they are deciding merely raises questions of interpretation? For example, when the Supreme Court decides on the specific case of a mayor of a town cutting the water supply to people who have not paid a specific tax,[11] an individual ruling is issued, based on a general norm that assumes a particular interpretation of the offence of coercion, in which 'violence' includes intimidation. This interpretation is based on arguments concerning the ordinary meaning of the term and the protection of the legal interest in question. Does the foregoing imply the creation of law?[12]

The question may seem strange, since interpretation and the creation of law are normally contrasted. Even those realists who emphasize that there are always several possible

---

precedentes, precedentes interpretativos' in S Agüero and G Ratti (eds), *La escuela genovesa en Chile* (Tirant Lo Blanch 2022) 99–122.

[8] The article on coercion of the Spanish Penal Code (1995) refers to someone who, without being legitimately authorized, prevents another person *with violence* from doing something not prohibited by law, or compels them to do something they do not want to do.

[9] e.g. according to the Spanish Supreme Court (STS 23 November 1989), feinting to run someone over with a car constitutes a form of violence and is therefore a crime of coercion, even if there is no physical attack or assault. For decisions relating to the interpretation of the word 'violence' in the article on coercion, see L Ramírez-Ludeña, 'La irrelevancia de la violencia en el delito de coacciones' (2021) 3 InDret Penal 344–58.

[10] Here I leave aside the problems relating to the internal and external justification of the factual premise of the syllogism.

[11] STS 458/1983 (24 March 1983).

[12] I am not referring here merely to the fact that texts are one thing and their interpretation another. Rather, I am referring to the creative activity that often involves this interpretative activity in the context of the justification of a judicial decision. I understand then that there could be situations where this creative activity does not occur, e.g. because different methods of interpretation lead to the same reading of the relevant rules. See JJ Moreso, *Indeterminacy and Legal Interpretation* (Kluwer 1998) 131–71. In my view, what is sometimes called 'understanding' (and contrasted with interpretation) may involve identifying one norm among others, and is thus a creative activity in the legal field.

interpretations distinguish the set of possible interpretations from the creation of law.[13] By means of some semantic distinctions, I would like to show here that although we can still distinguish between interpretation and the creation of law, in many cases where the judges interpret, they carry out an important activity that can be considered creative. This makes it possible to speak of genuine precedents in these areas, which do not limit themselves to reproducing the applicable law, but rather select a norm (instead of alternative possible norms). At this point, I want to remain neutral with respect to whether the selection is in the strong sense (the other options are wrong) or the weak sense (selecting one because it is considered to be preferable). As I will try to show, this may depend not only on the kind of interpretative problem involved but also on the theory of law that is considered the right one.

Unless some form of naive descriptivism is assumed, combined with the idea that meanings are fixed once and for all, it is hard to deny that very often doubts arise in relation to the normative premise of a judicial decision. The view that within and outside the legal realm, descriptions are available to us that are transparent and determine what we refer to represents an idealized and implausible vision of our language.[14] This has led some authors to understand the relevant descriptions as more sophisticated, for example by resorting to clusters of socially determined descriptions, which can give rise to doubts and errors.[15] And it has led proponents of theories of direct reference to reject that descriptions play a central role in explaining how we refer and what we refer to.[16] Following Putnam's well-known example, imagine that the term 'water' was introduced by pointing to specific occurrences of the substance in a lake. These initial instances are considered paradigmatic instances and then other instances are classified according to their similarity to the paradigms. What makes a sample of a substance water, and what the correct application of the term 'water' depends on, may not be accessible to people. In fact, it is the molecular structure H_2O that determines whether something is water or not, and thus determines the domain of application of the term 'water'. But the discovery of the nature of water occurred long after the term was used. And this in turn can raise doubts and misconceptions about the relevant similarity.[17] In the legal sphere, this is precisely what has happened with terms such as 'marriage'. Adèle Mercier, who acted as an expert witness in Canadian courts, giving evidence on behalf of gay couples seeking the right to marry, considers a semantic argument according to which the characteristic features that define a marriage (commitment to a shared life, respect, trust, etc) are present in both heterosexual and same-sex unions, so that same-sex marriage has always been covered by the term 'marriage'.[18] To understand that non-descriptivist theories of reference provide a good account of what happens, at least in some cases, is to admit that judges, in adopting

[13] R Guastini, 'A Sceptical View on Legal Interpretation' (2005) Analisi e diritto 139–44.

[14] In countries such as Spain, rote-based education often favours judges having such a vision about the language and the language of law, as is evident in many of their references to literal meaning. This view is intuitive because it is how we learn and teach the use of many terms, and because it gives us a clear explanation of why terms refer to some objects and not others. And in the legal field, to understand that we decide to regulate in a certain way, which means that we decide that certain situations with certain characteristics entail certain legal consequences, seems particularly plausible. It may be arguable that my analysis starts by taking into account semantic considerations, ignoring the particularities posed by the legal field; however, I believe that semantic considerations shed light on our understanding of the problem, although its impact depends on legal issues, as I will try to show later. See L Ramírez-Ludeña, 'The Meaning of 'Literal Meaning''(2018) 1 Analisi e Diritto 83–101.

[15] J Searle, 'Proper Names' (1958) 67 Mind 166–73.

[16] L Ramírez-Ludeña, *Diferencias y deferencia. Sobre el impacto de las nuevas teorías de la referencia en el derecho* (Marcial Pons 2015).

[17] G Martí and L Ramírez-Ludeña, 'Legal Disagreements and New Theories of Reference' in A Capone and F Poggi (eds), *Pragmatics and Law* (Springer 2016) 121–37.

[18] G Martí and L Ramírez-Ludeña, 'Tolerance, Flexibility and the Application of Kind Terms' (2021) 198 Synthese 2973–86.

422   LORENA RAMÍREZ-LUDEÑA

certain interpretative decisions, do not confine themselves to describing the law, and that therefore precedents in these areas make a difference. This is so even though they are expected to find out the *true* meaning of the term and not to change its domain of application.

Secondly, problems may arise when our usage of the terms is tolerant, that is, when several uses coexist which divide approximately the same domain of application in different ways.[19] In this respect, judges often choose one of these uses when deciding a case. It seems difficult to deny that this involves creative activity on the part of the judge, even though they are pre-existing uses from which the judge chooses. To return to the example of 'violence', when the issue of coercion was raised, a strict legal use of the term that distinguished violence from intimidation and the use of force existed alongside the broader ordinary use of the term. The Judges then chose to understand the term 'violence' in the context of the offence of coercion in a broader sense, opting for one of the already existing uses. Again, this involves creative activity and lends significance to precedents in this area, as judges do not limit themselves to describing pre-existing law.

Let us now turn to the widespread assumption that meanings are fixed once and for all. It seems hardly debatable that the meaning of a word determines its domain of application, that is, what it should or should not be applied to. But the aforementioned has often been understood in a robust way, assuming that it is determined, for any past, present, or future object, whether or not it belongs to the extension of the term.[20] This robust reading can be challenged by the following thought experiment.[21] Suppose Olympia is a member of a community living in isolation on an island where the class of birds and the class of flying things are coextensive. In this community, they use the term 'bird' to refer to objects in these coextensive classes and have beliefs such as 'only birds can fly' and 'birds are living things' that apply to the island birds. One day, Olympia sees airplanes in the sky for the first time and easily classifies them as birds. Later, when she sees a plane land, she comes to the belief that not all birds are living beings. Let us assume that the practice of applying 'bird' to planes ends up being established in the community. Despite the initial lack of clarity, due to the fact that the community had different beliefs about birds, they all consider that they have always used 'bird' to refer to things that fly and realize that some of the beliefs they had previously about birds (e.g. that they were all living things) were wrong. Suppose instead that Olympia had initially seen planes on the ground without knowing that they could fly. She could then have classified them as non-birds. And if she had seen them take off later, she would have concluded that not all things that fly are birds. If we assume that this other practice is common in the community, they will probably also think that 'bird' had always referred to birds, realizing that some of their earlier beliefs (e.g. that only birds could fly) were wrong. In neither scenario do community members think that they have changed the meaning of 'bird'; they understand that the current usage follows naturally from the previous usage.

This shows that it does not seem to be fixed from the outset whether planes are in the extension of 'bird' or not, which challenges the robust version of the principle that meaning determines extension. Certain accidental events concerning how members of the community first encountered planes had a decisive influence on the adjustment of beliefs in the

---

[19] In ibid we characterize as 'semantic tolerance' the acceptance of such partly overlapping uses in the speakers' community. When the coexistence of different uses is not tolerated, the semantics of the term is *strict*.

[20] This does not mean ignoring the fact that there are cases that raise doubts, but it is generally understood that when an answer is given in cases of vagueness, a change in meaning occurs, something that I will question here.

[21] On this example, inspired by that of Mark Wilson, see Martí and Ramírez-Ludeña, 'Tolerance and Flexibility' (n 18).

community. And it seems wrong to speak of a change in meaning, because the two options (including or excluding planes) seem equally consistent with the way the term was used by the community.[22] This suggests that the semantics of some terms is flexible in the sense that, at any given time, when the question of whether to classify an object under the term arises, there may be more than one course of action open that is arguably compatible with the meaning of the term, and is a continuation of its previous use.

Whether or not the semantics of a term are flexible depends on many factors, including the intentions and interests of the speakers, and what might be at stake in keeping the extension fixed. On the other hand, admitting semantic flexibility leads to the question of what makes the history of the use of a flexible term go one way or another. Many and varied factors may play a role: economic considerations, social pressures, and moral issues, among others. In the legal field, when doubts arise regarding terms that are used in a flexible way, it is important to note that there are not two current uses in the community, but two possibilities, compatible with the pre-existing use, between which the judge chooses. These *alternative equilibria*, in Jackman's words,[23] involve different domains of application of the term, thus involving creative activity, although none of them involve a break with the current use. Continuing with the example of violence in the offence of coercion, once the ordinary meaning is considered the correct one, which is flexible, it has been debated what to do in cases where there are two alternatives that seem to be compatible with the previous usage. In this respect, the Supreme Court has considered deleting data on the cloud pertaining to an ex-partner as being constitutive of the offence of coercion (and so, violent).[24]

The fact that there is creative activity in the situations just described does not mean that this activity, which is interpretative, cannot be distinguished from the creation of law *stricto sensu*. In the case of words used according to the view provided by non-descriptivist theories of reference, there may be disagreements about the relevant similarity, about which we may even be completely wrong. Indeed, mistakes can occur not only when the relevant similarity is misidentified, but also when the term is assumed to work in a different way (according to the transparent beliefs of certain individuals). In the case of terms used in a tolerant manner, the court can make a mistake and create law if it assigns a meaning to the term different from those that are considered legitimate. As for flexibility, if judges opted for an unavailable equilibrium, they would be making a mistake and creating law.

However, the distinction between interpretation (even if it involves a creative activity) and creation is far from straightforward, for it is not only semantics that matter for the purposes of the distinction: the vision one has about which theory of legal interpretation and which theory of law are correct becomes crucial. For example, Dworkinians and Hartians offer different characterizations of when judges create or interpret law and of what kinds of considerations are relevant to understanding whether they interpret rather than create law.[25]

This can be illustrated by the example of violence in coercion. It can be debated whether, depending on the context, only one of the uses of 'violence' that coexisted in the community

---

[22] For other examples that are not as fictitious as the 'bird' example, such as the inclusion of e-sports as an Olympic sport, see ibid.

[23] H Jackman, 'We Live Forwards but Understand Backwards: Linguistic Practices and Future Behavior' (1999) 80 Pacific Philosophical Quarterly 157–77.

[24] STS 421/2020 (20 July 2020).

[25] See G Martí and L Ramírez-Ludeña, 'On Whales and Fish. Two Models of Interpretation' (2020) 11 Jurisprudence 73–75.

was correct. We have already seen that the Supreme Court moved to a so-called 'spiritualiza-tion' of the term 'violence'. This seemed to contradict a systematic interpretation because if the legislator had wanted to do so they could have used the term 'intimidation' or the expression 'use of force' in the offence of coercion, as it is the case with other offences in the same penal code. This broad understanding of 'violence' can be seen as a mistake if one adopts a Dworkinian framework and gives priority to evaluative considerations in connection with the principle of legality. For according to this view, what happened with the term 'violence' in the case of coercion would mean an extension by analogy that exceeds the limits of interpretation. Things are different if one adopts a Hartian framework that would grant relevance (based on conceptual considerations) to ordinary meaning. Or perhaps (in a Hartian framework) the existence of different possible interpretations is recognized when controversy arises. In any case, according to this view, the Supreme Court's solution does not constitute a case of prohibited analogy.

The incidence of the theory of interpretation and of the theory of law does not exclude the possibility that interpretation and creation may continue to be differentiated if a particular theory is adopted or if the various possible theories all agree in their understanding of particular cases.

The fact that there are rules, in a given legal system, that refer to vertical precedents does not seem to alter to any relevant degree the creative activity of judges in the field of interpretation that has already been highlighted. However, it does allow the highest judges to play an important role in the evolution of the meaning of terms in the legal community and, in many cases, in society in general. In the case of the term 'marriage', for example, although Spanish society was highly polarized before the change in the law and the judicial decision, the law had a major impact on society's perception of marriage in Spain.[26]

Thus, although these decisions are interpretations of certain terms and provisions rather than genuine creation, this does not mean that they are mere descriptions of the law. They involve important creative activity and add something new to the law, so they can constitute genuine precedents.[27]

3. The Binding Force of Precedent

A different question from the previous one is that of the binding character of those interpretations. When analysing the degree of bindingness of precedents, several factors are usually considered.[28]

---

[26] L Ramírez-Ludeña, 'Interpretación evolutiva y tolerancia. Un análisis crítico de la Sentencia del Tribunal Constitucional Español sobre matrimonio entre personas del mismo sexo' (2018) 22 Discusiones 153–88. Precisely for this reason, judges seem to perform a significant role in conceptual engineering: the use of some terms is deliberately specified, and this impacts the way in which we use it.

[27] I do not want to deny that a particular precedent may be a genuine precedent even if it does not add anything to the law, in the sense that its content overlaps with another source. What is necessary is that the precedent involves a creative activity providing an interpretation of statutory law, even if it does overlap with another source (e.g. a custom) that provides that very interpretation. In a similar vein, Hafsteinn Dan Kristjánsson argues that even though a precedent can depend on the underlying source, this does not mean that it does not add to the law: a precedent can concretize, clarify, or settle. See the contribution to this volume by Hafsteinn Dan Kristjánsson (Chapter 6).

[28] The normative force of precedents is normally assumed to be gradual in the sense that it is not a matter of all or nothing, but may be more or less robust depending on several elements I will briefly analyse in the text. I realize that the binding force of precedents in a given legal system may vary depending on the groups or individuals being analysed. In this chapter, I will focus on judges, in particular those belonging to hierarchically inferior

First, a relevant issue is whether precedents must always, or only sometimes, be considered, or if their mention is even forbidden. The more precedents are to be taken into consideration, the more robust their binding character. Beyond that, it is important to specify what it means to take them into account. It might mean merely citing them, just looking at them even though they do not have to feature as explicit premises of the reasoning, incorporating them into the reasoning even if they are not crucial for the decision, or adopting them as a normative premise for subsequent decisions. The latter seems to indicate that precedents are weightier, especially if what must be followed is the same norm, instead of a norm axiologically consistent with the norm adopted by higher courts.

Another relevant element is whether it is necessary to provide other arguments supporting the same interpretation, or whether additional arguments must be provided to justify the adoption of the higher court's interpretation; if precedents can be considered autonomously and additional arguments are not needed for adopting the precedent, their binding force seems more robust. And as far as the interpretation and the application of precedents is concerned, their binding force is more robust when there is less discretion in determining the *ratio decidendi* (and in distinguishing it from *obiter dicta*) and when phenomena such as distinguishing and overruling are not allowed.[29]

All this depends on the way in which the (contingent) rules of adjudication regulate the binding force of precedents, rules that depend on the actual practice and may even contradict explicit rules.[30]

Surprisingly, if we take the afore-mentioned factors into account, we can see that the binding force of precedents is quite robust in civil law systems such as the Spanish system. Decisions of the Spanish Supreme Court that contain a certain interpretation of a legal text are normally taken into account when that legal text is mentioned. In this sense, precedents seem to have the same force as the text they interpret,[31] and are considered whenever that text is relevant. In addition, judges do not provide arguments for adopting the interpretation of the Supreme Court, and no other interpretative arguments are usually provided to justify that interpretation.[32] The interpretation adopted by the Supreme Court is frequently

---

courts. People in general and the higher courts may themselves feel less bound by precedents, which may mean that the higher courts change their decisions quite often and that lawyers challenge the decisions of the lower courts despite the precedent being generally respected. In any event, the fact that the higher courts frequently change their position may make it difficult, and even impossible, for the lower courts to determine and apply *a* precedent.

[29] See Á Núñez Vaquero, MB Arriagada Cáceres, and I Ampuero Hunter (eds), *Teoría y práctica del precedente* (Tirant 2021) 333–418; A Peczenick, 'The Binding Force of Precedent' in DN MacCormick and RS Summers (eds), *Interpreting Precedents* (Ashgate 1997) 461–79.

[30] I do not want to reject the idea that rules of adjudication may be statutory rules themselves, but instead to emphasize that the binding force of precedents depends on how they are practised. I do not want to deny either that precedents may be sources of law and that may be part of the rule of recognition. In any case, the rule of recognition is related to the identification of the law and the rules of adjudication to its application. See JM Vilajosana, 'Social Facts and Law: Why the Rule of Recognition is a Convention' in L Ramírez-Ludeña and JM Vilajosana (eds), *Legal Conventionalism* (Springer 2019) 89–107.

[31] Strictly speaking, we cannot say that they do have the same force if the relevance of those precedents could be eliminated by introducing a new law that prohibits the use of precedents, for example. They can also be considered subordinate because, as we have seen, they have to be an interpretation (not a creation) of the law, and also inasmuch as particular precedents can be invalidated when statutory law changes.

[32] I am focused on vertically binding precedents and not on how the precedents bind the Supreme Court itself. Indeed, in the Spanish legal system, the higher courts can and often do deviate from their previous decisions even without explicitly presenting arguments to justify the change. See M Gascón, *La técnica del precedente y la argumentación racional* (Tecnos 1993). In any case, the existence of several precedents, which may contradict each other, does not prevent precedents from being considered binding in common law systems.

followed by the lower courts without any hesitation or controversy as to its content. Indeed, the Spanish Supreme Court sometimes does not provide a comprehensive justification for its decision, which makes it difficult to question the decision.[33] Moreover, the lower courts do not seem to have large margins of discretion in determining the *ratio*, and in distinguishing it from *obiter dicta*. Therefore, precedents are not only normally cited but also incorporated without question as part of the normative premise when the provision is relevant to resolve a case, especially in certain branches of the law. And precisely because the existence of binding precedents is not explicitly recognized, a culture of their application (with phenomena such as distinguishing or overruling) has not been developed, hence they are rarely altered by the lower courts.[34]

For all these reasons, it can be argued that despite what is frequently said and theorized, the binding nature of vertical precedents can actually be quite strict in countries with a continental tradition such as Spain. This is one of the consequences of the hierarchical structure of the Spanish legal system, which is made evident by elements such as the existence of a judicial career and the system of appeals in Spain.[35] Moreover, the assumption that judges merely apply the law helps to explain why the higher courts do not provide detailed reasoning that is later questioned by other courts lower in the hierarchy. To provide detailed reasoning would be to admit that all judges, and the Supreme Court in particular, play a central role in interpreting and applying the law. And as I mentioned earlier, all this reinforces and is reinforced by the absence of a culture of precedent, which means that phenomena such as distinguishing or overruling do not occur at the level of the lower courts.

Thus, the lower courts in countries with a civil law tradition like Spain do not generally deviate from the decisions of the higher courts. It might be emphasized, however, that this responds only to matters of prudence and convenience, and that precedents are only de facto binding. In other words, in systems like the Spanish system, there are no *legally* binding precedents. However, if being legally binding requires the formal existence of sanctions for deviations from the precedent, then it becomes clear that even in common law systems, where the existence of precedents is uncontroversial, there are no such sanctions.[36] In countries such as Spain, judges regularly invoke Supreme Court precedents, regardless of why they do so (formal justice, decisional economy, etc), and officials understand that judicial decisions are *properly* reasoned when this is done.[37] Moreover, according to some of the rules of the system, departing from precedent can lead to invalidating the decision, therefore judges tend to adopt the decisions (including amendments of previous decisions) of the Supreme Court in an uncritical way, in order to avoid reversal on appeal.[38] Thus, it does not seem justified to claim that precedents are not legally binding on judges.

---

[33] e.g. in the decision STS 421/2020 mentioned earlier (n 24), in which the Supreme Court considered deleting data on the cloud pertaining to an ex-partner as being constitutive of the offence of coercion, the court did not provide any argument to defend that the conduct was violent.

[34] For an explanation of the Spanish legal system, see A Ruiz Miguel and FJ Laporta, 'Precedent in Spain' in MacCormick and Summers (n 29) 259–91. The incidence of precedents in some branches such as criminal law has considerably increased in recent years, which, in my view, depends on what occurs in legal practice and not just on the explicit legal changes in regulation that have taken place.

[35] As Ferreres suggests, these elements may have made unnecessary the formal recognition of binding precedents. See V Ferreres, 'Sobre la possible fuerza vinculante de la jurisprudencia' in V Ferreres and JA Xiol (eds), *El carácter vinculante de la jurisprudencia* (Fundación Coloquio Jurídico Europeo 2010) 51–56.

[36] See, e.g., Z Bankowski, DN MacCormick, and G Marshall, 'Precedent in the United Kingdom' in MacCormick and Summers (n 29); RS Summers, 'Precedent in the United States (New York State)' in ibid.

[37] In this sense, in order to evaluate their legally binding character, it is important to consider not only what happens when precedents are not followed but also what happens when they are followed. See Á Núñez Vaquero, 'Constitutive Rules of Precedent. A Non-Prescriptivist Account of *Stare Decisis*' (2022) 46 Revus (in press).

[38] In any case, what matters is how these rules play out in practice, rather than their mere formal recognition.

We have seen that interpretation does involve some creative activity, but this can be distinguished from a genuine creation of law. But what happens when the higher courts exceed their interpretative limits so that, by hypothesis, they create law instead of interpreting it?

In fact, in systems such as the Spanish system, the lower courts tend to adopt the decisions of their superiors without reflecting deeply on the distinction between interpretation and creation. Far from being merely persuasive, they normally take precedents as authoritative regardless of their content (content-independent), taking them into account without challenging them. In view of legal practice, the binding force of precedents does not seem to depend on whether they offer an adequate characterization from another source, that is, whether they involve an interpretation and not a creation *stricto sensu*. The lower courts quote fragments of Supreme Court decisions verbatim or simply indicate the relevant decisions (date and number) without disputing what is said or expressing doubts as to the determination of the content.

But then, it would seem that precedents in systems such as the Spanish one can be truly creative, going beyond the mere interpretation of statutory law. This, however, is contrary to the common view that it makes sense to distinguish between interpretation and creation, and that hierarchically superior courts, although they make final decisions, can be mistaken. However, this tension is only apparent and is explained by the fact that the question of the binding force of precedents is not distinguished from the question of whether precedents are a source of law, which I will discuss in section 4.

4. But are They a Source of Law?

According to legal practice in systems such as the Spanish one, it is plausible to argue that Supreme Court precedents are sources of law, in the sense that they become the basis for determining what legal norm is expressed by the statute. But we have already seen that it is often denied that they have this character, since it is understood that the source is the statute, the interpretation of which the court merely ascertains or discovers. I have tried to show here that there is some creative activity whenever an interpretation is chosen, and this is so even when that reading of the rule, that semantic usage, may be said to already exist.[39]

In section 3, I argued that the lower courts are bound by precedents even when the court that decided the precedent engaged in genuine creation. This seems to suggest that the Supreme Court's interpretations are not only sources of law but also infallible. However, at the same time I have argued that (at least in certain areas and assuming certain theories of interpretation and of law) the Supreme Court can be wrong. In this respect, in Spain the decisions of the Supreme Court may be invalidated by the Constitutional Court if they have provided an interpretation contrary to the Spanish Constitution.[40] The seemingly paradoxical situation is highlighted when we make certain distinctions.

In line with what I have said about the justification of judicial decisions, judges establish general norms, and in this sense their decisions can be a source of law. And they are so identified, according to legal practice. Moreover, given the rules governing the application of precedents that were mentioned in section 3, according to legal practice, precedents from the Supreme Court are considered binding for the judges in the lower courts. However, this does

---

[39] On the notion of 'source', see J Aguiló, *Teoría general de las fuentes del Derecho (y del orden jurídico)* (Ariel 2000); J Cueto Rúa, *Fuentes del derecho* (Abeledo-Perrot 1961).

[40] Miguel (n 34).

not prevent it later being found (e.g. in Spain, by the Constitutional Court) that one of the interpretations of the Supreme Court is invalid because it violates other rules. The same applies to legislation, which is in general considered a source of law even if a particular statute can later be declared invalid because it contradicts the Constitution—even if it is never declared invalid (despite it being so) and remains applicable for judges.

Precedents are thus identified as a source of law in a way that depends on their treatment of the underlying source. If an interpretation of a legal provision does not accord with the interpretative standards of the system, then it is not identified as a source in systems such as that in Spain.

Nothing precludes, however, the possibility that a *particular* norm, invalid according to the interpretative practices of the legal system, might be applied over a period of time. I think that may involve a change in the law, but not in the general criteria of validity to the extent that, according to the system, the Supreme Court may still, in general, be legally wrong. On the other hand, if the violation were *systematic*, two situations could arise. First, there could be a change in the rule of recognition, understanding that the norms determined by the Supreme Court are law (whether or not the Supreme Court deviates from the interpretative standards of the system). Secondly, it could be assumed that the Supreme Court's interventions no longer involve the application of pre-established general rules. All of this is contingent, of course.[41]

If it is reiterated at this point that precedents are not sources of law because they are merely an interpretation of sources, then there is nothing left but to emphasize again what was said earlier: their important role in identifying the norm expressed by a legal provision when there are alternatives. In the absence of a precedent, we would not be able to say that a particular norm (and not others) belongs to the legal system in question. *Stricto sensu*, precedent is the source whose interpretation allows us to identify the *ratio decidendi*, which is the interpretation of another source, the statute. To claim that precedent is not a source because it is in fact only a logical consequence of pre-existing norms is to ignore the important creative activity that I have described.[42]

Finally, in Spain it is sometimes denied that precedents are a source of law because it is thought that judicial independence would then be compromised, and to protect independence judges are forbidden from giving instructions to subordinates. However, this argument seems to beg the question: if precedents determine the content of the law, this does not seem to affect the independence of judges in the lower courts who, after all, apply the very norms of the system in the light of precedents. And, in any event, the fact that precedents may affect judicial independence cannot undermine their character as a source, but only makes it desirable that they should not be regarded as sources.[43]

---

[41] A different question I will not address here is whether it is explicitly understood that judges (at least some) are competent to create general norms, and to create invalid norms. See J Ferrer, *Las normas de competencia* (Marcial Pons 2000).

[42] Following Guastini's distinctions, precedents in the Spanish system can be considered a source of law, both in the formal sense, which refers to the general norms of legal production of the system, as well as in the material sense, which aims to identify certain acts or facts as a source by their content or normative result, when they produce general and abstract norms. And given the *erga omnes* effects of the *ratio decidendi*, they would be sources of law in a third sense outlined by Guastini. See R Guastini, *Las fuentes del derecho. Fundamentos teóricos* (Raguel Ediciones 2016).

[43] For arguments rejecting the claim that precedents entail giving instructions, Ferreres (n 35) 60.

5. Final Remarks: Predictability and Adaptability

In the civil law tradition, precedents have often been viewed with suspicion. It has been assumed that the creation of law by judges can undermine the predictability of the law, and that predictability is preserved when the legislature determines the law and judges merely apply it. Moreover, the existence of precedents is also viewed with suspicion because it means being bound by past decisions, which precludes the adaptability of the law to new realities. In contrast, those who advocate the consolidation of a system of precedents in the civil law tradition argue that it would contribute to the predictability of the law and its adaptability to a complex and changing reality. If we take into account what has been presented in this chapter, the existence of binding judicial decisions seems, in principle, to increase the predictability of judicial decisions and allow the system to adapt to new situations without the need for difficult change.[44]

The previous statement, however, must be qualified. If we pay attention to what has occurred in relation to terms such as 'violence', we can see that the existence of binding jurisprudence favours predictability and adaptability only in some cases. If the court initially extended the scope of the term to include cases of psychological coercion, this can be seen as a response to society's growing demand for recognition that violence is not necessarily physical. However, whether a judicial change in the law successfully responds to a social demand is entirely contingent, and jurisprudence can move away from the current view. The relation between binding jurisprudence and predictability, too, is contingent: whether the law becomes more predictable depends on the decision of the court, which may in fact opt for a broad understanding that only increases uncertainty. I think this has happened in the case of coercion in Spain, for example when the Supreme Court considered cutting the water supply to people who had not paid a specific tax as an instance of violence without providing a detailed justification.[45]

In addition, the predictability and adaptability of precedents largely depends on other contingencies of the legal system. Thus, we have already seen that in systems such as the Spanish one, there is a rather robust system of precedents, which is related to the role attributed to judges, limited to the application of the law. Often judges only explain their decisions by citing the text of a rule, giving the impression that there is a single solution that follows from the normative text without any creative activity on their part. And practices such as distinguishing are absent. If the interpretation that is implicit in such a decision is then uncritically adopted, predictability seems to be enhanced. Moreover, the determination of the *ratio decidendi* is usually not that complex, in an area where legal doctrine also helps to clarify the interpretations established by the courts.[46]

However, the Spanish Supreme Court is still widely seen as a court of appeal rather than an instrument for providing a unified interpretation of the law; therefore the court resolves

---

[44] See MI Garrido Gómez, 'La predecibilidad de las decisions judiciales' (2009) 15 Ius et Praxis 55–72; G Rosado Iglesias, 'Seguridad jurídica y valor vinculante de la jurisprudencia' (2006) 28 Cuadernos de Derecho Público 83–123, defending the view that the existence of precedents promotes values such as predictability.

[45] See n 11.

[46] Although I will not deal with this issue here, it is usually emphasized that this also responds to the lesser importance of the facts in civil law: the *ratio decidendi* is related to the interpretation of the law and neither the doctrine nor the jurisprudence mention the facts when they extract and refer to the *ratio decidendi*. Other aspects, such as the fact that the judges agree on a single decision (unique collective decision, even if there are *votos particulares*) and individual judges do not make independent decisions, also facilitate the identification of the interpretative decision. On the other hand, the fact that two or more concurring decisions are required may make it more difficult to identify the *ratio*.

a very large number of disputes.[47] This does not favour predictability, because it makes it harder to identify the higher courts' interpretative choices, and it is easier for their position to change. And, as far as adaptability is concerned, explicit and detailed reasoning and phenomena such as distinguishing (elements that do not seem to be very prominent nowadays in the Spanish system) can favour the emergence of dialogue between the judges, which may favour decisions that are consistent with new circumstances.[48]

In short, it cannot be argued that the existence of precedents hinders predictability and adaptability. Nor can it be conclusively argued that precedents promote predictability and adaptability. It all depends on complex and contingent circumstances.

---

[47] The Spanish Supreme Court, composed of almost of a hundred judges divided into five chambers that are divided into sections of five judges, issues more than 25,000 decisions per year. See Miguel (n 34) 262.

[48] As Duxbury points out, the fact that they are aware of their relevance improves the decision and its justification and makes them more accountable. See N Duxbury, *The Nature and Authority of Precedent* (CUP 2008) 96. In fact, the explicit use of good arguments by judges creates a tendency towards unification when the lower judge and the Supreme Court itself cannot find better arguments, and that can also lead to decisions becoming more predictable.

32

The Oracles of Codification

Informal Authority in Statutory Interpretation

Nils Jansen

1. Introduction

Since 1945, the existence of case law and the authority of precedents have been among the most contested, and indeed difficult, theoretical topics discussed among civilian legal scholars in general,[1] and in Germany in particular.[2] The reason for those difficulties has been that, according to orthodox doctrine, there simply is not, and cannot be, a genuine doctrine of (binding) precedents in a codified legal system. Only legislation and (though of little relevance) customary law are recognized as legitimate sources of the law.[3] Judges are not empowered to make the law, but rather have to apply it.[4]

At the same time, however, it has been increasingly difficult to deny that the codifications have been complemented with thick layers of case law.[5] Jurists therefore began to analyse judge-made law as a social fact; they have been reluctant, however, to acknowledge it as a source of law in any sense, or as some sort of binding legal authority. Until the end of the twentieth century, many German jurists would even avoid the use of the concept of *Richterrecht* (judge-made law) altogether, or use the word only in quotes.[6] Indeed, the authors of leading textbooks on the methods of legal interpretation (*Juristische Methodenlehre*) assumed that the purpose of those methods was to bind judges to legislation and to limit

---

[1] In what follows, the term 'civil law' refers to continental codified legal systems, such as Germany, France, or Austria. Yet, it is not based on a full comparative survey and does not include, in particular, the Nordic legal systems.

[2] For a historical introduction, see J Schröder, *Recht als Wissenschaft. Geschichte der juristischen Methodenlehre in der Neuzeit (1500–1990)*, vol 2 (3rd edn, CH Beck 2020) 149–60.

[3] K Larenz, *Methodenlehre der Rechtswissenschaft* (6th edn, Springer 1991) 431f; K Larenz and C-W Canaris, *Methodenlehre der Rechtswissenschaft* (students' edition) (3rd edn, Springer 1995) 255f. Apparently, many authors even today stick to this, see B Rüthers, 'Fortgesetzter Blindflug oder Methodendämmerung der Justiz? Zur Auslegungspraxis der obersten Bundesgerichte' (2008) *Juristenzeitung* 446–51; C Hillgruber, "Neue Methodik'— Ein Beitrag zur Geschichte der Rechtsfortbildung in Deutschland' (2008) *Juristenzeitung* 745–55. For similar discussions by the French exegetical school, see JP Dawson, *The Oracles of the Law* (University of Michigan Law School 1968) 392ff; for discussions during the twentieth century, see 'The Enigma of Judge-Made Law' in ibid 416ff.

[4] See, generally, M Payandeh, *Judikative Rechtserzeugung. Theorie, Dogmatik und Methodik der Wirkungen von Präjudizien* (Mohr Siebeck 2017) 112ff.

[5] Dawson (n 3) 432, 461ff: 'Germany's case-law revolution'; for France, see ibid 375, 386f, 397ff. See also R Zimmermann and N Jansen, 'Quieta Movere. Interpretative Change in a Codified System' in P Cane and J Stapleton (eds), *The Law of Obligations: Essays in Celebration of John Fleming* (OUP 1998) 285–315, 287ff, 296ff; N Jansen, 'Codifications, Commentators, and Courts in Tort Law: The Perception and Application of the Civil Code and the Constitution by the German Legal Profession' in M Lobban and J Moses (eds), *The Impact of Ideas on Legal Development* (CUP 2012) 186–203.

[6] Schröder (n 2) 151; see, as examples, P Badura, 'Grenzen und Möglichkeiten des Richterrechts— Verfassungsrechtliche Überlegungen' in *Rechtsfortbildung durch die sozialgerichtliche Rechtsprechung. Verhandlungen des Deutschen Sozialgerichtsverbades; 1. Deutscher Sozialgerichtstag 1972* (1973) 40–57, 40; Larenz (n 3) 429; F Bydlinski, *Juristische Methodenlehre und Rechtsbegriff* (Verlag Österreich 1982) 501; *Entscheidungen des Bundesgerichtshofs in Strafsachen* (BGHSt) 40, 138, 167 (1994).

Nils Jansen, *The Oracles of Codification* In: *Philosophical Foundations of Precedent*. Edited by: Timothy Endicott, Hafsteinn Dan Kristjánsson, and Sebastian Lewis, Oxford University Press. © Nils Jansen 2023. DOI: 10.1093/oso/9780192857248.003.0033

judicial power.[7] At best, precedents have been treated as 'epistemic' sources (*Rechtserkenntnisquelle*).[8] But that meant reading decisions of a highest court like decisions of any other court or as academic articles and thus could not account for the prominent role of decisions of the highest courts in legal practice.[9] It is only a fairly recent development that judge-made law has been discussed in a more open way and that jurists have begun to analyse and understand the specific features of precedents in a civilian legal system. Although the 'nature' of precedent necessarily depends on the positive law of a specific legal system,[10] some aspects of those discussions may be interesting beyond the narrow civilian context. In what follows, I will therefore first give a brief overview of the history of judge-made law in the codified legal systems and then analyse the specific authority of precedents today.

2. The Rise of the Courts

Wherever legislation does not provide an absolutely clear, unambiguous answer to a legal issue, jurists will assume that courts follow prior decisions; hence, wherever courts have their decisions published, they become unofficial law-makers.[11] Yet, while English judges from early on had reported cases and treated them as sources of the law,[12] such reporting was not practised on the continent before the seventeenth century.[13] Indeed, German courts did not begin to formalize and control the publication of their own decisions before 1800.[14] Similarly, after 1830, learned practitioners in France began to develop new forms of publication such as the encyclopaedia or *répertoire* and techniques such as analytical notes to make accessible to practical lawyers the Cour de cassation's jurisprudence (namely, case law).[15] It is, hence, a fairly recent development that the judiciary has assumed an active role in the development of the law.[16] With the increasing complexity of society and of the law, it was generally felt that such a more active role was necessary;[17] accordingly, Bernhard Windscheid began to analyse

---

[7] H-P Haferkamp, 'Zur Methodengeschichte unter dem BGB in fünf Systemen' (2014) 214 *Archiv für die civilistische Praxis* 60–92; cf also R Alexy and R Dreier, 'Precedent in the Federal Republic of Germany' in DN MacCormick and RS Summers (eds), *Interpreting Precedents* (Routledge 1997) 17–64, 42f.

[8] Larenz (n 3) 432 with references to many other authors.

[9] Of course, every academic writing or judicial decision on any legal issue is an 'epistemic source' in that it may be particularly convincing and therefore may be used when making a legal argument or justifying a legal decision. It will be seen, however, that not every such decision and writing is authoritative. Texts become authorities if the legal profession accepts a citation of such text as a valid legal argument, independently of its content, and if such texts therefore can *replace substantive legal argument*.

[10] See the contribution to this volume by Hafsteinn Dan Kristjánsson (Chapter 6).

[11] N Jansen, *Recht und gesellschaftliche Differenzierung* (Mohr Siebeck 2019) 280; N Jansen, 'Methoden, Institutionen, Texte. Zur diskursiven Funktion und medialen Präsenz dogmatisierender Ordnungsvorstellungen und Deutungsmuster in Recht und Religion' (2011) 128 *Zeitschrift der Savigny-Stiftung für Rechtsgeschichte (Germanistische Abteilung)* 1–71, 35ff.

[12] On the bureaucratization of the king's court, see J Hudson, *The Oxford History of the Laws of England*, vol 2, 871–1216 (OUP 2012) 523, 851; for the early reporting of cases, see J Baker, *An Introduction to English Legal History* (5th edn, OUP 2019) 188ff.

[13] For details, see H Coing, *Europäisches Privatrecht, vol 1: Älteres Gemeines Recht (1500–1800)* (CH Beck 1985) 125f; F Ranieri, 'Kasuistik und Regelbildung bei der Rechtsfindung im europäischen Ius Commune des 16.–17. Jahrhunderts' in G Essen and N Jansen (eds), *Dogmatisierungsprozesse in Recht und Religion* (Mohr Siebeck 2011) 153–87, 174ff.

[14] Dawson (n 3) 432ff; Ranieri (n 13) 174ff.

[15] Dawson (n 3) 389, 397ff, 400ff.

[16] H-P Haferkamp, 'The Science of Private Law and the State in Nineteenth Century Germany' in N Jansen and R Michaels (eds), *Beyond the State? Rethinking Private Law* (Mohr Siebeck 2008) 245–67, 257f; cf K Kroeschell, *Deutsche Rechtsgeschichte, vol 3. Seit 1650* (5th edn, Böhlau 2008) 171f.

[17] Jansen, *Differenzierung* (n 11) 281f.

the relevant case law in his leading textbook on national (Roman) German law.[18] With the creation of a German Supreme Court (Reichsgericht; since 1950 Bundesgerichtshof),[19] the ground was laid for the uniform judicial development of German law.[20]

The creation of the Reichsgericht was part of the unification of German law in the early days of the German Reich. That was the heyday of the codification movement, however, when jurists generally believed that all law derived from the state's legislation,[21] and that the state's power was vested in the parliaments, on the one hand, and in the kings' governments, on the other. Indeed, nineteenth-century constitutions had little to say on the judiciary; accordingly, constitutional theory did not usually analyse the judiciary as an independent power in the state.[22] Rather, the declaratory theory of legal judgments prevailed according to which judges would find and apply, rather than make, the law as laid down in legislation.[23] As a matter of principle, any judicial law-making was illegitimate.[24] All of these assumptions have long prevented legal scholars from taking an unbiased look at judge-made law.[25]

Legal practitioners, however, knew better. When at the turn of the nineteenth to the twentieth century they began to write commentaries on the new national codifications, they used this new form of literature specifically to inform practising lawyers about the courts' interpretations of the codifications.[26] Rather than asking for the best interpretation of the code's provisions, they therefore primarily restated the courts' readings of the law wherever that was relevant.[27] Thus, Adolf Baumbach, a presiding judge in the Court of Appeal in Berlin, who is commonly regarded as an intellectual 'father' of the modern German commentary,[28] programmatically wrote in 1924: 'I had to restrict myself to giving the answer that the courts over the years have found and established as correct.'[29] With the increasingly thick glosses of case law complementing the codifications, this understanding has gained ground

---

[18] B Windscheid, *Lehrbuch des Pandektenrechts* (7th edn, Rütten & Loening 1891).

[19] In 1869, the Reichsoberhandelsgericht, a supreme court for commercial cases, was established (originally as the Bundesoberhandelsgericht) in Leipzig; in 1878, when it was decided to unify all private and criminal law, it was replaced with, or rather transformed into, the Reichsgericht (which later became the Bundesgerichtshof).

[20] Payandeh (n 4) 86f.

[21] R Zimmermann, 'Codification: History and Present Significance of an Idea' (1995) 3 *Eur Rev Private L* 95–120, 96–103; R Zimmermann, 'Codification. The Civilian Experience Reconsidered at the Eve of a Common European Sales Law' (2012) 8 *Eur Rev Contract L* 367–99, 374ff; N Jansen and R Michaels, 'Private Law and the State Comparative Perceptions and Historical Observations' (2007) 71 *Rabels Zeitschrift für ausländisches und internationales Privatrecht* 345–97.

[22] For a detailed analysis, see Payandeh (n 4) 92ff, 102ff. The best-known exception was O von Bülow, *Gesetz und Richteramt* (Duncker & Humblot 1885) 41ff and passim.

[23] The leading authority was O Mayer, *Deutsches Verwaltungsrecht*, vol 1 (Leipzig 1895) 84 (courts did nothing but declare the law's will). For the declaratory theory in general, see FC von Savigny, *System des heutigen Römischen Rechts*, vol I (Veit 1840) 13ff, 45ff, 83ff; Windscheid (n 18) 36ff, 50ff (§§ 14ff, 20ff); on those latter two authors, see A Brockmöller, *Die Entstehung der Rechtstheorie im 19. Jahrhundert in Deutschland* (Nomos 1997) 89ff, 93, 108ff. In more recent times, declaratory theories of the law have been held by leading scholars such as E Picker, 'Richterrecht oder Rechtsdogmatik—Alternativen der Rechtsgewinnung' (1988) *Juristenzeitung* 1–12, 62–75, 62f; C-W Canaris, *Systemdenken und Systembegriff in der Jurisprudenz* (2nd edn, Duncker & Humblot 1983) 67ff.

[24] Alexy and Dreier (n 7) 47.

[25] ibid 42f.

[26] See E Rabel, 'Review: J v Staudingers Kommentar zum BGB' (1915) 7 *Rheinische Zeitschrift für Zivil- und Prozeßrecht* 508–15, 512; for a historical analysis, see D Kästle-Lamparter, *Welt der Kommentare. Struktur, Funktion und Stellenwert juristischer Kommentare in Geschichte und Gegenwart* (Mohr Siebeck 2016) 215ff; N Jansen, 'Vom Aufstieg des Kommentars und Niedergang des Lehrbuchs' in D Kästle-Lamparter, N Jansen, and R Zimmermann (eds), *Juristische Kommentare. Ein internationaler Vergleich* (Mohr Siebeck 2020) 25–44, 30ff.

[27] For a more detailed analysis of the leading early commentaries (such as *Planck*; *Staudinger*; *Oertmann*; *Warneyer*; *Baumbach*), see Jansen, 'Aufstieg des Kommentars' (n 26) 36ff.

[28] Kästle-Lamparter (n 26) 71f, 224ff, 256f; Jansen, 'Aufstieg des Kommentars' (n 26) 33.

[29] A Baumbach, *Taschenausgabe der neuen Zivilprozeßordnung* (CH Beck 1924) III (Preface): 'Ich musste mich damit begnügen, … die Antwort zu geben, die Rechtsprechung im Laufe der Jahre als richtig erkannt und festgestellt hat.'

also in academia. Meanwhile, the conviction that it is for the courts to finally determine the meaning of legislation is shared by jurists working in all different parts of the legal system. Indeed, there can no longer be any doubt that a comprehensive picture of the law can only emerge by 'reading together' legislation and relevant case law; and that the significance of case law has increased with the growing number of precedents.[30]

Today, such a view of the law also determines the self-understanding of Supreme Courts. Federal judges quite confidently claim to shape the law's development; they assume that their decisions have a significance beyond their decision of an actual case. Indeed, the Bundesgerichtshof describes its judgments regularly as *Richterrecht* (judge-made law);[31] and as far as the judicial control of unfair contract terms is concerned, the court even explicitly equates its case law with legislative prohibitions on specific terms.[32] Accordingly, the court protects the reliance of citizens on its case law by means of quite different doctrinal techniques and instruments,[33] including prospective overruling[34] and *obiter dicta*. Thus, where a defendant causes damage despite acting in accordance with established standards of care and where the Federal Supreme Court then introduces stricter duties regarding such a danger, the defendant may be excused by reason of an unavoidable *error iuris*.[35] Similarly, the court may interpret a contract term in the light of precedent even if, in the case at hand, the court establishes a new, different interpretation of that term for the future.[36] Or the court may protect a party's reliance on previous case law on the basis of the principle of good faith in § 242 BGB (Civil Code).[37] Similar observations hold true in administrative and in criminal law, where courts usually require governmental bodies, including public prosecutors, to follow and apply relevant precedents.[38] And, of course, solicitors and other lawyers are bound to the relevant judge-made law; they may be liable if they do not treat relevant precedents as if they were binding law.[39] All in all, the legal practical *effect* of precedents in the codified legal systems of Europe is today quite similar to the effect of precedents in the common law world, where precedents are regarded as binding law.[40] This does not mean, however, that

---

[30] A Heldrich, '50 Jahre Rechtsprechung des BGH—auf dem Weg zu einem Präjudizienrecht?' (2000) *Neue Juristische Wochenschrift* 497–500.

[31] *Entscheidungen des Bundesgerichtshofs in Zivilsachen* (BGHZ) 121, 13, 18 (1992); Bundesgerichtshof (2014) *Neue Juristische Wochenschrift* 1168 (2013); Bundesgerichtshof (2006) *Neue Juristische Wochenschrift, Rechtsprechungs-Report* 107, 108 (2005).

[32] BGHZ (n 31) 121, 13, 18 (1992); Bundesgerichtshof (n 31) (2014) *Neue Juristische Wochenschrift* 1168 (2013).

[33] For a comprehensive picture, see Payandeh (n 4) 330ff.

[34] BGHZ (n 31) 150, 1, 5 (2003); BGHZ 154, 370, 377f (2003); see K Langenbucher, 'Rechtsprechung mit Wirkung für die Zukunft' (2003) *Juristenzeitung* 1132–40.

[35] N Jansen, *The Structure of Tort Law* (OUP 2022) 333f; see, e.g., Bundesgerichtshof (1985) *Neue Juristische Wochenschrift* 620, 621 (1984); Bundesgerichtshof (1995) *Neue Juristische Wochenschrift* 2631, 2632 (1995).

[36] Zimmermann and Jansen (n 5) 308f.

[37] Bundesarbeitsgericht (Federal Court of Labour Law) (1991) *Der Betrieb* 915ff (1990); BGHZ (n 30) 114, 127, 136f (1991); BGHZ 150 1ff (2002); BGHZ 154, 370, 377f (2003). In those cases, the court specifically asks whether one party in fact relied on its previous case law, and whether such reliance was justified. Where this is not the case, or where the relying party's interests do not outweigh the other party's interests, the court departs from precedent without further ado.

[38] BGHSt (n 6) 15, 155, 158ff (1960); Oberlandesgericht (Court of Appeal) Zweibrücken (2007) *Neue Zeitschrift für Strafrecht* 420. Details are disputed: prosecutors have to press charges if, according to precedent, the accused is likely to be convicted; they may, however, express their views of the law in their pleadings and thus, indeed, plead acquittal.

[39] Bundesgerichtshof (1993) *Neue Juristische Wochenschrift* 3324: 'In view of the significance of supreme-court decisions in legal practice, a lawyer is always required to follow this case law when acting on behalf of a client.' See also C Grüneberg in *Grüneberg* (formerly *Palandt*). *Bürgerliches Gesetzbuch: BGB* (81st edn, CH Beck 2022) § 280, para 68.

[40] R Cross and JW Harris, *Precedent in English Law* (4th edn, OUP 1991) 39ff.

their legal *nature*, namely, the legal rules applying to precedents, may be equated with those in the common law.

3. The Authority of Precedent

This short historical survey suffices to point out the difficulties for jurists in a codified legal system in formulating a consistent and appropriate doctrine of precedent. The basic reason was clearly the set of jurisprudential assumptions connected with the declaratory theory of judicial decisions and the narrow doctrine of sources of the law.[41] Those assumptions have never allowed civilian jurists to develop anything similar to a rule of *stare decisis*. In fact, apart from a very limited set of exceptions (such as decisions of the Federal Constitutional Courts nullifying statutory legislation), courts are not formally bound by precedent:[42] neither by a prior decision of the same court nor by decisions of superior courts.

Although courts are thus free, as a matter of principle, to ignore precedents, there are procedural provisions aiming to ensure coherence and unity among those courts that have to make final decisions.[43] What is more, in actual legal practice, courts usually do follow precedents. Following precedents makes their legal reasoning much easier, decisions are likely to be reversed on appeal if a court does not follow precedents, and it would be regarded as (morally) inappropriate if a court simply ignored a reference by a party to a precedent.[44] Yet, as a matter of abstract legal principle, every judge is free to ignore judicial authorities or even to deviate from a firmly established line of precedent and follow his or her better interpretation of the law. In Austria, this is even laid down in Article 12 of the Allgemeines Bürgerliches Gesetzbuch (ABGB; Civil Code).[45] Thus, absent a legal obligation of courts to follow precedents, most German writers have concluded that the binding effects of precedents were merely a matter of fact without any normative, legal meaning.[46] They therefore described the bindingness of precedents, somewhat misleadingly,[47] as 'de facto validity (*faktische Geltung*)'.[48] The problem with such views is that they cannot account for the fact that following precedents is today generally regarded as legitimate, that there is a normative expectation that officials will follow precedents, and that citizens may assume that precedents give expression to the law. Precedents do have a normative meaning.

A. Rules of Argumentation, or Burdens of Argument?

Since the 1970s, a group of modern authors have tried to give expression to the increasing normative significance of precedents by means of prescriptive rules of argumentation. Those theories argued that there should be a presumption of reasonableness in favour of

---

[41] At nn 20–25.

[42] Alexy and Dreier (n 7) 26f.

[43] ibid 31ff.

[44] One factor relevant in this context is probably the fact that judges in civilian legal systems are expected to know and apply the law (*iura novit curia*) to the facts presented to them, while judges in the common law will usually be confronted with relevant precedents through the argument of counsel for the parties.

[45] Art 12 ABGB: 'Judicial decisions never have the force of law and must not be extended to other cases or other parties.'

[46] Larenz and Canaris (n 3) 255.

[47] Alexy and Dreier (n 7) 28.

[48] Larenz and Canaris (n 3) 255.

436 NILS JANSEN

precedents,[49] or that precedents should be followed where the law is unclear,[50] or that precedents set burdens of argument for those intending to deviate from them.[51] All those theories seemed to accord with arguments made by courts according to which the weight of precedents depended on the force of their arguments and their competence,[52] or that precedents should be followed unless 'clearly outweighing reasons' were offered.[53] The problem with such approaches, however, was that they did not address the basic weakness of the German doctrine of legal sources, which does not contain a middle category between strictly binding legislation ('formal sources') and non-binding arguments ('material sources').[54] Moreover, those authors did not appropriately distinguish the differences of legal bindingness vis-à-vis different groups (such as courts, advocates and other lawyers, public prosecutors, or civil servants in the public administration).[55]

On the one hand, the legal nature of precedents in Germany cannot appropriately be described in terms of a rule of argumentation, as far as courts are concerned, because there simply is no such rule. Strictly speaking, the law does not oblige judges to follow, or even to consider, relevant precedents; hence, *courts are simply not bound* by case law—not even in a weak sense. An appeal cannot be based on the allegation that a court ignored relevant precedents;[56] and judges, unlike lawyers, will not have to pay damages if they do so. Citizens thus do not have a 'right' vis-à-vis a court that the judges in fact consider relevant case law. Only in exceptional cases can an appeal be brought on the basis that different courts held diverging views about a relevant issue,[57] and even in those cases courts are not legally required to actually discuss the divergent rulings of other courts.

On the other hand, however, as has already been shown, citizens may nevertheless rely on case law. Indeed, precedents *are binding on all other actors* in the legal system, such as public officials, public prosecutors, as well as solicitors and lawyers in general.[58] All those lawyers are bound in their professional practice to consider—and in fact usually to follow— precedents. At the same time, the German Supreme Courts consider themselves bound to earlier judgments and will depart from precedent only on the basis of very strong, usually new, arguments.[59] In addition, where a departure from precedent has retroactive effect, judges are usually prepared to protect a party's reliance on previous case law by means such as *error iuris* or good faith.[60] From the citizens' perspective, there is hence no significant difference between case law and legislation; from their point of view, precedents have a normative significance and justify the assumption that precedent gives expression to the actual law.[61] Precedents in a codified legal system may thus be analysed as permissive sources of the law, in a rather strong sense.[62] The unifying perspective of citizens makes it possible to

---

[49] M Kriele, *Theorie der Rechtsgewinnung* (Dunker & Humblot 1976) 243ff.

[50] Bydlinski (n 6) 506ff; F Bydlinski, 'Hauptpositionen zum Richterrecht' (1985) *Juristenzeitung* 149–55, 152f; H-M Pawlowski, *Methodenlehre für Juristen* (2nd edn, Müller 1991) paras 519ff.

[51] R Alexy, *A Theory of Legal Argumentation* (OUP 1989) 274ff; Alexy and Dreier (n 7) 30: 'between binding force and mere illustrativeness'; H Koch and H Rüßmann, *Juristische Begründungslehre* (Beck 1982) 186ff.

[52] *Entscheidungen des Bundesverfassungsgerichts* (BVerfGE) 126, 369, 395 (2010).

[53] See BGHZ (n 30) 85, 64, 66 (1982).

[54] Alexy and Dreier (n 7) 46.

[55] At nn 31–39.

[56] See, with more detail and many references, Payandeh (n 4) 297ff.

[57] On the relevant provisions, see Alexy and Dreier (n 7) 31f.

[58] At nn 31–39.

[59] Payandeh (n 4) 309ff.

[60] See nn 34–37.

[61] cf Payandeh (n 4) 125ff.

[62] On the concept of permissive authorities, see HLA Hart, *The Concept of Law* (2nd edn, OUP 1994) 294 (note to p 101); L Green, 'Positivism, Realism, and Sources of Law' in T Spaak and P Mindus (eds), *The Cambridge Companion to Legal Positivism* (CUP 2021) 39–59, 51–54 (I am grateful here to Hafsteinn Dan Kristjánsson for

analyse the civilian law of precedent in terms of a single coherent model, even if different rules apply for different groups of legal actors, such as lawyers, attorneys, or judges.

Nevertheless, the concept of a burden of argument seems to be too strong as far as the effect of precedents on courts is concerned, and too weak to describe their effect on non-judicial actors in the legal system. In what follows, I will therefore switch from the prescriptive perspective of the *Juristische Methodenlehre*[63] to a more descriptive, Weberian point of view and focus on how precedents are actually used and understood by jurists working in a codified legal system. In essence, it will be seen first that precedents are interpretative authorities and, secondly, that their nature is rather informal[64] (as opposed to strictly binding, formal authorities,[65] namely, exclusionary, or pre-emptive reasons[66]). Texts such as judicial decisions, commentaries, or textbooks are authoritative in this sense, if jurists accept them as content-independent, ultimate arguments, namely, as sources of the law, without requiring further legal reasons to do so.[67] Whereas legislation is formally binding in that jurists and citizens do not have discretion whether to apply a provision (as long as it is valid), judicial authorities are permissive sources of the law (as explained earlier)[68] of a more informal nature. In particular, neither their coming into existence nor their authoritative substance are determined by any formal element, as their authority emerges in subsequent processes of reception, interpretation, and recognition.[69] Both from the judges' and the citizens' perspective, they *may be relied* on in legal discourse, but there is *no obligation* to rely on them. Where conflicting authorities are present, such as divergent decisions by different courts of appeal, their use in legal discourse depends on, and at the same time determines, their relative weights.

---

very helpful advice). While Hart describes such permissive authorities as 'good reasons' and distinguishes them from merely historical sources of the law, the point here is that although courts are not obliged to follow precedents, citizens may nevertheless rely on such precedents and will be legally protected in that reliance. This would not be the case with what Hart and Green address as permissive sources, such as foreign judgments, or institutional or Roman writers. Thus, precedents in civil law are particularly weighty reasons, or, as I will explain, authorities.

[63] At n 7.

[64] See the more detailed account in Payandeh (n 4) 142ff, 145ff, 277ff.

[65] For such a concept of authority, see N Roughan, *Authorities: Conflicts, Cooperation, and Transnational Legal Theory* (OUP 2013) 19ff. Like many English-writing authors since Hobbes, Roughan describes authorities as powers; which accords well with Hobbes' theory, where *authoritas* describes the legitimate political power of the 'authorized' representative of a *civitas*: T Hobbes, *Leviathan* (N Malcolm ed) in N Malcolm and others (eds), *Clarendon Edition of the Works of Thomas Hobbes*, vol 2 (OUP 2012) 244 (cap 16): 'Repraesentans Actor, Repraesentatus Author dicitur, ut cujus authoritate Actor agit. ... Et ut Ius habendi, Dominium, ita Ius agendi, Authoritas dicitur'; see generally Q Skinner, 'Hobbes on Representation' (2005) 13 *Eur J Philosophy* 155–84, 156ff, 166 ff. In classical Latin, such authority would not have been *auctoritas* but rather *potestas*: R Geuss, 'Zwischen Athen und Rom' (2010) 4 *Zeitschrift für Ideengeschichte* 23–40, 26ff. My concept of authority accords with the original Latin concept, as it was understood by continental jurists and is today used to describe the nature of precedents by German authors; Jansen, *Differenzierung* (n 11) 214f, 222ff, 227ff; Payandeh (n 4) 142ff, 147ff, 277ff.

[66] J Raz, 'On the Nature of Law' in J Raz, *Between Authority and Interpretation* (OUP 2009) 91–125, 109f; Raz, 'The Problem of Authority: Revisiting the Service Conception' (2006) 90 *Minn L Rev* 1003–44, 1018ff.

[67] See n 72; N Jansen, *The Making of Legal Authority. Non-legislative Codifications in Historical and Comparative Perspective* (OUP 2010) 42ff. Of course, there may be political, prudential, moral, or other reasons for recognizing such a text as legal authority. But such reasons are not part of the legal system. Their place is rather 'before', or 'outside', the law; cf Hart (n 62) 107f.

[68] At n 62.

[69] cf generally P Atiyah and RS Summers, *Form and Substance in Anglo-American Law. A Comparative Study of Legal Reasoning, Legal Theory, and Legal Institutions* (OUP 1987). While the formal validity of statutes depends on formal factors such as procedure, promulgation, and countersigning, and while the binding nature of common law precedents derives from the rules of *stare decisis* and from the *ratio decidendi* of the relevant decision, the authority of civil law precedents is independent of any such element of legal formality. Absent such formality, it is not possible to identify a 'valid', strictly binding rule or principle in a civil law precedent; hence, civil law precedents are described in this chapter as informal authorities.

B. Interpretative Authority

The starting point for such an analysis of precedents is that all legal decisions and arguments need to be based on the law, and that means, in a codified legal system, on the applicable legislative sources. The task of jurists is to apply those sources in a methodologically correct way. Thus, jurists have to interpret relevant norms by means of semantic, genetic, historical, systematic, and teleological arguments;[70] and they have to take into account general doctrinal knowledge.[71] All those arguments offer *substantive*, that is, content-dependent, reasons supporting a specific interpretation I_a of a legal provision's requirement R.

Obviously, methodologically correct substantive interpretations of legal provisions are frequently burdensome, as jurists have to consider a wide range of different arguments, often pointing in different directions. The jurist's task is much easier if he or she can rely on some interpretative authority. Interpretative authorities support, or even replace, substantive legal arguments concerning the interpretation of a legal provision with a content-independent justification. Thus, a text T (a textbook, a commentary, or a judicial judgment) stating that

T: *The requirement* R_p *of provision* P *is to be interpreted in accordance with interpretation* I_a.

is authoritative in this sense if (and only if) the legal profession accepts that statement as a good argument justifying the interpretation I_a of R_p in P without requiring further reason to do so,[72] and without requiring further substantive reason for I_a. The point of precedents in a codified legal system is thus that they replace substantive arguments with content-independent, authoritative interpretative statements. Jurists relying on precedent do not explain *why* some proposition correctly interprets a specific legal provision, but rather state *that* this is the case. An example is the following proposition, taken from the *Grüneberg* (formerly *Palandt*), the most important (and in itself highly authoritative) standard commentary on the German Civil Code.[73]

> The right to one's own body is a legally specified part of the general right of personality. The protected interest is the physical existence and self-determination of the person, which is embodied in a man's physical condition(BGH **124**, 52).[74]

Here, while '(BGH **124**, 52)' refers to a decision of the Federal Supreme Court published in the 124th volume of the court's official collection of cases, this citation is exemplary for the use of precedents in Germany. Of course, the first important aspect to note is the precedent's *interpretative* nature. The violation of a 'right to one's own body'—which in itself is used to concretize the requirement of 'injury to life, limb, or health'[75]—is a requirement of a delictual claim under § 823 (1) BGB (Civil Code); and the precedent thus relates to the interpretation of a legal provision of the formally binding codification. The precedent is thus

---

[70] For a formal analysis of those arguments, see Alexy (n 51) 234ff.

[71] ibid 250ff.

[72] See n 67.

[73] See Jansen, *Making Legal Authority* (n 67) 121–26.

[74] 'Das Recht am eigenen Körper ist ein gesetzlich ausgeformter Teil des Allgemeinen Persönlichkeitsrechts. Schutzgut ist das Seins- und Bestimmungsfeld der Persönlichkeit, das sich in der körperlichen Befindlichkeit verwirklicht (BGH **124**, 52)': *Grüneberg*/Sprau (n 38) § 823, para 4.

[75] § 823 (1) BGB: 'Wer … das Leben, den Körper, die Gesundheit … verletzt.'

not authoritative as a decision on a specific set of facts, as a statement of the law *tout court*, or of a legal rule. Rather, it is authoritative as far as it is used to interpret (an element of) a legislative provision ('injury to life, limb, or health') or otherwise restates the law (e.g. an underlying doctrinal assumption). Therefore, its use in legal discourse is highly abstract. As the example shows, jurists in civilian legal systems usually cite precedents without giving any information about the facts of the case and without discussion of detail.[76] Indeed, civilian legal systems usually neither have a specific doctrine of *ratio decidendi*[77] nor any technique of distinguishing.[78] From a German jurist's perspective, a judicial decision is a precedent not because the facts of the case are similar to a new case, but rather because the judges' views on the interpretation of an act of legislation or on a related issue of legal doctrine expressed in that case are relevant for the case at hand. Thus, the relevant feature of a precedent is not the court's decision on the facts but rather its interpretation of legislation or its views on underlying doctrine. Precedents are usually not independent (permissive) sources[79] of the law, beside legislation, but rather authoritative interpretations of such legislation. Hence, they are not applied by analogy but rather as an element of statutory interpretation.[80]

The second aspect to note is that the citation of precedent usually replaces substantive interpretative arguments. In our example, the author of the commentary obviously does not feel obliged to explain why their specific interpretation of 'injury to life, limb, or health', namely, 'right to one's body' is correct or preferable to other possible views. Indeed, they do not add any further argument to support their statement. Rather, the reference to the decision by the Federal Supreme Court is meant to replace all further arguments. This is an expression of the precedent's content-independent, authoritative nature in general and of its specific weight in particular. The author of the commentary expects that readers (i.e. mainly legal practitioners) will accept the reference to such a precedent as a sufficient argument justifying the author's interpretation of the provision in question. Of course, authors may alternatively rely on precedents to support their content-related arguments on some issues of legal interpretation; they may thus complement substantive with authoritative arguments. The important point, nevertheless, is that jurists habitually accept reference to precedents as a sufficient argument supporting an author's, and likewise a court's, interpretation of a legal provision.[81] Even if judges are not required to consider precedent, citing a precedent therefore suffices to justify the specific interpretation of legislation or to justify a conclusion on some other abstract issue of law. Thus, the general normative significance of precedents: while judges are free, as a matter of principle, to ignore or to deviate from relevant precedents, citizens may nevertheless rely on case law, because appeals can be based on the allegation that the court misinterpreted the law, and this allegation may be supported mainly, or even exclusively, by reference to relevant case law.

---

[76] Alexy and Dreier (n 7) 24.

[77] ibid 48f.

[78] ibid 54f.

[79] At n 62.

[80] However, they are not simply interpretative factors like *travaux préparatoires* but rather themselves authoritatively state the (statutory) law in question.

[81] Jansen, *Differenzierung* (n 11) 285. Cf, e.g., Bundesgerichtshof (2014) *Neue Juristische Wochenschrift* 2568, para 28: 'In its decision of 17.7.2008 …, however, the court departed from its older, restrictive line and held that § 167 Code of Civil Procedure will regularly be applicable also to deadlines that may be observed by extrajudicial action.' After a short recapitulation of this interpretation of § 167 Code of Civil Procedure, the court simply applies the rule, which it had stated there, to the present case.

C. The Emergence of Authority

Now, although precedents are authoritative in codified civilian legal systems, it is still true that judges are not empowered to decree general rules;[82] hence, the absence of anything like *stare decisis*. In such systems, case law is not regarded as judge-made law but as jurists' law (*Juristenrecht*); it is therefore never a direct result of a court's judgment. Civilian case law cannot be enacted or made, but only emerges in subsequent processes of reception, interpretation, and recognition of judgments,[83] with the result of such processes being that jurists assume that they are expected by the law to apply precedents so far as they are relevant. The underlying social mechanism is not fundamentally different from the mechanism underlying a legal system's rule of recognition and ultimately the social reality of every institution.[84] Yet, such recognition does not relate to a legal system as a whole, but rather directly to particular judgments, and it vests those decisions not with formal but rather with informal authority.[85] Thus, it is not the individual judgment that creates new law. Case law rather emerges as a result of the court binding itself to this judgment, on the one hand[86]—for example, by citations—and as a result of other courts citing it affirmatively and of the relevant commentaries treating it as authority, on the other hand.[87] In such reception processes, judicial rulings are recognized—in whole or in certain aspects—as authoritative interpretations of legislation. Case law in civilian legal systems thus emerges in informal discourses among courts and in doctrinal literature: *ceteris paribus*, a consolidated line of decisions is of higher authority than an isolated judgment;[88] and the first case in such a line may later become a 'leading case'.[89] Although courts are certainly able to influence such reception processes, for example by means of public communication through press offices and through extrajudicial statements of judges, they can never control those informal processes.

The factors determining the weight of judicial authorities cannot appropriately be formulated in normative, prescriptive terms.[90] Of course, the force of a decision's arguments and the competence of the ruling court are important factors as far as the reception and recognition of a judicial decision is concerned.[91] Other factors, however, which explicitly or tacitly inform legal discourse and control the reception of case law, may include conceptually and systematically stabilized doctrinal expectations prevailing among jurists, on the one hand, and convictions of justice—often habitual— and political biases of the lawyers involved, on

---

[82] H Kelsen, *Reine Rechtslehre* (2nd edn, University of California Press 1960) 255ff; P Hilbert, 'An welche Normen ist der Richter gebunden?' (2013) *Juristenzeitung* 130–36, 134.

[83] Jansen, *Differenzierung* (n 11) 290–97; M Albers, 'Höchstrichterliche Rechtsfindung und Auslegung gerichtlicher Entscheidungen' (2012) 71 *Veröffentlichungen der Vereinigung der Deutschen Staatsrechtslehrer* 257–95, 266ff, 286f; cf also Zimmermann and Jansen (n 5); Payandeh (n 4) 267ff.

[84] For the social mechanisms underlying such processes of recognition, namely, authorization, see Jansen, 'Methoden, Institutionen, Texte' (n 11) 36–40; PL Berger and T Luckmann, *The Social Construction of Reality* (Anchor Books 1966) especially 48, 119; K-S Rehberg, 'Institutionen als symbolische Ordnungen' in G Göhler (ed), *Die Eigenart der Institutionen* (Nomos 1994) 47–84, 58; K-S Rehberg, 'Weltrepräsentanz und Verkörperung' in G Melville (ed), *Institutionalität und Symbolisierung* (Böhlau 2001) 3–49. The basic mechanism is that lawyers believe that other lawyers expect them to treat precedents as authorities, and they regard such expectations as legitimate.

[85] F Schauer, 'Authority and Authorities' (2008) 94 *Va L Rev* 1931–96, 1956.

[86] cf N Duxbury, *The Nature and Authority of Precedent* (CUP 2008) 116: 'strategy of self-binding'.

[87] U Wesel, 'hM' (1979) 56 *Kursbuch* 88–109, 89f, 97f, 104ff; Kästle-Lamparter (n 26) 322, with detailed further references.

[88] Alexy and Dreier (n 7) 50f; Payandeh (n 4) 477ff.

[89] Alexy and Dreier (n 7) 54.

[90] But see ibid 34ff.

[91] BVerfGE 126, 369, 395 (n 51).

THE ORACLES OF CODIFICATION   441

the other. The reception processes determining the authority and the weight of precedents in a civilian legal system are part of, and give expression to, the law's positive, contingent nature.

4. Legislation and Case Law

During the twentieth century, discussions concerning the legitimacy of judicial law-making and the relationship between legislation and case law usually relied on the metaphor of 'gaps (*Lücken*)' in the codifications and statutory law. The underlying idea was that the methods of legal interpretation could and should bind judges as closely as possible to legislation,[92] yet that there were, unfortunately, cases in which the legislation did not determine the decision of a legal case with sufficient clarity. These were gaps in the law, and only with regard to those gaps could the assumption of binding precedents be legitimate.[93] Case law was thus assigned a subsidiary function vis-à-vis legislation.

The problem with such approaches is the underlying concept of law and the law's boundaries. The meaning of all legislation, as with every act of communication, is open to interpretation; laws have an 'open texture' which cannot be fixed by the methods of interpretation or other techniques.[94] Correspondingly, the metaphor of 'gaps' is often misleading as it presupposes the possibility of clearly determining the boundaries of the legislature's determinations of the law. Indeed, case law is relevant not only where Parliament left an issue undecided but also with issues which have in fact been regulated by legislation, as it is not the legislature but rather the judges who finally have to 'sing the law's carol'.[95] Of course, this does not mean that legislation was ultimately 'empty' or meaningless.[96] As with music, there are usually correct and incorrect interpretations—Mozart's *Jupiter Symphony* must not be played like a symphony by Brahms or Mahler; and it would be wrong to extend the meaning of 'injury to life, limb, or health' to include insults. Nonetheless, it is impossible to determine which of many possibly correct interpretations is the only right one; moreover, it is often not possible to draw a clear line between 'correct' and 'incorrect' interpretations. Even if it was agreed that the interpretation of baroque and classical composers should be performed in a historically informed way, the existing discography proves that there remains ample space for interpretation. Similarly, the interpretation of legislation, and thus the final determination of what the law is, is unavoidably the responsibility of the community of jurists in general and in particular of judges.[97]

Beginning with Oscar von Bülow (writing as early as 1885),[98] scholars have therefore increasingly emphasized that all legislative law-making is unavoidably under the proviso of being concretized by the judiciary. Modern scholars therefore describe the relationship between legislation and case law no longer with the metaphor of 'gap-filling', but rather as a

---

[92] See, for a comprehensive analysis, Haferkamp, 'Methodengeschichte unter dem BGB' (n 7).

[93] See the references at n 50.

[94] Hart (n 62) 123, 128ff, 272ff (Postscript); MT Fögen, *Das Lied vom Gesetz* (Carl Friedrich von Siemens Stiftung 2007) 29–41, 84ff. Cf also M Klatt, *Making the Law Explicit: The Normativity of Legal Argumentation* (Hart 2008); M Klatt, 'Die Wortlautgrenze' in KD Lerch (ed), *Recht verhandeln. Argumentieren, Begründen und Entscheiden im Diskurs des Rechts* (De Gruyter 2005) 343–68. Although Klatt insists on the normativity of semantics, he admits that this only exceptionally limits the judicial interpretation of legislation.

[95] Fögen, *Lied vom Gesetz* (n 94) 47.

[96] But see ibid 93, 99.

[97] M Auer, 'Der Kampf um die Wissenschaftlichkeit der Jurisprudenz' (2015) 23 *Zeitschrift für Europäisches Privatrecht* 773–805, 794ff, referring to G Flavius, *Der Kampf um die Rechtswissenschaft* (H Kantorowicz ed, Nomos 1906).

[98] von Bülow, *Gesetz und Richteramt* (n 21) 41ff and passim; cf Alexy and Dreier (n 7) 45.

closely knit fabric of legislative and adjudicative threads of the law.[99] With such metaphors, case law is seen as a prolonged arm of legislation:[100] it is for judges to ultimately determine what the legislature decreed. This is obvious in those parts of the law where legislatures have consciously left issues undecided. Thus, in tort law, in the field of unjustified enrichment, or with labour law and fundamental rights, answers to quite fundamental questions can sometimes not be found in legislation, but have been authoritatively determined by case law.[101] This is clearly visible where a court departs from a previously acknowledged interpretation of legislation; indeed, the German Federal Constitutional Court has even been considered a 'constitution-changing power' in the state.[102] Yet the observation that the meaning of all acts of legislation is ultimately determined by the community of interpreters, and thus in particular by the judiciary, holds true for all parts of private and public law. This is the reason why nearly all court decisions cite precedents.[103] They thereby show that they follow established paths of interpretation.

5. Conclusion

Although codified civil law systems do not acknowledge precedents as formal sources of law, case law has nevertheless become an omnipresent feature and, indeed, a specific characteristic of civil law. Judicial interpretations of legislation are commonly regarded as informally authoritative statements of the actual law; yet, they are not authoritative as decisions on the actual facts but rather as interpretations of the law. Precedents are thus informal, interpretative authorities. From the practical lawyer's perspective, this means that the law cannot be gauged from the code or a statute alone; hence, lawyers must always take the relevant case law into consideration when applying legislation. Even if courts are thus not bound by precedents, citizens may actually rely on case law.

---

[99] J Esser, *Vorverständnis und Methodenwahl in der Rechtsfindung* (Athenäum 1970) 187; Albers, 'Höchstrichterliche Rechtsfindung' (n 83) 260ff, 266ff; Payandeh (n 4) 17ff and passim; Jansen, *Differenzierung* (n 11) 282ff.

[100] J Esser, 'Richterrecht, Gerichtsgebrauch und Gewohnheitsrecht' in J Esser and H Thieme (eds), *Festschrift für Fritz von Hippel* (Mohr Siebeck 1967) 95–130, 113ff, 116ff, 118 (judge-made law not 'secondary' but rather a 'continuum of legislation'); Esser, *Vorverständnis und Methodenwahl* (n 99) 75f.

[101] U Volkmann, 'Verfassungsänderung und Verfassungswandel. Beobachtungen zum Verhältnis von Stabilität und Dynamik im Verfassungsrecht der Bundesrepublik Deutschland' (2018) *Juristenzeitung* 265–71, 269f (constitutional law); N Jansen, 'Gesetzliche Schuldverhältnisse: eine historische Strukturanalyse' (2016) 216 *Archiv für die civilistische Praxis* 112–233 (unjust enrichment and tort law).

[102] L Michael, 'Die verfassungswandelnde Gewalt' (2014) 5 *Rechtswissenschaft* 426–80.

[103] Alexy and Dreier (n 7) 23.

33
Predictability and Precedent

Hillary Nye[*]

1. Introduction

One argument that is often given for the value of respecting precedent involves a rule-of-law sort of justification: that we ought to respect precedent because that will make the law predictable for those who are subject to it. There are, of course, many other justifications for precedent, such as treating like cases alike, and so on.[1] But here I want to focus on the importance of predictability and reliance.[2]

I will assume that predictability is valuable, even if it is not the only thing at stake in a given situation. It is important to respect the legitimate expectations of those who may rely on the law.[3] But predictability does not seem to be a value in its own right.[4] It might instead be seen as an instrumental value. It is important because it promotes other values. One of the most commonly mentioned is liberty; the closely related value of autonomy is also often

---

[*] I would like to thank all the participants at the authors' workshop for this volume in October 2021 for excellent questions and comments, and Timothy Endicott, Hafsteinn Dan Kristjánsson, and Sebastian Lewis for organizing the workshop and bringing together this volume. I want to give particular thanks to my commentator at that workshop, Emily Kidd White, for her astute and insightful comments, which greatly improved the chapter. I also presented a version of this chapter at the Alberta Early Career Legal Scholars Workshop, and am very grateful to all the participants at that event for their thoughtful engagement with it. Thanks also to Grace Nye for helpful discussions and for keeping me on track with Zoom writing sessions.

[1] On treating like cases alike, and for some criticism of this idea, see TM Benditt, 'The Rule of Precedent' in L Goldstein (ed), *Precedent in Law* (Clarendon Press 1987) 89, 90–91; see also F Schauer, 'Precedent' (1987) 39 Stan L Rev 571, discussing treating like cases alike at 595–97, and discussing a wider range of justifications for precedent at 595–602. Jeremy Waldron lists a wide variety of justifications, including 'the importance of stability, respect for established expectations, decisional efficiency, the orderly development of the law, Burkean deference to ancestral wisdom, formal or comparative justice, fairness, community, integrity, the moral importance of treating like cases alike, and the political desirability of disciplining our judges and reducing any opportunity for judicial activism'. J Waldron, '*Stare Decisis* and the Rule of Law' (2012) 111 Mich L Rev 1, 3.

[2] Waldron notes that certain of the justifications for precedent are connected to the rule of law, and not others. Ones that do have rule of law implications are 'the quest for constancy and predictability in the law, and the importance of generality and treating like cases alike', ibid. 'There is a cluster of considerations commonly cited in support of the system of precedent that seems to invoke rule-of-law values. These include the importance of certainty, predictability, and respect for established expectations.' ibid 9. Benditt discusses predictability as one justification for precedent: 'Another sort of consideration supporting precedent has to do with the idea of promoting stability in a legal system. Here we are to note that people rely on past decisions in the sense that they make decisions and commit resources based on them. People enter into contracts expecting certain legal rules to be applied to them.' Benditt (n 1) 91. Benditt notes, however, that flexibility in a legal system is also important, and balance is required.

[3] Expectations must, of course, be distinguished from legitimate expectations. '[I]t is important to bear in mind that it is only legitimate expectations which need to be considered in decision-making, not any expectation which someone forms. The mere fact that a decision was made in the past provides no reason in itself to expect that it will be followed in the future, and certainly creates no entitlement to expect that it will be followed.' G Lamond, 'Precedent and Analogy in Legal Reasoning' (2006) Stanford Encyclopedia of Philosophy 26. Legitimacy, Lamond says, is tied to whether there are in fact good reasons for following the prior decision, or whether there is a practice of following those decisions, ibid 27. I will discuss the distinction between legitimate expectations and expectations generally, in section 2, as well as in section 3.C.

[4] I thank Emily Kidd White for pressing me on this point, and I'm also grateful for discussion of the issue at the authors' workshop for this volume in October 2021.

Hillary Nye, *Predictability and Precedent* In: *Philosophical Foundations of Precedent.* Edited by: Timothy Endicott, Hafsteinn Dan Kristjánsson, and Sebastian Lewis, Oxford University Press. © Hillary Nye 2023. DOI: 10.1093/oso/9780192857248.003.0034

444   HILLARY NYE

raised as a justification for ensuring predictability. '[P]redictability ... is supposed to make it easier for people to exercise their liberty (i.e., their autonomous powers of planning and action).'[5] I will say more about this later.

So, I begin by taking seriously the fact that predictability is important, even if it is not the only value, and even if it is not best characterized as a value in and of itself at all. But I want to argue that, despite its importance, it is sometimes raised as a justification in cases where it does not belong. I want to draw attention to situations in which predictability is not at stake, though it may mistakenly be thought to be. If I am right, this will help to redirect our reasoning in such cases, so that we focus on what other justification might exist (if any) for following precedent in such cases. With predictability out of the way, we can see more clearly what the true justification might be, or we can see that in fact there is no justification for following precedent in such cases.[6]

2. Precedent and the Value of Predictability

First, what is predictability? Predictability is one of the most prominent rule-of-law desiderata. The rule of law demands that law be made and applied in a way that is predictable, thereby enabling people to plan their lives in accordance with it. Lon Fuller emphasized the fact that people need to know what the law expects of them so that they can conform their behaviour to it and not be blindsided by official action after the fact. As Fuller states, 'the citizen cannot orient his conduct by law if what is called law confronts him merely with a series of sporadic and patternless exercises of state power'.[7] The aim of the rule of law is to avoid this kind of unpredictable projection of power against the legal subject and ensure that any governmental interference they may experience can be expected and worked into their life plans. Fuller's view is rich, and predictability is only one aspect, but it is a central element. It is also clearly connected to underlying values of dignity and autonomy. Fuller presents a vision of human beings according to which they are capable of exercising autonomy, and to fail to recognize this is to infringe their dignity. Departures from the principles of the 'inner morality of law'[8] are 'an affront to man's dignity as a responsible agent'.[9]

Joseph Raz also focuses on predictability and behaviour-guidance. According to Raz in his canonical work 'The Rule of Law and its Virtue', the fundamental idea of the rule of law is 'that people should be ruled by the law and obey it, and ... that the law should be such that people will be able to be guided by it'.[10] His list of principles shares much in common with Fuller's, and adds procedural elements. He ties virtually all of these principles to the value of

---

[5] Waldron (n 1) 9.

[6] It might be asked why I am focusing on these cases since it is also true that we can point to competing values even in cases where predictability *is* at stake. What do we gain by looking at cases where predictability drops away? I thank Emily Kidd White for raising this in her comments. There is an analytic clarity that comes from looking at pure cases where a consideration, usually considered central, is absent. We then see more clearly what other considerations look like. Weighing values is notoriously difficult, and so it seems to me we can helpfully evaluate something when we see it highlighted on its own, without the challenge of weighing it against something else. But this choice is also a practical one: I think there is a tendency in the literature and in case law to overstate the importance of predictability. It is too often raised and treated almost as a trump. I aim to prompt us to stop and look more closely, and I think finding cases where predictability is not at stake is a helpful way to do this.

[7] LL Fuller, *The Morality of Law* (Yale UP 1964) 110.

[8] The inner morality of law is Fuller's term for the 'eight distinct standards by which excellence in legality may be tested', ibid 42. See ibid 39 for his description of the principles. There is debate about whether these principles are best described as a 'morality', but most theorists take them to form part of the core of the rule of law.

[9] ibid 162.

[10] J Raz, 'The Rule of Law and its Virtue' in *The Authority of Law* (2nd edn, OUP 2009) 213.

behaviour-guidance.[11] We strive to guide behaviour in ways that ensure that people can predict the use of state power and plan their lives around it.

This is again connected to autonomy and dignity. As Raz puts it:

> observance of the rule of law is necessary if the law is to respect human dignity. Respecting human dignity entails treating humans as persons capable of planning and plotting their future. Thus, respecting people's dignity includes respecting their autonomy, their right to control their future.[12]

We value predictability for its influence on people's ability to act autonomously. I will focus throughout the chapter on this idea of enabling planning and ensuring people are treated as autonomous agents who are able to form a plan of life and carry it out without their intentions being frustrated.

So, it is clear that predictability, because of its implications for behaviour-guidance, is an important part of the rule of law, and that this is because of the fact that predictability promotes liberty, dignity, or autonomy. In many cases, this connection is made explicit, though sometimes it is merely implicit. Generally, however, predictability is not valued for its own sake but because it is a way of respecting one or more of these values.

Turning, then, from the rule of law to precedent, we can see that one of the central justifications for precedent has much in common with this rule-of-law ideal of predictability aimed at protecting autonomy. Frederick Schauer treats predictability as an important justification for precedent.[13] 'When a decisionmaker must decide this case in the same way as the last, parties will be better able to anticipate the future.'[14]

Others too tie precedent to predictability. Neil Duxbury says:

> when acting and planning we want to be able to foresee the consequences of our actions, and so we may find it useful to know that if problem X arises because of what we do then the court, given how it has consistently handled this problem in the past, will rule A.[15]

Duxbury also ties this to the kind of agency we value being able to exercise in our lives: the ability to order our affairs.[16] Once these kinds of expectations are generated, then there is a standing reason for courts to hesitate to depart from their prior decisions, because parties who have used them to predict the future 'will suffer considerable reliance loss'.[17] The general idea behind the predictability argument for precedent is that it is good for people if the law is predictable. Predictability enables people to know what will happen to them, plan their lives, and confidently execute those plans. Knowing that precedents will be upheld contributes to that predictability.[18]

---

[11] ibid 214–18.
[12] ibid 221.
[13] Schauer (n 1) 597–98.
[14] ibid 597.
[15] N Duxbury, *The Nature and Authority of Precedent* (CUP 2008) 160.
[16] ibid 161.
[17] ibid 162.
[18] When we think about predictability, one context that immediately comes to mind is that of hard cases—cases where there is no clear legal outcome. But as many have acknowledged, in hard cases we may worry *less* about predictability. In such cases, the judge's decision does not cause uncertainty, because there is *already* uncertainty in the law. See HLA Hart, *The Concept of Law* (2nd edn, OUP 1994). In a hard case, the law is unsettled, and both parties have some reason to think their view may prevail, but also some reason to be less than sanguine about the likelihood of success. The decision can only go one way, and one or the other party is going to have their expectations

But although predictability is important and valuable, there arises a potential tension. The fundamental dilemma of the predictability argument for Schauer is put thus:

> To what extent is a decisionmaking environment willing to tolerate suboptimal results in order that people may plan their lives according to decisions previously made?[19]

Schauer argues that 'the value of predictability is really a question of balancing expected gain against expected loss'.[20] Duxbury similarly notes that not all expectations are worthy of protection,[21] and that judges have to balance the harm that individuals may suffer with 'the possibility that following the precedent might not be in the broader public interest'.[22] And as Lamond says:

> In an institutionalised system with many decision-makers and a heterogeneous group of legal materials there is a tension between decision-making being relatively predictable for those to whom it will apply and the law being morally improved.[23]

In other words, the value of predictability—or, rather, the value of autonomy or liberty that appears to underpin calls for predictability—must be weighed against other values. A law that is predictably terrible might not be worth keeping in place; we may wish to accept the costs of change in order to improve the law. John Gardner puts this well when he says that 'Not every manifestation of justice is an act of following a sound rule'.[24] We cannot reduce all just acts to the form of rules. Gardner goes beyond this to say that justice doesn't always favour catering to the expectations of the parties—or, in other words, doing what is predictable. Indeed, 'were the expectations morally abhorrent ones, justice might be in favour of *maximizing* frustrated expectations on both sides'.[25] This is true and important. The balance between predictability and its attendant promotion of autonomy, on the one hand, and justice, on the other, is no doubt challenging to strike, and there is much that could be said about how we should draw that line. But in this chapter I am not concerned with teasing out the precise balance that should be struck in those cases. What I am interested in are times when that tension disappears. There are situations where we can focus on the value on the

---

upset. But both parties know this, so we might think uncertainty is not really the key worry here. The litigation in hard cases is going to settle the uncertainty in law rather than create it. (There are different versions of hard cases as well, such as when the law is 'clear', but in tension with another law, or viewed as unfair, etc. In that case, the predictability worry may be more or less present, depending on how widespread the belief is that there is unfairness warranting change.) What I will discuss in rest of the chapter is not hard cases, but cases where there are other reasons to think that change in the law is unproblematic or that there was no reliance.

[19] Schauer (n 1) 597.
[20] ibid 598.
[21] Duxbury (n 15) 164.
[22] ibid 163.
[23] Lamond (n 3) 38. Waldron advises caution here. The tension may not be as great as it seems. If a judge disregards a precedent, this 'no doubt diminishes predictability, but it need not ruin it altogether. It does not make it impossible for people to form and act on expectations about future legal decisions; it just adds an element of uncertainty to their calculations. How much uncertainty—how much damage it does to the basis of predictability—is a matter of degree and depends on all sorts of surrounding circumstances, such as the congruence of the change with existing business practices, et cetera.' Waldron (n 1) 12.
[24] J Gardner, 'The Virtue of Justice and the Character of Law' in *Law as a Leap of Faith* (OUP 2012) 254. I thank my commentator, Emily Kidd White, for drawing my attention to the relevance of this chapter for the argument here.
[25] Gardner (n 24) 258.

other side of the balance (fairness, justice, or whatever it is that is at stake) without struggling with the tension just elaborated because there is no predictability concern in the balance. There are times, I will argue, where the predictability concern carries no weight, even though there is a dramatic change in what is done.

The argument I want to put forward here is that there are situations, which often go unnoticed, where there is little or nothing to be gained on the predictability side of things by keeping the law the same. There is an assumption at play in many discussions of precedent that any change in the law always comes with some amount of loss in predictability. But I want to show that there are certain contexts in which this is not the case. I will make this argument in the context of contract law, though it may have broader implications.

3. Expanding the Scope of Law-Compliant Behaviour

I will use the Canadian case of *Rosas v Toca*[26] as a vehicle to explore situations where a change in a precedent, even a seemingly dramatic one, may not be problematic, due to the change expanding the scope of behaviour that counts as compliance with the law. The argument I want to make here is that there are cases where a change in the law will not interfere with predictability or reliance because it amounts to a lowering of the standards of what is expected of the parties in terms of meeting the tests for legal enforcement.

I begin with a brief summary of the facts. *Rosas* is a decision full of human drama. It is extremely interesting from the point of view of reflecting on how ordinary subjects of the law plan and order their affairs. It involved two friends: Ms Rosas and Ms Toca. Ms Rosas won the lottery and subsequently offered a loan of $600,000 to Ms Toca, which was to be repaid in one year. She extended the time frame for payment of the loan several times.[27]

Eventually, their friendship broke down and Ms Rosas wanted to recover the money she had loaned to Ms Toca.[28] She sued and came up against a limitations clause: it appeared that her suit to recover the money would be barred due to the passage of time.[29] However, if each of the extensions of the loan renewed the clock on the limitations clause, then her suit would still be in time. The problem was that these extensions were post-contractual variations without consideration. Each time Ms Rosas extended the date for payment, Ms Toca gave nothing in return. They were therefore unenforceable due to the general rule that consideration is required in order for variations of contracts to be enforceable.[30] If that general rule—a very old and established rule—remains the law, then Ms Rosas cannot recover the money she loaned to her friend, and it would seem that she is prevented from doing so due to her own generosity in extending the loan so many times.

The rule on post-contractual variations is an important and long-standing part of contract law. In light of this, an argument might be raised that reasons of predictability justify leaving the rule in place. For example, Marcus Roberts has argued that this constitutes a major change: 'Far from incremental, the effects of this decision may be far-reaching and may indeed have "uncertain ramifications".'[31] He continues:

---

[26] *Rosas v Toca* 2018 BCCA 191.

[27] ibid [2].

[28] ibid [9].

[29] ibid [17].

[30] *Stilk v Myrick* (1809) 2 Camp 317, 170 ER 1168, SC 6 Esp 129 (Eng KB).

[31] M Roberts, '*Rosas v Toca*—Asses and "Incremental Changes" to Consideration' <https://ssrn.com/abstract= 3347371> 10, accessed 31 May 2021.

448   HILLARY NYE

There is a danger that we could look back on decisions like *Rosas v Toca* as opening the door to the abolishment of consideration. Is removing an element of contract law that has existed for at least 400 years from one type of contract really 'incremental'? Are the ramifications of the decision truly not 'uncertain'? Just because the Court of Appeal said so does not make it true.[32]

This kind of argument, sometimes explicitly stated, and other times lurking under the surface, seems to be one of the reasons courts have been so hesitant to make changes in the area of consideration.

In *Rosas*, the court determined that the rule should be reformed, so that consideration is no longer required in cases of post-contractual variation. The court puts it as follows:

> When parties to a contract agree to vary its terms, the variation should be enforceable without fresh consideration, absent duress, unconscionability, or other public policy concerns, which would render an otherwise valid term unenforceable. A variation supported by valid consideration may continue to be enforceable for that reason, but a lack of fresh consideration will no longer be determinative.[33]

This appears to be a foundational change in the law, given the fundamental importance and longevity of the doctrine of consideration in contract law.[34] However, I want to argue that it is not a change that affects predictability. This is because it widens the scope of what will count as law-compliant behaviour. It does not turn expectations upside down by demanding something new of the parties; rather, it requires less of them in order to meet the demands of the law. If they are to make a legally enforceable contract, they can now still do what they did previously, but they can also do less—they can simply not give consideration, as long as their intentions are clear, and their bargain will still be upheld. Thus, the scope of compliant behaviour is wider: it is now the case that a larger group of people will meet the test for a legally enforceable contract.[35]

To examine whether it is really right to say that there is no predictability concern here, we can look at a range of different affected parties in different situations. We should ask what reliance on the pre-existing duty rule would have looked like, depending on the different positions of each party and their respective understandings of what the law is:

(1) Both parties knew about the law and relied upon it/complied with it.
(2) Both parties did not know about the law, or thought it was different than it actually was.
(3) One party knew about the law and one did not.

Table 33.1 sets out these possibilities. I will examine each of these in turn in sections 3.A–C.

---

[32] ibid 11.

[33] *Rosas* (n 26) [183].

[34] It should be noted that this decision does not change the core requirement for consideration in the formation of new contracts; it merely alters the conditions under which a variation of an already existing contract will be found to be binding.

[35] The idea that less is demanded of the parties is not the same as the idea that there are no winners and losers, or that one party is not worse off ultimately. I discuss this in section 4.A. It also doesn't yet show that there are no predictability concerns. I aim to demonstrate that in sections 3.A–C.

PREDICTABILITY AND PRECEDENT   449

Table 33.1 Parties' knowledge of the law

	Party 1 knows	Party 1 doesn't know
Party 2 knows	Both know; both comply	One party knows and the other does not; whether they comply or not will depend on what suits the party with knowledge
Party 2 doesn't know	One party knows and the other does not; whether they comply or not will depend on what suits the party with knowledge	Neither know; neither comply

A. Both Parties Knew the Law

In this category, we imagine that both parties knew about the law and relied upon it or complied with it. In the case of the post-contractual variation rule, that would mean that they paid consideration in order to ensure that their bargain would be legally enforceable. In situations like this, if the law is changed, these parties are not disadvantaged because their bargains are still enforced. I will argue that there is no predictability problem if the law is changed to be wider, because their situation is still captured.

A person who knew about the rule and relied on it would have taken it into account in structuring their affairs, and would have paid or insisted their contracting party paid consideration for the variation. We can assume that a reasonable party who can properly be said to be relying on that rule did in fact do just that (or, at the very least, had the opportunity to do so). They relied on it and therefore they structured their contractual relationships such that they would be enforceable. If all of those unknown parties—we are thinking not of Ms Rosas and Ms Toca here but others who might be affected by the change in the law—knew about the rule and relied on it, they would have complied with it. What happens to them when the law changes? In fact, nothing. The new rule in *Rosas* does not reverse the situation so that those who paid consideration now no longer have their bargain enforced. Rather, it simply widens the category of enforceable bargains such that more bargains are included, while continuing to enforce the bargains of those who did provide consideration. In this sense, I have described it as expanding the scope of compliant behaviour because it places fewer demands on the parties in order to meet the criteria of enforceability. This means that a larger group of people will be in compliance with the law. Parties have to do less to have an enforceable bargain. But those who did more—who complied with the rule and gave consideration—also have their bargains upheld. So, if the court enforces Ms Rosas and Ms Toca's bargain, it does no damage to the bargains of those who did rely on and follow the rule: their bargains remain enforceable.[36]

---

[36] One might object that there is a harm to these parties: they paid consideration when they need not have. This is an economic loss. I thank Hafsteinn Dan Kristjánsson for raising this point. This is an important worry. I don't deny that they may be worse off. But I am concerned here with the specific worry about predictability. In order to see whether this is able to be framed as a predictability concern, we need to examine the parties' expectations. Did they expect to have an enforceable bargain? If so, that expectation is upheld. Could it be said that they expected to have their bargain upheld and to not pay consideration? No, because at the time that was not the law. Their position is more analogous to the shopper who buys an item and later finds that it has gone on sale. This is a disappointment, certainly, but it is not a case of frustrated expectations.

Contrast this with a situation where the opposite occurs: the court's new decision *adds to* rather than reducing the burden on parties to comply with the law. Let's say they change the law so that consideration must be given for variations *and* it must be more than nominal consideration. A peppercorn will no longer do.[37] This would be a change that would clearly implicate reliance. It would mean that people who are not parties to the case at bar would have their expectations frustrated. Those who had varied their contracts and followed the rule and given consideration, but only nominal consideration, would now find that their contracts were unenforceable, and this would upset their reliance on the law.

We might, however, imagine a different case where both parties know the law. Previously, we were envisioning a situation where both parties know the law and desire to create a contract; they therefore comply and give consideration in order to create an enforceable bargain. But what about a situation where the parties knew about the law and wanted to *avoid* legal consequences? We can imagine that because of their desire to not have legal consequences attached to their agreement, they will choose not to give consideration in order to ensure their bargain is simply treated as a friendly agreement and not a legally enforceable one. Some parties might have known about the rule requiring consideration for variations, and specifically chosen not to give consideration in order to ensure that the agreement is treated as merely an agreement between friends and not a legally enforceable agreement. Will such parties be disadvantaged? A change like the one in *Rosas* might then affect these parties' reliance; people in such a situation might then be captured by the new, more relaxed, consideration rule, when they did not expect or intend to be.

Looking to the specifics of the change in *Rosas*, there are ways in which this is avoided: the new rule is designed to capture cases where the parties demonstrated a genuine intent to alter their agreement. The court emphasizes that since we are dealing with variations, we are already in a situation where the parties intended to be bound. 'Further, as with any bargain, certainty of terms and proof of mutual intention to be bound will have to be proved by the party seeking to rely on the variation agreement.'[38] So, the court would be looking for evidence that the parties did in fact intend to vary the terms of the contract. In the hypothetical case raised as an objection here, we have parties who both intend not to create an enforceable variation, and presumably the court will take that intention seriously.

But abstracting from the details of the change in *Rosas*, does this worry more generally have force? We are concerned with situations where the parties know the law, and try to arrange their affairs to avoid it, but are subsequently captured by a change in the law that expands what counts as compliance. Mindy Chen-Wishart argues that we should be careful about not ensnaring people in legal obligations:

> In general, transactions in the private domain should remain free *from* contract, and transactions in the market domain—where reciprocity, trust and social sanctions are not implicit—should only attract state enforcement where the parties' dealings are marked by mutual respect. Consideration marks the boundary between the two.[39]

---

[37] The classic 'peppercorn principle' in contract law states that consideration need not meet any test of sufficiency; even a peppercorn is adequate. 'The amount of consideration paid on a contract can be as minimal as a peppercorn or a penny': *Portfolio Acquisitions Canada Inc v Salamona* (2008) CarswellOnt 3446 (Ont SCJ) [11].

[38] *Rosas* (n 26) [180].

[39] M Chen-Wishart, 'In Defence of Consideration' (2013) 13 Ox U Commw LJ 209, 238.

This is an important observation. I do not wish to encourage judges to alter the law in ways that will problematically ensnare unsuspecting people into contractual obligations. It is hard to grapple with this worry in the abstract, but my sense is that judges would generally take the approach in *Rosas*, of searching for a genuine intention to be legally bound and, absent that, will not find legal obligations. To put the point more broadly, we might say that predictability worries will not arise in cases of overturning precedents when the court is widening the scope of legally compliant behaviour, as long as the court is conscious of just how wide the new boundaries are. Where the requirements of law are technical, and parties may have done something close but insufficient, courts may with caution consider some lesser action as sufficient for meeting the legal test. They might stretch the boundaries to include those who have done something close to the technical requirement, but not so wide that they ensnare those who have no intention of acquiring legal obligations. The court may require *less* of the parties, but it should not require *nothing*. What this looks like in a given situation will take careful, case-by-case examination, but there is room for widening the scope of what counts as legal compliance before we reach the point where *just anything* counts as legal compliance.[40]

B. Both Parties Were Mistaken About the Law

In this situation, we are envisioning that both parties were unaware of the law, or thought it was different to what it actually was. The outcome here will depend on what their mistaken view was, but in the case of the pre-existing duty rule, we can use a perhaps simplistic binary: the parties either thought they had to give consideration for a variation or thought they did not. If they thought they did, then they are in the first category. But if they thought they did not, then what is their position? They will have attempted to vary their contract and failed to do so. They will have disappointed expectations because they did not know about this legal requirement. They wanted to secure the protection of the law, and they thought that they did so. But they did not do everything that was required to make this the case, and so they have been unsuccessful in varying their contract.

What happens to such parties if the law is now brought in line with what their prior belief was? If the judge loosens the rule such that consideration is no longer required, then the law is brought in line with their previous understanding of it. People in this position will therefore not have a predictability problem. The revised law will now match their expectations. By expanding the scope of what counts as legal compliance, the revised law now includes them, and the therefore have their contract upheld. Here, since we are dealing with parties who share the same misunderstanding about the law, a dispute requiring enforcement is unlikely; rather, both parties will be glad that the law now matches their expectations. The case may be different with parties who have opposing views about the law, as section 3.C discusses.

---

[40] How this would play out in other contexts is beyond the scope of the chapter. There may be other technical requirements, such as limitations periods, that the court would have to consider whether to uphold. It would be necessary to consider the predictability effects on all parties in more detail to determine whether these cases would count as cases where the scope of law-compliant behaviour is widened without causing a predictability concern.

C. Parties Had Opposing Views About the Law

In this category, we can imagine that the parties' understandings of the law diverged. One knew that the law required consideration for contractual variations, and the other did not. We now imagine that the parties purport to vary their contract without providing consideration. (If they vary it and do provide consideration, no problem arises.) In this situation, the party who does have knowledge is best described as exploiting their superior knowledge of the law. They wish to give the impression that they are promising to vary the contract in a legally enforceable way while not in fact doing so. They know consideration is required, but keep that information to themselves in order to ensure their varied bargain will not be enforceable, presumably so that they can get out of it if they so choose. They are taking advantage of the fact that the other party is ill-informed about the law.

The problem here is the mismatch between expectations. One party thinks they are making a contract and the other knows they are not. Here the key will be the *legitimacy* of these expectations.[41] Are the expectations of the party with knowledge, that the court will refrain from upholding the bargain, legitimate expectations that deserve protection? I think not. As noted earlier, many authors accept that not all expectations are worthy of protection. In particular, if we have to choose between one set of expectations and another, then it seems plausible to show hesitation in upholding expectations that appear to be exploitative. If we see predictability as instrumentally valuable, as I have suggested we should, it makes sense to say that not every expectation deserves protection. In determining which expectations are legitimate, we should look to whether the underlying value—dignity, liberty, autonomy, and so on—is promoted.

But put to the side the legitimate expectations point—we can sidestep that complex question. Here I am concerned to make a different, and narrower, point. In this situation, predictability is, essentially, a wash. One party thinks one thing, and the other thinks something different. It is impossible to satisfy both sets of expectations. One party will have their expectations frustrated either way. We might think, then, that predictability cannot be a determining factor here. There might appear to be a predictability problem for the party with knowledge: their expectations will be overturned. But if the judge is to provide predictability for that party, they will in so doing create unpredictability for the other party. Thus, predictability doesn't point us in either direction here, and we can safely set it aside to look at other reasons to apply or overturn the precedent.

On the other hand, one might think that it is not evenly balanced, and that we should prioritize the expectations of the person who actually knows the law.[42] We are familiar with the idea that ignorance of the law is no defence. That principle makes sense in the criminal law, but in the context of private law disputes it seems less essential to demand that the parties know the law. In private law, more than criminal law, there are often multiple reasonable positions, and it may make sense to provide some space for the expectations of those who do not understand the technical nuances of the rule.

---

[41] See Lamond (n 3). As noted earlier, Lamond ties legitimacy to whether there are 'good reasons' for following the decision. This, of course, raises the question of what a good reason is—a question too large to answer here. I will simply say that asking judges to consider this does not go beyond what they paradigmatically do as judges. Engaging with concepts like 'legitimacy', 'reasonableness', and 'goodness' is a standard part of judicial decision-making.

[42] I thank Hafsteinn Dan Kristjánsson for raising this point.

(i) When should we assess knowledge?

Should we assess the parties' knowledge at the time of contracting, or later, when seeking legal remedies? In principle, it makes sense to examine intentions at the time of formation of the contract, as that is the point in time at which expectations are set. But we can look at both stages to see what conclusions we might draw.

If we focus on expectations at the time of contracting in *Rosas*, Ms Rosas and Ms Toca will both be in category (2), where both parties are mistaken about the rule. It seems reasonably clear that at the time of their bargain, neither of them was aware of the pre-existing duty rule or took it on board in their deliberations. In that case, as we have already seen, they do not have a predictability-based objection, because the change brings the law in line with what they expected.

If we focus instead on expectations at a later stage, once lawyers have informed the parties of all their rights, then our assessment may be different. The parties will be similarly situated to parties in category (3). There is not, strictly speaking, an information mismatch, because both parties are now fully informed of their legal rights. But Ms Toca (or rather, her lawyer) is now exploiting a mismatch in their previous understanding of the law. She knows that Ms Rosas did not know about the pre-existing duty rule before, and now she wishes to get out of a bargain on the basis of this information which benefits her vis-à-vis Ms Rosas. If we think about this in terms of legitimate expectations, again, there is no reason to think that Ms Toca had a legitimate expectation that the agreement would not be enforced. Indeed, she had no such expectation, legitimate or not, until this later stage where she is informed of the legal argument available to her. When assessing expectations at this later stage, there may be other considerations, but there are no predictability concerns, properly understood.

4. Objections

A. Does Ms Toca Still Lose Something?

I have argued that there is no predictability worry here. But we might be uncomfortable with the idea that this change to the law is permissible. Gardner warns us that it is not just expectations that matter. It is a mistake to ignore 'the other things that must still be allocated apart from the frustrated and fulfilled expectations (such as the losses and the penalties)'.[43] The law inevitably creates winners and losers.[44] We might say that Ms Toca is on the losing end of a change in the law. Certainly, her position is worse after the court's decision. She no longer gets to keep the $600,000 that she would have if the court decided differently. Perhaps I am being too quick in saying that this change is permissible.

It is important to be clear: I am not saying that no one is disadvantaged here. I am saying that there is no argument founded on predictability that tells us not to overturn the precedent. The predictability worry drops out of the picture for parties in all three categories— whether they knew the law, were both mistaken about it, or had mismatched understandings. And so we should not use predictability to prevent change in the law. We can instead turn to other values. Here we are able to ask about the harm to Ms Toca, as well as to Ms Rosas. Certainly, one of them will be on the losing end in terms of practical outcomes. But we can

---

[43] Gardner (n 24) 258.
[44] ibid 261.

454   HILLARY NYE

assess that in terms of the relevant values, without worrying about predictability. That is the core of my claim here.

B. Systemic Implications

An objection might be raised that the view I put forward here neglects the systemic implications of legal change. I have attempted to carve out a category of cases where there is no predictability implication for the parties, or for other parties facing similar legal questions (e.g. whether or not to provide consideration). But we might wonder whether this is too narrow a focus. Should we not worry that the overturning of a precedent signals a broader readiness to change the law?[45] In other words, can we really draw a conclusion by looking at individual cases, or do we need to think about broader systemic implications?

My answer, in short, is that systemic predictability is compatible with a general cautiousness about reliance on precedents. But that cautiousness will be limited to a fairly small range of cases. We should think about the message that would be sent to the public by the kind of approach I suggest here. Parties would know that predictability is generally important to courts. They would learn that precedents are sometimes overturned, but they would also see that the decision to overturn a precedent is sensitive to whether it has been relied on. They will note that this approach does not counsel overturning a precedent in a way that will undermine reliance broadly speaking, though it may counsel overturning a precedent when the person relying on it is doing so in an exploitative way. I am comfortable with endorsing a view that might have a chilling effect on exploitative behaviour. I think that may be the case here. Someone who wants to rely on a precedent that they know the other person is unaware of might rightly learn to be cautious about taking such an approach. But ordinary reliance behaviour should not be chilled by this kind of approach.

5. Conclusion

I have argued that certain kinds of changes do not implicate predictability. What might be a dramatic and substantial change in the law might nevertheless fail to upset predictability for those who have an interest in the outcome. I outlined one particular context in which we should be live to the possibility that predictability is not at stake. (There may be others.) That is, I looked at situations where overturning a precedent will expand the scope of behaviour that counts as compliant with the law. The change will not increase the burden of compliance but rather lessen it. In such situations, those who did follow the law will not be disadvantaged by the change. The predictability worry drops out of the picture because we are still able to predict, for example, that a variation for which consideration was given will be enforced, and so we do not upset the expectations of those who did give consideration. We have simply enabled another subset of people to also take the benefit of the law, by expanding what counts as compliance.

We can see, then, that overturning precedents might in some situations be unproblematic from a predictability standpoint—and this might extend to precedents that have stood for hundreds of years, and are deeply imbedded elements of the law. Even in such cases, where

---

[45] I thank Emily Kidd White for raising this objection.

the rule appears to be foundational, changing it in a way that expands the scope of legal compliance can be permissible from a predictability point of view. Others who knew about the rule will have taken it into account in their behaviour, and they will still meet the bar for what the law requires—they will simply have gone above and beyond. But that is no problem. The problem truly arises when the law is changed such that someone is now required to have done more than before. In cases where the bar for compliance is lowered, predictability concerns carry no weight.

I have argued here that we must look more closely to see when predictability is important. There is value in predictability, and it hinges on the idea that we ought to respect people as autonomous agents. But we should not be too quick to cry 'predictability' when a precedent is overturned. There are situations in which predictability is not at stake. In such situations, we can put aside the predictability worry, and then we can see more clearly whether there are other considerations that favour keeping the precedent in place, or whether this is a situation where overturning a precedent entails no loss.

The upshot of all of this is that we should pay attention to context. Predictability is hugely important, but it is not always at stake. Arguments about when a precedent should or should not be overturned must be sensitive to the presence or absence of predictability implications for legal subjects. If there are such implications, then, of course, they must be weighed in the balance. But we should be careful not to manufacture a predictability concern to be weighed against the reasons that favour change, if no such concern exists.

PART V

EFFECTS OF PRECEDENT IN MORALITY AND LAW

34
Precedent Slippery Slopes

Katharina Stevens

1. Introduction

In *Texas v Johnson*, the US Supreme Court ruled that burning the American flag was protected speech under the First Amendment of the US Constitution. The case is famous for its contribution to US law about the freedom of speech. It is also famous (at least in legal-reasoning circles) because of Justice Brennan's justification. One part of his opinion reads as follows:

> To conclude that the government may permit designated symbols to be used to communicate only a limited set of messages would be to enter territory having no discernible or defensible boundaries. Could the government, on this theory, prohibit the burning of state flags? Of copies of the Presidential seal? Of the Constitution? In evaluating these choices under the First Amendment, how would we decide which symbols were sufficiently special to warrant this unique status? To do so, we would be forced to consult our own political preferences, and impose them on the citizenry, in the very way that the First Amendment forbids us to do.[1]

Brennan can be interpreted as using a *slippery slope argument*. Under this interpretation, he argues that deciding to count flag-burning as the desecration of a venerated object will make it likelier that other expressive acts will also be so classified.[2] This will lead to a slippery slope with the abhorrent result that government decision-makers habitually use their political preferences to decide what kinds of expressive acts are forbidden.

Several authors note that slippery slopes appear in precedent opinions especially often—both as part of a decision's justification and as an objection that needs to be answered.[3] For example, in another famous case, the Canadian Supreme Court decided that limiting the freedom of expression to prevent hate speech was constitutional. The court paraphrased possible slippery slope worries in order to answer them later:

> Additionally, condoning a democracy's collective decision to protect itself from certain types of expression may lead to a slippery slope on which encroachments on expression central to s. 2 (*b*) values are permitted. To guard against such a result, the protection of communications virulently unsupportive of free expression values may be necessary in

---

[1] *Texas v Johnson* 491 US 397 (1989).

[2] I thank Timothy Endicott for pointing out that Brennan might also be arguing that it would no longer be possible to reject such prohibitions on free-speech grounds without inconsistency. Then Brennan's argument would be a *logical* slippery slope (see section 2 for definitions).

[3] See, e.g., E Lode, 'Slippery Slope Arguments and Legal Reasoning' (1999) 87(6) Cal L Rev 1469; F Schauer, 'Slippery Slopes' (1985) 99(2) Harv L Rev 361; E Volokh, 'The Mechanisms of the Slippery Slope' (2003) 116(4) Harv L Rev 1026.

Katharina Stevens, *Precedent Slippery Slopes* In: *Philosophical Foundations of Precedent*. Edited by: Timothy Endicott, Hafsteinn Dan Kristjánsson, and Sebastian Lewis, Oxford University Press. © Katharina Stevens 2023. DOI: 10.1093/oso/9780192857248.003.0035

order to ensure that expression more compatible with these values is never unjustifiably limited.

Importantly, slippery slope arguments also seem to be *stronger* in contexts of precedent. For example, van der Burg distinguishes various kinds of slippery slope arguments but dismisses most.[4] One exception is slippery slopes in the context of precedent, which receive a much more positive treatment. Walton includes the 'precedent slippery slope' as a special type in his book-long analyses of slippery slope arguments.[5]

However, as a reviewer points out, Walton fails to explain how precedent slippery slopes are structured differently than other types.[6] And in later work, Walton merely classifies precedent as a factor that makes it harder to resist the slide down the slope.[7] Finally, Govier argues that precedent slippery slope arguments are always weak.[8]

Is it true that slippery slope arguments are stronger in the context of precedent? And if so, why? One possibility is Schauer's suggestion that the importance of slippery slope arguments in the law may be due to the allegiance that legal decisions owe to the past in determining the future.[9] Another is van der Burg's idea that each common law precedent makes the next judge feel committed to making the next step down the slope.[10] These explanations are useful when discussing slippery slopes generally, and they point in the right direction. But I think they paint only part of a picture that needs completion.

Here, I want to concentrate on the relationship between reasoning about setting precedents and slippery slope arguments. Their connection is important enough to warrant identifying a special argument type, the precedent slippery slope. This argument type has its own inner structure, which distinguishes it from other kinds of slippery slope arguments. However, I do not believe it likely that precedent slippery slope arguments will be strong often enough to be solely responsible for the special strength of slippery slopes in the context of precedent. I argue that not all slippery slopes that are used in the context of precedent are precedent slippery slopes—many of them are slippery slope arguments of another type. Understanding how precedent slippery slope arguments work also allows us to understand that and why *empirical* slippery slope arguments are stronger in the context of precedent. Taking slippery slope arguments seriously is therefore not just a strange quirk of common law judges. They should take them seriously, at least if they are interested in making good decisions from the point of view of political morality.

The chapter is divided into four sections. In section 2, I explain different types of slippery slope argument and Walton's attempt at establishing the precedent slippery slope. Then I discuss the peculiarities of reasoning with precedent that create the relationship between precedent and slippery slopes in section 3. Finally, in section 4, I present my argument for the existence of precedent slippery slope arguments as a special argument type. I explain the added strength that empirical slippery slope arguments have in the context of common law precedent.

---

[4] W van der Burg, 'The Slippery Slope Argument' (1991) 102(1) Ethics 42.

[5] D Walton, *Slippery Slope Arguments* (Clarendon Press 1992).

[6] W van der Burg, 'Walton`s Slippery Slope Arguments' (1993) 15(3) Informal Logic 221.

[7] D Walton, 'The Basic Slippery Slope Argument' (2015) 35(3) Informal Logic 273.

[8] T Govier, 'What's Wrong with Slippery Slope Arguments?'(1982) 12(2) Can J Philosophy 303; T Govier, 'The Famous, or Infamous, Slippery Slope' (2005) 38(152) Humanist in Canada 34.

[9] Schauer, 'Slippery Slopes' (n 3).

[10] van der Burg, 'Slippery Slope Argument' (n 4).

2. Slippery Slope Arguments

Slippery slope arguments are a kind of argument from consequences.[11] Specifically, they support rejecting some decision φ. This decision is admitted to be innocuous or beneficial by itself. The argument then shows that making it will lead to a further decision φ1 (by the decision-maker or someone else). This will lead to decision φ2, and so on, all the way down to decision ψ. ψ is clearly detrimental or even catastrophic. The argument then cites the ψ's detrimental nature as a reason not to make decision φ to begin with.

Theorists have discussed several versions of this argument type. The distinction between the logical and the empirical slippery slope is most generally accepted.[12] The difference lies in the mechanism explaining *why* decision φ will set the domino effect of later decisions in motion.

A. Logical Slippery Slope Arguments

Logical slippery slope arguments typically rely on *sorites*-style vagueness problems.[13] They claim that the slide down the slope must happen because there is no specific point for which a change in decision-making can be justified.[14] An example is the slippery slope argument about abortion.[15] The argument points out that the development of the fetus is incremental. Therefore, it is impossible to determine the point at which the fetus changes from a being that can permissibly be killed to a person who cannot. Once the abortion of a very young embryo has been permitted, it will be impossible to find a point at which the change to forbidding abortion can be justified. According to the argument, by allowing any abortions, one also commits to allowing the abortion of older and older fetuses, all the way to birth.

This example shows that the logical slippery slope argument works via the claim that making decision φ *logically* commits the decision-maker to also making the detrimental decision ψ. She will be led down a slope and, at any point, she will be unable to justify refusing the next decision on pain of inconsistency.

The logical slippery slope argument is often considered fallacious. This is because its users seemingly ignore that while no *specific* stopping point can be uniquely justified, it is easily justifiable to stop *somewhere* on the slope. Further, because stopping at all is justifiable and no specific stopping point stands out, it is also justifiable to select a random stopping point. Decision-makers can locate this point somewhere in the 'grey area' where it is hard to say whether making the next decision is beneficial or detrimental.[16] Therefore, logical slippery slope arguments, by themselves, hardly ever provide strong reasons. Generally, a strong slippery slope argument needs to have an empirical component.[17]

---

[11] Walton, 'Slippery Slope Arguments' (n 5); Walton, 'Basic Slippery Slope Argument' (n 7).

[12] The distinction is not universally accepted (see, e.g., M Hinton, 'Slippery Slopes and Other Consequences' (2017) 27 Logic and Logical Philosophy 453.

[13] An example of a *sorites*-style vagueness problem is the problem that would arise if one attempted to determine the exact point at which a person would become 'bald' if their hair was removed one hair at a time.

[14] Govier, 'What's Wrong' (n 8); van der Burg, 'Slippery Slope Argument' (n 4); Walton, 'Slippery Slope Arguments' (n 5); J Whitman, 'The Many Guises of the Slippery Slope Argument' (1994) 20(1) Social Theory and Practice 85.

[15] P Devine, 'On Slippery Slopes' (2018) 93(3) Philosophy 375.

[16] See, e.g., van der Burg, 'Slippery Slope Argument' (n 4).

[17] See, e.g., Govier, 'What's Wrong' (n 8).

B. Empirical Slippery Slope Arguments

Empirical (or causal) slippery slope arguments cite some contextual factor related to the issue about which the decision is made. They claim that because of this factor, making the decision φ will *cause* decision-makers to become more likely to make the decisions φ1, φ2, and so on, all the way to ψ.[18]

Williams distinguishes between having a *reasonable* justification for the claim that there is a relevant difference between two cases and being able to defend it *effectively*.[19] It is possible that a *reasonable* argument for a relevant distinction between two cases exists and can justify interrupting the descent down the slope. But the argument will not be *effective* if the distinction is not understood by the relevant decision-makers. Because of this lack of effectiveness, decision-makers will make decision φ1, φ2, and so on without noticing that a justification for deciding otherwise was available. They will *fail to distinguish* between distinguishable cases (I take this term from Enoch).[20]

Accordingly, empirical slippery slope arguments are strong when some factor can be identified which makes it likely that decision-makers will not recognize and make reasonable distinctions. Empirical slippery slope arguments can be defeated by showing that this factor is absent or not very strong. Volokh has produced a detailed analysis of many such causal mechanisms.[21] The list includes: each decision along the slope lowers the cost of making the next; each decision alters the decision-makers' attitudes to the next; each decision exploits the decision-makers' tolerance for small changes for the worse.

I want to point out that causal slippery slope arguments can include reference to *sorites*-style vagueness. In empirical arguments, vagueness is used as evidence that decision-makers will fail to notice when their decisions go too far. Here, the slippery slope argument uses the *sorites* problem as a causal factor, and is therefore an empirical argument. So, the mechanism behind the logical slippery slope can be a causal factor in an empirical slippery slope. This point will become important later.

There is, then, an important difference between logical and empirical slippery slope arguments which justifies treating them as two separate types. Logical arguments aim to show that making decision φ *commits* decision-makers to also making decision ψ. By contrast, empirical arguments aim to show that making decision φ, together with some contextual factors, will *cause* decision-makers to make decision ψ because of their *failure to distinguish*. Is there a similar difference between these two types and slippery slope arguments that use precedent?

C. Precedent Slippery Slope Arguments

Walton adds the precedent slippery slope to his book-length discussion.[22] This type of argument warns against making decision φ because it will set a precedent, leading to decisions φ1, φ2, φ3 …, and finally ψ. Van der Burg, reviewing the book, shows that Walton does not explain how the precedent slippery slope operates *differently* from the others.[23]

---

[18] cf van der Burg, 'Slippery Slope Argument' (n 4); Walton, 'Slippery Slope Arguments' (n 5); Whitman (n 15).

[19] B Williams, *Making Sense of Humanity and Other Philosophical Papers* (CUP 1995).

[20] D Enoch, 'Once You Start Using Slippery Slope Arguments, You're on a Very Slippery Slope' (2001) 21(4) OJLS 629.

[21] Volokh (n 3).

[22] Walton, 'Slippery Slope Arguments' (n 5).

[23] van der Burg, 'Walton's Slippery Slope Arguments' (n 6).

What could the distinguishing factor be? Walton's discussion does reveal something special about the precedent slippery slope. He points out that decision-makers use this argument to defend themselves against someone about whom they are deciding and who advocates for making decision φ. In the same passage, he discusses when arguments accusing decision-makers of inconsistency are cogent. The connection is clear. The decision-maker argues against φ via a slippery slope argument that predicts that should she later resist ψ, she will be accused of inconsistency because she refuses to follow her own precedent. Accordingly, the distinguishing feature of the precedent slippery slope argument is that it is interpersonal. It is based on the worry that the decision-maker will not be able to justify her refusal to make a decision further down the slope *to others*.

Walton claims that precedent slippery slope arguments are often successful. By contrast, Govier argues that these arguments are bound to fail.[24] This is because precedents allow for *distinguishing*. Precedent decisions must only be followed in situations that are similar in *all* relevant respects to the precedent. If the decision-maker can point to a difference, she may distinguish the precedent instead of following it. Even though it *seems* that the two situations are relevantly similar, the relevant difference shows that they are not. But if decision φ really is beneficial, and decision ψ really is detrimental, then there must be a difference between them that justifies stopping somewhere on the slope.

Therefore, others might *try* to accuse the decision-maker of inconsistency if she resists making further decisions down the slope. But the decision-maker is in fact not deciding inconsistently. Govier goes on to admit that sometimes slippery slope arguments using precedents *can* succeed.[25] However, this requires support from evidence that later *decision-makers* will fail to notice important distinctions. The precedent must become a causal factor in an empirical slippery slope argument.

3. Common Law Precedent

Govier's argument seems convincing, but I believe that she relies too heavily on distinguishing. The interpersonal factor that Walton points out has weightier implications for precedent than either author acknowledges. I will argue that this interpersonal factor destabilizes Williams's distinction between being able to provide a reasonable justification for distinguishing and being able to defend it effectively.[26] It makes the solution of *distinguishing* a precedent less available for escaping a slippery slope than Govier thinks.

My argument is especially strong in the context of common law precedent.[27] It relies on the justification for treating precedent as authoritative in the law. This justification has implications for what counts as good reasoning with precedent and what counts as a good justification for distinguishing, at least from the point of view of political morality. These implications are what makes precedent slippery slopes possible. Therefore, I must begin by explaining where the normative force of precedent comes from.

First, however, I should point out that any argument about precedent is complicated by the debate about what kind of inference grounds reasoning by precedent. The most

---

[24] Govier, 'What's Wrong' (n 8); Enoch (n 21) repeats this argument.

[25] Govier, 'What's Wrong' (n 8).

[26] Williams (n 19).

[27] I think the argument I present also works for precedent in non-legal contexts, in situations in which precedent has force because the precedent decisions created reasonable expectations.

popular contenders are the rule-based and the analogy-based approaches. For the sake of brevity, I cannot present my argument twice, once in the language of rules and once in that of analogies. I have decided to adopt an analogy approach for this chapter, largely because distinguishing plays a central role in my argument. Distinguishing is based on the identification of relevant differences. Only very few rule-based approaches suggest a rule-based way of dealing with distinguishing.[28] Most accept it as an aspect of reasoning with precedents that is concerned with analogical reasoning.

A. The Strange Force of Precedents

The difference between a precedent-setting decision φ and a decision α that does not set a precedent is that φ seems to create a *new reason* merely by existing.

Take the non-precedent-setting decision α. It can be used in an argument for repeating α in relevantly similar cases. However, this argument has to show that α was a good decision in its original case to provide *evidence* that making the decision α again would also be good, given the similarity of the two cases. The argument does not use the mere *existence* of α as a reason for repeating it.

This is different when it comes to a precedent-setting decision φ. The mere *existence* of φ is a reason for making the same decision in a case that is relevantly similar. In fact, in common law jurisdictions, where the principle of *stare decisis* makes precedents *binding*, this reason is a protected reason. In addition to providing a (first-order) reason *for* making the decision φ, it also provides a (second-order) reason excluding certain reasons that speak against decision φ.[29] If a *precedent-setting* decision φ exists, then the fact that it turned out to be wrong does not prevent using φ's existence as a reason to repeat it. And where precedent is binding, the wrongness of the decision cannot even be counted against repeating φ.

That a precedent-setting decision φ creates a reason for repeating it in relevantly similar cases is strange, as Schauer points out.[30] It suggests that precedent-setting decisions can *make* a later decision correct by existing. But surely the mere performance of an otherwise all-things-considered wrong action should not make that action *less wrong* in the future.

Elsewhere I have argued that this puzzle cannot be solved by pointing to the famous principle that *like cases should be treated alike*.[31] Nor do precedent decisions magically turn wrong actions into right ones. Rather, I argue that a decision (legitimately) becomes a precedent when certain *second-order reasons* apply that justify treating the decision as a precedent.

According to Joseph Raz, we can distinguish two kinds of reasons.[32] First-order reasons weigh directly on whether to make the decision φ. By contrast, second-order reasons are reasons for or against treating certain facts *as* first-order reasons. Certain kinds of second-order reasons can justify treating certain decisions as reasons to make them again in relevantly similar cases—that is, as precedents. For example, a decision-maker might make

---

[28] In K Stevens, 'Reasoning by Precedent—Between Rules and Analogies' (2018) 24(3) Legal Theory 216, I suggest that Horty and Bench-Capon's account could be read as integrating distinguishing into a rule-based approach; see J Horty and T Bench-Capon, 'A Factor-Based Definition of Precedential Constraint' (2012) 20(2) Artificial Intelligence and Law 181; J Horty, 'Rules and Reasons in the Theory of Precedent' (2011) 17(1) Legal Theory 1. Some reject distinguishing as a legitimate part of reasoning by precedent for this reason (see, e.g., L Alexander and E Sherwin, *Demystifying Legal Reasoning* (CUP 2008).

[29] G Lamond, 'Do Precedents Create Rules?' (2005) 11(1) Legal Theory 1.

[30] F Schauer, *Thinking Like a Lawyer: A New Introduction to Legal Reasoning* (Harvard UP 2012).

[31] K Stevens, 'Case-to-Case Arguments' (2018) 32(3) Argumentation 431.

[32] J Raz, *Practical Reason and Norms* (OUP 1999).

decision φ in a context where they can expect people to form reasonable expectations about their future behaviour on its basis. These expectations are important because there are moral reasons against disappointing reasonable expectations that one has allowed to form.[33] So, making the decision φ in those circumstances gives the decision-maker an additional reason to repeat φ in similar circumstances. In sum, as I see it, the normative force of precedent decisions originates from second-order reasons.

B. Precedent in the Law and the Principle of *Stare Decisis*

What does all this have to do with slippery slopes? I argue for a connection between what it means to reason *well* with common law precedent and the need to take the risk of slippery slopes seriously. I believe that this connection stems from the kinds of second-order reasons that give common law precedent its force. Therefore, I must now identify these second-order reasons.

One might think that the legal validity of the principle of *stare decisis* in common law jurisdictions is what gives common law precedent its force. No further inquiry is necessary. Indeed, in earlier work, I have said that the existence of this authoritative rule is the second-order reason that turns common law decisions into binding precedents.[34] For the purposes of that paper, this answer was sufficient. However, in this chapter, I am supporting a claim about how judges *should* reason from the point of view of political morality. Slippery slope arguments are usually about where judges *should* take the law with their decisions. They are warnings that decisions might have unintended, bad consequences. It is not enough to refer to the legal principles which give common law precedents their force. Those could at most tell us how judges must reason in order to generate legally valid precedents. If the goal is to argue about how judges should reason to make *good* precedent-setting decisions, then I need to show which reasons justify adopting the principle of *stare decisis* in the first place.

For this, I follow those who argue that the principle of *stare decisis* is justified through two kinds of rule-of-law considerations.[35] First, the requirement that people should be able to form reliable expectations about how state power will be wielded. Secondly, the requirement that people should not become, or have reason to think of themselves as, subject to the arbitrary power of individuals. I call the first requirement that of *reliability*. I follow Lewis in calling the second the requirement of *equality*, because it preserves the equality between the judge and the legal subject.[36]

I do not want to claim that these are the only reasons justifying the adoption of *stare decisis*. Other reasons have been discussed. For example, there are reasons having to do with the epistemic advantages of trusting earlier, good-faith, intelligent deliberators.[37] But I believe that rule-of-law reasons are central and therefore have an important impact on what it means to reason well with precedent. My argument does not rely on assuming that rule-of-law considerations are the only source of the force of precedent, only that they are a central source.

---

[33] cf T Scanlon, 'Promises and Practices' (1990) 19(3) Philosophy & Public Affairs 199.

[34] Stevens, 'Case-To-Case' (n 31).

[35] e.g. J Waldron, '*Stare Decisis* and the Rule of Law: A Layered Approach' (2012) 111(1) Mich L Rev 1; S Lewis, 'Precedent and the Rule of Law' (2021) OJLS 873.

[36] ibid.

[37] See, e.g., N Duxbury, *The Nature and Authority of Precedent* (CUP 2008); D Strauss, 'Common Law Constitutional Interpretation' (1996) 63(3) U Chi L Rev 877.

(i) The reliability requirement

The rule of law requires that the law be prospective, promulgated, clear, consistent, and relatively stable. All this is necessary so that legal subjects can reliably plan their lives within the boundaries of the law. It protects them from being uncertain whether the state may foil their plans at any juncture, or from being afraid that their actions may surprisingly be treated as illegal.[38]

However, there is not a jurisdiction where there is a promulgated, obvious legal answer to every possible question. At least the explicitly promulgated law has gaps. Therefore, judges find themselves with cases where the promulgated law does not explicitly determine their decision and they have discretion.[39] Judges may try to preserve their role as appliers of the law in these situations by deciding according to their interpretation of what the surrounding law implies. Nonetheless, their decision remains one that *manifests* the law *while* it applies it.[40] With respect to these kinds of decisions, the subjects of the law are not able to confidently form reliable expectations beforehand. They may be surprised.

Admittedly, this friction with the rule of law is unavoidable. It is impossible to make promulgated law that explicitly determines the outcome for every possible case. Nonetheless, the rule of law demands that public agencies *strive* to enable the formation of reliable expectations. And one way to limit the amount of discretion needed is by requiring judges to follow the decisions of earlier judges. That way, each decision made with discretion reduces the number of decisions that will be unpredictable from the legal subject's point of view. This is especially effective if lines of precedent establish common law rules that are more general and easier to understand than single precedents. This too is enabled by *stare decisis*. According to this argument, *stare decisis* is justified because it reduces the amount of discretion that judges use, enhances predictability, and diminishes uncertainty.

(ii) The equality requirement

Waldron points out that predictability can be accomplished in different ways.[41] Theoretically, if legal subjects know their individual judges well enough, even the judgments of a tyrannical judge-king become predictable. Predictability, to Waldron, is therefore not the main rule-of-law value. Instead, what Waldron focuses on is that legal subjects should be subject to the *law*, not to powerful people. And they should have assurance of this. The rule of law preserves people's dignity as equals even to those who will decide their case.

As before, a problem arises from the gaps in the promulgated law. Judges need to make decisions that are underdetermined by legal sources. Waldron argues that the rule of law requires judges to let their decisions be guided by any applicable legal reasons available, even if they are not binding. When judges preside over cases, they are not there as individuals with their own opinions. If they were, they would have personal power over legal subjects, which is unacceptable. Rather, they must be there as members of the court, an institution that applies the law, *not* an institution that realizes the preferences of the individual judge. They have to present their reasoning in a way that shows that they were trying to *apply* the law even if they needed to use discretion. In order to show that they did not take the opportunity to decide according to their own lights, they need to refer to *general legal* reasons. This

---

[38] cf, e.g., L Fuller, *The Morality of Law* (Yale UP 1964); J Raz, *The Authority of Law: Essays on Law and Morality* (Clarendon Press 1979).

[39] Depending on the legal theory you ascribe to, this might be strong or weak discretion.

[40] Or, if you are one of those who believe that the law already has an answer to any question, they identify law that is so hard to identify that it may come as a surprise to everyone.

[41] Waldron (n 35).

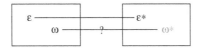

Figure 34.1 Is the similarity relevant?

enables the legal subjects whose case is being decided to recognize themselves as subjects of the law, not as persons subjected to the individual judge.

Importantly, when a later judge is confronted with a case similar to the earlier judge's, she *also* has to act as a member of the court. And the court already acknowledges the general legal reasons which determined the earlier case. The later judge, therefore, must convincingly show that she has followed the law as identified in the precedent, which requires either following the precedent or showing that distinguishing is appropriate. Doing otherwise would turn the idea that it was the law that decided the earlier case into a lie. Or it would mean that the present judge would rather realize her personal opinions by deciding the new case differently. Therefore, according to Waldron, the equality requirement justifies the principle of *stare decisis*.

C. Second-Order Reasons, *Stare Decisis*, and Relevant Similarities

I have shown that rule-of-law reasons play an important part in justifying the adoption of *stare decisis* and in giving precedent its force in common law jurisdictions. Now I argue that they do more than that. They *also* partake in determining *which* later cases are impacted by this force. This is because they contribute to determining which cases count as being similar to the precedent case *in all relevant respects*. Thereby, they impact what can count as a *good* reason for distinguishing. As I will argue later, this leads to the breakdown of Williams's distinction between reasonable and effective justifications for distinguishing and makes precedent slippery slopes possible.[42]

Once more: precedents apply to cases that are similar to them in *all relevant respects*. They do not apply to all cases that are similar to them *simpliciter*. All cases are *in some way* similar to each other. It is therefore important to know how to identify relevant similarities and differences between a present case and a precedent. When thinking about precedent from the analogy approach's point of view,[43] I believe the best solution to this problem comes from Juthe's account of what constitutes a relevant similarity in an argument by analogy.[44]

Arguments by analogy typically cite similarities between two cases to support the claim that there is a further similarity. Say that there is a similarity constituted by an element ε belonging to the earlier case and an element ε* belonging to the present case. The argument claims a further similarity between an element ω known to belong to the past case and an element ω* *claimed* for the present case (see Figure 34.1). For precedents, this further similarity would be the need for the decision φ. How do we determine whether the similarity between ε and ε* is relevant for the claimed similarity between ω and ω* and therefore for the existence of ω* in the present case?

---

[42] Williams (n 19).
[43] See the introduction to section 2 for an explanation for why I choose to approach this problem from the analogy-approach's point of view.
[44] A Juthe, 'Argument by Analogy' (2005) 19(1) Argumentation 1–27.

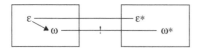

Figure 34.2 It is if there is an inferential connection in the earlier case

The answer is that the similarity between ε and ε* is relevant if, and only if, in the earlier case element ε was part of what determines that it had element ω. ε must have something to do with the existence of ω in the earlier case. Only then can the fact that the present case has ε* be a reason to expect that the present case has ω* (see Figure 34.2). The term Juthe uses for this is that there must be a *determining relation* between ε and ω.[45] Importantly, the kind of determining relation that is needed depends on the context in which the analogy is supposed to provide a reason. Probable, causal, epistemic, normative, evaluative, resultant, or supervenient relations could all be required.

Earlier I said that when it comes to reasoning by precedent, the feature ω from the precedent case that is supposed to be transferred into the feature ω* in the present case is the necessity of the precedent decision φ, which is supposed to be repeated in the present case.[46] I therefore ask: what kind of determining relation is needed between an element ε in a common law case and its precedent decision φ, so that the similarity between ε and a new case's ε* is relevant and gives a reason for making decision φ* in the present case?

A first option might be that the relation must be one of justification. The similarities between elements in the present case and those elements of the precedent case that *justified* the precedent decision are relevant. If factor ε justified decision φ in the precedent, then having ε* is a reason to make decision φ* in the present case. After all, if element ε was a reason for making decision φ in the past, it is still a reason for making φ in a later case. But that cannot be it. The fact that a precedent-setting decision φ exists gives a reason to make decision φ again in relevantly similar cases even if decision φ was *unjustified*. So we cannot rely on what justifies decision φ when determining relevant similarities. Even if there is nothing that justifies the precedent decision, there can be relevantly similar cases where the decision has to be repeated.

A second option is that the precedent judge must have *considered* element ε to be part of the justification for decision φ. After all, the principle of *stare decisis* requires that decisions are left to stand. Presumably, if a judge makes decision φ on the basis of elements ε1, ε2, ε3, and so on, then it is the combination of these elements and the decision that must be left standing. But this does not work either. What if the judge made the decision based on one set of elements but then justified it, in their opinion, with another set? Common law judges look at the precedent *opinions* to identify the meaning of a precedent. More importantly, *stare decisis* would not be justifiable on rule-of-law grounds if it required judges to follow a precedent judge's potentially secret ideas about what justified their decision. Then legal subjects could neither form reliable expectations nor would they be given good reason to believe that

---

[45] A very simple example: 'Dogs are like cats. Both are affectionate. Dogs are good pets. Therefore, cats are good pets.' That both cats and dogs are affectionate is a relevant similarity with respect to the conclusion *only* because in dogs getting attached to their owners *contributes* to their being good pets.

[46] Elsewhere, I have given a more complex and more accurate description of the analogical argument by precedent, according to which the conclusion of the analogical argument actually is that the precedent and the present case are 'legally the same', i.e. can be mapped for every legally relevant feature and do not have any legally relevant differences. Here, I have simplified the matter at the cost of slight inaccuracy in order to save space and to make the idea easier to understand. However, the interested reader can find the more complex account in Stevens, 'Between Rules and Analogies' (n 28).

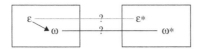

Figure 34.3 Should a similarity be recognized?

the law rather than the judge's idiosyncrasy was the basis for the decision.[47] So, at least from the point of view of political morality, judges should not determine relevant similarity by asking what the precedent judges *believed*.

This brings us to the third option: element ε must have been included in the precedent opinion as part of the basis on which the decision φ was made. Then and only then is the similarity between the precedent's element ε and the present case's element ε* relevant. This option has the advantage of explaining relevant similarity even where the precedent decision φ was unjustified. And because it requires judges to attribute relevant similarity if and only if the present case shares those elements that have been promulgated as the basis for the precedent, legal subjects can use precedent opinions to reliably predict which cases will be decided by application of the precedent. In addition, once their case has been decided, they can see that their judge decided for reasons that already belonged to the law, not their own. Therefore, from the point of view of political morality, there are strong reasons for judges to take this route: it preserves rule-of-law values and thereby the justification for adopting *stare decisis* in the first place.

We have seen that second-order rule-of-law reasons contribute to determining whether a similarity between a precedent and a new case is relevant. But they do more: they also contribute to whether two factors in a precedent and a new case count as similar. Let's say that there is an element ε in a precedent case which is included in the arguments supporting the decision φ, and described in a certain way. And let's say that a present case has an element ε* that *might or might not* be similar. How should a judge decide whether to count ε and ε* as a similarity (see Figure 34.3)? If there are several options for interpreting the description of ε, then the judge has to choose one of them to determine whether to treat ε* as being similar. What should that choice of interpretation be guided by?

Again, the second-order reasons that justify the normative force of precedent come into play. The interpretation of ε's description cannot aim at which interpretation would make the justification best. There might not be a good justification for the precedent, and still it exerts its force. And the interpretation cannot aim at what the precedent judge might have *meant* by the words she wrote. After all, legal subjects should not have to guess at the potentially idiosyncratic ways in which past judges would interpret their own words. That would undermine the rule-of-law justification for *stare decisis*. Rather, the interpreting judge must aim at identifying what can be considered to have been promulgated to the legal subjects.

How can the judge do this if she is faced with words vague enough that it is in question whether ε, which they describe, and the present case's ε* are relevantly similar? Well, the goal is to preserve the law's predictability and the legal subject's justified impression of being subject to the law instead of powerful individuals. Therefore, the judge must aim to identify the interpretation that she can reasonably expect an averagely reasonable (and adequately legally educated) legal subject would have expected to see.[48] If this legal subject can

---

[47] This worry applies, to a lesser degree, also to the first option.
[48] By a 'reasonable legal subject', I do not mean a person who embodies some abstract, *true* reasonableness. Rather, I have in mind a subject who recognizably belongs to the group of people who are actually governed by the law in question, who does not subscribe to false beliefs that would be idiosyncratic in this group, and who has

470 KATHARINA STEVENS

be reasonably expected to think that element ε* of the new case is similar to element ε of the precedent case, then the judge should treat them as similar. Or at least, that is what the second-order rule-of-law reasons justifying the principle of *stare decisis* counsel her to do.[49]

D. Distinguishing

Having said all this, I can finally talk about distinguishing. As I explained earlier, a common law judge can avoid following an apparently applicable precedent by distinguishing it. Govier argued that a decision-maker will always be able to do so to avoid a slippery slope:[50] A genuine difference in the normative desirability of two decisions must be based on a relevant difference between the two cases.

What I said about the impact that the second-order rule-of-law reasons have on the identification of relevant similarities has implications for distinguishing. Distinguishing is possible when two cases *look* like they are relevantly similar, but there is a relevant difference. I want to discuss two kinds of differences that may justify distinguishing.

First, the difference may be found between an element ε of the precedent case and what appears to be a similar element ε* of the present case. The opinion describes ε in a certain way. ε* *might* be considered similar to ε, but this is in question. The judge may then conclude that elements ε and ε* are not similar after all because some aspect of ε* makes them relevantly different. My earlier arguments about determining similarity apply to this situation. The second-order reasons justifying *stare decisis* direct the judge to identify a difference only if she can expect that a reasonable legal subject would expect that element ε and element ε* might not be considered similar.

Secondly, the difference may be identified when the present case has an unshared element ϋ, there is no description of a relevant element ε that might also fit ϋ in the opinion, and ϋ speaks against making the decision φ. When should a judge distinguish based on ϋ? Again, the second-order reasons justifying the principle of *stare decisis* play some role. Unexpected distinguishing disrupts the predictable working of the law that *stare decisis* sets up, and interrupts the implicit assurance that it is the law, not judges, that exerts power. Therefore, the judge should give some weight to whether a reasonable (and adequately legally educated) legal subject could be expected to realize that element ϋ could be used for distinguishing. At least, a judge should be concerned that a reasonable legal subject would easily understand why there is a basis for distinguishing once it is explained. If the judge expects that a reasonable legal subject would be very surprised and/or couldn't understand an explanation for distinguishing, then distinguishing undermines the rule-of-law justification for *stare decisis*. Therefore, the second-order reasons that justify the principle of *stare decisis* give rather weighty reasons against surprising distinguishing. Common law judges who want to make decisions that are good from the point of view of political morality have weighty reasons, ultimately stemming from rule-of-law considerations, to make decisions that they think these

a general knowledge and capacity for reasoning that is about average for this group. My notion of a reasonable subject is heavily influenced by Tindale's notion of the idealized audience (C Tindale, *Acts of Arguing: A Rhetorical Model of Argument* (State University of New York Press 1999)).

[49] I have debated whether I should say that if such a subject would not expect the interpretation, the judge should at least be able to expect that the subject would easily understand an explanation of why the interpretation is correct. This would still preserve the equality requirement but would not preserve the predictability requirement.

[50] Govier, 'What's Wrong' (n 8).

subjects will expect, or at least that they believe they can easily explain. Of course, sometimes judges might realize that the resulting decision would be manifestly unjust or unwise. It may cause enough harm or indignity to outweigh the rule-of-law reasons pulling the judge towards it. If that happens, good decision-making from the point of view of political morality may require a judge to distinguish unexpectedly.[51] The rule-of-law reasons that support the practice of precedent are outweighed. But this does not change the fact that their force exists in the application of precedent and must be overcome if unexpected or hard-to-understand distinguishing is to be justified.

4. Precedent Slippery Slope Arguments and Slippery Slope Arguments in the Context of Precedent

Why all this talk about judges who apply precedent? What does all of this have to do with slippery slope arguments, which are addressed to judges who decide whether to *set* a precedent?

Slippery slope arguments concede the goodness of decision φ but warn of its consequences for later decisions. When making precedent-setting decisions, judges have to think both about their present case *and* about implications for later cases. For common law precedent, later decisions are made by later judges. So, whether a slippery slope argument is successful depends on these later judges. I argue that there are slippery slope arguments in the context of common law precedent that work differently than their logical and empirical counterparts. This is because of the effect that the second-order rule-of-law reasons have on how later judges should make their decisions.

A. The Nature of Precedent Slippery Slope Arguments

The precedent-setting judge may worry about the later judges' failure to see the relevant differences between cases on the slope and fear a slippery slope because of this. However, then she is simply worrying about *empirical* slippery slopes that exist *in the context* of precedent. This comes down to what Enoch calls a decision-maker's 'failure to distinguish' between cases that should have been distinguished.[52] Our judge distrusts the later decision-makers, the later judges.

However, in the case of common law precedent, there is an additional worry: the weight of the second-order rule-of-law reasons may pull later judges down the slippery slope by committing them to the respective next step.

As I explained earlier, Williams points out that sometimes making a distinction between two cases can *reasonably* be defended, in that there is a good argument available for why the decision φ should be made in the first case but the decision φ_1 should not be made in the second case.[53] But for some audiences, such an argument might be too complex or require too fine-grained an understanding of the issue. As a result, the distinction cannot be defended *effectively*. Even though there is a good argument for making the distinction, people

---

[51] Similarly, good decision-making may sometimes even require decisions that go against what the law explicitly demands, as, e.g., Brand-Ballard argues (J Brand-Ballard, *Limits of Legality: The Ethics of Lawless Judging* (OUP 2010)).

[52] Enoch (n 20).

[53] Williams (n 19).

472 KATHARINA STEVENS

will not understand its basis. As discussed in section 1.2, this insight is important for explaining empirical slippery slope arguments, which are based on this *failure to distinguish* by decision-makers. But in the case of common law precedent, Williams's insight explains more.

Remember Govier's argument against the viability of precedent slippery slope arguments.[54] *If* decision φ is desirable but decision ψ is undesirable, then there has to be some difference between case φ and case ψ, and between φ and φ_1, φ_2, and so on. Such a difference allows distinguishing, which results in avoiding the slippery slope.

If Govier is correct, then a judge in a new case who is fully reliable in identifying relevant differences never makes a decision that goes too far down a slope. This is because she never misses reasons to distinguish. She recognizes them no matter how complex the arguments for them. She is in no danger of sliding down a slippery slope because of her own failure to distinguish. However, against Govier, I want to argue that even such an amazing judge could find herself making decisions that lead too far down a slope.

There is a set of cases in which this amazing judge would realize that an argument is available which successfully shows that a relevant distinction between the cases exists. Following the precedent would be going too far down the slippery slope. However, there is also an important subset to this set where the judge realizes that while *she* can see why distinguishing is warranted, a reasonable legal subject would probably not. The legal subject would *fail to distinguish* because the successful argument is too complex for her, or the required background knowledge too hard to acquire. For this subset of cases, the amazing judge sees that the distinction between precedent and the present case is reasonable but, with respect to the *audience of reasonable legal subjects*, not effective. Therefore, distinguishing would undermine the predictability of the law and the legal subject's confidence that they are being judged by the law, not the judge.

The amazing judge then has to do a calculation of harms: will it cause more harm to take one more step down the slope? Or will it cause more harm to disappoint reasonable expectations and make subjects feel that they were judged according to the personal opinions of the judge? In some cases, the balance of reasons would counsel our judge to make the next decision φ_1 down the slope. This can happen even though, without the additional reasons based on the rule-of-law requirements, φ_1 would not have been the right decision. The amazing judge finds that a combination of the existence of the precedent decision φ and the likely *failure to distinguish* by the reasonable legal subject, *commits* her to making the next step down the slope.

The more a precedent is cited and followed, the more legal subjects tend to form expectations on its basis and the greater the harms when these expectations are disappointed. Therefore, it is possible that once our judge has decided *not* to distinguish, the case for distinguishing further down the slope becomes more difficult. As the expectations of legal subjects become more assured, and as more legal subjects start acting on their reasonable assumptions, the weight of the rule-of-law reasons increases. When the question whether to make decision φ_2, or even decision ψ, comes around, moving further down the slope is again the lesser of two evils.

So, where the second-order rule-of-law reasons outweigh the reasons for distinguishing, a present judge can find that she *should* take that next step. And her taking the next step can strengthen these second-order reasons so that the judge in a later case may face the same

---

[54] Govier, 'What's Wrong' (n 8); Govier, 'Famous Slippery Slope' (n 8).

situation. When the precedent-setting judge made the first precedent-setting decision φ, she *committed* later judges to making the decisions φ_1, φ_2, φ_3, and finally ψ.

Therefore, the precedent slippery slope is its own type of slippery slope argument, complete with its own unique mechanism. Like the logical slippery slope argument, it is based on the worry that making the first decision φ will *commit* later decision-makers to the decisions φ_1, φ_2, φ_3, ..., ψ. And, like the empirical slippery slope argument, it relies on the insight that some distinctions between cases can be *reasonably* but not *efficiently* defended. However, the resulting *failure to distinguish* lies with legal *subjects*. Their expectations weigh on which decision should be made, changing the balance of reasons in favour of moving down the slope.

B. The Added Potency

My argument may have succeeded in showing that precedent slippery slope arguments are their own *kind* of arguments; but does this explain why slippery slope arguments are often stronger in the context of precedent? How often should we expect that the situation I described sustains itself long enough that an innocuous decision φ results in a slide to ψ? To be honest, I would be surprised if this happened very often. So, I do not think that the existence of precedent slippery slopes alone explains the strength of slippery slope arguments in the context of precedent.

However, I *do* think that understanding precedent slippery slopes allows us to understand this extra strength. Recall the connection between logical slippery slope arguments and empirical slippery slope arguments from the beginning of the chapter. The *sorites*-style vagueness problems that drive the logical slippery slope can *also* become a factor in empirical slippery slopes. This happens when the logical slippery slope argument fails—the decision-maker is *not* logically committed to the steps down the slope—but the decision-maker does not notice the failure. In this case, the *sorites*-style vagueness becomes the causal factor in an empirical slippery slope.

In the context of precedent, there is a similar connection between precedent slippery slopes and empirical slippery slopes. Real judges are, in fact, *not* as amazing as the amazing judge. They make mistakes, including ones in the estimation of how important it is to avoid further steps down a slippery slope, and how important it is to avoid disappointing reasonable expectations. Judges are usually concerned with rule-of-law values, or at least they have good reason to appear concerned with them.[55] If judges want to avoid seeming activist, they may be overly hesitant to distinguish surprisingly, and they may overestimate what will surprise legal subjects. This is especially likely when other conditions for slippery slopes exist. When confronted with factors that increase the likelihood of a slippery slope, judges must not only escape the causal mechanisms pulling them down the slope. They must also consider the likelihood that legal subjects may form expectations based on *their* failure to distinguish. Even when judges *should* conclude that this likelihood is not too great, they may not. Even when the precedent slippery slope argument fails, its mechanism may contribute to an empirical slippery slope. So the mechanism behind precedent slippery slopes routinely makes empirical slippery slopes slipperier in the context of precedent. That, together with the existence of genuine precedent slippery slopes, is why slippery slope arguments in the context of precedent are stronger than in other contexts.

---

[55] cf R Posner, 'What Do Judges and Justices Maximize? (The Same Thing Everybody Else Does)' (1993) 3 SCER 1.

5. Concluding Remarks

The slippery slope argument is often considered a fallacy. Those who subscribe to this view are prone to dismiss it upon identification. But as I have shown, there is good reason to take the argument seriously in the context of precedent. Judges are right to address slippery slope arguments in their opinions, to consider their strength in their decisions, and to try to cut off slopes before they can develop, for example by suggesting a stopping point to prevent the formation of expectations. Reasoning about whether to set a precedent, and how to present precedent decisions in opinions, should include consideration of slippery slopes and how to deal with them.

35

'A Previous Instance'

Yamamoto and the Uses of Precedent

Jeremy Waldron

1. Introduction

When an action takes place and it is controversial, people sometimes point to a version of it that was done some time before (perhaps long before). They call that a *precedent* and, despite the fact that the relation between the two events has little in common with the jurisprudential principle of *stare decisis*, they seem to imagine that the sheer fact of this event's having occurred in the past should help to allay misgivings about its present counterpart.

So, for example, the practice we call 'targeted killing' (used in the war against terrorism) is controversial. The US maintains a list of people (names, photos, dossiers, known whereabouts) associated with international terrorism. From time to time, names are downloaded from that list and a decision is made to act against the named individuals. They are hunted down, one by one, and killed either by drone strikes or by teams of special forces on the ground. Some of the targets are high-profile individuals, like Osama bin Laden, who was tracked down and killed in Pakistan in 2011. (I will mostly concentrate on this case in the discussion that follows). Many other targets—thousands, in fact—are foot-soldiers or relatively minor functionaries in terrorist groups whose names have come to the notice of US counter-terrorist forces in one way or another. Are all these targeted killings lawful? Are they morally justified? Should we be comfortable with the use of 'death squads' in the war against terrorism? Is it permissible to target individuals by name? Can high commanders be killed in this way, even away from the battlefield? Isn't that assassination? These questions continue to be debated and I have participated in those debates.[1] For the purposes of the present discussion, however, I will treat it as a rich and suggestive domain in which to explore the informal significance of precedent.

So let's consider something that is supposed to have set a precedent for targeted killing. In March 2015, US Attorney-General Eric Holder said this in an address to the Northwestern University School of Law:

> [I]t is entirely lawful … to target specific senior operational leaders of al Qaeda … This is not a novel concept. … [D]uring World War II, the United States tracked the plane flying Admiral Isoroku Yamamoto—the commander of Japanese forces in the attack on Pearl Harbor and the Battle of Midway—and shot it down specifically because he was on board. As I explained to the Senate Judiciary Committee following the operation that killed Osama bin Laden, the same rules apply today.[2]

---

[1] See, e.g., T Meisels and J Waldron, *Debating Targeted Killing: Counter-Terrorism or Extrajudicial Execution?* (OUP 2020).

[2] *Attorney General Eric Holder Speaks at Northwestern University School of Law* (5 March 2012) <http://www.justice.gov/iso/opa/ag/speeches/2012/ag-speech-1203051.html> accessed 10 March 2022.

Jeremy Waldron, *'A Previous Instance'* In: *Philosophical Foundations of Precedent*. Edited by: Timothy Endicott, Hafsteinn Dan Kristjánsson, and Sebastian Lewis, Oxford University Press. © Jeremy Waldron 2023. DOI: 10.1093/oso/9780192857248.003.0036

476 JEREMY WALDRON

Holder echoed a defence that had been offered by former Yale Law School Dean Harold Koh when, as Legal Adviser at the State Department, he defended targeted killing in a March 2010 address to the American Society of International Law:

> During World War II ... American aviators tracked and shot down the airplane carrying the architect of the Japanese attack on Pearl Harbor, who was also the leader of enemy forces in the Battle of Midway. This was a lawful operation then, and would be if conducted today.[3]

And by John Brennan, President Obama's Assistant for Homeland Security and Counterterrorism, at the Woodrow Wilson Center in April 2012:

> In this armed conflict, individuals who are part of al-Qa'ida or its associated forces are legitimate military targets. We have the authority to target them with lethal force just as we targeted enemy leaders in past conflicts, such as German and Japanese commanders during World War II.[4]

The story of Isoroku Yamamoto's targeting in April 1943 is well known.[5] A high-ranking admiral, he was responsible—and notoriously so—for planning and directing the Japanese Navy's attack on Pearl Harbor. A year or two later, during the Guadalcanal campaign, American codebreakers discovered that Yamamoto would be flying from New Britain (in the western Pacific) to visit bases on Bougainville Island. A force was sent to intercept the flight and Yamamoto's aircraft was shot down, killing all those on board including Yamamoto himself. This was a grievous blow to Japan and a source of considerable celebration for the Americans involved.

Now, our interest today is *precedent* and the question I want to raise in order to cast light on the uses of precedent is this: what is the significance of the Yamamoto killing supposed to be in twenty-first-century arguments about the targeted killing of terrorists and their leaders? Some scholars refer to the Yamamoto attack as '[a] valuable *case study*'.[6] Others say it is just an *illustration* of our practice. These characterizations are bland and non-committal. Still others, less cautiously, describe the Yamamoto attack as a sort of *precedent*. Robert Turner maintains that during wartime states may lawfully kill enemy combatants and their leaders, and he says: 'To mention but one precedent, during World War II the United States intentionally targeted an aircraft carrying Admiral Yamamoto.'[7] Jennifer Daskal uses the same term:

---

[3] H Koh, *The Obama Administration and International Law* (2010) American Society of International Law, Proceedings of the Annual Meeting 207–21.

[4] J Brennan, 'The Ethics and Efficacy of the President's Counterterrorism Strategy' (*Lawfare*, 30 April 2012) <https://www.lawfareblog.com/2012/04/brennanspeech/> accessed 10 March 2022.

[5] There is a good account of the Yamamoto operation in ALK Wey, 'Special Operations by Air Power' (2017) 64 Air Power History 33. See also R Cargill Hall (ed), *Lightning over Bougainville: The Yamamoto Mission Reconsidered* (Smithsonian Institution Press 1991); B Davis, *Get Yamamoto* (Random House 1969).

[6] TB Hunter, 'Targeted Killing: Self-Defense, Preemption, and the War on Terrorism' (2009) 2 J Strategic Security 1, 9–10 (emphasis in original).

[7] R Turner, 'An Insider's Look at the War on Terrorism' (2008) 93 Cornell L Rev 471, 487.

[T]he main precedent upon which the United States relies to justify its lethal-targeting operations is the killing of Admiral Isoroku Yamamoto ... who was shot down over the Pacific while en route to several forward-operating bases.[8]

So, what should we think? Is the Yamamoto attack a precedent? Do/can/should US counter-terrorism forces rely on it? If it isn't a precedent, might it nevertheless work *like* a precedent in some ways? What aspects of it help to justify our present practice? What sort of reliance is involved?

At the very least, there is a parallel. It is not hard to configure the dramas, respectively, of the Yamamoto attack and the bin Laden attack to make the analogy evident.[9] As Rachel VanLandingham put it in 2015, 'Reasoning by example, or making legal assessments by highlighting similarities and differences among examples, seems to dominate the Obama Administration's discussions of the legality of its armed response to al Qaeda and its associates.'[10] And she thinks that this resort to analogy is 'not surprising, given this method of reasoning's relative ubiquity not only in the canons of traditional legal reasoning, but in daily life as well'. But the popularity of analogy as a form of argument is inversely proportional to the articulation of how it's actually supposed to work. Just saying 'analogous' doesn't yet connect to the issue of justification. The force and structure of analogical argument is seldom explicitly discussed by those who talk this way; and, until it is, we will not get much illumination of our practice of precedent from the utility of examples like this.

2. A Legal Precedent?

If the Yamamoto attack is a precedent, it is not so in any juridical sense.[11] The decision to attack Admiral Yamamoto was taken by high American military commanders, including President Roosevelt, not by a judge. The question of its justifiability was never brought to or tested in a court in April 1943 (or before or since).

Compare the case of Richard Quirin, a German saboteur of German extraction who was executed in the electric chair in Washington DC in August 1942. Quirin was tried by a military tribunal set up under President Roosevelt's authority. When he complained that he was entitled as a US citizen to trial by a civilian court, the US Supreme Court turned him down, holding that '[c]itizenship in the United States of an enemy belligerent does not relieve him from the consequences of a belligerency which is unlawful because in violation of the law of war'.[12] So the case of *Ex parte Quirin* became available for citation as a precedent seventy years later when 9/11 terrorists made similar complaints about military tribunals at Guantanamo Bay.[13] Nothing like that happened in the case of Yamamoto.

---

[8] JC Daskal, 'The Geography of the Battlefield: A Framework for Detention and Targeting outside the "Hot" Conflict Zone' (2013) 161 U Pa L Rev 1165, 1213. See also J Steinberg and M Estrin, 'Harmonizing Policy and Principle: A Hybrid Model for Counterterrorism' (2014) 7 J National Security Law & Pol'y 161.

[9] M Hasian, 'American Exceptionalism and the Bin Laden Raid' (2012) 33 Third World Quarterly 1803, 1816: 'In the same way that US flyers had once "legally" downed the aircraft carrying Admiral Yamamoto Isoroku in 1943, the Navy seals *could be configured* as warriors in a legal armed conflict who were defending their nation from continuous and imminent attacks' (emphasis added).

[10] R VanLandingham, 'Lost in Translation? The Relevancy of Kobe Bryant and Aristotle to the Legality of Modern Warfare' (2015) 42 Pepperdine L Rev 393, 394–96.

[11] T Meisels, 'Reply to Professor Waldron' in Meisels and Waldron (n 1) 262: 'Of course this occurrence cannot in itself be taken as anything like a precedent, establishing a new rule of conduct.'

[12] *Ex p Quirin* 317 US 1, 37 (1942).

[13] See, e.g., *Hamdi v Rumsfeld* 542 US 507, 519, 523 (2004).

There is a tiny bit of case law in and around the Yamamoto incident. *Barber v Widnall (Secretary of the Air Force)*, in 1996,[14] concerned a pilot who wanted to receive all rather than just some of the credit for the attack. He questioned the Air Force's determination of attack credit in the federal courts. Sometimes in the law review literature, *Barber* is cited just in order to make the attack itself look like a judicial precedent.[15] But really *Barber* had nothing to do with the justifiability of killing Yamamoto. It was about the vanity of Lieutenant Barber, who believed that post-attack reports had been cooked to make it look as though Thomas Lamphier unjustly shared his (Barber's) credit for shooting down the plane with the admiral on board.[16]

However, the lack of any juridical context for the Yamamoto decision need not mean that important arguments usually associated with *stare decisis* were not canvassed at the time. Some could not have been. The argument in *Federalist* 78 that the system of precedent is justified because it disciplines and constrains judges can have no justification because there were no judges to discipline in this way.[17] Binding President Obama to a rule accepted by President Roosevelt is another thing altogether. Nor could we use the arguments about the importance of *stare decisis* to judicial legitimacy set out in *Planned Parenthood v Casey*.[18] But other precedent-related ideas may work in an informal way. Elsewhere I have argued that the juridical operation of *stare decisis* needs to be understood in terms of an earlier court presenting a perhaps-novel decision in a principled light and looking forward to its being accepted as such—and the underlying principle being accepted as such—by other courts in similar subsequent cases as a requirement of the rule of law.[19] There is no reason something like this could not take place informally outside the juridical context.

Our records of the Yamamoto decision are not perfect, but there appears to have been some discussion of whether this killing could be viewed as an instance of a principle. And some historians write as if its significance as a possible precedent might have been considered at the time in a forward-looking way:

> Clearly, killing him in the way we did led to an immediate military advantage, but by establishing a precedent in terms of which members of the supreme military command of a nation can expect to be targets at any time and in any place, did we restrict the future capacity of our own military commanders to exercise leadership?[20]

There was some consciousness that the decision might represent a watershed in our attitudes towards what otherwise may be regarded as assassinations. In his history of the Pacific War, Ian Toll argues that it represented the repudiation of 'a conventional understanding of military chivalry. ... Under no conceivable circumstance would George Washington have ordered a hit on William Howe or Robert E. Lee on Ulysses S. Grant.'[21] Joseph Dawson reminds

---

[14] *Barber v Widnall (Secretary of the Air Force)* 78 F3d 1419 (USCA 9th Cir, 1996).

[15] See, e.g., R Barnidge, 'A Qualified Defense of American Drone Attacks in Northwest Pakistan under International Humanitarian Law' (2012) 30 Boston U Int'l LJ 409, 437 fn 133.

[16] As well as the 9th Circuit decision, there is also a report of the decision of a 1985 Victory Credit Board of Review, in Hall (n 5) 190–95.

[17] L Goldman (ed), *The Federalist Papers* (OUP 2008) 385 (Alexander Hamilton: 'A view of the constitution of the judicial department in relation to the tenure of good behavior').

[18] *Planned Parenthood v Casey* 505 US 833 (1992).

[19] See J Waldron, '*Stare Decisis* and the Rule of Law: A Layered Approach' (2012) 111 Mich L Rev 1.

[20] M Davenport, 'The Killing of Yamamoto viewed as Ethically Wrong' in Hall (n 5) 54.

[21] I Toll, *The Conquering Tide: War in the Pacific Islands, 1942–1944: Vol II of The Pacific War Trilogy* (Norton 2015) 204.

us that the Duke of Wellington is reputed to have been aghast at the suggestion that Napoleon should be specifically targeted at Waterloo once his subordinates claimed they had him in their sights. This, he says, is 'the prime nineteenth century example of one senior officer who would not order disciplined troops to fire upon the known location of a senior enemy leader, while simultaneously efforts were underway to kill or maim hundreds or thousands of other enemy soldiers on the same battlefield'.[22] From Emer de Vattel in the eighteenth century[23] to the Israeli War Manual,[24] the custom of not targeting kings and generals had been recognized and affirmed.[25] The usual view is that such customs were abandoned after the end of the nineteenth century, with the increased barbarism of war.[26] And the Yamamoto attack stands as an icon of such abandonment. It might register then as a marker of what had become or was becoming a new era of total war.

If precedent were involved, we would have to consider too the possibility of distinguishing the two cases. Though both cases involved the killing of enemy commanders well away from the actual field of combat,[27] the Yamamoto killing attended the admiral's performance of command duties in and around an active theatre of war; he was travelling to visit bases in Bougainville that were important in a ferocious ongoing conflict. The bin Laden killing, by contrast, tracked the erstwhile al Qaeda leader down to something like his retirement home in Abbottabad, from which it was by no means clear that he was continuing to perform command functions in anything like a declared war. I guess one should say that whether this disanalogy is important depends on our securing a relatively precise sense of the principle that was supposedly established in 1943. But, of course, in the informal realm of 'precedent'—especially where, as in this case, the earlier decision is separated from the later one by seventy years and massively different circumstances—that is exactly the difficulty.

3. Customary Law?

I have said that the technical idea of precedent doesn't really apply to the relation between the Yamamoto attack and the 2011 targeting of Osama bin Laden. But there is one other technical legalism that might be relevant here.

We might say that the Yamamoto decision instantiates state practice for the purposes of customary international law (CIL).[28] 'Practice in war reflects the widespread acceptance of this.'[29] Harlan Grant Cohen says that international lawyers 'cite the United States'

---

[22] J Dawson, 'Targeting Military Leaders: A Historical Review' in Hall (n 5) 35.

[23] E de Vattel, *The Law of Nations* (first published 1760, B Kapossy and R Whitmore eds, Liberty Books 2008) 565–66 (book III, ch 8, §159).

[24] *Israeli Manual on the Laws of War*: 'An attempt on the lives of enemy leaders (civilian or military) is forbidden', cited by N Melzer, *Targeted Killing in International Law* (OUP 2008) 48.

[25] Some deny that this was ever a real principle. But those who insist that such attacks were *always* accepted as OK mostly mention the vulnerability of high commanders in battle 'leading from the front' rather than the separate issue of their being tracked down and targeted. See also Hall (n 5).

[26] Toll (n 21) 204.

[27] For consideration of this, see M-E O'Connell, *The Choice of Law against Terrorism* (2010) 4 J National Sec L & Pol'y 343, 361.

[28] M Lewis, 'Responses to the Ten Questions' (2011) 37 Wm Mitchell L Rev 5021. Patricia Zengel calls the Yamamoto killing an application of customary law in P Zengel, 'Assassination and the Law of Armed Conflict' (1992) 43 Mercer L Rev 615, 627. Zengel says the Yamamoto killing 'clearly was permissible under international law' (ibid).

[29] B Ross, 'The Case for Targeting Leadership in War' (1993) 46 Naval War College Rev 73, 81.

480   JEREMY WALDRON

assassination of Japanese General [sic] Yamamoto during World War II for evidence of the rules on targeted killing and the geographic scope of the battlefield'.[30]

But even if Yamamoto is analysed in these terms, it is hardly enough by itself to constitute or furnish anything like conclusive evidence in regard to the status of targeted killings of commanders in international humanitarian law. There are a number of difficulties. To be evidence of state practice for the purposes of CIL, the killing of Yamamoto would have to stand alongside lots of other instances (in and around 1943), including the practice of other states. Also, it is not clear that Yamamoto instantiates the appropriate kind of normativity: at best, it represents the US taking upon itself a licence to kill rather than constraining its conduct pursuant to the recognition of an international obligation. And, finally, there is precious little in the way of *opinio juris* to complement the sheer fact of the 1943 decision. Though—as I pointed out in section 2—there was some canvassing of alternative possible positions, it is not clear that there was enough in the way of legal/normative analysis for the purpose of the formation of CIL.

4. Non-Judicial Precedent?

Let's return to precedent. Certainly it is true that the idea of precedent can be used loosely as well as in the strict juridical sense. The *Oxford English Dictionary* gives as its first definition 'A previous instance taken as an example or rule by which to be guided in similar cases or circumstances; an example by which a comparable subsequent act may be justified.' This is an entirely non-technical idea.

Some legal scholars speak of 'non-judicial precedents', referring to the ability of institutions other than courts to settle issues by their actions for subsequent decision-makers, or, as Michael Gerhardt puts it, 'the constitutional significance of precedents made by public authorities other than courts'.[31] Gerhardt has made a study of non-judicial precedent, mostly in constitutional matters, where issues that appeared to be left open or uncertain by the constitutional text and/or by the array of existing judicial decisions were settled by a decision of some institution other than a court. So, for example, the death of President William Henry Harrison in 1841 left it unclear whether his Vice President (John Tyler) was supposed to succeed to the presidency itself under Article II of the Constitution or was simply entitled to exercise presidential powers until a successor was elected. The matter was settled finally and definitively in 1967 by the Twenty-Fifth Amendment, but in the intervening 126 years it was governed by the decisions of Tyler himself and the Senate in 1841 in resolutions referring to Tyler as President of the US. Those determinations settled the matter for all practical purposes and governed the succession to the highest office of seven other vice-presidents (the last being Lyndon Johnson).[32] As Gerhardt puts it:

> Tyler's succession to the presidency became a precedent because of the concerted efforts of Tyler and other national leaders to make it one. They knew that people facing the same circumstances in the future would seek guidance from what Tyler did immediately after

---

[30] HG Cohen, 'The Primitive Lawyer Speaks! Thoughts on the Concepts of International and Rabbinic Laws' (2020) 64 Vill L Rev 665, 668.
[31] MJ Gerhardt, 'Non-Judicial Precedent' (2008) 61 Vand L Rev 713, 715. See also M Gerhardt, *The Power of Precedent* (OUP 2004) ch 4.
[32] Gerald Ford's succeeding Richard Nixon took place under the auspices of the Twenty-Fifth Amendment.

Harrison's death; thus, they took great pains to construct a precedent that would withstand the test of time.[33]

Does the slaying of Admiral Yamamoto fit the bill of a non-judicial precedent as Gerhardt understands it? Certainly that is how it would have to be regarded if the term 'precedent' attached to it were not to be a complete misnomer. But 'non-judicial precedent' is so far just a negative idea, it doesn't offer much for the affirmative part of our analysis.

To the extent that Gerhardt adds affirmative content, it seems to revolve around two ideas of intention and discoverability. Non-judicial precedents, he says, 'are past constitutional judgments or activities of non-judicial actors in which public authorities try to invest normative authority'.[34] They are recognizable as embodying such an intention and readily discoverable for anyone who subsequently faces an issue of the same kind. It's a little unclear, but I suspect that Yamamoto falls short on both these criteria. Though, as I have said, the likely precedential effect might have been mentioned in the planning of the Yamamoto attack,[35] the decision to go ahead was not publicly represented as the selection of a principle to govern future cases of that kind. And really Yamamoto came into its own as a precedent only seventy years later when Obama Administration officials required some 'authority' to defend their practice of targeted killing, and rooted around for what they hoped would be a disarming and persuasive analogy. Now Gerhardt has largely worked alone in this field and his characterization of non-judicial precedent should not be regarded as the be-all and end-all. But apart from providing useful terminology, he really doesn't make a case that can be applied to the relation between the Yamamoto and the bin Laden attacks.

5. Showing vs Creating Permissibility

Still, we ought to persevere because Yamamoto may be a precedent in some other sense. Let me approach the matter as follows. When I see the Yamamoto attack being cited in debates about targeted killing, I am never sure whether

(a) the attack is being cited as something that was already evidently permissible in 1943, so that later cases supposedly analogous to it (our targeted killings) get the benefit of that manifest permissibility,

or whether

(b) the Yamamoto example is being cited as something that makes a twenty-first century targeted killing permissible by providing a precedent for it even though that precedent decision was not in and of itself so evidently justifiable as the instances that are now supposed to 'follow' it.

This is a subtle but important distinction. Juridical precedent is characteristically understood in the second way, (b). A case arises whose proper disposition is unclear or unsettled in law; a court nevertheless decides that case in one particular way; and afterwards, the fact

---

[33] Gerhardt, *Non-Judicial Precedent* (n 35) 722.
[34] ibid 783.
[35] See n 20 and accompanying text.

482   JEREMY WALDRON

of it having done so makes it settled law that any subsequent case should be decided in the same way. The court in the earlier case did not have the benefit of such a precedent. So, the later cases are on a surer footing than the earlier one; but they are so precisely by virtue of the precedent that the earlier case establishes. Most precedents in the law reports work like this.

6. Controversy at the Time

But arguments of type (a) are not unknown, especially in informal cases. Often the logic is: Yamamoto's killing was *obviously* permissible at the time; and killing bin Laden now is like killing Yamamoto; so the earlier case shows that the practice currently in question never really was troublesome. It dispels any aura of controversy.

'Yamamoto' might be operating here like the word 'Hitler'—as a sort of conversation stopper. When people bring up Adolf Hitler in debates about targeted killing, they say it is just obvious that targeting Hitler would have been permissible, and since bin Laden is in the same league, morally, as Hitler, no one can object to bin Laden being targeted.[36] Now actually Isoroku Yamamoto was in many ways an honourable man, but at the time he was demonized as a cunning and treacherous savage.[37] And so the attack on him could be presented as manifestly justifiable, and that manifest justifiability projected forwards to the killing of Osama bin Laden. Since killing Yamamoto was obviously right, who can deny that killing bin Laden was right also? The use of the word 'surely' is often a marker of the supposed force of this reasoning:

> If it is moral and legal to individually target uniformed enemy military officers, surely the same goes for leaders of terrorist organizations. It cannot be the case that law and morality give the latter greater protection than the former.[38]

Or it can be phrased as a rhetorical question. Homeland Security Secretary Jeh Johnson asked, in a speech delivered at Yale:

> Should the legal assessment of targeting a single identifiable military objective be any different in 2012 than it was in 1943, when the U.S. Navy targeted and shot down over the Pacific the aircraft flying Admiral Yamamoto, the commander of the Japanese navy during World War II, with the specific intent of killing him?[39]

Analogy is important in this rhetoric. But it is not operating to *construct* a sense of rightfulness in the later attack. Instead, it is operating to make vivid what we are all supposed to have already known then and can be reminded that we know now about the targeting of

---

[36] See the discussion in Meisels and Waldron (n 1) 201–02.

[37] Thomas Lamphier, one of the pilots who shot down Yamamoto's aircraft, said this in the *New York Times* in 1945: 'Yamamoto! All the cunning and power-madness of his race embodied in one man, the epitome of every brutal, strutting little savage he commanded. From infancy ... he lived out every day of his vengeful life ... in anticipation of the moment when he would stand with his foot upon the throat of the United States and lay down the Emperor's dictates for its bondage', quoted in Hall (n 5) xi.

[38] I Somin, 'Admiral Yamamoto and the Justification of Targeted Killing' (*The Volokh Conspiracy*, 13 May 2011) <http://volokh.com/2011/05/13/admiral-yamamoto-and-the-justification-of-targeted-killing> accessed 10 March 2022.

[39] J Johnson, 'National Security Law, Lawyers, and Lawyering in the Obama Administration' (2012) 31 Yale L & Pol'y Rev 141, 147.

scoundrels like this. Thus, it is sometimes said that because it never occurred to anyone in 1943 to challenge the Yamamoto attack, we can project that clear sense of justifiability from the 1940s onto targeted killings in the present-day war against terrorism.[40]

In fact, the decision to kill Admiral Yamamoto was actually quite controversial in 1943. According to Craig Symonds's authoritative naval history, *World War II at Sea*, it was controversial on tactical grounds because it might disclose the codes the Americans had broken.[41] And it was also controversial in principle. Admiral Nimitz questioned its legality and rumour has it that the query went up to President Roosevelt who made the final decision. Symonds adds: 'And finally, there was the moral issue. Men died in combat every day, but to target a specific individual like this seemed more like assassination. Did the United States want to do that?' John Paul Stevens, until recently an Associate Justice on the US Supreme Court, was one of the codebreakers who secured the information that formed the basis of the Yamamoto attack. He was troubled by the prospect at the time and talked of it later. According to Diane Amann, 'Stevens affirmed that the Yamamoto incident led him to conclude that "[t]he targeting of a particular individual with the intent to kill him was a lot different than killing a soldier in battle".'[42]

The controversy presented itself as an issue about assassination. On the one hand, scholars say that 'the weight of history has never viewed the Yamamoto ambush as an illegitimate assassination'.[43] On the other hand, an unpleasant 'vibe' of assassination seems to linger:

Even the lawful targeting of leaders during wartime, which is not properly considered assassination at all, has been rare because of the strength of the norm against assassination itself. In effect, the norm appears to 'spill over' to create a stigma against such actions. . . . And although willingness to target opposing leaders during hostilities seems to be increasing, the association of this practice with assassination continues to render it ethically problematic, irrespective of its legality.[44]

Perhaps it is prudent to say with Rick Pildes and Sam Issacharoff that '[t]argeting critical enemy leaders is a longstanding, *if delicate*, facet of warfare'.[45]

7. Traditional Arguments for Precedent

I distinguished two uses of 'precedent'—(a) an earlier case which shows in itself that the conduct in question is obviously justified; and (b) an earlier case in which the justifiability of

---

[40] See, e.g., R Delahunty and J Yoo, 'What Is the Role of International Human Rights Law in the War on Terror?' (2010) 59 DePaul L Rev 803, 808, say of strikes like that against Yamamoto that 'their legality has been accepted without significant controversy'. See also G Blum and P Heymann, 'Law and Policy of Targeted Killing' (2010) 1 Harv National Security J 145, 150, where they talk of 'the uncontroversial targeted killing of Japanese Admiral Isoroku Yamamoto'.

[41] C Symonds, *World War II at Sea: A Global History* (OUP 2018) 410ff.

[42] D Amann, 'John Paul Stevens, Human Rights Judge' (2006) 74 Fordham L Rev 1569, 1583. See also J Rosen, 'The Dissenter: Justice John Paul Stevens' (*New York Times*, 23 September 2007) <https://www.nytimes.com/2007/09/23/magazine/23stevens-t.html> accessed 10 March 2022 for further dimensions of Stevens's concerns.

[43] T Yin, 'Broken Promises or Unrealistic Expectations: Comparing the Bush and Obama Administrations on Counterterrorism' (2011) 20 Transnt'l L & Contemporary Problems 465, 486.

[44] W Thomas, 'Norms and Security: The Case of International Assassination' (2000) 25 Int'l Security 105, 114–15.

[45] S Issacharoff and R Pildes, 'Targeted Warfare: Individuating Enemy Responsibility' (2013) 88 NYU L Rev 1521, 1570.

484 JEREMY WALDRON

the conduct wasn't already settled, but whose settlement in that case has begun the process of treating later instances as justified. I now want to turn to (b), for the among the arguments that conform to this model are found many of the considerations associated with *stare decisis* in modern jurisprudence. I have in mind:

- arguments about the fairness of treating like cases alike;
- arguments about predictability, expectations, and reliance;
- arguments about the importance of institutional settlement and repose;
- arguments about the conservation of epistemic effort; and
- Burkean arguments about the desirability of doing things the same way over and over again, while resisting the unseemly charms of innovation.

None of these is ever laid out fully in the Yamamoto literature. But there are shreds and inarticulate hints of these arguments here and there—which in my opinion is typical of the informal use of precedent in circumstances of great controversy. People just spout phrases which they think might lend some credibility to their position or at least silence an opponent. That's how argument goes in public life, by and large.

The other thing about the these 'arguments', when you list them as I have done, is the remarkable variety of considerations associated with *stare decisis* that might conform to the (b)-type logic. Consider, for example, the argument from consistency and comparative justice. It's an argument that rests on the idea of the fairness of treating like cases alike. It begins with the decision in the earlier case, which might have gone either way. But having been made, that decision lays down a marker that can then be taken up on behalf of one of the parties in the later case. That party might be in danger of having their conduct judged wrongful in the later case. But they plead that that would be unfair. In the earlier case, an equivalent party was exculpated or vindicated. Tom Lamphier was not condemned as an assassin for his attack on Yamamoto. So it would be unfair to condemn the Navy SEALs in 2011 as assassins for their attack on Abbottabad.

It's a bit far-fetched, reaching back as it does almost seventy years for 'the like case' that it says now should be treated alike. There has been an awful lot of water under the bridge in those seventy years, ranging from the massive assassination programme associated with Operation Phoenix in Vietnam through the Castro and Trujillo attempts to the US executive orders of 1976 and 1981 prohibiting any person employed by the US government from engaging in (or conspiring to engage in) assassination.[46] One can't help noticing the element of cherry-picking as people reach back into history to find a precedent that they can demand consistency with as a matter of fairness. One can't help thinking that a good lawyer would have a field-day 'distinguishing' the two cases that are supposed to be bound together by fairness.

Of course, it need not be the actual killers who are supposed to benefit from like cases being treated alike. Maybe it's unfair to criticize the government's actions in 2011 when 'like' actions were approved in 1943. Or maybe the point of the consistency argument was to show that there is nothing in our history for bin Laden in fairness to claim the benefit of.

---

[46] For the Phoenix Program, see S Hersh, 'Moving Targets' (*New Yorker*, 15 December 2003) <https://www.newyorker.com/magazine/2003/12/15/moving-targets> accessed 10 March 2022; D Andrade, *Ashes to Ashes: The Phoenix Program and the Vietnam War* (Lexington Books 1990). For the US regulation, see US Executive order 12333 (1981) §2.11, and the discussion in Meisels and Waldron (n 1) 199–202.

Yamamoto had no legitimate complaint in 1943 and so it would be unfair to ascribe such a complaint to the leader of al Qaeda in 2011.

Sometimes the argument about fairness is connected to the importance of predictability and reliance on settled expectations. In principle, they are distinct: the comparative justice argument we have just been considering is supposed to work whether its beneficiaries were induced to rely on the earlier decision or not.[47] But the SEALs who attacked the compound in Abbottabad (and those who sent them) might say that they were entitled to rely on an expectation of legitimacy arising out of the decision-making associated with the Yamamoto attack. They might say that operatives need such islands of predictability as they organize their plans and actions and navigate around legal and moral constraints in these troubled times. Unless prior events like the Yamamoto attack are treated as precedents, it might be said, our forces will be operating in a sea of uncertainty with no established landmarks. Again, one may wonder about the picking-out of landmarks from a seventy-year-old history, but the argument has something to it.

Pulling back further yet from the dictum 'Treat like cases alike', it may be argued that *the law itself* requires this issue to be settled, whether this settlement is a matter of fairness or reliance in regard to the parties involved or not. As at the end of the nineteenth century, there was simply uncertainty surrounding the issue of targeting enemy leaders—a grey area between combat and unlawful assassination. Going ahead with the Yamamoto attack, despite whatever controversy was involved, might be taken to have settled that, and once settled it should not lightly be allowed to become undone.[48]

The settlement idea might imply that it doesn't matter how the issue was decided so long as it was settled. Any certainty, any repose in the back-and-forth over an issue like this, is worth it, no matter how arbitrary. An altogether different argument under model (b) points to the method by which the matter was settled. True, the issue was uncertain as the earlier case (Yamamoto in our paradigm) came up for decision. But as it cropped up, people thought long and hard about the issue that arose. And a lot of hard work in figuring it out was done in reaching the earlier decision. Now we have the advantage of that for our future decisions, at least if the decision we face now is configured in broadly the same way as the decision that was figured out then. There is no need to repeat the process; no need to reinvent the wheel.

In a way, this is a Burkean argument: it is wrong for us to try and figure everything out for ourselves. At least sometimes we should rely on the wisdom of our ancestors. In 1943, we had the benefit of the wisdom of the greatest generation; in 2011, we have nothing but the pert loquacity of paper theorists. We want to get the matter right, but figuring it out anew for ourselves may not be the best plan. Why not? Perhaps, as Burke puts it, we should hesitate 'to put men to live and trade each on his own private stock of reason; because we suspect that this stock in each man is small, and that the individuals would do better to avail themselves of the general bank and capital of nations, and of ages'.[49]

Again, I don't know how far these considerations appealed or ought to have appealed to those who directed the targeting of members of al Qaeda. Epistemic humility was not really the hallmark of the Obama Administration. Perhaps, given the seriousness of the matter, involving as it did the targeting and killing of individuals, it was reassuring to be able to say to

---

[47] See the attempt to untangle considerations of consistency, predictability, and reliance in Waldron, '*Stare Decisis* and the Rule of Law' (n 19).

[48] For the principle of institutional settlement, see H Hart and A Sacks, *The Legal Process: Basic Problems in the Making and Application of Law* (W Fricke and P Eskridge eds, Foundation Press 1994) 1–9.

[49] E Burke, *Reflections on the Revolution in France (1790)* (CUP 2013) 129.

ourselves that there was not really any innovation involved. Officials could say that 'the notion of targeted killing using military force [was] not a novel concept'.[50]

> The use of drone strikes against Al-Qaeda does not mark the first time the United States has engaged in targeted killing during wartime. During World War II, President Roosevelt authorized a mission to shoot down Japanese General Yamamoto's plane after learning of his flight plans. Thus, ... precedent exists for targeting individuals for death during wartime.[51]

This precedent might afford some sort of psychological comfort in troubling times, an island of reassurance—this is business as usual—amidst otherwise extraordinary measures that have had to be taken.

8. Just Something to Say

And, in the end, that might be all we can really say about the precedential character of the Yamamoto attack. It hints at various considerations, and makes them available as one-liners in the political rhetoric of officials like Koh and Holder and Brennan. But, out of the judicial context, they are but shards and shreds of argument. We may say to ourselves that there is something here, but it might be in a rather anxious and half-hearted spirit: 'These fragments I have shored against my ruins'.[52] We want to have something to say, in defence of targeted killing, and we want it to sound impressive. But we are nervous about simply asserting in our own voice, in moralistic mode, that we think it is a good idea.

I am reminded of an observation by Justice Scalia on the quite different topic of the citation of foreign law in American judicial opinions, which, he thought, might help to rescue an activist judge from a feeling of naked embarrassment as he goes about inventing new constitutional restrictions:

> Let's face it. It's pretty hard to put together a respectable number of pages setting forth (as a legal opinion is supposed to do) analytical reasons for newly imposed constitutional prescriptions or prohibitions that do not at all rest (as the original Bill of Rights did not rest) upon logic or analysis, but rest instead upon one's moral sentiments, one's view of natural law, one's philosophy, or one's religion. ... [W]ithout something concrete to rely upon, judicial opinions will be driven to such philosophic or poetic explanations as 'At the heart of liberty is the right to define one's own concept of existence, of meaning, of the universe, and of the mystery of human life'. Surely not a happy state of affairs for a court of law. It will seem much more like a real legal opinion if one can cite authority to support the philosophic, moral, or religious conclusions pronounced. Foreign authority can serve that purpose.[53]

---

[50] J Bennett, 'Exploring the Legal and Moral Bases for Conducting Targeted Strikes outside of the Defined Combat Zone' (2012) 26 Notre Dame J L Ethics & Pub Pol'y 549, 556.

[51] L Kwoka, 'Trial by Sniper: The Legality of Targeted Killing in the War on Terror' (2011) 14 U Pa J Const L 301, 304.

[52] TS Eliot, *The Wasteland* (Boni and Liveright 1922), line 430.

[53] A Scalia, 'Foreign Legal Authority in the Federal Courts' (2004) 98 Am Society of International Law Proceedings, 305, quoted in J Waldron, *Partly Laws Common to All Mankind: Foreign Law in American Courts* (Yale UP 2012) 51.

One dredges up a decision by a Canadian court, or the ECHR, or by a court in India or Zimbabwe. One puts that into one's opinion, and '[b]y God it looks lawyerly'.[54]

Well, similarly here. In the debate about targeted killing, officials had to defend Obama Administration policy on the hunting down and killing of high-ranking terrorist leaders. They were legal officials and so they would be self-conscious about saying, 'Well, it just seems the right thing to do.' So they reached back seventy years to a decision—in some ways similar, in other ways quite different—that was made during the Second World War, not by a court but also (as their decision was) by military and administration officials. But they called it a *precedent*, gleaning a suggestion of some extra layer of technical and lawyer-like respectability. It didn't really amount to much more than pointing, in the words of the *Oxford English Dictionary*, to 'a previous instance'. There were a few bits of 'chaff and rags and paltry blurred shreds of paper',[55] alluding to the force that a precedent might have. But did it add anything beyond, 'We did this before, and—lo!—we can do it again'? Not much, I fear.

9. Conclusion

If you have read this far, I am grateful to you for indulging me in the rather peculiar method of this chapter. It has brought together a few quite disparate elements of my scholarly interests: an abstract analysis of arguments that lie behind the idea of *stare decisis*,[56] the normative controversy over targeted killing in the modern war against terrorism, and some rich detail on the killing of Admiral Isoroku Yamamoto and the political use of that killing to shore up our sense of the legitimacy of modern-day targeting.

One might have pursued the topic of the informal use of precedent in purely analytic terms, using algebra to distinguish a precedent decision, D_1, from a subsequent one, D_2. And so on. I did that in '*Stare Decisis* and the Rule of Law',[57] and I came close to it again in the distinction between models (a) and (b) of the precedential argument in section 3 of this chapter. But I thought the piece could be livened up with a bit of thick description in order to show some of the indeterminacies and uncertainties that surround the real-world uses of precedent, especially when their historical significance is invoked in informal political contexts.

The downside of this approach is that our conclusions about the use of Yamamoto's killing as a precedent might not generalize to other cases in which informal and non-judicial precedents are invoked. I don't want to denigrate the analytical argumentation that might be required to see if this is so. But we can only pursue those analytical arguments if we have a reasonably rich sense of the messiness—in general—of real-life cases. And the best way to get that is to explore the messiness of one or more cases in particular.

---

[54] Justice Scalia as quoted by Rachel Morris as quoted in turn by Waldron (n 19) 251 fn 22.

[55] Burke (n 49) 128.

[56] Waldron, '*Stare Decisis* and the Rule of Law' (n 19); Meisels and Waldron (n 1) particularly 210–13 (on the Yamamoto killing).

[57] Waldron, '*Stare Decisis* and the Rule of Law' (n 19).

36

Consistency in Administrative Law

Adam Perry[*]

1. Introduction

In 1978, thirteen-year-old Carl Bridgewater was murdered during a burglary at Yew Tree Farm in the West Midlands, UK. Jim Robinson and Vincent Hickey were charged with the murder. Although they insisted they were innocent, both men were convicted and sentenced to life in prison. The two men were still in prison, eighteen years later, when it was revealed that the police had fabricated the evidence against them. Robinson and Hickey were released, and the Secretary of State accepted that there had been a miscarriage of justice.

There is a right to compensation for miscarriages of justice under section 133 of the Criminal Justice Act 1988. The amount of compensation is fixed by an independent assessor, who must consider 'any other conviction of the person and any punishment resulting from them' when fixing compensation for non-pecuniary losses, such as loss of reputation. The assessor assigned to Robinson's case, Sir David Calcutt QC, deducted 10 per cent from the compensation otherwise due to him because of his long criminal record. The assessor assigned to Hickey's case, Lord Brennan QC, deducted 25 per cent from the compensation otherwise due to Hickey considering his long criminal record. Hickey's criminal record was, however, no longer, or worse, than Robinson's.[1]

Hickey appealed. Like cases had been treated unalike, he said. He and Robinson had like criminal records, yet Robinson had been treated better than him. At trial, the judge in *O'Brien v Independent Assessor*[2] thought that two things were 'incontrovertible':

> First, if the same assessor had determined ... [both] cases, he would not have made such different deductions ... Secondly, when considered individually ... [the Hickey deduction] cannot be said to be irrational or otherwise open to challenge.[3]

The assessments were collectively inconsistent, but individually reasonable. This second point was decisive:

> [The assessor for Hickey] simply disagreed with the 10% deduction which ... had been made in *Robinson*. Was he to make what he believed (and, in my judgment, permissibly believed) to be the correct decision or was he bound to allow himself to be influenced by

---

[*] I would like to thank Thomas Adams, Kate Greasley, Hafsteinn Dan Kristjánsson, Sandy Steel, and especially Andrew Currie for comments on drafts of this chapter and a related article. Thanks also to participants in seminars at Queen's University and Oxford University.

[1] Indeed, Hickey's record was not as bad as Robinson's. See *O'Brien v Independent Assessor* [2007] UKHL 10 [24].

[2] *O'Brien v Independent Assessor* [2003] EWHC 855 (Admin). Robinson's and Hickey's claims were heard along with others challenging decisions in respect of compensation for miscarriages of justice. One of these other claims was brought by Michael O'Brien.

[3] ibid [44].

an award with which he disagreed? In my judgment it was neither irrational nor otherwise unlawful for [the assessor] to apply deductions ... which were in all other respects un-objectionable. He was not bound by any principle of consistency because there was good reason in his permissible judgment to depart from Sir David's approach.[4]

An assessment that would be lawful, taken on its own, does not become unlawful because it is inconsistent with another lawful assessment.

Hickey's appeals to the Court of Appeal and House of Lords also failed. Lord Bingham, in the House of Lords, explained:

[T]he assessor's task in this case was to assess fair compensation for each of the appellants. He was not entitled to award more or less than, in his considered judgment, they deserved. He was not bound, and in my opinion was not entitled, to follow a previous decision which he considered erroneous and which would yield what he judges to be an excessive award.[5]

Even though Sir David and Lord Brennan disagreed as to the appropriate deduction, each acted reasonably and, hence, lawfully.

Many claimants have tried, as Hickey did, to convince a court that an administrative decision in their case was unlawful simply because it was less favourable than a decision in a previous and like case.[6] Had these claimants succeeded, there would be something akin to a system of administrative precedent. The decision by an executive official in one case would bind an official in a later and like case, even if the official in that later case believed that the earlier decision was erroneous. The 10 per cent deduction in Robinson's case would dictate the permissible deduction in Hickey's case, for example, even though the assessor in Hickey's case was convinced 10 per cent was too low.

In general, English courts have rebuffed these attempts, as the courts rebuffed Hickey's attempt.[7] I want to know whether they are right to do so. I won't defend the claim that an official should decide a case as an official decided a previous and like case. I'm sure that claim is false, for reasons I explain in section 3. But I shall defend a similar claim:

Consistency Where A and B are officials, A should decide a case as B decided a like case, unless A is more likely to decide the case correctly than B.

This claim holds true, I'll say, even when the official in the later case believes that the earlier case was decided incorrectly. This claim is relatively modest, but it is practically important. It suggests, for instance, that Lord Brennan was wrong to deduct 25 per cent from Hickey's award and that he should have deducted 10 per cent instead, as Sir David did. I shall also defend:

---

[4] ibid [47].

[5] *O'Brien* (n 1) [30].

[6] See, e.g., *R (Gallaher Group Ltd) v The Competition and Markets Authority* [2018] UKSC 25 [24] ('the domestic law of this country does not recognise equal treatment as a distinct principle of administrative law') (Lord Carnwath). There are helpful overviews in K Steyn, 'Consistency—A Principle of Public Law?' (1997) 2 Judicial Review 22; J Randhawa and M Smyth, 'Equal Treatment and Consistency Before and After *Gallaher*' (2018) 23 Judicial Review 159.

[7] English courts have been more amenable to the argument that the treatment of a case is unreasonable due to the different treatment of a previous and like case. But on this approach, 'differential treatment of like cases per se is insufficient to invalidate a decision': Randhawa and Smyth, ibid 162.

Enforcement	It should be unlawful for A not to decide a case as B decided a like case, unless A is more likely to decide the case correctly than B.

Essentially, it should be unlawful to breach consistency. Based on this claim, I shall suggest, tentatively, that the courts should have held that Lord Brennan's decision to deduct 25 per cent from Hickey's award was unlawful. I defend these claims with respect to England and English law, though I believe that appropriately modified versions would hold true more generally.

2. Consistency

I want to start by clarifying the relevant notion of consistency.

One type of consistency is consistency between a decision in a case and a prior commitment. A 'commitment' includes a policy and a promise as to how a case, or cases of a class, will be decided. If an official adheres to a commitment when deciding a case addressed by that commitment, then the official's decision is consistent with that commitment. Consistency with prior commitments is required, under some conditions, by the doctrine of legitimate expectations.[8] If, for example, Lord Brennan had promised Hickey that he would deduct only 10 per cent from his compensation, then Hickey could rely on the doctrine of legitimate expectations to challenge Lord Brennan's deduction of 25 per cent.

It is an interesting question whether the law should require consistency with prior commitments and, if so, why. I suspect that the answer will appeal to practical rationality. Commitments such as policies and promises can be understood as, or involving, plans or intentions. One is rationally required to follow through on one's plans or intentions unless one reconsiders them.[9] Reconsideration is rational only under special circumstances, such as when one is presented with new evidence.[10] By insisting that officials follow through on their commitments, absent special circumstances, the law upholds the rational requirements applicable to officials. Much more would have to be said to substantiate this suggestion, of course, but I shall not try to do that here. My interest is not consistency with commitments.

A second type of consistency is between the decisions in, or treatment of, two cases.[11] Let us say that the decisions in two cases are consistent if and only if the cases are alike and the decisions are alike. The decisions are inconsistent if and only if the cases are alike and the decisions are different. When are two cases 'alike'? Not when they are identical. No two cases are identical. Even though Robinson and Hickey were convicted of the same murder and spent the same number of years in prison, for example, their cases were different in many respects. The parties were different, the cases were heard at different times, and so on. Let us say, instead, that two cases are alike if and only if their fact patterns are the same.[12] Robinson's and Hickey's cases share a fact pattern, despite differing in many particulars.

---

[8] See, e.g., *R v North and East Devon Health Authority, ex p Coughlan* [2001] QB 213 (CA). For a discussion of the doctrine, see F Ahmed and A Perry, 'The Coherence of the Doctrine of Legitimate Expectations' (2014) 73 CLJ 61.

[9] T Scanlon, 'Reasons: A Puzzling Duality?' in RJ Wallace, P Pettit, and S Scheffler (eds), *Reason and Value: Themes from the Moral Philosophy of Joseph Raz* (OUP 2004) 244.

[10] M Bratman, 'Planning and the Stability of Intention' (1992) 2 Minds and Machines 1, 4–8.

[11] H Wilberg, 'A Duty of Consistency? The Missing Distinction Between Its Two Forms' (UK Constitutional Law Blog 27 February 2020) <https://ukconstitutionallaw.org/2020/02/27/hanna-wilberg-a-duty-of-consistency-the-missing-distinction-between-its-two-forms/>.

[12] J Brand-Ballard, *The Limits of Legality* (OUP 2010) 256.

Within the category of consistency between cases, we can draw a further distinction. Like cases could be decided at the same time or at different times. There is synchronic inconsistency if like cases are decided differently at the same time.[13] If a single official makes synchronically inconsistent decisions, then that official will normally hold inconsistent beliefs. The official believes that a case with a certain fact pattern merits one type of treatment and, at the very same time, believes that it does not merit that type of treatment but some other type of treatment instead.[14] Many philosophers think that it is irrational to hold contradictory beliefs at the same time.[15] If the law should uphold the rational requirements applicable to officials, then there may be a simple argument for the unlawfulness of certain types of synchronic inconsistency between cases. My concern is not synchronic consistency between cases, so I shall not pursue this possibility further.

Diachronic inconsistency—inconsistency between cases decided at different times—is trickier. Even when two cases were decided by one official, and even when that official holds inconsistent beliefs, we still cannot infer any irrationality if the cases were decided at different times. Yesterday I believed that Johannesburg is the capital of South Africa. Today, having thought better, I instead believe that Johannesburg is not the capital of South Africa. These beliefs are inconsistent, but I am not irrational for holding both if I hold them at different times. It is not irrational for me to change my mind. The same is true of officials. So, the irrationality of inconsistent beliefs does not explain what, if anything, is wrong with diachronic inconsistency between cases.

My interest, going ahead, is diachronic inconsistency between cases. This is the more common type of inconsistency between cases; most cases are not decided at the same time. It is also the only type of inconsistency at issue in Robinson's and Hickey's cases. There was no policy or promise in these cases, and they were decided at different times by different officials. I want to know what, if anything, is wrong with this type of inconsistency and what, if anything, judges should do about it.

When two cases are alike, I shall sometimes refer to the decision in the earlier case as a 'precedent'. If the official in the later case makes a like decision, then he or she 'adheres to' precedent; otherwise, he or she 'departs from' precedent. This is just a convenient shorthand. By using these terms, I do not mean to propose that administrative law should incorporate the equivalent of the common law doctrine of precedent, with all its elaborate distinctions and rules.

3. Fairness

My argument starts with the principle that like cases should be treated alike, which I term the 'fairness principle'.[16] I then show how to move from the fairness principle to consistency.

---

[13] See, e.g., *R (Middlebrook Mushrooms Ltd) v Agricultural Wages Board of England and Wales* [2004] EWHC 1447 (Admin) (holding that the differential treatment of mushroom pickers and other agricultural workers in the same legislation was unreasonable).

[14] This assumes that the official believes that the fact pattern *uniquely* merits one type of treatment and a different type of treatment.

[15] See, e.g., J Broome, *Rationality Through Reasoning* (John Wiley & Sons 2013) 155.

[16] Others also characterize the principle as part of fairness, including R Dworkin, *Taking Rights Seriously* (OUP 1978) 113. But the principle is also claimed on behalf of other normative domains. See, e.g., *Matadeen v Pointu* [1999] 1 AC 98, 109 ('treating like cases alike and unlike cases differently is a general maxim of rational behaviour') (Lord Hoffmann); *AM (Somalia) v Entry Clearance Officer* [2009] EWCA Civ 634 [34] (the principle is 'perhaps the most fundamental principle of justice').

492   ADAM PERRY

Much of this section summarizes and refines an argument that I have developed elsewhere for precedent following in the judicial context.[17]

A. Fairness Principles

Formulating a plausible version of the fairness principle is not easy. Here is a first attempt:

Strong Fairness Principle   For any two like cases c_1 and c_2, where c_1 is earlier than c_2, if you treat c_1 in some way, then fairness provides a decisive reason to treat c_2 alike and reason not to treat c_2 unalike.

To say that there is a decisive reason for you to do something is another way of saying that you should or ought to all-things-considered do it. To decide a case differently than a like case would be to act contrary to a decisive reason were the strong principle sound. Lord Brennan decided Hickey's case differently than Sir David decided a like case. So, Lord Brennan would have acted wrongly were the strong principle sound.

The strong principle is not sound, however. Deciding a case incorrectly does not make it right to decide a like case incorrectly. Imagine that Sir David erred by deducting a mere 10 per cent from Robinson's compensation. Lord Brennan should not repeat that mistake. Any principle that tells us otherwise is a bad principle.[18]

We can avoid this objection by weakening the fairness principle. Here is one way to weaken it:

Moderate Fairness Principle   For any two like cases c_1 and c_2, where c_1 is earlier than c_2, if you treat c_1 in some way, then fairness provides a *pro tanto* reason to treat c_2 alike and reason not to treat c_2 unalike.

According to the strong principle, fairness provides a *decisive* reason to treat like cases alike. The moderate principle is weaker because it says that fairness provides merely a *pro tanto* reason to treat like cases alike. *Pro tanto* reasons can be outweighed. Perhaps the reason provided by the moderate principle *is* outweighed when it favours an otherwise incorrect decision. Lord Brennan would have a reason of fairness to make the same decision as Sir David, even if Sir David erred. If he erred, though, then Lord Brennan would have an even stronger reason to make the correct decision instead.

Much of the difficulty remains, however. It is simply not true that a wrong decision in one case is *any* reason, of any weight, to treat a like case wrongly as well. Robinson was imprisoned even though he was innocent. That fact does not provide even the slightest support for imprisoning the equally innocent Hickey, for example.[19]

So, the strong and moderate principles are not appealing. Before we abandon the idea that it is fair to treat like cases alike, it is worth reflecting a little more on our intuitions. Imagine that an immigration officer reviews our visa applications. Our applications are alike. Both should be rejected. And, indeed, mine is rejected. Yours, however, is granted. I cannot

---

[17] A Perry, 'Precedent and Fairness' (unpublished manuscript, available on request).

[18] P Montague, *Comparative and Non-Comparative Justice* (1980) 30 Philosophical Quarterly 131, 133; L Alexander, *Constrained by Precedent* (1989) 63 So Cal L Rev 1, 10; G Lamond, 'Precedent and Analogy in Legal Reasoning' in EN Zalta (ed), *Stanford Encyclopedia of Philosophy* (2016).

[19] Alexander (n 18) 10; L Alexander, 'Precedent' in D Patterson (ed), *A Companion to Philosophy of Law and Legal Theory* (John Wiley & Sons 2010) 495. I offer additional objections to the Moderate Fairness principle in Perry (n 17).

object that I have been treated incorrectly; after all, the correct decision *was* to reject my application. But there is still something objectionable here. What is objectionable—what is unfair—is that you have been treated better than me even though we are no different.[20] A good principle would accommodate this intuition without committing the same mistakes as the strong and moderate principles.

Here is a principle that can do so:

Weak Fairness Principle   For any two like cases c_1 and c_2, where c_1 is earlier than c_2, if you treat c_1 correctly, then fairness provides a *pro tanto* reason for you to treat c_2 alike and not to treat c_2 differently.[*]

The condition does not apply if an earlier case was decided incorrectly. As a result, the weak principle does not demand that we repeat our errors, unlike the strong and moderate principles. The condition *is* satisfied when the earlier decision was decided correctly, so it explains why it was unfair to correctly refuse my visa application and grant yours. The Weak Fairness Principle gives us everything we need in a principle of fairness. I shall treat it as true in what follows.

B. Fairness to consistency

There is, of course, a big difference between the Weak Fairness Principle and our target claim, Consistency. Now I want to bridge that gap.

If the Weak Fairness Principle is sound, and officials in like cases at different times disagree as to the correct decision, then there is an asymmetry between:

- the two officials deciding differently when the official in the later case is correct; and
- the two officials deciding the same way when the official in the earlier case is correct.

In the first scenario, if the later official decides differently than the earlier official, then the later official decides correctly. But he or she does not decide fairly. He or she does not decide unfairly either. Fairness is simply not at issue.[21] In the second scenario, if the later official decides in the same way as the earlier official, then the later official decides correctly *and* fairly.

Suppose that the two officials are equally likely to reach a correct decision. Following and departing from precedent have the same probability of yielding a correct decision. But following precedent has a greater probability of yielding a decision that is also fair. So, following precedent is the weakly dominant alternative: it is better in one respect (the value realized) and worse in no other (including the probability of realizing a value). To illustrate, suppose that Sir David and Lord Brennan are equally likely to arrive at a correct assessment. Since Lord Brennan is more likely to decide fairly by following Sir David's decision than by departing from it, he should follow Sir David's decision. Lord Brennan should therefore deduct a mere 10 per cent from Hickey's award.[22] In essence, Lord Brennan is faced with a tie between his view and Sir David's, which fairness breaks in favour of following Sir David's.[23]

---

[*] This formulation appears, with slight changes, in Perry (n 17).

[20] D Lyons, 'Formal Justice' (1972) 58 Cornell L Rev 833, 843.

[21] At least, by virtue of any principle of fairness about the like treatment of like cases.

[22] Does it matter if there was more than one correct decision available? No. As long as the initial decision was correct the Weak Fairness Principle favours its repetition—even if there was an alternative, equally correct decision.

[23] I thank Andrew Currie for help with this argument.

494 ADAM PERRY

Here is an analogy. You can play on either of two pinball machines. You have the same odds of winning on either machine. If you win on either, then you will receive a free turn. But if you win on the left-hand machine, it will give you a second free turn. On which machine should you play, all else being equal? The answer is, of course, the left-hand machine. The probability of a payoff is the same, but the payoff is larger. Similarly, if Lord Brennan is equally likely to decide correctly whether he makes a like or unalike decision, but he obtains the 'fairness bonus' only if he makes a correct and like decision, then he should make a like decision.

It is easy to see that the same reasoning applies with even greater force when the earlier official is *more* likely to decide correctly than the later official. In that case, following precedent is strictly dominant: it is better than departing from precedent in every respect. There is a higher probability of realizing some value *and* the value realized is greater.

If the earlier official is not more likely to decide correctly than the earlier official, nor are they equally likely to decide correctly, then only one possibility remains: the later official is more likely to decide correctly. So, another way to state the conclusion is that a later official should follow precedent unless he or she is more likely to decide correctly than the earlier official. And this, of course, is just consistency.

4. Enforcement

With my argument for consistency in hand, I turn to enforcement. Enforcement, to recall, is the claim that it should be unlawful for officials not to decide cases as earlier officials decided like cases, unless the later officials are more likely to decide correctly. In other words, there should be a legal requirement to adhere to consistency. By a 'legal requirement', I mean a judicially enforceable requirement.

My argument for enforcement is simple:

P1   There is a reason to legally require officials to do what a moral requirement directs them to do if they would be more likely to satisfy that requirement as a result.

P2   Officials would be more likely to satisfy consistency were they legally required to do so.

C   So, there is a reason to legally require officials to satisfy consistency.

I shall treat P1 as given. It follows from a general understanding of judicial review as a set of requirements aimed at bringing officials into greater conformity with the moral and rational requirements already applicable to them.[24] The conclusion states only that there is a reason for it to be unlawful to violate consistency. It does not state that this is what should be done overall or all things considered; that is a stronger claim, which may be correct but which I shall not argue for here. I shall focus instead on P2.

---

[24] For some initial efforts in this direction, see A Perry, 'Plan B: A Theory of Judicial Review' (unpublished manuscript, available on request).

A. The Help that Doctrine Can Provide

To establish P2 it is necessary to show three things:

- that officials would sometimes violate Consistency left to their own devices;
- that judges can force officials to change their decisions; and
- that judges can identify would-be violations of consistency.

The first condition is obviously true. Officials are neither saints nor paragons of rationality. There is probably no moral or rational requirement that they fully adhere to, and consistency is no exception. Hickey's case, and others like it, confirm the point.[25] Nor does much need to be said on the second point: judges have a suite of orders and remedies designed to bring recalcitrant officials into line with the law. The third condition, however, requires explanation.

To reliably identify would-be violations of consistency, judges must be able to do two things. One is to identify when like cases are alike. The other is to work out whether a later official is more likely to decide a case correctly than an earlier official. I do not minimize the challenges involved here; at the same time, these are challenges which judges are well equipped to meet.

Start with identifying whether two cases are alike. This is what judges do every time they decide whether a judicial precedent is distinguishable. Indeed, a common law judge's greatest claim to expertise is working out whether cases are alike. Of course, there are differences between the judicial and administrative contexts. It can be difficult to identify what exactly are the reasons in administrative matters. And there may be no detailed explanation of those reasons. On the other hand, judges already review administrative decisions to determine whether they are based on all relevant 'considerations' (meaning, reasons). Indeed, this ground is the 'bread and butter' of judicial review.[26] The implication is that judges are competent to identify reasons in administrative contexts.

Turn now to identifying whether a later official is more likely to make a correct decision. In general, agents are equally likely to decide a matter correctly if they have:

- the same ability to evaluate evidence on a matter; and
- the same evidence on the matter.

Conversely, an agent is more likely to be correct than another agent on a matter only if he or she has a greater ability to evaluate evidence, greater evidence, or both.[27] By the 'same ability to evaluate evidence', I mean to describe an equivalent overall ability, which can be the result of different inputs. Two officials can be equally able, for example, even though one is more intelligent and the other is more experienced. And by the 'same evidence' I do not mean evidence of the same particular facts. The evidence before Sir David was about Robinson whereas the evidence before Lord Brennan was about Hickey. In some sense, they did not have the same evidence. What matters for our purposes is whether there is evidence that establishes the same fact pattern.

---

[25] For many examples along the same lines, see the discussions in K Steyn, 'Consistency—A Principle of Public Law?' (1997) 2 Judicial Review 22; Randhawa and Smyth (n 6).

[26] M Elliott and J Varuhas, *Administrative Law* (OUP 2017) 237.

[27] SE Bokros, 'A Deference Model of Epistemic Authority' (2021) 198 Synthese 12041, 12049.

As with determining likeness across cases, comparing evaluative abilities and access to evidence is familiar work for judges. Sometimes judges compare their own abilities and access to those of other bodies. This is what judges do every time they decide whether to defer to the opinion of an executive official or legislature on epistemic grounds, for example.[28] Sometimes, judges must compare two other bodies' abilities and access. If there are competing expert witnesses at trial, for instance, the judge must decide who is more likely to come to a correct opinion of a factual issue, based on the witnesses' qualifications, track records, access to the scene, familiarity with the lay witnesses, and so on.

In summary, if the argument for enforcement is controversial, it is because P2 is controversial. And if P2 is controversial, it is because that premise requires judges to identify would-be violations of consistency. However, identifying would-be violations of consistency merely requires judges to perform tasks that are analogous to tasks they already perform, and which it is generally accepted that they are competent to perform. That is enough to show that P2, and hence the argument for enforcement, is plausible.

To be clear, I mean only that judges are competent to work out whether cases and officials are alike. I do not mean that they are necessarily more competent than anyone else. If a later official thinks that he or she is better able to assess evidence or has better access to evidence than an earlier official, then it may be appropriate for a judge to take that view into account.

B. Rules and Exceptions

If my argument for enforcement is right, then judges should review official decisions for consistency. Generally, the burden to prove that an administrator has acted unlawfully lies with the claimant. Suppose that a claimant can show that his or her case is like an earlier case, which was decided more favourably. Should the claimant also need to show that the later official is not the superior of the earlier official?

No. When there is no evidence as to which of two events occurred, a rough-and-ready rule is to assign the same probability to each event.[29] If I flip a coin, and you have no reason to think it landed one way over the other, you should assign a 0.5 probability to the event of it landing heads and a 0.5 probability to the event of it landing tails. By the same reasoning, if a court has no evidence as to which official decided correctly, then it should proceed on the basis that it is equally likely that each official decided correctly. So, in the absence of any reason to think that one of these officials is more accurate than the other, the court should treat the officials as equally likely to have decided correctly.

The implication is that if a claimant can prove that two cases are alike, then the claimant should prevail, in the absence of evidence that the earlier official was more likely to have decided correctly. The claimant need not demonstrate anything else for a court to be able to conclude that consistency has been violated. The burden does indeed lie with the claimant to show that like cases were treated differently. Once that burden is satisfied, though, the

---

[28] See, e.g., *Huang v Secretary of State for the Home Department* [2007] UKHL 11 [16] (the court should give 'appropriate weight to the judgment of a person with responsibility for a given subject matter and access to special sources of knowledge and advice'); *R (Begum) v Headteacher and Governors of Denbigh High School* [2006] UKHL 15 [34]; *International Transport Roth GmbH v SSHD* [2002] EWCA Civ 158 [87].

[29] This is the principle of indifference. As formulated, the principle is too simple. Exactly how to correct for its flaws is a matter of intense philosophical debate. For an overview and a possible solution, see M Huemer, *Paradox Lost* (Palgrave Macmillan 2018) c 8.

burden shifts to the official to bring forward evidence that he or she is more likely to have decided correctly than the earlier official.

When the burden of proof shifts in this way, it is appropriate to distinguish a rule from its exception.[30] Enforcement therefore favours this doctrinal structure:

Rule   It is unlawful for an official to decide a case differently than an earlier official decided a like case.

Exception   There is an exception to this rule if the later official is more likely to decide the case correctly than the earlier official.

It would be for the claimant to show that the rule applies. It would then be for the official to bring themselves within the scope of the exception.

C. The Difference that Doctrine Can Make

Let me explain how these points could apply in practice. In Hickey's case, the burden would lie on him to show that his case is like Robinson's and that he was treated worse than Robinson. This would have been an easy burden for him to meet. It was obvious to the courts that Robinson's and Hickey's cases were alike.

The burden would then shift to Lord Brennan (more precisely, to the Office of the Independent Assessor) to show that the exception applies. That would mean showing that Lord Brennan is more likely to decide Hickey's case correctly than Sir David was to decide Robinson's case correctly. This would have been a difficult burden to meet. Before serving as independent assessors for miscarriages of justice, both Sir David and Lord Brennan had long and distinguished careers as barristers.[31] Both served as Chairman of the Bar of England and Wales. Both argued many high-profile cases, built diverse legal practices, served on varied committees and boards, and so on. Their biographies are hardly identical. No doubt the two were able in different ways. But there is no evidence, as far as I can see, that one assessor is better than the other at evaluating evidence relevant to compensation for miscarriages of justice. Moreover, both assessors had access to the same information about the same murder as well as the criminal records of the claimants. It is plausible, as a result, that Sir David and Lord Brennan were equally likely to reach a correct decision. Certainly, there appears to be no reason to believe that Lord Brennan would have been more likely to decide correctly.

If Lord Brennan failed to discharge his burden, either because there was no evidence of his superiority or that the evidence was insufficient, then Hickey should prevail. As a result, it is plausible that the ground of review that I have outlined would have led to a different result in *O'Brien*.

---

[30] For a sophisticated account of exceptions consistent with this proposal, see L Duarte d'Almeida, 'A Proof-Based Account of Legal Exceptions' (2013) 33 OJLS 133.

[31] 'Lord Daniel Brennan QC' (*The Legal 500*) <https://www.legal500.com/firms/9227-matrix-chambers/9227-london-england/lawyers/628816-daniel-brennan-qc/> accessed 27 January 2022; J Morton, 'Sir David Calcutt' The Guardian (17 August 2004) <https://www.theguardian.com/media/2004/aug/17/guardianobituaries.pressandpublishing> accessed 17 January 2022.

37
Escaping Precedent

Inter-Legality and Change in Rules of Recognition

Nicole Roughan[*]

1. Introduction

Avoiding a precedent does not typically alter a legal system's ultimate rules of recognition.[1] Individual precedents are binding on their particular facts, but may be straightforwardly overruled, distinguished, found to be *per incuriam*, or unworkable, without unsettling the recognition of sources of valid law in that system. The present chapter examines how, in contrast to such avoidance, an escape from precedent is effected through changes in a legal system's ultimate rules of recognition.[2] While a doctrine of precedent provides tools for avoiding a particular precedent, an escape from precedent operates, more fundamentally, to escape the doctrine of precedent itself. The escape examined in this chapter arises from the interaction of legal orders (or 'interlegality'),[3] which confronts state legal systems with the legal orders of supranational, transnational, international, or sub-national law. In contexts of interlegality, the operation of precedent can—perhaps perversely—provoke changes to a legal system's rule of recognition.

The challenge that interlegality poses to rules of recognition is familiar from cases involving hierarchical interactions of state and international or regional law, as well as horizontal interactions between state systems that are managed through the techniques of conflict of laws. Although both conflict of laws and theories of state–supra-state relations reveal some of precedent's provocative characteristics, the focal category examined here is the interaction of state and Indigenous legal orders in common law settler states. Within that category, it draws out relations between state law and *tikanga Māori*[4] in Aotearoa New

---

[*] I would like to thank Gabriella Keys and Sophie Bijl-Brown for research assistance supported by a Rutherford Discovery Fellowship from the Royal Society Te Apārangi, and Timothy Endicott for his feedback. Errors remain my own.

[1] I adopt the plural conception of rules of recognition, following the explanations given by J Raz, *The Authority of Law* (OUP 1979) 95; J Gardner, *Law as Leap of Faith* (OUP 2012) 101. Cf G Lamond, 'Legal Sources, the Rule of Recognition, and Customary Law' (2014) 59 Am J Juris 25 on the singularity of an ultimate rule of recognition, which maps Hart's original account in HLA Hart, *The Concept of Law* (3rd edn, OUP 2012).

[2] This terminology tracks lawyerly usage, in which 'avoidance' straightforwardly nullifies a precedent. Escape, as conceived here, amounts to a trickier, more unusual, and more controversial manoeuvre.

[3] The term comes from B de Sousa Santos 'Law: A Map of Misreading. Toward a Postmodern Conception of Law' (1987) 14 J Law Soc 279, 288. Interlegality may be met with recognition of versions of legal plurality, or with efforts at integrating legal orders. On legal plurality, see N Roughan and A Halpin, *Pluralist Jurisprudence* (CUP 2017) 1–19.

[4] Tikanga Māori encompasses 'Māori law' and is not reducible to 'mere' custom or 'lore'. See, e.g., J Williams, 'Lex Aotearoa: An Heroic Attempt to Map the Māori Dimension in Modern New Zealand Law' (2013) 21 Wai L Rev 1. Tikanga is widely recognized and invoked in official practice, and (to an increasing extent) across the wider community as a complex system of principles, rules, and institutions, varying among different hapū or iwi groups but with a common identifiable core. See E Durie, 'Maori Custom and Values in NZ Law' (Study paper No 9, New Zealand Law Commission Wellington 2001).

Nicole Roughan, *Escaping Precedent* In: *Philosophical Foundations of Precedent*. Edited by: Timothy Endicott, Hafsteinn Dan Kristjánsson, and Sebastian Lewis, Oxford University Press. © Nicole Roughan 2023. DOI: 10.1093/oso/9780192857248.003.0038

Zealand, to show how escapes from precedent involve changing the ultimate rule(s) of recognition either to reject or to give effect to the content of Indigenous law, to the authority of Indigenous legal officials, or to the sources of Indigenous legalities.

Although Indigenous claims challenging past or continuing injustices may raise specific aspects of more general tensions surrounding precedent's relation to justice, the present claim is not that justice requires the revision of earlier precedents that have failed to recognize Indigenous law.[5] The claim is that where precedents in common law settler states recognize or refuse to recognize Indigenous law, such precedents stake out the response to interlegality within the settler state's rule of recognition. Such precedents, however, are not the end of the matter. Instead, the continuing presence (and pressure) of an Indigenous legal order's claims to legal authority, and its confrontations with state law, mean the courts are asked to confront precedent with some regularity. In contexts of interlegality, the role of precedent amplifies the deliberate contribution of judges to reaffirming or reforming rules of recognition.[6]

Interlegality thus brings to a head the relationship of precedent to rules of recognition. The argument to come accepts the basic truth of some account of a Hartian rule of recognition, arising from the practices of legal officials, as a customary rule of that group. Precedent's confrontation with interlegality, however, offers a reason to reject conceptions of a rule of recognition as an 'accidental' customary rule among officials. Instead, consistently with a more reflective account of customary normativity,[7] courts are provoked to revise and either reaffirm or reform what they see themselves as bound to recognize as law.

The argument proceeds in section 2 with analysis of: (i) the relation of precedent and change, feeding in to (ii) the uncomfortable fit between precedent and a customary rule of recognition. Section 3 then: (i) summarizes an account of precedents of interlegality provoking developments in rules of recognition in New Zealand; and (ii) draws out thematic impacts of interlegality's confrontation with precedent.

2. Precedent and Rules of Recognition

A. Precedent, Identity, and Change

Examining the operation of precedent in cases involving the interaction of legal orders highlights the role of precedent in effecting a legal system's identity, and its role in managing one legal order's responses to another. While particular precedents can point in either the direction of one legal order's openness or closure to another—towards one legal order's embrace or rejection of the application of another legal order—a doctrine of precedent has an identity-protecting character for the particular common law system in which it operates. Through both its empowering and constraining aspects,[8] the operation of precedent helps

---

[5] Such an argument is ultimately inextricable from claims to the recognition of Indigenous law. Recognition of tikanga Māori is often treated as an aspect of 'Treaty justice', guaranteed under art 2 of the Treaty of Waitangi. See, e.g., C Jones, *New Treaty, New Tradition: Reconciling New Zealand and Māori Law* (UBC Press 2016). In other work, I have suggested that recognition of the status of law is itself a matter of justice. See N Roughan, 'Honing our Jurisprudence' [2022] NZ L Rev (forthcoming).

[6] Such developments in the rule of recognition marry aspects of both change and continuity in the officials and institutions claiming law's authority. These are not the 'revolutionary' changes that accompany regime change, with its complete overhaul of both the sources and objects of recognition.

[7] See, e.g., G Postema, 'Custom, Normative Practice, and the Law' (2012) 62 Duke LJ 707.

[8] See the contribution to this volume by Grant Lamond (Chapter 2).

to support a legal order's identity—its distinction from other legal orders.[9] That a rule is laid down in a decision of an earlier/higher court in this legal system is a reason to apply that norm in this legal system, while norms from other systems don't get a look in, being merely illustrative or persuasive.

The general means of avoiding a precedent is by distinguishing—that is, showing that an earlier *ratio* does not apply to the instant case because of its materially different facts. Some jurisdictions also add more 'evolutionary' bases for avoiding precedent, allowing that significant social or juridical changes may warrant movement away from (much) older precedents.[10] A doctrine of precedent determines that what has gone before and/or above binds what follows, unless there are particular (limited) reasons to delve back into the first-order legal question, that is, reasons discrediting the authority of its resolution.[11] A court may thus avoid precedent by finding its own earlier decision to be *per incuriam*—failing to attend to relevant applicable law.

Neither orthodox nor evolutionary practices of precedent disrupt the recognition of sources of law. Precedent's content-independence protects the content of rulings, while projecting the court's recognition of the sources of that content. This chapter explores one scenario in which both the content of a precedent and the recognition of its underlying sources of law matter, contrary to orthodoxy. Perhaps unsurprisingly, cases that directly contest the recognition of sources of law generate *rationes decidendi* that express practices giving content to a rule of recognition. The content of such cases means that their impact as precedents have a particular effect on rules of recognition. An earlier case may have been decided in accordance with a different rule of recognition, which is (directly) challenged in the instant case.

A more indirect avenue of confrontation with rules of recognition may be revealed through extending the *per incuriam* avenue for avoiding precedent. Given that a precedent is treated as having been decided correctly on its facts, a *per incurium* decision is no precedent at all. What does this mean for a case decided not simply in ignorance of the applicable law, but with an ignorant or careless recognition (or non-recognition) of sources of law? Could these provoke a more fundamental escape from precedent?

Individual precedents that contest rules of recognition (directly or indirectly) may also highlight how precedent itself functions as both a practice that is part of a rule of recognition and a secondary rule of both adjudication and change. A doctrine of precedent operates as a second-order rule establishing how some law is to be changed: by being overruled or narrowed by later/higher courts.[12] It also operates as a second-order rule about the adjudication of disputes (requiring that adjudicators follow applicable precedent only in materially similar cases). More broadly, however, a *practice* of precedent in common law systems is an aspect of a system's rule(s) of recognition. It entails that judicial decisions are (subject to particular conditions) sources of valid law that lower/later judges—*qua* legal officials—are bound to follow.

---

[9] For analysis of validity-based, purposive, or political conceptions of law's identity, see C Mac Amhlaigh, 'Taking Identity Seriously: On the Politics of the Individuation of Legal Systems' (2021) 42 OJLS 1.

[10] e.g. in New Zealand, see the discussion of a fourth 'evolutionary' category in *Singh v Police* [2021] NZCA 91.

[11] L Alexander, 'Constrained by Precedent' (1989) 63 SCLR 1 on precedent's content-independence. Content-independent authority is not conclusive authority. See G Postema, 'On the Moral Presence of Our Past' (1991) 36 McGill LJ 1153 on the limits of the moral force of precedent.

[12] As a secondary rule of change, a doctrine of precedent empowers judges to change the law by match-making rules and principles with wider, narrower, or analogous fact scenarios.

If a system contains both a doctrine of precedent and a practised rule of recognition that recognizes the authority of precedents, judges of those systems are empowered and bound both by the doctrine and by the rule of recognition. The empowering effect of precedent, as a doctrine, gives higher judges a protected say on what the law is. The empowering effect of a practice of precedent within a rule of recognition, however, gives higher judges a protected say on what the rule of recognition is.

Although a rule of recognition in Hart's sense depends on wider normative practices among officials, not just judges, a system embracing precedent empowers judges so that what they recognize as law, leading to their development of the reasons for their decisions that are applied as precedents, is protected within their own sub-category of legal officials. Where a doctrine of precedent empowers the courts in this way, it doubles down on—and may protect—what the rule of recognition among officials establishes. It lays a legal doctrine on top of a customary rule. A precedent that directly reflects on the rule of recognition therefore gives judges a special and protected opportunity to say what the rule of recognition is.

That claim requires closer examination of the customary character of rules of recognition and the uncomfortable relation of precedent to such custom.

B. Precedent in a Customary Rule of Recognition

For the purposes of this chapter, the idea of a rule of recognition is treated as basically sound, capturing that certain normative practices of officials generate a rule binding each other to apply norms derived from the sources of law they recognize.[13] Contemporary work on the character of the rule of recognition has sharpened the account of law's normativity through a conception of a rule of recognition as a 'customary rule'.[14] Such work, offered on the back of challenges to the idea of a 'conventional' rule of recognition,[15] aims to settle both the 'chicken-and-egg' problem of how law makes officials and officials make law, and the question of how a rule of recognition is normative for officials.[16] As explained in work from Gardner and Macklem:

[13] In other work, I have argued that the normativity of a rule of recognition lies not in the rule itself but in the relation of the roles of official and subject. N Roughan, 'Official Point of View and the Official Claim to Authority' (2018) 38 OJLS 191.

[14] A customary rule is kind of social rule. Endicott explains that to have a social rule is 'to use a behavioural regularity as a guide to behaviour'. T Endicott, 'Are There Any Rules?' (2001) 5 J Ethics 199–220, 214. The question is what kind of social rule is custom? Here I follow Postema, 'Custom' (n 7) in treating a customary rule having at least some reflective character, belonging to a community in which participants treat the regular behaviour as the right (not merely rational) thing to do. This entails a critical reflective attitude towards the rule, as well as what Postema terms 'reciprocally oriented' conduct. Draft work from Penner criticizes Postema's more demanding conception that custom entails 'discursive' practice. See JE Penner, 'Why is Understanding Customary Law So Difficult?' (Unpublished manuscript on file with the author).

[15] A conventional rule is a rule that is followed, at least in part, for the reason that others (will) also follow it. Hart's 'Postscript' subscribed him to a conventionalist account, but explained a rule of recognition as 'a form of judicial customary rule', risking a conflation of customary and conventional rules. Hart (n 1) 256. See J Dickson, 'Is the Rule of Recognition Really a Conventional Rule' (2007) 27 OJLS 373; L Green, 'Positivism and Conventionalism' (1999) 12 Can J L & Juris 35. The differences are matters of technicality that are not always helpful, as Tucker argues. (See A Tucker, 'Uncertainty in the Rule of Recognition and in the Doctrine of Parliamentary Sovereignty' (2011) 31 OJLS 61.) Social rules may also combine conventional and customary aspects. A simplified distinction might be illustrated by the social rule, 'When in Rome, do as the Romans do', which might be read as a convention—a pragmatic instruction to 'fit in' by coordinating one's behaviour with the locals, not drawing attention, or causing disorder. Alternatively, it may be read to require respect for local custom, which should be followed because that is the right (i.e. polite) thing to do. Such custom may even be ostentatiously respected. Only the latter reading is, in Postema's sense, 'reciprocally oriented' (Postema, 'Custom' (n 7)).

[16] Discussed further in Roughan, 'Official Point of View' (n 13). Cf Lamond (n 1) arguing that a rule of recognition is not an official customary rule, but 'customary law *in foro*', i.e. the customary law of officials.

[The rule of recognition] is a customary (or social) rule. A group of people (thereby rendered 'officials') regard themselves as bound to follow the practice of their own group in treating certain of their own ('official') actions and activities as creating binding norms. ... One implication is that the ultimate rule of recognition is, to a very large extent, accidentally made. Each official takes himself or herself to be merely following the practice of his or her peers, when in fact he or she is helping to constitute that practice and thereby to shape the rule. The rule changes precisely as it was born, mainly by mistake—that is to say, by successive attempts merely to follow it that in fact contribute to its development.[17]

Gardner separately offered several different formulations of the customary character of the ultimate rule of recognition, as well as the implications of its customary status for the prospect of change. He argued:

[A]ny change in this rule [of recognition] depends on the usually unforeseeable actions of many other law-applying officials, usually no single judge is in a position to intend to change it either. And yet as a law-applying official each single judge is part of the official population whose social rule constitutes the legal rule, and as part of this population he can contribute to changing the rule. It follows that a single judge can readily be an accidental participant, but only rarely an intentional participant, in a change of customary law.[18]

The customary account specifically relies upon the absence and/or irrelevance of precedent in setting out the content of the rules of recognition. Gardner argued that rules of recognition (along with other constitutional rules in England) are 'made and sustained accidentally by the judicial custom of following them. When at long last these rules are challenged in court, there is often no previous case law on point.'[19] Moreover, Gardner suggested, when a court does get to express the content of the rule of recognition, their 'formulations of it cannot be more than mere commentary or gloss.'[20] An authoritative rule expressed in a precedent may be laid down upon the customary rule, without replacing the customary rule. The practice and evolution of the rule may be influenced (but is not determined) by such formulations.

The impact of precedent, and its empowerment of judges, suggests that judicial pronouncements in cases contesting rules of recognition (including cases of interlegality) are more than mere gloss. The specific matter of change provoked by the confrontation of precedent and interlegality, however, is best illustrated alongside broader strengths and difficulties of the customary conception of the rule of recognition.

The customary account of the rule of recognition well captures the integration of behaviour and attitudes into normative social practices (unlike more reductive notions of both belief and habit),[21] the communality and normative impact of those practices , and the importance of custom's gradual evolution and extension across time[22] It offers a genealogical and normative account of the role of officials in generating, sustaining, and changing rules of

---

[17] J Gardner and T Macklem, 'Legality: Reviewed' [2011] NDPR <https://ndpr.nd.edu/reviews/legality/> accessed 18 April 2022.

[18] Gardner, *Leap of Faith* (n 1).

[19] ibid 83–84. Gardner offers the doctrine of *stare decisis* itself as an example of such a rule sustained by judicial custom.

[20] J Gardner, 'Interview: Law as a Leap of Faith' in R Marshall, *Ethics at 3:AM: Questions and Answers on How to Live Well* (OUP 2017).

[21] For a richer engagement with habit's normative and ethical potential, see S Delacroix, 'Law and Habits' (2017) 37 OJLS 660.

[22] e.g. Postema, 'Custom' (n 7).

recognition.[23] However, the 'rare' prospect of individual judges changing a customary rule of recognition invites further elaboration of what this might look like, when it may be permissible or even justified, and what its impact could be.

It is part of rule of recognition orthodoxy that judges cannot wilfully set out to change that rule. This claim is not based on (though it can be related to) some normative theory about the limits of the judicial role, rather it is an analytic point about the rule of recognition itself. The rule simply is an expression of what legal officials take themselves to be bound to apply (not what they wish they were bound to apply). The accidental conception holds that, ordinarily, an individual judge's impact leading to change is only accidental, through errors that get carried forwards. More rarely, there may be 'wilful misrepresentations' of the rule, which may be sufficiently influential as to become the rule.[24]

As Raz and others have set out in more detail (and as Hart's formulations at times suggested), although judges as law-applying officials have a key role in forming and reforming the rule of recognition, the rule of recognition does not belong to judges to change.[25] Ordinarily, one judge is just one among many judges, and judges are just one class of officials among many. To characterize such diluted impacts as 'accidental', however, devalues the power that precedent gives to judges, not only to formulate but also to reformulate and reform rules of recognition.

A customary rule of recognition across a community of legal officials may span the practices of multiple (general and specialist) courts, legislative assemblies, local governance bodies, and a range of executive agencies. In such a diffuse 'community', the difference between following an existing customary rule and creating a new one is indeterminate.[26] Individual judges may think they are pinpointing emergent custom, conscious that it may not map exactly on to all aspects of current official practice. Is that a misrepresentation of the customary rule? Would it not, conversely, be a misrepresentation for a judge to stick steadfastly to an older rule of recognition amid emergent changes by which they are surrounded? Neither 'accident' nor 'wilful misrepresentation' accurately characterizes the activities of a judge who consciously positions a decision (or series of decisions) as moving a rule of recognition along in the direction in which they take it already to be moving, consistent with the evolutionary nature of custom.

A doctrine of precedent then embeds authority uncomfortably into such custom, provoking reflection on the rule of recognition. Precedent operates as something of a beacon, signalling and projecting not only what courts have decided earlier but also what they have earlier treated as rules of recognition. In its forward-looking aspect, however, precedent offers an opportunity to reformulate those rules in ways that will influence future practice. This interrupts the notion of accidental, casual, mistaken, or misrepresentative development of customary rules of recognition, highlighting that a customary rule of recognition is quite unlike a primary customary law. While primary custom may be subject to accidental

---

[23] In Hartian accounts, officials themselves 'come to be' through recognition, which may be unplanned but not accidental. The alternative—that there is a planned project among elite persons to mutually treat each other as officials—may ring true for critical approaches but is not part of either Hart's or Gardner's account of how officials come to be officials.

[24] e.g. see Gardner, 'Interview' (n 20).

[25] Raz (n 1); Hart (n 1).

[26] This is different from claiming that the rule of recognition itself is indeterminate or contested. Gardner's own account of the impact of disputes or divergences over the rule of recognition argues that the key to the rule is not its extension, but its intentional element. So long as judges maintain the internal point of view, seeing themselves as following the rule, the fact that they change its extension in the process, (e.g. to recognize new sources of law) is not itself problematic. Gardner, *Leap of Faith* (n 1).

generation and regeneration, accidental changes to rules of recognition are made less likely by the operation of precedent, insofar as a doctrine of precedent not only protects an individual decision but also projects, for all to see and reflect upon, the recognized sources of valid law on which the decision is based (which may include precedent itself).

Precedent's provocation of intentional pressure upon rules of recognition emerges most prominently when judges question the sources of law underlying a precedent that they cannot avoid through the usual means. Such individual reflection and effort to reform the rule of recognition is far from accidental, and if it effectively influences other officials (either gradually or immediately, as in the case of a judge influencing his or her colleagues on the bench to recognize or reject a source of law), it may contribute to a change in the rules of recognition.

A conception of accidental rules of recognition characterizes such individual intentional efforts to develop the underlying rules of recognition as wilful misrepresentations of what the current rules actually are. It treats deliberate efforts to deviate from the rule of recognition as breaches of a duty to apply (only) those sources of law that the rule of recognition picks out. The backward-looking temporal element of precedent, however, harbours the possibility of a change in rules of recognition intervening between the earlier and the instant cases. A judge may develop a rule of recognition, without wilfully misrepresenting it, by reflecting on what an earlier court was bound to recognize as valid law according to the rule of recognition prevailing at that time, and what the instant court is bound to recognize as valid law according to the current rule of recognition. There may have been an evolution in rules of recognition, in between the two times, that distances the instant case from the earlier case. The forward-looking temporal aspect of precedent, moreover, may be taken to empower the individual judge, so that one who seeks to formulate the changes is not wilfully misrepresenting the rule of recognition, but suggesting the current direction of its development as they see it.

The evolution of rules of recognition is perhaps most familiar from analyses of changes in sovereignty arising from revolutionary or major evolutionary change.[27] When cases raise justiciable questions regarding the continuity of precedents from an old order, they are often treated as questions about continuity or dependency between the earlier system and the new system's rules of recognition. Such cases—which may be among the 'rare' instances of deliberate change that the accidental conception expressly permits—reveal quite straightforwardly the provocative role of precedent.

Such revolutionary cases, however, are not matters of interlegality, though they may leave interlegality in their wake. Newly independent legal orders are often left to grapple not only with questions of continuity or discontinuity of a prior legal order but also with ongoing and regular contests over the prior and continuing interactions of Indigenous law with any remaining (reformed or re-recognized) colonial legal institutions. The practices of precedent that provoke deliberation over the rule of recognition are more jurisprudentially complex (and more practically significant) for such newly independent systems than for those of the colonial powers.[28] Local judicial responses to such interlegality can be drawn out as instances of the ways in which a doctrine of precedent both provokes and empowers judges—within

---

[27] To isolate one example, see *Madzimbamuto v Lardner-Burke* [1968] UKPC 18.

[28] Oliver suggests that these cases are mostly of interest to legal historians. C Oliver, 'Change in the Ultimate Rule of a Legal System: Uncertainty, Hard Cases, Commonwealth Precedents and the Importance of Context' (2015) 26 King's LJ 367–411.

the matrix of officials whose practices generate a legal system's rules of recognition—to engage in practices that contribute to reforming the rule of recognition itself.

3. Precedents of Interlegality

The constraints of space preclude a full cross-jurisdictional study of the impact of precedent in relating settler state legal orders to Indigenous legal orders. Instead, this section details the impact of precedent on interlegality between state and Indigenous law in Aotearoa New Zealand, drawing out key thematic aspects of precedent's impact upon formulating, reformulating, and reforming rules of recognition.[29]

A. Interlegality in Aotearoa New Zealand

Different jurisprudential narratives have been used to explain and analyse shifting trends in the interlegality effected by the arrival of English laws in Aotearoa New Zealand.[30] Extracting one such narrative does not seek to engage the technicalities of different doctrines of recognition or non-recognition.[31] Nor is this a legal historian's account (which would insist upon more contextual detail and nuance); nor that of a comparativist (which might emphasize distinctive aspects of New Zealand's largely customary constitution). The present point is to show how the meeting of tikanga Māori and settler law, through precedents, has provoked shifts in rules of recognition.

A brief account of the history of interlegality in the state courts highlights how early precedents recognized prior and continuing Māori 'customary' legal orders, most notably through respect for existing property rights.[32] This was pragmatically necessary in the nascent state institutions, and was in line with prevailing colonial law and policy as well as both common and international law protections for continuity of property and local law upon acquisitions of sovereignty. However, after the violence of war in the 1860s, and against the backdrop of anxiety over the security of land transactions on which the growing settler colony relied, the infamous 1877 decision *('Wi') Parata v Bishop of Wellington*[33] changed course by finding that

---

[29] To avoid entirely isolating the state–Indigenous context, consider the illustration of interlegality contested in *R (Miller) v The Secretary of State for Exiting the European Union* [2017] UKSC 5, which expressly confronted the impact of the relationship between UK and EU law on rules of recognition in the UK. Cf analyses from T Poole, 'Devotion to Legalism: On the Brexit Case' (2017) 80 MLR 696–710; G Philipson, 'EU Law as an Agent of National Constitutional Change: *Miller v Secretary of State for Exiting the European Union*' (2017) 36 Yb Eur L 46.

[30] See Williams, 'Lex Aotearoa' (n 4), which starts with Kupe's law, which predated the arrival of settler law. This analysis has been influential in both scholarship and in the courts. See, e.g., *Re Edwards (Te Whakatōhea No 2)* [2021] NZHC 1025. The relation of tikanga to state law is a key feature of both practical and theoretical jurisprudential interest in New Zealand, reignited by the resurgence of claims to the application of tikanga before the courts, and its increasing presence in legal education. See, e.g., J Ruru and others, 'Inspiring National Indigenous Legal Education for Aotearoa New Zealand's Bachelor of Laws Degree' (Borrin Foundation 2020). The present chapter does not examine the practice of interlegality seen from within tikanga or the role of precedent or rules of recognition therein. It is in that sense an incomplete account.

[31] cf PG McHugh, *Aboriginal Title: The Modern Jurisprudence of Tribal Land Rights* (OUP 2011).

[32] See, e.g., *R v Symonds* (1847) NZPCC 387 (though the report of the case was not printed until 1938); *Re Lundon and Whitaker's Claims Act 1871* (1872) 2 NZCA 41. Both confirmed the continuity of Indigenous property and the existence of common law Aboriginal title as a burden on the Crown's title.

[33] *('Wi') Parata v Bishop of Wellington* (1877) 3 NZ Jur (NS) SC 72. Normally referred to as *Wi Parata*. The judgment delivered by Prendergast CJ describes New Zealand as 'a territory thinly peopled by barbarians without any form of law or civil government' (77) (Prendergast CJ). The case is infamous for its declaration that the Treaty of Waitangi was 'a simple nullity' (78). See D Williams, *A Simple Nullity? The Wi Parata Case in New Zealand Law and History* (Auckland University Press 2011); JW Tate, 'The Privy Council and Native Title: A Requiem for *Wi*

Māori had no customary law that could be recognized through the common law, and that the statutory framework requiring cognizance of such custom 'cannot call what is non-existent into being'.[34] Any Crown declarations about native title, moreover, were 'acts of State' in which the Crown was rightly 'sole arbiter of its own justice'.[35]

Despite its apparent disregard for precedent and legislation, indeed disregard for the prevailing rule of recognition, *Parata* was applied by the Court of Appeal as precedent in *Nireaha Tamaki v Baker*, which on appeal to the Privy Council generated that court's criticism that it was 'rather late in the day' for the New Zealand courts to deny the existence and recognition of Māori custom, in the light of numerous statutory recognitions.[36] That decision had little impact in New Zealand,[37] and when the issue came before the Privy Council again shortly afterwards, it inflamed matters with strong language suggesting that the New Zealand courts were too close to the executive.[38] This prompted an official protest by the New Zealand judges—the 'Protest of Bench and Bar', which worked indirectly to reaffirm the New Zealand courts' non-recognition of Māori customary law in order to avoid its impact on land tenure.[39]

This narrative may sound like a matter of early common law history in the New Zealand colony, but it had lasting impacts through the twentieth century. The *Parata* position, backed by concentrated expansion in the number and breadth of the settler state institutions, as well as concerted assimilation polices aimed at the destruction of Indigenous identities, practices, and laws, resulted in a settled (settler) rule of recognition with no place for Indigenous law as an independent source of law. The present claim is that the line of authority was not only a 'serious legal mistake'[40] but also projected a rule of recognition that did not treat Māori customary law as law. Thus, in addition to the immense substantive impact on Māori land retention, the impact of the precedents' shift away from recognizing Māori customary law came to alter the rule of recognition.[41]

The non-recognition of customary law was relied upon in the 1963 decision of *In re Ninety-Mile Beach*,[42] and was not challenged in substance until the mid-1980s.[43] It was not

---

Parata?' (2004) 12 Waikato L Rev 101 argues that only the failure to recognize customary law found traction as a precedent from the case. See also J Evans, 'Reflections on *Nireha Tamaki v Baker*' (2006) 2 Te Tai Haruru J 9.

[34] *Parata* (n 33) 79.
[35] ibid 78. The court's confidence in the Crown continued: 'it cannot be questioned, but must be assumed, that the sovereign power has properly discharged its obligations to respect, and cause to be respected, all native proprietary rights' (79).
[36] *Nireaha Tamaki v Baker* [1901] AC 561.
[37] Evans (n 33) argues that the judgment failed to correct the mistaken and aberrant judgment of *Parata*. A later Privy Council decision, *Mana Kapua v Para Haimona* [1913] AC 761, correctly identified the existence of customary title prior to its recognition by statute, but apparently went unnoticed in New Zealand.
[38] *Wallis v Solicitor-General* [1903] AC 173. The court offered its own incorrect reasoning that Māori customary rights were sourced in the Treaty of Waitangi.
[39] Tate (n 33).
[40] Evans (n 33) argues that 'for eighty-five years after the decision in *Nireaha Tamaki,* New Zealand courts, its administrators, and its politicians continued to deal with issues of native title on the basis of a serious legal mistake'.
[41] L Fraser and J Wall, 'Ngāti Apa: A Counter Reformation' (2007) 1 NZLSJ 279 argued that the rejection of Privy Council authority itself can be interpreted as a reformation of the rule of recognition, followed by a counter-reformation in *Ngāti Apa*. Respectfully, insofar as the courts (and other officials) continued to follow Privy Council precedent in other respects (up until the formal split from that court and instigation of the New Zealand Supreme Court), the substantive division over native title does not appear to have upset the rule of recognition.
[42] *In re Ninety-Mile Beach* [1963] NZLR 461.
[43] Both *Te Weehi v Regional Fisheries Officer* [1986] 1 NZLR 680 and *Huakina Development Trust v Waikato Valley Authority* [1987] 2 NZLR 188 (HC) confirmed that Māori customary laws could be recognized within the common law, subject to evidence. The latter applied *Nireaha Tamaki* (n 36), and reached back to *Public Trustee v Loasby* (1908) 27 NZLR 801 (SC) which had applied a version of the general common law test for recognition of custom derived from the *Case of Tanistry* (1608) Dav 28, 80 ER 516.

until 2003 that both *Parata* and the (directly applicable) *Ninety-Mile Beach* decisions were overruled, in *Attorney-General v Ngati Apa*.[44] In that case, the court (and in particular Elias CJ) criticized *Ninety-Mile Beach* for following the 'discredited authority' of *Parata*, which had been 'revolutionary' in its time, and reiterated the earlier line of authority that had recognized Māori custom.[45]

The precedents established and rejected are not the only contributors to rules of recognition surrounding interlegality in New Zealand. General and special legislation offers prominent and powerful expressions of tikanga, thereby recognizing sites of Māori authority, through co-management or co-governance, interpretation, expertise, and rule-making.[46] The *Ngati Apa* case itself triggered a major legislative intervention, to subdue popular backlash over its perceived implications.[47] The resulting framework for the recognition of customary rights gives substantive (though incomplete) recognition to tikanga and invites the courts to seek guidance from pūkenga (court-appointed experts in tikanga) or binding opinions from the specialist Māori Land Court.[48] Claims under the new framework are now working their way through the courts, providing fresh opportunities for the courts to reformulate the recognition of tikanga.[49]

The contemporary chapter of this recognition narrative offers striking efforts by the courts to clarify the status of tikanga, provoked by the limitations of earlier precedents. Rather than seeking specific doctrinal recognitions akin to aboriginal title, these include reaching for expressions of tikanga's independent authority within some sense of genuinely interactive legal ordering. Some of these forms were contested (but not decided) in *Takamore v Clarke*,[50] including treating tikanga as one consideration in discretionary decision-making; mediating the recognition of tikanga through a common law test (including substantive 'reasonableness');[51] or treating tikanga more broadly as 'part of the values of the common law'.[52] The unclear range of options prompted the lower courts to continue grappling with these and other forms of recognition for tikanga, including lengthy discussions of the history of interlegality itself.[53]

A more recent New Zealand Supreme Court reflection was offered in *Trans-Tasman*,[54] finding that where relevant, tikanga is to be taken into account as 'other applicable law', and offers an independent source of 'existing interests', in respect of resource consent decisions

---

[44] *Attorney-General v Ngati Apa* [2003] 3 NZLR 643 (CA). The case preserved the prospect of a claim to customary title in the foreshore and seabed, and the role of the courts in hearing such a claim. Foreshadowed in *Te Runanganui o te Ika Whenua Society v Attorney-General* [1994] 2 NZLR 20 (CA).

[45] *Ngati Apa* (n 44) citing *Symonds* (n 32); *Re Lundon* (n 32) and *Nireaha Tamaki* (n 36). For an argument that *Ninety-Mile Beach* was *per incuriam*, see R Scragg, 'The New Zealand Court of Appeal and the Doctrine of *Stare Decisis*' (2003) 9 Canterbury L Rev 294.

[46] I have elsewhere examined these legislative references, in N Roughan, 'The Association of State and Indigenous Law: A Case Study in Legal Associations' (2009) 59 UTLJ 135. Other official (and officials') practices of recognition cannot be examined here.

[47] For an argument that recognition of Māori law would require a change in the rule of recognition including a challenge to parliamentary sovereignty, see J Dawson, 'The Resistance of the New Zealand Legal System to Recognition of Māori Customary Law' (2008) 12 J South Pacific L 56.

[48] Marine and Coastal Areas (Takutai Moana) Act 2011, s 99. Opinions of the Māori Land Court bind the High Court, following a procedure established earlier by the Te Ture Whenua Maori Act 1993, s 61.

[49] See, e.g., *Re Edwards* (n 30), which used the pūkenga procedure.

[50] *Takamore v Clarke* [2012] NZSC 116, [2013] 2 NZLR 733. This case involved a conflict between burial rules under tikanga, and common law rules leaving burial decisions to an Executor.

[51] Citing the 1908 effort to analogize Indigenous custom to general custom, in *Public Trustee v Loasby* (n 43).

[52] N Coates, 'Recognition of Tikanga in the Common Law of New Zealand' [2015] NZ L Rev 1.

[53] *Re Edwards* (n 30).

[54] *Trans-Tasman Resources Ltd v Taranaki-Whanganui Conservation Board* [2021] NZSC 127 [169] (William Young and Ellen France JJ), [237] (Glazebrook J), [296]–[297] (Williams J), and [332] (Winkelmann CJ).

under the Exclusive Economic Zone Act. The court specifically rejected the applicant's argument (and the High Court's finding) that tikanga was not an independent source of law.[55] This position builds on earlier dicta from former Chief Justice Elias that 'rights and interests according to tikanga may be legal rights recognised by the common law and, in addition, establish questions of status which have consequences under contemporary legislation'.[56]

Amidst all this recognition and effort to clarify the status of tikanga, it is also striking that the courts, even at the highest level, seldom pronounce on the content of tikanga, which is acknowledged to be a matter for 'those who have been tasked or honoured with the mātauranga of their tīpuna—the knowledge and wisdom passed down to them by their ancestors'.[57] Such deference was on display in *Ellis v R*, in which the Supreme Court interrupted its proceedings in order to seek guidance on the application of tikanga to the question of whether a non-Māori person's claim to overturn his conviction should be continued after his death.[58] A joint statement of tikanga, prepared after discussions among leading experts, was presented by both parties to the court, to assist them with this question. While the full judgment is yet to be delivered, this procedural novelty, along with the courts' general reluctance to impose their interpretations of tikanga itself, suggests (re-)emerging recognition of a degree of independence in the authority of tikanga, even when it is invoked and relied upon by the courts.

In summary, the interlegality narrative here shows developments that first recognized the independence of Māori customary law, then mediated recognition for customary law through common law doctrines. The *Parata* precedent then rejected mediated recognition, but the 1980s–2013 cases reinstated it,. From *Takamore* to the present the courts have been experimenting with forms of unmediated recognition that appear to point once again to recognizing the independence of tikanga Māori as a source of law.

B. Forming and Reforming Rules of Recognition

Unlike claims to Indigenous *rights* that are massaged through common law doctrines, direct claims to the authority of Indigenous *law* press the common law's reliance upon precedent into a corner, requiring courts to draw a precise line around rules of recognition. Cases invoking the application of Indigenous law specifically challenge precedents that have subordinated Indigenous claims to legality by treating them as mere matters of fact which, if proven, are subjected to common law tests for recognition. Courts must then examine not only the sources of law within the system, but also what counts as law and what does not—as well as what (if any) rules apply to the interactions of the legal orders. In doing so, they must also examine the claims to the enforcement of exclusivity or supremacy of one order's legal authority, over others.[59]

Challenges to precedents such as *Parata* or *Ninety-Mile Beach* offer something more foundational than finding them to be *per incuriam* because the exclusion of a source of law is not a matter of carelessness—in the way of overlooking a relevant statute or prior judgment

---

[55] ibid [169].

[56] *Ngāti Whātua Ōrākei Trust v Attorney-General* [2018] NZSC 84, [2019] 1 NZLR 116 (partially dissenting).

[57] *Re Edwards* (n 30).

[58] *Ellis v R* [2020] NZSC 89. For commentary, see M Stephens, 'Rāhui, mana, and Peter Ellis' (E-Tangata 2020) <https://e-tangata.co.nz/comment-and-analysis/rahui-mana-and-peter-ellis/> accessed 18 April 2022.

[59] Discussed further in N Roughan, *Authorities: Conflicts, Cooperations, and Transnational Legal Theory* (OUP 2013).

stating the content of the law. Exclusion involves not ignorance but non-recognition of an independent source of law.

Alongside the direct questions of the recognition of Indigenous law as law, the pressure posed by interlegality may drive reformulation of the limits of legality in constraining political power. While the non-recognition of Indigenous legalities had long operated alongside non-justiciability doctrines to leave the Crown fettered only by moral and political obligations towards Māori, the renewed recognition of customary law operates in tandem with enhanced legal supervision of aspects of relations between Crown and Māori.[60] Putting the two developments together may approach justiciability's 'third rail'—too fraught to directly confront—by examining the very sovereignty of the state legal order, and the courts' role within it.[61]

Such reflection on interlegality disrupts any comfortable circularity of the customary conception of a rule of recognition. When there is a challenge about the rule of recognition itself, there can be no accident in its continuation or variation. Unlike other changes in rules of recognition, interlegality entails a meeting point between legal orders, or, more precisely, confronts one legal order with the officials, institutions, rules, claims to authority, and coercive enforcement of another order. While a precedent in a legal order might rule out another legal order's operation, or filter that operation through its own forms and techniques of recognition, its underlying rules of recognition remain susceptible to pressure posed by the other legal order upon its broader recognitive practices. In cases of state–Indigenous interlegality, where the intersection entangles proximate persons and places, such pressure may generate officials' practices, as well as wider social acceptance, that redistribute recognition, and rescind earlier inclusions or exclusions of Indigenous law.[62]

In this sense, changes in the recognition of sources of law offer not an avoidance but an escape from precedent, through a trapdoor to the underground current of a customary rule of recognition. Such escape contributes to reforming not only the rules of recognition operated by a system's officials but also the recognition of officials. A customary rule of recognition is deeply entwined with (and dependent upon) deliberate practices around the recognition of officials, mutual recognition between officials, and the recognition that is built into the idea of the official.[63] These implicate broader social practices of recognition including complex relations of recognition between officials and subjects. If those practices of recognition change, so that new officials are recognized and/or old officials lose that status, the content of the rules of recognition among officials may also be altered.

Efforts to give legal effect to the determinations of Indigenous authorities may amount to their recognition as officials of law, whose practices can affect the reformation of rules of recognition.[64] Recognition of such officials is probably necessary to address the concern that the recognition by state courts (or individual judges therein) of tikanga as a source of

---

[60] The Supreme Court in *Proprietors of Wakatū and Others v Attorney-General* [2017] NZSC 17 found (for the first time) that the Crown had breached a specific fiduciary duty, not merely a 'political trust'.

[61] My interpretation of the precedents is that none so far touch this third rail, but *Trans-Tasman* establishes that other officials are required to apply tikanga as required by the EEZ Act. If the forthcoming *Ellis* judgment gives effect to the content of statement of tikanga, it may send a similar message to the lower courts.

[62] On the emergence of broader social recognition for aspects of tikanga as a regulator of behaviour, see Stephens (n 58).

[63] On the practice of recognition built into the idea of officiality, which is reflectively and not accidentally sustained, see N Roughan, 'From Office-Holding to Officiality' (2020) 70 UTLJ 231.

[64] The *Ellis* procedure, which may be conceived as a determination not only of the content of tikanga but also its applicability as a source of law, arguably treats the authorities on tikanga as officials.

law is a veiled or inadvertent re-colonizing mission.[65] Such controversies remind us that the redistribution and reform of recognition of sources of law (and officials of law) in contexts of interlegality may not always be justifiable or popular. They can generate push-back both among communities of officials and across broader communities—creating dissatisfaction among both proponents and sceptics of Indigenous–state interlegality. Tracking those evaluative responses, however, and engaging the justificatory challenges they raise, are necessarily matters for separate work.

4. Conclusion

Drawing upon shifting rules of recognition in the New Zealand context of state–Indigenous interlegality, this chapter has examined how the interaction of legal orders can provoke escapes from precedent through changes to rules of recognition. While individual precedents can operate to keep legal orders apart, to preserve one's domination over another, or to weave them together, the underlying customary rule of recognition can be revised and reformed in the light of the pressure posed by one legal order on another's recognitive practices. These shifts and developments reveal how practices of precedent challenge the idea that rules of recognition are made and sustained by accident. Questions of continuity and change are confronted deliberately wherever the existence of precedent requires the courts to commit either to a fading or an emerging rule of recognition.

---

[65] See A Sykes, 'The Myth of tikanga Māori in Pākehā law (Nin Thomas Memorial Lecture, Faculty of Law, University of Auckland, 5 December 2020; E-Tangata <https://e-tangata.co.nz/commentand-analysis/the-myth-of-tikanga-in-the-pakeha-law/>.

38
Hoary Precedents

Matthew H Kramer[*]

Hoary precedents are rulings or sets of rulings which were issued by courts many decades ago and have never been overturned subsequently. Can it ever be the case that a hoary precedent, invoked as legally binding by judges and other legal-governmental officials in numerous contexts, is not in fact legally binding? This chapter will argue that the answer to such a question is affirmative, and that the affirmative answer is entirely consistent with the resistance of legal positivists to the proposition that law is an inherently moral phenomenon. That affirmative answer will be reached through some reflections on the metaphysics of legal objectivity. One's grasp of the differences among the types of mind-independence delineated in section 1 below is crucial for one's recognition of the possibility that a precedent long perceived by judges and other officials as established law is in fact an excrescence which certain jurists are both legally obligated and legally permitted to nullify.

1. Types of Mind-Independence

We need first to attend to some distinctions among the ways in which the norms of a legal system are mind-dependent or mind-independent.[1] One such distinction lies between (i) beliefs held by any particular individual and (ii) beliefs held in common by individuals who collaborate in the running of a legal system or in some other collective enterprise.[2] Sometimes when theorists affirm the mind-independence of certain matters, they are simply indicating that the facts of those matters transcend the beliefs or attitudes of any given individual. They mean to allow that those facts are derivative of the beliefs and attitudes and behavioural patterns shared by individuals who interact as a group (such as the judges and other legal officials who together conduct the operations of a legal system). These theorists contend that, although the views of any single individual are not decisive in ordaining what is actually the case about the matters in question, the understandings which individuals share in their interactions as a group are indeed so decisive. Let us designate as '*weak* mind-independence' the type of objectivity on which these theorists insist when they ascribe a dispositive fact-constituting role to some group of individuals while denying any such role to each separate individual. That modest species of objectivity is obviously to be contrasted with '*strong* mind-independence', which obtains whenever the nature or existence

---

[*] I thank Sebastian Lewis and Hillary Nye for their comments, which helped me to improve an earlier draft of this chapter.

[1] In some paragraphs in this section, I draw quite heavily—albeit with many significant modifications—on M Kramer, *Objectivity and the Rule of Law* (CUP 2007) 3–12.

[2] Of course, the views held in common by the people who undertake some collective enterprise are often not merely held in common but are also complicatedly interlocked. Very frequently, a key reason for the harbouring of such views by each participant in a collaborative endeavour is his or her sense that virtually every other participant harbours them and expects him or her to harbour them.

Matthew H Kramer, *Hoary Precedents* In: *Philosophical Foundations of Precedent*. Edited by: Timothy Endicott, Hafsteinn Dan Kristjánsson, and Sebastian Lewis, Oxford University Press. © Matthew H Kramer 2023. DOI: 10.1093/oso/9780192857248.003.0039

of some phenomenon is determined neither by the views of any separate individual nor by the common views and convictions that unite individuals as a collectivity. Insofar as strong mind-independence prevails within a domain of enquiry, a consensus on the bearings of any particular state of affairs in that domain is neither necessary nor sufficient for the actual bearings of the specified state of affairs. How things are, in that domain, is independent of how they are thought to be.

Before we turn to a second major division between types of mind-independence, a brief clarificatory comment is advisable. When some phenomenon is weakly mind-independent, its existence or nature is ordained by the beliefs and attitudes (and resultant patterns of conduct) that are shared among the members of a group. However, the beliefs and attitudes need not be shared among *all* the members of a group. In any large-scale association or community, very few beliefs and convictions will be shared by absolutely everyone. What typically underlies the existence of a weakly mind-independent entity—an entity that can equally well be characterized as 'weakly mind-dependent'—is not some chimerical situation of unanimity but instead a situation of convergence among *most* of a group's members. Consider, for example, the diffuse group of people throughout Canada who competently use the English language. If most of those users of the language regard the employment of 'ain't' as improper in any formal speaking or writing (except when the term is deliberately wielded for comical effect), and if most of them accordingly forgo the use of that slang term in formal contexts, then Canadian English includes a weakly mind-independent rule proscribing the employment of 'ain't' in formal discourse. Probably, some competent users of the English language in Canada do not eschew 'ain't' in formal contexts. Such a fact, if it is a fact, is perfectly compatible with the existence of the aforementioned rule. Indeed, the exact difference between the status of some entity X as a weakly mind-independent phenomenon and the status of some entity Y as a strongly mind-*dependent* phenomenon is that the existence or nature of X (unlike the existence or nature of Y) is not ordained by the outlook of any particular individual. Instead, it is ordained by the outlooks and conduct that prevail among most of the members of some group. Typically, convergence among a preponderance of a group's members—which falls short of convergence among all of those members—will be sufficient to ground the existence or to establish the nature of some weakly mind-independent phenomenon. Note furthermore that, when there is very little convergence among a group's members on some proposition, and when the lack of convergence negates the existence of some weakly mind-independent entity X (such as a linguistic norm that allows the use of 'ain't' in formal contexts), the weakly mind-independent character of X is evidenced by the very inexistence of such an entity. Precisely because X is weakly mind-independent rather than strongly mind-independent, the meagreness of the convergence among the outlooks of the group's members is something that matters to X's existence.

Now, before we can come to grips with the question whether legal norms are strongly mind-independent or weakly mind-independent (or neither), we need to attend to another major dichotomy: the dichotomy between existential mind-independence and observational mind-independence. Something is *existentially* mind-independent if and only if its occurrence or continued existence does not hinge on the existence of some mind(s) and the occurrence of mental activity. Not only are all natural objects mind-independent in this sense, but so too are countless artefacts such as pens and houses. Although those artefacts would never have materialized as such in the absence of minds and mental activity—that is, although in their origins they were existentially mind-dependent—their continued existence does not similarly hinge on the presence of minds and the occurrence of mental activity. A house would persist for a certain time as the material object that it is, even if every being with a mind were magically and permanently whisked out of existence.

Something is *observationally* mind-independent if and only if its nature (comprising its form and substance and its very existence) does not hinge on how any observer construes that nature. Whereas everything that is existentially mind-independent is also observationally mind-independent, not everything that is observationally mind-independent is existentially mind-independent. Consider, for example, an intentional action. The occurrence of any such action depends on the existence of a mind in which there arises the intention that animates the occurrence, yet the nature of the action does not hinge on what any observer(s)—including the person who has performed the action—might believe it to be. Even if every observer thinks that the action is of some type B, it may in fact be of some contrary type C.

The four categories resulting from these two dichotomies are summarized in Table 38.1:

Table 38.1 Varieties of mind-independence

	Existential	Observational
Weak	The occurrence or continued existence of something is not dependent on the mental activity of any particular individual.	The nature of something is not dependent on what it is thought to be by any particular individual.
Strong	The occurrence or continued existence of something is not dependent on the mental functioning of any members of any group individually or collectively.	The nature of something is not dependent on what it is thought to be by any members of any group individually or collectively.

When pondering the mind-independence of laws, then, we should be attuned to both the strong/weak distinction and the existential/observational distinction. A bit of reflection on the matter should reveal that, if the *existential* status of laws is our focus, most general legal norms are weakly mind-independent while most individualized legal directives are not even weakly mind-independent. Quite evident is the fact that most general legal norms are at least weakly mind-independent existentially. The continued existence of those norms does not stand or fall on the basis of any individual's mental activity; it is not the case that the cessation of the mental processes of any particular individual brings about the disappearance of general legal norms. Whereas someone's beliefs and fantasies and attitudes and convictions are existentially dependent on the mind of the particular individual who harbours them, the existence of any general legal norm differs in not being radically subjective. (There can be exceptions in rather unusual circumstances. In a monarchy, the officials might adhere to a practice whereby some general laws go out of existence whenever the mental activity of the reigning king or queen has permanently ceased. Such an arrangement would be peculiar, but it would plainly be possible. Still, in a legal system that is to endure beyond a single person's lifetime, the incidence of any general laws that existentially are strongly mind-dependent would have to be highly circumscribed.)

When we move away from general laws and concentrate on individualized legal directives, we seldom find any existential mind-independence. Typically, if not always, an order addressed to a particular person—by a judge or some other legal official—will not remain in effect as such if its addressee's mental activity permanently ceases. If the result sought through the issuance of the individualized order is to be achieved, it will usually have to be pursued through some other means (perhaps through the issuance of a directive to some alternative individual or set of individuals who will act in lieu of the original addressee).

514   MATTHEW H KRAMER

Typically, then, an individually addressed legal requirement is strongly mind-dependent existentially; its continued existence as a legal requirement hinges on the occurrence of mental activity in a particular person's mind.

By contrast, the continuation of the operativeness of general legal norms will almost always transcend the mental functioning of any given individual. Even so, the existential mind-independence of such norms is weak rather than strong. They cannot persist in the absence of all minds and mental activity. They abide as legal norms only while certain people (most notably, judges and other legal officials) collectively maintain certain attitudes and beliefs and behavioural patterns concerning them. Unless legal officials converge in being disposed to treat the prevailing laws as authoritative standards by reference to which the juridical consequences of people's conduct can be gauged, those laws will cease to exist. Of course, some of the general mandates within a functional legal system—such as ordinances that prohibit jaywalking—can continue to exist as laws even though they are invariably unenforced. The requirements imposed by such mandates are not backed up by the prospect of sanctions, but they remain legal obligations. However, the very reason why such legal duties continue to exist as legal duties is that myriad other legal obligations are quite regularly given effect through the activities of legal officials, who converge in being disposed to treat those other obligations as enforcedly binding requirements. Only because those manifold other legal requirements are regularly given effect, does a system of law exist as a set of functional institutions. In the absence of the regularized effectuation of most mandates and other norms within a legal system of governance, the system and its sundry components will have gone by the wayside. In sum, the continued existence of laws (including unenforced laws) as laws will depend on the decisions and endeavours of legal officials. Yet, because those decisions and endeavours inevitably involve the beliefs and attitudes and dispositions of conscious agents, the continued existence of laws as laws is not strongly mind-independent. The existential mind-independence of general legal norms is only weak.

Let us now investigate the observational mind-independence of legal norms. Is their observational mind-independence strong or only weak? We can know straightaway that general legal norms are at least weakly mind-independent observationally. After all, as has already been remarked, everything that is existentially mind-independent is also observationally mind-independent. The outlooks and mental processes and behavioural patterns that constitute the existence of a legal system are those shared by many officials in their interactions with one another. The nature of any of those outlooks and mental processes and behavioural patterns is manifestly independent of what any particular individual takes their nature to be.

Matters become more intricate, however, when we turn from inquiring whether legal norms are observationally mind-independent to inquiring whether their observational mind-independence is strong or weak. Here we come back to the conundrum that has occasioned this whole discussion of mind-independence—a conundrum that can now be addressed rigorously. As has been suggested near the outset of this chapter, of key importance for one's coming to grips with the problem of hoary precedents is one's recognition of the difference between the weakness of the existential mind-independence of legal norms and the strongness of the observational mind-independence of those norms. Quite a few legal philosophers, such as Andrei Marmor, have had no doubt that the observational mind-independence of laws is merely weak. Marmor first notes that, when a concept pertains to something that is strongly mind-independent observationally, 'it should be possible to envisage a *whole community of speakers* misidentifying [the concept's] real reference, or extension'.[3] He then declares: 'With respect to concepts constituted by conventional practices [such as the operations of a legal system], however, such comprehensive mistakes about their reference [are] implausible. If a given concept is constituted by social conventions, it is impossible for the pertinent community to misidentify its reference.'[4] He emphatically proclaims: 'There is nothing more we can discover about the content of the [norms of our social practices] than what we already know.'[5] Actually, however, things are more complicated than Marmor suggests. His comments are not completely wrong, but they are simplistic. (In the following ruminations on the strong observational mind-independence of laws, there is no need for me to distinguish between general norms and individualized directives. In each case, the observational mind-independence is always strong.)

On any matter of law, the whole community of legal officials in some jurisdiction can indeed be mistaken. Legal officials can collectively as well as individually be in error about the attitudes and beliefs—concerning some matter of law—which they themselves share. They can collectively be in error about the substance and implications of those shared beliefs and attitudes, and can therefore collectively be in error about the nature of some legal norm(s) which those beliefs and attitudes sustain. To assume otherwise is to fail to differentiate between (i) their harbouring of the first-order attitudes and beliefs and (ii) their second-order understandings of the contents and products of those first-order mental states. The fact that the officials share certain attitudes and beliefs and behavioural patterns in regard to the existence and content of some legal norm is what establishes the existence and fixes the content of that norm; but the officials can collectively misunderstand what has been established and fixed by the attitudes and beliefs and behavioural patterns which they share. A gap of misapprehension is always possible between people's first-order beliefs and their second-order beliefs about the contents and implications of those first-order beliefs.

Indeed, Marmor's elision of the first-order/second-order distinction will land his analysis in incoherence when it is applied to many credible situations. Suppose that the courts in some jurisdiction declare that their previous interpretation of a particular law was incorrect. They now maintain that that law should have been understood and applied (and will henceforth be understood and applied) in some alternative way. They affirm that, had the earlier interpretation been correct at the time of its adoption, it would still have been correct now; however, it was mistaken at the time of its adoption and is mistaken now. If the members of the judiciary are collectively infallible at the current juncture when they pronounce on this matter of legal interpretation, then they were fallible at the earlier juncture when they espoused the now-disowned reading of the specified law. Conversely, if they were collectively infallible at that earlier juncture, then they are currently mistaken when they deem themselves to be rectifying an error. However Marmor might try to analyse such a situation, he will be led to the conclusion that legal officials have collectively erred about a matter of legal interpretation. His insistence on the officials' collective infallibility will have undermined itself.

The observational mind-independence of legal norms is therefore strong rather than weak. Nevertheless, Marmor is not flatly incorrect. If the legal officials in a jurisdiction do collectively err in their understanding of the substance and implications of some legal norm(s) which their own shared beliefs and attitudes and behavioural patterns have brought into being, and if they do not correct their misunderstanding, then in most cases

---

[3] A Marmor, *Positive Law and Objective Values* (OUP 2001) 138 (emphasis in original).
[4] ibid.
[5] ibid.

their misunderstanding will thenceforth be determinative of the particular point(s) of law to which it pertains. It will in effect have replaced the erstwhile legal norm(s) with some new legal norm(s). Such an upshot will be especially plain in any portions of a country's law that are covered by doctrines of precedent akin to those in Anglo-American jurisdictions, but it will ensue in other areas of the law as well. The new legal norm(s) might be only slightly different from the previous one(s)—the differences might lie solely in a few narrow implications of the norm(s)—but there will indeed be some differences, brought about by the legal officials' mistaken construal of the substance and implications of the superseded norm(s). Subsequent judgments by the officials in accordance with the new legal standard(s) will not themselves be erroneous, since those judgments will tally with the law as it exists in the aftermath of the officials' collective misstep. The officials go astray in perceiving the new legal standard(s) as identical to the former legal standard(s); but, once their error has brought the new standard(s) into being, they do not thereafter go astray by treating the new standard(s) as binding. (There can be limited exceptions to this general point. If the officials in a legal system adhere to a norm requiring them to undo any mistaken judgment whenever they come to discern their mistake within a certain period of time, and if they comply with that norm in most circumstances to which it is applicable, then their non-conformity with it in some such set of circumstances would temporarily vitiate the new legal standard that has been engendered by a misstep which they have acknowledged but not corrected. However, the additional error of non-conformity will itself quickly be absorbed into the workings of the legal system—along with the now-acknowledged but uncorrected misstep—as something that is binding on the officials.)

Of course, a new legal norm engendered by the officials' collective misunderstanding of a pre-existent legal norm may itself become subject to misapplication in the future. If it does indeed undergo distortion in that manner, it will have been displaced by some further legal norm that is the product of the distortion. Such a process in its general contours, through which a collective error on the part of the officials has led to the supersession of some legal standard(s) by some other legal standard(s), is open to recurring indefinitely. Legal change can occur by many routes, but a succession of errors is one of them.

Thus, although Marmor is incorrect in contending that the observational mind-independence of legal norms is weak rather than strong, his remarks can serve to alert us to the fact that the *existential* mind-independence of those norms is never strong. Legal officials can collectively be wrong about the implications of the laws which their own shared beliefs and attitudes and behavioural patterns sustain, but typically their errors (unless subsequently corrected) enter into the contents of those laws and thereby become some of the prevailing standards. Moreover, we should note that—in the remarks quoted earlier—Marmor does not initially assert that community-wide mistakes about the extensions of conventional concepts are impossible. He initially asserts merely that they are implausible. Such an assertion is overstated, but it is not entirely misguided. There is some truth in the thesis that our epistemic access to the products of our own practices is more intimate than our epistemic access to the phenomena of the natural world. Though that thesis should never obscure the possibility of disaccord between people's first-order beliefs and their second-order beliefs about the contents and implications of those first-order beliefs, it aptly suggests that we should often feel greater confidence in our grasp of our own ideas than in our grasp of entities which we have not fashioned. Within limits that prevent it from hardening into a dogma about the infallibility of our apprehension of our own practices, a tenet about relative levels of confidence is pertinent. That tenet is particularly germane in connection with very narrowly and precisely delimited conventions such as the rules of chess, but it also has some force in connection with conventions that are more diffuse—such as those that make up a large legal system.

In short, when we ponder whether the general norms of a legal system are objective in the sense of being mind-independent, we should arrive at a complex conclusion. Such norms are both existentially and observationally mind-independent, but their existential mind-independence is weak, whereas their observational mind-independence is strong. Though discrepancies between officials' perceptions and the actualities of the norms can arise because of the norms' strong observational mind-independence, the weakness of the norms' existential mind-independence minimizes those discrepancies. It does so not by ensuring that the officials who run a legal system are collectively infallible in their interpretations of legal materials, but by ensuring that most of their uncorrected errors will quickly be incorporated into the law of the relevant jurisdiction. In other words, most incongruities between the officials' collective perceptions and the substance of the law are quite rapidly removed through the recurrent reshaping of the substance in accordance with the perceptions. Furthermore, because legal officials are so familiar with their own practices and the products of those practices, any incongruities between what is collectively perceived and what is actual should be relatively uncommon.

Many philosophers appear to assume that, if there is widespread disagreement or uncertainty among the legal officials in a given jurisdiction about the content and very existence of a determinately correct answer to some legal question, there cannot be any such answer to that question. An assumption along those lines would be well-founded if the observational mind-independence of legal norms were like the existential mind-independence thereof in being only weak. In fact, however, although legal norms are constitutively underlain by the shared first-order beliefs and attitudes of legal officials, they are endowed with contents and implications that can exceed the officials' own second-order grasp. Think, for example, of a constitutional provision or some other legal norm that prohibits the infliction of severely cruel punishments. Legal officials will need to reflect on the tenor of that norm in order to ascertain how it bears on various punitive measures. In so doing, the officials might disagree with one another intractably about the legitimacy of some specific type of punishment, or most of the officials might feel deeply uncertain about the matter. Nonetheless, there may well be uniquely correct answers to many of the questions about which the officials disagree or about which they feel uncertain. Their wrangling or perplexity over some of the implications of a legal norm—a norm that exists because of their law-creating activities—is not a bar to the determinacy of those implications.

HLA Hart described the distinction between the weak existential mind-independence and the strong observational mind-independence of laws. Though he did not analyse that distinction with the precise and somewhat technical philosophical categories which I have employed here, he perceptively understood that the *finality* of the decisions rendered by the topmost court in a legal system does not amount to the *infallibility* of those decisions.[6] Like the other officials who run a system of legal governance, the officials who occupy positions on the topmost court can collectively be mistaken about the contents and implications of the laws which they apply. By powerfully insisting as much, Hart evinced his awareness of the difference between the weak existential mind-independence and the strong observational mind-independence of those laws. On the one hand, every law in a jurisdiction possesses its status as such through the practices whereby the legal-governmental officials

---

[6] HLA Hart, *The Concept of Law* (2nd edn, OUP 1994) 141–47.

there collectively identify the norms that belong to their system of governance as laws. Those norms belong to that system because they are treated as belonging thereto by the officials, whose practices of law-ascertainment uphold the standards of legal validity—including most notably the ultimate standards in the Rule of Recognition—under which the norms are endowed with the status of laws. On the other hand, although the very existence of laws as laws is due to the collective endeavours of the officials in sustaining and applying the aforementioned standards of legal validity, the officials collectively as well as individually can go astray when construing the standards of legal validity or when construing any of the laws that are recognized as such by reference to those standards. Hart was correct in his stance on this point; he was right to deny that legal-governmental officials are ever collectively infallible in their interpretations of legal norms. By proleptically rebutting Marmor's contrary stance on the matter, Hart implicitly apprehended the contrast between the weak existential mind-independence and the strong observational mind-independence of legal norms.

2. Long-Standingness and Moral Egregiousness

As is evident, my affirmation of the possibility of collective mistakes by legal-governmental officials in their pronouncements on the contours or implications or existence of legal norms is coupled with my recognition that the erroneous determinations of the officials will typically become absorbed into the law of their jurisdiction. Very often, any subsequent decisions that accord with their missteps are not themselves legally erroneous, for those subsequent decisions can be reflective of the fact that the law has been modified—perhaps slightly or perhaps more far-reachingly—by the missteps. This point is especially pertinent in relation to common-law systems with their generally strong doctrines of precedent, but it applies in varying degrees to civil-law systems as well.

In some fascinating recent ruminations on mistaken judgments by the US Supreme Court with regard to matters of American constitutional law, Brian Bix quotes from Antonin Scalia's dissenting opinion in *Obergefell v Hodges*—the 2015 case in which the Court concluded that same-sex couples have rights under the US Constitution not to be excluded from the marriage laws of American states. Scalia wrote sardonically as follows:

> The five Justices who compose today's majority are entirely comfortable concluding that every State violated the Constitution for all of the 135 years between the Fourteenth Amendment's ratification and Massachusetts' permitting of same-sex marriages in 2003. They have discovered in the Fourteenth Amendment a fundamental 'right' overlooked by every person alive at the time of ratification, and almost everyone else in the time since. They see what lesser legal minds—minds like Thomas Cooley, John Marshall Harlan, Oliver Wendell Holmes, Jr., Learned Hand, Louis Brandeis, William Howard Taft, Benjamin Cardozo, Hugo Black, Felix Frankfurter, Robert Jackson, and Henry Friendly— could not.[7]

Scalia's fulminations prompt me to emphasize that the extent to which the mistaken judgments of legal-governmental officials become ensconced in the law of their system of

---

[7] *Obergefell v Hodges* 135 S Ct 2584, 2629 (2015) (Scalia J, dissenting) (footnote omitted), quoted in B Bix, 'Objectivity, Conventions, and the Possibility of Universal Error' in V Kurki and M McBride (eds), *Without Trimmings: The Legal, Moral, and Political Philosophy of Matthew Kramer* (OUP 2022) 120–21.

governance is a matter that varies from one jurisdiction to the next. It is a matter that hinges on the content of the Rule of Recognition in each jurisdiction, and that content is of course contingent on the actions and dispositions of the officials therein. *Pace* Scalia, then, there is ample room for a system of governance in which the overruling of some hoary decisions and doctrines can be a way of reasserting the law as it has always fundamentally been.

Is there a strong moral case for a Rule of Recognition under which the reversal of some hoary precedents can be a way of reasserting the law as it has fundamentally been? In a system of governance like that of the United States, where some constitutional provisions articulate standards for legal validity that are overtly moral, the Rule of Recognition should both authorize and obligate the topmost adjudicative officials to overturn hoary judgments (as well as more recent judgments) that are morally egregious. Insofar as those officials act correctly in accordance with that authorization and that obligation, they are reasserting the law as it has always fundamentally been. If the Rule of Recognition in the United States is accurately understandable along these lines,[8] then *Obergefell v Hodges* and *Brown v Board of Education* are properly classifiable as reassertions of the Equal Protection Clause of the Fourteenth Amendment in the US Constitution. Each of those decisions served to correct decades of misrepresentations of that clause. Because the overturning of those misrepresentations has always been not only legally possible but also legally permissible and legally obligatory for the topmost court of the land (if the Rule of Recognition in the United States is along the lines suggested in this paragraph), the overturning in each case is a restoration. It returns the law to a state of affairs where the full-blown Equal Protection Clause in relation to a certain matter is legally binding on all adjudicative and governmental officials in the jurisdiction, rather than solely on the topmost adjudicative officials there. Thitherto, since the mistaken decision by the topmost court that has now been undone, the lower-tier adjudicators had been legally bound to effectuate not the full-blown Equal Protection Clause but instead that clause as it was erroneously construed in the mistaken decision. Henceforth, with the erroneous construal removed, the lower-tier adjudicators will be legally bound to effectuate the full-blown Equal Protection Clause just as the adjudicators on the topmost court have always been so bound.

Probably, the preceding paragraph has accurately recounted the way in which the overruling of morally egregious hoary cases is handled under the Rule of Recognition in the United States. Even if the paragraph is not fully accurate in application to the Rule of Recognition there, it has tersely limned the way in which the reversal of morally egregious long-standing judgments can and should be handled under a credibly possible Rule of Recognition. Despite Scalia's ranting, there is nothing silly or preposterous in the notion that those morally grotesque judgments have always been legally mistaken and have never fully entered into the law of the jurisdiction where they have been rendered. Under the Rule of Recognition that prevails in this or that particular jurisdiction, the notion denounced by Scalia—the notion that some judgments of the topmost court which have gone unreversed for many decades are nonetheless such that the topmost court is both legally permitted and legally obligated to set those judgments aside as null and void—can be true there.

Are my remarks here compatible with the resistance of legal positivists to the proposition that law is an inherently moral phenomenon? They are patently consistent with Inclusive

---

[8] I think that the Rule of Recognition in the United States is indeed along these lines, but the content of the Rule of Recognition in any jurisdiction is partly a complex empirical matter into which I do not wish to sally forth here. Thus, I frame this point as a conditional proposition in order to avoid making anything hinge on that complex empirical matter.

Legal Positivism, for they have been framed explicitly with the terms and concepts that would be employed by Inclusivists.[9] My ruminations are also compatible with at least some versions of Exclusive Legal Positivism, since some Exclusivists allow that a substantive legal norm or a criterion for legal validity can have the content of a moral principle if the norm or criterion has been enacted or affirmed in some empirically ascertainable source such as a constitutional provision.[10] In my reflections here, I have therefore deliberately concentrated on a criterion for legal validity that was enacted or affirmed in the Fourteenth Amendment to the US Constitution.

3. Legally Valid and Not Legally Valid

My discussion in section 2 leads us into a crux that surfaces repeatedly in the fine recent paper by Bix from which I have just been quoting. Bix himself encapsulates that crux in a pithy formulation at the end of his paper, as he declares that 'law is not an area of clear bivalence; we can sensibly say that, at a given point, "*Plessy* both is and is not the law".[11] His invocation here of the logical law of bivalence, which maintains that every proposition is either true or false, is inapposite. Were there any logical difficulty in the situation to which he is adverting, the relevant principle of logic would be either the law of excluded middle— which maintains that it can never be the case that neither a proposition p nor the negation of p is true—or the law of non-contradiction, which maintains that it can never be the case that both p and the negation of p are true. In any event, there is no logical conundrum in the situation to which Bix is referring. We can recognize as much when we keep in mind what has been said in section 2.

To facilitate my engagement with Bix's example of *Plessy v Ferguson*, I will assume here that the Rule of Recognition in the United States is as I have indicated that it might be in section 2. (If that assumption is inaccurate, then my present discussion pertains to a credibly possible system of legal governance rather than to the actual system of legal governance in the United States.) We have seen in section 2 the sense in which the 1896 ruling by the US Supreme Court in *Plessy* did enter into the law of the United States, and the sense in which it did not. That ruling never fully entered into the law of the United States, because the Justices on the Supreme Court from 1896 onward were legally authorized and legally obligated under the prevailing Rule of Recognition to overturn *Plessy* at any time. Had the decision in *Plessy* gone against racial segregation rather than in favour thereof, it would have entered fully into American law—in which event the Justices on the Supreme Court would thereafter have been neither legally permitted nor legally obligated to overrule that decision. However, since the *Plessy* ruling in fact upheld the practice of racial segregation in public facilities, the Justices were thenceforward both legally obligated and legally permitted to undo that ruling as null and void.

We have likewise seen in section 2 the sense in which the *Plessy* judgment did enter into the law of the United States. Although that judgment was voidable by the US Supreme Court

---

[9] For my principal defences of Inclusivism and Incorporationism, see M Kramer, *Where Law and Morality Meet* (OUP 2004) 2–9, 17–140. For a landmark book-length treatment of the topic, see WJ Waluchow, *Inclusive Legal Positivism* (OUP 1994).

[10] S Shapiro, 'The Difference that Rules Make' in B Bix (ed), *Analyzing Law* (OUP 1996) 57, 58–59.

[11] Bix, 'Objectivity' (n 7) 124. *Plessy v Ferguson* is the infamous 1896 case in which the US Supreme Court held that racial segregation in the provision of public transportation did not contravene the Equal Protection Clause of the Fourteenth Amendment to the US Constitution.

from the moment it was rendered, and although the voiding of it by the Court was both legally obligatory and legally permissible, it was not voided until it was overruled nearly six decades later.[12] As a consequence, for nearly six decades the administrators and lower-echelon adjudicators in the American system of governance were legally obligated to treat that judgment as an authoritative part of the law in their jurisdiction. They were not legally at liberty to perform their roles in ways that were inconsistent with the terms of the *Plessy* decision (for example, by issuing directives to public bodies requiring those bodies to deseg-regate their facilities). In precisely this manner, that decision figured alongside the countless other rulings of the Supreme Court as a legally binding basis for the determinations of ad-ministrators and lower-tier adjudicators in their capacities as public officials.

Now, the sense in which the *Plessy* judgment and other morally outrageous judgments of the US Supreme Court entered into the vast matrix of legal norms in the American system of governance is entirely consistent with the sense in which the *Plessy* judgment and the other morally outrageous judgments did not enter into that vast matrix. Whereas the former sense pertains to what was legally binding on administrators and lower-echelon adjudicators in the American system of governance, the latter sense pertains to what was legally binding on the Justices of the US Supreme Court. Whereas the Justices were legally bound to orient them-selves toward the Equal Protection Clause *simpliciter*, the administrators and lower-tier ad-judicators were legally bound to orient themselves toward the Supreme Court's misconstrual of the Equal Protection Clause. Hence, contrary to what Bix suggests at the end of his paper, we do not encounter any logical mystery with regard to the place of *Plessy* in the law of the United States during the first half of the twentieth century.

Bix quotes a statement by Connie Rosati that might seem to uncover a different crux. Meditating on the possibility of a world in which the *Plessy* decision would never be over-ruled, Bix writes as follows:

> One can then imagine an alternative version of American legal history, one where *Plessy v Ferguson* was never overruled by *Brown v Board of Education*, or any other case. Relating to that alternative legal history, Rosati comments: 'It seems decidedly odd to say that people never discovered what the law really is, that they didn't know and never will know that the law is not *Plessy*'.[13]

On the one hand, the counterfactual scenario conjured up here by Rosati is indeed odd. On the other hand, it is not imponderable. If the Rule of Recognition in the counterfac-tual United States is the same as what my present section has assumed to be the Rule of Recognition in the actual United States, and if the *Plessy* ruling in the counterfactual history would indefinitely persist without being deemed by the US Supreme Court to be null and void, then the people in the counterfactual United States would indeed never discover what the law on segregation in public education there really is. To be sure, we might conclude that the Rule of Recognition in the counterfactual United States is very likely not the same as the Rule of Recognition which I have tentatively ascribed to the actual American system of governance in this section. Still, such a conclusion is not forced upon us as it would be if

---

[12] Like Bix, I here assume that *Plessy* was overruled outright by *Brown v Board of Education*—though, discon-certingly, the *Brown* judgment did not state explicitly that it was overruling *Plessy* altogether.

[13] Bix, 'Objectivity' (n 7) 121, footnote omitted, quoting C Rosati, 'Some Puzzles about the Objectivity of Law' (2004) 23 Law and Philosophy 273, 292.

the proposition broached by Rosati—her proposition about never discovering what the law really is—were thoroughly outlandish.

To see why the proposition which she floats is not ridiculous, we should attend to the distinction between the property of being unknowable and the property of being unknown. In the sentence which Bix quotes from Rosati, her wording can easily incline readers to think that she envisages a situation in which the veritable content of the Equal Protection Clause is not only unknown in the counterfactual United States but also unknowable there. Such a situation would indeed be preposterous. As I have argued elsewhere,[14] all basic principles of morality and most derivative principles of morality are always knowable by human beings even if some of the principles are unknown in this or that particular society. Hence, were Rosati contemplating a scenario in which the true content of the Equal Protection Clause is unknowable rather than merely unknown, we would be justified in dismissing that scenario. Instead, however, the counterfactual situation which she ponders is one in which that true content would remain unknown indefinitely but would not be unknowable. Consequently, although that situation is odd (as Rosati says), it is to be taken seriously as a possibility.

[14] M Kramer, *Moral Realism as a Moral Doctrine* (Wiley-Blackwell 2009) 51–56.

39

Partnering with the Dead to Govern the Unborn

The Value of Precedent in Judicial Reasoning

*Heidi M Hurd**

> A dead man sits on all our judgment-seats; and living judges do but search out
> and repeat his decisions. … Whatever we seek to do, of our own free motion, a
> dead man's icy hand obstructs us! … And we must be dead ourselves, before we
> can begin to have our proper influence on our own world, which will then be no
> longer our world, but the world of another generation, with which we shall have
> no shadow of a right to interfere.[1]

The fruits of the rule of law—liberty, fairness, cooperation, and equality—are typically
thought to entail that those living today must be judged by the dictates of those who have
long been dead. While it is important not to take for granted the political stability and economic security that appear to be the fruits of governing today by the decisions of yesterday
and tomorrow by the decisions of today, we surely have to question the often-unquestioned
necessity of letting dead men sit on our benches. Can we give good reasons for the judicial
perpetuation of precedents? And since the justification for relying upon and extending good
precedents is given by their goodness (however one cashes that out), the more perspicacious
question is why judges should rely upon and further entrench bad precedents. What could
justify a judge in applying a common law rule or a particular interpretation of a statutory or
constitutional rule laid down in a series of past cases that was conceptually, morally, or legally unjustified at the time it was announced, or that now fails to square with what the judge
would decide if it were a case of first impression?

Inasmuch as I have authored books and articles that have been confused with manifestos
on anarchy,[2] it will come as a surprise to many to learn that in the quest to justify the judicial reliance on precedent, I believe we can take valuable instruction from the timeless work
of Edmund Burke—the flagbearer of conservatism whose jurisprudential views were themselves inspired by a great fear of anarchism. I, of course, find it far less obvious than Burke did

---

* I would like to thank Nina Varsava for her insightful critique of this piece at the authors' workshop for this
volume in October 2021. She identified further problems with a Burkean conception of precedent that together
amounted to an astute critique of my thesis that Burkean conservatism is a fruitful source of arguments for teth-
ering our future to the choices of the past.

[1] N Hawthorne, *The House of the Seven Gables* (Walter Scott 1851) 192 <https://babel.hathitrust.org/cgi/pt?id=
uva.x000936852&view=1up&seq=198&skin=2021&q1=a%20dead%20man> accessed 24 September 2021.

[2] See, e.g., HM Hurd, *Moral Combat* (CUP 1999); HM Hurd, 'Why You Should be a Law-Abiding Anarchist
(Except When You Shouldn't)' (2005) 42 San Diego L Rev 75–84; HM Hurd, 'Challenging Authority' (1991) 100
Yale LJ 1611–77.

Heidi M Hurd, *Partnering with the Dead to Govern the Unborn* In: *Philosophical Foundations of Precedent.* Edited
by: Timothy Endicott, Hafsteinn Dan Kristjánsson, and Sebastian Lewis, Oxford University Press. © Heidi M Hurd 2023.
DOI: 10.1093/oso/9780192857248.003.0040

that our judges should be constrained by precedents that do not embody the rules we would have them write today were they free to author our future as we would want it authored. But it is because Burke was so convinced that there is value today in repeating the past that I am eager to survey his famous arguments for a judicial conservatism that is dispositionally foreign to my general jurisprudential tastes.

Let me begin by situating this inquiry. Concerns about the role of precedent traditionally fall into two categories. Some critics worry about whether and how content can be extracted from past judicial decisions and made relevant to present and future decisions. These worries can take numerous forms. Can singular legal propositions be true or false? Can general legal propositions to be true or false? Can interpretive propositions be true or false? Can propositions of value be true or false? And can analogical claims about the similarities between cases—empirical, legal, and normative—be true or false? Other critics assume that we can make sense of the claim that past decisions can constitute precedents for present and future ones but worry, instead, about the normative force of those past decisions. Their questions go not to how precedents can be thought to be precedents but to why judges ought to follow precedents when precedents are thought to be available. This chapter constitutes a contribution to the literature on this second topic. My interest is in extracting, taxonomizing, and preliminarily exploring four categories of arguments—conceptual, psychological, moral, and aesthetic—that can be teased out of Burke's writings for why decisions made in the past properly constrain our futures.

It is impossible to evaluate the merits of the arguments that we can borrow from Burke without appreciating their place in Burke's larger social and political theory, and so, section 1 will provide an exegetical summary of what I take to be the ten central commitments of Burkean conservatism. Section 2 will take up the conceptual claim that to be governed by law at all entails that we be governed by precedent. Section 3 will assess Burke's conviction that the use of precedents can overcome a host of epistemic limitations and cognitive biases that beset both judges and citizens and that constitute threats to the rule of law. Section 4 will work through a series of normative claims that appear implicit in Burke's defence of precedent, some metaethical, some of a first-order sort. Finally, section 5 will explore justifications for projecting the past into the future that rely on aesthetic claims rather than conceptual, psychological, or moral ones.

1. The Central Tenets of Burke's Conservatism

For the sake of both brevity and clarity, it is useful to enumerate ten tenets that constitute the load-bearing beams of Burke's social and political edifice. First and very importantly, Burke was unimpressed by the powers of human reason and sceptical of prospects for its improvement.

> We are afraid to put men to live and trade each on his own private stock of reason, because we suspect that this stock in each man is small and that the individuals would do better to avail themselves of the general bank and capital of nations and of ages.[3]

---

[3] E Burke, 'Reflections on the Revolution in France' (1791) in J Waldron (ed), *Nonsense Upon Stilts: Bentham, Burke, and Marx on the Rights of Man* (Methuen 1984) 96–118.

Second, he conceived of human society as a fragile achievement that is delicately comprised of relationships that are held together by social rules, reciprocal conventions, cultural traditions, collective expectations, personal loyalties, economic forces, religious beliefs, and shared myths. In Burke's view, these complex components of human cooperation both individually and collectively defy human comprehension, let alone systematization.

Third, as a result of the first two convictions, Burke vested little stock in abstract theory that purported to advance universal moral or political truths. As JGA Pocock explains:

> [Burke's] account of political society ... endows the community with an inner life of growth and adaptation, and it denies to individual reason the power to see this process as a whole or to establish by its own efforts the principles on which the process is based.[4]

Fourth, while Burke was unimpressed with the power of individual rationality, he vested considerable faith in what he called society's 'prejudices'—'the unexamined wisdom accumulated over generations'.[5] As Burke wrote: 'The individual is foolish. The multitude, for the moment, is foolish ... but the species is wise, and when time is given to it, as a species, it almost always acts right.'[6]

Fifth, Burke's conviction that a society's 'habits' reflect the organic accumulation of rational capital motivated him to insist that we are bound by a 'social contract'. But the social contract he imagined was altogether unlike the real or hypothetical consensual agreements imagined by liberal social contract theorists. For Burke, the social contract is a 'partnership' between the dead, the living, and those of future generations, the continuance of which 'is under a permanent standing covenant'.[7] In Burke's view, the terms of this covenant are given by 'natural law'—not by the consent of those subject to it nor by the will of the majority. As Burke wrote:

> Men without their choice derive benefits from association; without their choice they are subjected to duties in consequence of these benefits; and without their choice they enter into a virtual obligation as binding as any that is actual.[8]

Sixth, precisely because Burke was convinced that progress is a product of organic change, he was appalled by revolutionary efforts to make wholesale social changes in the pursuit of abstract ideals.

> It is with infinite caution that any man ought to venture upon pulling down an edifice which has answered in any tolerable degree for ages the common purposes of society, or on building it up again, without having models and patterns of approved utility before his eyes.[9]

---

[4] JGA Pocock, 'Burke and the Ancient Constitution—A Problem in the History of Ideas' in *Politics, Language and Time: Essays on Political Thought and History* (Methuen 1971) 202, 203.

[5] E Young, 'Rediscovering Conservatism: Burkean Political Theory and Constitutional Interpretation' (1994) 72 N Carolina L Rev 619, 648.

[6] E Burke, 'Speech on the Reform of the Representation in the House of Commons' (1782) in HG Bohn (ed), *The Works of the Right Hon. Edmund Burke*, vol 2 (Henry G Bohn 1841).

[7] E Burke, 'An Appeal, from the New to the Old Whigs' (1791) in ibid vol 1.

[8] ibid.

[9] Burke, 'Reflections' (n 3) 106.

526 HEIDI M HURD

Seventh, despite his distaste for utopian efforts at radical reform, Burke was not opposed to social and political change, and he himself carried impressive reformist credentials.[10] It was his method for achieving change, not his opposition to it, that marked Burke as a conservative, for he believed that the only kind of good change was slow change. Progress could only be made through evolution, never revolution. The present must be able to justify itself by its incremental innovations on the past, and the future must unfold by analogy to the present. We must, he insisted:

> derive all we possess as an inheritance from our forefathers. All the reformations we have hitherto made, have proceeded upon the principle of reference to antiquity; and I hope ... that all those ... hereafter, will be carefully formed upon analogical precedent, authority, and example.[11]
>
> By a slow but well-sustained progress, the effect of each step is watched; the good or ill success of the first, gives light to us in the second; and so, from light to light, we are conducted with safety through the whole series.[12]

Eighth, on the basis of his faith in progress by precedent, Burke advocated the political leadership of traditional elites. His argument went beyond the hypothesis that those new to political power would exalt in its use. His claim was instead an aretaic one—that those who are born to the ruling class will more likely possess the virtues needed to manage change gradually (dispositional traits of modesty, patience, caution, prudence, and respect for the past).[13]

Ninth, Burke was convinced that there is no substitute for virtuous character in a nation's political leaders. In his view, James Madison was wrong to believe that the threat of tyranny can be eliminated by creating institutional checks and balances that can corral the ambitions of those whose appetite for power is self-serving.[14] In Burke's view, those who are not disposed to abide by the constraints of law cannot be constrained by it, and thus the rule of law depends on a society's ability to imbue its rulers with civic virtue.

Tenth, Burke further believed that citizens cannot be ruled by law if they are not predisposed to abide by its demands. While laws can guide conduct, the only thing that guarantees that people will be inclined to be so guided is their possession of dispositional virtues that make them aspire to honourable dealings with others. In Burke's view, such traits of character develop out of an 'affection' for one's society and for its institutional and cultural trappings. As he insisted, '[t]o make us love our country, our country ought to be lovely', and the loveliness of a country lies not in its geography but in its entrenched traditions, socially reinforced and reinforcing manners, institution-affirming pageantry, and moralized social myths. As Burke maintained, '[t]hese public affections, combined with manners, are required sometimes as supplements, sometimes as correctives, always as aids to law'.[15] To

---

[10] For a summary of Burke's vigilant efforts to end the oppression of Catholics in Ireland, the slavery of African Americans in the US, and the exploitation of Indians by the British East India Company, see Young (n 5) 653–54.

[11] Burke, 'Reflections' (n 3) 81.

[12] ibid 217.

[13] For a thoughtful discussion of how the other components of Burke's conservatism bolster this eighth tenet, see DI O'Neill, 'Burke on Democracy as the Death of Western Civilization' (2004) 36 Polity 201–25.

[14] See, e.g., J Madison, 'The Same Subject Continued with the Same View and Concluded' in M Pelof (ed), The Federalist 2, Paper No 51 (1987) 265.

[15] Burke, 'Reflections' (n 3) 110.

unsettle the traditions and degrade the manners that are foundational for civic virtue is to erode the ability to rule a society by law.

From these ten tenets it is possible to tease out a quite extensive set of conceptual, psychological, moral, and aesthetic defences for deciding cases in the present in the same way that similar cases were decided in the past. The task in the coming four sections is to critically examine this menu of rationales so as to assess the strength of the case for constraining the discretion of living judges by the decisions of judges long dead, and particularly to ask whether they provide convincing reasons for judges to perpetuate rules they deem today to be in error.

2. The Conceptual Case for Perpetuating Precedents

The most robust defence of precedent-governed decision-making that might be garnered from Burke's conservatism is a conceptual one. It is the claim that only if judges, and therefore citizens, are bound by precedent does a nation live under the rule of law at all. To be constrained by law simply is to have one's liberty limited by rules laid down by long-dead law-makers who could not have known the ways in which those rules would be ill-suited to changed times. When judges substitute their own judgments concerning how texts ought to best be interpreted or how legal relations ought to be arranged for those made by judges of a past era, they abandon the rule of law altogether.

This understanding of precedent is standardly thought to be coextensive with an originalist theory of interpretation. As Jeffrey Goldsworthy insists, any argument against an originalist theory of interpretation:

> is really an argument against having a constitution, or indeed any law, at all, since it is of the essence of law that decisions are governed by norms laid down in the past. Taken to its logical extreme, it is an argument not only that judges should ignore the law, but also that everyone else should ignore the judges, who owe their authority to laws laid down by 'the dead hand of the past.'[16]

On this view, judges should judge us by the values of the past, not by those of the present; they should seek to realize the goals of those who crafted our constitutional and statutory texts and our common law rules, not the ends which those might now be made to serve. As Laurence Lessig writes, judges must resolve cases 'as if the political presuppositions were as they were when the text being applied was authored—willfully blind to the currently best moral theory, and embracing instead the original moral or political theory'.[17]

If the very concept of law entails adherence to precedent, and if a judge only adheres to precedent by vigorously applying an originalist theory of interpretation, then one might think that little more needs to be said in defence of the view that the challenges of the present ought to be managed by the decisions of judges who knew nothing of them. But while the rule of law might conceptually imply that the choices made by judges and citizens are constrained in a way they would not be otherwise, such constraints are made possible by theories of interpretation that are thoroughly indifferent to the intentions with which laws were originally authored, the values of those who wielded those pens, and the goals that motivated

---

[16] J Goldsworthy, 'Originalism in Constitutional Interpretation' (1997) 25 Fed'l L Rev 1, 27.
[17] L Lessig, 'Fidelity in Translation' (1993) 71 Tex L Rev 1165, 1260.

their rule-making. Judges who are faithful to the rule of law certainly cannot think of themselves as umpires who maintain that 'it ain't nothin' 'til I call it'. They must, rather, think of themselves as akin to the umpires who are intent to 'call it as I see it'— who presupposes that there is some fact of the matter to be called, the measure of which is antecedent to the call itself. But all of the major non-originalist theories of interpretation purport to constrain judges so as to prevent them from acting as mini legislatures. If judges must interpret the texts and decisions of earlier law-makers and adjudicators according to their plain meaning, as measured by conventional understandings,[18] then they are constrained from realizing their own values. If they must interpret legal decisions and texts in accordance with their 'spirit'—so as to serve the highest and best ends those rules can be thought to serve within the existing fabric of the legal system[19]—then judges are estopped from pursuing their own ends. And if judges must interpret legal texts by consulting our best moral and scientific theories concerning the nature of the things to which legal language refers,[20] then judges are prevented from thinking of themselves as inventors, rather than discoverers.

Judges thus need not be originalists in order to be constrained by precedent. And if they are not originalists, the alternative theories of interpretation available to them will permit the kinds of incremental changes that allow legal precedents to evolve organically in ways that preserve law while allowing for the kind of 'growth and adaptation' that Burke thought essential. Burke may have been right that the only kind of legal change that leaves intact the governance of the law is slow change. But law surely must permit change over time, and such a concession dooms any argument for precedent that insists that change is conceptually inconsistent with law. As Burke wrote of the necessity of legal evolution, 'Nothing in progression can rest on its original plan. We may as well think of rocking a grown man in the cradle of an infant.'[21] In other words, we had better have an account of the value and force of precedent that both demands judicial allegiance to rules that compel unfortunate results, while permitting the gradual reformulation of those rules so as to minimize such results.

3. The Psychological Case for Perpetuating Precedents

Let us turn then to four distinct psychological justifications that Burke's conservatism offers for the judicial perpetuation of precedents even when they are inconsistent with rules that judges would otherwise craft. The first two lean on the claim that the judicial use of precedent can help to overcome epistemic deficiencies, while the second two stress the ways in which the judicial reliance on precedent can correct for cognitive biases that may otherwise motivate both judges and citizens to scoff at the law.

The first epistemic defence of precedent that can be extracted from Burke's writings targets the cognitive limitations to which judges are thought to be subject. According to this argument, the past provides a reliable heuristic for what is optimal in the present. Tradition constitutes the wisdom that a society has acquired over time—the accumulated experiences of the many that the few thwart at their peril. If two heads are better than one, then the judgments of generations can be expected to be more reliable than the judgments of individuals

---

[18] For a well-known defence of this view, see F Schauer, 'Statutory Construction and the Coordinating Function of Plain Meaning' (1990) Sup Ct Rev 231; D Strauss, 'Why Plain Meaning?' (1997) 72 Notre Dame L Rev 1565.

[19] For a famous articulation of this theory of interpretation, see LL Fuller, 'Positivism and Fidelity to Law: A Reply to Professor Hart' (1958) 71 Harv L Rev 630.

[20] For a defence of this view, see MS Moore, 'A Natural Law Theory of Interpretation' (1985) 58 So Cal L Rev 277.

[21] E Burke, 'Letter to the Sheriffs of Bristol' (printed for J Dodsley 1777).

or small groups of elites. It follows from this that judicial determinations that have been re-fined by repetition over time provide judges with the best indication of what is practically workable, legally harmonious, and morally optimal in the present. They ought to defer to precedent because they can expect that so doing will yield more right results than will their independent judgment.

The problem with this argument is that it appears to buck the hypothetical that has in-spired our inquiry. Our interest is in why judges should perpetuate precedents that they rightly believe are *not* practically workable, legally harmonious, or morally optimal in the present. Judges do not need reasons to defer to precedent when they have good epistemic reasons to think it provides good advice; they need reasons to defer to precedent when they have good epistemic reasons to think it provides bad advice. If their goal should be to maxi-mize the number of right decisions over the course of their judicial careers, then judges may do well to give substantial epistemic weight to precedent and to defer to it in circumstances of doubt; but they ought to set it aside when they are epistemically justified in believing that so doing will enable them to reach a better result, all things considered. In short, the epi-stemic case for judicial deference to precedents will only be as good over time as are those precedents. Since two wrongs rarely make a right, a judge who is not in doubt about what would be the best decision in a case derives no reason to defer to a contrary precedent that was wrongly set and wrongly replicated.

The second epistemic argument that might be elicited from Burke's conservatism draws on the cognitive limitations that can be assigned to citizens, rather than judges. On this ar-gument, courts can command the allegiance of citizens only if citizens understand and en-dorse the wisdom of judicial decisions. The psychology of citizens, however, is such that they cannot readily appreciate anything that is new if it is not put in terms of what is familiar. Hence, judges must cleave to precedents, making incremental changes in ways that leave in-tact the relationship between the law of the present and the law of the past. Notice that this argument does not lean on the claim that because citizens rely on precedent, courts ought to follow it so as not to thwart reliance interests in ways that unfairly leave citizens worse off than they would have been if they had not abided by precedent.[22] The argument here is a purely epistemic one: citizens themselves employ precedent as a heuristic means of under-standing the law's requirements, and thus judges themselves should be loath to part ways from precedent so as to avoid creating gaps between the law itself and citizens' beliefs about the law.

The problem with this argument is that while citizens surely look to legal precedents as a means of predicting whether and when the law will attach consequences to their conduct, it is hard to understand why we would value widespread knowledge of, and continued adher-ence to, unfortunate rules more than we would value recalibrating the law so that it demands right action, even as we can predict a certain amount of confusion during a transitional period. One has to be able to justify the claim that the confusion caused by substituting good rules for bad ones will generate so many bad actions that these will trump the value of the right actions that can be expected to occur once the new rule is widely known. Were change so frequent and radical as to cause citizens to lose faith in the law's ability to guide right action, perhaps this thesis could be sustained. But unless the law currently compels wide-spread wrong action, it seems hysterical to suggest that judicial departures from precedents

---

[22] I shall come to the reliance-based argument in section 4 when considering moral arguments for abiding by precedent.

in cases in which those precedents compel wrong actions will so unsettle citizens' faith in the judicial system as to cause anarchy.

Let me now turn to two arguments that exploit the role that the cognitive biases of citizens might play in justifying judicial deference to precedent. Burke, of course, cast such concerns in less modern terms, but his point was that judicial conservatism can be a tonic for motivational ills. The first of these arguments holds that citizens cannot be subjectively motivated to abide by the law absent 'affection' for the traditions that are generated by the exercise of legislative and judicial powers. As Burke insisted, 'These public affections, combined with manners, are required sometimes as supplements, sometimes as correctives, always as aids to law.'[23] To command the obedience of citizens, legal changes must incorporate enough of the old to generate a kind of 'carry-over affection' for the new. On this account, judges must perpetuate rules and cleave to past legal interpretations that preserve public perceptions of historicity so as not to cut emotional ties that motivate the allegiance of those governed to those whose rules govern them.

It is hard to deny that many find change itself disruptive and dispiriting, but this argument succeeds only if change is harder on citizens than are the results of the wrong rules perpetuated by judicial adherence to bad precedents. Surely the 'affection' that citizens have for the law is ultimately best purchased by ensuring that the law is the best it can be, rather than perpetuating laws that lead to consequences that are unjust, inefficient, or otherwise unfortunate. It is an odd argument to insist that people will bear more allegiance to the law if they do not face the risk that bad laws will give way to better ones, but instead can count on bad laws living on indefinitely into the future.

We come considerably closer to our goal of understanding why judicial conservatism might correct for cognitive biases when we turn to the second motivational argument that can be derived from Burke's conservative jurisprudence. On this argument, the role of law is to solve the problem of weakness of will. Citizens are, by their nature, susceptible to temptations to abandon their long-term interests for short-term gratifications. It is the task of law to prevent these short-sighted trades. Judges must thus frequently refuse to make legal changes that accord with the popular will on pain of violating the trust vested in them by a citizenry that self-paternalistically looks to the law's incentive-altering effects to counteract the whims of temptation.

It is possible to distinguish two versions of this general thesis that paternalism demands conservatism. On the first version, paternalism is properly exercised by constitution drafters, legislators, and judges at the time that constitutional provisions and statutory rules are codified and common law rules are crafted (and by judges at the time that constitutional and statutory provisions require interpretation) so as to guarantee that citizens cannot pursue short-term goals at long-term cost. On the second version, citizens engage in wise self-paternalism when they tie themselves to the mast of the past by refusing to depart from rules entrenched by precedent, despite present temptations to pursue current, possibly short-sighted, goals that would depend for their validation on the willingness of judges to overrule precedent.

Justice Scalia appeared to champion the first of these two versions when he observed that:

---

[23] Burke, 'Reflections' (n 3) 110.

The purpose of constitutional guarantees … is precisely to prevent the law from reflecting certain changes in original values that the society adopting the Constitution thinks fundamentally undesirable.[24]

But if past constitutional framers, legislators, and judges knew our own interests better than do we today, then this argument collapses into the previous epistemic claim that past rules are very likely to be right, rather than wrong. To the fear of ignorance on the part of both judges and citizens, this argument adds the fear that citizens will be weak of will and will thus lean either towards interpreting rules or seeking their revision so as to permit their substitution of short-term gratifications for long-term welfare. Moreover, this argument again bucks the hypothetical that drives our inquiry. When it is crystal clear that the iterative application of a rule will not lead to right action over the long run, what, if anything, might speak in favour of reiterating that rule in a fresh case? *Ex hypothesi* the answer cannot be that deference to the rule will keep in check motivational forces that will otherwise incline citizens to wrong action so that, over time, judicial conservatism will yield more right action than wrong action.

We come away from the epistemic arguments for reliance on precedent without a convincing account of why precedents should command our allegiance, especially in cases in which they appear manifestly at odds with what a judge would and should decide on the merits. Let us then leave behind arguments that rest on concerns for the epistemic and motivational deficiencies that citizens and judges might be thought to have, and seek, instead, overtly normative arguments for the role and weight of precedent.

4. The Moral Case for Perpetuating Precedents

There are at least five normative theses suggested by Burke's political conservatism that might lend justificatory support for judicial reliance on precedent. The first is a metaethical one that draws on the fact that while Burke frequently employed the language of natural law, there are numerous passages in his work that suggest that Burke was a metaethical conventionalist.[25] One can certainly understand his exaltation of tradition if he in fact believed that what is morally right just *is* what society conventionally believes to be right. Enduring traditions would then plausibly both cause and reflect a society's moral convictions, and lawmakers who seek to marry law to morality would be wise to craft and interpret laws so as to capture and extend existing traditions. To part with precedent would be to part with morality, for by definition, it would be unconventional.

While metaethical conventionalism might explain Burke's fidelity to time-honoured traditions and rules, those who flirt with this argument as a philosophical rationale for perpetuating precedents are committing themselves to defending a form of moral relativism that I have argued at length is indefensible.[26] Since I'm not going to argue against myself, I will simply suggest that we will do better to leave behind Burke's unfortunate metaethics for the first-order arguments that he makes, several of which offer substantially more insight into

---

[24] A Scalia, 'Originalism: The Lesser Evil' (1989) 57 Cin L Rev 849, 862.

[25] See the discussion of Burke's apparent moral relativism in the introduction to Waldron (n 3) 94.

[26] See HM Hurd, *Moral Combat* (CUP 1999) 27–61; HM Hurd, 'Relativistic Jurisprudence: Skepticism Founded on Confusion' (1988) 61 So Cal L Rev 1417, 1459–505.

why judges do right to hold us to rules that may demand of us what would be wrong in the absence of those rules.

The second argument rests on the claim that deference to the past protects substantive rule-of-law values. If liberty is chilled whenever the consequences of conduct are unpredictable; if fairness demands the protection of citizens' reliance interests; if equality demands the like treatment of like cases over time; and if coordination problems can only be solved by solutions made salient by long-term stability; then the law should be changeless, or at least very slow to change. Radical changes, and even the prospect thereof, makes laws unpredictable and unreliable and scrambles the criteria that specify who deserves to be treated alike.

That the rule-of-law values appear to depend upon law's long-term stability is surely a powerful reason to believe that judges should be reluctant to part ways with past precedents. If law is made less certain and if reliance interests are thwarted when judges substitute new rules for old ones, when they alter the connotation of legal terms between cases, when they apply rules in ways that create confusion about the goals that they serve or the spirit that makes best sense of them, then judges have good reasons to perpetuate precedents into the future, even when better rules could be crafted if the slate of expectations and reliance interests could be wiped clean. But of course, as we concluded earlier, law is not conceptually inconsistent with innovation, and its values have to be balanced against the values served by adjusting its demands in the light of changed circumstances and enlightened values.

The third normative thesis that one occasionally glimpses in the tenets of Burke's conservatism is that of the utilitarian: law-makers should seek to maximize social utility by summing the preferences of their citizens and satisfying those that are collectively the weightiest. In Burke's hands, this thesis translates as follows: given their settled expectations, citizens are made happiest by slow change rather than revolutionary change; and this is true even if the system that results would have made everyone happier sooner had it been possible to adopt it whole cloth. Such a claim is reminiscent of RM Hare's argument that utilitarianism often requires the perpetuation of institutions and cultural trappings that do not maximize happiness, because the transitions to arrangements that would better secure happiness are more costly than the incremental gains that would result.[27]

Like any utilitarian argument, the proof for this one is in the empirics. To invoke utilitarianism in defence of the thesis that it is generally good for judges to abide by bad precedents, one will have to defend the claim that people are in fact made happier by denying them what they think will make them happy (namely, rapid judicial innovations that would promote present conceptions of welfare maximization) in favour of enforcing against them arrangements that promoted the happiness of people in the past. The defence of such a counter-intuitive claim runs the risk of necessitating familiar, but troubling, methods of laundering citizens' preferences so as to substitute those they should have for those they think they do have. Those who are not eager to join modern-day utilitarians in their efforts to insist that 'nudging' citizens to have wants that they do not have can be both true to the tenets of utilitarianism and defensibly non-paternalistic[28] are likely to find this avenue of argumentation unattractive.

---

[27] RM Hare, 'What is Wrong with Slavery?' (1979) 8(2) Phil and Pub Affairs 103.

[28] See, e.g., RH Thaler and CR Sunstein, *Nudge: Improving Decisions About Health, Wealth, and Happiness* (Penguin 2008); CR Sunstein, *Why Nudge: The Politics of Libertarian Paternalism* (Yale UP 2014); CR Sunstein, *Choosing Not to Choose: Understanding the Value of Choice* (OUP 2015). See also HM Hurd, 'Fudging Nudging: Why "Libertarian Paternalism" is the Contradiction It Claims It's Not' (2016) 14 Geo J Law and Pub Pol'y 703.

The fourth normative thesis suggested by Burke's conservatism holds that honouring tradition is a crucial means of enforcing the terms of the social contract. Recall that Burke rejected the liberal view that the terms of the social contract are those to which citizens have agreed or would agree.[29] In his view, its content is given by principles of natural law that are best evidenced by the traditions that are enduringly capable of uniting past, present, and future generations. It follows from this view that judges honour the social contract if, but only if, they attend to and advance enduring social traditions.

One might think that one gets as strong an argument for judicial allegiance to precedent from the more traditional liberal conception of the social contract without having to shoulder the hefty metaphysics that underly Burke's natural law-based social contract. On this view, once defended by Richard Posner, judges should read and enforce all laws as they would read and enforce all voluntary contracts, implementing the expectations of those who authored them.[30] But those who are bound by laws are not analogous to those who are bound by contracts; for how can persons who were not in fact party to the drafting of laws be bound by their terms in the same way as are those who in fact entered into consensual agreements? Contractarian liberals have, of course, laboured long and hard to make the metaphor do moral work. Some have invoked Lockean claims of implied consent,[31] others have mustered Platonic duties of gratitude,[32] and still others have summoned Rawlsian obligations of reciprocity.[33] If any of these arguments can be sustained, they would seemingly lend useful support to a strong theory of precedent. But I have never managed to conjure the moral magic of consent from constructions of hypothetical consent or other such forms of philosophical legerdemain, and thus I am leery of efforts to justify the judicial perpetuation of bad rules by claims that such rules enjoy 'consent-lite'.

So, let us return to Burke's unconventional conception of the social contract as a covenant that unites past, present, and future generations through timeless traditions. Burke wrote:

> [W]herein by the disposition of a stupendous wisdom, moulding together the great mysterious incorporation of the human race, the whole, at one time is never old, or middle-aged, or young, but in a condition of unchangeable constancy, moves on through the varied tenor of perpetual decay, fall, renovation, and progression. Thus, by preserving the method of nature in the conduct of the state, in what we improve, we are never wholly new; in what we retain we are never wholly obsolete.[34]

This view that those who administer state functions ought to engage in a form of biomimicry,[35] crafting institutions that organically permit evolution through time so as to maximize their adaptation (but not their 'speciation'), provides a powerful reason for adhering to precedents, changing them incrementally rather than ever overruling them. As a means of honouring commitments to those in the past, judges are obligated to implement the rules past judges laid down (as those judges were themselves obligated, on this theory, to honour the decisions of those who came before them). But as a means of honouring

---

[29] See n 8 and accompanying text.

[30] See, e.g., RA Posner, 'Bork and Beethoven' (1990), 42 Stan L Rev 1365.

[31] See J Locke, *The Second Treatise on Government* (JW Gough ed, Basil Blackwell 1976) 61.

[32] See Plato, 'Crito' in E Hamilton and H Cairns (eds), *The Collected Dialogues of Plato* (H Tredennick tr, Princeton UP 1961) 27.

[33] See J Rawls, 'Justice as Fairness' (1958) 67 Phil Rev 179–83.

[34] Burke, 'Reflections' (n 3) 100.

[35] See JM Benyus, *Biomimicry: Innovation Inspired by Nature* (HarperCollins Perennial 2002).

commitments to those in the present and future, judges must incrementally accommodate laws to present needs and anticipated future changes. Deference to precedents, coupled with a creative willingness to alter those rules at the margins so as to reduce their tension with the rules that would be best crafted were they cases of first impression, permits judges to reconcile the obligations they owe to past generations with the obligations they owe to present and future generations.

As poetically appealing as this argument is, one has to be able to make more than metaphorical Burke's claim that there is a non-consensual covenant between generations that requires judges to honour the rules announced by past judges while making room for incremental innovations that meet the needs and values of current and future citizens. I would not know how to move from metaphor to metaphysics here, for it seems to me that to talk of a non-consensual covenant is as oxymoronic as to talk of hypothetical consent. It wraps a moral claim about the content of that covenant (or the hypothetically consensual arrangement) in the clothing of an agreement, contract, consensual arrangement, or shared understanding that really draws its normative force from an entirely different and undefended source.[36]

The final normative thesis that might be extracted from Burke's conservatism concerns the importance of cultivating virtues and suppressing vices in citizens and judges alike. In Burke's view, as we saw,[37] certain virtues of character accrue only by means of repetitive behaviours that are cultivated by traditional practices and rituals. The abandonment of traditions imperils the cultivation of important character traits on the part of those who govern and those who are governed. In turn, '[t]he worst of the politics of revolution is this: they temper and harden the breast, in order to prepare it for the desperate strokes which are sometimes used in extreme occasions' so that 'the mind receives a gratuitous taint'.[38]

This notion that adherence to tradition breeds virtue, while rapid change breeds vice, appears a promising basis both for demanding judicial allegiance to precedent and for insisting that such allegiance is consistent with incremental improvements in the law. Habits are best cultivated by judicial conformity to stable and enduring laws, and laws are made most stable by a judicial allegiance to a strong theory of precedent. Yet the process of inculcating particular character traits may be impervious to small or incremental changes in the legal order. Indeed, it may be integral to breeding virtue that one permits those who acquire its attributes to seek incremental improvements in imperfect human institutions; for one could not possess the virtue of justice without seeking to alter legal and political institutions in ways that better realize its demands. Thus, one might plausibly argue that so long as habits of *character* are preserved, habits of *conduct* can (and must) change. Of course, inasmuch as the former are contingently dependent upon the latter, revolution and even judicial activism of a sort that works wholesale changes remain inconsistent with the goal of inculcating virtue through habit. But inasmuch as legal evolution may be consistent with the cultivation of virtuous dispositions, the best theory of legal evolution may be one that both preserves elements of the past and permits changes in the present and future.

---

[36] Nina Varsava astutely recognized that this argument, like many others that can be teased from Burke's conservative jurisprudence that vest the value of precedent in the value of history, fails to provide any reason why a judge ought to abide by a precedent laid down yesterday.

[37] See the tenth tenet of Burke's conservatism in section 1.

[38] Burke, 'Reflections' (n 3) 102.

I take it that the worry with this Burkean line of argument is that it appears to commit proponents to a perfectionist theory of law—a theory that takes the cultivation of virtue and the suppression of vice to be the proper role of government. While such a goal might make plausible a strong theory of precedent, its defence on its merits is no small philosophical matter. Beyond that of Burke himself, one would surely enjoy some distinguished company were one to embrace political perfectionism en route to predicating judicial deference to precedent on the need for the state to cultivate virtue;[39] but the price for this justification would extend far beyond the costs of declaring oneself a Burkean conservative.

5. The Aesthetic Case for Perpetuating Precedents

We come then to a final category of justifications that Burkean conservatism might afford a theory of precedent—a category comprised not of conceptual, psychological, or moral claims, but of aesthetic ones. Burke's conservatism appears particularly indebted to aesthetic considerations, for Burke frequently insisted that the legal system of Britain deserved deference in perpetuity just because it possessed important aesthetic qualities. As he maintained, it provided 'a decent drapery for life'; it fostered 'pleasing illusions which made power gentle'; it 'harmonized the different shades of life and … by a bland assimilation, incorporated into the politics the sentiments which beautify and soften private society'; it 'cover[ed] the defects of our naked shivering nature'; and without it, citizens would sadly come to know that 'a king is but a man; a queen is but a woman; a woman is but an animal; and an animal is not of the highest order'.[40]

Burke was surely right that traditions and pageantry adorn both public and private life in ways that provide aesthetic experiences that are valuable in their own right. Our affection for public rituals such as standing for national anthems, reciting pledges of allegiance, honouring twenty-one-gun salutes, holding large public inaugurations of heads of state, conducting broadly publicized state funerals, turning out for parades, and holding firework displays on national holidays attests to the fact that traditions are valued, in part, solely for their aesthetic enrichment and expression. But Burke may have been right in believing that traditions do more than adorn our lives; they may positively display attributes of our national character and institutions of which we are rightly proud. He may thus have been right to fear that sweeping social reforms by both legislatures and judges might also sweep away traditions that are valuable aspects of our lives, leaving us poorer for the loss of sources of ritual and pageantry.

It may be that the aesthetic motivation for honouring the past best explains the conservative psyche and the sometimes-quaint nostalgia that seems characteristic of those who are anxious to ensure that the future does not dismantle the past. The philosophical burden of such a defence of precedent would be to make sense of conceiving of the law as an instrument of aesthetic expression. It would surely be tempting to convert the aesthetic argument for living in the past into a psychological or moral one—to elevate as aesthetically worthy those legacies that bolster psychological virtues (e.g. courage, generosity, the capacity for delayed gratification) or advance conditions of justice (e.g. eliminating wealth disparities,

---

[39] See, e.g., J Raz, *The Morality of Freedom* (Clarendon Press 1986); T Hurka, *Perfectionism* (OUP 1993); G Sher, *Beyond Neutrality: Perfectionism and Politics* (CUP 1997); M Nussbaum, 'Perfectionist Liberalism and Political Liberalism' (2011) 39 Phil and Pub Affairs 3.

[40] Burke, 'Reflections' (n 3) 110–11.

reducing racial discrimination). But to convert the aesthetic justification into either a psychological or moral one returns us to previous arguments and previous challenges. If the aesthetic interpretation appeals at all, it should be defended as a free-standing justification for the adoption of a jurisprudence that attends to our aesthetic satisfaction, quite apart from our psychological and moral flourishing.

6. Conclusion

I have canvassed a lengthy menu of arguments for the importance of judicial adherence to precedent that can be culled from Edmund Burke's timeless philosophical conservatism. Precisely because I do not share Burke's conservative predilections, I have reached to his impassioned arguments as an honest means of exploring just what can be said for binding ourselves to rules laid down by dead men, and for binding those who will live long after us by legal innovations designed to serve our needs and not theirs. However, each of the justificatory arguments with which Burke might arm a proponent of a robust account of the role and value of precedent comes at a philosophical price. As I have illustrated, to choose from this philosophical menu may well require one to defend a preference-laundering version of utilitarianism, or sign onto Burke's idiosyncratic non-consensual social contract theory, or embrace a form of political perfectionism, or predicate one's account on the sheer aesthetic benefits that may be the reward of requiring those within a society to adhere to judicially tempered traditions.

40
Emotions and Precedent

Emily Kidd White[*]

1. Introduction

The philosophy of emotion raises complications for theories of precedent. Philosophers of emotion have drawn multifaceted maps of the various ways that emotions interact with evaluative judgments,[1] or more generally, with thick concepts.[2] I will argue that it is productive to think of the effect of some precedents as facets of legal reasoning that are related to the use and understanding of legal concepts as thick concepts.[3] In legal reasoning, precedents are routinely invoked to explicate, and/or clarify, the content of legal concepts that are at issue in a case.[4] Some invocations of precedent aim to provide a more robust, detailed—or thicker—understanding of a legal concept by detailing its prior, and at times paradigmatic, applications. The multiplicity of ways that emotions interact with thick concepts pose challenges for any general theoretical account of precedent in legal reasoning and bringing these distinctions to light illuminates the difficulty of deciphering the sub-surface work of emotions in public-facing legal reasons. In at least some cases where a precedent is invoked to thicken the understanding of a legal concept at issue in a case, variations in the emotional architecture associated with that invocation will come in direct tension with the legal concept under examination, or with other legal values and principles that pertain to equality, and equal treatment under law.

2. Emotions and Thick Concepts

In 1972, Bernard Williams published 'Morality and the Emotions' in a small volume of philosophical papers.[5] Williams's explicit aim in the paper, delivered as his inaugural lecture

---

[*] I would like to thank the volume editors, Timothy Endicott, Hafsteinn Dan Kristjánsson, and Sebastian Lewis for the rewarding two-day workshop for this volume in October 2021, and Timothy especially for offering such constructive comments on an early draft. The chapter benefited greatly from the USC Legal Theory Workshop convened by Felipe Jimenez and Gregory Keating. I thank them and Marcela Prieto Rudolphy for their superb and challenging questions and comments. My warm thanks as well to Jeremy Waldron and Frederick Wilmot-Smith for invaluable feedback on earlier work that influenced the writing of this chapter.

[1] RC Solomon, *Not Passion's Slave: Emotions and Choice* (OUP 2003); R de Sousa, *The Rationality of Emotion* (MIT Press 1997); M Craven Nussbaum, *Upheavals of Thought: The Intelligence of Emotions* (CUP 2008); SR Leighton, 'A New View of Emotion' (1985) 22 American Philosophical Quarterly 133.

[2] B Williams (ed), 'Morality and the Emotions' in *Problems of the Self: Philosophical Papers 1956–1972* (CUP 1973); P Goldie, 'Thick Concepts and Emotion' in D Callcut (ed), *Reading Bernard Williams* (Routledge 2009).

[3] See, e.g., E Kidd White, 'Replaying the Past: Roles for Emotion in Judicial Invocations of Legislative History, and Precedent' (2019) 9 Oñati Socio-legal Series 577.

[4] The question of whether and how precedents might constrain judicial reasoning is here purposefully left open. The narrow claim is only that in at least some instances judges have discretion about the applicability, meaning, reach, and force of past precedents. See, e.g., M Del Mar, *Artefacts of Legal Inquiry: The Value of Imagination in Adjudication* (Hart 2020).

[5] Williams, 'Morality' (n 2).

Emily Kidd White, *Emotions and Precedent* In: *Philosophical Foundations of Precedent.* Edited by: Timothy Endicott, Hafsteinn Dan Kristjánsson, and Sebastian Lewis, Oxford University Press. © Emily Kidd White 2023. DOI: 10.1093/oso/9780192857248.003.0041

at Bedford College, London, was to steal from the ruins of emotivism to say something about the relationship between emotions and normative judgment.[6] On Williams's view, emotivism's mistake was evaluating the relationship at too general a level. Emotivism for Williams 'offered a connexion between moral language and the emotions as straightforward and as general as could be conceived in the form of the thesis that the function and nature of moral judgment was to express the emotions of the speaker and to arouse similar emotions in his hearers'.[7] Stated as such, the significance of emotions to normative judgment was either easily disproven (and frequently lacking explanatory power when faced with counter-examples) or—more important to Williams—impossible to grip at such a high level of generality.

Williams argued that it would be more useful either to analyse the ways that at least some sentences semantically incorporate expressions of emotion[8] or, more central to the present chapter's claim, to consider the ways that 'a speaker's expressing emotions should be regarded as a necessary condition of his utterance's counting as the making of a moral judgement'.[9] This latter path draws from the speech–act view of emotivism, which, as Williams writes, leads to questions of when it might not be possible to disentangle emotions from an evaluative judgment,[10] for the reason that at least some evaluative judgments rely on ideas about sincerity (including of belief, and, subject to some qualifications, commitment) which, for Williams, implicate emotions. As Williams argues, it is not always possible to disentangle the emotional aspects of an evaluative judgment without a loss of meaning, or texture.[11] Thick concepts are those in which emotions, evaluations, and thick descriptions are irrevocably bound up with one another.[12] The position is that, in at least some cases, the emotional aspects of the evaluative judgment at hand are neither secondary, nor severable, and one consequence of this view is that evaluative judgments are distinguishable based on the emotional aspects they possess.

Williams's arguments in 'Morality and the Emotions' were given careful attention, and extension by his former student Peter Goldie in 2009 in a paper entitled 'Thick Concepts and Emotions',[13] which sought to bring its insights to bear on neo-sentimentalist theories, which generally claim the position that it is appropriate to feel certain emotions when particular forms of evaluation are called for.[14] Goldie revises this position by placing emphasis on the work of emotional dispositions in order to make sense of examples where the characteristic emotion that is thought to be intrinsic to the judgment is not present in an individual instance, though it tends to be embedded in the actor's ways of seeing, being, and valuing. On this view, for example, you might know that it is right to feel outrage at certain political facts and yet fail, for reasons good or bad, to experience that emotion. We can think, for example, of teaching about a past atrocity and having the work of choosing words carefully come to obscure or quiet the anger that one might otherwise find appropriate, or of the way that grief can stay the feeling of joy that might otherwise surface upon the hearing of good news. Emotional dispositions are important for Goldie because emotions relate to each other,

---

[6] ibid 208–09.

[7] ibid 208.

[8] ibid 212.

[9] ibid 214.

[10] ibid.

[11] See, e.g., E Kidd White, *Emotions in Legal Reasoning* (OUP forthcoming).

[12] Williams, 'Morality' (n 2).

[13] Goldie, 'Thick Concepts and Emotion' (n 2).

[14] Goldie cites a formulation from Justin D'Arms and Dan Jacobson, which is that 'to think X has some evaluative property Φ is to think it appropriate to feel F in responses to X': ibid 99.

reasons, and values in complex and often protean ways.[15] Political and ethical outlooks are revealed in the tendency to feel emotions with respect to certain others and situations, not in their presence or absence at a particular moment in time.

Thick concepts for Williams and Goldie are ones that have more, rather than less, descriptive content (distinguishing them from thin concepts, including thin evaluative concepts such as good or right). Thin concepts operate at a higher level of abstraction than thick ones. For example, the concept of betrayal is thicker and includes more detail than the concept of wrongness. In addition to this descriptive content, thick concepts possess evaluative content that presents as 'keyed in to approval (or disapproval)' [16] of the descriptive content giving us a thick-textured 'idea of the character of the person, object, or action, so characterized'.[17] By contrast, 'thin concepts although clearly evaluative, are thought not to have much or any descriptive conceptual content: we get little if any sense of what the object is like beyond the fact that the user likes (or dislikes) it, and thinks others should do the same, and so on'.[18] Examples of thin evaluative concepts are *good*, *bad*, and *right*. Such concepts are 'very abstract vehicles of commendation or disparagement that can be attached to an almost unlimited range of actions or states of affairs'.[19] Thick concepts are specific and evaluative. *Gentleness*, *cruelty*, and *patience* are examples. Applications of a thick concept will vary across contexts. Gentleness with respect to one's newborn child differs from the gentleness that one might show a teenager, with differing approaches, modes, and aims operating in each instance of the application of the thick concept. As Goldie explains, finding an activity to be cruel attributes a certain wrongness to that activity, such that the finding of cruelty 'cannot be disentangled from its evaluative content'.[20] To apply a thick concept like *discriminatory*, for example, to an action is to evaluate that action and condemn that action. As with all thick concepts, the application relies on a judgment about certain facts, which if they turn out to be false or ill-founded, undermine the application of that concept.[21]

A final characteristic of a thick concept as described by Williams in *Ethics and the Limits of Philosophy*[22] is that they are both *world guided* and *action guiding*. *World-guided* concepts are ones that 'might be rightly or wrongly applied' and *action-guiding* concepts are ones that tend to be related to reasons for action, which is not to say they cannot be defeated by other reasons, including value-based and/or pragmatic reasons for action.[23] *Action-guiding* concepts for Goldie and Williams are sometimes wielded unconsciously or spontaneously, and at other times after considered thought. Significantly, and of central importance to the following argument, these two features can come apart in the application of thick concepts. *World-guiding* concepts can be applied by 'insightful observers' who don't share the values or ways of seeing implied by the concept.[24] Those observers might well predict, for example, how someone who holds the concept as an *action-guiding* concept, might think, or act. They

---

[15] Some philosophers of emotion describe being in the grip of a strong emotion as being in an emotional state (e.g. of grief, fear, or rage). For discussions on this, on relations between emotions and reasons, and the ways that different emotions interact with, or even potentially preclude, one another, see Leighton, 'New View' (n 1); W Lyons, 'On Emotions as Judgments' in S Leighton (ed), *Philosophy and the Emotions: A Reader* (Broadview Press 2003); J Robinson, *Deeper than Reason: Emotion and Its Role in Literature, Music, and Art* (Clarendon Press 2005).

[16] S Kirchin, *Thick Concepts* (OUP 2013) 1–2.

[17] ibid.

[18] ibid.

[19] R Dworkin, *Justice for Hedgehogs* (Belknap Press 2011) 181.

[20] Goldie, 'Thick Concepts and Emotion' (n 3) 95.

[21] AW Moore, 'Maxims and Thick Ethical Concepts' (2006) 19 Ratio 129, 135.

[22] B Williams, *Ethics and the Limits of Philosophy* (Harvard UP 1985).

[23] Goldie, 'Thick Concepts and Emotion' (n 2) 96.

[24] Williams, *Ethics* (n 22) 141–42. Cited also in Goldie, 'Thick Concepts and Emotion' (n 2) 96.

540 EMILY KIDD WHITE

might apply the thick concept to deliberations and activities in ways that they discern others expect, or they might publicly exclaim and showcase their *world-guided* (but not *action-guiding*) application of the thick concept for other reasons. These *world-guided* applications, however, remain distinguishable from an *action-guiding* application of a thick concept, and it is questions about sincerity and emotion, for Goldie, which work best to explicate this distinction. Williams writes, 'that reference to a man's emotions has significance for our understanding of his moral sincerity, not as a substitute for, or just in addition to, the considerations drawn from how he acts, but as, on occasion underlying our understanding of how he acts'.[25] Williams continues:

> what is relevant to our understanding of his moral dispositions is not whether there are (in our view) grounds or reasons for action of that sort, but whether he sees the situation in a certain light. And there is no reason to suppose that we can necessarily understand him as seeing it in that light without reference to the emotional structure of his thought and action.[26]

3. Roles for Emotion in *Fully Engaged* Applications of Thick Concepts

Within the field of the philosophy of emotion, it is a long-abandoned view that emotions are beyond judgment, or political evaluation, though this is often the stated rationale for the call to disentangle legal reasoning from emotion.[27] Emotions have affective and cognitive aspects that relate closely to one another.[28] Emotions involve a judgment or evaluation about an object or an event, and an affective or physiological aspect (that can be broadly characterized as a pain or a pleasure), which works to establish their characteristic constituent desires for action,[29] and, ultimately, differentiates them from other modes of thought or experience.[30] Shame, for example, has a negative, painful orientation, and its constituent desire is to make oneself small or disappear.[31] Williams rejects the Kantian view, which sees emotions as 'capricious', 'passive', and, as the 'product of natural causation', 'fortuitously distributed'.[32] Such a view, for Williams, 'suggest[s] a crude view of emotions themselves' and implies 'that

---

[25] Williams, 'Morality' (n 2) 222.

[26] ibid.

[27] A burgeoning field of law and emotion literature begins from this premise. See, e.g., SA Bandes and others (eds), *Research Handbook on Law and Emotion* (Edward Elgar 2021); TA Maroney, 'A Field Evolves: Introduction to the Special Section on Law and Emotion' (2016) 8 Emotion Rev 3; A Amaya and M Del Mar (eds), *Virtue, Emotion and Imagination in Law and Legal Reasoning* (Hart 2020).

[28] Leighton, 'New View' (n 1); Solomon, 'Not Passion's Slave' (n 1); RC Solomon, *The Passions: Emotions and the Meaning of Life* (Hackett 1993); Nussbaum (n 1).

[29] J Gardner, 'The Logic of Excuses and the Rationality of Emotions' (2009) 43 J Value Inquiry 315.

[30] Within the philosophy of emotion, there are wide-ranging views on how best to describe the relationship between the physiological and cognitive aspects of an emotion. Questions about sequence and rank abound. For cognitivists, like Martha Nussbaum, certain emotions tend to follow from the holding of particular evaluative judgments. Others, like William James, find that physiological responses precede and assist in forming the cognitive aspects of an emotion. See, e.g., Nussbaum (n 1); W James, 'What Is an Emotion?' (1884) 9 Mind 188. Others find a strong distinction between these two aspects superficial, with some drawing on contemporary research in neuroscience to put pressure on both sorts of causal accounts. See, e.g., Robinson (n 15); M Gendron, 'The Evolving Neuroscience of Emotion: Challenges and Opportunities for Integration with the Law' in S Bandes and others (eds), *Research Handbook on Law and Emotion* (Edward Elgar 2021).

[31] Solomon, *The Passions* (n 28); see, in particular, ch 8, 'The Emotional Register'.

[32] Robinson (n 15).

EMOTIONS AND PRECEDENT   541

there is no way of adjusting one's emotional response in the light of other considerations, of applying some sense of proportion, without abandoning emotional motivation altogether.'[33]

Individual emotions relate to facts and beliefs that can be subject to scrutiny, standards of evidence, and rational judgment. Subject to some qualification, emotions are answerable to reasons.[34] They are evaluative in the sense that they reveal to some extent what an individual finds important.[35] It is for this reason that Robert Solomon describes them as 'eudemonistic', and as 'engagements with the world'[36] for their tendency to reveal deep and personal understandings of value (for good or ill), and, at times even, a (well-placed or not) sense of justice. Given that emotions are evaluative in this sense, it is possible to press both upon the facts or beliefs underlying an emotion and upon the judgment motivating an emotion.[37] As emotions are object-directed, new information about an object can work to revise an emotional state[38] (though not always for some emotions can prove resistant, or irrational).[39] Further, as emotions reflect evaluative judgments, they are open to probing questions about the status of the value underlying one's emotional concerns.

To move deeper into the distinction outlined earlier concerning the *world-guided* and *action-guiding* aspects of thick concepts, Goldie draws on a paper by Adrian Moore on the difference between *understanding* a concept and being *fully engaged* with a concept. As Moore wrote:

> Thick ethical concepts can be grasped in two ways, an engaged way and a disengaged way. To grasp a thick ethical concept in the disengaged way is to be able to recognize when the concept would (correctly) be applied, to be able to understand others when they apply it, and so forth. To grasp a thick ethical concept in the engaged way is not only to be able to do these things, but also to feel sufficiently at home with the concept to be prepared to apply it oneself, where being prepared to apply it oneself means being prepared to apply it not only just in overt acts of communication but also in how one thinks about the world and in how one conducts one's affairs.[40]

Emotions play a role with respect to both *understanding* and being *fully engaged* with a thick concept. In terms of the former, understanding a thick concept often means understanding something about its emotional architecture, including features of the emotions that it engages (including their cognitive and physiological aspects, dominant metaphors, and constituent desires for action)[41] that characteristically apply with respect to them. In terms of the latter, however, emotions and emotional dispositions play a significant and non-severable role in the *full engagement* of a concept. They do so in complex, typically potent, fluid, and sometimes elliptical ways. In many cases, what makes the *living by* the thick concept in question sincere is an emotional disposition, which entails the tendency to emotionally engage with circumstances involving its relevant applications.

Thick concepts don't exist in a vacuum. They have, as Goldie puts it, a *focus* and a *stance*. The focus is the object of concern, and the stance is the 'emotional "attitude"' held towards the

---

[33] Williams, 'Morality' (n 2) 224.
[34] Gardner (n 30); Williams, 'Morality' (n 2).
[35] Nussbaum (n 1).
[36] Solomon, *Not Passion's Slave* (n 1); Solomon, *The Passions* (n 28).
[37] Nussbaum (n 1).
[38] ibid; Solomon, *The Passions* (n 28).
[39] Williams, 'Morality' (n 2) 224.
[40] Goldie, 'Thick Concepts and Emotion' (n 2) 96. Citing Moore (n 21) 137.
[41] Solomon, *The Passions* (n 28).

focus'.[42] Sincerity, for Williams and Goldie, becomes an important facet of the application of a thick concept because the expression of a judgment will only constitute *fully embracing* or *living by* a concept where the person in question 'shares (subject to the above qualifications) the feelings and emotions that give application of the concept its point'.[43] These sincere views stemming from *living by* and *fully embracing* a thick concept tend, then, subject to some qualifications, to motivate action, ways of seeing, and patterns of reasoning.[44] This, for Goldie, is the deep connection between thick concepts and emotion, that is, that a sincere full engagement with a concept implicates character and emotional dispositions.

4. Problems for Precedent with Thick Legal Concepts and Emotion

Invocations of precedent can contribute additional layers of meaning and detail to legal concepts, a process which, drawing from the field of ethical theory, reflects the notion of *thickening*.[45] This is a backward-looking process that engages prior uses of a legal concept, across differing contexts, to build a better grip on its meaning and implications for the case at bar. Often the process flags paradigmatic examples or circumstances which engage the concept.[46] Similar to the view held here, Maksymilian Del Mar argues that it is useful to think of precedents as 'thick resources', the 'dynamic content' of which is to some extent constrained by stabilizing practices (e.g. textbooks, restatements of the law), but nevertheless never so constrained as to be incapable of being construed as relevant in a novel way.[47] References to precedent in the explication and use of legal concepts are a constitutive aspect of the practice of common law legal reasoning, which is not to say that anything about the use of particular precedents or a more general theory on the level of constraint they supply is uncontested.[48] The work of finding and using precedents in legal reasoning has never lacked a politics.[49]

Judges can invoke precedents as applications of thick concepts in *world-guided* and/or *action-guiding* ways. Whether and how judges use precedents to *fully engage* with an application of a legal concept can have an impact on legal reasoning. A *fully engaged* application of a thick legal concept requires the use of precedent that reflects an emotionally inflected stance towards a focus (i.e. an object of concern) that depends upon a particularized and sincere form of valuing, or way of seeing, which concerns that focus. The possibility of a *fully engaged* application of a thick legal concept immediately raises sceptical questions about what precisely at the level of theory is required by judges in their applications of thick legal concepts, and so too, about the self-awareness of judges, and the ability of judges (or anyone) to either fully understand and/or manage their own emotionally imbued set of value commitments and ways of seeing.[50]

---

[42] Goldie, 'Thick Concepts and Emotion' (n 2) 105. The contents of this emotional attitude can shift depending on the circumstances. When we value someone, we can feel angry when they are disrespected, concerned when they are sick, happy when they are happy, etc.

[43] ibid.

[44] ibid.

[45] Williams, *Ethics* (n 22); S Scheffler, 'Morality Through Thick and Thin a Critical Notice of Ethics and the Limits of Philosophy' (1987) 96 The Philosophical Review 411.

[46] Kidd White, 'Replaying the Past' (n 3).

[47] M Del Mar, 'What Does History Matter to Legal Epistemology?' (2011) 5 J Philosophy of History 383, 386.

[48] E Kidd White, 'Notes on a Supreme (Legal) Fiction' (2022) 47 J Legal Philosophy.

[49] ibid.

[50] ibid.

Leaving aside questions concerning the scope of the discretion permitted to a judge in the use of precedent, the claim here is that legal concepts can exude a certain thinness that references to precedent can work to supplement.[51] Precedents can be used to *fully engage* with an application of a legal concept, they can be used to give the appearance of this full engagement, they can be applied by a judge acting in the manner of an 'insightful observer', or by a judge wishing to present themselves as an 'insightful observer' applying the concept. Given the existence of these distinct possibilities, even where the discretion of the judge to use precedent to *thicken* the legal concept at issue seems limited, the challenges outlined later pose deep problems for theories of precedent that profess the normative value of public reason, or other substantive rule-of-law values, such as the commitment to equal treatment under the law. Depending on the theory of legal interpretation at play, casting light on these distinctive possibilities seems to require either that judges always (under an account where moral or evaluative reasoning is part of legal reasoning) or never (under an account where moral or evaluative reasoning is excluded from legal reasoning) —without exception—show a sincere full (i.e. *action-guiding*) engagement with a legal concept in the application of a precedent.[52]

A. The Difficulty of Distinguishing between World-Guided and Action-Guiding Applications of a Legal Concept

The practices associated with the use of precedents in common law judicial reasoning make it difficult to discern instances where legal concepts are being applied in *world-guided* but not *action-guiding* ways. It is difficult to discern on the face of a written judgment when a judge is *using* a legal concept but not *embracing* or *fully engaging* with that concept. In several instances, this might not matter to the case outcome, and it may or may not be decipherable on the face of the judgment's reasoning. And yet, the roles that emotions play with respect to *world-guided* and *action-guiding* applications of a thick concept are quite distinct. This is significant because it is not clear that a legal concept will be applied as vigorously or searchingly where it is not *action guiding*. And so, too, because the implications of this focus on emotion for accounts of legal reasoning are stark and demanding. In what follows, I raise two distinct issues which suggest that, in at least some instances, the role emotions play with respect to some thick legal concepts impact judicial reasoning.

(i) Emotions as aids to understanding

In the pages of a 1979 *New Yorker*,[53] Grace Paley's short story 'Love' ends with the protagonist blowing through the aisles of a grocery store before running into an old friend with whom she'd had a terrible argument years before. They had long since stopped speaking. Seeing her friend's lovely face, a face that she had previously delighted in, she finds her own hand advancing to this woman's hand, taking it up and giving it a kiss. Her friend smiles at the gesture, rearranging the past, and settling into place a new range of possibilities.

Paley here gives us an inroad into a discussion on the epistemic benefits of emotions in judicial reasoning. Crucially, the use of the term 'epistemic' here pertains to the cognitive

---

[51] For an argument on the interpretation of thin legal concepts, see C McCrudden, 'Human Dignity and Judicial Interpretation of Human Rights' (2008) 19 Eur J Int'l L 655.

[52] I thank Felipe Jimenez for pushing me to clarify this implication of my argument.

[53] G Paley, 'Love' *The New Yorker* (8 October 1979).

process of understanding[54] in relation to the construction of legal arguments and findings, not to ascertainment of anything like an objective moral fact.[55] As in Paley's story, emotions move and motivate us; they can rearrange our understandings of pertinent facts and highlight certain features of a situation that are important to us.[56] Emotions have epistemic functions even where they do not ground our evaluative judgments. They can startle and 'capture and consume our attention, [thereby] facilitating a reassessment or reappraisal of the evaluative information that emotions themselves provide'.[57]

Emotions can serve epistemic functions, allowing us to focus on features of the world that we consider important or, conversely, to identify threats to those persons, things, or values that we hold dear.[58] When we value something, certain features of the object of our value (a landscape, an event, even an idea) can stand out to us.[59] Emotions can play positive (or negative) epistemic roles in judicial reasoning by gripping and focusing the attention[60] of the presiding judge or judicial panel, thereby prompting a re-evaluation of the impugned law, of the legal dispute, or of the transactions and relations involved in the case.

For good or ill, emotions at work in the application of a legal concept 'can motivate the search for reasons that bear on the accuracy of their own initial assessment of some object or event, and thus motivate the rational reappraisal or reassessment of that object or event'.[61] It is significant to note here that the attention-directing features of emotions are far from apolitical, and raise a series of questions about whose emotions are legible to those in power, whose emotions are perceived to be legitimate, compound, deeply felt, or authentic,[62] and which harms, wrongs, or interferences warrant emotional concern.[63]

Emotions can work to focus critical attention on the object of emotion, or on a line of reasoning that engages that object, inviting a process of cognitive reflection[64] that can work to diffuse, intensify, or change the emotion (e.g. we can think of fear moving to indignation, or to laughter upon further reflection)[65] or, more broadly, one's understanding of the matter at hand. Jenefer Robinson's understanding of emotions as process underscores the ways emotions might contribute to motivation and understanding:

> When human beings have an emotional response to something in the (internal or external) environment, they make an affective appraisal that picks that thing out as significant to me (given my wants, goals, and interests) and requiring attention. This affective appraisal causes physiological changes, action tendencies, and expressive gestures, including characteristic facial and vocal expressions, that may be subjectively experienced as feelings, and the whole process is then modified by cognitive monitoring.[66]

---

[54] See, e.g., CZ Elgin, 'Emotion and Understanding' in G Brun, D Ulvi, and D Kuenzle (eds), *Epistemology and Emotions* (Routledge 2016).

[55] See, e.g., T Nagel, 'Types of Intuition' (2021) 43 London Review of Books.

[56] CZ Elgin, 'Impartiality and Legal Reasoning' in A Amaya and M Del Mar (eds), *Virtue, Emotion and Imagination in Law and Legal Reasoning* (Hart 2020).

[57] MS Brady, *Emotional Insight: The Epistemic Role of Emotional Experience* (OUP 2013).

[58] See, e.g., L Blum, 'Iris Murdoch' in EN Zalta (ed), *The Stanford Encyclopedia of Philosophy* (Summer 2022, Metaphysics Research Lab, Stanford University).

[59] E Kidd White, 'Till Human Voices Wake Us: The Role of Emotions in the Adjudication of Dignity Claims' (2014) 3 J Law, Religion and State 201.

[60] Brady (n 57) 13.

[61] ibid.

[62] Bandes, 'Remorse and Criminal Justice.' (2016) 8 Emotion Rev 14.

[63] E Kidd White, 'On Emotions and the Politics of Attention in Judicial Reasoning' in Amaya and Del Mar (n 56).

[64] See, e.g., Robinson (n 15).

[65] P Goldie, 'Narrative Thinking, Emotion, and Planning' (2009) 67 J Aesthetics and Art Criticism 97, 10.

[66] Robinson (n 15) 113.

As Robinson emphasizes, these various elements are 'interconnected': 'physiological responses reinforce attention'; 'action tendencies and behavior may change the environment so that the emotional situation changes or dissipates'; and '[c]ognitive monitoring may confirm or disconfirm affective appraisals'.[67] Emotions direct our attention to various features and attributes that resonate with us. Emotions motivate the finding of evidence and analogies that appear relevant to the legal question before the court, and, so too, for good or ill contribute to the smoothing out of various disanalogies and/or evidentiary hurdles that might otherwise present. Emotions have attention-capturing shortcutting functions (fear is the usual example as it inspires a response often before a full cognitive appraisal has had time to form).[68] Emotions often work as shorthand in this regard; they can be fast-working, motivating processes (we can even think of the names of certain precedents themselves carrying tone-filled, emotional weight, which is not to say well-known precedents won't conjure up even radically different associations across groups).

For Williams, it is possible to understand correct applications of a thick concept without embracing that concept. In support of this argument, Goldie raises Moore's example of the concept of the *Sabbath* suggesting that 'this is a concept whose correct application is readily grasped by those who do not embrace the concept in an engaged way'.[69] I am not sure this always holds. Even with respect to the example at hand, the *Sabbath*, it is not clear that there isn't some lack, or difference, of understanding that might translate into a different emphasis, a difference in tone, weight, or considered detail (including the ability to grip some of the concept's more ineffable aspects) that might lead to an inapt application in particular circumstances. Emotions signal that something is important to an agent and in a particular way. Emotions are important to value-directed practices not only for reasons of authenticity and sincerity but also for understanding.

As stated earlier, 'insightful observers' will often be able to perform, or give heed to, any expected emotional aspects that would be involved in *fully embracing* a legal concept (e.g. a particular conception of liberty), for this is precisely what it means to apply a thick concept in a *world-guided* way. If, however, I am correct that there remains some difference, in at least some cases, in the understanding and application of thick legal concepts through precedent when judges apply them in a *world-guided* but not in an *action-guided* way (with the difference having to do with an emotional engagement that is either live in the particular instance or present at a dispositional level), then this poses a challenge to existing theories of legal reasoning. As Moore writes, 'to "embrace" a concept is to grasp it in the engaged way. It is to enter into the spirit of the concept, to have whatever outlook gives the concept its point, to *live by* the concept.'[70] There is a difference between chronicling emotions and experiencing emotions.[71] There is a difference between using emotion words because they appear appropriate to the task, like empathy and compassion, and experiencing either of these things.[72]

I have written in the past of the concern that judges might employ disordered or false versions of empathy in their legal reasoning practices, drawing on the language of the claimant, without real efforts to understand their station or point of view.[73] The concern here is how judges might employ precedents to signal a *fully engaged* application of a thick legal concept

---

[67] ibid.
[68] Leighton, 'New View' (n 1).
[69] Goldie, 'Thick Concepts and Emotion' (n 2) 96.
[70] Moore (n 21) 157.
[71] Kidd White, 'On Emotions' (n 63).
[72] Kidd White, *Emotions in Legal Reasoning* (n 11).
[73] Kidd White, 'On Emotions' (n 63).

while only drawing on precedents in a *world-guided* manner to serve their own political outlooks and intuitions (or more perniciously, their own stereotypes and prejudices) about the claimant and the case, thereby failing to give the legal concept full weight, and, so too, offering a false public account of their own reasoning process (i.e. an insincere performance of full engagement). This is not an argument in favour of sincere, *fully engaged* applications of thick legal concepts, which can obviously be objectionable at the level of substantive politics (we know all too well the problem of sincerely held bad politics).[74] It is the clarification that given the motivating and epistemic features of emotions, there is reason to believe that the use of precedent will differ across *world-guided* and *action-guiding* applications of the thick legal concept at issue in a case. The earlier concern could, notably, also run in the opposite direction, with a judge purporting to use precedent to apply a thick legal concept in a *world-guided* way (aiming, perhaps, for the cloak of authority associated with a cool, emotionally disengaged application) when in fact they are using precedent to apply a thick legal concept in a *fully embraced* and sincere *action-guiding* way (whether they are sufficiently self-aware to know this or not).

(ii) In at Least Some Cases, the Law Seems to Require that a Thick Legal Concept be Applied in an Action-Guiding Manner, Drawing on Certain Emotions (While Resisting Others)

The idea of sincerity that is so important to Williams takes on additional complex dimensions when we enter the terrain of legal reasoning. Sincerity might operate, or fail to operate, at multiple levels with respect to the practice of legal reasoning. Insincerity might signal a chasm between the private normative and/or political views of the judge, and their pronouncement on the status of a particular precedent as binding. Or, as set out earlier, the difference between a legal concept that is applied via precedent in a *world-guided* but not an *action-guiding* manner.

One response to the foregoing might be to say that while judges must draw on precedents to provide a thicker understanding of a legal concept, they are never required to *fully engage* with the legal concepts that they apply to the case at bar. Judges in common law legal systems must look to precedents to thicken their understanding of the *world-guided* aspects of the legal concept under examination before applying it in ways that might be defended as correct. The demands of the judicial role do not include sincerity, nor the emotional engagement that sincerity sometimes requires. Judges are meant to take on the role of the 'insightful observer', charged with the task of understanding the legal concepts that are relevant to the present case and applying them regardless of their own political commitments or sense of justice and so on.

This is one description of the role that seems fair to defend though it remains, at times, somewhat incongruent with at least some expectations surrounding substantive rule-of-law norms, and also with respect to at least some aspects concerning the judicial role itself (sincerity in taking up the role, or feeling the political and moral weight of the role).[75] The writing styles of common law judges varies widely.[76] Common law judges sometimes write judgments as if there is space between their own political views and what they take the law

---

[74] Much will depend here on the theory of legal interpretation at play and whether there are thought to be resources within that theory to correct for injustice.

[75] TA Maroney, 'The Persistent Cultural Script of Judicial Dispassion' (2011) 99 Cal L Rev 629.

[76] Del Mar, Artefacts of Legal Inquiry (n 4).

to require, but not always.[77] And yet, with respect to at least some legal concepts and values, something seems awry in requiring too strict a separation between the legal concepts and values that require application through the strictures of legal reasoning and those that might be privately held by the judge or judicial panel.[78] It is not altogether clear that judges aren't meant to feel the weight of some thick legal concepts, like dignity, for example.[79]

A cold distance is, as John Gardner wonderfully put it, not an unemotional stance, it is just another emotional disposition, and one that itself reveals value commitments or the lack of value commitments.[80] In at least some cases, something at the level of value commitment and at the level of legal interpretation appears awry where a judge experiences no emotions with respect to the use, description, or interpretation of precedents (or when visiting certain facts within them),[81] or where they display the wrong emotions when using precedent to thicken a legal concept. At times, a cold distance is the inapt or wrong emotional response. As John Gardner memorably wrote, 'there is no general or default answer to the question of whether a sober appreciation of reasons for action is more reasonable than an emotionally-charged appreciation of those same reasons for action. Being cool, calm, and collected is just another place on the emotional map, with no special claim to rational efficiency.'[82] He continues, 'Neither the passionate nor dispassionate among us has any a priori claim to be generally more effective in acting in conformity with reasons about value. ... Sometimes, surely, a cold calculation is just the opposite of what is called for.'[83] Emotions are, in Gardner's terms, precisely those that are called for in the practice of a value. As Michael Stocker and Elizabeth Hegemon write:

> Emotions may show valuings rather than value: how a person values something, not the value something has or the value the person takes it to have. Sometimes people have emotions that contain and reveal valuings, not values; and sometimes people have emotions that reveal a lack of valuing, even in the face of acknowledged value ... I may not value, or may barely value, what I know has great value. For example, I may not value or may barely value a given school of music, even though I know—and know directly, for myself, not just by being told by those I know do know—that it is of the very highest value.[84]

In at least some cases, applications of a legal value will appear inapt where a judge appears not to have the requisite emotions when drawing on various precedents, or interpretation of precedents, or, in the alternative, where they display the wrong emotions.[85] Martha Nussbaum, for example, argues that disgust has no place in legal reasoning because no other emotion paints its object in such a negative and contemptuous light.[86]

---

[77] ibid; Maroney, 'Persistent Cultural Script' (n 75); Kidd White, *Emotions in Legal Reasoning* (n 11).
[78] Kidd White, 'Replaying the Past' (n 3).
[79] Kidd White, 'Till Human Voices Wake Us' (n 59).
[80] Gardner (n 29).
[81] See, e.g., B Zipursky, 'DeShaney and the Jurisprudence of Compassion (Case Note)' (1990) 65 NYU L Rev 1147.
[82] Gardner, 'The Logic of Excuses and the Rationality of Emotions', 349.
[83] ibid.
[84] M Stocker and E Hegeman, *Valuing Emotions* (CUP 1996) 158.
[85] Kidd White, 'Till Human Voices Wake Us' (n 59).
[86] Nussbaum (n 1).

B. The Concern Over Inconsistent or Unequal Applications of Action-Guiding Concepts

The final critique of the neo-sentimentalist position in Goldie's paper also stems from a concern about generality in the theoretical construction of the relationship between emotions and thick concepts. Here, Goldie addresses Moore's revision to the neo-sentimentalist's position, critiquing that it does not account 'for a limited domain of a fully engaged application of a thick concept'.[87] Goldie draws upon an example from RM Hare of an aggressive and demeaning initiation ceremony for recruits at a military academy taking place under the authority of an official who knows perfectly well how to *fully engage* with the concept of *cruelty* when it comes to his own children. Goldie notes how the official might withhold the use of the thick concept of *cruelty* in judgments about what had been done to the recruits,[88] or, more subtly, use the term knowing how it applies in the usual case while recasting some of its implications ('the ceremony was *cruel* but entertaining'). In the second case, we could say that this official was not *fully engaged* with the concept in this context though they are in other parts of their life. As Goldie writes, '[s]uch a person is by no means inconceivable nor unimaginable'.[89] Summarizing the argument, he writes, that 'for any particular person, full engagement with a thick concept, and correlatively its action-guidedness in application by that person, need not apply across all domains. One can be fully engaged in a concept here but not there.'[90]

In the field of legal reasoning, this insight translates into a concern that judges use precedent to *fully engage* in the application of a legal value when certain issues are at stake, or more perniciously, when the rights or interests of certain groups are at stake, but not always, and not across all of the applicable domains.[91] Like the official just mentioned, they also might not see how they have carved out a space where they simply won't recognize the application of the thick concept as apt, or they will readily (and not always self-knowingly) craft narratives as to why certain suspensions, revisions, qualifications, or provisos to the concept's application are appropriate. The philosophy of emotion here elicits this deep criticism of judicial reasoning that is otherwise difficult to pinpoint because, on the face of the legal reasoning in question, the applicable legal concepts will either be seen as non-applicable, or they will be referenced but only in a superficial or lifeless manner. Susan Bandes has, for example, written of how the emotion of remorse implicates something of a future gaze, and a promise of better behaviour. She finds, devastatingly, that judges are often less apt at reading a concrete future (full of family, success, education, etc) for poor and/or racialized defendants, and hence are less likely to attribute to them the emotion of remorse, a factor which has concrete consequences in terms of sentencing.[92] Cast in more general terms, the concern is with a legal test applied in seeking and searching ways for some claimants but not others, or with respect to some legal rights and not others, with precedents marshalled to give apparent warrant to such disparate results, obscuring the structured inequality at play.[93]

---

[87] P Goldie, *The Mess Inside: Narrative, Emotion, and the Mind* (OUP 2012) 100.

[88] Goldie, 'Thick Concepts and Emotion' (n 2) 100–01.

[89] ibid 101.

[90] ibid.

[91] Kidd White, 'On Emotions' (n 63).

[92] SA Bandes, 'Remorse and Demeanor in the Courtroom: Cognitive Science and the Evaluation of Contrition' in *About the Integrity of Criminal Process: From Theory into Practice* (Hart 2016).

[93] On the indeterminacy of legal language serving the interest of some while giving legal warrant for dispossession and violence against others, see, e.g., Kidd White, 'Notes on a Supreme (Legal) Fiction' (n 48); R Knox, 'Haiti at the League of Nations: Racialisation, Accumulation and Representation' (2020) 21 Melbourne J Int'l L 1; N Tzouvala, *Capitalism As Civilisation: A History of International Law* (CUP 2020).

This is a powerful challenge for theories of judicial reasoning that encompass the use of precedent. Masked by the *world-guided* applications of legal concepts (which might even evince the appearance of the right and requisite emotional stances—outrage at cruelty, anger at discrimination, etc), the legal reasoning might look defensible on its face, but it will lack the *fully engaged* application of the concept. A masked, bloodless application.

We know all too well in our political life about half-hearted attributions of rights, for example to refugees and migrants.[94] Some legal concepts get applied in highly motivated ways and others not, and with respect to some interests and not others. These uneven *fully engaged* applications can at times undermine the legal value in question (a value like human dignity that is meant to be attributed equally to all human beings), and so too the principles and norms of application concerning equality and equal treatment before the law.

5. Conclusion

> She felt a warning tremor as she spoke, as though some instinct deeper than reason surged up in defense of its treasure. But Darrow's face was unstirred save by the flit of his half-amused smile.[95]

Embedded in the context of legal reasoning, the core insight in the previously referenced papers by Williams and Goldie—that one must avoid the risk of oversimplifying or overgeneralizing the relationship of emotions to thick evaluative concepts—seems as fruitful as ever. A focus on emotion illuminates some of the more subtle ways in which judicial uses of precedent reveal held values, ways of seeing, and political commitments, and so, too, some of the stark demands placed on the judicial role by various theories of judicial reasoning and precedent.

A focus on emotions in the use of precedent in the application of legal concepts reveals a distinction between full engagement and something less than full engagement, that might otherwise be difficult to ascertain. This distinction can work to derogate from commitments to both substantive and procedural equality and equal treatment under the law. Nothing in this chapter constitutes an argument in favour of all legal concepts being applied in a *fully engaged* manner. This is a separate question of ethics, and politics. The question, however, of whether this is what the law calls for remains a pressing, critical, and uncomfortable one. Questions about judicial sincerity and self-knowledge seem overly intimate and yet highly relevant.

Gerry Simpson writes that one motivation for his recent book that details some of the sentimental aspects of international law is 'the hunch that most of what is interesting in life occurs off-screen'.[96] This hunch is here shared and taken as a warning that much of the work of emotions in legal reasoning is sub-surface, impacting our understanding of legal questions in myriad ways. Legal concepts will be *fully embraced* at the service of some goals, and persons, and ways of life but not others. The deeper-than-reason political outlooks of judges

---

[94] See, e.g., I Mann, *Humanity at Sea: Maritime Migration and the Foundations of International Law* (CUP 2016).
[95] E Wharton, *The Reef*, cited as an epigraph in Robinson (n 15).
[96] G Simpson, *The Sentimental Life of International Law: Literature, Language, and Longing in World Politics* (OUP 2021).

shape reasoning efforts and case outcomes in ways that are, at times, hard to ascertain and hold to account. This isn't necessarily a fatalistic conclusion. Rather, it is a call for sub-surface emotional dispositions, and the politics they reveal, to be drawn out and subjected to critique. Or, more broadly, a call to question whether present processes of adjudication are constructed to deliver on the norms and commitments they profess.

Index

For the benefit of digital users, indexed terms that span two pages (e.g., 52–53) may, on occasion, appear on only one of those pages.

Tables and figures are indicated by *t* and *f* following the page number

abduction *see* contest and precedent
administrative law 488–97
  consistency 490–91
    diachronic inconsistency 491
    synchronic consistency 491
  enforcement 494–97
    difference that doctrine can make 497
    help that doctrine can provide 495–96
    legal requirement to adhere to consistency 494
    rules and exceptions 496–97
  fairness principles 492–93
  Hickey case 488–90
aesthetic considerations and precedent 535–36
AI and law 72–74
American legal realists *see* legal realists
analogy/analogical reasoning and precedent 135–38, 160–68
  analogical thinking in law: characteristic form 229–30
  analogies and precedent-following 235–36
    analogical thinking saving time 235
    analogies as source of both principles and policies 235
    avoiding hubris by resort to decided cases as analogies 235
    commitment to consistency and equal treatment 235
    facilitating agreement 235–36
    fostering planning, maintaining predictability, and protecting expectations 235
  analogies outside of law 227–28
  confusion in analogical reasoning 233–34
  decision by analogy 160–68
    analogy as deduction of 'legal reasons' from prior decisions 166–68
    analogy as incompletely theorized decision-making 161–62
    analogy as intuition of similarity 160–61
    analogy as mapping 162–65
  distinguishing application of precedent and analogous use of precedent 152–54
  erotetic account of legal analogy 124–25
  extending precedent by analogy 135–37
  features of analogy 230–31
    focus on particulars 230–31
    incompletely theorized judgments 231
    principled consistency 230

principles operating at low or intermediate level of abstraction 231
fixed points, precedents or judgments as 231–32
law-applying arguments and legal analogies 125–26
legal analogy 123–24
norms of change 83
objections to method of analogy 236–39
  excessive conservatism 236–38
  unreliability of method of analogy 236
precedent-based analogies 123–26
precedents as rules and analogies 232–33
  precedent as a rule 232
  precedent as analogy 233
reconstructing scheme of arguments by analogy 136–37
applicability, norms of 87
Aristotle 90
artefactual theory of precedent 268–80
  common law as artefact 3, 268, 275
  customs as artefacts 271–73, 279
  law as genre of artefact 269–71
  institutionality of precedent 278–80
    institutionality of law 279
    institutions as artefacts 278–79
    lack of consciousness in design 5
artificial intelligence, law and 72–74, 187
  machine-learning predictive programs 72–73
  potential influence of AI 72
  predictively valuable rules 73
  programs modelling more detailed determinations 73
  trend towards granular representations including factual rules 73–74
Austin, John 36–37, 244

bare precedents 149–50
Bentham, Jeremy 2–3, 36–37, 296
  analogical reasoning 236, 237–38
  attacks on the common law 238–39
  customary law 28–29
bidirectional model 180–81, 288–90
bin Laden, Osama 475, 477, 479, 481, 482, 484–85
Brazil *see* civil law systems
Burke, Edmund 298
  analogical reasoning 236
  balancing of principles as source of judicial obligation 342–43

552 INDEX

Burke, Edmund (*cont.*)
  bindingness of legal rules 342–43
  conservatism, and 523–24, 527
    affection for one's society 526–27
    central tenets of 524–27
    human society as fragile achievement 525
    judicial perpetuation of precedents, and 528–31
    progress as product of organic change 525–409
    progress only through evolution/slow change
      526, 528, 532, 534
    reliance on wisdom of ancestors 236, 485, 524
    rule of law dependent on rulers having civic
      virtue 526, 534
    social contract, non-consensual 525, 533,
      534, 536
    society's prejudices, faith in 525
    value in repeating the past 484, 524
  horizontal precedent 298–99
    strong theory of 298–99, 339–41, 342–45,
      346, 348
    weak theory of 339
  metaethical conventionalist, as 531–32
  overruling on basis of weighted balance of
    reasons 344
  psychological case for perpetuating precedents 528
    cognitive limitations of citizens 529–30
    cognitive limitations of judges 528–29, 530–31

ceteris paribus 40, 440
change, norms of 82–83
  analogy from precedents 83
  examples of 82
  power conferred by 82, 83
  striking down unconstitutional statutes 83
civil law systems 331, 418–30
  binding precedent/*stare decisis* 268, 321–22, 323,
    331–34, 424–27, 442
  Brazil 333–34
  cases giving rise to binding rules 324
  predictability and adaptability of
    precedent 429–30
  Spain 418, 419, 422–23, 425–325
  whether precedents must always or sometimes be
    considered 425
  interpretation and creation of law 419–24
    creative activity on part of the judge 420–21,
      422, 423, 424
    different meanings of 'creation' 420
    distinction between interpretation and
      creation 423–24
    doubts arising in relation to normative premise
      of decisions 421–22
    semantic flexibility 422–23
  mistaken judgments 518
  ratio decidendi 352–53
  Supreme Court precedents as sources of law 427–28
    judges establishing general norms 427–28
    Spain 427, 428
    treatment of underlying source, and 428

codification 431–42
  case law historically 431–32
  legislation and case law 441–42
  precedent, authority of 435–41
    difficulties in formulating consistent doctrine of
      precedent 435
    emergence of authority 440–41
    interpretative authority 438–39
    procedural provisions to ensure coherence and
      unity 435
    rules of argumentation 435–37
  rise of the courts 432–35
    commentaries on new national
      codifications 433–34
    declaratory theory of legal judgments prevailing
      433, 435
    judge-made law 434–35
    legal effect of precedents in the codified legal
      systems 434–35
  publication of decisions 432–33
  rules of argumentation 435–37
    courts not bound by case law 436
    precedents as interpretative authorities 437
    precedents binding on all other actors in legal
      system 436–37
cognitive science 248–51
common law
  binding precedent see *stare decisis*
  constraint, and see precedential constraint
  customary law, and
    common law as customary law 54–55
    customs as sources for decisions 273–74
    weight/bindingness afforded to precedent
      273, 274
  doctrine of precedent as fundamental part of 21
  function of courts to resolve disputes between
    parties 23
  incremental development of judicial precedents,
    evolving through 154
  individual court decisions as law-creating 22–23
  judicial decisions as evidence of common law 23
  normal science, and 90
    necessity of agreement in science and
      common law 97
    normal science operating by accumulation
      within a fixed paradigm 90
    scientific paradigm acting like a precedent 90
  other common law jurisdictions
    persuasive authority from 23
  precedent as independent and dependent source of
    law in 22
  precedents in common law 149–56, 352–53
    bare precedents 155–56
    creation of precedents in common law 156–57
    customary law, and 273
    precedents as holdings in reasons of
      decisions 150–55
    precedent in common law: slippery slope
      arguments 463–71

INDEX

statutes presumed not to change common law 3–4
consistency 490–91
  administrative law, in *see* administrative law,
    consistency in
  analogical reasoning, and
    commitment to consistency and equal
      treatment 235
    principled consistency, 230
  as mere enabler 141–42
  consistency with past cases as mere enabler 141–42
constructive interpretation 283, 285–88, 318
contest and precedent 198–213
  agonies of argument in *Monge* trilogy 201–4
    Cloutier v The Great Atlantic & Pacific
      Tea Co 201
    Howard v Dorr Woolen Co 201
    Monge v Beebe Rubber Co 200
  agonies of legal precedential argument from
    logocratic viewpoint 210–13
  logocratic abduction of abduction 204–10
    goals, purposes, and truth 205–7
    interpretive abduction 207–10
    logocratic enterprise conception of
      explanation 204–5
  Logocratic Method of argument 199, 205–6
    abduction 205, 206–7, 209, 210–11
    agonophilic approach to argument, as 199
    dialectical-rhetorical referee 207
    identification and evaluation of arguments as
      core of 209
    interpretive process, nature of 209–10
    legal arguments represented as deductions 210
    philosophical anthropology of argument
      208, 210
  precedented contests in legal argument 198–200
    legal arguments from precedent taking place in
      contests 198–99
    logocratic agonophilic explanation of legal
      argument by precedent 199
    'reason', in the form of arguments making
      law 198–99
  precedential arguments in *Monge* trilogy 203–4
constitutional conventions 32–33
constructive interpretation 283, 285–88
customary law
  change in 381
  common law, and *see* common law
  doctrine of precedent as part of 28–33
  in foro 28–29
  in pays 28–29
  nature of 54–55
  practice in war 479–80
  rule of recognition as form of 29–30, 33–34
  social rules as 54–55

Dancy, Jonathan 354–58, 362–63
defeasible rules, supplanting 101–14
  motivation for adopting a defeasible rule
    model 102

  problem of indeterminacy 102–6
  salience account 109–14
  salience account as replacement for defeasible rule
    model 113–14
  no single defeasible rule emerging from source
    case 112
Del Mar, Maksymilian 542
dictum, dicta 37, 70, 140–41, 333
  holding, *dicta* and factual precedent 70–71
Dindjer, Hasan 47
distinguishing 3, 23–24, 150–51, 214–26, 300, 345–
  46, 353
  all courts having power of distinguishing 185
  approach of courts to 345–46
  definition 216
  distinguishing rules not a legitimate practice 160
  factual differences, insufficiency of 346
  judicial reasoning
    based on rules, and 345
    non-positivist in character 346
  law-amendment, as 300
  legal certainty 214, 215
  lower courts 300, 301–2
  meaning of 300, 345, 500
  morally plausible manner, distinguishing
    in 345–46
  presumption against distinguishing, courts
    and 345–46
  Raz, and 300–2
    conditions for distinguishing 301, 302
  salience account as replacement for defeasible rule
    model 113–14
  structure of distinguishing 220–25, 221*f*, 223*f*, 224*f*
doctrine of precedent 21–25
  components of 21–25
    courts 'bound' by higher courts' decisions and
      own decisions 24–25
    independent and dependent source of law,
      precedent as 22
    individual precedents as sources of law 22–23
    judicial decisions creating law 23–24
  justifying 347–48
  Kuhn's definition of precedent 89, 92–94
    more stringent conditions 93–94
    precedents as objects for further
      articulation 92–93
    precedent as specification 93
  legal power, and 392–96
  legal status of 28–34
    customary law *in foro*, doctrine of precedent as
      part of 28–33
    rule of recognition as form of customary law (*in
      foro*) 29–30
  nature of 25–34
    concept of legal precedent 76–79
    content of precedent, meaning of 394–95
    doctrine of precedent in rule of
      recognition 26–28
    legal doctrine, as 28

554 INDEX

doctrine of precedent (*cont.*)
  legal force of precedent 395–96
  operation of precedent dependent on good faith
      of judge 51–52
  see also *stare decisis*
Dworkin, Ronald
  bindingness of legal rules 342–43
  constructive interpretation 283, 285–88, 318
  elements of precedent having gravitational
      force 50–51
  equality 281, 283, 284
  erroneous decisions, gravitational force of 284
  integrity 36–37, 39–40, 46–47, 281, 282–83, 285–
      86, 288
  'justification' standing alongside 'fit' in legal
      reasoning 54–55
  law itself as interpretive concept 295
  legal positivism 296–97
  legal principles 168–69
  metaphor of the chain novel 277, 282
  moral and legal practice on a continuum 37
  moral principles courts are legally obligated to
      consider 341
  one system view 35–36, 39–40, 45–48
    neutrality, importance of 45, 46–47
    questions of law as moral questions 45
    rejecting two-systems approach to
        jurisprudence 45–46
  positivism 45
  precedent 17, 282–83, 340–43
    balancing of principles as source of judicial
        obligation 342–43
    second-order reasons 342
    set of principles judges weigh in general balance
        of principles 341–42
    value of precedent as equality or formal
        justice 281
  realism, and 318–19
  rules and principles 296–97, 298, 341, 343
  unfair surprise in process of adjudication 293

elements of precedent 75–88
  application of norms of legal method 79–87
    norms of applicability 87
    norms of change 82–83
    norms of institutional decision-making 83–86
    norms of interpretation 86–87
    norms of recognition 79–82
    norms of subsumption 87
  legal effects of precedent 88
  legal material as (written) precedent, nature
      of 76–79
    concept of legal precedent 76–79
    law used as source of law 78–79
    precedent as source of law 77–78
  legal method and significance of precedent 75–76
    authoritative and persuasive precedents 75
    legal method, elements of 76
    legal method, nature of 75

precedents binding *de jure* or *de facto* 75
emotions and precedent 537–50
  emotions and thick concepts 537–40
    action-guiding concepts 539–40
    emotivism, nature of 537–38
    thick concepts, nature of 538–40
    thin concepts, nature of 539
    world-guided concepts 539–40
  problems for precedent with thick legal concepts
      and emotion 542–49
    concern over inconsistent/unequal applications
        of action-guiding concepts 548–49
    difficulties distinguishing world-guided and
        action-guiding legal concepts 543–47
    emotions as aids to understanding 543–46
    law requiring thick legal concept to be applied in
        action-guiding manner 546–47
  roles for emotion in fully engaged applications of
      thick concepts 540–42
    emotions answerable to reasons 541
    emotions having related affective and cognitive
        aspects 540–41
    evaluative nature of emotions 541
    understanding and being fully engaged with
        thick concept 541
    world-guided and action-guiding aspects of thick
        concepts 541
Endicott, Timothy 65, 387, 459
equality 283–85
  Dworkin 281, 283, 284
  integrity and judicial decisions 283–85
  rule of law, and 39–40, 42
  slippery slope arguments 466–67
  value of precedent, as 281
exemplarity and imitation 171–84
  exemplarism, nature of 171, 177
    'dogmatic exemplarism' and 'critical
        exemplarism' 174
    examples as embodying distinctive kind of
        normativity 172–73
    exemplars as pedagogical tools 176–77
    exemplars central to identity-formation of
        individuals and communities 176–77
    'exemplary superprecedents' 174
    illustrative and injunctive exemplarity 171–72
    landmark precedents 176
    legal exemplars 174
    ordinary and extraordinary exemplarity 173–74
    precedents as a kind of exemplar 171–72, 175
    public exemplarity 174–75
    Roman discourse of exemplarity 174
    subject and object exemplarity 171–72
    typical and unique examples 173–74
    virtue-based approach to exemplarity 172
  exemplary cases and development of law 181–84
    fossilized exemplars 183
    hidden exemplars 182
    mixed exemplars 183
    negative exemplars/anti-exemplars 182–83

INDEX 555

unconceived exemplars 183–84
imitation 177–81
adaptative and formal imitation 179
evolution of legal culture driven by
imitation 181–82
exemplars as objects of imitation 177
imitation as driving force of human culture
181, 184
imitation as collective process 178
imitation of precedent as complex, reasoned-
guided process 180–81
imitative reasoning as matter of analogy 176–78
reasoning by precedent as following an
example 177
self-referential imitation 180
expiscation *see* legal principles, expiscation of

fairness
categorical moral duty to treat like cases alike 353–
54, 491–94
fairness principles 492–93
fairness and consistency 493–94
notice and fairness 293–94
stare decisis, as reason for 353–55, 484
universalizability, and 353–54
Ferrara, Alessandro 174–75
Finnis, John 107
future decisions 281–95
bidirectional model 288–90
integrity and judicial decisions 282–88
objections to aiming for consistency with future
decisions 290–94
epistemic asymmetry 292–93
feedback and tradition 294
notice and fairness 293–94
redundancy 291–92
strategic decision-making 290–91

generalized second-order reasons, precedent as 335–49
Dworkin on precedent 340–43
Germany *see* codification
Goldie, Peter 538–42
Goodhart, Arthur 105
determining *ratio* of a case 244–46, 249
groupthink 58–59

Hart, HLA 298, 299
legal positivism 296–97, 298, 311
mind-independence of laws 517–18
precedent 393
communicating general standards of
behaviour 403
court's discretionary decision-making 298
doctrine of precedent as legal doctrine 28
permissive and non-mandatory legal source 43
relevant similarity 315
rule of recognition 21, 25–28, 29–44
foundations of law lying in official acceptance
407, 413

plurality of rules of recognition 407
rules of change, and 406, 410, 417
vehicles in the park 43
hermeneutics of legal precedent 143–57
analytical reconstruction of legal
hermeneutics 144–46
intentionalist conception of meaning and
interpretation 144–45, 146
legislative intent 145–46
hermeneutics of precedent 147–56
collective intentionality of courts 147–48
precedents in common law 149–56
precedents on statutory law 148–49
hoary precedents 511–22
definition 511
legal validity 520–22
long-standingness and moral
egregiousness 518–20
types of mind-independence 511–18, 513*t*
Hobbes, Thomas
legal positivism 296
precedent 36–37
holdings 70–71, 150–55
designated holding having rule-like character 150
formulation and semantics of holding not
necessarily the holding 152–53
holding of a precedent conditioned by the
facts 150–52
indeterminacy 153–54
horizontal precedent 11, 241, 262–63
benefits of courts being constrained by 12
legal positivism, and 297–99
strong Burkean version of 298–99
vertical precedent, and 41–43
see also *stare decisis*
Horty, John 168
House of Lords Practice Statement 1966 24, 41–42,
84, 322, 371

imitation *see* exemplarity and imitation
inference to best legal explanation 126–28
informal use of precedent 475–87
customary international law, Yamamoto killing
and 479–80
arguments as to possible precedent 478–79
lack of any juridical content 478
non-judicial precedent 480–81
permissibility, showing vs creating 481–82
institutional decision-making, norms of 83–86
concerning role of a particular institution 83–84
institutional considerations 86
institutional unification 2
stare decisis, and 84–86
intention
imputed intent 382–83
legal hermeneutics 144–46
complications arising with required intentional
subject 145–46
collective intentionality of courts 147–48

556 INDEX

intention (*cont.*)
   intentionalist conception of meaning and
      interpretation 144–45, 146
   legislative intent 145–46
  specific convergence, intentional choice and 43–44
interlegality and rules of recognition 498–510
  challenge interlegality poses to rules of
     recognition 498–99
  precedent and rules of recognition 499–505
    precedent, identity, and change 499–505
    precedent in customary rule of
      recognition 501–5
  precedents of interlegality 505–10
    forming and reforming rules of
      recognition 508–10
    interlegality in New Zealand 505–8
interpretation
  constructive interpretation 283, 285–88, 318
  innovative techniques of interpreting precedents 3
  intentionalist conception of meaning and
     interpretation 144–45, 146
  interpretation and creation of law in civil
     systems 419–24
  interpretive abduction 207–10
  law as interpretive concept 295
  mistakes in applying principles of statutory
     interpretation 369–70
  norms of 86–87
    'foreign' precedents 87
    precedent as an interpretive factor for another
      precedent 86
    precedent as interpretive factor for other types of
      sources 86–87
    regulating legal interpretation or interpretation
      of a source 86
  precedent, interpretation of 328–29

judges
  collective intentionality of courts 147–48
  constructive interpretation 283, 285–88, 318
  decisions *see* judicial decisions
  fallibility of judicial decisions 2–3
  having a rule in mind when deciding to act 134
  influenced by own backgrounds, training, and
     experience 251
  judicial reasoning *see* reasoning
  law-making *see* law-making powers and precedent
  maverick judges 51
  motivation of 51–52, 57
    desire to be acknowledged by groups as
      successful 57
  multiple audiences, judges speaking to 51–52
  operation of precedent dependent on good faith
     of 51–52
  outcome preferences 247–48, 250–51
  reputation 56–57
  social group member, as 52–53
    conflicting rules in groups, risk of 53
    group membership in private capacity 53

    groups shaping judge's reasoning 52
    techniques for making precedent more just 3
judicial law-making 23–24
  law-making constrained by issues before the
     court 23
  precedents able to be distinguished by later
     courts 23–24
  precedents deciding issues by reference to existing
     law, not *de novo* 23
  reactive role of courts 23
judicial techniques for making precedent more just 3
juries
  determination of negligence as jury question 66
  juries not bound by past decisions 63
  jury determinations treated with deference 65–66
  verdicts having no precedential value 65–66
jurisprudence constante 22–23, 323–24, 389
justice
  precedent, and 2, 4
  rule of law, and *see under* rule of law

Köpcke, Maris
  specific convergence 42–44
Kuhn, Thomas *see* paradigm and precedent

Lamond, Grant 16, 102–4, 150–52, 166, 167–68, 187,
    300, 345–46, 387, 390, 446
landmark cases 172, 174–75, 176–77, 324, 485
law–fact distinction 64–66
  judge's role as fact-finder 65–66
  jury determinations treated with deference 65–66
  jury verdicts having no precedential value 65–66
  only conclusions on law treated as precedent 64
law-making powers and precedent 380–91
  judicial power 387–90, 392, 393, 403
    England 387–88, 390
    France 387, 389
    Germany 389
    US 388–89
  legal powers
    action counting as exercise of legal
      power 381–82
    exercises of legal powers as 'acts-in-the-law' 380–81
    law-making acts as exercises of 392
    legal validity, and 395–96
    nature of 380–82, 393
    precedent, and 392–96
  precedent, features of 396–99, 402–3
    act setting precedent having degree of publicity
      or recognizability 397
    act setting precedent is intentional 397–98
    act within relationship governed by fairness
      397, 399
    benefit-conferring precedents 398
    continuity in the relevant relationship 397
    performing the act once provides reason to
      perform it again 399
legal argument
  contests, and *see* contest and precedent

uses of precedent, and *see* uses of precedent and
legal argument
legal certainty
civil law 214, 215
common law 215
legal creep and precedent 62–74
factors encouraging legal creep 69–74
findings of facts being treated as precedent 70–71
legal creep, objections to
bench trials applying different laws than jury
trials 63
degree of predictability, legal creep and 63–64
lower-level court is in better position to evaluate
evidence 63
rules carrying air of illegitimacy or
arbitrariness 63
transparency, legal creep contrary to the
value of 63
legal method
elements of
legal materials, practices, or factors on which law
based 76
legal reasons 76
norms of legal method 76
nature of 75
norms of legal method, application of 79–87
norms of applicability 87
norms of change 82–83
norms of institutional decision-making 83–86
norms of interpretation 86–87
norms of recognition 79–82
norms of subsumption 87
significance of precedent, and 75–76
legal orders, interaction of *see* interlegality and rules
of recognition
legal positivism 205–6, 268, 296–97
declaratory theory, and 147
exclusive positivism 297–99, 360, 361–62
inclusive positivism 360, 519–20
legal reasons as conventional reasons 351
nature of 45–46
precedent-based critique of 296–311
implications 310–11
legal positivism, horizontal precedent doctrine
and 297–99
legal positivism, vertical precedent doctrine and
299–302
separation thesis 359–60, 362
social thesis 360
theory of legal validity, as 362
theory of sources of law, as 362
legal powers *see* law-making powers and precedent
legal principles 138–42
construction of 168–70
criteria for 169
difficulty with 169–70
expiscation of 131–32
extending precedent by analogy 135–37
examples of 131

meaning of 'expiscate' 130–31
judges balancing competing principles 169
nature of 168–69
legal realists 247–48, 312–19
non-legal factors determining judicial
outcomes 247–48
outcome preferences of judges as dominant 247–
48, 250–51
precedent/precedential constraint 245–46, 312–19
rejoinder to realism about precedent 318–19
scepticism about constraint of precedent 313
similarity, question of 246
legal reasoning *see* reasoning
legislation
case law, and 441–42
law-making by courts, and 416
legislative facts and adjudicative facts 70–71
legislative intent 145–46
legislative override of precedents 376–77
overruling as authorized act of judicial
legislation 298–99
precedent, and 4
purposive way of making law, as 394
statutes presumed not to change common law 4
Lewis, Sebastian 465
like cases should be treated alike 2, 39–40, 156, 215,
216, 353–54, 464, 484, 491–92
Llewellyn, Karl 316–17
malleability of precedent 316
precedential constraint 245–46
scepticism about precedent binding courts 313
Logocratic Method of argument *see under* contest
and precedent
Lyons, David 39–40

MacCormick, Neil 117, 119, 120, 122–23, 130, 131–
32, 141–42, 147, 285, 321–22
mistaken statutory precedents 367–79
application of principles of statutory interpretation,
mistakes and 369–70
argument from parliamentary supremacy 375
qualifications to the argument 375–76
objections to the argument 376–79
adhering to precedents promotes certain
values 377–79
legislative override argument 376–77
tacit acquiescence arguments 376–77
whether courts should follow mistaken statutory
precedents 370–75
disagreement among judiciary 370–71, 372
judicial practice and its limits 370–72
morality/moral reasons, precedent and *see stare
decisis*

natural model of precedential constraint 12–13
negligence 66–68, 90–91, 94–95, 125, 127–28, 130,
134–36, 302–10
New Zealand 505–10
non-judicial precedent 480–81

obiter dicta 3, 36, 79, 123–24, 434–35
   ratio decidendi, and 41–42, 43–44, 118–19, 120, 143–44, 425
one system view 35–36, 39–40, 45–48
   Dworkin, and
      neutrality, importance of 45, 46–47
      questions of law as moral questions 45
      rejecting two-systems approach to jurisprudence 45–46
   law as moral system 35–36
   stare decisis, and 39–40, 45–48
overruling 3, 24, 300, 312, 315, 322, 330
   authorized act of judicial legislation, as 298–99
   courts' power to overrule own decisions 24
      grounds for overruling 24
   exclusionary understanding of judge-made law, requirement for 343–44
   higher courts overruling decisions of lower courts 24–25, 298–99
   highest court overruling own prior decision 298–99, 343–44, 346
   horizontal level, at 323, 331
   legal positivism, and 297–99
   only certain courts having authority to overrule earlier decisions 185
   overturned precedents a case of negative exemplarity 182–83
   permissible list of non-excluded reasons for overruling 343–44
   prior decision must be 'clearly wrong' 344
   ratio as summary proposition of the balance of various reasons in a judgment 344
   risks and rewards of overturning 96–99
      Dobbs v Jackson Women's Health Organization 97–99
      precedents overturned as 'malfunctions' of current paradigm 94
   'very good reason' to overrule, need for 344
   weighted balance of reasons, overruling on basis of 344, 345

paradigm and precedent 89–100
   common law and normal science 90
   scientific paradigm acting like a precedent 90
   Kuhn's definition of precedent 89, 92–94
      more stringent conditions 93–94
      precedents as objects for further articulation 92–93
      precedent as specification 93
   Kuhn on scientific progress 89
      common law, and 90
   precedent as paradigm 90–92
      precedents and paradigms not synonymous 90–91
   precedents overturned as 'malfunctions' of current paradigm 94–96
paradox of precedent 49–51
per incuriam rule 3, 81, 326–27, 373–74, 395, 402–3, 498, 500, 508–9

Perry, Stephen
   critique of Raz's exclusive positivism 296–99
persuasive authority 3
   authoritative and persuasive precedents 75
   nature of 76
   persuasive *rationes* of cases not formally binding 50–51
practical reason
   precedent, and 338–40
   Raz, and 336–38, 341
      acting on balance of reasons 337–38, 340–41
      exclusionary reasons 297–98, 299, 337, 338, 339–40, 343–44, 347
      exclusionary rules 338, 339, 343, 344, 346, 347, 348–49
      first-order reasons for action 336, 341
      modes of practical reasoning 339–40
      protected reasons 337, 340
      rules of thumb 337–38
      scope 337–38
      second-order reasons for action 336, 339–40, 342
      system of absolute discretion 339
precedent
   civil law systems *see* civil law systems
   constraint, and *see* precedential constraint
   contest, and *see* contest and precedent
   doctrine of *see* doctrine of precedent
   elements of *see* elements of precedent
   emotions, and *see* emotions and precedent
   escape from *see* interlegality and rules of recognition
   exemplarity, imitation seem exemplarity and imitation, precedent and 171–84
   formal bindingness 323
   fundamental norms of 240–42
   future decisions, gravitational force of *see* gravitational force of future decisions
   hoary precedents *see* hoary precedents
   informal use of *see* informal use of precedent
   interpretation of 328–29
   law-making powers, and *see* law-making powers and precedent
   legal creep, and *see* legal creep and precedent
   legal powers, and *see* law-making powers and precedent
   legal theory, and 343–47
   mistaken statutory precedents *see* mistaken statutory precedents, courts and
   non-judicial precedent 480–81
   paradigm, and *see* paradigm and precedent
   point of precedent 399–402
      deferred decisions, precedent enabling 401
      precedent creating a reason that did not exist before 399
      precedent-setting in face of underdetermination 399–400
      valuable control over guidance, precedent providing 401

practical reason, and 338–40
practices of 330–31
realists, and *see* legal realists
reasons for following see *stare decisis*
reasons holism, and *see* reasons holism and shared
    view of precedent
similarity, and *see* similarity and precedent
source-norm distinction, and *see* source-norm
    distinction, and precedent
theories of 71–72
    adjudicative model 71–72
    artefactual theory *see* artefactual theory of
        precedent
    facts-plus-outcome model 71
    necessity model 71–72
unprecedents 380, 384, 385
precedential constraint 36–37, 185–97
    basic concepts 188–90
    benefits of 12
    conceptual problems of 185–88
    constraint by reasons 190–94
        constraint 191–93
        decisions consistent with background case
            base 191–93
        domestic scenario 193–94
        priority ordering on reasons 190–91
    constraint in common law dependent on rules 185
    constraint, real mechanism of 194–97
        'The alligator and the ocelot' 194–95
        permissibility, formal and social notions of
            195, 196–97
    models of 12–17
        bidirectional model 288–90
        natural model 12–13
        reason model 187, 191–93
        result model 14–17
        rule model 13–14, 101, 328
        standard model 185
    priority ordering on reasons 190–91
    similarity and precedent *see* similarity and
        precedent
    statutes and constitutions, under 18
    strength of 18–19
    see also stare decisis
predictability 443–55
    analogical thinking, and 235
    autonomy, and 445, 446–47
    civil law systems 429–30
    importance of 444, 446
    legal creep and 63–64
    liberty, and 443–44, 445, 446–47
    predictability as important justification for
        precedent 445
        predictability as instrumental value 443–44
        value of predictability, and 444–47
    rule of law, and 443, 444
        autonomy and dignity 445
        predictability and behaviour-guidance 444–45
    stare decisis, and 353, 377, 378

value of autonomy or liberty weighed against other
    values 446–47
prestige impulse 2, 3–4
presumptive reasons and *stare decisis* 255–67
    horizontal precedent and presumptive
        reasons 262–67
    presumptive reasons, meaning of 255
    presumptive reasons for action 255–62
Priel, Dan 268–69, 271, 279

questions 133–35

ratio decidendi 3, 25, 27, 37, 117, 135
    authority of a past decision 344
    content of *ratio* determined by test of perceived
        moral salience 54
    courts refraining from giving *ratio* of
        decisions 134–35
    distinguishing relevant, irrelevant, and ambiguous
        factors 50
    general norm, as 352–53
    gravitational pull of precedent 55–57
        elements of past decisions possessing
            gravitational pull 50–51
        reputation of judges 56–57
    identifying *ratio* 49–50, 54
        reason leading to conclusion, *ratio* as 50
    left to be reconstructed by future courts 134–35
        interpretative exercise, as 135
    matter of judgment, extracting binding *ratio* and
        assessing scope as 51, 56–57
    nature of 350
    obiter dicta, and 41–42
    reach of *ratio* as ambiguous and disputed 50
    summary proposition of the balance of various
        reasons in a judgment, as 344
Rawls, John 40–41, 163–64
    justice, nature of 39
    obligations of reciprocity 533
    reasoning to reflective equilibrium 163–64
    stare decisis 40–41
Raz, Joseph 7
    distinguishing 13–14, 300–2, 310–11
        conditions for 14, 186–88, 194, 301, 302
    legal positivism 335, 338, 343
        exclusive legal positivism 296–99, 310–11
    overruling 297–99, 343–44
    practical reason 336–38, 341
        acting on balance of reasons 337–38, 340–41
        exclusionary reasons 297–98, 299, 337, 338,
            339–40, 343–44, 347
        exclusionary rules 338, 343, 344, 346,
            347, 348–49
        first-order reasons for action 336, 341
        modes of practical reasoning 339–40
        protected reasons 337, 340
        rules of thumb 337–38
        second-order reasons for action 336, 339–
            40, 342

560 INDEX

Raz, Joseph (*cont.*)
  precedent, doctrine of 343–44
  rule of law 444–45
    autonomy and dignity 445
    predictability and behaviour-guidance 444–45
  sources thesis 335–36
reason model of constraint *see under* precedential
    constraint, models of
reasoning 158–70
  analogical reasoning *see* analogy/analogical
    reasoning and precedent
  conventional reasons 352, 359, 361, 362
  distinguishing *see* distinguishing
  equilibrium, reasoning to 159–60
  genuine reasons 358–59
  groups shaping judges' reasoning 52
  imitation, reasoning by *see* exemplarity and
    imitation, precedent and
  judicial reasoning, value of precedent in 523–36
    aesthetic case for perpetuating
      precedents 535–36
    conceptual case for perpetuating precedents 527–28
    moral case for perpetuating precedents 531–35
    psychological case for perpetuating
      precedents 528–31
  'justification' standing alongside 'fit' in legal
    reasoning 54–55
  legal reasons
    element of legal method, as 76
    genuine or conventional 359–60
    nature of law, and 359–60
    ordinary legal reasons 361–62
  moral values giving rise to moral reasons 36–37
  presumptive reasons *see* presumptive reasons and
    stare decisis
reasons holism 355–57
  different types of considerations 355, 356f
  favourers and enablers 355–56, 357
  intensifiers and attenuators 356–57
  meaning of 350–51
  reasons atomism, and 355
  theory of genuine reasons, as 351, 358–59
recognition, norms of 79–82
  multiple precedents, effects of 80–81
  positive or negative 80
reliability
  slippery slope arguments, reliability requirement
    and 466
  unreliability of method of analogy 236
res judicata 11, 19, 78, 311
result model of precedent *see under* precedential
    constraint, models of
resultance and supervenience 354–56
royal prerogative 30
rule model of precedent *see under* precedential
    constraint, models of
rule of law
  autonomy and dignity 445
  demands of justice, and 3

  law-making discretion, and 417
  law must be clear, intelligible, and constant 96–97
  precedent, and 2–3, 4
  predictability and behaviour-guidance 444–45
  stare decisis, and 416
  values of stability, reliability, equality 39–40, 42
rules of recognition 21, 26–28, 360
  criteria for identifying binding legal considerations
    in judgments 26, 28
  customary law (*in foro*), as form of 29, 33–34
    official customary standards 29
  doctrine of precedent as part of 26–28
  forming and reforming 508–10
  foundations of law lying in official acceptance
    407, 413
  imposing a duty on officials 28
  interlegality, and *see* interlegality and rules of
    recognition
  legal standard, as 29–30
  per incuriam avenue for avoiding precedent 500
  precedent, and 500
    empowering effect of practice of precedent
      within rule of recognition 501
    individual precedents contesting rules of
      recognition 500
    precedent in customary rule of
      recognition 501–5
    source of law 26, 500
  rules of change, and 406, 410, 412, 417
  social rules, as 28, 407, 415–16
  US, in *see* United States (US)

Schauer, Frederick 39–40, 43
separation thesis 351
  application of 362
  no necessary connection between content of law
    and true morality 359–60
  non-positivist theories rejecting 351, 360
shared view of precedent 350
similarity and precedent 240–51
  determining relevant similarity: cognitive
    science 248–51
    cognitive realism 249
    judge's outcome-and policy-independent
      judgments 249–51
    judge's outcome preferences 247–48, 250–51
  fundamental norms of precedent 240–42
  relevant similarity 244–48
    legal realist challenge 245–46
    traditional views 244–45
Simpson, AWB
  authority of cases 344
  common law as customary law 54–55
  conditions for later modification of an earlier
    rule 186–88, 194
  distinguishing cases 195
  judges having 'a rule in mind' 134
  legal obligation to follow precedent 38
  permissible decisions 195

slippery slope arguments 459–74
 common law precedent 463–71
  distinguishing 470–71
  force of precedents 464–65
 nature of slippery slope arguments 461–63, 471–73
  empirical slippery slope arguments 462
  logical slippery slope arguments 461
  precedent slippery slope arguments 462–63
 precedent, and 471–73
social model of precedent 51–58
 implications of social model 58–60
  legal rules of precedent complemented by non-legal social rules 51–52
  operation of precedent dependent on good faith of judge 51–52
  persuasive *rationes* of cases not formally binding 50–51
  judges as insiders talking to fellow group members 52
  social groups and social rules 52–53
  shared beliefs about morality taking form of social rules 54
source-norm distinction 324–26
 'binding-versus-persuasive' distinction, caveats about 320, 321–22
 formal bindingness 323
 implications of distinction 326–27
 precedent and underlying source, relationship between 80–82
 precedent as source, precedent as norm 328–34
sources of law 22, 500
 precedent as source of law 77–78, 392
  common law, in 22
  independent and dependent source of law, precedent as 22
  individual precedents as sources of law 22–23
  permissive and non-mandatory legal source, precedent as 43
Spain *see* civil law systems
standard model of precedential constraint *see under* precedential constraint, models of
stare decisis 11
 affecting legal rights and obligations of non-parties 39
 applying to courts' determinations of law 11
 civil law systems, in 331–34
 institutional decision-making, and 84–86
 legal creep, and *see* precedent and legal creep
 legal doctrine of 38–44
  legal output 42–44
  moral input 38–42
 major systemic implications of 38–39
 moral and juridical approaches 36–38
  juridical approach 37–38
  moral values giving rise to moral reasons 36–37
  moral values outweighing moral costs 40–41
 nature of 11, 35–48, 241, 297

courts 'bound' by higher courts' decisions and own decisions 24–25
 involving issue of law not fact 64
 norm of adjudication, *stare decisis* as 84
one-system view objection 45–48
overruling *see* overruling
precedential constraint, nature of *see* precedential constraint
presumptive reasons, and *see* presumptive reasons and *stare decisis*
reasons for 11–12, 360–61, 483–86
 desirability of doing things the same way over and over 484
 duty to give effect to the law 35
 Dworkinian integrity 36–37, 39–40, 46–47, 168–69
 efficiency reasons 39
 epistemic considerations 39, 484
 fairness 353–55, 484
 hierarchy of courts, preserving 11
 institutional settlement and repose 484
 like cases should be treated alike 2, 39–40, 464, 484, 491–92
 moral reasons 35–36, 38–42
 pragmatic considerations 13
 predictability 353, 377, 378, 484
 reliance interests 377, 378, 484
 rule-of-law values of stability, reliability, equality 39–40, 42, 353, 377, 378
 slippery slope arguments *see* slippery slope arguments
 specific convergence 42–44
 see also doctrine of precedent
statutory law, precedents on 148–49
Stevens, Katherina
 amended rule model 101
 analogical mapping 162–63, 164–65
 binding precedent 38
subsumption, norms of 87
 past decisions, and 87
 regulating application of a legal norm to the facts 87
Summers, Robert 321–23, 324
Sunstein, Cass 161, 163–64
supervenience 354
 meaning of 354
 resultance, and 354
 treating like cases alike as regards their supervenience bases 354–55
 universalizability, and 354

targeted killings, use of *see* informal use of precedent

United States (US)
 American legal realists *see* legal realists
 constitutionally erroneous Supreme Court precedent 407–11, 412–16, 518–20
 Dobbs v Jackson Women's Health Organization 97–99, 198, 200, 211
 judicial law-making 388–89

562 INDEX

United States (US) (*cont.*)
  landmark precedents 176
  legal creep 62–63
    factual precedents, lower courts increasing
      use of 70
    increasing numbers of court cases and
      opinions 69
    law–fact distinction 62, 64–65
    legislative facts 71
    negligence, and 66, 68
  Monge v Beebe Rubber Co 200–4
  New York v United States 315–17
  overruling 331
  Payne v Tennessee 198, 200
  rules of legal change 410, 412
  rules of recognition 408, 410, 412, 415–16
    hoary precedents, and 519, 520–22
    social rules 415–16
    US rules of legal change, and 412
  slippery slope argument: *Texas v Johnson* 443–44
  stare decisis 263–67
    function of 416
    mere error not sufficient ground for overruling
      407, 409
    practical effect of constitutional *stare decisis* in
      Supreme Court 406
    Supreme Court, and 405–17
    systemic implications of 38–39
  Supreme Court
    appointments of new justices, effects of 415
    Constitution conferring 'judicial power' on 408
    constitutional-law-making institution, as 406,
      407, 412
    justices forming ad hoc coalitions 415
    lower courts, and 412–14, 416–17
    not bound by erroneous constitutional
      precedents 405–6, 409, 411, 412
    role in constitutional cases 416

  rule of recognition and US rules of legal
    change 412
  status and weight of constitutionally erroneous
    precedent 407–11
  targeted killings *see* informal use of precedent
universalizability 360–61
  conditional moral duty to treat like cases
    alike 353–54
  fairness, and 353–54
  meaning of 354
  supervenience, and 354
unprecedents 380, 384, 385
uses of precedent and legal argument 117–29
  applying precedent 118–23
    conceptual apparatus and vocabulary 118–19
    legal syllogism model 119–23
    meaning of 118
  argument and precedent 128–29
  inferences to best legal explanation 126–28
    structure of 126–27
  precedent-based analogies 123–26
    erotetic account of legal analogy 124–25
    juridical consequences of decisions 123–24
    legal analogy 123–24

vertical precedent 41–42
  absolute strength of 11, 24, 262–63, 266
  benefits of 11
  distinguishing, and 266
  horizontal precedent, and 41–43
  justification for 43
  legal positivism, and 299–302
  nature of 11, 240–41

Williams, Bernard 462, 463, 467, 471–72, 537–42,
  545, 546, 549

Yamamoto, Isoroku *see* informal use of precedent